GUIDE TO

Grantseeking on the Web

2003 EDITION

Kief Schladweiler, Editor

Contributors

This edition of *The Foundation Center's Guide to Grantseeking on the Web* is the result of the hard work of the following individuals, and of their considerable experience exploring the World Wide Web.

Claire Acher
Jennifer Allen
David L. Clark
Sarah Collins
Phyllis Edelson
Susanne Leigh Goddeau
Bruce Gumm
Christine Innamorato
David G. Jacobs
John Kendzior
Kevin Kinsella
Thomas Lam
Cheryl Loe
Judith B. Margolin
Beverly McGrath
Lorna Aikman Mehta
Kelly Miniter
Margaret Morth
Mitch Nauffts
Anita H. Plotinsky
Paul Schlotthauer
Maria Serapiglia
Megan Steintrager
Achala Wali
C. Renée Westmoreland

Printed and bound in the United States of America.

Library of Congress Cataloging-in Publication Data

The Foundation Center's guide to grantseeking on the Web / Kief Schladweiler, editor.— 2003 ed.
p. cm.
Includes bibliographical references and index.
ISBN 1-931923-67-1 (pbk. : alk. paper)
1. Fund raising—Computer network resources—Directories. 2. Endowments—Computer network resources—Directories. 3. Web sites—Directories. I. Title: Guide to grantseeking on the Web. II. Title: Grantseeking on the Web. III. Schladweiler, Kief. IV. Foundation Center.
HV41.2.F68 2003
025.06'65815224—dc22

2003015342

TABLE OF CONTENTS

FOREWORD

A few years ago, management guru Peter Drucker declared the 20th century "the century of business" and predicted that the 21st century would be "the century of the social sector." Drucker's prediction was based on two assumptions: one, that what he called the 20th-century "mega-state" had failed, in both its totalitarian and democratic versions, to deliver on a single one of its promises; and two, that the 21st century, at least in its early decades, would continue to be one of social, economic, and political turmoil—turmoil that would demand the emergence of a strong, independent social sector, innovative leadership, and cross-sectoral collaboration.

While it's too soon to say whether Drucker's bold prediction will come to pass, it is increasingly evident that the "third sector" has become a vitally important part of American society. In field after field, nonprofit organizations funded by private foundations, government, and/or business are in the trenches, battling disease, protecting the environment, striving to improve education, delivering services to the poor and disadvantaged—doing, in other words, what Drucker argued is their primary task: creating human health and well-being.

Technology, especially in the last decade or so, has given a huge assist to these efforts. Far from being the quaint rustics often portrayed in the media, third sector leaders and managers have embraced the Internet, e-mail, and the Web to deliver services more efficiently, improve fundraising results, and extend the reach of their organizations. Moreover, as the ability to aggregate online audiences inexpensively has become a reality, the sector has begun to move beyond issues of reach and efficiency to focus on Web-enabled models of collaboration, knowledge management, and communities of practice.

Regardless of how social and economic forces play out over the next few decades, the culture of the Web is likely to remain ideally suited to the purposes of the nonprofit community. With our many Web-delivered resources and services—and now with the fourth edition of this guide—the Foundation Center remains committed to the idea that a networked nonprofit sector is a vibrant and effective nonprofit sector. We encourage you to visit our Web site at http://fdncenter.org, and we hope that it—and the book in your hands—opens many doors for you as *you* get down in the trenches and work to make your goals and dreams a reality.

INTRODUCTION

Scope

The Foundation Center's Guide to Grantseeking on the Web, 2003 edition, is intended as a selective rather than a comprehensive index of available philanthropic sites on the Web. (We do, however, include an extensive listing of private foundations, grantmaking public charities, corporate grantmakers, and related nonprofit Web sites in the appendices at the back of the book.) Since no one source can cover all philanthropic Web sites that exist, it would be foolhardy to try. Besides, the fluid nature of the Internet ensures that sites can and will be established, shut down, or moved to a new URL location overnight.

Our aim with this guide is to provide you with an introduction to the most useful Web sites and to deliver some solid advice about how to get the most out of your online funding research time. The Foundation Center is in a unique position to offer these suggestions, since Center staff has been scouring the Web in search of useful information since 1994, when the Center launched its own Web site. We hope that this selective approach will facilitate your ability to find pertinent information quickly on grantmakers on the Web while still encouraging you to explore on your own.

The Web sites referred to as examples throughout this guide cover a wide range of subject areas aimed at a broad audience. Some are specialized sites, focusing on a specific topic, while others are portal sites with information and links that span any number of topics. Some exist for one purpose only (e.g., to raise money for a particular cause). Others have a variety of features (such as news, grants announcements, e-mail notifications, software downloads, interactivity, or organizational information). But all of the sites included in this guide share one thing in common. They provide information and tools for finding potential funders, learning about the nonprofit sector, conducting statistical research, and connecting grantseekers and others through electronic communication, and they offer useful content.

If you are interested in the world of philanthropy, this guide will lead you to appropriate resources. With our own Web site, the Foundation Center has created a specialty portal for grantseekers and others. We continue to develop and expand our online offerings while keeping pace with the burgeoning Internet. Once you have become familiar with the Web resources available in your area(s) of interest, we invite you to visit our Web site (http://fdncenter.org) and follow the paths that open up to you.

Features and Arrangement

This edition of *The Foundation Center's Guide to Grantseeking on the Web* employs a number of devices to make it easier for you to find the information you need. The links and abstracts to the Web sites mentioned in the book are found in the appendices at the back of the book. This should help provide you with an uninterrupted reading experience while still delivering the information you need to locate specific Web sites and resources. Also in the 2003 edition you will find a new chapter (Chapter 10) focusing on e-learning for the nonprofit sector. All eleven chapters combined round out a complete approach to grantseeking on the Web that includes independent foundations, community foundations, public charities, corporate funders, government funding, and individual donors.

As in prior editions, screen shots of featured Web sites help you to visualize the sites and will prepare you for when you actually visit them. (But be forewarned: Some of the sites may look different by the time you get to them, due to the nature of the ever-changing Web.) Look for sidebars throughout the text providing concise tips and easy-to-read clarification. This edition also provides a combined proper name and subject index. If, for example, you're interested in Web sites mentioned in the book regarding the environment, you can look up the term "environment" in the index. Or if you have the name of a specific Web host, look that organization up in the index. This edition also has a glossary of terms relating to the Internet that may be unfamiliar to someone new to the process of grantseeking on the Web.

Chapter 1 is a survey of the range of information and services available at the Foundation Center's Web site (http://fdncenter.org). We reorganize and redesign

Tips When Grantseeking on the Web

To find a word or phrase within the Web page you currently have open, use your browser's "Find" option ("Ctrl+F" in most cases). This is especially useful when you are confronted with a page that contains quite a bit of text. The "Find" option lets you quickly jump to that section of the page where your word or phrase occurs so that you can judge the usefulness of the site much sooner.

As you conduct your research on the Web, it is a good idea to bookmark pages that you think you will return to again. If you are using Netscape, you will find the heading "Bookmarks" at the top of the screen; if you are using Internet Explorer, you will find the heading "Favorites." When you come across a page you'd like to bookmark, click Bookmarks/Favorites and then select Add Bookmark/Add to Favorites from the pull-down menu.

our Web site on a continuous basis to accommodate the growing amount of information. Most recently we created a directory for individual grantseekers and launched personalization software that allows information to be targeted to users who have registered a profile on the site. The Center's Web site is now organized with a focus on providing specific useful tools and directed information according to the needs of each visitor. Especially for first-time visitors, reading this chapter may make navigating our site even easier. And remember, the Web is vast; if you get lost following a trail of links, you can always return to http://fdncenter.org to pick up the trail afresh.

In Chapter 2 we discuss various approaches that independent (or private) foundations are taking in utilizing the Web. From simply providing basic information to actively championing the use of new communication technologies and trying to ensure equal access for all, foundations increasingly are getting involved with the Web. You can now find independent foundations that offer annual reports, grants guidelines, grants listings, and grant application forms. In some cases, foundations have taken the next step and are now providing grant application forms on the Web that can either be downloaded and filled out by grantseekers or, in some cases, submitted directly to the funders online. While recent innovations such as these make it easier to apply for a grant, being successful at grantseeking on the Web still requires "old-fashioned" research, hard work, and patience.

The Foundation Center takes great pains to present an accurate picture of U.S. philanthropy. In doing so we make a distinction between private foundations and public charities, sometimes known as "public foundations." In Chapter 3 we present those public charities on the Web that we have identified as having grantmaking programs. This group includes community foundations, a growing segment of U.S. philanthropy. Information is not available as systematically for the great variety of public charities as it is for private foundations. It is our hope that highlighting grantmaking public charities in this way will stimulate more of them to provide us with detailed information about their grantmaking activities.

Chapter 4 surveys the online world of corporate philanthropy, in addition to suggesting strategies for finding corporate funding information on the Web. Corporations describe their giving programs in a variety of ways and to varying degrees, so creativity and persistence come into play when conducting corporate giving research on the Web. This chapter stresses the need to consider the different motivations and goals of corporate givers and how these can affect your funding approach. This chapter also distinguishes between corporate foundations and direct giving programs, since understanding such distinctions will have an impact on your funding research.

There is a tremendous amount of government information on the Web. Chapter 5 attempts to make sense of this vast amount of information by pointing you to selected sites at the many levels of government that describe a variety of assistance programs. Unlike corporations, where you may need to sift through general information on the company to find information specifically about its giving programs, there is a wealth of information available on the Web about government funding, much of it overlapping and duplicative. People both inside and outside of government have tried to organize this information for you. This chapter reviews the many sites detailing specific support programs as well as sites that can lead you to useful information. Exploring these sites will help you understand how government agencies and funding programs are organized and can reveal a lot about their relationship to the nonprofit sector.

What to Look for on Grantmaker Web Sites

When visiting grantmaker Web sites, you will want to obtain answers to the following questions:

- *Does the grantmaker fund projects similar to yours?* Most grantmaker Web sites explicitly state the sort of projects that are funded. Go through the site thoroughly to get a sense of the funder's mission, who its founders were, and its history.
- *Does the Web site offer a listing of recently awarded grants?* If such a list is not apparent, see if the grantmaker has posted its annual report on the site. Often, annual reports contain grants lists and relevant financial data. Some grantmakers' Web sites provide links to their grantees' Web sites. Exploring these Web sites will provide you with additional information about the kinds of projects and organizations funded by the grantmaker.
- *Does the grantmaker accept applications?* Some grantmakers consider projects by invitation only.
- *What are the application guidelines?* This information, provided on most grantmaker Web sites, will tell you in the clearest terms whether or not a project such as yours would be considered for funding. Guidelines will provide you with application procedures and deadlines and inform you as to whether you should apply directly or first send a letter of inquiry. Some grantmaker Web sites have application forms that you can download or print from the screen. A few will allow you to apply online.
- *Are there funding restrictions?* These are usually stated explicitly, often in the application guidelines.
- *How do you contact the grantmaker?* Note the correct address, phone number, and e-mail address. Before you contact a grantmaker, become familiar with that grantmaker's preferred means of approach. Some accept e-mail inquiries and respond to phone calls, but the majority will require that you send a formal letter or proposal by post.
- *Who are the officers, trustees, and staff?* If this information is available, you will be able to address your inquiry to the correct person, not to an institution, when you contact the grantmaker.

Note: It is always important to try to ascertain how recently the information you are looking at was posted to the Web site. If the content is vague or not dated, you will need to confirm the data you have gathered from another source or directly from the grantmaker.

Chapter 6 reveals strategies and resources for finding support from individual donors. You may already know that identifying individual donors is somewhat difficult because, unlike foundations, individuals are not required to disclose to the public their financial and philanthropic activities. Approaching wealthy public figures is often an unsuccessful strategy. Most celebrities are inundated with requests for money, and they may have no particular connection to the activities or location of your nonprofit organization. This chapter provides recommendations and links to relevant Web sites that help you find information on individual donors. It also tackles thorny issues like privacy on the Internet and fundraising ethics, and it offers a prospect worksheet for use in researching individual donors online.

Chapter 7 surveys a variety of sites—hosted in diverse settings—that offer searchable databases that may help Web users identify potential sources of assistance or general information. Wherever possible, we have divided the world of searchable databases into the two major categories of "for-free" and "for-fee." There is some overlap of this chapter with the subject matter of other chapters because the databases covered are often within corporate, government, and nonprofit organization settings, including a few on foundation Web sites.

Chapter 8 chronicles "other" useful Web sites, many of them hosted by nonprofit organizations. These are sites that Foundation Center staff has found to be the most useful and descriptive of the nonprofit sector, including some sites concerned with philanthropy in other countries. Many of the sites covered in this chapter will provide you with links to other resources you may find useful. This sampling of sites is organized according to the subject categories used at the Center's Web site to provide ready access to this growing number of resources.

Chapter 9 is a comprehensive, selected listing of online publications (with abstracts for each) concerned with philanthropy and the nonprofit sector. Included are many field-specific newsletters and other online publications that describe the current trends and policy context for various nonprofit activities. Here you will find online journals that have print counterparts and those that offer unique content available only on the Web. Use this chapter to identify the online publications that will keep you up-to-date concerning your particular field and interests.

As noted, Chapter 10 is new to the 2003 edition of this book. Though nonprofits in general have been slow to adapt to the potential of e-learning (as compared to the academic or for-profit arenas), there is now an increased interest among nonprofits that wish to assist staff and volunteers in developing new skills and in learning online about the multi-faceted world of fundraising and nonprofit management. This chapter reviews e-learning sites designed specifically for nonprofit organizations, as well as general e-learning sites that can be adapted by the nonprofit community.

Chapter 11 illustrates how interactive communication is used to build communities on the Web. The simple but powerful interactivity of Internet e-mail, electronic mailing lists, and Web boards allows communities of Web users to define themselves online and to establish dialogues and conversations, both private and public, that can advance their work or inform their interests. This chapter surveys a number of the community-building services available for grantseekers and other nonprofit practitioners, and it provides tips on how to begin participating in these various forums.

There is also an extensive set of appendices.

Appendix A provides a brief introduction to general search engines that we hope will equip you with the additional tools you need to be successful at grantseeking on the Web.

Appendices B–F list the many links to private foundations, grantmaking public charities, community foundations, corporate givers, and nonprofit organizations that will be found at the Center's Web site (http://fdncenter.org). Brief abstracts are also provided so that you will have an idea in advance about what is available on these sites. (The Foundation Center updates grantmaker links and abstracts continually, so be sure to check the Finding Funders area of our Web site for the latest listings.) Readers can save time by familiarizing themselves with the world of foundations on the Web, programs of individual foundations, and basic Web offerings by referring to these appendices prior to going online.

Appendix G is a bibliography of print and other resources about the Internet that may be of interest to nonprofit practitioners. It is a compilation drawn from the Foundation Center's Literature of the Nonprofit Sector Online (LNPS), a database you can search for free by visiting http://lnps.fdncenter.org.

Appendix H is a glossary of selected Internet-related terms that you are likely to come across in your research. It is offered here to help clarify jargon and explain technical terminology that may be unfamiliar to you.

The Foundation Center's Web site is a specialty portal dedicated to "Helping grantseekers succeed, helping grantmakers make a difference." This guide is in one sense the static form of this specialty portal. It is full of specific information about Web sites that may be useful in your grantseeking efforts. We invite you to use both this guide and our Web site in conjunction with one another as a way to get your online grantseeking efforts off to a flying start.

CHAPTER ONE

A Guided Tour of the Foundation Center's Web Site

The Foundation Center is the nation's leading authority on philanthropy and is dedicated to serving grantseekers, grantmakers, researchers, policymakers, the media, and the general public. The Foundation Center's mission is to support and improve philanthropy by promoting public understanding of the field and helping grantseekers succeed. To achieve its mission, the Foundation Center collects, organizes, and communicates information on U.S. philanthropy, conducts and facilitates research on trends in the field, provides education and training on the grantseeking process, and ensures public access to information and services through our World Wide Web site, print and electronic publications, five library/learning centers, and a national network of Cooperating Collections. The Center uses various media, increasingly media that is electronic in nature, to achieve its mission. The Center's Web site gives visitors around-the-clock access to objective and incisive coverage of the news of philanthropy, current data on grantmakers and their giving, and how-to resources on grantseeking and the use of Center resources. It enables us to provide education in grantseeking and authoritative information on philanthropy to a variety of audiences, unlimited by geography.

Technology Used on the Center's Web Site

In order to reach the widest possible audience, the Foundation Center's Web site is designed for anyone with access to the Internet, from high-level computer users to novices. Dynamic HTML (DHTML) and JavaScript are used to enhance site navigation via drop-down and expanding menus, floating windows, and graphical effects. Interactive features (such as specialized search engines and automated listserv subscription forms) and sophisticated, secure e-commerce software are used to expedite the delivery of information and goods to our visitors. We use special software allowing visitors to register and provide information that is used to personalize their visit by delivering content based on their interests and role in the philanthropic field. The Foundation Center is also in the process of making its Web site more accessible to those with disabilities. While the site has been designed to accommodate as many visitors as possible, across as many computer platforms as possible, we recommend using the latest version of either Microsoft's Internet Explorer or Netscape's Navigator to browse the site.

An Overview of the Foundation Center's Web Site

The Foundation Center's Web site (http://fdncenter.org) greets you with an informative and attractive home page designed to quickly guide you to the information you seek. As our tagline, "Helping grantseekers succeed; helping grantmakers make a difference," states, the site is designed to aid grantseekers and grantmakers by providing specific tools and directed information according to the needs of each visitor.

Orientation Tools on the Center's Web Site

To familiarize yourself with the layout of our site and to find the specific information you're looking for, you may find it helpful to click one of our three site orientation tools: the Guided Tour of the Foundation Center's Web Site, the Site Map, and the Site-Wide Search.

The Guided Tour of the Foundation Center's Web Site can be found in the Virtual Classroom section of the Learning Lab directory. This feature, complete with screen shots of the site's main pages, provides an overview of what you can expect to find throughout our site. Visitors can choose to view the information either in a few small, sequential steps or in a print-friendly format with all of the content appearing on a single page.

The Site Map, which is accessible from the left menu and the bottom of almost every page of the site, presents the layout of the site at a glance. Each main directory and its associated subdirectories are listed, including the individual Web sites of each of the Center's five libraries.

The Site-Wide Search is located at the bottom of the right column of the Center's home page. It is also in the SearchZone, which is accessible from the left menu and the bottom of almost every page on the main site. The Site-Wide Search function enables you to enter a word or phrase in a search window. The search engine will search all the text on the Center's site (with the exception of *PND* and the Marketplace, which have their own search functions) for the keywords you entered and display the results as links with summaries.

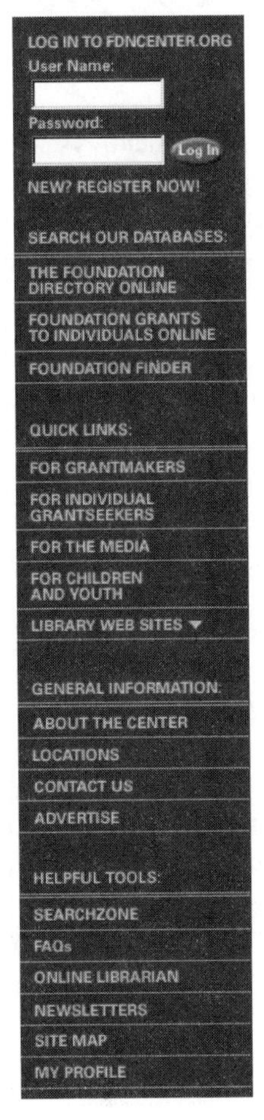

Links to the five main directories of the site—*Philanthropy New Digest (PND),* Finding Funders, Learning Lab, Researching Philanthropy, and Marketplace—are located in the gray menu at the top of the page. Placing your cursor over the name of each directory on the top navigation bar will open a drop-down menu of more specific areas within that directory. You can either click on the name of the directory heading itself, which will take you to that directory's main page with an index of links for the content within the directory, or click on one of the specific areas from the drop-down menu, which will take you directly to that area. Once you travel to a particular directory, the first menu in the left column will pertain to that specific directory, but the navigation bars at the top of the page will remain the same. Exceptions to this are *PND* and the Marketplace, which are self-contained sites, each with its own navigational framework. Both of these areas have links back to the Foundation Center's main site, indicated as FC Home.

At the top of the left-hand column of our home page, you will find a log-in box and a link to our new registration area. Registered visitors who are logged into the Center's Web site will find content delivered to them based on their interests, location, and role in the field of philanthropy. Visitors who are logged in will see their name displayed instead of the log-in box. Registration is free and takes only a few moments. If you have "cookies" enabled in your Web browser, you will be automatically logged in to our Web site the next time you visit using the same computer. More details about the new personalized features of our Web site will be described as we continue our tour of the Center's Web site in this chapter.

Below the log-in box, you will find links to some of the most widely used and essential features of our site, such as *The Foundation Directory Online* and *Foundation Grants to Individuals Online*, our fee-based subscription services, and our free Foundation Finder lookup tool. The left menu also includes Quick Links to areas of the site created for specific audiences: For Grantmakers, For Individual Grantseekers, For the Media, and For Children and Youth. Clicking on Library Web Sites will expand a menu of links to the Web sites of each of the five Foundation Center libraries and our Cooperating Collections (libraries around the country that collaborate with us by making copies of the Foundation Center's key research tools available to the public). The Quick Links menu appears on nearly every page of the site.

General Information links—About the Center, Locations, Contact Us, and Advertise—provide access to key information for those seeking more details about the Foundation Center.

The last grouping of links in the left menu is another universal set of links appearing on nearly every page of the main Web site. These links are designed to aid your general understanding of our work and our site, and they include: SearchZone, FAQs, Online Librarian, Newsletters, Site Map, and My Profile. The SearchZone provides access to all search mechanisms on the Center's Web site from a central location. In addition to providing visitors with the ability to search our Web site using the Site-Wide Search, we have created a number of specialized tools to aid you in finding the information you need. The FAQs (Frequently Asked Questions) link provides access to the answers to more than 125 questions about funding research, nonprofit management, the Foundation Center, and more, with the 15 most frequently asked questions listed first. First-time visitors will find this area especially valuable. If you are unable to find the answer to a question, you can contact the Online Librarian, a free service that responds to reference questions via e-mail. Visit our Newsletters subscription page to subscribe to the Center's various free electronic newsletters, and check the Site Map if you are having difficulty locating a particular piece of information. Follow the My Profile link to update your personalization profile or to register, if you haven't done so already.

The Foundation Center's home page not only provides quick navigation to the rest of the site, but also offers a wealth of information that is continually changing. Registered visitors will find a personalized greeting and a special navigation box guiding them to helpful areas of the site based on their registration information. The home page also announces the latest developments at the Foundation Center, such as research findings, new products and services, and upcoming training programs for grantseekers, which are personalized, if possible, to your profile. Daily highlights from *Philanthropy News Digest* include the latest headlines, requests for proposals, and job opportunities in the nonprofit sector. If you have registered, you will also find a link to My PND, which delivers the latest news and special features pertaining to your areas of interest and geographic location. Finally, our Fact of the Day offers an interesting and informative new fact about philanthropy with related links each day. Following the links in any of these sections will take you to more detailed information.

A menu appears at the bottom of every page with links back to the main sections of the site. In this menu, you will also find a Feedback link. If you are a first-time visitor to the site or have an observation to share, follow this link and fill out a form to send an e-mail to the Center's Web Services staff.

Most visitors to the Foundation Center's Web site have a particular question in mind that they hope will be answered over the course of their online research. In the remainder of this chapter, we'll address many of these questions and point out the best places on the Center's site to find answers.

"I'm new to the grantseeking process. How do I begin?"

The Learning Lab (http://fdncenter.org/learn) should be your first stop if you want to learn about the grantseeking process—or simply brush up on your fundraising skills.

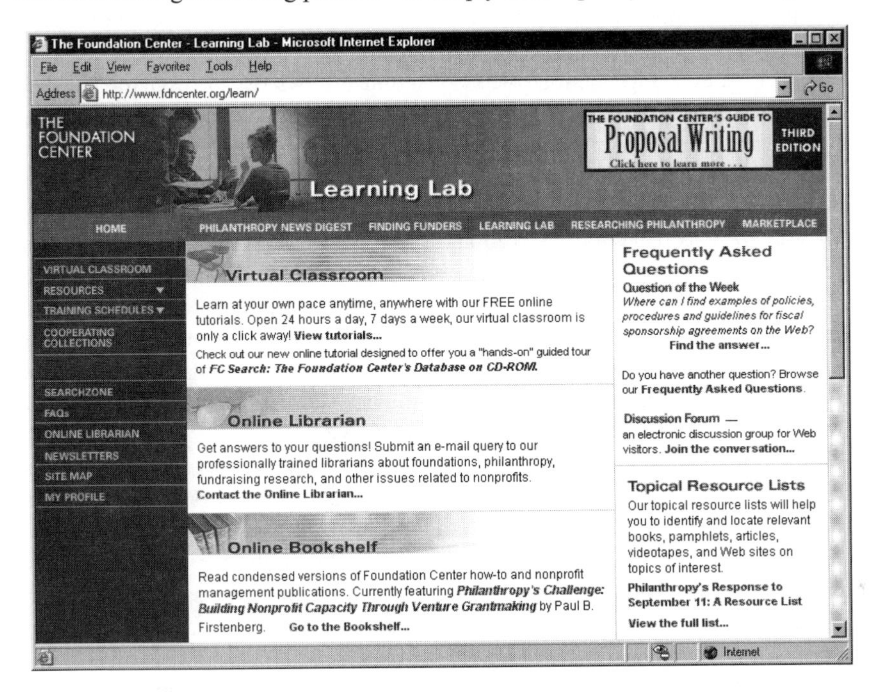

The Learning Lab area of the Center's Web site is an important venue for providing this education. While our libraries provide training to thousands of grantseekers each year, our Web site provides valuable education on philanthropy to many more, regardless of their geographic location. In addition to educational resources designed especially for grantseekers, our Web site also contains material that is helpful to grantmakers and the general public.

One of the Learning Lab's main offerings is the Virtual Classroom, where site visitors can take advantage of a variety of Web-based tutorials. If you are new to our site, start with the Guided Tour of the Foundation Center's Web Site. It provides a quick overview of the main directories of the site.

Also in the Virtual Classroom are two resources that new grantseekers will find particularly useful. These are the Online Orientation to the Grantseeking Process and the Guide to Funding Research. The Online Orientation to the Grantseeking Process introduces you, step by step, to the process of seeking funding from foundations. The Orientation is designed in a linear format with a clear beginning and end, with links that guide you through it page by page; it will acquaint you with the following topics:

- What the Foundation Center is and the services we offer
- What a foundation is and how foundations typically operate
- Three approaches to funding research
- Who gets foundation grants
- What funders look for in a grantee
- What types of support grantmakers typically give
- How to establish a nonprofit organization
- How to find support available to individuals
- Effective tools for funding research
- Hints on proposal writing

After a general introduction, the Orientation follows two divergent paths: for individual grantseekers and for nonprofit organizational grantseekers. Following those paths, it branches further into specific tools, skills, and topics of interest. The Orientation provides several resources for further research on the Internet, as well as printed materials.

If you are familiar with the Web and the grantseeking process or have completed the Orientation, the Guide to Funding Research is a good refresher and reference as you conduct your research. The Guide to Funding Research contains much of the same information as the Orientation but offers more information on Foundation Center resources. The Guide to Funding Research also has a glossary of common terms you may encounter in the course of your foray into funding research. From its table of contents, you can choose just the subjects you want to review. In the contents, you will also see that you can print or view a single text file of the entire Guide. If you don't have regular access to a computer, you may want to consider printing the file for future reference.

Both the Orientation and the Guide to Funding Research offer a brief introduction to proposal writing, which is elaborated on in the Proposal Writing Short Course, also found in the Virtual Classroom. Use the Proposal Writing Short Course tutorial, also available in a Spanish language version, to get you through what can be a daunting process, and consider bookmarking it or saving it in your "favorites" so that you can refer to it each time you need to write a new proposal.

In the Virtual Classroom, you'll also find several other tutorials on more specific topics:

- Proposal Budgeting Basics—The basics of developing a project budget, an important component of the grant proposal.
- Demystifying the 990-PF—An overview of the content, accessibility, and value of Form 990-PF, the tax return filed by private foundations.
- *FC Search* Interactive Tour—A "hands-on" guided tour of *FC Search: The Foundation Center's Database on CD-ROM. FC Search* is a comprehensive, searchable CD-ROM database of active U.S. foundations, corporate giving programs, and grantmaking public charities and their associated grants.
- *FC Search* Guided Tour—Learn how *FC Search* can help you to target funding prospects from among the universe of U.S. grantmakers.

- Advanced *FC Search*: Strategies & Techniques—This online course is geared for advanced users of the Foundation Center's database of private U.S. funders. Learn how to create effective strategies and uncover hidden tips and little-known tricks that will maximize search results.
- Establishing a Nonprofit Organization—Learn 12 key tasks of establishing a nonprofit organization.
- Foundations Today Tutorial—Gain a better understanding of the foundation world through the use of statistical information.
- *LNPS* Online Guided Tour—*Literature of the Nonprofit Sector: The Foundation Center's Online Catalog with Abstracts (LNPS)* is a searchable database of the books, articles, and nonprofit resources on philanthropy, the foundation world, the nonprofit sector, voluntarism, and charitable giving, giving users unique access to the contents of the Center's five libraries.

In addition to the courses in the Virtual Classroom, the Learning Lab offers User Aids, practical guides listing print and electronic resources for nonprofit and individual grantseekers; the Online Bookshelf with condensed versions of Center publications available for free; Topical Resource Lists, which list timely resources on a variety of topics drawing from the Center's library collections and Web resources; and Training for Grantseekers, which provides links to the educational opportunities and training schedules at the Center's five libraries. Many of these classes are free. If you have a question, check the FAQs (Frequently Asked Questions). You may find that your question has already been answered here. Our more than 125 FAQs cover a wide variety of philanthropy- and fundraising-related subjects and provide references to useful print and electronic resources.

If you still haven't found the information you need, you can submit a question to the Online Librarian, a free service staffed by professionally trained librarians who will answer your questions about foundations, philanthropy, fundraising research, and other issues related to nonprofits. You will receive a response to your query via e-mail within approximately two business days.

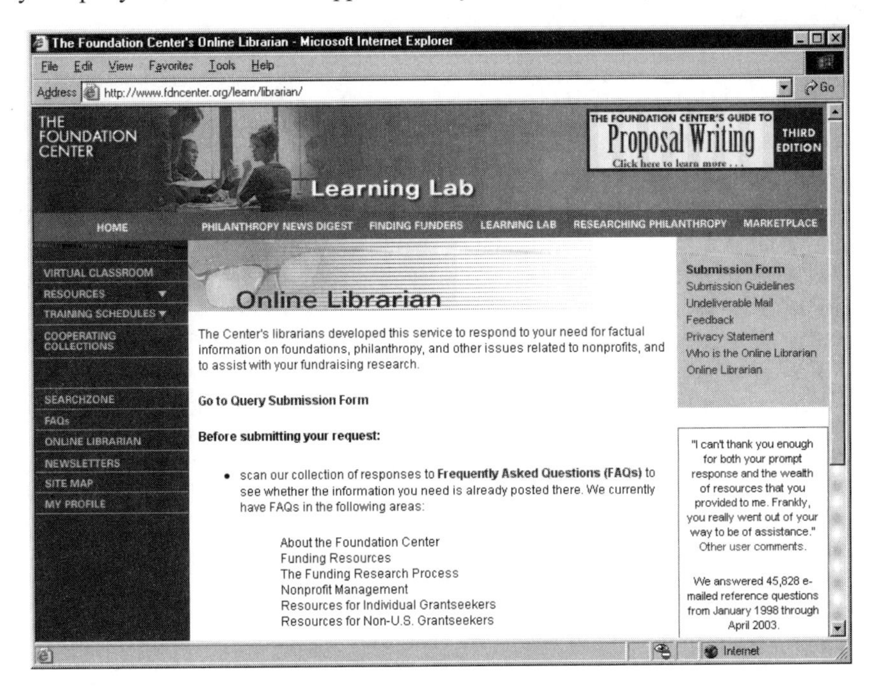

"How can I find information on the grantmakers that will fund me?"

If you are conducting research on potential funders, the Finding Funders directory (http://fdncenter.org/funders) is a natural place to start.

The Finding Funders directory provides you with the most current and accessible information about grantmakers. This information takes several forms and is based on data that is either gleaned from questionnaires sent to grantmakers by the Center, IRS returns, grantmaker publications, or culled from grantmaker Web sites. The various presentations of grantmaker information accommodate different research styles and needs.

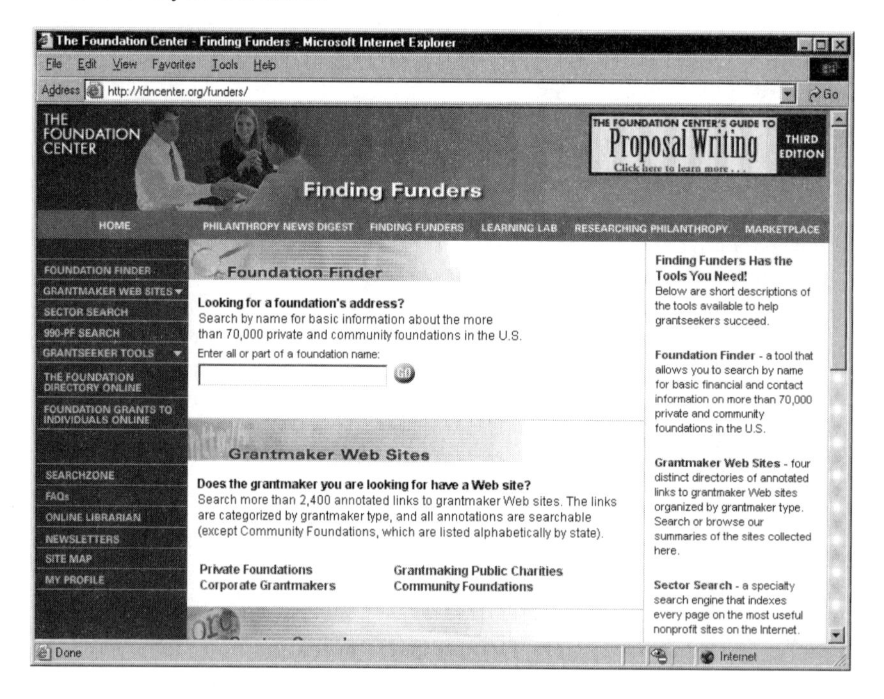

If you need information about a particular foundation, use Foundation Finder to look up basic information on more than 70,000 private and community foundations. In Foundation Finder, you must search for a foundation by entering its name or a portion of its name. Foundation Finder contains basic information extracted from the Center's comprehensive database of foundations—address, contact person, telephone number, fax number, e-mail address, Web address, basic financial data, type of foundation, and a link to its most recent Form 990-PF or private foundation tax return filed with the IRS. (Note: Not all elements will be available in each entry. For instance, a Form 990-PF or Web site may not be available for a particular grantmaker.) Foundation Finder also provides an update form allowing grantmakers to correct any outdated or erroneous information in their entries.

Detailed information about a particular grantmaker may be obtained by examining its Form 990-PF through Foundation Finder. The Form 990-PF is most useful for small or local foundations that do not have Web sites or printed guidelines, since private foundations are required to provide a complete grants listing in this return. Follow the PDF link in the Most Recent IRS Filing field of a foundation's entry, and then select the year of the Form 990-PF you would like to view. Returns will be downloaded as an Adobe PDF (Portable Document Format) file. To view these files it will be necessary to have the Adobe Acrobat Reader software (available as a free download at http://www.adobe.com/products/acrobat/readstep2.html). Since the length of a foundation's return can be several pages or several hundred pages, it might take a considerable time to download.

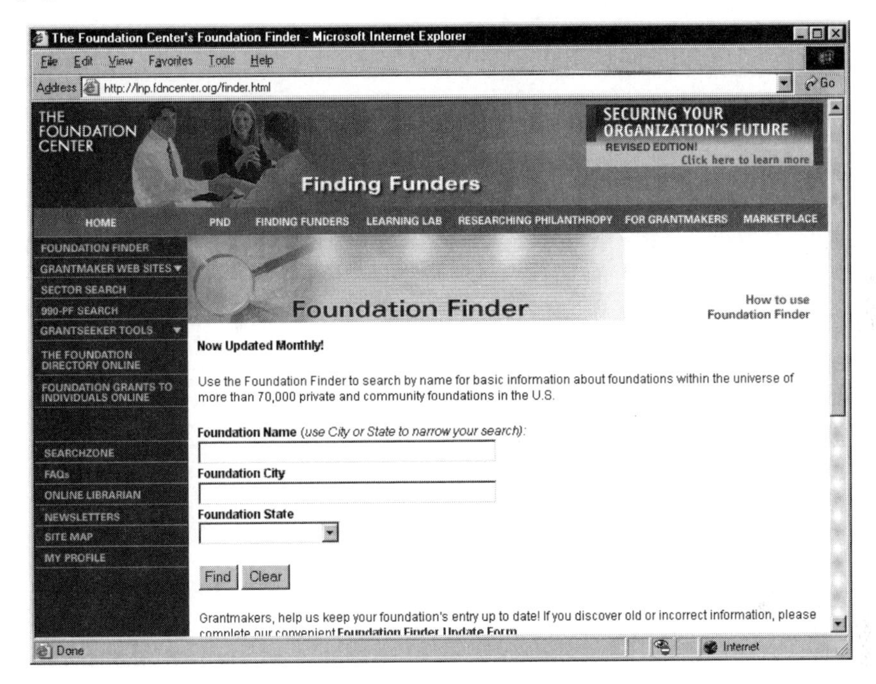

In addition to providing a link to a foundation's Form 990-PF in Foundation Finder, the Foundation Center's Web site provides links to these returns in individual *Foundation Directory Online* records and through 990-PF Search, which allows you to search by foundation name or employer identification number (EIN). Grantmaking public charities and community foundations (which are included in *The Foundation Directory Online,* but are technically public charities) do not file the Form 990-PF, so their returns are not available through the Foundation Center's Web site, though this may change in the future. A link to a diagram of the Form 990-PF, detailing where to find important information, can be found under Grantseeker Tools in the left menu of all pages in the Finding Funders directory and in Foundation Finder and 990-PF Search. A corresponding tutorial, Demystifying the 990-PF, can be found in the Learning Lab's Virtual Classroom.

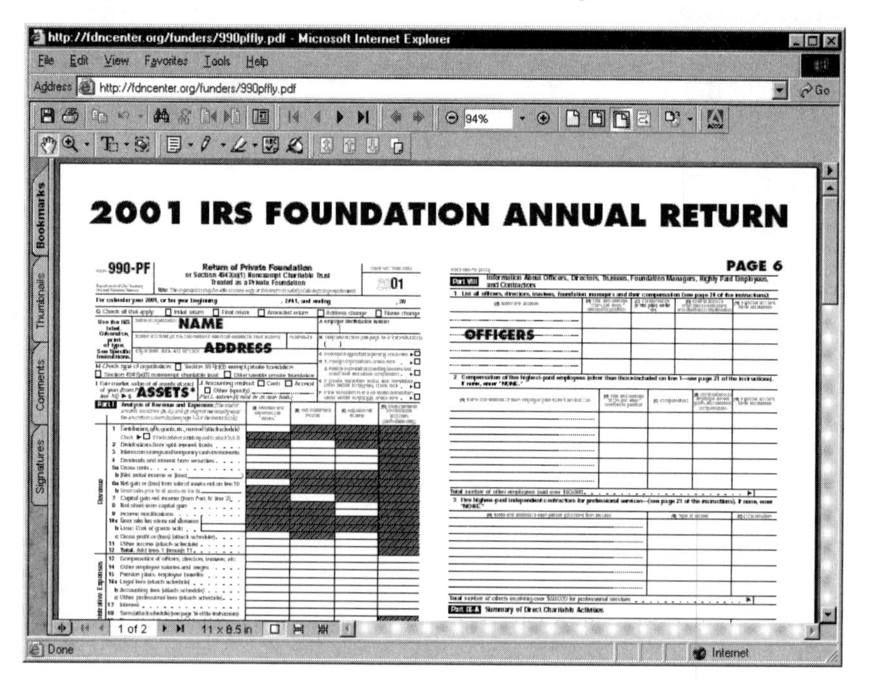

In the Finding Funders directory we also provide grantmaker information through Grantmaker Web Sites, a compendium of annotated links. Each grantmaker Web site is explored by a Foundation Center staff member, who then writes brief descriptions of the grantmakers' missions and Web site offerings. These sites are organized into four grantmaker types: private foundations, corporate grantmakers, grantmaking public charities, and community foundations. The first three categories offer alphabetical and searchable listings, and the fourth, community foundations, is organized by state. Searches of our annotated links will provide you with a list of grantmakers whose Web sites might warrant a visit in the course of your research. Links in Grantmaker Web Sites are updated at regular intervals, and new sites are added as we learn about them. For a complete listing of our annotated grantmaker links, see Appendices B, C, D, and E.

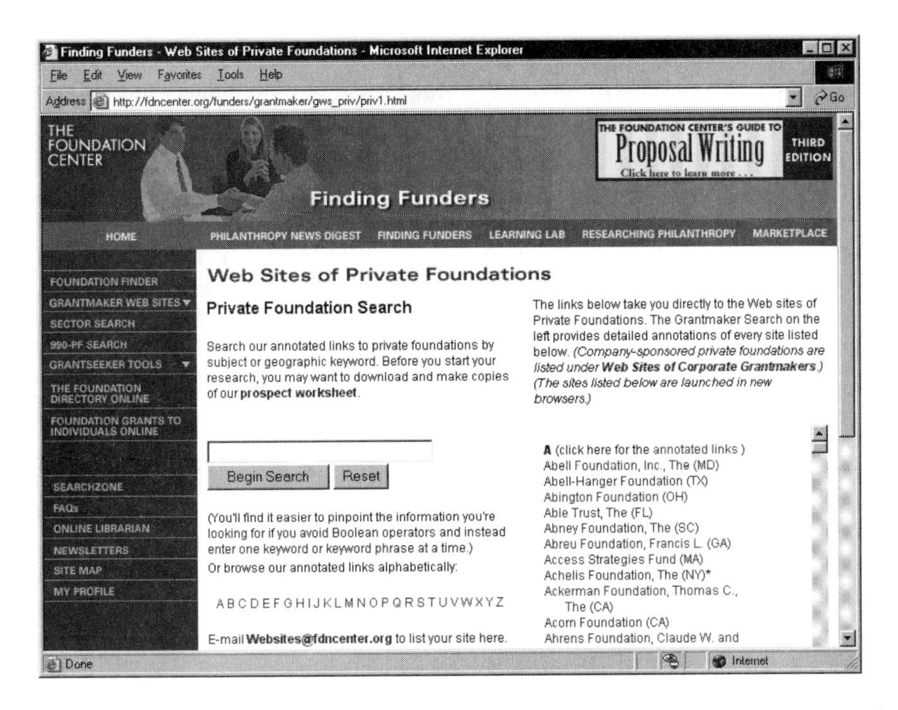

The layout of pages listing the Web sites of private foundations, corporate grantmakers, and grantmaking public charities is identical, and the same research strategies can be used in each section. If you are familiar with a particular grantmaker and would like to visit that grantmaker's Web site, the alphabetized name list on the right side of the screen provides direct links. If you have heard of a grantmaker but would like some preliminary information before visiting its Web site, select the first letter of the grantmaker's name from the alphabetical string in the middle-left of the page. From here you will find an alphabetical listing of grantmakers (whose names begin with the letter you have chosen), descriptions of the organizations and Web content, and links to their Web sites.

If you are looking for funders focusing on a particular subject area or geographic location, you will find the search feature most helpful. Enter keywords in the search box that describe the type of project you are seeking to fund, or enter the geographic location of the project, and click Begin Search. A list of grantmakers whose annotations contain the words that were searched on will be returned on the right side of the page. When you click on a grantmaker name in the search results list, you will find a description of the grantmaker and a link to its Web site. Click on the grantmaker name to visit its Web site.

Because community foundations offer grants within specific geographic regions, the foundations in this directory are organized by state. You should be able to identify easily those foundations in your geographic location.

Using our Sector Search you have the ability to search grantmaker and other Web sites themselves. With Sector Search, the Foundation Center has created an application that indexes information gathered from *only* the most useful nonprofit Web sites. Instead of trying to retrieve useful information from a search of the entire Web, we have programmed this software to search only the Web sites we have identified. Searches can be limited to the organization type you specify (private foundations, corporate grantmakers, grantmaking public charities, community foundations, nonprofits, or government resources), thus significantly increasing your chances of finding the information you are looking for. In addition to its usefulness for finding information on potential funders, Sector Search can also be used to find documents and resources used by other nonprofit organizations that can be adapted to meet your own needs. These documents and resources can include employee manuals, business plans, sample proposals, and more. You can search across all categories of organizations or narrow your search to just one category. For the greatest number of results, use broad search terms and conduct your search across all organizational categories. To narrow your search, use more specific search terms and select one organizational category within which to conduct your search. Since Sector Search will likely return a greater number of results than the annotation-based search of Grantmaker Web Sites, you may find you need to narrow your search terms when using this engine. Use the advanced search option or the Help File to help focus your search.

Both Sector Search and Grantmaker Web Sites will provide you with a list of grantmakers on the Web that are potential funders for your organization or project, although a final determination about that will require additional research. You should also be aware that you will likely need to consult additional resources, as only about three percent of grantmakers currently have Web sites. However, these research tools are quite useful if you have identified particular funders and you wish to explore their Web offerings.

To compile a more comprehensive and targeted list of potential funders, you might consider subscribing to either *The Foundation Directory Online* or *Foundation Grants to Individuals Online,* our searchable databases of the nation's foundations, corporate giving programs, and grantmaking public charities.

The Foundation Directory Online (http://fconline.fdncenter.org) allows searches across various indexed fields in conjunction with plain text searching to return targeted lists of funding prospects. Searches return grantmaker profiles that include address and contact information; Web site links (if available); fields of interest; types of support; names of donors, officers, trustees, and staff; financial information; links to Forms 990-PF; and more. *The Foundation Directory Online* is available in four subscription levels. The first level of service, *The Foundation Directory Online Basic,* contains current descriptions of 10,000 of the largest foundations in the United States. The second level of service, *The Foundation Directory Online Plus,* includes access to the database of 10,000 foundations, plus access to a grants database of information on more than 250,000 grants made by the top 1,200 foundations. In addition to searching grantmaker profiles, you can search the grants database to find grant recipient profiles including recipient, recipient location, recipient type, grantmaker, grant amount and description, and more. The third level, *The Foundation Directory Online Premium,* provides access to the grants file plus a database of the 20,000 largest foundations in the nation. The most comprehensive level of service, *The Foundation Directory Online Platinum,* provides access to the grants database, plus the Center's entire database of more than 74,000 grantmakers, including foundations, grantmaking public charities, and corporate givers. There are varying subscription fees for the different levels. Subscriptions to *The Foundation Directory Online* are offered at monthly and yearly rates.

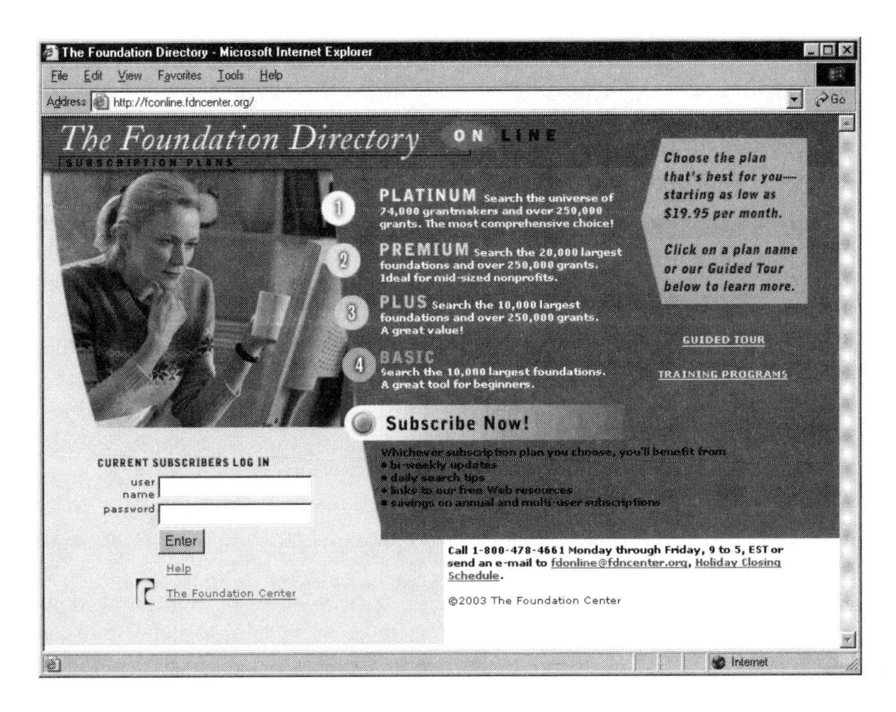

Foundation Grants to Individuals Online (http://gtionline.fdncenter.org) provides individual grantseekers with access to a database of more than 5,600 foundation and public charity programs that fund students, artists, researchers, and other individual grantseekers. If you are seeking funding for yourself, this unique online database will help you to compile a prospect list from a list of grantmakers that offer educational support (scholarships and student loans); arts and cultural support; awards, prizes, and grants by nomination; funding for international applicants and company employees; research and professional support; and assistance for general welfare and special needs. *Foundation Grants to Individuals Online* subscriptions are offered at monthly, three-month, and yearly subscription rates.

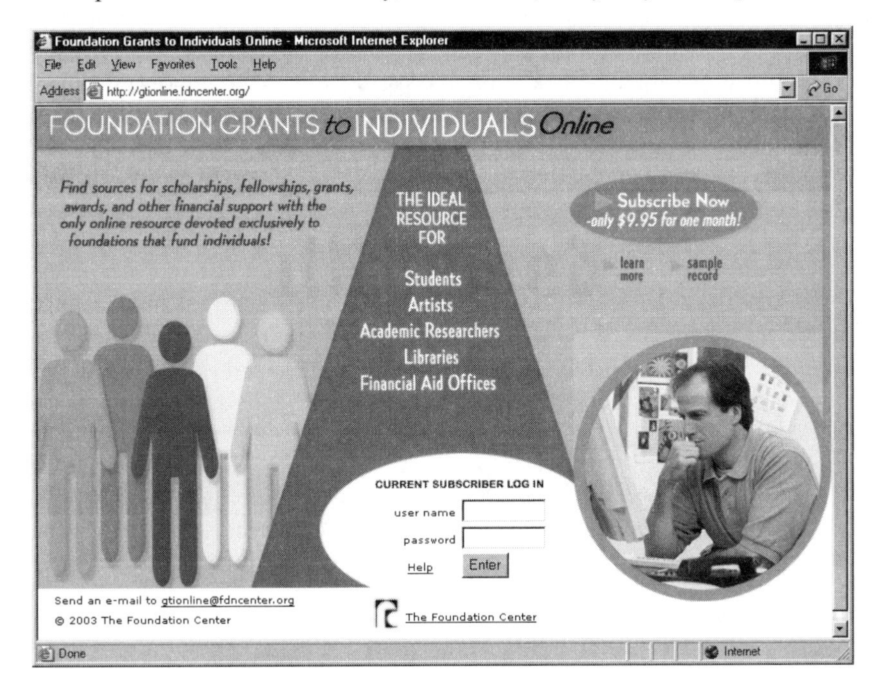

In the left menu of the Finding Funders directory, you will find Grantseeker Tools to help you organize your funding research. This expandable menu contains links to Common Grant Applications, Diagram of Form 990-PF, Prospect Worksheets, and the Proposal Writing Course (in English and in Spanish).

Common Grant Applications provides links to standard application forms used by grantmakers in various states or regions of the United States. The common grant application format has been adopted by groups of grantmakers to allow grant applicants to produce a single proposal for a specific community of funders, thereby saving time. Before applying to any funder that accepts a common grant application form, be sure to ascertain whether your project matches the funder's stated interests and whether the funder would prefer a letter of inquiry in advance of receiving an application form. Also be sure to check whether the funder has a deadline for proposals, as well as whether it requires multiple copies of your application.

As mentioned earlier, our Diagram of Form 990-PF shows you at-a-glance what information you will find on a foundation's tax return and where key information is located.

The Prospect Worksheets are simple forms to download before starting your research to help keep you organized and focused. We have provided versions of the worksheet for prospecting institutional and individual donors, and each is available in a format convenient to you. Forms to fill in on your computer are provided in Rich Text Format, Microsoft Word 95, and Microsoft Word 2000 formats. Forms to print out, copy, and complete by hand are provided in Adobe PDF format. As you locate funders whose priorities seem to closely match your project, fill out a prospect worksheet for each one. The prospect worksheet will help you match the goals and needs of your project with the goals and interests of funders. Use this tool to record financial data; subject focus; geographic limits; types of support; populations served; the names of officers, donors, trustees, and staff; application information; sources from which you gathered information about the funder; notes; and follow-up communications.

The Proposal Writing Short Course will help you through the process of writing your proposal once you've identified a list of prospective funders. Although we've provided a link to the course in Finding Funders for convenience, it is actually located in the Learning Lab's Virtual Classroom. Further information about instruction in proposal writing can be found in our libraries and the Marketplace.

One final resource you may wish to consult when seeking potential funders is the RFP Bulletin in *Philanthropy News Digest.* RFPs (requests for proposals) are often made by grantmakers who wish to attract applicants with specific types of projects they are interested in funding. New RFPs are posted to the site daily. Each listing provides a brief overview of a current funding opportunity—including application deadline and a link to the full RFP description—offered by a foundation or other grantmaking organization. Interested applicants should read the full RFP at the grantmaker's Web site or contact the grantmaker directly for complete program guidelines and eligibility requirements before submitting a proposal. In addition to being posted online, the content of the RFP Bulletin is available in the form of a free, weekly electronic newsletter. If you would like to subscribe, you may do so by entering your e-mail address in the subscribe box of any page of the RFP Bulletin or by clicking on the Newsletters link on the main Foundation Center Web site.

"How can I keep current with what's happening in philanthropy today?"

Philanthropy News Digest (*PND*) (http://fdncenter.org/pnd) is the Foundation Center's online news journal offering daily philanthropy news, interviews, book and Web site reviews, nonprofit spotlights, a conference calendar, requests for proposals, and nonprofit job opportunities.

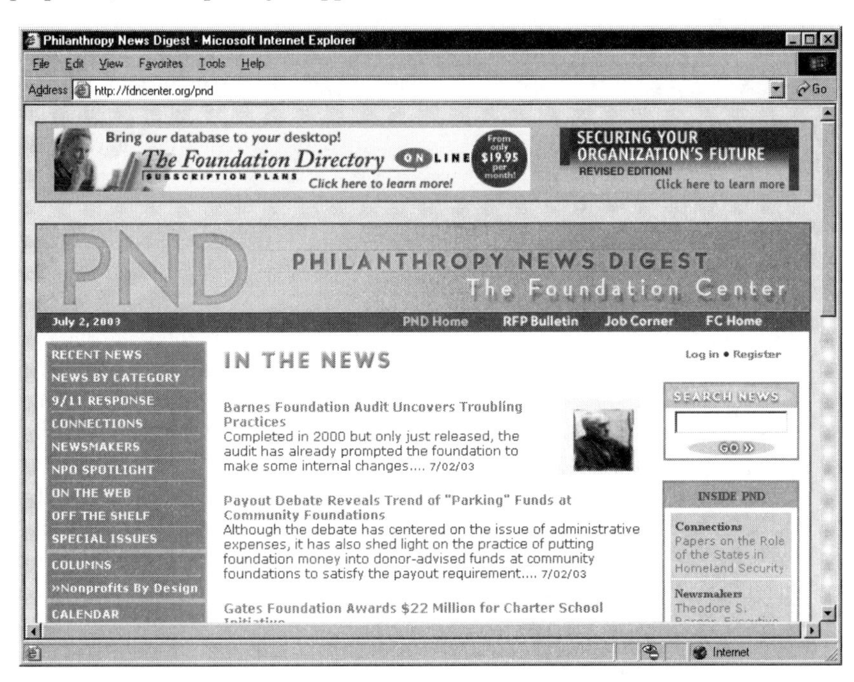

The *PND* home page features the top two or three philanthropy news stories of the day followed by news headlines sorted by subject area from the previous four days. Menus at the top and left of the page provide navigation to the RFP Bulletin, Job Corner, and other *PND* features. Log In and Register links are provided for visitors interested in viewing *PND* news and features pertaining to their interests and location; a search box allows searching of news and special features; and Inside *PND* offers highlights of what you'll find in *PND* on any given day.

PND's news service is a compendium of philanthropy-related articles and features culled from print and electronic media outlets nationwide. News articles are posted daily on the Web site. Clicking on a news headline takes you to an abstracted version of the story, with a citation to the print or electronic source. If you would like *PND* delivered to your e-mail box every Tuesday evening, just enter your e-mail address into the subscription box provided on each *PND* page and click the Add Me button.

In addition to the news service, *PND* offers a wealth of information about philanthropy and the nonprofit sector. *PND*'s Newsmakers column features interviews with influential figures in the field of philanthropy. NPO Spotlight highlights the interests and activities of a different nonprofit organization each week. Connections presents links to the best the Web has to offer on issues related to the changing world of philanthropy. (*Connections* is now available as a biweekly e-mail newsletter.) 9/11 Response features 9/11-related philanthropy news items, interviews, and more. People seeking to continue their professional development, network with other nonprofit representatives, or learn more about the field of philanthropy may find it worthwhile to visit the Conference Calendar, which gives the location, date, and Web address of various philanthropy-related events. Finally, *PND*'s Off the Shelf (book reviews) and On the Web (Web site reviews) sections provide recommendations of the latest online and print offerings in the nonprofit field.

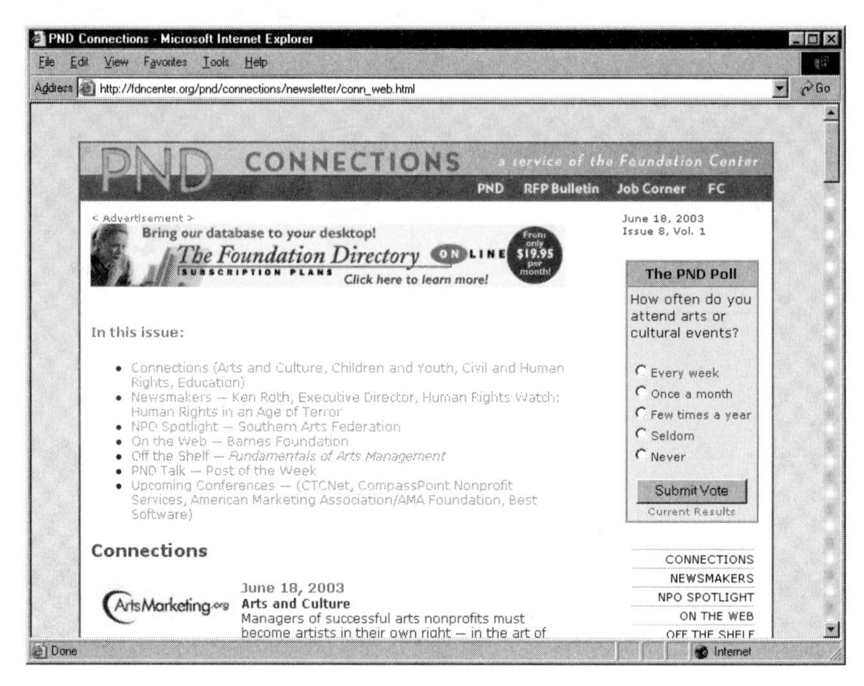

Visitors who have registered and are logged in to the site will find a My PND menu item on the *PND* home page. Follow the My PND link to view links to news, RFPs, job listings, and other content that relates to your top areas of interest and your geographic location. You can easily change your specified interest by clicking Edit Profile on the My PND page.

PND news and features from January 2001 to the present can be searched by entering a keyword in the search box that appears on every page of *PND*. Results of your search will list the titles of abstracts in which your search terms appear, in chronological order (from most recent to oldest). Follow the Archives link to search a separate historical archive of news from January 1995 to December 2000.

PND also publishes periodic special issues focusing on particular topics of interest to nonprofit organizations. Past topics have included international philanthropy, health, organizational effectiveness, arts, children and youth, celebrating philanthropy, and technology. And you can share opinions, insights, and questions related to the field of philanthropy with your peers on the PND Talk and ArtsTalk discussion boards.

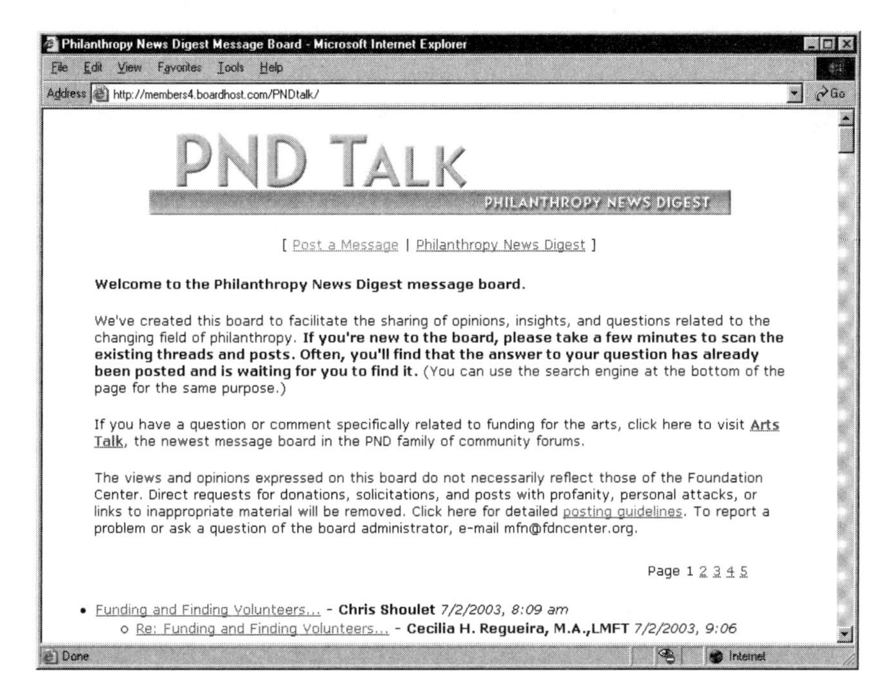

Nonprofit job seekers will find it very helpful to visit the Job Corner, which announces current full-time job openings at U.S. foundations, grantmaking public charities, and other nonprofit organizations. Jobs can be searched by organizational type, job function, state, or keyword. The Job Corner is also available via free subscription as a weekly electronic newsletter.

"I'm looking for statistics on foundation giving. Where can I find this information?"

Many excellent resources focusing on foundation giving can be found in the Researching Philanthropy directory (http://fdncenter.org/research) of the site.

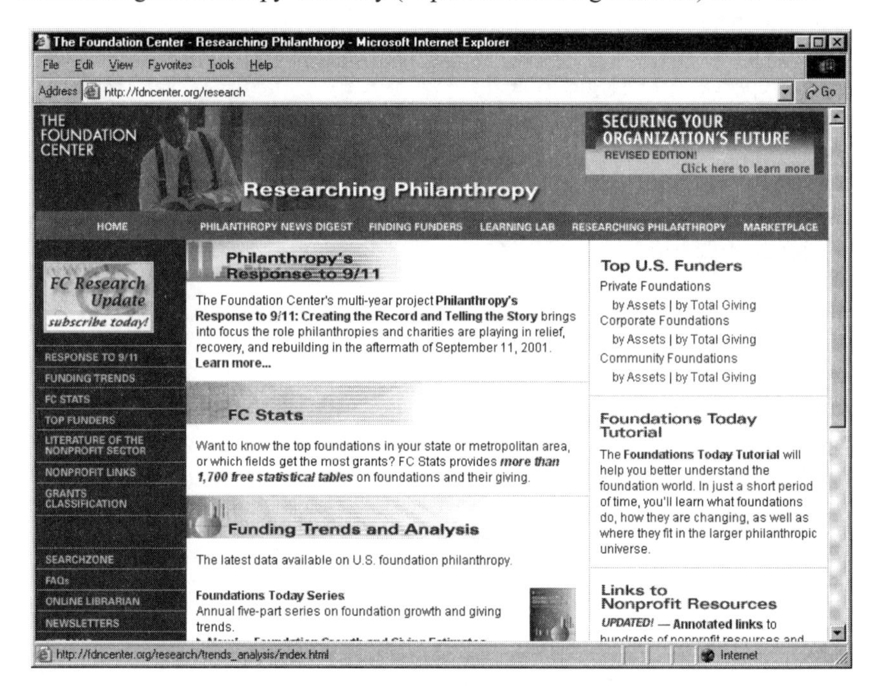

One of the most useful tools in the Researching Philanthropy directory is FC Stats, a free resource that provides a wealth of statistical data on U.S. private and community foundations and their funding patterns. FC Stats is produced from the Center's research database, the authoritative national statistical data source on grantmaking foundations. FC Stats currently offers close to 2,000 data tables available only from the Foundation Center going back to 1997 (1997 tables are grantmaker statistics only). These tables and ranked lists provide the most frequently requested types of summary financial data on foundations. FC Stats contains a menu of the broad categories of grantmaker and grant statistics available on our Web site. To view a list of available statistics, make a selection from the menu, which includes a link to the full listing of available tables. Some menu selections (e.g., geographic or subject areas) will display additional lists from which to choose the appropriate data table. Tables are available as Adobe PDF files. The Foundation Center also offers fee-based custom statistical searches of our research database to grantmakers, journalists, academic researchers, and others who are seeking tailored information on trends in the foundation field. To find out more about ordering a customized search, select About FC Stats.

The Funding Trends and Analysis area within the Researching Philanthropy directory will help to familiarize you with the foundation world and broad giving trends. For instance, information in this directory will give you a sense of what percentage of foundation funding is going to organizations in your area of interest or geographic location. In the Funding Trends area you can find and view highlights and excerpts of Center research publications, like the *Foundations Today* series, a yearly five-part series on foundation growth and giving trends, and other special reports. All are available in PDF format, and press releases are also available.

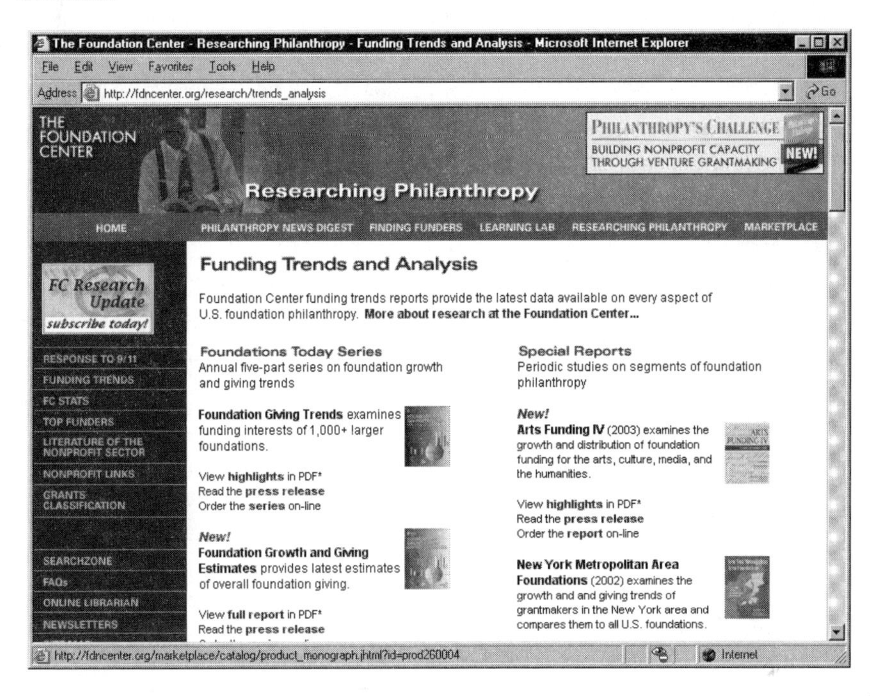

Visitors to the Researching Philanthropy directory can also view our Top U.S. Funders lists, which include snapshot rankings of U.S. grantmakers pulled from the most current information available in the Center's database. Updated quarterly and sorted by asset size as well as by total giving, lists are provided of the top 100 private foundations, the top 50 corporate grantmakers, and the top 25 community foundations.

Another valuable research tool is the *Literature of the Nonprofit Sector (LNPS). LNPS,* an online version of the Center's library catalog, is a searchable database of the literature of philanthropy, and comprises the holdings of the Foundation Center's five libraries. *LNPS* contains some 22,000 full bibliographic citations, of which more than two-thirds or 14,500 have descriptive abstracts, and is updated on a continuous basis as our libraries' holdings are updated. *LNPS* also includes links to the full-text of selected journal articles. To further assist you in your research, there are New Acquisitions lists by subject—including books, articles, videos, and other resources recently added to our collections. The following screen shot shows what a search might look like if you wanted, for example, articles from our New York library, published since 2000, on collaboration among nonprofit organizations.

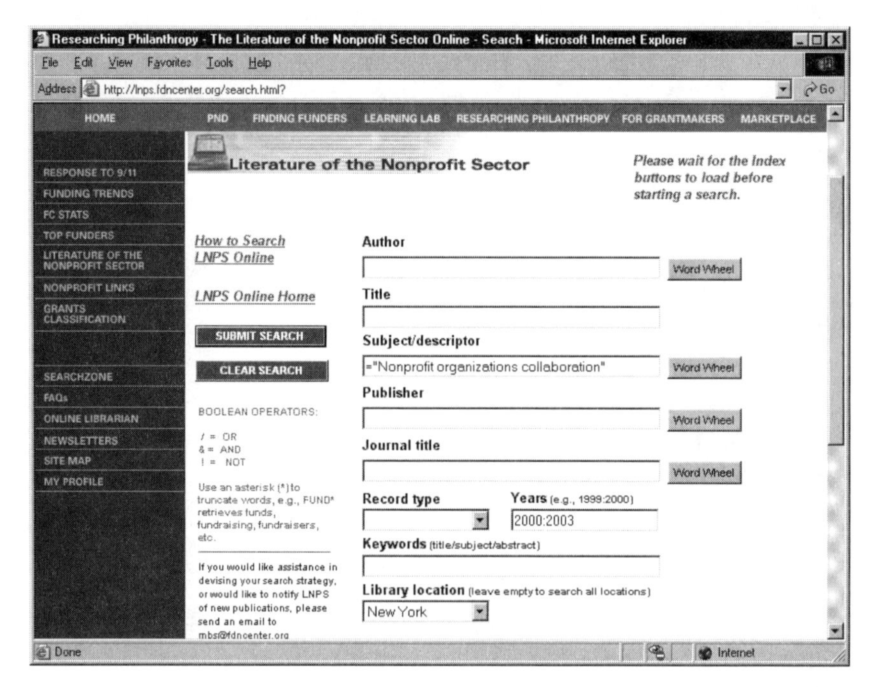

In Researching Philanthropy's Links to Nonprofit Resources, we have selectively gathered and annotated links to the most useful Web sites serving the nonprofit sector. The links include information and resources on the topics of philanthropy, fundraising, nonprofit news, nonprofit management, technology, public interest and policy, government, and international philanthropy. You will also find a listing of nonprofit organizations specializing in specific program areas. See Chapter 8, "Other Useful Sites for Grantseekers," for a sampling of some of the sites contained in the Center's Links to Nonprofit Resources section, and see Appendix F for a complete listing of these sites.

Finally, the Researching Philanthropy directory houses our Grants Classification Manual, which describes our grants indexing procedures in detail. In 1989, the Foundation Center adopted a classification system derived from the National Taxonomy of Exempt Entities (NTEE), a comprehensive coding scheme developed by the National Center for Charitable Statistics. NTEE establishes a unified national standard for classifying nonprofit organizations; it also provides a more concise and consistent hierarchical method to classify and index grants. NTEE uses two- or three-character alphanumeric codes to track institutional fields and entities, governance or auspices, population groups, and religious affiliations. The universe of institutional fields is organized into 26 "major field" areas. While based on NTEE, the Foundation Center's grants classification system added indexing elements not part of the original taxonomy, including sets of codes to classify types of support, population groups served, and for international grants, geographic focus, and recipient country.

"I'm seeking funding for myself as an individual, where do I look?"

While the vast majority of foundation grants are awarded to nonprofit organizations rather than to individuals, individual grantseekers make up approximately 20 to 30 percent of visitors to our Web site and libraries. To assist them with their research, we have created an area of our site called For Individual Grantseekers.

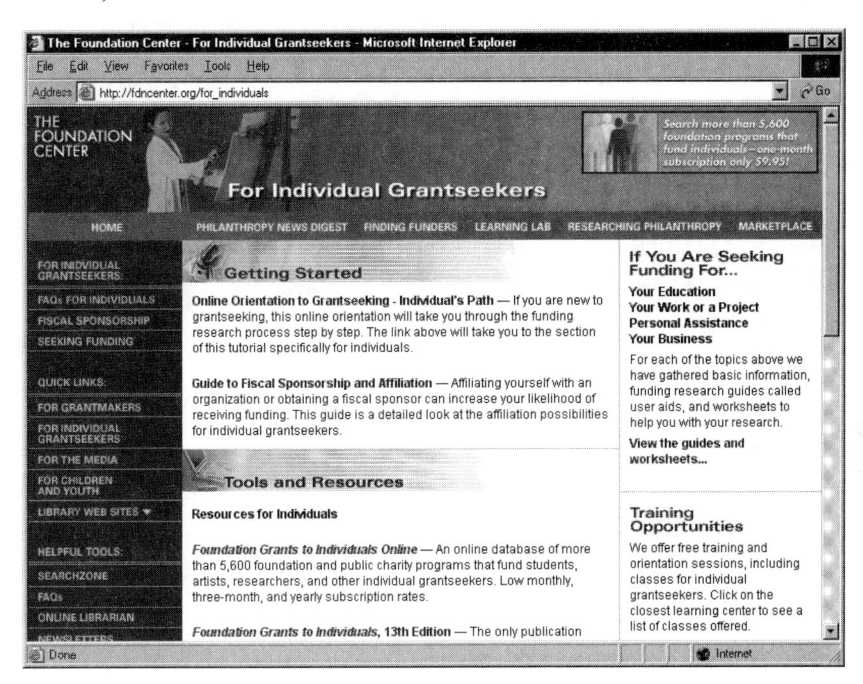

In this special new directory, we have organized and provided direct links to the relevant materials available at our site for individuals. For Individual Grantseekers provides direct access to three key tools: our Online Orientation to the Grantseeking Process, which has a learning path specifically for individuals; *Foundation Grants to Individuals Online,* an online database of more than 5,600 foundation and public charity programs that fund students, artists, researchers, and other individual grantseekers; and an online guide, excerpted from Judith B. Margolin's *The Individual's Guide to Grants,* about fiscal sponsorship and affiliation, which can be a crucial part of an individual's strategy in seeking funding.

This new area of our Web site also answers frequently asked questions and provides information on the various kinds of funding individuals seek, along with links to User Aids listing resources for individuals in specific populations or professions. Individual grantseekers will also find links, tools, and worksheets that will add structure to their funding research; information about free training for individuals in our libraries; and information about what sort of funding is likely (or unlikely) to be available to them.

"I represent a grantmaking organization. What does the Center's site offer me?"

While many of the Foundation Center's resources and services cater to grantseekers, grantmakers are an important audience as well. If you represent a grantmaking organization, our For Grantmakers directory (http://fdncenter.org/for_grantmakers) will answer your questions and help you to stay current, spread the word about your organization, direct you to services designed to assist you in your work, and refer your grantees to appropriate resources. Several of the key elements in the directory are described here.

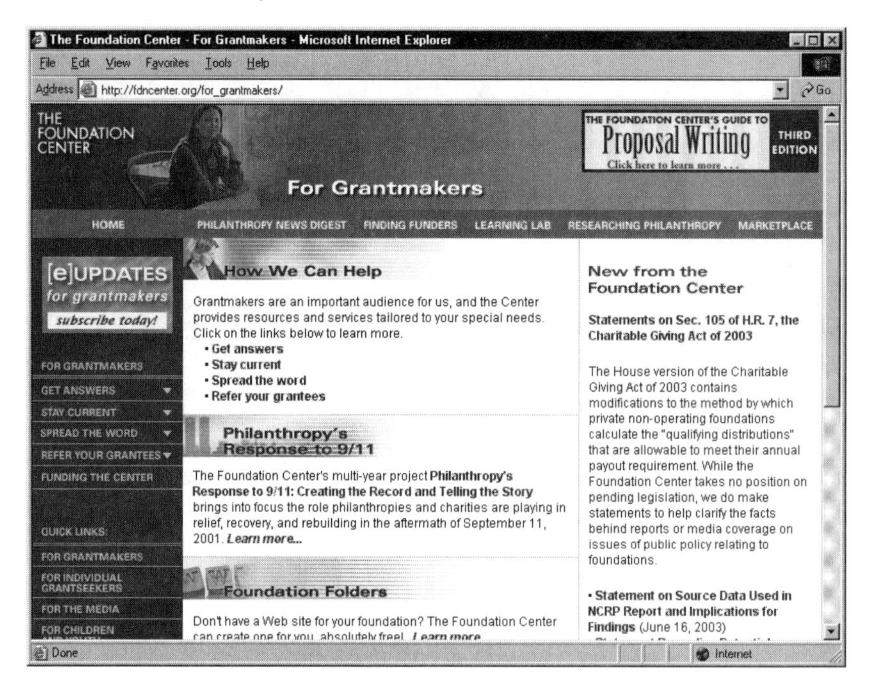

GET ANSWERS

To answer your questions about the Foundation Center and its offerings, we have compiled a special list of Grantmakers' FAQs that may prove useful to you. You may also e-mail reference questions to our Online Librarian, who will respond to you, typically within one to two business days. Or you can call our Grantmaker Services hotline at 1-212-807-2446.

The Foundation Center also offers custom searches of our research database, designed according to your specifications. These searches can help you prepare a report for your board, identify funding partners, research philanthropic assets and giving in your locality, investigate possible new areas of funding activity, and identify potential grantees. There is a charge for this service based on the data requested and staff time required. Donors to the Foundation Center receive a discount.

We have also compiled a list of Web-based resources for grantmakers in our Other Helpful Links. This is a series of annotated links sorted into categories, such as philanthropy resources, nonprofit resources, and government resources. Web sites of regional associations of grantmakers (RAGs) and other grantmaker membership organizations are accessible from this listing.

STAY CURRENT

E-Updates for Grantmakers is a free service exclusively for grantmakers that delivers news of particular interest directly to your computer. This monthly e-mail update features new publications and research reports, links to articles and resources, and announcements of upcoming events.

The Center's research studies will keep you current about the activities of your fellow grantmakers and trends in the field. Our annual five-part series of reports, *Foundations Today,* provides the latest information on foundation growth and trends in foundation giving. The Center also issues reports on grantmaking in specific subject areas and on regional giving. You can review key findings and excerpts of our research studies online or order the complete reports in the Marketplace.

SPREAD THE WORD

The Foundation Center is the place to find information and to communicate about philanthropy. Our materials are used by grantseekers, the media, policymakers, and researchers to learn about funding programs and activities. As part of your efforts to present the work of your grantmaking organization, we encourage you to send us information about your funding programs and grants for distribution through our print and electronic publications and our Web site.

From your desktop, you can update the information about your grantmaking organization seen by the thousands of Web visitors who use Foundation Finder or who subscribe to *The Foundation Directory Online.* Our *Foundation Directory Online* Updater can be accessed by selecting the Update Your Own Info link under Spread the Word from the menu on the left of the For Grantmakers directory.

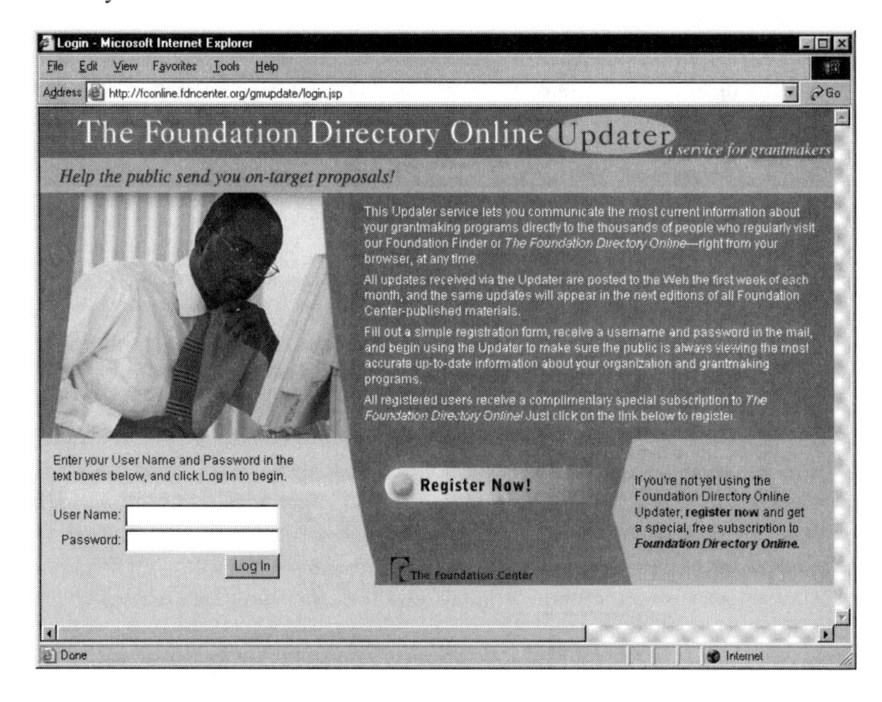

Electronic grants lists are an efficient way to send us specific grants information as it is described in your own systems. Several commercial software vendors have grants-tracking products that fully support our electronic grants reporting standard, but we can accept a variety of other electronic formats as well. If you are preparing to convert to a new system, we can also advise you on how to join with other foundations in adopting our classification system for your own grant records. To find out more about electronic reporting or grants classification, click on the Send E-Grants Lists link under Spread the Word from the left menu.

To help foundations spread information in their own words and make funding information accessible to a wider audience, the Foundation Center creates free Web sites for eligible grantmakers as part of our Foundation Folders initiative. Any domestic independent, community, or company-sponsored foundation can have a Web site (a.k.a., Foundation Folder) hosted on the Center's Web server at no charge. At this writing, the Foundation Center maintains sites for more than 100 grantmakers. At a foundation's request, we will also scan and post its Form 990-PF, helping the foundation meet IRS regulations for making this document widely available to the public. (For more information on the Foundation Center's Foundation Folders initiative, see p. 40.) The following screenshot shows a Foundation Folder Web site created and hosted by the Foundation Center.

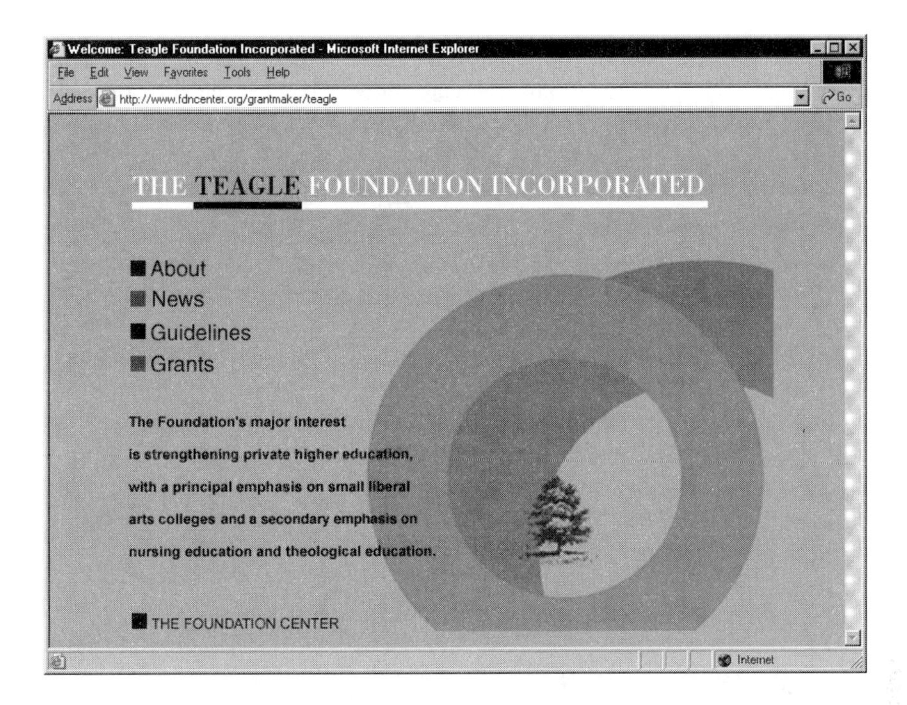

Other services that will help you get the word out include mailing labels (available at a reasonable fee) to help you distribute materials, such as annual reports and press releases, to other grantmakers. As part of *PND's* RFP Bulletin, the Center will post your requests for proposals, which are organized on our site by subject area and are removed automatically when the deadline has passed. *PND* also features a Job Corner where you can list current full-time job openings at your organization. Instructions for submitting RFPs or job opportunities are posted in *PND.*

REFER YOUR GRANTEES

We encourage you to refer nonprofit organizations to our Web site or to our libraries for information and education about grantseeking and related topics. The For Grantmakers directory provides direct links to full descriptions of the services provided in our libraries and in our vast nationwide network of Cooperating Collections—libraries that provide free use of core Center materials to those outside the locations where we have libraries. Included among those services are a variety of training and education programs to instruct grantseekers in the funding research process.

Free brochures describing our extensive services to grantseekers are available for you to send on to applicants whose projects your foundation is unable to fund or to grantees that need to research additional funding sources.

The For Grantmakers area also provides information on how grantmakers can help the Foundation Center continue to carry out its mission. For this purpose, we have developed an area called Funding the Center that contains information about the Center's operations, services, and resources we provide to the nonprofit field. While we cover more than half of our operating budget through earned income, approximately 600 foundations and corporations provide annual support, which enables us to sustain and strengthen our existing programs. About 200 of our annual donors designate their gifts for one of our four regional offices. Special project grants permit us to develop new capacities for service.

"How can I learn about and/or purchase Foundation Center products?"

In addition to operating libraries that provide directories of grantmaker information, nonprofit literature collections, and other tools to assist grantseekers, the Foundation Center publishes and sells print and electronic publications and data about grantmakers, grantmaking in specific subject fields, nonprofit management, fundraising, and philanthropy, all of which can be ordered from the Marketplace (http://fdncenter.org/marketplace).

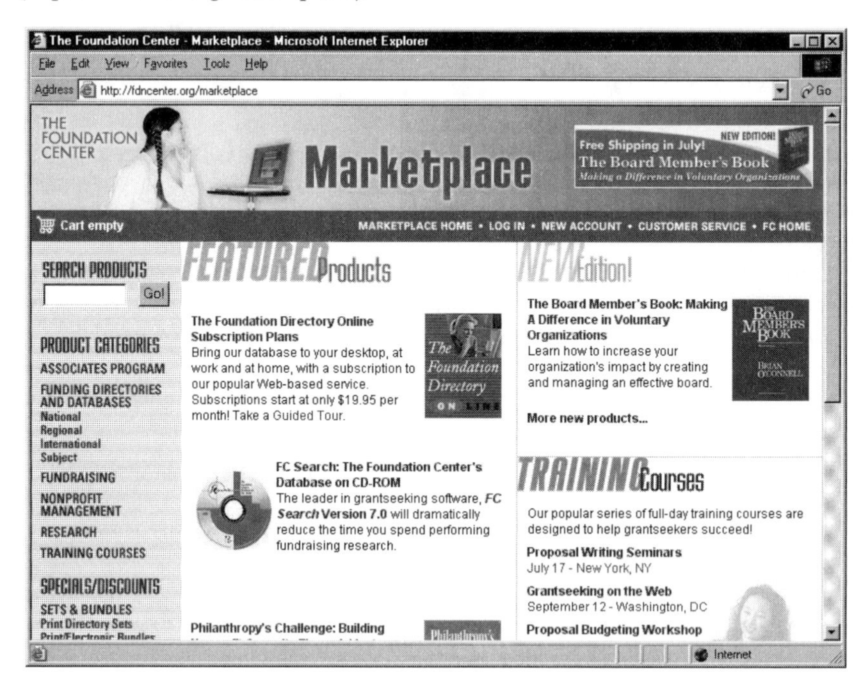

If you are not near a Center library or Cooperating Collection, or if you have an ongoing need for information on grantseeking, you may want to purchase Center products to continue your research. The Marketplace enables visitors to our Web site to review detailed descriptions of print and electronic products published by the Foundation Center.

If you have a particular title, author, or subject in mind, you can search our entire publications catalog by entering keywords into the Search Products box at the top of the left menu. Search results retrieved in response to the keywords you entered will take you directly to the categories and products whose descriptions best match your search terms. You can also browse listings by product category—Associates Program, Funding Directories and Databases (National, Regional, International, and Subject), Fundraising, Nonprofit Management, Research, and Training Courses.

Select the Training Courses link to learn about our full-day training programs. Online registration is available for all fee-based programs, which are offered in various cities throughout the country. Full-day training programs offered by the Center include:

- Proposal Writing Seminars
- Foundation Fundraising: An Introductory Course
- Developing a Fundraising Plan: Securing Your Organization's Future
- The Foundation Center's Proposal Budgeting Workshop
- Grantseeking on the Web Hands-on Introductory Training Course
- Evaluating Funding Prospects: Strategies for Finding a Match
- Funding Research with *FC Search* Training Course
- Finding Funding Prospects with *The Foundation Directory Online*

Grantseekers who desire assistance from the Center with custom prospect research may wish to consider joining our Associates Program. Associates Program membership is a cost-effective way to supplement your staff with additional fundraising support services. Our expert researchers access the most up-to-date information in the Center's publishing and Form 990-PF databases and in many other resources. To find out more, click on Associates Program at the top of the left menu.

Once you click on a product name, you will see a detailed description of the product along with its price and an Add to Cart button that lets you place the product in your Shopping Cart. The Shopping Cart holds all the items you put aside to purchase until you have finished shopping, and it lets you pay for them all at once via credit card on a secure server. You may change the desired quantity of each item in your shopping cart, and you may also remove an item by clicking the Remove box. Once you have completed any changes, click Recalculate before checking out.

Providing you with a secure online shopping experience is important to the Foundation Center. We recognize that security is an essential aspect of any online transaction, and we want to assure you that your credit card and personal information are safeguarded. To protect your credit card transaction, the Foundation Center uses industry-standard encryption software.

If you have a question while you are shopping or checking out, follow the Customer Service link in the menu at the top of the page. You will find information on how to place an order, registration, shipping, returns, and privacy and security; FAQs; and contact information for the Center's customer service department.

The menu at the top of the page also has a New Account link, which changes to My Account once you have registered and logged in. Once registered, you can follow this link to edit information pertaining to your customer account.

"What do the Center's five libraries offer to nonprofits in their regions?"

If you live near one of the Center's five libraries in Atlanta, Cleveland, New York, San Francisco, or Washington, D.C., you may want to visit that library's own Web site to find out about hours, local services, and upcoming events, including short classes, full-day seminars, and workshops. Links to each of the library sites are accessible from the left menu on the Center's home page under Library Web Sites.

At our five Foundation Center libraries, we offer free and for-fee educational programs on the fundraising process, proposal writing, grantmakers and their giving, and on other related topics. On the home page of each library Web site, you'll find links to a three-month training and education calendar. By clicking on a program in the calendar, you can view a detailed description and register online. You may wish to subscribe to the free e-mail newsletter of the Center library nearest you for announcements of upcoming events and training sessions. To do this, enter your e-mail address in the input box at the top of the left menu on that library's home page.

Each library's Web site also serves as a source of news about local grantmaking and nonprofit activities. In Talking About Philanthropy, a magazine-like feature, you'll find relevant articles that are posted on a monthly basis about grantmakers and successful nonprofits, as well as news from the Foundation Center.

Talking About Philanthropy leads with a featured article from the Center's monthly library newsletter. The full newsletter can also be viewed in PDF format. Spotlight On describes the activities of different nonprofit organizations serving the regional area in which each Center library is located. To ensure the broadest possible representation of the region's nonprofit sector, the selection of organizations for Spotlight On is based on criteria such as programmatic interests, geographic focus, and size. Grantmakers in the News highlights grantmaking organizations in each location that have undertaken new endeavors, experienced changes in their program focus or staff, or announced their most recent award recipients. And Grants That Make a Difference features success stories—grants given to local nonprofits that have helped make a difference in people's lives.

The Web sites also offer information about new additions to the libraries' collections, links to community resources, and a bulletin board with general announcements.

Conclusion

The Foundation Center's Web site is a vital vehicle for disseminating the information on philanthropy that we have been providing through other means for more than 45 years. It is also a multiple-access gateway to the foundations and other grantmakers who share your interests. You should leave the Center's Web site closer to your goal of finding the funds or information you seek to carry out your work. The Center's site, through its information resources and organized Web links, will also inform a variety of audiences about the philanthropic field in general. With an ever-increasing number of interactive features, the Foundation Center's Web site is a communication system for the field of philanthropy.

CHAPTER TWO

Independent Foundations on the Web

In 1999, 70 percent of the 100 largest foundations and roughly 400 of the more than 50,000 independent foundations in the United States had a Web site or "presence"—and only a handful of these foundations accepted proposals or applications online. At the beginning of the year 2003, approximately 81 percent of the 100 largest foundations and more than 1,600 of the more than 59,000 independent foundations had Web sites.

The stream of electronic communication, via e-mail, has also become a very important tool for both foundations and grantseekers. E-mail has made it easy for people in different locations to come together in ways that were not thought possible only a short time ago. More than 2,100 foundations have e-mail addresses through which general questions and application inquiries can be submitted. In many instances, the e-mail address belongs to a grant administrator or an information specialist.

Even with the technological strides made by private foundations in the last few years, the philanthropic field still lags behind the private sector. This is especially evident among newly established independent foundations. The majority of foundations have yet to take full advantage of the possibilities that the Web has to offer in terms of exposure, marketing, and public relations. In the past two years, more than 8,100 independent foundations have been established, the majority with no Web presence. Factors such as inadequate funds or lack of resources may account for the fact that many newly established foundations have yet to take full advantage of the Internet. Yet, newly established independent foundations are probably among the best candidates to call upon the Web as an effective instrument for communication and exposure of their grant initiatives.

Many of those foundations that have taken advantage of the Internet are starting to utilize their Web sites in constructive, truly communicative ways. A number of foundations now post their quarterly and annual reports, newsletters, guidelines, grants listings, and even interactive application forms online. In this chapter, we'll look at independent foundations that are using their Web sites in unique ways to delineate their mission and services more effectively to grantseekers. Our review isn't meant to be comprehensive, nor is it intended as the final word on the subject. Our intent is to inform rather than critique, while at the same time highlighting practices and trends that seem to hold promise for foundations, the nonprofit sector, society in general, and grantseekers in particular.

Grants Information on Independent Foundation Web Sites

In the past few years there has been an increase in the number of independent foundations that list some or all of their recent grants on their Web sites. Some sites offer grants information in the form of browsable listings. Several foundations offer grants information through searchable databases accessible directly from their sites, while others provide both. The following examples should give you a better idea of how various foundations are using the Web to communicate to grantseekers more effectively about their funding areas of interest.

Information on grantees of the Seattle-based Bullitt Foundation (http://www.bullitt.org) can be browsed by alphabetical listing, geographic funding area, program priority area, or by issue. Grantee profiles include a description of the organization and contact information, including address, phone and fax numbers, e-mail addresses, and URL. A description of the grant itself is also provided.

The Web site of the J. Paul Getty Trust (http://www.getty.edu/grants/awards) makes available browsable listings of recent grants going back to 1995.

Two examples of searchable grants databases can be found on the Web sites of the W.K. Kellogg Foundation and the Graham Foundation for Advanced Studies in the Fine Arts.

One of the main functions of the Kellogg Foundation's Web site (http://www.wkkf.org) is to "provide Web access to an extensive database of information related to the grants we fund." In support of this end, the W.K. Kellogg Foundation has created a searchable grants "Knowledgebase" organized around four different search approaches. By selecting Search Grants Files, you are taken to an online form where you can enter your search terms. You may also choose to browse the database by programming category, geographically (United States, Latin America and the Carribean, and Southern Africa), or alphabetically by recipient name. Selecting programming category allows you to browse through grants that share the same "coding" within the Kellogg Foundation's system. Selecting by geographic region lets you browse according to grantee location. An advanced search option is also available, allowing you to search the text of the grant record by status (active or closed), Kellogg Foundation contact person, award start and end date, and by range of the grant amount. Listed grants date back to 1991.

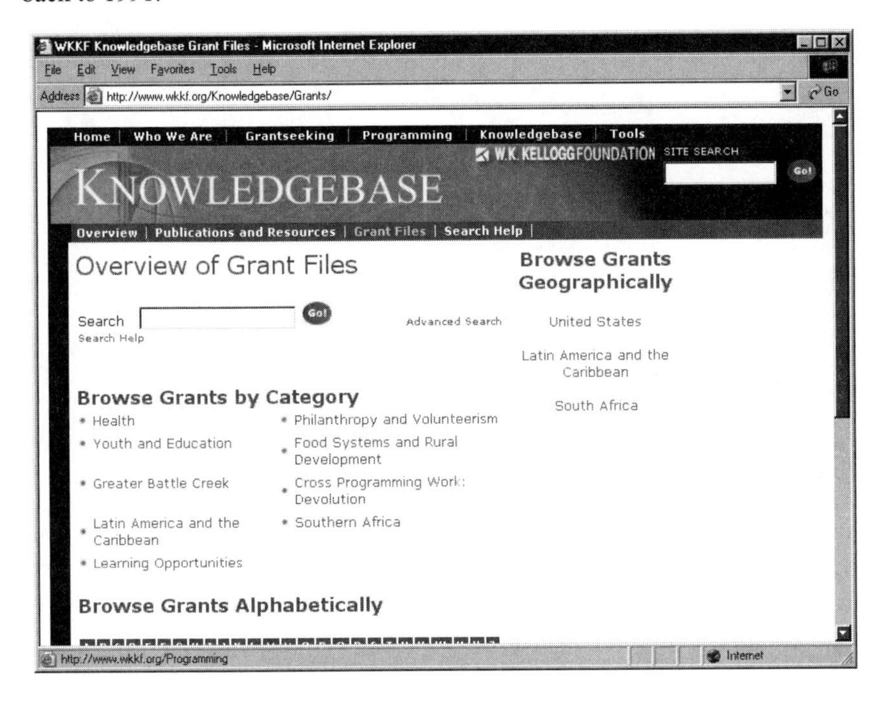

The Chicago-based Graham Foundation for Advanced Studies in the Fine Arts (http://www.grahamfoundation.org) clearly states the goals for its new searchable grants feature: "We have put this [grants] data online in a searchable form because we intend these abstracts to be utilitarian data rather than only historical records." The searchable grants database allows the grantseeker to search by keyword or to browse by subject, medium, or year (back to 1996).

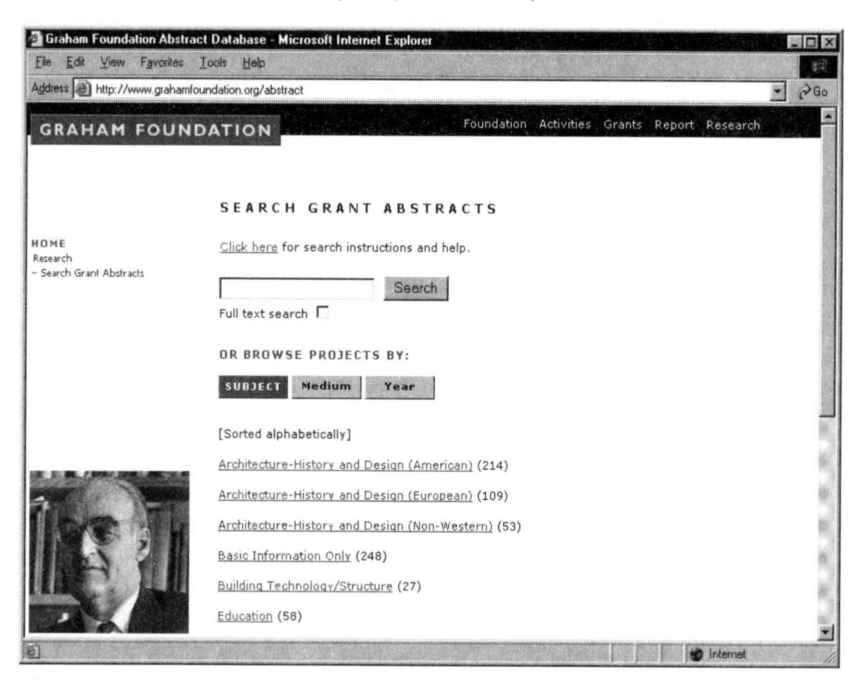

The Ford Foundation (http://www.fordfound.org) and the Charles Stewart Mott Foundation (http://www.mott.org) are among other major foundations that offer searchable grants databases on their Web sites. The Pew Charitable Trusts' site (http://www.pewtrusts.com) allows you to browse by program category. You can then see an overview of that program, including an historical record of giving and recent grants. Links are also available to grantee Web sites. The search area of the site also lets you search for grants by program area and date range.

Many foundations provide their grants listings online through an electronic version of their annual report. A good example of this approach can be found at the Web site of the Bradley Foundation (http://www.bradleyfdn.org). This foundation offers its listings of grants awarded from 1997 through 2002 through downloadable annual reports in PDF format. Grants lists are also available as an online (HTML) Schedule of Grants and a browsable, alphabetical listing. This Web site also offers press releases and downloadable publications spotlighting recent grant awards.

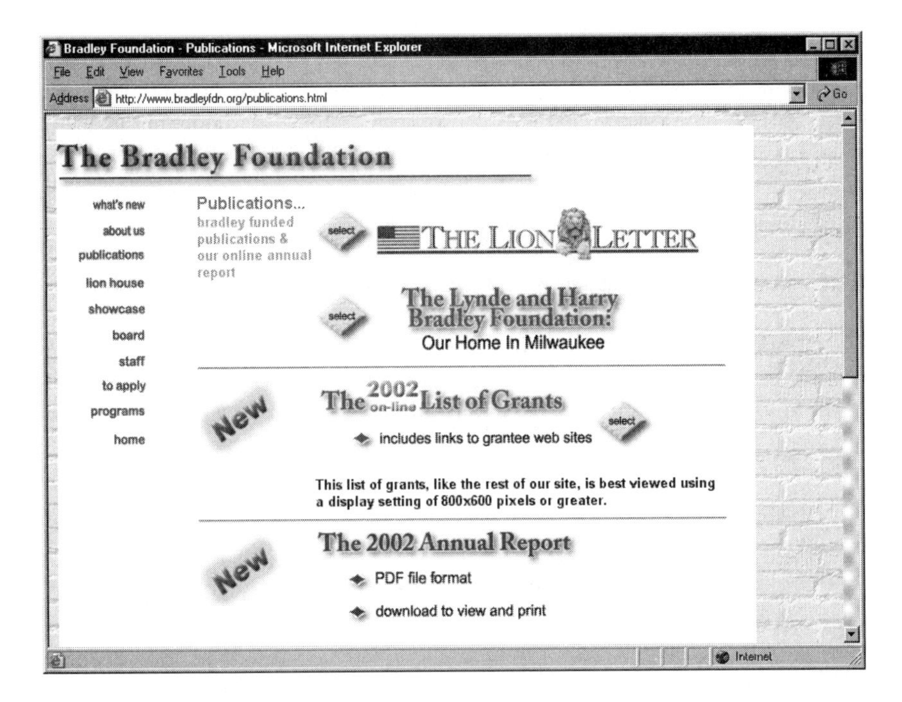

When you come across foundation Web sites in the course of your funding research, check to see whether there is a browsable or searchable grants database, an online annual report with grants information, or a Form 990-PF. (For more information on the Form 990-PF, see page 52.) Information from these sources can help you quickly determine whether your organization's needs match the giving patterns of the foundation you are interested in approaching.

The Application Process Online

In addition to grants listings, foundations today are beginning to call upon the capabilities of their Web sites to facilitate the application process. Some foundation Web sites offer downloadable application forms, which can be printed out, filled in, and then mailed, faxed, or sent to the foundation via e-mail. Others have an interactive Web form that can be filled out online and submitted directly from the site. Still others have an interactive eligibility quiz that asks a series of questions to determine eligibility based on program and geographic areas *before* revealing the application information. Most foundation Web sites that have application materials online also make a great deal of other information available regarding their past giving, program areas, and limitations to their grant programs. This helps to provide grantseekers with a clearer view of who is eligible for funding and who should proceed by submitting an application. In most cases, the online application form serves more as a letter of inquiry than it does as a full proposal. But it helps the grantmaker quickly determine whether you have done your homework and checked the guidelines and eligibility criteria made available on its site before submitting a full proposal. The following is a sampling of foundation Web sites that illustrate the variations you may encounter regarding the application process.

When GTE and Bell Atlantic merged to become Verizon, a new foundation was launched to serve the nonprofit community—the Verizon Foundation (http://foundation.verizon.com). The Verizon Foundation was the first foundation to accept proposals and application forms online. Upon entering the foundation's Web site, you are given the option of viewing the foundation's grantmaking areas and public information in either English or Spanish, demonstrating the foundation's awareness of the diverse communities it serves. The Web site also offers a Nonprofit Search tool that allows grantseekers to check to be sure that their organizations are eligible 501(c)(3) entities.

Verizon's full application is available as a Web form in the Partnership Opportunities area and can be completed in approximately 45 minutes, according to the instructions. Look carefully at the grants guidelines, which provide information on eligibility criteria, how and when to apply, and a helpful hints and suggestions list. Before submitting the application form, you should take Verizon's interactive eligibility quiz. FAQs are also available to help you find the answers to basic questions.

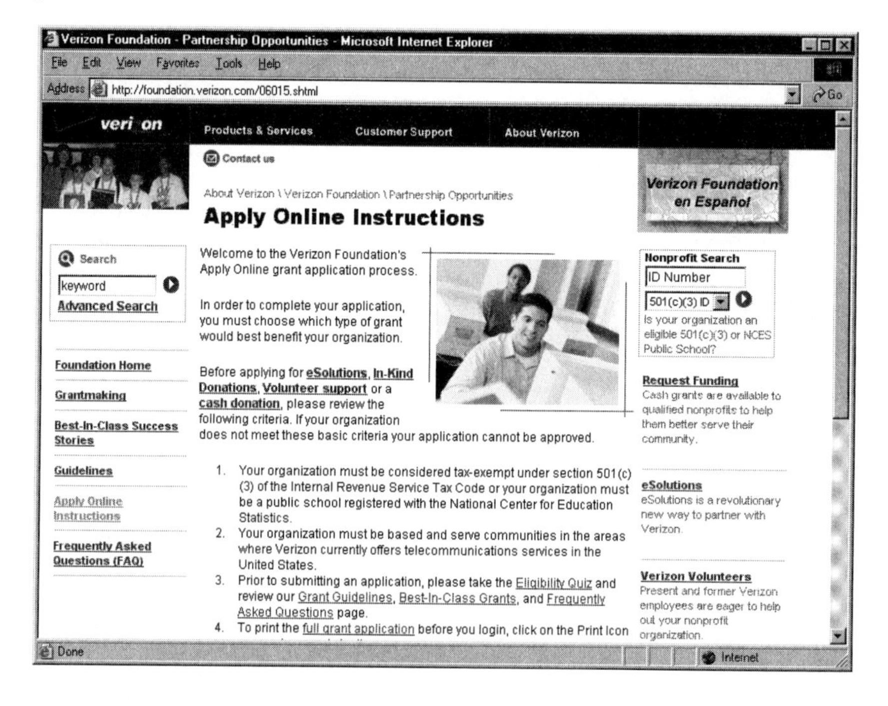

In Your Community is an interactive section of the Verizon site where you can learn about the foundation's support in your area by entering your zip code. You will find contact information for a local Verizon Foundation Director of Community Affairs, a listing of grants and in-kind donations made in your specific community, and a quick form you can fill out to join an e-mail service notifying you of news, events, and special invitations to programs in your geographic area.

The Verizon Foundation has five priority funding areas: basic and computer literacy, workforce development, community technology development, employee voluntarism, and a program that recycles old phones to benefit victims of domestic violence. The foundation also offers four different types of support: eSolutions, in-kind donations, volunteer support, and cash grants. Technological training and support solutions for major national nonprofits with multiple points of operation throughout the United States is in eSolutions. This grantmaking program gives the nonprofit community new tools for innovative philanthropic solutions, including a needs analysis tool, which measures an organization's technology needs, and "e-trainings," which are designed to close the digital divide through live training programs. Services of eSolutions also include network design and intranets, desktop applications, and Web site hosting services. Organizations interested in e-trainings must submit to a review by the foundation.

The Chowdry Family Foundation (http://www.chowdryfoundation.org) of Lakewood, Colorado, does not have its own application form, but it does accept the Colorado Common Grant Application Form. Along with its program area information and grant guidelines, its Web site includes a link to its preferred application form. Applicants can either fill in an electronic version of the form online and print it out for mailing to the foundation, or they can download the document for later modification in either ZIP or PDF format. In addition, the Web site offers a listing of the Chowdry Family Foundation's most recent grant recipients.

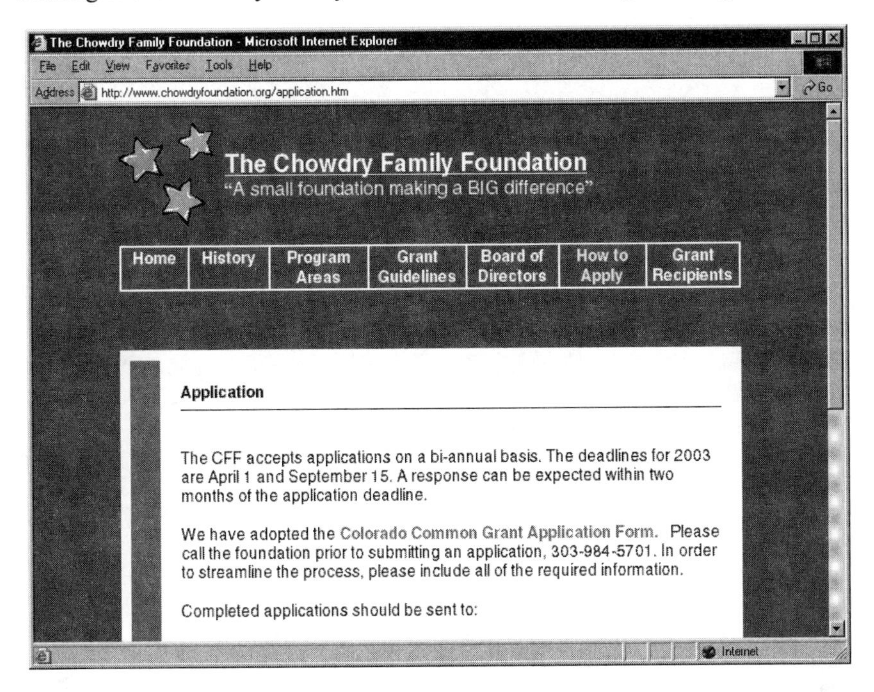

The Edmund F. Maxwell Foundation (http://www.maxwell.org) offers several printable forms on its Web site, including application guidelines, a financial aid worksheet for scholarship applicants, and the application form itself.

The California Endowment (http://www.calendow.org), of Woodland Hills, California, offers on its Web site an applicant cover sheet and a sample budget format for use in an application, in GIF and PDF formats. There is also an online form to request the foundation's application information and annual report by mail, as well as a mechanism for sending feedback. In addition, the foundation now offers a database of grants awarded since 1999 that is searchable by keyword, program area, or geographic location.

The Edward E. Ford Foundation (http://www.eeford.org), of Washington, D.C., keeps its online application information in a password-protected area on its site. Instructions read: "Schools and associations which have secured a place on an agenda for consideration by the Board of the Foundation will be issued a password to be entered below to access specific directions and necessary forms for submitting a proposal." Check the guidelines, annual report, or programs of interest to help determine your organization's eligibility.

The Web site of the Livermore, California-based Fannie and John Hertz Foundation (http://www.hertzfndn.org) offers an interactive application form that states, "Applications are normally submitted in electronic form via the Internet. Paper application materials for those lacking Internet access may be obtained (without prejudice) from the Foundation by telephonic request." To begin the application process, registration is required.

Foundation for the Future (http://www.futurefoundation.org), of Bellevue, Washington, makes a preliminary application form available on its Web site. According to its site: "Eligible applicants will be provided with a copy of the Foundation's Grant Announcement and Invitation."

Another Washington State-based grantmaker, the Glaser Progress Foundation (http://www.glaserprogress.org), offers three ways for grantseekers to apply. First, an online grant application form is available that can be submitted immediately to the foundation upon completion. Those who can't complete the application form immediately can use the outline, featuring information to be included in an application (available in Word and PDF formats). You can also e-mail an electronic version of the application to the foundation or produce a hard copy and send it in via ground-based mail. The foundation will acknowledge receipt of the application within one week.

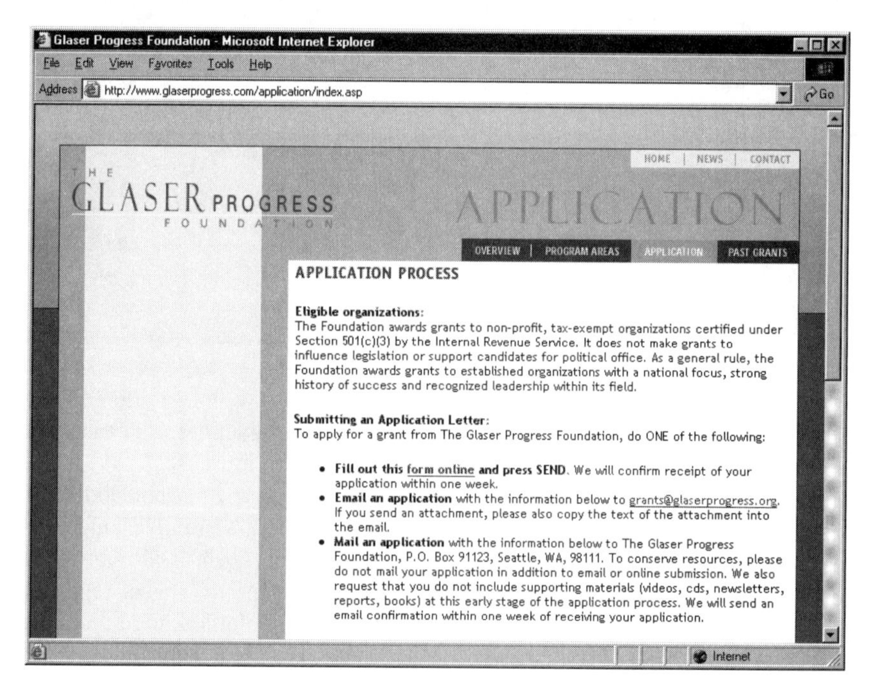

The Frank Stanley Beveridge Foundation's Web site (http://www.beveridge.org) is designed "to determine whether your organization is eligible to receive grants from the Foundation and to permit you to initiate a grant application." The site has an interactive survey you can take to help determine your eligibility. Because the Westfield, Massachusetts, foundation has geographic limitations, grantseekers are asked to click on a map of the United States to determine if they fall within the foundation's geographic guidelines. The next step is to enter your zip code. If you are geographically eligible, you will be queried as to the type of support requested. If you qualify, you are taken to an electronic preliminary grant proposal form. If approved, a printed grant proposal abstract and guidelines will be mailed to you. If you do not qualify, you will receive notification to that effect.

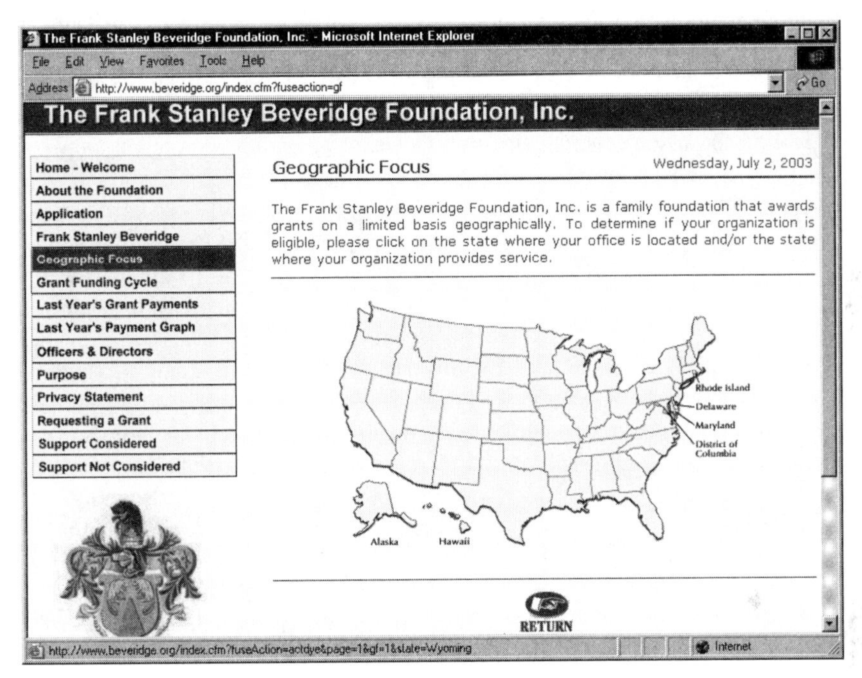

The Foundation Center's Foundation Folders Initiative

The Foundation Center develops free Web sites for foundations through its Foundation Folders initiative (http://fdncenter.org/grantmaker/folders.html). Each foundation that participates receives a "folder" or directory on the Foundation Center's Web site that holds its own materials for posting on the Web. From its beginnings in 1997, the program has had two goals: to provide private, community, and company-sponsored foundations with an immediate, low-cost presence on the Web and, in the process, help them become familiar with some of the issues surrounding the rapid evolution of communications technologies and media; and to make information about foundations accessible to a wider audience. Also, starting in 2001, the program was opened conditionally to public charities with grantmaking programs and grantmaker affinity groups.

The Foundation Folders service enables eligible grantmakers to post online public information materials (mission statements, program descriptions, application guidelines, grants lists, financial statements, contact information, annual reports, PDF files of Form 990-PFs, and more). More than 100 folders are currently online, and more than 140 have been created to date. One useful benefit of this initiative is that these sites can be updated quickly, so foundations that revise their information can get the changes out to the general public in a timely and effective manner. Once a grantmaker in the program decides to establish and maintain a site on its own (under its own unique domain name—for example, http://www.myfoundation.org), its folder on the Center's site is "retired."

A list of Foundation Folders is available in the For Grantmakers directory (http://fdncenter.org/grantmaker/foldermenu.html). Private foundation sites are organized into three categories: total giving over $10 million, total giving between $500,000 and $10 million, and total giving up to $500,000. Within these categories, the sites are further organized alphabetically by state. There are separate categories for community foundations, public charities, and affinity groups. In addition, you can also view an alphabetic list of all Foundation Folders.

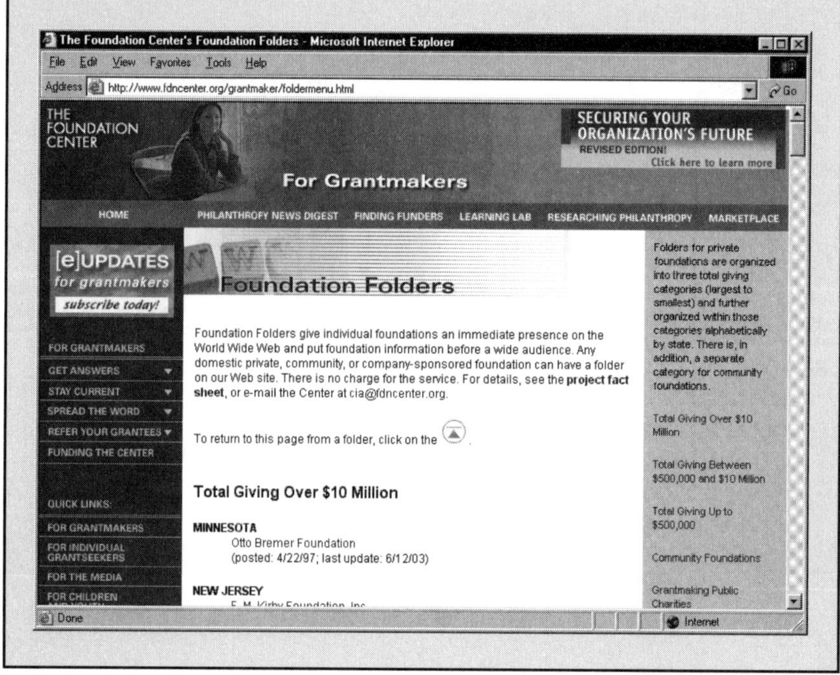

A link to and a description of each of the Foundation Folder Web sites is also listed in the appropriate section (e.g., Grantmaker Web Sites and Sector Search) of the Finding Funders Directory.

Foundation Folders come in a variety of formats, from one-page fact sheets—see the site for the Daughters of the Cincinnati (http://fdncenter.org/grantmaker/cincinnati), based in New York City—to fairly elaborate, multi-tiered sites. Examples of the latter include the sites for the St. Paul-based Otto Bremer Foundation (http://fdncenter.org/grantmaker/bremer) and the New York-based Doris Duke Charitable Foundation (http://fdncenter.org/grantmaker/dorisduke).

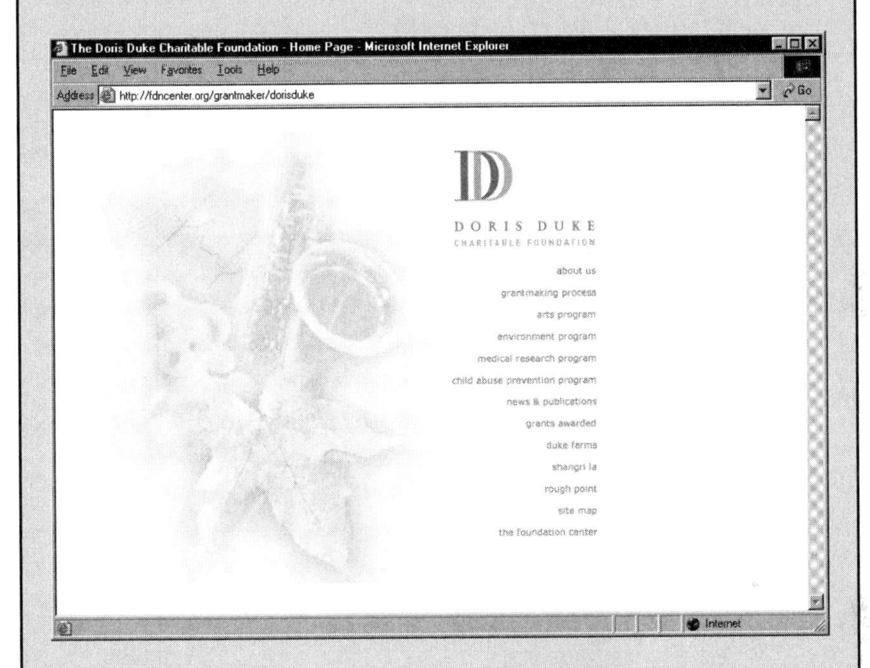

Whether a site comprises a single page or an entire array of informational materials, the end result is the same: the information can be viewed by anyone, anywhere, who has Internet access and a Web browser. At a minimum, posting public information to the Web ensures that these materials can be found and indexed by Web-based search engines. (See Appendix A for a listing and description of some popular general search engines.) The search engines, in turn, retrieve that information, with varying degrees of effectiveness, whenever it is requested. As the information is disseminated in ever wider circles, the chances of other individuals and organizations finding and creating links to it increase. In the final analysis, it's the very simple but powerful hyperlinking capabilities of the medium that enables webs of common interest to be created and that drives the exponential growth of the Web itself. The opportunity to deliver information free on the Internet presents grantmakers—especially smaller grantmakers—with a host of challenges and is likely to profoundly reshape the way most funders communicate with their constituencies in the next decade.

Portals, Content Aggregators, and Information-Rich Sites

A number of foundations have developed Web sites that go well beyond presenting information about their own programs. These sites offer educational and advocacy materials in support of the causes that the foundation's leadership cares about.

In the field of healthcare, for example, the Princeton, New Jersey-based Robert Wood Johnson Foundation (http://www.rwjf.org); the Henry J. Kaiser Family Foundation (http://www.kff.org) in Menlo Park, California; and the New York City-based Dana Foundation (formerly The Charles A. Dana Foundation) (http://www.dana.org) use their sites to inform people about issues addressed by their grantmaking programs. The Dana Foundation's Web site, for instance, offers extensive information about programs, activities, and foundation publications and serves as a "gateway to brain information." The Web site offers access to general information about the brain and current brain research, including publications, links, and even a children's section. The Dana BrainWeb is a directory of links to Web sites in multiple categories related to brain diseases and disorders. Additional links are added quarterly.

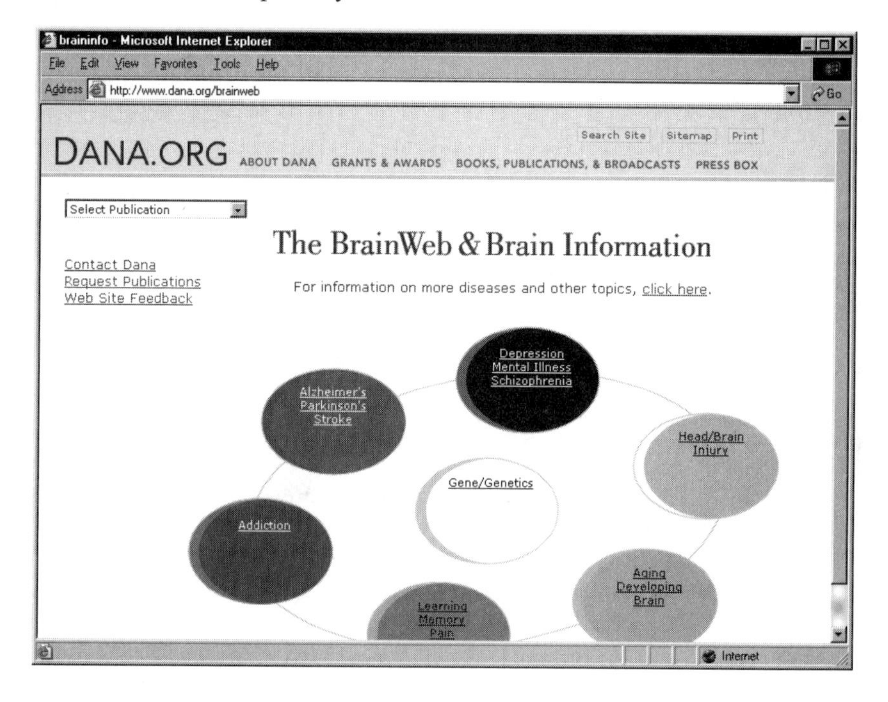

In another type of Web presentation, the Baltimore-based Annie E. Casey Foundation's Web site (http://www.aecf.org) provides a range of interactive features for those who serve disadvantaged children. The KidsCount section of the site offers statistical data in state-by-state profiles, graphs (state indicators graphed over time), maps, rankings, and raw data downloadable in a number of file formats. In 2003, the foundation added a new feature to KidsCount called the CLIKS system. This system "brings together data on the well-being of children collected by KidsCount grantees from state and local sources." You can search the data to generate customized statistical reports and color-coded maps on a state, county, city, and community level. The Family to Family initiative offers tools for meeting the challenges of the child welfare system. Resource tools include a fact sheet, a multi-page summary, a full implementation guide (requires registration), and an online publications order form for obtaining print copies. In addition to the Family to Family initiative, visitors can also access information on a range of other Casey Foundation initiatives.

The Web site of the Washington, D.C.-based Benton Foundation (http://www.benton.org) is designed to connect people to the information and resources they need to make a difference in their communities and to use information technologies more effectively. The Benton Foundation's site offers headlines, a "virtual library" of foundation publications and online resources browsable by subject, and links to e-newsletters and discussion groups, all designed to assist nonprofit organizations in their work. The foundation offers separate sites that provide information on its many program areas. These include Capacity Building, Communications Policy, Connect for Kids, Digital Divide Network, Digital Opportunity Channel, OneWorld U.S., and Sound Partners for Community Health.

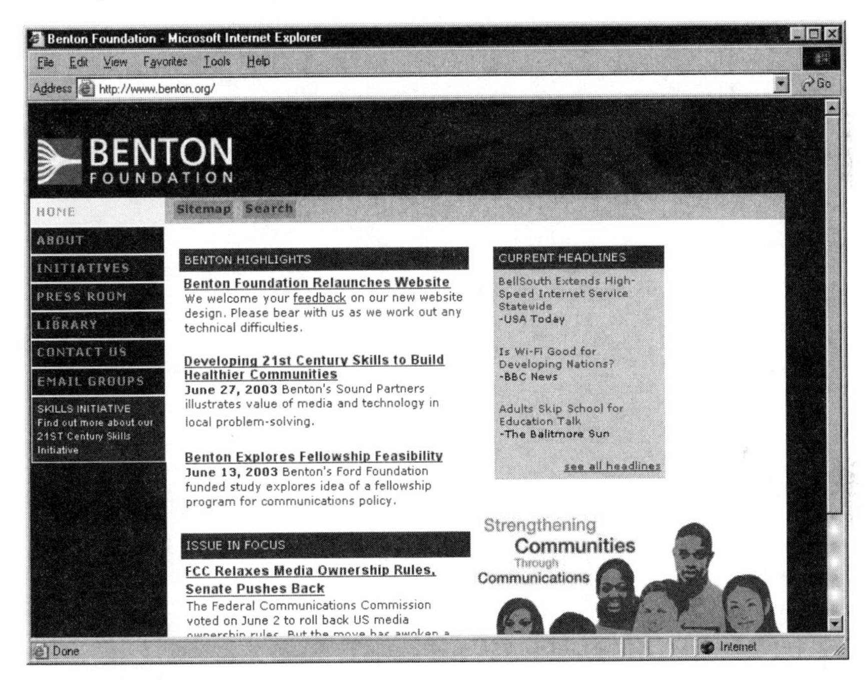

These are but a few examples of today's foundation Web sites that go beyond the mere provision of basic information about the grantmakers themselves. These sites demonstrate the trend of a growing number of foundations that are truly committed to using the Web to enhance their relationships with grantees and potential grantees and to use this vast worldwide platform to educate the public about specific issues or areas of concern.

Online Resource Information Centers

The Internet has revolutionized the availability of information to educate and inform the public about the activities of foundations. The Web sites included in this section are those of philanthropic infrastructure organizations, grantmaker associations, or other membership groups. They offer useful tools for unearthing information on foundations, understanding how they work, and learning more about the people who manage them.

The Council on Foundations (http://www.cof.org), a nonprofit membership association of grantmaking foundations and corporations, offers comprehensive philanthropic information on foundations geared to the interests of its grantmaking audience. The mission of the council is to serve the public good by promoting and enhancing responsible and effective philanthropy. For more than 50 years, the Council on Foundations has helped foundation staff, trustees, and board members in their day-to-day grantmaking activities. Through one-to-one technical assistance, research, publications, conferences and workshops, legal services, and a wide array of other services, the council addresses the important issues and challenges that face foundations and corporate funders.

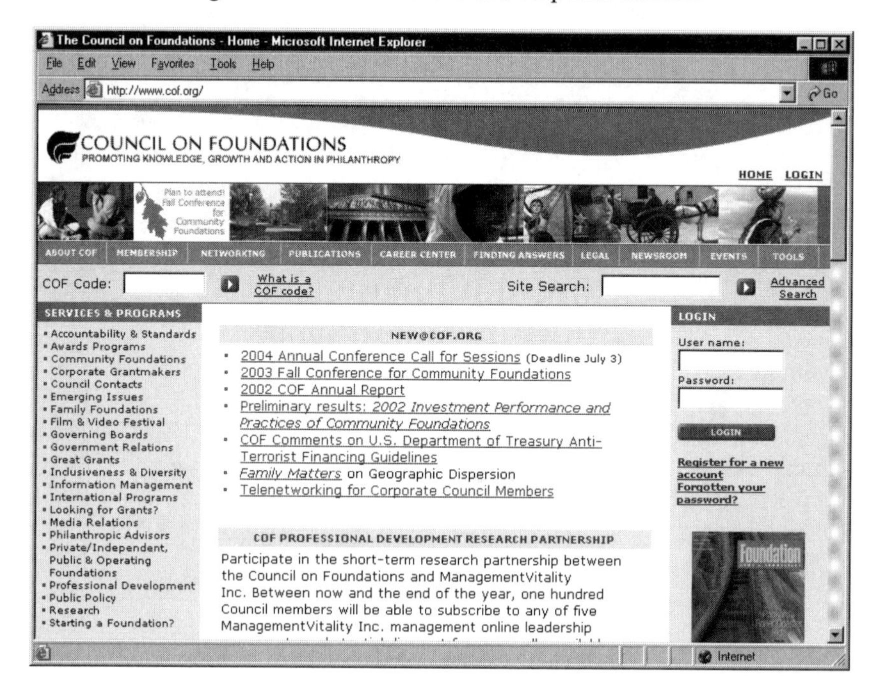

The council maintains an informational Web site geared toward its grantmaker audience that highlights the primary types of nonprofit philanthropic organizations: community foundations, corporate foundations/giving programs, family foundations, private/independent and private operating foundations, public foundations, and non-U.S. foundations. The site is user-friendly, with targeted links focusing on foundations and their operations. At the council's site you will find information on networking, council publications, job listings, FAQs, legal information, news, events listings, and tools for grantmakers to assist them in their daily work. There is also information on accountability, emerging issues, governing boards, government relations, inclusiveness and diversity, information management, media relations, philanthropic advisors, professional development, public policy, research, and resources for starting a foundation. Much of the site is available only to council members, but some sections are open to everyone.

Each year the council organizes conferences, workshops, and lectures aimed at the grantmaking public. Among the conferences offered by the council are the Family Foundations Virtual Conference, the Conference for Community Foundations, and its Annual Membership Conference. Major speeches from council events and activities can be found under Speeches of Note in the About COF section of the site.

Grantmaker associations are another important source of information. Generally organized along regional or state lines, the Web sites of these associations contain contact and other useful information about grantmaking foundations in their areas.

The Forum of Regional Associations of Grantmakers (http://www.rag.org) is a national membership organization of 28 of the nation's largest regional associations of grantmakers (RAGs). RAGs themselves are associations of area grantmakers, representing more than 4,000 local grantmakers nationwide, that affiliate with other member grantmakers to enhance the effectiveness of private philanthropy in their regions. The forum conducts research and studies of interest to those seeking information on new ventures in charitable giving. The forum's Web site serves as a national network for other colleague organizations that collaborate with RAGs around the country. The forum helps RAGs in providing local leadership to grantmakers in several important areas. One such area, New Ventures in Philanthropy, provides initiatives to help promote the creation of new foundations and corporate giving programs and to encourage new donors to endow philanthropic funds, the income and/or principal of which will be used for grantmaking. It does so in part by developing tools and approaches to promote philanthropy and by awarding grants to coalitions or organizations that promote the full range of options available for establishing foundations, giving programs, and other grantmaking funds. Another important area, Public Policy, helps alert grantmakers to new challenges and changes in the philanthropic world that may impact the breadth and scope of giving. On the site, you will also find a complete list of RAGs in the United States, giving resources, and common grant application/report forms used by member RAGs.

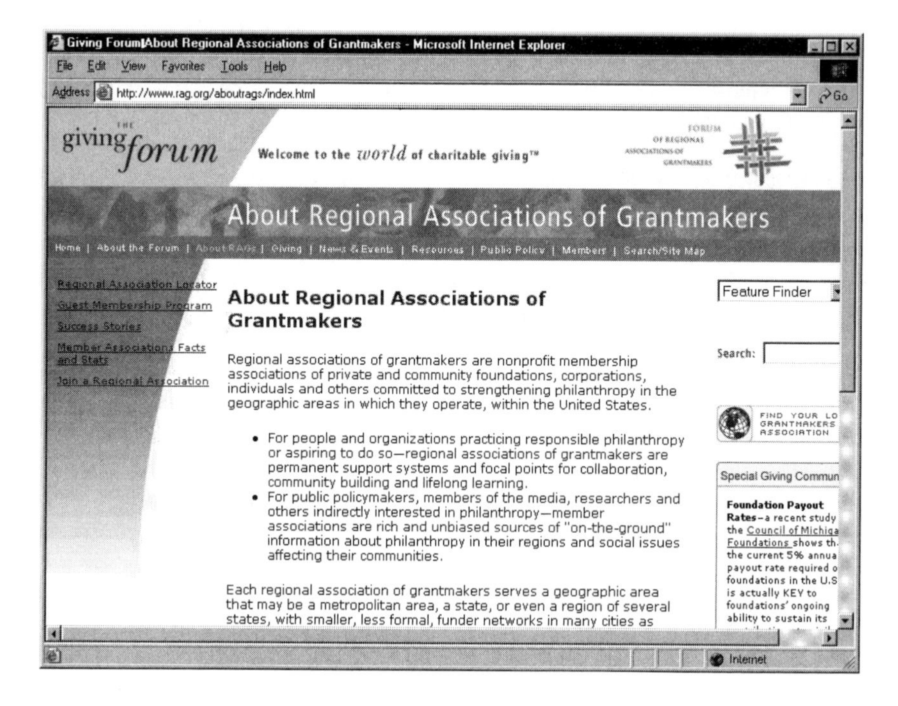

The Association of Small Foundations (ASF) (http://smallfoundations.org), based in Bethesda, Maryland, is a membership organization of nearly 2,800 small foundations, committed to building and strengthening small foundation philanthropy by providing top quality, timely, practical, member-driven programs to all foundations with few or no staff. Members have access to the many programs offered by ASF, including a quarterly newsletter; an annual member survey; a directors and officers liability insurance policy at reduced rates; full access to the members-only ASF Web site with hundreds of downloadable articles, sample grant guidelines, job descriptions, request-for-proposal letters, and grant agreement letters; guides to colleagues and programs of other foundations that may be doing similar work to their own; national and regional meetings; discounted periodicals and software programs; answers to questions submitted by other members; trustee leadership meetings; and Foundations in a Box, a comprehensive resource (in electronic or print formats) containing more than 2,000 pages of expertise from more than 140 different authors on topics such as investment management, tax and legal guidelines, grantmaking, board issues, and small office management. New foundations may be eligible for complimentary membership.

GrantSmart (http://www.grantsmart.org) is an informational and interactive resource center for and about the nonprofit community. Operated by Canyon Research and funded by the J.C. Downing Foundation, GrantSmart has gathered data about private foundation activities that may be of interest to grantseekers, philanthropic organizations, and individual donors. Its searchable online database allows users to access IRS Forms 990-PF filed by private foundations. You can search more than 60,000 returns by name, location, or asset size of the organization. GrantSmart also hosts a complete database of all Section 527 organizations that have filed IRS Form 8871, "Notice of Section 527 Status for Political Organizations," which lists contribution and expenditure information for political organizations.

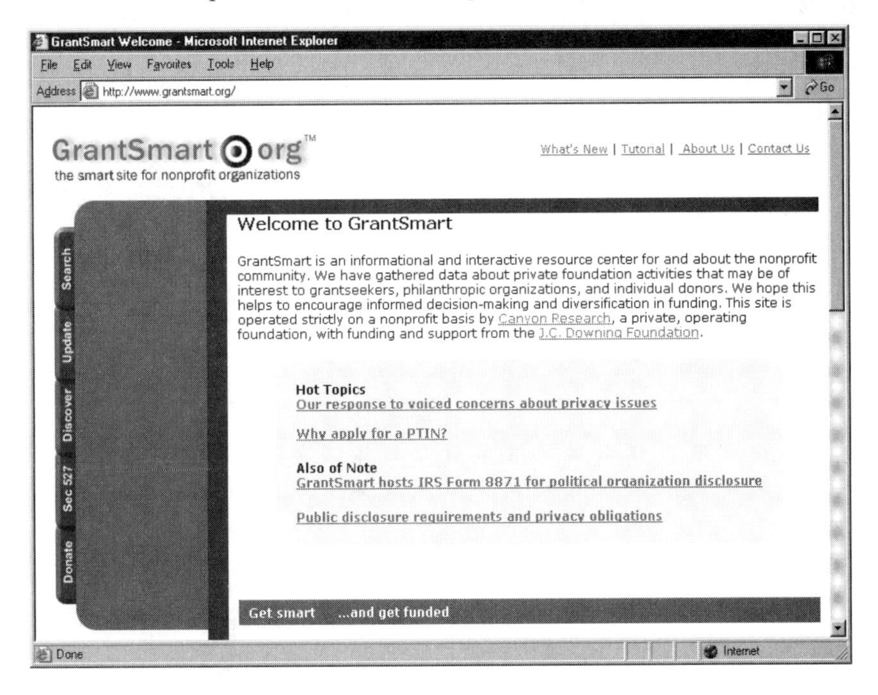

Seeking 9/11 Giving Information on the Web

The tragic events of September 11, 2001, resulted in an unprecedented surge in philanthropy. From individual donors giving to relief organizations, to corporations making multi-million dollar donations, the flow of money contributed for relief and recovery efforts was massive. The following is a sampling of Web sites providing information on charitable giving in the aftermath of 9/11.

THE FOUNDATION CENTER: PHILANTHROPY'S RESPONSE TO 9/11: CREATING THE RECORD AND TELLING THE STORY

Immediately following September 11, 2001, the Foundation Center embarked on an effort to create the definitive record of philanthropy's response to the events of that day, capturing not only the dollars pledged and distributed for relief and recovery, but also telling the human aspect of the story. This effort evolved into a multi-year project that has garnered the support of foundations and corporations.

The Foundation Center's Philanthropy's Response to 9/11: Creating the Record and Telling the Story (http://fdncenter.org/research/911), available on our Web site, offers a comprehensive database of institutional donors and recipients, reports analyzing the response, and an archive of 9/11-related news and original interviews.

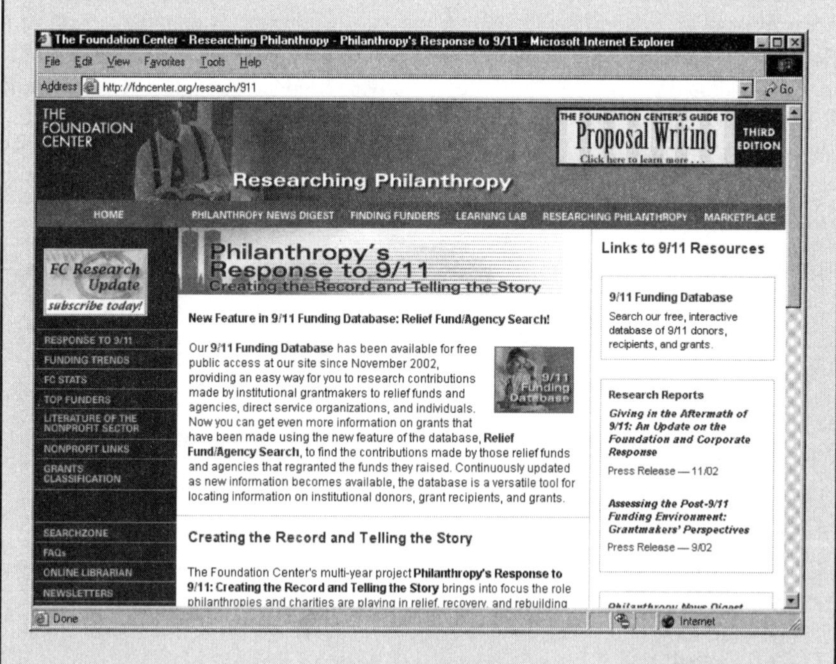

The 9/11 Funding Database, available in two different views, is a free, interactive tool for retrieving information on institutional donors, grant recipients, and grants made following September 11, 2001. In the first view you can search the database for contributions made by institutional grantmakers (foundations, corporations, and public charities) by grantmaker type, grantmaker state, recipient state, and recipient type. The second view allows users to access information on the efforts by relief funds and agencies that acted as regrantors for funds they received from institutional and individual donors, and is searchable by relief fund/agency, relief fund/agency state, recipient state, recipient type, and sponsoring organization. The data on 9/11-related funding is provided as it is reported to keep the information current.

Also available from Philanthropy's Response to 9/11 are free downloads of Center research reports and press releases regarding the foundation and corporate response to 9/11, including the Center's first report, *Giving in the Aftermath of 9/11: Foundations and Corporations Respond,* and the follow-up, *Giving in the Aftermath of 9/11: An Update on the Foundation and Corporate Response.* A subsequent report will be issued in 2003, and a final summary will be incorporated into a compendium volume in 2004.

After 9/11, our *Philanthropy News Digest (PND)* editors conducted more than a dozen interviews with key figures involved in the relief and recovery, including Lorie Slutsky, president of the New York Community Trust; Clara Miller, president of the Nonprofit Finance Fund; and Joshua Gotbaum, executive director and chief executive officer of the September 11th Fund. A complete archive containing each interview is provided from the Philanthropy's Response to 9/11 page. From here you can also access a compilation of these interviews, *September 11: Perspectives from the Field of Philanthropy,* which can be viewed online in PDF format or ordered free of charge from the Web site. A second *Perspectives* volume was issued in September 2003 and is also available in PDF format at our Web site. Links are also provided to 9/11-related news originally published in *Philanthropy News Digest.*

OTHER SOURCES OF 9/11-RELATED GIVING INFORMATION

The 9/11 United Services Group, a consortium of 13 New York City human services organizations involved directly with recovery efforts, has an extensive list of 9/11-related reports and studies, including a section for Philanthropic/Disaster Response Reports (http://www.9-11usg.org/index3.asp?page=REPSTUDIDX#philanthropic).

GuideStar's Web site (http://www.guidestar.org/news/features/table_rescue.stm) features a table listing participating GuideStar organizations that provide disaster relief and assistance, many of which have contributed to the September 11 relief effort. This table is browsable by state or alphabetically, and it provides links to the appropriate IRS Form 990 or 990-PF in the GuideStar database. Free registration is required to view the Forms 990 and 990-PF.

The Better Business Bureau's Disaster Response Information page (http://bbb.blenderbox.com/disasterrelief) is one of the primary resources allowing individuals to look up charities involved in the post-9/11 relief and recovery efforts. Among other resources, there is a National 9/11 Charity Database that can be searched by name or keyword, or by charity focus. You can also view charities by alphabetical listing.

The IRS has also tracked new charities founded specifically in response to 9/11 and has added a listing of them as an addendum to IRS Publication 78 (http://www.irs.gov/charities/article/0,,id=96140,00.html).

Conducting Online Funding Research Using the Foundation Center's Web Site

In order to facilitate your online funding research, the Finding Funders section of the Foundation Center's Web site offers several search features you can use to identify and locate potential funders that have Web sites. Two of the more useful are the Grantmaker Web Sites and Sector Search features. Grantmaker Web Sites and Sector Search offer two similar, yet distinct, ways of finding potential funders active on the Web. Both are searchable databases of the more than 2,400 grantmakers that currently have Web sites, and both allow you to search by grantmaker type.

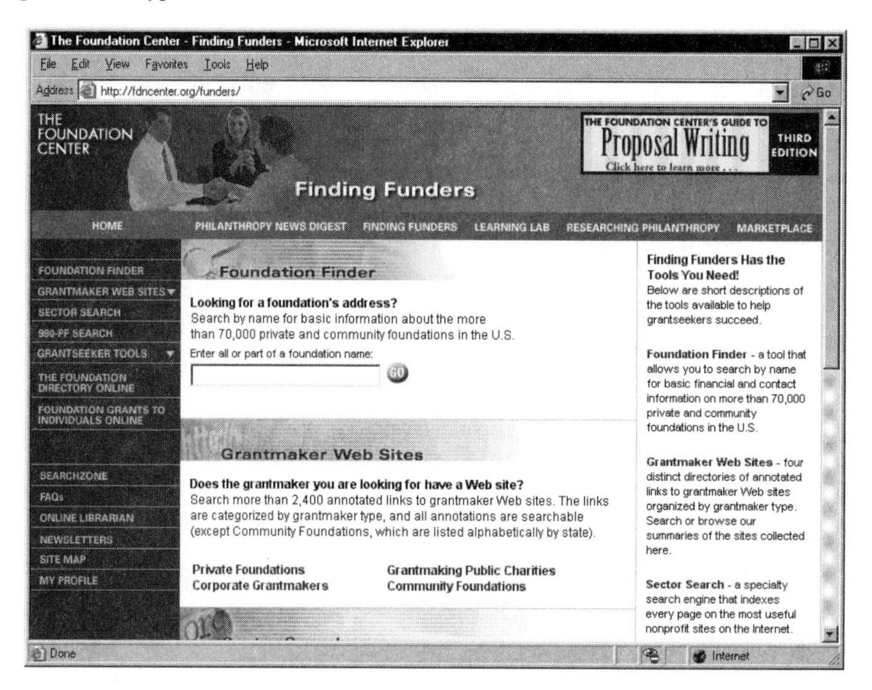

Grantmaker Web Sites offers annotated links to thousands of grantmaker Web sites, divided into three searchable categories: private independent foundations, corporate grantmakers, and grantmaking public charities. The grantmaker search engine in each category allows you to search annotations created by Center staff for grantmakers by subject and geographic keyword, making it possible for you to assemble a preliminary list of grantmakers on the Web that may be able to address your specific funding needs. A fourth category, community foundations, is organized alphabetically by state.

Sector Search, by contrast, is similar to a general search engine, in that it lets you search for keywords on individual Web pages. You can tailor your search to a specific grantmaker type, or you can use the Advanced Search feature for a higher degree of specificity. Sector Search also allows you to search nonprofit and government Web sites in addition to the four grantmaker types found in Grantmaker Web Sites.

Remember, however, that even though these two tools represent the most complete listing of foundations on the Web, your search will be restricted to those funders with some sort of Web presence—currently, around 2,400 grantmakers of the more than 74,000 tracked by the Foundation Center. In other words, unlike the information in the Center's print directories, *FC Search: The Foundation Center's Database on CD-ROM,* and *The Foundation Directory Online,* the comprehensiveness of the annotations in the Grantmaker Web Sites and Sector Search directories depends solely on the availability and breadth of the online resources themselves. Because of this, going directly to individual foundation Web sites is most useful if you have already identified them as potential funders of your work. Of course, as more grantmakers join the online community, the Center will continue to expand its list of searchable site annotations.

(See Chapter 1 for a more complete description of Grantmaker Web Sites, Sector Search, and all of our other Web site features.)

Foundations on the Web: Levels of Engagement

We've already made note of the fact that even with the technological strides made by private foundations in the last several years, the philanthropic field as a whole still lags behind the corporate sector, where utilization of the Web in fulfillment of day-to-day operations is concerned.

In this section, we explore the very broad spectrum of user engagement available at foundation Web sites. By "engagement," we are referring to the degree to which a particular foundation's Web site communicates useful information to the visitor by means of its content offerings, interactivity, and overall design. The level of engagement the grantseeker encounters at a particular Web site should not be taken as a true reflection of that funder's commitment to its grantees and grant applicants, however. This is because, as we know, technology is expensive, budgets may be tight, and it takes a while for some foundation board members to become convinced that a fully-developed Web site will, in fact, enhance rather than detract from efforts aimed at their core business—philanthropy. In most instances, from the grantseeker's perspective, even a "plain vanilla" Web site is better than no Web site at all, as long as it's been updated within the past year.

In the area of content, grantmaker Web sites offer varying levels of information that can be viewed along a continuum (see figure on page 54). At one end of the continuum, this might include simple information about the foundation and its mission, contact information, and perhaps an e-mail address—the kind of thing one would expect to find in a brief fact sheet. Further along the continuum one might encounter such items as guidelines, grants listings, annual reports, and even some financial information (including in a few instances the most recent Form 990-PF available). Still further along the continuum more user-friendly sites provide links to proposal writing resources, samples of successful proposals that the foundation has funded, and application forms that may be viewed online, downloaded, or printed out.

Interactivity is another element that serves to make grantmaker Web sites engaging for the visitor. At the most basic level, a foundation may offer a simple HTML listing of grants. At the next level the visitor might actually find a searchable database of prior grants awarded. As we've seen, some sites, in addition to

What Are Forms 990-PF and Where Can I Find Them?

To find detailed information on foundations that do not have Web sites or issue annual reports (and most do not), you will need to refer to their IRS returns, Forms 990-PF. The IRS requires that every private foundation file a Form 990-PF each year. IRS returns provide comprehensive financial data, a complete grants list, the names and remuneration (if any) of the foundation's trustees and officers, and other information on the foundation. The Form 990-PF may be the only source where you will find complete grants lists for smaller foundations. The amount of detail provided on each grant will vary from foundation to foundation.

In March 2000, new disclosure regulations went into effect that require foundations to provide, at a "reasonable fee," photocopies of their three most recent tax returns—including Form 990-PF and Form 4720 ("Return of Certain Excise Taxes on Charities and Other Persons Under Chapters 41 and 42 of the Internal Revenue Code")—as well as their original application for tax-exempt status to anyone who requests them in person or in writing. As with other tax-exempt organizations, the requirements can be satisfied by private foundations making the documents "widely available" over the Internet. Unlike other tax-exempt organizations, however, private foundations *are* required to make the names and addresses of their donors available to the public. Foundations will not be required to fulfill requests when they are determined to be part of a campaign of harassment.

The Foundation Center offers online access to more than 100,000 Forms 990-PF in Adobe PDF format. (Multiple years are provided where available.) You will need to download Adobe's free Acrobat Reader software—if it is not already installed on your computer—in order to view the returns (http://www.adobe.com/products/acrobat/readstep2.html). Returns can be found using Foundation Finder, 990-PF Search, *The Foundation Directory Online*, and *FC Search: The Foundation Center's Database on CD-ROM.* Forms 990-PF are updated at the Center's Web site with new returns approximately every four to six weeks.

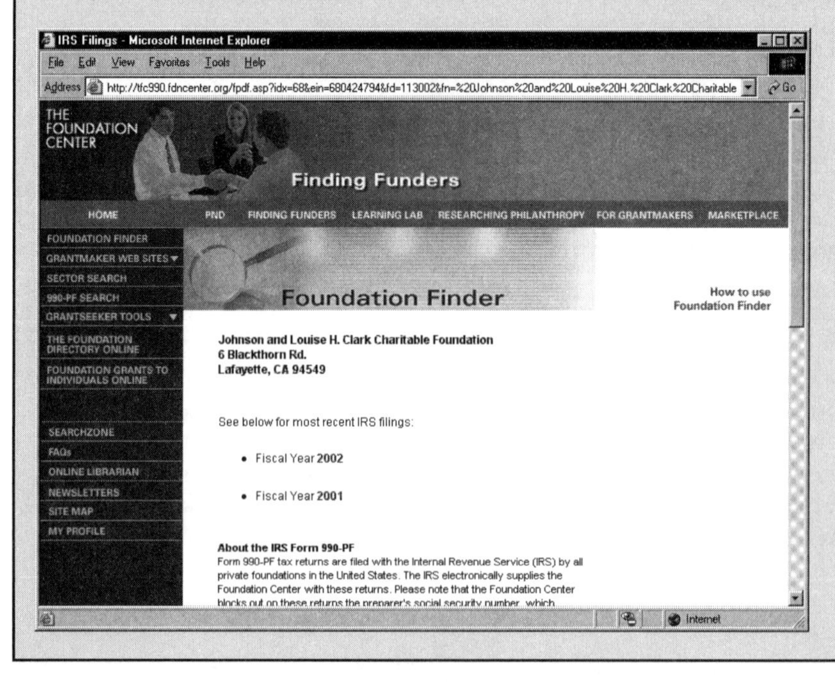

enabling the visitor to search in a variety of ways, provide online application forms. (While the online application is a definite trend, grantmakers who use them struggle with the requirement that certain supporting documents, such as the IRS determination letter and audited financial statements, still need to be submitted by "snail" mail and somehow attached to the proposal that already came in online.)

As new technology has become available, some grantmaker Web sites now offer interactive eligibility self-tests that pose a series of questions to help the grantseeker determine if he or she should pursue this particular funding prospect or not. Most recently a few foundation Web sites have begun to take the element

Photocopies of private foundation returns may also be requested from the IRS via the Web (http://www.irs.gov/pub/irs-pdf/f4506a.pdf), by fax (801-620-6671), or by writing to the Ogden Service Center, P.O. Box 9941, Mail Stop 6734, Ogden, UT 84409. Include the foundation's full name and the city and state where it is located. The IRS will bill you for the cost of the copies.

State attorneys general (http://www.naag.org/ag/full_ag_table.php) may have copies of Form 990-PF returns for foundations in their states as well. For instance, if the organization you are looking for is in California, the State Attorney General's office of California (http://caag.state.ca.us/charities) posts California charity and foundation tax returns (Forms CT-2, 990, 990-EZ, and 990-PF) on its Web site.

GuideStar (http://www.guidestar.org), an online database of information on the activities and finances of more than 850,000 nonprofit organizations, run by Philanthropic Research Inc., makes nonprofit tax returns, including foundation Forms 990-PF, accessible via the Internet. To search by EIN on GuideStar, simply click on the Advanced Search option and you will see an EIN search field. Free registration is required in order to view Forms 990-PF.

How soon will a foundation's 990-PF be available for public scrutiny?

The typical IRS filing deadline for most foundations is approximately six months after the end of the foundation's fiscal year, assuming no filing extension is granted. It then takes another few months for the IRS to process and scan the Forms 990-PF into a digitized format. For example, if a foundation's fiscal year ended on December 31, 2002, you can expect its Form 990-PF to become available sometime in the fall of 2004. Of course, foundations may also request filing extensions from the IRS, which can lead to further delays in the Form 990-PF becoming publicly available. For more information, see our FAQ "What is the lag time between the close of a foundation's fiscal year and the date a copy of its tax return is available in a Foundation Center library or on its Web site?" (http://fdncenter.org/learn/faqs/lag_time.html).

All five Center libraries and some Cooperating Collections offer assistance to visitors on effective utilization of the 990-PF as part of the funding research process. Center libraries offer a free class, Guide to the Resources on the Foundation Center's Web Site, that includes a segment on finding relevant information on the 990-PF. There is also an online tutorial, Demystifying the 990-PF, in the Virtual Classroom on the Foundation Center's Web site (http://fdncenter.org/learn/demystify/index.html).

of interactivity to a new level by adding "personalization" software that enables the grantseeker to create a customized profile, reflecting the kind of information he or she seeks. The next time (and every time thereafter until the visitor modifies his or her user profile) the gransteeker logs in to this particular site, the information on the screen will be tailored to his or her area(s) of interest, geographic location, level of expertise, and so on.

The design elements one encounters at foundation Web sites will, of course, vary greatly from site to site. Some are little more than electronic versions of pamphlets that are regularly distributed to grantseekers, while others employ the latest innovations to make their Web sites not only useful, but a pleasure to look at as well.

LEVELS OF ENGAGEMENT AT GRANTMAKER WEB SITES: A CONTINUUM

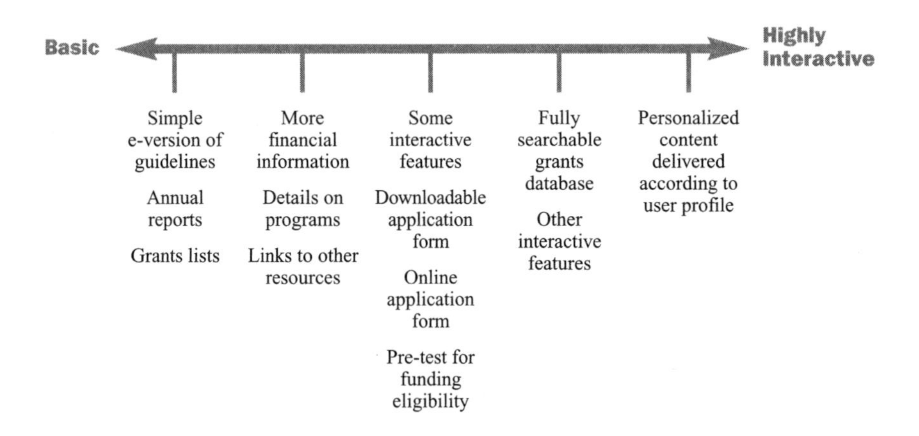

ALONG THE ENGAGEMENT CONTINUUM: EXAMPLES OF FOUNDATION WEB SITES

The Bayport Foundation of Minnesota (http://www.scenicriver.org/bp/) has a very basic Web site. The home page has contact information and a short, one-paragraph description of its funding interests and geographic giving area. There are also links to the Minnesota Common Grant Application Form used by the foundation, the foundation's Forms 990-PF, the requirements for a submitted proposal, and a listing of deadlines and board meeting dates.

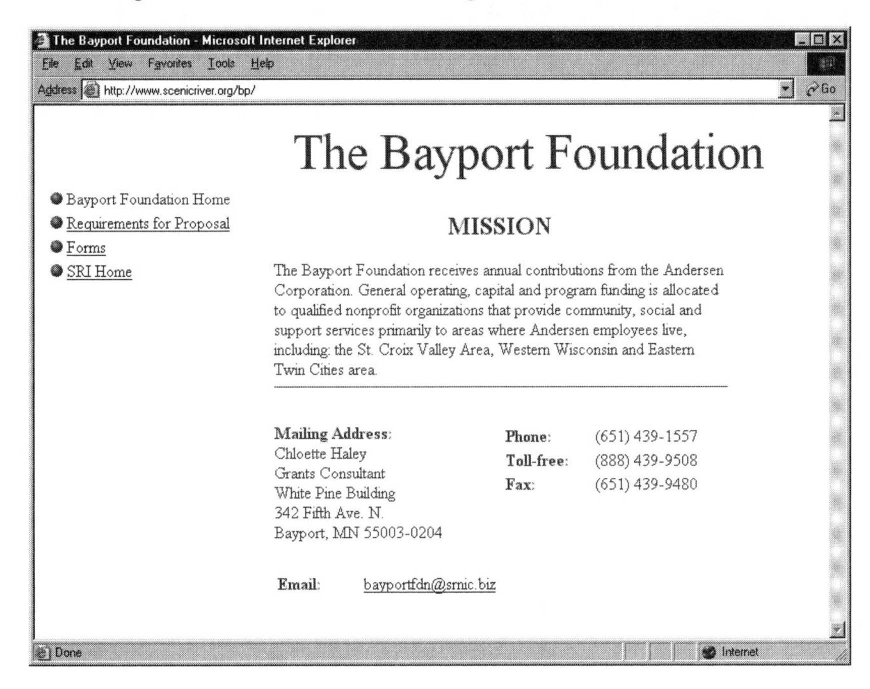

The Web site of the Starr Foundation of New York (http://fdncenter.org/grantmaker/starr), which makes grants in a number of areas, including education, medicine and healthcare, public policy, human needs, culture, and the environment, has a simple look and offers information on the history of the foundation, describes its program areas, an e-mail address, and links to several years' worth of its Form 990-PF.

Another example of a rather straightforward site is that of the Carnegie Hero Fund Commission of Pittsburgh, Pennsylvania (http://www.carnegiehero.org). This site contains a useful collection of links that take you to general information, requirements and nominations, a list of recent awardees, and contact information.

The Walton Family Foundation (http://www.wffhome.com), of Bentonville, Arkansas, has a Web site that provides a fair amount of information in an accessible and direct manner. Here you can find information on the background of the foundation, the focus of the foundation's program areas, funding guidelines, restrictions, application procedures (including HTML versions of a proposal cover sheet with an outline and a project report outline), descriptions of exemplary programs that have been funded in the past (with links to recipient Web sites), and a 2001 listing of grant recipients and amounts arranged by subject area.

The Walton Family Foundation Web site is an example of a site that provides a wealth of content in a rather simple design format.

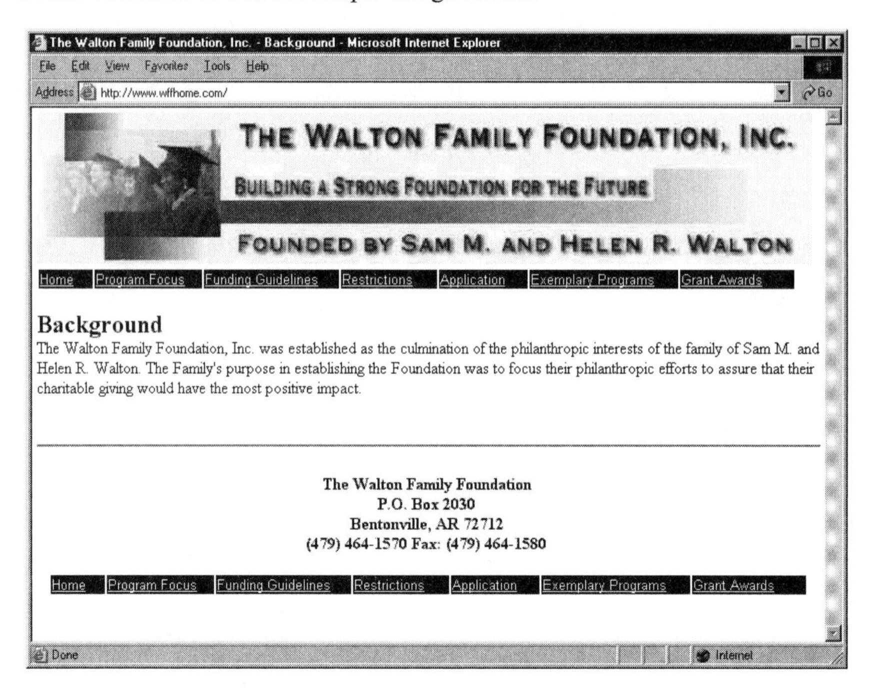

The James Ford Bell Foundation, established in Minneapolis, Minnesota, in 1955, gives high priority to projects with historical connections to the Bell Family. From the home page of its Web site (http://www.fpadvisors.com/jamesfordbell.htm) you will find biographical information about James Ford Bell, founder of General Mills, Inc., and historical information about the foundation itself. Links from the home page take you to brief but important information on guidelines, limitations, application procedures, and deadlines. Also available are a grants listing from 1998, a grant application cover page, and 1999 and 2000 annual reports. This Web site provides useful, if slightly dated, information for grantseekers and serves the needs of the foundation's relatively narrow funding interests.

Moving along the continuum just a bit, you'll find the Web site of the Andrew W. Mellon Foundation (http://www.mellon.org). The New York City-based foundation, one of the largest private foundations in the country, was created in 1969 by the merger of two smaller foundations established in the 1940s by Paul Mellon and Ailsa Mellon Bruce, son and daughter of Andrew W. Mellon, the American financier and patron of the arts. The foundation makes grants in six core program areas: higher education, museums and art conservation, performing arts, population, conservation and the environment, and public affairs. On the foundation's Web site you will find a good deal of information useful to grantseekers organized in an easily understandable fashion, such as contact information, history of the foundation, grants guidelines, and listings of trustees and staff. Detailed information about the foundation's history and program areas is also provided, including selected Mellon program essays and annual and special reports. In the Annual Reports section, you can select elements of past annual reports from a series of drop-down menus. You can select presidents' reports back to 1979, program essays back to 1988, grants lists back to 1987, and full annual reports back to 1997. Some of these elements are available in HTML format, while others are available as PDF files. Select Recent Grants for quarterly listings of grants organized by program area. The Publications area contains book reviews and selected reports available in PDF format. Though it is not likely you will get lost on this well-designed site, a site-wide search engine is also available.

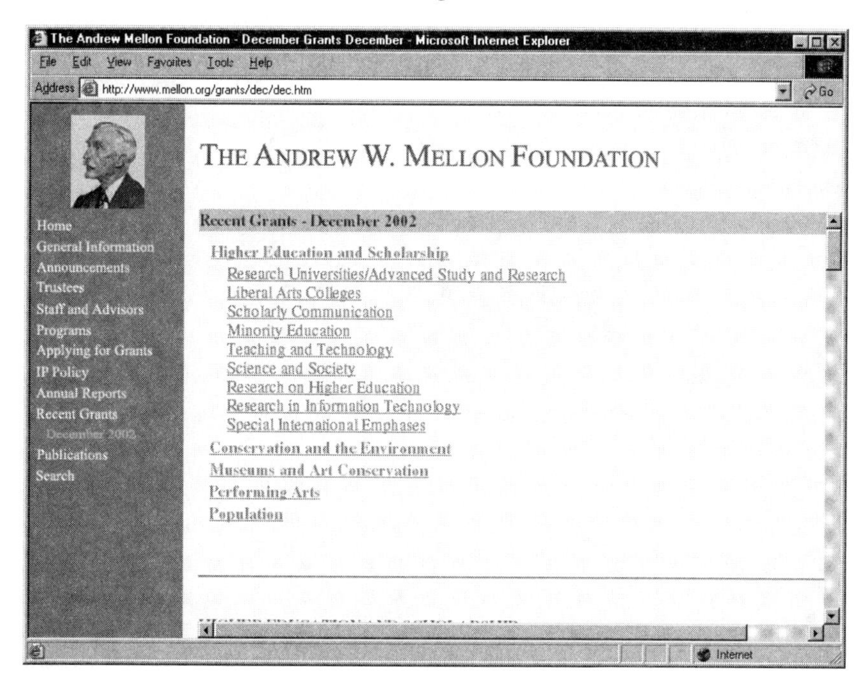

The Annenberg Foundation's Web site (http://www.annenbergfoundation.org) clearly reflects the St. Davids, Pennsylvania-based foundation's willingness to engage grantseekers directly. The foundation was established in 1989 as the successor corporation to the Annenberg School at Radnor, Pennsylvania, founded in 1958 by Walter H. Annenberg, publisher (*TV Guide, Seventeen*) and philanthropist. The Annenberg Foundation is best known for its $500 million (now $1.1 billion with challenge grant funds included) K-12 "Annenberg Challenge" grant program, which has its own Web site (http://www.lessonsandreflections.org). Through its 18 locally-designed Challenge Sites, it has awarded 21 challenge grants to reform-minded school districts, local governments, and/or nonprofit stakeholders affecting 2,400 public schools that served more than 1.5 million students and 80,000 teachers. A goal of the program is to replicate successful school reform programs throughout the country. One way of doing that, as the foundation's site demonstrates, is to use the Internet's capabilities to engage people in dispersed locations, connecting them to different ideas and experiences by providing links to other sites—in this case, links to the Web sites created by the individual Challenge Site locations.

The Annenberg Foundation also uses its main Web site to engage its audience and make grantmaking procedures more transparent to grantseekers. The foundation's site provides background information on the foundation, its founder, sister organizations, and trustees and staff. There is also information on grants awarded by the foundation, including a history of past grants available in table, graph, and chart formats; information on the foundation's major grant initiatives; application guidelines; detailed samples of selected past grants in PDF format; funding restrictions; and information on what to include in a letter of inquiry or a full proposal. The Press Room area makes available press releases, as well as grant overviews and program information (separate links are available for overviews and program information for each of the foundation's major programs). While none of the items mentioned above is searchable on its own, there is a site-wide search engine provided.

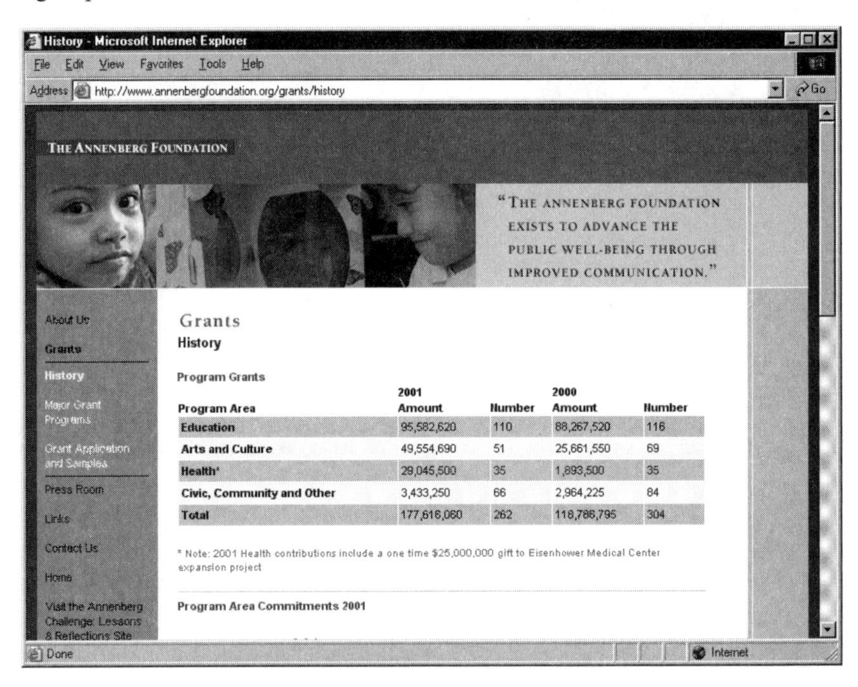

The last few years have seen a number of very sophisticated foundation Web sites come online with meticulously designed, database-driven capabilities. We now turn our focus to those foundation Web sites that can be placed on the upper ranges of the engagement continuum.

Grantseekers can see a fine example of a sophisticated, yet content-rich and Web-friendly design by visiting the Web site of the Chicago-based John D. and Catherine T. MacArthur Foundation (http://www.macfound.org). Several assumptions underlie the policies of the MacArthur Foundation, the most important being that the "Foundation's effectiveness depends in part on its capacity to learn from others." This indicates a willingness to engage its audience and is reflected throughout its Web site.

In the About Us section, the MacArthur Foundation provides an overview of its four major programs—the Program on Human and Community Development, the Program on Global Security and Sustainability, the General Program (providing support mostly for public-interest media projects and other changing special interest areas), and the MacArthur Fellows Program (the so-called "genius" awards). The foundation also makes program-related investments (PRIs) that support its goals. The information available in the About Us section and a brief financial snapshot are available for download in PDF format (and are available in Spanish and French as well). More extensive information on the major program areas is also available in HTML and PDF formats.

Recent Grants offers a browsable database of past grants made by the MacArthur Foundation going back to 1999. To navigate the grants listings, select the appropriate year from the program area you wish to view. Once in a grants listing for a particular program area in a given year, you can select a Strategy (or major category) from a drop-down menu to gain access to an even more focused grants list. (A sub-category drop-down menu is also offered for most Strategies to allow for the most relevant grants listings.) For instance, in the Human and Community Development program area, you can select the Strategy "Individuals and Society" from the drop-down menus provided, and then choose "Juvenile Justice" or "Mental Health" from the sub-categories. Each Strategy has its own essay describing the purpose, funding strategy, research accomplishments, and funding and contact information for each grantmaking program.

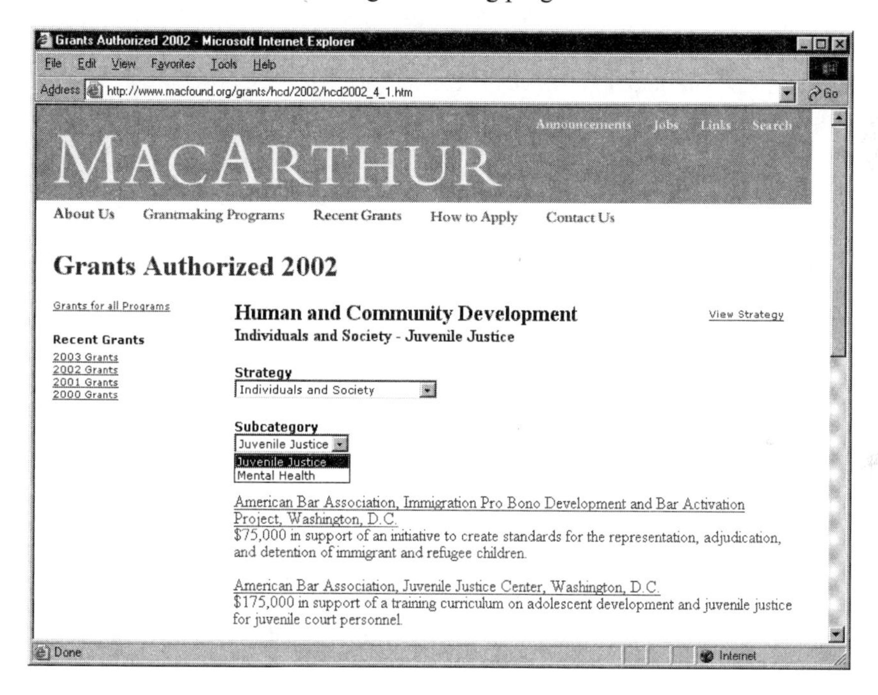

Also available on the site are speeches, papers, and presentations given by MacArthur Foundation staff or from its International Lecture Series on Population Issues. A collection of special reports commissioned by the foundation can be found here, as well as a listing of foundation publications that can be ordered by phone or that are available for download in PDF format directly from the Web site. Links to the MacArthur Foundation India (in English) and MacArthur Foundation Russia (in Russian) Web sites are also available from the home page.

The Bill & Melinda Gates Foundation (http://www.gatesfoundation.org) is dedicated to improving people's lives by sharing advances in health and learning with the global community. Co-chaired by Bill Gates' father, William H. Gates, Sr., and Patty Stonesifer, the Seattle-based foundation has an endowment of approximately $24 billion, making it the largest private foundation in the world. The foundation makes grants in four major program areas: Global Health, Education, Libraries, and the Pacific Northwest. Special projects that do not fall within these program areas are also funded, but only to pre-selected organizations.

The Web site for the Bill & Melinda Gates Foundation is a highly engaging one for all three elements we've discussed: content, interactivity, and design. It includes extensive information on the program areas mentioned above and also provides grants eligibility and guidelines, grants listings back to 1994 (with links to the Web sites of funded organizations), and tables and graphs giving a breakdown of Gates Foundation giving overall and by program area. Annual reports, fact sheets, newsletters, program publications, and other materials are also readily available, many in PDF format. The foundation also takes full advantage of its close relationship with the Microsoft Corporation. Among the more interactive features on the foundation's Web site are slide shows on the history of the Bill & Melinda Gates Foundation and profiles of exceptional programs funded by the foundation and the successes and challenges its leaders faced. (More of these profiles can be found in the Story Gallery.) Speeches by Bill Gates, Melinda Gates, William H. Gates, Sr., Patty Stonesifer, and individuals from the foundation's program areas can be found in the Media Center. Speeches are presented in full-text format, and many also have video and audio files that can be viewed or heard through Windows Media Player or Real Player.

Elsewhere on the site, you can find other interactive features, such as the World AIDS Day 2002 Interactive Documentary or audio versions of press releases from the foundation. The Bill & Melinda Gates Foundation Web site's ease of use, its attention to telling the full story behind the foundation's grantmaking, and its interactive features all contributed to its winning the 2002 silver medal of the Council on Foundations' Wilmer Shields Rich Award for a Web site in the "Independent, Family and Operating Foundations, Assets More Than $55 Million" category.

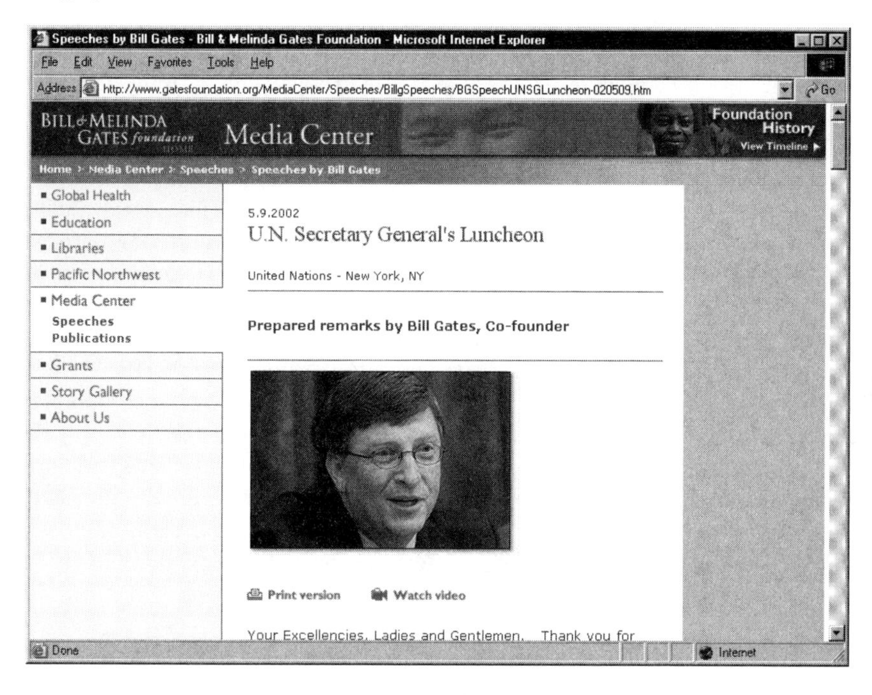

The mission of the Gill Foundation (http://www.gillfoundation.org) of Denver, Colorado, is to secure equal opportunity for all people, regardless of sexual orientation or gender identity. It is the country's largest funder of lesbian, gay, bisexual, and transgender organizations. The Gill Foundation's Web site has a searchable grants database and information on its programs, including an interactive eligibility quiz that asks the grantseeker a series of questions to determine whether or not his or her organization falls within the foundation's funding guidelines. The foundation's Web site takes engagement and information provision to the highest level by providing training and technical assistance materials, including information on fundraising fundamentals, board development, special events, corporate sponsorship, and capital campaigns. The site also provides proposal writing workshop information, news releases and publications, donor and employment resources, and sample documents on employment non-discrimination policy and fiscal sponsorship.

New to the Gill Foundation's Web site is a personalization feature that tailors the information you see to your own grantseeking needs. There are two personalization options at the site. First, you can register your personal profile with the site, including name (optional), contact or geographic information, audience type, gender, sexual orientation, and areas of interest. You are also asked to submit a username and password you will use to log in to the Web site when you return. The other personalization choice is to select the Change Your Audience Option to choose the audience term that best describes you (potential grantee, donor, media, grantee, training participant, or activist). In this way you can have news and other information that relates to your particular interests brought to your desktop automatically (without having to log on to the Web site with a username and password). Both features represent highly interactive ways to tailor what the visitor sees to the most relevant information based on his or her interests.

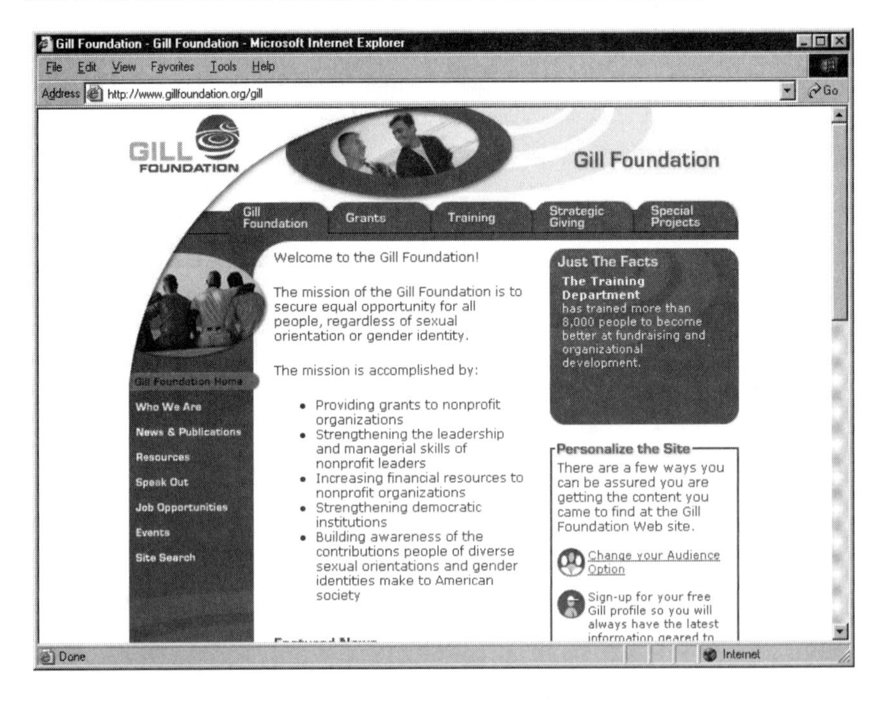

Schwab Learning (http://www.schwablearning.org/index.asp), an initiative of the Charles and Helen Schwab Foundation of San Mateo, California (http://www.schwabfoundation.org), advocates and educates in support of the foundation's mission by providing free information, resources, publications, and support to parents of children with learning differences and to children with learning disabilities themselves. The frustrating lack of information on dyslexia when Charles and Helen Schwab's son was diagnosed with the learning disorder was the inspiration behind the creation of the Schwab Learning program/Web site. Main directories include: Identifying (resources for understanding learning differences and recognizing a child's strengths and needs), Managing (resources to help manage issues that arise from having a child with learning differences), Connecting (resources for exchanging knowledge with the experts and gaining support in the SchwabLearning.org community), and Resources (easy-to-use, interactive tools and practical publications and resources to help children and parents of children with learning differences).

SchwabLearning.org totally engages its audience through a wide variety of means, including polls, quizzes, newsletters on the Web and via e-mail; the Parent to Parent Message Board; resources in Spanish; a Don't Panic, Get Help button; My Page personalization software (that will target news and information based on your personal interests, needs, and profile); and most importantly, through its overall assistance in connecting users with resources and information about learning differences.

In recent years, many foundations have transformed their plain Web sites into more appealing and complex sites. Examples of stellar Web content, interactivity, and design now abound. But it also has been instructive to observe the steady increase in the number of small- and medium-sized foundations that have been able to leverage modest new media budgets into excellent examples of the ways in which a Web site can further the mission of a foundation by engaging its audience through content, interactivity, and design.

Conclusion

This brief introduction to the world of independent foundations on the Web is designed to give you a taste of the wealth and scope of information to be found on the various types of grantmaker sites you are likely to encounter. We invite you to explore the full range of grantmaker sites available using the various search tools offered on the Foundation Center's Web site or by other means, such as general search engines. A complete list of annotated URLs for independent foundations will be found in Appendix B and on the Center's Web site.

CHAPTER THREE

Grantmaking Public Charities and Community Foundations on the Web

Although community foundations technically are public charities, they differ from other public charities in many respects. There is much information on the Web that can provide a clear explanation of the differences. In short, for grantseekers, it is best to keep in mind that public charities usually have very narrowly defined interests and are not tied to a specific geographic area, while community foundations have broad interests but tend to concentrate on specified regions. Both types of public charities file Form 990 with the IRS, while private foundations file Form 990-PF. For practical purposes, paying attention to the unique features of each type of public charity can expedite grantseeking on the Web. Thus, a grant application to a public charity should emphasize the defined purpose of the project, while a grant application to a community foundation should also focus on the geographic area specified by that foundation.

What Is a Public Charity?

There are approximately 850,000 public charities registered with the IRS under Section 501(c)(3) of the Internal Revenue Code. This is more than ten times the number of private foundations. Most, of course, are not grantmakers. The relatively small number of grantmaking public charities (sometimes referred to as "public foundations") that the Center has been able to uncover differ from private foundations in several ways, primarily in their sources of support. Private foundations typically draw their funds from a single source, either an individual, a family, or a company. With the exception of those few that are endowed, the majority of public charities are supported by contributions from multiple sources, including individuals, foundations, religious organizations, corporations, and government agencies. In some cases, income is generated from activities related to their charitable purposes.

There are several ways a nonprofit organization can meet the IRS definition of a public charity. One, called the "public support test," means that the organization must: a) receive no more than one-third of its support from gross investment and unrelated business income and b) receive at least one-third of its income from the public in contributions, fees, and gross receipts related to the organization's exempt purpose. A second way is for the organization to claim Automatic Public Charity Status. This status is given to schools, religious organizations, hospitals, or similar organizations that meet certain criteria. A typical example would be a religious organization that maintains a facility for worship. The third way to obtain public charity status is by establishing what is called a supporting organization, or one that is organized for, and controlled by, a designated public charity (or charities). Supporting organizations have existed since 1969. They have become more popular recently because a supporting organization is not subject to the excise taxes and penalties that apply to private foundations and because the tax code provides a more liberal deduction for donations made to such an organization.

Because public charities are accountable to a broad support base, the regulations and reporting requirements for them are less stringent than they are for private foundations. Gifts to public charities are commonly eligible for maximum income tax deductibility, whereas those to private foundations are limited. Furthermore, public charities and private foundations follow different annual IRS reporting requirements.

It is important to remember that most grantmaking public charities are by definition grantseekers as well, since gifts to them receive the full tax deductibility just mentioned. Another characteristic of grantmaking public charities is that their giving interests typically are very specific, addressing a narrow or single field of interest, a specific population group, or a limited geographic community (the latter is true for community foundations, of course). For the public charities listed in this chapter, their grantmaking activity may be only a small part of their overall charitable program.

Because the primary activity of community foundations is grantmaking, traditionally, the Foundation Center has included them in its statistical analyses and reference works about private foundations. The formal grantmaking operations and grant-reporting capabilities of most community foundations allow them to be represented logically and systematically in our databases and publications. Now that the Center is identifying and tracking other grantmaking public charities, for definitional clarity we can present community foundations as a group within the grantmaking public charity universe. The Center's links to community foundation Web sites are organized by state, since most community foundations are focused principally on a specific geographic area.

In recent years, the Foundation Center has identified more than 2,400 public charities, over and above the approximately 600 community foundations, that have some sort of grantmaking program. We will not attempt to present a complete picture of the grantmaking public charity universe in this chapter. At this time there is no simple way to systematically identify those non-private foundation charities that in fact do operate clearly defined giving programs. The Form 990 is not intended for this purpose and is only marginally helpful in this regard. We hope that our continued efforts to gather information on grantmaking public charities will stimulate those organizations that believe they qualify to be included in Center listings to contact us or forward information concerning their grantmaking programs.

Donor-Advised Funds

Most community foundations, in addition to their general funds, have donor-advised funds, which permit the donors to make recommendations as to where the donated money might be directed. Most community foundations and some public charities include this type of fund, which has been in existence for some time. Donor-advised funds managed by financial institutions, on the other hand, are relatively new and of increasing importance in the field. In fiscal year 2001, the Fidelity Investment Charitable Gift Fund (http://www.charitablegift.org) was the largest donor-advised fund in the United States. Similar charitable gift funds have been established by other investment groups.

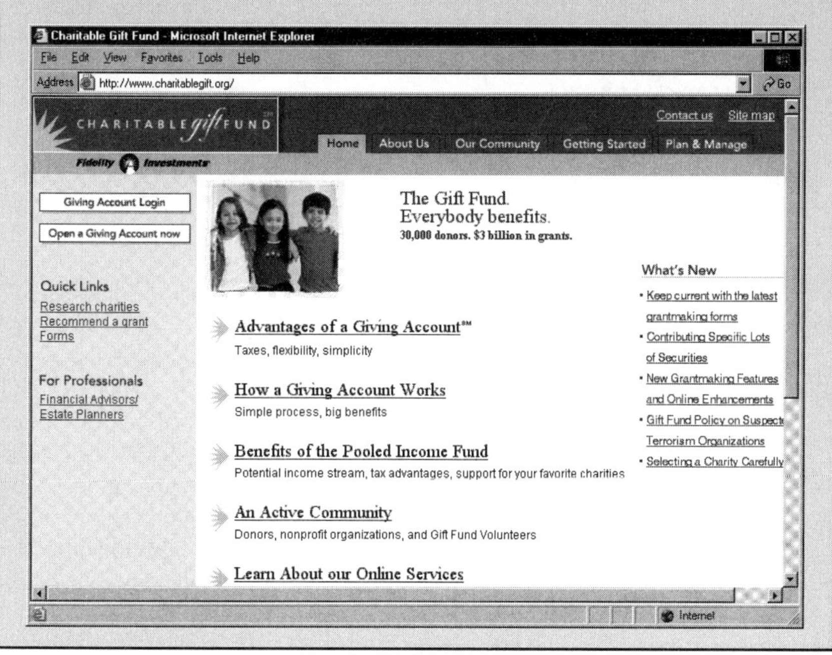

A Sampling of Useful Web Sites

There are a number of Web sites that aggregate information about the public charity universe. They are often the best starting points for your research because they present lists of useful Web links all in one place. Here are some examples that will help you access information. Sometimes the links will take you to a charity Web page, other times to a specific Web site focused on a particular aspect of your search.

The Alliance of Artists' Communities (http://www.artistcommunities.org) is a national service organization that supports artists' communities and residency programs. Click Links on the menu, and a list of organizations will be presented.

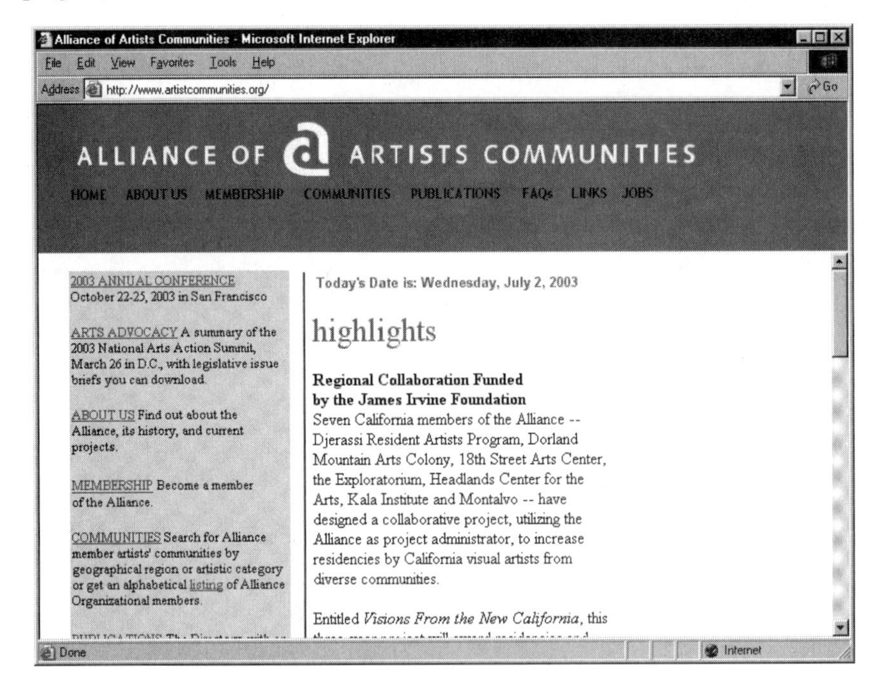

Community Foundation Locator (http://www.communityfoundationlocator.org/search/index.cfm), sponsored and maintained by the Council on Foundations, is an excellent tool for finding community foundations. Begin by clicking on a state or selecting from search options provided on the locator page. In addition to this page, the council's Web site (http://www.cof.org) provides a wealth of information about all types of grantmakers.

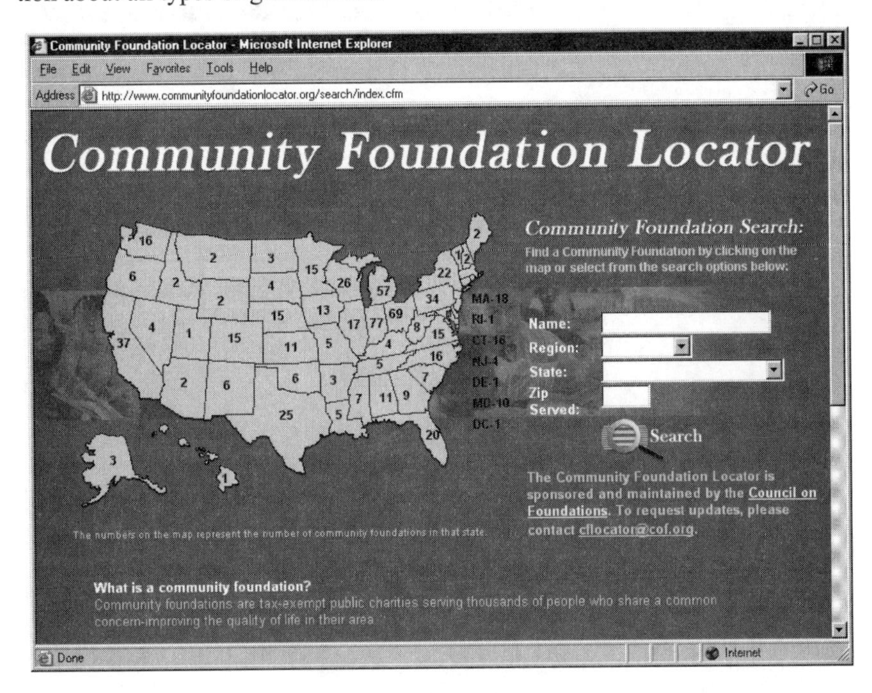

Foundations On-Line (http://www.foundations.org), a service of the Northern California Community Foundation, Inc., provides a list of links to community foundations, public charities, and additional sites to browse.

GrantsNet (http://www.grantsnet.com), sponsored by the Howard Hughes Medical Institute and the American Association for the Advancement of Science, is a free service and an excellent source to find funding for training in the biomedical sciences and undergraduate science education.

Grantmakers in Health (http://www.gih.org) is a very good source of charity listings for grantseekers focused on health-related giving.

The National Endowment for the Humanities (http://www.neh.gov/whoweare/statecouncils.html) provides listings of the humanities councils maintained by all 50 states and U.S. territories. The listings are extremely useful because they describe what projects are being funded within each state or territory. Most of these sites have links that lead to other charities.

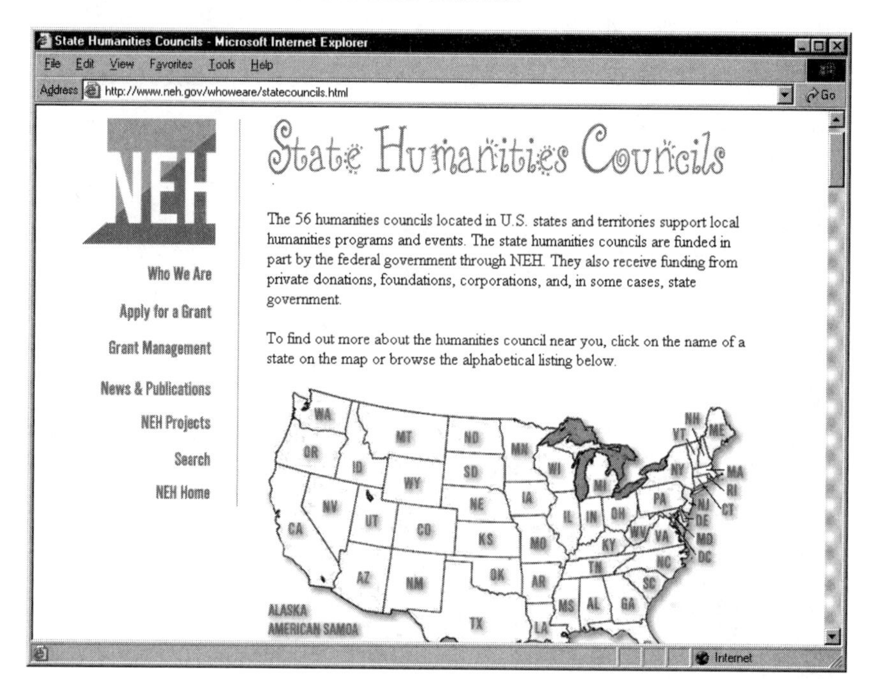

U.S. Nonprofit Organization's Public Disclosure Regulations Site (http://www.muridae.com/publicaccess) provides useful information about the regulations governing public disclosure of IRS forms concerning nonprofit organizations. It explains the different rules governing various types of nonprofits. Many areas of this site are free, but some require that you subscribe.

Looking for Funders

USING THE SEARCH CAPABILITY AT THE FOUNDATION CENTER'S WEB SITE

On the Foundation Center's Web site it is possible to do structured searching for information concerning grantmaking public charities on the Web.

Grantmaker Web Sites

In Grantmaker Web Sites, every grantmaking public charity and community foundation listed on the Foundation Center's Web site is annotated with general information about the charity and its Web site. In the Grantmaking Public Charities section, the time-saving Grantmaker Search feature lets you search the text of abstracts written by Center staff. These abstracts help you to learn the program interests of the charities and to become familiar with the contents of the sites without having to take the time to explore the sites yourself. Community foundations are listed alphabetically by state.

Let's say, for example, that you are interested in conservation issues and are looking for public charities or community foundations that make grants in this subject area. On the Center's Web Site, click on the Finding Funders directory and then on the left side of the following page, click on the section entitled Grantmaker Web Sites. From the expanded menu, select Grantmaking Public Charities or Community Foundations. Your search begins here.

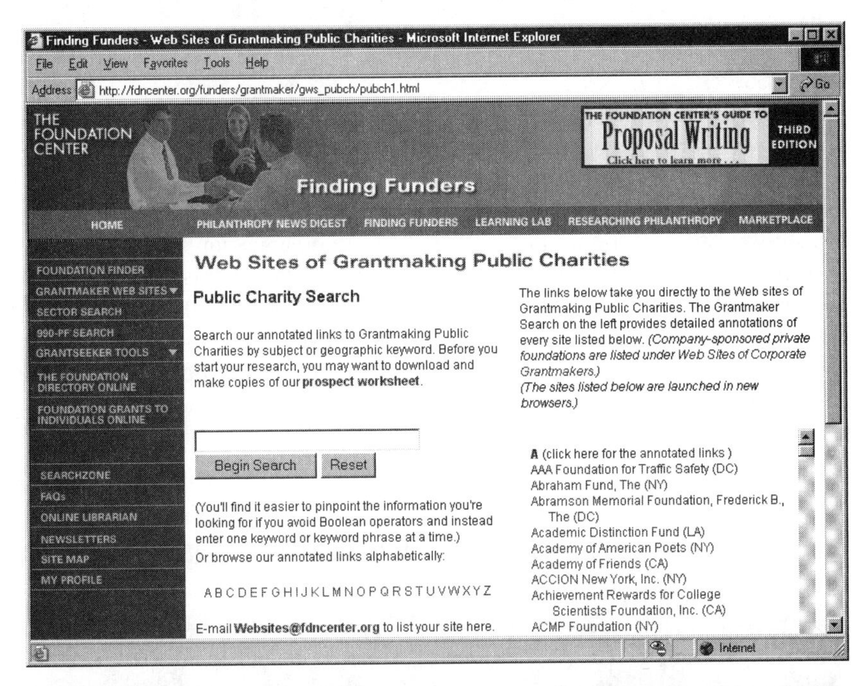

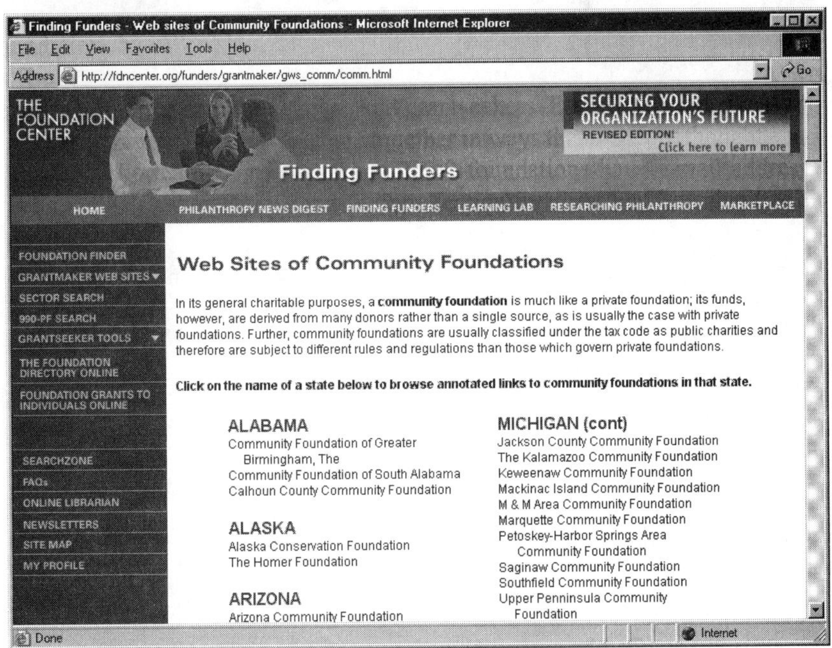

You can search grantmaking public charities by entering a keyword(s), or you can simply browse the links alphabetically. Because you are interested in conservation issues, enter the term "conservation" into the search box and click the Begin Search button to perform the search. A numbered list of results will appear. Clicking on the name of any grantmaking public charity from this list will take you to the Center staff-written abstract, with a description of the charity and a link to its home page.

Sector Search

The Foundation Center also offers Sector Search (http://www.fdncenter.org/funders/web_search/web_search.html), a search engine that indexes information gathered only from the most useful nonprofit Web sites. Instead of trying to retrieve useful information from a search of the entire Web, we have programmed this software to search only the Web sites of the organization type you specify (private foundations, corporate grantmakers, grantmaking public charities, community foundations, nonprofits, or government resources), thus significantly increasing your chances of finding the information you are looking for. To search for grantmaking public charities and/or community foundations only, simply de-select the grantmaker types you wish to exclude from your search by removing the check marks from the boxes next to those categories of grantmakers. The following screen shot shows that only the Community Foundations box remains checked.

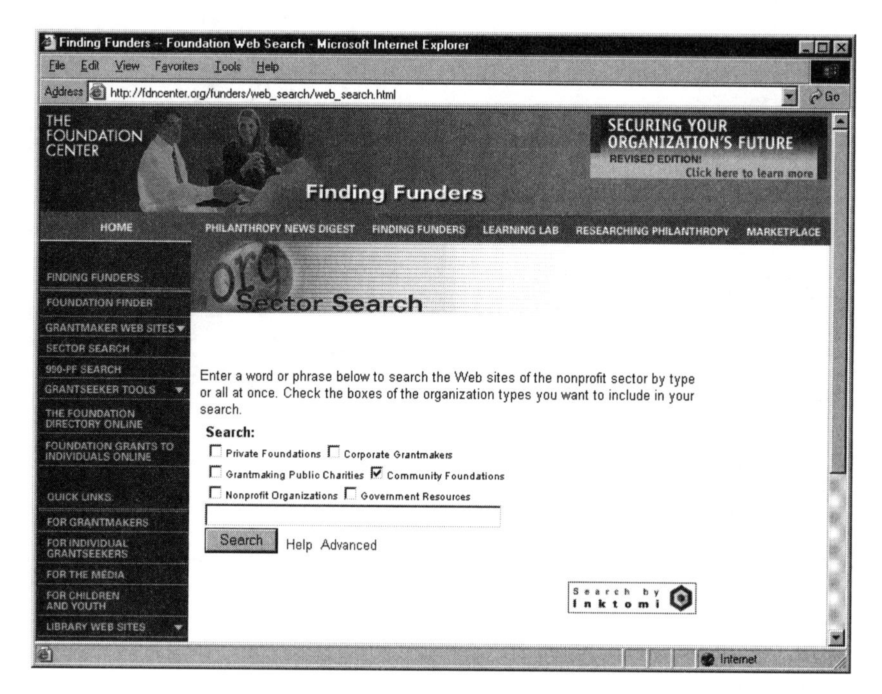

The Foundation Directory Online

For subscribers to *The Foundation Directory Online* (http://fconline.fdncenter.org), community foundations will be found in all of the Foundation Center's family of *Foundation Directory Online* products, while other grantmaking public charities are covered only in the Foundation Center's *Platinum* online subscription service.

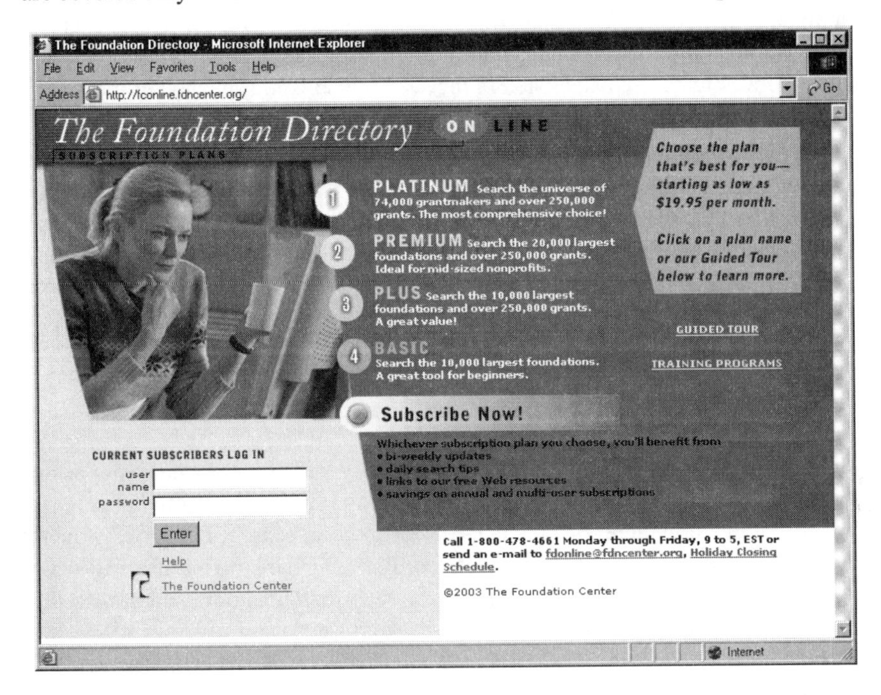

As noted, the Foundation Center continually strives to identify and describe public charities that operate grantmaking programs along with their other activities. Be sure to check the Grantmaker Web Sites, Sector Search, and *The Foundation Directory Online* areas of our Web site frequently for the latest updates. Also see Chapter 1 for a fuller description of these and all Center Web site resources.

USING A SEARCH ENGINE

An important point to keep in mind as a novice grantseeker is that searching the Web does not proceed in a straight line from point A to point B. It is very likely that in the beginning you will spend a lot of time getting used to the layered approach that is required. Eventually, you will develop search strategies that suit your specific needs.

Because all search engines are not alike, it makes sense to familiarize yourself with the capabilities of each one. Where one does not provide enough information, another might. Where one delivers few "hits," another may produce thousands. When using any search engine, enter terms that best specify what you are looking for. Try to be as specific as possible. For example, if you represent an arts organization and are looking for funding for a theater, you might enter keywords such as "theater funding" or "dramatic arts" into the search box. Or you might enter "public charity" or "women's charity" as keywords if you are seeking funding for a program benefiting women. Remember, the broader the term you enter, the greater the number of search results you will receive. Because there is no immediate way to identify a grantmaking public charity on the Web, it will be necessary to add terms such as "grants" or "funding" in your searches, or you will need to investigate each site listed in the search results to see whether the organization actually awards grants.

If the search engine you use does not produce a satisfactory list of Web sites, you can try again, either by entering different terms or by using a different search engine altogether. Experience will teach you which approach and which search engine best meet your specific research needs.

There is no substitute for a well thought-out plan for searching the Web. Discipline and persistence are required to navigate through the seemingly endless possibilities available. There are, however, several good search engines that can help you define and streamline your searches (see Appendix A).

Suggested Search Terms

Here are some specific words or phrases you may wish to include in your search strategies. Type them either separately or with another defining word in the search box. But don't stop there. Be creative. Customize your search. Think of synonyms and broader terms. As you become more familiar with the kind of information you are searching for and the unique features of each search engine, add those words that appear on a regular basis to your list. You might want to begin with words such as these:

- association
- public charity
- Form 990
- fund
- community foundation
- 501(c)(3)
- arts council
- application form
- annual report
- grants list

New IRS Disclosure Rules

Revised regulations regarding the IRS Form 990 took effect on June 8, 1999. The new disclosure rule requires nonprofit organizations to respond to public requests for information by making copies available of their Forms 990 for the past three years. An organization is also required to provide a copy of its application for tax exemption (Form 1023 or 1024), if the organization filed for exemption after July 1987 or possessed a copy of its exemption application on that date. All attachments and associated schedules to the forms must be included, although nonprofits do not have to provide the listing of their donor names.

Federal law used to require that most tax-exempt nonprofit organizations allow public inspection of recent, annual tax returns. As a result of this new ruling, however, public access has been expanded. Copies of Forms 990 must be made readily available to anyone making a request in person to an organization's management or administrative personnel. Requests in writing must be answered within 30 days unless the organization makes these documents widely available (such as on the Web).

Organizations must comply with the regulations or face penalties. The rules also define in detail the offices of an organization to which a request may *not* be made, list circumstances under which a response can be delayed for several days, and define a circumstance of harassment (requests made to interfere with an organization's work) under which a response can be withheld.

As we just mentioned, the regulations also provide that nonprofit organizations can satisfy the "widely available" requirement by posting their Forms 990 on the Web. If an organization posts its tax return on the Web, it is free from the requirement to provide the form when requests are made in person or by mail. Because the tax form itself must be presented in its original format, most 990 documents are presented in PDF format, making the return appear as if it were a photograph on your screen. To view PDF files it will be necessary to have the Adobe's Acrobat Reader software, which is available as a free download at http://www.adobe.com/products/acrobat/readstep2.html, if it is not already installed on your computer.

A Form 990 and the application for tax-exempt status are not alternatives to an annual report or an accounting audit, however. They are not intended to assist the grantseeker in any way. Forms 990 are primarily used to help the IRS determine whether an organization qualifies for tax exemption. Secondarily, they fulfill a legal requirement for accurate financial data that is publicly available. These two legal requirements offer the public the opportunity to examine a nonprofit's financial and operational activities and heighten public accountability. Guidestar.org is one of the best places to search for a charity's Form 990.

New Health Foundations

The dramatic increase of health conversions in the last two decades has resulted in the establishment of 163 new health foundations. These entities were established from the sale or merger of a nonprofit hospital, health plan, or health system with another entity to become a public charity, a private foundation, or a social welfare organization. More than 45 percent of the new health foundations are public charities. The majority of these charities focus their giving on the health-related or social welfare needs of specific populations in the community that for many years were served by the facility before its conversion. For grantseekers interested in funding within the healthcare sector of philanthropy, the Grantmakers In Health Web site (http://www.gih.org) provides a link to potential funders. On the tool bar, across the top of the page, click on Links, then click Health Grantmakers, and finally select GIH Funding Partners for an alphabetical listing of organizations that offer unrestricted support to Grantmakers In Health.

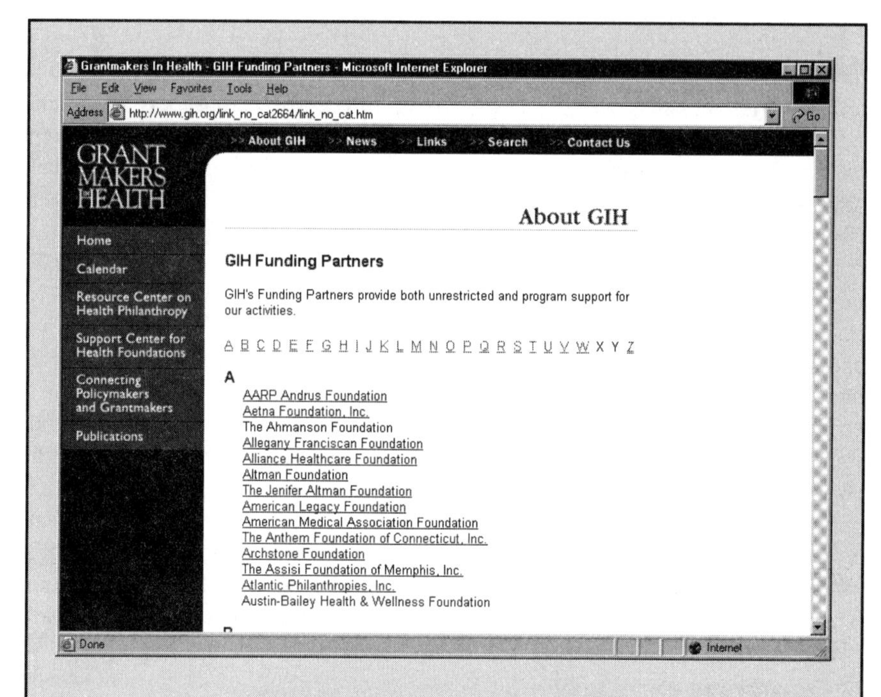

The St. Luke's Health Initiatives (http://www.slhi.org) of Phoenix, Arizona, is one example of a health conversion foundation with a well-developed site index. Select the Site Index from the top of the page for a complete listing of the Web site's contents. You will find listings of recent and past grant recipients and descriptions of current programs. In order to find the initiatives' fiscal information for the latest tax year, you will need to refer to its Form 990, which is not available on the site.

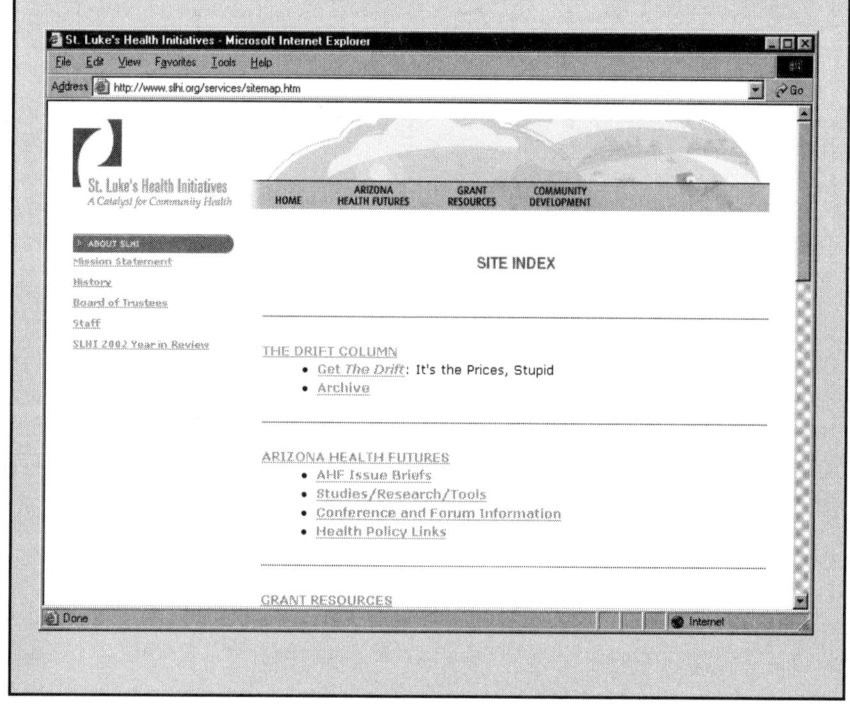

USING GUIDESTAR.ORG

Finding grant money is far from easy. It usually takes many searches to find a public charity that is a grantmaker, that meets your funding criteria, and that will select your organization as an eligible recipient. You can use GuideStar to help you identify these organizations.

GuideStar (http://www.guidestar.org) gathers and distributes data on more than 850,000 nonprofit entities. Financial information is included, and for some charities program information is also included. In 2000, GuideStar made all available IRS Forms 990 for public charities accessible on its site as PDF files. Basic information can be viewed directly online, but as of mid-2003, registration is now required to view Forms 990 on GuideStar (there is no charge to register). It is the site most commonly used by grantseekers and others seeking information on public charities.

Click on Advanced Search to use GuideStar to search by the name of a public charity or by its EIN (Employer Identification Number). You can also limit your searches by city and state, zip code, category, nonprofit type, income range, or NTEE code. Press Enter or click Search to submit your search, and a list of search results will appear. You may need to scroll down through a list of similar sounding names to find the specific charity you are interested in, since several organizations may match your search criteria. When the search results page appears on the screen, you will notice five symbols in a legend across the top. When these symbols appear next to an organization's name, it indicates whether there is information available in the form of a complete report, financials, Form 990, old reports and financials, and whether the organization has a Web site. Don't rely on these notations entirely, however. If you do not see a WWW icon next to the name of an organization in GuideStar, you still might want to use a search engine to try to find its Web address.

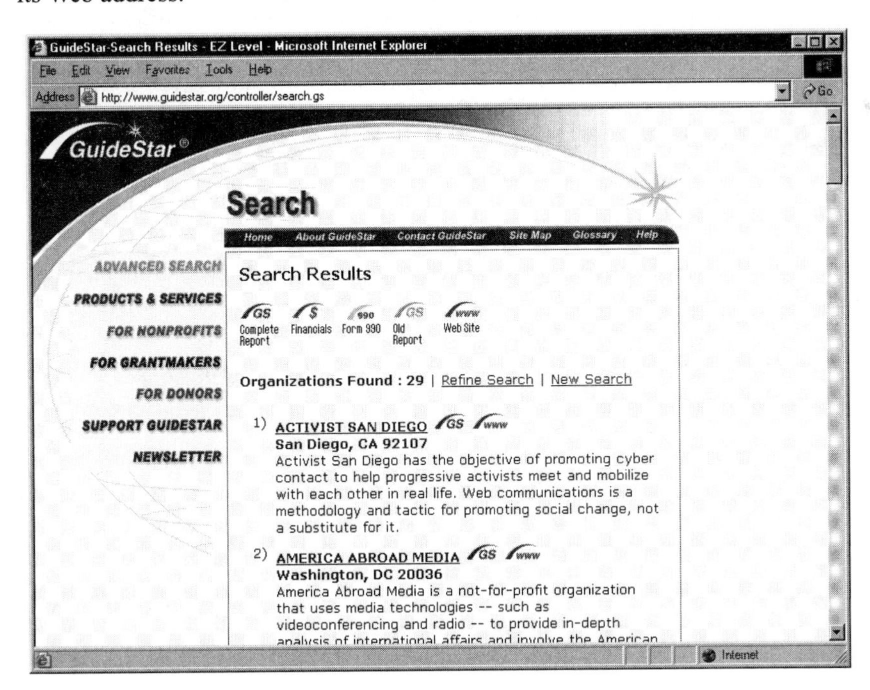

Once you select an organization from the list of results, look on the left side of the page for a menu. The Form 990, if available, is listed there. When using GuideStar, fill in as many of the search boxes as necessary. For example: to find a public charity that is an arts organization giving between $25,000 and $100,000 in New York City, the entry will look like the screen shot below. You can adjust the criteria in the search boxes to broaden or narrow your search.

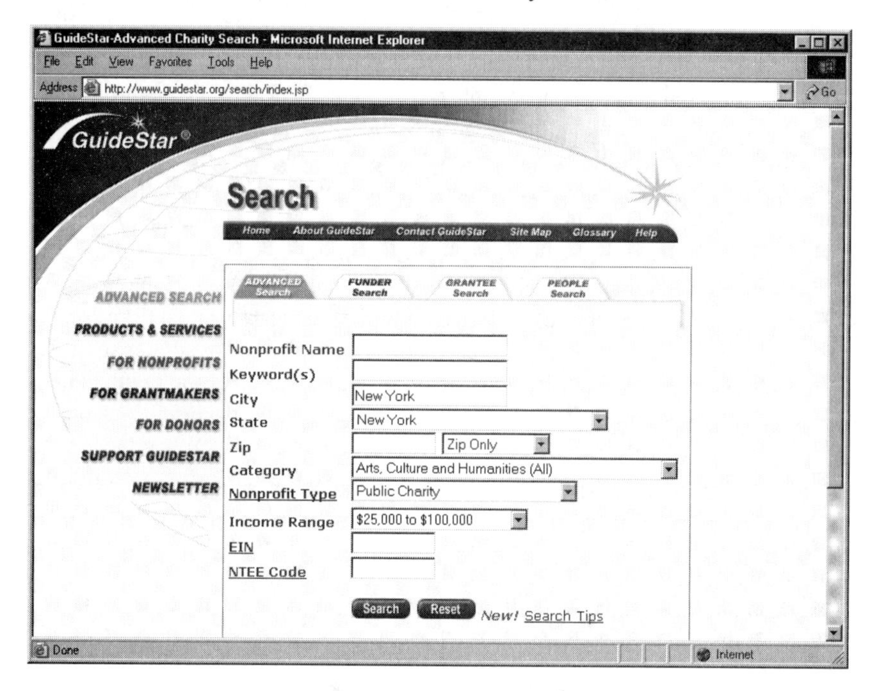

Finding Useful Information on Grantmaking Public Charity Web Sites

WEB SITE INFORMATION

When you visit a public charity's Web site, an easy way to determine whether it is a grantmaker or not is to check whether there is a grant application form or grants list on the site. But don't jump to conclusions. If there is no application form or grants list, the mission or program descriptions of the organization may also indicate whether or not it makes grants.

For public charities that appear to be grantmakers, check the annual report, if available, on the site. The type of funds that the organization provides will give you an idea of your chances for getting a grant. Most money awarded to grantseekers comes from unrestricted funds of the grantmaking organization. Grants made from restricted funds, e.g., donor-advised or other funds, may not meet your needs. If there is no clear indication that grants are awarded, do not be deterred. Use GuideStar to access the Form 990, since it might contain the information you are looking for. Or check other Web sites to obtain additional information. Once you have determined that the public charity is indeed a grantmaker, but the charity states "applications not accepted," you may not want to spend further time researching this particular organization. And if it's clear from posted guidelines on the Web that you don't qualify, it goes without saying that you shouldn't apply.

On the other hand, if it seems that you might qualify and there is an online application form, you should take this as a very good sign. The Web site should also give more detailed information about the sort of programs that are likely to be funded and the size of the grants that the organization will typically give. The preferred method of contacting the organization—by letter, e-mail, or telephone—should be noted as should the application deadline. In some cases, application forms can be downloaded, printed, or filled in from the Web site, like the form made available on the Web site of the Muskegon County Community Foundation (http://www.cffmc.org/teacherminigrants.htm).

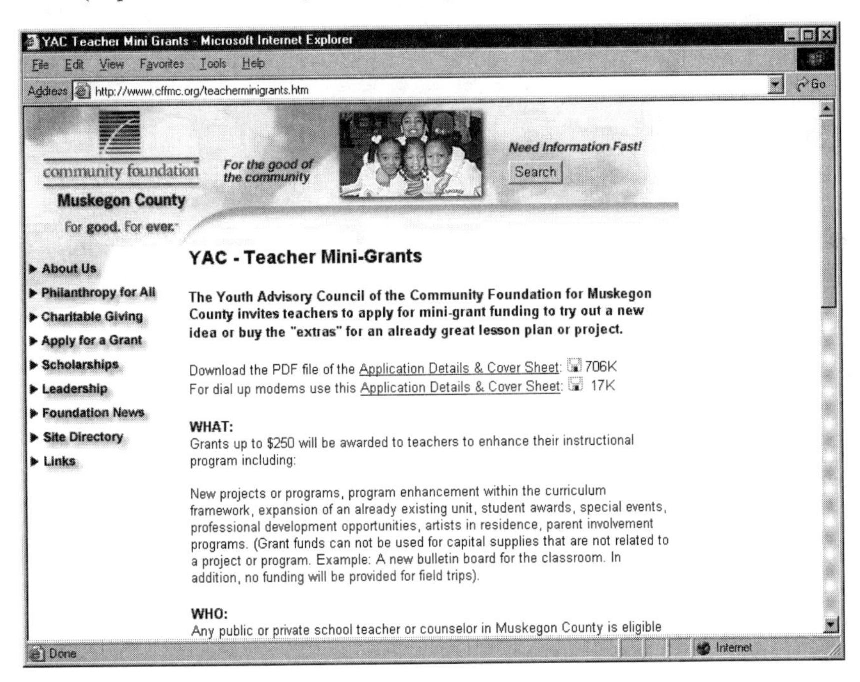

Be sure to scan the charity's board of directors or staff listing. You should do this for two reasons. The first is to assess the credibility and stature of the organization. The second reason is that you may recognize the name of someone with whom you have had contact in the past. A personal connection can be valuable. A telephone call or a preliminary letter of inquiry with a succinct description of your program's needs is definitely worthwhile. Indeed, that approach enhances your chance for eventual funding, and it will also help when it comes time to submit a full proposal. The following screen shot shows a list of board members for the Humanities Council of Washington, D.C. (http://www.wdchumanities.org), with brief biographical information on each board member.

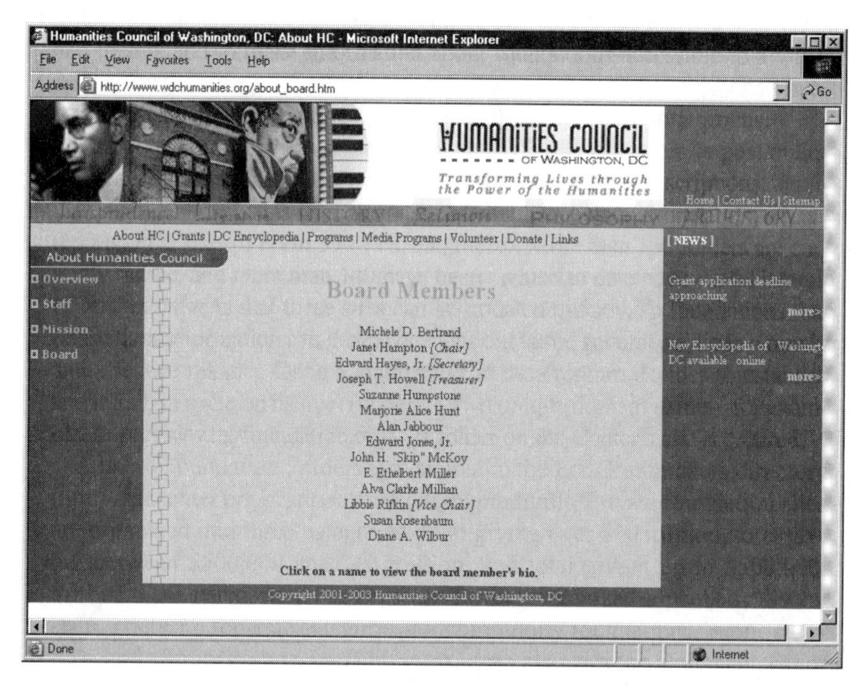

Before you exit a Web site be sure to click on any available links, which may direct you to *other* Web sites that could be useful and should be explored. Some charities print a "last updated" line at the bottom of their Web pages. If the site is not current, use caution when relying on the information provided.

THE FORM 990—AN IMPORTANT PART OF YOUR RESEARCH

More often than not, fiscal information for a nonprofit organization will not be included on its Web site. Even an annual report may not include financial data. This kind of information, however, is a very important part of your research.

All public charities over a certain minimum size file an IRS Form 990, which provides information about whether the charity makes grants. Check the charity's Web site to see if it posts its Form 990. This is the best way to get the most current information. The Tides Foundation (http://www.tidesfoundation.org) of San Francisco, California, for example, offers its Form 990 and recent grants lists on its site. If the charity you are investigating does not provide a copy of its 990 on its site, you may want to use GuideStar.org (see above) to obtain that information.

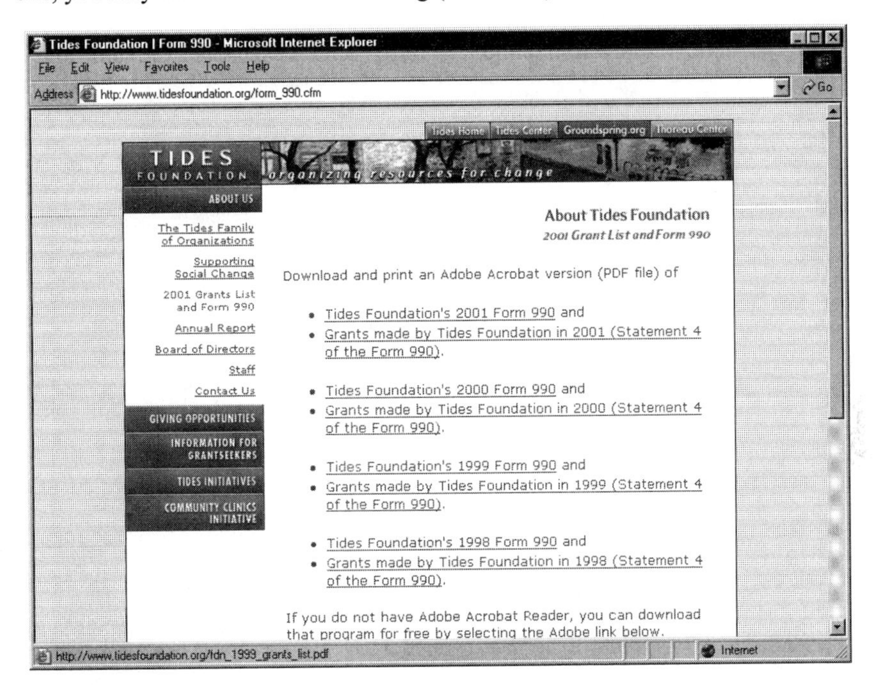

A word to the wise: If there is a current tax return listed as well as a prior year's return, and the more current fiscal data does not show evidence of grantmaking, check the prior year's return. Sometimes the more recent return has not been fully completed or was inaccurately filled out. Checking earlier returns may provide the information you seek.

To verify the grantmaking status of the organization, turn to page 2, Part II of the Form 990. Lines 22 and 23 will state the dollar amount of grants provided for that tax year. If these lines do not give the information, line 43 may have information on awards, prizes, scholarships, etc. Read the statement attached to this line. It will say whether there were any grants, scholarships, or loans to individuals or organizations for that tax year. If the information is still not available, refer to Schedule A, Part IV, line 3A to see if the organization provides grants for scholarships, loans, and the like. Again, look for a corroborating statement(s): e.g., the explanation of exempt purpose or explanation of the program achievements noted on the return.

As an illustration, the following screen shot shows the top of page 2, Part II of the Three Guineas Fund's (http://www.3gf.org) Form 990 for 2001. By looking at line 22, you can see that $180,000 was given in grant support for that tax year. By looking further down the page to Part III, "Statement of Program Services Accomplishments," you will find that the total grants amount constituted nine separate grants in support of the fund's mission of "advanc[ing] social justice for girls and women."

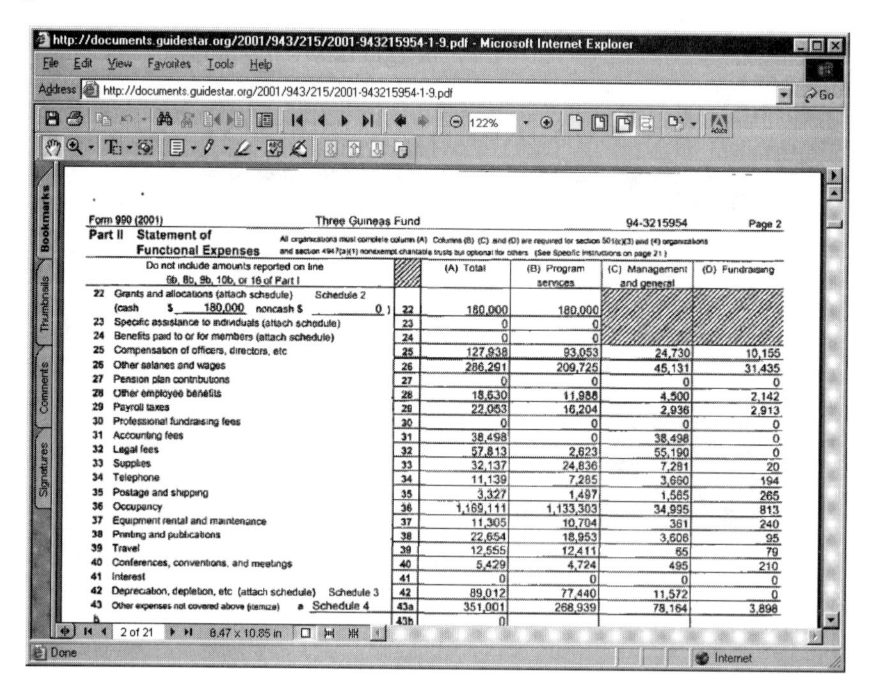

Form 990 (2001) Three Guineas Fund 94-3215954 Page 2

Part II Statement of Functional Expenses All organizations must complete column (A). Columns (B), (C), and (D) are required for section 501(c)(3) and (4) organizations and section 4947(a)(1) nonexempt charitable trusts but optional for others. (See Specific Instructions on page 21.)

Do not include amounts reported on line 6b, 8b, 9b, 10b, or 16 of Part I		(A) Total	(B) Program services	(C) Management and general	(D) Fundraising
22 Grants and allocations (attach schedule) Schedule 2 (cash $ 180,000 noncash $ 0)	22	180,000	180,000		
23 Specific assistance to individuals (attach schedule)	23	0	0		
24 Benefits paid to or for members (attach schedule)	24	0	0		
25 Compensation of officers, directors, etc	25	127,938	93,053	24,730	10,155
26 Other salaries and wages	26	286,291	209,725	45,131	31,435
27 Pension plan contributions	27	0	0	0	0
28 Other employee benefits	28	18,630	11,988	4,500	2,142
29 Payroll taxes	29	22,053	16,204	2,936	2,913
30 Professional fundraising fees	30	0	0	0	0
31 Accounting fees	31	38,498	0	38,498	0
32 Legal fees	32	57,813	2,623	55,190	0
33 Supplies	33	32,137	24,836	7,281	20
34 Telephone	34	11,139	7,285	3,660	194
35 Postage and shipping	35	3,327	1,497	1,565	265
36 Occupancy	36	1,169,111	1,133,303	34,995	813
37 Equipment rental and maintenance	37	11,305	10,704	361	240
38 Printing and publications	38	22,654	18,953	3,606	95
39 Travel	39	12,555	12,411	65	79
40 Conferences, conventions, and meetings	40	5,429	4,724	495	210
41 Interest	41	0	0	0	0
42 Depreciation, depletion, etc (attach schedule) Schedule 3	42	89,012	77,440	11,572	0
43 Other expenses not covered above (itemize) a Schedule 4	43a	351,001	268,939	78,164	3,898
b	43b	0			

Aside from this information, the Form 990, although filers are not mandated to do so, may sometimes have grants lists attached, giving you an idea of the number and type of grants and amount of money awarded.

Once you have established that an organization is a grantmaking charity in your area of interest, you should make sure that you have all the information needed to meet the requirements. The more information you have that corresponds to the organization's grantmaking guidelines and procedures, the greater your chances of targeting the right funders and of obtaining funding. To avoid wasted effort, requests are best limited to the most likely organizations. To help you determine whether there is a match, you may want to print out and use the Foundation Center's Prospect Worksheet, available in the Finding Funders section of the Center's Web site.

Residencies

The majority of grantmakers provide cash grants to nonprofit organizations. A typical pattern for some grantmaking public charities, however, is to give an award or awards each year directly to individuals in specific fields. Many also provide individuals with non-monetary support. Some grantmaking public charities that support individual artists, for example, provide both cash grants and residencies, while others provide only residencies. Residencies are non-monetary grants that cover workspace, food, housing, and other expenses for the duration of the residency. If the organization you are researching appears to offer only residencies, refer to the Form 990 and/or the Web site to determine if cash grants are also given.

The Djerassi Resident Artists Program (http://www.djerassi.org) is an example of a public charity that provides only residencies. You may check the Form 990 or the Web site for further information. Here is what you will find.

If you examine the 2001 Form 990 (available at Guidestar.org), you will notice that there is no entry on Part II, line 22 or 23 for grants, but Part III, "Statement of Program Services," points you to Attachment D, where you will find a listing for its Resident Artists Program and a dollar amount for the expenses. On the tax return you will also find a list of grantees and statistical breakdowns of residencies awarded by discipline, gender, and geography. This is the kind of detective work you will need to engage in if you want to use the Web to research funding opportunities at grantmaking public charities.

In another part of the Djerassi Resident Artists Program's Web site, you will see several categories listed on the menu on the left side of the home page. Select Residencies to find out about the program. Go into Applications to find information on how and when to apply and to find the application form itself (to be printed out and mailed in). The information contained here should help you decide whether this is a good prospect for you or not.

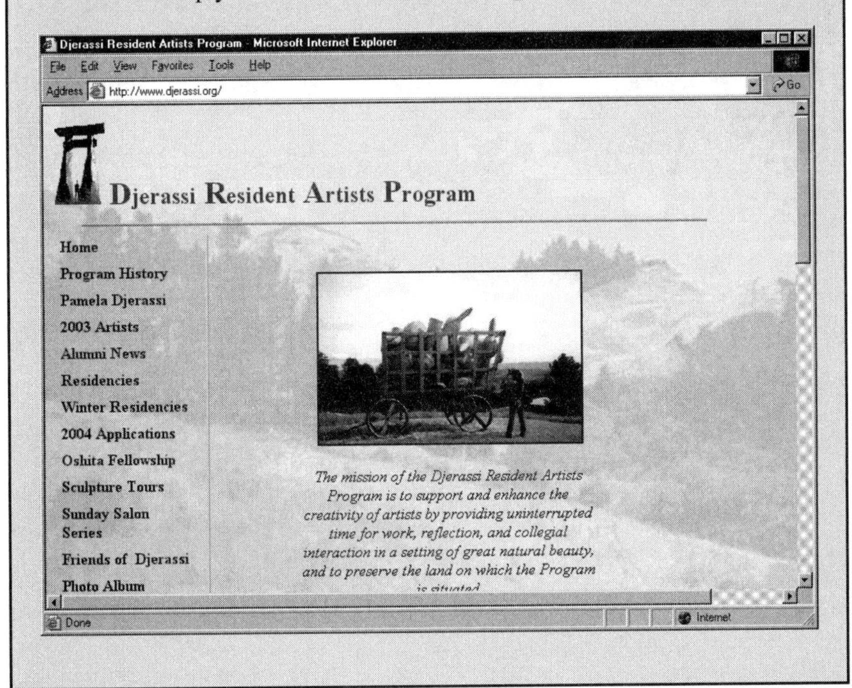

Some Examples of Grantmaking Public Charity and Community Foundation Web Sites

Below are examples of several well-developed grantmaking public charity and community foundation Web sites. Please note that these are large organizations whose grantmaking programs focus on specific subject fields or geographic areas.

Ms. Foundation for Women (http://www.ms.foundation.org)
The Ms. Foundation for Women, based in New York City, has a Web site that helps promote the foundation's charitable purpose. From the Publications area of the site, you can access the foundation's annual report (with grants listings), grants guidelines, and a list of funding opportunities. The Ms. Foundation for Women operates programs in the following areas: Women's Economic Security; Women's Health and Safety; and Girls, Young Women, and Leadership.

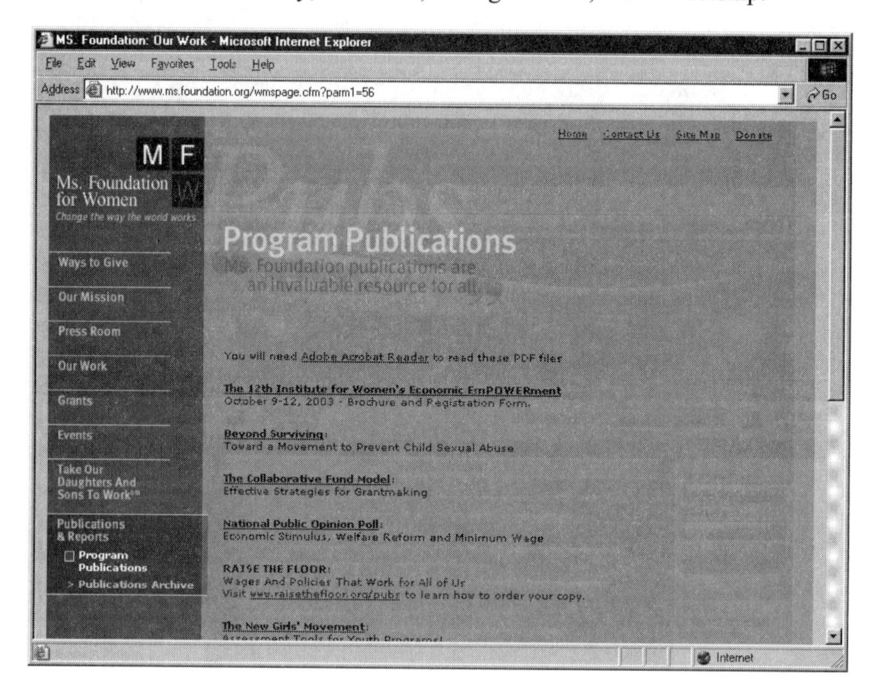

The Howard Hughes Medical Institute (http://www.hhmi.org)

The Howard Hughes Medical Institute is based in Chevy Chase, Maryland, and its mission is to support science education from the earliest grades through advanced training. Its Web site will take some time to explore thoroughly. While this site contains a wealth of information, it is necessary to click through several screens to find what you need. To find the application information, select Grants and Fellowships from the top of the home page. If you explore some of the program information in the Obtaining Funding section, you will find application guidelines and forms in PDF and Word formats. There are many additional pages that provide relevant information for the grantseeker.

The Pinellas County Community Foundation (http://fdncenter.org/grantmaker/pinellas)

The Web site of the Clearwater, Florida-based Pinellas County Community Foundation was developed by the Foundation Center as part of its Foundation Folders initiative. (See page 40 for more information on the Foundation Center's Foundation Folders Initiative.) On the left side of the page is a table of contents that makes it possible to see at a glance the topics covered. The menu includes information about the foundation, its history, a grants list, guides for donors, and a list of supporters.

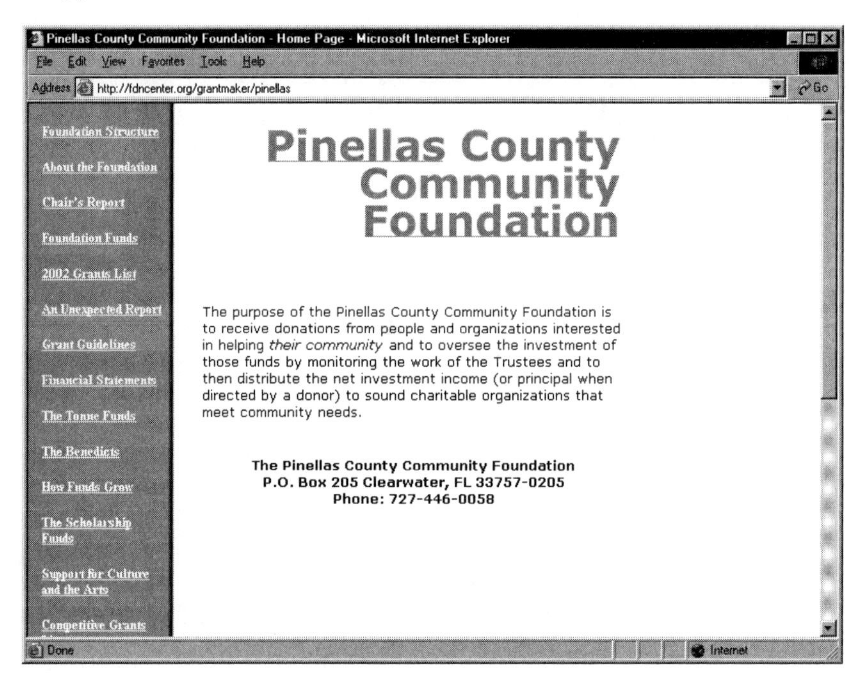

The Cleveland Foundation (http://www.clevelandfoundation.org)
Based in Cleveland, Ohio, the Cleveland Foundation is America's oldest community foundation. The site provides access to numerous forms, including the foundation's grants guidelines in PDF format and a grant request cover sheet and grant reporting form, which are both available as Word documents. You can enter your information directly into the forms and then save them to your computer. Similarly, a project budget form, available as an Excel file, lets you enter your project budget information directly into the appropriate areas and can then be printed out or downloaded.

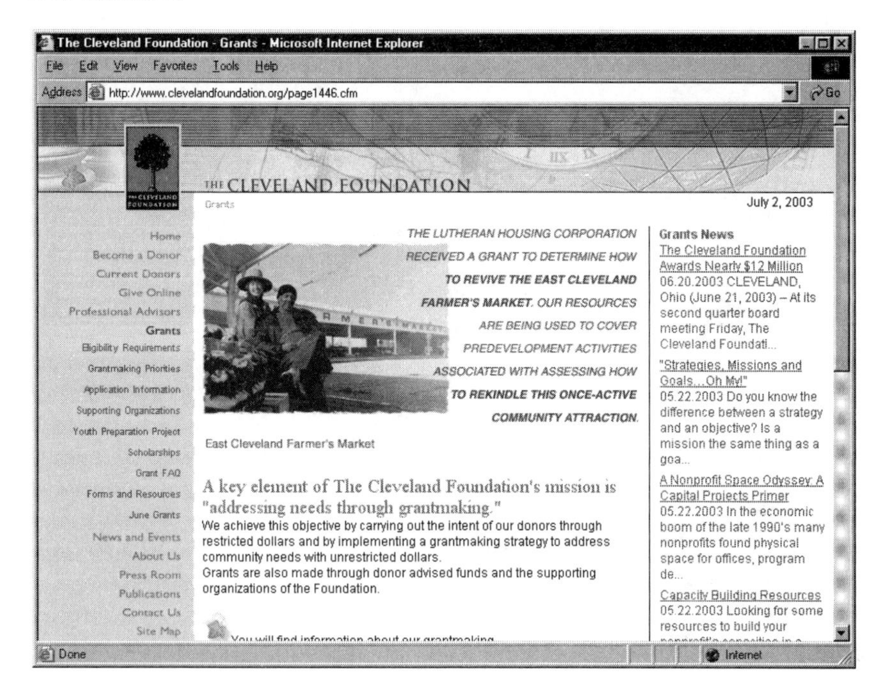

The Robin Hood Foundation (http://www.robinhood.org)

The Robin Hood Foundation's goal is to eliminate poverty in New York City. Its Web site provides a great deal of information about the foundation's giving. Select the Program topic from the tool bar across the top of the page, and you can view a list of the five Core Fund Recipients in alphabetical order by program area. The program areas are divided into the following categories: early childhood, education, job training, survival, and youth and after-school programs. There are also descriptions of successful ongoing programs, a description of the foundation's funding priorities, and information on the foundation's 9/11 Relief Fund recipients.

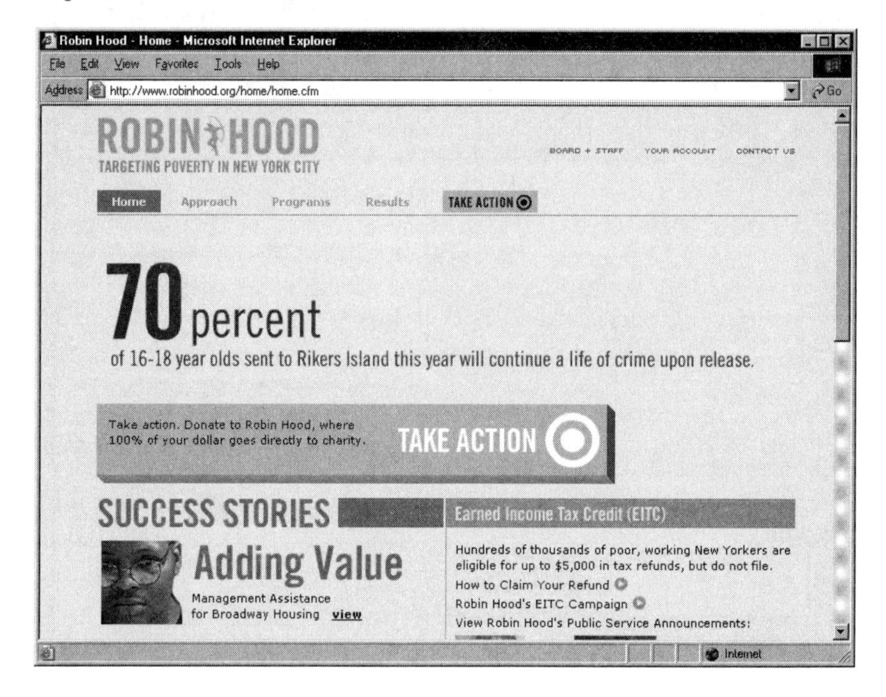

Conclusion

Grantmaking public charity and community foundation Web sites generally provide detailed information about a charity's purpose: for example, whether it makes grants on a broad basis or exists for the benefit of a specific organization(s). Most Web sites have internal search capabilities that will yield even more detailed information. If the description does not make it clear whether the organization gives grants, a careful look at its Form 990 can provide that information. In some cases, an even more detailed description of giving policies can help you select likely prospects and eliminate unlikely sources of funding.

Inspection of a charitable organization's Web site will help indicate whether or not it could be a source of funding for your project. One important key phrase to look for is a description saying that the charity has "unrestricted funding." That phrase shows that the charity's leadership, independent of any advice from donors, decides where at least a portion of its funding will be directed.

To select a likely public charity for support of a given project, check on the amount and direction of funding that the charity typically awards. A list of the charity's recent grants will produce much of this information. The wording of the program or mission statement of the funder should be studied, to help guide the writing of a proposal or submission of an application. Directions for submission formats and any deadlines should be observed carefully, as should any special instructions. For example, some funders require multiple copies of your proposal.

While submitting a number of applications to a range of different grantmaking organizations may seem to be an attractive strategy, this scatter-shot approach typically does not yield results. It is best to concentrate on meeting as closely as possible the precise criteria outlined in the guidelines of a specific public charity or charities. One well-aimed proposal can be more effective than a number of less targeted applications.

CHAPTER FOUR

Corporate Giving Information on the Web

Corporate Giving: An Overview

The motivations behind the giving policies of individual corporations vary widely and can be complex. Before delving into corporate giving research on the Web, a brief description of why and how corporations give will offer grantseekers a better understanding of what to look for when undertaking online investigation into corporations as possible sources of funding.

Corporate giving usually entails a combination of altruism and self-interest. Unlike foundations and other charitable agencies, philanthropy is at best a minor sideline for most corporations. Their main obligations are to their customers, employees, shareholders, and the "bottom line." They give to support employee services, guarantee well-trained potential employees, build both local and national community relations, enhance their image, return favors, secure tax deductions, and influence policy and opinion makers.

Companies understand the power of publicity and that charitable giving helps build a strong public image. Some enlightened companies view giving as essential for good corporate citizenship. However, corporations expect concrete rewards in return for their generosity.

Many companies today use the Internet as a means to promote their philanthropic activities. By posting information about their charitable endeavors on the Web, companies make the public aware that they are involved in improving the quality of life, particularly in areas of company operations. This exposure gives the company a positive image and improves public relations, which ultimately translates into increased profits.

TRENDS IN CORPORATE GIVING

In recent years corporations have reshaped their giving programs, narrowing their focus to specific objectives, carefully examining how grants are used, and rethinking their possible benefits. Many also have developed additional non-cash giving programs.

Companies often favor high-profile causes such as improving our nation's education system, with a focus on math, science, opportunities for minorities, and school reform. Environmental issues, low-income housing, and preventive health maintenance also are popular areas of corporate giving.

In addition, companies strive to maximize the impact of their giving. Direct involvement with students and teachers, in projects such as adopt-a-school and other tutoring and mentoring programs, is one approach. More and more companies also seem to be fostering collaborative donor and nonprofit efforts and taking on long-term projects. In a bid for enhanced community standing, they also support voluntarism among their employees.

COMPANY-SPONSORED FOUNDATIONS AND DIRECT CORPORATE GIVING PROGRAMS

Companies provide support to nonprofits through private "company-sponsored" foundations, direct corporate giving programs, or both. Company-sponsored foundations are legally separate entities that usually maintain close ties with the sponsoring companies, and typically their giving directly reflects their "parents'" interests. Most maintain relatively small endowments and rely on annual contributions from the company to support their programs. Some corporations build their

The Community Reinvestment Act

The Community Reinvestment Act (CRA), a federal law passed in 1977, requires banks to help meet the credit needs of their entire communities, including low- and moderate-income neighborhoods. Banks failing to do so may be denied permission by the government to expand their business locations, buy or merge with other banks, or engage in interstate banking. Grantseekers looking for loans rather than cash or in-kind gifts, therefore, might begin by seeking out banking firms in their own communities. Whether CRA loans represent a form of corporate giving is a hotly debated topic within the philanthropic community, but some companies do regard these loans, which generate interest on the companies' investment, as part of their total charitable giving.

The Community Reinvestment Act does not require banks to make unsound business decisions. Banks are not obligated to make loans to organizations or individuals believed to be a risk. The CRA points banks in a general direction in order to serve the needs of the community in which they are located, rather than directing them to make specific loans. The CRA stimulates banks to make loans for low-income family housing, to invest in community development, and to support small businesses.

foundations' endowments in "fat" years and tap into them in "lean" ones so that giving levels remain fairly consistent. For others, there is a direct relationship between the state of the economy, the value of company stock, and corporate philanthropic coffers, so giving can vary greatly from year to year depending on economic conditions.

Company-sponsored foundations must adhere to the appropriate regulations governing all private foundations, including filing a yearly IRS Form 990-PF, which includes a report on contributions. As with all Forms 990-PF, these returns are publicly available on a number of Web sites, including the Foundation Center's site. These returns can be very helpful in researching individual corporate foundations and their giving.

For all other charitable activities not conducted by a company's foundation, there is much less government regulation. Corporations are not required to publicize direct corporate giving programs or to sustain prescribed funding levels. They also support nonprofits in a variety of other ways out of operating funds, and these expenditures won't show up in their giving statistics, if such numbers are made available at all. For a variety of procedural, policy, and/or legal reasons, a corporation may not be able to contribute directly to a worthy organization and will choose to provide support in some other way. This is often treated as a business expense. For these reasons, finding information on direct corporate giving programs can be challenging.

"In-kind" gifts, such as donated products or loaned employee services, comprise an estimated 20 percent of corporate giving, although these numbers may be inflated due to the fact that many companies report their in-kind donations at market value rather than at cost. Whatever the true percentage of corporate giving they represent, in-kind gifts are sometimes overlooked by organizations seeking corporate support.

Direct corporate giving by public companies has been a topic of controversy within the business community for some time now. Especially in lean times, shareholders sometimes complain that corporate profits belong to them and not to charity. While big business tends to agree, many enlightened CEOs realize that the long-term interests of a company and its shareholders are best met by a reinvestment of some corporate funds back into the community. Only through a healthy community, they say, can business flourish. This doesn't mean, however, that a company will not attempt to hide some or all of its charitable endeavors from the public.

For the reasons noted above, most of the corporate giving information available on the Web concerns company-sponsored foundations. Foundations usually provide much more specific information concerning their grantmaking activities, including information on address and contact persons, geographic limitations, fields of interest, types of support offered, application procedures, and so on. One of the advantages for a company that uses a direct giving program rather than a company-sponsored foundation is precisely that the company need not disclose how much or to whom it contributes. Therefore, when researching direct corporate giving programs online, grantseekers must use a little more ingenuity and adopt a well-honed and discerning selection process.

A barrier to uncovering useful giving information on the Web is that companies tend to use their Web sites primarily as public relations tools. They may post little more than several pages concerning some of the high-profile grants they have made in the recent past. Unfortunately, this kind of Web presentation can lead grantseekers to believe that they may be eligible for a grant, when in fact they are not. Sites like these often generate hundreds, if not thousands, of applications to companies that do not accept unsolicited applications or do not support the causes these proposals address.

How to Find Corporate Funders

As already noted, most corporate giving coincides closely with other corporate activities and usually is limited to the geographic areas where companies conduct business, including headquarters and plant and subsidiary locations. The grantseeker's search should focus on local businesses as well as on major corporations that operate in their neighborhood. Corporate directories and corporate giving studies are key resources.

In addition to the Web strategies outlined below, grantseekers should also consult public libraries for regional and business indexes. The local Chamber of Commerce and Better Business Bureau also may have such guides. Do not overlook the yellow pages and local community newspapers. In corporate grantseeking, personal contacts are essential. A grantseeker should consider board members, volunteers, and staff as assets who may have important contacts with corporate funders. These people should be encouraged to share their knowledge and to think about whom they may know who can help secure corporate funding.

UTILIZING THE WEB AS A SEARCH TOOL

All of this having been said, many companies now maintain a presence on the Web. With a little ingenuity on the grantseeker's part, these sites can become important potential sources of information about corporate community involvement and grantmaking activities.

Searching: Secondary Corporate Giving Resources

Several portal sites are good starting points for grantseekers in search of corporate giving programs and company-sponsored foundations. Primary among these are the Foundation Center's Web site (http://fdncenter.org/funders/grantmaker/gws_corp/corp1.html), the U.K.-based Charities Aid Foundation's CCInet (http://www.ccinet.org/search.cfm), and the CSC Non-Profit Resource Center (http://home.attbi.com/~cscunningham/Corporate.htm). These sites have extensive lists of links to corporate giving programs and company-sponsored foundations.

The Foundation Center's Web Sites of Corporate Grantmakers (http://fdncenter.org/funders/grantmaker/gws_corp/corp1.html) is a listing of corporate givers that can be browsed alphabetically or searched by subject or geographic keyword. (For more on this and other Center Web site features, see Chapter 1.)

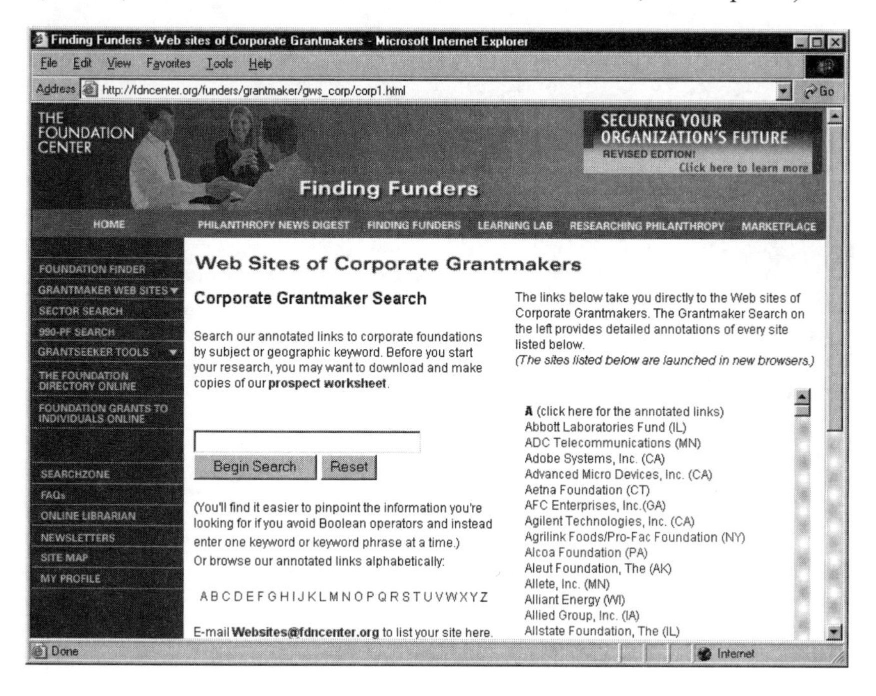

The Charities Aid Foundation's CCInet (http://www.ccinet.org), a corporate community involvement site, hosts a searchable database of more than 270 companies that offer some form of charitable giving. CCInet is based in the UK but includes American companies in its database. You can search alphabetically or by keyword, country, grantmaker type, grant type (or type of support), grant area (or field of interest), online report type, or business type. Entries in your search results indicate which companies have earned the CCInet Gold or Silver Hallmark Award, which are benchmarks for corporate giving. A useful key also lets you quickly identify the availability of ethics reports, social responsibility reports, environmental audits, and foundation reports.

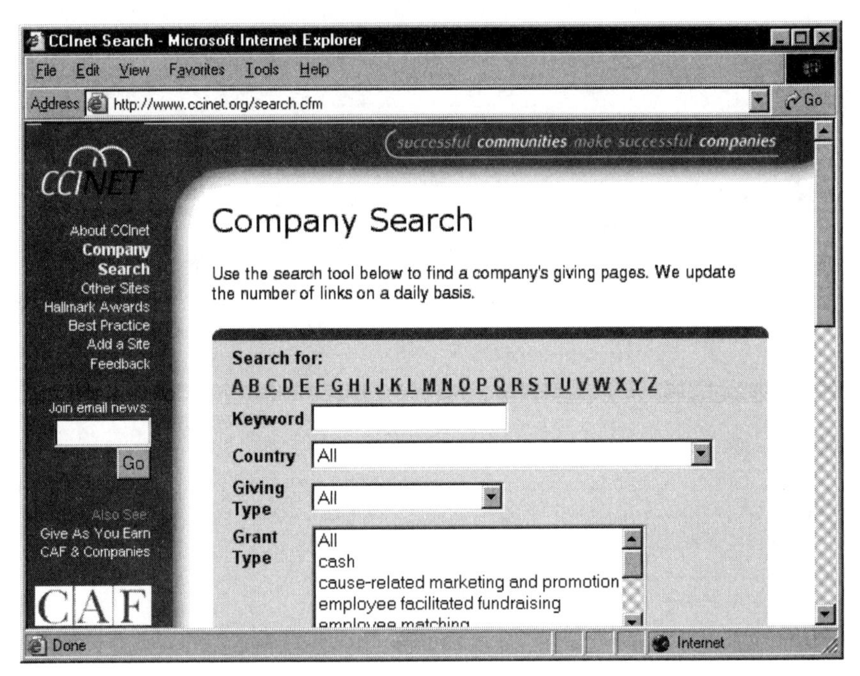

The CSC Non-Profit Resource Center's Web site (http://home.attbi.com/~cscunningham/Corporate.htm) has an informative listing of links to corporate givers. Hundreds of links are coded with subject headings to identify funding areas. An icon identifies recently added links.

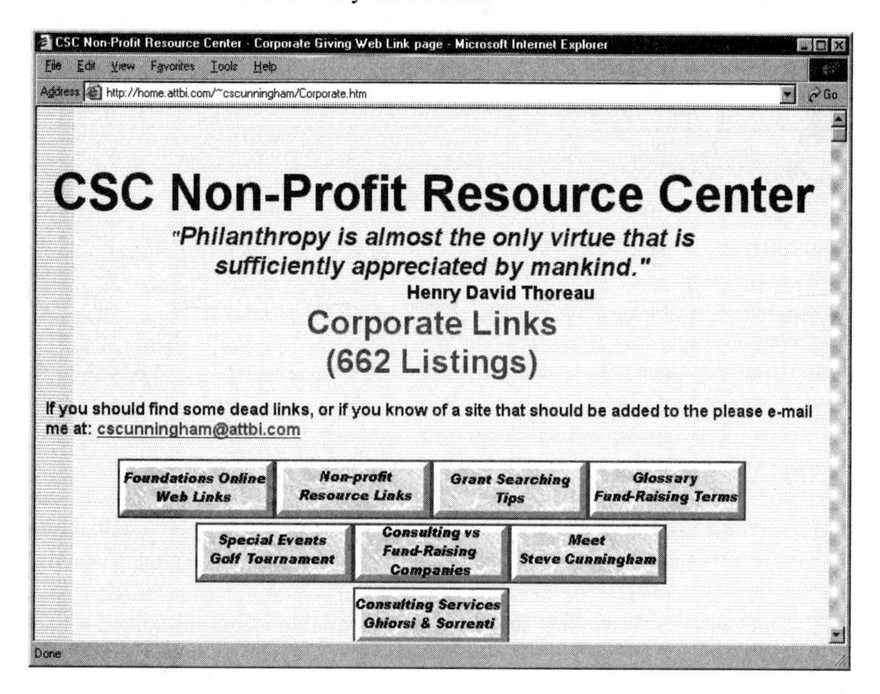

Searching: Doing It Yourself Using a Search Engine

Another way to find corporate giving information on the Internet is to use a search engine. See Appendix A for brief descriptions of some of the most useful ones. If you're new at this, try each one out to see which search engine has the features you like best. The key to retrieving a reasonable number of hits that contain useful information on corporate giving, rather than a list of thousands of irrelevant Web sites, is choosing the proper search terms and knowing the rules and limitations of the search engine you are using. There are differences in how search engines work and what results you can expect from them.

The search terms you select can greatly improve your search results. Try to search initially with broad phrases such as "corporate giving," "community relations," or "company contributions." Once you have an idea about what kind of information is available by means of a particular search engine, you may be able to further narrow your searches by adding words more specific to your needs (e.g., "arts corporate giving"). You may also want to try the same search using various search engines; you will often get vastly different results. Other terms to try are "in-kind gifts," if looking for product donations, or "community reinvestment act," for those seeking loans.

Searching: Uncovering Giving Information on Corporate Web Sites

A different strategy is required to research the corporate giving policies of a specific company. Often there is no "search" option on a particular corporate Web site, although gradually this feature is becoming more available. You must be on the lookout, therefore, for broad categories that may lead you to the information you seek. Often you will find these categories among a menu containing items such as Products and Services, Investor Relations, and so on. The categories most likely to contain information on the giving policies of the company typically are found under headings such as Community Relations, Public Affairs, Corporate Information, or About Us.

Frequently, corporate giving information is contained on a "page within a page." In other words, you have to delve deeply, or in the case of a Web site, click often, to get to it. The best way to circumvent this sometimes tedious process is to use the site map, if one is available. A good site map will list most or all of the pages contained on the Web site. These listings are usually the simplest way to move to the subject you are looking for and are often more reliable than the hit-or-miss process of clicking from page to page.

RESEARCHING CORPORATE INFORMATION

You may want to begin with basic information about the company itself, including the areas of company operations, the products and services the company provides, a list of corporate officers, and fiscal information.

A good place to start when looking for information about a public company (that is, a company whose stock is traded publicly) is the Securities and Exchange Commission's EDGAR Database (http://www.sec.gov/edgar/searchedgar/webusers.htm). This is a text-only database that contains an archive of all the financial documents filed with the SEC since 1994.

Corporate Information: What To Look For

Annual report
Business statement
Executive officers
Press releases
Product listings
Worldwide locations

You should read whatever material the company provides carefully and then determine whether your organization is a logical candidate for a particular program. An inappropriate application is a waste of time for both the candidate and the corporation.

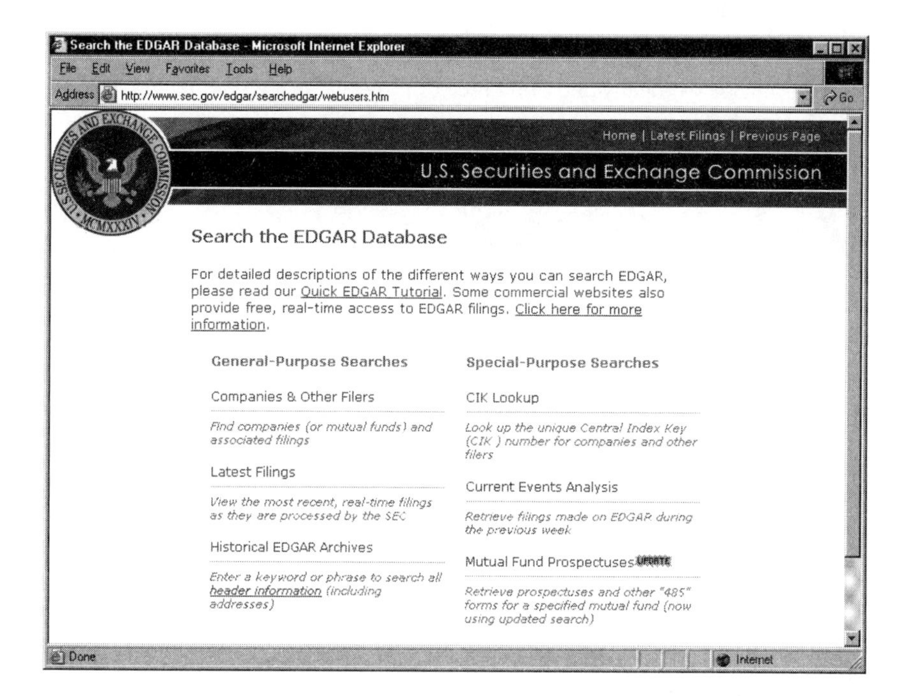

This site contains extensive information about every public company and its operations. Most of the basic information about a company can be found in an annual filing called a 10-K. The main challenge is digging through a lot of material that is irrelevant in order to find the information you need. This requires patience and persistence.

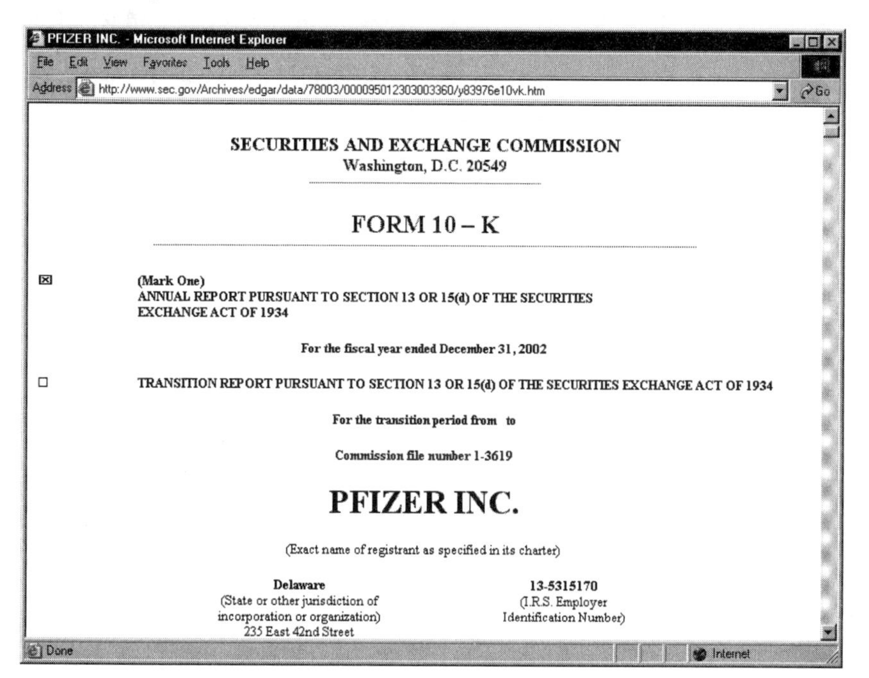

SECURITIES AND EXCHANGE COMMISSION
Washington, D.C. 20549

FORM 10 – K

☒ **(Mark One)**
ANNUAL REPORT PURSUANT TO SECTION 13 OR 15(d) OF THE SECURITIES EXCHANGE ACT OF 1934

For the fiscal year ended December 31, 2002

☐ **TRANSITION REPORT PURSUANT TO SECTION 13 OR 15(d) OF THE SECURITIES EXCHANGE ACT OF 1934**

For the transition period from to

Commission file number 1-3619

PFIZER INC.

(Exact name of registrant as specified in its charter)

Delaware
(State or other jurisdiction of incorporation or organization)
235 East 42nd Street

13-5315170
(I.R.S. Employer Identification Number)

Another valuable site to consider when researching corporate information is the Yahoo! Finance Company and Fund Index (http://biz.yahoo.com/i). This site provides a searchable database of information on more than 9,000 public companies in the United States.

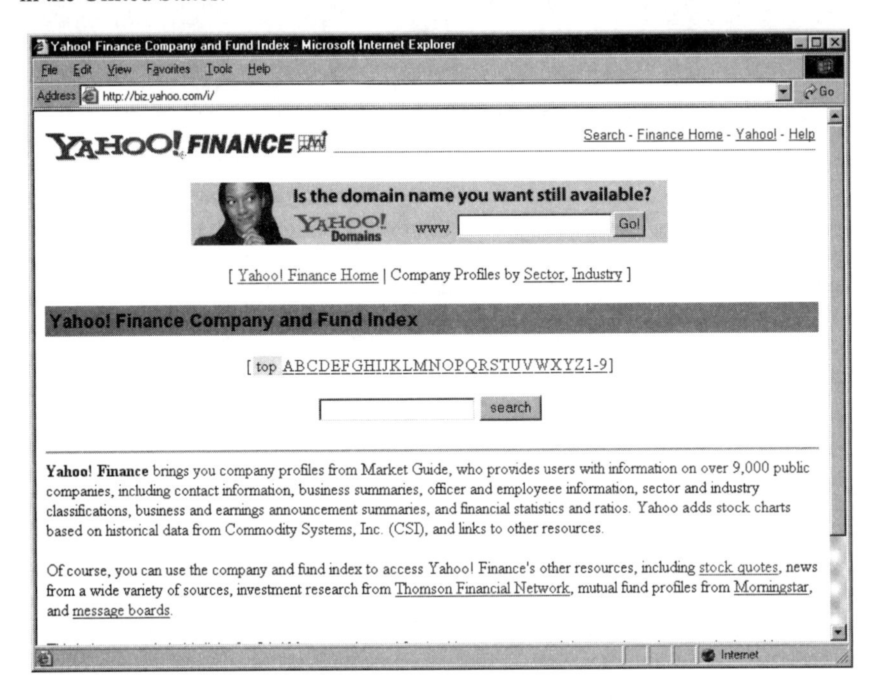

One of the most comprehensive sites for corporate information on public and private companies, not only in the United States but abroad, is Hoover's Online (http://www.hoovers.com). Hoover's boasts access to records on millions of companies, although a subscription is needed for full access.

Helpful pages for information about businesses on other Web sites include Internet Prospector's Corporations page (http://www.internet-prospector.org/company.html) and the Companies and Executives section of David Lamb's Prospect Research Page (http://www.lambresearch.com/CorpsExecs.htm). Both sites have links to corporate directories and other sources of business information, and either is a good starting point when looking for corporate information. Those wishing to receive or view corporate annual reports may want to visit the Investor Relations Information Network (http://www.irin.com). Here, annual reports for more than 3,000 companies can be accessed in PDF format.

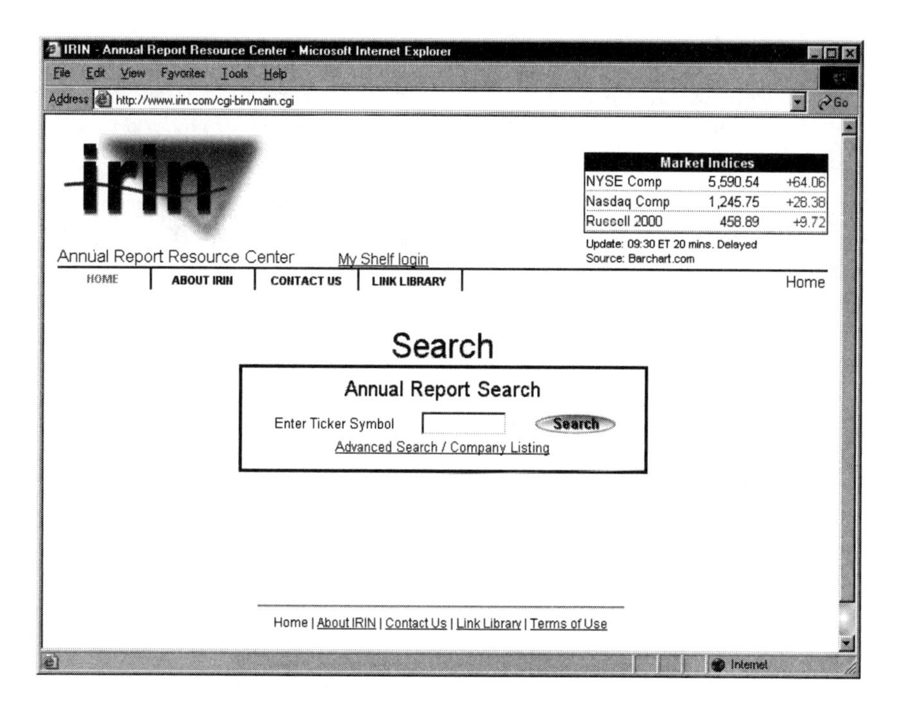

Most of the information available on these sites concerns publicly traded companies. Finding information on privately held corporations requires more research and ingenuity and may also necessitate using a search engine to look up the company in question to see if it's on the Web.

Perhaps the quickest and easiest way to find a public or private corporation's information is to simply type the name of a company into your browser's location bar and hope for success. Many companies have set up Web sites that can be accessed by the most obvious "http://www.companyname.com" format.

For example, Verizon Communications' Web site can be found at http://www.verizon.com. By clicking on the link called About Verizon, a wealth of corporate information becomes available. The company's annual report and press releases can be found in the Investor Information section of this page.

Sara Lee's Web site can be found at http://www.saralee.com. By selecting Our Company, one can access corporate facts and figures, including a listing of company leaders in Corporate Officers, an historical summary in History/Timeline, and correspondence data in Contact Us.

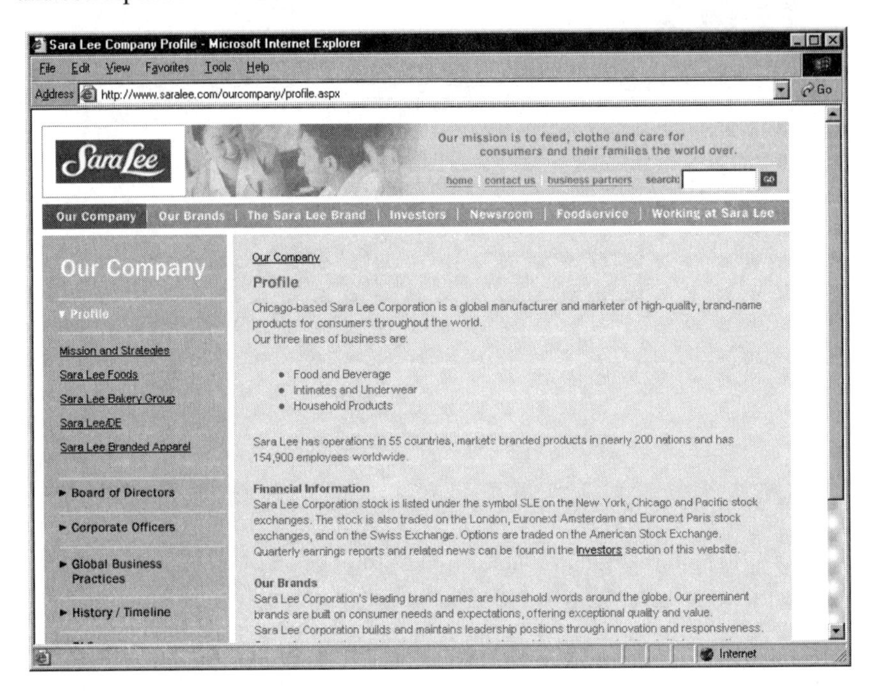

If you encounter difficulties locating corporate Web sites, try different variations of a company's name. For example, the Web site for 3M can be found alternately at http://www.3m.com and at http://www.mmm.com.

FINDING PHILANTHROPIC INFORMATION ON INDIVIDUAL CORPORATE WEB SITES

Corporations on the Web present their giving information in widely varying formats. Some companies provide easy access to their philanthropic activities directly from their home pages, while others may have information on their grantmaking programs buried within other sections. Some companies provide no giving information at all on their Web sites, while others combine direct corporate giving program information with foundation information on a single page. Grantseekers must be diligent in order to find the information they need on a corporate Web site. You should examine the information provided on a corporate site very carefully before applying for a grant.

Hidden Information

As previously mentioned, it is often the case that a company provides giving information within a section called Corporate Information or About Us. An example of a Web site containing "buried" corporate giving information is Hewlett-Packard's site (http://www.hp.com).

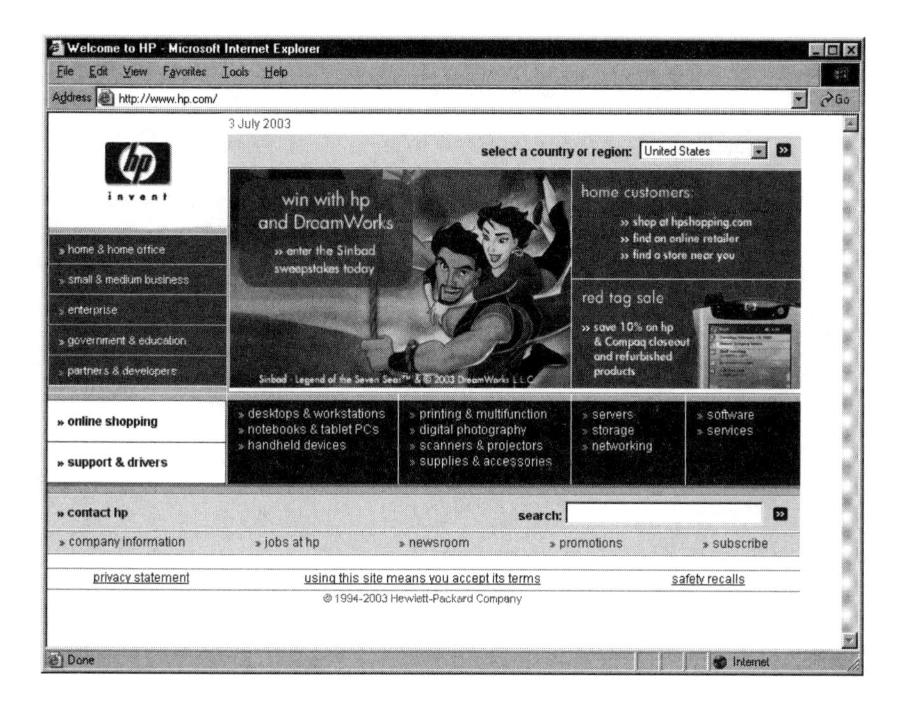

The details on the corporation's grantmaking activities will be found in the section called Global Citizenship (http://www.hp.com/hpinfo/globalcitizenship), which is itself in the area called Company Information. The links easily can be followed from the company's home page, but no reference to this path is provided. Less Web-savvy grantseekers could very well visit Hewlett-Packard's Web site and entirely miss the fact that philanthropic information is available there.

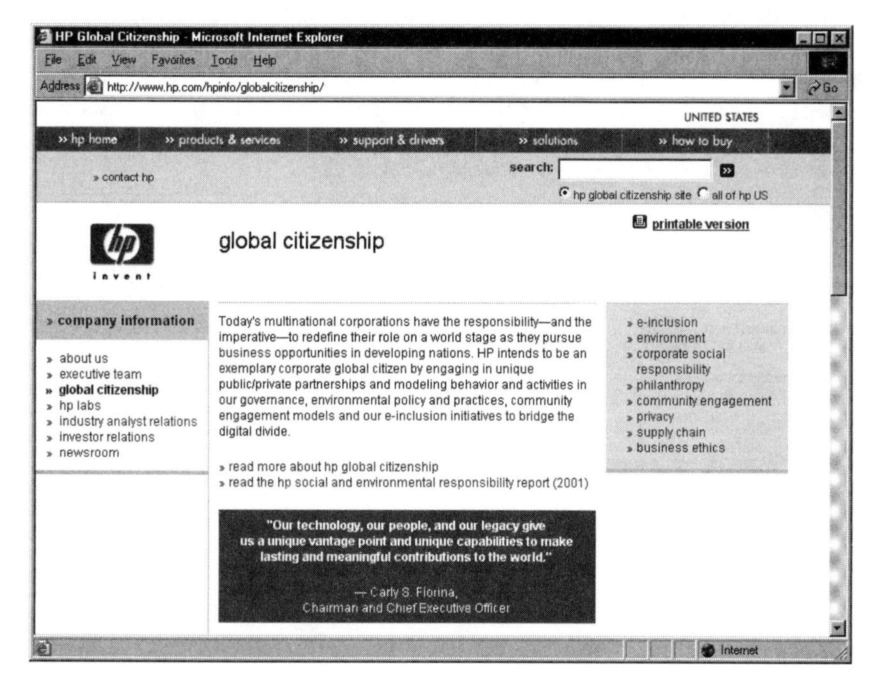

Like Hewlett-Packard, the philanthropic information on Eli Lilly's Web site (http://www.lilly.com) is hard to uncover.

It is in the section called Community Service (http://www.lilly.com/about/community/index.html), which is itself in the About area. To make matters more difficult for the grantseeker, the heading for the Community Service page is not among the broad categories listed in the right-hand margin of the page, where it would be expected. Instead, it's located near the top, in smaller letters. Once again, the information is readily uncovered if you know where to look, but Eli Lilly provides no reference on its site that this specific sequence of links must be followed.

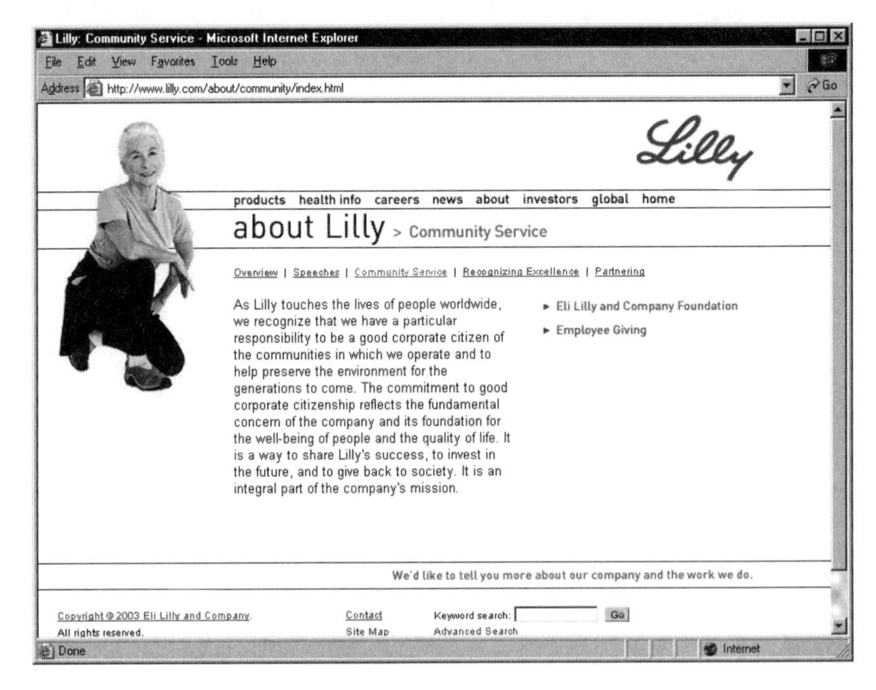

Some companies provide site maps, which can be used as a guide to finding a hidden page. For example, Clorox's home page includes a link to its site map, which clearly shows that the company has dedicated a page to its philanthropic activities (http://www.clorox.com/sitemap.html). Community Involvement is listed in the section called Company Information and can be accessed easily with a click of the mouse directly from the site map.

Thankfully, many companies are taking advantage of advances in Web site design and technology to make hidden pages more obvious. You'll sometimes notice that rolling your mouse over a broad subject heading will automatically provide you with a listing of the pages that can be found in that section.

More Transparent Sites

Other corporate Web sites make your search for giving far easier. For example, Northrop Grumman's home page has a direct link to its Community Relations page (http://www.northropgrumman.com/com_rel/community_main.html). This is the area containing information on its charitable contributions and exemplifies the kind of information a grantseeker hopes to find on a corporate Web site.

Northrop Grumman provides links to its guidelines for grantseekers, a message from its chairman, and its formal Community Report.

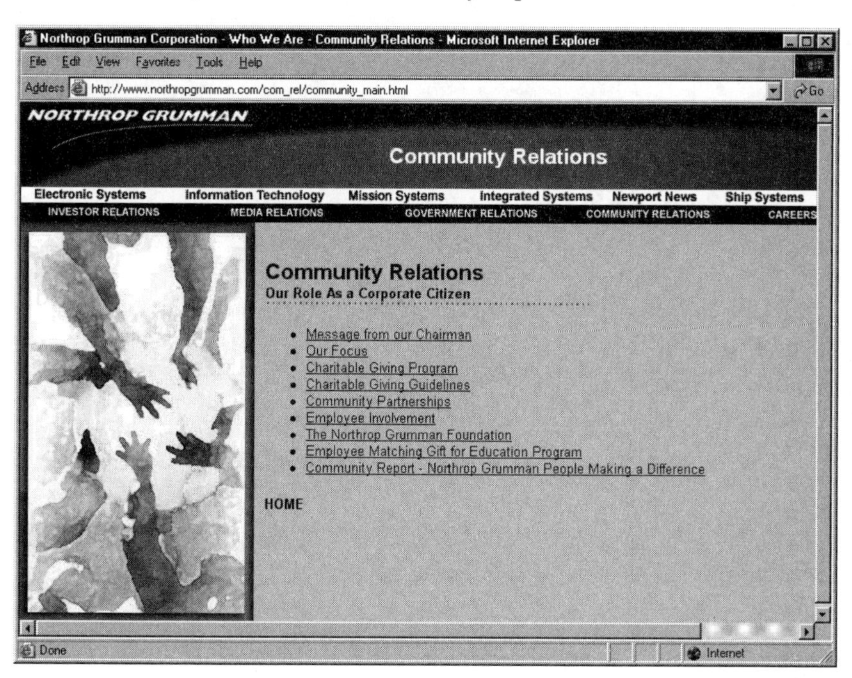

Liberty Bank provides a link to its foundation (http://www.liberty-bank.com/Foundation) directly from its home page. Links to company-sponsored foundations are usually easier to spot than those to the more general, and informal, direct corporate giving pages. In this case, the heading Liberty Bank Foundation leaves no doubt as to the type of information that awaits you.

The Liberty Bank Foundation's page includes links to its grantmaking guidelines, an application form, a list of recently awarded grants, and even a listing of resources for nonprofits. This is an excellent example of a well-organized corporate giving page that provides virtually all of the information that a grantseeker would need to determine whether a company might be an appropriate source of support.

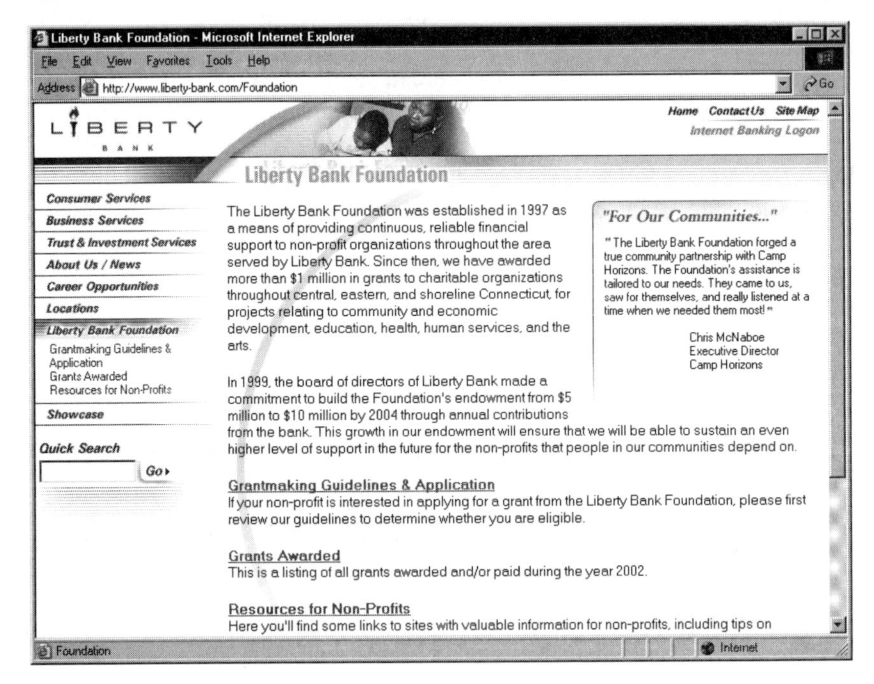

It should be noted that many companies provide information regarding their environment-, health- and safety-related initiatives on their Web sites. But this is not necessarily grantmaking information. Although many companies do indeed make grants to environmental organizations or to those that promote health and safety within their community, the material posted on the Web usually refers to a company's efforts to reduce its negative impact on the local environment or to improve health and safety conditions for its employees. Use your best judgment in deciding whether the information provided is of relevance to you as a grantseeker for environmental or health causes.

Combination Sites: Company-Sponsored Foundations and Corporate Giving Programs

As noted, many companies make charitable contributions both directly and through a company-sponsored foundation. Often, information on both arms of a company's charitable giving efforts is combined on the Web, making it difficult for the grantseeker to differentiate between the two separate grantmaking bodies. Grantseekers need to proceed with caution when visiting such sites and to conduct further research to determine the appropriate approach. Sometimes both programs are administered out of the same office and by the same staff, while at other times they function completely independently of one another. In some cases they each require separate proposals. Very often, the types of support provided and the geographic limitations established vary widely. For instance, cash donations might be supplied by the foundation, while in-kind support is handled exclusively by the company.

CIGNA's Web site (http://www.cigna.com/general/about/community) contains information on both a company-sponsored foundation and a direct corporate giving program. In fact, the company announces this fact at the bottom of the last page of its Contributions Report, something many companies neglect to make so obvious. There is valuable information here on CIGNA's philanthropic endeavors, but one can't tell for sure whether the information reflects donations made by the CIGNA Foundation or by the company itself. When in doubt, a telephone call to the company is probably the grantseeker's best bet.

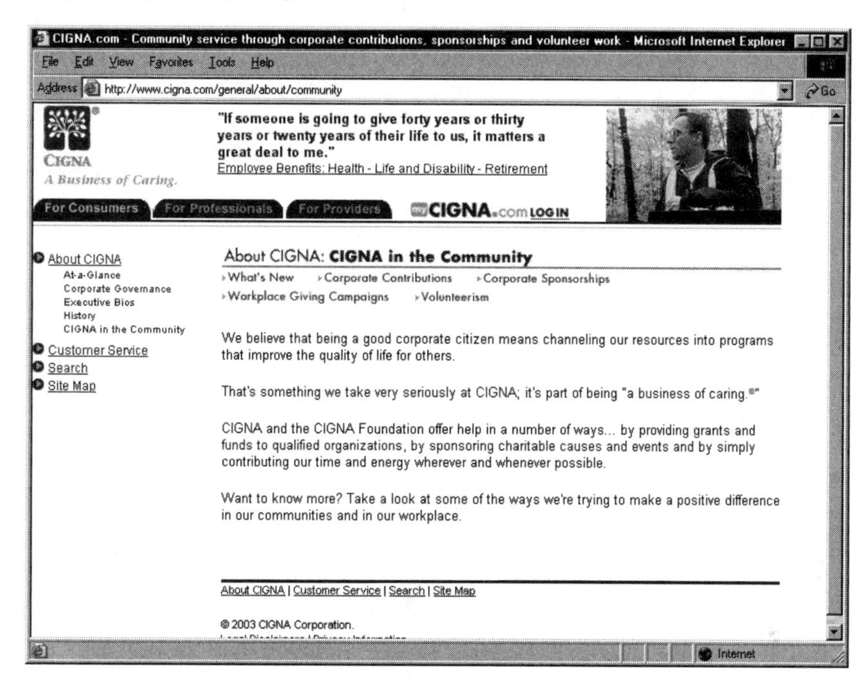

Making the Best Use of Available Resources

THE SUBJECT, GEOGRAPHIC, AND TYPE OF SUPPORT APPROACHES TO CORPORATE GRANTSEEKING

There are several tried-and-true approaches to corporate grantseeking research, each appropriate for a different situation. The subject approach leads grantseekers to corporations with an interest in funding programs in certain fields and to businesses whose activities are related to their nonprofit programs. Some nonprofit/corporate common interests will be obvious: A sporting goods manufacturer expresses interest in an athletic program for disadvantaged youth; a musical instruments manufacturer supports a primary school music appreciation program; a pharmaceutical company or alcoholic beverage supplier funds a drug education program. Because most corporate giving programs are limited to giving in communities where the company operates, a grantseeker's research should focus on a company's areas of operation, including corporate headquarters, subsidiaries, divisions, joint ventures, and local plants and offices. A company will often support programs that provide direct service to employees and other community residents, have potential for public recognition, and improve customer relations in specific geographic areas. A type of support approach can be equally productive. Corporations will often provide funds in a few highly specific ways, such as for capital improvements, operating budgets, and by matching employee donations.

NON-CASH OR IN-KIND GIFTS

Many companies also make non-cash contributions. For example, a clothing manufacturer may have "irregulars" or extra clothing to donate to a homeless shelter. It's important to note that non-cash or in-kind giving often is accomplished through an intermediary. Charities such as Gifts In Kind International (http://www.giftsinkind.org), Share Our Strength (http://www.strength.org), Volunteers of America (http://www.voa.org), and New York's City Harvest (http://www.cityharvest.org) act as pass-through organizations for corporations wishing to provide in-kind gifts while ensuring that donations reach those who need them most in an efficient manner. Visiting these intermediaries' Web sites is a worthwhile endeavor for those seeking in-kind support.

DO YOUR HOMEWORK

It is critical that you learn as much as you can about a corporation's funding patterns *before* submitting a request. The funder may have an annual report or printed guidelines as well as information about the company and its giving on a Web page. These will help you target your appeal. Business reports present company philosophy and describe company plans for the community, providing vital background in linking a grant request to company interests. Economic conditions and business news also should be followed. A company laying off employees or running a deficit may not be the best one to ask for a donation.

PERSONAL CONTACTS

In terms of corporate grantseeking, how important is it to "know someone"? In the electronic age, real human contact is becoming less prevalent. With e-mail, fax machines, voice mail, and the Web all competing for attention, it is sometimes difficult to get in touch directly with someone you know, much less a stranger. Personal contacts can help, but their impact varies from corporation to corporation. Seeking grants from company foundations and direct corporate giving programs with designated philanthropy personnel and explicit guidelines for grantseekers is unlikely to require personal contacts. Personal contacts may be more important when seeking support from companies with more informal giving programs and no formal guidelines or staff to process requests. It never hurts, however, if someone on your board either works at a corporation or knows the CEO.

PRESENTING YOUR IDEAS TO A CORPORATE GIVER

Most corporate givers will expect you to submit a proposal or a preliminary letter of inquiry by mail. A few have application forms you'll need to fill out. Even fewer have online applications. Be sure to find out in advance what is required. A proposal must be clear, concise, and appropriate in tone. Draw up a realistic budget, and be prepared to divulge all sources of income and how that money will be used, since corporate grantmakers emphasize the bottom line. Many ask for evidence of fiscally responsible, efficient management. Be explicit. State program or agency goals, a plan of action, a timetable, and a method of evaluation. Be sure to submit a detailed and reasonable budget. Be brief but comprehensive.

First and foremost, the grantseeker should always consider the funder's motivation for giving. Establishing the connection with a corporate grantmaker's goals is the grantseeker's key to success. Focus on company self-interest more than benevolence. For example, a corporate giver may want to develop a trained pool of potential employees, support research for future products, expand its markets, respond to related social issues, ward off criticism of company policies, and, of course, increase sales. Consider what a business stands to gain from your program. Point out the potential benefits to the company as well as to your nonprofit and the audiences you serve.

Getting corporate support demands creativity, ingenuity, and persistence. Competition will be stiff, but gradually, the Web is making it easier for the grantseeker to put his or her best foot forward.

CHAPTER FIVE

Government Funding Resources on the Web

Grantseekers looking for federal government funding will be pleased with the wealth of resources on the Internet. Because printed government documents and information tend to be dense and laborious to read through, the Web is the ideal place to conduct research into federal grant programs. Online government resources of interest to grantseekers include general information about government agencies, databases and statistics about philanthropy, legal and financial information, funding availability announcements, and guides to proposal writing.

Although government resources on the Internet are so plentiful as to be potentially overwhelming, a number of Web sites exist whose creators—often at universities or nonprofit organizations—have culled, categorized, organized, and annotated government and government-related sites to make things easier for the uninitiated. These sites vary greatly in design, amount and type of information, and in their usefulness to grantseekers. This chapter is intended to suggest starting points and to help identify the essential sites for uncovering government funding information.

Begin at the Top

The top is a logical place to start to get the broadest possible view of resources. The executive, legislative, and judicial branches of the federal government have Web sites, as do many federal departments and agencies and state and local governments. You may want to start with the White House's Cabinet and Government Web site (http://www.whitehouse.gov/government/index.html), which provides access to information from the White House, the president's cabinet, independent federal agencies and commissions, and the legislative and judicial branches.

The House of Representatives site (http://www.house.gov) and the Senate site (http://www.senate.gov) allow you to connect to your state representative or senator. These sites also include access to information about legislation recently passed and under consideration.

The frequently updated databases of THOMAS (http://thomas.loc.gov), offered by the Library of Congress, provide searchable information about the U.S. Congress and the legislative process. Included is information on congressional activity and committee reports.

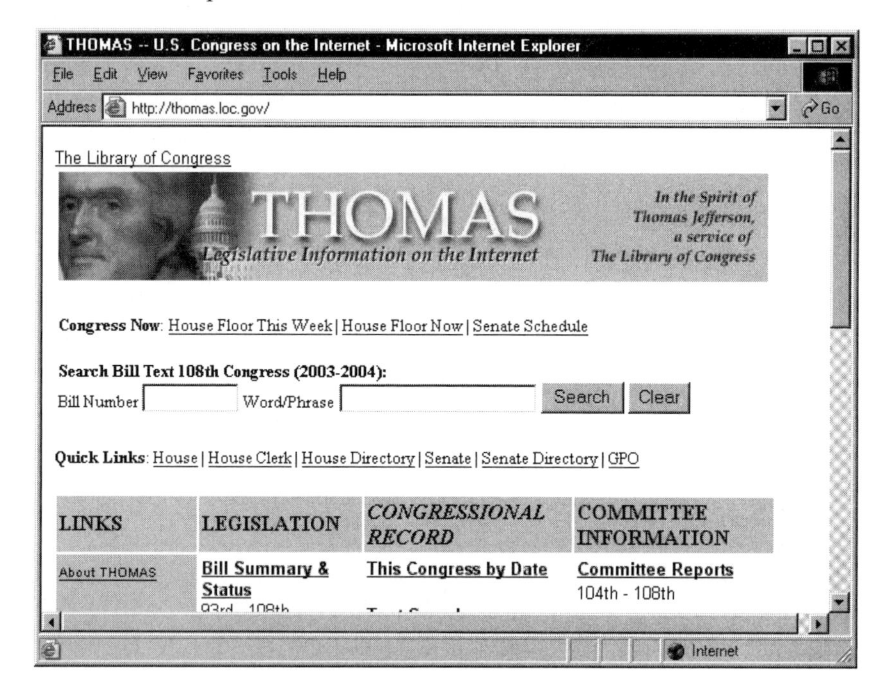

GENERAL GOVERNMENT INFORMATION SITES

In addition to the official government branch home pages, many government departments and non-governmental organizations compile links to government and related sites. One of the Library of Congress Internet Resource Pages (http://lcweb.loc.gov/global/executive/fed.html), for example, has a comprehensive set of executive branch links organized by department and agency.

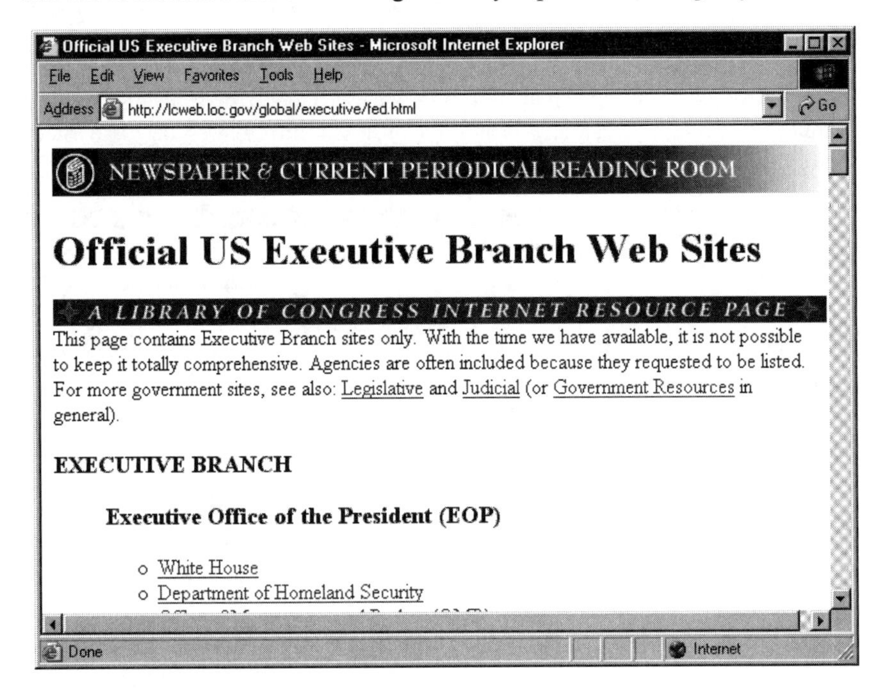

Here are some other good places to begin your search for information on government funding on the Web:

FirstGov (http://www.firstgov.gov)
FirstGov is an initiative administered by the U.S. General Services Administration. It bills itself as "the official U.S. gateway to all government information" and has a powerful search engine that can search 51 million pages of government information. For example, to search for information on funding for the arts, simply enter "art grants" in the search field. Your search will return more than 1,000 relevant results. You can target your searches to federal or state resources or search them both. You can also browse government information on FirstGov by topic, such as Federal Benefits and Grants.

GovSpot (http://www.govspot.com)
GovSpot, a portal to online government information, is a well-organized site produced by StartSpot Network. The main pages of the site are listed topically. For example, you can link to the FBI in the Crime/Justice link under the heading Justice & Military or the Department of Commerce under Matters of Money. To locate a complete list of federal agencies or state government information, look under Shortcuts. Other interesting sub-categories include You Asked for It, Do You Know?, and In the Spotlight. To find the answer to the frequently asked question, "How do I get a government grant?" look in the Miscellaneous category under You Asked for It. Simple navigation and use of colorful graphics make GovSpot an excellent Web site for the novice grantseeker interested in locating government information.

Federal Gateway (http://www.fedgate.org)

Federal Gateway is a search engine that includes links to federal, state, and local government sites and unabashedly states that "the entire official United States Government is here." It includes a useful section on commonly used government abbreviations and acronyms. An area called Key Federal Documentation is meant to assist you in searching for basic U.S. government information, including some unique approaches.

FedWorld (http://www.fedworld.gov)

Sponsored by the National Technical Information Service, FedWorld is a portal site that emphasizes access to technical and scientific government information. It is a comprehensive, easy-to-use gateway to government Web pages, including U.S. government job announcements and other general government Web sites.

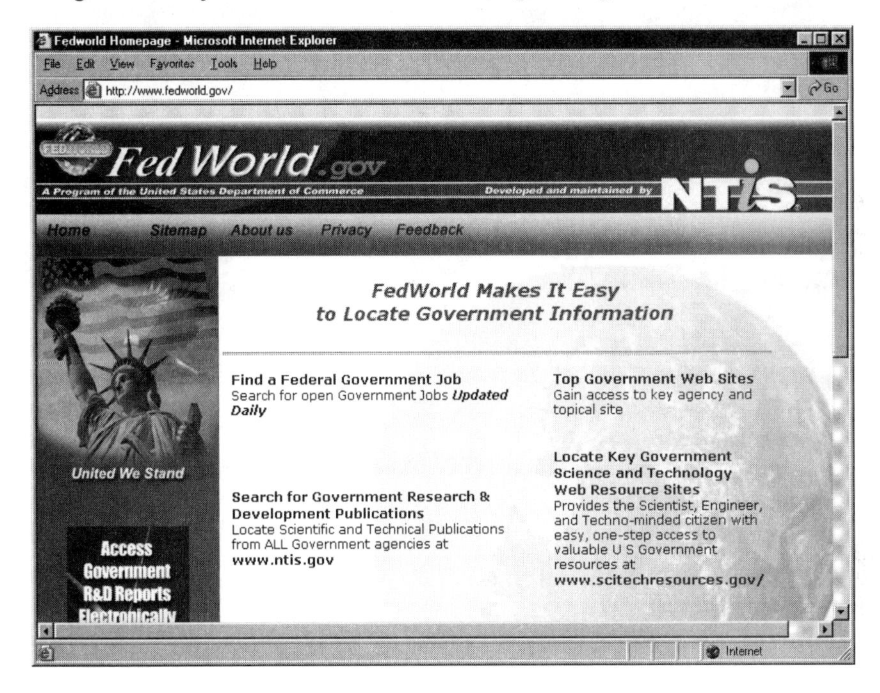

The Foundation Center's Links to Nonprofit Resources—Government (http://fdncenter.org/research/npr_links/npr07_gov.html)

The Government area of the Links to Nonprofit Resources in the Foundation Center's Researching Philanthropy directory provides easy access to most of the sites highlighted in this chapter, in addition to several specific federal and state agencies of interest to grantseekers and nonprofit organizations. (See Chapter 8 for more on the Center's Links to Nonprofit Resources.)

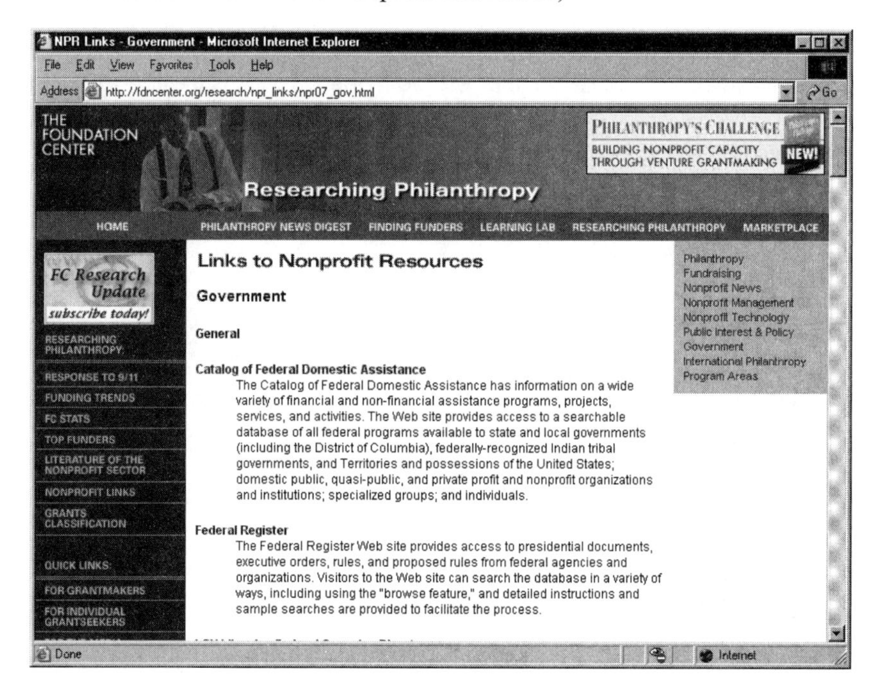

The Foundation Center's Sector Search—Government Resources (http://fdncenter.org/funders/web_search/web_search.html)

You can search for government information on the Internet by using the Foundation Center's Sector Search and de-selecting all but Government Resources. Enter a keyword or phrase to retrieve all relevant pages on these government sites. Results can be sorted by relevancy or date. Use the advanced search feature for more finely tuned search results.

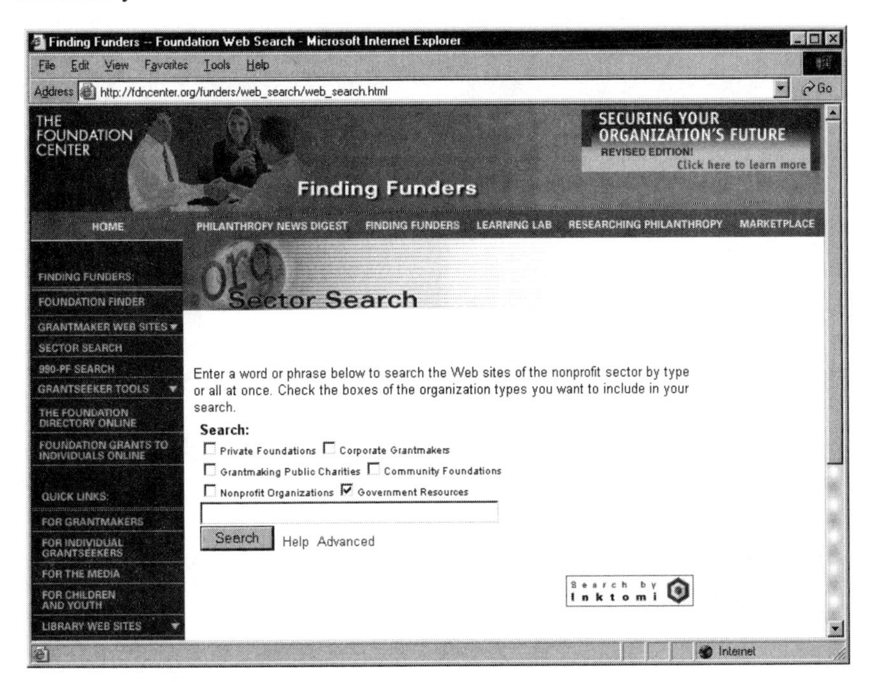

Louisiana State University's Libraries Federal Agencies Directory (http://www.lib.lsu.edu/gov/fedgov.html)

Organized very similarly to Yahoo!, Louisiana State University's Libraries Federal Agencies Directory provides a comprehensive list of links to federal government departments, agencies, and related organizations, such as boards, commissions, and committees, right on its main page so that you can simply search or scan for relevant words or appropriate departments. A complete hierarchical and alphabetical listing of U.S. federal government agencies is also available.

Federal Acquisition Jumpstation (http://prod.nais.nasa.gov/pub/fedproc/home.html)

Although Federal Acquisition Jumpstation, a portal that links to federal procurement information, is designed for the business community, it is relevant to grantseekers as well because it delineates how the government spends its money. It also includes links to procurement information for specific government agencies.

The Federal Citizen Information Center's National Contact Center (http://www.info.gov)

The National Contact Center's site, offered by the Federal Citizen Information Center, provides information about federal agencies, programs, and services. It includes comprehensive answers to often-asked questions about federal loans, grants, and assistance. Each FAQ links to general resources and specific government agencies and includes contact information. Geared toward the individual as opposed to the nonprofit organization, the site provides a toll-free number (1-800-FED-INFO) for members of the public to ask questions of FCIC's knowledgeable staff.

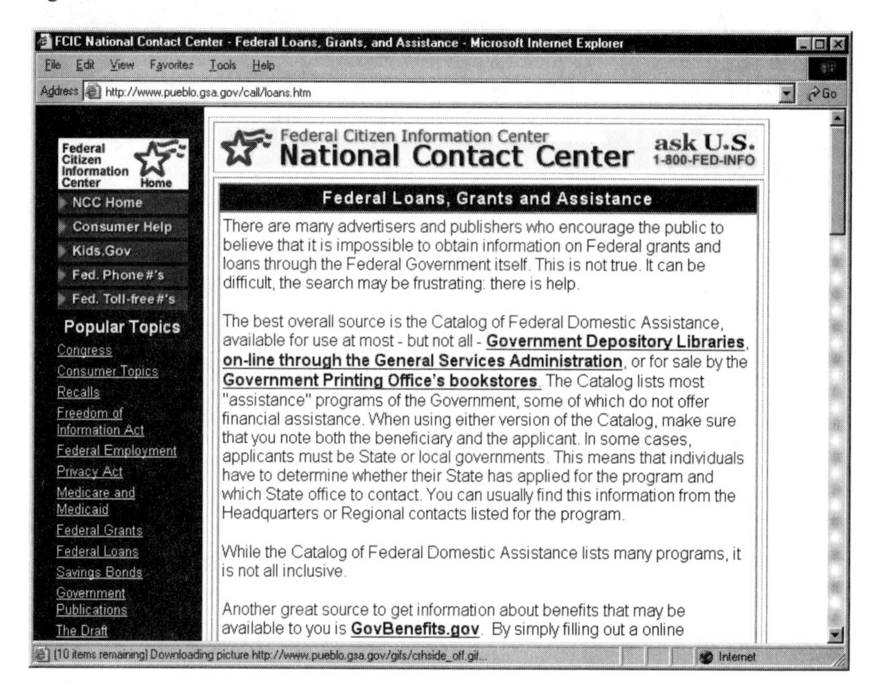

U.S. State and Local Gateway (http://www.firstgov.gov/Government/State_Local.shtml)

The U.S. State and Local Gateway Web page, part of FirstGov.gov, gives employees of state and local governments easy access to federal information to assist them in their service to their constituencies. Its links to grants, contracts, and assistance programs are organized by subject category in an easy-to-read chart.

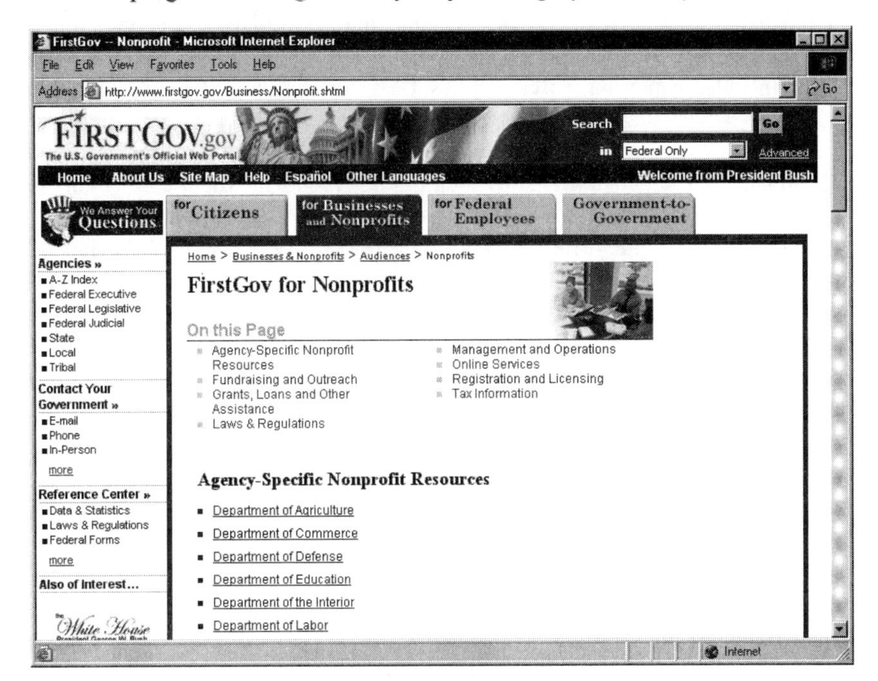

Focusing Your Research on Government Funding

Government-related sites tend to contain an enormous amount of information, much of it not very useful to the grantseeker looking for funding in a specific field. As with corporate Web sites, funding information is often buried deep within a government site and can be easily missed. In addition, funding information may not be situated in one area of the site but dispersed by department or categorized by subject matter. Because most of these sites are so information-rich, many of them have internal search engines. Grantseekers should make it a habit to use them when available. By entering the search terms "grants," "funding," "opportunities," or even "research and development," in addition to keywords describing the particular subject for which funding is sought, you are less likely to miss relevant information.

The majority of grants offered by the government—especially at the federal level—are in the fields of education, health and scientific research, human services, the environment, agriculture, industry, historical research, arts, and the humanities, though not limited to these categories. Looking at the more specialized departments, grants are awarded in a wide range of disciplines. Federal funders generally prefer projects that serve as prototypes or models for others to replicate, whereas local government funders look for strong evidence of community support for your project.

Though a fair number of awards to individuals exist, as with foundation funding, the majority of government grants are awarded to eligible nonprofit organizations rather than directly to individuals. Most government support for individuals is in the form of loans, primarily to students.

GENERAL GOVERNMENT GRANT INFORMATION SITES

There are a number of sites that focus specifically on government funding opportunities for nonprofit organizations, researchers, and educators. These sites offer a direct avenue to federal grant information, through structured indexes or by means of site search engines.

Catalog of Federal Domestic Assistance (http://www.cfda.gov)

The Catalog of Federal Domestic Assistance (CFDA) is probably the government resource most familiar to grantseekers. Its Web site is part of the General Services Administration and provides information on a wide variety of financial and other assistance programs, projects, services, and activities. The CFDA uses "assistance" in a generic sense. In addition to grant programs, you will also find information on other forms of aid, such as loans, surplus equipment, and training.

You can submit a simple query and receive clear, detailed information, including eligibility requirements, application procedures, and examples of funded projects. New users are advised to read through the First Time User's Guide and the FAQs before beginning. Other choices from the main page are Browse the

Catalog, which will lead you to Catalog Contents and Find Assistance Programs. You'll probably want to start with Find Assistance Programs, but the Contents section is worth coming back to. It contains more details on how to use the CFDA, the very informative Developing and Writing Grant Proposals, and other useful links.

There are many options for searching and browsing the Catalog from the Find Assistance Programs page. You can view lists of programs by agency and sub-agency (e.g., go directly to entries for the Department of Housing and Urban Development), or by applicant eligibility. Many of the assistance programs listed may be only for state and local governments, so it can be helpful to limit your search to programs for which nonprofit organizations are eligible. If you're trying to plan ahead, you can even view listings arranged by application deadline.

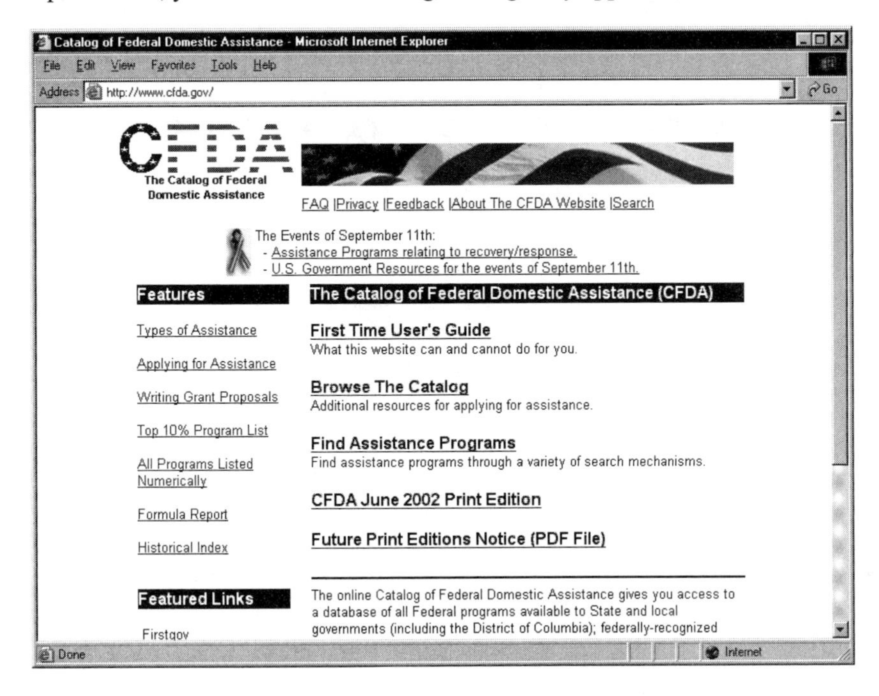

If you're not sure what to look for first, try the simple Keyword Search, which will bring up any listings in the Catalog with your keywords. The phrase "at-risk youth," for example, brings up 275 listings, each of which includes information on the sponsoring agency, program objectives, and details on eligibility and how to apply. If a free-text search isn't specific enough for you, try the Find a Grant section, which narrows your search to only direct grant programs. In this section, once you click on a general heading, such as Environmental Quality, you can then view the sub-categories (Water Pollution, Air Pollution, etc.) and link directly to the grant information on each federal agency's Web site. For example, under the Water Pollution category, you will find links for grant programs under the auspices of the Commerce Department, Department of the Interior, and the Environmental Protection Agency, among others. For each topic heading you will view listings of grant opportunities only, so you don't need to wade through listings for other types of assistance, such as loans. Or for a completely different approach, try the Top 10 Percent of Programs link, which shows you the most frequently viewed Catalog programs. In addition to the directory of grant information, this site offers links to sites of interest to current government grantees, such as the Payment Management System and the Automated Standard Application for Payment.

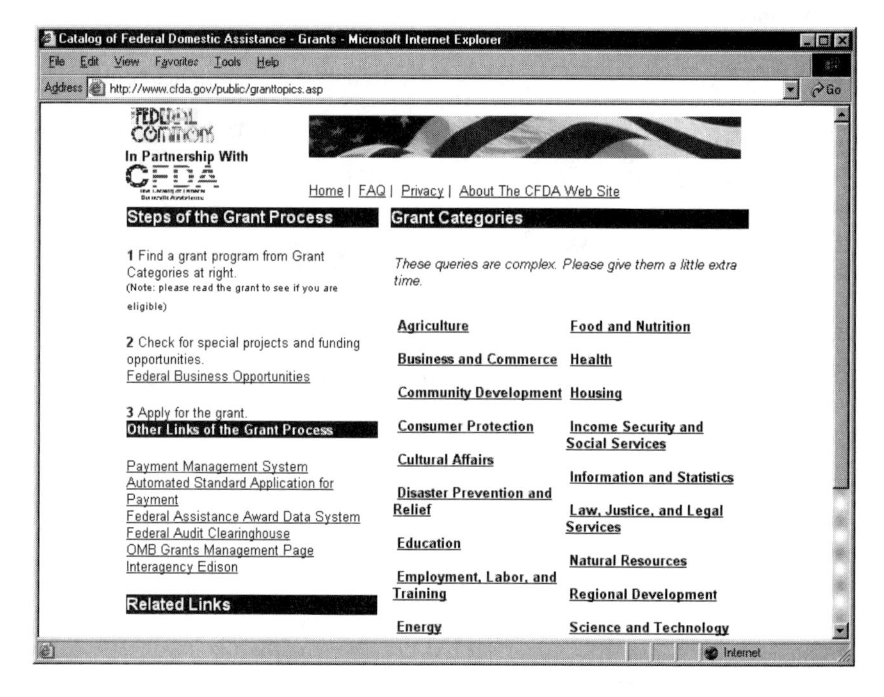

Grants.gov (http://www.grants.gov)

Grants.gov is a new comprehensive site that calls itself "the electronic storefront for Federal grants." Managed by the U.S. Department of Health and Human Services, it brings together 11 departments and agencies "for the development of a one-stop electronic grant portal where potential grant recipients will receive full service electronic grant administration."

Grant topics are divided into categories such as agriculture, education, and housing. A click on Arts will lead you to Web pages of the National Endowment for the Arts, Institute of Museum and Library Services, and others, where you can find guidelines and grant applications online. There are also links to the Catalog of Federal Domestic Assistance and other key government funding sites.

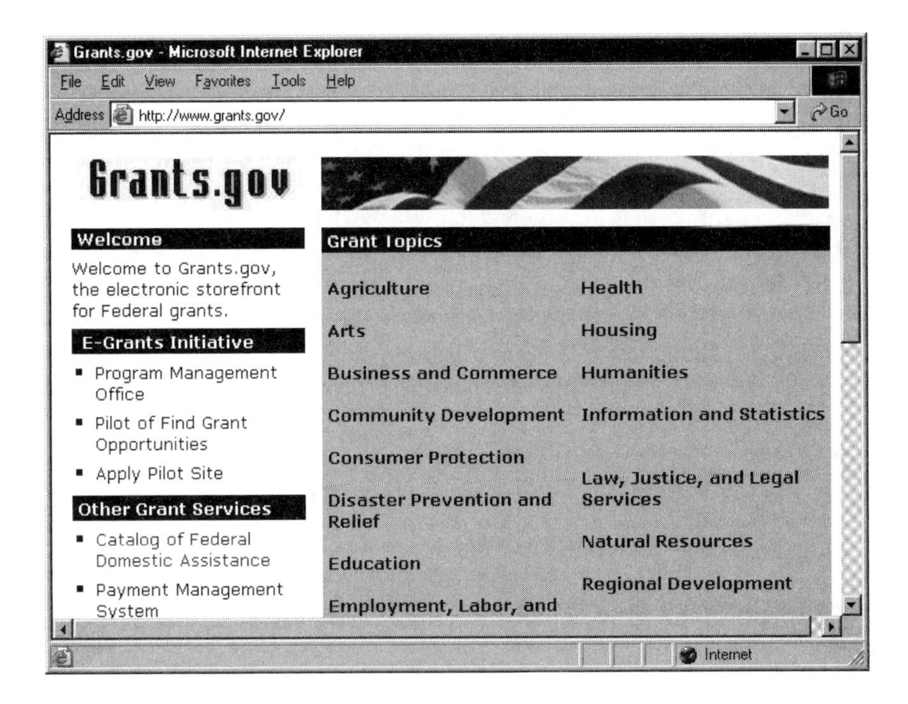

***Federal Register* (http://www.gpoaccess.gov/fr/index.html)**

The *Federal Register* is the official daily record of the federal government, and as such it has the most current and comprehensive information regarding government-funded projects and funding availability. You can also find postings of proposed regulations and agency meetings here. The *Federal Register* is an essential stopping point in the grantseeker's journey because it provides information on government funding availability and new grant programs. Many government agencies often link to this site because their own grants information may not be as up-to-date.

You can search the full-text of the *Federal Register* in a variety of ways, guided by detailed instructions and sample searches. Although there is no section devoted exclusively to grants or notices of funding availability (NOFAs), grantseekers can enter keywords to generate a list of potential funding notices. The NOFA can be a very detailed document that outlines the criteria for funding, guidelines for applications, and relevant deadlines. You will also find a contact name for the funding agency.

Grantseekers can search the *Federal Register* back to 1994. The default is to search the current year only, but you can select to search multiple years. In Advanced Search, you can limit your search to the Notices section only by selecting it; add a date range if desired (keeping in mind that the *Federal Register* is published every business day); then enter search terms describing your program interests. To narrow your search to NOFAs, use the phrase "notice of funding availability" or the words "grants" or "funds" among your search terms. When viewing the results, you will note that your search terms are bolded, which makes it easier to see how relevant the notice may be.

An additional feature is the ability to browse the daily tables of contents of the *Federal Register* back through 1998, or you can sign up to receive a free daily e-mail featuring the table of contents. This can be very useful if you are looking for notices from a specific department or agency (the table of contents is listed alphabetically by government agency). When scrolling through the table of contents, look under the department/agency name for the heading NOTICES: Grants and cooperative agreements; availability, etc.

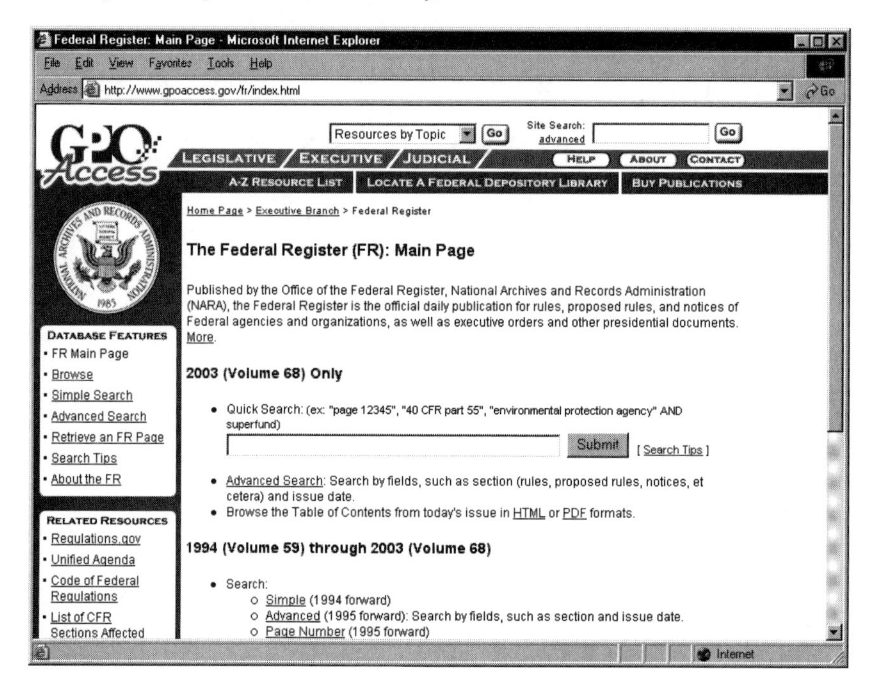

FirstGov for Nonprofits (http://www.firstgov.gov/Business/Nonprofit.shtml)
This is a "one-stop shopping" point for federal information related to nonprofit organizations, including funding information. This site provides extremely valuable information and services from federal agencies. You'll find links to many of the other sites discussed in this section, so this is a good site to bookmark.

The site is divided into a number of categories: Grants, Loans and Other Assistance for Nonprofits; Fundraising and Outreach; Tax Information for Nonprofits; Registration and Licensing for Nonprofits; Management and Operations; Laws and Regulations; More Information, by Topic; Online Services; and Agency Specific Nonprofit Resources.

If there is a specific government department or agency you're looking for, start with the Agency Specific Nonprofit Resources section. Many departments have created their own Web sites geared to nonprofits with their relevant information, including grant and funding opportunities, all in one place. For example, if you're working for a charter school and want to see whether the Department of Education has any applicable funding programs, you could click on Education and go right to the grant information.

The table of contents will lead you to some of the key clearinghouse sites for government information, including funding sources. We refer to many of these sites, such as FedWorld, the *Federal Register,* and the Catalog of Federal Domestic Assistance, throughout this chapter.

NON-GOVERNMENTAL SITES

Federal Information Exchange (http://content.sciencewise.com/fedix/index.html)

Seven federal agencies contribute content to the Federal Information Exchange (FEDIX), providing access to information on government funding opportunities for research and education organizations. Listings are arranged by participating agency: the Agency for International Development, Air Force Office of Scientific Research, Department of Agriculture, Department of Defense, National Aeronautics & Space Administration, National Institutes of Health, and Department of Transportation.

Listings are taken primarily from *Federal Business Opportunities* (regarding government contracts) and the *Federal Register,* among other sources. You can also obtain information about each agency's ongoing funding programs. Each listing includes a summary of the original posting, with links back to the sponsoring agency's pages. Your results list is displayed in order by expiration date.

You can also connect to MOLIS (http://content.sciencewise.com/molis/index.htm), the Minority Online Information Service, which serves minority populations in the education and research communities. You can search past grant awards and current opportunities offered by federal agencies to minority-serving organizations. Of special interest to individual grantseekers is a searchable database of minority scholarships. By using MOLIS you will focus on opportunities specifically for minority groups. As of the writing of this chapter, the FEDIX and MOLIS Web sites are being redesigned.

Grants Web (http://www.srainternational.org/newweb/grantsweb/index.cfm)
Created by the Society of Research Administrators International, Grants Web is a comprehensive site that highlights government grantmaking areas with links to federal agencies and their funding programs. Although you cannot search this site for grant opportunities, it does provide detailed lists of government funding resources and links to specific agencies' application forms.

University of Michigan Documents Center (http://www.lib.umich.edu/govdocs/fedgt.html)
The annotated links at the University of Michigan Documents Center's Web site provide access to some of the major government databases and funding and contract acquisition sites, such as the Catalog of Federal Domestic Assistance, a few searchable university databases, Department of Education grant opportunities, and so on. This site provides access to most of the aforementioned sites, but it is well organized and worth visiting.

TRAM (Research Funding Opportunities and Administration) (http://tram.east.asu.edu)
TRAM offers a variety of useful resources on its Web site, which was initially developed by the Texas Research Administrators Group and is now hosted by Arizona State University East. One of the most interesting features is the Electronic Agency Forms section, where you can download copies of application forms accepted by certain government agencies in Word, PDF, or iPDF formats (iPDF is an interactive PDF document allowing you to enter your information directly onto the form for printing or saving at a later time). TRAM also provides links to federal agencies that have made their forms available on their own Web sites.

Office for Faith-Based and Community Initiatives

On January 29, 2001, President George W. Bush issued an executive order creating the White House Office for Faith-Based and Community Initiatives (OFBCI) and directed five government agencies (the Dcpartments of Justice, Education, Labor, Health and Human Services, and Housing and Urban Development) to establish their own respective offices, or "Centers," within 45 days of his order. On December 12, 2002, President Bush further ordered the Department of Agriculture and the U.S. Agency for International Development to develop OFBCI offices within 45 days.

President Bush's initiative is intended to identify and eliminate regulatory, contracting, and other obstacles to the participation of faith-based groups in the delivery of social services. In part, the OFBCI's function is to knock down "unnecessary legislative, regulatory, and other bureaucratic barriers that impede effective faith-based and other community efforts to solve social problems." The OFBCI also drafts new legislation and generally acts as an advocate for the cause.

Further information on this initiative can be found at the White House Office of Faith-Based and Community Initiatives site at http://www.whitehouse.gov/government/fbci.

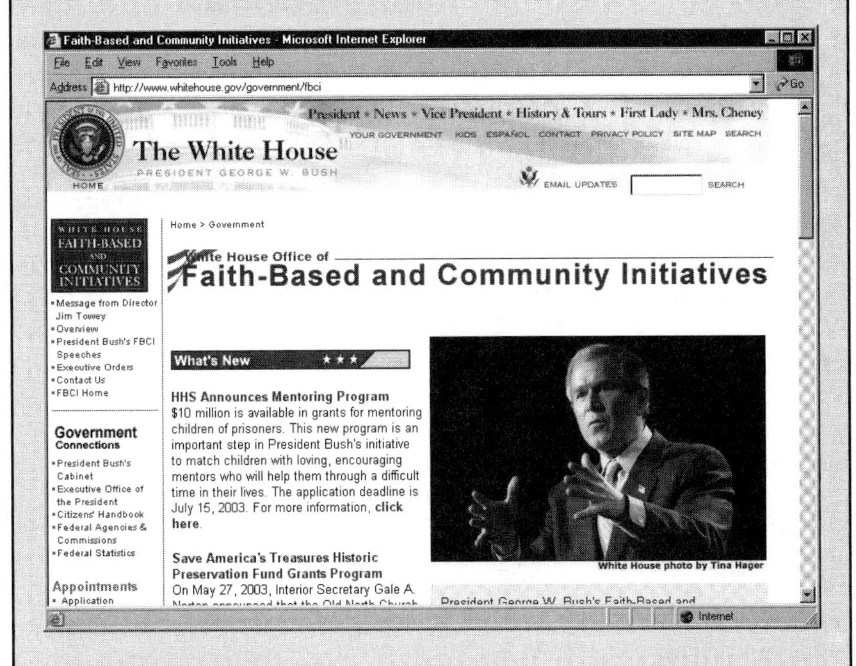

Faith-based organizations interested in applying for federal funding should contact the agency running the program directly. All of the government agencies directed to establish OFBCI Centers have established Web sites focusing on faith-based initiatives:

- Department of Justice (http://www.ojp.usdoj.gov/fbci)
- Department of Education (http://www.ed.gov/faithandcommunity)
- Department of Labor (http://www.dol.gov/cfbci)
- Department of Health and Human Services (http://www.hhs.gov/fbci)
- Department of Housing and Urban Development (http://www.hud.gov/offices/fbci/index.cfm)
- Department of Agriculture (http://www.usda.gov/fbci/index.html)
- The U.S. Agency for International Development (http://www.usaid.gov/our_work/global_partnerships/fbci)

A list of more than 100 programs of interest to small faith-based and community groups, representing $65 billion in federal grant opportunities from several federal agencies, is available at http://www.whitehouse.gov/government/fbci/grants-catalog-index.html.

Specific Subject Areas

Grantseekers with a clearly defined project in a specific discipline or subject area may choose to go directly to the government department or agency that is most likely to offer them funding. A grant project may even be developed with a particular funder in mind. The Web sites of most government agencies have some information about funding. They also usually provide links to the general grant information sites described in the previous section. The following are some of the federal government departments, independent agencies, subordinate agencies, state and local government sites, and other government sites that typically provide funding assistance and/or information. (URLs indicate grants/funding information pages, not the departmental home page.)

U.S. DEPARTMENTAL WEB SITES

Department of Agriculture
(http://www.reeusda.gov/1700/funding/ourfund.htm)
The Cooperative State Research, Education, and Extension Service (CSREES) of the Department of Agriculture administers a variety of grant programs available to researchers, educators, and small businesses.

Department of Education
(http://www.ed.gov/topics/topics.jsp?&top=Grants+%26+Contracts)
The Grants and Contracts section of the Department of Education's Web site contains information on student financial assistance and links to a host of grants and contracts information.

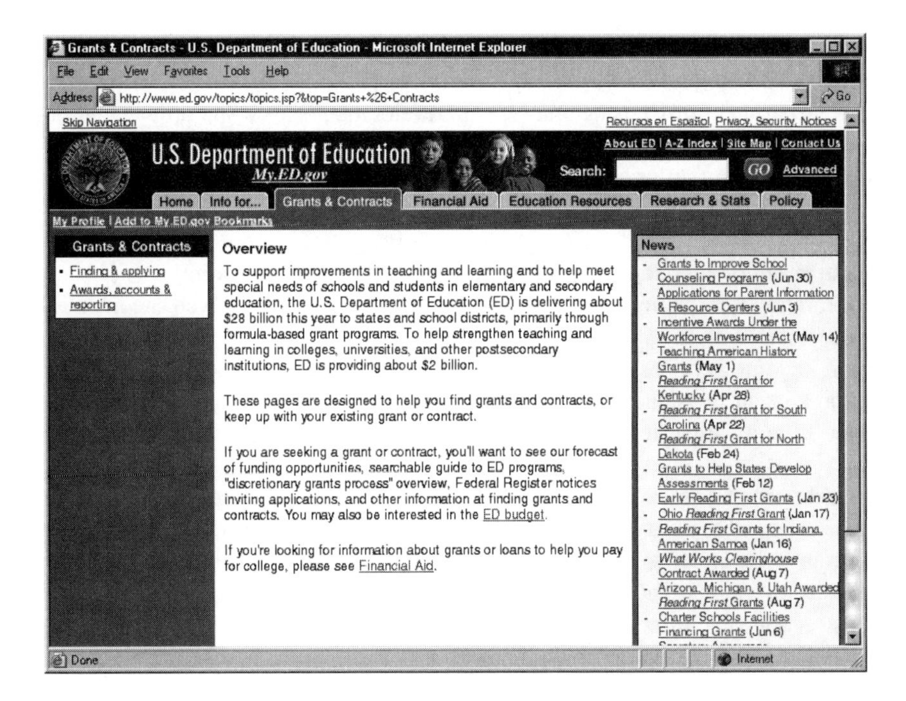

Department of Health and Human Services (http://www.hhs.gov/grantsnet)
The Department of Health and Human Services (HHS) has an exemplary Web site for grantseekers. Visitors can go straight to the Electronic Roadmap to Grants, a visual representation of the grants process that includes links to information on HHS funding opportunities, how to write grant proposals, HHS standard application forms, and many other topics.

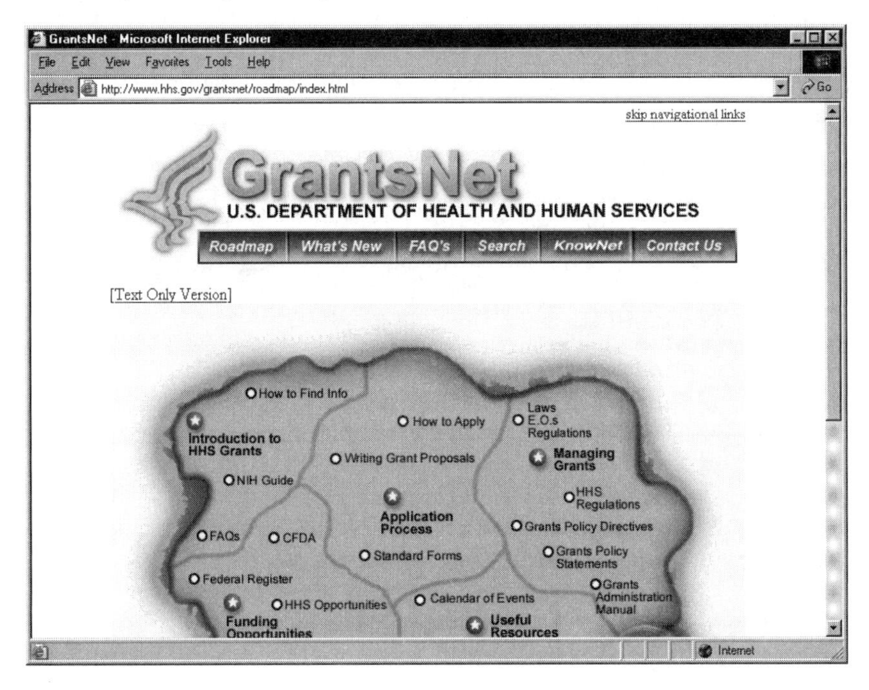

Department of Housing and Urban Development (http://www.hud.gov/fundopp.html)
This Department of Housing and Urban Development's Web site provides information about various types of grants through "SuperNOFAs," including community development, affordable housing, and research. Application and other forms are available in PDF format.

Department of Justice (http://www.usdoj.gov/10grants/index.html)
The funding information offered on the Department of Justice's Web site includes grants offered by the Office of Justice Programs (OJP) and the Community Oriented Policing Services (COPS). Click on Funding Opportunities at OJP for application kits, current funding opportunities listed by source, and a Grants Management System with a step-by-step guide to applying for grants online.

Department of Transportation (http://www.dot.gov/ost/m60/grant)
This section of the Department of Transportation's Web site provides information on grants, generally made to state and local governments (with some to Indian tribes, universities, and nonprofit organizations), for the planning, design, and construction of transportation improvements. There also is information on the limited amount of funding available for research and development projects.

INDEPENDENT AGENCIES

Environmental Protection Agency (http://www.epa.gov/ogd)
The Grants and Debarment section of the Environmental Protection Agency's (EPA) site offers information on funding opportunities for environmental causes, such as pollution prevention, environmental education, and environmental justice. Information on past EPA grants is available and searchable by applicant name, award date, grant, geography, or keyword. There is also information on how to apply, grant application forms in PDF format, an EPA grant-writing tutorial, and links to EPA grants offices in your region.

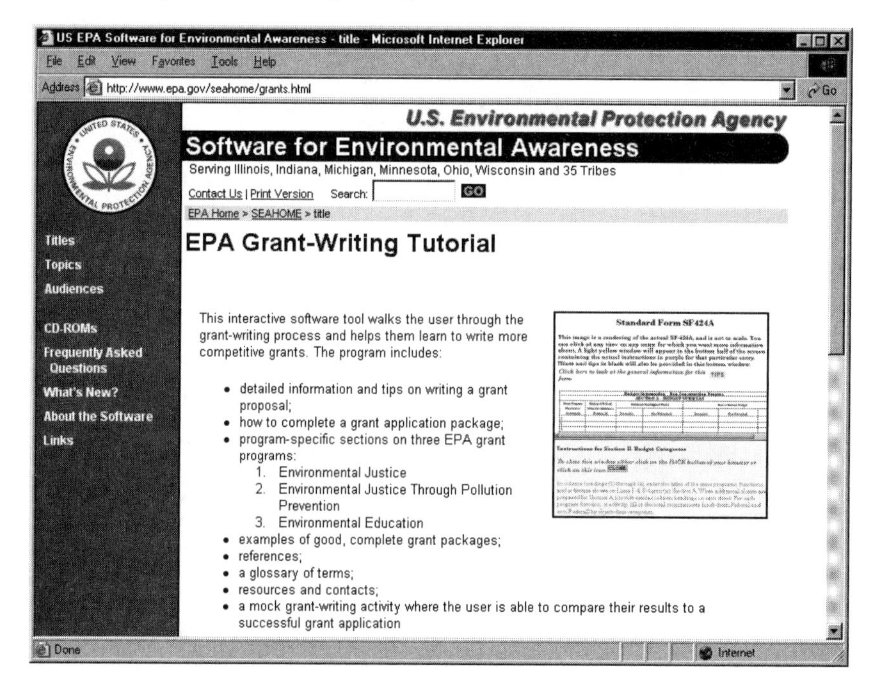

National Historical Publications and Records Commission (http://www.archives.gov/grants/index.html)

The National Historical Publications and Records Commission (NHPRC) of the National Archives and Records Administration makes grants to archives, educational organizations, libraries, historical societies, and other nonprofit organizations aimed at identifying, preserving, and providing public access to records, photographs, and other materials that document American history. This site features information on NHPRC grant programs, details on how to apply, and application forms, reports, and publications in PDF format.

Institute for Museum and Library Services (http://www.imls.gov/grants/index.htm)

This site for the Institute for Museum and Library Services includes information on applying for grants and awards for museum and library programs, with deadlines, application forms in PDF format (that can be printed out or filled in online), and information on how professionals in the field can serve as peer reviewers for submitted applications.

National Endowment for the Arts (http://arts.endow.gov)

This often-visited site for the National Endowment for the Arts describes federal funding opportunities available for arts projects through national, state, and local funding programs. From the home page, click on Cultural Funding: Federal Opportunities for further information on government programs. Click on Apply for a Grant for grant guidelines and application forms for specific programs in Word and PDF formats. You will also find RFPs and listings of past grants.

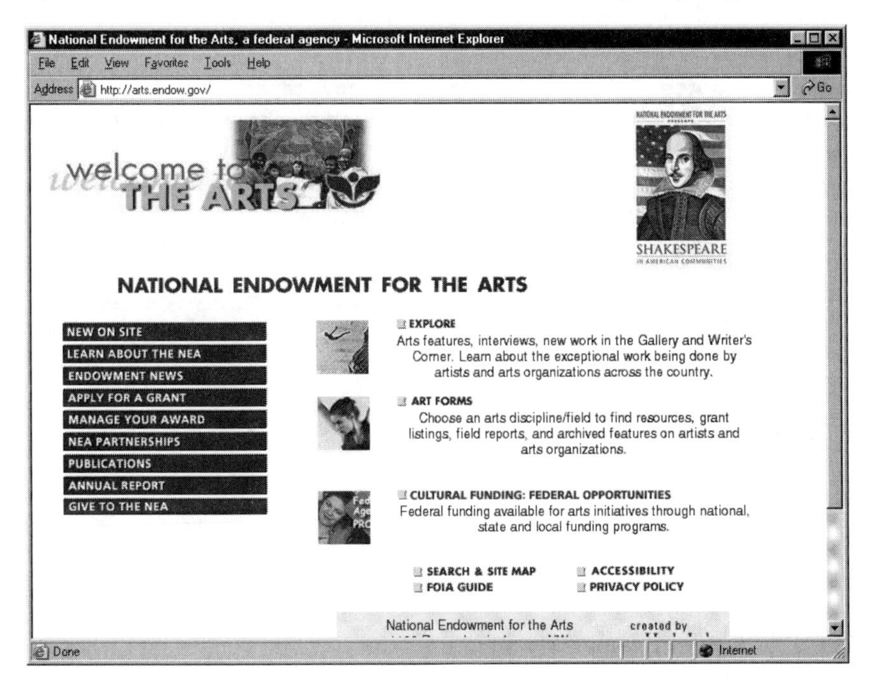

National Endowment for the Humanities (http://www.neh.gov)
The National Endowment for the Humanities supports research, education, preservation, and public programs in the humanities. Click on Apply for a Grant to find information and application materials for these highly competitive grantmaking programs. The site also lists recent endowment awards.

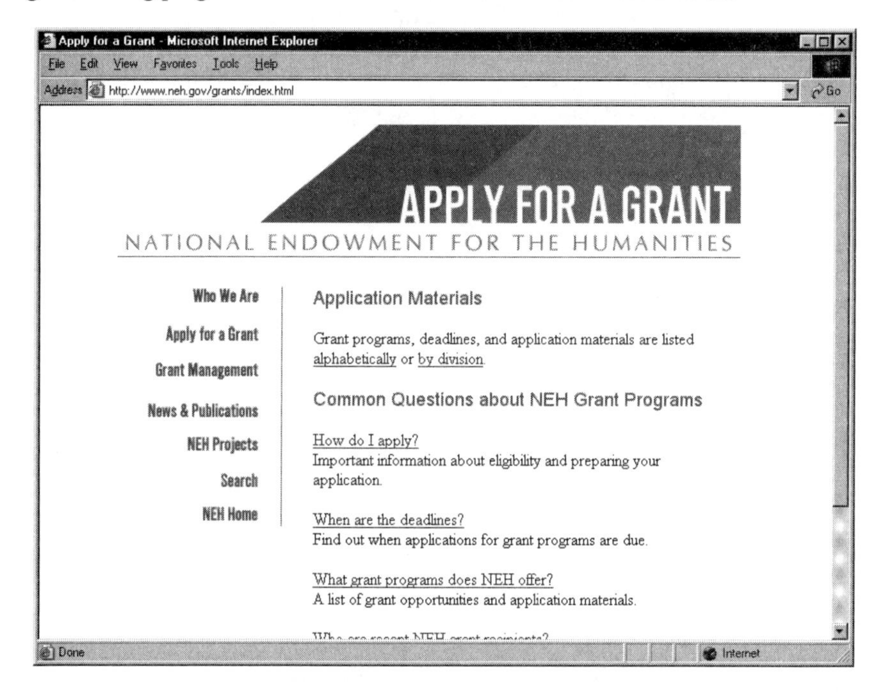

National Institutes of Health (http://grants.nih.gov/grants/index.cfm)
The National Institutes of Health's (NIH) easy-to-use site features clear information about research contracts (including RFPs and information on preparing proposals), research training opportunities, and NIH grant fellowship programs. The Computer Retrieval of Information on Scientific Projects (CRISP), a searchable database of federally funded biomedical research projects, is accessible on the site.

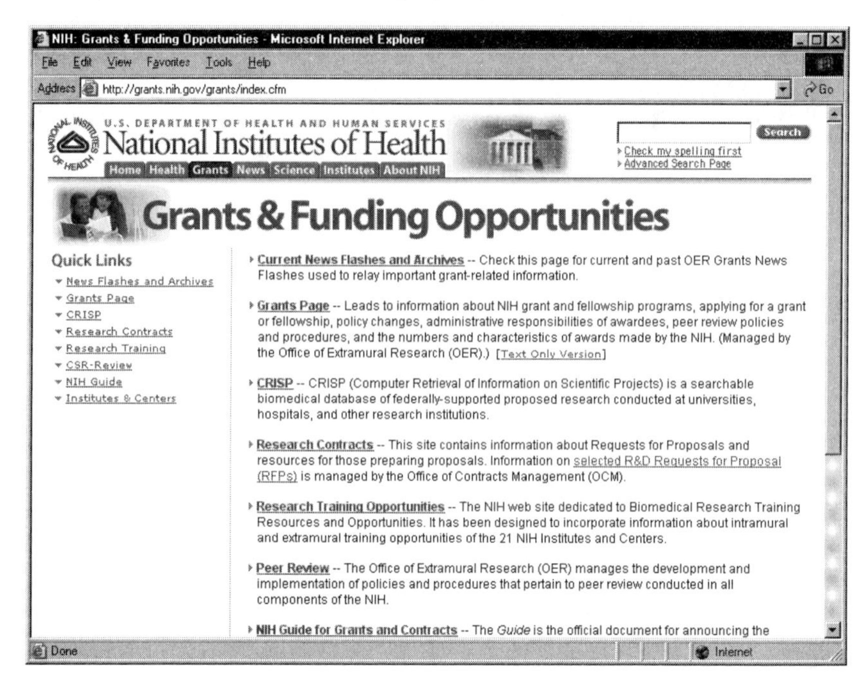

National Science Foundation (http://www.nsf.gov/home/grants.htm)
The National Science Foundation is an independent U.S. government agency responsible for promoting science and engineering through research and education projects. From the home page, you can easily find information on funding opportunities, proposal preparation, grants awarded, and more.

National Telecommunications and Information Administration (http://www.ntia.doc.gov)
The National Telecommunications and Information Administration (NTIA) site offers information on grants and research services in the telecommunications arena. The NTIA administers two programs: the Public Telecommunications Facilities Program and the Technology Opportunities Program, an umbrella program under which most of the federal government's digital divide initiatives fall.

Corporation for National and Community Service (http://www.cns.gov)
The Corporation for National and Community Service encompasses Americorps, Senior Corps, Learn and Serve America, and a variety of other programs. Click on Funding & Initiatives for notices of funds available, or on eGrants, the corporation's online grant application and management system. Assistance with the application process is easy to access, and there's an area where you can practice entering and submitting an application or act as a peer reviewer of other grant applications.

Small Business Administration (http://www.sbaonline.sba.gov)
The Small Business Administration is a well-known independent governmental agency that assists small businesses through a variety of programs. You can easily navigate the site by using its search engine or by clicking on a topic such as Starting Your Business. Here you will find a startup kit, an outline for a business plan, and additional resources. Other areas of interest on the site include Financing Your Business and Business Opportunities.

Smithsonian Institution (http://www.si.edu/ofg)
The Smithsonian Institution's Office of Fellowships site offers information on its pre-doctoral, post-doctoral, and graduate student fellowship programs, including the Minority Internship Program and the Native American Awards Program. Application forms are also available in PDF format.

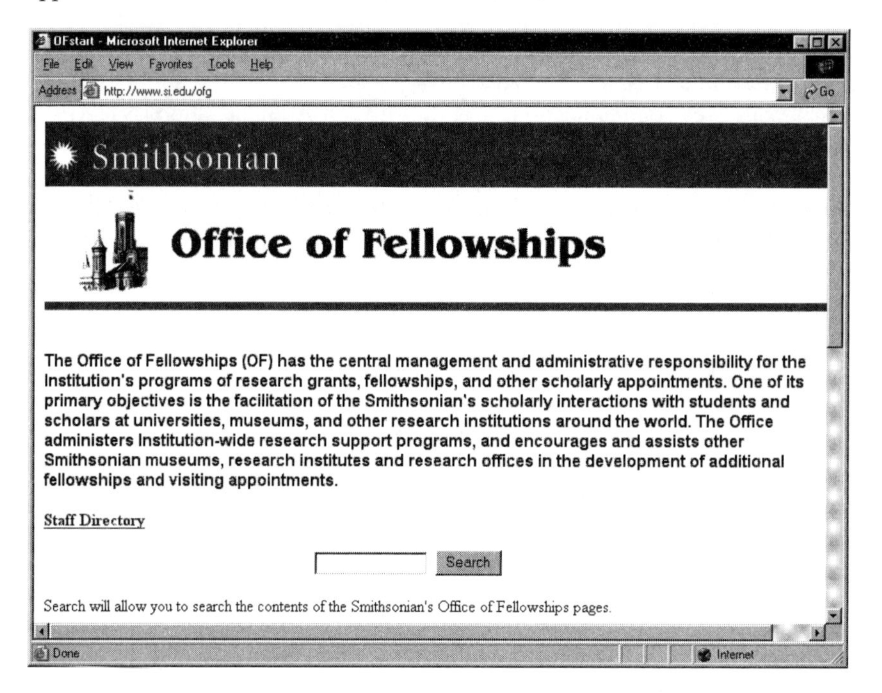

SUBORDINATE AGENCIES

Agency for Healthcare Research and Quality (http://www.ahcpr.gov/fund)
The Funding Opportunities page of the Agency for Healthcare Research and Quality's Web site describes its research agenda and financial assistance for research projects. The focus primarily is on opportunities for investigator-initiated research grants.

EZ/EC Community Toolbox (http://www.ezec.gov/Toolbox)

This site, developed by the Rural Empowerment Zone and Enterprise Community Program Offices of the U.S. Department of Agriculture's Office of Community Development, is designed to provide effective and sustainable community and economic development. Resources are targeted toward the Community Empowerment Initiative's four key principles: Economic Opportunity (for business development), Sustainable Community Development, Community-Based Partnerships, and Strategic Vision for Change. Also provided are links to helpful information on implementing these strategic plans, including financing, methods, and information on how to start and manage a nonprofit organization.

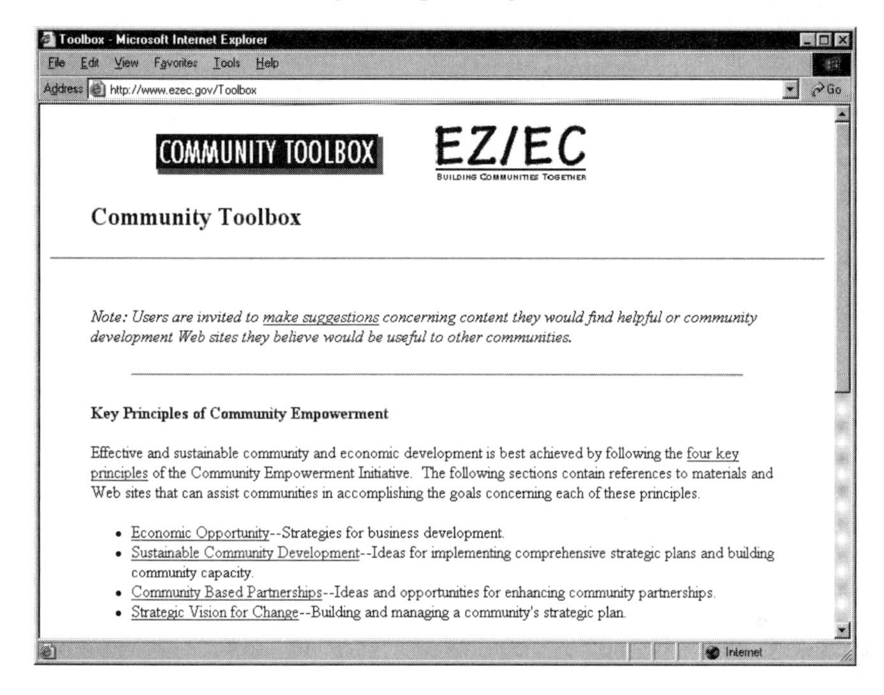

Office of Juvenile Justice and Delinquency Prevention (http://ojjdp.ncjrs.org)

This site offers comprehensive information on the grants and funding process of the Office of Justice and Delinquency Prevention, as well as statistics, publications, and national resources on juvenile justice issues.

Office of Minority Health Resource Center (http://www.omhrc.gov/OMHRC/index.htm)
The Office of Minority Health Resource Center's Web site includes a searchable database of funding and grant resources for minority health projects.

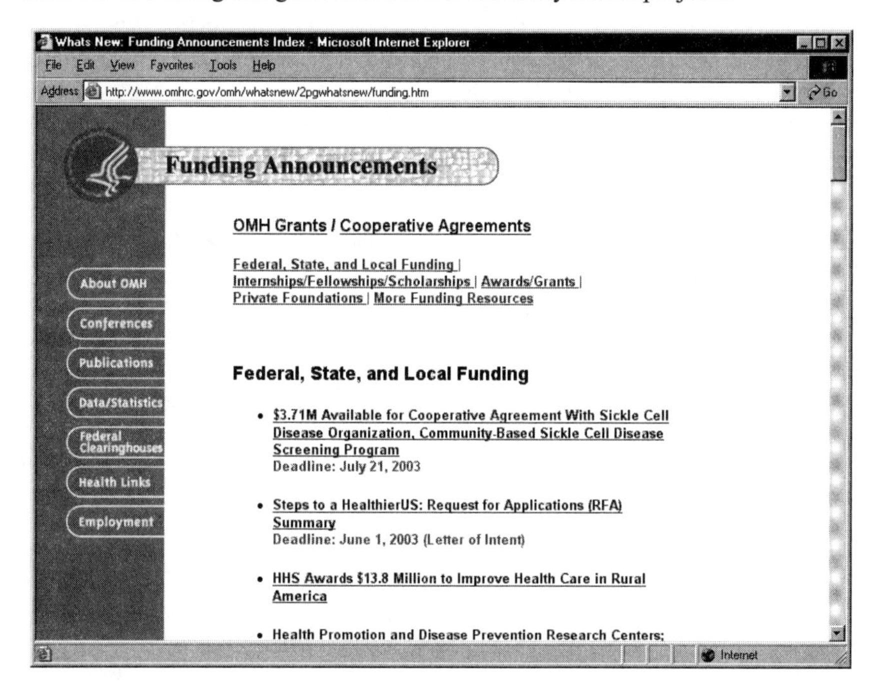

Substance Abuse and Mental Health Services Administration (http://www.samhsa.gov/grants/grants.html)
The Substance Abuse and Mental Health Services Administration's (SAMHSA) Web site has an electronic version of *Online Tips for SAMHSA Grant Applicants* (in Help with Grant Applications), the booklet used in SAMHSA's Grant-Writing Technical Assistance Workshops. It also has ample information on several programs offering discretionary grants.

STATE AND LOCAL GOVERNMENT INFORMATION SITES

Since virtually every branch of government—be it national, state, or local—has some sort of Internet presence, you can delve even deeper in your prospect research if you know what you're looking for and where to look. To find state and local government resources, try these sites:

State and Local Government on the Net (http://www.piperinfo.com/state/index.cfm)
State and Local Government on the Net consists of links to each state and territory (plus tribal governments). In turn, each state page provides links to the governmental branches, departments, counties, cities, boards, and commissions that have Web sites. It can be helpful in searching for local grantmaking bodies, such as arts councils.

NASCIO State Search (http://www.nascio.org/statesearch)
State Search, offered by the National Association of State Information Resource Executives, is "designed to serve as a topical clearinghouse to state government information on the Internet." Linking to one of its 32 categories, such as Arts Commissions, State Libraries, or Education, generates a list of links (by state) to the Web sites of all departments involved in that subject area.

Library of Congress: State and Local Governments (http://lcweb.loc.gov/global/state/stategov.html)
The Library of Congress State and Local Governments Page offers links to meta-indexes of state and local government information—for example, the National City Government Resource Center, a site that provides access to cities' government information—national state centers such as the Council on State Governments, and links to governmental Web pages for each state.

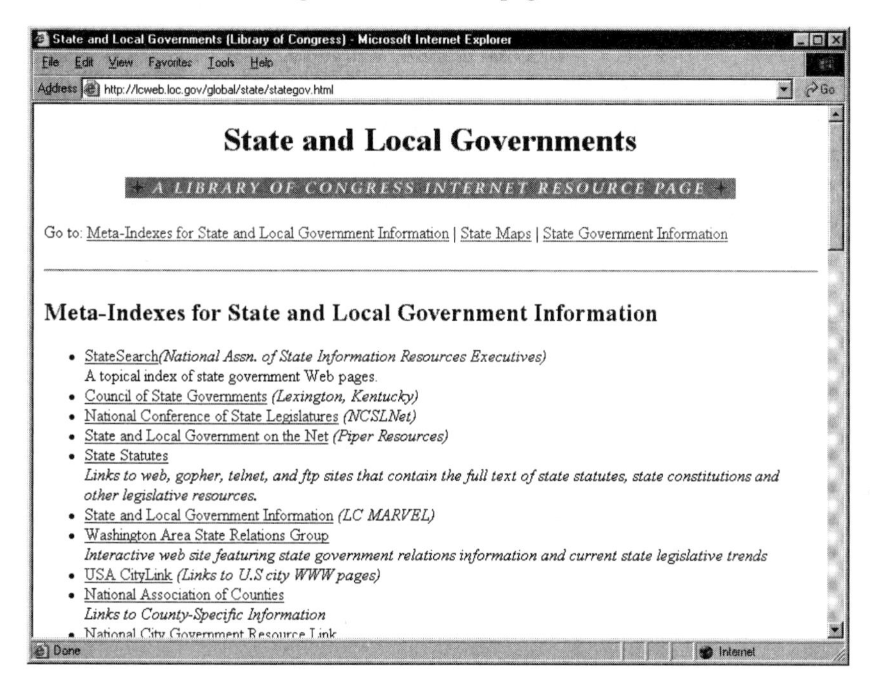

Grants Action News **(http://assembly.state.ny.us/gan)**
Grants Action News is a monthly Web publication of the New York State Assembly. Each issue lists funding opportunities at both the state and federal levels and provides you with eligibility requirements, funding availability, deadlines, and contact information. Each issue also features listings of learning opportunities.

OTHER GOVERNMENT RESOURCES

In the miscellaneous category, you may find government-related sites useful both in your grants search and in gaining a better understanding of the nonprofit sector and its relationship to government.

FedStats (http://www.fedstats.gov)

FedStats provides a variety of statistics produced by more than 100 agencies of the federal government, including the National Center for Education Statistics and the Health Resources and Services Administration. It provides links to statistics by topic or state and statistical agencies by subject or name.

Internal Revenue Service—Tax Information for Charitable Organizations (http://www.irs.gov/charities/charitable/index.html)

The IRS's Tax Information for Charitable Organization's page contains very useful tax information as it relates to the nonprofit sector. You can learn about the various types of exempt organizations, the requirements for exemption, the annual filing requirements for tax-exempt entities, and disclosure and substantiation requirements for contributions to nonprofit organizations. Links are provided to relevant forms and publications throughout this section of the IRS's site.

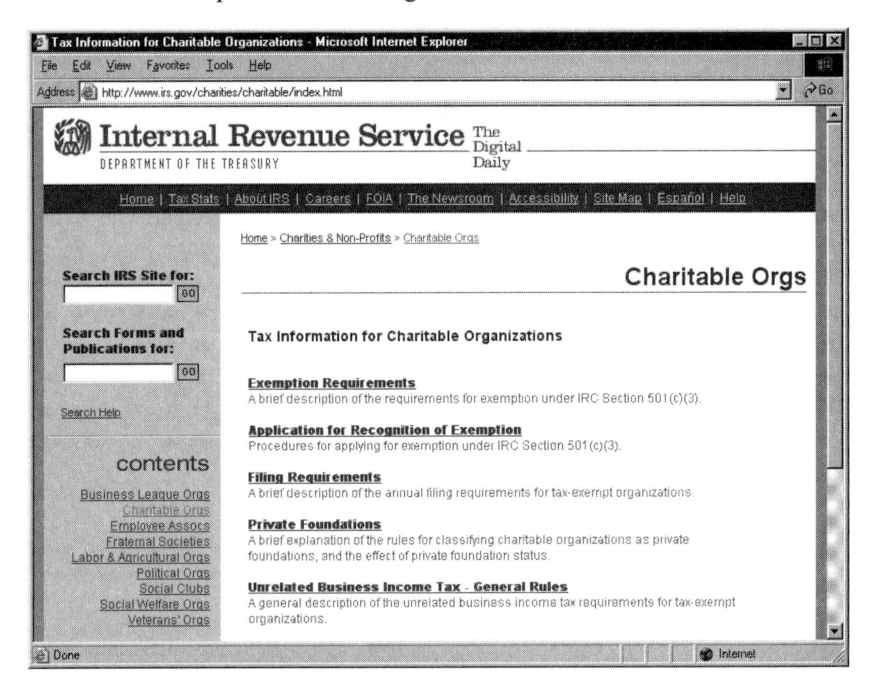

State Agencies that Monitor Charities (http://philanthropy.com/free/resources/general/stateags.htm)

The Chronicle of Philanthropy provides a directory of Web sites entitled State Agencies that Monitor Charities, for the various national and state agencies that regulate charities and fundraising within their states.

National Association of Attorneys General (http://www.naag.org/ag/full_ag_table.php)

The Web site for the National Association of Attorneys General lists the attorneys general of all 50 states. Attorneys general are often charged with regulating charitable activities in their respective states. You may be able to access Forms 990-PF and Forms 990 through your state's attorney general's office.

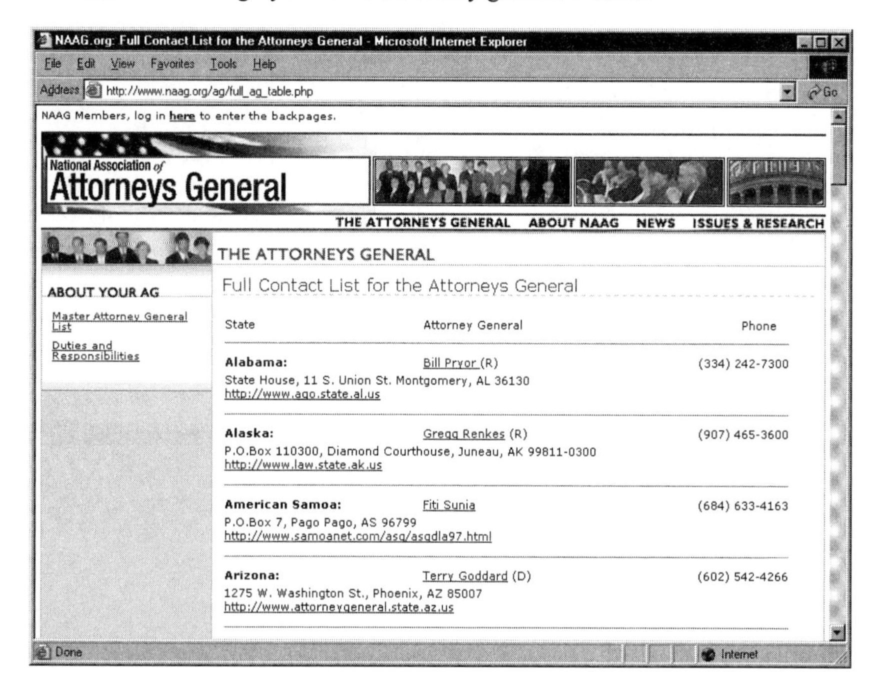

The Federal Election Commission (http://www.fec.gov)

The Federal Election Commission's Web site offers a wealth of information on contributions to presidential and congressional campaigns. You can view reports and data on campaign finance disclosure filings going back to 1993. You can also search a database of selected contributions by individual contributor (by name, city, state, zip code, principal place of business, date, and amount) or by Political Action Committees (PACs) (by state, party, office, or name), for the last two congressional election cycles. This Web site is especially useful for grantseekers researching an individual's giving patterns related to politics.

Office of Management and Budget Grants Management Page (http://www.whitehouse.gov/omb/grants/index.html)

The Office of Management and Budget (OMB) develops policy to ensure that grants are managed properly and that federal dollars are spent in accordance with applicable laws and regulations. Although OMB does not award grants, its Web site links to the Catalog of Federal Domestic Assistance and other useful sites. The site also provides links to numerous grants management forms that may be of interest to grantseekers.

U.S. Census Bureau (http://www.census.gov)

A wealth of statistical information about the United States, its people, communities, businesses, and geography can be found on the U.S. Census Bureau's site.

This is particularly useful as a source of data that can enhance and support a grant proposal.

Conclusion

The list of resources provided in this chapter is by no means exhaustive. Rather, it is a guide to some of the more user-friendly stopping-off points for government grantseeking on the Web. As with any search for funding, it is essential to start with a clear idea of what you are looking for. This proves especially true when combing through the profusion of government resources. As a rule, to supplement what you've discovered on the Web, it is also a good idea to contact by phone or e-mail the agency to which you are considering applying in order to obtain the most up-to-date information on its programs and procedures.

CHAPTER SIX

Online Prospecting for Individual Donors

The Internet is a veritable goldmine for prospect researchers. In fact, the advent of such an enormous compendium of information on virtually any subject readily available at the click of a mouse has totally revolutionized the strategies used by those seeking to raise funds from individuals. Unfortunately, there is no central database or single source of information listing the giving interests of individuals. Unlike foundations, private citizens, no matter how wealthy, are not required to disclose personal financial information or giving histories to the public. Individuals give in ways that reflect their unique interests, and these may change over time. Moreover, even if you are lucky enough to find information on an individual's philanthropic interests and financial status, you will not find "application guidelines" for approaching this individual. Therefore, you will need to gather information from a variety of sources. In this chapter we will look at some of the most useful Web sites to build your prospect files and, more important, to uncover relevant background information on each of your prospective donors. As a grantseeker you will find that the Internet is much more helpful for the latter function because the basic tenet of fundraising still prevails: the closer an individual is to your organization to begin with, the more likely that person is to give you money.

What Is Prospect Research?

As a prospect researcher you are looking for individuals who have the capacity and willingness to give to your organization and an interest in your cause or project. The research part of the equation involves gathering as much useful and relevant information as you can to measure the three factors noted above. What are the benefits of prospect research? First, it will provide details on the person's wealth so that you can gauge his or her ability to give. Second, it will provide insight into the person's background, interests, and hobbies, which will help you determine potential interest in your cause or organization. It may also help you shape your presentation when "making the ask"; you will feel more confident approaching an individual about whom you've already discovered some basic information. Third, prospect research can often uncover connections either to other individuals already affiliated with your organization or to relatives, colleagues, and friends who may also be potential prospects.

Another key concept to keep in mind is that in order to be efficient while conducting Web research, you need to be selective. There is so much information out there that you may find yourself suddenly lost in cyberspace. That is, you may waste enormous amounts of time coming up with Web sites that produce duplicative information or, even worse, conflicting information, so you have no idea what to believe.

Also, there may be missing items, such as a phone number, salary figure, or record of a recent contribution, that you really need in order to complete your prospect picture but that elude your best online detective work. Or you may be stymied in your efforts to prove or confirm a family relationship between two prospects. You may encounter contradictory information and need a "third opinion" or one from an authoritative source to say which is correct. While the process of researching individuals on the Web can be all-absorbing, it can also be quite frustrating. Remember that prospect research is rather like a jigsaw puzzle: there is no truly irrelevant information because you never know how one piece of information will fit with another until you've reached the end of the research process.

As you begin your Web journey, you will discover that it takes a great deal of discipline to stay on track. Many of the sites we'll look at in this chapter offer truly fascinating information, and it's very easy to get sidetracked. For example, when you click on a site that helps you find out about real estate holdings of your prospect, the next thing you know, you may find yourself checking on the assessed value of your neighbor's house. Unless you have unlimited time at your disposal (and what grantseeker has that luxury?), you will need to constantly remind yourself of the task at hand and continuously refocus your efforts.

Research Strategies

You might begin with a prospect worksheet that lays out the essential elements for a thorough inquiry of any individual donor. You should fill one out for each prospect on your list. We've created one for you to use (on page 144) that includes many of the elements you will need. This worksheet is available in rich-text, Word 95, Word 2000, and PDF formats online at http://fdncenter.org/funders/wrksheet/index.html.

The worksheet we've provided is very comprehensive. You may find that not all categories apply to your particular Web search, so you may want to adapt this worksheet for your own needs or create your own. The purpose of such a research tool is to force you to be consistent and to keep a detailed history of URLs and citations to other sources you've consulted so that you can always retrace your steps. If you find yourself filling in the same or similar information repeatedly, you will need to narrow your search to Web sites with more targeted or up-to-date content. Or you may decide that perhaps you've done all you can for this particular prospect and move on to either the next step (cultivation or direct appeal) or to another prospect.

We recommend a three-pronged approach when researching individuals on the Web: compile, investigate, and analyze.

Compile

Much of the prospecting part of your research goes on at this earliest stage. While some prospect identification will actually take place online (and we'll show you how to use various Web sites to do that later in this chapter), most of the names on your initial prospect list will come from other sources. As noted earlier, it simply stands to reason that someone *already* involved with your organization or cause is your best source for future gifts. The greater the level of involvement (e.g., board member, volunteer, or past donor), the more likely the contribution. By the same token, the more tenuous the connection (a friend of a staff member, someone who has given to an agency similar to yours, or someone whose colleague died from the disease your agency seeks to cure), the less likely and the smaller the gift. It goes without saying that someone with absolutely no connection to your organization or cause whatsoever is highly unlikely to contribute without extensive cultivation over a period of time, even if he or she has the capacity to do so.

You'll want to compile as comprehensive a list of prospects as possible before you begin. Your list might be extensive, since it may include all alumni from your college for the past ten years or everyone who gave more than $500 to your local symphony, for example. (Competitors' Web sites, if they happen to include donor lists, are certainly a good place to look for your own prospects.) You may well use the Web to help compile such master lists. For efficiency's sake you will want to spend the greater portion of your time, however, researching those prospects with the closest ties to your organization.

Investigate

While this may seem paradoxical, it is a tried and true fundraising technique: learn as much as you can about those prospects you already know. You can never tell when a seemingly minor detail you uncover will make or break your appeal. Is it possible that you'll actually encounter new prospective donors in the course of your Web research? Absolutely. Every fundraiser has a tale to tell regarding how he or she suddenly and unexpectedly came across the perfect donor in the least likely place. And the nature of the Web, with its multiple access points, interfaces, and links at all levels makes the "eureka!" phenomenon even more likely.

Nonetheless, most of your online research time will be spent using various Web sites and search engines to find out as much as possible about names you've already gathered. Here's where your prospect worksheet will come in handy. It will ensure that you don't overlook a key element or fact, and it will help you avoid retracing your steps to check or verify information at a later time when you may be up against a deadline.

Analyze

The Internet belongs to everyone and to no one. There is no Webmaster in the sky, no content manager you can rely on to exercise overall editorial control to ensure that what you find will be up-to-date or even accurate. For this reason we

Prospect Worksheet—Individual Donors

Basic information:

Name (first, middle, last) ______________________

Title (Mr., Ms., Mrs., Dr.) ______________________

Former or maiden name or nickname______________________

Address ______________________

____

Phone number(s) ______________________

Alternate address ______________________

____

Employment information:

Place of employment ______________________

(Web site, if any) http:// ______________________

Address ______________________

____

Work phone number ______________________

Work e-mail address ______________________

Position (title) ______________________

Since (date) ______________________

Salary and other benefits (estimated)______________________

Other relevant employment-related data (former employment)______________________

____

Personal information:

School(s) attended ______________________

Board affiliation(s)______________________

Foundation affiliation(s) (if any)______________________

____

Civic/volunteer interests ______________________

Social (include club memberships) ______________________

____

Hobbies ______________________

Giving history (include large gifts, dates, etc.) ______________________

____

Assets (real estate, stock, etc.)______________________

____

Other wealth indicators______________________

____

Family information (if applicable):

Spouse's name ___

Spouse's occupation ___

Spouse's affiliation(s) ___

Spouse's philanthropy ___

Children's school(s) ___

Other (siblings, parents, etc.) ___

Connection to your organization:

Board member (dates) ___

Volunteer (current?) ___

Current or past donor (amount and other details) ___

Friend of board member or staff (provide contact name) ___

___

Other (shared interests, etc.) ___

Area(s) of commonality with the prospect:

Prior giving history ___

Geography ___

Subject field ___

People ___

Other ___

Sources consulted (provide URLs, dates, and other details):

Search engines (terms used) ___

Web sites ___

Databases ___

___

Contributions lists ___

Directories ___

Newspapers ___

Other ___

History of past cultivation (if any):

Type (letter, call, invitation, meeting, etc. and dates) ___

___

Recommended next step(s):

(Indicate deadlines) ___

___

___

recommend that you seek out the most authoritative sources possible. There's no guarantee, for example, that what you find on Hoover's reputable business information site (http://www.hoovers.com) is totally correct or current, but it's far more likely to be than what you come across on the Web site of some online business-related newsletter you have never heard of before.

A healthy dose of skepticism is the online prospector's best friend. If you uncover "facts" about your prospect on the Web that seem too good to be true, they may well be. The best way to protect yourself is also a favorite requirement of many newspaper editors: confirm *all* critical data in at least one other reliable source before you accept any information as valid. When visiting a Web site for the first time, *always* check to see who the host is. There's usually an About Us section that can be more or less informative. Look for information that indicates when a site was last updated, as we've mentioned earlier. This is essential for time-sensitive materials. The more experience you have with this type of analysis, the more it will become second nature to you. Eventually you will get to the point where you can almost sense whether the information you've gathered is adequate to proceed with an appeal or whether you need to keep on digging to compile more data.

At the end of the analysis stage, you will want to rate your various prospects to coincide with your plans to approach them. Depending on the nature of your project, you may have a different means of approach in mind for each one (e.g., a phone call for one, a visit from a board member for another, and a letter of endorsement for a third). Or you may be making a mass appeal to a wider list (e.g., a brochure mailing, a telethon, or an invitation to a gala). Once again your prospect worksheet will come in handy. If filled in properly, it should enable you to arrange all your prospects or groups of prospects in priority order and according to the next steps you plan to take.

TIPS TO SPEED YOU ON YOUR WAY

When researching an individual on the Web or elsewhere, clearly it is critical to be sure you're looking up the right person. The spelling or alternate spellings, nicknames, middle names, initials, or such suffixes as "Jr." or "III" are all very important for you to know *before* you begin your research. Of course, if one form of a person's name doesn't work, you can always try another with very little time or effort expended.

Geographic locations, including where the person lives (including multiple residences), works, or where he or she vacations, can be helpful as well. It's also good to know women's maiden or former names. All of these elements will help prevent you from going down some blind online alleys before you hit on the right source.

We mentioned relevance earlier. This is an important rule of thumb to keep in mind: if you've found nothing useful after 20 minutes or so of searching, it's probably time to move on to a different site or to perform a new search on a different prospect.

Have a specific strategy in mind before you get started. How much time do you plan to spend on the Web as opposed to other, more traditional resources? While this guide is about conducting research on the Web, the Internet is not the be-all and end-all of research tools. There may well be magazines, newspapers, or print or electronic directories that have the information you require. And don't overlook the value of the "invisible network," that is, people who know something about someone that might be useful to you. Lastly, that wellspring of helpful information, your local librarian, can be a wonderful resource for those seeking relevant information on prospective donors, particularly those who are famous or prominent only in your own locale.

A WORD ABOUT ETHICS

Unlike other types of grantmakers covered in this book, in this chapter we are talking about individuals—people just like us—who might feel a bit uncomfortable, at a minimum, about their privacy being invaded by someone looking to solicit them for a charitable gift. While privacy matters have always been of concern to prospect researchers, the Web has made it incredibly easy to uncover information that in the past only the most persistent and creative fundraiser would have been able to unearth. Horror stories abound about very private information, such as medical histories, banking records, or legal matters, being readily accessible on the Internet to those with access to someone's Social Security number. As a grantseeker you need to be highly sensitive to the appropriateness of what you uncover. First, you may not want to let your prospect know how deeply you've been delving into personal matters; but secondly, you may not want to let yourself get involved with his or her information beyond your own comfort level. If you work for a large nonprofit development office, your own organization should have standards regarding what is appropriate and what is not in terms of respecting a prospect's privacy.

In response to the many issues raised regarding privacy rights and readily available, free online information on individuals, the Association of Professional Researchers for Advancement (APRA) has posted a Statement of Ethics on its Web site (http://www.aprahome.org/advancement/ethics.htm).

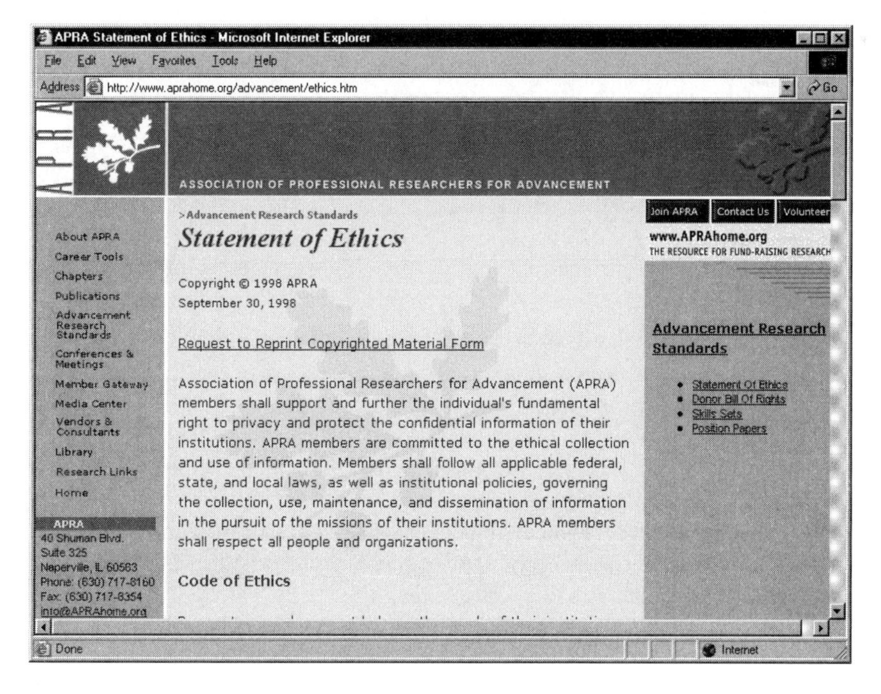

The Association of Fundraising Professionals (AFP) also posts ethical standards and a statement of principles on its site (http://www.afpnet.org/ethics), and the ePhilanthropy Foundation has posted a code specifically related to ethical online practices on its site (http://www.ephilanthropyfoundation.org).

Search Engines

The first and most obvious place to search for online information on an individual whose name you already have is by means of a general search engine. See Appendix A for an annotated list of several of these. Be sure to follow the advice we've provided regarding correct names and forms of names and trying your search several different ways. For example, if you use Google (http://www.google.com) to find information on Brooke Astor as a prospective donor, here's what your results might look like. (Note: we got the best hits by typing "brooke astor" into the search box; we could also have tried searching on "mrs. vincent astor.")

Each search engine has its own criteria for generating results and its own syntax for constructing your search queries. For some it's best to put the name inside quotation marks, as in "brooke astor." For others you will want to try +brooke+astor. Each search engine has its own idiosyncrasies that you will need to learn. For example, for some, the plus sign tells the search engine that each term you've listed must be present in your results list but not necessarily immediately adjacent to one another. This feature helps narrow your search to only the individual you have in mind, while at the same time covering variants of the name. You should also try nicknames and alternate spellings.

In AltaVista (http://www.altavista.com) you can search for exact phrases by clicking on Advanced Search and entering terms into the field labeled, "this exact phrase." A search for Brooke Astor using this method yields the following results:

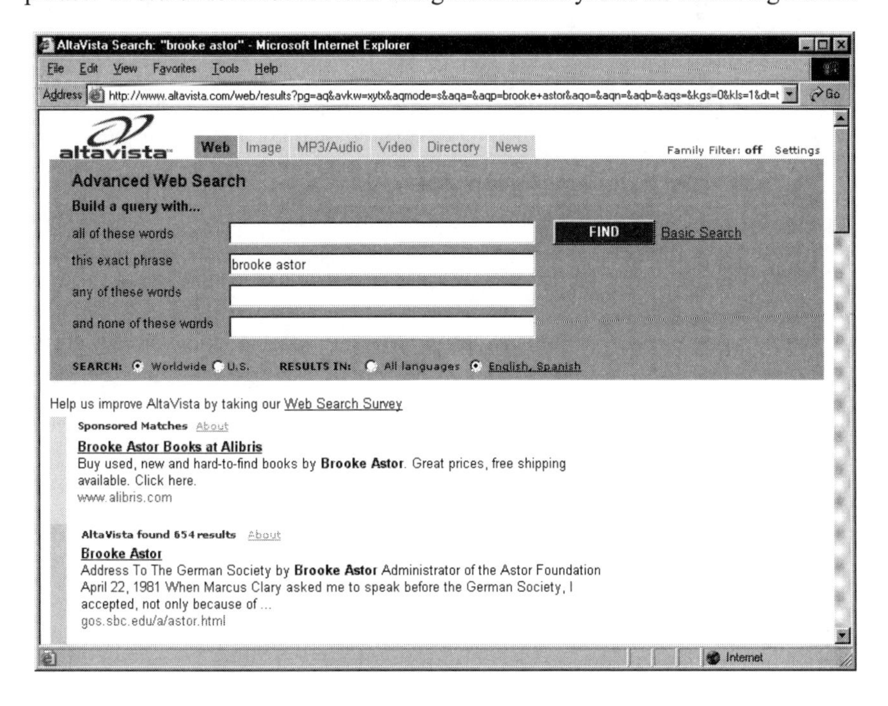

You will find that some of the hits that come up are different from those generated by the Google search. This is a good example of why it is recommended that you try more than one search engine.

Be sure to learn the advanced search features of your favorite search engines and the correct search syntax for each in order to yield the most relevant results.

Incidentally, there is no foolproof way to use the Web to determine whether Mrs. Astor is a foundation's donor or board member, at least not for free. Of course, you can use a search engine and hope that her name comes up that way. You can also use Foundation Finder on the Foundation Center's Web site. However, this works only if the name of the foundation is the same as that of the individual, since you need to type in all or part of a foundation's name to search via this feature. If you subscribe to *The Foundation Directory Online,* you can click on the Trustees, Officers, and Donors index and select Brooke Astor to determine if she is affiliated with a foundation. Depending on whether you subscribe to *The Foundation Directory Online Basic, Plus, Premium,* or *Platinum,* you will be searching the largest 10,000, 20,000, or all U.S. foundations (including grantmaking public charities and corporate givers at the Platinum level). If you visit a Foundation Center library, you can perform a comprehensive search for free, using the Trustees, Officers, and Donors index on *The Foundation Directory Online* or *FC Search: The Foundation Center's Database on CD-ROM.*

NEWSPAPER AND MAGAZINE SEARCHES

Online newspaper and magazine resources can be useful for anecdotal information and for biographical information not available elsewhere. It goes without saying that more prominent individuals will be covered in the larger, national news sources, and the less prominent in local media. There are a variety of online sites that cover both kinds of media. If you're extremely lucky, you'll encounter an online magazine article that provides a full biographical portrait of your prospect.

For prospects active in business or finance, you might want to start with bizjournals.com (http://www.bizjournals.com). This free online resource searches some 40 business journals for articles printed within the last several years, and it has a very simple search interface you can use by typing in the individual's name. Free registration is required to read the articles.

There are also more general news search services, such as FindArticles.com (http://www.findarticles.com), that cover a variety of media. At the top of the search screen for FindArticles.com, you can select the View By Subject and View By Name features to see what publications are included, either by subject or alphabetically by newspaper name.

You may want to try more than one of these search engines. Read each home page description carefully to determine what kinds of news media are covered and how long items are archived. You may also find that "current" articles (those that are up to 30 to 60 days old) may be free, whereas older articles are available only to registered members or for a fee.

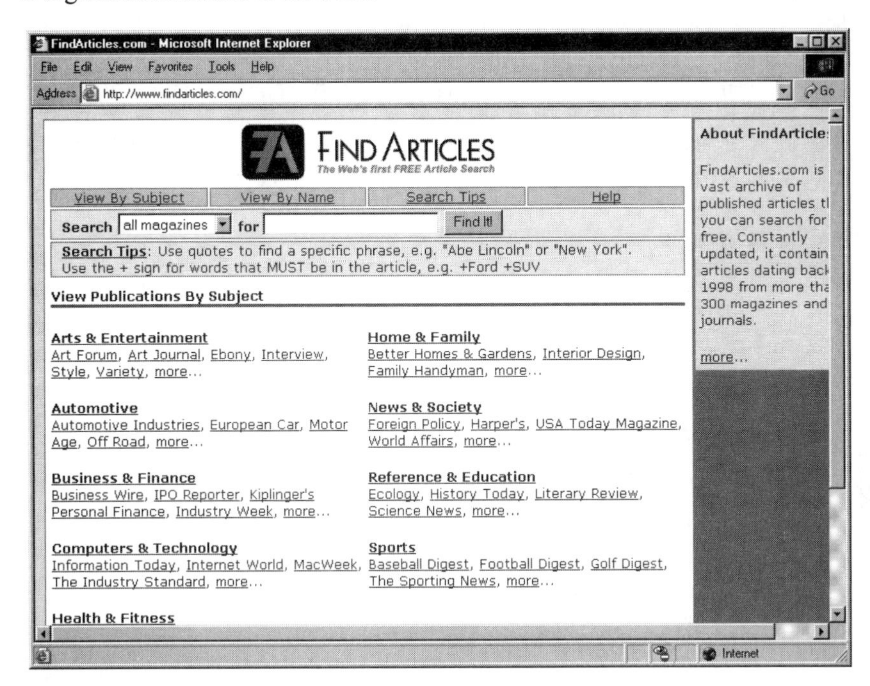

We mentioned the "eureka!" phenomenon earlier. By this we mean the fortuitous way in which one Web link suddenly and quite unexpectedly leads to another. For example, on FindArticles.com, in the search results for FedEx CEO Frederick W. Smith, one of the hits links to an article on the Nature's Best and CEMEX International Awards, which honor wildlife and nature photographers. We learn that *Nature's Best Magazine,* which promotes nature photography and conservation, has established the Nature's Best Foundation, and that Frederick W. Smith is on the board. This tiny nugget of information may be just the type of thing you are looking for to complete your profile of Mr. Smith's interests. Up until now it's possible you didn't even realize that he was interested in environmental causes.

This is also a good time to illustrate how readily one can get sidetracked. For a moment you may forget the task at hand. You might well be tempted to begin exploring the other board members of the Nature's Best Foundation or contributors to *Nature's Best Magazine.* This side expedition may make sense as a next step, or it may not. You need to ask yourself what is the best use of your time. Perhaps you want to proceed with checking more Web sites for information on Frederick W. Smith first, while making a note to return to *Nature's Best Magazine* and the Nature's Best Foundation at a later time. This is particularly true if you already have reason to believe that Mr. Smith is a likely prospect, while you have no idea whether this is the case for the other people on the board or contributions list.

The Internet Prospector Web site (http://www.internet-prospector.org) is also a very useful online source for news on individuals. In fact, this is a wonderful site for varied content, and each month there are new links to resources grouped under general categories, such as Corporations, Foundations, People, News Online, International, and Tools. The People section has extensive biographical sources. If you click on News Online, you will find such things as business news, fundraising news, meta-indices to the foreign press (useful when researching executives of international companies), and a variety of news-only search engines. Finding your way around this particular site is well worth the investment of your time, though you can also save time by subscribing to an e-mail version. Be sure to use the site-wide search engine to find the exact information you are looking for.

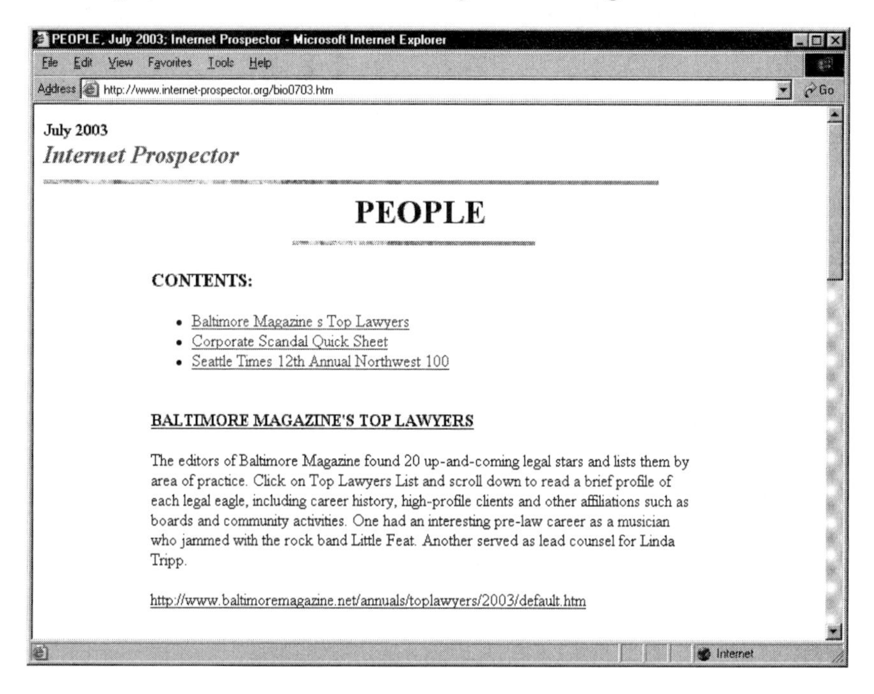

Sometimes you will be seeking information on a very recent newsworthy event, such as the appointment of a new CEO or a large, just-announced gift to a university. PR Newswire (http://www.prnewswire.com) is a useful source for these kinds of breaking news stories. Under News & Information, select a country. Then click on Advanced Search, where you will find three search options: all press releases for the past 30 days; a topical search by industry, subject, state, or company name; and a keyword search. In addition, it is possible to search the archive for 2,000 companies included in the Company News on Call subscriber database. You can further narrow your search by state, company name, or within the last three business days. The results list you receive will be weighted by relevancy.

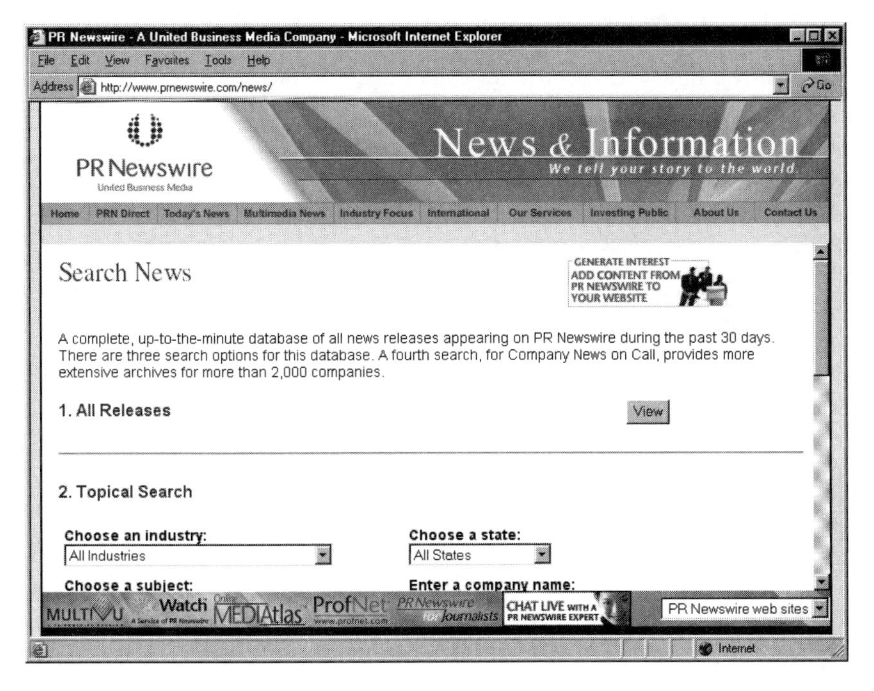

Many of the larger metropolitan newspapers have their own online search services. *The New York Times* (http://nytimes.com) and *The Washington Post* (http://www.washingtonpost.com) are chief among them. Searches for current articles generally are free, whereas searches for articles more than a week or a month old may entail a fee. To access some of these, you will need to become a registered online subscriber, but generally this service is free of charge and simply requires you to fill out a brief online questionnaire and to select a username and password. In addition to some of the media meta-search engines and large metropolitan newspaper sites, a search of the local hometown paper for your prospect is always worthwhile. For information on CNN's Ted Turner, for example, you might visit *The Atlanta Journal-Constitution*'s Web site (http://www.ajc.com). Here you can search staff-written and selected articles since 1985 in "the stacks" (the archive). In any search you do you're likely to find substantial hits on Ted Turner.

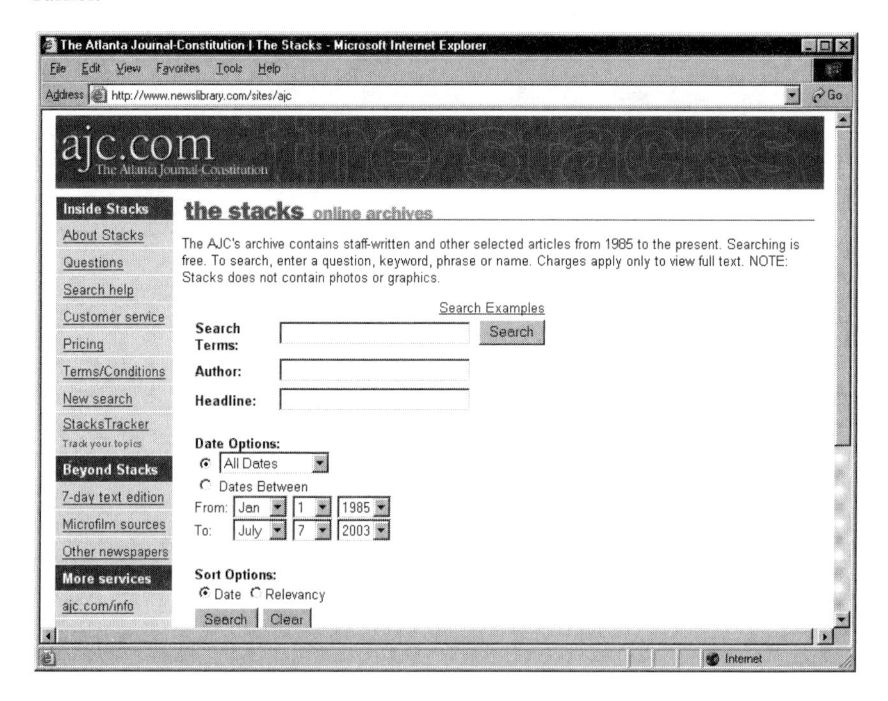

For national or international "breaking" news items, don't overlook CNN's Web site at http://www.cnn.com. The content changes every 15 minutes or so.

MagPortal.com (http://www.magportal.com) allows you to select from Free Magazines in 200 categories or the fee-based Feeds, which offer more traditional online magazines and more custom search engine features. As an important step in the research process, it is always worthwhile to check to see who the online provider is and to determine their guidelines for inclusion or exclusion in the database. This will take a few minutes, but it will save you time in the long run.

A click on the Free Magazines section of the MagPortal.com site yields magazine titles in an alphabetical list with first and last publication date displayed. Included in this list are such magazines as *The American Prospect* and *Boardwatch,* both of interest to the prospect researcher. Search results can be arranged by quality of the match, date, publication title, and category. A recent search for Microsoft's Bill Gates yielded more than 1,100 hits. For articles from magazines with unfamiliar titles, be sure to investigate the publisher to check for authenticity and to see if they may have a particular axe to grind or viewpoint to put forward.

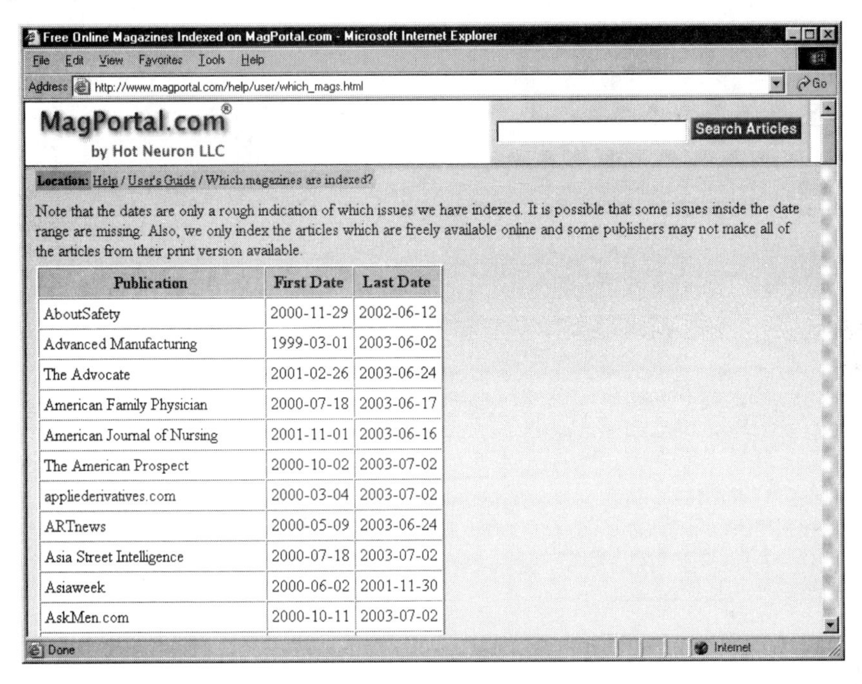

Publication	First Date	Last Date
AboutSafety	2000-11-29	2002-06-12
Advanced Manufacturing	1999-03-01	2003-06-02
The Advocate	2001-02-26	2003-06-24
American Family Physician	2000-07-18	2003-06-17
American Journal of Nursing	2001-11-01	2003-06-16
The American Prospect	2000-10-02	2003-07-02
appliederivatives.com	2000-03-04	2003-07-02
ARTnews	2000-05-09	2003-06-24
Asia Street Intelligence	2000-07-18	2003-07-02
Asiaweek	2000-06-02	2001-11-30
AskMen.com	2000-10-11	2003-07-02

For prospect researchers, the major business publications, such as *The Wall Street Journal, Fortune,* and *Forbes,* each provide excellent online search features on their Web sites. Most are free or free once you register. Most also offer the options of a basic search or advanced search. For those you plan to return to frequently, it's probably worthwhile to learn the ins and outs of the advanced search features, since this will make you more efficient each time you visit the site.

On the Forbes.com site (http://www.forbes.com), you can search for information in various categories, such as Business, Technology, Markets, Work, Lists (Forbes 500s, World's Richest People, 400 Richest Americans, etc.), Personal Finances, and Lifestyle, and you can search by a person's last name and/or by a company's stock symbol. The last name search is a little time-consuming because you need to scroll down an alphabetical list. However, it yields specific information as to an individual's precise title and company affiliation.

An all too often overlooked resource may be your local public library's Web site, particularly if you live in a major metropolitan area. Many libraries provide free access, by means of a public library card, to a vast array of online newspaper and magazine resources, some of which would otherwise be available only on an expensive fee-for-service basis. For instance, Proquest Direct, offered by a number of library systems, is an online database of more than 3,500 newspapers and periodicals, ranging from titles as specific as *Accountancy Ireland* to the more general news, business, and public interest magazines. These days even some smaller public libraries have Web sites that provide access to various CD-ROM and other online periodical databases. It's worth checking to see whether your local library provides these services.

PEOPLE, FAMOUS AND NOT-SO-FAMOUS, INCLUDING THEIR CHARITABLE GIFTS

The Church of Jesus Christ of Latter-day Saints (the Mormons) has been incredibly industrious in gathering information related to genealogy on millions of family names. Its FamilySearch Web site (http://www.familysearch.org) enables you to search a vast collection of records to determine family histories and connections. An online Social Security death index is also available at this site. Morbid as this may sound, prospect researchers frequently must determine the date of an individual's death, and this is one way to do so. This is one of those Web sites where you can easily become distracted and spend hours investigating your own and others' ancestors, rather than your prospect's. If you stick to the task at hand, fascinating connections between families may emerge that are very useful for the grantseeker to know about.

An excellent resource for finding women philanthropists will be found on the University of Michigan's Web site. Entitled Women in Philanthropy (http://www.women-philanthropy.umich.edu), this resource includes specific information on gifts from generous women in Women Donors. While not comprehensive, there is a lot of information included for the online grantseeker. To search for a particular prospect, select a letter corresponding to that individual's last name.

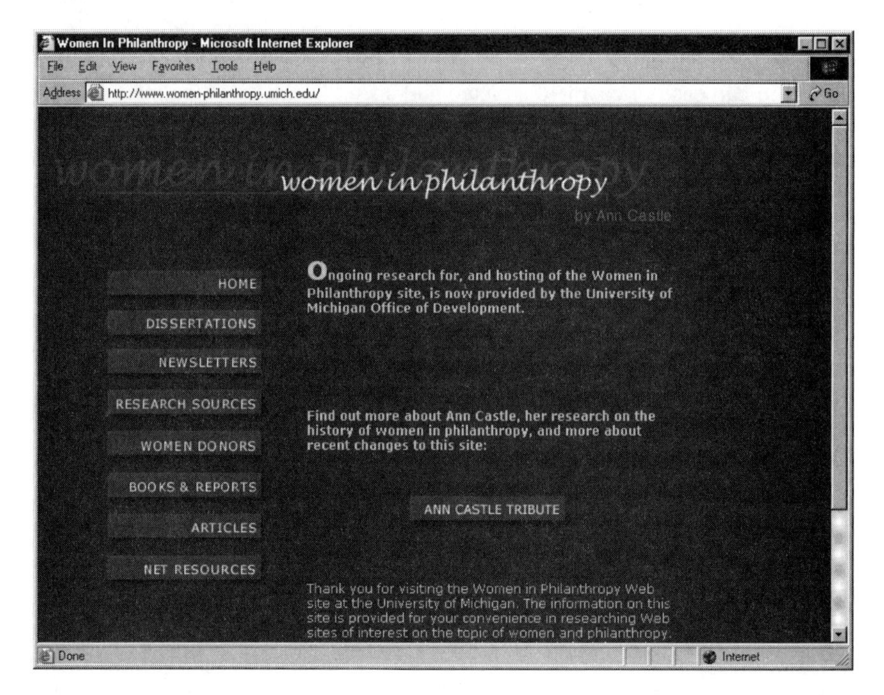

Celebrities

Celebrities are very involved in charitable endeavors these days. Some have their own foundations. Others support various causes in a variety of ways, ranging from merely lending their name to very publicly endorsing an organization or effort. There are a number of Web resources to help find out about celebrities' charitable activities.

While many of these grantmaking organizations are seeking funds as well as operating their own programs, it may be a safe bet that the celebrities involved may also be interested in supporting your program or cause, if it relates to—but doesn't compete with—their interests. Your job as a grantseeker would then be to conduct further research and determine the best means of approach.

The Giving Back Fund (http://www.givingback.org) is a pooled-asset community foundation primarily serving the philanthropic interests of athletes and entertainers. Its home page includes a Philanthropy Hall of Fame and the opportunity to donate to one of the charitable organizations featured on the site. Here you will find such charities as the Jon Seda Foundation, which funds research into the causes of and cures for Reflex Sympathetic Dystrophy Syndrome, and the Jorge Posada Foundation, which supports athletic programs for children in New York and Puerto Rico. A click on the Nancy Kerrigan Foundation, for example, yields a great deal of information on the Olympic ice-skating champion's charitable interests.

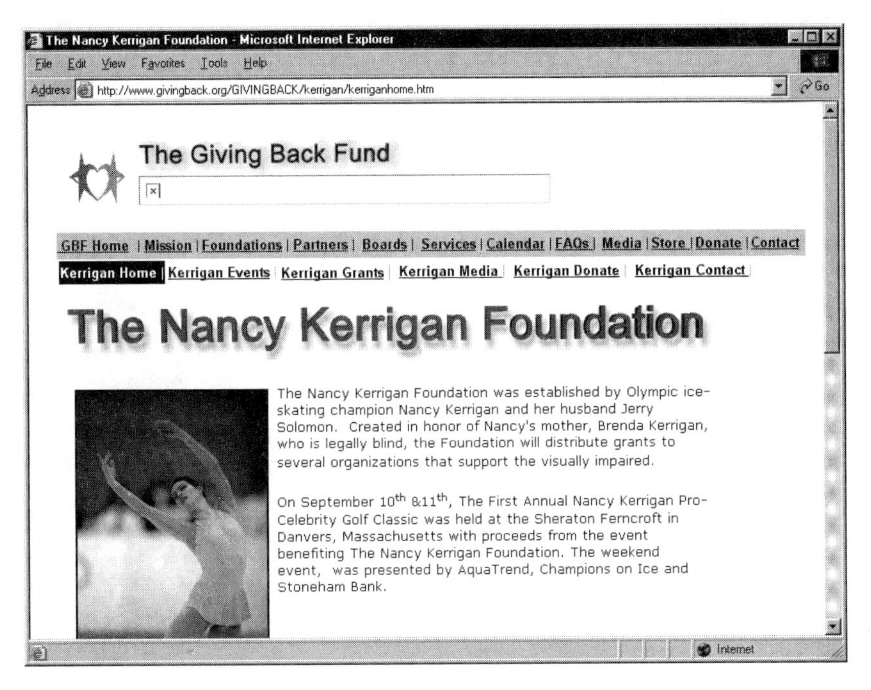

You can also conduct more general searches using various online search engines. A search on the Forbes.com Web site (http://forbes.com), for example, using the term "celebrity charities," yields 124 documents listed by date, all of which describe celebrity charities covered by *Forbes.*

If you visit the Lists directory on Forbes.com, you can click on the Forbes Celebrity 100 list (http://www.forbes.com/static_html/celebs/2002.html). You can browse a list of the top 100 celebrities according to their "power" rank, money rank, earnings, press clips, Web hits, magazine covers, TV/radio hits, and so on. You can also search the full list by name or category. This is all in good fun, but it also includes useful information for those seeking to solicit donations from celebrities.

Another useful Web site is the Hollywoodreporter.com (http://www.hollywood-reporter.com/thr/people/index.jsp). Here you will find a Philanthropic Directory, "an A to Z resource guide to charity organizations with significant entertainment-industry involvement." While the subject matter may appear glamorous, the information seems to be accurate and the intent—to highlight charitable activities of Hollywood celebrities—is serious.

On the Foundation Center's Web site, in the new Youth and Philanthropy area, you will find a Famous and Celebrity Philanthropists sub-directory at http://fdncenter.org/focus/youth/kids_teens/youth_celebrity.html, with brief descriptions and links to celebrity foundations set up by athletes, entertainers, and wealthy individuals. There are also profiles of famous philanthropists of the past.

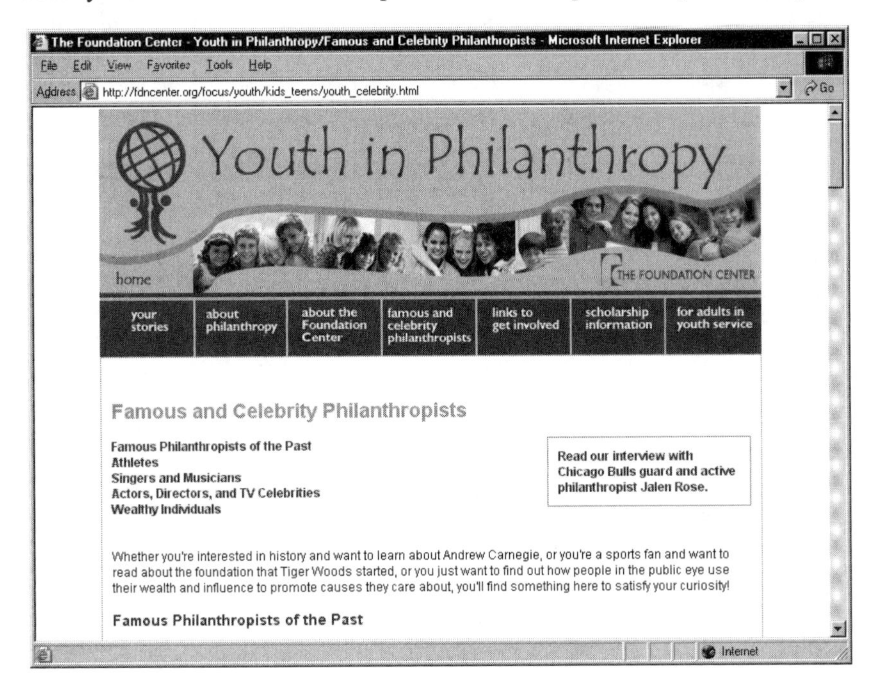

Biographies

Biography.com (http://www.biography.com), one of the Arts and Entertainment (A&E) Network's Web sites, offers a BioSearch feature covering a truly remarkable 25,000 personalities. The emphasis is clearly on celebrities, but others are here as well. For example, one search yielded information on Douglas Taylor Ross, founder of SofTech. Another search for Michael J. Fox yields a well-written and comprehensive biography of this star, who has recently redirected much of his time to research on Parkinson's disease. Many of the individuals covered are deceased, of course, but that is true of most of the general biographical sites.

Speaking of the deceased, another Web site, Lives, the Biography Resource (http://www.amillionlives.com), covers only those who are no longer with us, including "individual lives of the famous, the infamous, and the not so famous." As with the Mormons' death index, this site can provide very useful background information for the prospect researcher, particularly when you are trying to track down historical and family connections.

Sometimes all you are looking for on a particular individual is an address and/or phone number. The Ultimate White Pages (http://theultimates.com/white) Web site may be able to help you there. This is a meta-search engine that covers six different directories all at once. It does not include unlisted phone numbers, however.

Corporate Heavy Hitters

By far the easiest category of individuals to research on the Web is corporate executives. The reason for this is that the Internet is a virtual treasure trove of information on companies and those who run them. In fact, there is so much available online today regarding corporate executives that you can easily come up with highly duplicative information in the course of visiting just a few Web sites. The best advice we can provide to grantseekers scoping out those who run our nation's corporations as possible sources of individual contributions is to find those sites most useful to you and stick to them, particularly once you've gained enough experience to know that a given Web site consistently provides up-to-date and accurate information and is relatively easy to search.

One resource that's very popular with prospect researchers is the Biography section on CEO Central's site (http://www.surferess.com/CEO/html/biographies.html). This Web site provides not only biographies but "interesting facts and statistics" (e.g., an executive's golf handicap) and photos of America's CEOs. Listings of past CEOs are also available. Some of what you encounter here may come across as a rather breathless paean to captains of industry. Nonetheless, this is a useful source to become familiar with. The home page features a list of the top CEOs. Click on any of the names, and you will find a thorough, well-researched biography of a corporate luminary such as Warren Buffet of Berkshire Hathaway.

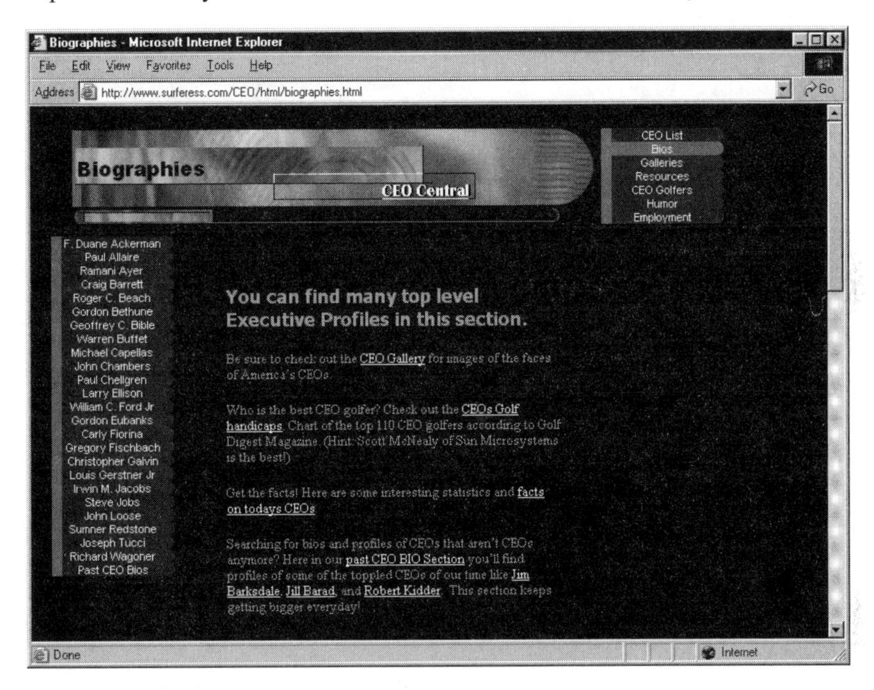

Forbes magazine's Web site (htttp://www.forbes.com) is a highly useful resource on corporations and those who run them. As described in the earlier celebrity section, the People search feature on this Web site is equally useful for those in the business sector. A search for Apple Computer's Steve Jobs, for example, yields 178 documents in the database, arranged in reverse chronological order, each with its own brief abstract. It is also possible to see the person's cash compensation, stock options, and investments in other companies, though in many cases this information, or elements of it, will not be available.

The Forbes.com Web site also boasts its frequently clicked-on Forbes 400 Richest Americans list. This is divided into yearly online segments, going back a number of years. Results can be sorted by rank, worth, age, marital status, residence, and source. A click on any of the top 400 richest listings provides you with a concise but information-packed biography of the individual in question, including an estimate of his or her net worth and a brief history of employment. Similar information is provided, along with biographical links, on Forbes' World's Richest People list, dating back to 1996. Many are U.S. executives.

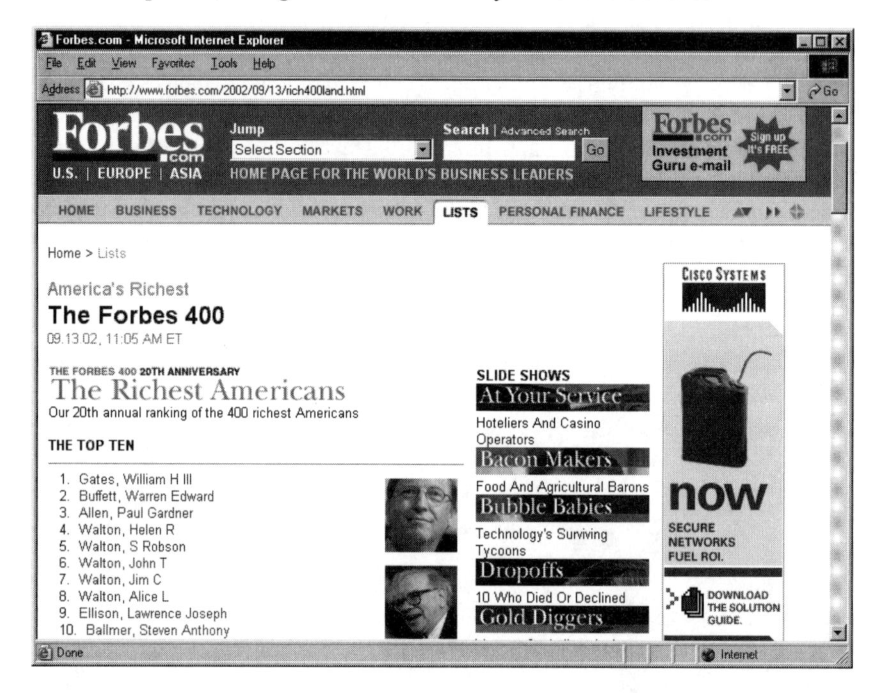

Forbes.com also offers a People Tracker service, whereby you can sign up for free membership and receive customized e-mail alerts on changes in an individual's title, compensation, stock options exercised, or "breaking news" for 120,000 executives. This service might make even the most seasoned fundraiser breathe a sigh of relief, since it could save an enormous amount of effort keeping track of those in your "live" prospect file whom you are trying to monitor over a period of time.

Forbes' chief competitor, *Fortune* magazine, offers its own lists and biographical information on its Web site at http://www.fortune.com. This site includes a list of America's Forty Richest Under 40 that can be sorted by rank, name, age, company, and net worth. Online biographical sketches are available for those on the list. In addition there are numerous other searchable lists on Fortune.com, including Most Powerful Women in Business (the Power 50), All-Star Analysts, Most Powerful Black Executives, and Washington Power 25. It's likely that one or another of your prospects might appear on at least one of these lists, if you are searching for those involved in industry or politics.

Another online source for biographical snapshots of financial people is Wall Street Reporter at http://wallstreetreporter.com/html2/main.htm.

There is also a Web site for Canadian business leaders at http://www.canadianbusiness.com. This site hosts a special list of Canada's Rich 100.

There are more specialized Web sites as well. One example is GoldSea 100 (http://goldsea.com/Profiles/100), which provides a list of America's top Asian-American professionals.

If none of these Web sites pans out, you might try a large portal site such as CEOExpress at http://ceoexpress.com. Here you will find a meta-index of daily newspapers, business newspapers and magazines, technology and lifestyle magazines, newsfeeds, and Internet search engines. You can search by name, company name, or stock symbol.

One final tip: If you are searching for information on an individual, and you know what corporation he or she heads or works for, try going right to that company's Web site. For example, a visit to the Barnes & Noble corporate Web site (http://www.barnesandnobleinc.com) can uncover a highly informative resume of its CEO, Leonard Riggio. If he were among your top prospects, the information included here would get you well on your way to filling out your prospect worksheet.

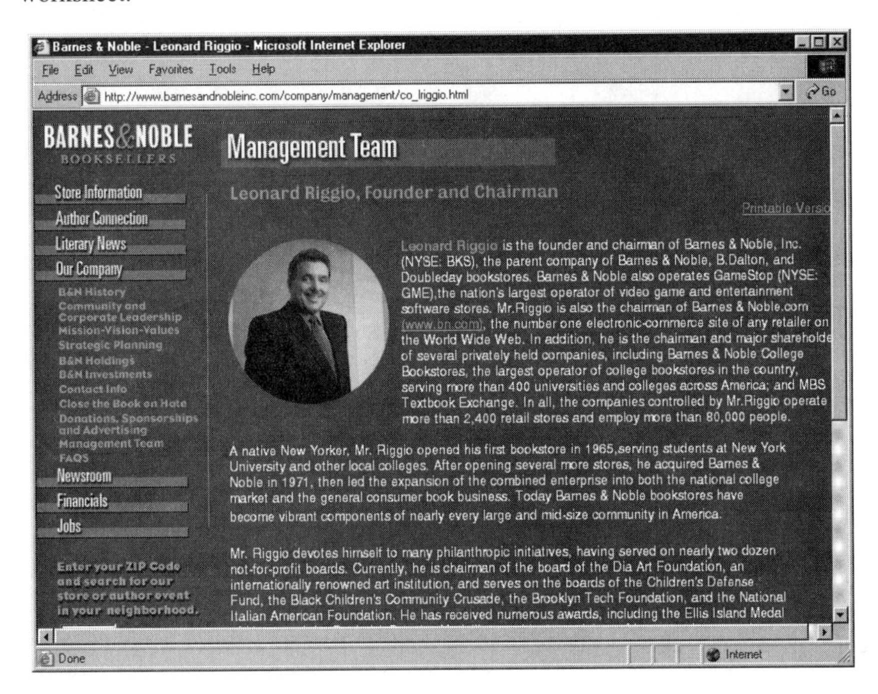

CAPACITY TO GIVE—SALARIES, ASSETS, AND RECENT GIFTS AWARDED

When researching those in the corporate sector you will want to determine their capacity to give your organization a substantial gift. One way to do this is to look at salary information. Although most executives' salary tells only part of the story, it is a good place to start. Salary surveys abound on the Internet. When referring to any of these sites, be sure to check the last date updated. Particularly in times of uncertain stock prices and company layoffs, today's millionaire could easily be tomorrow's unemployed. So it is critical to refer to the most current and trustworthy source available.

One salary survey is in the Pay & Perks link in the Careers section of *Business Week* magazine's site (http://businessweek.com), which posts articles and reports on executive pay as well as several tables, including one on the top-paid chief executives. Still another source of salary surveys is the SiliconValley.com Web site (http://www.siliconvalley.com/mld/siliconvalley), focusing on executive salaries at Silicon Valley companies.

An additional source for salary information is the huge labor union AFL-CIO's Web site (http://www.aflcio.org/corporateamerica/paywatch), where you will find a feature called Executive Paywatch. This site promises you will "learn how to track down CEO pay." We mentioned previously that it's critical that you understand whether a particular site's host may have a certain slant or perspective on the data it provides. This site is a good example, since it also has features such as Does the CEO Deserve That Big Pay Package?

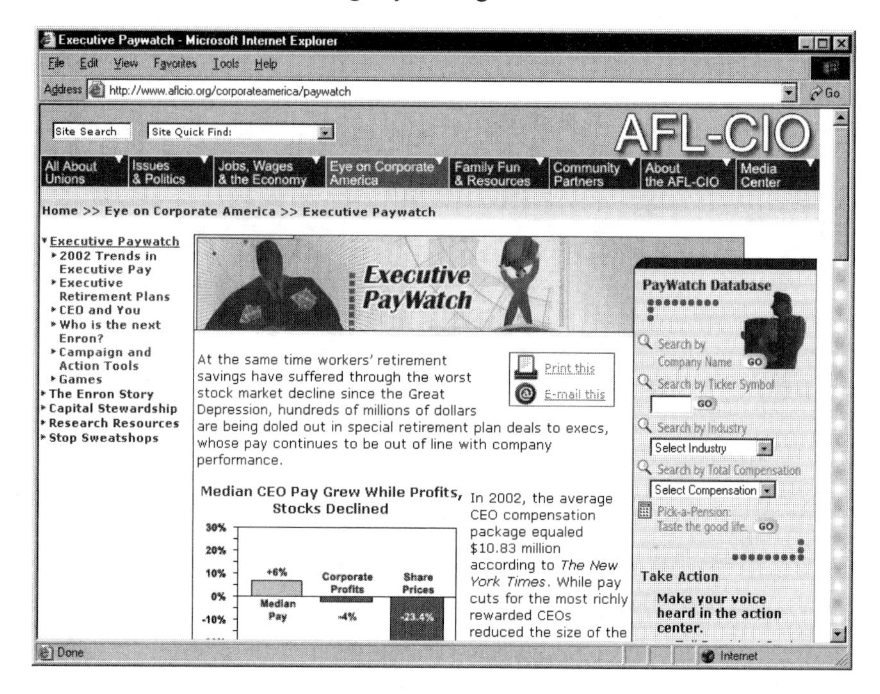

For salary information on those in the nonprofit sector, there are a number of resources. Be forewarned, however, that since most of these derive from public information returns filed with the IRS, the data you uncover may be up to two years old. This is when it is advisable to try to refer to other resources as well, in order to determine an individual's capacity to give. A basic resource for executives of the nation's 62,000+ private foundations is the Form 990-PF that each foundation is required to file with the IRS. On this form the foundation is required to list its top officers, directors, trustees, and foundation managers, along with their compensation.

You can access Forms 990-PF readily from the Foundation Center's Web site via Foundation Finder, *The Foundation Directory Online,* or 990-PF Search, all found in the Finding Funders directory. Multiple years are provided where available. 990-PF Search allows you to search by name or Employer Identification Number (EIN). Forms 990-PF are also available on GuideStar (http://www.guidestar.org), a database profiling more than 850,000 U.S. nonprofit organizations. You will need to go through a free registration process in order to view the Forms 990-PF on GuideStar.

The Chronicle of Philanthropy issues an annual salary survey for nonprofit executives that can be found on its Web site at http://philanthropy.com. The information is arranged by category of nonprofit and is eagerly awaited each year by those in the sector seeking to compare and contrast compensation information. Much of the data comes from direct surveying rather than the Form 990 or other public documents, so it tends to be relatively up-to-date. The *Chronicle* also publishes the names of those organizations that refuse to cooperate with its survey. Access to this part of the site is available only to *Chronicle* subscribers.

GuideStar has posted a nonprofit compensation report, compiled from Form 990 data, at its Web site, http://www.guidestar.org/services/compstudy2.stm. This study, available in several formats at various prices, includes at least one paid position at 75,000 nonprofit organizations in 14 job categories.

On its Web site, *The NonProfit Times* (http://www.nptimes.com) issues an annual salary survey as a special report and another special report, the NPT Power and Influence Top 50, which profiles the nation's top nonprofit executives.

The Foundation Center's FAQ "Where can I find information on employee compensation in the nonprofit sector?" (http://fdncenter.org/learn/faqs/html/emp_comp.html) provides links to other print and electronic resources for determining compensation in the nonprofit sector.

An excellent resource on companies and those who manage them, including their compensation and stock holdings, are filings with the Securities and Exchange Commission (SEC). If you are interested in compensation information on Martha Stewart, for example, you can perform a search for her at the SEC EDGAR site (http://www.sec.gov/edgar.shtml). Begin by clicking Search for Company Filings and then Companies & Other Filers. In this case, since her name is part of the company name, Martha Stewart Living Omnimedia, Inc., you can enter her name in the Company Name field. You will then find a list of documents filed by her conglomerate in the last several years. To access her compensation information, including salary, bonus, and stock options—as well as those for the other officers and directors of her company—you will want to look for Form DEF 14A (or what is commonly called a proxy statement). Select DEF 14A and then click on Document 1 (the first link provided). Learning to read the Form DEF 14A takes a bit of getting used to, but for top corporate executives at public companies whose salary information is not readily available elsewhere, it is well worth the effort.

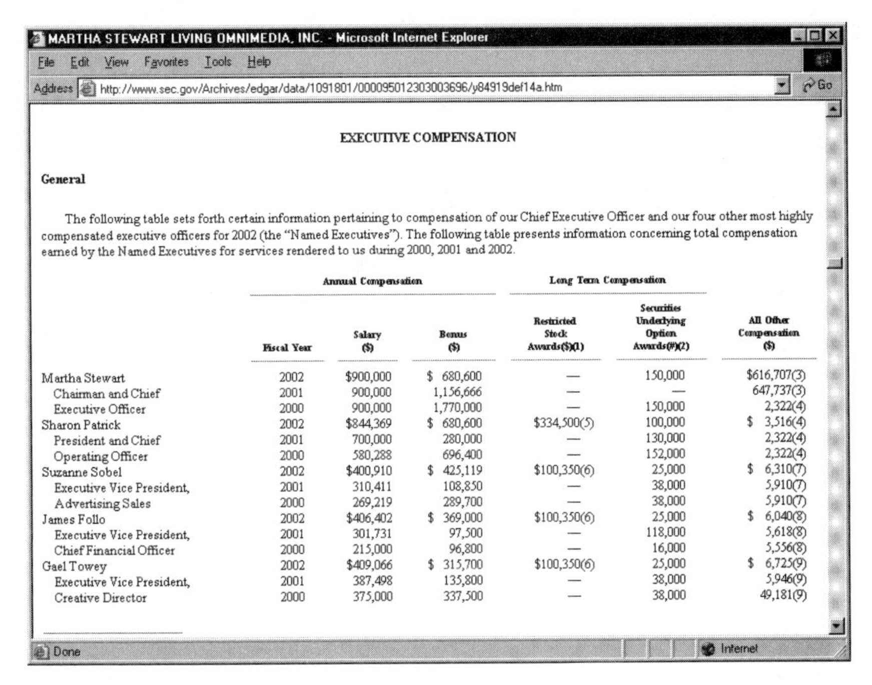
MARTHA STEWART LIVING OMNIMEDIA, INC. - Microsoft Internet Explorer

File Edit View Favorites Tools Help

Address http://www.sec.gov/Archives/edgar/data/1091801/000095012303003696/y84919def14a.htm Go

EXECUTIVE COMPENSATION

General

The following table sets forth certain information pertaining to compensation of our Chief Executive Officer and our four other most highly compensated executive officers for 2002 (the "Named Executives"). The following table presents information concerning total compensation earned by the Named Executives for services rendered to us during 2000, 2001 and 2002.

		Annual Compensation		Long Term Compensation		
	Fiscal Year	Salary ($)	Bonus ($)	Restricted Stock Awards($)(1)	Securities Underlying Option Awards(#)(2)	All Other Compensation ($)
Martha Stewart	2002	$900,000	$ 680,600	—	150,000	$616,707(3)
Chairman and Chief	2001	900,000	1,156,666	—	—	647,737(3)
Executive Officer	2000	900,000	1,770,000	—	150,000	2,322(4)
Sharon Patrick	2002	$844,369	$ 680,600	$334,500(5)	100,000	$ 3,516(4)
President and Chief	2001	700,000	280,000	—	130,000	2,322(4)
Operating Officer	2000	580,288	696,400	—	152,000	2,322(4)
Suzanne Sobel	2002	$400,910	$ 425,119	$100,350(6)	25,000	$ 6,310(7)
Executive Vice President,	2001	310,411	108,850	—	38,000	5,910(7)
Advertising Sales	2000	269,219	289,700	—	38,000	5,910(7)
James Follo	2002	$406,402	$ 369,000	$100,350(6)	25,000	$ 6,040(8)
Executive Vice President,	2001	301,731	97,500	—	118,000	5,618(8)
Chief Financial Officer	2000	215,000	96,800	—	16,000	5,556(8)
Gael Towey	2002	$409,066	$ 315,700	$100,350(6)	25,000	$ 6,725(9)
Executive Vice President,	2001	387,498	135,800	—	38,000	5,946(9)
Creative Director	2000	375,000	337,500	—	38,000	49,181(9)

Done Internet

Regarding stock holdings, a very useful site is CNET.com (http://investor.cnet.com). Here you will find a feature called CEO Wealthmeter that provides an alphabetical list by company and includes the CEO's name, the value of his/her holdings, today's change (up or down), and the CEO's latest fiscal year compensation. This is an excellent source for identifying companies' stock symbols, since a number of business sites are arranged so you can search by symbol. One other interesting feature of this site is Today's Top 5 Gainers (on the stock market) and, of course, Today's Bottom 5 Losers. The latter might be of interest to refer to just before you approach a CEO for a substantial gift.

Another online research strategy for determining capacity to give is to search by profession. For doctors, lawyers, and others, there are Web sites that have searchable directories. While these sites rarely provide any specifics on individuals' earnings, they do have useful biographical and other information. Two of these are Martindale-Hubbell's site at http://martindale.com (for attorneys) and the American Medical Association's site at http://www.ama-assn.org. Another is CareerJournal.com (http://www.jobstar.org/tools/salary/sal-prof.htm), which is intended for those entering various fields. This site provides access to 300 general salary surveys, as opposed to specific individuals' salaries, but is useful if you can't find the information you need elsewhere. Here you can search by profession, such as accounting, public relations, and so on. Occasionally you may be searching for information on prospects and donations in the political arena. Or you may be considering asking a local politician to lend his or her name to an event your nonprofit is planning, and you want to check out who's been supporting him or her in advance. A good Web site for this kind of data is Open Secrets at http://www.opensecrets.org. Here you will find a Donor Lookup feature that includes individual and "soft money" contributions.

Another way to estimate capacity to give is an obvious one: recent gifts awarded. *Slate* (http://slate.msn.com) posts a list of the Slate 60: the 60 largest American charitable contributions of the year from the country's top philanthropists. This is fascinating and pertinent reading for those seeking major gifts for their own institutions.

The Foundation Center's *Philanthropy News Digest* (*PND*) (http://fdncenter.org/pnd) is an excellent source for current media coverage of large gifts, not only by grantmaking organizations but also by individuals. You can search the *PND* archive by an individual's name as far back as 1995. Links to relevant organizations are provided.

The SearchZone (http://fdncenter.org/searchzone) on the Foundation Center's Web site is a good way to research recent gifts and affiliations of individual prospects. Here you will find 990-PF Search, Foundation Finder, and *PND* Search mentioned above. You will also find Sector Search, a search engine that limits its searches to only Web sites across the nonprofit sector; Grantmaker Web Sites, which searches annotations of grantmaker Web sites written by Center staff; and the fee-based subscription service, *The Foundation Directory Online.*

If you click on Sector Search, for example, and enter "George Soros" in the search box, you receive 494 results, sorted by relevance. Many of the hits discuss causes that he has funded.

An additional resource available on the Foundation Center's Web site in the Researching Philanthropy area is *Literature of the Nonprofit Sector Online* (http://lnps.fdncenter.org). This bibliographic database, which can also be accessed through SearchZone, contains some 22,000 records, many of which are extensively abstracted. Nearly 80 percent are from periodical articles in the fields of philanthropy and nonprofit management. A recent search on Bill Gates yielded 24 hits, a number of which provided valuable insights into Mr. Gates and his charitable initiatives.

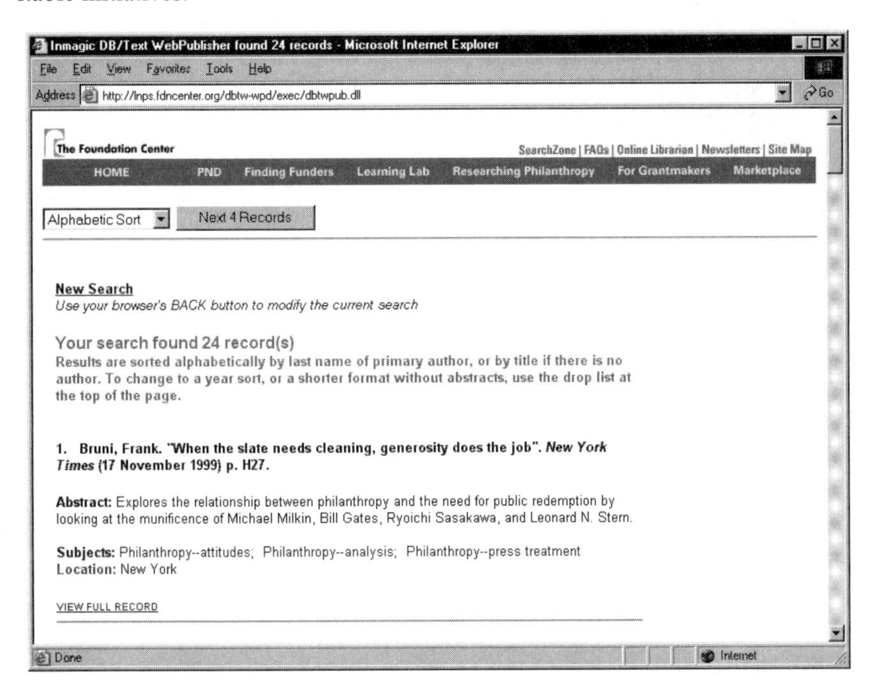

Philanthropy News Network (PNN) is another source of information on individual gifts and pledges. You can search for people and their giving at the PNN site (http://pnnonline.org) to find details on large gifts derived from other sources.

In determining an individual's capacity to give, in addition to salaries, stock holdings, and records of recent gifts, other types of assets and their value also are of interest. Real estate, yachts, and airplanes are the three types of assets about which online information is most often available. The University of Virginia's Portico has a popular feature on its Web site (http://indorgs.virginia.edu/portico/personalproperty.html), whereby you can check property assessments arranged by geographic region of the country. This area of the Portico site also provides other useful links, including real estate listings more specific to local areas, sites for determining airplane ownership, airplane registrations, and even yacht ownership.

GATEWAYS TO PROSPECT RESEARCH

Not surprisingly, the Web sites of various university development offices throughout the country provide excellent entrees to the world of prospect research. Most are organized in highly systematic ways by topic and provide an array of links to other sites that have proven of use to university development staff over the years. It is truly amazing and of enormous benefit to the grantseeker that so much of this information is available online for free by visiting these sites, since their developers have generously decided to share their research expertise with others.

The Princeton University Web site, for example, offers an extensive list of resources its development staff has found useful in determining an individual's assets and unearthing biographical information (http://www.princeton.edu/one/devres/netlinks.html).

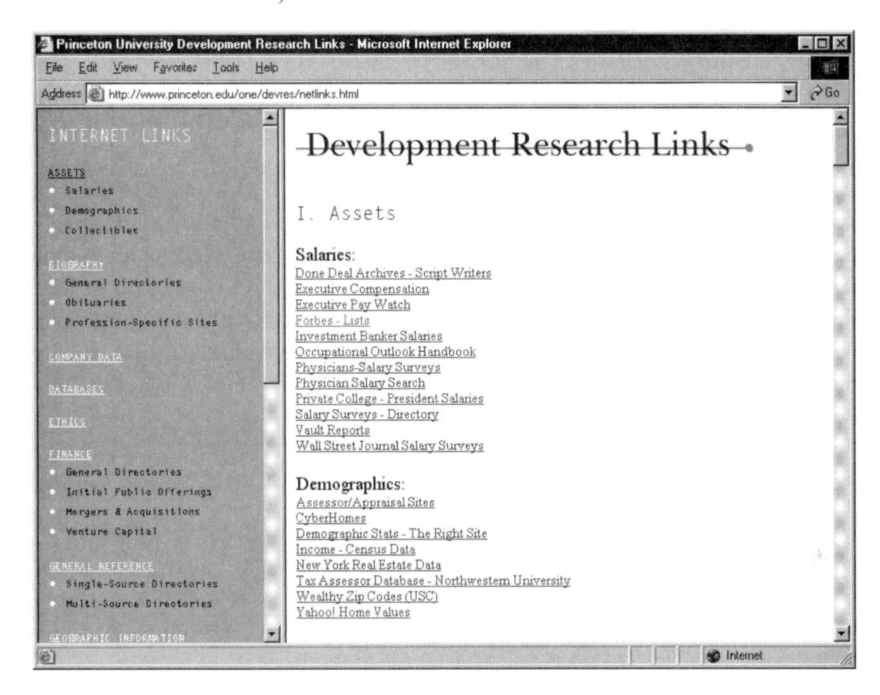

Another useful resource will be found on Syracuse University's Web site at http://web.syr.edu/~dekelley/hotlist.html. Here you will find Dorry Kelley's favorite prospect research links—"and *not* the golf variety."

Northwestern University posts its research bookmarks in a variety of categories on its site at http://pubweb.acns.nwu.edu/~cap440/bookmark.html. Categories include Alumni Directories, Mergers and Acquisitions, Tax Assessor Database, and so on.

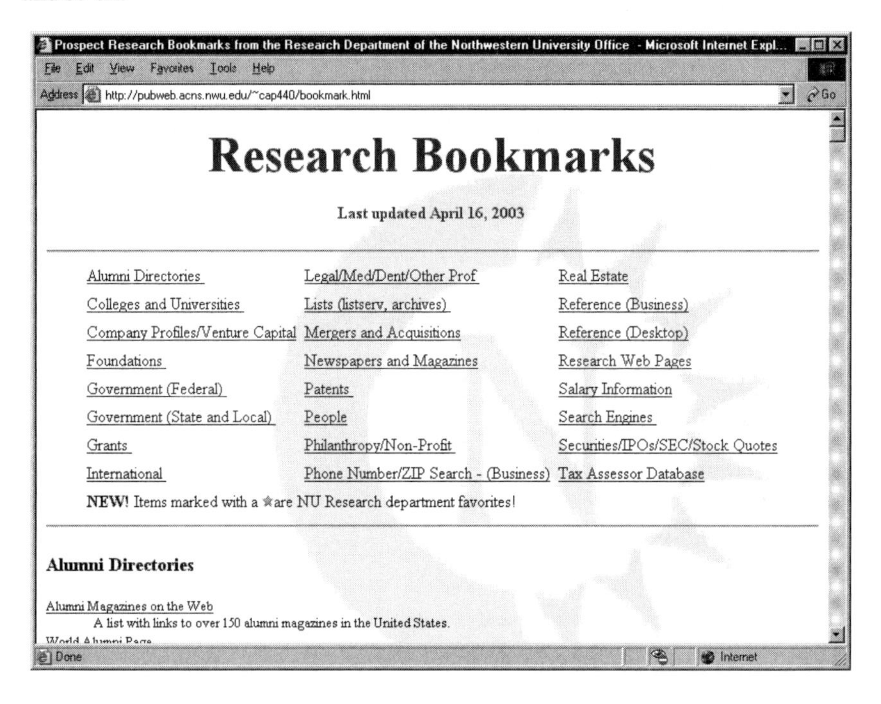

We've already mentioned the University of Virginia's Portico Web site and its prospect research area (http://indorgs.virginia.edu/portico). On this site you will find a series of links, compiled in a very logical way (Biographical, Personal Property, Salaries, etc.), and links to other online resources that are extremely helpful in estimating net worth and determining capacity to give.

Another useful gateway resource to many of the Web sites featured in this chapter is the Association of Professional Researchers for Advancement's Web site, mentioned earlier for its statement of ethical standards. Here you will find Web Resources for Advancement Research (http://www.aprahome.org/researchlinks/index.html), which is extremely well put together and definitely worth a visit by anyone seeking information on individual donors, especially those whose online detective work has not yet yielded much useful information.

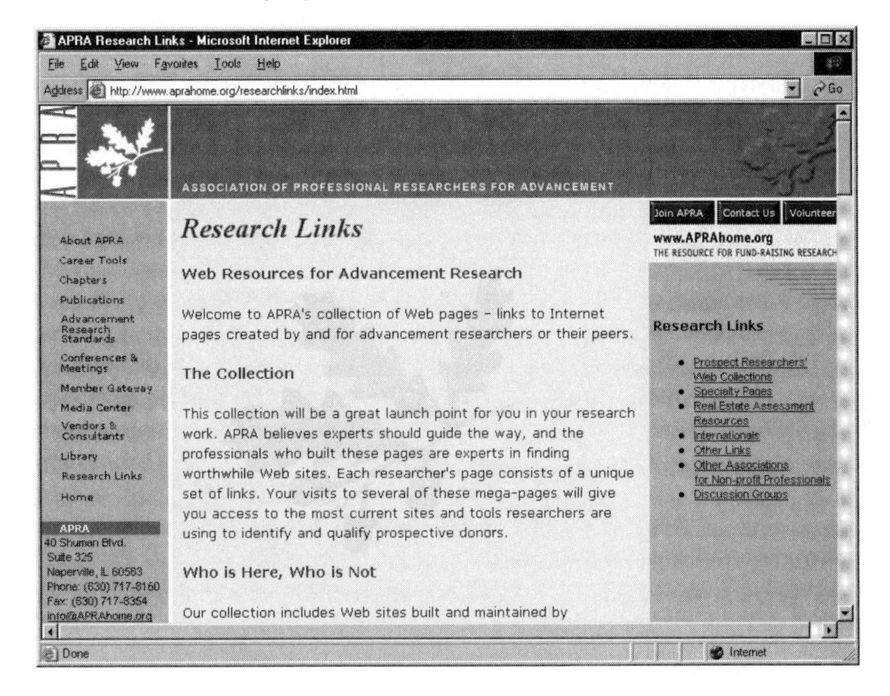

Last but certainly not least when it comes to gateways is David Lamb's Prospect Research Page (http://www.lambresearch.com), the name of which is a little deceiving, since it is certainly more than a single page. David Lamb, former director of prospect research at the University of Washington and Santa Clara University, is considered by many to be the "Web guru" of online prospect research. The site includes categories such as Corporations/Executives, Public Records, Professionals, and others. This Web site is an attempt to "separate the wheat from the chaff when it comes to research resources on the Internet." These are David Lamb's personal recommendations of Web sites to visit, and since he is the expert, you may want to take the time to fully explore them.

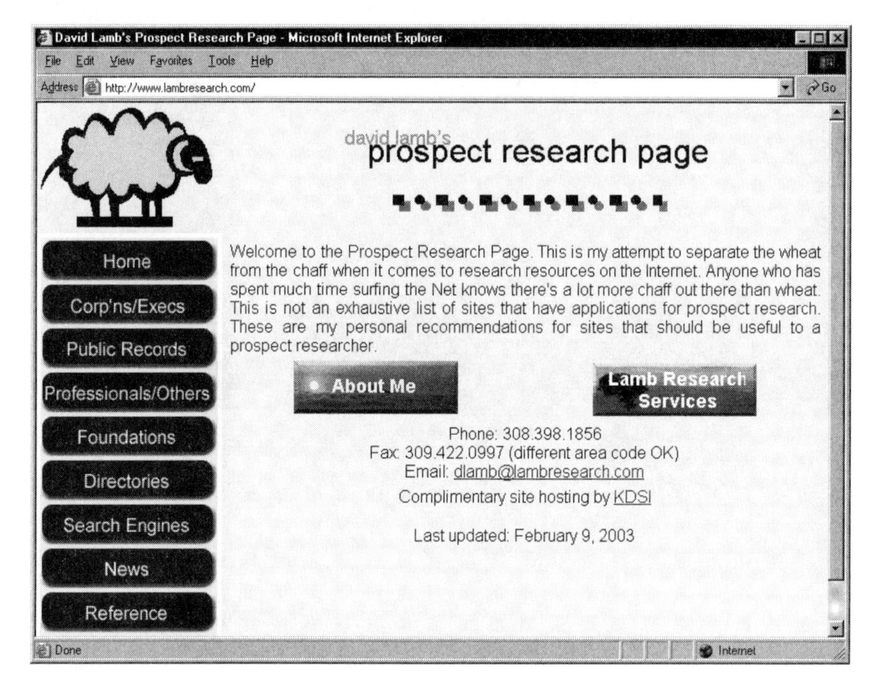

Fee-Based Services

In this chapter we have focused primarily on Web resources that are available for free or for a small subscription fee to anyone seeking information on potential individual donors. We would be remiss, however, if we did not at least mention the availability of online services that provide extensive information and search capabilities on individual donors for a more substantial fee. Most require annual subscriptions or membership, and there may be individual online search charges as well. For larger organizations and those engaged in intensive campaigns to raise funds from individuals, these may be worth investigating.

Chief among these are Dialog (http://www.dialog.com), which is one of the original online database providers, with access to databases in business, government, medicine, intellectual property, and many others, and Lexis-Nexis (http://www.lexis-nexis.com), which has more than 30,000 searchable databases in multiple disciplines including many databases for researching individuals.

A fee-based service called Prospect Research Online (PRO) provides a compilation of publicly available information on individuals and institutional donors on a subscription basis. For more information, visit its Web site at http://www.rpbooks.com. WealthEngine.com (http://www.wealthengine.com) mines data from a variety of online sources, such as Dun & Bradstreet, Disclosure Insider Trading, and Marquis Who's Who, and provides concise, integrated reports disclosing information on business affiliations, stock transactions, pension holdings, and giving histories of prospective donors. The Foundation Center's aforementioned family of fee-based subscriptions services, *The Foundation Directory Online,* will provide you with information on grantmakers with which your prospects are affiliated. Another fee-based service, Target America (http://www.tgtam.com), purports to contain records on the top five percent of the wealthiest and most generous people in the nation. A helpful annotated list of fee-based prospect research services has been published in the May/June 2002 issue of *Currents,* the online journal of the Council for Advancement and Support of Education (CASE), and may be found on the CASE Web site at http://www.case.org/currents/2002/may/conley.cfm.

And finally, the Foundation Center's Associates Program (http://fdncenter.org/marketplace; click on Associates Program), while geared to delivering information about institutional grantmakers, also provides Associate members with telephone and e-mail reference services on individual donors and offers a service whereby members can request biographical searches on individual prospects. The Associates Program also provides members with access to its own extranet—a Web site available to members only.

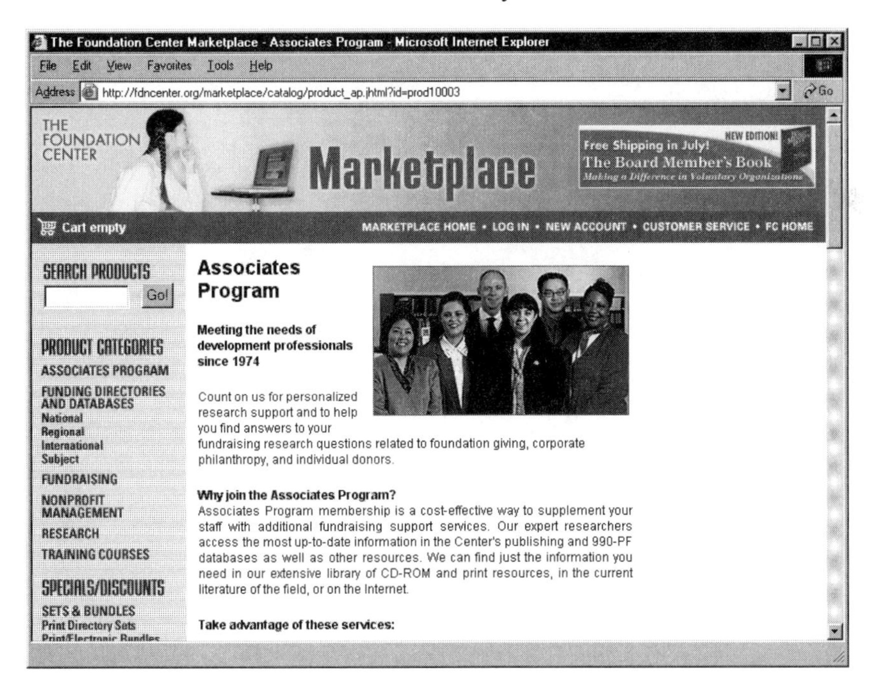

Conclusion

In summary, the resources on the Web for researching individuals are quite extensive. Most of the resources you will encounter as a grantseeker are available free of charge or at minimal expense. While in this chapter we have just scratched the surface of what is out there, we have tried to provide a selective list of some of the better sites, guidance on the best approach to these Web sites, and recommendations on research strategies to adopt. Our best advice is to utilize the individual prospect worksheet we provided as a research tool and maintain your critical eye as you visit each site. Your most valuable resource as a grantseeker is your own time. To preserve this resource you need to adhere to the disciplined approach we described earlier. And keep in mind that the best prospects you'll uncover online have the capacity to give, an interest in your cause, and a connection to your organization.

CHAPTER SEVEN

Searchable Databases on the Web

With each passing day, more grantseekers are using Web-based search engines as essential, time-saving tools in their funding research. Because much of the Web itself is indexed by search engine services, you could say that it is a sort of giant database, albeit sprawling and without the important control and consistency provided by a single-source database. The good news for grantseekers, however, is that a vast number of well-organized databases are available on the Web, some of them completely free.

As you read this chapter, please bear in mind that the list of sites within is by no means comprehensive. This is intended, rather, as a selection of suggested starting points for the grantseeker looking for searchable, Web-based information. These sites represent only a tiny fraction of the sites you can find on your own once you get started.

Publicly accessible databases generally offer keyword searching in one or more searchable fields and can be used effectively, even by those with little or no prior experience with online research. Other good news is that many veteran information service providers, some of whom have employed database technology for decades, are now making their databases available online via the Web, often modifying their search technology in the process to facilitate access by novice researchers. Because of the modifications to these Web-based tools, database searching has become an option for an increasingly wide and varied audience of grantseekers. In short, the Web has brought the search and retrieval of organized data sets within reach of anyone who has access to the Internet.

Databases on the Web of interest to grantseekers cover a wide spectrum—from the funding-specific that let you search for potential donors, to the more general and news-oriented types, which may not help you find potential donors but which can complement your research on the prospects you have identified from other sources. In this chapter, we describe various databases that are of particular interest to grantseekers, as well as databases of more general interest to the philanthropic community and to those who work for and run nonprofits.

Please note that we have differentiated between databases that are free and those that are not. Valuable information can be obtained from both categories, and you shouldn't necessarily assume that information that you pay for is more useful than what's available for free. Each grantseeker must evaluate these sites on a case-by-case basis to determine how useful the information provided is going to be to his or her specific funding research needs.

Nonprofit and Foundation Databases

The Web provides access to a wide variety of databases containing information on nonprofit organizations and foundations that can be very useful to the grantseeker, especially in providing names, addresses, and financial information. The primary source of information for some of these services is the IRS, which makes that information available to the public for free. (See Chapter 5 to learn more about the wealth of government information available on the Web.) Listed below are some of the free and fee-based foundation and nonprofit databases that you may find helpful in your funding research.

FREE DATABASES

Idealist (http://www.idealist.org)

Idealist, a project of Action Without Borders, is a nonprofit organization that promotes the sharing of ideas, information, and resources to "help build a world where all people can live free and dignified lives." The site is available in English, Spanish, French, and Russian. Through the site's searchable indexes, visitors can access a global directory of more than 35,000 nonprofit and community organizations in 165 countries. Visitors to the site can search by organization name, location, or mission keyword. Idealist also includes separate databases of nonprofit news sites, job and volunteer opportunities, resources for nonprofit managers, and more.

The Foundation Center's Foundation Finder (http://lnp.fdncenter.org/finder.html)

More of a look-up tool than an searchable database, Foundation Finder serves as a quick reference for basic foundation information. If you know the name or partial name of any of the more than 70,000 private and community foundations in the United States, Foundation Finder will provide you with that foundation's address, contact person, and a basic financial profile, as well as a link to its Web site, if there is one, and its most recent IRS Form 990-PF filing (in a downloadable PDF file format).

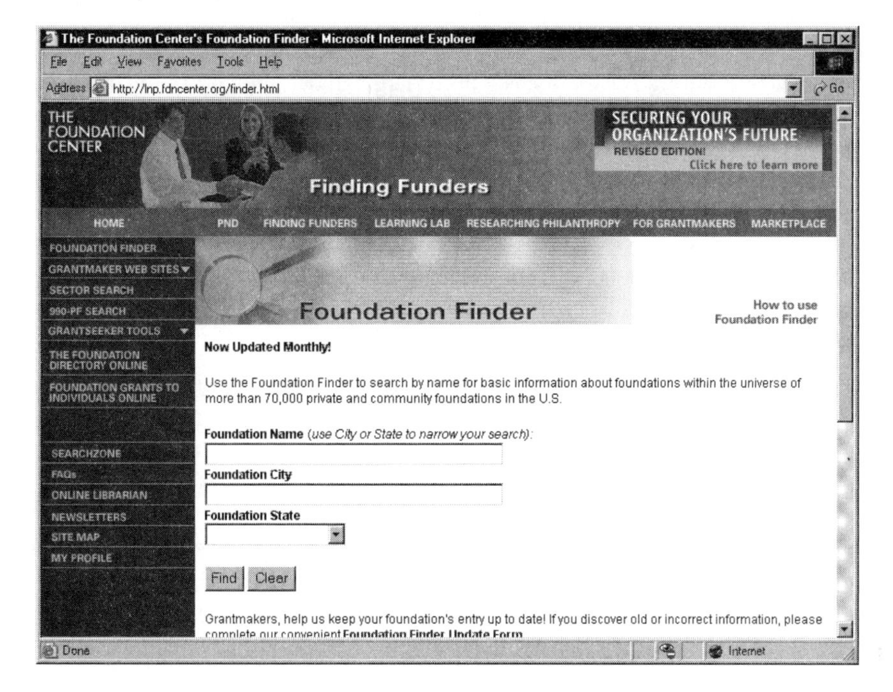

GuideStar (http://www.guidestar.org)

The GuideStar Web site is produced by Philanthropic Research, Inc., a 501(c)(3) public charity. GuideStar's stated mission is to "revolutionize philanthropy and nonprofit practice with information." Its free database includes information on all IRS-registered 501(c)(3) nonprofit organizations (the organizations to which donations are tax-deductible). Currently, there are more than 850,000 organizations in the database, including public charities and private foundations. GuideStar's advanced search engine allows you to search for an organization by keyword or name, activity, city, state, zip code, nonprofit type, revenue range, Employer Identification Number (EIN), or National Taxonomy of Exempt Entities (NTEE) code. Both Forms 990 and 990-PF are available on this site. GuideStar EZ allows access to basic information about a nonprofit organization, but you will need to register at the GuideStar Plus level to access Forms 990 and 990-PF and organizational, mission, program, goal and result, financial, and leadership information. GuideStar has also added for-fee services to its site (GuideStar Products), such as subscription-based Analyst Reports, which offer detailed financial analyses of individual public charities, and Charity Check, which allows grantmakers to see an organization's Publication 78 record, listing the organization's name, city, and current tax-exempt status, including what percentage of contributions to it are tax deductible.

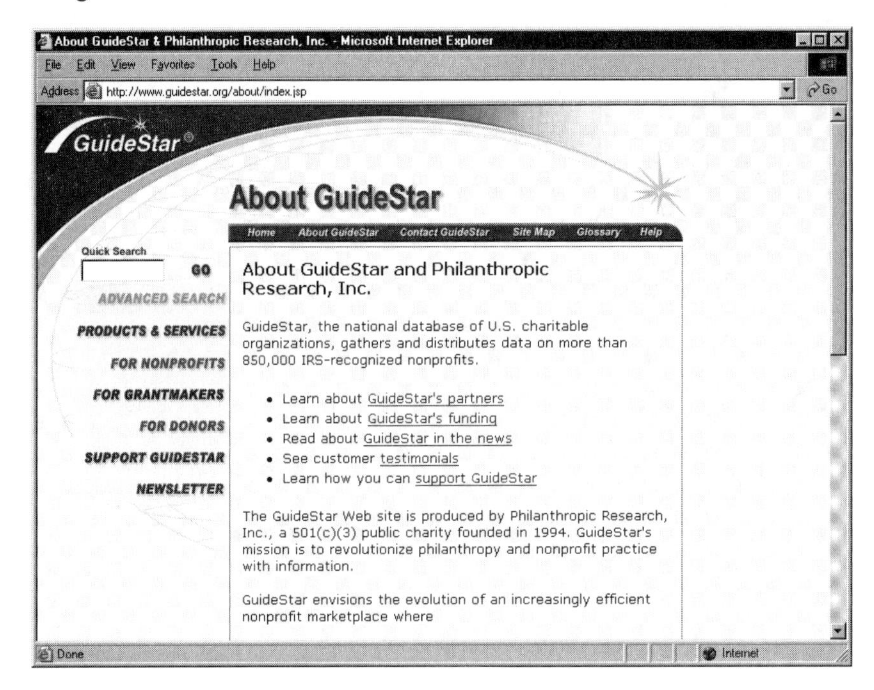

FinAid (http://www.finaid.org)

Launched in 1994, the FinAid site has a reputation for thoroughness. The site caters to high school, college, and graduate students and contains information about scholarships, fellowships, loans, and military aid. In addition to its free databases, FinAid offers a variety of useful tips, making it a helpful place to start a scholarship search on the Web.

NYFA Source (http://www.nyfa.org/nyfa_source.asp?id=47&fid=1)

The New York Foundation for the Arts (NYFA), a nonprofit arts service organization, provides grants and services to individual artists and arts-related organizations in all artistic disciplines in the United States. At its site you will find NYFA Source, an extensive national database of awards, services, and publications for artists of all disciplines. Here artists, arts organizations, and the general public can access information on more than 3,400 arts organizations, 2,800 award programs, 3,100 service programs, and 900 publications for individual artists nationwide, with more programs added every day.

FEE-BASED AND MEMBERSHIP DATABASES

The Foundation Directory Online **(http://fconline.fdncenter.org)**

The Foundation Directory Online is a subscription-based service, offering four levels of access to information from the Foundation Center's database. *The Foundation Directory Online Basic* service includes access to profiles of the 10,000 largest foundations in the United States, based on annual giving. *The Foundation Directory Online Plus* service includes access to those 10,000 profiles, plus a grants database of information on more than 250,000 grants made by the top 1,200 funders in the nation. *The Foundation Directory Online Premium* service provides access to the grants file plus profiles of the 20,000 largest foundations in the country. And the most comprehensive level of service, *The Foundation Directory Online Platinum,* provides access to the grants database, plus the Center's entire database of more than 74,000 foundations, grantmaking public charities, and corporate giving programs (the latter two of which are available only at the Platinum level).

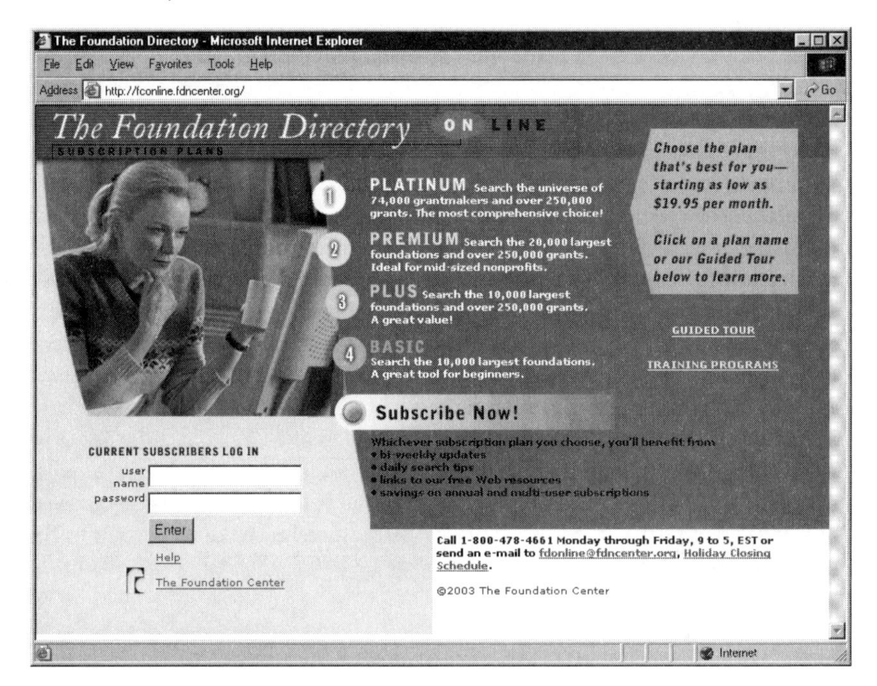

By entering specific search criteria in up to 11 fields, subscribers can perform targeted searches that identify prospective funding sources. The information available through the service is updated twice a month and, like Foundation Finder, includes access to the most recent Forms 990-PF for private foundations, as well as daily search tips, links to free Foundation Center resources, a members-only message board, a free electronic newsletter with information relevant to subscribers, and a Help file that includes search tutorials and instructions on basic and advanced search techniques. Subscriptions are available on a monthly or annual basis.

European Foundation Centre (http://www.efc.be)

The European Foundation Centre (EFC) promotes and supports the work of foundations and corporate funders active in and with the European community. A nonprofit organization established in 1989 by seven of Europe's leading foundations, the EFC today serves a core membership of more than 200 members, associates, and subscribers; 250 community philanthropy initiatives; and serves an additional 48,000 organizations linked through a network of information and support centers in 37 countries worldwide.

The three core functions of the centre are to represent the interests of member organizations at the level of third parties, such as national governments and European Union institutions; to convene and coordinate meetings and facilitate networking; and to provide a relevant and current information base to reinforce member organizations' programs and initiatives. The Orpheus database contains more than 650 profiles of foundations and corporate funders active in Europe. Of those, there are some 475 profiles available on the EFC's free database, Funders Online (http://www.fundersonline.org). This site also includes a newsroom and a variety of other free resources for grantseekers.

Canadian Centre for Philanthropy (http://www.ccp.ca)

The Canadian Centre for Philanthropy is a national charitable organization dedicated to advancing the role and interests of the voluntary sector for the benefit of Canadian communities. The online version of the *Canadian Directory to Foundations and Grants* (the "Online Directory") contains information on more than 1,700 active grantmaking foundations in Canada. The database is limited to subscribers; members receive a discount on annual subscriptions.

FOUNDATION GRANTS DATABASES—FREE

A number of foundations offer fully searchable Web sites. The Ford Foundation, W.K. Kellogg Foundation, Charles Stewart Mott Foundation, and Pew Charitable Trusts have gone a step further and provide grantseekers with specialized online databases of their recent and past grant awards.

Ford Foundation Grants Database (http://www.fordfound.org/grants_db/view_grant_detail1.cfm)

The Ford Foundation's database covers all grants made by the foundation since 1999 and is updated on a quarterly basis, making it one of the most current sources of information on the Ford Foundation's grantmaking activities. To access the database, click the For Grantseekers link on the top bar of the Foundation's home page, then select Grants or View Grants Database. You can search the database by program area, grant year, and keyword. The results deliver descriptive text detailing the grants, including who received the grant, how much it was for, and its purpose. Other information on Ford grants and new grantmaking initiatives can be found on its Web site in the Annual Report, the quarterly Ford Foundation Report, and the foundation's press releases.

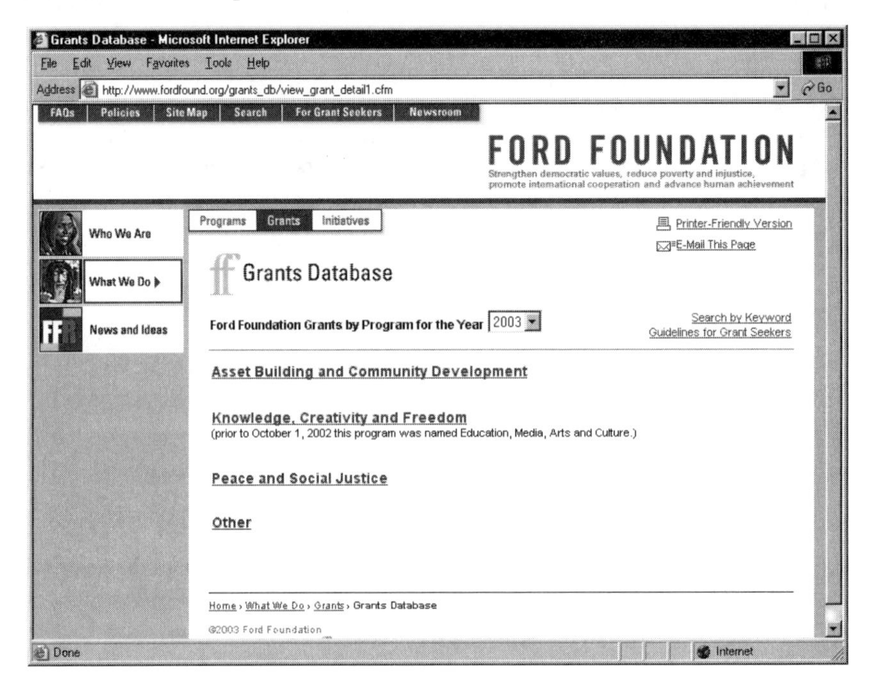

W.K. Kellogg Foundation Knowledgebase Grant Files (http://www.wkkf.org/Knowledgebase/Grants)

The W.K. Kellogg Foundation's grants database, which is updated on a daily basis, includes all of Kellogg's grants since 1991 and is the most current source of information on the foundation's grantmaking activities. To access the database, visitors to the home page should select Knowledgebase at the top and then Grants File from the next page. The grants database is organized around the Kellogg Foundation's program interests—Health, Youth and Education, Greater Battle Creek, Latin America and the Caribbean, Learning Opportunities, Philanthropy and Volunteerism, Food Systems and Rural Development, Cross Programming Work: Devolution, and Southern Africa. You can browse by geographic location, by program category, or alphabetically by recipient. You can also conduct an advanced grants search of the database by text, status, foundation contact, start date, end date, and amount of grant.

Charles Stewart Mott Foundation Grant Database (http://www.mott.org/grants.asp)

The Charles Stewart Mott Foundation Grant Database contains detailed information on grants dating back to 1993. The data is updated frequently and is the most current source of information on the foundation's grantmaking activities. Two means are provided to search for specific grant information. The first allows users to search information about the grantee by keyword, name, city, state/province, or country; the second allows users to search on specific grant details with fields such as program area, year of the grant, subject, geographic focus, and dollar amount range.

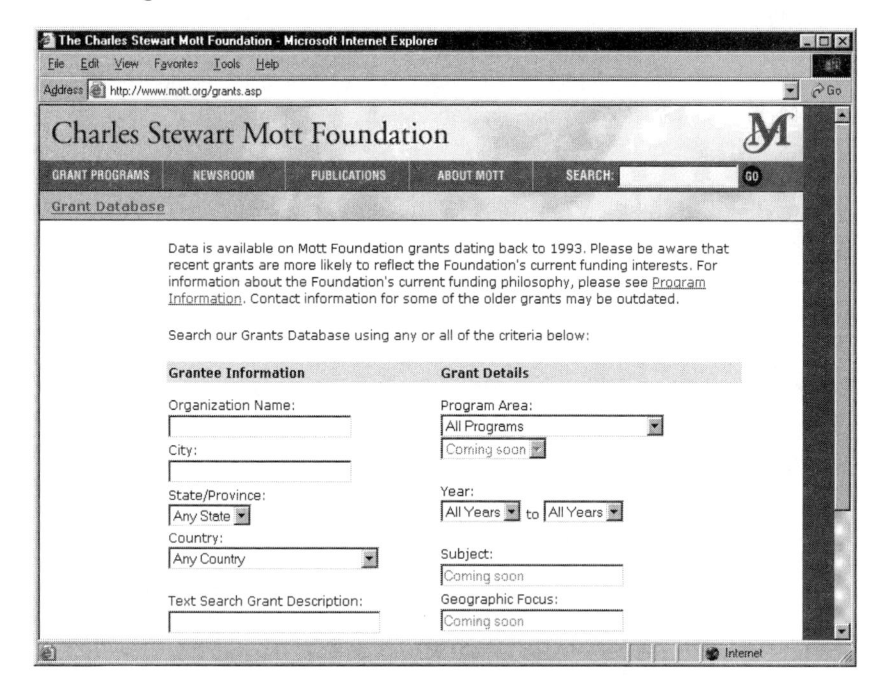

Pew Charitable Trusts' Grants Database (http://www.pewtrusts.com/search)

The Pew Charitable Trusts' Web site allows visitors to search selected grants dating back to the 1980s. A synopsis of the purpose(s), the amount, and the recipient of each grant is provided, including contact information, e-mail address, and a link to the recipient's Web site. To search the database by program area or date range, select Search from the tool bar at the top of the home page.

REGIONAL FOUNDATION DATABASES

Regional databases can be particularly useful to grantseekers looking for funding from grantmakers whose giving programs are locally focused. Here we'll explore several regional databases as examples of available resources. To identify resources in your region of the country, contact a regional association of grantmakers (RAG) (see the RAG Forum Web site's Regional Association Locator at http://www.rag.org/ralocator.html) or community foundation in your area (see the Council on Foundations' Community Foundation Locator at http://www.communityfoundationlocator.org/search/index.cfm). Some of the following databases are free, while others are available only to members or for a fee.

Greater Kansas City Council on Philanthropy (http://www.kcphilnet.org)

The Greater Kansas City Council on Philanthropy has provided a local forum for the exchange of information on philanthropy and fundraising since 1975. The site offers fee-based access to a database of foundation information; a regularly updated, cross-referenced directory of approximately 600 foundations making grants in the Kansas City region; and a searchable database of information on corporate giving in the area.

Donors Forum of Chicago—Illinois Funding Source (http://ifs.donorsforum.org)

The Donors Forum of Chicago (http://www.donorsforum.org) is an association of Chicago-area grantmaking institutions promoting effective and responsive philanthropy through its educational, collaborative, and networking efforts. The Forum's Illinois Funding Source (IFS) offers three fee-based annual subscription options, providing access to two searchable databases. FoundationSource comprises a directory of more than 2,600 Illinois foundations, and GrantSource indexes more than $2.5 billion in grants dollars awarded by local funders. Updated monthly, IFS delivers details on newly established foundations, changes in foundation contacts and priorities, and updated grants lists. A free three-day trial is available.

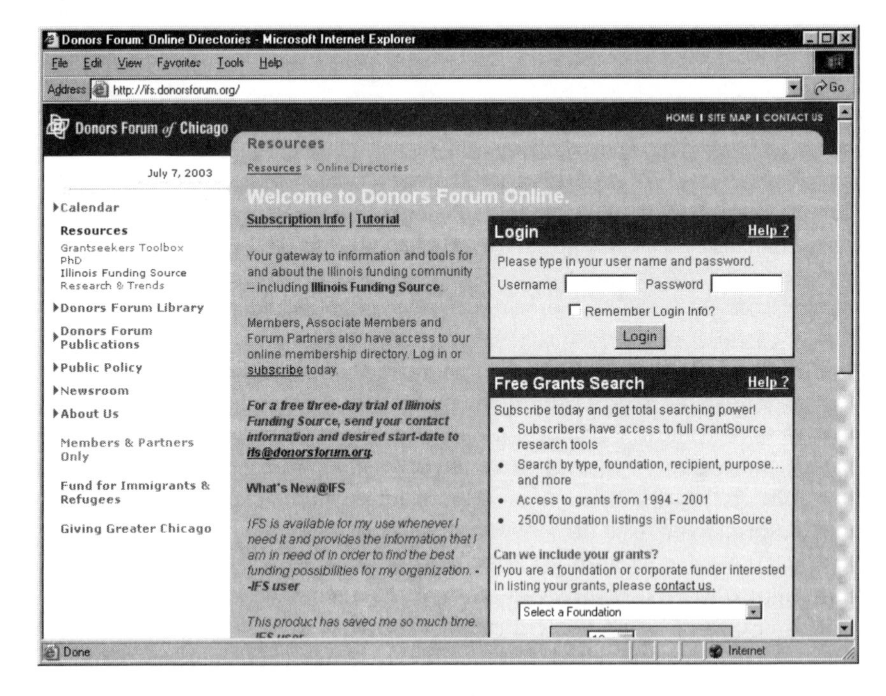

Associated Grant Makers (http://www.agmconnect.org/agmwebmanager.nsf)
Associated Grant Makers (AGM) is a regional association of grantmakers in Massachusetts, New Hampshire, and Rhode Island supporting foundations, corporate giving programs, and other organized donor institutions. AGM also supports nonprofit organizations engaged in corporate and foundation fundraising. The AGM Web site offers detailed descriptions of the services provided to grantmakers and nonprofit organizations, common proposal and reporting forms in HTML and PDF formats, information on events of interest to grantseekers and grantmakers, a catalog of AGM books and videos for sale, and extensive links to online nonprofit and philanthropic resources. This site also includes a members-only, searchable database. It contains more than 500 grantmakers and gives these organizations the opportunity to describe, in their own words, the goals and the limitations of their grantmaking programs. The database was designed to help fundraisers begin the process of learning about the major grantmakers based in Massachusetts, New Hampshire, and Rhode Island.

DATABASE SERVICES FOR GRANTSEEKERS—FEE-BASED

There are a small number of commercial database services specializing in information for grantseekers. The ones described here focus on nonprofits and database management software and offer electronic services geared to the needs of grantseekers and charitable organizations.

BIG Online (http://bigdatabase.com)
Featuring profiles of more than 67,000 foundations and corporate funders in the United States and Canada, BIG Online provides searchable access to funding histories, funding analysis by sector, contact information, giving preferences, and biographies of key grantmaker personnel. Located in Vancouver, Canada, BIG Online was initially focused domestically but now has a separate site for U.S. customers. The BIG Online offerings include information on more than 1,400 U.S. federal government funding programs, more than 7,000 of the largest U.S. foundations, and more than 3,500 of the largest giving corporations in the nation. Also available are links to some 60,000 U.S. foundation IRS filings (Forms 990-PF) and Foundationsearch.com, which purports to allow keyword searching of these tax returns. Customer consultants provide subscription information and offer free guided tours of the site.

Prospect Research Online (http://www.iwave.com/pub/about_pro.shtml)
Prospect Research Online (PRO 2.0) is a database designed specifically for nonprofit organizations offered by online business research provider iWave. PRO 2.0 provides detailed information on individuals, foundations, and corporations for organizations to use in fundraising. Subscribers receive unlimited database access plus a weekly What's New report and five complimentary custom research consultations each month.

GrantSelect (http://www.grantselect.com)
Universities, libraries, school districts, community nonprofits, and researchers use GrantSelect to search an extensive database of funding opportunities. Offering more than 10,000 funding opportunities and a large collection of sponsored research opportunities, GrantSelect has a range of pricing options. An e-mail alert

service delivers funding information—including information from state and federal governments, corporations, foundations, and associations—to users. A free seven-day trial option is available. You can choose to subscribe to the entire database or select from seven customized segments.

Corporate Financial Information

Hoover's Online (http://www.hoovers.com)
Hoover's Online is an easy-to-use site with links to corporate Web sites in its Company Capsules. Enter an organization's name in the entry box on the home page for free Company Capsules to view news and information—company profile, key personnel, full stock quote, and selected press coverage—on public and private enterprises. Subscribers get the same information but in much greater depth and detail. There are four paid-subscription options available. Hoover's also contains Capsules of a number of large non-publicly traded U.S. enterprises, including foundations and other nonprofits, healthcare companies, cooperatives, and universities.

SEC Filings & Forms (EDGAR) (http://www.sec.gov/edgar.shtml)
The Securities and Exchange Commission (SEC) requires all public companies (except foreign companies and companies with less than $10 million in assets and less than 500 shareholders) to file registration statements, periodic reports, and other forms electronically through EDGAR. Anyone can access and download this information for free. Here you'll find links to a complete list of SEC filings available through EDGAR and instructions for searching the EDGAR database.

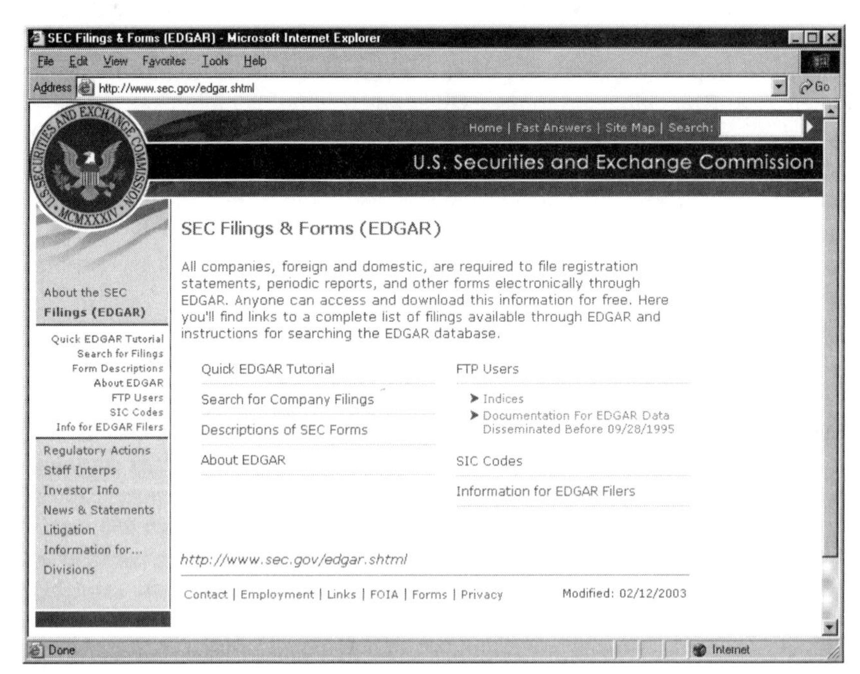

EDGAR Online (http://www.edgar-online.com/start.asp)
EDGAR Online is the same database as described above, but the interface is more user-friendly, and there is a fee to use EDGAR Online.

Inc. Online (http://www.inc.com/home)
Inc. Online is an information resource for entrepreneurs and small business owners who wish to grow their businesses. In addition to the most recent edition of *Inc.* magazine and an archive of articles dating back to 1986 on a wide variety of topics, the site also offers a searchable database of Inc. 500 lists, America's 500 fastest-growing companies, and so on, going back to 1982.

CORPORATE NEWS ONLINE

Business Wire (http://www.businesswire.com)
The Business Wire site includes company press releases. Search by date, industry, subject, or geography, or select Company News Archives for all of a company's press releases. It includes links to corporate profiles, electronic media kits, and corporate URLs where available.

PR Newswire (http://www.prnewswire.com)
PR Newswire provides comprehensive news targeting, distribution, and measurement services on behalf of some 40,000 organizations worldwide that seek to reach the news media, the investment community, and the general public with full-text news developments. This site is especially useful for uncovering corporate intelligence.

***Forbes*—Lists (http://www.forbes.com/lists)**
Forbes magazine has made available in database format a variety of its lists of wealthy individuals and companies, including the Largest Private Companies in the United States, the World's Richest People, the Richest Americans, and more. (See Chapter 6 for more information on Forbes.com.)

Newspaper Searching

Newspaper Web sites are generally searchable by keyword. Articles are available until the source site deletes or archives them. Archived information past a certain date is generally available only for a fee from the source publication or an online vendor. Many regional business newspapers are now available online (indexed at most of the major news sites) and provide excellent information on local philanthropists, corporate giving, family foundations, and so on.

American Journalism Review (http://www.ajr.org)
The American Journalism Review site includes worldwide links to thousands of news organizations online. You can browse or search links to daily, non-daily, campus, major metropolitan, national, alternative, specialty, business, and international newspapers. You can also search magazines, broadcasters, and news services, including pre-selected top sites.

***The Chronicle of Philanthropy* (http://philanthropy.com)**
The Chronicle of Philanthropy is an important news source for charity leaders, fundraisers, grantmakers, and other people involved in the philanthropic enterprise. In print, the *Chronicle* is published biweekly, except for the last two weeks in June and the last two weeks in December (a total of 24 issues a year). A subscription includes full access to this Web site and news updates by e-mail. The Web site offers the complete contents of the latest issue, an archive of articles since October 16, 1997, and grant listings from 1995—all fully searchable.

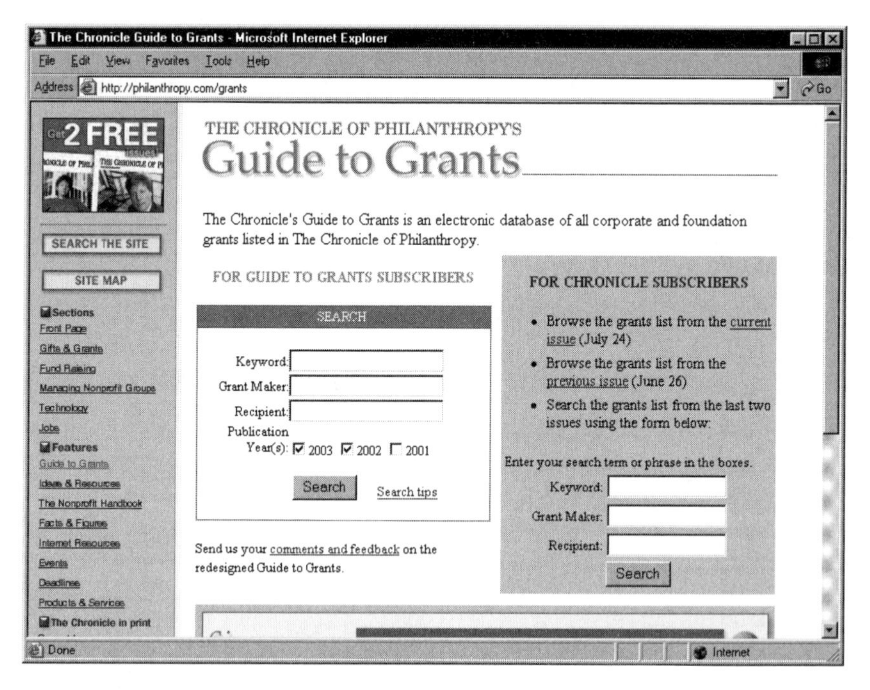

The *Chronicle*'s Guide to Grants is an electronic database of all corporate and foundation grants listed in *The Chronicle of Philanthropy* since 1995. One drawback is that the date grants were awarded does not appear—only the date when grants were published in the *Chronicle*. Subscriptions are available for periods of one week to one year. There is a significant discount if you are also a subscriber to the print journal.

General Information Databases

A wide range of vendors offer fee-based access to an enormous variety of Web-based databases. Most for-fee information vendors, including those that specialize in funding information, offer their database information in a variety of pricing structures. Web-based database vendors usually offer pricing options that can be tailored to a user's particular needs.

Web access offers users a great deal of flexibility. For-fee database searches can, however, be quite expensive, even on the Internet. Bear in mind that the Web has expanded rapidly, and the cost of data now varies greatly. While fee-based services are often comprehensive and efficient, the same information can sometimes be found through other sources at a lower cost or even for free if you take the time to search for it.

Another benefit of these databases is that they are updated on a regular basis, some as frequently as daily, or even hourly. The larger database vendors tend to simplify their search structures for Web presentation, gearing them toward a broad user audience as opposed to the specialized advanced researcher.

General information databases offer a wide spectrum of resources, such as legal and government documents; newspaper and periodical articles; a variety of corporate information, including company profiles; and information on almost any topic you can think of. Oftentimes, it is possible to search a single database or multiple sources at once.

The Dialog Corporation (http://www.dialog.com)

The Dialog Corporation has been a source for online information for more than 30 years and is now one of the businesses of the Thomson Corporation. It offers hundreds of databases representing a broad range of disciplines, company directories, news sources, general reference, and biographical information. Dialog can guide you to more than 50,000 of the most objective and respected publications and more than 800 million unique records of key information documents available online.

Dialog's Files 26 and 27 relate exclusively to the world of philanthropy, with database information provided by the Foundation Center. The Foundation Directory (File 26) provides profiles of more than 74,000 independent, company-sponsored, operating, and community foundations. The Foundation Grants Index (File 27) provides information on grants that have been awarded by more than 1,200 of the nation's largest funders beginning in 1989 through the present.

Dialog provides its services in three different platforms: Web-based, Intranet, and Desktop Solutions. Dialog's information is grouped into four different product lines: Dialog, Dialog DataStar, Dialog Profound, and NewsEdge. The information in these product lines can be accessed by subscribing to Dialog and setting up an account, or they may be accessed directly on a per-use basis, via a credit card.

An example of just a few of the content areas are business, chemical, energy, food, government, intellectual property, medical, news, pharmaceuticals, reference, and technology to more than 7,000 global newspapers, newswires, trade journals, magazines, and more.

A complete listing of online databases is available at Dialog (http://www.dialog.com/products). The online access rates vary by database and in some cases by output, search time costs, and telecommunications charges (depending on the access options you have chosen). Training is provided as online tutorials and/or guided tours.

DialogWeb (http://www.dialog.com/products/dialogweb)

This is a tool for novice and experienced online searchers alike. DialogWeb provides easy access to more than 600 databases through the convenience of a Web browser. In addition to an enhanced Web interface, there are some features unique to DialogWeb, including a free database directory that lets you browse Dialog databases by subject. A free preview and tutorial are available.

LexisNexis (http://www.lexisnexis.com)

LexisNexis, the global, legal, and information division of Reed Elsevier, provides online access to legal, news, public records, and business information services. The Lexis service contains major archives of federal and state case law, continuously updated statutes of all 50 states, state and federal regulations, and an extensive collection of public records from U.S. states and larger counties. These include regional, national, and international newspapers, newswires, magazines, trade journals, and business publications. Nexis offers brokerage house and industry analyst reports; business information from Dunn & Bradstreet; public records such as corporate filings, company records, and property records; and tax information. The two services combined offer access to more than 30,000 databases.

From the LexisNexis home page, you can select Products & Services from the menu at the top of the screen or through the View drop-down menus located on the left side of the screen. You can then browse the product name index or select the tabs at the top to view resources by industry, occupation, or task. Within the Industry section, you can select Not For Profit (http://www.lexisnexis.com/fundraising), or in the Occupation section, you can select Fundraising/Donor Researchers (http://www.lexisnexis.com/fundraisingpro). Selecting one of these options will bundle databases and information of interest to nonprofit organizations. These databases allow you to search for individual contact information, company data and background, foundation affiliations and giving history, individual and corporate giving histories, and media references for companies, foundations, and individuals of interest.

Factiva (http://factiva.com)

Factiva, a Dow Jones & Reuters Company, provides content from nearly 8,000 sources, including the Dow Jones and Reuters Newswires and *The Wall Street Journal.* The Factiva database includes articles from major newspapers worldwide, business and trade magazines, television and radio transcripts, and content from more than 120 wire services. Factiva also offers multiple language interfaces and content from 118 countries in 22 languages.

ProQuest Direct (http://www.il.proquest.com)

ProQuest Direct provides access (mostly through libraries and universities) to more than 4,000 newspapers and periodicals, more than a million dissertations, and a wide range of other content. The ProQuest brand encompasses more than 100 products and services for research and learning at all levels, including ABI

Inform, which contains content from thousands of journals that help researchers track business conditions, trends, management techniques, corporate strategies, and industry-specific topics worldwide. Free trials are available.

H.W. Wilson Company (http://www.hwwilson.com)
Primarily serving librarians and researchers, H.W. Wilson offers more than 40 full-text, abstract, and index databases over the Web and on CD-ROM. Database subjects range from applied science and technology to social sciences. H.W. Wilson also contains an extensive group of biographical databases. Free database trials are available.

Gale Group (http://www.galegroup.com)
The Gale Group is a unit of the Thomson Corporation, an e-information publisher for libraries, schools, and businesses, among others. Best known for its authoritative reference content and its helpful organization of full-text magazine and newspaper articles, the company creates and maintains more than 600 databases that are published online, in print, and in microform. In addition to serving the library community, Gale also licenses its proprietary content for integration within Web-based information services.

Target America (http://www.tgtam.com)
Target America offers fee-based databases containing information on the top five percent of the wealthiest and most generous people in the nation, in terms of income, assets, and philanthropic history. Ninety-four percent of individuals in the database give more than $5,000 a year to charities. Target America allows you to research major gift prospects by providing access to comprehensive personal profiles, including relevant business and financial information, and relationship reports.

Database Services for Academic Professionals

There are a number of grants databases, primarily intended for academics, that offer access to a variety of government and private funding sources. These services charge a fee, but some also offer free information as well.

Illinois Researcher Information Service (http://www.library.uiuc.edu/iris)
The Illinois Researcher Information Service (IRIS) is a unit of the University of Illinois Library at Urbana-Champaign. The IRIS office compiles the IRIS Database of funding opportunities, which is updated daily and contains records on more than 8,000 federal and private funding opportunities in the sciences, social sciences, arts, and humanities.

Community of Science, Inc. (http://www.cos.com)
Community of Science, Inc. (COS) is an Internet site for the scientific research and development community that brings together scientists and researchers from more than 1,600 universities, corporations, and government agencies worldwide. Notable for grantseekers is the COS Funding Opportunities database, an extensive source of funding information on the Web. The database is updated daily and

currently contains more than 23,000 records, representing some 400,000 funding opportunities, worth more than $33 billion.

InfoEd International (http://www.infoed.org)
InfoEd International provides information and management software systems and services for the academic, medical, and scientific research and development communities. These integrated software solutions span proposal development, proposal tracking, project management, compliance systems, clinical trials management, and technology transfer and are used by more than 600 institutions worldwide.

A FEW THOUGHTS ABOUT GENERAL SEARCH ENGINES

Keep in mind that you can and should also use general search engines, such as Google or Yahoo! Try keyword and phrase searching to see what you come up with when you enter relevant terms in the search box such as "grants," "foundations," "fundraising," "philanthropy," and so on. You may locate a lot of useful information that can supplement your other funding research nicely. (See Appendix A for descriptions and tips on using general search engines.)

Conclusion

Initial exploration and assessment of the usefulness of Web databases will require an investment of your time and perhaps money—if you choose to sign up for subscription-based services. In conjunction with the other Web resources covered in this guide, however, you should be able to find a great deal of useful information by means of these databases. And don't forget, in addition to your Web-wide database research, including *The Foundation Directory Online*, you can benefit from the wealth of free resources available at the Foundation Center's Web site. Try starting out with an exploration of *Philanthropy News Digest,* Finding Funders, Learning Lab, and Researching Philanthropy. (See Chapter 1 for a full description of the resources on the Center's Web site.)

CHAPTER EIGHT

Other Useful Sites for Grantseekers

This chapter presents a sampling of some of the unique and more useful Web sites available in the Links to Nonprofit Resources (Nonprofit Links) section of the Foundation Center's Web site (http://fdncenter.org/research/npr_links/index.html). In general they are organized in the same way as the Web links, though a few of the categories you will find at our site are absent from this condensed version. See Appendix F for a full category listing.

A Selection of Useful Sites

In this chapter, we present a selective list of unique and useful Web sites with annotations. These sites can be utilized whether you are looking for information on charity monitoring organizations, online giving, program evaluation, issue advocacy, nonprofit boards, nonprofit management, program areas (arts, education, the environment, health, science, women and girls, etc.), international resources, or resources for individual grantseekers, among many other purposes. In collecting and providing annotations to these sites, the Foundation Center continues to function as a specialty portal, "Helping Grantseekers Succeed, Helping Grantmakers Make a Difference."

Center staff continually adds to our lists of Web sites and prepares annotations for them to aid in your online exploration of funding opportunities and helpful resources. Below are our recommendations of useful Web sites for grantseekers, grantmakers, and others. Since many nonprofit Web sites could fit in a number of categories, placement here in one or another category is to a certain extent arbitrary. That is, many of the resources could fit into two or more categories, based on their features and content, since more and more sites offer multiple services and resources to nonprofit organizations and grantseekers in general. What these sites have in common is that they reward deeper investigation. They are resources that you'll want to return to time and again in searching for online information about foundations, grants, fundraising, and nonprofit management. Our goal is *not* to be comprehensive—which is impractical when dealing with the Web—but to point the way to a manageable number of useful sites that are representative or unique.

Philanthropy

Council on Foundations (http://www.cof.org)
The Council on Foundations (COF) is a membership organization for grantmakers that serves the public good by promoting and enhancing responsible and effective philanthropy. It provides leadership expertise, legal services, and networking opportunities—among other services—to more than 2,000 members and to the general public. The COF Web site offers a wealth of information for and about foundations. Site features include: Networking, including links to member Web sites, colleague organizations, and affinity groups; Publications; Career Center, with job postings and resources; Finding Answers, where you can search the council's FAQs; Legal, which includes excerpts from select publications and special articles offering advice on legal issues of concern to foundations, as well as legislative analysis, IRS regulations, board issues, grantmaking legal issues, and international legal information; the Newsroom, featuring news, press releases, media alerts, and issue papers; Events, announcing council conferences and workshops; and Tools, featuring a collection of resources helpful to the work of grantmakers.

Criteria for Inclusion in the Foundation Center's Links to Nonprofit Resources

If you know of a Web site (whether your own or others) that you would like to see included in the Foundation Center's Links to Nonprofit Resources, please read our inclusion criteria below:

To be listed, a Web site must provide information that is useful to our audiences either about a particular nonprofit organization or the nonprofit sector as a whole. Web sites of for-profits generally are not included, but exceptions are made on a case-by-case basis for those offering a significant resource to the nonprofit sector.

If your Web site meets these criteria, please e-mail your link with a short description of your site to Links@fdncenter.org.

Under Services and Programs you will find additional resources and information on accountability and standards, community foundations, corporate grantmakers, emerging issues, family foundations, governing boards, government relations, inclusiveness and diversity, information management, international programs, media relations, philanthropic advisors, private/independent and operating foundations, professional development, public policy, research, and starting a foundation.

Foundation News & Commentary, COF's flagship magazine, and Breaking News, a current awareness service, are also available from the council's site. Much of the site is for members only, and members are required to register to obtain a username and password.

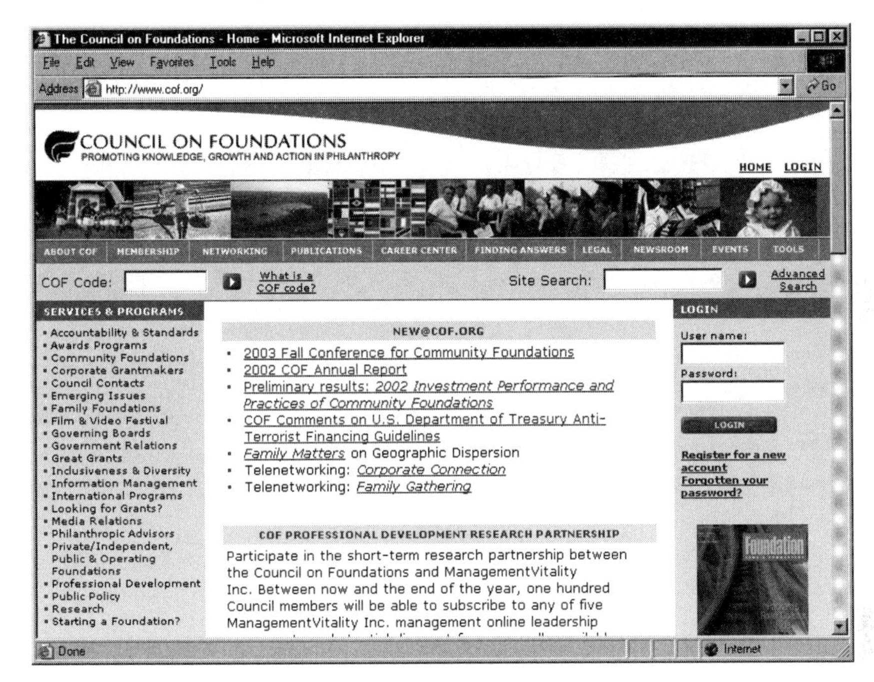

Forum of Regional Associations of Grantmakers (http://www.givingforum.org)
The Forum of Regional Associations of Grantmakers (RAGs) is a membership association of the nation's largest RAGs across the country that help more than 4,000 local grantmakers practice more effective philanthropy in their communities. The forum assists RAGs in providing local leadership to grantmakers on issues of public policy, promoting the growth of new philanthropy, technology, and measuring effectiveness and impact. The forum's Web site includes the Regional Association Locator (http://www.givingforum.org/ralocator.html), which lists contact information for each individual RAG in the United States.

INDEPENDENT SECTOR (http://www.independentsector.org)
The INDEPENDENT SECTOR (IS) is committed to promoting, strengthening, and advancing the nonprofit and philanthropic community to foster private initiative for the public good. The Web site provides an overview of IS programs in the Issues section, including the Three Sector Initiative, Corporate-Nonprofit Partnerships (Mission and Market), Emerging Leadership, Giving and Volunteering, Tax Policy, Nonprofit Advocacy and Lobbying, Accountability, Civil Society Education, and Faith-Based Organizations in the Nonprofit Sector. The Research directory includes the Nonprofit Almanac and Desk Reference, which provides facts and figures on the size and scope of the nonprofit sector; Giving and Volunteering in the United States, which covers the giving and volunteering habits of individuals; and the Measures Project, which focuses on measuring the impact of the third sector on society. IS's Public Affairs program advocates on behalf of the nonprofit sector in areas such as tax issues, nonprofit advocacy and lobbying, government funding, accountability, and public policy. Click on GiveVoice.org to connect with your legislators and government officials about issues affecting the nonprofit sector. The NonProfit Pathfinder, designed for scholars, researchers, practitioners, funders, and the media, gathers and organizes online information on philanthropy, the nonprofit sector, and civil society organizations.

Quality 990 (http://www.qual990.org)

Quality 990, sponsored by the National Center for Charitable Statistics, INDEPENDENT SECTOR, the Association of Fundraising Professionals, and the National Council of Nonprofit Associations, was created to serve organizations and individuals concerned with improving the quality of financial reporting in the nonprofit sector. It is dedicated to improving the quality of IRS Forms 990 filed by nonprofit organizations. With new regulations and wider, simpler access to a nonprofit's tax form, this site offers many resources to assist the community involved in filing this form. There is information on forming or joining a Nonprofit Accountability Collaborative (990 NAC), which are forums consisting of accountants, nonprofit managers, regulators, and the general public. Local 990 NAC activities fall under two main categories: education and recommendations. Comprehensive guides to the form are available, along with links to information that help in understanding the form itself and the rules to its disclosure.

Fundraising

GENERAL

David Lamb's Prospect Research Page (http://www.lambresearch.com)

Lamb, a former development officer at the University of Washington and Santa Clara University, has attempted to "separate the wheat from the chaff" in describing truly useful Internet sites for researching corporations, foundations, and individual donors. David Lamb's Prospect Research Page includes links to directories of doctors, judges, lawyers, and airplane owners; online news sources; and corporate and public records databases. What's nice about this site is that Lamb has distilled the vast number of potential sources of information on the Internet into a relatively small selection of annotated sites.

Internet Prospector (http://www.internet-prospector.org)
Internet Prospector is a nonprofit service to the prospect research community, produced by volunteers nationwide who "mine" the Web for prospect research "nuggets." Although designed for nonprofit fundraisers, anyone seeking tools for accessing corporate, foundation, biographical, international, and online news sources will find this Web site useful. You'll find an online newsletter and an archive of past issues. A search engine is also provided, allowing you to quickly search for information from back issues located on the site. An option to subscribe to the free monthly newsletter is also available.

Michigan State University Grants and Related Resources (http://www.lib.msu.edu/harris23/grants/grants.htm)
The amount of information available through the Michigan State University Grants and Related Resources Web site is nearly overwhelming, but Jon Harrison of the University of Michigan Library System has created a site that is well organized and cleanly designed. Start by clicking Grants for Nonprofits. Most valuable are the annotated lists of resources (print, electronic, and online) for grant information in particular subject areas, from Arts and Cultural Activities to Religion and Social Change. For each subject area, Harrison provides abstracts of useful print resources, descriptions of databases, and links to online information. There is also a substantial section on grants to individuals, including financial aid. Harrison has even assembled an impressive bibliography, with links, on grantsmanship techniques, including lots of information on fundraising research and proposal writing.

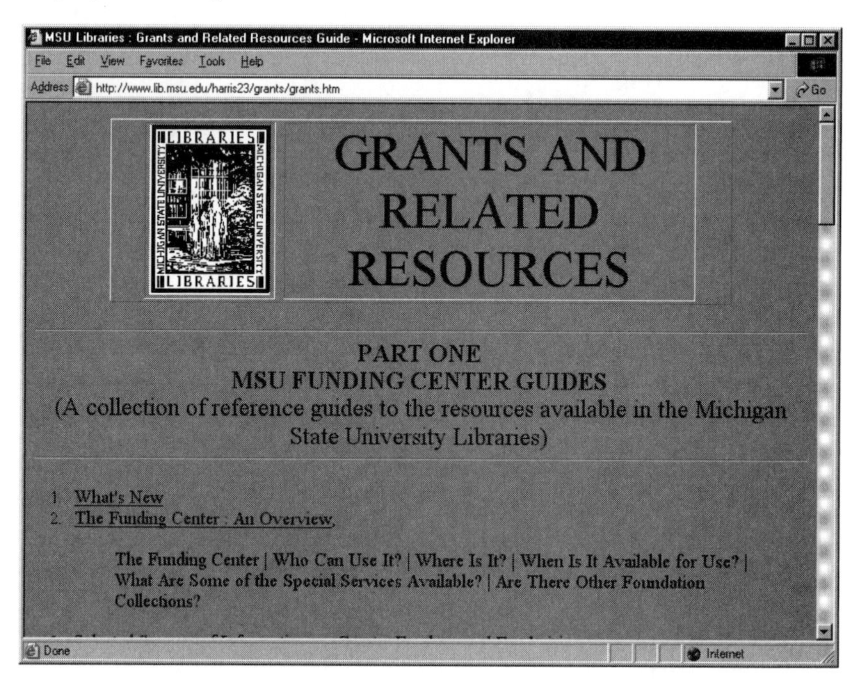

Portico (http://indorgs.virginia.edu/portico)

Portico is a collection of Web sites, containing publicly available information, compiled for the use of the advancement and fundraising communities. The Portico Web site has a comprehensive set of links to sites that provide information on biographies of individuals, occupations, personal property, salaries, stocks, businesses, media, nonprofits, international, and other resources. The site also has resources for and about the nonprofit community, nonprofit and philanthropy news, state and regional resources and databases, science and medical-related funding opportunities, and sources related to the international philanthropic community. The Other Resources section has links to prospect research pages, professional organizations, electronic libraries, and periodicals.

CHARITY-MONITORING ORGANIZATIONS

BBB Wise Giving Alliance—Give.org (http://www.give.org)

The BBB [Better Business Bureau] Wise Giving Alliance collects and distributes information about the programs, governance, fundraising practices, and finances of hundreds of charitable organizations that solicit nationally and are the subject of donor inquiries. Besides providing reports on specific charities, the Give.org Web site has news and alerts and several "Tips On..." publications, including one on standards for charitable solicitations and used car donations. The site also offers an area where you can inquire or complain about a charity.

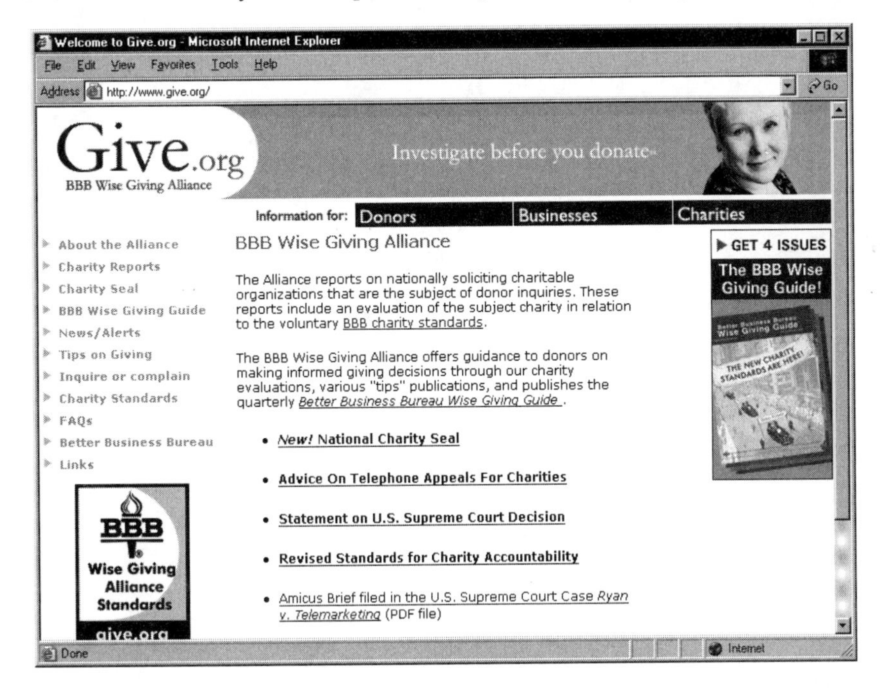

ONLINE GIVING

e-Philanthropy (http://www.actknowledgeworks.net/ephil/index_html)

e-Philanthropy is the Web site for the W.K. Kellogg Foundation report, e-Philanthropy v.2.001, which documents the phenomenon of interactive online services for philanthropy and voluntarism. This site allows you to access the report and a database of information related to e-philanthropy, which can be browsed by name or primary focus (shopping and profit sharing, fundraising services, knowledge and capacity building, donor services, auctions/events, advocacy, giving time/volunteering, and full service portals), or searched by name keyword.

Groundspring.org (http://www.groundspring.org/index_gs.cfm)
Created in 1999 by the Tides Foundation as eGrants.org, Groundspring.org is a forward-looking nonprofit that works to help progressive nonprofits increase their financial support through online fundraising. Groundspring.org's tool, DonateNow, allows organizations to accept credit card donations through online transactions. EmailNow gives nonprofits an affordable, ad-free tool to send e-newsletters, raise money online, and communicate with supporters. Groundspring.org also recently acquired ebase, a free community relationship management database developed by TechRocks. A workshop calendar is also available.

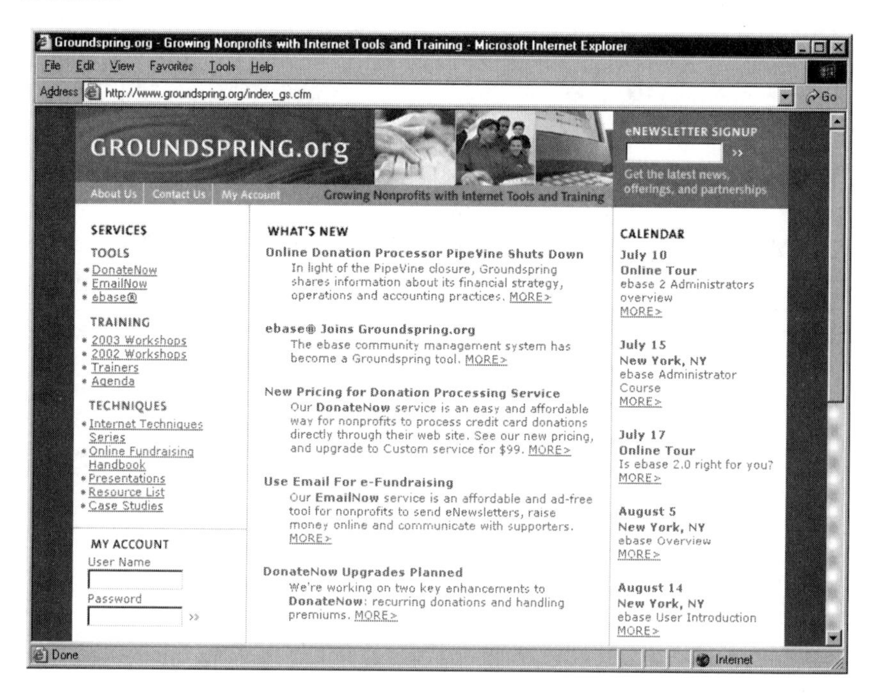

Independent Givers of America (http://www.givedirect.org)
The Independent Givers of America (IGA) is a nonprofit organization whose mission is "to bring together generous people and deserving causes, principally but not exclusively by developing Internet-based systems that reduce the cost and increase the productivity of charitable solicitation." Its Web site gives philanthropists the opportunity to set up a personal, private, online foundation; accept e-mail proposals at any time; find an IGA-recommended charity; and contribute to any IRS-recognized charity, church, or school.

Nonprofit News and Publications

***The Chronicle of Philanthropy* (http://philanthropy.com)**
Like its biweekly print analog, *The Chronicle of Philanthropy*'s Web site is full of useful information for fundraisers, grantmakers, nonprofit managers, and others. The site is organized into broad topic areas—Gifts and Grants, Fund Raising, Managing Nonprofit Groups, Technology, and Jobs. It includes a summary of the contents of the *Chronicle*'s current issue, with an archive of articles since 1987; a database of all corporate and foundation grants listed in the *Chronicle* since 1995; a listing of award and RFP deadlines; surveys conducted by the *Chronicle* and reports of other surveys conducted by other organizations; job opportunities in the nonprofit sector; a listing of upcoming conferences and workshops; and annotated links to other nonprofit resources on the Internet. In-depth information on nonprofit employers, technology companies, fundraising service companies, consultants, and direct-marketing service companies is also available. Visitors can sign up for free e-mail updates about changes at the site as well as breaking news stories. Some of the material is available only to *Chronicle* subscribers.

Internet Nonprofit Center (http://www.nonprofits.org)
A project of the Evergreen State Society in Seattle, Washington, the Internet Nonprofit Center is oriented toward providing information to and about nonprofit organizations. The Web site has an extensive Nonprofit FAQ section, with information on a wide range of topics of interest to leaders and managers of nonprofit organizations; a Library that offers longer essays, bibliographies, practical guides, and analysis of the nonprofit sector; and current nonprofit news. The Recent Changes link provides you with a list of the 50 most recent revisions and additions to the site. You can also sign up for the free weekly e-mail publication, Nonprofit Online News.

Nonprofit Management & Staffing Resources

GENERAL

Association of Fundraising Professionals (http://www.afpnet.org)
The Association of Fundraising Professionals (AFP) consists of 26,000 individual members in 169 chapters throughout the United States, Canada, and Mexico, working to advance philanthropy through advocacy, research, education, and certification programs. Visitors to AFP's Web site will find extensive information on nonprofit philanthropy and AFP activities and publications, AFP's professional advancement programs and course information, the full text of its Code of Ethical Principles and Standards of Professional Practice, and the Principles of an E-Donor Bill of Rights, created to address concerns and challenges arising from Internet charitable giving. In addition, job opportunity and member services modules are made available to AFP members. You can sign up for free e-mail updates on professional advancement and public policy.

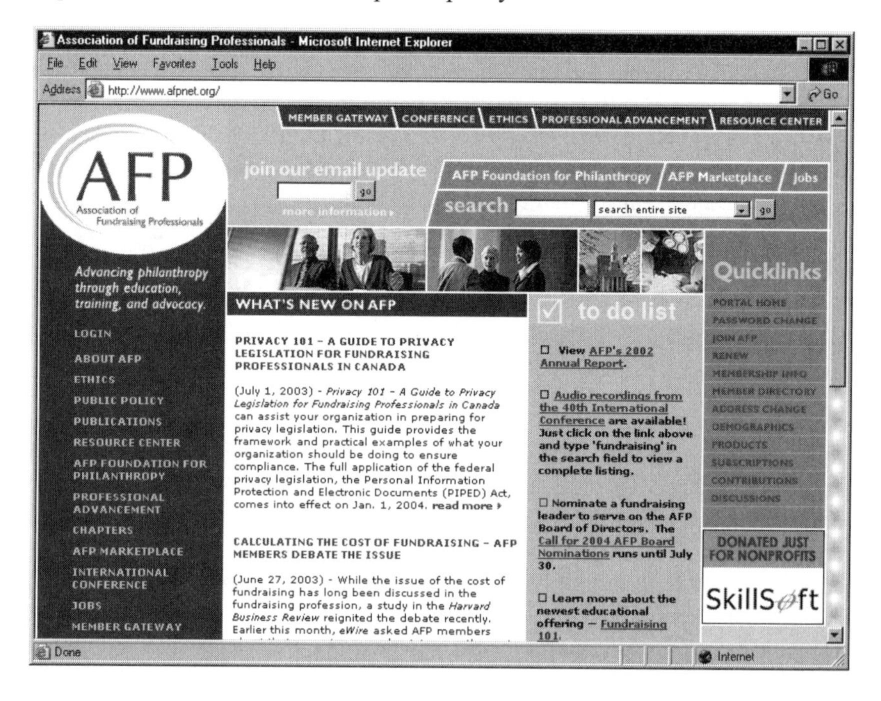

The Grantsmanship Center (http://www.tgci.com)
The Grantsmanship Center (TGCI) is a clearinghouse of fundraising information and provides training in grantsmanship and proposal writing for nonprofit organizations and government agencies. In addition to training program and schedule information, TGCI's Web site offers grant source information on community foundations and federal, state, and international funding; current *Federal Register* grant funding information, including a daily summary; *TGCI Magazine,* an online publication; and a listing of publications for fundraisers, including TGCI proposal writing guides. This site also has a new resource, Winning Grant Proposals Online, with examples of effective proposal writing models for designing programs, consisting entirely of recent federally funded, top-ranked grant proposals in a wide variety of subject areas.

InnoNet (http://www.innonet.org)
InnoNet (Innovation Network, Inc.) is dedicated to building evaluation and learning skills, knowledge, and processes within public and nonprofit organizations through the use of participatory evaluation. The Web site of InnoNet provides a free, innovative Workstation tool to guide nonprofits and public agencies through a planning and evaluation process, resulting in a blueprint for designing, evaluating, and implementing a successful program, with a corresponding work plan. InnoNet also provides information on its consulting services and workshops, and it provides a wealth of evaluation resources in its Resource Center. The InnoNetworking section connects you to a message board, discussion group, news, and an opportunity to sign up for e-mail updates.

BOARDS

***Board Café* (http://www.boardcafe.org)**
Board Café, published by CompassPoint Nonprofit Services, is a monthly electronic newsletter for members of nonprofit boards. Each issue includes board information, opinions, news, and resources, with a "Main Course" article that can be applied to board work. The Web site also has access to past issues of the newsletter dating back to 2001.

BoardSource (http://www.boardsource.org)
BoardSource, formerly the National Center for Nonprofit Boards, provides practical information, tools and best practices, training, and leadership development for board members of nonprofit organizations worldwide. BoardSource also publishes material on nonprofit governance, including more than 100 booklets, books, videos, and audiotapes. Visitors to the Web site will find feature articles; information on membership, consulting and training, and board resources; Boardtalk, a listserv for BoardSource members that explores governance issues; and *Board Member Online,* an abridged version of *Board Member,* the members-only periodical of BoardSource.

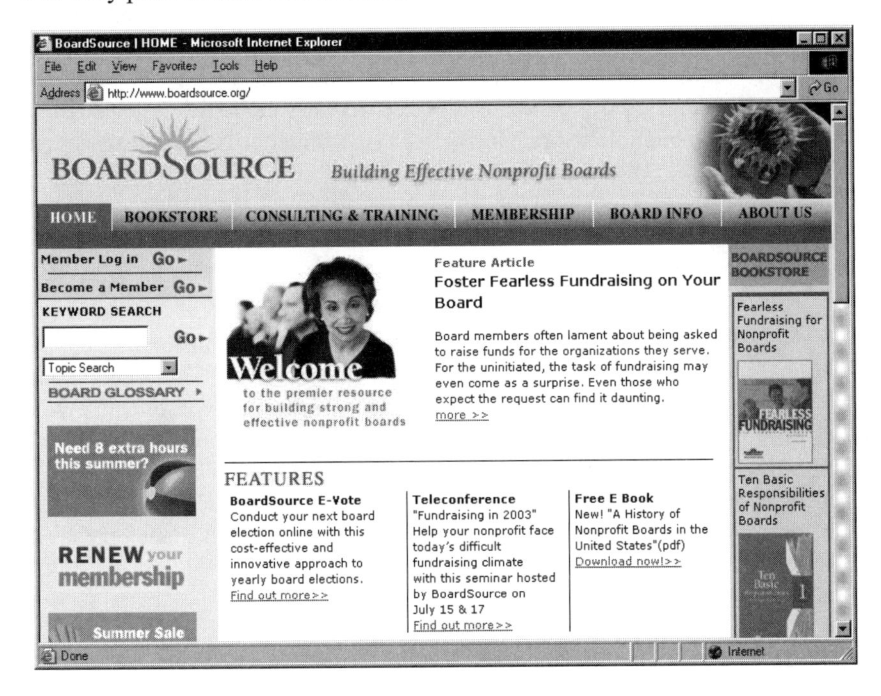

JOB OPPORTUNITIES

CharityChannel—Career Search Online (http://charitychannel.com/careersearch)
CharityChannel's Career Search Online allows you to search for jobs by location, classification, title, organization, keyword, and just submitted items. You can also search listings of executive recruitment firms.

The Foundation Center's Job Corner (http://fdncenter.org/pnd/jobs)
The Foundation Center's Job Corner features some 500 current full-time job openings at U.S. foundations, corporate grantmakers, educational institutions, nonprofit infrastructure organizations, grantmaking public charities, and other nonprofit organizations. Jobs are searchable by organizational type, job function, state, and keyword. The Job Corner is also available as a free weekly e-mail bulletin.

Idealist—Nonprofit Jobs (http://www.idealist.org/ip/jobSearch?MODULE=JOB)
Idealist, a project of Action Without Borders, has a Nonprofit Jobs Web site that provides a searchable database of nonprofit jobs around the world. Visitors can search the database by geography, area of focus, or job category, and can subscribe to a free daily, personalized job e-mail list. Nonprofits can register and post job openings at no charge.

PROGRAM EVALUATION

American Evaluation Association (http://www.eval.org)
The American Evaluation Association (AEA) is an international professional association of evaluators who assess the effectiveness of nonprofit programs, policies, personnel, technology products, and organizations. The AEA Web site has a variety of evaluation-related resources, including information about the association's annual conference and other related events, topical interest groups, published books and journals, the full text of key documents for evaluators, a list of job postings and training institutions in the field, links to other sites of interest, a listing of ongoing degree programs of relevance to evaluation, and the EVALTALK Listserv, a discussion list devoted to issues in the field of evaluation. The AEA member newsletter, first published in the winter of 2001, is also accessible from the site.

VOLUNTARISM

Energize, Inc. (http://www.energizeinc.com)
Energize, Inc. is an international training, consulting, and publishing firm, specializing in voluntarism "especially for leaders of volunteers." The Web site has Hot Topics, a monthly essay by voluntarism expert Susan J. Ellis; Collective Wisdom, offering success stories and advice; a volunteer management library of articles and books; voluntarism information sources and links, with listings of conferences, classes, resource centers, Web sites, magazines, products, and services; and listings of paid volunteer management jobs, internships, and exchange opportunities.

Volunteer Match (http://www.volunteermatch.org)
Volunteer Match helps individuals nationwide find on-site volunteer opportunities posted by local nonprofit and public sector organizations. Volunteers can search an online database of thousands of one-time and ongoing opportunities—including walk-a-thons, beach day cleanups, tutoring, home building, meal deliveries, and more—by zip code, distance, category, and duration, then sign up automatically by e-mail for those that fit their interest and schedule. The Web site also has an online newsletter, and a listing of "virtual volunteering" opportunities for individuals, including those with disabilities, who wish to contribute their time via computer. Community service organizations with volunteer opportunities can also post their information with VolunteerMatch.

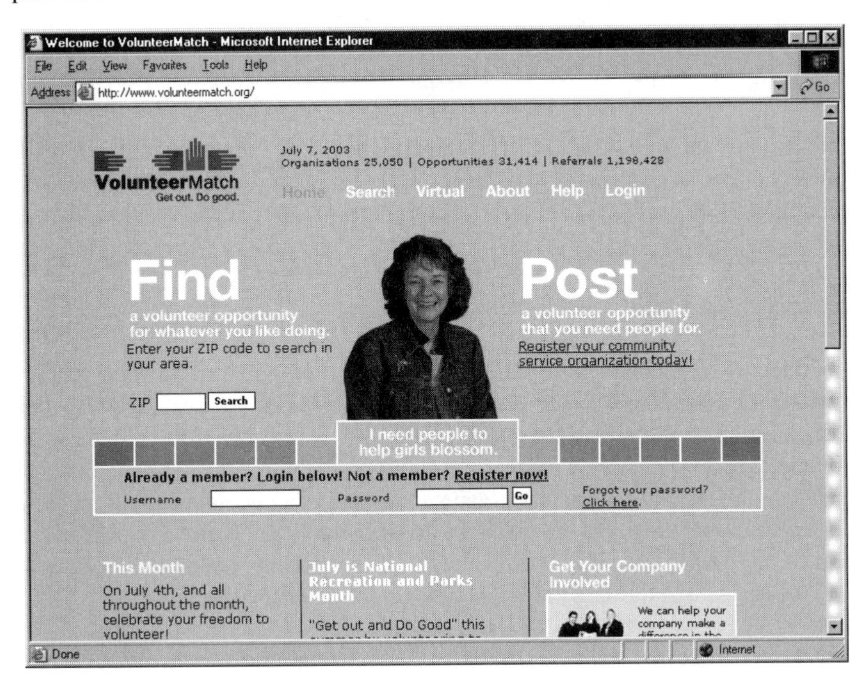

NPO MEMBERSHIP ORGANIZATIONS

National Council of Nonprofit Organizations (http://www.ncna.org)
The National Council of Nonprofit Organizations is a network of dozens of state and regional associations ranging from large to small, well-established to just starting up, in all fields, including social service, education, health, and cultural activities. The council's Web site contains information on the various state associations, conferences and meetings, job listings, and projects with which the council is currently involved.

Nonprofit Coordinating Committee of New York (http://www.npccny.org)
The Nonprofit Coordinating Committee of New York (NPCC) is a membership organization dedicated to protecting and helping the nonprofit community of the New York metropolitan area. The committee's Web site provides Peter Swords' "How to Read the IRS Form 990 & Find Out What It Means," an employee benefits survey, and Who Does What?, a searchable database of nonprofits that offer

technical assistance to other nonprofits. There are also links to the Government Grants Information Service (an alert service for grants at the federal and New York state and city levels) and *New York Nonprofits* (with online versions of selected articles from the print publication, available only to NPCC members). A workshop calendar is also available online.

Nonprofit Technology

Benton Foundation (http://www.benton.org)
The Benton Foundation works to bring together philanthropy, public policy, and community action in the promotion of digital media to bring about social change. The foundation's Web site offers a virtual library with information on a range of issues, such as health, education, and industry, and their roles in the information age. Visitors to the site can sign up for electronic news services, order and view publications, and join online discussion groups, all focusing on a variety of technology and social change-related issues. Links to numerous foundation initiatives, including the Digital Divide Network, Connect for Kids, and OneWorld U.S., are also provided.

CompuMentor (http://www.compumentor.org)
CompuMentor works to provide technology resources—person-to-person services, low-cost software, and online resources—to nonprofits and schools serving low-income communities. The Web site has a link to DiscounTech, which offers software packages that can be ordered online for a fraction of the retail cost to organizations that qualify; a mentor matching program that matches skilled technical volunteers with community organizations and schools; a consulting program that includes technology planning for small and mid-size nonprofits; and information for nonprofits interested in developing a Community Technology Center to provide access and training to low-income or disadvantaged communities.

TechSoup—Recycled Hardware (http://www.techsoup.org/recycle/index.cfm)
TechSoup's Recycled Hardware page is a great place to go if you are looking for usable recycled computers for your nonprofit organization or if you are looking for a place to donate your old computer. There is a list of recycling/refurbishing organizations, tips on donating a computer, featured articles and resources, and a message board.

ebase (http://www.ebase.org)
Now part of Groundspring.org, ebase is an integrated database designed to help nonprofits effectively manage interactive communications with their members, donors, citizen activists, volunteers, and clients. The database is available for downloading free of charge from the Web site.

Gifts In Kind International (http://www.giftsinkind.org)
Gifts In Kind International links corporations (including 40 percent of Fortune 500 companies) and their product donations and services—including software and computer training—with a network of more than 50,000 nonprofit organizations. Nonprofit organizations with 501(c)(3) status (or an international equivalent), tax-exempt educational organizations, and U.S. Indian reservations are eligible to register with Gifts In Kind for donated products and discounted services. A Special Needs section is also available for individuals with disabilities. Gifts In Time, a free global online system, matches company volunteers with nonprofits needing assistance, in areas such as community rebuilding, mentoring, coaching, technology planning, and other critically needed support.

NPower (http://www.npower.org)
NPower, which started in Seattle, Washington, but now has expanded to more than 60 communities nationwide, helps other nonprofits use technology to better serve their communities. NPower offers a variety of technology-related services to area nonprofits, including technology assessments and planning, hands-on help with network implementation, database management, technology training classes, print and electronic technology resource libraries, and short-term technology project assistance. NPower's Tech Surveyor enables an organization to assess hardware, software, and staff technology skills. TechAtlas, co-developed with TechRocks, is a step-by-step Web-based planning tool that nonprofits can use to assess their current technology use and to receive recommendations on how to better implement technology to achieve their mission.

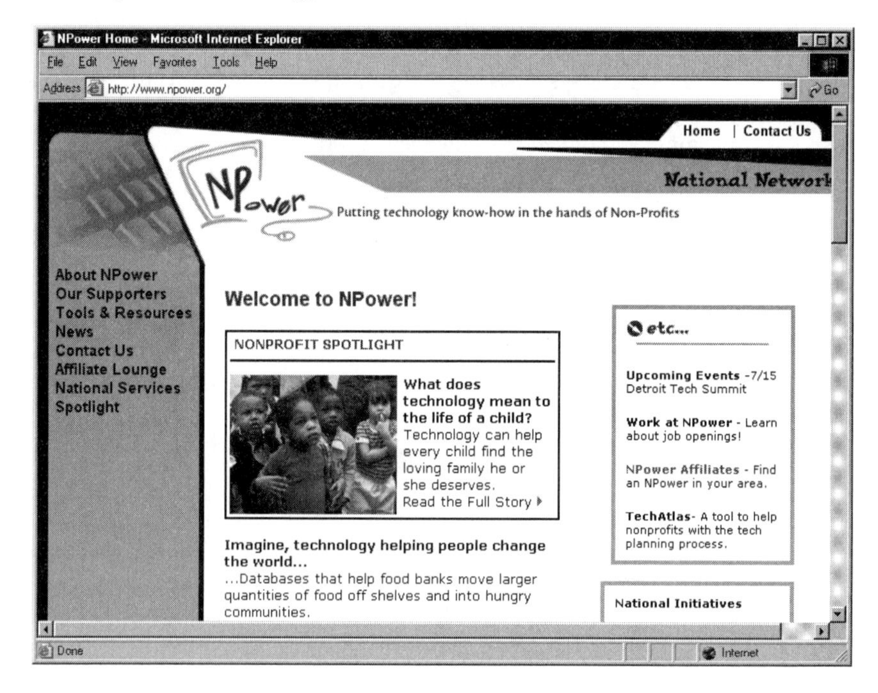

TechRocks (http://www.techrocks.org)
TechRocks encourages and enables foundations, advocacy groups, and activists to use technology to achieve their goals. Visitors to the TechRocks Web site will find ebase, described above, and TechAtlas, co-developed with NPower, which provides context specific technology recommendations and step-by-step guides to assist organizations with their individual technology issues. Various case studies and TechBits, two- to three-page primers on topics that organizations consistently have questions about, are also available.

TechSoup (http://www.techsoup.org)
TechSoup, "powered by CompuMentor," is a Web-based resource center that offers technology assistance and solutions for small to mid-size nonprofit organizations. The site offers nonprofit technology articles and news and information on where to find donated or discounted software and equipment through its companion site, DiscounTech. Also available is information on computer training; advice on technology funding; information on technology planning; listings of available

volunteers and consultants; and detailed information on recycled hardware, including how to find it. The Web site also has a free monthly publication, *By the Cup,* with features articles related to nonprofit technology.

Technology Tip Sheets for Nonprofits (http://www.coyotecommunications.com/tips.html)

Technology Tip Sheets for Nonprofits was created by Jayne Cravens, of Coyote Communications, to help nonprofit and public sector organizations reap money-saving, program-enhancing benefits from technology. In these Tip Sheets you will find advice, help, support, and strategies for incorporating technology into your nonprofit organization. Most of the information is geared to community-serving organizations, but some materials are for a broader audience. The Web site includes a What's New section for frequent visitors.

Public Interest and Policy

HandsNet (http://www.handsnet.org)

HandsNet is a membership organization of more than 5,000 public interest and human services organizations. Web site features include articles and alerts, providing daily news updates on human services issues and legislation; the WebClipper news and delivery service, with human services headlines from hundreds of Web sites that can be tailored to your interests; and information on training and capacity building programs, including a Mobile Technology Classroom, and information consulting and knowledge-management services.

NetAction (http://www.netaction.org)

NetAction is dedicated to promoting the use of the Internet for effective grassroots citizen action campaigns and to educating the public, policymakers, and the media about technology policy issues. Its site provides the Virtual Activist, an online training program for Internet outreach and advocacy; NetAction's Online Buyer's Guide; additional reports focusing on cyber action issues; and the report, "Our Stake in Cyberspace: The Future of the Internet and Communications As We Know It."

USC Center on Philanthropy and Public Policy (http://www.usc.edu/schools/sppd/philanthropy)

The USC Center on Philanthropy and Public Policy works to promote effective philanthropy and strengthen the nonprofit sector through research that informs philanthropic decision making and public policy. It brings together philanthropic, nonprofit, policy, business, and community leaders through a variety of activities, including a Distinguished Lecture Series, roundtable discussions, and periodic research seminars. In addition to reports and research papers (in PDF format), the Web site has links to Academic Research Centers that focus on nonprofits, public policy, or the study of philanthropy.

International Philanthropy

GENERAL

Grantmakers Without Borders (http://www.internationaldonors.org)

Grantmakers Without Borders, a collaborative project of the Tides Center and the International Working Group of the National Network of Grantmakers, works to expand and enrich progressive international philanthropy and to support international projects by providing free advice, alternative sources of information, and increased opportunities for communication among donors. The Web site has an annotated set of links to resources for international philanthropy, organized by donor organizations, organized philanthropy, international news, economics and finance, statistics, and think tanks.

Idealist (http://www.idealist.org)

Idealist, a project of Action Without Borders, is available in English, Spanish, French, and Russian. It has a searchable database of more than 35,000 nonprofit and community organizations in 165 countries, which can be searched or browsed by name, location, or mission; a searchable list of volunteer opportunities; hundreds of job, consultant, and internship listings; and listings of events, programs, and publications. News articles, commentary, reports, and essays related to NGOs are updated frequently. My Idealist allows you to register for personalized e-mail updates, job and volunteer information, and connections to others with similar interests.

CANADA

Canadian Centre for Philanthropy (http://www.ccp.ca)

The Canadian Centre for Philanthropy's mission is to "advance the role and interests of the charitable sector for the benefit of Canadian communities." Web site resources include a foundation and grants directory of more than 1,700 foundations that are actively granting in Canada; information about centre publications; membership information, including the centre's annual symposium; an overview of the centre's Imagine initiative, which promotes public and corporate giving, volunteering, and community support on a national level; and results of various research studies, including volunteering statistics, trends, and comparative studies, mostly through the centre's sister sites, Nonprofitscan.ca and Givingandvolunteering.ca.

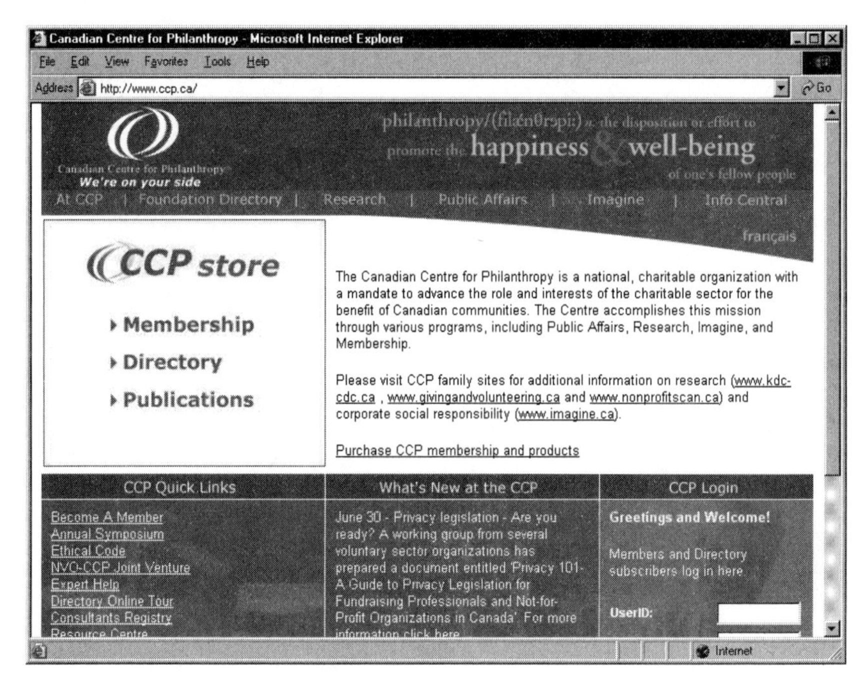

EUROPE/EURASIA

European Foundation Centre (http://www.efc.be)

The European Foundation Centre (EFC) promotes and underpins the work of foundations and corporate funders active in and with Europe. Established in 1989 by seven of Europe's leading foundations, the EFC today has a membership of more than 200 members, associates, and subscribers; 250 community philanthropy initiatives; and serves a further 48,000 organizations linked through networking centers in 37 countries across Europe. The Web site also has a listing of member events; information on EFC's projects, activities, and publications; and EFC newsletters, including *Newsline.*

ISRAEL

Giving Wisely: The Internet Directory of Israeli Nonprofit and Philanthropic Organizations (http://www.givingwisely.org.il)
The Giving Wisely Web site is the online companion to the print directory, *Giving Wisely*. The site has browsable listings of Israeli foundations, trusts (*Hekdeshot*), and nonprofit organizations (*Amutot*). In addition to browsing, you can use the searchable database to view foundation or nonprofit profiles in full or partial format. The search feature works in both Hebrew and English.

MIDDLE EAST

Foundation for Middle East Peace (http://www.fmep.org)
Established in 1979, the Washington, D.C.-based Foundation for Middle East Peace (FMEP) works to promote a just solution to the Israeli-Palestinian conflict that brings peace and security to both peoples. In addition to its role as an information clearinghouse, FMEP awards grants to organizations and projects that contribute significantly to a solution to the Israeli-Palestinian conflict. The bimonthly *Report on Israeli Settlement in the Occupied Territories* reports on Israeli settlement policies and negotiations with the Palestinians.

UNITED KINGDOM

Charitynet.org (http://www.charitynet.org)
Charities Aid Foundation, a British nonprofit whose aim is to encourage charitable giving in the United Kingdom as well as internationally, sponsors the Charitynet Web site, "designed to benefit anyone with an interest in philanthropy, wherever they are in the world." The site includes contact information for thousands of charities and serves as a technical assistance provider to both funders and nonprofits. Use the search engine to search more than 2,000 charity and nonprofit Web sites by keyword, country, theme, or category. Or click on one of the following categories for a quick listing of available sites: Charities and Nonprofits, Government and Public Sector, IT and Internet, Jobs and Human Resources, Foundations, Information Providers, E-zines and News, Financial Services, Education and Training, Legal and Professional, and Media and Marketing. Charitynet.org also provides a news service of current happenings in philanthropy and can be customized to your program and geographic interests when you register with the site.

Nonprofit Resources, By Program Area

ARTS

***Art Deadlines List* (http://www.xensei.com/users/adl)**

Art Deadlines List is a monthly Web and e-mail newsletter listing art contests and competitions, scholarships, fellowships, and grants; juried exhibitions; jobs and internships; calls for entries/proposals/papers; writing and photo contests; residencies; design and architecture competitions; auditions; casting calls; festivals; and other funding opportunities (including some that take place on the Web) for artists, art educators, and art students of all ages. Two versions are available, free and paid subscription. *Art Deadlines List Blog* provides listings in Web log format so you can see the announcements as they become available.

Arts & Business Council Inc. (http://www.artsandbusiness.org/home.htm)

Through its local and national programs, the Arts & Business Council Inc. promotes mutually beneficial partnerships between corporations and nonprofit arts groups. The council's signature program, Business Volunteers for the Arts, places corporate executives as *pro bono* management consultants with nonprofit arts groups. The Web site includes information about programs and services, including a link to ArtsMarketing.org, a national arts marketing site addressing arts organizations' daily marketing needs and longer-term marketing issues. The *Arts & Business Quarterly* provides updates on happenings at the council; social, economic, and political trends affecting the arts; reviews of new publications and technology; and general news from the arts community.

National Assembly of State Arts Agencies (http://www.nasaa-arts.org)
The National Assembly of State Arts Agencies (NASAA) is the membership organization of America's state and jurisdictional arts agencies. The Web site's Arts Over America section provides a directory of links to state arts agencies and regional arts organizations, an annotated list of arts-related Web sites, and links to major funders in the arts. The Artworks section has information on trends, issues, and activities influencing decision makers in the arts and government. The Web site also has a News from NASAA section, featuring news and legislative updates, and Publications, including a strategic planning toolkit.

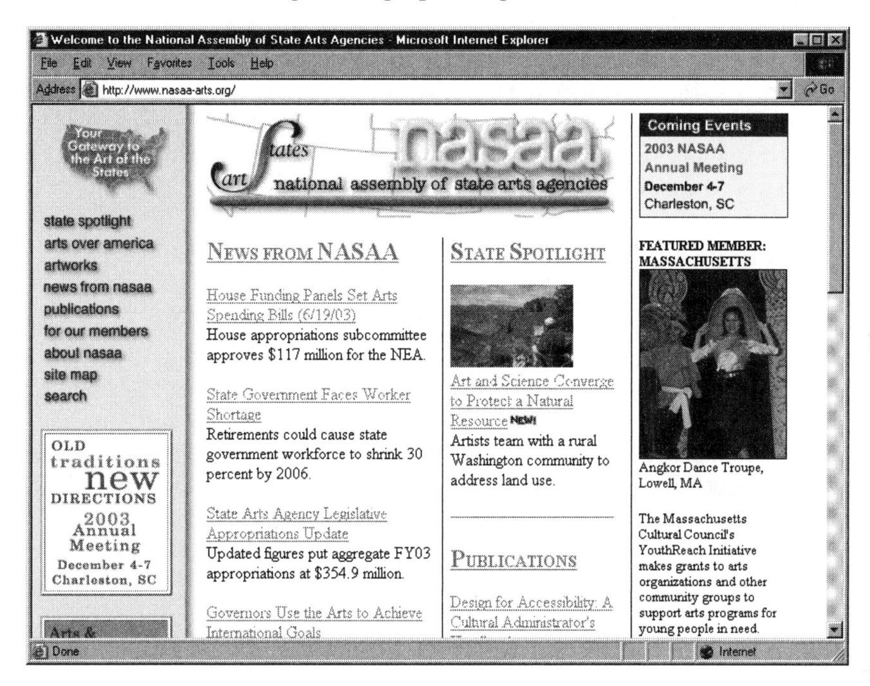

Volunteer Lawyers for the Arts (http://www.vlany.org)
Established in 1969, the New York City-based Volunteer Lawyers for the Arts works to help the New York arts community understand and deal with its legal problems, including through the provision of *pro bono* legal services. The Web site provides information on the group's educational and advocacy work, as well as a schedule of upcoming seminars, a publications listing, news, and contact information for a legal advice hotline.

CHILDREN, YOUTH, AND FAMILIES

Connect For Kids (http://www.connectforkids.org)
Connect For Kids (CFK), a project of the Benton Foundation, was developed for parents, educators, and policymakers. It provides solutions-oriented coverage of critical issues for children and families covering 20 topics, including arts and youth development, out-of-school time, foster care, community building, kids and politics, and volunteering and mentoring. The Web site has a free weekly e-mail newsletter, *Connect for Kids Weekly,* with a news archive; Connections, a monthly highlight of articles, profiles, and interviews from CFK; and a New on the Site

area. CFK also offers resources for volunteering, a list of organizations working on behalf of children and families (searchable by name, topic, and geographic scope), a calendar of events, and a list of resources by state.

COMMUNITY DEVELOPMENT

National Congress for Community Economic Development (http://www.ncced.org)

The National Congress for Community Economic Development is a membership organization of more than 3,600 community development corporations (CDCs), which support their communities' economic development through grants, loans, donations, and income-generating projects. The Funding section of the Web site provides links to government funding opportunities and awards programs, and the State Associations section gives contact information for state-based coalitions of CDCs across the nation.

CRIME PREVENTION

Join Together Online (http://www.jointogether.org)

Join Together Online, a project of the Boston University School of Public Health, is a national resource for communities working to reduce substance abuse and gun violence nationwide, through the dissemination of public policy and community action information. The Web site offers news releases, funding news, grant announcements, resources (including a searchable and browsable resource database), facts, and Web links related to both substance abuse and gun violence. You can also sign up for *JTO Direct,* a free e-mail newsletter with news, alerts, and funding headlines. Daily and weekly versions are available.

DISABILITIES

Disability Resources Monthly (DRM) Guide to Disability Resources on the Internet (http://www.disabilityresources.org)

This nonprofit Web site, staffed by volunteers, provides an extensive online guide to information resources—searchable by state and by subject—designed to help people with disabilities live independently. The site also includes funding sources (click on Grants & Grant-Writing). The print newsletter, *Disability Resources Monthly,* is available by subscription through the site.

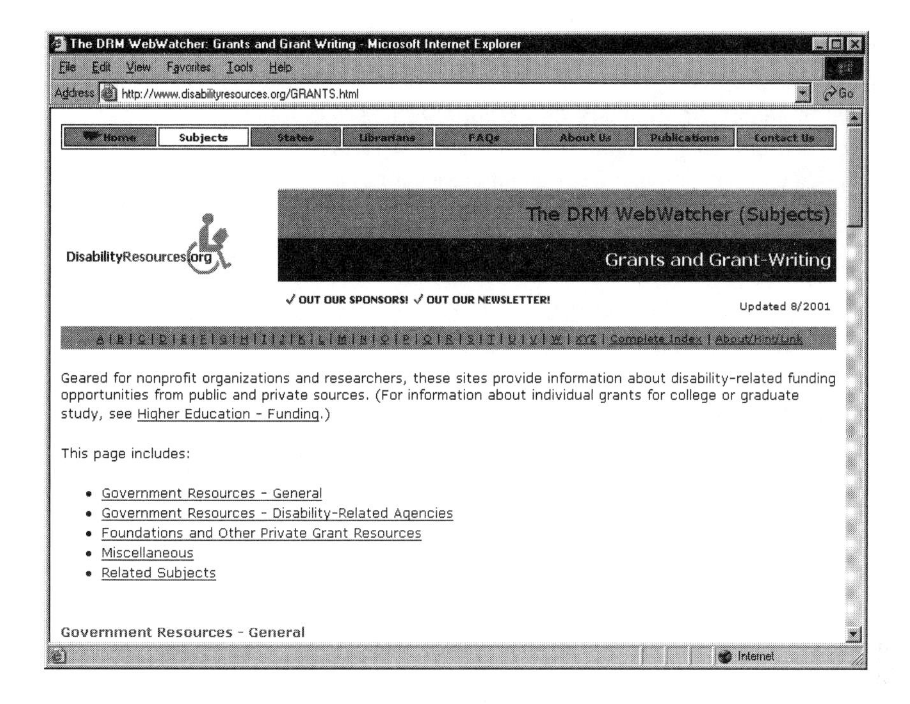

EDUCATION—GENERAL

The Council for Advancement and Support of Education (http://www.case.org)
The Council for Advancement and Support of Education (CASE) is an international association of education advancement officers, including alumni, administrators, fundraisers, public relations managers, publications editors, and government relations officers at more than 3,000 colleges, universities, and independent elementary and secondary schools. The CASE Web site contains job postings; discussion groups; information about CASE's awards and fellowships, training courses, member services, and related merchandise; the online magazine, *CURRENTS;* a matching gifts clearinghouse database; and news about issues related to institutional advancement at colleges, universities, and independent schools around the world.

EDUCATION—ELEMENTARY AND SECONDARY

Computers 4 Kids (http://www.c4k.org)
Computers 4 Kids accepts donated computers, refurbishes them, and donates them to schools and organizations in need. The Web site has a list of needed equipment, grant information, downloadable application forms, and news of upcoming events.

ENVIRONMENT

Environmental Grantmakers Association (http://www.ega.org)
The Environmental Grantmakers Association (EGA), an affinity group of the Council on Foundations, is a voluntary association of foundations and giving programs concerned with the protection of the natural environment. The Web site provides brief information on membership, EGA working groups, and member-initiated projects.

MULTICULTURAL/MINORITIES

Office of Minority Health Resource Center (http://www.omhrc.gov/OMHRC/index.htm)
The Office of Minority Health (OMH) Resource Center offers a large amount of easily navigable material including news releases, online publications, OMH funding announcements, a searchable funding database, requests for proposals, requests for applications, internship awards program announcements, listings of additional funding resources, and OMH's newsletter, *Closing the Gap.*

Grants to Individuals

Michigan State University Grants and Related Resources—Grants for Individuals (http://www.lib.msu.edu/harris23/grants/3subject.htm)
Already cited in the Fundraising Resources section of this chapter, the MSU site includes a separate section for individuals that covers Web sites, databases, and print resources, including links to many federal, state, and university-based funding sources. Resource listings are organized by academic type, population group, and subject.

NYFA Interactive: For Artists (http://www.nyfa.org/level1.asp?id=1)
The New York Foundation for the Arts (NYFA), a nonprofit arts service organization, provides grants and services to individual artists and arts-related organizations in all artistic disciplines in the United States. This site includes information on fellowship opportunities in writing and the visual arts and on fiscal sponsorship. NYFA also provides access to NYFA Source, an extensive national database of awards, services, and publications for artists of all disciplines. Artists, arts organizations, and the general public can access information on more than 3,400 arts organizations, 2,800 award programs, 3,100 service programs, and 900 publications for individual artists nationwide, with more programs added every day. You can also access *NYFA Current,* a weekly digest of news in the arts, which often contains information on grants and funding and is also available via an electronic mailing list.

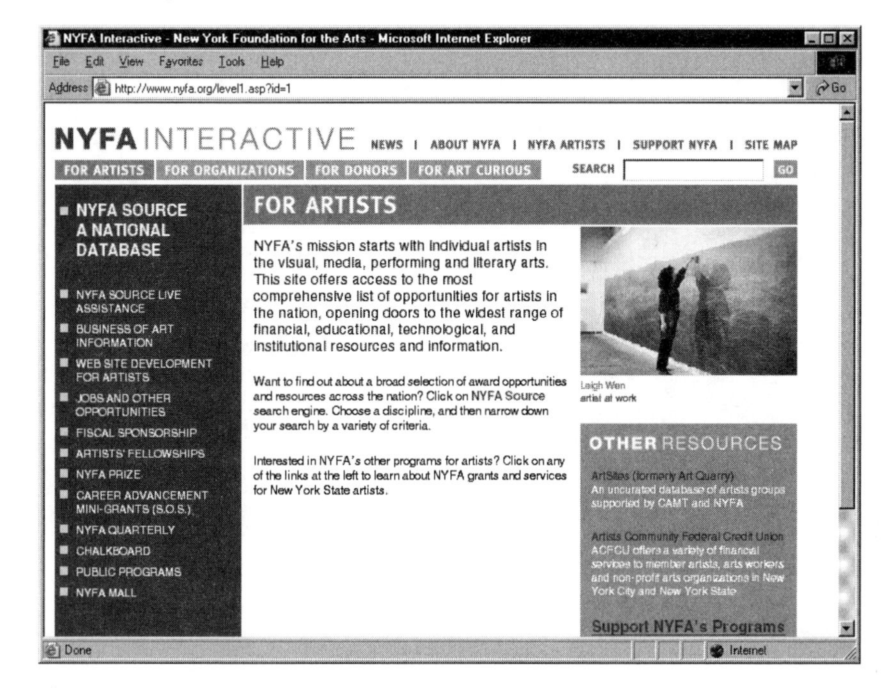

FinAid (http://www.finaid.org)

FinAid, "The SmartStudent Guide to Financial Aid," offers a number of useful features, including FastWeb, a free scholarship search engine that lets you enter information about yourself and your area of study and then responds with an appropriate list of available scholarships. FastWeb's database contains information on more than 600,000 scholarships. (Free registration is required in order to use FastWeb.) FinAid also has links to government funding sources, financial aid offices, information for international students, and other sites of interest to those seeking financial aid.

Conclusion

The Internet is growing so rapidly that just keeping current with what's available could be a full-time job. Surfing for new Web sites, while time consuming, is an essential part of that process. Many of the sites we've reviewed will help keep you informed about new online resources, but it's important not to understate the value of simply spending time on the Web yourself. The Links to Nonprofit Resources section of the Foundation Center's Web site is a great starting point for further exploration and will continue to inform you about new sites of interest as well as changes to some of your old favorites.

CHAPTER NINE

Online Journals

In today's fast-paced, information-based world, it is increasingly important for grantseekers to keep informed of recent developments in philanthropy. One way to do this is by reading nonprofit journals, newsletters, and other publications. An array of online philanthropic journals, news awareness services, and electronic publications make it easier than ever to keep your finger on the pulse of developments affecting your fundraising efforts. The range of current information now available on the Web is vast and growing daily.

Electronic publications are useful for grantseekers in a variety of ways. These resources can make a real difference in helping you stay better informed, whether you are seeking the latest information about a particular funder, grants listings, information on nonprofit management, or the latest news about individual movers and shakers in the field. Content ranges from well-researched, in-depth features to abstracts of notable articles and current news headlines. Although some publications require a username and password, most are open for unrestricted access.

The electronic publications described in this chapter present their information in a variety of forms. There are electronic publications that mirror their print counterparts and that post all (or nearly all) of their content online. Some journals and newsletters have created information available exclusively on the Web, while others operate e-newsletters that exist only in the form of an e-mail sent directly to your inbox. Still others are current awareness vehicles, providing headlines on philanthropy or on programmatic areas of interest to nonprofits. Some deliver only sample articles or content as a sort of marketing tool designed to sell subscriptions to print editions. Any one of these electronic publications may also be directed toward a specific audience, subject area, or geographic focus, whether local, national, or international.

You'll find foundation-sponsored publications; government-sponsored journals relating to the federal, state, and local levels; and newsletters researched and issued by private companies and individuals. Some online publications are posted daily, some biweekly, some monthly, and some several times a year. (Most indicate prominently how often the content is updated.) More and more frequently these online publications offer the same or similar content through e-mail listservs. This means you don't have to visit a Web site regularly to find new content. If you have an e-mail address, you can subscribe to the publication directly from the Web site (or by sending your e-mail address to a specified e-mail address) to receive messages ranging from notification that new content has been added to a site to the full text of the publication itself. (See Chapter 10 for more on joining online mailing lists.)

What follows is a selective listing of some of the philanthropy-related journals now on the Web, with a brief description of each. We have organized these sites into categories for ease of reference (electronic counterparts of print publications, e-newsletters, current awareness/alert services, online exclusives, selected articles with subscription information, local/regional, international, and online directories of journals and newsletters). Since many online journal sites could fit into a number of categories, placement here in one or another category is to a certain extent arbitrary. A more comprehensive listing is available at the Foundation Center's Web site (http://fdncenter.org/research/npr_links/npr03_news.html). Some sites containing these journals are also mentioned in other chapters, but here we focus on the content, features, and usefulness of the online journals themselves. A note of caution: in this fast-changing environment, last week's e-journal may be gone this week, or it may have changed its title or focus.

Electronic Counterparts of Print Publications

***The Chronicle of Philanthropy* (http://philanthropy.com)**

This is the online version of the biweekly print publication, *The Chronicle of Philanthropy,* considered "the newspaper of the nonprofit world." Visit the Web site and you'll find a newspaper-like layout with news photographs and headlines from feature articles in the print edition of the *Chronicle.* There is a site-wide search engine and links to articles, grants listings, and current job listings from the site's main sections: Gifts and Grants, Fund Raising, Managing Nonprofit Groups, Technology, and Jobs. Other features include the Guide to Grants (an electronic database of all corporate and foundation grants listed in the *Chronicle* since 1995), Ideas and Resources, the Nonprofit Handbook, Facts and Figures, Internet Resources, Events, Deadlines, Products and Services, and more. This comprehensive site also has listings of upcoming conferences in the field, news of workshops and seminars, and links to other philanthropic Internet sources. Under the Chronicle in Print heading, you can browse the titles of articles from the current and previous issues. Much of this site is available only to subscribers of the print version, although there are selected articles available for free. You can also search the job listings from the previous issue at no cost. To obtain access to the entire site, you can subscribe via e-mail, snail mail, phone, fax, or Web form. You can also obtain a separate subscription to the *Chronicle*'s Guide to Grants on a weekly or yearly basis, with *Chronicle* subscribers receiving a discount. Subscribe to the *Chronicle*'s free e-mail list to receive updates on what's new in the newspaper and on the site, plus special bulletins when major philanthropic news stories break.

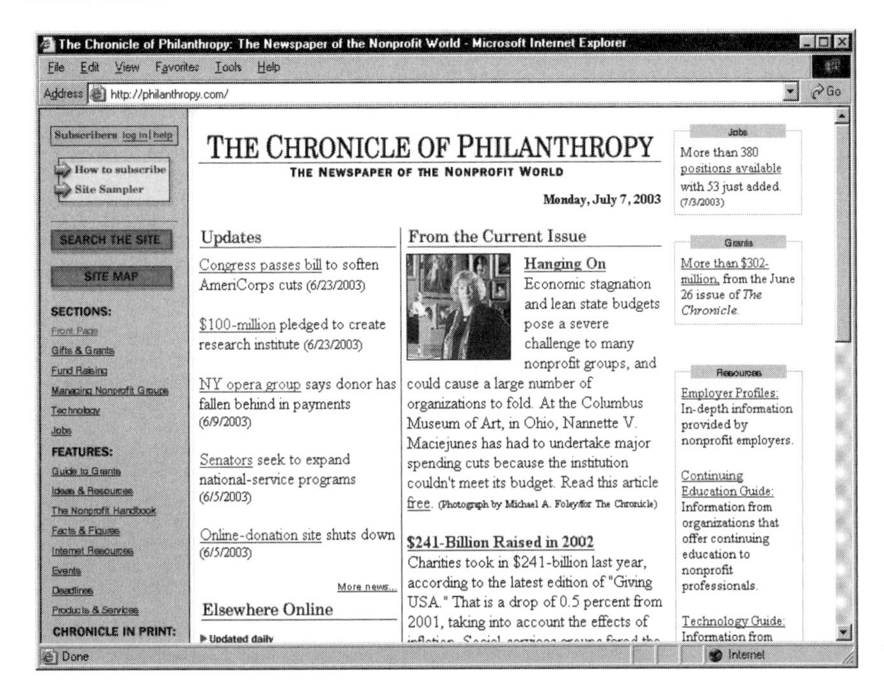

Common Wealth (http://www.movingideas.org/commonwealth)
Common Wealth is the Web site companion to the print publication, *The American Prospect (TAP)*. Online, you will find the Common Wealth Series, which consists of full-text articles dating back to 1993 on nonprofit organizations, philanthropy, and civil society. The *Common Wealth* site features nonprofit news and research, an archive of past *TAP* articles, links to special reports on issues affecting the nonprofit community, original articles available only online, and links to Web sites of other organizations. *Common Wealth* is updated weekly.

***CURRENTS* (http://www.case.org/CURRENTS)**

CURRENTS, published by the Council for Advancement and Support of Education, focuses on educational issues with special features on fundraising. Most articles are available in full text online with an archive dating back to 1999. The archive is browsable by date, article title, and author. It also provides access to the *CURRENTS* Index 1975—1998, which is browsable by author and topic. Get Your Own Issue provides information on how to obtain a specific issue or article from *CURRENTS* as well as subscription information for the print edition. Talk To Us gives contact information for the publication, while the Jobs section offers job postings in development, alumni relations, communications, government relations, student recruitment, and advancement services and information systems.

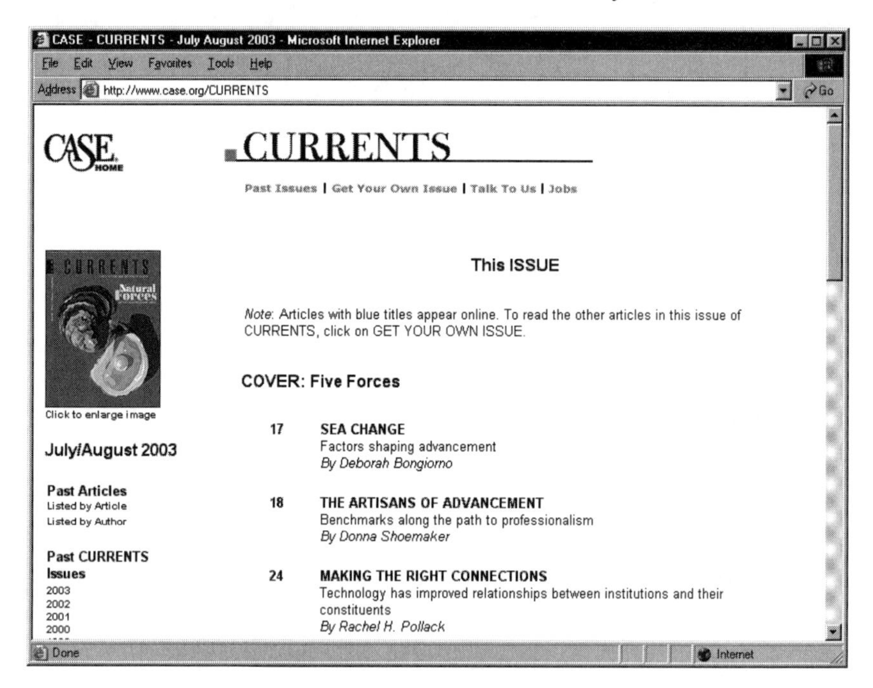

***eSchool News Online* (http://www.eschoolnews.org/resources/funding)**

The journal, *eSchool News Online,* "Where K—20 Education and Technology Meet," hosts a Funding Center where users can find the latest information on grant programs, funding sources, and technology funding information for education. The site, which is updated daily, features educational technology funding news; a column by Deborah Ward, an independent proposal writing consultant; upcoming grant deadlines; ongoing grant opportunities; a link for posting grant opportunities; recent grant awards; *eSchool News* forums; and funding publications. The site also provides subscription information about other print publications published by *eSchool News.* Free registration is required for some areas of the site.

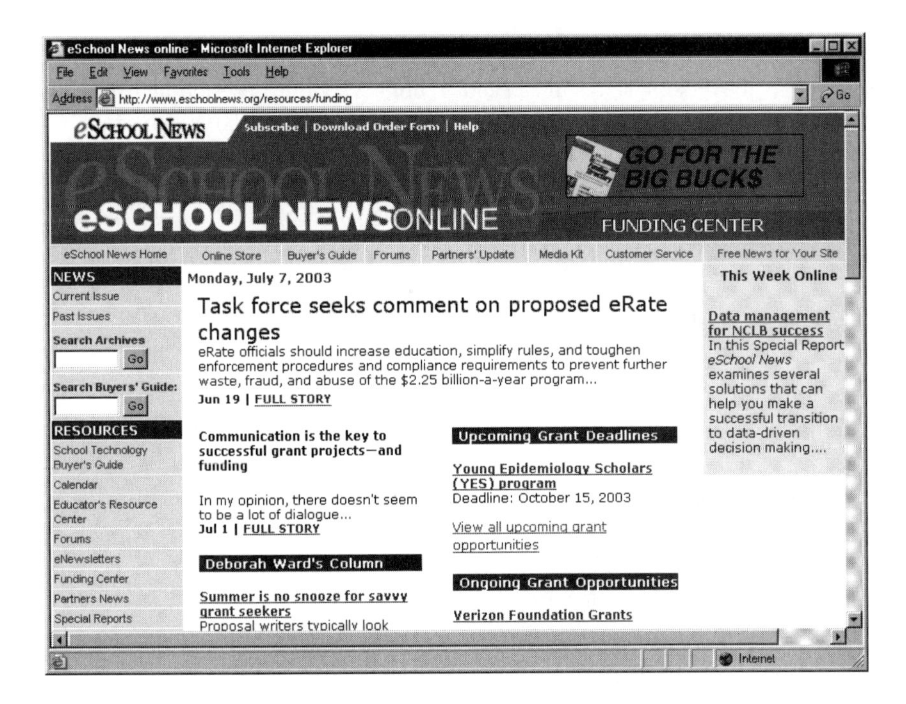

***Foundation News and Commentary* (http://www.foundationnews.org)**

Foundation News and Commentary is a bimonthly print publication published by the Washington, D.C.-based Council on Foundations (COF), a membership organization for grantmakers. It has a target audience primarily comprised of grantmakers (trustees and staff of donor organizations) but is also read by grantseekers, financial advisers, policymakers, and anyone interested in the philanthropic field. When coming to the Web site, you will see highlights from the current issue's table of contents and the full text of selected articles. Subscribers to the print edition receive access to the full Web content. An archive, available for subscribers, dates back to 1997.

Editorial content focuses on the grantmaking community and includes round-ups of trends and news in the philanthropic field, along with interviews with leaders in the nonprofit arena. It also offers analysis, commentary, and ideas—all conducive to effective grantmaking. Web content includes the cover story, special features, and research. The Departments section, which vary from issue to issue, includes news from Affinities (special interest groups within COF) and RAGs (regional associations of grantmakers). You'll also find a helpful Government Update section and the People section, which details job changes in the foundation world. Columns include At Issue and Of All Things, a collection of foundation news stories. *FN&C Now,* a free e-mail newsletter published "as news breaks," is also available. The *FN&C Now* archive dates back to its first issue in 2000.

The Job Bank link takes you to the council's Career Center where there are searchable job postings, resumes, and a library of job description templates. Non-members pay a small fee to post a job listing or resume, but it is free to COF members.

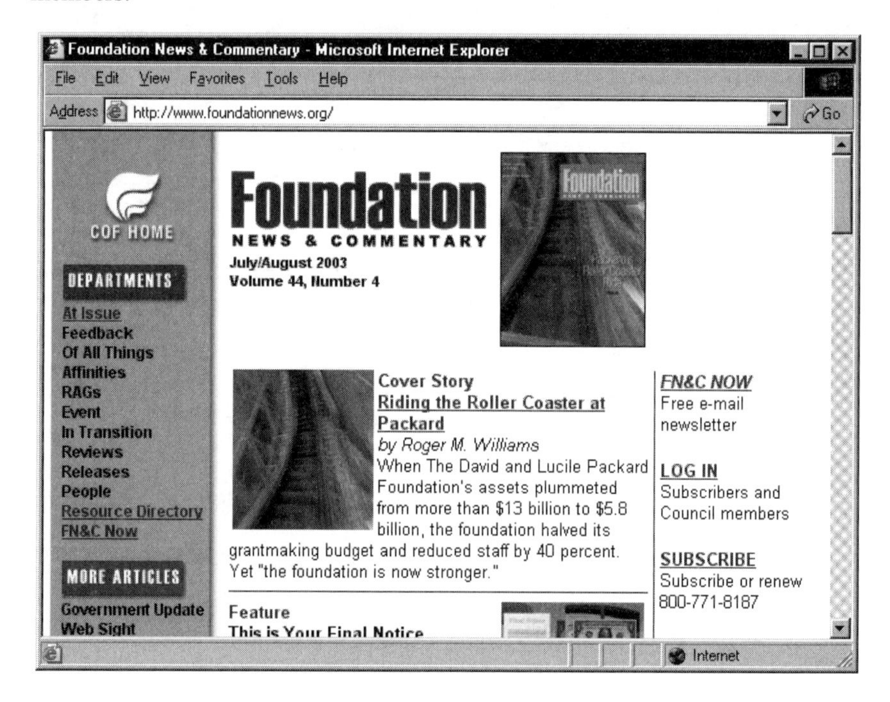

Grantmakers in Health Bulletin
(http://www.gih.org/info-url2678/info-url_list.htm?attrib_id=3319)

Grantmakers in Health Bulletin is a biweekly newsletter, published by Grantmakers in Health (GIH), a Washington, D.C.-based organization. GIH has a mission of helping foundations and corporate giving programs improve the nation's health by building the skills, knowledge, and effectiveness of grantmakers in the field of health philanthropy. Through its work, GIH fosters communication and collaboration among grantmakers and others.

The *Bulletin* features breaking news in health philanthropy, including New Grants and Programs and Awards. You'll also find Surveys, Studies and Publications (linking to health-related reports), People (detailing recent appointments and promotions), Meetings (listing conferences and other gatherings of interest to health-related grantmakers), Online (reviewing new and interesting health-related Web sites), and Positions Available (listing job openings at grantmaking health organizations). Once a month, in Grantmaker Focus, the activities and accomplishments of a "founding partner" are profiled. Issue Focus, also a monthly feature, examines a single health issue or philanthropic strategy and its implications for health grantmakers. In addition, you can access PDF files of the current issue or past issues back to October 1998.

Health Affairs (http://www.healthaffairs.org)

Health Affairs provides access to the editor's choice of selected articles on the healthcare system from a variety of viewpoints and includes GrantWatch, focusing on foundations and the field of health philanthropy. Subscribers to the print edition can log on to access full-text articles. Single articles or issues can be purchased through the Web site. Each issue provides a full table of contents and an archive that dates back to 1982, searchable by keyword, year, issue, and volume and number.

The NonProfit Times (http://www.nptimes.com)

The NonProfit Times bills itself as "the leading business publication for nonprofit management" and targets its content to nonprofit executive managers (nonprofit executives can qualify for a free subscription). This Web newsletter, issued 24 times a year, including six *Direct Marketing* and six *Financial Management* editions, presents the table of contents and selected full-text articles from its print counterpart.

The home page provides selected headlines linked to complete nonprofit news features. There also are special reports available, including three popular reports issued annually. The Salary Survey, published in February, provides a summary of nonprofit compensation information and information on ordering the full report and a downloadable PDF chart. The NPT 100, issued in November, examines and ranks America's largest nonprofits and includes information on how to order the full report and a downloadable PDF chart. The third special report, the NPT Power and Influence Top 50, issued in August, profiles the nation's top nonprofit executive leaders with a PDF version of the full report available. You can also view the NPT Executive of the Year in December. NPT Guides, available from the home page, offers guides on nonprofit products and services. Sign up for *NPT Weekly* for a free weekly e-mail full of news and management tips. Past tips are also available by category.

The full table of contents and the full text of selected articles from the latest issues of *Financial Management Edition (FME)* and *Direct Marketing Edition (DME)* also are available from the home page. In the Issue Library, you'll have access to tables of contents and full-text lead stories from back issues dating to January 1999. The Resource Directory, updated 24 times a year, provides links to nonprofit resources. NPT Jobs, in the Resource Directory, is a good place to find job listings in the nonprofit sector. Full issues of *The Nonprofit Times* are available only through print subscriptions (information and subscription form available online).

Philanthropy **(http://www.philanthropyroundtable.org)**

Philanthropy is a bimonthly magazine located on the site of the Philanthropy Roundtable, a Washington, D.C.-based national association of individual donors, corporate giving representatives, foundation staff and trustees, and trust and estate officers. The Philanthropy Roundtable supports the notion that "voluntary private action offers the best means of addressing many of society's needs, and that a vibrant private sector is critical to creating the wealth that makes philanthropy possible." Click on Philanthropy Magazine to review the magazine's full content, which includes full-text features, reviews, commentary, grants announcements, staff changes, interviews, and donor Q&A. Access to the complete content of past issues dating to winter 1997 is provided. In addition, you can sign up for an e-mail notification service, which provides news briefs on issues of interest to donors and alerts to upcoming Philanthropy Roundtable meetings. You can subscribe to the print edition through an online shopping cart.

E-Newsletters

Board Café **(http://www.boardcafe.org)**
You can subscribe online to this electronic newsletter, "exclusively for members of nonprofit boards of directors," to have it delivered to you by e-mail the second week of each month. It is published by CompassPoint Nonprofit services, a consulting and training organization with offices in San Francisco and San Jose, California, and has a regional focus with a national reach. Content ("short enough to read over a cup of coffee") includes news, opinions, and information to help board members contribute and get the most out of their board service. The archive contains issues dating back to November 1997. PDF versions of past issues (to 2001) are also available.

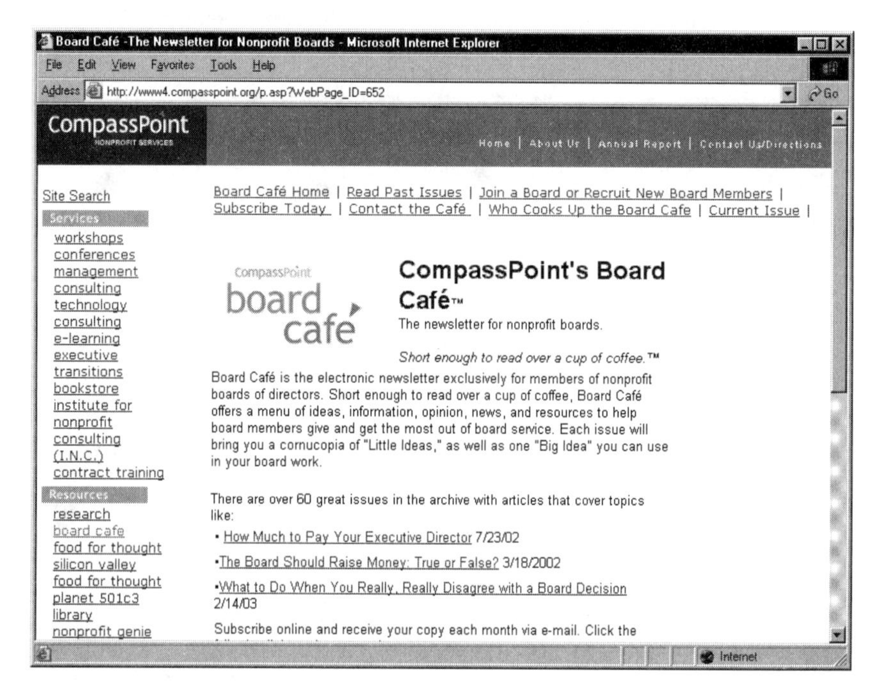

By the Cup **(http://www.techsoup.org/sub_btc.cfm)**
TechSoup.org, "the technology place for nonprofits," publishes the monthly e-mail newsletter, *By The Cup,* which is archived here. Each issue has nonprofit technology news, discounted software alerts, feature articles, tips and resources, and highlights of the TechSoup.org Web site. To receive the most current issue, sign up for a free subscription.

Dot Org **(http://www.dotorgmedia.org/Team/Involved.cfm)**
Dot Org is a free, bimonthly e-newsletter that serves as a practical guide, providing tips, tools, techniques, and case studies, to help nonprofits make effective use of the Internet and other technologies. *Dot Org* is published by technology and Internet strategy consultants Michael Stein and Marc Osten. Back issues can be accessed in HTML format.

***DRG Memo* (http://www.drgnyc.com/list_serve/index.htm)**

The Development Resource Group (DRG), publishers of the *DRG Memo,* is a national executive recruiting firm working exclusively within the nonprofit sector. *DRG Memo* reviews best thinking and practices within professional staff recruitment and development in the nonprofit sector.

***Internet Prospector* (http://www.internet-prospector.org)**

Internet Prospector, "a nonprofit service to the prospect research community," is produced by volunteers nationwide who "mine" the Web for prospect research "nuggets." It is primarily intended for nonprofit fundraisers, but anyone seeking tools for accessing corporate, foundation, biographical, international, and online news sources will find this resource useful.

Each month's newsletter includes reviews of and annotated links to resources organized under the headings Corporations, Foundations, News, People, International, and Tools. In addition, there is an archive of past issues and a search engine provided. You can subscribe to an e-mail version of the newsletter that is sent during the first week of each month or to PRSPCT-L, a heavily trafficked listserv for prospect researchers that incorporates *Internet Prospector* in its postings.

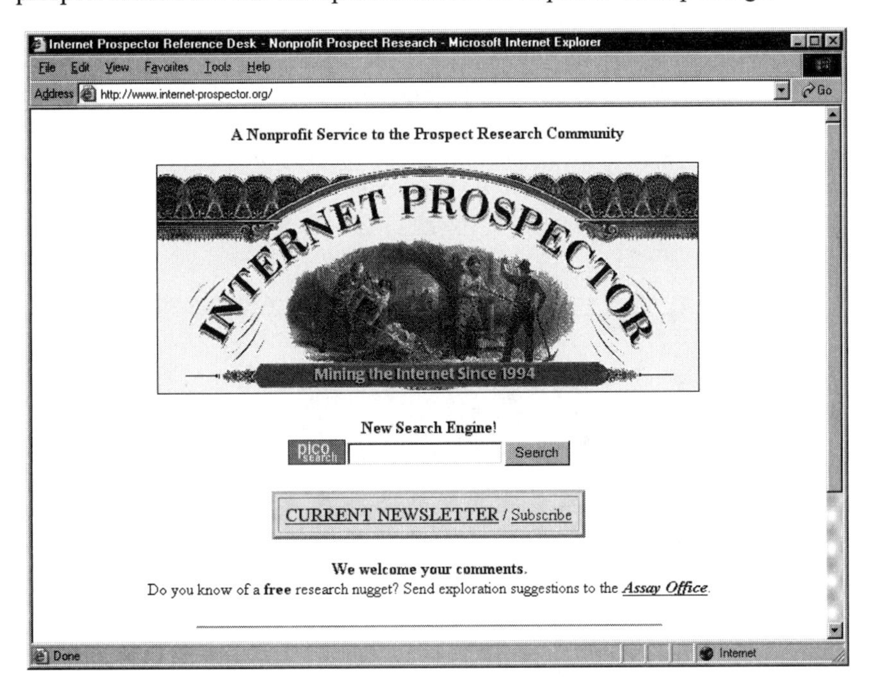

KDV Free Newsletter Subscriptions (http://www.kdv.com/newsletters.html)

Kern, DeWenter, Viere, Ltd. (KDV), a financial consulting group, offers three free e-mail subscriptions on its Web site. *Insight on Estate Planning* (bimonthly) features tips for reducing estate and gift taxes, marital and retirement planning, creating wills, and protecting assets. Articles present strategies for leveraging gifts, using insurance, creating trusts, timing retirement plan distributions, transferring wealth between spouses, and making charitable gifts to take maximum advantage of certain tax breaks. *Nonprofit Agendas* (bimonthly) focuses on new regulations, tax legislation, finance and governmental issues, management, fundraising, technology, and employee compensation for the nonprofit sector. *Tax Impact* (bimonthly) is designed to help inform individuals and businesses of changing tax laws. Topics include donor-advised funds, minimizing the tax burden, creating financial plans for the future, succession plans, and tax reduction strategies.

***Tech4Impact* (http://www.coyotecommunications.com/tech4impact.html)**
Tech4Impact, an e-mail newsletter, is less about techno-jargon and more about the human factors in using technology to benefit people, communities, and the environment. The newsletter is hosted by Yahoo! Groups and is sent out on the second Tuesday of the month. *Tech4Impact* is produced by Jayne Cravens, creator of coyotecommunications.com and contributor to the Virtual Volunteering Project and the United Nations Volunteers program. Selected articles are available from this page, as is a link to an archive of all past issues.

Current Awareness/Alert Services

***onPhilanthropy* (http://www.onphilanthropy.com)**
Presented by Changing Our World Inc., a national philanthropic services company for nonprofit corporations and individuals, the *onPhilanthropy* Web site offers analysis, commentary, interviews, and profiles on issues and people in the world of philanthropy. Select News, Technology, or Corporate Giving for more specific articles and information on those topics. This site also offers five free e-newsletters: *Observations in Philanthropy, Today's Fundraiser, Inside Corporate Philanthropy, The Wired Nonprofit,* and *Nonprofit Jobs Report,* which can be subscribed to easily from the home page. NPO Today, a free daily "news feed," is also available for free.

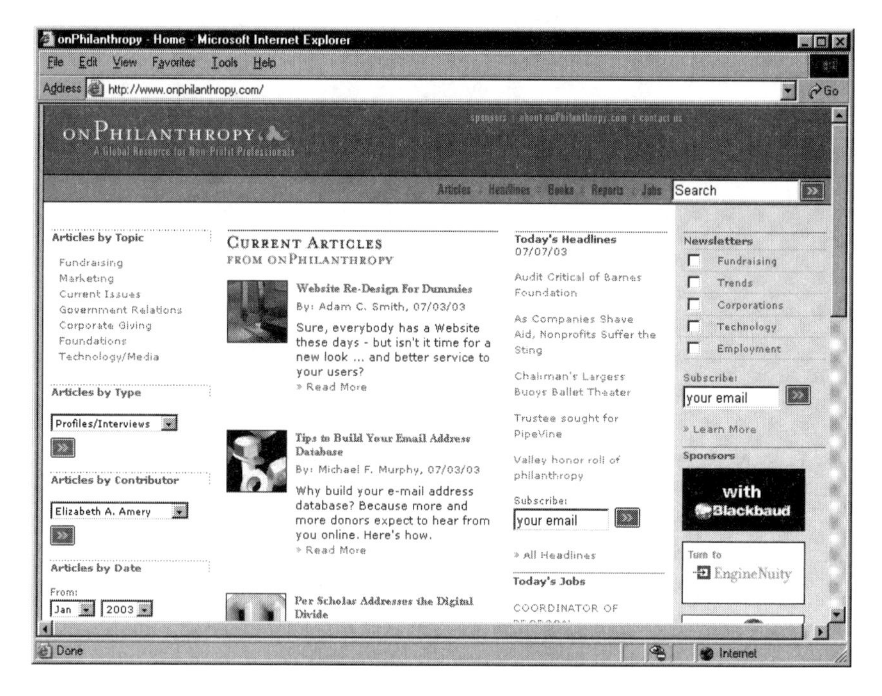

CharityNews-USA (http://charitychannel.com/charitynews-usa.shtml)
CharityChannel was established in 1992 as a volunteer-driven online community of voluntary-sector professionals. Today the community consists of more than 100,000 participants, with nearly 35,000 direct subscriptions to CharityChannel's forums and eNewsletters. *CharityNews-USA* is a daily compilation of news and commentary affecting the philanthropic sector. Visit the *CharityNews-USA* site every day or let them send you the daily news of the U.S. nonprofit sector Monday through Friday, via e-mail. Also available are free e-mail subscriptions to *CharityNews-Canada, CharityNews-International, CharityNews-UK, CharityWire* (which currently allows nonprofits to issue their press releases through *CharityWire*, at no charge), *E-Philanthropy Review, Grants and Foundations Review, Major Gifts Review, Nonprofit Boards and Governance Review, Nonprofit Consulting Review,* and many more.

HandsNet (http://www.handsnet.org)
Washington, D.C.-based HandsNet works to "empower organizations to effectively integrate new online strategies, strengthening their program and policy work on behalf of people in need." The Web site includes news headlines and features on timely surveys, data, legislation, and budget issues ranging from managed care and welfare reform to HIV prevention and neighborhood preservation. There also are alerts on pending legislation, with links to pertinent sites and direct e-mail links to relevant sources. The fee-based WebClipper Service sends members daily e-mail updates on issues they specify, ranging from affordable housing to welfare reform. There also is a Publications area where you can view reports on the Web, discussion groups, funding pages, action alerts, and a conference calendar. You can sign up online for a free 30-day trial of WebClipper.

***Harvest Today* (http://www.harvesttoday.org)**

Harvest Today's Web site re-posts breaking news from 200 leading philanthropy news and information sources and syndicates this content to for-profit and nonprofit subscribers and to subscribing individuals. *Harvest Today*'s news feeds are updated daily and are organized by topic into news channels, including U.S. Philanthropy News, Global Philanthropy News, Boards & Governance, Charitable & Tax Policy, Estate Planning, Fundraising, Gifts & Grants, Nonprofit Innovations, Managing Nonprofits, Technology & Philanthropy, Philanthropy Reports, and Volunteerism. The service is free of charge, and you can also sign up for e-mail alerts at no charge. There is a fee, however, to syndicate the information to make it available directly at your own Web site.

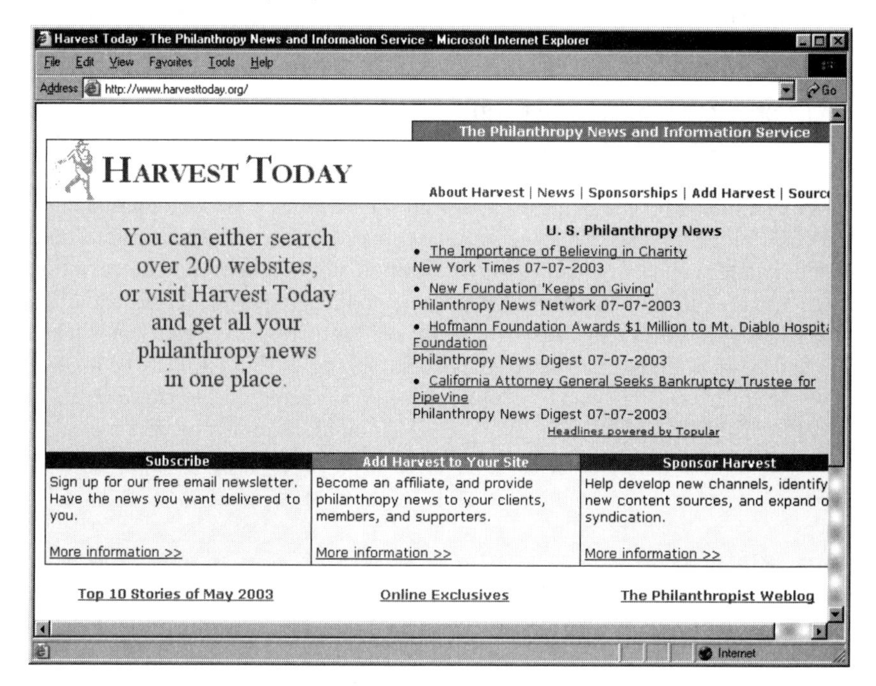

Join Together Online (http://www.jointogether.org)
A national resource center and meeting place for communities working together with the goal of reducing substance abuse (e.g., illicit drugs, excessive alcohol, and tobacco) and gun violence, Join Together Online is a project of the Boston University School of Public Health.

The main page offers current news releases, feature articles, links, and funding news about substance abuse and gun violence. But each topic also has its own page with its own information. On each individual home page you will see the top news stories and, most relevant for grantseekers, selected funding-specific news stories and resources. Once in either the substance abuse or gun violence pages, go to the bottom of the screen, where you will find: Issues, featuring background information on substance abuse and gun violence; News, featuring funding news and grants announcements, newswire stories, original features, press releases, research, and commentary; Take Action, which includes the Legislative Action Center where you can keep up with the latest legislation on hot issues; Resources, with a resources database, an events calendar, and facts; and Find Help, featuring resources for substance abusers and victims of gun violence.

You can also subscribe to *JTO Direct's* News and Alerts or Funding News e-mails, which offer digests of important national news, funding news, and funding and legislative alerts, delivered via e-mail five days a week or once weekly.

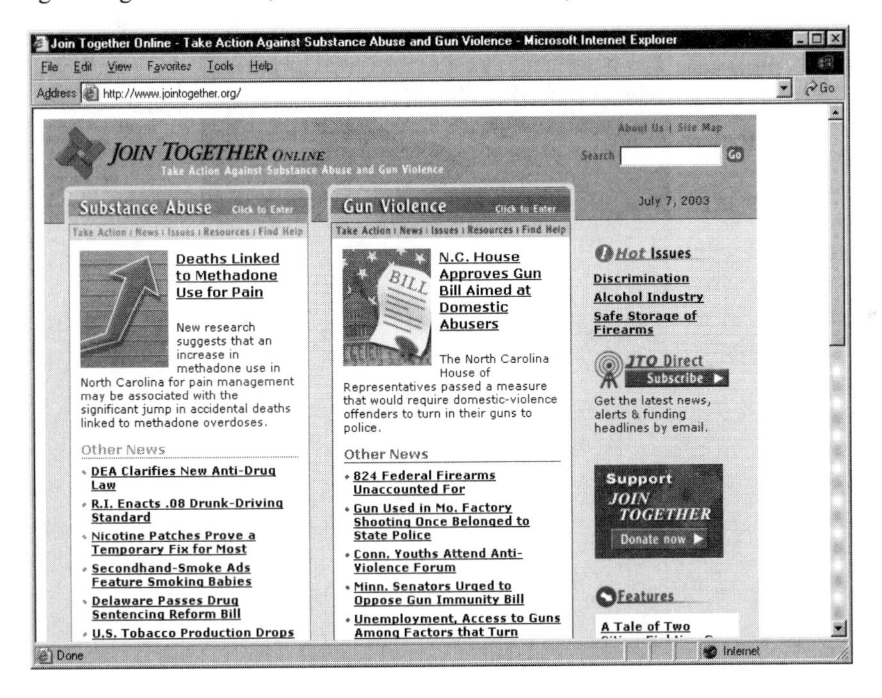

***Nonprofit Online News* (http://news.gilbert.org)**
Nonprofit Online News, a compilation of current news and feature articles on the nonprofit sector, is a program of the Seattle-based Gilbert Center, which works "to support and empower the people and organizations who are changing the world for the better." Feature Articles includes opinions and observations by Michael Gilbert, a nonprofit communications consultant and former nonprofit executive and board member. News items range from announcements of upcoming conferences and speakers to notes about interesting features on philanthropic sites, news reports and surveys, books, and links to relevant articles and sites. The news follows a "Weblog model of short, readable items delivered on a regular basis." You can subscribe to a weekly e-mail version of the news site, and you can access the archive back to 1997. For recent news, use the calendar to search by the date that items were posted.

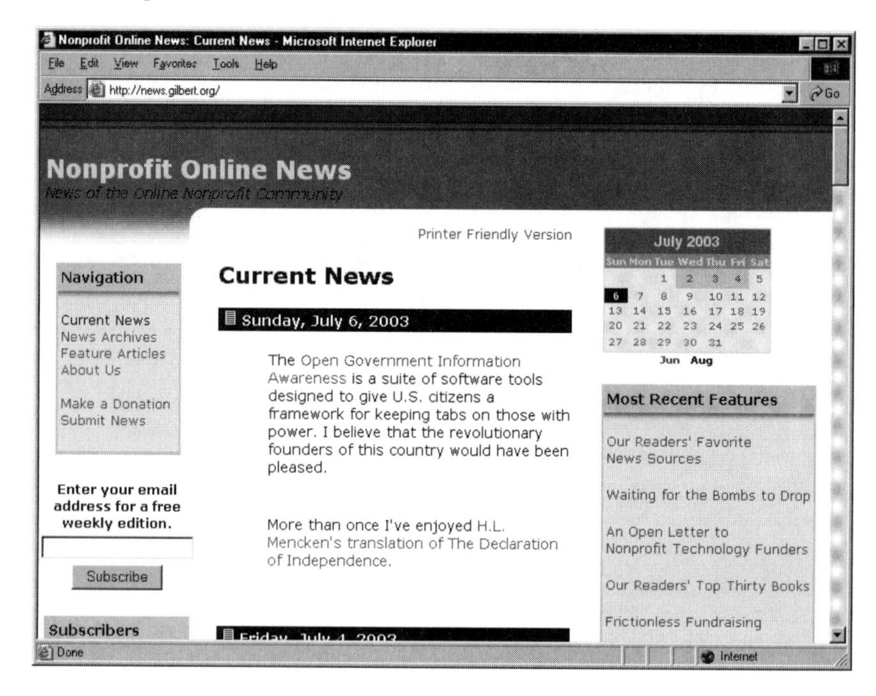

***Philanthropy Journal* (http://www.philanthropyjournal.org/front.asp)**
Philanthropy Journal is an online nonprofit news awareness publication, sponsored by the A.J. Fletcher Foundation of North Carolina that "helps people understand, support, and work in the nonprofit and philanthropic world." The site focuses on nonprofit news in North Carolina, the United States, and abroad. News items are posted daily, and its archive is searchable by date, field of interest, and keyword. The site also has a searchable Announcements section, where you can find conference calendar listings, profiles of people and groups, and fundraising results. Visitors can also search through jobs listings by geographic region, title, or field of interest and can sign up for a free weekly e-mail newsletter.

***Philanthropy News Network Online* (http://www.pnnonline.org)**
This daily Web news service is part of the Philanthropy News Network (PNN), whose mission is to deliver "news, information, and resources to all segments of the nonprofit world in order to help them better achieve their goals."

PNN Online features daily national news summaries, organized by subject area (arts, culture, and humanities; education; the environment; health; human services; public works and advocacy; and general fundraising). An archive in each subject area allows readers to access articles from the past three months. Users can post reactions or comments to the Web board thread available for each story. Select Archive for articles at least one year old and dating back to 1997. There are listings of conferences and nonprofit jobs as well.

Philanthropy News Digest (PND) (http://fdncenter.org/pnd)

A free online journal offered by the Foundation Center, *Philanthropy News Digest (PND)* is a compendium, in digest form, of philanthropy-related articles and features gathered from print and electronic media outlets nationwide. The most recent philanthropy-related articles can be found on the *PND* home page organized by topic, and items older than a week can be accessed from the News by Category menu.

PND features include the Job Corner, with searchable listings of job openings at U.S. foundations and other nonprofit organizations, and the RFP Bulletin, a weekly listing of current funding opportunities offered by foundations and other grantmaking organizations. You'll also find 9/11 Response, featuring 9/11-related philanthropy news items, interviews, and more; Connections, which offers fresh links to the "best the Web has to offer" on issues related to the changing world of philanthropy; Newsmakers, featuring conversations with nonprofit executives and leaders; the NPO Spotlight, highlighting the activities and interests of a different nonprofit organization every week; and a Conference Calendar, listing conferences taking place across the nation. *PND*'s Off the Shelf (book reviews) and On the Web (Web site reviews) features provide recommendations on the latest online and print offerings in the nonprofit field. And the *PND* message boards, PND Talk and ArtsTalk, let users share opinions, insights, and questions related to philanthropy with a large and growing community of consultants, development professionals, fundraisers, grantseekers, artists, and others.

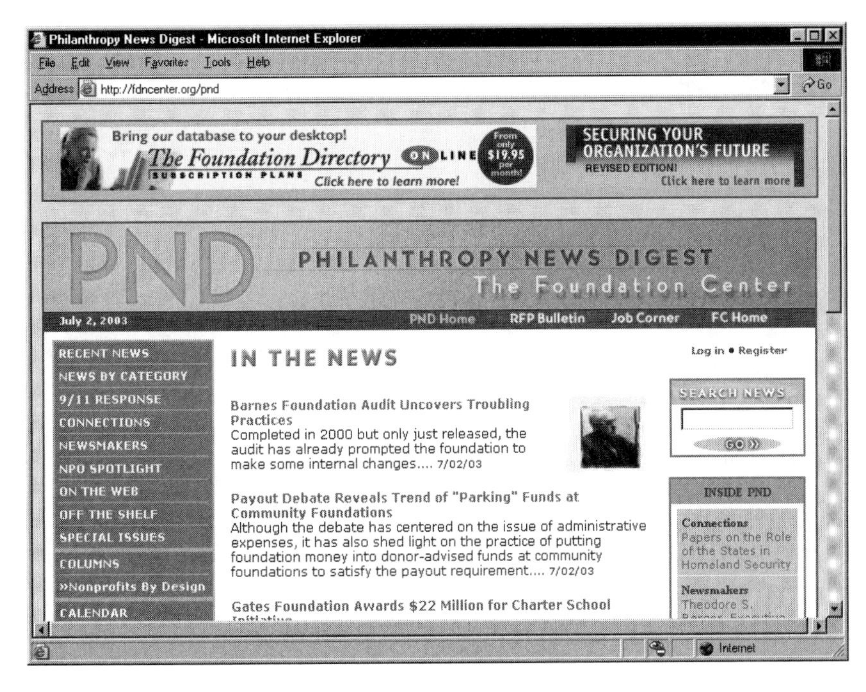

Visitors who have registered and are logged in to the site will find a My PND menu item on the *PND* home page. Once registered, follow the My PND link to view links to news that relates to your top areas of interest and your geographic location. You can easily change your specified interest by clicking Edit Profile on the My PND page.

The *PND* search engine allows you to perform keyword searches of past issues dating back to January 2001. Select PND Archives to access a separate searchable database of *PND* issues dating back to 1995. By selecting Special Issues you can also access *PND* special quarterly issues focusing on topics, such as Funding for the Arts, Funding for Children & Youth, and Technology Resources for Nonprofits. Subscribe to *PND* for free by entering your e-mail address into the subscription box provided on any page of *PND*. You will receive the journal via e-mail every Tuesday evening. You can also subscribe to *Job Corner Alert, RFP Bulletin,* or *Connections* at the Center's Newsletters page (http://fdncenter.org/newsletters).

Pulse! **(http://www.allianceonline.org/pulse.html)**

Pulse! is a national online newsletter described as "The Online Newsletter of the Nonprofit Management Support Community." *Pulse*! is delivered every month or two via e-mail, providing readers with a timely summary of what's happening in the nonprofit sector and the management support community. Content includes a brief digest of current happenings within the sector, new ideas, conferences, awards, and postings on relevant books, videos, and Web sites.

The newsletter is a free service of the Alliance for Nonprofit Management, the Washington, D.C.-based organization whose mission is to "increase the effectiveness of individuals and organizations that help nonprofits build their power and impact." You can subscribe to a free e-mail edition of the newsletter or submit news items to the site. A complete archive of back issues dates back to January 1997.

Online Exclusives

Arts Funding Watch (http://fdncenter.org/profile)

Arts Funding Watch, a monthly electronic newsletter of arts-related news and information, is a publication of the Foundation Center. The newsletter includes news updates, job postings, funding opportunities, and other special features relating to the arts. Arts Funding Watch is available exclusively to registered visitors of the Foundation Center's Web site who indicate an interest in the arts. To sign up, simply choose Arts & Culture as one of your interests in the My Profile section of the Foundation Center's Web site.

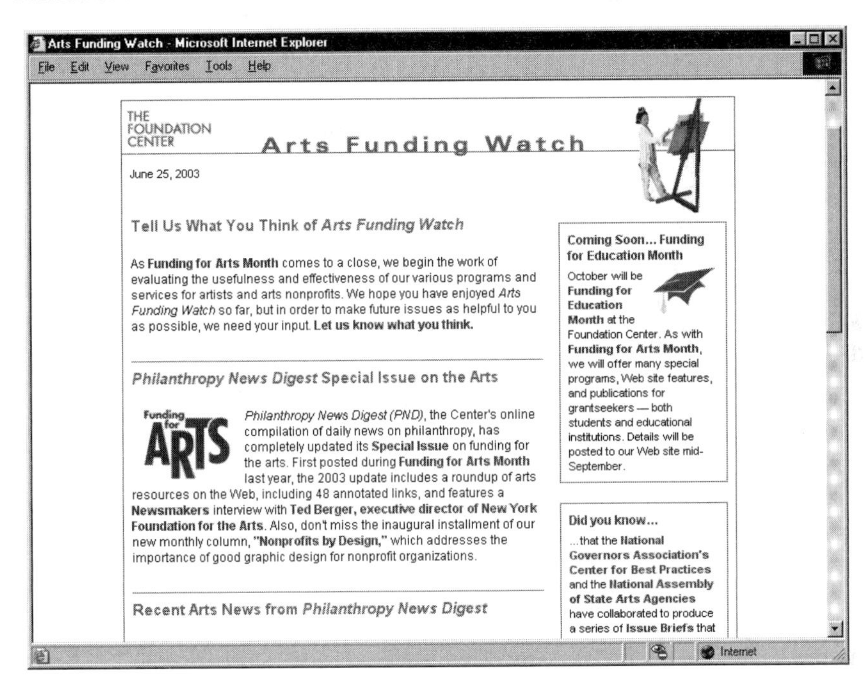

Foundation Watch **(http://www.capitalresearch.org/pubs/pubs.asp)**

Foundation Watch is a monthly newsletter published by the Washington, D.C.-based Capital Research Center (CRC), a conservative group that focuses on "reviving the American traditions of charity, philanthropy, and voluntarism," and "identifying private alternatives to government welfare programs." CRC's research is channeled into four newsletters, including *Foundation Watch* (select this option from the drop down menu), which monitors and examines the grantmaking activities of private foundations and analyzes their impact on American society. Online you'll find selected articles dating back to January 1998.

NYFA Current **(http://www.nyfa.org/level2.asp?id=17&fid=6&sid=105)**
NYFA Current, a weekly online journal of arts news and funding notices, is a project of the New York Foundation for the Arts (NYFA). The journal includes news updates on philosophical, political, social, and economic issues affecting the arts and culture community. Also featured are Current Web Reports, notices of funding opportunities for artists, opportunities for organizations, arts events (with descriptions of events, time, date, place, and contact information), and arts-related job opportunities. A free subscription is available via e-mail.

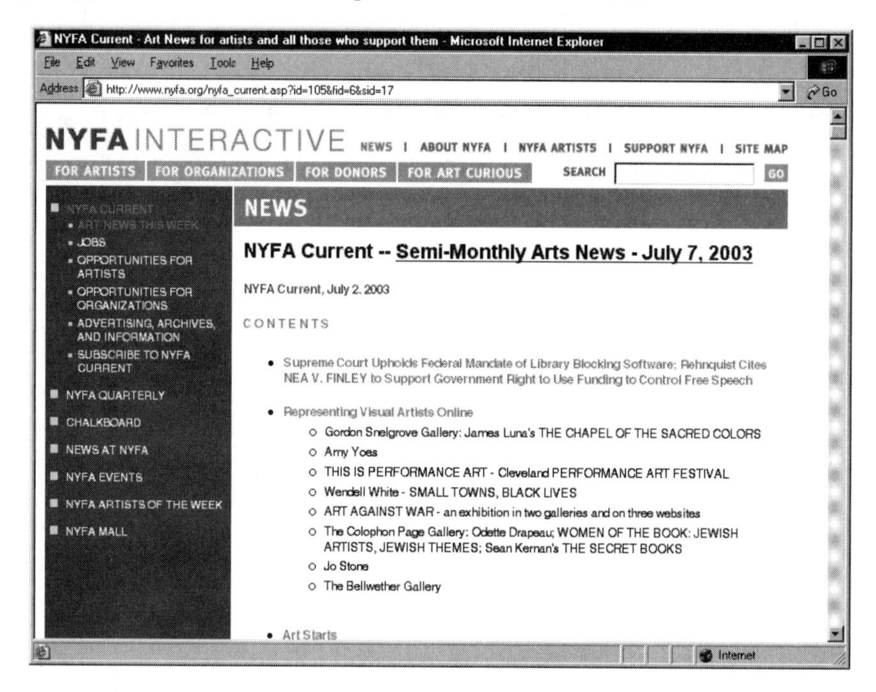

Planet 501c3 **(http://www.planet501c3.org)**
Miriam Engelberg's *Planet 501c3* is hosted by Compass Point Nonprofit Services in San Francisco. This monthly cartoon series takes a humorous look at the nonprofit world.

***Volunteer Today* (http://www.volunteertoday.com)**

Described as "the Electronic Gazette for Volunteerism," *Volunteer Today* is a monthly online newsletter directed at those interested in volunteer management. It serves two purposes: first, to build the capacity of individuals to organize effective volunteer programs, and second, to enhance the profession of volunteer management. Regular features include News, Recruiting and Retention, Management and Supervision, Training, Ask Connie (a volunteer manager/consultant/trainer who responds to e-mail questions), Tech Tips, the Volunteer Program Evaluations Series, and Boards and Committees. You also can find listings of Internet resources, volunteer opportunities, a calendar of events, and a bookstore. Register online and receive an e-mail "heads-up" called *VT News,* which lets you know when each new newsletter is posted.

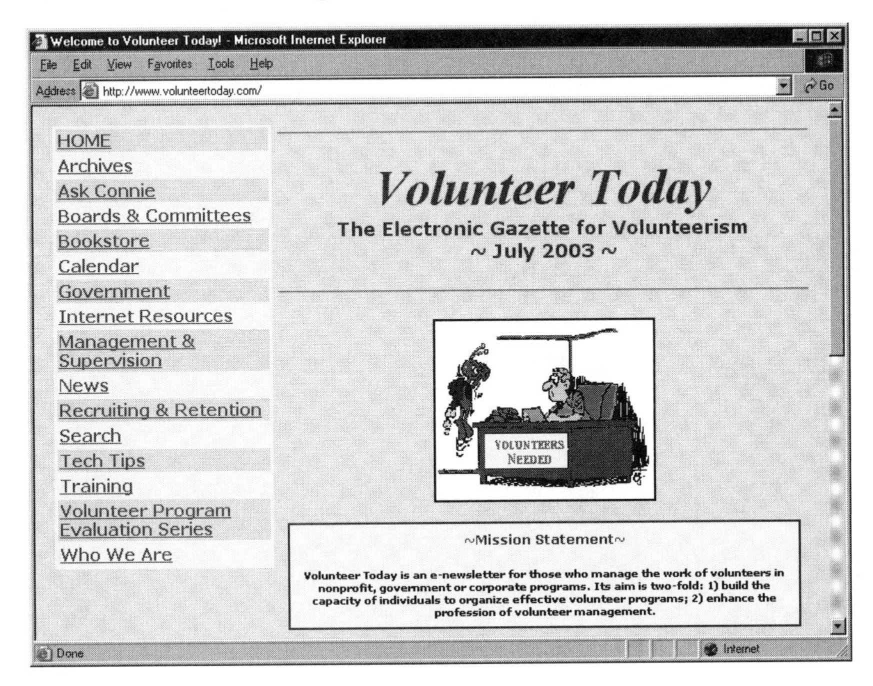

Selected Articles with Subscription Information

Advice at GrassrootsFundraising.org (http://www.grassrootsfundraising.org/advice/index.html)
This area of the GrassrootsFundraising.org Web site provides links to numerous useful resources and other information. There are more than 50 complete *Grassroots Fundraising Journal* articles and sample book chapters available here. You can download individual past articles as PDF files or order back issues for a fee. In addition, you can sign up for Chardon Press' free monthly newsletter that includes funding tips and the *Grassroots Fundraising Journal* column, Dear Kim Klein, which is also available as a searchable archive here. You can even post a question using an online form or find a public workshop near you.

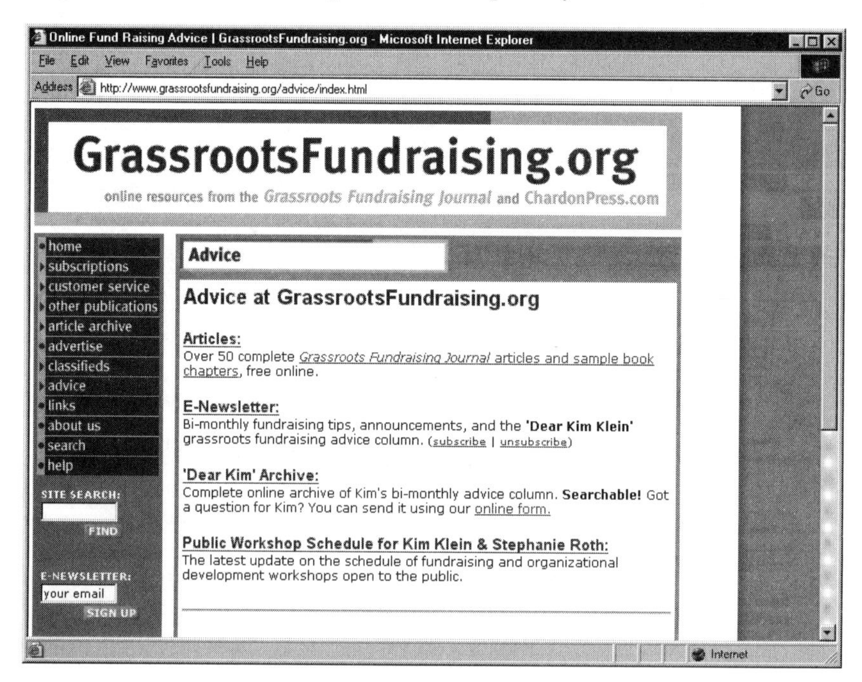

Board Member Online **(http://www.boardsource.org/bmoarchive.asp)**
Board Member Online, published ten times a year by BoardSource (formerly the National Center for Nonprofit Boards), is designed to give you highlights of each new regular issue of *Board Member* and to serve as a ready archive of past issues. The online version of *Board Member* offers access to the "members only" print publication, presenting abbreviated introductions to feature articles, departments, and case studies where, each month, three experts in the field offer possible solutions to challenges facing real board members. You must be a BoardSource member to access full-text articles. Members have access to the archive dating back to 1998. *Board Member Online* also offers information on how to submit articles for publication.

Don Kramer's Nonprofit Issues **(http://www.nonprofitissues.com)**
Don Kramer's Nonprofit Issues is a bimonthly print newsletter, edited by Don Kramer and based in Dresher, Pennsylvania, of "Nonprofit Law You Need to Know." Content is targeted to nonprofit executives and their advisers and includes

current issues and news about federal and state cases and recent regulations and rulings affecting the work of nonprofit organizations. Specifically, you'll find coverage of federal tax law, employment law, board liability, volunteer law, corporate governance, foundation rules, charitable giving, insurance, and copyright/trademark issues. Online, you'll find tables of contents and highlights featuring full-text articles from the current issue. Ready reference pages (e.g., articles summarizing rules and regulations that control nonprofit activity) are available as PDF files for a fee. Subscriptions to *Nonprofit Issues* are available in print and PDF formats. You can register for Thursday with the Editor, a fee-based monthly seminar conference call with the publication's editors, to discuss topics in the current issue or any other relevant subject matters. You can also subscribe online to an e-mail update or mailing list, which alerts you to site changes, new publications, and other offers. A two-issue trial offer is available.

Leader to Leader
(http://www.josseybass.com/WileyCDA/WileyTitle/productCd-LTL.html)
Published by Jossey-Bass, *Leader to Leader* is a quarterly report sponsored by the Leader to Leader Institute (formerly the Peter F. Drucker Foundation for Nonprofit Management) and written by top executives, authors, consultants, and social thinkers, with an interest in issues related to nonprofit management, leadership, and strategy. Content offers an insight into what nonprofit leaders are planning for, what they see as the challenges ahead, and how they are dealing with change. From this site you can access the full text of selected articles in PDF format dating back to the winter 2001 issue. The tables of contents are available for issues dating back to the winter 2000 issue, and individual issues can be ordered dating back to the summer 1996 issue. Information on how to subscribe to the print edition is also available online.

***The Nonprofit Quarterly* (http://www.nonprofitquarterly.org)**
The Nonprofit Quarterly is a publication of Third Sector New England, a Boston-based nonprofit organization "dedicated to capacity building and promoting active democracy." Visitors to this Web site can access the full table of contents of the current issue and selected full-text articles. An archive is available back to the fall 1998 issue. A free monthly e-newsletter is also available and is archived back to June 2001. Selected issues have Discussion Guides to help start and focus discussions around topics covered in the publication. Click on NPQ Learning Center to join moderated discussions supporting the mission of *The Nonprofit Quarterly.* Links to articles under discussion are included, and you can join the discussion via a Web board or an e-mail listserv. Visitors also can subscribe to the print edition online or via e-mail, fax, or telephone.

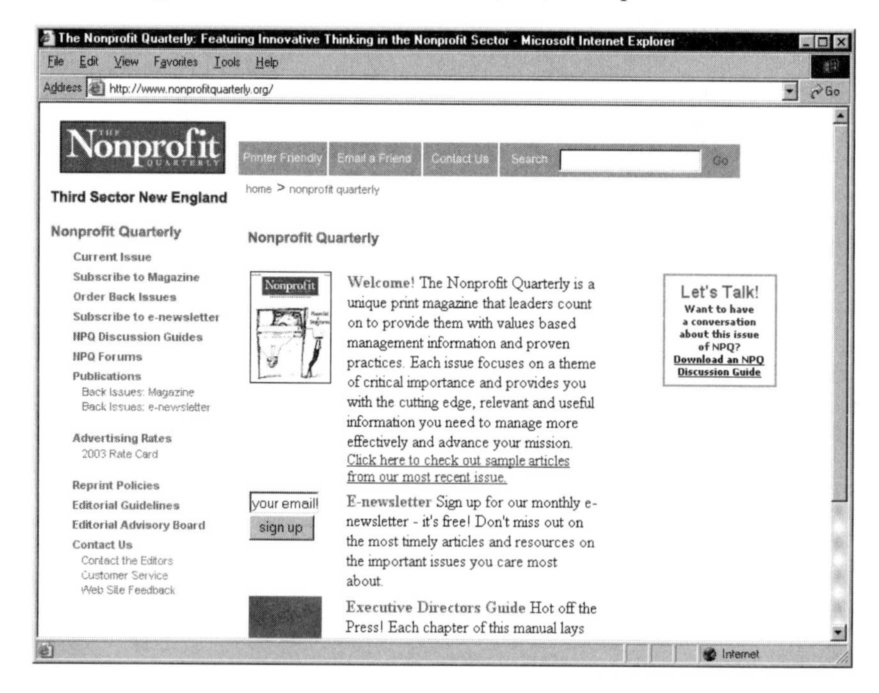

Poets & Writers Online **(http://www.pw.org/mag/index.htm)**
The companion Web site for *Poets & Writers Magazine,* published six times a year, offers the full text of selected feature articles and news from the print edition as well as exclusive online content. Most important to grantseekers is the Grants & Awards section. It includes Deadlines, a listing of grant competitions and contest awards that offer at least $1,000 and for which deadlines are fast approaching (with contact information); a two-month Submission Calendar that lists upcoming award deadlines; Recent Winners, announcing recent grants and awards winners, including description, contact information, and links to relevant Web sites; and Conferences and Residencies, which lists conferences, literary festivals, residencies, and colonies of interest to poets and writers. Direct Quotes features interviews with writers available exclusively online, and the Classifieds sections features contests, conferences, jobs, workshops, publications, calls for manuscripts, and more. An archive with selected full-text articles is available back to January/February 1996.

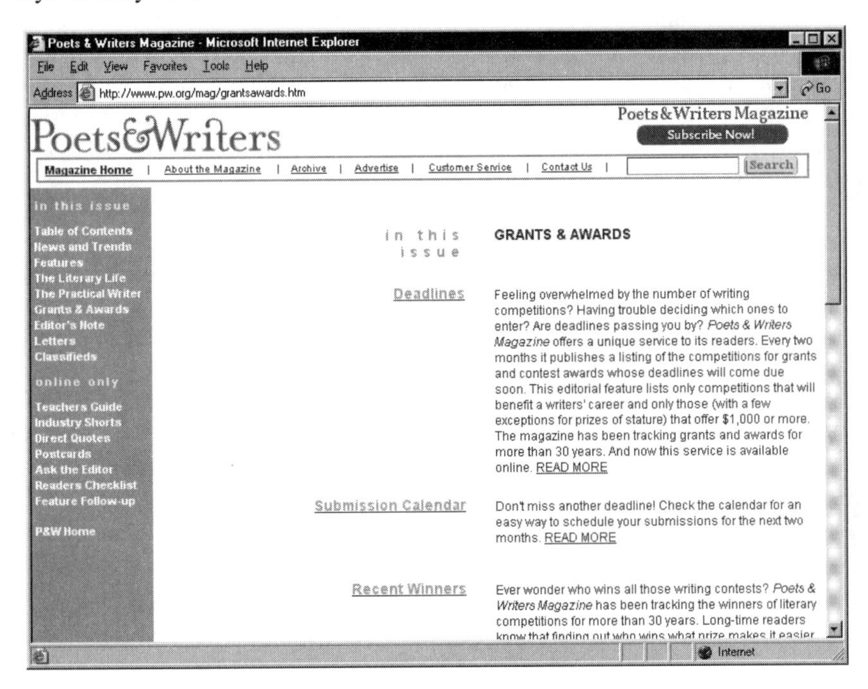

Trusts and Estates (http://www.trustsandestates.com)
Trusts and Estates, a magazine for estate planning and wealth management professionals, has been published monthly since 1904. Here you will find selected full-text feature articles and tables of contents from recent issues of the publication. Other site features include information on how to subscribe to the print edition, guidelines for submitting articles for publication, an editorial index covering the years 1993 to 2000, a calendar of events, information about the magazine itself (including how to order back issues), and information for advertisers. You can also sign up for the *Wealth Management Letter,* a free weekly e-mail newsletter. The ability to browse back issues is currently listed as "coming soon."

Local/Regional

***Giving Forum Online* (http://www.mcf.org/mcf/forum/index.html)**
Giving Forum Online is a free quarterly newspaper published by the Minnesota Council on Foundations, a regional association of grantmakers based in Minneapolis. Content includes information and news on Minnesota philanthropy, current giving issues, and grantmaking research. You'll find highlights of the latest issue plus the full text of selected articles, arranged topically, dating back to 1995. What's New (http://www.mcf.org/mcf/whatsnew/index.html) links to the weekly *Minnesota Giving News.* Here you will find the weekly features, News in Brief, Grants of Note, Jobs, Media Clippings, and People (providing recent news on people in Minnesota grantmaking). There is also a calendar of Minnesota grantmaker deadlines and upcoming training programs, links to Minnesota grantmakers, and press releases. You can sign up for a free weekly e-mail alert, or you can subscribe to the quarterly print newspaper for free, using an online form. A searchable news archive dates back to 1995.

***Grants Action News* (http://assembly.state.ny.us/gan)**
Grants Action News is a monthly publication of the New York State Assembly. Each issue lists funding opportunities at the state and federal levels and from local foundations and organizations. Each listing provides you with eligibility requirements, funding availability, deadlines, and contact information. Issues also feature proposal writing training opportunities.

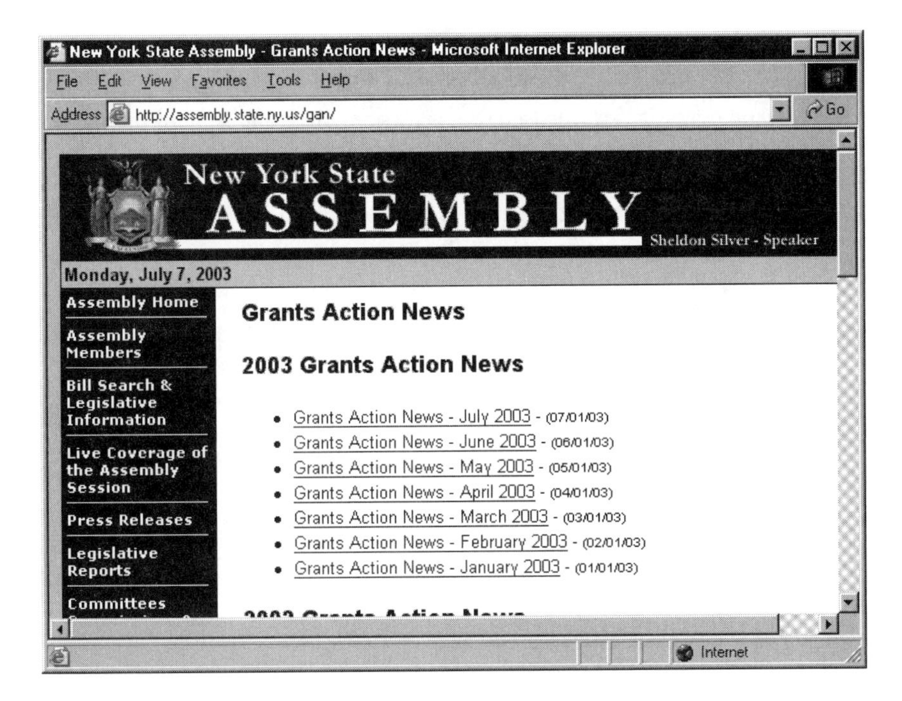

International

International Dateline **(http://www.cof.org/index.cfm?containerID=45&)**
International Dateline is a quarterly newsletter published by the Council on Foundations that provides grantmakers and their associations with information and resources regarding domestic giving on international themes, U.S.-based cross-border grantmaking, and the development of philanthropic structures around the world. Recent features of the newsletter include News and Announcements; A Conversation With . . . , which includes interviews with foundation and program representatives; a link to a conference calendar; and Legal Dimensions, an insert covering legal aspects of international grantmaking. Past issues are available for approximately two years in PDF format.

International Journal of Not-for-Profit Law
(http://www.icnl.org/journal/journal.html)
The *International Journal of Not-for-Profit Law,* a quarterly publication of the International Center for Not-for-Profit Law, is available as a free e-mail subscription. It "provides up-to-date information on legal and regulatory developments affecting the not-for-profit sector in countries around the world." Articles, country reports, case notes, and book reviews are available. The most recent issues are thematically focused, with several articles in each issue addressing a single broad topic. The online and e-mail articles are condensed versions of the print publication. However, country reports feature links to supplementary information. Archived issues date back to September 1998.

Social Economy and Law **(http://www.efc.be/publications/sealabstract.html)**
Published by the European Foundation Centre, *Social Economy and Law* (*SEAL*) is a journal on nonprofit law focused primarily on Central and Eastern Europe and the newly independent states, with expanding coverage of the European Union. The journal seeks to promote an "enabling environment for the social economy (foundations, associations, and other nonprofit organizations) and to enhance the process of legal reform by improving the knowledge of current legal developments throughout Europe." The SEAL initiative is supported by the Charles Stewart Mott Foundation and the Open Society Institute-Budapest. You can browse country reports, editorials, and other features back to the summer 1998 issue.

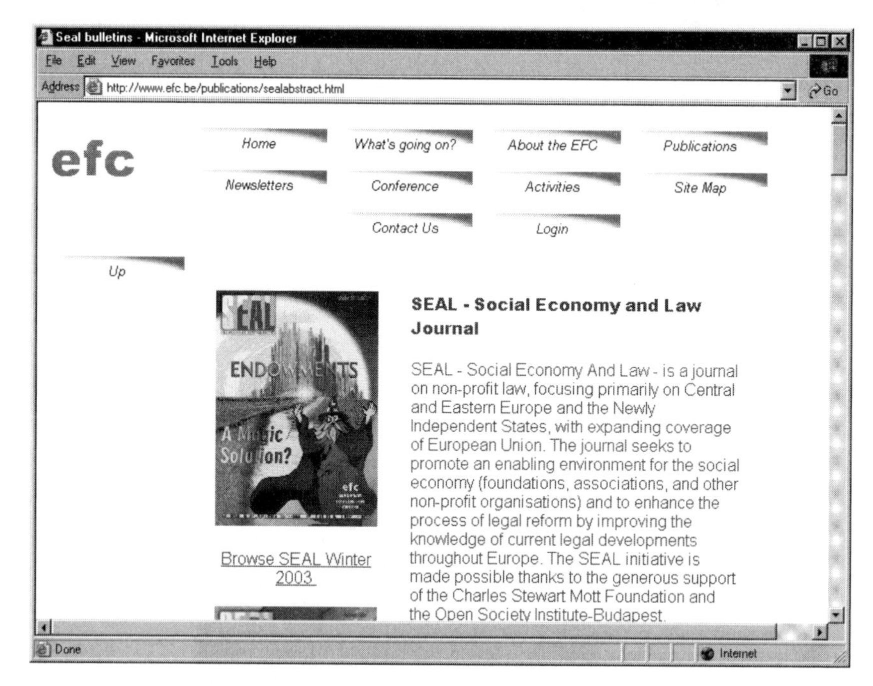

UK Fundraising **(http://www.fundraising.co.uk)**
UK Fundraising provides daily summaries of news items from a variety of sources. The site also has listings of job openings, events, and suppliers, as well as a discussion forum. Though not quite qualifying as full personalization, if you read a news item on a particular topic, links from that page to other resources (jobs, events, books, and so on) will reflect that subject matter.

Online Directories of Journals and Newsletters

Charity Village—Online Publications for the Nonprofit Community (http://www.charityvillage.com/charityvillage/ires2.asp)
Charity Village, an Ontario, Canada-based Web site, presents this alphabetical listing of e-newsletters and other online publications that are useful to nonprofits. The scope is local, national, and international. A maple leaf icon indicates those online publications with a Canadian focus.

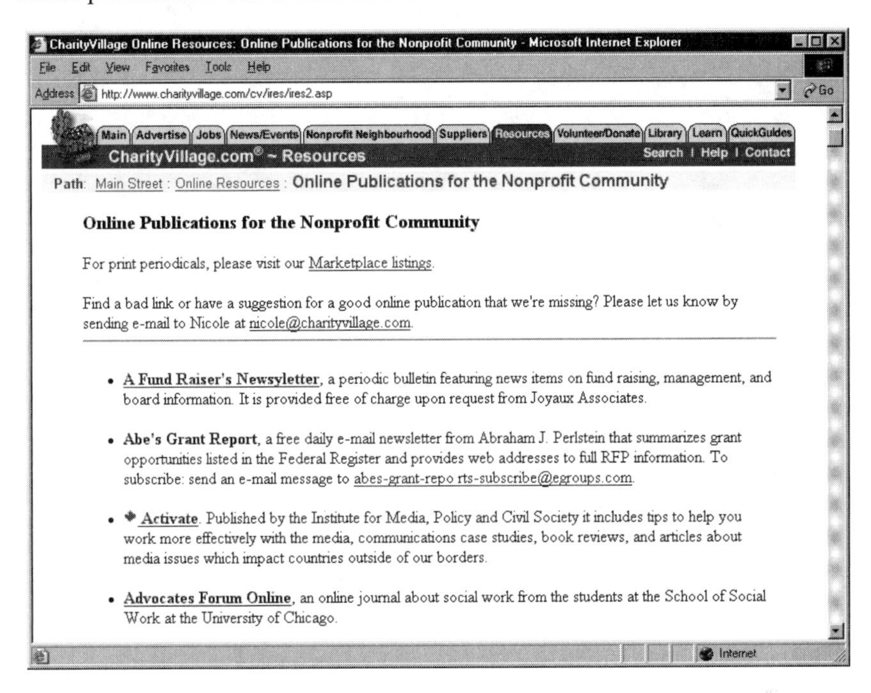

The Foundation Center—*Literature of the Nonprofit Sector Online* (http://fdncenter.org/research/lnps/list.html)
Literature of the Nonprofit Sector Online (*LNPS*), the Foundation Center's online catalog of the Center's library holdings, has a separate, alphabetical list of more than 100 periodicals and newspapers. Links are provided to those publications with online content or information.

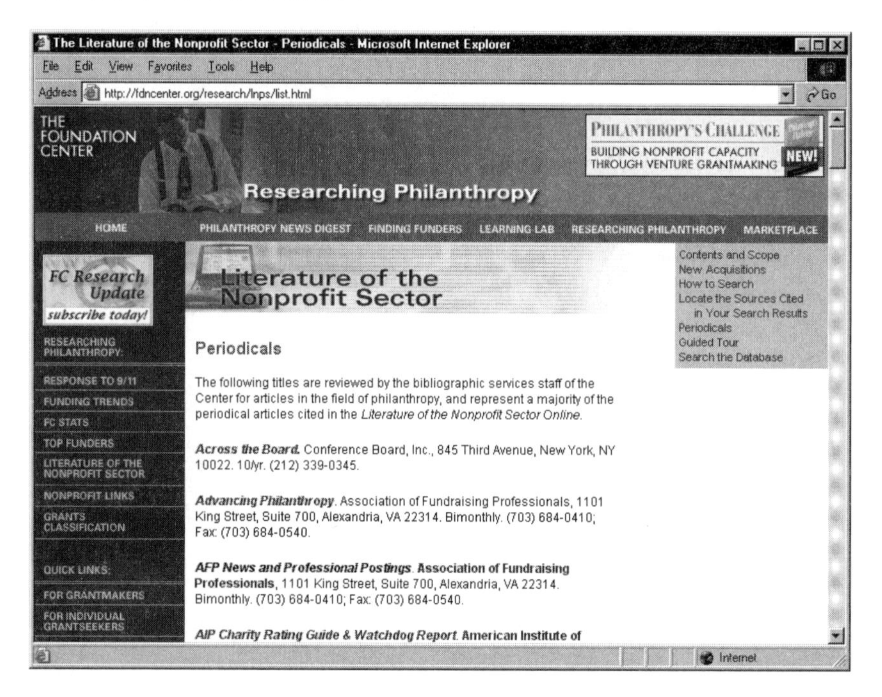

Michigan State University Libraries—Nonprofit Newsletters and Current Awareness Services (http://www.lib.msu.edu/harris23/grants/percat2.htm)
This valuable section of the Michigan State University Libraries' Web site provides a listing of nonprofit newsletters and current awareness services arranged alphabetically.

Conclusion

The overview of nonprofit sector online journals and news services provided in this chapter should be thought of as an introduction only. A curious mind and a focused strategy will assist you in finding additional information and/or the electronic publication that is right for you. Most of the online journals listed here, and many others that you may discover on your own, have an archive of past issues and articles for you to view. Take the time to peruse these archives to find out if a particular publication is right for your needs. If there is an e-mail subscription option, you might want to subscribe to an issue or two to get a feel for the type of content provided. (You can always unsubscribe later if you need to.) To assess a publication's information and its relevance to you or your organization, ask the following questions: How current is the information? How much does a subscription cost? How easy is it to unsubscribe? Is there an archive of past issues? What individual or group is behind it, and do my or my organization's views, politics, and goals mirror theirs? As always, close reading and a critical eye are necessary for evaluating the information you seek and receive online.

The Foundation Center regularly looks for new nonprofit information and news services on the Web and posts new links and annotations to the Links to Nonprofit Resources—Nonprofit News and Publications section of our Web site (http://fdncenter.org/research/npr_links/npr03_news.html). Please check back often to see what new online journals have appeared on the scene that can help keep you well informed.

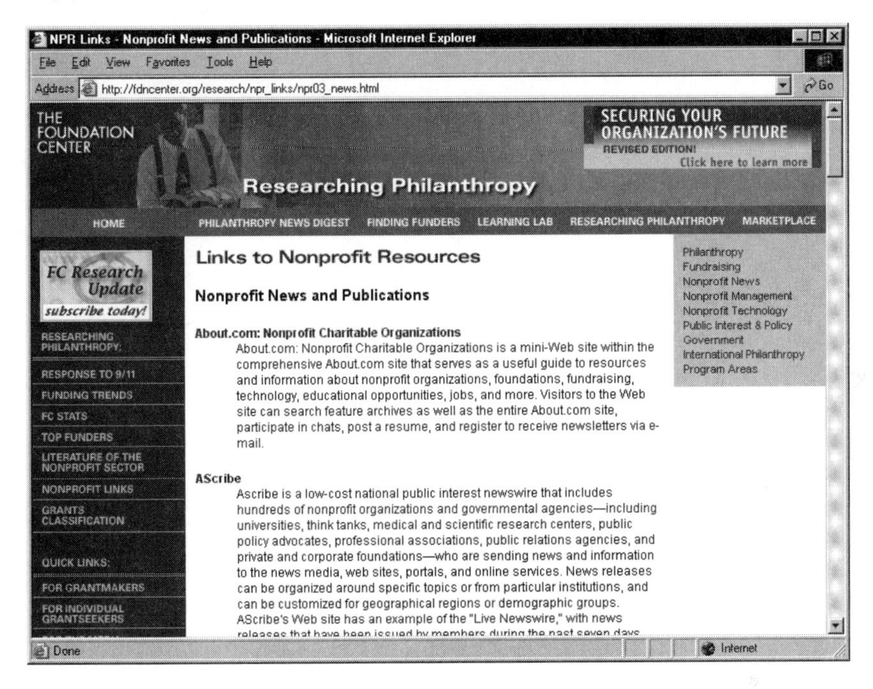

CHAPTER TEN

E-Learning for the Nonprofit Sector

Introduction to E-Learning

In this chapter we will explore the current status of e-learning in the nonprofit sector. As an efficient and relatively inexpensive means of training large groups of far-flung employees, particularly in technical matters, national and multi-national corporations have adopted e-learning with alacrity. Universities have also jumped on the e-learning bandwagon as both a source of additional revenue for non-degree courses and as a way to broaden their student bodies to include those who have day jobs and prefer to take classes on their own schedules at night or on weekends. Nonprofit organizations have been slower to embrace Web-based technology in general and e-learning in particular. But the past few years have born witness to more and more nonprofit Web sites being used to solicit donations, market goods, and serve as informational vehicles about community services and projects. And gradually the number of e-learning opportunities is beginning to proliferate as nonprofits exploit the potential of this new platform to assist staff and volunteers in developing new skills and in learning the many "tricks of the trade" of fundraising and nonprofit management.

It is now possible, for example, to earn a Certificate in Nonprofit Management from the Center on Philanthropy at Indiana University (http://www.philanthropy.iupui.edu), to further professional development by taking a CFRE-accredited Online Course in Fundraising from the Association of Fundraising Professionals (http://www.afpnet.org/professional_advancement/online_education), or to take online tutorials from Neighborhood Networks, which cover topics such as technology, proposal writing, and partnership development (http://wbt.neighborhoodnetworks.org). The Foundation Center's Virtual Classroom (http://fdncenter.org/learn/classroom/index.html) also offers a number of free tutorials and other online learning modules, including a Proposal Writing Short Course in English and in Spanish. (See Chapter 1 for a full description of the Center's Virtual Classroom.)

Some Definitions

"Distance learning" is a very broad term and refers to any and all educational endeavors that utilize CD-ROMs, videotapes, audiotapes, closed-circuit television, radio broadcasting, satellite transmission, online training, and other formats to facilitate learning when student and instructor are separated in time and/or space. Distance learning has a long history, of course, going back to correspondence classes completed through the mail or radio in the mid-20th century. With the rapid growth of the World Wide Web, distance learning has taken on entirely new dimensions. Although used interchangeably with such terms as Web-based learning, online learning, or distributed learning, the term "e-learning," as we'll employ it in this chapter, is primarily associated with activities involving computers and interactive networks. The Web-based environment, with its 24/7 access, speed, and multiple modes of communication is fully exploitable to both complement and extend distance learning efforts. And it enables students to have a variety of truly interactive experiences outside the traditional classroom setting. E-learning also breaks down geographic barriers so that students in rural outposts and overseas can participate as well.

Other terms to become familiar with when embarking on a discussion of e-learning include "synchronous" learning, "asynchronous" learning, "blended" learning, "brick and click" schools, "virtual" classes, online "chat," "application sharing," and "threaded" discussions.

Synchronous learning takes place over the Internet in real time. For example, all students taking a given class may simultaneously view a video stream of a professor delivering a lecture from a remote location and then participate in an online chat with that professor. On the other hand, in an asynchronous mode, a student/learner may log in to a discussion forum after reading lecture notes posted to a Web site earlier in the week and then respond through the forum according to his or her own time schedule. A threaded discussion is simply a version of a regular classroom discussion on a particular topic or topics, except that it is posted to the Web or through e-mail. Blended learning takes advantage of both real-time interactions and asynchronous interaction to create the most flexible learning environment. And in the same vein, brick and click schools combine traditional classroom options with Web-based learning modules.

To further understand these and other terms, visit the glossaries of e-learning terms that can be found on the United States Distance Learning Association Web site (http://www.usdla.org/html/resources/dictionary.htm) or in the American Society for Training & Development's online publication, *Learning Circuits* (http://www.learningcircuits.org/glossary.html).

E-learning has been criticized for being "lonely" for the student. But far from having a solitary experience, e-learners actively engage in creating "learning communities." Loosely analogous to a group of students in a traditional classroom, such electronic communities are built by means of chat rooms, discussion forums, e-mail, and other interactive modes of Web-based communication. Web-based learning communities are especially attractive vehicles for nonprofit organizations to consider as extensions of their traditional services and communication efforts. Information technologies offer new opportunities for nonprofits to network, strengthen ties to the communities they serve, foster collaborations, and build new audiences.

Let's take a look at some of the resources currently available to nonprofit e-learners.

INFORMATION PORTALS

The following Web sites are gateways to information related to distance education and e-learning available on the Web. These sites include links to white papers, educational opportunities, journals, discussion forums, and so on.

AskERIC—Distance Education (http://www.askeric.org/cgi-bin/res.cgi/Educational_Technology/Distance_Education)

AskERIC is a service of the Educational Resources Information Center (ERIC) (http://www.eric.ed.gov), a national information system funded by the U.S. Department of Education that provides, through its 16 subject-specific clearinghouses, a variety of services and products on a broad range of education-related issues. The ERIC database is a high quality information resource that indexes and abstracts many journals and periodicals in the field of education and in related fields. AskERIC's page on distance education primarily focuses on resources for educators interested or engaged in implementing distance education and includes selected Internet resources, online communities, organizations, and ERIC resources.

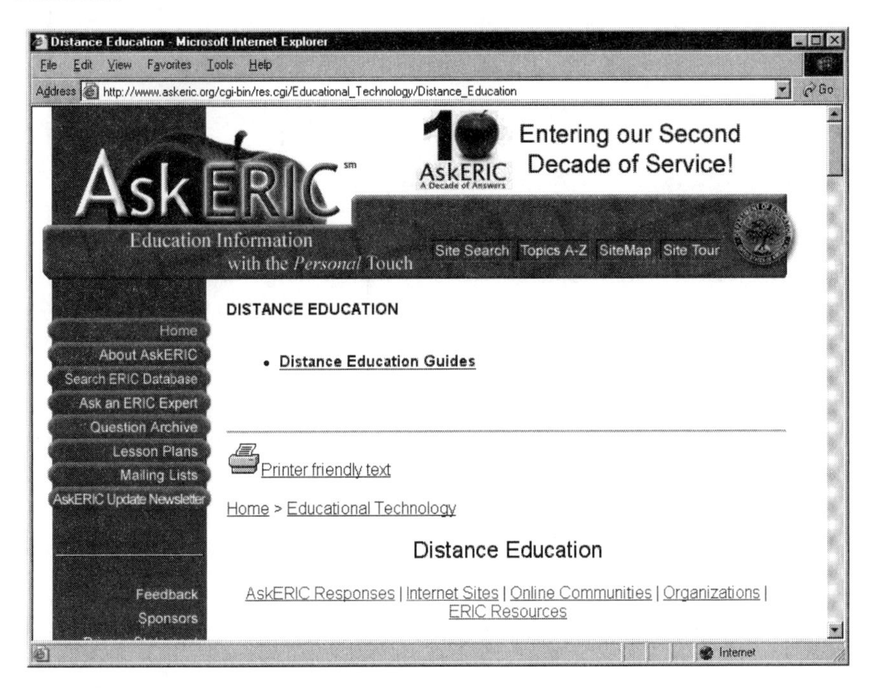

Distance Education Clearinghouse (http://www.uwex.edu/disted/home.html)
Managed and maintained by the University of Wisconsin-Extension, in cooperation with its partners, the Distance Education Clearinghouse is a comprehensive and widely recognized site that brings together distance education information from Wisconsin, national, and international sources. Features include the Keeping Current section, with links to journals, headlines, and conferences and events. The Policies and Guidelines section provides links to Web sites that concentrate on issues such as accessibility, legislation, funding resources, and intellectual property and copyright laws. Other sections include Introducing Distance Education; Programs and Courses; Technology, Teaching, and Learning; Research; Distance Education Community; and Learning Environment.

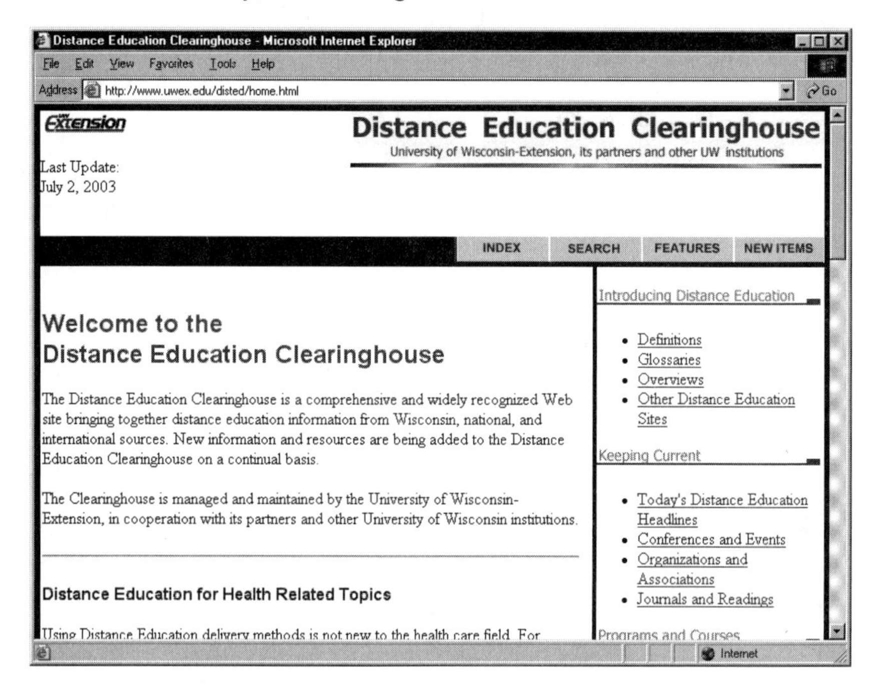

Distance Learning Resource Network (http://www.dlrn.org)
The Distance Learning Resource Network (DLRN) is the dissemination project for the U.S. Department of Education's Star Schools Program, a federally funded distance education program. This site is designed to provide information about Star Schools' projects, courses, and resources, including general information about distance education, how to find online courses, certification for online teaching, instructional methods and strategies, and online tools to assist with designing courses for Web-based instruction (including examples of existing online courses). It also provides networking opportunities through listservs geared toward K-12 students, adult learners, and educators.

elearnspace (http://www.elearnspace.org)
This site is managed by George Siemens, an instructor at Red River College in Winnipeg, Manitoba, Canada. Although unaffiliated with an institution, elearnspace is useful for the range of links it provides that relate to developing instructional technology. It also has many resources for beginners, including resources on the pros and cons of e-learning. The main feature of this site is the

elearnspace blog. Short for Web log, a "blog" consists of regular updates, links, and news posted on a personal site. There are a variety of blog links posted to this site, and they include feature articles, news, trends, and information related to the e-learning industry.

Free Management Library—On-Line Learning (http://www.mapnp.org/library/trng_dev/methods/on_line.htm)

The Free Management Library is a highly integrated library of resources for nonprofit and for-profit organizations. The site is designed to be as user-friendly as possible, with a focus on providing free, online management resources to organizations. It includes a directory of links to specific resources on online education. Categories include Evaluating Online Learning; Learning Portals; Online Discussion Groups; Newsletters, etc.; and Related Library Links.

Peterson's Distance Learning (http://www.petersons.com/distancelearning)

Peterson's Distance Learning, a portal to information on college resources, includes information on distance learning opportunities. From the distance learning page you can search more than 1,100 distance learning programs (select Nonprofit/Public Management from the Course of Study drop-down menu for courses relevant to the nonprofit field) and take a self-assessment quiz to determine whether distance learning or a more traditional educational model is better suited to your learning style. In a unique offering, by means of the appropriately named DistanceLearningProgramsWantYou, the site also allows you to register your personal profile and then permit distance learning programs to contact you.

Seton Hall University—Nonprofit Management Education: Current Offerings in University Based Programs (http://pirate.shu.edu/~mirabero/Kellogg.html)
Based on a study conducted to examine the impact of nonprofit management education programs, Nonprofit Management Education: Current Offerings in University Based Programs, compiled by Seton Hall University faculty, allows you to search for more than 240 colleges and universities with courses in nonprofit management. A listing of six degree-granting nonprofit management programs that are offered online is included.

TeleCampus—Online Course Directory (http://courses.telecampus.edu/subjects/index.cfm)
From New Brunswick, Canada, comes TeleCampus, an exhaustive searchable database of for-fee and free online learning courses around the world. Although registration is recommended, it is not required to use the general search engine for finding online courses. Try typing in the term "nonprofit" in the Search Courses field and you will find close to 100 online courses aimed at e-learners from nonprofit organizations.

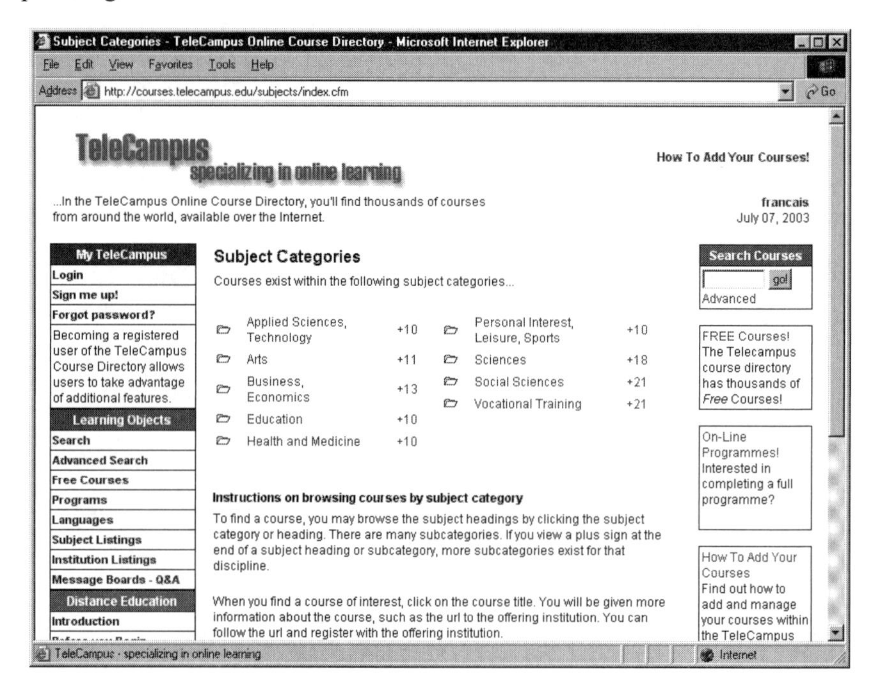

TeleEducation NB's Learning Support— Online Learning: Before You Begin (http://teleeducation.nb.ca/english/article.cfm?sbsec_ID=64&sec_id=9)
TeleEducation NB (New Brunswick) has an online tutorial for new distance learners (http://teleeducation.nb.ca/content/web-guides/english/evaluation), which in addition to orienting the newcomer to e-learning, is a relatively painless way to take your first online learning course. The tutorial helps answer questions such as, "What is distance learning all about?," "How do I choose the right course?," and "Am I ready to be a distance learner?"

United States Distance Learning Association (http://www.usdla.org)
The United States Distance Learning Association's (USDLA) mission is, in part, to provide national leadership in the field of distance learning and to advocate for the growth and use of distance learning. It is an excellent source of general information about distance learning, e-learning, and related resources, including breaking news, the *USDLA Journal,* and distance learning training programs.

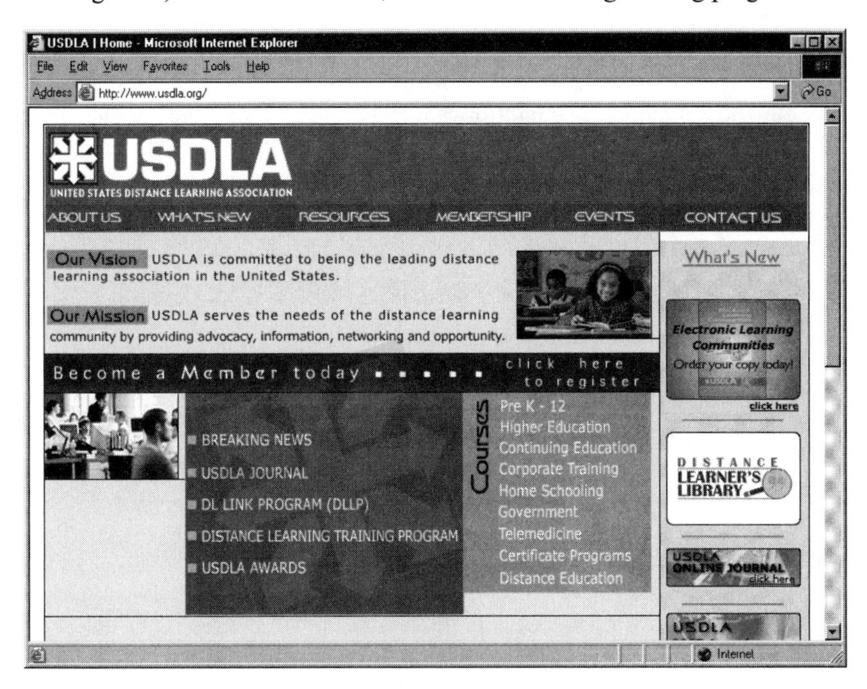

E-LEARNING SITES FOR NONPROFITS

Lack of technological capabilities and limited funding are major drawbacks facing nonprofits interested in e-learning. However, the following Web sites reflect the diverse array of nonprofit e-learning opportunities available, many targeted to specific audiences or subgroups within the nonprofit sector. They include both certificate and non-certificate programs, as well as courses that are free and those that require a fee. Most of the hosting organizations are nonprofit, but a few are not. These sites can be viewed as both resources for e-learners and as a sampling of the ways nonprofit organizations are exploring e-learning. They display varying degrees of sophistication in their level of interactivity and their utilization of the e-learning tools currently available.

Association of Fundraising Professionals—First Course in Fundraising (http://www.afpnet.org/professional_advancement/online_education)
The Association of Fundraising Professional's First Course in Fundraising gives professionals a fundamental understanding of the entire development process. This Web-based "streaming video" course, consisting of eight self-paced modules, covers the basics of managing a fundraising program and provides an overview of fundraising techniques, including annual campaigns, capital campaigns, grant support, and major gifts. The First Course in Fundraising is available both to

association members and non-members for a fee. A brief, free demonstration can be viewed in the Windows Media Player.

Council on Foundations—Grantmaking Basics Online
(http://www.cof.org/Content/General/Display.cfm?contentID=124&)
The Council on Foundations is a membership organization that assists foundation staff, trustees, and board members with their grantmaking activities. Grantmaking Basics Online is an adaptation of the council's print publication, *Grantmaking Basics: A Field Guide for Funders,* with one new chapter written specifically for the Web. Though mostly a straightforward text presentation, some interactivity is evident, primarily through the use of study guides, brief quizzes, and e-mail updates. The Grantmaking Basics Online Mentor Program pairs a beginning grantmaker with an experienced grantmaker (based on similar interests and values). Mentor and mentee work together to achieve the learning objectives of Grantmaking Basics Online.

The Foundation Center's Virtual Classroom
(http://fdncenter.org/learn/classroom/index.html)
The Foundation Center's Virtual Classroom has a number of free online tutorials including Proposal Budgeting Basics, Establishing a Nonprofit Organization, Orientation to the Grantseeking Process, and more. The Virtual Classroom's newest training module, the *FC Search* Interactive Tour, offers an interactive, "hands-on" guided tour of *FC Search: The Foundation Center's Database on CD-ROM.* Based on the content of some of the free classes offered at Foundation Center libraries, the tutorials in the Virtual Classroom are extremely useful to gain an understanding of how to use essential funding resources and the fundamentals of the foundation fundraising process. Coming soon to the Center's Web site will be its first multi-session, interactive Web-based course on proposal writing.

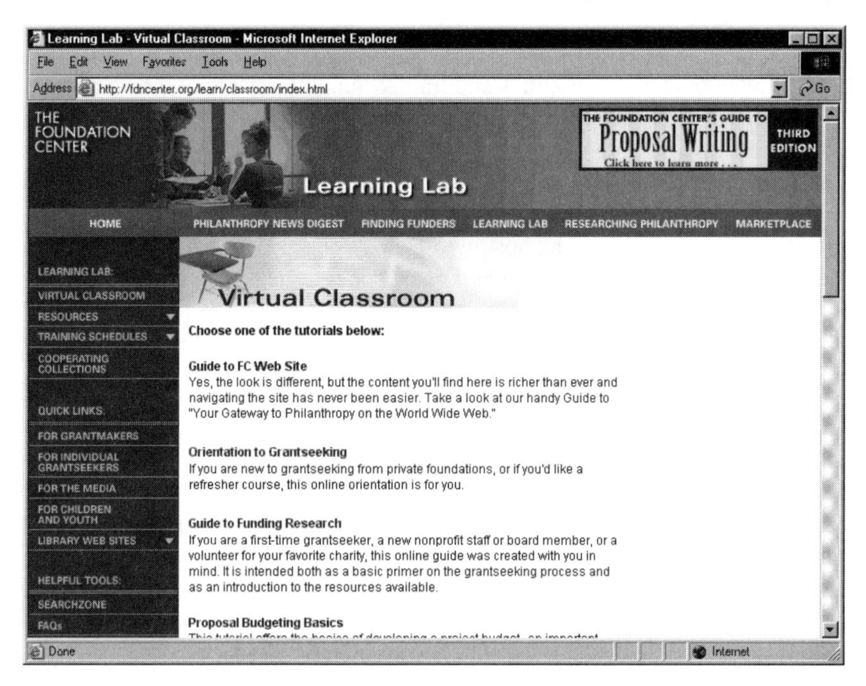

World Wide Learn—Non-Profit & Fundraising Training (http://www.worldwidelearn.com/business-course/nonprofit-fundraising-course.htm)

World Wide Learn is one of the largest Web-based directories of online courses covering more than 150 subject areas, including accredited degree programs, continuing education, and other online training. The Non-Profit & Fundraising Training category provides information and links to online courses on topics such as proposal writing, fundraising basics, community development, business planning, not-for-profit accounting, volunteer management, and more.

Benton Foundation—Open Studio: The Arts Online (http://www.benton.org/openstudio/home.html)

The Benton Foundation, based in Washington, D.C., "seeks to shape the emerging communications environment in the public interest," and to help "nonprofit organizations enhance the impact of their work through strategic use of communications technologies and digital media." One of the foundation's initiatives is Open Studio: The Arts Online. In partnership with the National Endowment for the Arts, this initiative seeks to provide Web access and training to artists and arts organizations to ensure and expand their presence on the Internet.

Free Management Library—Free, On-Line Nonprofit Organization and Management Development Program (http://www.managementhelp.org/np_progs/org_dev.htm)

The Free Management Library, a project of the Management Assistance Program for Nonprofits (http://www.mapfornonprofits.org), offers 13 learning modules in its On-Line Nonprofit Organization and Management Development Program (the Free Nonprofit Micro-eMBA). Modules include Understanding Your Nonprofit, Developing Your Strategic Plan, Developing Your Fundraising Plan, and Designing Your Program Evaluation Plans. These very basic self-paced modules, though not really interactive, do provide in-depth information on each topic, including links to further resources, suggested learning activities, and toolkits.

Leader to Leader Institute (http://www.leadertoleader.org)
The Leader to Leader Institute (formerly known as Peter F. Drucker Foundation for Nonprofit Management) offers a number of online courses. One of the newest is Meeting the Collaboration Challenge Workshop (http://www.leadertoleader.org/collaboration/challenge/workshop/faq.html), which covers the preparation, planning, and development required for successful nonprofit and business alliances. The workshop follows an essentially synchronous model, with telephone conferencing and a small amount of self-paced instruction and homework required in preparation for the conference calls.

nonprofitlearning.com (http://www.nonprofitlearning.com)
The nonprofitlearning.com site is a Web-based delivery platform for online professional development courses for nonprofit executives, staff, and volunteers. Through a collaboration with its partners, nonprofitlearning.com offers a series of four-week, fee-based courses, entitled Fundraising on the Internet: How to Succeed (soon to be available in Spanish), The Medium & the Message: Maximizing Your Online Marketing, Harnessing the Net: Realizing Your Organization's Online Potential, and If You Build It . . . How to Make a Better Nonprofit Web Site. Following the blended model, class formats combine live chat class time, structured Web tours, and collaborative group work, with individual offline readings and assignments.

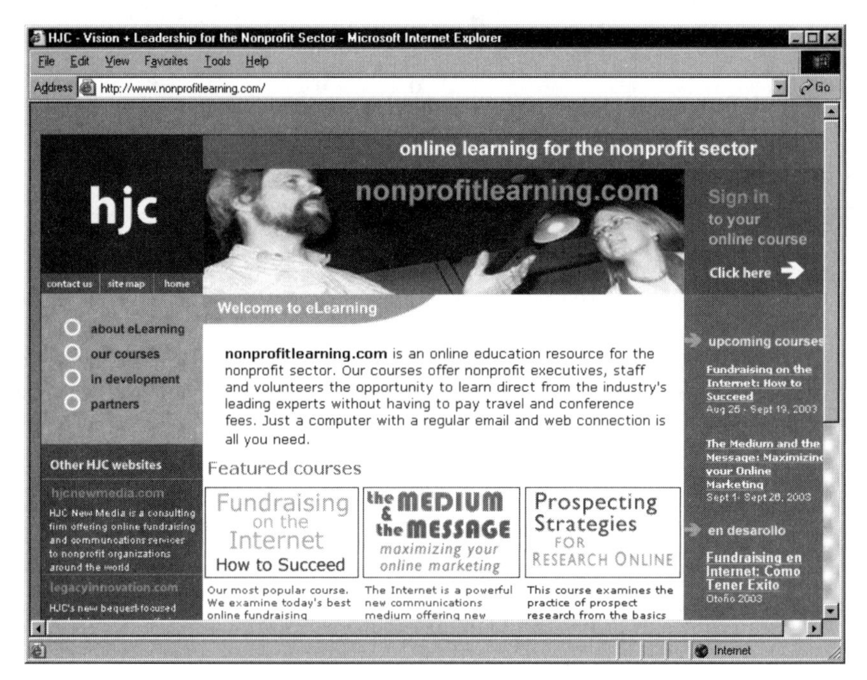

Nonprofit Risk Management Center—Risk Management Tutorials (http://www.nonprofitrisk.org/training/train.htm)

The Nonprofit Risk Management Center provides assistance and resources for community-serving nonprofit organizations. The center has developed several free online tutorials, including the No Surprises Volunteer Risk Management Tutorial, which is designed as a risk assessment guide for managers of volunteer programs, and the Accident Preparation and Response Tutorial, designed to help nonprofits prepare for, and respond to, workplace-related accidents. These online tutorials, while not highly interactive, are a good example of how to provide essential instruction over the Web.

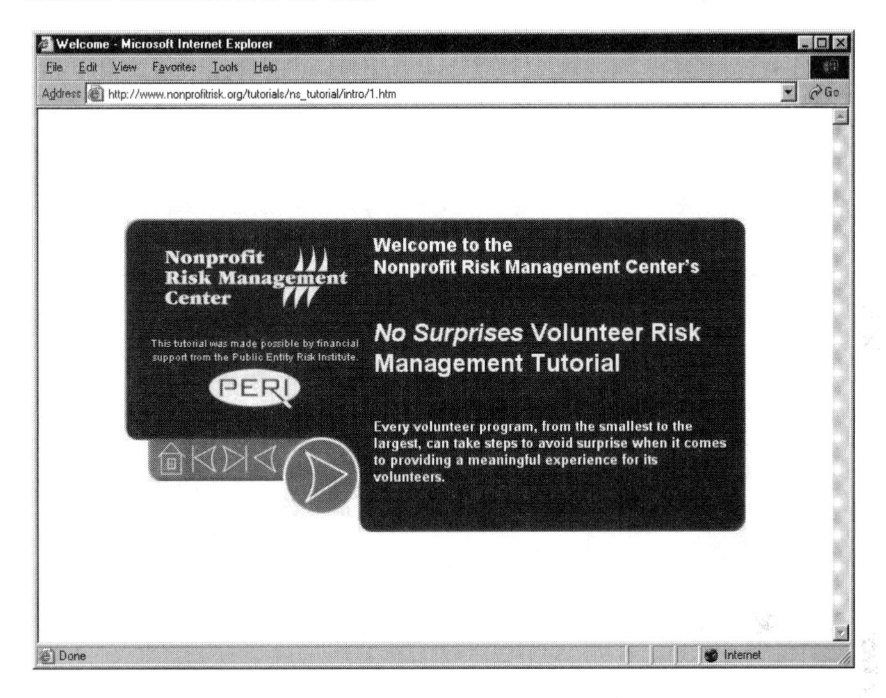

Isoph Institute (http://www.isoph.com)

The Isoph Institute is a for-profit company that assists nonprofit organizations with integrating learning technologies into their programs and is a good source of information on these issues. Isoph provides e-learning authoring tools, a free mini-consultation on e-learning strategy, and online courses exclusively for nonprofit organizations and socially focused organizations. The Isoph Institute recently merged with SmarterOrg (http://www.smarterorg.com) to pool their collective resources and expertise to better serve their customers. Course demonstrations are available after a free registration procedure at the site.

Strategic Press Information Network—SPIN Tutorials (http://www.spinproject.org/resources/tutorials.php3)

The Strategic Press Information Network (SPIN) Project provides comprehensive media technical assistance in the form of training, intensive media strategizing, and resources for nonprofit community organizations across the country. The SPIN Tutorials are a collection of online tutorials aimed at teaching nonprofits effective media strategies and tactics to support social change work. Online tutorials include Strategic Media Plans, News Hooks, Cultivating Relationships with

Reporters, Making News with Your Report, Internet PR, Photo Ops and Media Events, Media Lists, Working with PR Consultants, Setting Up Shop, and a Clips Tipsheet. The tutorials offer candid observations and straightforward suggestions throughout. They are self-paced and rely on text and colorful graphics to carry the weight of the instruction.

TechSoup: Articles—Training
(http://www.techsoup.org/articles.cfm?topicid=9&topic=Training)
TechSoup, a CompuMentor site, is a comprehensive source of technology information for nonprofit organizations. From TechSoup's Training page (in the Articles and News section) you can access a list of online training providers. Each entry is annotated (including contact information) and rated by TechSoup users. Also from the Training page, you can access a listing of online training courses, such as Beginning PC Maintenance, "donated" (read discounted) by SkillSoft, an e-learning solutions company.

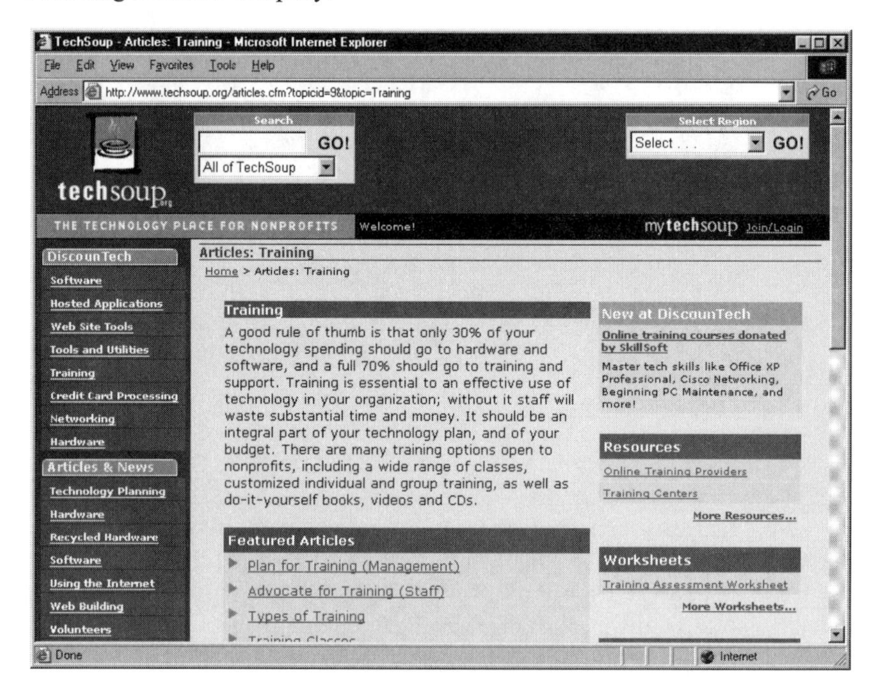

University of Illinois at Chicago—Online Certificate in Nonprofit Management (http://www.uic.edu/cuppa/gci/programs/profed/online/index.htm)
The University of Illinois at Chicago's Online Certificate in Nonprofit Management, a Web-based professional education program, is designed for nonprofit practitioners who want to enhance their knowledge, skills, and contacts. Certificate programs include Financial Management, Nonprofit Governance, Fundraising Management, Marketing Management, Strategic Management, and Operational Management. These courses give the student access to a wide array of online tools, such as Web conferencing, threaded discussions, and synchronous chat. Lectures, class work, and discussions are all posted online. This is a good example of a higher education institution moving into the e-learning field with a side benefit to the nonprofit community.

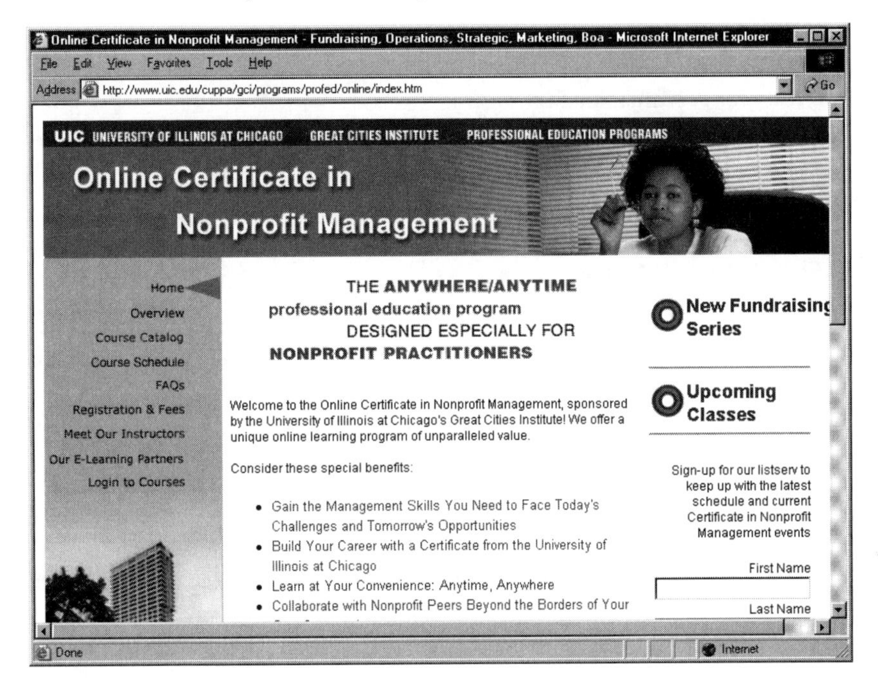

EVALUATION AND ACCREDITATION OF E-LEARNING PROGRAMS

For students pursuing an academic degree on the Internet at the undergraduate or graduate level, accreditation is a means of ascertaining if a Web-based educational program meets a set of standards established by recognized authorities in the field. The Distance Education and Training Council (DETC) (http://www.detc.org) is designated by the Department of Education as the "nationally recognized accrediting agency" under terms of Public Law. The Council for Higher Education Accreditation also recognizes DETC as an accreditation authority. (Both recognize DETC for post-secondary classes only.) An alphabetical listing of accredited institutions, annotated with year first accredited, year of next review, contact information, and programs offered, is available from DETC's site.

The United States Distance Learning Association has a useful, practical guide to understanding the accreditation process and its value (http://www.usdla.org/html/resources/certification.htm).

The *Virtual University Gazette* has an informative FAQ section on distance learning, accreditation, and college degrees (http://www.geteducated.com/articles/dlfaq.htm).

E-LEARNING JOURNALS

E-learning journals provide an excellent introduction to the field, and they are a good way to keep abreast of trends and current issues related to electronic distance learning. The journals listed here reflect just a sample of the variety of offerings currently available on the Web. Not all are exclusively targeted to nonprofits.

The Sophist (http://www.isophinstitute.com/sophist.aspx)

The Sophist is the online newsletter of the Isoph Institute. It is especially useful because it tracks e-learning initiatives in the nonprofit sector. Although only offered periodically, it contains articles on topics such as Web conferencing, synchronous learning, and online communities. You can sign up to receive this newsletter as a free e-mail, or you can access the archive of past issues.

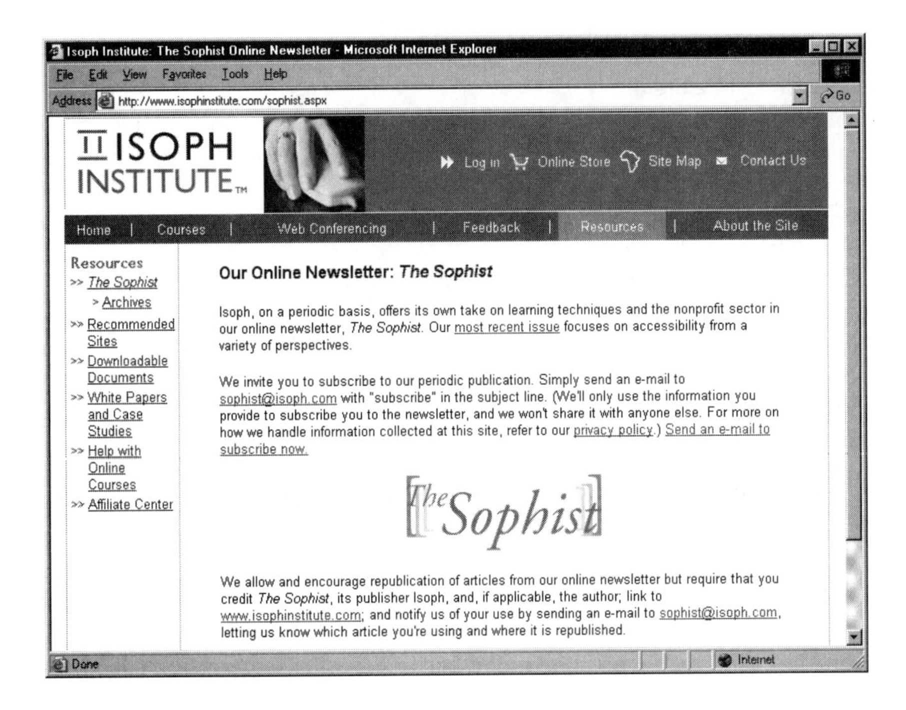

***USDLA Journal* (http://www.usdla.org/html/membership/publications.htm)**

The *USDLA Journal* is the official refereed publication of the United States Distance Learning Association (USDLA), published monthly online. The journal documents the latest developments in the field of distance learning, both in research and in practice, with full-text articles available online and an archive going back to 2000.

***Learning Circuits* (http://www.learningcircuits.org)**

Learning Circuits is the American Society for Training and Development's (http://www.astd.org/index_IE.html) online magazine "all about e-learning." It features articles that cover the latest distance learning technologies, industry news, and distance learning events. Primarily aimed at the distance education market, this magazine is a useful introduction to the universe of e-learning technology.

Association for the Advancement of Education—Digital Library (http://www.aace.org/dl)
Aimed at the academic community, the Digital Library is a valuable online resource of peer-reviewed and published international journal articles and proceedings papers on the latest research, developments, and applications related to all aspects of educational technology and e-learning.

Learning & Training Innovations **(http://www.ltimagazine.com/ltimagazine)**
Learning & Training Innovations, the online journal from Advanstar Communications, takes a somewhat technical approach to news and information about e-learning strategies, developments, and resources. It provides information on building and delivering advanced learning environments for business, government, and higher education, but can be adapted to the general nonprofit environment as well.

Virtual University Gazette **(http://www.geteducated.com/vugaz.htm)**
The *Virtual University Gazette (VUG)* is a free, monthly newsletter covering "the Internet University movement." *VUG* claims to serve more than 30,000 distance learning professionals and students at the adult and post-secondary levels. Written in an informal style, *VUG* offers articles on accreditation and student surveys and has free downloadable publications on a variety of topics, such as the *Best Distance Learning Graduate Schools* series. An archive is available back to 1998. *VUG* is also available as a free, monthly e-mail newsletter.

E-LEARNING LISTSERVS/DISCUSSION GROUPS

Online community forums for anyone involved with e-learning are good communication vehicles to directly connect with others in the nonprofit sector. (For general information on how listservs work, see Chapter 11.)

Learning Circuits (http://www.learningcircuits.org/links.html)

Learning Circuits offers a comprehensive set of links to discussion groups with brief capsules describing each one.

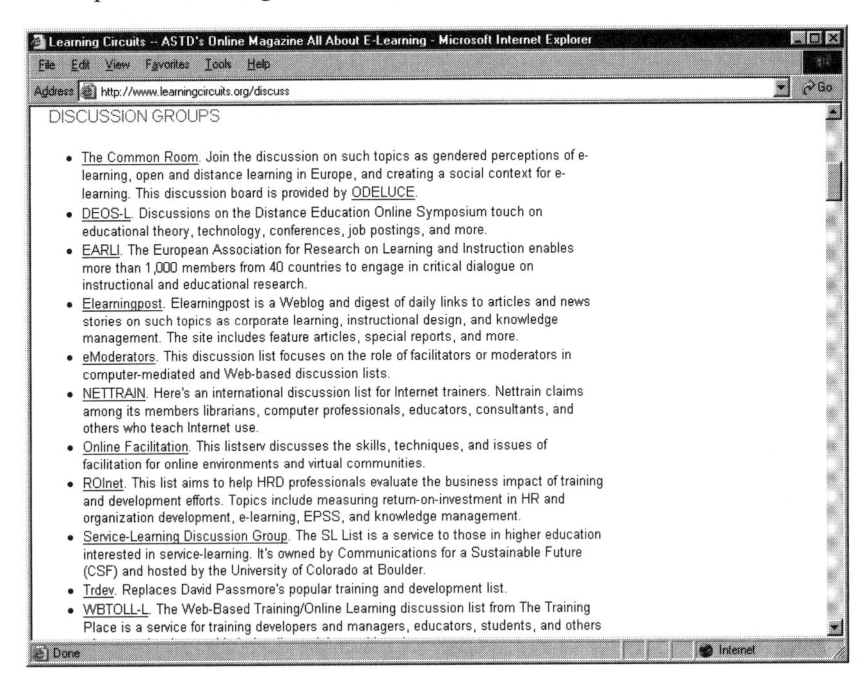

DEOS-L—The Distance Education Online Symposium (http://www.ed.psu.edu/acsde/deos/deos-l/deosl.html)

The DEOS-L listserv is run by the American Center for the Study of Distance Education, which is part of Penn State's College of Education. Discussions touch on educational theory, technology, conferences, job postings, and more. Commands for subscribing and unsubscribing are available on the site.

Elearningpost (http://www.elearningpost.com)

Elearningpost is a digest of daily links to articles and news stories about corporate learning, community building, instructional design, knowledge management, personalization, and more. Besides the daily links, this newsletter contains feature articles and related special reports on many of the above topics. *Elearningpost* is available as a free, daily e-mail newsletter.

Conclusion

Keep in mind that many of the Web sites we've looked at in this chapter include their own e-newsletters, journals, or discussion forums. It is always a good idea when you find a site that is particularly useful or relevant to your needs to browse further to see what features are available, to be sure that you don't miss anything critical.

We hope that the resources highlighted in this chapter will serve as a useful, if not comprehensive, introduction to emerging e-learning opportunities in the non-profit sector. As is obvious from the range of Web sites, e-learning is beginning to strike a positive chord with the nonprofit community.

CHAPTER ELEVEN

Building Community: Listservs, Discussion Forums, and Message Boards

Introduction

The use of the Internet has greatly advanced the ability of grantseekers to share information, advice, and prospecting and other techniques with colleagues. Like a conference that goes on continuously, participants of listservs, discussion forums, and message boards can learn efficiently from each other about useful directories, books and software, upcoming workshops and meetings, fundraising strategies, job announcements, and more. In effect, these interactive communication tools assist in the creation of an electronic learning community that helps users from anywhere in the world establish and strengthen ties, facilitate collaboration, disseminate knowledge, build new audiences, and inform others of the important work they are doing.

It is important to note that there are differences in the ways that members of a given online community interact with one another. These differences are often based upon the technology used and the level of interactivity allowed within a given community. This chapter deals exclusively with two-way communications that take place over the Internet (i.e., listervs, discussion forums, and message boards). These modes of communication allow users to send an e-mail (or submit a posting to a Web board) that is available for viewing by other members of that list (or Web board). Other users in that community can then contribute to the conversation by replying to the original message (or adding to the same "thread") or by starting their own conversation within the group. Two-way communication is integral to the development of an online community.

One-way communications (i.e., online journals, electronic newsletters, e-mail distribution lists, and so on) are not covered in this chapter. (For a discussion of online journals and newsletters, see Chapter 9.)

DEFINITIONS

Before we begin, we should first define some terms that will be used throughout this chapter. The terms "listserv," "discussion list," "discussion forum," "forum," and "discussion group" are common terms that are often used interchangeably to describe a community of subscribers to an electronic mailing list (via e-mail). For the purposes of this chapter, we primarily use the terms "listserv" and "discussion forum."

The terms "Web board" and "message board" are terms interchangeably used to describe interactive communication that takes place over the Web. This is an increasingly popular way to keep in touch with members of a given community because no e-mail account is required, and, therefore, one's e-mail box does not get overloaded with list postings. Web or message board postings are usually organized by topic and many require registration to participate.

"Newsgroups" or "Usenet newsgroups" are similar to listservs and message boards except that a special Newsreader software program is usually required to view and participate in ongoing discussions.

Listservs and Discussion Forums

THE BASICS

Grantseekers can communicate with each other on a wide range of non-profit-related topics by subscribing to relevant listservs or discussion lists. By simply e-mailing a command to the appropriate e-mail address or signing up at a Web site, a grantseeker may join a discussion group in progress and automatically begin to receive any messages posted to that list, as well as respond to messages and inquiries posted by others. Discussion forum management software (such as Listserv, produced by L-Soft International, and one of the most popular programs) is used by list managers to set up and administer lists.

Subscribers use simple e-mail commands to participate. Every listserv has at least two e-mail addresses. There are administrative addresses for subscribing, unsubscribing, and other useful commands, which will be described below. (When sending an e-mail to an administrative address, keep in mind that it is only being read by a computer. Although the commands are simple, misspellings and even slight deviations from the prescribed format will prevent your message from having the desired effect.) The second address is the one you use to send messages to the entire list of subscribers. Keep this important distinction in mind. If you wish to communicate directly with the person who manages the listserv—often referred to as the list "owner," "manager," or "administrator"—you will need to send your message to that individual's personal e-mail address.

Another important distinction in listservs relates to whether the list is moderated or not. Unless it is stated otherwise, it is safe to assume that a list is unmoderated. This means that there is no filter on what gets posted to the list. This does not, however, mean that anything goes. Most lists have a ban on advertising and other specific guidelines as to what constitutes suitable subject matter. Violate these rules, and you will likely hear from the list manager. You may also be barraged by criticism from other subscribers. If the violation is particularly egregious or persistent, the list manager can prevent you from having further contact with list members or can "unsubscribe" you.

If you subscribe to a moderated list, your messages are forwarded to the list "moderator," who then decides whether or not to post them. The moderator—who can be an individual or a committee, paid or unpaid—also reserves the right to edit your material. There are various reasons that lists may be moderated. Often, the list owner wants to keep the discourse tightly focused and seeks to ensure that no offensive messages are distributed to the list. Another reason might be that a list with heavy volume is receiving too many administrative commands, which are being sent mistakenly to the posting address for all subscribers to read. Subscribers may become annoyed and begin leaving the list as a result. A moderated list will involve a slight delay in posting of messages, though rarely more than one day.

HOW TO SUBSCRIBE

The subscribe command varies slightly depending on the listserv management software used by the list manager. The standard procedure to subscribe to most lists requires that you send an e-mail message to the list subscription address (administrative address) and leave the subject or "re:" line blank. In the body of the message, type "subscribe <list name>" (without the brackets or quotes). Some lists require that you include your first and last name after the list name. Others require that you enter the subscribe command in the subject field while leaving the body of the message blank. If you wish to subscribe to a mailing list, follow the specific instructions given by the list or by the referring source. Shortly after sending your subscription request, you will receive an e-mail acknowledging your subscription. You should read the instructions that you receive in the acknowledgement e-mail and save the e-mail or print it out as a paper file. It normally includes a description of the list, appropriate subject matter, rules, and additional commands that you may wish to use in the future—especially the unsubscribe command.

SENDING A MESSAGE: DO'S AND DON'T'S

When you subscribe to a new list, don't be in a hurry to post your first message. "Lurk" for a week or so; that is, read others' messages without posting your own for a while. One of the most valuable aspects of discussion groups is the fact that you have time to consider other postings and your own comments. Therefore, try to focus on sending concise, productive, and relevant comments or questions, not emotional ones. Be sure that your contribution is on target. Consider going to the list's archive, if it exists, to see if your topic has already been covered. Long-time subscribers can become impatient with novices who ask questions that have been thoroughly responded to in the past. If you are in a hurry, apologize up front before posting what could be an "old" topic and ask for advice about where to find the prior discussion.

Before responding to any posting to a list, think about whether you want to respond to an individual directly or post your response to the whole list. Hitting the reply button will normally mean that you are responding to the entire list. A typical mistake that a beginner makes is posting a private comment to the whole list. This can prove embarrassing. You can avoid embarrassment by making it a rule to keep personal comments or confidential information out of any e-mail. It may be unwise, for example, to send your resume over the Internet in response to job announcements that are frequently posted to mailing lists. We've seen people attach their resume and respond with the reply button, sending it to the entire list.

You should name the subject of your message carefully. Some lists have specific subject categories that you should use. These will be included in the initial instructions you receive upon acknowledgment of your subscription. Follow the rules. It will make it a lot easier for you and other subscribers to delete unwanted messages.

Most lists specifically forbid advertising, although a few lists actually invite it. Don't delude yourself into thinking that you're simply supplying information to a community of subscribers. An advertisement will always be recognized for what it is. If you are still unsure about how your communication will be construed, you can e-mail a message to the list owner in advance and ask if your message would be acceptable.

A few other tips that will help you be a productive member of your new list community include:

- If you ask a broad question, invite other subscribers to send their messages directly to you and offer to provide feedback to the list in the form of a summary.
- Be careful with humor. It is very easy to be misunderstood in this medium. You also risk being "flamed" or censured by the other subscribers if your comments are seen as off-base.
- Don't post irrelevant, inane comments. Other subscribers will resent receiving unwanted, seemingly frivolous messages in their e-mail boxes.

MANAGING YOUR MAIL

It's useful to familiarize yourself with some easy commands that will help you keep your mailbox from overflowing, find previous postings on a particular subject, and even protect your privacy by concealing your name and e-mail address on a list. As we've previously mentioned, when you subscribe to a mailing list, your subscription is usually acknowledged with an e-mail message containing the basic commands that you need. If that information is not sufficient, more information on list commands can usually be found by sending a message to the list's administrative address with the word "help" in the body of your message. Whichever list you use, be sure you follow directions carefully and to the letter. Misspellings or incorrect punctuation will result in errors.

A quick overview of the most useful Listserv brand software commands can serve here as an example of how to manage your mail. These commands include digest, postpone, index, and conceal. If you have subscribed to a Listserv list with fairly heavy volume, you may send an e-mail to the administrative address with "set <listname> digest" in the body of the message. This will allow you to receive batches of messages periodically rather than individually as they are posted. The list manager determines the interval at which the digest will be sent—often daily or weekly. To undo this command, send "set <listname> nodigest" in a message to the administrative address.

Lists that are handled by Listserv software also offer the option of postponing your mail if you will be away for a period of time. Send an e-mail to the administrative address with the following words in the body of your message: "set <listname> nomail." When you wish to receive messages once again, you must send a new command to the administrative address. The command for this in Listserv-managed lists is "set <listname> mail."

The index command, available for lists run by Listserv management software, allows you to obtain archive files for a particular list. Send an e-mail to the list's administrative address with the word "index <listname>" in the body of the message.

"Conceal" is a useful command to protect your privacy. Many listservs have a command whereby others may request that a list of subscribers be sent to them via e-mail. In most cases this includes the e-mail address and first and last name of the person (i.e., no more than the information you provide when subscribing). With Listserv brand software, you have the option of sending a "set <listname> conceal" command in order to conceal your address so that it will not be included in any subscriber lists that are requested by others. The command "set <listname> noconceal" will reverse this action.

FINDING LISTS

There are several ways to find suitable listservs. Once you are on a listserv, make sure to read about other related lists that may interest you. If you are seeking a list on a specific topic, and you are already on a related listserv, it is perfectly legitimate to query other subscribers about the best list for you. Listed below are directories of listservs and discussion forums of interest to grantseekers. You may use the indexes provided or try terms such as "fundraising," "foundations," "nonprofit," or "philanthropy" in keyword searches. The following sites may be helpful.

Yahoo! Groups (http://groups.yahoo.com)

Yahoo! Groups, hosted by the Internet company Yahoo!, is an increasingly popular site where users can join existing listservs or establish their own. Registration is required to get a Yahoo! ID and password needed to access forums on Yahoo! Groups. Use some of the terms listed above to search for relevant topics. Individual listings include a description of the forum and important e-mail addresses for subscribing, unsubscribing, posting messages, and the list owner. Most archives are available to members only, though some are accessible to the general public.

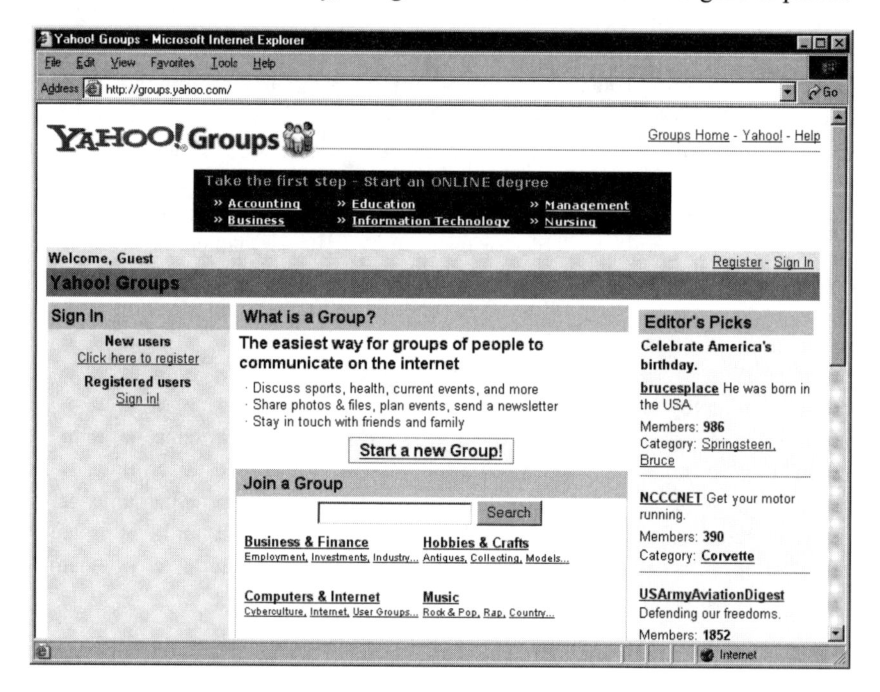

Topica (http://www.topica.com)

Topica.com hosts thousands of newsletters and discussion lists. Visitors can search the site or use the indexes to locate lists of interest. Topica's site makes it easy for readers to control their subscription options (e.g., subscribe, unsubscribe, and vacation hold), find e-mail content with a directory of newsletters organized by subject, or create a newsletter.

L-Soft CataList (http://www.lsoft.com/catalist.html)

L-Soft International is the company that produces and sells the Listserv brand software. Much as Kleenex has done with tissues, L-Soft's Listserv software has established itself as a brand name in the field. From L-Soft's CataList Web site, you can browse any of the more than 72,000 public Listserv lists on the Internet, search for mailing lists of interest, view them by host country or by number of subscribers, and get information about Listserv host sites. You can also subscribe to a list from this site. Available lists are generated automatically from Listserv's lists database, and it is, therefore, always up to date.

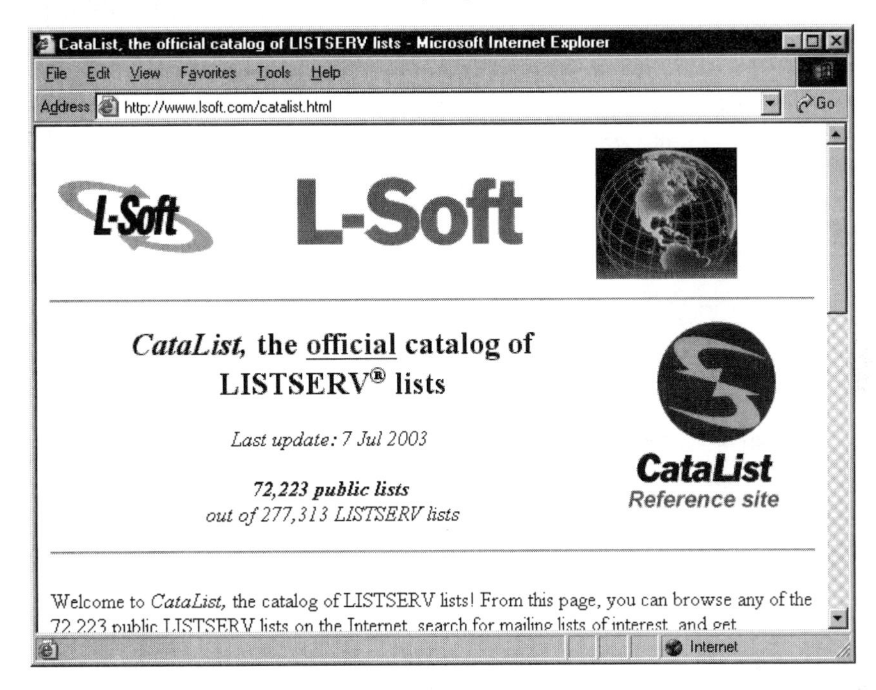

Tile.net (http://www.tile.net)

Tile.net, a part of List-universe.com's collection of Web sites, is designed to provide a comprehensive Internet reference to discussion lists, newsgroups, FTP sites, computer product vendors, and Internet service and Web design companies. You can search each category by keyword, or you can follow the menu-driven option to find the list you are looking for.

Grants and Related Resources—Mailing Lists and Discussion Forums (http://www.lib.msu.edu/harris23/grants/maillist.htm)

Jon Harrison, the Foundation Center Cooperating Collection Supervisor at Michigan State University, operates this site. This excellent Web site contains a listing of discussion lists (and some Web-based message boards) of specific interest to the nonprofit sector. These lists include the name of the list, a brief description, and the subscription and posting addresses for the list.

Charity Village—Online Discussions
(http://www.charityvillage.com/charityvillage/stand.html)
Charity Village, a Web site for Canadian charities and nonprofits, contains a valuable list of e-mail discussion groups, as well as lists of Usenet newsgroups, Web boards, and Internet Relay Chat (IRC) rooms/chatlines. Listings are for both U.S. and Canadian-based online discussion services.

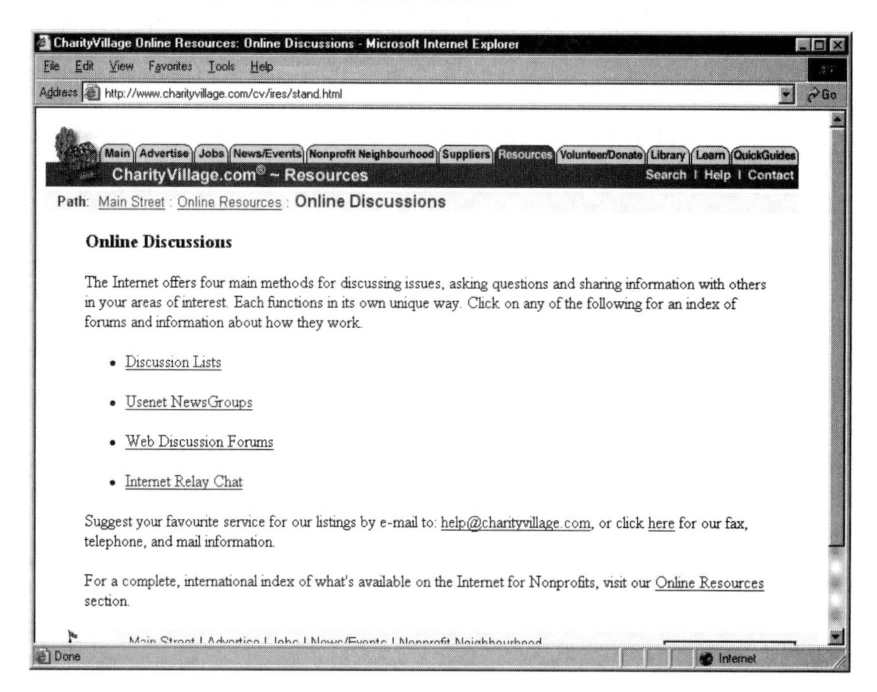

Listservs and Discussion Forums—Some Examples

CHARITYCHANNEL FORUMS

Grantseekers interested in participating in a community of fundraisers and nonprofit representatives via listservs or discussion forums for fundraising and nonprofit issues should not miss CharityChannel, which features an impressive collection of discussion lists for nonprofit professionals on its Forums page at http://www.charitychannel.com/resources/forums/index.html. Currently at CharityChannel Forums, there are more than 1.5 million postings each month on more than 150 moderated forums. With the help of many volunteers, Stephen Nill has developed and promoted these forums with clear instructions on how to use the lists, subscribe, unsubscribe, receive postings in digest forms, and access archives. (CharityChannel Forums use L-Soft's Listserv list management software and commands.) At CharityChannel's home page, you can simply click on the Forum Descriptions link for a list of forum categories. You may subscribe directly from the Web site or via standard e-mail commands. When subscribing to a CharityChannel Forum, always leave the subject line of your message blank.

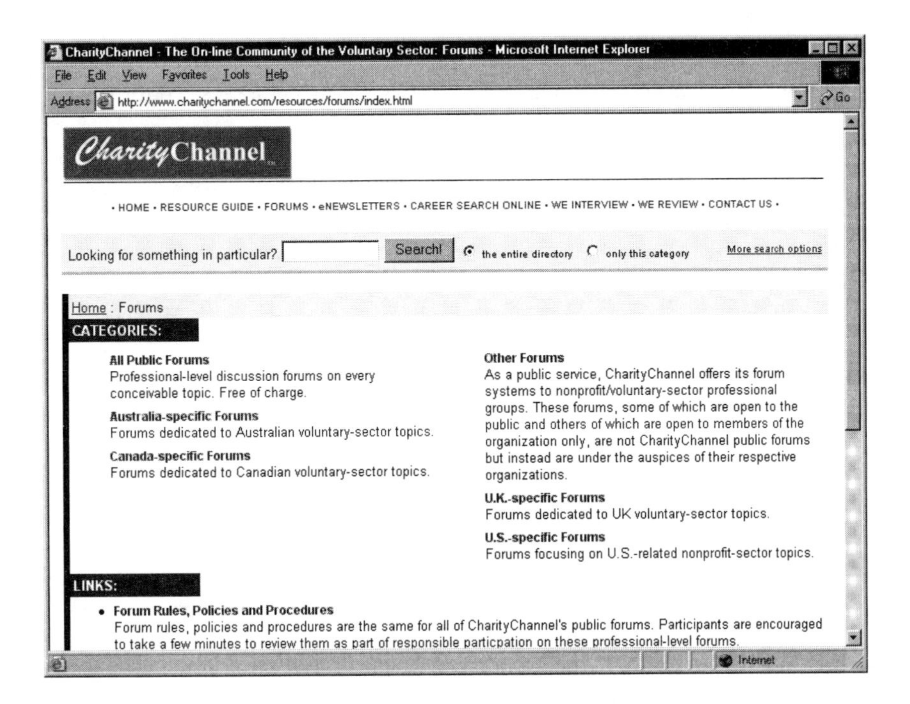

When you subscribe to a list from the CharityChannel Forum site, an e-mail will be sent to you asking you to reply by e-mail or to click on the URL in the message in order to verify the subscription. (This will prevent others from using your e-mail address to subscribe.) You will then receive a message indicating that your subscription has been accepted. From that point on, messages posted to the list will arrive in your e-mailbox. You don't need to go to the Web site to participate in the discussion forums, but you may want to visit the site for easy access to any of the lists' archives, to subscribe to other lists, or to see additional content. Additionally, like many message boards and newsgroups, CharityChannel discussion lists can be viewed on the Web exclusively if you'd like to keep your e-mail box clear of listserv postings.

Postings that promote a service, product, or other commercial interest are not permitted on CharityChannel Forums, but text-based classified ads are available for a fee.

Several of the CharityChannel lists are described below, along with a compilation of other discussion lists of interest to development professionals, prospect researchers, and grantseekers. Each example includes the name of the list, a brief summary of the kinds of topics addressed by the list community, subscription and posting addresses, archive address (if one exists), and other useful information, where available. All CharityChannel Forums are moderated lists to maintain the quality of the postings.

CHARITYTALK

This is CharityChannel's flagship discussion list, established in 1994 for those interested in hearing from people from a variety of specialties, not necessarily their own. CHARITYTALK, "The 'Big Tent' Discussion List of the Nonprofit World," invites people from every segment of the nonprofit sector to participate, with an emphasis on philanthropy. Fund development professionals, nonprofit

CEOs, college presidents, consultants, accountants, academics, and others are all encouraged to contribute their expertise on a wide range of topics. Traffic is fairly heavy on this list.

To subscribe to CHARITYTALK, use the Web form found at CharityChannel's Forums page or send an e-mail message to listserv@charitychannel.com. In the body of your message, type: subscribe charitytalk <your name>. To post a message to the list, send your e-mail to charitytalk@charitychannel.com. CHARITYTALK's archive can be found at http://charitychannel.com/archives/charitytalk.html.

CONSULTANTS

Originally established in 1997, CONSULTANTS is now among the CharityChannel forums. Its audience has remained stable—fundraising consultants or those interested in consulting. The purpose of the list is to discuss issues related to philanthropy and its associated services. Points of discussion may include such aspects of consulting to nonprofit organizations as marketing, client/consultant relations, fees and collection, ethics, strategies, and resources.

To subscribe to CONSULTANTS, use the Web form found at CharityChannel's Forums page or send an e-mail message to listserv@charitychannel.com. In the body of your message, type: subscribe consultants <your name>. To post a message to the list, send your e-mail to consultants@charitychannel.com. CONSULTANTS' archive can be found at http://charitychannel.com/archives/consultants.html.

GIFTPLAN

Established in March 1997, this discussion group is now among the CharityChannel forums. It focuses mainly on issues related to planned giving in the United States.

To subscribe to GIFTPLAN, use the Web form found at CharityChannel's Forums page or send an e-mail message to listserv@charitychannel.com. In the body of your message, type: subscribe giftplan <your name>. To post a message to the list, send your e-mail to giftplan@charitychannel.com. GIFTPLAN's archive can be found at http://charitychannel.com/archives/giftplan.html.

GRANTS

A popular list among development professionals and proposal writers, GRANTS focuses on all aspects of grants and foundations. Grantseeking in any field, foundation formation, foundation funding, and foundation administration are all suitable topics.

To subscribe to GRANTS, use the Web form found at CharityChannel's Forums page or send an e-mail message to listserv@charitychannel.com. In the body of your message, type: subscribe grants <your name>. To post a message to the list, send your e-mail to grants@charitychannel.com. GRANTS' archive can be found at http://charitychannel.com/archives/grants.html.

COUNCIL FOR ADVANCEMENT AND SUPPORT OF EDUCATION LISTSERVS

The Council for Advancement and Support of Education (CASE) owns and operates several mailing lists related to fundraising on its Listservs page at http://www.case.org/resources/listservs.cfm. Below we describe just a few of CASE's many listserv offerings.

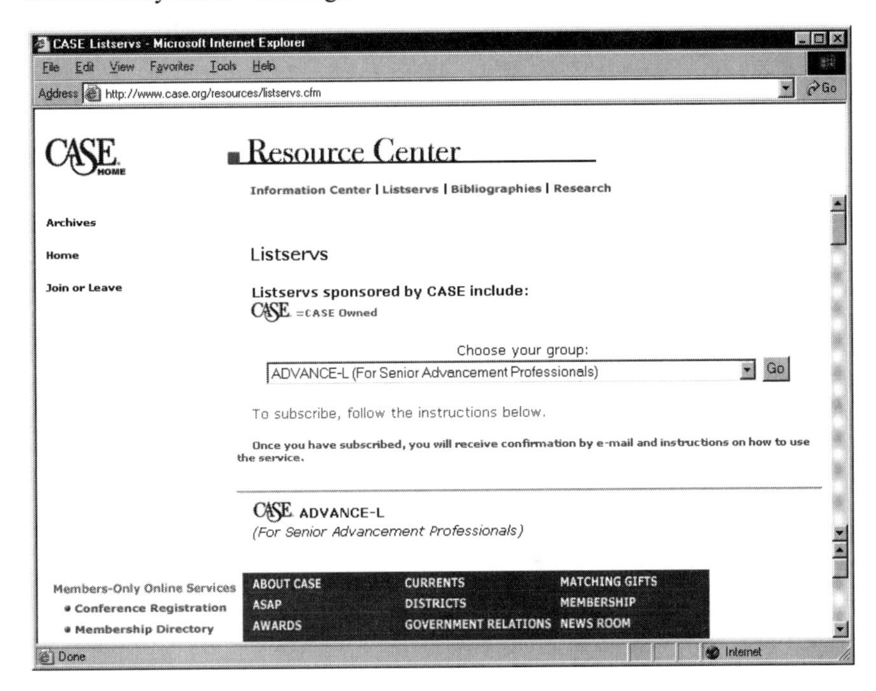

ALUMNI-L

This unmoderated list is dedicated to the interchange of ideas and information among alumni relations and professionals at colleges, universities, and independent schools. Topics include alumni education, working with boards and volunteers, alumni training and workshop programs, activities of the Council for Advancement and Support of Education, cooperation with one's development office, and more. Traffic is fairly heavy on this list. It is not unusual to receive multiple messages every day.

To subscribe to ALUMNI-L, use the Web form found at CASE's Listservs page or send an e-mail message to listserv@hermes.case.edu. In the body of your message, type: subscribe alumni-l <your name>. To post a message to the list, send your e-mail to alumni-l@hermes.case.edu. The address of the archive is http://hermes.case.org/archives/alumni-l.html. You will need to register in order to access it.

EPHILANTHROPY-L

This CASE list covers all aspects of fundraising over the Web. This includes setting up a donation service on nonprofit Web sites and information on how to conduct fundraising activities using online resources.

To subscribe to EPHILANTHROPY-L, use the Web form found at CASE's Listservs page or send an e-mail message to listserv@hermes.case.edu. In the body of your message, type: subscribe ephilanthropy-l <your name>. To post a message to the list, send your e-mail to ephilanthropy-l@hermes.case.edu. The address of the archive is http://hermes.case.org/archives/ephilanthropy-l.html. You will need to register in order to access it.

FUNDSVCS

This list is presented by CASE as a service to the advancement and gift processing professions. It is for fundraising services and related technical discussions only. Topics include fundraising software options; IRS, CASE, and FASB/GASB rules and regulations; and pretty much any topic of interest to the "back office" operation within a fundraising program. This list is maintained by John H. Taylor, director of Duke University's Office of Alumni and Development Records.

To subscribe to FUNDSVCS, use the Web form found at CASE's Listservs page or send an e-mail message to listserv@hermes.case.org. In the body of your message, type: subscribe fundsvcs <yourname>. To post a message to the list, send your e-mail to fundsvcs@hermes.case.org. The address of the archive is http://hermes.case.org/archives/fundsvcs.html. You will need to register in order to access it.

OTHER DISCUSSION FORUMS OF INTEREST

FUNDLIST

This list, operated out of John Hopkins University, is primarily for fundraising professionals whose emphasis is on education. FUNDLIST is heavily used, with a wide range of topics, including annual campaigns, planned giving, development, ethics, policy/procedures, and many others.

To subscribe to FUNDLIST, send an e-mail message to listproc@listproc.hcf.jhu.edu. In the body of your message, type: subscribe fundlist <your name>. To post a message to the list, send your e-mail to fundlist@listproc.hcf.jhu.edu.

PRSPCT-L

PRSPCT-L, hosted by Yahoo! Groups, is a highly popular discussion list for prospect researchers and development professionals in education and service organizations. Participants share resources and techniques on a wide range of topics, including rating prospects and products, fundraising, ethics, and job announcements. This is a busy, well-focused list, full of research leads.

To subscribe to PRSPCT-L, go to http://groups.yahoo.com/group/PRSPCT-L and register on the site. It is very convenient to sign up for this list on the Yahoo! Groups site, and you have the option either to receive messages directly in your e-mail box or to access them at the Web site. You can also view and search the archive on this Web site.

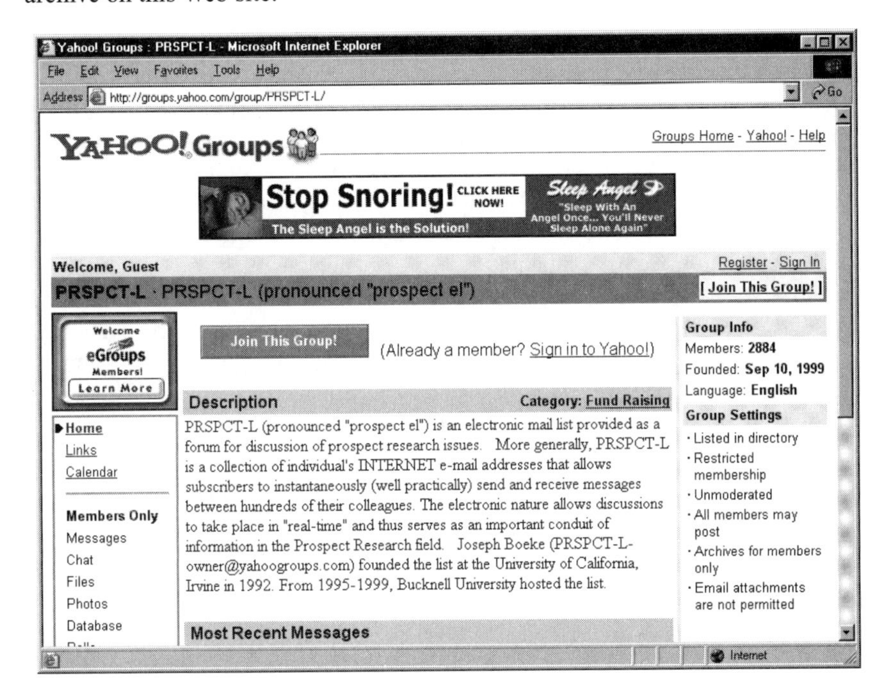

MESSAGE BOARDS AND NEWSGROUPS

Other examples of communities on the Internet available to the grantseeker take the form of message boards and newsgroups.

Message boards (or Web boards), available at some nonprofit-related Web sites, allow you to participate in ongoing discussions organized by topic. It is not necessary to have additional software other than your Internet browser in order to participate in such forums, though registration may be required. Web-based message boards can be very convenient. If you opt for one, your e-mail box won't fill up with messages that are not of interest to you. If you are seeking information or a dialogue on a specific subject, you can start your own thread or go to an appropriate message board to see if the topic has been covered.

Etiquette on message boards is very similar to that for listservs and discussion forums. Review the advice given in "Sending a Message: Do's and Don'ts" earlier in this chapter.

Since a critical mass of posters is essential to get a message board off and running and for it to be successful, its existence must be well publicized by the hosting individual or organization, through mailing lists and other promotional vehicles. Or the host's Web site must be compelling enough to attract repeat visitors.

The Foundation Center maintains two highly popular message boards in the *Philanthropy News Digest* area of its site (http://www.fdncenter.org/pnd). PND Talk (http://members4.boardhost.com/PNDtalk) is a very active forum where members of the nonprofit philanthropic community—development professionals, consultants, individual grantseekers, and others—share advice, insights, and questions related to the changing world of philanthropy.

Arts Talk (http://members5.boardhost.com/ARTStalk), the second *PND* message board, is devoted to questions and observations related to funding for the arts.

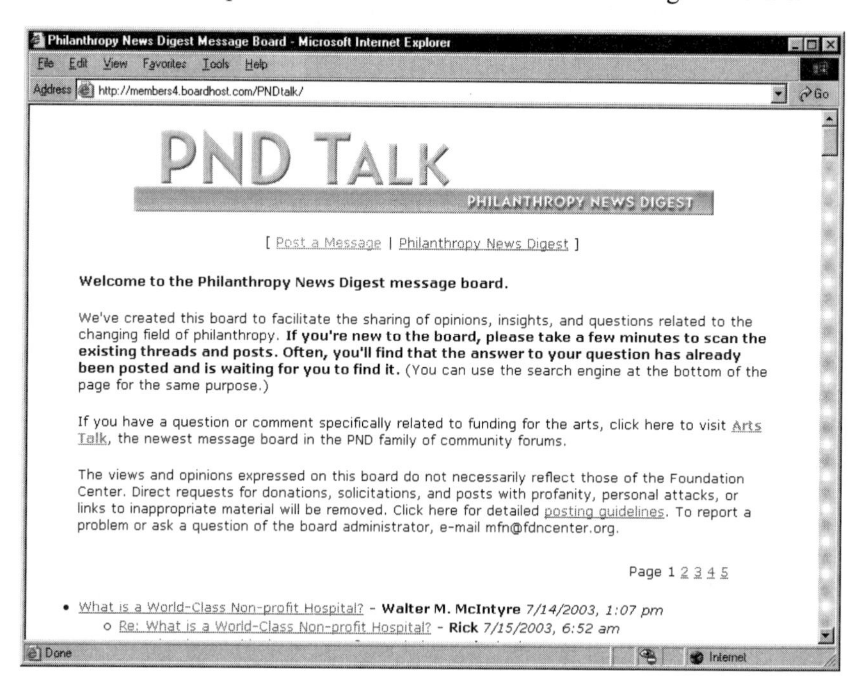

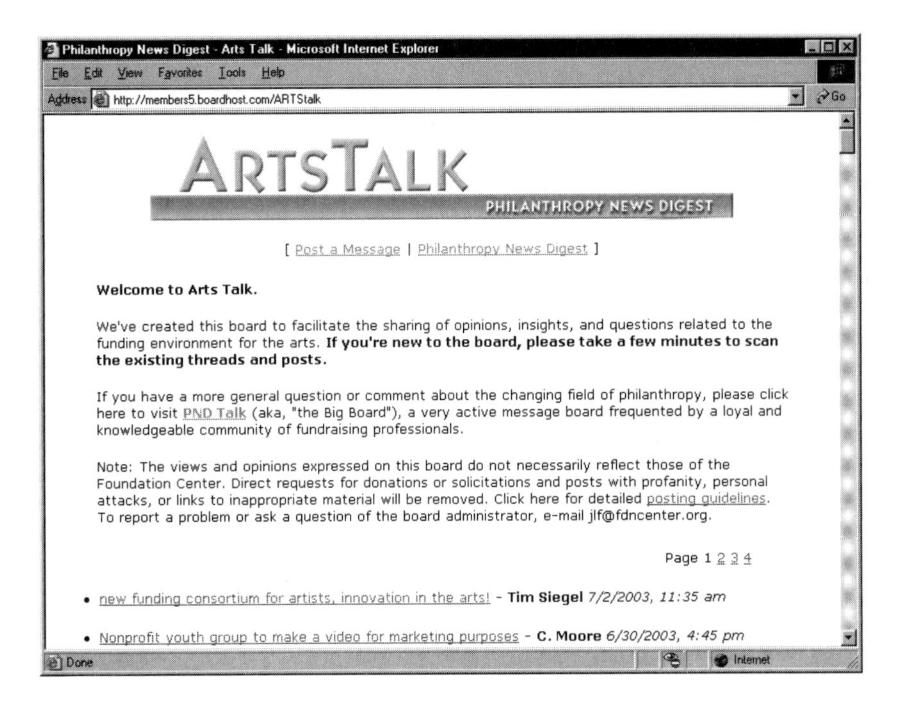

In Usenet newsgroups, people with similar interests chat about their favorite topic or exchange ideas, as they would on a discussion list. Newsgroups, however, do not operate by e-mail and are not moderated or owned by anyone. To access a newsgroup, you need Newsreader—software that is usually provided through your Internet Service Provider. You must then go to the Usenet group where you can view previously posted messages, which you will find organized by topic. To participate, simply post an article (message). Before starting a new thread (topic), you are advised to read the newsgroup's FAQs to see if the topic has already been thoroughly covered.

Each newsgroup usually has a name that signifies the subject matter covered. For example, newsgroups of interest to the nonprofit sector include soc.org.nonprofit, alt.activism, and alt.society.civil-liberties, to name just three. Usenet newsgroups are hosted by a wide range of organizations, from government agencies and large universities to high schools and businesses. Among the periodic postings in newsgroups, you will find listings of other active newsgroups. An official Usenet primer is available from Google Groups (http://groups.google.com/googlegroups/help.html), which features a searchable archive of hundreds of millions of messages to Usenet since 1981. You can also visit http://www.tile.net, the Web site discussed earlier, to search for newsgroups.

Conclusion

As a true nonprofit online learning community begins to take shape, grantseekers have numerous opportunities to take advantage of a variety of methods to interact electronically with one another. These interactions can be productive, inexpensive, and convenient. Some of the interactive capabilities not covered in this chapter (e.g., live chat and real-time conferencing) require more planning and organizing and may, therefore, be more suitable for specialty uses. However, many grantseekers and others have found that an easy way to get started communicating with colleagues is to subscribe to a discussion list or visit a message board. If you lose interest in a forum or message board, you can always unsubscribe and/or try another. Once you are involved in a discussion list or message board, you will find frequent postings from colleagues and other experts providing technical (and other) advice and pointing the way to the growing resources available over the Internet.

APPENDIX A

General Search Engines

Here is a brief introduction to thirteen sites (twelve search engines and one site *about* search engines), that we hope will provide you with additional information to be successful at grantseeking on the Web.

Each search engine offers different sets of parameters that you must follow in order to get the results you desire. While one search engine may automatically default to searching derivatives of a word (for example: fund, funds, funding, funder), others will not, and you will need to specify each form of a word separately. Still others will permit you to use the asterisk (*) to request all word endings after the root. Some permit you to indicate with a plus sign (+) which terms *must* be present in your results, while still others let you use the word "and." It is important to remember that search engines are not as smart as humans. That is, they don't really "know" what you are looking for or anything at all. They will only search for what you tell them to search for, within the confines of the software's programming. The burden is on you as the searcher to determine the best way to use a particular search engine. It is essential, therefore, to look for help files that are available at any search engine you visit, until you are fully familiar with its features and limitations.

In deciding which search engine to use, it is important to be aware that each employs a different methodology for organizing and locating material that will affect your results. Directory sites typically utilize human editors to index sites and organize them by categories. Crawler sites, on the other hand, search Web pages to locate matches for your search terms. Metacrawlers go a step further, actually utilizing several crawlers at once for a more comprehensive search. Directory sites can be useful early on in your search, especially if you have only a vague sense of your topic and are looking for help in narrowing it down. Category and subcategory listings can provide you with ideas about how to proceed with your searching.

Other differences you'll appreciate among search engines are in the amount of customization they provide and the presence of additional features and functionality that can assist your search. More and more search engines are adding features that extend your options for locating information, including the ability to search for a specific type of information, such as news, MP3 or audio files, video files, or images. We have noted these features and others in the listing below to give you a sense of the unique aspects of each site.

Once you find a search engine you like, you might be tempted to rely on it all the time, to the exclusion of others. This would be a mistake. Although there is substantial overlap, each search engine indexes only a fraction of the total content of the World Wide Web. More importantly, search engines may index different sets of Web pages. For this reason, it is important to utilize more than one search engine to ensure the most comprehensive search results. Sophisticated Web searchers use different search engines to generate different kinds of "hits," depending on whether they want to broaden or narrow their search, focus on private or government or international sites, and so on. As you become more familiar with search engines, no doubt you will come up with your own list of favorites, depending on the circumstances.

Search Engine Watch (http://www.searchenginewatch.com)
This is *the* place to go on the Internet to find information on search engines. Search Engine Watch has at-a-glance search tip charts, a searchable database of Web search engines, reviews and ratings, and links to topical articles. You can even subscribe to a free e-mail newsletter to keep up with the latest changes regarding your old favorites, while keeping an eye out for new ones. Separate browsable directories are available for major and specialty search engines. If you haven't yet found a search engine to your liking, consult Search Engine Watch to identify one. Try the First-Time Visit? link for a handy overview of what's on the site and how to use it.

About.com (http://about.com)

About.com is an Internet directory with hundreds of expert topic-specific "guides." Hundreds of subject areas are grouped into 23 channels, each administered by a guide who has formal training and life experience in his or her particular subject matter. Each guide provides links to hundreds of the best Web sites on the Internet, as well as original content.

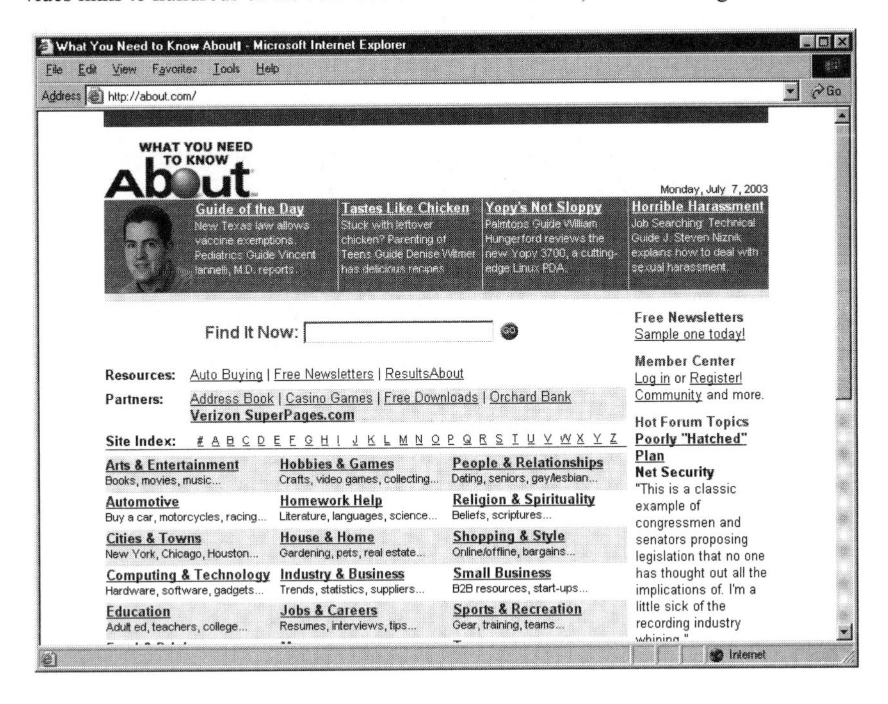

AlltheWeb.com (http://www.alltheweb.com)

AlltheWeb is known for the comprehensiveness and relevancy of results it returns. It's proprietary FAST technology allows you to use Boolean operators such as "and," "or," and "not" for greater precision in your searching. At AlltheWeb you can search Web pages or look specifically for pictures, news, videos, or MP3 or FTP files. The Advanced Search option lets you filter by domain (.org, .com, etc.), content, or other properties for a super-customized search. And the site offers several specialty search solutions, including Scirus science information search.

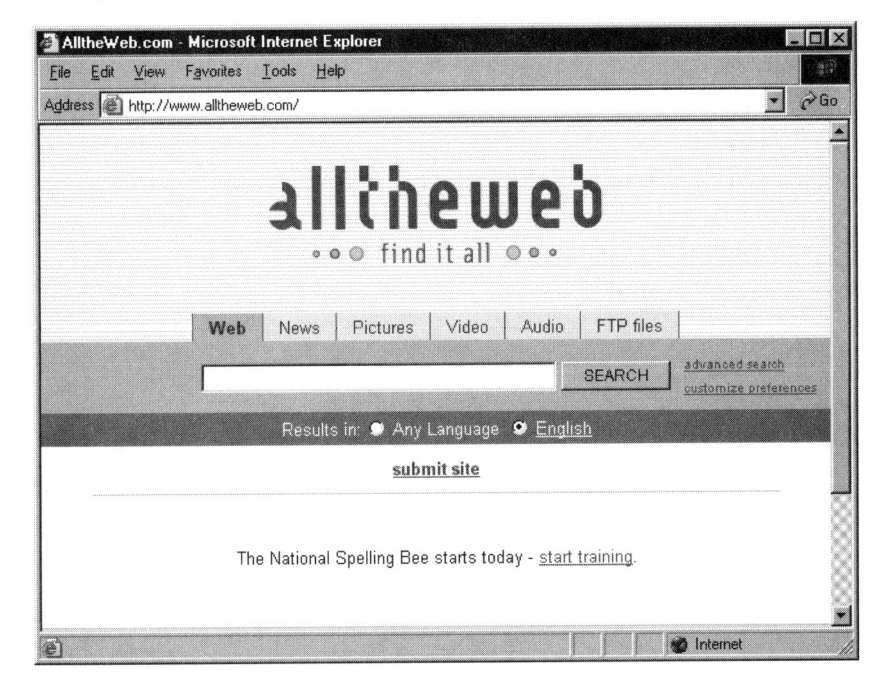

AltaVista (http://www.altavista.com)

AltaVista is known for having one of the largest collections of Web sites in its search engine. Take the time to learn its search commands, particularly in the advanced search mode, to take full advantage of the many options available for constructing highly specific searches. You can translate from multiple foreign languages into English from sites retrieved through your search, or you can translate your own text by using Babel Fish, a free language translation service. AltaVista also offers the option of using its directory to conduct subject-specific searches, and allows you to search specifically for images, video, MP3/audio files, or news articles.

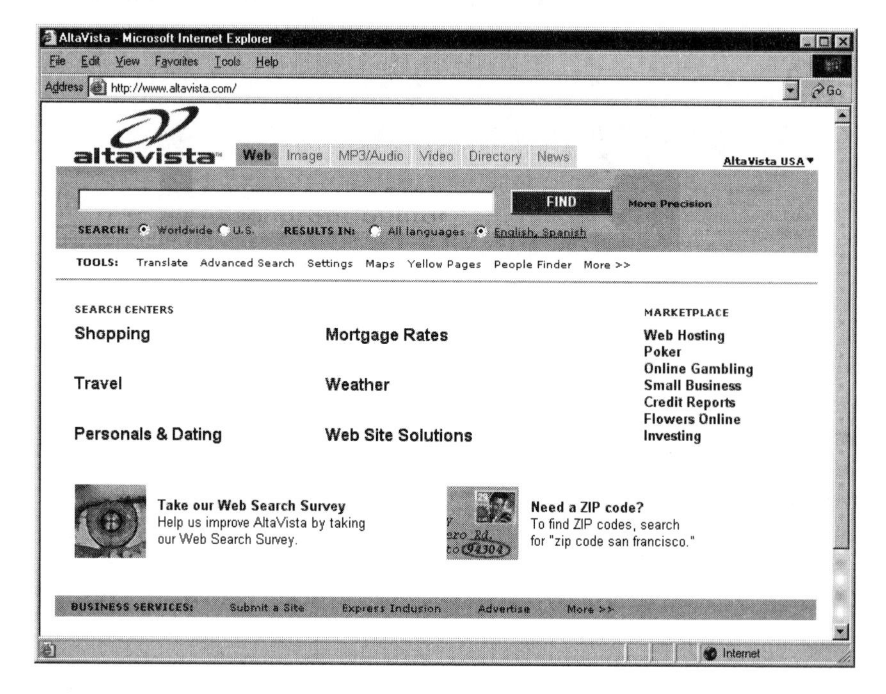

AOL Search (AOL users: http://aolsearch.aol.com)

AOL's search engine is now powered by the iconic Google, so if you're an AOL member, AOL Search will provide you with just about all of the Google results, plus results from AOL's own content pages as well. If you're a Google fan, however, you should be aware that AOL Search does not retain all of Google's functionality, such as the ability to cache Web pages.

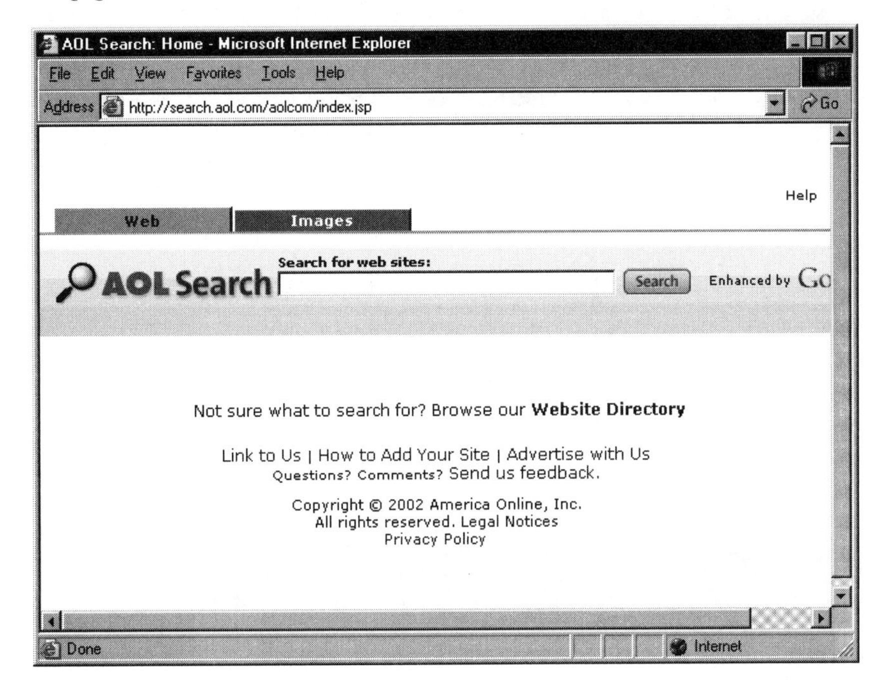

Ask Jeeves (http://www.ask.com)

Ask Jeeves lets you search for answers the way most people want to, by simply asking a question. Rather than having to figure out the most relevant key words, Ask Jeeves invites you to enter a specific question using "natural language," and then uses the words in context to help find you the information you're really looking for. The process can seem hit or miss, but more often than not, you'll retrieve links to relevant Web sites. Ask Jeeves also offers a Browse by Subject area that ranks Web pages according to how many other users have viewed them.

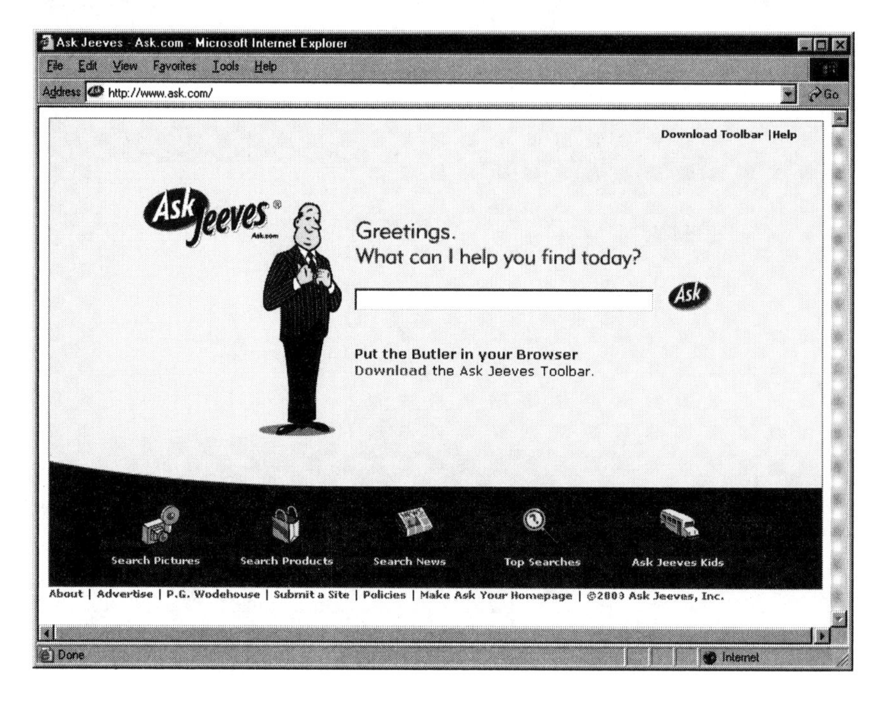

Google (http://www.google.com)

Google sports a simple design but packs a powerful punch. It uses a page rank system that usually brings you to what you are looking for within the first page of your search results, if not the very first link. (Click on I'm Feeling Lucky for the highest ranked choice.) According to its developer, Google's system works so well because it "interprets a link from page A to page B as a vote, by page Λ, for pagc B." Google additionally ranks and reviews the content of the site, casting its "vote" to ensure quality results. Other powerful Google options include the ability to search specifically for images, news items, or Usenet group posts related to your topic or to browse the subject directory. Google also offers another unique feature that lets you view a cached, or stored, copy of a Web site that acts as a snapshot of a specific moment in that site's history.

Hotbot (http://www.hotbot.com)

HotBot, operated by Lycos, includes four of the Web's major search engines—FAST, Google, Inktomi, and Teoma—providing access to four powerful search tools on the same page. HotBot's Custom Web Filters option allows you to search only within specific languages, regions, domains, or date ranges in order to tailor your search.

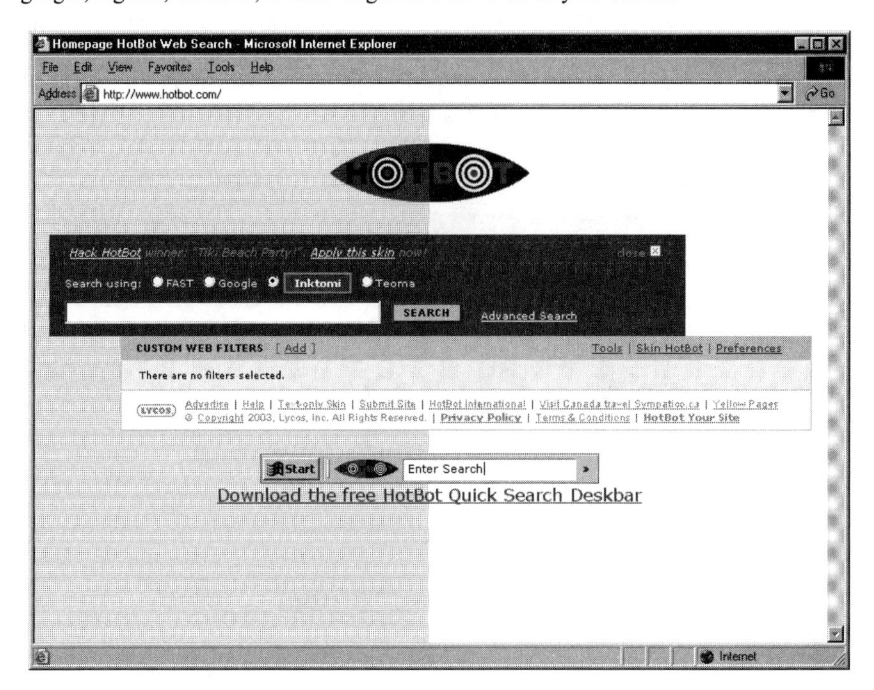

Lycos (http://www.lycos.com)

The Lycos search engine is powered by FAST. Its results, therefore, will be similar to AllTheWeb.com but it does offer some additional functionality to make your search go more smoothly. One of these is its Fast Forward feature, which lets you see results on one side of the screen and the actual Web pages on the other. Lycos also provides relevant categories from a human-compiled directory as well as a list of searchcs it judges to be relevant to yours.

Metacrawler (http://www.metacrawler.com)

As its name implies, Metacrawler is a meta-search engine that searches multiple other search engines (11 as of this writing) in one single search. Use the Advanced Search link to select which engines to include in your search as well as to customize the display of your results list. Metacrawler also allows you to limit your search to images, message boards, or MP3 files to increase your precision.

MSN Search (http://www.search.msn.com)

This Microsoft-run search engine uses LookSmart to search the Web, adding informed judgment of human editors to help determine relevancy and guide your search. In addition to providing a search results list, MSN Search editors also scan completed searches to provide a list of "popular topics" along with your search results. Added functionality includes the Search Preview function, which displays thumbnail pictures of your top page hits.

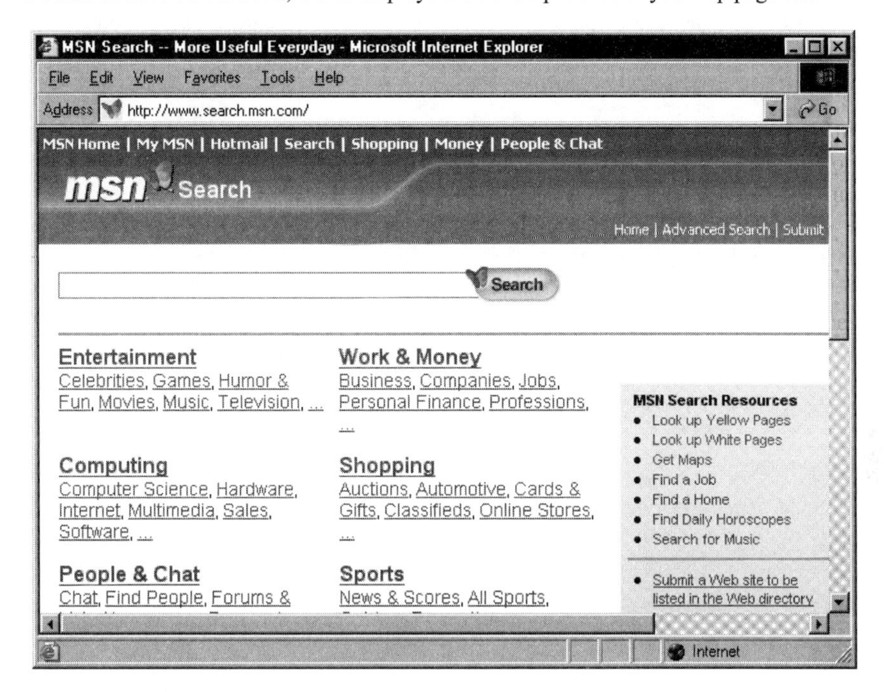

ProFusion (http://www.profusion.com)

ProFusion is a meta-search engine that also provides a topical directory listing of sites on the Web. To conduct a more structured search, click on the Advanced Search option to select which search engines you want ProFusion to use, including the "fastest five" or allowing the site to pick. ProFusion also offers a unique search feature that searches "invisible Web" PDF documents. An added bonus is the ability to customize your search by adding Customized Search Categories to your Profusion search page and setting Alerts, which provide e-mail notification with new search results for your favorite searches or when your selected Web sites have been updated.

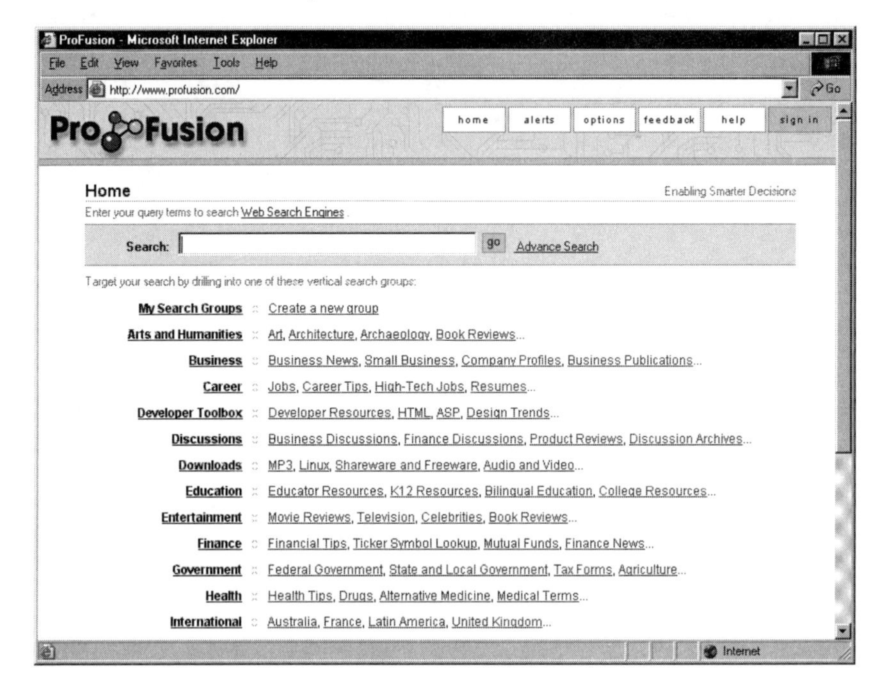

Teoma (http://www.teoma.com)

Teoma indexes fewer pages than some of the more powerful engines like Google or AllTheWeb, but it is known for providing relevant results and a few unique features to assist your searching. Two of these are the Refine button, which provides suggestions to narrow your search, and the Resources section, which lists links to pages that serve as information resources for your topic.

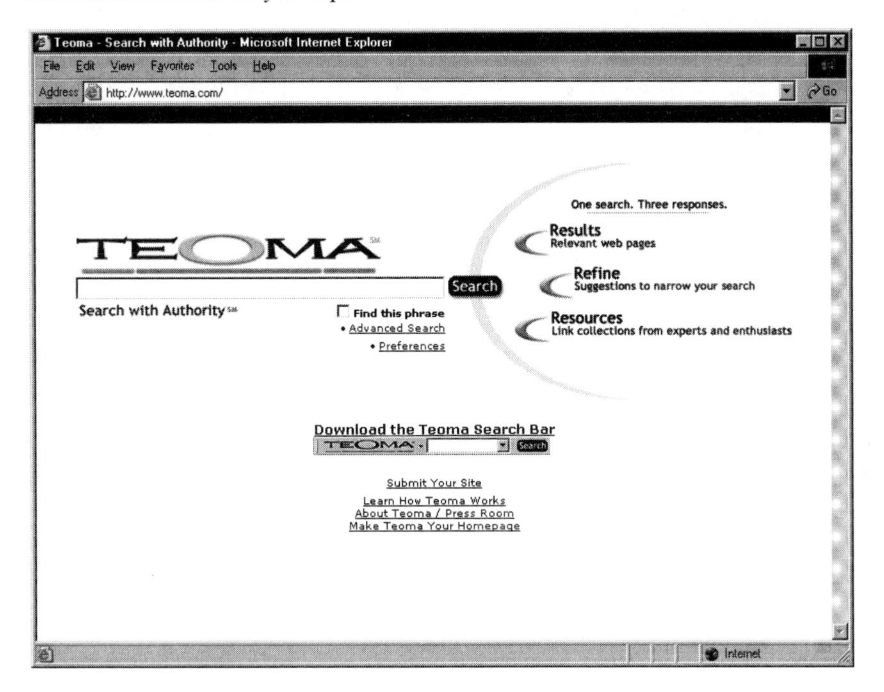

Yahoo! (http://www.yahoo.com)

Yahoo!, one of the most visited sites on the Web, utilizes a Google-powered search engine enhanced with its own directory categorization. In addition to getting Google search hits based on an electronic "crawl" of the web, Yahoo!'s search engine also provides matches to its own directory categories, which have been compiled by human editors. Alternatively, Yahoo! also offers the option to limit your search to its human-edited directory by going to http://dir.yahoo.com.

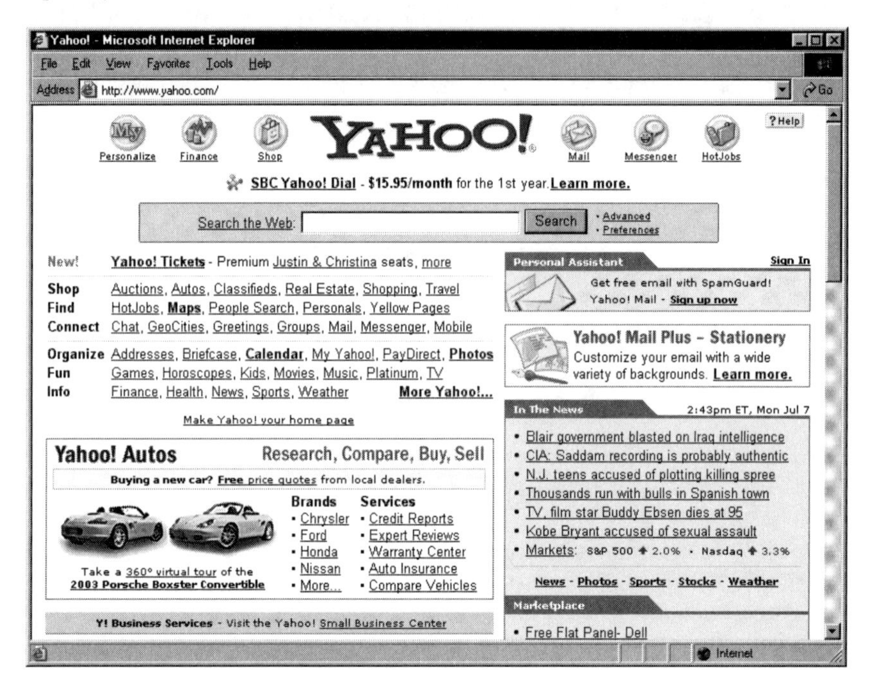

APPENDIX B

Private Foundations on the Web

Abell Foundation, Inc. (MD) (http://www.abell.org/)
The mission of the Baltimore-based Abell Foundation, Inc. is to improve the quality of life in Maryland, specifically in the Baltimore area. The foundation, established in 1953, focuses its grantmaking efforts on education, health and human services, workforce development, community development, arts and culture, and conservation and the environment. Visitors to the foundation's Web site will find in-depth descriptions of the foundation's funding interests, programs, and eligibility requirements; an extensive library of publications; a list of grantees; a detailed history of the foundation; a financial overview; and answers to frequently asked questions.

Abell-Hanger Foundation (TX) (http://www.abell-hanger.org/)
The Abell-Hanger Foundation was created by George T. and Gladys H. Abell, noted Midland, Texas philanthropists. Grants are made to nonprofit organizations whose projects involve the arts, culture, and humanities; higher education; health; human services; public/societal benefit; and religion. Funding is limited to Texas organizations and to national groups that have a significant presence in Texas. Visitors to the foundation's Web site will find grant criteria, proposal guidelines and deadlines, a financial summary, and a pre-proposal questionnaire to be e-mailed to the foundation for further information.

Abington Foundation (OH) (http://www.fmscleveland.com/abington)
The Abington Foundation, named for the place in New England where David Knight Ford's ancestors first settled, was created in 1983 to support the values that the senior Fords championed and which their descendants now uphold. The foundation focuses its grantmaking primarily on education (pre-primary and higher), healthcare (with an emphasis on geriatrics and nursing), economic independence (the promotion or sustaining of self-sufficiency), and cultural activities. Grants are primarily awarded in Cuyahoga County, Ohio. The foundation's Web site provides application guidelines, information about previous grants awarded, and the foundation's financials.

The Able Trust (FL) (http://www.abletrust.org)
The Able Trust, also known as the Florida Governor's Alliance for the Employment of Citizens with Disabilities, was created by the Florida legislature in 1990. Its mission is "to be the leader in providing Floridians with disabilities fair employment opportunities through fundraising, grant programs, public awareness and education." The trust provides grants to Florida nonprofits and to Florida citizens with disabilities. The trust's Web site includes a link to the Florida Business Leadership Network, whose hiring practices support people with disabilities; a Knowledge Center that provides advice to prospective grant applicants and to leaders of nonprofits and of programs in the disability area; the trust's Youth Leadership Forum, a leadership training program for high school juniors and seniors with disabilities; various other disability links and resources; grant information, events, and news; and a downloadable grant application with guidelines.

The Abney Foundation (SC) (http://www.abneyfoundation.org/)
The Abney Foundation was established in 1957 in Greenwood, South Carolina, by Susie Mathews Abney, the widow of the founder of Abney Mills. The foundation's mission is "to make grants for innovative and creative projects, and to programs which are responsive to changing community needs in the areas of education, health, social service, and cultural affairs." The foundation's primary focus is on higher education. All agencies funded by the Abney Foundation serve the citizens of South Carolina. The foundation's Web site contains grant application guidelines, a history of the foundation, a listing of colleges with scholarship endowments from the foundation, an In the Spotlight section that highlights one of these schools, links to philanthropy-related Web sites, and contact information.

Francis L. Abreu Charitable Trust (GA) (http://www.abreufoundation.org)
Located in Atlanta, Georgia, the Francis L. Abreu Charitable Trust was established under the will of May Patterson Abreu in honor of her husband, Francis, who died in 1969. The trust benefits others "by providing grants to arts and cultural programs, education, health associations, human services, and children and youth services." Grants are restricted to organizations exclusively within the Atlanta metro area. Forms of support awarded by the trust include capital campaigns, program development, seed money, and matching funds. To apply, interested parties must complete an application form, which may be printed from the trust's Web site, and attach supporting documentation. Details are provided online.

Access Strategies Fund (MA) (http://www.accessstrategies.org)
The mission of the Massachusetts-based Access Strategies Fund is "to help disenfranchised communities in Massachusetts harness their collective power to access and use the democratic process to improve their lives." The fund currently supports electoral reform/voting rights, political resources and tools, political participation of youths, connecting immigrant groups to political power, and voter mobilization. Visitors to the fund's Web site will find grant guidelines and deadlines, a list of previous grantees, news and events, resources and links, and travel directions to the fund's Cambridge office.

Achelis Foundation (NY) (http://fdncenter.org/grantmaker/achelis-bodman/)
Established in New York in 1940 by Elisabeth Achelis, a native of Brooklyn Heights and a founder of the World Calendar Association, the Achelis Foundation today concentrates its grantmaking in the greater New York City area. The foundation's funding interests include arts/culture, education/school reform, entrepreneurship/employment, environment/conservation, family preservation/civil society, health/rehabilitation/biomedical research, volunteerism/philanthropy, and youth services. Visitors to the foundation's Web site will find a brief history of the foundation; statements from the foundation's chairman, president, and executive director; application guidelines and procedures; recent grantees and a breakdown of grant distributions by program area; a listing of the foundation's trustees, officers, and staff; and a financial overview of the foundation. The Achelis Foundation is run in conjunction with the Bodman Foundation, making grants in many of the same categories. One application may be used to apply to both foundations.

Thomas C. Ackerman Foundation (CA) (http://ackermanfoundation.org)
The Thomas C. Ackerman Foundation was founded in San Diego, California, in 1991 after the death of lawyer Thomas C. Ackerman. The foundation seeks to support the interests of its benefactor and namesake by making grants to support education, programs for the prevention of child abuse and cruelty to animals, the local arts, the educational institutions that he attended, his church, and other endeavors relating to community development and to health and human services in the San Diego area. The foundation does not support projects that may lead to dependence on the foundation for the organization's continued existence. See the foundation's Web site for other exclusions and restrictions, a complete description of the application process, an online application, contact information, the foundation's latest fiscal information, a summary of recent grants, a history of the foundation, and a statement from its president.

Acorn Foundation (CA) (http://www.commoncounsel.org/pages/foundation.html)
Created in 1978, the Acorn Foundation is a member of the Common Counsel Foundation of Oakland, California. The Acorn Foundation "supports projects dedicated to building a sustainable future for the planet and to restoring a healthy global environment." The foundation primarily funds grassroots organizations implementing community-based projects that preserve and restore habitats supporting biological diversity and wildlife; advocate for environmental justice, particularly in low-income and indigenous communities; and prevent or remedy toxic pollution. Most Acorn Foundation grants are made in North America, though occasional grants are made in Latin America. Applications should be submitted to the Common Counsel Foundation and will be considered for all member foundations. The Common Counsel Foundation's Web site offers applications guidelines and deadlines, a list of exclusions, and a link to the National Network of Grantmakers Common Grant Application, which is also accepted.

Claude W. and Dolly Ahrens Foundation (IA) (http://www.ahrensfoundation.org)
The Claude W. and Dolly Ahrens Foundation was founded in 1992 by Claude W. Ahrens, who enjoyed a long and successful career in the Grinnell area and wanted to give back to his community. The foundation gives grants to nonprofit organizations in central Iowa that are requesting funds for specific projects to improve their community, especially relating to parks and recreation. To apply for a grant, organizations should send short letters of introduction describing their projects and their goals. Should the foundation be interested and request a full application, details about what to include in the application are listed on the Web site. The site also contains several lists of previous grantees.

Akonadi Foundation (CA) (http://www.akonadi.org)
Named after an oracle goddess of justice in Ghana, Africa, the Akonadi Foundation of Oakland, California, was established in 2000 to eliminate structural and institutional racism. To work towards its mission, the foundation supports a variety of programmatic approaches, including research, policy work, advocacy, litigation, organizing, media, arts, diversity training, education, and other tools that work toward eradicating racism. The Akonadi Foundation provides funding within the San Francisco Bay Area, as well as to organizations that are national in their scope and reach. The foundation's Web site includes application guidelines, a printable grant application, answers to FAQs, a listing of past grantees, and contact information.

The J.A. & Kathryn Albertson Foundation (ID) (http://www.jkaf.org)
Established in 1966 by Joe Albertson and his wife Kathryn, the J.A. & Kathryn Albertson Foundation which is based in Boise, Idaho, seeks to improve pre-K through grade 12 education in Idaho. The foundation does not accept unsolicited grant proposals. Funding is focused on creating high performance schools, promoting reading skills, fostering teacher excellence, utilizing technology in the classroom, and engaging parents and families in early childhood education. The foundation's Web site include descriptions of the foundation's initiatives, downloadable publications (newsletters, research studies, guides, and annual reports), and general contact information.

Alcoholic Beverage Medical Research Foundation (MD) (http://www.abmrf.org)
The Alcoholic Beverage Medical Research Foundation is "devoted solely to supporting research on the effects of alcohol on health, behavior and prevention of alcohol-related problems." The foundation funds innovative biomedical, behavioral, and social science research on alcohol consumption and abuse prevention. Headquartered in Baltimore, Maryland, the foundation was first established in 1969 as the Medical Advisory Group under the administrative auspices of the Johns Hopkins University School of Medicine; it then merged in 1982 with a parallel group in Canada. Subsequently, the foundation became completely independent of Johns Hopkins and was structured to ensure absolute scientific independence from financial contributors. The foundation evolved into the largest independent nonprofit foundation devoted to alcohol research in North America. The foundation's Web site includes a downloadable grant application form and guidelines; issues of its online journal; its annual report; a list of its other publications; summaries of recent meetings; a list of recent grantees; contact information; and related links. The site also contains short professional biography of each member of the foundation's management and board of trustees and of each member of the foundation's two advisory boards.

Allegheny Foundation (PA) (http://www.scaife.com/alleghen.html)
The Allegheny Foundation is one of the Scaife Foundations of Pittsburgh, Pennsylvania. It funds programs in the western Pennsylvania area that involve historic preservation, civic development, and education. The foundation's Web site instructs potential grantees to send an initial letter of inquiry and lists several specific required attachments. While grants are usually determined at a board meeting in November, proposals are accepted throughout the year and addressed as soon as possible. The foundation's annual report can be downloaded in Adobe Acrobat format.

Paul G. Allen Charitable Foundation (WA) (http://www.pgafoundations.com)
The purpose of the Seattle, Washington-based Paul G. Allen Charitable Foundation is "to promote the healthy development of vulnerable populations and strengthen families and communities in the Pacific Northwest." To that end, the foundation funds projects that improve the quality of life for disadvantaged children, youth and families, seniors, and people with special needs. See the foundation's Web site for eligibility requirements and restrictions. In addition to application guidelines, the site also provides case studies, a list of selected past grants, and an online application form.

Paul G. Allen Foundation for Medical Research (WA) (http://www.pgafoundations.com)
The purpose of the Seattle, Washington-based Paul G. Allen Foundation for Medical Research is "to support innovative programs and research that promote health, prevent disease, and improve practices and healthcare delivery." The foundation accepts applications by invitation only, and letters of inquiry are not reviewed. The site provides case studies and a list of selected past grants.

Allen Foundation for Music (WA) (http://www.pgafoundations.com)
The purpose of the Seattle, Washington-based Allen Foundation for Music is "to support creativity, innovation, and public participation in all forms of American popular music." The foundation funds endeavors in the Pacific Northwest that promote experimentation across disciplines, provide access to artists and art forms not readily available, develop new audiences for music, and encourage individuals to discover their own creativity. See the foundation's Web site for eligibility requirements and restrictions. In addition to application guidelines, the site also provides case studies, a list of selected past grants, and an online application form.

Allen Foundation for the Arts (WA) (http://www.pgafoundations.com)
The purpose of the Seattle, Washington-based Allen Foundation for the Arts is "to strengthen the Pacific Northwest's cultural community and encourage its creativity and vitality. " The foundation, which is interested in the visual, performing, new media, and literary arts, also supports entities that feature local, regional, and national artists in a variety

of disciplines and that encourage public participation and the promotion of critical thinking. See the foundation's Web site for eligibility requirements and restrictions. In addition to application guidelines, the site also provides case studies, a list of selected past grants, and an online application form.

Paul G. Allen Forest Protection Foundation (WA) (http://www.pgafoundations.com)
The purpose of the Seattle, Washington-based Paul G. Allen Forest Protection Foundation is "to protect and sustain the endangered forested ecosystems of the Northwest and Hawaii." Currently, the foundation is undergoing a strategic planning process to determine future funding priorities. As a result, its grantmaking is temporarily suspended. Once new guidelines are developed, they will be posted on the foundation's Web site. In the meantime, the site provides case studies and a list of selected past grants.

Paul G. Allen Virtual Education Foundation (WA) (http://www.pgafoundations.com)
The purpose of the Seattle, Washington-based Paul G. Allen Virtual Education Foundation is "to advance innovative and effective uses of information technology in K-12 education." The foundation is especially interested in projects that will help connect cognitive research to classroom applications. See the foundation's Web site for eligibility requirements and restrictions. Applications for funding are accepted by invitation only. The foundation does accept brief (one- to two-page) letters of inquiry regarding initiatives or projects that are consistent with the foundation's mission and funding priorities. In addition to application guidelines, the site also provides case studies and a list of selected past grants.

Allen Foundation, Inc. (MI) (http://www.tamu.edu/baum/allen.html)
Established in 1975 by agricultural chemist William Webster Allen, the Midland, Michigan-based Allen Foundation, Inc. makes grants to projects that benefit human nutrition in the areas of education, training, and research. Visitors to the foundation's Web site will find the foundation's policies, priorities, eligibility requirements, and deadlines; a biography of Mr. Allen; a listing of the foundation's board of trustees; an online grant application form; latest news; and a selection of past grants. Visitors may also access an archive of the foundation's most recent annual reports.

Alliance Healthcare Foundation (CA) (http://www.alliancehf.org/)
The San Diego-based Alliance Healthcare Foundation, established in 1988, funds healthcare programs for medically-underserved populations in southern California, primarily in San Diego County. Priority is given to programs that address the issues of restricted access to healthcare, substance abuse, communicable diseases, violence, and mental health. The foundation's Web site provides an overview of the foundation and its history; grantmaking guidelines, rules, and procedures; program descriptions and subject-specific research findings; a list of staff and board members; news and publications; profiles of past grantees; links to related organizations and resources; and contact information.

Altman Foundation (NY) (http://fdncenter.org/grantmaker/altman)
Philanthropist and department store owner Benjamin Altman founded the Altman Foundation in 1913 to serve New York City organizations committed to enriching the quality of life in the city. In particular, the foundation focuses on initiatives that help individuals, families, and communities achieve their full potential. The areas of primary interest to the foundation are education, health, community development, and arts and culture. The Altman Foundation's Web site provides downloadable financial statements and lists of recent grantees, as well as grant guidelines and application procedures. The foundation accepts the New York/New Jersey Area Common Application Form and has no submission deadlines.

Jenifer Altman Foundation (CA) (http://www.jaf.org)
Based in San Francisco, California, the Jenifer Altman Foundation was established in 1991, shortly before the death of its namesake, a health and environment researcher. The organization is committed to "the vision of a socially just and ecologically sustainable

future through program interests in environmental health and mind-body health." Grants are made primarily in these two categories. The foundation requests that interested nonprofits submit a concept letter before sending a full proposal. If it is decided that the project matches the foundation's interests, then the grantseeker will be given further instructions, which will include sending the application cover page that is available on the site. In addition to detailed information about the foundation, its funding interests, and application procedures, the foundation's Web site also lists past grantees. The Jenifer Altman Foundation is run in conjunction with the Mitchell Kapor Foundation and the StarFire Fund, making co-grants with each in some categories. One application serves to apply to all three foundations.

Amateur Athletic Foundation of Los Angeles (CA) (http://www.aafla.com)
The Amateur Athletic Foundation of Los Angeles was established to manage southern California's share of the surplus funds generated by the 1984 Olympic Games. The foundation focuses its grantmaking activities on sports programs for youth in Southern California's eight counties, and it gives special attention to groups and communities underserved by traditional sports programs, including girls, minorities, the physically challenged or developmentally disabled, and youth in areas where the risk of involvement in delinquency is particularly high. Visitors to the foundation's Web site will find detailed grant guidelines and application criteria, downloadable research reports, and a search engine for the Web site. The site also offers information on the foundation's own youth sports program, historic sports art and artifact collection, sports research library, and special events.

The Amerind Foundation, Inc. (AZ) (Operating foundation) (http://www.amerind.org)
Presently a nonprofit archaeological research facility and museum devoted to the study and interpretation of Native American cultures, the Amerind Foundation was founded by William Shirley Fulton in 1937 as a private, nonprofit archaeological research institution. Located in the Dragoon Mountains, in the southeastern corner of Arizona known locally as Texas Canyon, the foundation commits its resources to three main concerns: the conservation and preservation of material culture, research, and education. In addition to the museum, the foundation also has an archaeological library. Visitors to the Web site will find information on the foundation's history, a statement of purpose, contact and visitor information, seminars and exhibits, a photo gallery, publications information and an online order form, employment and volunteer opportunities, a site map, and a list of related links. However, no specific information is provided about grants.

Amy Foundation (MI) (http://www.amyfound.org)
The Amy Foundation was established by W. James Russell and his wife Phyllis in 1976 and was named after their daughter. The foundation, based in Lansing, Michigan, seeks to restore the spiritual and moral character of America by promoting the teaching of obedience to all of Christ's commands, thus making "disciples" of those who receive and take to heart this message. The foundation strives to reach its goal via its writing contest, church writing groups program, newsletter, and the dissemination of its brochure, "The United States: A Discipled Nation in this Generation," also available online. Visitors to the foundation's Web site will find writing award guidelines; newsletter issues; samples of past awarded writing; the Amy Internet Syndicate, which provides editorial opinion columns free of charge for use in any publication; an online feedback form; an online publications order form; a list of resources; and links to other sites.

The Hugh J. Andersen Foundation (MN) (http://www.scenicriver.org/hja/)
The Bayport, Minnesota-based Hugh J. Andersen Foundation's mission is to give back to its community "through focused efforts that foster inclusivity, promote equality, and lead to increased human independence, self-sufficiency, and dignity." The foundation requests that prospective applicants contact its grants consultant prior to submitting a proposal to determine if the program might be of interest to the foundation. Grants are restricted to Minnesota groups. Web site visitors will find downloadable application forms, proposal deadlines, a research survey, the foundation's Form 990-PF, and its annual report.

Angelica Foundation (CA) (http://www.angelicafoundation.org)
The Angelica Foundation, based in Racho Santa Fe, California, supports "progressive grassroots organizations that empower communities to become more environmentally sustainable, culturally rich, and socially just." Funding is restricted to nonprofit organizations in California, New Mexico, and Hawaii, as well as non-governmental organizations (NGOs) in Mexico and Central America; the funding location priority differs from year to year. The foundation makes program and initiative grants in the areas of the environment, social justice, and the arts and supports groups that work in drug policy reform. Both types of grants are by invitation only; the program grant is usually for a two-year funding period. The foundation posts complete application guidelines in English and Spanish on its Web site, along with a letter from the board of directors, and a recent list of grant recipients. Contact information is available online.

The Angels on Track Foundation (OH) (http://www.angelsontrack.org/)
Dennis and Vicky Moore established the Angels on Track Foundation after their son Ryan died in a collision between the car in which he was riding and a train at a railroad crossing. The mission of the foundation is to "provide the financial backing needed to improve railroad crossing safety throughout Ohio, and to educate local highway authorities on the various programs available through state and federal funding." Located in Canal Fulton, Ohio, the foundation aims to establish railroad safety task forces in all 88 counties in Ohio, establish a central statewide railroad safety task force, supply funding support for five upgrades each calendar year, and to "educate, save lives, and pursue all avenues available to ensure all railroad grade crossings are equipped with adequate safety devices." Consult the Web site for grant eligibility requirements; railroad safety-related articles, news, and links; information about the foundation's educational materials; and contact information.

Animal Welfare Trust (NY) (http://fdncenter.org/grantmaker/awt/)
Founded in New York in 2001, the Animal Welfare Trust is devoted to promoting the well being of the animal community. The trust's grant program seeks to assist organizations whose work can help alleviate animal suffering and/or raise public consciousness toward respecting animals. Although general organizational funding will be considered, preference will be given to well-defined projects with clear goals and objectives. Due to limited resources, local animal rescue/shelter and spay/neuter programs and wildlife management and conservation projects cannot be considered. Visit the trust's Web site to review funding priorities, application information, and sample grants.

Annenberg Foundation (PA) (http://www.whannenberg.org/)
The St. Davids, Pennsylvania-based Annenberg Foundation "exists to advance the public well-being through improved communication" and concentrates its grantmaking in education, culture, the arts, and community and civic life. It provides funding for programs likely to produce large-scale, beneficial change. Visitors to the foundation's Web site will find a biography of Walter H. Annenberg, founder/donor, former *TV Guide* publisher, and former ambassador to the Court of St. James; an overview of the foundation's grant programs; general information about independent organizations established by the foundation; a breakdown of grant distributions by program area and a list of sample grants; application procedures and proposal guidelines; and basic fiscal information.

The Anschutz Family Foundation (CO) (http://www.anschutzfamilyfoundation.org/)
Established in 1982, the Denver, Colorado-based Anschutz Family Foundation "supports Colorado nonprofit organizations that assist people to help themselves while nurturing and preserving their self-respect." The foundation encourages endeavors that strengthen families and communities and advance individuals to become productive and responsible citizens. There is a special interest in self-sufficiency, community development, and programs aimed at the economically disadvantaged, the young, the elderly, and the disabled. The foundation is also dedicated to funding efforts in rural Colorado. Visitors to the foundation's Web site will find grant guidelines, a list of sample grants, resources for capacity

building, a foundation history, contact information, and a message from the foundation's president.

The Ben Appelbaum Foundation (NY) (http://www.benappelbaumfoundation.org)
The Ben Appelbaum Foundation, based in New York City, is a mentoring organization that provides individuals in the greater tri-state metropolitan area with the inspiration, guidance, and practical assistance they need to undertake worthwhile entrepreneurial activities that offer long-range benefits to society. The foundation matches successful mentee candidates with a mentor based on the proposed venture. The mentor provides the mentee with advice, resources, and an extended network of other professionals who can foster the development of the enterprise. In addition, the Ben Appelbaum Foundation may offer resources through which possible financing may be obtained. The mentor-mentee relationship is monitored and evaluated by the foundation through quarterly meetings with both parties involved. Visit the foundation's Web site to find further information on applying as a mentee or mentor, application policies with downloadable application forms, news, events, success stories, and contact information.

Arca Foundation (DC) (http://fdncenter.org/grantmaker/arca/index.html)
Established in 1952 as the Nancy Reynolds Bagley Foundation, the Arca Foundation received its present name in 1968. The Washington, D.C.-based foundation is dedicated to the pursuit of social equality and justice, and its grantmaking focuses on empowering citizens to help shape public policy. The Arca Foundation has no standard application form, but requests that proposals include several specific components outlined on its Web site. The foundation's site also provides a recent grants list, a brief history, financial statements, a trustees list, and contact information.

Archstone Foundation (CA) (http://www.archstone.org)
Established in 1985 as the FHP Foundation and renamed in 1996, the Archstone Foundation has refocused its grantmaking activities on healthcare for the elderly and on the well-being of aging adults within their communities, with an emphasis on the southern California region. The Long Beach, California-based foundation's Web site provides information about application procedures and funding restrictions, online access to several of its publications, a searchable grants database, answers to FAQs, news, and links to aging-related resources.

Arcus Foundation (MI) (http://www.arcusfoundation.org)
The Arcus Foundation, located in Kalamazoo, Michigan, is a family foundation established in 1997 that seeks to "contribute to a pluralistic society that celebrates diversity and dignity, invests in youth and justice, and promotes tolerance and compassion," with an emphasis on southwestern Michigan. The Arcus Foundation is especially interested in programs and organizations that celebrate and serve members of the gay, lesbian, bisexual, and transgender communities. The foundation also funds programs that focus on youth, cultural enhancement, and environmental sustainability, and promotes and supports the rights of animals to live free of human cruelty and abuse with a special fund dedicated to sanctuaries and conservation of Great Apes. Those interested in applying for a grant should first send a letter of inquiry. Further information about application criteria can be found on the foundation's Web site, as well as an interview with the foundation's president, news items, descriptions and sample grants relating to the foundation's special funds, and background information.

Ethel Louise Armstrong Foundation (CA) (http://www.ela.org)
Located in Altadena, California, the Ethel Louise Armstrong Foundation was established in 1994. The organization's mission is "to promote, through grants and scholarships, the inclusion of people with disabilities in the areas of arts, advocacy, and education." The foundation annually awards scholarships to women with disabilities who are pursuing advanced degrees at schools in the United States. Grants are awarded to organizations that are either led by or that work to support adults—especially women—with disabilities.

Application guidelines and deadlines, eligibility requirements, and restrictions can be found on the Web site, along with a list of past grant recipients. The site also includes relevant news, profiles of the founders, and disability resources.

Arsalyn Foundation (CA) (Operating foundation) (http://www.arsalyn.org)
The nonpartisan Glendora, California-based Arsalyn Foundation was established in 1996 to address a decline in voter participation. The organization's mission is "to encourage young Americans to become informed and active participants in the electoral process." The foundation hosts meetings through its Technical Assistance Program and helps organizations working to enhance civic and political engagement among young people to acquire training and share experiences. Through its Peer Exchange Program, the foundation funds site visits between groups promoting youth civic and political engagement to assist in the spreading/sharing of models and methodologies. The foundation also hosts a national conference and helps cover the expenses of attendees. The foundation is open to being approached for special projects by like-minded organizations. The foundation's Web site includes rules and deadlines for applying to its participatory programs; an online application for the peer exchange program; relevant news, resources, and events; and contact information.

Artists' Fellowship, Inc. (NY) (http://www.artistsfellowship.com/home.html)
Originally established in 1859, Artists' Fellowship, Inc. of New York assists professional fine artists (painters, graphic artists, sculptors) and their families in times of emergency, disability, or bereavement. The organization does not accept applications from performance artists, commercial artists, commercial photographers, filmmakers, crafts persons, or hobbyists, and it does not award scholarship funds or fellowships for study, schooling, or travel. The fellowship's Web site provides detailed information on the application process, outlines desired qualifications of prospective applicants and the program's limitations, and provides a downloadable application, information about becoming a member, and the fellowship's history.

The Asbury-Warren Foundation (GA) (http://www.asburywarren.org)
The Asbury-Warren Foundation was established by Josephine Warren Asbury in memory of her parents, Charlotte and Richard C. Warren. SunTrust Bank serves as trustee of the foundation, in accordance with the founder's wishes. The foundation primarily funds educational and religious organizations in Appalachia. Visitors to the foundation's Web site will find application information, a downloadable grant application form, and contact information.

The Atlanta Foundation (GA)
(http://www.wachovia.com/charitable_services/atlanta_overview.asp)
The Atlanta Foundation was established in 1921 to improve the quality of life for residents of Georgia's Fulton and DeKalb Counties by promoting education, scientific research, healthcare, community enrichment, and social equality. Visit the foundation's Web site for grant guidelines, a list of past grantees, grant request statistics, and contact information.

The Lily Auchincloss Foundation Inc. (NY) (http://www.lilyauch.org)
Lily Auchincloss Foundation is dedicated to the enhancement of the quality of life in New York City. Areas of interest to the foundation include contemporary visual art, preservation, and community programs that serve to enrich the lives of the people of New York City. At this time, the foundation is not considering proposals for dance, film, music, or theater programs. In general, the foundation will not support research projects, mental health programs, medical services (including hospitals and nursing homes), substance abuse programs, or private schools. Visitors to the foundation's Web site will find application guidelines, lists of recent grantees, and contact information.

The Marilyn Augur Family Foundation (TX) (http://fdncenter.org/grantmaker/augur/)
The Marilyn Augur Family Foundation, inspired by the Biblical passage of Matthew 25:30-40, was established in 1995 and supports Dallas, Texas-area organizations that provide basic human needs—including food, shelter, clothing, and healthcare—and education to those living in poverty or in prison. The foundation places special emphasis on children's programs and on Christian organizations that minister to the needy. Visitors to the foundation's Web site will find a description of the foundation's funding priorities and application procedures, its history, a list of its trustees, and contact information.

Austin-Bailey Health and Wellness Foundation (OH) (http://fdncenter.org/grantmaker/austinbailey/)
The Austin-Bailey Health and Wellness Foundation was established in 1996 and strives to promote the physical well-being of the people of Ohio's Holmes, Stark, Tuscarawas, and Wayne Counties. This mission is realized by funding programs that address the "healthcare affordability concerns of the uninsured and underinsured, the poor, children, single parents, and the aging" and programs that address "the mental health needs of individuals and families, as well as those that address domestic violence." The foundation's Web site provides grant guidelines, eligibility requirements, and limitations, as well as a listing of previous grant recipients and the board of directors. The foundation's latest tax return and financial statements, as well as a summary of its health needs assessment study, are available as downloadable documents.

Mary Reynolds Babcock Foundation, Inc. (NC) (http://www.mrbf.org/)
The Babcock Foundation, Inc. was created in 1953 with a $12 million bequest from Mary Reynolds Babcock, a daughter of the founder of the R.J. Reynolds Tobacco Company. Based in Winston-Salem, North Carolina, the foundation concentrates its activities on community-building initiatives in the southeastern United States, placing a special emphasis on activities that seek to assure the well-being of children, youth, and families; bridge the faultlines of race and class; and invest in communities' human and natural resources over the long term. The foundation's current program, Building Just and Caring Communities, comprises three funding areas: the Organizational Development Program, which makes grants to help individual organizations in the Southeast implement concrete organizational development activities; the Community Problem Solving Program, which aims to support coalitions working on local community issues in ways that "build lasting capacity in their communities to solve problems"; and the Opportunity Fund, which provides core support to emerging organizations. Visitors to the foundation's Web site will find detailed descriptions of all three programs, a list of recent grants, a brief history of the foundation and a statement of its purpose and values, listings of the foundation's board and staff, and contact information.

Helen Bader Foundation, Inc. (WI) (http://www.hbf.org/)
The Milwaukee-based Helen Bader Foundation, Inc. supports innovative programs that advance the well-being of people and promote successful relationships with their families and communities. The foundation concentrates its grantmaking in five areas: Alzheimer's disease and dementia (geographic focus: national, with priority given to Milwaukee and Wisconsin), children and youth in Israel (geographic focus: Israel), economic development (geographic focus: Milwaukee), education (geographic focus: Milwaukee), and Jewish life and learning (geographic focus: Milwaukee and Delaware River Valley area). In addition to background information, press releases, and a biography of founder Helen Bader, the foundation's Web site provides general program information; application guidelines and downloadable application forms; recent grants list, grant summaries by program area, and profiles of featured grantees; and contact information.

The Francois-Xavier Bagnoud Foundation (NY) (http://www.fxb.org/index.html)
In 1989 Francois-Xavier, the Countess Albina du Boisrouvray, created the Bagnoud Foundation in memory of her only son, a helicopter pilot killed at the age of 24 in a crash in West Africa. The foundation "carries out various philanthropic activities"; among its programs

are five fellowships in the College of Engineering at the University of Michigan as well as the Francois-Xavier Bagnoud Aerospace Prize administered by the Aerospace Engineering Department at the University of Michigan. Also featured on the site is the Association Francois-Xavier Bagnoud, which, although funded by the foundation, is independent of the foundation's philanthropic activities and has at its disposal $5 million for "strictly humanitarian goals." The association is involved in "more than two dozen initiatives involving children's rights, health and human rights, and pediatric HIV/AIDS in 17 countries." The Web site contains information and guidelines for the Xavier-Bagnoud Aerospace Prize and information on past winners of the prize, detailed information on the association's work in each region around the world, news and press releases, a downloadable application for grantseekers, and an online contact form. Also available are a calendar of events, a search engine, and an archive of past news releases and information dating back to 1996, as well as links to related sites.

Bailey Family Foundation, Inc. (VA) (http://bailey-family.org/)
Established in 1997, the Bailey Family Foundation, Inc. of Virginia holds a mission of expanding the availability and enhancing the quality of post-secondary education. Based on set criteria, the foundation provides financial assistance to students for higher education. Visit the foundation's Web site to view the funding criteria, and to learn about the various programs, application procedures, the Bailey family, and contact information.

Banks Family Foundation (CA) (http://www.banksfamilyfoundation.org)
The Banks Family Foundation, located in Oakland, California, works to help children become responsible adults by supporting organizations that "benefit the health, education, and welfare of the children of Northern Alameda County." the foundation's Web site includes basic grant guidelines, recent grants awarded, a listing of affiliations and links, and contact information.

Baptist Community Ministries of New Orleans (LA) (http://www.bcm.org/)
Baptist Community Ministries (BCM) was endowed with the proceeds from the sale of Mercy + Baptist Medical Center in August of 1995. Its stated mission: "Baptist Community Ministries is committed to the development of a healthy community offering a wholesome quality of life to its residents and to improving the physical, mental, and spiritual health of the individuals we serve." This $150 million private foundation makes grants to qualifying charitable organizations in the five-parish region surrounding New Orleans. Its funding interests are primarily in education, health, public safety, and governmental oversight, and grantees and programs are "evaluated considering the religious history and mission of BCM." Awards range from $50,000 for one year to nearly $2 million over four years. The ministries' Web site lists goals for each funding area and provides grant information and guidelines, a summary of the grant review process, a listing of past grant recipients, and contact information.

The Barr Family Endowment Trust (WI) (http://fdncenter.org/grantmaker/barr/)
The Barr Family Endowment Trust was established to periodically provide awards to graduating high school seniors with overall grade point averages of 3.6 or higher (on a 4.0 scale) who have attended Homestead High School in Mequon, Wisconsin. Visitors to the trust's Web site will find contact information and a downloadable version of the trust's latest tax return.

William E. Barth Foundation (KY) (http://www.doddanddodd.com/foundation.htm)
Located in Louisville, Kentucky, the William E. Barth Foundation was established by two teachers in the Jefferson County School District in honor of their brother. The foundation supports charitable organizations in Louisville and Jefferson Counties, with a focus on programs that address the welfare of children. The foundation's Web site provides application guidelines, downloadable forms, and a listing of the charitable organizations that the foundation supports, and contact information.

Stockton Rush Bartol Foundation (PA) (http://www.bartol.org/)
The Stockton Rush Bartol Foundation was established in 1984 in Philadelphia, Pennsylvania, to assure the everyday existence of the arts in the city. The foundation provides financial and technical assistance to qualifying organizations. The foundation's priorities include organizations that: serve children through arts education programs that promote social and educational development; serve communities by providing broader access to high-quality arts experiences at the neighborhood level; and/or serve the arts community by supporting cultural organizations at critical junctures in their artistic or organizational development. The foundation does not support programs or organizations presented outside of the Philadelphia area. Visit the foundation's Web site to view other grant exclusions, application guidelines, a printable application, board/staff lists, and contact information.

The Bayer Institute for Health Care Communication (CT) (Operating foundation) (http://www.bayerinstitute.org)
The mission of the West Haven, Connecticut-based Bayer Institute for Health Care Communication is to enhance the quality of healthcare by improving the communication between the clinician and the patient through education, research, and advocacy. The institute is funded by the pharmaceutical division of the Bayer Corporation in the U.S. and the Healthcare Division of Bayer in Canada. The institute works with healthcare organizations to conduct research and provides educational opportunities for clinicians to develop effective communication skills. Up to five grants a year are made to investigators to develop new knowledge about clinician-patient communication. The institute also receives grants to support specific projects, enters into contracts with various organizations to develop and implement communication improvement programs, and sells materials to organizations conducting its programs. The institute's Web site contains application instructions for the grant program, information about workshops and continuing education opportunities, and contact information.

The Bayport Foundation (MN) (http://www.scenicriver.org/bp/)
Funded by Minnesota-based Andersen Corporation, best known for making windows and patio doors since the turn of the previous century, the Bayport Foundation supports the general operating, capital, and program funds to qualified nonprofit organizations that provide community, social, and support services to areas where Andersen Corporation employees live: the St. Croix Valley, western Wisconsin, and the eastern Twin Cities areas. Visitors to the foundation's Web site will find application criteria, deadlines, a downloadable copy of the Minnesota Common Grant Application Form, and contact information.

Charles T. Beaird Foundation (LA) (http://www.beairdfoundation.org)
The Charles T. Beaird Foundation, founded in 1960, is dedicated to "improving the Shreveport, Louisiana area through assisting organizations to add opportunity, freedom of action and choice, self-betterment, and a climate for change to the lives of the people they serve." The foundation supports small, local programs, which are "innovative and perhaps even unpopular," as well as larger national causes, such as the United Way and American Cancer Society. The foundation provides a brief history, mission statement, and contact information on its Web site.

Arnold and Mabel Beckman Foundation (CA) (http://www.beckman-foundation.com/)
The Arnold and Mabel Beckman Foundation makes grants "to promote research in chemistry and the life sciences, broadly interpreted, and particularly to foster the invention of methods, instruments, and materials that will open up new avenues of research in science." The Irvine, California-based foundation's Web site provides brief biographies of Arnold and Mabel Beckman; guidelines and downloadable application forms for the Beckman Young Investigators (BYI) Program, which provides research support to promising young faculty members in the early stages of academic careers in the chemical and life sciences, and the Beckman Research Technologies Initiatives; and links to Beckman Institutes/Centers at the University of Illinois at Urbana-Champaign, the California Institute of Technology, Stanford University, the Beckman Laser Institute, and City of Hope.

The Beim Foundation (MN) (http://www.beimfoundation.org)
Established in Excelsior, Minnesota in 1947, the Beim Foundation funds organizations primarily in Minnesota, sporadically funding in other parts of the upper Midwest as well. the foundation's interests lie in the arts, education, the environment, and human services. Visitors to the foundation's Web site will find an outline of project types that are considered, limitations to funding, past grant recipients, and contact information. Applications submitted via e-mail will not be considered, but the foundation provides application procedure guidelines for mailed applications.

Beldon Fund (NY) (http://www.beldon.org/)
The Beldon Fund is an environmental grantmaker headquartered in New York City. By supporting effective, nonprofit advocacy organizations, the Beldon Fund seeks to build a national consensus to achieve and sustain a healthy planet. The fund plans to invest its entire principal and earnings by 2009 to attain this goal. The Beldon Fund focuses project and general support grants in three programs. The Human Health and the Environment program seeks to add new, powerful voices to promote a national consensus on the environment and to activate the public on issues that matter to people in a deeply personal and potent way. The fund seeks proposals that engage new constituencies in exposing the connection between toxic chemicals and human health and in promoting public policies that prevent or eliminate environmental risks to people's health, particularly through application of the precautionary principle. The program focuses grant making in three areas: New Advocates (specifically doctors, nurses, public health professionals, health-affected people, parents, and teachers), Human Exposure to Toxic Chemicals, and Environmental Justice. The Corporate Campaigns program seeks to answer the constant and growing efforts by many corporations to block the development of a national consensus on the environment and the achievement of real, sustainable progress on the health of our planet. The Key States program focuses on particular states (currently Florida, North Carolina, Michigan, Minnesota, and Wisconsin) where the power of a growing, energized consensus for environmental protection can be organized and brought to bear on public policy and policymakers. The Beldon Fund's Web site features program guidelines and grant application procedures, the annual report, a list of recent grants, and contact information.

The James Ford Bell Foundation (MN)
(http://www.users.uswest.net/~famphiladv/jamesfordbell.htm)
Established in 1955 by James Ford Bell, the founder of General Mills, Inc., the James Ford Bell Foundation has a long-standing historical association with the Twin Cities of Minneapolis and St. Paul, Minnesota. The foundation is especially interested in funding projects that have historical connections to the Bell Family, such as the James Ford Bell Library, the James Ford Bell Museum of Natural History, the Delta Waterfowl Foundation, and the Minneapolis Institute of Arts. The foundation also considers funding in the environment, including preservation, education, and overpopulation and its impact; the arts, especially programs of historic interest to the foundation, as well as arts organizations active in the Twin Cities; social services, especially prevention and self-sufficiency in the Twin Cities; and education, consistent with the interests of the foundation. There is an extensive biography of James Ford Bell on the foundation's Web site which gives more detailed information on the foundation's main programs of interest. Also available on the site are grant guidelines and limitations, detailed application procedures and deadlines, a downloadable grant application cover page, and contact information.

Bella Vista Foundation (CA) (http://www.pacificfoundationservices.com/bellavista/)
The San Francisco, California-based Bella Vista Foundation helps to insure healthy emotional development in children during the first years of their lives. Qualified grantees are those organizations that offer education or social services, and that promote resource conservation. The foundation also plans to provide support for early childhood programs and environmental restoration. The foundation's Web site features information on areas that will not be considered, a board of directors list, contact information, and application procedures.

The Claude Worthington Benedum Foundation (PA) (http://fdncenter.org/grantmaker/benedum/)
The Pittsburgh, Pennsylvania-based Claude Worthington Benedum Foundation was established in 1944 to support the areas of West Virginia and Pittsburgh, Pennsylvania. Within each area, the foundation has distinct areas of interest. In West Virginia, areas of interest include education, health, human services, community development, economic development, and the arts. In southwestern Pennsylvania, areas of interest include regional economic development, support for business and education development in outlying counties, Pittsburgh cultural district, and the United Way. Visitors to the foundation's Web site will find specific program information; application guidelines; a listing of trustees; officers, and staff; a recent grants listing; restrictions; and contact information.

Benton Foundation (DC) (http://www.benton.org/)
The Benton Foundation seeks to shape the emerging communications environment and to demonstrate the value of communications for solving social problems. Its mission is to promote communication tools, applications, and policies in the public interest. Through its Communications Policy and Practice arm, the foundation supports nonprofits using communications to solve social problems and strengthen social bonds. Other projects of the foundation are Connect for Kids, an online resource for "helping Americans act on behalf of children"; Open Studio: The Arts Online, which provides community access to the arts on the Internet; and Sound Partners for Community Health, which awards grants to public radio stations that demonstrate how community-centered journalism can positively affect the ways in which local healthcare issues are addressed. The foundation has created the Virtual Library, which supplies dozens of papers and policy documents online. Visitors to the site will find useful communications technology "best practices," the Benton Foundation Library, hundreds of annotated links to nonprofit and telecommunications resources on the Internet, and a listing of the foundation's board members and staff.

H.N. & Frances C. Berger Foundation (CA) (http://www.hnberger.org/)
The H.N. & Frances C. Berger Foundation was created to provide people with the opportunity to improve their own situations, "to help people help themselves." Established as a private family foundation in 1961 by Nor and Frances Berger, the focus of the foundation's funding is on children and youth, in keeping with the Bergers' belief that the future rests in their hands. To that end, the establishment of college buildings and scholarships are among its charitable projects. The foundation, located in Palm Desert, California, supports a variety of civic, educational and community projects, with the majority of grants related to programs in the southern California area. The foundation prefers to seek out its own projects, and does not solicit grant proposals. However, "those with interest in a potential dialogue" are encouraged to submit a one-to two-page request for consideration, which should include a concise statement of intent and a brief history of the organization and its activities. The Web site contains an address for contact and brief biographies of the founders.

Viola W. Bernard Foundation (NY) (http://www.violawbernardfoundation.org/)
The Viola W. Bernard Foundation was established initially in 1968 as the Tappanz Foundation to provide seed money for innovative mental health programs with a particular emphasis on families and children. The mission of the Viola W. Bernard Foundation remains to support innovative programs that address the interplay between social conditions and the psychological health of children and families. Grants are generally limited to projects or programs for children and young people with a mental health component. Visit the foundation's Web site to learn more about Dr. Bernard, the mission of the organization, application guidelines, past grant recipients, and contact information.

The Grace and Franklin Bernsen Foundation (OK) (http://www.bernsen.org/)
The Grace and Franklin Bernsen Foundation was established in 1968 to fund nonprofit organizations in and around Tulsa, Oklahoma. The foundation funds grants supporting "religious, charitable, scientific, literary, or educational purposes, or for the prevention of cruelty to children." A biography of the founders on the Web site contains links to

recipients of the foundation's grants over the course of its history. the foundation's Web site also provides an annual report, grant guidelines, and contact information.

Frank Stanley Beveridge Foundation, Inc. (FL) (http://www.beveridge.org/)
The Florida-based Frank Stanley Beveridge Foundation, Inc. was established in Massachusetts in 1947 by Frank Stanley Beveridge, the founder of Stanley Home Products, Inc. Today the foundation considers grant proposals in some two dozen institutional/program activity areas, including animal-related, arts and culture, civil rights, community improvement, conservation/environment, crime, disasters/safety, diseases/medical disciplines, education, employment, food and agriculture, health (general/rehabilitative), housing, human services, mental health, crisis intervention, philanthropy/voluntarism, public affairs and society benefit, recreation, religion, science, social sciences, and youth development. The stated purpose of the foundation's Web site, however, is to determine whether potential applicants are eligible to receive grants from the foundation. In addition to a self-administered, interactive survey to help grantseekers determine whether they meet the foundation's basic eligibility requirements, visitors to the site will find a biography of Mr. Beveridge, a recent grants list, a listing of the foundation's officers and directors, and contact information.

Bicknell Fund (OH) (http://fdncenter.org/grantmaker/bicknellfund/)
The Bicknell Fund of Cleveland, Ohio, was established for the purpose of promoting the well-being of mankind. Areas of interest of the fund include support for the homeless and disadvantaged in the Cleveland area, education, civic and public affairs, and art and humanities. Visit the fund's Web site to view grant guidelines, proposal requirements, grant history, financials, board listing, and contact information.

F.R. Bigelow Foundation (MN) (http://www.frbigelow.org/)
The F.R. Bigelow Foundation was founded in 1946 by the president of the St. Paul Fire & Marine Company, an insurance company now known as The St. Paul Companies, Inc., to continue the philanthropic interests of his family. Serving the greater St. Paul metropolitan area (including Ramsey, Washington, and Dakota Counties, but giving preference to St. Paul-based organizations), the foundation centers its funding on education, human services, humanities, the arts, and community development. Visitors to the foundation's Web site will find an online annual report, the details of past grants, guidelines and limitations of grants, a downloadable grant application, and contact information.

William Bingham Foundation (OH) (http://fdncenter.org/grantmaker/bingham/)
The William Bingham Foundation was established in 1955 by Elizabeth Bingham Blossom in memory of her brother, William Bingham II, to continue the philanthropic tradition of the family. Initally, the foundation's grantmaking focused on educational, cultural, and health and human service organizations in the Cleveland area. Over the years, however, the foundation's objectives have broadened to reflect the needs of the communities in which its trustees reside. Today, the foundation contributes to a wide variety of organizations in the areas of the arts, education, and health and human services in those communities as well as nationwide. The foundation's Web site provides a brief history of the foundation, its program interests and grantmaking procedures, a list of grants paid in the latest year, and trustee, officer, and staff listings.

Birmingham Foundation (PA) (http://www.birminghamfoundation.org)
The Birmingham Foundation was established in 1996 to benefit the quality of life in south Pittsburgh, a community formerly known as Birmingham. The foundation focuses on health-related and human services grantmaking in a three zip code area of south Pittsburgh. Visitors to the foundation's Web site will find application guidelines and an outline for the initial letter of intent. The foundation accepts a Common Grant Application Format developed by Grantmakers of Western Pennsylvania, which can be accessed and printed online from a link to its Web site. Downloadable health assessment guides and service area

guides, recent and past grants lists, and contact information are provided online at the foundation's Web site.

Blakemore Foundation (WA) (http://www.blakemorefoundation.org/)
Based in Seattle, Washington, the Blakemore Foundation was established by Thomas and Frances Blakemore in 1990 to encourage the study of Asian languages at an advanced level and to increase the understanding of Asian art in the United States. The foundation makes approximately twenty grants each year for the advanced study of modern Chinese, Japanese, Korean, and Southeast Asian languages. These grants are intended for individuals successfully pursuing academic, professional, or business careers involving Asia who realize that language study abroad at an advanced level is essential to realize their goals. The grants cover tuition, related educational expenses, basic living costs, and transportation for a year of language study abroad. Grants to improve the understanding of Asian fine arts are made to museums, universities, and other educational or art-related institutions in the United States that have programs, exhibits, or publications dealing with the fine arts of Northeast, East, and Southeast Asia. Printable and downloadable application forms for the language grants can be found on the site. There are no formal grant applications for art grants. Visit the foundation's site for detailed grant guidelines and instructions, biographies of the foundation's founders, contact information, and links to universities in Asia.

Blandin Foundation (MN) (http://www.blandinfoundation.org/)
The mission of the Blandin Foundation is to strengthen rural Minnesota communities, with a special focus on the Grand Rapids community and Itasca County. To that end, the foundation sponsors conferences and leadership programs and provides approximately $12 million to Minnesota organizations annually. Outside of Itasca County, Blandin grants are restricted to the focus areas established by the foundation's board of trustees: education, cultural opportunities, community leadership training, environmental stewardship, safe communities, economic opportunity, and "convening." The trustees commit most of the foundation's grant dollars to its major partners, who have the responsibility of administering each focus area. Potential grant applicants are encouraged to review the foundation's current focus areas and then contact the appropriate partner organization, which can be done via e-mail through the foundation's Web site. The site also provides program descriptions, a list of grants made in the most recent year, and detailed grant restrictions.

The Arthur M. Blank Family Foundation (GA) (http://www.BlankFoundation.org/)
The Arthur M. Blank Family Foundation is "committed to supporting programs and organizations that create opportunity, enhance self-esteem, and increase awareness about cultural and community issues among young men and women." The Atlanta-based foundation provides funding in the following areas: arts and culture, athletics and outdoor activities, environment, fostering understanding between young people of diverse backgrounds, helping adolescents learn, and empowering young women and girls. The foundation's geographic focus includes Atlanta, New York City, Boston, and Los Angeles. Special consideration is given to organizations that are located in Atlanta, reach underserved youth, or improve the quality of public education. The foundation's Web site includes information about each funding area, grant application instructions and a description of the review process, a downloadable application, and a listing of grant limitations.

The Morton K. and Jane Blaustein Foundation (MD) (http://fdncenter.org/grantmaker/blaustein/)
The Morton K. and Jane Blaustein Foundation is a family foundation established to allow for people to achieve equal opportunities in education, access quality healthcare, and participate in a democratic society. Grants are made in the areas of education, health and human rights, and social justice. Visit the the foundation's Web site to view funding priorities, eligibility criteria, selected grants, and contact information.

Blowitz-Ridgeway Foundation (IL) (http://fdncenter.org/grantmaker/blowitz/)
Founded in 1984 with the proceeds from the sale of Chicago's Ridgeway Hospital, a psychiatric facility focusing on low-income adolescents, the Blowitz-Ridgeway Foundation continues the hospital's mission by making grants primarily for medical, psychiatric, psychological, and/or residential care, and research programs in medicine, psychology, social science, and education. Preference is given to organizations operating within the state of Illinois. Visitors to the foundation's Web site will find application guidelines and procedures and a listing of recent grants.

Bodman Foundation (NY) (http://fdncenter.org/grantmaker/achelis-bodman/)
The Bodman Foundation was established in 1945 by investment banker George M. Bodman and his wife, Louise Clarke Bodman, to distribute funds in the religious, educational, and charitable fields "for the moral, ethical, and physical well-being and progress of mankind." Today the foundation concentrates its grantmaking in New York City, with occasional grants directed to northern New Jersey. Areas of foundation interest include funding for youth, rehabilitation, biomedical research, child welfare, science education, major cultural institutions, health and hospitals, social services, welfare reform, alcohol and drug abuse, responsible fatherhood and father absence, and education (including charter schools, public school reform, and parental school choice). Other interests include voluntarism, literacy, homelessness, entrepreneurship and economic development, environment (science education and land conservation), and job training with employment in the private business sector. Visitors to the foundation's Web site will find a brief history of the foundation; a statement from foundation president John N. Irwin III; application guidelines and procedures; recent grants lists; a listing of the foundation's trustees, officers, and staff; and contact information.

The Boehm Foundation (NY) (http://members.aol.com/boehmfdn/)
The Boehm Foundation of New York was created to support grassroots groups in the United States and to support organizations working to advance democratic values, civil and economic rights, and to eliminate the root causes of conflict. The foundation makes grants in two program areas. Within these two areas the foundation places emphasis on organizations with limited access to financial and other resources and organizations working in and with low-income and immigrant communities and communities of color. Visit the foundation's Web site to view application procedures, an archive of recent annual reports, grants approved for the most recent year, and contact information.

Boettcher Foundation (CO) (http://www.boettcherfoundation.org/)
The Boettcher Foundation, established by the Colorado Boettcher Family in 1937, has been funding programs that promote the general well-being of Colorado residents for over 60 years. The foundation's four areas of giving are education, civic and cultural programs, community and social service, and hospital and health service. Additionally, the foundation provides merit-based scholarships for Colorado high school seniors to Colorado institutions of higher learning and a Teacher Recognition Award. Honorary and Memorial Grants, mainly in honor of former board members and executives of the foundation, are also available. Visitors to the foundation's Web site will find extensive information on all aspects of the granting process. Guidelines, past grants in each funding area, and grant distribution information; a description of the scholarship application; information on past scholars and their achievements; FAQs; financial information; and a biography of the Boettcher Family are all available online.

The Bogliasco Foundation, Inc. (NY) (Operating foundation) (http://www.liguriastudycenter.org)
The Bogliasco Foundation, Inc. is headquartered in New York City and grants semester-long fellowships for scholars or artists to work at the Liguria Study Center in Bogliasco, Italy, near Genoa. The fellowship is designed for advanced creative work or scholarly research in archaeology, architecture, classics, dance, film or video, history, landscape architecture, literature, music, philosophy, theater, or visual arts. Interested applicants must

submit a description of the project they will pursue while in Italy, which should result in a public presentation of some kind. The foundation's Web site provides an overview of the facilities and resources in Bogliasco at the Study Center, an online form to request application materials, and New York contact information.

The David Bohnett Foundation (CA) (http://www.bohnettfoundation.org/)
The Los Angeles-based, David Bohnett Foundation's mission is to improve society through social activism. Entrepreneur and co-founder of GeoCities, David Bohnett formed the foundation in 1999 after GeoCities became the largest community on the Internet. The grantmaking organization supports nonprofits in six key target areas, including gun control, voter registration activities, animal language research, development of mass transit and non-fossil fuel transportation, and lesbian and gay organizations that provide community based social services. The foundation encourages grant proposals from qualified nonprofit organizations with a mission that is closely aligned with the foundation's goals. The foundation makes grants for general operating, seed money, capital support, matching grants, and challenge grants. Upon entering the foundation's site, visitors can view recent grants and recipients, grant application information, proposal deadlines, and contact information.

Bonfils-Stanton Foundation (http://www.bonfils-stantonfoundation.org)
The Colorado-based, Bonfils-Stanton Foundation was established in 1963 by Charles Edwin Stanton following the death of his wife, Mary Madeline Bonfils, to support local organizations. Areas of interest of the foundation include arts and culture, community service, education, and science, including hospitals and health services. The foundation's Web site contains information on guidelines, deadlines, board and staff listings, and contact information.

Corella & Bertram F. Bonner Foundation (NJ) (http://www.bonner.org/)
The Corella & Bertram F. Bonner Foundation was established in 1989 with "the hope and, indeed the expectation, that the impact of their support would be far reaching in the areas of hunger and education." In the years since then, the foundation has provided $9.5 million in grants to thousands of religious, community-based hunger relief programs across the country through its Crisis Ministry Program. Over the same period the Bonner Scholars Program has awarded more than $12 million in scholarship support to more than 2,500 students at 24 colleges. The foundation's Web site provides general information on and application guidelines for both programs, including a downloadable grant application cover sheet, as well as highlights from the foundation's newsletter, a list of recent grants, board and staff listings, and contact information.

Mary Owen Borden Foundation (NJ) (http://fdncenter.org/grantmaker/borden/)
The Mary Owen Borden Foundation was founded by Bertram H. Borden in 1934 to honor his recently departed wife. In recent decades, the foundation has limited its new funding to New Jersey's Mercer and Monmouth Counties. Its current giving is focused on disadvantaged youth and their families, including needs such as health, family planning, education, counseling, childcare, substance abuse, and delinquency. Other areas of interest for the foundation include affordable housing, conservation and the environment, and the arts. The foundation's Web site provides general information, application guidelines and procedures, a summary of recent grants, a listing of the foundation's officers and trustees, and contact information.

The Bothin Foundation (CA)
(http://www.pacificfoundationservices.com/bothin/index.html)
The Bothin Foundation was established in California in 1917 to support the western Bay Area, including Sonoma, Marin, San Francisco, and San Mateo Counties. The foundation supports low income, at-risk children, youth, and families; the elderly; and the disabled. To a limited extent, grants may also be made to environmental agencies, arts organizations that predominately serve youth, and community-based capital campaigns. The foundation supports capital or building and equipment needs, but it does not support endowment drives or

general operating expenses. The Web site includes other explicit grantee exclusions, recent grants lists, staff/board list, application procedures, and contact information.

Robert Bowne Foundation, Inc. (NY) (http://fdncenter.org/grantmaker/bowne/)
Established in 1968 by Bowne & Co., Inc., and named in honor of the company's founder, Robert Bowne (1744-1818), the Robert Bowne Foundation, Inc. concentrates its grantmaking on out-of-school programs in New York City that address the issue of youth literacy. The foundation provides grants for special, advocacy, and research projects; general operating expenses of relevant programs; technical assistance in program design and reform; and evaluation studies. The foundation does not support in-school projects or projects following a traditional remedial model of instruction, nor does it award grants to religious organizations, primary or secondary schools, colleges, or universities (except when some aspect of their work is an integral part of a program receiving funding from the foundation). Visitors to the foundation's Web site will find a brief history of the foundation, a detailed description of its program and application procedures, recent grants lists, a listing of the foundation's trustees and staff, and contact information.

Lynde and Harry Bradley Foundation (WI) (http://www.bradleyfdn.org)
Established to commemorate Lynde and Harry Bradley, successful turn-of-the-century Milwaukee businessmen, the Lynde and Harry Bradley Foundation furthers the brothers' mutual interest in helping to improve the quality of life in the metropolitan Milwaukee area and to "preserving and defending the tradition of free representative government and private enterprise which has enabled the American nation to flourish intellectually and economically." Like the Bradley brothers, the foundation is "devoted to strengthening American democratic capitalism and the institutions, principles, and values which sustain and nurture it. Its programs support limited, competent government; a dynamic marketplace for economic, intellectual, and cultural activity; and a vigorous defense at home and abroad of American ideas and institutions." Recognizing that "responsible self-government depends on enlightened citizens and informed public opinion," the foundation also supports scholarly studies and academic achievement. The foundation's Web site provides passionate descriptions of the foundation's mission and driving philosophy, general information about its current program interests and grantmaking policies, and listings of the foundation's board, officers, and staff.

Brainerd Foundation (WA) (http://www.brainerd.org/)
The Brainerd Foundation is dedicated to protecting the environmental quality of the Pacific Northwest—Alaska, Idaho, Montana, Oregon, Washington, and the Canadian province of British Columbia—by supporting "grassroots-oriented projects that motivate citizens to get involved in efforts to protect the environment." The majority of the foundation's grants are awarded within one of three program areas: endangered ecosystems, toxic pollution, and communication strategies. The foundation also makes what it calls Emergency Grants, which range from $250 to $2,000. These grants are given to "organizations that are confronted with an opportunity to carry out important work—in a hurry." Visitors to the foundation's Web site will find detailed program guidelines and limitations, application procedures, lists of recent grant recipients, biographies of the foundation's directors and staff, and a number of links to community resources in the Pacific Northwest.

The Braitmayer Foundation (CT) (http://www.braitmayerfoundation.org)
The Connecticut-based Braitmayer Foundation is a third generation family foundation interested in supporting organizations and programs from across the United States that enhance the education of K-12 children. Areas of particular interest for the foundation include curricular and school reform initiatives; preparation of and professional development opportunities for teachers, particularly those that encourage people of high ability and diverse background to enter and remain in K-12 teaching; and local community efforts, including partnerships, that increase educational opportunities for students. The foundation's Web site includes grant guidelines, a selected list of recent recipients, information about the Braimayer family, trustee listings, and contact information.

Mary Allen Lindsey Branan Foundation (GA) (http://www.wachovia.com/charitable_services/branan_overview.asp)
The Mary Allen Lindsey Branan Foundation of Atlanta is a split-interest trust that supports public charities in Georgia through grantmaking. The foundation places special emphasis on capital improvement projects. Included are needs of the United Methodist Church and its agencies and affiliated programs. Visitors to the foundation's site will find grant guidelines, a grant application, financial information, recent grants awarded, a listing of committee members, and contact information.

Otto Bremer Foundation (MN) (http://fdncenter.org/grantmaker/bremer/)
The mission of the St. Paul-based Otto Bremer Foundation is "to be an accessible and responsible financial resource to aid in the development and cohesion of communities within the states of Minnesota, North Dakota, Wisconsin, and Montana, with preference given to those communities served by the affiliates of Bremer Financial Corporation." Within its geographic focus, the foundation makes grants in the areas of racism, rural poverty, community affairs, education, health, human services, and religion. Visitors to the foundation's Web site will find program and application guidelines, a summary of the foundation's grantmaking activities, and comprehensive grants lists in each program area.

Brentwood Foundation (OH) (http://www.southpointegme.com/frames_pages/)
The Brentwood Foundation was established in 1994 following the merger of Brentwood Hospital, which was an osteopathic hospital, with Suburban Hospital, now known as South Pointe Hospital. The foundation is a charitable trust "dedicated to the promotion and advancement of education, research, patient care and charity care in the field of osteopathic medicine." Specifically, the foundation's mission is to provide educational opportunities designed to strengthen the capabilities of students and practitioners in the osteopathic field, support research efforts that focus on osteopathic medicine, educate the public about services and trends in the field of osteopathic medicine, and initiate and promote activities designed to advance and improve patient care in osteopathic hospitals. The foundation limits its grants to organizations located in Ohio, particularly those organizations in northeastern Ohio area. Additionally, the foundation prefers to make grants for specific projects rather than for operating costs or capital. Details on how to submit an application, deadlines, and contact information are all available on the foundation's Web site.

Brico Fund, Inc. (WI) (http://bricofund.org/)
Founded in 1995, the Brico Fund, Inc. is a private foundation located in Milwaukee, Wisconsin, funding at both the local and national levels, with a mission to promote a just and equitable society, restore and sustain the earth's natural systems, nourish the creative spirit, and secure full participation in society for women and girls. Operating, program, capital and endowment grants have been made in the past years. Visit the fund's Web site to find a history of the organization, funding criteria, application procedures, grants listings, directors' listings, and contact information.

The Bright Mountain Foundation (CO) (http://fdncenter.org/grantmaker/brightmountain/)
Founded in 1999, the Bright Mountain Foundation of Colorado believes that "the heart of a community is based on how the community treats its more vulnerable members." The foundation is dedicated to helping children, senior citizens, and persons living with HIV/AIDS to enjoy safer, healthier, and more fulfilling lives in a way that promotes the potential of the individual. Visit the foundation's Web site to learn about grant programs, view grant guidelines and procedure, and access contact information.

The Broad Foundation (CA) (http://www.broadfoundation.org/)
The Broad Foundation, located in Los Angeles, California, was established in 1999. The foundation funds innovative efforts to dramatically improve governance, management, and labor relations in large urban school systems. The foundation is "dedicated to building K-12 educational leadership capacity, strengthening union-management relations and supporting aggressive, system-wide strategies to increase student achievement." To apply for a

grant, applicants send an initial concept paper to the foundation via e-mail. Contact information is listed on the Web site. The site also provides more specific information about the types of grants the foundation provides and the foundation's staff, founders, and program areas.

The Brookdale Foundation Group (NY) (http://www.brookdalefoundation.org)
Based in New York City, the Brookdale Foundation Group is comprised of The Brookdale Foundation, the Glendale Foundation, and Ramapo Trust. These three distinct entities have separate officers and boards of directors or trustees, but all are endowed by the Schwartz family and share a common focus: the needs and challenges of America's elderly population. The group has three major funding initiatives: the Leadership in Aging Program, a fellowship in the field of gerontology and geriatrics; the National Group Respite Program, which provides small seed grants and technical assistance to foster the development of dementia-specific, social model day-service programs to meet the needs of persons with Alzheimer's and their caregivers; and the Relatives as Parents Program, to establish community-based services to grandparents and other relatives who have assumed the responsibility of surrogate parent. However, the group will also consider new and innovative projects that will provide direct services and that will improve the lives of older people. Guidelines for the three funding initiatives and instructions for application are provided, as well as contact information for each program. Those interested in the Leadership in Aging Program can also find lists of participating institutions, members of the medical advisory and review boards who review applications, past fellows, and senior fellows on the site. For those who wish to submit proposals unrelated to the three major initiatives, the group provides suggestions for submission as well as a downloadable information cover sheet for general grant applications and contact information.

Gladys Brooks Foundation (NY) (http://www.gladysbrooksfoundation.org/)
The Gladys Brooks Foundation of New York makes grants to private nonprofit, publicly supported libraries, educational institutions, hospitals, and clinics. Generally, the board will only entertain grant applications from applicants located in Connecticut, Delaware, Maine, Massachusetts, New Hampshire, New Jersey, New York, Pennsylvania, Rhode Island, Vermont, the District of Columbia, Maryland, Virginia, West Virginia, Ohio, Indiana, North Carolina, and South Carolina. Visitors to the foundation's Web site will find a biography of Ms. Brooks, a grant history, recent annual reports, and a downloadable grant application.

The Brown Foundation (TX) (http://www.brownfoundation.org/)
Founded in 1951, the Houston-based Brown Foundation supports qualifying nonprofit organizations in Texas in the areas of public education at the primary and secondary levels, community service, and the arts. The foundation's Web site includes complete funding guidelines and limitations, along with information on the foundation's current funding interests, program guidelines, a downloadable annual report, FAQs, and contact information.

James Graham Brown Foundation, Inc. (KY) (http://www.jgbf.org/)
Established under a trust agreement in 1943 and formally incorporated in 1954, the James Graham Brown Foundation, Inc. is dedicated to fostering the well-being, quality of life, and image of Jefferson County and Kentucky. The foundation does this by actively supporting and funding projects in the fields of civic and economic development, education, youth, and health and general welfare. Since the death of its benefactor, James Graham Brown, in 1969, the foundation has awarded approximately 2,100 grants totaling more than $200 million—mainly in Kentucky, with a small percentage awarded in other parts of the Southeast. The foundation's Web site provides information about the foundation's proposal requirements and application procedures, a list of recent grant recipients organized by program area, and contact information.

Eva L. and Joseph M. Bruening Foundation (OH) (http://www.fmscleveland.com/bruening/)

The Eva L. and Joseph M. Bruening Foundation was established to support charitable organizations in Cuyahoga County, Ohio. The foundation supports programs that enhance the quality of community life by educating youth, comforting the aged, and encouraging the disabled and disadvantaged. Visitors to the foundation's Web site will find information on the application process, grant guidelines, a listing of recent grants, financial reports, and contact information.

Bruner Foundation, Inc. (MA) (http://www.brunerfoundation.org)

Based in Cambridge, the Bruner Foundation, Inc. administers the Rudy Bruner Award for Urban Excellence, created in 1986 by Simeon Bruner, and named in honor of his late father. The award was created by Mr. Bruner to "foster a better understanding of the role of architecture in the urban environment and has become one of America's leading forums for the discussion of issues related to urban architecture, planning, and revitalization." The Award celebrates and publicizes places that "are developed with such vision and imagination that they transform urban problems into creative solutions." The award seeks to promote fresh and innovative thinking about cities and "to encourage us all to demand—and build—excellence in the urban environment." The site contains instructions and guidelines for applying, a list with descriptions of past award winners, contact information, and a downloadable order form for the foundation's publications, which include in-depth, illustrated case studies of winner projects and a distillation of selection committee discussions on the nature of the urban excellence.

Frank H. and Eva B. Buck Foundation (CA) (http://www.buckscholarships.org)

The Vacaville, California-based Frank H. and Eva B. Buck Foundation is dedicated to supporting education. The foundation administers the Frank H. Buck Scholarship program, under which full scholarship support is awarded annually to students "who have an overwhelming motivation to succeed in all endeavors and who have demonstrated a commitment to themselves, their families and their communities." The foundation gives preference to scholars who live in California's Third Congressional District, as served by Frank H. Buck, which at that time included Solano, Napa, Yolo, Sacramento, San Joaquin, and Contra Costa Counties. Direct support is also sometimes given to educational institutions, libraries, and others in support of the foundation's main emphasis. The foundation also supports other charitable endeavors as determined from time to time by the board of directors. Scholarship applications may be obtained by writing, e-mailing, leaving a voice mail, or submitting a request online. In addition to scholarship guidelines, visitors will find a short biography of Frank H. Buck and contact information.

Temple Hoyne Buell Foundation (CO) (http://www.buellfoundation.org)

The Temple Hoyne Buell Foundation was established in 1962 to support the charitable interests of Temple Hoyne Buell, a noted architect and civic and business leader in Colorado. The foundation's funding priorities changed to focus on organizations that support youth, especially in the areas of "early intervention, prevention, and improving the social and educational systems critical to the well-being of Colorado's youngest citizens." the foundation's main areas of interest include early childhood development and education, education, the social and emotional development of children, and family stability for children. Visitors to the foundation's Web site will find detailed grant guidelines, downloadable applications, funding types, recent awards given, descriptions of the foundation itself, and contact information, among other resources.

Bullitt Foundation (WA) (http://www.bullitt.org/)

The Seattle-based Bullitt Foundation is committed to the protection and restoration of the environment of the Pacific Northwest. This commitment includes environmental problems that disproportionately impact low-income urban and rural communities. The foundation invites proposals from nonprofit organizations that serve Washington, Oregon, Idaho, British Columbia, western Montana (including the Rocky Mountain Range), and coastal

Alaska, from Cook Inlet to the Canadian border. Within these broad parameters, the foundation focuses its grantmaking activities in energy and climate change; forests and land ecosystems; growth management and transportation; public outreach, education, and capacity building; rivers, wetlands, and estuaries; sustainable agriculture; and toxic substances, mining, and radioactive waste. Visitors to the foundation's Web site will find program descriptions, grant application and final report instructions, printable grant applications, detailed grantee information, a report from the foundation's president (Denis Hayes, national coordinator of the first Earth Day in 1970), an FAQ section, board and staff listings, preliminary financial statements, and contact information.

Margaret E. Burnham Charitable Trust (ME) (http://www.megrants.org/Burnham.htm)
The Portland, Maine-based, Margaret E. Burnham Charitable Trust makes grants to organizations in or serving the state of Maine. The subject areas supported annually include community/social services, medical, education, arts/culture, and the environment. The trust is a member of the Maine Philanthropy Center. The trust's Web site also includes previous years' grants lists, grant application information, deadline information, a printable grant application, and contact information.

Burning Foundation (WA) (http://fdncenter.org/grantmaker/burning/)
The Burning Foundation of Seattle, Washington, is committed to three main interests. The environmental program is concerned with the preservation of the region's rivers, forests, fish population, and land. The conservation program for low-income children and youth provides grants to organizations that allow this population hands-on experience with protecting the environment in which they live. The foundation also supports teen pregnancy prevention through school-based health and education programs, mentoring projects, and community clinic programs. Visitors to the foundation's Web site will find further information on the foundation's programs, application guidelines, and contact information.

Burroughs Wellcome Fund (NC) (http://www.bwfund.org/)
Established in 1955 to advance the medical sciences by supporting research and other scientific and educational activities, the Burroughs Wellcome Fund today emphasizes "career development of outstanding scientists and advancing areas in the basic medical sciences that are underfunded or that have a shortage of qualified researchers." The fund makes grants in five focus areas: basic biomedical sciences, infectious disease, interfaces in science, science education, and transitional research. The fund's programs support middle and high school students and academic scientists through postdoctoral-faculty bridging awards, faculty awards, and institutional awards. The fund's Web site offers complete descriptions of the fund's programs; award eligibility requirements and guidelines; application deadlines; a listing of the fund's board of directors, officers, and staff; a fast-loading version of its most recent annual report; news briefs; and recent issues of Focus, the fund's newsletter.

The Bush Foundation (MN) (http://www.bushfoundation.org/)
Archibald Granville Bush and his wife, Edyth Bassler Bush, created the Bush Foundation in 1953 to encourage and promote charitable, scientific, literary, and educational efforts. The Bush Foundation, based in St. Paul, Minnesota, "is committed to enhancing the quality of life in Minnesota, North Dakota, and South Dakota by making grants to nonprofit organizations and providing fellowships to individuals in those states." The foundation's primary grantmaking areas are human services and health, education, and arts and humanities. Its fellowship program for individuals focuses on leadership, medicine, and arts. The foundation also supports out-of-region projects with historically black private colleges and fully accredited tribally controlled colleges. The Web site provides specific details on the types of grants awarded, previous grants, and what to include in each type of grant or fellowship application, as well as downloadable applications. Contact information is available on the foundation Web site.

Edyth Bush Charitable Foundation (FL) (http://www.edythbush.org)
The mission of the Edyth Bush Charitable Foundation is "grantmaking designed to help people help themselves." To that end, the foundation supports programs that "help underprivileged or needy people to improve themselves or relieve human suffering." The foundation makes grants to nonprofit organizations exclusively located and/or operating within a 100-mile radius of Winter Park, Florida, with special emphasis on Orange, Seminole, Osceola, and Lake Counties. The foundation, which was founded by the widow of Archibald G. Bush, a director and principal shareholder of the Minnesota Mining & Manufacturing Company, also has broad interests in human service, education, healthcare, and a limited interest in the arts. Visitors to the foundation's Web site will find a detailed account of the foundation's application policies and procedures, as well as recent grants lists by subject area.

Butler Family Fund (DC) (http://fdncenter.org/grantmaker/butler/)
The Butler Family Fund of Washington, D.C. has funding priorities focusing on homelessness and criminal justice reform. The fund is also concerned with global warming. Geographic areas of interest include California, Chicago, New York, Philadelphia, Wisconsin, Washington, D.C., and London. The fund does not accept unsolicited proposals. Visit the fund's Web site to find a history of the fund's grantmaking, board and staff lists, and contact information.

Byerly Foundation (SC) (http://www.byerlyfoundation.org/)
The mission of the Byerly Foundation is to "improve the quality of life in Hartsville, South Carolina by working with public and private interests to improve the education, economic and social needs of our citizens." the foundation's grantmaking is divided between the areas of education, economic development, and community life. Visit the foundation's Web site to find a listing of programs previously supported, further information on funding priorities, application policies, and contact information.

The Morris and Gwendolyn Cafritz Foundation (DC) (http://www.cafritzfoundation.org/)
The Morris and Gwendolyn Cafritz Foundation was established in 1948 by Morris Cafritz, a civic leader who raised money for numerous charities and community projects. This Washington, D.C.-based foundation was created with the goal of "improving the quality of life for residents of the Washington, D.C. area," and it currently funds projects in four areas: arts and humanities, education, health, and community service. The foundation concentrates its grantmaking on organizations whose project offer direct assistance to the District of Columbia and its environs." The foundation uses the Washington Regional Association of Grantmakers Common Grant Application, which can be downloaded from the foundation's Web site. Also available on the foundation's Web site are grant guidelines and restrictions, an annual report, contact information, information about grantees, and a list of linked resources for grantseekers.

The California Endowment (CA) (http://www.calendow.org/)
Established in 1996 as a result of Blue Cross of California's conversion from a nonprofit to a for-profit corporation, the California Endowment works to "expand access to affordable, quality healthcare for underserved individuals and communities, and to promote fundamental improvements in the health status of all Californians." Within this context, and as a new foundation keenly interested in delivering maximum benefit to its constituents, the endowment has two grant programs, as well as special projects. CommunitiesFirst focuses on three broad areas of interest: access, health and well-being, and multicultural health. The Local Opportunities Fund was created "to provide communities with resources to address important health issues on a local level." The endowment's Web site offers application procedures and a downloadable application, an online publications order form, staff and board listings, contact information, an electronic feedback form, and an extensive list of relevant Internet resources.

California Masonic Foundation (CA) (http://www.freemason.org/foundation/index.htm)
The California Masonic Foundation, located in San Francisco, California, awards scholarships to California high school students. The program is intended to assist exceptional California high school seniors who are seeking to attend a university or trade school within the United States. Scholarships are based on the whole person concept, with emphasis on academic performance and financial need. Scholarship manuals can be requested by mail or downloaded from the Web site. The foundation also sponsors the Masonic Student Assistance Program, a series of three-day workshops for California state educators, administrators, and support staff in schools from kindergarten through high school. These workshops teach participants how to identify kids at risk and help them on the road to a successful life. More information about the program and contact information is available on the site.

California Wellness Foundation (CA) (http://www.tcwf.org/)
The mission of the California Wellness Foundation is to improve the health of the people of California by making grants for health promotion, wellness education, and disease prevention. The foundation concentrates its grantmaking activities in eight areas: diversity in the health professions, environmental health, healthy aging, mental health, teenage pregnancy prevention, violence prevention, women's health, and work and health. It also makes grants through a Special Projects Fund for activities outside those eight areas. In addition to information about its general grants program and descriptions of strategic initiatives in each of its eight focus areas, the foundation's Web site provides a listing of latest grants, news, links to related Web sites, and the foundation's newsletter, downloadable in Adobe Acrobat format.

Louise P. and Wofford B. Camp Foundation (CA)
(http://fdncenter.org/grantmaker/camp/990pf.pdf)
View recent tax returns of the California-based Louise P. and Wofford B. Camp Foundation.

The Campbell Foundation (FL) (http://members.aol.com/campfound)
Based in Ft. Lauderdale, Florida, the Campbell Foundation was established in 1986 by the late Richard Campbell Zahn. "It was Mr. Zahn's wish that his foundation support other nonprofit organizations conducting clinical research into the prevention and treatment of HIV/AIDS, and related conditions and illnesses. The foundation's funding lies in alternative, nontraditional avenues of research." The foundation's Web site features grant application instructions, grants listings, and contact information.

James & Abigail Campbell Foundation (HI)
(http://www.kapolei.com/ejc/guidelines_fdn.htm)
Established in 1980, the James & Abigail Campbell Foundation is funded by Campbell family members and friends to perpetuate the memory of James and Abigail Campbell. The mission of the foundation is to strengthen families, create more effective educational programs, and improve the quality of life for Hawaii's people. Visitors to the foundation's Web site will find a brief history of the organization, further funding priorities, annual reports, grant application information, recent grants listings, and contact information.

Cannon Foundation (NC) (http://www.thecannonfoundationinc.org)
The Cannon Foundation was established in 1943 to support Cabarrus County and the State of North Carolina through philanthropy. Historically, grants have been made for healthcare, primarily in the local area, and education, especially to independent liberal arts colleges in the Piedmont and western regions of the state. In recent years, there has been an increase in grants to human and social service programs and organizations. A limited number of grants are made in the fields of arts and culture, historic preservation, and environmental concerns. Grants in the area of religion normally are reserved for local (Cabarrus County) churches and are restricted in amount. Visit the foundation's Web site to learn more about the mission, guidelines and application procedure, FAQs, grants listing, board and staff data, and contact information.

Iris & B. Gerald Cantor Foundation (CA) (Operating foundation) (http://www.cantorfoundation.org/)
Established in 1978, the Iris & B. Gerald Cantor Foundation is involved with the support and promotion of the arts. The goal of the foundation, which bears the names of its founders, is to "promote and encourage the recognition and appreciation of excellence in the arts; to enhance cultural life internationally through the support of art exhibitions, scholarship, and the endowment of galleries at major museums; and to support biomedical research." It has donated more than 450 Rodin sculptures to institutions throughout the world, funded and organized Rodin exhibitions, created a Rodin Research Fund at Stanford University, and given numerous endowments to major art museums. The foundation's support of biomedical research focuses on healthcare initiatives for women, with an emphasis on the early diagnosis and treatment of breast cancer. The foundation makes significant gifts to endow new patient facilities, laboratories, and research fellowships at hospitals and medical centers. Visitors will find a site mostly devoted to Rodin's life and work, a schedule of traveling Rodin exhibitions organized by the foundation, a suggested reading list on Rodin, the artist's bio, a virtual gallery and information on the foundation's activities and a biography of the founders.

Canyon Research (CA) (Operating foundation) (http://www.canyonresearch.org)
Canyon Research seeks to advance communications research and education by funding specialized research projects that focus on three areas of support: innovative, computer-related communications technology; public communications policy; and domestic communications regulatory issues. Canyon Research supports these three areas of research through grants and fellowships that allow researchers to develop new and innovative technologies that in turn will create breakthroughs in computer communications capabilities. There are currently no restrictions on grant amounts and no restrictions based on geography. Canyon Research periodically issues a call for applications that describe the targeted research and education projects funded; proposals that do not fall within the specified areas of support or that are not in response to a specific call for applications are unlikely to be funded. This Web site features a Call for Applications section, where the targeted research project is described; application procedures; grantmaking guidelines; areas of exclusion; contact information; and proposals, final reports, and descriptions of past and current projects.

Captain Planet Foundation, Inc. (GA) (http://www.turner.com/cpf)
Based in Atlanta, Georgia and established in 1991, the Captain Planet Foundation, Inc. is funded by a percentage of the licensing and merchandising revenue generated by the Captain Planet character, the animated television series, and other contributions. The mission of the foundation is to fund and support hands-on environmental projects for children and youths. Its objective is to "encourage innovative programs that empower children and youth around the world to work individually and collectively to solve environmental problems in their neighborhoods and communities." All prospective projects must promote understanding of environmental issues, focus on hands-on involvement, involve children and young adults ages 6-18, promote interaction and cooperation within the group, help young people develop planning and problem solving skills, include adult supervision, and commit to follow-up communication with the foundation. Visitors to the foundation's Web site will find an online proposal form, grant lists by state, environmental links, and contact information.

CarEth Foundation (MA) (http://www.funder.org/grantmaking/careth/)
The CarEth Foundation seeks to promote "a compassionate world of enduring and just peace with social, economic, and political equality for all." In support of its mission, the foundation is currently funding programs that promote the creation of a global community of peace and justice, democracy in the United States, and peaceful conflict resolution. The foundation is also currently interested in projects involving today's youth. Visitors to the foundation's Web site will find general descriptions of program goals, application

procedures and guidelines, and a list of recent grantees with links to all recipient organizations' Web sites.

CARLISLE Foundation (MA) (http://www.carlislefoundation.org)
Based in Framingham, Massachusetts, the CARLISLE Foundation evolved from CARLISLE Services, Inc., a grantmaking company founded in 1988 that acted as an intermediary between private donors and the human services community, soliciting and reviewing grant proposals, and presenting them to donors for consideration. In 1991, those same donors established the CARLISLE Foundation as a more efficient and effective means for continuing their philanthropic endeavors and as a statement of their continuing commitment. CARLISLE Foundation only funds programs operating within the six New England states and "attempts to promote creative problem solving and interventions." The foundation prefers to support new and innovative projects or those that demonstrate potential as models. Though it reviews a wide range of proposals, several areas have emerged as high priorities: substance abuse, domestic and community violence, homelessness/housing, economic development, and other services for children, youth, and families. In addition to grantmaking, the foundation provides free technical assistance or consultation to human services organizations. More information about this service and application and grant guidelines are available on the site. Also of interest are descriptions of programs currently funded, a list of organizations that received prior grants, and contact information.

Carnegie Corporation of New York (NY) (http://www.carnegie.org)
Carnegie Corporation of New York was created by Andrew Carnegie in 1911 to promote "the advancement and diffusion of knowledge and understanding." In addition to a brief history of Andrew Carnegie and his philanthropies and information about the foundation itself, the Web site of the Carnegie Corporation of New York gives visitors general information about the foundation's four currently supported program areas: education, international peace and security, international development, and strengthening U.S. democracy. Additional support is available through the Carnegie Corporation Scholars Program and the Special Opportunities Fund. The last affords the foundation an opportunity to make grants and appropriations outside its other defined program areas. Available as well are application guidelines and grant restrictions, a description of the foundation's initiatives, full-text versions of selected Carnegie publications, a listing of foundation officers and trustees, links to other foundation and nonprofit resources on the Internet, and contact information.

Carnegie Endowment for International Peace (DC) (Operating foundation) (http://www.ceip.org)
The Carnegie Endowment for International Peace was established with a gift from Andrew Carnegie in 1910. It conducts programs of research, discussion, publication, and education in international affairs and U.S. foreign policy and publishes the quarterly magazine *Foreign Policy.* The Endowment and its associates seek "to invigorate and extend both expert and public discussion on a wide range of international issues," such as worldwide migration, nuclear non-proliferation, and regional conflicts. It also "engages in and encourages projects designed to foster innovative contributions in international affairs." The Carnegie Endowment also has a public policy research center in Moscow to promote collaboration among scholars and specialists in the U.S., Russia, and other post-Soviet states. The Moscow Center holds seminars, workshops, and study groups and provides a forum for international figures to present their views to "informed Moscow audiences." The endowment has a Junior Fellows Program in which junior fellows work as research assistants to the endowment's senior associates. Fellows are uniquely qualified graduating seniors and individuals who have graduated during the past academic year and are selected from a pool of nominees. The Web site offers information on this program, as wells as information about the various projects within the Global Policy and Russia/Eurasia programs and links to the Carnegie Moscow Center and its magazine, *Foreign Policy.* A media guide, library, downloadable publications and book summaries, and lists of associates and their biographies, junior fellows, and board of trustees are also available.

The Carnegie Foundation for the Advancement of Teaching (CA) (Operating foundation) (http://www.carnegiefoundation.org)

Andrew Carnegie founded The Carnegie Foundation for the Advancement of Teaching in 1905, "to do and perform all things necessary to encourage, uphold, and dignify the profession of the teacher and the cause of higher education." Based in Menlo Park, California, the foundation is a major national and international center for research and policy studies about teaching. The foundation's work includes founding the Educational Testing Service and developing the Graduate Record Exam. It uses income from its endowment to support its research and publication activities and makes no grants. A small group of distinguished scholars generate, critique, and monitor advances in the theory and practice of education in the United States and worldwide. The foundation's mission is to address "the hardest problems faced in teaching in public schools, colleges and universities: how to succeed in the classroom, how best to achieve lasting student learning and how to assess the impact of teaching on students." The site contains an annual report, which further describes the work and programs of the foundation, including the Carnegie Academy for the Scholarship of Teaching and Learning, Preparation for the Professions Program, Higher Education and the Development of Moral and Civic Responsibility, and Cultures of Teaching and Learning in Higher Education. The site includes an online forum for conversations with teachers at all levels to converse about problems they have solved; press releases and articles; resource pages, with lists of publications, surveys, information on various facilities at the foundation, archives, and links; and contact information.

Carnegie Hero Fund Commission (PA) (Operating foundation) (http://www.carnegiehero.org/)

A coal mine explosion on January 25, 1904 near Harwick, Pennsylvania and the death of the two men who died trying to rescue those inside the mine inspired industrialist and philanthropist Andrew Carnegie to establish the Carnegie Hero Fund Commission. Within three months after the explosion that claimed 181 lives, Carnegie set aside $5 million under the care of a commission to recognize "civilization's heroes" and to carry out his wish that "heroes and those dependent upon them should be freed from pecuniary cares resulting from their heroism." Ninety-five years later, their mission is still the same: "to recognize acts of civilian heroism throughout the United States and Canada," and "to provide financial assistance to the awardees and the dependents of those awardees who are killed or disabled by their heroic actions." The Pittsburgh, Pennsylvania-based foundation awards a bronze medal, a $3000 grant, and scholarship eligibility to all cases considered worthy. Visitors to the Web site can read about the history behind the Commission and about past awardees; find award guidelines, application instructions, and contact information; peruse a bibliography for additional information about the Commission; and find links related to Andrew Carnegie.

The Kristen Ann Carr Fund (NY) (http://www.sarcoma.com)

Originally founded as a division of the T.J. Martell Foundation for Cancer, Leukemia, and AIDS Research, the Kristen Ann Carr Fund "provides grants for cancer research and seeks to improve all aspects of cancer patient life with an emphasis on adolescents and young adults." The Kristen Ann Carr Fund honors the life of Kristen Ann Carr (1971-1993), "a remarkable young woman who sought life and love," who herself had sarcoma. The New York City-based fund was established at her request and seeks to provide funding for research and treatment of sarcoma, provide funding for the education of young physicians, improve the quality of cancer patient life, and develop an adolescent care unit at Memorial Sloan-Kettering Cancer Center. Among the programs are the Sunshine Program, which attempts to grant the wishes of adolescent and young adult patients at Memorial Sloan Kettering, with a particular emphasis on and interest in the music and entertainment industries, and the Post-Treatment Resource Program, which is a resource center that offers a wide variety of services assisting people in their adjustment to life as cancer survivors. Visitors to the fund's Web site can find program information, links to related resources, news, and contact information.

Amon G. Carter Foundation (TX) (http://agcf.org/)

Established in 1945, the Amon G. Carter Foundation of Fort Worth, Texas, provides half of its annual grant budget to the Amon Carter Museum and the other half to general grants. Primary fields of interest include the arts, education, health and medical services, human and social services, programs benefiting youth and elderly, and civic and community endeavors that enhance quality of life. Visit the foundation's Web site to find a history of the organization and family, financial and grant information, application procedures, grants listings, and contact information.

The Carthage Foundation (PA) (http://www.scaife.com)

Based in Pittsburgh, Pennsylvania, the Carthage Foundation is one of the Scaife Foundations and confines most of its grant awards to programs that will address public policy questions concerned with national and international issues. There are no geographical restrictions, but the foundation does not make grants to individuals. Visitors to the foundation's Web site will find a downloadable annual report, which includes a grant list and financials; grant application instructions; links to other Scaife Foundations; and contact information.

Roy J. Carver Charitable Trust (IA) (http://www.carvertrust.org/)

The Roy J. Carver Charitable Trust was created in 1982 through the will of Roy J. Carver, an industrialist and philanthropist who died in 1981. Based in Muscatine, Iowa, "it is the largest private foundation in the state of Iowa," listing four funding areas: medical and scientific research, education, youth, and miscellaneous, which are grants that do no fall within the trust's four primary program classifications that have received special consideration because of their location." The majority of grants are awarded for initiatives in Iowa and a portion of western Illinois. Visitors to the trust's Web site will find information about each of the trust's five funding areas, grant lists, information about grant guidelines and application procedures, a downloadable application cover sheet, and contact information.

Mary Flagler Cary Charitable Trust (NY) (http://www.carytrust.org/)

The Mary Flagler Cary Charitable Trust is a New York City-based foundation that was created in 1968 by the will of its namesake, a great lover of music and the environment. The trustees work to continue supporting the interests of the founder and reevaluating what that means as times change. While much of the trust's assets are committed to the institutes now housing the family art collection, there are three unrelated grant programs. The Music Program "supports professional performance institutions that add to the vitality and diversity of New York City's musical life." There are also special, bi-annual funds that support the commission of new musical works and that support ensembles and nonprofit record companies to record living composers. The Urban Environment Program "supports grassroots groups and helps develop local leadership to work on environmental problems within low-income neighborhoods in New York City." This program has also established funds at the Citizens Committee for New York City and the Trust for Public Land. The Conservation Program primarily supports "collaborative efforts to protect natural resources, including barrier islands, estuaries and coastal wetlands at selected sites along the Atlantic coastline from Delaware to Florida." The trust's Web site specifies the areas that the trust funds and underlines that most awards go to local action groups or regional/national conservation groups that are active at these sites. Lists of trustees and staff, categorized lists of previous grantees, and basic financial information are provided online. The trust requests that interested applicants submit letters of inquiry.

Annie E. Casey Foundation (MD) (http://www.aecf.org/)

Established in 1948 by Jim Casey, one of the founders of United Parcel Service, and his siblings, the Annie E. Casey Foundation is dedicated to "fostering public policies, human service reforms, and community supports that more effectively meet the needs of today's vulnerable children and families." Working with neighborhoods and state and local governments, the foundation provides grants to public and nonprofit organizations to strengthen the support services, social networks, physical infrastructure, employment, self-determination, and economic vitality of distressed communities. Most grantees have been invited by the foundation to participate in these projects. The foundation does not make grants to individuals, nor does it support capital projects that are not an integral part of a foundation-sponsored initiative. Visitors to the foundation's Web site will find KIDS COUNT, an interactive database with national and state-level indicators of children's well-being; publications, including online newsletters and the foundation's magazine *AdvoCasey;* grant guidelines; and extensive information about its ongoing initiatives.

The Casey Family Program (WA) (Operating foundation) (http://www.casey.org)
Jim Casey, founder of United Parcel Service, created the Casey Family Program in 1966 to "provide planned, long-term out-of-home care to children and youth, with long-term family foster care as its core." Its mission is "to support families, youth, and children in reaching their full potential." The program, "through national and local community partnerships, advocacy efforts, and by serving as a center for information and learning about children in need of permanent family connection aims to positively impact the lives of children," in addition to those the Program directly helps with foster care. Headquartered in Seattle, Washington, there are field offices in Arizona, California, Colorado, Hawaii, Idaho, Louisiana, Montana, North Dakota, Oklahoma, Oregon, South Dakota, Texas, Washington, and Wyoming. Visitors to the program's Web site will find information on the organization, research services, annual reports, its strategic plan, locations, contact information, and links to sister organization and resources.

Harold K.L. Castle Foundation (HI) (http://www.castlefoundation.org/)
The Harold K.L. Castle Foundation, Hawaii's largest private foundation, was founded in 1962 by Harold Castle, the owner of Kaneohe Ranch. A significant portion of Mr. Castle's real estate assets were bequeathed to the foundation upon his death in 1967, and it is that asset base from which most of the foundation's grants are made. Historically, the foundation's priorities have been private education, youth, and health programs for windward Oahu, but the broad purpose of the foundation allows it to respond to any current community concern. In recent years, the foundation made grants in the areas of arts and culture, education, the environment, health and human services, science and technology, and youth services. The foundation is also one of the few private funders that still awards large capital improvement grants. The foundation's Web site provides a brief history of the foundation, an overview of its current priorities, proposal guidelines, a listing of recent grants, news briefs and related links, and contact information.

Samuel N. and Mary Castle Foundation (HI) (http://fdncenter.org/grantmaker/castle/)
For more than a century, the Samuel N. and Mary Castle Foundation and its precursor, the Samuel N. Castle Memorial Trust, have served the needs of the people of Hawaii. Over the years, the foundation's grantmaking has focused primarily on the support of early education and child care, private education (elementary and high schools, as well as colleges and universities), Protestant churches, and arts and cultural organizations with ties to the Castle family. In addition, through the Henry and Dorothy Castle Memorial Fund, the foundation supports the health and human services sector, concentrating its funds on agencies directly providing services to young children and their families. Because Hawaii's population is concentrated on O'ahu, preference is given to organizations whose programs are O'ahu-based. The foundation's Web site provides a history of the foundation and brief biographies of Samuel N. and Mary Tenney Castle, messages from the foundation's president and executive director, a rundown of its grantmaking policies and application procedures, a list of grants awarded in previous years, and contact information.

The Cleo Foundation (CA) (http://www.pacificfoundationservices.com/cleo/index.html)
The San Francisco-based Cleo Foundation (formerly the CAW Foundation) was established in 1997 to support public charities in surrounding counties (including limited funding for San Luis Obispo and Seattle, Washington). The foundation's interests include children, youth, and adults in areas such as education, human services, healthcare, and homelessness. While primarily focusing on capital improvements and equipment

acquisition, the foundation will consider support for specific projects. The foundation will not support annual appeals or endowments. At the foundation's Web site, visitors will find specific application procedures, recent grants list, and contact information.

Center for the Public Domain (NC) (http://www.centerforthepublicdomain.org/)
The Center for the Public Domain, located in Durham, North Carolina, "supports the growth of a healthy and robust public domain by establishing programs, grants, and partnerships in the areas of academic research, medicine, law, education, media, technology, and the arts." The center prioritizes the funding of collaborative projects. Funding guidelines, details of the application process, and descriptions of organizations the center has previously funded can all be found online, along with contact information for interested applicants. The center's Web site also serves as a reference on intellectual property and its applications.

Century Foundation (NY) (Operating foundation) (http://www.tcf.org/)
The Century Foundation (formerly the Twentieth Century Fund) was founded in 1919 and endowed by Edward A. Filene to "undertake timely and critical analyses of major economic, political, and social institutions and issues." The foundation is an operating rather than grantmaking foundation and does not award fellowships or scholarships, support dissertation research, or make grants to individuals or institutions. Similarly, it almost never supports large-scale data-gathering efforts or research designed primarily to develop theory or methodology. Currently, it welcomes proposals in four areas: improving living standards, restoring civil society and respect for government, reinvigorating the media, and identifying new foundations for American foreign policy. In addition to information on and excerpts from current and recently completed projects, visitors to the foundation's Web site will find a mission statement and history of the foundation; detailed program descriptions; proposal submission guidelines; the foundation's recent annual report; press releases and a publications catalog; listings of the foundation's board and staff; including e-mail links to staff members; links to sites of interest; and contact information.

The Ceres Foundation (CA) (http://fdncenter.org/grantmaker/ceres/)
The mission of the Ceres Foundation of Newport Beach, California, is "to provide the catalyst needed to mobilize human energies and talents that lie dormant." To accomplish this, the foundation strives to help "people in deprived conditions to develop the skills, motivation and teamwork they need to become productive contributors to society. This could include support for quality pre-schools, youth activities, mentoring programs, job training, rehabilitation, and other services which are not adequately provided." The foundation also helps "to create conditions in which people can make good use of their skills and motivation. This could include support for creation of job opportunities, resources for entrepreneurs, community networks, safe neighborhoods, and healthy environments." Visit the foundation's Web site to view grant guidelines and contact information.

Chahara Foundation (MA) (http://www.chahara.org)
The Chahara Foundation's mission is "to support radical grassroots nonprofits run by and for low income women in the greater Boston area" The foundation seeks to "amplify women's voices as they fight to shape public opinion and policy around the issue of economic oppression." The foundation targets organizations that provide service, outreach, advocacy and/or organizing training with particular emphasis on women/girls who have known and are trying to move out of poverty. The foundation's Web site features further information about the foundation's mission, news on the current grant cycle, recent grantees, a downloadable grant application, and contact information.

The Challenge Foundation (TX) (http://www.challengefoundation.org/)
Established in 1989, the Challenge Foundation supports "model educational initiatives that make it possible for every American child to attain a high school education that produces literate, factually aware, and thinking graduates second to none in the world." The primary vehicle for the foundation's grantmaking is through the Charter School Grantmaking Program, which supports model charter schools that embrace the foundation's mission. Visit

the foundation's Web site to find out more about its programs, view recent success stories, and obtain contact information.

The Champlin Foundations (RI) (http://fdncenter.org/grantmaker/champlin/)
The aim of the Champlin Foundations is "to provide funds to those tax-exempt organizations in Rhode Island who serve the broadest possible segment of the population." The Warwick, Rhode Island-based organization makes direct grants for capital needs, such as the purchase of equipment, construction, renovation, and purchases of real property. They do not provide funds for facilities or equipment for agencies who engage in "program activities," such as counseling and day care, and do not rely solely on applications to allocate grants. They identify and make grants to many organizations that have not applied, or may encourage those who have not to apply. Grantseekers can consult the foundation's Web site for guidelines and funding criteria, and find contact information, a list of members of the distribution committee, and a breakdown of previous grants.

Harry Chapin Foundation (NY) (http://fdncenter.org/grantmaker/harrychapin/)
The Harry Chapin Foundation, founded to "address the problems of the disadvantaged and promote educational programs that lead to a greater understanding of human suffering," provides funding for community education, arts in education, and agricultural and environmental programs. The foundation favors programs in the New York region, although it will consider national programs. The foundation's Web site provides funding guidelines and a contact for application requests, past grant recipients, a biography of Harry Chapin, and a listing of board members.

Charitable Leadership Foundation (NY) (http://www.charitableleadership.org/)
The Charitable Leadership Foundation of New York "supports programs/organizations that address problems in the areas of education, housing (especially low-income), [and] job skills/economic opportunities for low-income people." The foundation also supports initiatives in medicine and medical research that meet certain criteria. Visit the foundation's Web site to find a history of the organization, funding criteria, application procedures, grants listings, and contact information.

The Chiang Ching-kuo Foundation for International Scholarly Exchange (VA) (Operating foundation) (http://www.cckf.org/)
The Chiang Ching-kuo Foundation for International Scholarly Exchange is headquartered in Taipei, Taiwan, Republic of China, with a regional office in McLean, Virginia. The foundation was established in 1989 in memory of the late president of the Republic of China, Chiang Ching-kuo, who died in 1988. Its purposes are to promote the study of Chinese culture and society and to promote understanding between the Chinese and other people of the world, with the "ultimate goal of encouraging the integration of the best of Chinese culture with an emerging global culture." The foundation's programs are limited to the academic sphere, and the scope of its programs includes Chinese cultural heritage, classical studies, the Republic of China, Taiwan area studies, and China-related comparative studies. Grants are made in four international regions to institutions and individuals, for institutional enhancement, research, conferences and seminars, subsidies for publication, and fellowships for graduate students and post-doctoral research. Visitors to the Web site will find details of each of the foundation's funding categories and programs, grant guidelines and deadlines, downloadable applications, contact information, a list of the board of directors and officers, and grant recipients lists.

Chiesman Foundation for Democracy, Inc. (SD) (http://www.chiesman.org)
Philanthropist Allene R. Chiesman founded the Chiesman Foundation for Democracy to promote and support "greater awareness of democracy and democratic ideals by citizens." Based in Rapid City, South Dakota, the foundation supports institutes and programs that assist citizens to understand the meaning of American democracy; the importance of participatory citizenship; the principles of economic competitiveness and development and the role of government; scholars who research and publish results on sound government policy

options that promote economic growth and productivity, participatory government, and U.S. constitutional law; and universities and colleges that establish centers for civic education and law-related education and that establish forums for the education of students, faculty, and citizens. Visitors to the Web site will find more detailed information about the foundation's goals, purposes, programs, and endowments. Other points of interest are descriptions of the foundation's programs; a bio of the founder; the foundation's online publication, *Chiesman Quarterly;* a listing of civic education resources; and contact information.

The Christensen Fund (CA) (http://www.christensenfund.org)

Allen D. and Carmen M. Christensen formed the Christensen Fund in 1957 in Palo Alto, California. The fund is a private, independent foundation dedicated to assisting organizations in the visual arts, conservation science, and education. The fund has developed a new grantmaking program that combines "interests in arts, biological conservation science and education into a single approach." Funding is directed towards strengthening the understanding, appreciation, and creative persistence of biological and cultural diversity in four main geographic regions: the American Southwest and northern Mexico; central Turkey, Iran, and central Asia; the African Rift Valley (Ethiopia); and New Guinea and Aboriginal Northern Australia. San Francisco Bay Area-based organizations are considered as well. For more information regarding the fund's procedures and deadlines, visit the fund's Web site.

The CINTAS Foundation (NY) (http://www.iie.org/fulbright/cintas)

The CINTAS Foundation, located in New York City, was established with funds from the estate of the late Oscar B. Cintas, a former Cuban ambassador to the United States and a prominent industrialist and patron of the arts. The foundation awards fellowships annually to creative artists of Cuban lineage who currently reside outside of Cuba. Specifically, the fellowships are intended to acknowledge creative accomplishments and encourage the development of talented and creative artists in the fields of architecture, literature, music composition, the visual arts, and photography. The application form, recommendation form, and slide script form can all be downloaded from the Web site. Deadlines and application guidelines are posted on the site as is contact information and a list of previous fellows.

Frank E. Clark Charitable Trust (NY) (http://fdncenter.org/grantmaker/feclark/)

The New York-based Frank E. Clark Charitable Trust provides support to religious and charitable organizations that hold an interest in small churches in small communities and those that provide services to low-income adults. Geographic focus is placed primarily on organizations doing work in New York City. No grants are made to individuals or private foundations or for matching gifts or loans. Visit the trust's Web site to learn more about grant priorities, application procedures, and contact information.

Edna McConnell Clark Foundation (NY) (http://www.emcf.org/)

The Edna McConnell Clark Foundation seeks to improve conditions and opportunities for people who live in poor and disadvantaged communities. The foundation "has been shifting its focus and resources toward strengthening the field of youth development and assisting key organizations," with an "institution and field building approach to grantmaking. By 2004, the Program for Youth Development will become the sole focus of the foundation." The foundation is in the process of completing its work in its longstanding areas of focus: tropical disease research, justice, child protection, New York neighborhoods, and student achievement. Applicants may want to read the foundation's latest annual report to ensure that their projects fit within the above programs' very specific grantmaking strategies. Visitors to the foundation's Web site will find detailed program descriptions, application guidelines, a recent grants list organized by program area, a report from the foundation president, a list of foundation-sponsored publications that can be obtained free of charge, board and staff listings, and contact information.

Robert Sterling Clark Foundation, Inc. (NY) (http://fdncenter.org/grantmaker/rsclark/)
Incorporated in 1952, the Robert Sterling Clark Foundation, Inc. has provided financial assistance to a wide variety of charitable organizations over the years. At present, the foundation is concentrating its resources in the following areas: arts and culture—strengthening the management of New York cultural institutions, government accountability—improving the performance of public institutions in New York City and State, family planning-ensuring access to family planning practices. While most of its support will be allocated for these purposes, the foundation has also begun to make funds available to protect artistic freedom and to educate the public about the importance of the arts in our society. Visitors to the foundation's Web site will find program guidelines, application procedures, and contact information.

The Clipper Ship Foundation (MA) (http://www.agmconnect.org/clipper1.html)
Founded in 1979 by David Parmely Weatherhead, the Clipper Ship Foundation, based in Boston, Massachusetts, offers financial assistance to fulfill the goals and broaden the scope of human service organizations. "Priority is given to those organizations devoted to helping the homeless and ill-housed, the destitute, the handicapped, children and the aged, or addressing the needs of new immigrants and other needy communities and neighborhoods." The foundation favors grants that will be matched or will stimulate giving by other donors, and grants for the construction or renovation of physical facilities or other capital projects, over operating grants. In general, grants are limited to human service organizations whose majority of individuals served reside in the greater Boston area, but special consideration will be given to emergency disaster situations worldwide. Grants in support of the arts will be limited to those that expose children or disabled individuals to the arts without charge or at a significantly reduced cost. Visitors to the Web site will find information about the foundation, including application information, contact information, grant guidelines, and annual reports.

The Cloud Foundation (MA) (http://www.agmconnect.org/cloud.html)
The Boston-based, Cloud Foundation seeks to renew the confidence, ambition, and hope of youth at risk by supporting programs that provide immersion in a foreign culture and exposure to the arts in the rich mosaic of Boston, the United States, and the world. Major interests of the foundation include exposing youth to cross-cultural experiences that can deepen self-awareness through an understanding of themselves in their world and offering youth the opportunity to fully participate in the arts, including dance, drama, writing, music, and visual arts. The foundation prefers to support projects that actively seek to involve underserved youth, combine artistic challenge with exposure to new cultures, deepen awareness of one's self through exposure to another culture, involve immersion in a foreign culture, foster confidence and trust in participants, encourage development of artistic skills for the purpose of self-expression, seek to build new leaders in both the proposing organization and participant group, and are initiated or supported by local community groups. The Cloud Foundation's Web site includes lists of previous years' grants, specific information on areas funded, application deadlines, application information, and contact information.

The Clowes Fund, Inc. (IN) (http://www.clowesfund.org)
The Indianapolis, Indiana-based, Clowes Fund, Inc. seeks to "enhance the common good by encouraging organizations and projects that help to build a just and equitable society, create opportunities for initiative, foster creativity and the growth of knowledge, and promote appreciation of the natural environment." The fund makes grants in the arts, education, and social services in areas where the Clowes family and the fund's board members reside. Visitors to the fund's Web site will find more information about the fund's current mission, priorities, officers, members, and staff; a recent grants listing; and contact information.

Lynne Cohen Foundation for Ovarian Cancer Research (CA) (http://www.lynnecohenfoundation.org/)
The Lynne Cohen Foundation for Ovarian Cancer Research, of Santa Monica, California, is an organization created "in memory of a woman who dedicated her life to the well-being of others." The mission of the foundation is to continue Lynne Cohen's spirit of giving by supporting groundbreaking research to improve the survival rates for women with ovarian cancer. Visitors to the foundation's Web site will find a brief history of how the organization came to be, information about ovarian cancer, funding priorities, grant application information, a listing of the current research projects being funded, and contact information.

The Coleman Foundation, Inc. (IL) (http://www.colemanfoundation.org/)
The Chicago, Illinois-based Coleman Foundation, Inc. was established in 1951 by Mr. and Mrs. J.D. Stetson Coleman, entrepreneurs with various holdings including Fannie May Candies. Their desire was to "make the community aware of opportunities which could improve the quality of life." The foundation's major grantmaking areas are education; cancer research, care, and treatment in the Midwest; housing and education for the handicapped; and a wide range of other educational programs. The Coleman Foundation also considers "special needs associated with poverty and unemployment." Support is generally focused on organizations in the Midwest, particularly in the Chicago metropolitan area, although programs across the United States are considered. Proposals are not solicited, and grantseekers should first make contact through an inquiry letter. Visitors to the Web site will find information about the foundation's programs, grant eligibility, grant applications and procedures, grant lists, financial statements, and contact information.

The Collins Foundation (OR) (http://www.collinsfoundation.org/)
The Collins Foundation was established in 1947 with a mission to "improve, enrich, and give greater expression to the religious, educational, cultural, and scientific endeavors in the state of Oregon and to assist in improving the quality of life in the state." Visitors to the foundation's Web site will find submission guidelines, a helpful FAQ section about grantmaking activities, a statistical breakdown of grants by subject area, a listing of selected grants, an annual report, and contact information.

The Colorado Trust (CO) (http://www.coloradotrust.org)
Established in 1985, the mission of the Colorado Trust is to promote the health and well-being of the people of Colorado through the support of accessible and affordable healthcare programs and the strengthening of families. The trust employs an initiative framework in which it identifies objectives, establishes workable approaches, and recruits interested organizations to implement programs. Visitors to the trust's Web site will find descriptions of its initiatives in each of Colorado's counties, as well as information about its approaches to grantmaking. Special features of the site include a funding opportunities mailing list and a program evaluation section entitled "Lessons Learned at the Colorado Trust."

Columbia Foundation (CA) (http://www.columbia.org)
Madeleine Haas and her brother William, established the Columbia Foundation in 1940 "for the furtherance of the public welfare." This San Francisco-based foundation has had a long-standing interest in world peace, human rights, the environment, cross-cultural and international understanding, the quality of urban life, and the arts, though the board of directors set new priorities within these areas as conditions change. Currently, there are three program areas: arts and culture, whose goal is to enhance the quality of life through arts and cultural programs, with a geographic focus in the San Francisco Bay Area and London; human rights, whose goal is the protection of basic human rights for all, with a focus in the San Francisco Bay Area and national programs; and sustainable communities and economies, with the goal of "securing, within the means of nature, a quality of life that is just and equitable for all humanity and future generations, and to ensure the viability of other species," with a geographic focus on the San Francisco Bay Area. The foundation

also considers media projects. Its Web site provides grant and application guidelines, a summary of its screening process, information about its funding and project priorities, a printable application cover sheet, a downloadable application, grant lists, and contact information.

The Commonweal Foundation, Inc. (MD) (Operating foundation) (http://www.commonweal-foundation.org)

Founded in 1968, the Silver Spring, Maryland-based Commonweal Foundation, Inc. supports education and programs in the Maryland and Washington, D.C., metropolitan area, with a focus on educational assistance for disadvantaged, at-risk youth. Current programs of the foundation are Pathways to Success Boarding School Scholarship Program, which awards scholarships to boarding schools; Partners in Learning, providing reading and writing instruction to children in after-school or summer programs in high-risk Maryland neighborhoods; Community Assistance Grants, supporting a variety of social service endeavors; and Learning Disabilities Support Program, providing special educational services for students whose families cannot afford them or cannot obtain them in the public schools. Visitors to the foundation's Web site will find more detailed program information, application guidelines, a board list, and contact information.

Commonwealth Fund (NY) (http://www.cmwf.org)

Founded in 1918 by Anna Harkness, the Commonwealth Fund, a New York City-based organization, supports independent research on health and social issues and makes grants to improve healthcare practice and policy. The fund is "dedicated to helping people become more informed about their healthcare, and improving care for vulnerable populations such as children, elderly people, low-income families, minority Americans, and the uninsured." The Commonwealth Fund awards grants in four major areas: improving insurance coverage and access to care, improving the quality of healthcare services, international healthcare policy and practice, and improving public spaces and services. Details about each funding area are available on the fund's Web site. Prospective grantees should send a letter of inquiry via regular mail or e-mail. The fund's Web site provides a detailed history of the organization, links to annual reports, information about its staff and board of directors, and downloadable publications relating to the fund's work.

Community Memorial Foundation (IL) (http://cmfdn.org/)

The Community Memorial Foundation of Illinois was established in 1955 with the mission "to improve the health of the people who live and work in metropolitan Chicago with the primary focus on the western suburbs." Geographic focus of the foundation includes 27 communities in western Cook and southeastern DuPage Counties. Visit the foundation's Web site to find a history of the organization, grant information, an annual report, a board listing, application procedures, grants listings, and contact information.

Community Technology Foundation of California (CA) (http://www.partnership.pacbell.net/ctf.html)

Based in San Francisco, California, the Community Technology Foundation of California was established in 1998 to administer the $50 million Pacific Bell Community Technology Fund, a partnership between Pacific Bell and nine statewide community coalitions. The foundation was created to "ensure that all Californians have access to emerging technology." The grantmaking programs focus on three key areas: capacity building for community organizations, leadership development, and developing a technology user in every home. Aimed at bringing communications technologies to traditionally underserved populations, the programs target groups including low-income, inner-city, minority, disabled, limited-English speaking, and low-income senior communities. Funding may come in the form of matching or challenge grants or leveraged gifts. The foundation's Web site offers grant applications and guidelines only when the applications are being accepted. The site also provides information on the foundation's programs, a list of the board of directors, news and events, and contact information.

Compton Foundation, Inc. (CA) (http://www.comptonfoundation.org)
Established as a trust in 1946 by Dorothy Danforth and Randolph P. Compton, the Menlo Park, California-based Compton Foundation, Inc. converted to a foundation in 1973. The organization's original mission was to "build the foundations for peace and to help prevent another world war," and it has been expanded to include "support for welfare, social justice, and the arts in the communities where [Compton] family board members live." These goals are achieved through a grant program that emphasizes peace and security, population, and the environment as its major categories. The program encourages prevention and research by preferring projects involving public education, education of policy makers and the media, advocacy and public activism, replicable demonstration projects, scholarly research, and fellowships to promising young scholars at selected institutions. The Web site expands on the foundation's interests and involvement in each of the three major categories, offers a grant history, staff and board lists, financial statements, and application deadlines and guidelines, including a printable proposal outline form.

Connelly Foundation (PA) (http://www.connellyfdn.org)
Based in West Conshohocken, Pennsylvania, the Connelly Foundation develops programs with and directs its support to educational, human services, health, cultural, and civic organizations. Established in 1955 by Mr. and Mrs. John F. Connelly, its mission is to enhance the quality of life in the greater Philadelphia region. The foundation focuses its philanthropy on nonprofit organizations and institutions based in and serving the city of Philadelphia and the surrounding Delaware Valley region and prefers to support projects that receive funding from several sources. Of note is the founders' mandate, which specifies that a minimum sixty percent of funding be granted each year to organizations affiliated with the Roman Catholic Church or toward programs impacting its members. Visitors to the Web site will find application guidelines, grant summaries and a breakdown of grants by geographic concentration, staff and board listings, information on its founders, and contact information.

Conservation, Food & Health Foundation (MA) (http://www.grantsmanagement.com/cfhguide.html)
The primary purpose of the Massachusetts-based Conservation, Food & Health Foundation is "to assist in the conservation of natural resources, the production and distribution of food, and the improvement and promotion of health in the developing world." The foundation, incorporated in 1985, is especially interested in supporting projects that lead to the transfer of responsibility to the citizens of developing countries for managing and solving their own problems and in supporting self-help initiatives. Preference is given to organizations located in developing countries or to developed countries organizations whose activities are of direct and immediate benefit to developing countries. Visitors to the foundation's Web site will find detailed application guidelines and eligibility requirements, a recent grants list, a form for submitting a concept paper to the foundation (in advance of a final proposal), and contact information.

Cooper Foundation (NE) (http://www.cooperfoundation.org/)
Created in 1934 by Joe Cooper, the Nebraska-based Cooper Foundation restricts its support to organizations within its home state, primarily in Lincoln and Lancaster Counties. The foundation's mission is to support innovative ideas that "promise substantial impact and encourage others to make similar or larger grants." To that end, it funds programs in education, human services, the arts, and the humanities. It does not fund individuals, endowments, private foundations, businesses, health or religious issues, travel, or organizations outside of Nebraska, and most of its grants are for program funding rather than general operating support. Visitors to the foundation's Web site will find a brief history of the foundation, grant guidelines, program priorities, financial reports, and contact information.

The Cooper Institute (FL) (Operating foundation) (http://www.cooperinstitute.org)
The Cooper Institute, based in Naples, Florida, is a nonprofit educational foundation established in 1974 by Irving S. Cooper, who was an internationally renowned neurosurgeon,

teacher, and author. The Institute is focused on the interests and well being of healthcare consumers and "dedicated to advancing the understanding of the relationship between living habits and health, and to providing leadership in implementing these concepts to enhance the physical and emotional well being of individuals." The institute's goal is that patient education will create choice and also encourage patient input in the debate over medical quality improvement. Visitors to the Web site will find information about the institute and its founder, links to databases of physician profiles, training and certification information, links to related products, links to sites about healthcare policy, and contact information.

The Aaron Copland Fund for Music, Inc. (NY) (http://www.amc.net/resources/grants)
The Aaron Copland Fund for Music, Inc. is one of the grant programs administered by the American Music Center (AMC), based in New York City. Aaron Copland was one of the founders of AMC in 1939, whose original mission was to "foster and encourage the composition of contemporary (American) music and to promote its production, publication, distribution and performance in every way possible throughout the Western Hemisphere," and whose contemporary mission now is "building a national community for new American music." There are two programs under the Aaron Copland Fund for Music, Inc.: the Performing Ensembles Program and the Recording Program. The objective of the Performing Ensembles Program is to "support organizations whose performances encourage and improve public knowledge and appreciation of serious contemporary American music." The objectives of the Recording Program are: "to document and provide wider exposure for the music of contemporary American composers; to develop audiences for contemporary American music through record distribution and other retail markets; and to support the release and dissemination of recordings for previously unreleased contemporary American music and the reissuance of recordings no longer available." Visitors to the Web site will find eligibility information, funding provisions, selection criteria, application instructions, downloadable brochures and applications, contact information for the two programs, links to other grant programs administered by AMC, and information about AMC.

Mary S. and David C. Corbin Foundation (OH) (http://fdncenter.org/grantmaker/corbin/)
The Mary S. and David C. Corbin Foundation was established "to help enrich the lives of the people of Akron and Summit County, Ohio." Areas of interest to the foundation include arts and culture, civic and community, education, environment, healthcare, housing, human and social services, medical research, and youth. Visitors to the foundation's Web site will find grant guidelines, a downloadable grant application, a trustees listing, and contact information.

Corman Foundation, Inc. (AL) (http://www.touch1.com)
The Corman Foundation, Inc. of Atmore, Alabama, was created in 1989 by Jim and Jane Corman, the founders of the Touch 1 telecommunications company. The foundation's goal is "to glorify God and make Christ known through effective stewardship of the resources entrusted to the foundation." The organization supports evangelical Christian groups with money, time, oversight, prayers, and encouragement. Grants are given to help efforts directly "aimed at securing the salvation of individuals, and providing for the discipleship and training of God's people for Christian witness." Groups that primarily address physical needs may apply if they have a strong secondary component that meets the description above. Visitors to the foundation's Web site will find information on the foundation's mission, grant guidelines and procedures, a list of currently supported organizations, FAQs, and contact information.

S.H. Cowell Foundation (CA) (http://www.shcowell.org/)
The S.H. Cowell Foundation of San Francisco, California, was established in 1956. The organization's goal is "to improve the quality of life of children living in poverty in northern California by making grants that support and strengthen their families and the neighborhoods where they live." The foundation has four program areas: affordable housing,

family resource centers, K-12 public education, and youth development. The foundation also provides emergency funds and supports building efforts. Visitors to the site will find program guidelines and restrictions, a description of the application process, information on recent grants, and lists of the staff and the board of directors.

Jessie B. Cox Charitable Trust (MA)
(http://hemenwaybarnes.com/privatesrv/jbcox/cox.html)
Jessie B. Cox, noted for her philanthropy, established the Jessie B. Cox Charitable Trust to continue that tradition following her death in 1982. The Boston, Massachusetts-based trust funds projects in New England in the areas of health, education, environment, and development of philanthropy, with a particular interest in projects that will primarily benefit underserved populations and disadvantaged communities, as well as projects that focus on prevention rather than remediation. The trust also has an interest in fostering collaboration among nonprofit organizations in New England and welcomes collaborative concept papers. The trust's Web site provides grant guidelines and policies, exclusions, application procedures, annual reports and grants lists, and contact information.

Crail-Johnson Foundation (CA) (http://www.crail-johnson.org/)
The Crail-Johnson Foundation of San Pedro, California, seeks to "promote the well being of children in need, through the effective application of human and financial resources." Priority is given to organizations and projects of benefit to residents of the greater Los Angeles area. In addition to awarding cash grants, the foundation also provides technical assistance to select community-based projects benefiting children and families. Current areas of emphasis are health and human services, education programs, and neighborhood and community. Visitors to the foundation's Web site can access the foundation's annual report, grant application guidelines and limitations, a financial statement, information on selected grants, and a listing of officers and staff. The Web site also provides links to other grantmakers online, detailed descriptions of special foundation projects, and contact information.

Crotched Mountain Foundation (NH) (http://www.cmf.org/)
The Crotched Mountain Foundation is an umbrella organization comprised of the Crotched Mountain School and Rehabilitation Center and the Crotched Mountain Community Based Services, which extends throughout New Hampshire and into Maine and New York. Founded by businessman and philanthropist Harry Alan Gregg, the foundation traces its origins back to the New Hampshire Society for Crippled Children, which was established in 1936. Its mission is to "promote, encourage, and sponsor charitable health, rehabilitative, and educational services on behalf of children, adults, and elderly persons." The foundation "enables and empowers persons with physical, developmental, emotional, or other health-related considerations to pursue their highest degree of physical, emotional, and social independence as may be individually possible." The foundation's Web site contains information on the foundation's history and its programs for the disabled and elderly, a search engine for the Web site, links, and contact information.

Nathan Cummings Foundation, Inc. (NY) (http://www.ncf.org/)
Established by Nathan Cummings, noted philanthropist and founder of the Sara Lee Corporation, the Nathan Cummings Foundation is "rooted in the Jewish tradition and committed to democratic values, including fairness, diversity, and community." The foundation "seeks to build a socially and economically just society that values nature and protects the ecological balance for future generations; promotes humane healthcare; and fosters arts and culture that enriches communities." To that end, the foundation focuses its grantmaking activities in five program areas: arts, environment, health, Jewish life, and "interprogram," which reinforces connections among the foundation's core areas. Visitors to the foundation's Web site will find detailed guidelines, grants lists for each program area, links to grantee Web sites, application procedures, staff and trustee listings, and various reports and publications, including the foundation's most recent annual report.

Charles A. Dana Foundation, Inc. (NY) (http://www.dana.org/)
The Charles A. Dana Foundation, Inc. is a private philanthropic foundation with principle interests in science, health, and education, with a strong focus on neuroscience. Visitors to the foundation's Web site will find grantmaking policies and procedures; detailed application and program information, including recent major grants; information about the Charles A. Dana Awards, which honor innovators in neuroscience and education reform; the Dana Alliance for Brain initiatives, a nonprofit dedicated to educating the public about the benefits of brain research; a publications archive which includes the foundation's most recent annual reports; Dana BrainWeb, annotated links to Web sites devoted to specific brain disorders, general health, and neuroscience; a listing of the foundation's directors, officers, and staff; and press and contact information.

Donahue Foundation (CO) (http://www.donahuefoundation.org)
Established in Denver, Colorado, in 1990, the Donahue Foundation provides tuition assistance to the young and economically disadvantaged. The foundation only makes grants to qualified nonprofit organizations that support a non-public school. Visit the foundation's Web site to view grantmaking priorities, the foundation's most recent grants, application guidelines, the foundation's most recent tax return, and contact information.

Lucy Daniels Foundation (PA) (http://www.ldf.org/)
The Lucy Daniels Foundation's goal is to "foster personal development, emotional freedom, and a deeper understanding of creativity through programs of psychoanalytic treatment, education, and research." Lucy Daniels also heads the Lucy Daniels Center for Early Childhood, which applies psychoanalytic understanding to early childhood education. The foundation is especially interested, however, in the treatment and research into the psychoanalysis of creative people; this project comprises the foundation's central work. Although there is no specific information related to grants on the foundation's Web site, there is an overview of the foundation's programs and events, as well as resource links and contact information.

Daughters of the Cincinnati (NY) (http://fdncenter.org/grantmaker/cincinnati/)
The Daughters of the Cincinnati was incorporated as a society in 1894 to "advance and encourage investigation and study of the history of the American Revolution, and to instill into the minds of the rising generations, a knowledge of, and reverence for, the inspired wisdom, and unswerving determination which successfully carried on the struggle for Liberty." The organization provides individual scholarships to daughters of career officers commissioned in the regular U.S. Army, Navy, Air Force, Coast Guard, or Marine Corps. Visitors to the foundation's Web site will find further details on program interests, application information, and contact information.

The Davidson Foundation (NV) (http://www.davidsonfoundation.org/)
Located in Incline Village, Nevada, the Davidson Foundation was founded in 1997 by Bob and Jan Davidson and their children, Liz, Emilie, and John. Its mission is to "advance learning, enhance human potential and empower people to live lives of achievement and service," with a focus on supporting exceptionally gifted young people. To that end, one of the foundation's programs is the Davidson Young Scholars Pilot Program, whose mission is to "recognize, nurture and support the special needs of exceptionally gifted children." The program was launched in the spring of 1999 and provides a variety of resources, such as needs-assessment, personal planning, funding, mentoring, and fellowship to children between the ages of 4 and 12. The foundation states that it is proactive in its grantmaking, seeking out and investigating grantmaking opportunities with nonprofit organizations whose work supports the mission. It does not accept unsolicited grant proposals. Consult the foundation's Web site to learn more about the foundation, its focus on exceptionally gifted children, the Davidson Young Scholars Pilot Program, application procedures, information on exceptionally gifted children, its annual report, grants lists, and contact information.

The Ken M. Davis Foundation (TX) (http://fdncenter.org/grantmaker/davis/)
The Ken M. Davis Foundation of Fort Worth, Texas, supports charities that directly provide for human welfare for basic needs and quality of life. Specific areas of interest include food, shelter, clothing, healthcare, disabilities, and childcare. The foundation's geographic focus is the areas of Midland-Odessa, and Fort Worth, Texas. Visitors to the foundation's Web site will find application information, a downloadable application, a copy of the foundation's most recent tax return, and contact information.

Arthur Vining Davis Foundations (FL) (http://www.jvm.com/davis/)
The Arthur Davis Vining Foundations provide support nationally for five primary program areas: private higher education, secondary education, religion (graduate theological education), healthcare (caring attitudes), and public television. The foundations do not make grants to individuals; institutions or programs outside the United States and its possessions; publicly governed colleges, universities, or other entities that are supported primarily by government funds (except in healthcare and secondary education programs); or projects incurring obligations extending over several years. Visitors to the foundations' Web site will find descriptions of each program area, a recent grants list organized by program area, application procedures, a brief FAQ, and contact information.

Dr. G. Clifford & Florence B. Decker Foundation (NY) (http://www.pronetisp.net/~deckerfn/index.html)
The Dr. G. Clifford Decker & Florence B. Decker Foundation was established in 1979 to assist charitable organizations servicing the residents of Broome County, New York. Located in Binghampton, New York, the foundation focuses its grantmaking in education, medical and medical research institutions, and cultural and human service organizations. Grants may be used for capital projects or new and innovative projects and programs. In general, it does not provide continuing or regular operating support, as its efforts are "directed toward helping organizations provide programs to earn income and thus become self-sufficient." Grant applications can be requested by phone, mail, or e-mail. Visitors to the Web site will find grant application guidelines, the Deckers' and foundation's history, annual reports, a list of the board of directors, links to institutions that have received Decker Foundation grants, and contact information.

The Robert N. DeBenedictis Foundation (NY) (http://fdncenter.org/grantmaker/rnd/)
The Robert N. DeBenedictis Foundation is committed to supporting gay and lesbian and animal rights start-up and grassroots organizations in New York and Florida that attempt to fulfill the needs of their constituencies. Visitors to the foundation's Web site will find a brief biography of Mr. DeBenedictis, a projected budget for the current year, the organization's by-laws, and contact information.

Ira W. DeCamp Foundation (NY) (http://fdncenter.org/grantmaker/decamp/)
Established in 1970, the New York-based, Ira W. DeCamp Foundation focuses its grantmaking in three areas: community-based healthcare, foster care, and workforce development in the New York metropolitan area. No grants are made to individuals, private foundations, or for matching gifts or loans. No grants are made to endowments, scholarships, or fellowships. Visitors to the foundation's Web site will find detailed grant guidelines, proposal requirements, a grants listing, and contact information.

The Dekko Foundation, Inc. (IN) (http://www.dekkofoundation.org)
Chester E. Dekko created the Dekko Foundation, Inc. in 1981 as a way to give back to the communities that had bred his success. He learned that education, hard work, and leadership could provide economic freedom for any individual that desired it; accordingly, the mission of his foundation is to "foster economic freedom through education." The foundation's two broad program areas are education and community, with a geographic focus in communities where Group Dekko International had plants or where Mr. Dekko had a presence prior to his death in 1992. Grant proposals are considered from counties in Indiana, Iowa, and Alabama. Based in Kendallville, Indiana, its educational priorities are public and

private schools and early childhood education; its community priorities are community foundations, libraries, museums, parks, festivals, summer camps, youth organizations, and organizations for the needy and disabled. In addition to these funding areas, the foundation also considers proposals in three areas: early childhood development, child-centered education, and sustainability of youth-serving organizations. The foundation's grantmaking is limited to programs that support children from birth to age 18. Visitors to the foundation's Web site will find further information on the funding areas, geographic focus, grant guidelines, application instructions and an online application, the history of the foundation and a biography of its founder, and contact information.

The Barbara Delano Foundation, Inc. (CA) (http://www.bdfoundation.org)
The Barbara Delano Foundation, Inc. is a San Francisco-based foundation devoted to the protection of wildlife and its habitats and improving humankind's treatment of animals. The foundation was established in 1985 by Barbara Delano Gauntlett, granddaughter of Dr. William E. Upjohn, founder of the Upjohn Company, as an expression of her life-long commitment to conservation and the survival of local people and communities. The foundation currently considers applications for the support of the conservation and habitat protection of bears, elephants, exotic birds, great apes, large cats, marine mammals, marine turtles, rhinos, and sharks. The foundation also works for the humane treatment of domesticated animals. It seeks to assist grantees in obtaining further funding and with objective advice on campaigning and project management, and it offers to assist other foundations and private individuals in selecting international conservation programs to support. The foundation offers monitoring and on-site visit reports to donors without administrative charge. The site contains proposal guidelines, a grant recipient list, links to projects supported by the foundation, and contact information.

Gladys Krieble Delmas Foundation (NY) (http://www.delmas.org/)
The Gladys Krieble Delmas Foundation promotes "the advancement and perpetuation of humanistic inquiry and artistic creativity by encouraging excellence in scholarship and in the performing arts, and by supporting research libraries and other institutions that preserve the resources which transmit this cultural heritage." The foundation sponsors four distinct grantmaking programs: humanities, performing arts, research libraries, and Venetian research. Foundation trustees may also award discretionary grants outside of these specific programs. Visitors to the foundation's Web site will find descriptions and recent grants lists for each program area, a list of grants for Independent Research in Venice and the Veneto, application procedures and eligibility requirements, and a listing of the foundation's trustees, staff, and advisory board members.

The DeMatteis Family Foundation (NY) (http://fdncenter.org/grantmaker/dematteis/)
Founded in 2001, the DeMatteis Family Foundation of New York sets as its mission "to make life better by serving human needs through support to institutions involved in: education, health and human services, medical research, social services, and the arts," with a focus on the New York metropolitan area. Visitors to the foundation's Web site will find the foundation's policies and grant application instructions.

DENSO North America Foundation (MI) (http://www.densofoundation.org/)
The DENSO North America Foundation of Michigan was established in 2001 to provide skills and resources to assist communities prosper through the development of a skilled work force. The foundation supports educational institutions and universities located throughout North America, with an emphasis on engineering and technology. Types of support funded by the foundation include: capital campaigns, scholarships, student projects, and undergraduate research. Visitors to the foundation's Web site will find a listing of previous grants, an online application form, press releases, and contact information.

The Rene & Veronica di Rosa Foundation (CA) (Operating foundation) (http://www.dirosapreserve.org)

The Rene & Veronica di Rosa Foundation operates the di Rosa Preserve, the vision of two devoted patrons of the arts, Rene and Veronica di Rosa. The preserve is the public exhibition space for the di Rosa art collection, which consists of art produced in the greater San Francisco Bay Area during the latter part of the 20th Century. Visitors to the foundation's Web site can view a selection of images from over 1,600 works of art in the di Rosa Preserve. The site also contains short biographies of the founders, contact information, links related to art and the Napa, California area, where the preserve is located.

DJ & T Foundation (CA) (http://www.djtfoundation.org)

Television personality Bob Barker, of *The Price is Right* fame, established the Beverly Hills, California-based DJ & T Foundation in 1995, in memory of his wife, Dorothy Jo, and his mother, Matilda (Tilly) Valandra, who both loved all animals. Its goal is to help relieve animal overpopulation by funding low cost or free spay/neuter clinics all over the United States. The foundation assists all qualified spay/neuter clinics, but is most committed to making grants at the grassroots level to under-funded clinics that provide free or low cost spay/neuter services. Grantseekers can download an application or request one in writing after reading the grant guidelines and the FAQ sheet on the foundation's Web site.

Geraldine R. Dodge Foundation, Inc. (NJ) (http://www.grdodge.org/)

Founded in 1974, the Geraldine R. Dodge Foundation, Inc.'s mission is to "support and encourage those educational, cultural, social, and environmental values that contribute to making our society more humane and our world more livable." The foundation makes grants in five major areas: elementary and secondary education; arts, with a primary focus on New Jersey and on programs that seek to establish and improve education in the arts, foster conditions that promote public access to the arts, recognize the critical role of the individual artist, enable developing institutions to gain stability, and help major institutions realize long-term goals; welfare of animals, especially projects with national implications that encourage a more humane ethic and lower the violence in the way we treat animals; public issues, with a particular interest in New Jersey and the Northeast and focusing on ecosystems preservation, energy conservation, pollution prevention and reduction, education and communication efforts that lead to enlightened environmental policy, and projects that address population growth and family planning; and local projects in Morris County, New Jersey. The foundation's Web site provides concise program descriptions, application guidelines, a brief history of the foundation, and contact information.

The Patrick and Catherine Weldon Donaghue Medical Research Foundation (CT) (http://www.donaghue.org)

The Patrick and Catherine Weldon Donaghue Medical Research Foundation, based in West Hartford, Connecticut, was created in the will of Ethel Frances Donaghue in memory of her parents. One of Connecticut's first woman lawyers, she dedicated her substantial fortune to providing "financial assistance for research in the fields of cancer and heart disease and/or other medical research to promote medical knowledge which will be of practical benefit to the preservation, maintenance, and improvement of human life." The foundation began in 1991 with three grant programs that focused on postdoctoral fellows and new investigators doing basic and pre-clinical research in cancer and heart disease, and it has since expanded to include research in community health, epidemiology, and health services. It also "invites grant applications from investigators in mental health and neurodegenerative illnesses." There are currently three types of grant awards: Research in Clinical and Community Health Issues, the Donaghue Investigator Program, and the Practical Benefits Initiatives. The foundation focuses funding of research to health-related institutions and organizations located in Connecticut. Visitors to the Web site will find downloadable applications; information on its funding areas, grant award types, and grant guidelines and instructions; the founders' biographies and the foundation's history; highlights of its grantmaking and financial information; members of its advisory boards; a downloadable newsletter, a FAQ sheet, and contact information.

Gaylord and Dorothy Donnelley Foundation (IL) (http://www.gddf.org)
The Chicago, Illinois-based Gaylord and Dorothy Donnelley Foundation "supports efforts that create healthy human communities and natural environments in the Chicago region and the Lowcountry of South Carolina." The grant program awards funding to organizations working in the environment and conservation and in special projects in education and community welfare. While the foundation prefers requests for specific projects, those for general operating support are accepted. The foundation application can be downloaded in Adobe Acrobat format and includes guidelines and deadlines. The foundation's Web site includes lists of board and staff members and lists of past grantees, grouped by the year that the grant was awarded.

William H. Donner Foundation, Inc. (NY) (http://www.donner.org/)
The William H. Donner Foundation, Inc., a small, family foundation based in New York City, was created in 1961 with the endowment originally established by Mr. Donner for the International Cancer Research Foundation, which he founded in 1932 to honor his son's memory after his death from cancer. In January 1999, the foundation adopted a policy that it would no longer accept unsolicited proposals; only applications invited by the foundation are considered. In its grantmaking, the foundation follows two philanthropic principles of its founder: "acceptance of clearly defined risks and the judicious use of incentive grants to advance thoughtful, creative projects." the foundation's Web site contains a biography of its founder, a statement of its grantmaking policy, a listing of foundation officers and staff, and contact information.

Dorot Foundation (RI) (http://www.dorot.org/)
Based in Providence, Rhode Island, the Dorot Foundation is a charitable family foundation with a strong tradition of commitment to Israel, the Jewish community in North America, and nurturing the relationship between them both. The foundation sponsors the Dorot Fellowship in Israel, created to help build a knowledgeable and impassioned lay leadership for the Jewish community. Open to American Jewish college graduates below the age of forty, it is a full-year fellowship made up of four major components: Hebrew studies, Jewish studies, engagement with and volunteer service to the community, and monthly seminars. The foundation seeks to provide fellows with opportunities for development in the following areas: Hebrew competence, personal contact with Israelis and other future lay leaders, knowledge of Israeli society and institutions, leadership skills, and understanding of issues vital to the Jewish community in Israel, North America, and throughout the world. In addition to the fellowship program, the foundation provides travel grants to accredited colleges and universities. Visitors to the site will find fellowship information and application instructions, a downloadable application, contact information, and information on other educational programs in Israel.

Do Right Foundation (CA) (http://www.doright.org/)
The mission of the Do Right Foundation is to "address some of the current obstacles to a more joyful and rewarding society," and the foundation's Web site is devoted to explaining this philosophy as it relates to the grantseeking process. The foundation does not except uninvited grant applications, nor does it respond to unsolicited grant inquiries. Visitors to the site will find a biography of Dr. W. Edwards Deming, upon whose management concepts the foundation's philosophies are based. Grants lists and contact information are also available.

J.C. Downing Foundation (CA) (http://www.jcdowning.org/)
Founded in 1990, the San Diego-based J.C. Downing Foundation supports innovative efforts and original projects in five program areas: education and human development, environmental research and preservation, fine arts, sports and athletics, and technology and communications. The foundation awards grants to qualified nonprofit organizations with explicit, identifiable needs, and it does not place geographic or dollar restrictions on its grants. The foundation's Web site provides grantmaking guidelines and areas of exclusion, application procedures, a list of selected grants the foundation has made since 1990, and a

Resource section, which includes information about the grantseeeking process, a recommended reading list, and links to Web sites of interest.

Drachen Foundation (WA) (Operating foundation) (http://www.drachen.org/)
The Drachen Foundation is a non-profit educational corporation, founded in Seattle, Washington, in 1994 for "the purpose of facilitating educational projects concerning historical, cultural, and artistic areas of kiting." Primary focus includes artist-in residence programs, historical and cultural research, and educational publications. Awards for projects brought forth by the board of directors or advisory board are given based on the value and merit of the project. The Drachen Foundation does not solicit funding requests. The foundation operates the Drachen Study Center in Seattle; funds kite research globally; publishes books, a journal, and a newsletter; sponsors national and international exhibitions, conferences, and workshops, and collects and conserves kites. The foundation's Web site includes a brief history of kiting, a board/staff listing, links to affiliates, and contact information.

Draper Richards Foundation (CA) (http://draperrichards.org/)
The Draper Richards Foundation of San Francisco, California, provides "funding and business mentoring to social entrepreneurs as they begin their non-profit organizations." The foundation accepts proposals for a variety of public service areas, including, but not limited to, education, youth and families, the environment, arts, health, and community and economic development. Visitors to the foundation's site will learn more about the organization, its programs, and a few past grant recipients; brief biographies of the staff; and contact information.

Camille and Henry Dreyfus Foundation, Inc. (NY) (http://www.dreyfus.org/)
Established in 1946 by Camille Dreyfus as a memorial to her brother Henry, the principal aim of the Camille and Henry Dreyfus Foundation, Inc. is to "advance the science of chemistry, chemical engineering, and related sciences as a means of improving human relations and circumstances around the world." To that end, the foundation makes grant awards to academic and other eligible institutions for the purposes of sponsoring qualified applicants in their education and research. The foundation's Web site provides detailed descriptions of various programs, including eligibility requirements, application and nomination procedures, and a listing of recent grantees.

Jean and Louis Dreyfus Foundation (NY) (http://fdncenter.org/grantmaker/dreyfus)
The New York-based, Jean and Louis Dreyfus Foundation was established in 1979 to enhance the quality of life of New Yorkers, particularly the aging and disadvantaged. The foundation makes grants mainly within the five boroughs of New York City, primarily in fields supportive of aging, arts-in-education, education and literacy, and social services. Visitors to the foundation's Web site will find application procedures, recent grants lists, trustee and staff listings, and contact information.

Joseph Drown Foundation (CA) (http://www.jdrown.org)
Joseph Warford Drown was involved with the hotel industry, notably as owner of Hotel Bel-Air in Los Angeles. He formed the Los Angeles, California-based Joseph Drown Foundation in 1953 to provide an organized means of charitable giving, both during his lifetime and after his death in 1982. The goal of his foundation is "to assist individuals in becoming successful, self-sustaining, contributing citizens," and the foundation is interested in programs that break down barriers that prevent growth and learning. The foundation has five main funding areas: education, community health and social services, arts and humanities, medical and scientific research, and special projects, which are at discretion of the board but still related to the mission of the foundation. Programs in the area of medical and scientific research are initiated by the foundation; arts and humanities programs are a lesser priority and concentrate on outreach and education. Most of its grantmaking is limited to programs and organizations in California. Consult its Web site for more information about each funding area, as well as the grant application procedure, a list of sample grants, contact information, and related links.

The Dudley Foundation (WA) (http://www.dudleyfoundation.org)
Based in Bellingham, Washington, the primary goal of the Dudley Foundation is "to help alleviate unnecessary present and future suffering of all sentient beings by attempting to address its environmental and social roots." The foundation's focus is on "human overpopulation, wanton consumption of resources (greed), ecological degradation, and intolerance/injustice." The site contains application instructions and criteria, a printable application page, a description of the evaluation procedure, a list of organizations funded, biographies on staff who evaluate proposals, and contact information.

Doris Duke Charitable Foundation (NY) (http://fdncenter.org/grantmaker/dorisduke/)
The New York-based Doris Duke Charitable Foundation was created in 1996, in accordance with the terms of the will of Doris Duke, to improve the quality of people's lives by preserving natural environments, seeking cures for diseases, and nurturing the arts. The foundation currently pursues its mission through four grantmaking programs: the Arts Program, the Environment Program, the Medical Research Program, and the Child Abuse Prevention Program. The foundation's Web site describes these programs in detail and provides guidelines to the grantmaking process. Visitors to the site will also find grants lists, information about the foundation's three non-grantmaking operating foundations, and a listing of trustees and staff.

The Duke Endowment (NC) (http://www.dukeendowment.org/)
The Duke Endowment, a charitable trust established in 1924 by North Carolina industrialist James Buchanan Duke, continues its founder's philanthropic legacy of giving to "educate students and teachers, to heal minds and bodies, to nurture children, and to strengthen the human spirit." As a trust, the Duke Endowment differs from a private foundation in that its principle donor named specific organizations or individuals eligible to receive funding. In the case of the endowment, these are nonprofit healthcare organizations in North and South Carolina; nonprofit child care institutions in North and South Carolina; rural United Methodist churches and retired ministers in North Carolina, and Duke, Furman, and Johnson C. Smith Universities; and Davidson College. Program areas are education, healthcare, childcare, and rural churches. The endowment's Web site provides general program descriptions and application procedures, a grants list organized by area of interest, links to resources and grantee organizations, a searchable online catalog of library materials (the endowment's library houses a Foundation Center Cooperating Collection), financial statements, a listing of endowment trustees and staff, and contact information.

Jessie Ball duPont Fund (FL) (http://www.dupontfund.org/)
The Jessie Ball duPont Fund, a national foundation having a special, though not exclusive, interest in issues affecting the South, makes grants "to a defined universe of eligible institutions"—that is, any institution that received a contribution from Mrs. duPont between January 1, 1960 and December 31, 1964 (approximately 350 in total). Proof of eligibility is determined by the fund from examination of Mrs. duPont's personal or tax records or by the applicant presenting written verifiable evidence of having received a contribution during the eligibility period. The fund's mission, "to address broad-based issues of communities and of the larger society that have regional, national, and international relevance," is achieved through programs in arts and culture, education, health, historic preservation, human services, and religion. Visitors to the fund's Web site will find detailed program information and eligibility guidelines, annual reports, a statement of the fund's mission and core values, a biography of Mrs. duPont, and contact information. The fund also posts excerpts from *Notes from the Field,* its publication devoted to philanthropic "best practices," in the following areas: access to healthcare, affordable housing for low-income families, inclusiveness in institutions of higher education, taking action and seeking justice, and creating healthy outcomes for children.

Durfee Foundation (CA) (http://www.durfee.org/)
Named in honor of the late Dorothy Durfee Avery who, with her husband, the late R. Stanton Avery, founded the Avery Dennison Corporation, a multinational manufacturing

concern, the Durfee Foundation has awarded more than $13 million in grants since 1960 in the areas of arts and culture, education, history, and community development, primarily in southern California. Programs currently supported by the foundation include arts programs: Durfee Artist Awards, ARC (Artists' Resource for Completion), and Master Musician Fellowships; the Durfee Sabbatical Program; Student Challenge Awards; and the Durfee Community Fund. Although the foundation does not review unsolicited proposals, one-page letters of introduction are welcomed. Visitors to the foundation's Web site will find program descriptions and criteria, project proposal guidelines, financial statements and a summary of grants from the foundation's most recent annual report, a listing of the foundation's trustees, and contact information.

The Dyer-Ives Foundation (MI) (http://www.dyer-ives.org)
The Dyer-Ives Foundation was established in 1961 as a private charitable organization that makes grants to support social, educational, environmental, and cultural initiatives that build a sense of community, primarily in Grand Rapids, Michigan. The foundation supports two types of grantmaking: the Small Grants Program which provides funding for projects originating in the community, and the Neighborhood Initiative, which is an ongoing grant program initiated by the foundation's program goals. Visit the foundation's Web site to find further information on the organization's programs, a helpful FAQ sections, financial information, a staff and trustee listing, and contact information.

The Dyson Foundation (NY) (http://www.dysonfoundation.org)
The New York-based, Dyson Foundation was established in 1957 to support innovative programs and compelling causes. The foundation focuses much of its grantmaking on child welfare; however it also makes grants for specified areas in New York. The Dyson Initiative provides training services to pediatric professionals to help better serve their patients within the community. The foundation also makes less specific grants to the Mid-Hudson Valley area, in the areas of social services, education, health, community development, and arts and cultural programs. The foundation's Web site includes recent grants, explicit application information, staff/board lists, financial data, and contact information.

The Eagle Sky Foundation, Inc. (CO) (Operating foundation)
(http://members.aol.com/_ht_a/eagleskyf/myhomepage/index.html)
The Eagle Sky Foundation, Inc. was established "to create and build very high quality Christian Challenge Camp and Conference Centers in some of the most scenic areas of America, such as the Heart of the Rockies and the Ozarks." The foundation is a non-denominational Christian organization whose mission is to encourage Christians in their spiritual growth and development, which, the foundation believes, is "more easily accomplished in certain environments." Eagle Sky Christian Challenge Camp and Conference Center will be open to all Christians, churches, and denominations. The Eagle Sky of the Rockies' Ranch is located in the northern third of the Tennessee Park Valley in Lake County, Colorado.

The Cyrus Eaton Foundation (OH) (http://www.deepcove.org)
The philanthropic arm of the Eaton Corporation, a diversified industrial manufacturer based in Cleveland, Ohio, the Cyrus Eaton Foundation funds matching gifts, education, community involvement programs, and the United Way. The foundation's overall goal is to support quality of life improvements in the communities that the Eaton Corporation serves. Funding is provided in the following priority areas: arts, conservation, education, health and social welfare, public affairs, and science. An application can be downloaded in Microsoft Word or text format. Visitors to the foundation's Web site will find more detailed program information, lists of previous grants, a biography of Cyrus Stephen Eaton, downloadable versions of the foundation's most recent tax return, financial statements, and contact information.

Echoing Green Foundation (NY) (http://echoinggreen.org)
New York City-based Echoing Green Foundation was founded by venture capitalist Ed Cohen, who, along with a group of investors, created an organization that "applies venture capitalist principles to a social change sphere." The Echoing Green Foundation, named after a poem by artist William Blake, is a nonprofit foundation that offers full-time fellowships to emerging "social entrepreneurs." The foundation applies a venture capital approach to philanthropy by providing seed money and technical support to individuals creating innovative public service organizations or projects with goals of positive social change. The foundation also provides organizations with support to help them grow beyond a start-up. The fellowship includes a two-year $60,000 stipend, healthcare benefits, online connectivity, access to the foundation's network of social entrepreneurs, training, and technical assistance. Proposed organizations and projects can be domestic or international and in all public service areas, including but not limited to the environment, arts, education, youth service, civil and human rights, and community and economic development. Consult the foundation's Web site for information about the foundation and how to become a fellow, news and events related to the foundation, a resource center covering topics from organizational development to attracting resources related links, a public forum for dialogue about fellows and projects, profiles of fellows, and contact information.

Edah, Inc. (NY) (Operating foundation) (http://www.edah.org)
The mission of Edah, Inc. is to "give voice to the ideology and values of modern Orthodoxy and to educate and empower the community to address its concerns." Edah "focuses its efforts on Education, Leadership Training, Advocacy, and Communications." Visitors to the Web site will find information about past and current events and programs, news, community information, an Orthodox library, and contact information.

The Educational Foundation for America (CT) (http://www.efaw.org/)
The Westport, Connecticut-based, Education Foundation for America, was established in 1959 by Richard Prentice Ettinger and his wife, Elsie P. Ettinger. Mr. Ettinger was one of the founders of Prentice Hall Publishing. The foundation is based on five principles that Mr. Ettinger felt were the most important to philanthropy: take risks, think globally, focus grants sharply, make grants short-term, and know how and where the money will be used. Areas of interest include, but are not limited to, the environment, energy, the crisis of human overpopulation and reproductive freedom, Native Americans, the arts, education, medicine, and social services. Visitors to the Web site will find background information on the founders, letter of inquiry submission guidelines, deadlines, grants lists by area, board and staff listings, and contact information.

O.P. and W.E. Edwards Foundation, Inc. (NY) (http://fdncenter.org/grantmaker/edwards/)
The O.P. and W.E. Edwards Foundation, Inc. is located in the heart of New York City. Grants from the General Fund are made in annual support grants and trustee-directed grants to organizations serving children, youth, and their families who are severely disadvantaged economically. Grants from the W.E. Edwards Fund are distributed to organizations designated in the donor's will. The Arts and Astronomy Funds are donor-directed funds. The foundation also makes investments in organizations committed to economic development, including community development banks and loans for low-income housing. The foundation's Web site provides the foundation's grant and investment policy and an extensive list of previous grant recipients. The small, unstaffed foundation does not accept unsolicited proposals.

EGBAR Foundation (CA) (http://www.egbar.org)
Located in Huntington Beach, California, the EGBAR Foundation was established by Sunshine Makers, Inc, the manufacturers of Simple Green, an all-purpose cleaner, in 1989. The foundation's mission is to "create an appreciably cleaner environment by instilling in young people throughout the world, the importance of Making a Difference, one park, one neighborhood, one community at a time." More specific goals include educating children internationally on recycling and being environmentally conscious and addressing

community clean-up needs. One way that the foundation addresses these goals is through the EGBAR Environmental Curriculum, a collection of lessons and projects, many working in conjunction with newspapers, to enhance science classes for fourth through ninth graders and is available online for download. Participants in the curriculum are encouraged to take part in the annual EGBAR Clean-up Challenge and to submit essays to the EGBAR Environmental Essay Contest. The foundation also distributes over 400,000 Family Environmental Surveys and then posts the results and analysis on the site. The site includes related games and activities, a set of links, and information on selected staff and board members.

El Pomar Foundation (CO) (http://www.elpomar.org/)
Founded in 1937 by copper mining magnate Spencer Penrose and his wife, Julie, the El Pomar Foundation is one of the largest and oldest foundations in the Rocky Mountain West. The foundation makes grants throughout the state of Colorado in the areas of human services, community development, the arts, healthcare, amateur athletics, and education. In addition to grant application guidelines and summary financial information for the latest year, visitors to the foundation's Web site will find general information about the foundation and its many operating programs: Fellowship in Community Service, a program designed to develop future leaders among recent college graduates; El Pomar Youth in Community Service; El Pomar Awards for Excellence, which reward outstanding nonprofit organizations in Colorado; the foundation's Education Initiative; and El Pomar Center, which is dedicated to the recognition and promotion of excellence within the nonprofit community.

The Nell Warren Elkin & William Simpson Elkin Foundation (GA) (http://www.elkinfoundation.org)
The Nell Warren Elkin & William Simpson Elkin Foundation of Georgia was created as a memorial by Miss Margaret R. Warren, Miss Charlotte L. Warren, and Mrs. Josephine Warren Asbury, sisters of Nell Warren Elkin. Visitors to the foundation's Web site will find average grant ranges, a listing of charities with similar missions to those supported by the foundation, application information and submission dates, a downloadable application, and contact information.

Ellie Fund (OH) (http://www.fmscleveland.com/ellie)
The Ohio-based, Ellie Fund "seeks to better the lives of disadvantaged children in Cuyahoga County by supporting programs that aspire to meet basic human needs, heal wounds, and open doors." Priorities of the fund include crisis intervention, literacy, mental health, physical health, safety, and shelter. The fund's grants are directed to organizations located in Cuyahoga County, Ohio whose activities benefit the county's residents. The fund's Web site features information on the application process, grant guidelines, financial data, and contact information.

The Ellison Medical Foundation (MD) (http://www.ellison-med-fn.org/)
Headquartered in Bethesda, Maryland, the Ellison Medical Foundation funds basic biomedical research in multiple disciplines related to gerontology, the science of aging, through four programs. The New Scholars in Aging Program accepts applications by invitation only. The Senior Scholar Program, given to an established investigator, requires a letter of intent and cover page. There are listings of previous awardees of the Conferences and Workshops Program and the Infrastructure Award Program on the foundation's Web site. Details of restrictions, deadlines, and terms of funding through these four programs; contact information; and a general discussion of current research in gerontology are also available on the foundation's Web site.

Energy Foundation (CA) (http://www.energyfoundation.org/)
Created in 1991 under the auspices of the MacArthur Foundation, the Pew Charitable Trusts, and the Rockefeller Foundation, the mission of the Energy Foundation is "to assist in the nation's transition to a sustainable energy future by promoting energy efficiency and

renewable energy." Visitors to the foundation's Web site will find program descriptions, application guidelines, lists of recent grant recipients, and downloadable application forms for each of the foundation's seven program areas: utilities, buildings, transportation, renewable energy, integrated issues, U.S. Clean Energy Program, and the China Sustainable Energy Program. Also available online are essays on the foundation's mission, a section for special Foundation reports, and a list of annotated links to energy-related Web sites.

Engineering Information Foundation (NY) (http://www.eifgrants.org)
The Engineering Information Foundation began its long philanthropical history as a public foundation indexing and abstracting engineering and technical literature in 1934. In 1994, the foundation restructured itself as a private foundation dedicated solely to making grants to qualified nonprofit organizations. Based in New York City, the foundation's mission is to "improve worldwide engineering education and practice through information technology and the recruitment of women." To this end, the foundation has three fields of interest: availability and use of information, women in engineering (projects directed by engineering educators), and developing countries. The foundation's Web site outlines funding desires and limitations, as well as specific grant guidelines, criteria, terms, and conditions. Recent grants are posted by year and program area. The site also includes contact information and resources to facilitate communication among scholars with similar engineering interests.

Lois and Richard England Family Foundation, Inc. (DC)
(http://fdncenter.org/grantmaker/england/index.html)
Created in 1994, the Lois and Richard England Family Foundation, Inc. is "committed to improving the lives of those in need in the Washington metropolitan area." Toward that end, the foundation's grantmaking focuses on local human services, education, and arts and culture. The foundation also supports programs to strengthen Jewish life and institutions locally, nationally, and in Israel. Currently, the foundation is not accepting unsolicited applications. In addition to mission and goal statements, the foundation's Web site provides grant guidelines, an archive of grants lists, a listing of the foundation's trustees, and contact information.

The Florence C. and Harry L. English Memorial Fund (GA)
(http://www.englishmemorialfund.org)
The Florence C. and Harry L. English Memorial Fund was founded in 1964 to honor the son of Capt. James Warren English, Civil War hero and former mayor of Atlanta. The fund benefits nonprofit organizations in the metropolitan Atlanta community. Brief grant guidelines and limitations are provided online, along with a downloadable grant application form. The foundation's fund is administered by the SunTrustBank in Atlanta, and contact information can be found online.

The Environmental Trust (CA) (http://www.tet.org)
Located in La Mesa, California, the Environmental Trust exists to "protect and preserve our natural resources for future generations, by acquiring land, establishing land banks and facilitating the monitoring and management of lands identified and set aside by individuals, agencies, and developers for protection." The trust achieves its mission through varied means, from grants of money and land to facilitating the development of land bank systems and the management of property set aside as preserves or open space. Projects of interest focus on sensitive land planning concepts, the acquisition of natural lands and habitats for the enjoyment of Californians, and assisting every agency level in locating appropriate habitats for endangered species of plants and animals. The trust's Web site includes information on present and planned projects, a board list, and information on contributing to the trust.

Esquel Group Foundation, Inc. (DC) (http://www.esquel.org)
Esquel Group Foundation, Inc. (EGF) is the U.S.-based member and coordinator for regional programs of the Grupo Esquel Network, a group of nonprofit, non-governmental

organizations dedicated to promoting "alternative policies and programs which strengthen the role of civil society" and to promoting sustainable and equitable development in South America. The Washington, D.C.-based EGF provides a variety of services, including research, advocacy, technical cooperation, and extensive advice regarding development in Latin America to non-governmental organizations, foundations, private corporations, and international development agencies working in Latin America and the Caribbean. The foundation also works in collaboration with private sector entities to improve public policy for sustainable development, with political, economic, social, and natural resource considerations in mind. Grupo Esquel has five priority areas: legal framework for civil society; environment, especially in semi-arid and arid zones; rural development and agriculture; children and youth at risk; and "microenterprise development." Visitors to the foundation's Web site will find reports on the group's work, lists of publications and conferences participated in and organized by EGF, contact information for members of the EGF network, board and staff member profiles, a history of the foundation, and information on its internship program.

Eustace Foundation Trust (PA) (http://fdncenter.org/grantmaker/eustace/)
The Eustace Foundation Trust of Pennsylvania supports religious or educational organizations affiliated with the Roman Catholic Church. The trust supports small, local charities and organization in the Northeast as well as worldwide organizations. Visit the trust's Web site to view the it's latest tax return and contact information.

The Fales Foundation Trust (WA) (http://fdncenter.org/grantmaker/fales/)
The Fales Foundation Trust was established in 1985 by Gilbert R. Fales, a long-time Seattle resident. The trust was established to provide financial support to social service agencies addressing issues of homelessness and hunger and to artistic and cultural organizations in the city of Seattle. Visit the trust's Web site to find specific information on the foundation's areas of interest, policies, application procedures, and contact information.

Fassino Foundation (MA) (http://www.fassinofoundation.org/)
The Fassino Foundation supports community-based organizations in the Boston area by aiding homeless, abused, and disabled children and their families. The foundation also gives scholarships to specific area high schools. Visitors to the Fassino Foundation's Web site will find grant guidelines and application long forms for both smaller and larger grants available. Guidelines for attachments and contact information are also provided online.

Edward Fein Foundation (NV) (http://fdncenter.org/grantmaker/fein)
The Edward Fein Foundation, located in Glenbrook, Nevada, was established in 1965 to promote innovative educational activities. The foundation makes both academic grants to individuals and qualified organizations. Foundation support goes to a number of unique programs that promote excellence in students. The foundation also provides financial incentives to the best and brightest instructors. The incentives encourage the instructors to stay enthusiastically involved in the teaching profession. Visitors to the foundation's Web site will find grant guidelines and requirements, application information, and contact information.

Samuel S. Fels Fund (PA) (http://www.samfels.org)
Samuel S. Fels was a Philadelphia philanthropist and civic leader who was president of Fels & Company, which manufactured Fels Naptha, a popular household soap. On December 17, 1935, the Samuel S. Fels Fund was incorporated to initiate and support projects of "a scientific, educational, or charitable nature which tend to improve human daily life and to bring the average person greater health, happiness, and a fuller understanding of the meaning and purposes of life." Its mission is also to support projects "which prevent, lessen, or resolve contemporary social problems." Based in Philadelphia, the foundation has four funding categories: arts and humanities, education, community programs, and health. Grants are restricted to organizations located in the city of Philadelphia or are focused on local issues. An "ideal proposal to Fels is one that addresses positive social

change." Visitors to the foundation's Web site will find detailed grant application guidelines, a printable proposal cover sheet, a recent grants list, lists of trustees and staff, and contact information.

Hugh & Jane Ferguson Foundation (WA) (http://fdncenter.org/grantmaker/ferguson/)
The Hugh & Jane Ferguson Foundation, founded in 1987, is a family foundation that supports nonprofit organizations in the Pacific Northwest and Alaska. The foundation is dedicated to the preservation and restoration of nature, including wildlife and their required habitats. It also supports the institutions that present nature and our rich cultural heritage to the public. Areas of interest of the foundation include community-based projects working to restore habitat and wildlife by activating volunteers and local residents, collaborative and coalition projects involving a number of organizations working together to share strengths and maximize effectiveness, cultural and natural history institutions exploring the history and traditions of the greater Puget Sound area, and projects from Native American communities throughout the Northwest. Visitors to the foundation's Web site can view application guidelines, a listing of recent grantees, and contact information.

John E. Fetzer Institute (MI) (Operating foundation) (http://www.fetzer.org/)
The John E. Fetzer Institute of Kalamazoo, Michigan, was founded by its namesake, a broadcasting pioneer, to support "research, education, and service programs exploring the integral relationships among body, mind, and spirit." The institute usually does not accept unsolicited applications; instead it works with other organizations, institutions, and individuals on various projects. A limited number of funding opportunities are available, however, in the Announcements section of the institute's Web site. The institute has a special interest in "how individuals and communities are influenced by the interactions among the physical, psychological, social, and spiritual dimensions of life, and how understandings in these areas can improve health, foster growth, and better the human condition." The institute maintains funding programs in science, education for fellows and senior scholars, and emerging communities. Information on programs the institute supports and works with, as well as scholarly public grants, are available online along with contact information.

FHL Foundation (NM) (http://www.fhlfoundation.com)
Located in Albuquerque, New Mexico, the FHL Foundation is a small family foundation. Its mission is "providing collaborative support in the areas of discovery, education, and service, all with a focus on eliminating abusive systems which support abuse and oppression towards people and animals." The foundation has specific guidelines and limitations for funding, which are described on its Web site. Grants are made in the general areas of education, discovery, and service, all relating to the subjects of abuse and oppression. Grants are limited, in general, to New Mexico and Colorado. The grant request process begins with the "first-step survey form," which is available on-line, as are the deadlines for grant requests and grant application guidelines.

The Field Foundation of Illinois, Inc. (IL) (http://www.fieldfoundation.org/)
The Field Foundation of Illinois, Inc. was established in 1940 to provide support for community, civic, and cultural organizations in the Chicago area. The Field Foundation makes grants in six program areas: community welfare, culture, education, the environment, health, urban, and community affairs. The foundation awards grants only to institutions and agencies operating in the fields of urban and community affairs, culture, education, community welfare, health, and the environment, primarily serving the people of the Chicago metropolitan area. Visitors to the foundation's Web site can find detailed information about the specific grantmaking programs, restrictions, recent grants lists, officers/director/staff listings, and contact numbers.

Fields Pond Foundation, Inc. (MA) (http://www.fieldspond.org)
Created in 1993, the Fields Pond Foundation, Inc. of Waltham, Massachusetts, works to "provide financial assistance to nature and land conservation organizations which are community-based and which serve to increase environmental awareness by involving local

residents in conservation issues." Grants are made in four primary areas: trail making and other projects that give the public access to conservation lands, land acquisition for conservation, endowments to fund stewardship of conservation areas, and educational programs and publications. The foundation does consider loan requests for the purpose of acquiring conservation lands or projects with a "demonstrated local impact in precollegiate education." The site offers full application guidelines and deadlines for download. There are also lists of previous grants and links to related resources. The foundation accepts the Common Proposal Format of the Associated Grantmakers of Massachusetts, for which there is a link on the Web site.

The Film Foundation, Inc. (NY) (http://www.cinema.ucla.edu/education/education_f.html)
Incorporated in New York City in 1990, the Film Foundation, Inc. is headed by Martin Scorcese and nine other equally eminent directors. The group is "committed to fostering greater awareness of the urgent need to preserve motion picture history" and to "encouraging cooperative preservation projects between the archives and the industry and seeking to ensure that reliable preservation practices are in place for future productions." Funds are raised through national efforts and then distributed to the member archives and affiliated organizations. The site offers a list of the board of directors, links to each member archive and affiliated organization, a list of films preserved or restored as a result of foundation funds, and a list of the Advisory Council.

First Fruit Inc. (CA) (http://www.firstfruit.org)
First Fruit Inc., located in Newport Beach, California, "grants to Christian ministries in the developing world in the areas of leadership development, evangelism, and wholistic ministry." The organization does not fund individuals, nor does it consider sustained support. First Fruit's Web site provides Mandate and Trends That Guide Us sections, which allow visitors to examine the organization's guiding mission. No grant guidelines are available; instead, the organization requests that interested applicants send a two page letter of inquiry. Letter guidelines and First Fruit's contact information are provided online.

The James Marston Fitch Charitable Foundation (NY) (http://www.fitchfoundation.org/)
The James Marston Fitch Charitable Foundation was established in 1988 to "advance the study and the practice of the preservation of the historic architectural heritage of the United States." The foundation awards research grants to mid-career professionals who have an advanced or professional degree and at least ten years experience in historic preservation or related fields, including architecture, landscape architecture, architectural conservation, urban design, environmental planning, archaeology, architectural history, and the decorative arts. Visit the foundation's Web site to find out more about the grant program and view a history of recipients. Contact information is also available.

The Fitzpatrick Foundation (CA) (http://www.fitzpatrickfoundation.com/)
The Fitzpatrick Foundation of Burlingame, California is primarily interested in supporting elementary and secondary school programs for students and educators, with a particular emphasis on programs serving economically disadvantaged youth in the San Francisco Bay Area. The foundation supports a number of activities for students, including in-school and after-school programs that enhance academic achievement, arts education, athletics and recreation, technology skills, and leadership development. The foundation concentrates its support on programs that support contemporary visual and performing arts, improve or save lives of domestic animals and endangered species, enhance family life and health, and foster advances in technology. The foundation's Web site provides detailed information on the individual programs, grant guidelines, and contact information.

Flinn Foundation (AZ) (http://www.flinn.org/)
The Phoenix-based Flinn Foundation primarily awards grants in the fields of health and healthcare, but it also sponsors a scholarship program for higher education and supports Arizona's arts organizations (by invitation only). The foundation takes a proactive approach in its grantmaking; most grant recipients are chosen through requests for

proposals or by invitation. The foundation's activities are limited to the state of Arizona. In addition to brief biographies of foundation founders Dr. Robert Flinn and his wife, Irene Pierce Flinn, visitors to the foundation's Web site will find program descriptions, grant application procedures, a downloadable annual report, links to online resources, a publications order form, a listing of the foundation's trustees and staff, and an online contact/grant proposal inquiry form.

The Ford Family Foundation (OR) (http://www.tfff.org/)
The Ford Family Foundation, of Eugene, Oregon, was created in 1956 to return good fortune to the community of southwest Oregon. The organization is committed to "helping individuals, through organized learning opportunities, to be contributing and successful citizens; and to supporting non-profit activities, agencies, and projects, with particular emphasis on midsize and small communities in the State of Oregon and Siskiyou County, California." Grants are made in four major categories: arts and culture, civic and community betterment, health and human services, and education. The foundation prefers to support projects from well-established organizations that have already secured at least 50 percent of the necessary funding. Besides the grant program, the foundation also awards scholarships. The Ford Scholars Program, the Ford Opportunity Scholarship Program for Single Parents, and the Scholarship Program for Sons and Daughters of Employees of Roseburg Forest Products Company each have their own guidelines and restrictions. Although the foundation requires a pre-application letter for the grants program, the Web site does include application guidelines.

Ford Foundation (NY) (http://www.fordfound.org)
Founded in 1936 by Henry and Edsel Ford and operated as a local philanthropy in the state of Michigan until 1950, the Ford Foundation has since expanded to become a leading force in the world of national and international philanthropy. The foundation's broadly stated goals are to "strengthen democratic values, reduce poverty and injustice, promote international cooperation, and advance human achievement." To realize these goals, the foundation focuses its grantmaking in three program areas: asset building and community development; knowledge, creativity, and freedom; and peace and social justice. The foundation's Web site provides visitors with grant guidelines; application procedures; a searchable grants database; worldwide contact and program information; numerous publications to view online, including the foundation's most recent annual report and its quarterly magazine; and an online form through which to order copies of print publications.

Edward E. Ford Foundation (DC) (http://www.eeford.org/)
Established in 1957 by Edward E. Ford, an IBM director and independent businessman, the Edward E. Ford Foundation is dedicated to encouraging and improving secondary education as provided by independent schools in the United States. The foundation does not make grants to individuals. The initial step in the process of filing an application with the foundation is to contact the Office of the Executive Director in Washington, D.C., for a preliminary telephone interview. The foundation's Web site provides a brief history of the foundation, proposal guidelines for schools and associations, a list of recent grants, a one-page financial statement, and contact information.

Thomas B. Fordham Foundation (DC) (http://www.edexcellence.net)
Thomas B. Fordham was a successful industrialist and prominent civic leader in Dayton, Ohio, who passed away in 1944. In 1953, his widow, Thelma Pruett Fordham, established the Thomas B. Fordham Foundation in his memory. During her lifetime, the foundation aided diverse charitable organizations and educational institutions in the Dayton area, but upon her death in 1995, the trustees determined that reform of elementary/secondary school education would be the foundation's sole focus. To that end, the Thomas B. Fordham Foundation supports research, publications, and action projects of national significance in elementary/secondary education reform and significant education reform projects in Dayton, Ohio area. The Washington, D.C.-based foundation does not support unsolicited projects or consider unsolicited proposals. It is primarily interested in "projects leading to

information that advances knowledge of effective education reform strategies consistent with the foundation's principles." Visitors to the Web site will find further information on the foundation's mode of operation, information on its national reform issues, links, viewable and downloadable publications and articles, ordering information, bibliographies of recommended books, and contact information.

Fortune Family Foundation (WA) (http://www.fortunefoundation.org/)
The Fortune Family Foundation is located in Kirkland, Washington, and is committed to serving "organizations which seek to foster self-sufficiency in those individuals and families who have committed to attaining it" in the Puget Sound area of the state. The foundation's Web site provides detailed application guidelines and procedures, an overview of the organization, a Frequently Asked Questions page and a feedback form. Interested applicants should e-mail the foundation for further information.

Foundation for Child Development (NY) (http://www.ffcd.org/)
The New York City-based Foundation for Child Development is dedicated to the principle that all families should have the social and material resources to raise their children to be healthy, educated, and productive members of their communities. The foundation makes grants nationally to nonprofit institutions for research, policy analysis, advocacy, leadership development, and a small number of program development projects. Three cross-cutting themes guide the founation's work: linking research on children and families to formation of relevant programs and policies, identifying fresh approaches to crafting sound social strategies for children and families, and nurturing new generations of leaders in child development research and policy. The foundation does not consider requests for scholarships or grants to individuals, capital campaigns, or the purchase, construction, or renovation of buildings. The foundation's Web site offers a brief history of the foundation, its mission statement and application instructions, a searchable grants database, downloadable versions of the foundation's Working Paper Series, listings of the foundation's board and staff, and contact information.

Foundation for Deep Ecology (CA) (http://www.deepecology.org)
Located in Sausalito, California, the Foundation for Deep Ecology operates under an awareness of the current environmental threat to human life and to the lives of all species of plants and animals, as well as the health and continued viability of the biosphere. The foundation's belief that current environmental problems are rooted in overpopulation, loss of traditional knowledge, economic development of the modern world, and technology worship guide the organization's funding strategies in the areas of: Biodiversity & Wildness, Ecological Agriculture, and Megatechnology & Economic Globalization. The foundation's Web site provides extensive details on each area of funding interest, along with a more expansive explanation of the groups philosophy and mission. Interested applicants should prepare a letter of inquiry as outlined on the Grant Guidelines page. Additional publications, conference news, event listings, and contact information are also posted online.

The Foundation for Hellenic Culture, Inc. (NY) (Operating foundation) (http://www.foundationhellenicculture.com/)
The New York City branch of the Foundation for Hellenic Culture, Inc. was established in 1995, while the headquarters, in Athens, Greece, was created in 1992. The organization's goal is to "promote and disseminate Greek culture and language outside of Greece." The foundation sponsors art exhibitions, film screenings, concerts, lectures, theatrical productions, readings, and educational programs. The Web site includes a list of many of the sponsored activities in North America, the activities that are currently happening, and contact information for all of the foundation's branches.

Foundation for Middle East Peace (DC) (http://www.fmep.org)
Located in Washington, D.C., the Foundation for Middle East Peace (FMEP) was created in 1979. The group is committed to "inform[ing] Americans on the Israeli-Palestinian conflict and assist[ing] in a peaceful solution that brings security for both peoples." The four

main programs within the foundation are the Speakers Progam, the production of publications, media outreach, and grantmakers. The grantmaking program provides support for organizations and individuals working toward a resolution of the Israeli-Palestinian conflict. The Web site serves as a resource for those interested in the issue. There are electronic versions of many publications, maps, charts, and a searchable database of statistics. See the About FMEP section for information on the grants program.

Foundation for Seacoast Health (NH) (http://www.ffsh.org)
The Foundation for Seacoast Health, created in 1985, has become the largest private charitable foundation in New Hampshire. Its mission is to "support and promote healthcare in any one or more of the cities and towns in the New Hampshire/Maine Seacoast area and do any and all things in furtherance thereof, including providing goods, services, and programs and fostering the provision of goods, services and programs and the study, promotion, demonstration, and dissemination of ideas that promote public health and well-being." The foundation accepts grants from both individuals and nonprofit organizations located in the foundation's community. A "Request for Proposal" brochure, explaining the grant application procedure, can be obtained by calling, e-mailing, or writing the foundation. The foundation also has a scholarship program, which offers scholarships to assist qualified students who are residents of the foundation's community and are pursuing a degree program in health-related fields of study at an accredited institution of higher learning. Scholarship applications can be requested from the foundation. Deadlines for both grant and scholarship applications are posted on the Web site.

Foundation for the Advancement of MesoAmerican Studies, Inc. (FL) (http://www.famsi.org)
Based in Crystal River, Florida, the Foundation for the Advancement of MesoAmerican Studies, Inc. was created in 1993 to foster increased understanding of ancient MesoAmerican cultures. The foundation aims to assist and promote qualified scholars who might otherwise be unable to undertake or complete their programs of research and synthesis. Projects in the following disciplines are urged to apply: anthropology, archaeology, art history, epigraphy, ethnography, ethnohistory, linguistics, and related fields. Grant applications may be requested in writing or downloaded from the Web site, and visitors to the site will find grant reports, a summary of funding, and grant recipient lists. The archives and a bibliography devoted to MesoAmerican studies can be accessed from the foundation's Web site. The site also contains conference reports, links to PreColumbian sites, and contact information.

Foundation for the Future (WA) (http://www.futurefoundation.org)
In 1996 Walter Kistler established Foundation for the Future, in Bellevue, Washington. He is founder of Kistler Instruments Corporation, a world leader in the development of quartz sensors, and he is also the co-founder and Chairman Emeritus of Kistler Aerospace Corporation. The foundation is focused on the long-term survivability of humanity and supports research and symposia whose purpose is to identify the most critical factors that may affect future human life on Earth. To that end, the foundation has a research grant award program, the biannual Kistler Prize, and the Humanity 3000 symposium and seminars. The research grant award program provides financial support to scholars for research that is directly related to a better understanding of the factors affecting the quality of life for the long-term future of humanity. The Kistler Prize is awarded every other year to individuals and organizations for "outstanding achievement in identifying the genetic factors that may have a decisive impact on the survivability of a human population." Visit the Web site for more information about the foundation's programs, application procedures, newsletter, links to other futurist organizations, and contact information. The site also has online preliminary application, feedback, and information request forms.

The Fourjay Foundation (PA) (http://www.fourjay.org)
The Fourjay Foundation, based in Willow Grove, Pennsylvania, supports organizations whose chief purpose is to improve health and/or promote education within Philadelphia, Montgomery, and Bucks Counties in southeastern Pennsylvania. The foundation has a

Cardiology Research Grant, which is open to cardiology fellows in training and faculty at the rank of Associate and Assistant Professor level. Areas of focus include: congenital heart disease in the adult, regression of arteriosclerosis, new technology applications in the diagnosis of heart disease, early detection and/or prevention of stroke, and new advances in the treatment of hypertension. Application procedures, grant recipient lists, and printable application materials are available on the foundation's Web site. The site also provides information on the foundation's Healthlink Medical Center initiative. The center is an organization of volunteer physicians, dentists, nurses, dental hygienists, social service workers, and pharmacists who will provide free primary medical and dental care to individuals and families who are employed but without health insurance, who live in Bucks and Montgomery Counties.

John Edward Fowler Memorial Foundation (DC) (http://fdncenter.org/grantmaker/fowler/)
The John Edward Fowler Memorial Foundation of Washington, D.C., was created in 1964 in memory of John Edward Fowler, a northern Virginia businessman. The foundation is particularly interested in providing operating support in the areas of homelessness, hunger, at-risk children and youth, adult literacy, free medical care, seniors, and job training and placement. The foundation prefers to support smaller, grassroots, neighborhood-based organizations. The foundation prefers to focus its giving on organizations that serve disadvantaged people who live in the inner-city of Washington, D.C., and the close-in suburbs of Maryland and Virginia. Visitors to the foundation's Web site will find specific information on the foundation's areas of interest, recent grants listings, recent financial statement, application procedures, printable application, and contact information.

The William and Eva Fox Foundation (NY) (http://thefoxfoundation.org/)
The William and Eva Fox Foundation of New York is committed to the artistic development of theater actors as a strategy to strengthen live theater. The foundation is the largest grantmaker solely dedicated to the artistic and professional development of theater actors, and it is one of very few that provides direct support to individual actors. The foundation awards its fellowships to recent graduates of five elite drama schools to support periods of intensive training to develop particular aspects of their craft related to theatrical performance. Visit the foundation's Web site to learn more about the unique grantmaking provided through the organization, FAQs, further information on the individual fellowship programs, and contact information.

The Francis Families Foundation (MO) (http://www.francisfoundation.org)
The Francis Families Foundation of Missouri was originally established as the Parker B. Francis Foundation to serve the greater Kansas City area. In 1989, the Parker B. Francis Foundation merged with the Parker B. Francis III Foundation to become the Francis Families Foundation. The foundation's priorities include the Parker B. Francis Fellowship Program, a national post-doctoral program in pulmonary research, and support of educational and cultural programs located within the greater Kansas City area. Since the merger, however, the foundation has narrowed its focus within the educational component to give primary consideration to child and youth development at all levels, from early care through higher education. Visitors to the foundation's Web site will find further information on the grantmaking programs and geographical limitations.

Regina B. Frankenberg Foundation (NY) (http://fdncenter.org/grantmaker/frankenberg/)
The New York-based, Regina B. Frankenberg Foundation maintains an interest in programs that promote the care, conservation, treatment, well being, and prevention of cruelty to animals. General funding will be considered to organizations nationally, including U.S. organizations with international programs. With respect to companion animals, preference is given to organizations serving New York City and neighboring counties. Visit the foundation's Web site to learn more about grant priorities, application procedures, and contact information.

Freedom Forum, Inc. (VA) (http://www.freedomforum.org)
Dedicated to "free press, free speech, and free spirit for all people," the mission of the Freedom Forum, Inc. is to help the public and the news media to better understand one another. Primary areas of interest include First Amendment rights, journalism education, newsroom diversity, professional development of journalists, media studies and research, and international journalism programs. The forum does not accept unsolicited grant applications and only makes limited grants in connection with its programs. Its Web site offers a range of information and features, including detailed descriptions of the forum's programs and history; articles drawn from various Freedom Forum publications; links to the Gannett Center for Media Studies and dozens of related online resources; an online version of the forum's most recent annual report, with grant "highlights" organized by month; and a listing of the trustees and officers.

Frey Foundation (MI) (http://www.freyfdn.org)
As heir to Union Bank and Trust and founder of Foremost Insurance Company, Edward Frey accumulated considerable wealth, which he and his wife Francis believed should be reinvested in the community. As a means to carry out their charitable interests, they established the Frey Foundation, based in Grand Rapids, Michigan. The Frey Foundation is "committed to working together to make a difference in the lives of individuals, families, organizations, and communities," and states that "as we strive to make a meaningful impact on the lives of people, we encourage creativity and excellence and expect accountability of ourselves and others." The foundation has five funding categories: enhancing the lives of children and their families, protecting the environment, nurturing community arts, encouraging civic progress, and strengthening philanthropy, as well as two special initiatives: Revitalizing Our Community and Supporting Our Children. Support is primarily given to the western side of Michigan's lower peninsula, with special emphasis on the greater Grand Rapids area and Charlevoix and Emmet Counties. Consult the foundation's Web site for more details about each funding category, grant application instructions, financial statements, available publications, contact information, and links to other organizations in the community.

Friedman Family Foundation (CA) (http://www.friedmanfamilyfoundation.org)
The Friedman Family Foundation's mission is to "fund programs that attempt to end the cycle of poverty." Priority is given to organizations in the nine counties of the San Francisco Bay Area. The foundation believes in a "respect for the capabilities and dignity of all people, a belief in the power of ideas and in individual empowerment, a commitment to systemic change, a reverence for learning, faith in the ability to create a better world, and an obligation to the San Francisco Bay Area." Visitors to the foundation's Web site will find grant guidelines, application information, a history of grantees, staff and board information, and contact information.

The Frist Foundation (TN) (http://www.fristfoundation.org)
Formerly known as the HCA Foundation, the Nashville-based Frist Foundation was established in 1982 by Hospital Corporation of America (HCA). Following the merger of HCA with Columbia Healthcare Corporation in 1994, the foundation became fully independent of the company. In 1997 it changed its name to honor the philanthropic influence of its founding directors: Dr. Thomas F. Frist, Sr., gifted cardiologist, businessman, and philanthropist, and Dr. Thomas F. Frist, Jr., who still serves as chairman. The Frist Foundation continues its mission to invest its resources in select nonprofit organizations in metropolitan Nashville in order to strengthen their ability to provide services. The foundation's activities are mostly grantmaking, but it has also initiated special programs to enhance the community, some of which awards grants. Grants are awarded to a variety of organizations in the fields of health, human services, civic affairs, education, and the arts and generally fall into three categories: sustaining (operating support), project and program, and capital. Consult the foundation's Web site for more information on the foundation's special programs guidelines, funding guidelines, lists of directors and staff members, annual report, grant recipient lists, and contact information.

Frog Rock Foundation (NY) (http://www.frogrockfoundation.org/)
Founded in 2000, the Frog Rock Foundation of Westchester County, New York, helps children and young adults overcome economic disadvantages affecting education, healthcare, recreation, and physical and psychological well being. The foundation currently services family support, education, victims of violence, arts and recreation, and advocacy. Visit the foundation's Web site to find a grant history, application information, eligability requirements, and contact information.

Lloyd A. Fry Foundation (IL) (http://www.fryfoundation.org/)
The mission of the Lloyd A. Fry Foundation is to improve the quality of life for Chicago's disadvantaged residents by promoting solutions to problems associated with urban poverty. The Lloyd A. Fry Foundation was established in 1983 following the death of its founder and namesake, an entrepreneur in the roofing industry. Grants are made in the following fields: education, civic affairs and social service, arts and culture, and health. Grantseekers will find grant application guidelines, foundation history, board and staff listings, grants by area, the latest copy of the foundation's annual report, and contact information.

Helene Fuld Health Trust (NY) (http://www.fuld.org/)
Dr. Leonhard Felix Fuld and his sister, Florentine, created a foundation in honor of their mother in 1935, which was converted to the Helene Fuld Health Trust in 1965. This New York City-based foundation, administered by HSBC Bank USA, is dedicated to supporting and promoting the health, welfare, and education of student nurses. It's funding priority is financial aid to nursing students by establishing endowed scholarships at select nursing schools and by awarding grants to leading nursing schools and other organizations undertaking innovative programs designed to develop and expand the professional and leadership skills of nursing. The trust does not accept unsolicited grant proposals or financial aid requests. Visitors to the Web site will find detailed program guidelines and answers to FAQs.

The Fuller Foundation (NH) (http://www.fullerfoundation.org/)
Alvan T. Fuller, state legislator, member of Congress, Lieutenant Governor, and two-time Governor of Massachusetts, founded the Fuller Foundation in 1936. This Rye Beach, New Hampshire-based foundation supports nonprofit agencies that work to improve the quality of life for people, animals, and the environment. It also funds the Fuller Foundation of New Hampshire, which supports horticulture and education programs for the public at Fuller Gardens, which is what remains of Fuller's summer estate. The Fuller Foundation funds programs focused on at-risk youth, wildlife and endangered species, and the arts, predominantly in the Boston area and the immediate seacoast area of New Hampshire. New and "seed" organizations that do not have financial histories will also be considered for support, as long as they have sound financial plans. The foundation's Web site offers details on focus areas, guidelines, application procedures, and contact information.

Fund for Astrophysical Research (NY) (http://fdncenter.org/grantmaker/fundastro/)
The New York-based Fund for Astrophysical Research makes small grants to support research in astronomy and astrophysics. Founded in 1936 by Charles G. Thompson and Alice Bemis Thompson, the fund has supported astronomical and astrophysical projects in the United States, Australia, and New Zealand through loans and gifts of funds and optical equipment. Grants are awarded for the acquisition of astronomical equipment, and computer hardware or software that will be used in research. The fund's Web site contains a brief history of the fund, grant guidelines and recipients, a listing of officers and trustees, and a biography of Theodore Dunham, Jr., the fund's founding scientific director.

The Fund for New Jersey (NJ) (http://www.fundfornj.org)
Founded in 1958 under another name, The Fund for New Jersey continues to issue grants that directly address today's problems. The fund makes grants to qualifying organizations in New Jersey, with particular attention given to projects seeking to affect public policy. Formal programs include: Social and Economic Opportunity, Environment and Land Use,

Public Policy in New Jersey, and Agenda New Jersey. Visitors to the fund's Web site will find specific details about the grantmaking programs, application information, staff/trustee listings, and contact information.

Fund for the City of New York (NY) (Operating foundation) (http://www.fcny.org/)
The Fund for the City of New York is an independent private operating foundation whose mandate is "to respond to the opportunities and problems of New York City; to improve the performance of the city's government and the quality of life of its citizens." The fund's five primary grantmaking areas are children and youth, AIDS, community development and housing, the urban environment, and government and technology, but it also makes a limited number of grants that do not fall neatly into any of the above categories. Grants awarded are generally between $5,000 and $10,000, and the fund provides both general and project support. It also operates the Cash Flow Loan Program, the Nonprofit Computer Exchange, and the Management Initiative, all of which address "the importance of this type of funding to maintain the management infrastructure needed to support an agency's programs." Visitors to the fund's Web site will find detailed information on all of the fund's programs and initiatives, as well as contact information.

Fund for Nonviolence (CA) (http://www.fundfornonviolence.org/)
The Santa Cruz-based Fund for Nonviolence was founded in 1997 to benefit "community based efforts whose aim is significant social change which moves humanity towards a more just and compassionate coexistence." In general, the fund supports nonviolence in work for progressive social change, especially in the areas of women in poverty, children (with an emphasis on girls), and challenging state-sponsored violence (such as militarization and the death penalty). Funding priorities are for groups that focus on structural changes to root causes of injustice, reflect the spirit of nonviolence in their organizational structure and process, and demonstrate a vision grounded in reflective thought on actions taken. The fund's Web site provides details about its priorities, its current funding programs and limitations, guidelines for letters of inquiry, a list of grantees, and contact information.

Gaia Fund (CA) (http://www.gaiafundsf.org)
Based in San Francisco, California, the Gaia Fund was established in 1994 to support the environment and Jewish life. The fund places preference to organizations in the San Francisco area. Visit the fund's Web site to find funding priorities, grant application procedures, and contact information.

The Gar Foundation (OH) (http://www.garfdn.org)
The Gar Foundation was established in 1967 to support organizations located in Summit County, Ohio. Organizations in Cuyahoga, Medina, Portage, Stark, and Wayne Counties are given secondary consideration. Interests of the foundation include education, arts, social services, and other areas that are deemed supportive to communities. Visit the foundation's Web site to find out how to apply for support. The foundation's Web site also contains guidelines for applying, a helpful FAQs section, information about special initiatives, and contact information.

Bill and Melinda Gates Foundation (WA) (http://www.gatesfoundation.org/)
The William H. Gates Foundation and the Gates Learning Foundation merged in August 1999 to become the Bill and Melinda Gates Foundation and ranks as one of the wealthiest private foundations in the world. Established by the Microsoft co-founder and CEO, the Seattle-based foundation is dedicated to improving people's lives by sharing advances in health and learning with the global community. The foundation provides support for global health, education, libraries, nonprofit organizations in the Pacific Northwest, and special projects of the Gates family. Visitors to the foundation's Web site will find detailed descriptions of the foundation's various initiatives, grantmaking guidelines, press releases, complete grantee lists, and contact information.

Gates Family Foundation (CO) (http://www.gatesfamilyfdn.org)
The Denver, Colorado-based Gates Family Foundation was established in 1946 by Charles C. Gates, Sr., founder of the Gates Corporation, which began as a rubber company. Its purpose is to "enhance the quality of life of those who live and work in Colorado through activities that promote broad education, self-sufficiency, connection to nature, and cultural appreciation." The foundation primarily supports institutions, projects, and programs in the state of Colorado, with special attention paid to the Denver metropolitan area. Consult the foundation's Web site for further details on the foundation's major areas of funding interest, guidelines, application instructions, the latest annual report, with grant lists, projects funded, resource links, and contact information.

Fred Gellert Family Foundation (CA) (http://fdncenter.org/grantmaker/fredgellert/)
The Fred Gellert Family Foundation was founded in 1958 by a San Francisco Bay Area homebuilder. The foundation makes grants to organizations in the areas of "arts, education, environment, health, and social service, and on projects that link two or more of these areas," primarily serving communities in Marin, San Francisco, and San Mateo Counties. The foundation's Web site includes more detailed descriptions of these areas, as well as grant guidelines, application procedures, recently awarded grants, and contact information.

Carl Gellert and Celia Berta Gellert Foundation (CA) (http://home.earthlink.net/~cgcbg/)
Based in San Francisco, the Carl Gellert and Celia Berta Gellert Foundation promotes religious, charitable, scientific, literary, and educational activities in the nine counties of the greater San Francisco Bay Area (i.e., Alameda, Contra Costa, Marin, Napa, San Francisco, San Mateo, Santa Clara, Solano, and Sonoma Counties). Visitors to the foundation's Web site will find a mission statement, application guidelines, an online application request form, grant recipients, and contact information.

General Service Foundation (CO) (http://www.generalservice.org/)
The General Service Foundation, based in Aspen, Colorado seeks to address the global issues of international peace, reproductive health and rights, and resources. The foundation's International Peace Program addresses the need for stable communities mainly in Mexico, Central America, and the Caribbean; its Reproductive Health and Rights Program supports reproductive health services for women and adolescents in the United States and Mexico; and the Western Water Program supports the preservation of aquatic and riparian ecosystems in Idaho, Montana, Wyoming, Colorado, New Mexico, Utah, and Arizona. the foundation's Web site provides descriptions of its programs, grant guidelines and limitations, grantee lists in each area, application procedures, and contact information.

The George Foundation (TX) (http://www.thegeorgefoundation.org)
Based in Richmond, Texas, the George Foundation was established as a "trust for religious, charitable, scientific, literary and/or educational purposes" to benefit the citizens of Fort Bend County and to preserve the heritage of the area. Funding is directed towards programs in early childhood development and education. The foundation also offers scholarships and student loans for Fort Bend County students attending Texas colleges and universities, as well as scholarships for high school students. The George Foundation set aside land for the George Ranch Historical Park, where the authentic activities of a working Texas ranch are relived. It serves as a center for community activities, a place for agricultural research, a site for cultural and charitable events, and a resource for research and education about Fort Bend County. Visitors to the foundation's Web site will find grant application guidelines, scholarship opportunities, grant lists, and grantee report forms.

The George Family Foundation (MN)
(http://www.users.uswest.net/~famphiladv/george.htm)
The Minneapolis-based George Family Foundation considers its mission "to foster human development—spiritual, intellectual, physical and psychological—and to enhance the work of people and organizations devoted to exemplary service in the community." Its funding interests lie in five main categories: integrated healing (mind, body, heart, and

spirit), educational opportunity, youth development, overcoming barriers for women and people of color, and collaboration between people and organizations to address community needs. The foundation's Web site includes application guidelines and limitations, a downloadable grant application cover page, grant recipient lists, and contact information.

The Gerber Foundation (MI) (http://www.gerberfoundation.org/)
The mission of the Gerber Foundation is to "enhance the quality of life of infants and young children in nutrition, care, and development." The foundation, located in Freemont, Michigan, was established in 1952 as the Gerber Baby Foods Fund by Dan Gerber and the Gerber Products Company. Since 1994, the Gerber Foundation has been a separately endowed, private foundation. The foundation makes grants to national programs focusing on pediatric health, pediatric nutrition, and projects that evaluate the effects of environmental hazards on infants and young children. It also runs two scholarship programs for students in Newaygo County, Michigan and select surrounding areas. Information on how to apply for a grant or scholarship, the foundation's history, annual report, and trustees list can be found on the foundation's Web site.

Wallace Alexander Gerbode Foundation (CA) (http://fdncenter.org/grantmaker/gerbode/)
The Wallace Alexander Gerbode Foundation supports programs in the San Francisco Bay Area and Hawaii in the areas of arts and culture; environment; population; reproductive rights; citizen participation, building communities, and inclusiveness; and strength of the philanthropic process and the nonprofit sector. In addition to general application and fiscal information, the foundation's Web site provides an archive of grants, listed by program area and most recent financial information.

Benjamin S. Gerson Family Foundation (OH) (http://www.fmscleveland.com/gerson)
Located in Cleveland, the Benjamin S. Gerson Family Foundation was established in 1973. It funds organizations in greater Cleveland (with an emphasis on Cuyahoga County) focused on expanding opportunities for the economically disadvantaged and other marginalized groups in society, promoting family preservation, and nurturing creativity as an essential component of public and personal growth. The foundation's Web site includes funding guidelines, details on the application process, information on the foundation's recent grants, a financial report, and a contact information.

J. Paul Getty Trust (CA) (Operating foundation) (http://www.getty.edu/grants/index.html)
The J. Paul Getty Trust, a private operating foundation dedicated to the visual arts and humanities, comprises a museum, four institutes, and a grant program. The purpose of the latter is to strengthen the fields in which the trust is active by funding exceptional projects throughout the world that promote research in the history of art and related fields, advance the understanding of art, and conserve cultural heritage. The Getty Grant Program provides support to organizations and scholars in the areas of research, conservation, and leadership and professional development. The Grant Program section of the trust's Web site provides a general overview of its grantmaking activities, extensive program information and guidelines, a list of grants recently awarded, and application and contact information.

Addison H. Gibson Foundation (PA) (http://www.gibson-fnd.org)
Addison H. Gibson, a pioneer in the oil and gas industry during the early twentieth century, specified in his will that the majority of his fortune be used to help improve quality of western Pennsylvanians' higher education and medical care. The Pittsburgh-based Addison H. Gibson Foundation has an education loan program and a medical trust that provides medical treatment to needy, self-supporting patients who otherwise cannot afford the required medical aid. Visitors to the foundation's Web site will find further information on its programs, residency requirements, application information, a trustee and staff listing, and contact information.

Rosamund Gifford Charitable Corporation (NY) (http://www.giffordfd.org)
The Rosamond Gifford Charitable Corporation of New York is dedicated to addressing the educational, scientific, social, and religious needs of Syracuse and Onondaga Counties. The foundation supports organizations engaged in system change, empowering youth, and those who serve underrepresented and marginalized groups. Visitors to the foundation's Web site will find grant guidelines, grant histories, financial statements, staff and board listings, and contact information.

The Harry Bramhall Gilbert Charitable Trust (VA) (http://fdncenter.org/grantmaker/gilbert/)
The Harry Bramhall Gilbert Charitable Trust supports nonprofit organizations that contribute to the health, education, and cultural life of the Tidewater, Virginia region. The trust currently and funds nonprofits based in Norfolk, Chesapeake, and Virginia Beach, Virginia. Visitors to the trust's Web site will find downloadable tax returns, foundation establishment documents, and contact information.

Price Gilbert, Jr. Charitable Fund (GA) (http://www.wachovia.com/corp_inst/charitable_services/0,,3298,00.html)
The Price Gilbert, Jr. Charitable Fund, based in Atlanta, Georgia, was founded in 1973 to support charitable and educational institutions in the metropolitan Atlanta area, focusing on capital needs. Visitors to the fund's Web site will find grant guidelines, an application form, a listing of recent grants, grants statistics, and a listing of distribution committee members.

The Gill Foundation (CO) (http://www.gillfoundation.org)
Based in Colorado Springs, Colorado, the Gill Foundation seeks to secure equal opportunity for all people, regardless of sexual orientation or gender identity. The foundation primarily accepts grant proposals from gay, lesbian, bisexual, transgender, and allied organizations outside major metropolitan areas in states other than Colorado. Through the Gay and Lesbian Fund for Colorado, the foundation also funds nonprofit organizations in Colorado in the areas of arts and culture; children, youth, and families; civic participation; leadership; development; public broadcasting; and social justice. Visitors to the Web site will find more details about each grant program area, guidelines, application instructions, and an online eligibility quiz. The foundation also offers online information and resources about its efforts to strengthen nonprofit organizations and democratic institutions, as well as its efforts to build awareness of the contributions people of diverse sexual orientations and gender identities.

The Howard Gilman Foundation Inc. (NY) (http://www.howardgilman.org)
Based in New York City, the Howard Gilman Foundation Inc.'s mission is to support philanthropic programs in the areas of the performing arts, wildlife conservation, and cardiovascular diseases. The foundation provides residencies at the White Oak Plantation and grants to performing artists, primarily in dance and theater. It also supports research on cardiovascular diseases at the Howard Gilman Institute for Valvular Heart Diseases at Cornell University. Visitors to the foundation's Web site will find further details about the foundation's programs and guidelines, a brief biography of Howard Gilman, information about the White Oak Plantation, a list of recent grants, and contact information.

Irving S. Gilmore Foundation (MI) (http://www.isgilmorefoundation.org/)
The Irving S. Gilmore Foundation was established in Kalamazoo, Michigan, in 1972 to sustain and improve the cultural, social, and economic life of greater Kalamazoo. The foundation's funding priorities are the arts, culture, and humanities; human services; education and youth activities; community development; and health and well-being. The foundation's Web site provides a brief history of the foundation and a description of its involvement in the community, grant application guidelines and procedures, and contact information.

Bernard F. and Alva B. Gimbel Foundation (NY) (http://www.gimbelfoundation.org)
The Bernard F. and Alva B. Gimbel Foundation of New York was created in 1943. Grants are made in the areas of education, social welfare, the environment, and reproductive rights. In most program areas, the foundation seeks to fund both organizations offering direct services and those working to influence public policy. Grantmaking for direct services is focused almost entirely on organizations based in New York City. Visit the foundation's Web site to find proposal requirements and procedures, a list of recent grants, board and staff lists, and contact information.

The Frank Hadley and Cornelia Root Ginn Charitable Trust (OH) (http://www.ginnfoundation.org)
Established in 1991, the Frank Hadley and Cornelia Root Ginn Charitable Trust addresses educational and community-based healthcare needs through supporting effective programs and services that bring about long-term solutions for individuals and the community, principally in Cuyahoga County, Ohio. The trust also supports nonprofit organizations in building internal capacity in such areas as fundraising, technology, infrastructure, and staff development to meet their goals. Visit the trust's Web site for an overview of the grantmaking process, application information, grants listings, and contact information.

Glaser Progress Foundation (WA) (http://www.glaserprogress.org/)
The Glaser Progress Foundation was established by Rob Glaser, CEO and founder of RealNetworks, Inc., in Seattle, Washington. The foundation's efforts are focused on improving understanding and measurement of human progress; making animal treatment a crucial consideration in business, policy, and personal decision-making; and strengthening democracy by making independent voices heard. The foundation's Web site describes these initiatives and provides an online grant application, lists of previous grant recipients, and contact information.

Glazer Family Foundation (FL) (http://www.glazerfamilyfoundation.com/)
The Glazer Family Foundation, located in Tampa, Florida, works with nonprofit organizations in west central Florida that create programs supporting positive social and economic development in youth and families. It gives preference to programs focused on youth and families in the areas of general health, safety, education, and recreation. The foundation's Web site provides descriptions of its programs, application guidelines, an application form, and recent news.

The Gleitsman Foundation (CA) (http://www.gleitsman.org)
The California-based Gleitsman Foundation was established in 1989 to encourage leadership in social activism worldwide. The foundation makes grants to individuals through three distinct award programs. The Citizen Activist Award is presented every other year to worthy recipients in the United States that have challenged social injustice. The International Activist Award is presented in alternate years to recognize the achievements of individual activism internationally. The foundation also presents monthly awards of achievement to activists who have made a difference in their respective communities. Visitors to the foundation's Web site will find further details on the various awards, along with nomination and deadline information. Also available is a printable nomination form; a board of directors listing, with brief biographies; and a list of previous award recipients.

Glenn Foundation for Medical Research, Inc. (CA) (Operating foundation) (http://www.glennfoundation.org)
The California-based Glenn Foundation for Medical Research, Inc. hopes to "extend the healthful productive years of life through research on the mechanisms of biological aging." The foundation supports grant programs for post-doctoral fellows and scholars in collaboration with the American Federation for Aging Research (AFAR). Application information is available through AFAR (http://www.afar.org/). The foundation's Web site offers an overview of the foundation's mission, lists of fellows and scholars, and links to other organizations involved in research on aging.

Goizueta Foundation (GA) (http://www.goizuetafoundation.org)
The Atlanta-based Goizueta Foundation was established in 1992 by Roberto C. Goizueta, chairman and CEO of Coca-Cola. The foundation provides assistance for all levels of education, youth and family development, youth homes, immigrant/refugee services, services for people with disabilities, and pre-selected arts and culture organizations. The types of programs funded include institutional strengthening, organizational and program development and expansion, and organizational and project planning. The foundation's Web site provides detailed guidelines for grantseekers, resources for grantseekers, and additional information about the foundation and its founder.

The Golden Rule Foundation, Inc. (TX) (http://www.goldrule.org)
The Golden Rule Foundation, Inc. is dedicated to the American dream of self help. It does not fund unsolicited applications. The foundation's Web site provides downloadable forms for invited applicants, a listing of recent grants, and contact information.

Goldman Environmental Foundation (CA) (http://www.goldmanprize.org)
The Goldman Environmental Foundation, based in San Francisco, was founded by Richard N. Goldman. It has awarded the Goldman Environmental Prize since 1990 to demonstrate the international nature of environmental problems, to draw public attention to global issues of critical importance, to reward individuals for outstanding grassroots environmental initiatives, and to inspire others. The foundation awards $125,000 annually to six environmental heroes, who are nominated by a network environmental organizations and a confidential panel of experts. Recipients are chosen for their sustained and important efforts to preserve the natural environment. Visitors to the site will find recipient lists, a list of nominating organizations, press releases, and an online version of the foundation's newsletters.

Richard & Rhoda Goldman Fund (CA) (http://www.goldmanfund.org/)
The Richard & Rhoda Goldman Fund was established in 1951 to improve the quality of life in the San Francisco Bay Area, protect the environment, and promote a more just and sustainable world. The fund is interested in supporting programs that will have a positive impact in an array of fields, including the environment, population, violence prevention, Jewish affairs, children and youth, the elderly, social and human services, health, education, democracy and civil society, and the arts. While the fund is primarily interested in organizations and projects that have an impact on San Francisco and local Bay Area communities, it will consider inquiries from domestic organizations that provide support to Israel and national and international projects that address environmental and population issues. The fund's Web site provides lists of grants awarded; information on how to apply; detailed information about the fund and its programs, including a link to the Goldman Environmental Prize Web site (http://www.goldmanprize.org/); news and publications; and contact information.

Grable Foundation (PA) (http://www.grablefdn.org)
The Pittsburgh, Pennsylvania-based Grable Foundation was established in 1976 "to help children and youth become independent, caring, contributing members of society by supporting programs critical to a child's successful development." The foundation focuses its giving in three areas: improving educational opportunities, supporting community efforts, and strengthening families. Visitors to the foundation's Web site will find brief descriptions of its funding priorities, application guidelines, grants lists, information about the foundation, and contact information. The foundation accepts the Common Grant Application for Grantmakers of Western Pennsylvania and includes a link to this form on its site.

Bill Graham Foundation (CA) (http://www.billgrahamfoundation.org/)
Formed in 1991, the Bill Graham Foundation of California makes grants primarily in the areas of music, the arts, and education, while also supporting social work, environmental protection, and spiritual and compassionate projects in its community. The primary geographic focus of the foundation is the Bay Area and Northern California. Visit the foundation's Web site to learn more about Bill Graham and his life. Also available on the site are

application guidelines, a list of recent recipients, grant restrictions, and contact information.

Graham Foundation for the Advanced Studies in the Fine Arts (IL) (http://www.GrahamFoundation.org/)
The Graham Foundation for the Advanced Studies in the Fine Arts was established in 1956 in Chicago, Illinois. The foundation awards grants to individuals and institutions in support of activities that focus on architecture and the built environment and that lead to the public dissemination of ideas through publication, exhibition, or educational programming. In addition to its general grantmaking program, the foundation also offers the Carter Manny Award, which supports doctoral candidates in their research for academic dissertations directly concerned with architecture. The foundation's Web site provides detailed information about the foundation's programs and activities, grant descriptions and application instructions, lists of past recipients, its annual report, and a searchable database of grant abstracts.

William T. Grant Foundation (NY) (http://www.wtgrantfoundation.org/)
The William T. Grant Foundation seeks to help create a society that values young people and enables them to reach their full potential by investing in research, marketing and communications disciplines, and youth development and mental health. The foundation is especially interested in interdisciplinary research, including policy analyses and strategic communications research. Additionally, the foundation supports the development of promising junior scholars in tenure-track positions through its William T. Grant Scholars Program and youth-serving organizations in the New York City metropolitan area through its Youth Service Grants. The foundation's Web site offers information about the foundation, its active grants and funding opportunities, news, and a searchable database of resources relating to the foundation's interests.

The Grass Foundation (MA) (http://www.mbl.edu/labs/grassfdn/)
Based in Braintree, Massachusetts, the Grass Foundation supports independent research by young investigators in the field of neuroscience. The foundation provides fellowships for scientists at the beginning of their careers, has supported programs such as courses and lectureships, and has made grants to qualified institutions. The Grass Fellowship in Neuroscience supports research in neurophysiology, membrane biophysics, integrative neurobiology and neuroethology, neuroanatomy, neuropharmacology, cellular and developmental neurobiology, cognitive neuroscience, and computational approaches to neural systems. Visitors to the site will find information about programs supported by the foundation; detailed information about the Grass Fellowship, including application forms and past fellows and lecturers; and general foundation information.

William Casper Graustein Memorial Fund (CT) (http://www.wcgmf.org/)
The New Haven, Connecticut-based William Casper Graustein Memorial Fund was founded by Graustein's brother to continue the Harvard math professor's work in education reform. The fund's current mission is to "work collaboratively to improve education for Connecticut's children by supporting school change, informing the public debate on educational issues, and strengthening the involvement of parents and the community in education." The three key funding areas are policy research and advocacy, community engagement and parental involvement, and educational change in schools. The last is administered by the Connecticut Center for School Change. Application instructions for the other two programs can be found at the fund's site, along with grants lists, contact information, program reports, an online request form for free copies of assorted policy and research reports, and its most recent biennial report.

Great Bay Foundation (ME) (http://www.greatbayfoundation.org/)
The Portland, Maine-based, Great Bay Foundation's mission is to increase individuals' self-reliance by encouraging principle-based social entrepreneurs. The foundation supports programs that result in job creation or training; new goods, products, or services; and lead

to program participants' economic self-sufficiency and self-reliance. Grantmaking is usually focused on programs in the small cities, towns, and rural areas of northern New England. Visit the foundation's Web site to find links of programs previously supported, further information on funding priorities, application policies, and contact information.

Green Mountain Fund, Inc. (VT) (http://homepages.together.net/~gmfps/)
Located in Westford, Vermont, the Green Mountain Fund, Inc. supports organizations that actively organize for radical social change in Vermont and the Champlain Valley watershed of New York. The fund is "committed to revolutionary transformation toward a socialist-feminist society," which "requires the elimination of all oppressions (such as oppressions by race, sex, class, sexual orientation, age, ability, or species) and their basis in patriarchal, capitalist, and imperialist structures." To be eligible, organizations must have tax-exempt status, and no significant portion of their budgets can come from government agencies, religious institutions or "establishment foundations." Consult the fund's Web site for a complete listing of the causes it supports, application guidelines and instructions, an application form and coversheet, contact information for each board member, grant lists, and links to other resources.

The Greene-Sawtell Foundation (GA) (http://www.greenesawtellfoundation.org)
The Georgia-based Greene-Sawtell Foundation was established by Mr. Forest Greene and Mrs. Alice Greene Sawtell, who, during their lives, acted as the foundation's advisory committee. SunTrust Bank Atlanta, as trustee, now determines which charitable, religious, and educational organizations will receive support from the foundation. Visitors to the foundation's Web site will find average grant ranges, a listing of charities with similar missions to those supported by the foundation, application information and submission dates, a downloadable application, and contact information.

Greenville Foundation (CA) (http://fdncenter.org/grantmaker/grnville/)
The Sonoma, California-based Greenville Foundation provides support for special projects in the following areas: education, the environment, human and social issues, international, and religion. The foundation does not make grants for scholarships, individuals, venture capital, capital improvements, endowments, general classroom-based environmental education programs, individual species preservation, health, food banks, or temporary shelter. Because it is located in the West, "practicality dictates that proposals for domestic projects be located west of the Rockies," although a limited number of grants may be made outside the region. Grants for international programs are made only through U.S.-based or affiliated nonprofit organizations. The foundation's Web site provides program descriptions, recent grants lists in each program area, application guidelines and procedures, a downloadable application cover sheet, a financial report for the latest year, and contact information.

The Greenwall Foundation (NY) (http://www.greenwall.org/)
The Greenwall Foundation was established in 1949 by Frank and Anna Greenwall of New York City in honor of their daughter and other family members. The foundation mainly supports work in medicine, education, and the arts and humanities, while also providing limited support for basic research in insulin dependent diabetes mellitus. These interests break down into three specific program areas. The Interdisciplinary Program in Bioethics funds micro and macro bioethics issues, especially pilot projects, and can include programs that are sensitive or controversial in nature. The Education Program is geared toward the professional development of New York City schoolteachers. The Arts and Humanities Program provides funds for innovative and creative projects in visual, performing, and literary arts to encourage the growth of New York City as a cultural center. The foundation's Web page includes application procedures and guidelines, as well as a listing of past grants for each of these programs. Applicants are encouraged to contact the foundation well in advance of the grant due date.

The Grotto Foundation, Inc. (MN) (http://www.grottofoundation.org/)
The Grotto Foundation, Inc. was established in 1964 by Louis Warren Hill Jr., eldest grandson of James J. Hill, the railway baron known as "The Empire Builder." Located in St. Paul, Minnesota, the foundation works with communities of different ethnic groups and cultures that are "inspired by their sense of vision and possibility" and assists these communities as they move forward in the course they have determined for themselves. Its formal mission is "to benefit society by improving the education and the economic, physical, and social well-being of citizens, with a special focus on families and culturally diverse groups." It is further interested in "increasing public understanding of the American cultural heritage, the cultures of nations, and the individual's responsibility to fellow human beings." Visit the Web site for grant guidelines and instructions, a downloadable application, biographies of the founder and founding director, recent grants lists, financial information, list of board and staff members, contact information, and links to other resources.

Harry Frank Guggenheim Foundation (NY) (http://www.hfg.org/)
The Harry Frank Guggenheim Foundation sponsors scholarly research on problems of violence, aggression, and dominance and encourages related research projects in neuroscience, genetics, animal behavior, the social sciences, history, criminology, and the humanities. The foundation also awards research grants to established scholars and dissertation fellowships to graduate students. (Institutions, programs, and pure interventions are not supported.) Visitors to the foundation's Web site will find a section on its research priorities, detailed application guidelines and procedures, a comprehensive listing of recent grants and fellowships, and an interactive form for requesting written application guidelines, and the foundation's most recent annual report.

John Simon Guggenheim Memorial Foundation (NY) (http://www.gf.org/)
The John Simon Guggenheim Memorial Foundation awards fellowships for advanced professionals in all areas of the natural sciences, social sciences, humanities, and creative arts (except the performing arts). The foundation selects its fellows on the basis of two separate competitions, one for the United States and Canada, the other for Latin America and the Caribbean. Only professional individuals are eligible for awards; the foundation does not support students, organizations, or institutions. The foundation's Web site provides general information about its programs, fellowship eligibility requirements, and application deadlines in English, Spanish, and Portuguese. Also available is a listing of recent Guggenheim Fellows, a helpful FAQ, an interactive form for ordering application forms, a listing of foundation officers and trustees, and contact information.

Josephine S. Gumbiner Foundation (CA) (http://www.gumbiner.com/jsgf/)
The Josephine S. Gumbiner Foundation was established in 1989 by Josephine Gumbiner, a noted philanthropist with an educational and professional background in social work. The foundation strives to support nonprofit organizations that benefit women and children in the Long Beach area of southern California. Program areas that the foundation considers for funding include day care, education, housing, recreation, the arts, and healthcare, with a special emphasis on intervention, prevention, and direct service. New and existing programs, general operating expenses, and technical assistance grants are most likely to be funded by the foundation. Visitors to the Web site will find application guidelines, instructions, and a downloadable application form. The foundation also provides an online copy of its latest tax return, a review of the funding process, a list of past grantees, and an online e-mail response form.

George Gund Foundation (OH) (http://www.gundfdn.org/)
The George Gund Foundation was created in 1952 by Cleveland banker and businessman George Gund, who believed the private foundation structure provided the most positive, far-sighted vehicle for intelligent underwriting of creative solutions to social ills in a manner that would not be limited to his own lifetime. Today, the foundation makes grants quarterly in the areas of education, economic development and community revitalization, human services, arts, environment, and civic affairs. Grants are not made to individuals.

The foundation's Web site offers a biography of George Gund, program descriptions, grant application instructions and restrictions, contact information, and links to a handful of related Web sites.

Gunk Foundation (NY) (Operating foundation) (http://www.gunk.org/)
The Gunk Foundation is a charitable operating foundation established in 1994 "to provide a counterbalance to the recent, disturbing trends in funding for intellectual endeavors." It does this by supporting two types of projects: public arts projects, which are funded through the foundation itself, and scholarly/artistic publications. Visitors to the foundation's Web site will find grant and proposal guidelines and a downloadable application form.

Stella and Charles Guttman Foundation (NY) (http://fdncenter.org/grantmaker/guttman/)
The Stella and Charles Guttman Foundation of New York was established in 1959 to "improve and benefit mankind and the alleviation of human suffering." The foundation supports qualifying organizations interested in education, health and social services in New York City, and that support Israel. Visitors to the foundation's Web site will find detailed grant guidelines, directors/officers/staff listings, recent grants lists, and contact information.

Walter and Elise Haas Fund (CA) (http://www.haassr.org/)
The Walter and Elise Haas Fund was created in 1952. Walter Haas was president and later chairman of Levi Strauss and Co. The San Francisco-based fund was created to provide support projects that demonstrate an ability to have wide impact and that demonstrate creative approaches toward meeting human needs. An overall goal is the development of leadership and professional competence in the fields of human services, arts, environment, professional ethics, education, Jewish life, citizenship and civic education, and the Creative Work Fund, which the Elise Haas Fund, along with three other organizations, support the collaboration between artists and nonprofit organizations to create new work. Each field of support has funding and geographic priorities, which are listed in the grant guidelines. Consult the fund's Web site for grant guidelines; application instructions; grant request cover sheet; link to the Creative Work Fund, which has its own separate site and application instructions; grants lists; the president's statement and executive director's report; list of staff; and contact information.

Hagedorn Fund (NY) (http://fdncenter.org/grantmaker/hagedorn/)
The New York-based Hagedorn Fund supports religious or charitable organizations with interest in health, gardens, social services, youth, education, senior services, and housing and community development. Geographic focus is placed primarily on New York City organizations. Visit the fund's Web site to learn more about grant priorities, application procedures, restrictions, and contact information.

Hagen Family Foundation (MI) (http://www.hagenfamilyfoundation.org)
The Hagen Family Foundation, located in Dearborn, Michigan, is a private family foundation established in 1999 for the purpose of operating and acting exclusively for charitable, religious, literary, or scientific purposes, and/or to lessen the financial burdens of government by carrying out a grant-making program in support of other tax-exempt organizations. The foundation prefers to fund programs that seek start-up costs for creative new strategies, identify on-going means for being self sustaining; promote prevention of social problems, demonstrate inter-agency cooperation; and/or empower targeted populations to meet their own needs more effectively. Interested parties should first send a letter of intent, a form for which can be printed directly from the site. Should the letter of intent be received favorably by the board of directors, organizations will be asked to submit a grant application which can be downloaded from the Web site. Deadline and contact information can also be found on the site.

Halcyon Hill Foundation (NY) (http://www.hhf.org)
Established in 1992, the Halcyon Hill Foundation, located in Webster, New York, is a family foundation dedicated to the well-being of young children in Monroe County, New York and in areas where the directors live. Grants are made to programs and agencies that support and encourage education, health, justice, and the arts for pre-school age children. Grants to religious organizations are made only for nonsectarian programs, and no grants can be made to individuals. Visitors will find application procedures and a grant list.

The James H. Hall Eye Foundation (GA) (http://fdncenter.org/grantmaker/jameshall/)
The James H. Hall Eye Foundation, established in 1979, is a non-profit organization with a proud tradition of blindness detection and prevention. The foundation's mission is to diagnose eye diseases that damage and destroy sight and to prevent blindness in newborns and children through early intervention. The foundation provides free and immediate medical or surgical intervention to visually impaired children without financial resources, coordinates a community network to serve children who are not eligible for Medicaid or state programs, addresses important visual needs of underserved newborns and children in urban and rural areas of Georgia, underwrites educational programs through a post-doctoral fellowship approved by the American Association for Pediatric Ophthalmology and Strabismus, creates a cohort of pediatric ophthalmologists that continues in community service throughout members professional lives, and conducts innovative research to meet clinical needs in the field of pediatric ophthalmology and strabismus. Visit the foundation's Web site for information on the foundation's mission, grant guidelines, a copy of the most recent tax return, and contact information.

Hall-Voyer Foundation (TX) (Operating foundation) (http://www2.1starnet.com/hallv)
The Hall-Voyer Foundation, originally established in 1940 as the David Graham Hall Trust and Foundation, bases its philanthropic activities in the community of Honey Grove, Texas. As an operating foundation, the organization does not make grants; instead it supports a number of institutions. The foundation's projects of interest have changed over the years, but currently it is focused on the operation of the Bertha Voyer Memorial Library, St. Mark's Episcopal Church, Hall-Voyer Exhibits Hall, and maintenance of the Bertha Voyer Park, all in Honey Grove, Texas. The foundation's Web site gives a lengthy history of the foundation and its members, information on past projects, its financial status, and contact information.

Phil Hardin Foundation (MS) (http://www.philhardin.org/)
The Phil Hardin Foundation was created in 1964 by Mississippi businessman Phil Hardin, who wanted to give something back to the people of the state. From the outset, the focus of the foundation was on education. In 1997 it decided to further concentrate its efforts and resources on four goals: strengthening the capacity of communities in the state to nurture and educate young children, strengthening the capacity of higher education institutions to renew communities and their economies, strengthening the capacity of communities for locally-initiated educational improvement and economic development, and strengthening policy and leadership at local and state levels. Visitors to the foundation's Web site will find detailed information about the foundation's goals, programs, and strategies; application guidelines and a downloadable application form; a comprehensive set of links to related education resources; and contact information.

The Hartford Courant Foundation (CT) (http://www.hartfordcourantfoundation.org/)
The Hartford Courant Foundation of Connecticut "seeks to make a sustainable impact on the vitality of Connecticut's capital region by being a catalyst for hope, inspiration and creativity and by improving the lives of its people, especially its children." The foundation makes grants primarily in support of education, the arts, community development, and health and social services, with an emphasis on programs benefiting children, youth, and families. Visitors to the foundation's Web site will find information of the board and staff, grant guidelines, a listing of recent grants, information on the foundation's grants program, a downloadable copy of the latest tax return, and contact information.

John A. Hartford Foundation, Inc. (NY) (http://www.jhartfound.org/)
Established in 1929 by John A. and George L. Hartford, former chief executives of the Great Atlantic and Pacific Tea Company, the John A. Hartford Foundation, Inc. is concerned with the improvement of healthcare in America. The foundation focuses its grantmaking activities in the areas of aging and health and healthcare cost and quality, and it generally makes grants by invitation. Grantseekers are encouraged to familiarize themselves with the foundation's program areas and guidelines—detailed information about which can be found at its Web site—before submitting a letter of inquiry. The Web site also provides the foundation's most recent annual report, application information, a report from the chairman, a list of foundation trustees and staff, and contact information.

Charles Hayden Foundation (NY) (http://fdncenter.org/grantmaker/hayden/)
The New York City-based Charles Hayden Foundation seeks to promote the mental, moral, and physical development of school-aged youth in the New York and Boston metropolitan areas—the former defined as New York City and Nassau County, the southern portion of Westchester County and, in New Jersey, all of Hudson and Essex Counties and the contiguous urban portions of Union, Passaic, and Bergen Counties; the latter as the City of Boston and adjacent municipalities located on the east side of an arc from Salem to Quincy that is roughly delineated by Route 128. Priority is given to institutions and programs serving youth most at risk of not reaching their full potential, especially youth in low-income communities, and that continuously provide opportunities and support over many years. Visitors to the foundation's Web site will find a mission statement, recent grants lists, detailed application guidelines, and contact information.

John Randolph Haynes and Dora Haynes Foundation (CA) (http://www.haynesfoundation.org/)
Established in 1926, the John Randolph Haynes and Dora Haynes Foundation supports study and research in political science, economics, public policy, history, social psychology, and sociology, favoring projects with specific application to California and, more particularly, the Los Angeles region. The foundation also provides undergraduate scholarships, graduate fellowships, and faculty research fellowships in the social sciences to colleges and universities in the greater Los Angeles area. All support is made directly to institutions; no grants are awarded to individuals. A searchable bibliography of publications resulting from 75 years of foundation support is available at the foundation's Web site, along with detailed program information, recent grants lists, application guidelines, a listing of the foundation's board of trustees and staff, and a history of the foundation and the Haynes family.

Edward W. Hazen Foundation, Inc.(NY) (http://www.hazenfoundation.org)
The Edward W. Hazen Foundation, Inc. of New York City was established in 1925 by Edward W. Hazen, a New York State senator and retired publishing executive. The foundation is committed to "assisting young people, particularly minorities and those disadvantaged by poverty, in achieving their full potential as individuals and as active participants in a democratic society." The grantmaking program focuses on public education and youth development. Within public education, grants are awarded to programs that deal with parent and community organizing, advocacy, and training and leadership building. The youth development program addresses youth organizing and leadership development, innovative programs at youth-service organizations, and school-based leadership development programs. Interested applicants first submit a letter of inquiry and then may receive the foundation's application form in the mail. Application guidelines and lists of previous grantees can be viewed online or downloaded from the foundation's Web site. The site also includes trustee, board, and staff lists; links to related resources; and a list of FAQs.

The Health Foundation of Greater Cincinnati (OH) (http://www.healthfoundation.org)
The Health Foundation of Greater Cincinnati is committed to "promoting the health of the people of Cincinnati and the surrounding counties in Ohio, Kentucky, and Indiana through investing in enduring projects that improve community health status, healthcare delivery,

and access to healthcare for all." The grantmaking program is divided into five categories: primary care for the poor, children's health, substance abuse, severe mental illness, and other health related issues. Most funding in the first two categories goes toward strengthening primary care providers for the poor and school-based child health intervention. Eligible programs address issues including the following: the improvement and stimulation of healthcare delivery, the coordination and creation of community health services, the education of healthcare providers, and the public's awareness of and access to community health services. Each of the five main categories has its own area on the foundation's Web site that includes program reports, requests for proposals, and deadline information. Nonprofits within the twenty county service areas interested in applying for a non-specified grant should call the foundation with an initial inquiry before submitting a full proposal. Visitors to the Web site will find lists of each department's staff and the board of trustees. There are also lists of recent grants, and a section with health statistics.

Healthcare Foundation of New Jersey (NJ) (http://www.hfnj.org/)

The Healthcare Foundation of New Jersey is firmly rooted in the strong tradition of delivering the highest standards of medical care, a tradition established by the Jewish community in Newark, New Jersey and that began with the inauguration of the Newark Beth Israel Hospital in 1901. Formerly known as the NBI Healthcare Foundation, the private grantmaking foundation was founded in 1996 to alleviate the suffering of the most vulnerable members of the community. Its goal is to strengthen existing healthcare programs and provide seed money for innovative projects that address unmet healthcare needs. The foundation is interested in health-related proposals that address one of its four priority areas: vulnerable children and families of Newark, especially the South Ward; vulnerable members of the MetroWest Jewish community of northern New Jersey; medical education and humanism in medicine; and clinical research, especially at the Newark Beth Israel Medical Center. Consult the foundation's Web site for grant guidelines, instructions, information on programs, grants lists, and contact information.

Healthcare Foundation for Orange County (CA) (http://www.hfoc.org)

Based in Santa Ana, California, the Healthcare Foundation for Orange County was formed by the acquisition of United Western Medical Centers (UWMC), a nonprofit hospital system, by OrNda Healthcare, a for-profit company. Funds in excess of UWMC's departments and other obligations were placed in the foundation, the mission which is to improve the health of the neediest and most underserved residents of Orange County, with particular emphasis on UWMC's historic service area of Central Orange County. One of its major initiatives is "Healthy Orange County," which is aimed toward programs that will improve maternal, child, and adolescent health through increased access to prevention and primary care services. Funding emphasizes expanding and developing services for low-income families in Santa Ana, Tustin, Orange, and Anaheim. Preference is given to programs that maximize existing resources and enable individuals and communities to take charge of their own health. The searchable Web site provides grant application guidelines, a printable application cover page, information request form, and press releases.

William Randolph Hearst Foundations (NY) (http://hearstfdn.org)

The Hearst Foundation, Inc., was founded in 1945 by publisher and philanthropist William Randolph Hearst. In 1948, Hearst established the California Charities Foundation, the name of which was changed to the William Randolph Hearst Foundations after Mr. Hearst's death in 1951. The charitable goals of the two foundations are essentially the same, reflecting the philanthropic interests of William Randolph Hearst: education, health, social service, and culture. The foundations' proposal evaluation process is divided geographically: organizations east of the Mississippi River must apply to the foundations' New York offices, while organizations west of the Mississippi are asked to apply through the foundations' San Francisco offices. In addition to their grantmaking activities in the four program areas mentioned above, the foundations make grants to students through the Hearst Journalism Awards Program and the United States Senate Youth Program. Visitors to the foundations' Web site will find program guidelines, funding policies and limitations, a listing of recent grants, application procedures, and descriptions of both awards programs.

The Heinz Endowments (PA) (http://www.heinz.org/)
The Pittsburgh-based Heinz Endowments, comprised of the Howard Heinz and the Vira I. Heinz Endowements, support the efforts of nonprofit organizations active in the areas of arts and culture, education, children, youth, and families, economic opportunity, and the environment, with an emphasis on programs either in southwestern Pennsylvania or of clear benefit to the region. The endowments' Web site offers a range of information, including broad and program-specific statements of philosophy; information about goals, grants, projects, and staff in each program area; application guidelines; FAQs; news; and brief biographies of Howard Heinz and Vira I. Heinz, as well as various program officers and directors.

Clarence E. Heller Foundation (CA) (http://cehcf.org)
Founded by Clarence E. Heller in 1982 in San Francisco, the Clarence E. Heller Foundation's mission is "to protect and improve the quality of life through support of programs in the environment, human health, education, and the arts." In the area of the environment and health, the foundation concentrates on programs that address the health risks of toxic substances and environmental hazards; the Management of Resources program focuses on the viability of communities and regions and sustainable agriculture; music programs promote symphonic and chamber music; and education programs strive to give elementary and secondary students opportunities. The foundation also funds select special projects. Visitors to the Web site will find past program highlights, list of past grants, application guidelines, and contact information.

The F.B. Heron Foundation (NY) (http://fdncenter.org/grantmaker/fbheron/)
The F.B. Heron Foundation was created in 1992 with the mission of helping people and communities to help themselves. The foundation is interesting in helping low-income people to create wealth and take control of their lives. The foundation also makes program related investments (PRIs). Visitors to the foundation's Web site will find detailed information on the foundation's grant and PRI programs; application procedures; a copy of the latest annual report and tax return, a listing of the current directors, officers, and staff; and contact information.

Hershey Foundation (OH) (http://fdncenter.org/grantmaker/hershey/)
Founded in 1986 by Jo Hershey Selden, the Hershey Foundation was established in honor of her late husband, Alvin A. Hershey. Located in Concord Township, Ohio, the foundation is dedicated to providing "bridges of opportunity for the children of northeast Ohio." The foundation aims to help schools, museums, cultural institutions, and other nonprofits develop and implement innovative programs that will improve quality of life, build self-esteem, enhance learning, increase exposure to other cultures and ideas, and encourage the development of independent thinking and problem-solving skills. Support is given to pilot projects that can be replicated in other settings, with priority given to alternative educational programs; arts, cultural, and science programs; and early childhood education programs. Grants are given for program development and special projects, equipment that brings new capabilities to an organization (but not computers), capital campaigns, and endowment of special projects. Visitors to the Web site will find grant guidelines and procedures, grants lists, financial information, and a history of the Hershey Foundation.

Fannie and John Hertz Foundation (CA) (http://www.hertzfoundation.org)
The Fannie and John Hertz Foundation was founded in 1957 by John Daniel Hertz, an Austrian immigrant who lived the American Dream. The foundation, based in Livermore, California, is an expression of his gratitude for the country that afforded him so many opportunities. The foundation provides fellowships for graduate work leading to a Ph.D. from three dozen universities in applications of the physical sciences: applied physics, chemistry, mathematics, modern biology, and all areas of engineering. Although a list of fields of

study is provided on the Web site, it is up to the individual applicant to advocate his or her specific field of interest as an "applied physical science." Consult the foundation's Web site for information and application instructions for the Graduate Fellowship program. Visitors to the Web site will also find a history of the foundation and a biography of John Hertz and his wife Fannie, a FAQ page, links to other resources, and contact information.

William and Flora Hewlett Foundation (CA) (http://www.hewlett.org/)
The broadly stated mission of the William and Flora Hewlett Foundation, established by Palo Alto industrialist William R. Hewlett (of Hewlett-Packard fame), his late wife, Flora Lamson Hewlett, and their eldest son, Walter B. Hewlett in 1966, is "to promote the well-being of mankind by supporting selected activities of a charitable nature, as well as organizations or institutions engaged in such activities." The foundation concentrates its resources on activities in the areas of education, performing arts, population, environment, conflict resolution, family and community development, and U.S.-Latin America relations, which is an outgrowth of the foundation's long-standing interest in U.S.-Mexico relations. The foundation's Web site provides detailed program descriptions and application guidelines, a board and staff listing, a list of grants organized by program area, an online version of the foundation's annual report, and contact information.

Colin Higgins Foundation (CA) (http://www.colinhiggins.org/)
The San Francisco-based, Colin Higgins Foundation was established in 1986 to further humanitarian goals. The foundation is particularly interested in assisting organizations that have a significant impact in areas such as AIDS education and advocacy and the empowerment of gay men, lesbians, bisexual, and transgendered peoples. The foundation also maintains the Courage Awards program to honor ordinary but remarkable individuals whose courage helped to educate and enlighten others about the gay, lesbian, bisexual, and transgender communities. The foundation's Web site provides information on grant guidelines, a list of past recipients, and contact information.

Allen Hilles Fund (PA) (http://www.dvg.org/Hilles)
The Allen Hilles Fund, located in Philadelphia, provides financial support in the areas of education, women's issues, economic development in disadvantaged communities, and activities of the Religious Society of Friends. The fund was established by Edith Hilles Dewees in memory of her father, Thomas Allen Hilles, and began operation in 1983. Grants focus on the cities of Philadelphia and Chester, Pennsylvania and Wilmington, Delaware. Visitors to the site will find a history of the founder, guidelines, recent grants lists and statistics, the fund's tax return, a downloadable application form, and contact information.

Conrad N. Hilton Foundation (CA & NV) (http://www.hiltonfoundation.org/)
The Conrad N. Hilton Foundation was founded in 1944 by hotel entrepreneur Conrad N. Hilton and is based in Los Angeles, California, and Reno, Nevada. The foundation's mission is to "alleviate the suffering of the world's most disadvantaged, with a special emphasis on children and support for the work of the Roman Catholic Sisters." This cause manifests itself through eight project areas: blindness, early childhood development, substance abuse, water development, domestic violence, the Roman Catholic Sisters, mentally ill homeless, and the College of Hotel and Restaurant Management. The foundation also awards the Conrad N. Hilton Humanitarian Prize of $1 million to a nonprofit organization that has made an extraordinary contribution in alleviating human suffering. Additionally, the foundation supports the Conrad N. Hilton Fund, a nonprofit organization that makes grants to specific organizations delineated in its charter, but it does not accept unsolicited proposals. The foundation's Web site supplies further information on its finances, past recipients of the Humanitarian Prize, information on the process of nomination, a downloadable nomination form, news, conferences, a biography of Mr. Hilton, and links to priority grantee organizations.

HKH Foundation (NY) (http://www.hkhfdn.org)
The New York-based HKH Foundation focuses its attention on protecting civil liberties, protecting the environment, and reversing the arms race. The foundation funds organizations that seek to change the terms of debate and work to address the source of a problem rather than ameliorating its symptoms. The foundation maintains a Disarmament Directory, listing the organizations across the nation dedicated to peace and disarmament. Visit the foundation's Web site to learn more about the foundation's mission and to find online resources and contact information.

Hoblitzelle Foundation (TX) (http://home.att.net/~hoblitzelle/)
The Hoblitzelle Foundation, based in Dallas, Texas, was founded by Karl Hoblitzelle in 1942. Karl Hoblitzelle had a successful entertainment business and investments in the oil, gas, real estate, and banking industries in Texas. The foundation focuses its grantmaking on specific, non-recurring needs of educational, social service, medical, cultural, and civic organizations in the state of Texas, particularly within the metro Dallas area. Consult the Web site for application guidelines, links to additional information, a short bio of its founder, a listing of directors, grants lists, and contact information.

The Hoglund Foundation (TX) (http://www.hoglundfdtn.org)
Established in 1989, the Hoglund Foundation uses the "resources and abilities of the extended family of Forrest E. Hoglund and Sally R. Hoglund to generate and/or support activities that can make a positive difference in the lives of others." The primary focus of the Dallas-based foundation is to "promote interests and entities in education, health science and services, social services, and children's health and development." Priorities are organizations and programs that nurture, recognize, and reward individual initiative and responsibility; are innovative and promote creative solutions; have sound management and are efficient in the management of funds; and are collaborative in nature so that resources are shared and the impact of the grant is multiplied in the community. The foundation's geographic focus is primarily Dallas and Houston, Texas, but grants are made outside of this area. Visit the foundation's Web site for grant application guidelines, contact information, and links to other resources.

Horizon Foundation (MA) (http://www.horizonfoundation.org)
The Horizon Foundation is located in Ipswich, Massachusetts, and was founded in 1997. The foundation supports "non-profit organizations that affect positive change among children, the adults who work with them, and the communities in which they live. Horizon supports projects and organizations that teach respect and care for the natural environment, encourage an appreciation and understanding of the significance of the arts and history, and promote leadership skills." The foundation will only consider grant proposals from nonprofit organizations that support projects in Cumberland, Franklin, Lincoln, and York Counties in Maine; Barnstable, Essex, and Middlesex Counties in Massachusetts; and Mercer County in New Jersey. The foundation will consider proposals for youth-focused programs for children of elementary and secondary school age in the areas of the arts, the environment, history, education, and leadership training. Information about restrictions, grants sizes, and types of funding is available on the foundation's Web site, as is a list of previous grants awarded. The foundation does not accept unsolicited applications, but interested organizations may submit a letter of inquiry. Guidelines for the letter and the full proposal can be found on the site, along with deadline information.

Houston Endowment, Inc. (TX) (http://www.houstonendowment.org)
Founded in 1937 by Jesse H. Jones and Mary Gibbs Jones, and today the largest private philanthropic foundation in Texas, the Houston Endowment, Inc. is dedicated to the support of charitable undertakings serving the people of the greater Houston area and the state of Texas. It contributes to a broad spectrum of programs in education, healthcare, human services, cultural arts, and other areas. In addition to general information about the foundation and its founders, visitors to the Web site will find descriptions of the foundation's programs and grant eligibility criteria, scholarship information, application procedures, online

versions of the foundation's annual reports, recent grants lists, board and staff listings, and contact information.

HRK Foundation (MN) (http://www.hrkfoundation.org/)
HRK Foundation seeks to promote healthy families and communities, enhance the quality of and access to education, and improve the fabric of our society. The foundation's grantmaking interests center on the arts, health, community building, and education. While, historically, the foundation's geographic service area has included the Twin Cities metro area, the St. Croix Valley, and Ashland and Bayfield Counties in Wisconsin. In evaluating new requests, the board's primary focus is St. Paul. Visitors to the foundation's Web site will find grant guidelines, more geographic limitations, a listing of selected grants, contact information, and a downloadable grant application.

The Agnes B Hunt Trust (GA) (http://www.agnesbhunttrust.org)
The Agnes B. Hunt Trust was established in 1948 under the will of Robert G. Hunt of Spalding County, Georgia. Mr. Hunt was a generous man, establishing several charitable trusts, including the Agnes B. Hunt Trust, named in honor of his mother. Upon his death in 1950, the Agnes B. Hunt Trust began supporting "exclusively charitable and educational purposes" in Griffin and Spalding Counties, Georgia. Visitors to the foundation's Web site will find average grant ranges, a listing of charities with similar missions to those supported by the foundation, application information and submission dates, a downloadable application, and contact information.

Hunter's Hope Foundation, Inc. (NY) (http://www.huntershope.org/)
Created in 1997 by Former Buffalo Bills quarterback Jim Kelly and his wife after their son was diagnosed with Krabbes disease, Hunter's Hope Foundation, Inc. seeks to find a cure for all forms of leukodystrophies. Krabbes, a specific form of leukodystrophy, is caused by an error in the genes that does not allow for proper nerve development in the brain, affecting breathing and body temperature—those things the body regulates automatically. The foundation provides grants in three areas: post-doctoral fellowships are provided for those individuals who are within five years of receiving their degrees studying Krabbes or other leukodystrophies; pilot studies support researchers testing new concepts and ideas to fight the disease; and major research grants are awarded to senior investigators who are studying either basic mechanisms or treatment approaches to Krabbes disease. Visit the foundation's Web site to learn more about Krabbes Disease, obtain specific information on the foundation's giving program and contact information.

Huntingburg Foundation, Inc. (IN) (http://www.huntingburg.org/foundation.htm)
The Indiana-based, Huntingburg Foundation, Inc. was established in 1977 with a commitment to the past, present, and future needs of the community. The foundation maintains a number of institutional funds to support the town of Huntingburg, as well as scholarship funds to help local students find their way to higher education. Visitors to the foundation's Web site will find information regarding the endowment funds, scholarship information, grant and scholarship applications, information on grant deadlines, and contact information.

Hut Foundation (CA) (http://www.hutfdn.org)
Based in San Francisco, the Hut Foundation was established in 1998 and funds projects in the areas of education, humanitarian issues, and the environment. The foundation also seeks "to promote respect for others and to develop our commitment to family." Hut Foundation funds are used to target educational programs that serve children and young adults and strengthen families. Within the area of education, the Hut Foundation's primary funding interests include: children with autism and their families; animal assisted therapy for children and adults with disabilities; arts education, with an emphasis on populations that are culturally, economically, or physically disadvantaged; and environmental education for children and young adults. Programs which encourage the development of self-esteem and independence are preferred over direct-service programs. The Hut Foundation offers grants

to nonprofit organizations within the geographic areas where foundation members live and work: the San Francisco Bay Area, (San Francisco, Alameda, Marin, and Sonoma Counties), Maryland, (Montgomery and Prince Georges Counties), the District of Columbia, and Virginia. The format for letters of inquiry may be printed from the site; letters of inquiry may also be submitted electronically at their site. Visitors to the site will also find grant lists and contact information.

Hutton Foundation (CA) (http://www.huttonfoundation.org)
Betty L. Hutton founded the Hutton Foundation in 1980 to support educational, health, and community organizations and acts as a catalyst to encourage development of new programs and services for future generations. Primary areas of focus include education; health and human services; child, youth and family services; arts and culture; women's services; and civic and community development. Funding is primarily awarded to organizations in Orange, Riverside, and Santa Barbara Counties in California, with select international awards. In addition to donations and grants, the foundation also offers Program Related Investments (PRIs), which are loans to purchase buildings, make major tenant improvements on buildings owned by nonprofit organizations, and refinance existing real estate or construction loans. The foundation is headquartered in Santa Barbara, California, with an additional office in Orange County. Visit the Web site for grant application guidelines and instructions, further information about PRIs, information about the review and selection process, recent grants lists, and contact information.

Hyde and Watson Foundation (NJ) (http://fdncenter.org/grantmaker/hydeandwatson/)
Formerly the Lillia Babbitt Hyde Foundation and the John Jay and Eliza Jane Watson Foundation, which were consolidated in January 1983, the Chatham Township, New Jersey-based Hyde and Watson Foundation supports capital projects such as purchase or relocation of facilities, building improvements, capital equipment, instructive materials development, and certain medical research areas. Broad fields include health, education, religion, social services, arts, and humanities. Currently grant support is focused primarily in the New York City metropolitan area and Essex, Union, and Morris Counties in New Jersey. The foundation's Web site provides a history of the foundation, grant guidelines, grants lists, financial statements, and information about the foundation's management.

The i2 Foundation (TX) (http://www.i2foundation.org)
The mission of the Texas-based i2 Foundation is to "promote advancements in education, technology, environmental practices, medicine, and economic opportunity through programs that improve the quality of life and create a healthier society." Created in 1997 by employees of i2 Technologies, the purpose of the foundation is to give back to the community where the company operates. The major priorities of the foundation include the development and education of children and youth; however it also considers issues related to poverty, hunger, illiteracy, education, youth violence, violence against women, early child development, environmental preservation, scientific research, and improved healthcare. Visit the foundation's Web site to find information about the i2's mission, a FAQ page, grant application information, and contact information.

I Have a Dream Foundation (NY) (Operating foundation) (http://www.ihad.org)
The I Have a Dream Foundation (IHAD) was started by Eugene Lang, a New York businessman who in 1981 made an extraordinary offer to a group of sixth graders at the east Harlem elementary school he had once attended. He promised partial college scholarships if they finished high school. In 1986, Eugene Lang organized the national I Have a Dream Foundation to help launch a new generation of IHAD projects across the country. Today, the foundation helps "children from low-income areas become productive citizens by providing a long-term program of mentoring, tutoring, and enrichment, with an assured opportunity for higher education." Its goal is to see that all children graduate from high school "functionally literate and prepared either for fulfilling employment or further education." The foundation provides partial financial assistance for college, university, or accredited vocational school. Visit the foundation's Web site for further information on the

foundation's program, including a history of the foundation, a FAQ sheet, locations and contact information for local projects, and information about how to get involved.

Institute of Current World Affairs, Inc. (NY) (Operating foundation) (http://www.icwa.org)
Established in 1925, the Institute of Current World Affairs, Inc. of New York City is funded by its own Crane-Rogers Foundation and two other trusts. The organization's purpose is to "provide talented and promising individuals with an opportunity to develop a deep understanding of an issue, country, or region outside the United States and to share that understanding with a wider public." The institute offers two-year fellowships to people under 36 years of age for advanced study overseas. The organization's Web site offers all that an applicant needs. There is a list of current fields of interest and information on fellowships available each year, sometimes including additional specialized programs. There are application instructions and deadlines and a list of past fellows. Visitors will also find trustee and staff lists and contact information.

Institute of Mental Hygiene (LA) (http://www.imhno.org)
Created in 1937, the Institute of Mental Hygiene (IMH) is located in New Orleans, Louisiana. The IMH is committed to "investing in children through its grantmaking programs, active involvement with grantees, and leadership in improving mental health programs and policies." Nonprofits in New Orleans are eligible to apply to three different grant programs. The Children's Mental Health Grants Program funds the testing of new ideas, works to ensure that effective programs are replicated, addresses critical or emerging issues, and provides core support to reputable organizations. Programs involving very young children are especially encouraged to apply. The Early Childhood Mini-Grants Program supports organizations working with very young children and their families. Awards go toward seed money, leadership and training in the field, engaging parents as educators, and raising public awareness, among other issues. The Technical Assistance Grants Program makes grants to support management and capacity building in organizations. The institute's Web site includes more specific program descriptions and application deadlines. Grant guidelines and applications can be downloaded. The site also includes contact information for select staff members and a list of previous grantees. The institute's evaluation guidelines can also be viewed online.

Institute of Turkish Studies, Inc. (DC) (http://www.turkishstudies.org)
Created in 1982, the Institute of Turkish Studies, Inc. is located at the Edmund A. Walsh School of Foreign Service at Georgetown University in Washington, D.C. The organization is "devoted solely to supporting and encouraging the development of Turkish Studies in American higher education through an annual grant program." The institute supports the work of individuals and universities in the field of Turkish studies, the publication of books and journals that bring the field to the American population, and serves as a resource center on the history and current events of Turkey. The grant program offers scholarships and makes awards to institutes of higher learning. Individual awards include travel-research grants in Turkey for post-doctoral scholars, pre-dissertation graduate fellowships, dissertation writing grants, and teaching aid grants for the development of resources. Institutions may receive library support, matching grants for conferences and lecture series, and matching seed money for new faculty positions. There is a page with specific application instructions, deadlines, and restrictions for each of the awards. The site also includes a list of publications and information on public programs.

James Irvine Foundation (CA) (http://www.irvine.org/)
The San Francisco-based James Irvine Foundation was established in 1937 as the charitable trust of James Irvine, a California agricultural pioneer, to promote the general welfare of the people of California. Today, it is dedicated "to enhancing the social, economic, and physical quality of life throughout California, and to enriching the State's intellectual and cultural environment." Within this broad mandate, the foundation makes grants in seven program areas: the arts; children, youth and families; civic culture; health; higher education; sustainable communities; and workforce development. The foundation also makes

room for special projects. In the recent past the foundation has made a commitment to effective management and governance of nonprofits, initiated support for community foundations, and enhanced the capacity of organized philanthropy. Visitors to the foundation's Web site will find detailed program information, including priority goals and recent grants in each funding area, application guidelines, board and staff listings, numerous links to grantee organizations, a feedback area, and contact information.

Irvine Health Foundation (CA) (http://www.ihf.org/)
Established in 1985, the Irvine Health Foundation provides support for prevention, service, research, and policy activities related to the health and wellness of the Orange County, California, community. The foundation's Web site offers a mission statement, a listing of directors and staff, FAQs, press rcleases, grant highlights, a For Your Health feature, highlights from the foundation's lecture series, grant application procedures with FAQs, staff/board listings, and links to numerous related sites.

Irwin Foundation (MI) (http://comnet.org/irwin/)
The Irwin Foundation is located in Southfield, Michigan, and received its nonprofit status in 1996. It provides funding for scholarships in veterinary education. Its mission is "the promotion of veterinary education, including the funding of student funding in schools, departments, or units accredited in veterinary medicine of veterinary technology, within a major university structure." The foundation provides funding only to accredited schools within major universities. However, scholarship recipients are chosen by the universities themselves; the Irwin Foundation does not participate in, nor interfere with, the selection process. The Web site provides information about the future of the foundation, as well as links to information about the veterinary field.

Ittleson Foundation, Inc. (NY) (http://www.IttlesonFoundation.org)
Henry Ittleson, founder of CIT Financial Corporation, established the Ittleson Foundation, Inc. in 1932. The New York City-based foundation seeks to fund pilot, test, and demonstration projects and applied research that would inform public policy. "Such projects should be of significance beyond the local area of implementation and should result in an outcome of some consequence in the real world." Areas of particular interest are mental health, AIDS, and the environment; although it funds broadly in each area, there are specific concerns of interest. In the area of mental health, the foundation prefers projects that "cut across the entire field and those that address underserved populations." In the area of the environment, it seeks to educate a new generation of environmentalists, and it has interests in urban environmental issues and efforts at resource protection. For AIDS, the foundation focuses on prevention and mental health consequences of the disease. Visit the Web site for further information on each grantmaking area, application guidelines, grants lists and summaries, a downloadable annual report, guidelines, and contact information.

Caroline Lawson Ivey Memorial Foundation, Inc. (AL) (http://www.mindspring.com/~climf/index.html)
Located in Auburn, Alabama, the Caroline Lawson Ivey Memorial Foundation, Inc. was established in 1986 by Oliver Turner Ivey, a professor of history, to honor his wife. The organization works to "encourage, promote, and sponsor the discipline of Social Studies at all grade levels, with special emphasis being placed on the preparation of persons who plan to enter the teaching profession." This is accomplished through the distribution of scholarships and grants and the sponsorship of workshops. Scholarships are offered to college juniors and seniors who are pursuing careers of teaching social studies in middle or secondary grades. The grants are also offered to teachers in Alabama and west Georgia for curriculum planning and development, in-service training, the development of instructional materials for use in elementary and secondary schools, and other projects that focus on the cultural approach method of teaching. The foundation's Web site includes information on the foundation's methodology, biographical information on the founder and his wife, and a list of board members.

Janx Foundation (NJ) (http://fdncenter.org/grantmaker/janx/)

Based in Newark, New Jersey, the Janx Foundation funds programs that encourage the education of America's youth, especially in urban areas. It strives to provide "urban, underprivileged youth with positive opportunities to make evident to the world that they are productive, responsible members of society" in school, the workplace, and in life in general. To this end, the foundation prefers to fund nonprofits with youth development programs and gives preference to organizations in the greater New York and New Jersey metropolitan areas. The foundation's Web site provides an extensive explanation of its mission and goals. Grantseekers will also find letter of inquiry guidelines, grant submission guidelines, and contact information.

The Jaqua Foundation (NJ) (http://fdncenter.org/grantmaker/jaqua/)

The Jaqua Foundation of New Jersey is interested in collegiate education, welfare of animals, and the performing arts. The foundation does not make grants to individuals. Visitors to the foundation's Web site will find a copy of the foundation's latest tax return and contact information.

Martha Holden Jennings Foundation (OH) (http://www.mhjf.org)

The Martha Holden Jennings Foundation, founded in 1959, is dedicated to fostering "the development of young people to the maximum possible extent through improving the quality of education in secular elementary and secondary schools in Ohio." To that end, the Cleveland-based foundation is eager to explore new frontiers in Ohio schools and to promote more effective teaching in those schools. The foundation offers two specific grants programs, Grants-to-Administrators and Grants-to-Teachers, as well as an Open Grants program. Guidelines and limitations of these grants can be found on the foundation's Web site. Visitors to the site will also find downloadable versions of the foundation's bulletins, publications, and contact information.

Jerome Foundation (MN) (http://www.jeromefdn.org/)

The St. Paul, Minnesota-based Jerome Foundation promotes the careers and work of emerging artists in Minnesota and New York City through its support of programs in dance, literature, media arts, music, theater, performance art, visual arts, multidisciplinary work, and arts criticism. The foundation places the emerging creative artist at the center of its grantmaking and gives funding priority to programs and projects that are artist-driven. The foundation's Web site provides program guidelines; application requirements and procedures; full descriptions of every grant awarded in recent years, arranged alphabetically, by program area, or by date; answers to FAQs; financial statements; and contact information.

Jewish Foundation for Education of Women (NY) (http://www.jfew.org/index.html)

The Jewish Foundation for Education of Women provides financial aid for higher education to women within the New York City metropolitan area. The foundation is the successor to the historic Lower East Side Hebrew Technical School, and it provides two direct grant programs and numerous collaborative programs. The foundation's direct grant programs are the Fellowship Program for Émigrés Training for Careers in Jewish Education and Scholarships for Émigrés in the Health Professions, both of which are for émigrés from the former Soviet Union. Collaborative grants are made through partnerships with various organizations in New York City. The foundation's Web site provides more information on these grants and partnerships, as well as eligibility, a short application guide, a history of the foundation, and contact information.

Jewish Healthcare Foundation (PA) (http://www.jhf.org)

The Jewish Healthcare Foundation continues the tradition of its predecessor, Montefiore Hospital, a high-quality teaching hospital that pioneered advancements in medicine and public health and that provided medical care in a kindly environment with an understanding of Jewish people and their needs. In 1990, the board of trustees of Montefiore Hospital adopted a "plan of division" that separated the newly created Jewish Healthcare Foundation from the hospital. The mission of the foundation is to "foster the provision of healthcare services, healthcare education, and when reasonable and appropriate, healthcare research, and it shall respond to the health-related needs of the elderly, underprivileged, indigent and underserved populations in western Pennsylvania." The Pittsburgh, Pennsylvania-based foundation also supports and sometimes produces the research and publications necessary to inform others about new approaches to health problems. Grantmaking priorities are giving children the physical and mental health to succeed, preventing disease and disability, building healthy neighborhoods and communities, and improving public policies and systems of care. Visit the foundation's Web site for specific information on each grantmaking priority and for funding guidelines and application instructions.

Johnson Foundation, Inc. (WI) (Operating foundation) (http://www.johnsonfdn.org/index.html)
The primary activity of the Wisconsin-based Johnson Foundation, Inc. is planning and co-sponsoring conferences of public interest at Wingspread—its Frank Lloyd Wright-designed headquarters and conference center in Racine. The foundation encourages conference proposals from nonprofit organizations in six areas of interest: supporting sustainable development; enhancing learning productivity at all educational levels; building civil and civic community; encouraging constructive adult engagement in the lives of children and youth; Keland Endowment conferences on the arts, the environment, and persons with disabilities; and southeastern Wisconsin. The foundation does not award grants, fund programs, sponsor retreats or fundraisers, or rent its facilities. Visitors to the foundation's Web site will find a brief history of the foundation and its mission, general descriptions of its program interests, a searchable Virtual Library with online versions of recent annual reports and conference proceedings, dozens of links organized by program interest, and detailed information about proposing a conference.

Helen K. and Arthur E. Johnson Foundation (CO) (http://www.johnsonfoundation.net)
The Denver, a Colorado-based Helen K. and Arthur E. Johnson Foundation was established in 1948 in memory of Arthur E. Johnson, Colorado oil entrepreneur, and his wife Helen, both noted philanthropists in the area. The foundation strives to relieve suffering, provide basic human needs, promote self-sufficiency, and enrich the quality of life in local Colorado communities. The foundation's Web site provides application guidelines, contact information, board listings, and a brief biography of the Johnson family.

Robert Wood Johnson Foundation (NJ) (http://www.rwjf.org/)
The mission of the Robert Wood Johnson Foundation is to improve the health and healthcare of all Americans. The foundation's main funding goals are to assure that all Americans have access to basic healthcare at reasonable cost, improve the way services are organized and provided to people with chronic health conditions, and reduce the harm caused by substance abuse—tobacco, alcohol, and elicit drugs. The foundation's Web site is a guide to its programs and activities and a substantial resource for the healthcare field. Visitors will find detailed program descriptions and application guidelines, grant outcomes and related publications, information about the foundation's own programs and projects, a library of publications, current calls for proposals, and press releases and other media-related information.

Walter S. Johnson Foundation (CA) (http://www.wsjf.org/)
The Walter S. Johnson Foundation supports programs in northern California and Washoe County, Nevada that "help children and youth meet their full potential and rise to the challenges of our diverse and changing society." The foundation's grants program is focused on three primary goals: ensuring the well-being of children and youth, strengthening public education, and assisting young people in the transition to adulthood. Within these broad goals, the majority of grants are likely to focus on positive youth development, the professional development of educators, or the transition from school to career. Grants are also made for families in crisis and for integrated services, family support, and neighborhood development. The foundation's Web site provides grantmaking guidelines and grants lists

for each program area, as well as application procedures, and a listing of the foundation's trustees and staff.

JoMiJo Foundation (CA) (http://www.jomijo.org/)
The JoMiJo Foundation's mission is to "aid disenfranchised persons or communities through targeted funding of grassroots projects that improve the quality of people's lives or preserve the earth's natural environment." To achieve this, the foundation supports economically disenfranchised people and communities; provides aid in education and welfare of children, including those at risk; and supports social and economic justice for women and minorities. The foundation currently supports organizations in the San Francisco Bay Area, Denver, and Chicago. Visitors to the foundation's Web site will find examples of projects that have earned program support, as well as organizations and areas that are not supported; application information; an online letter of intent form; contact information; and links to a variety of local, regional, national, and Internet organizational resources.

Daisy Marquis Jones Foundation (NY) (http://www.dmjf.org)
The Daisy Marquis Jones Foundation, located in Rochester, New York, was established in 1968 by Daisy Marquis Jones and Leo Marquis Lyons as a way of giving back to the community. The foundation is "dedicated to improving the well-being of residents in Monroe and Yates Counties by funding programs that aid disadvantaged children and families." The foundation grants time-limited support to nonprofit organizations with programs or projects that provide access to healthcare, attend to the needs of young children or help families, and develop economic security. The Web site provides more detailed information about the types of programs the foundation funds and gives a list of previous grants. Applicants must fill out an inquiry form, which can be submitted through the Web site. Those who complete the form will receive a follow-up e-mail that details the next steps. The annual report and contact information also can be found on the foundation's Web site.

Joukowsky Family Foundation (NY) (http://www.joukowsky.org/)
The Joukowsky Family Foundation of New York was established in 1981 with a primary purpose of supporting education. Other interests of the foundation include cultural, social, archaeological, and historical activities. Visitors to the foundation's Web site will find information on the board, grant guidelines, a listing of recent grants, information on the foundation's scholarship program, a copy of the latest tax return downloadable, and contact information.

The Joyce Foundation (IL) (http://www.joycefdn.org)
Beatrice Joyce Kean, whose family's wealth came from the lumber industry, established the Joyce Foundation in 1948. The foundation supports efforts to protect the natural environment of the Great Lakes, reduce poverty and violence in the region, and ensure that its people have access to good schools, decent jobs, and a diverse and thriving culture. It also supports efforts to reform the system of financing election campaigns. Currently, the foundation's program areas are education, employment, the environment, gun violence prevention, money and politics, and culture. The Chicago-based foundation gives preference to organizations based in or who have a program in the Midwest, specifically the Great Lakes region: Illinois, Indiana, Iowa, Michigan, Minnesota, Ohio, and Wisconsin. Consult the Web site for further information on each program area and for grant application information and deadlines. The Web site also features a downloadable application form with guidelines, a newsletter, and annual report; grants lists and links to grantee organizations; a site search function; announcements and press releases; a listing of officers, directors, and staff; and contact information.

Henry J. Kaiser Family Foundation (CA) (http://www.kff.org)
The Henry J. Kaiser Family Foundation is an independent philanthropy that seeks to be an independent, trusted, and credible source of information, analysis, and balanced discussion on the field of health, which the foundation recognizes as being otherwise dominated by large interests. The foundation seeks to be this source of information to policymakers, the

media, and the general public. The foundation's work is focused on three main areas: health policy, media and public education, and health and development in South Africa. The foundation's Web site features information resource in its program areas, health-related news, reports, and fact sheets. The foundation makes few grants, but information about applying can be found in the "About KFF" section of the site.

Kansas Health Foundation (KS) (http://www.kansashealth.org/)
Established with the proceeds from the sale of the Wesley Medical Center in 1985, the Kansas Health Foundation makes grants to health organizations throughout the state aimed at improving the quality of health in Kansas. Although the majority of the foundation's activity centers around foundation-initiated partnerships and programs, it does provide funding each year through its Recognition Grant Program, which "supports grass-roots organizations doing creative and innovative work to improve the health of Kansans." Recognition Grants fall into five primary categories: primary care education, rural health, health promotion and disease prevention, public health, and health policy and research. In addition to general information about the foundation and its programs, visitors to the foundation's Web site will find Recognition Grant Program descriptions and funding guidelines.

The J.M. Kaplan Fund (NY) (http://www.jmkfund.org/)
The J.M. Kaplan Fund was established in 1944 to protect and support New York. The fund's grant program focuses on city life, conservation, historic preservation, migrations, and publishing. Specific interests include: art, architecture, publishing, and design; preservation of land and buildings; policy analysis and discussion of civic issues; microfinance and community economic development; and human rights and social justice. Visitors to the fund's Web site will find further information about areas of interest, geographic restrictions, staff information, grant guidelines, grants listings, and contact information.

Mitchell Kapor Foundation (CA) (http://www.mkf.org/)
The Mitchell Kapor Foundation, based in San Francisco, California, pursues its grantmaking with the mission of "improving human well-being and sustaining healthy ecosystems that support all life on earth." Established by Mitchell Kapor, the founder of the Lotus Development Corporation, the foundation centers its funding interests in the areas of human health, the environment, and the impact of information technology on society. The foundation's Web site provides detailed background descriptions of its two main grants: the Environmental Health Program and the Program on the Impact of Information Technology. The latter does not accept outside funding requests; it is chosen on foundation initiative. The former currently focuses on the issue of chemical contamination, and application instructions can be found through a link to the Jenifer Altman Foundation Web site. Contact information for the Kapor Foundation is provided online.

The Karma Foundation (NJ) (http://www.karmafoundation.org/)
The New Jersey-based Karma Foundation was established in 1996 to provide grants to support organizations engaged in activities and programs in the areas of arts and culture, education and literacy, health and human services, and the development and enrichment of Jewish life. Grants are made to local organizations in New Jersey's Middlesex, Union, Mercer, and Somerset Counties. The foundation's Web site provides grant guidelines, application procedures, restrictions, sample grants, a listing of foundation trustees, and contact information.

Ewing Marion Kauffman Foundation (MO) (http://www.emkf.org)
The Kansas City-based Ewing Marion Kauffman Foundation is a grantmaking foundation with special interests in entrepreneurial leadership and youth development. In making grants, the foundation aims to support "sustainable programs and projects that will lead to individual, organizational, and community self-sufficiency." The foundation accepts direct inquiries but does not seek unsolicited proposals. Features of its Web site include program

descriptions and application criteria, grant guidelines, contact information, and a brief biography of Ewing Kauffman.

The Kawabe Memorial Fund (WA) (http://fdncenter.org/grantmaker/kawabe/)
The Washington-based Kawabe Memorial Fund is a private foundation established under the will of Harry S. Kawabe. The foundation awards grants in the areas of human services, religious institutions, and scholarships directed towards students graduating from Seward High School. Visit the foundation's Web site to find specific information on the foundation's areas of interest, policies, geographical restrictions, application procedures, and contact information.

The Calvin K. Kazanjian Economics Foundation, Inc. (PA) (http://www.kazanjian.org)
The Calvin K. Kazanjian Economics Foundation, Inc. was founded in 1947. A business owner for thirty years, Mr. Kazanjian believed that social and political difficulties could be traced to economic illiteracy and that if people understood the basic facts of economics, "the world would be a better place in which to live." Therefore, the mission of the foundation is "to help bring greater happiness and prosperity to all through better understanding of economics." Based in Dallas, Pennsylvania, the foundation is interested in projects that present economics in an effective, thoughtful, and understandable way; encourage measurement of economic understanding more often and/or more effectively; help otherwise disenfranchised youth and/or adults learn to participate in the economic system; and distribute high-quality economic education materials to regions of the world with emerging markets, though such projects represent a small portion of the annual grants budget. The foundation is primarily interested in proposals that are national in scope, and it usually does not support regional or statewide programs. Visitors to the foundation's Web site will find application guidelines and procedures, information about the founder, links to other economic education resources, descriptions of some projects funded, and contact information.

The W.M. Keck Foundation (CA) (http://www.wmkeck.org/)
Established in 1954 by William Myron Keck, founder of the Superior Oil Company, the W.M. Keck Foundation focuses its grantmaking on the areas of medical research, science, and engineering. The foundation also maintains a program for liberal arts colleges and a Southern California Grant Program that provides support in the areas of civic and community services, healthcare and hospitals, precollegiate education, and the arts. According to the foundation's guidelines, eligible institutions in the fields of science, engineering, medical research, and liberal arts must be "accredited universities, colleges, medical schools, and major, independent medical research institutions." For the Southern California Grant Program, "only organizations located in and serving the population of southern California are eligible for consideration." Visitors to the foundation's Web site will find general program descriptions, application criteria and guidelines, the foundation's most recent annual report, grants lists organized by program, a page devoted to the W.M. Keck Observatory on Hawaii's Mauna Kea volcano, and contact information.

W.K. Kellogg Foundation (MI) (http://www.wkkf.org/)
The mission of the W.K. Kellogg Foundation is to "help people help themselves through the practical application of knowledge and resources to improve their quality of life and that of future generations." The foundation awards grants in the three following regions: the United States; Botswana, Lesotho, South Africa, Swaziland, and Zimbabwe; and Latin America and the Caribbean. The U.S. program areas include health, philanthropy, and voluntarism; food systems and rural development; youth and education; and support for greater Battle Creek, Michigan. In addition to program descriptions, application guidelines, and the foundation's latest annual report, the foundation's Web site offers a variety of useful features, including a searchable grants database, an electronic version of the *International Journal* of the W.K. Kellogg Foundation, and individual listings of resources of interest in the foundation's various program areas.

Henry P. Kendall Foundation (MA) (http://www.kendall.org/)
The Henry P. Kendall Foundation, based in Boston, Massachusetts, is dedicated to restoring and maintaining the ecological integrity of terrestrial, aquatic, and marine systems in the northeast and northwest regions of North America. The foundation's current programs are focused on the "desire to integrate good science and local knowledge into environmental decision-making, to build capacity for sustained protection of natural resources, and to connect people and place by fostering stewardship of those resources." The foundation's Web site includes application guidelines, downloadable versions of recent annual reports, a publication listing, staff and trustee listings, and contact information.

Joseph P. Kennedy, Jr. Foundation (DC) (http://www.familyvillage.wisc.edu/jpkf/)
The Joseph P. Kennedy, Jr. Foundation has two major objectives: "to improve the way society deals with its citizens who have mental retardation, and to help identify and disseminate ways to prevent the causes of mental retardation." To that end, the foundation provides seed funding that encourages new methods of service and supports, and through the use of its influence to promote public awareness of the needs of persons with mental retardation and their families. The foundation does not participate in capital costs or costs of equipment for projects or pay for ongoing support or operations of existing programs. Visitors to the foundation's Web site will find information on the foundation's various funding and award programs, detailed application guidelines, and an extensive lists of links to other online resources for mental retardation.

Kentucky Foundation for Women (KY) (http://www.kfw.org/)
Established in 1985, the mission of the Kentucky Foundation for Women is "to change the lives of women by supporting feminist expression in the arts in Kentucky." The primary goal of the foundation's grants program is to support the work of individual artists who live or work in Kentucky and "whose work embodies a feminist consciousness." Grants may also be awarded to organizations and for special collaborative projects that share the foundation's goals. In addition to general foundation information, application guidelines and procedures, and a list of recent grant recipients, visitors to the foundation's Web site can learn about the foundation's literary journal, *The American Voice,* and Hopscotch House, its rural retreat for women.

Charles F. Kettering Foundation (OH) (Operating foundation) (http://www.kettering.org/)
Established in 1927, the Charles F. Kettering Foundation's objective is "to understand the way bodies politic function or fail to function." The foundation does not make grants. It sponsors its own programs and participates in collaborative research efforts with other organizations to address the roles of politics and institutional structures as a dimension of everyday life. The results of the foundation's research are published in study guides, community workbooks, and other endeavors to help the public act responsibly and effectively on its problems. In addition to general information about the foundation's activities and publications, a listing of the foundation's trustees, and contact information, visitors to the foundation's Web site can access a searchable database of more than 3,500 non-evaluative summaries of books and articles in the subject areas of governing, community, education, international, science, policy, and political philosophy.

Kettering Family Foundation (CO) (http://www.ketteringfamilyfoundation.org)
Located in Denver, Colorado, the Kettering Family Foundation was established in 1955 and currently is composed of 12 family members who elect 13 trustees annually. Priority is given to trustee-sponsored requests. Unsolicited proposals will be considered only after trustee-sponsored requests have been reviewed and funded. The foundation considers unsolicited requests that fall under the following areas of interest: cultural/arts, education, the environment, medical/health, and social/human services. Information about how to apply and where to send applications is available on the site. Deadlines, lists of previous grantees, and the foundation's financial information are all available on the Web site.

The Kimball Foundation, Sara H. and William R. (CA) (http://www.pacificfoundationservices.com/kimball/index.html)
Founded in California in 1997, the Sara H. and William R. Kimball Foundation is committed to helping at-risk and disadvantaged individuals in the San Francisco Bay Area to achieve the highest possible quality of life. Major program interests include education and the arts. Within the education program, the foundation focuses on higher education (undergraduate and graduate programs), specifically in areas of youth development, academic enrichment, tutorials, outdoor education, leadership development, vocational training and employment, learning disabilities, and sports/recreational activities for low-income youth. The arts program primarily focuses on youth groups. The foundation also holds an interest in animal welfare and historic preservation, as well as capital support. The foundation's Web site features most recent grants lists, contact information, a list of the board of directors list, and application procedures.

The Sidney Kimmel Foundation for Cancer Research (PA) (http://www.kimmel.org/)
Located in Philadelphia, Pennsylvania, the Sidney Kimmel Foundation for Cancer Research is dedicated to "improving our basic understanding of cancer biology and to developing new methods for the prevention and treatment of cancer." The foundation supports the research of those who concentrate on basic cancer research, the rapid translation of basic science concepts into potential therapeutic applications, and/or clinical research with innovative treatment strategies. Grant recipients are chosen by a medical advisory board made up of distinguished cancer researchers. The foundation's Web site explains all of the grant guidelines and restrictions, as well as the rules and regulations. Each application must include a cover page, which can be printed from the site. Contact information, a list of FAQs, and lists of previous grant recipients are all available on the site.

The Kimsey Foundation (DC) (http://www.kimseyfoundation.org)
Established in 1996 by James V. Kimsey, the Kimsey Foundation's mission is to level the playing field for economically disadvantaged Washington, D.C. youth. Subject areas of interest to the foundation include education, computer technology, arts and culture, and domestic and international affairs. The foundation primarily funds programs that benefit children in the Washington, D.C. area. The foundation makes operating grants but prefers to fund established programs. Visit the foundation's Web site to find information on areas not supported by the foundation, grant application guidelines, and contact information.

Charles and Lucille King Family Foundation, Inc. (NY) (http://www.kingfoundation.org)
The Charles and Lucille King Family Foundation, located in New York City and established in 1989, provides scholarships for undergraduate and graduate students in film and television production. Undergraduates must be entering their junior or senior year and demonstrate academic ability, financial need, and professional potential. Normally, outstanding undergraduate and graduate students at New York University, the University of California–Los Angeles, and the University of Southern California, among other schools, receive funding of up to $2,500 per year. The foundation's Web site provides an FAQ, a list of past scholarship winners, and contact information.

Stephen and Tabitha King Foundation (NY) (http://www.stkfoundation.org/)
The Stephen and Tabitha King Foundation promotes strengthening and supporting communities and draws upon the values and spirituality of its founders. The foundation has a special interest in organizations and people who have less recourse to usual channels of resources, focusing on community-based initiatives, especially in the state of Maine. Visit the foundation's Web site to find further information about the grant process, a downloadable application, grant guidelines, and contact information.

F.M. Kirby Foundation (NJ) (http://fdncenter.org/grantmaker/kirby)
The New Jersey-based F.M. Kirby Foundation believes that "private philanthropy, at its best, if provided compassionately and prudently, encourages self-reliance and diminishes government's role." The foundation makes support mainly in the geographic areas of

interest to the Kirby family and for education, health and medicine, the arts, and religious, welfare, and youth organizations. Visitors to the foundation's Web site will find more specific information on the foundation's areas of interest, application procedures, and specific restrictions; a listing of directors and officers; and contact information.

Kirlin Foundation (WA) (http://www.kirlinfoundation.org/)
The Kirlin Foundation is committed to "protecting and fostering the creative imagination, self-worth, and happiness of young people by addressing, among other things, the current and future state of education in its many forms." The foundation participates in creating venture philanthropy in the Puget Sound area of Washington State. Visit the foundation's Web site for more information on the organization's mission, venture philanthropy, and how to become involved.

The Klingenstein Third Generation Foundation (NY) (http://www.ktgf.org/)
Established in 1993 by the grandchildren of Joseph Klingenstein, one of the founding partners of Wertheim & Company (now Schroder & Company, Inc.), the Klingenstein Third Generation Foundation focuses its funding interests in the areas of childhood and adolescent depression and attention deficit/hyperactive disorder (ADHD). Its grants primarily fall under the categories of intervention and referral, prevention, public education/training, and infrastructure. The foundation also awards a postgraduate research fellowship in clinical or basic research of depression. Letters of inquiry regarding grants may be sent via e-mail, though the foundation does not accept unsolicited applications for the fellowship. Its Web site includes information on application procedures, a list of recent grants, articles published by grantees, information on its funding philosophy, contact information, links to mental health associations for grantseekers, a mission statement, and information on its selection process for the fellowship.

John S. and James L. Knight Foundation (FL) (http://www.knightfdn.org/)
Established in 1950, the John S. and James L. Knight Foundation focuses its grantmaking activities on journalism, education, and arts and culture. The foundation also supports organizations in 26 communities where the communications company founded by the Knight brothers publishes newspapers, and it "remains flexible enough to respond to unique challenges, ideas, and projects that lie beyond its identified program areas, yet would fulfill the broad vision of its founders." Visitors to the foundation's Web site can access an array of information about the foundation and its programs: application guidelines and restrictions, including a sample proposal and downloadable proposal cover sheet; foundation news, including the foundation's most recent annual report; a listing of recent grants by program area; and a FAQ section.

Marion I. & Henry J. Knott Foundation (MD) (http://www.knottfoundation.org)
The Marion I. & Henry J. Knott Foundation was established in 1977 to nurture family unity in its founders' Maryland Roman Catholic community. The foundation today provides funding in five areas: arts and humanities, Catholic activities, education (Catholic and nonsectarian private schools), healthcare, and social and human services. Grants are limited to organizations in Baltimore City and Allegany, Anne Arundel, Baltimore, Carroll, Frederick, Garrett, Harford, Howard, and Washington Counties in Maryland. The foundation's Web site has a complete guide to its grant applications, including application guideline and limitations and a downloadable application form. The foundation also provides a listing of previous grants and a balance sheet of its assets.

Koinonia Foundation (MD) (http://www.koinoniafoundation.org/)
The Baltimore-based Koinonia Foundation supports projects that are consistent with its values of "a belief in oneness of life; a belief in the spiritual nature of the human individual, with respect for the integrity and wholeness of the person and the human race; a belief in the existence of a spiritual order designed and ordained by God, with a recognition of the wholeness and holiness of God's creation." Its funding priorities are grassroots programs and actions that work for systemic change, empower small group action to influence large

movements, and articulate a clearly defined goal or activity as part of a larger project or organizational effort. The foundation's Web site features detailed support guidelines, printable application forms, a listing of grant recipients, and contact information.

Kongsgaard-Goldman Foundation (WA) (http://www.kongsgaard-goldman.org)

The Kongsgaard-Goldman Foundation was formed in 1988 by Martha Kongsgaard and Peter Goldman. The Seattle-based private foundation supports a wide range of nonprofit organizations in the Pacific Northwest, specifically in Washington, Oregon, Idaho, Alaska, Montana, and British Columbia, Canada. Primary funding areas are human rights, civic development, environmental protection and restoration, and arts and humanities. Another funding area, but of low priority, is technical assistance. Within these funding areas, the foundation favors projects that reflect "a deep and broad level of citizen participation and leadership." Its priority is to help "fund the building of grassroots organizations with the power to change their communities and improve their lives." Visitors to the foundation's Web site will find further information on each funding area, downloadable guidelines, application instructions, grants lists, links to related sites, and contact information.

Koret Foundation (CA) (http://www.koretfoundation.org/)

Founded in 1979, the Koret Foundation's areas of funding interest include: San Francisco Bay Area Jewish community projects (Jewish identity, linking Bay Area Jewry to Israel, enhancing Jewish communal organizations, Jewish education/Jewish studies, and émigré resettlement), San Francisco Bay Area community development and support (K-12 public education, cultural/community development, higher education, and public policy), and Israel and international Jewish organizations (economic development/free market initiatives in Israel, higher education in Israel, and Jewish educational, cultural, and communal activities in the former Soviet Union). Recipient organizations in the San Francisco Bay Area must serve the needs of one or more of the following Bay area counties: San Francisco, Alameda, Contra Costa, Marin, San Mateo, or Santa Clara. In the area of Jewish funding, the foundation will consider grant applications from northern California and nationally on a selected basis. The San Francisco-based foundation also has the Koret Jewish Book Awards, in cooperation with the National Foundation for Jewish Culture, which serve to heighten the visibility of the best new Jewish books and authors. Visitors to the site will find downloadable guidelines and submission forms for the Jewish Book Awards, a printable letter of inquiry coversheet, application instructions, financial information, selected grants lists, an archive of news and press releases, and contact information.

The Emily Davie and Joseph S. Kornfeld Foundation (NY) (http://fdncenter.org/grantmaker/kornfeld/index.html)

Established in 1979, the Emily Davie and Joseph S. Kornfeld Foundation focuses on bioethics, palliative care, medical research, and education. Current program areas are fellowships in bioethics, palliative, and end-of-life care; the Center for ALS Research at Johns Hopkins Hospital; and literacy enrichment programs for New York City public school children. For further information, visit the foundation's Web site.

The Koussevitzky Music Foundations (NY) (http://www.koussevitzky.org)

The Koussevitzky Music Foundations of New York is a joint commissioning program of the Serge Koussevitzky Music Foundation in the Library of Congress and the Koussevitzky Music Foundation. The foundations consider applications from performing organizations for the joint commissioning of compositions designed primarily for orchestras and chamber groups that have a record of excellence in the performance of contemporary music. Visitors to the foundations' Web site will find grant guidelines, downloadable application forms, a listing of previous grants, and contact information.

The Paul Kowal Charitable Foundation (CA) (http://fdncenter.org/grantmaker/kowal/)

The purpose of the Paul Kowal Charitable Foundation is to receive and administer funds for religious, scientific, educational, and charitable purposes. Visitors to the foundation's Web site will find recent tax returns available for download and contact information.

Kresge Foundation (MI) (http://www.kresge.org)
Sebastian S. Kresge, founder of the S.S. Kresge Company that is now known as Kmart, established the Kresge Foundation in 1924. Its mission is "to promote the well-being of mankind." The Kresge Foundation makes grants to build and renovate facilities, challenge private giving, and build institutional capacity among nonprofits, with goals of strengthening the capacity of charitable organizations to provide effective programs of quality. Located in Troy, Michigan, the foundation has national and occasionally international geographic scope, and it supports a range of organizations "reflecting almost the entire breadth of the nonprofit sector." Currently, there are five programs: Bricks and Mortar, which is a grant program to build facilities and challenge private giving and which makes up the majority of the foundation's grantmaking; Science Initiative, a challenge grant program to upgrade and endow scientific equipment; Detroit Initiative, a grant program to support strategic investment in Detroit and southeastern Michigan; the Kresge Foundation Partnership to Raise Community Capital, a five-year grant program to develop permanent endowment assets for community foundations and nonprofit organizations; and the Kresge Foundation HBCU initiative, a five-year grant program that helps develop fundraising capacity at historically Black colleges and universities. Visit the foundation's Web site for detailed information on each program and its application guidelines, the foundation's latest annual report, a FAQ page, a history of the foundation, staff listings, and contact information.

Samuel H. Kress Foundation (NY) (http://www.shkf.org)
Samuel H. Kress, who made his fortune from S.H. Kress & Co. variety stores, established the Samuel H. Kress Foundation in 1929. With his fortune from his stores, Samuel Kress amassed a collection of over 3,000 works of art, which he then donated to more than 90 institutions in 33 states. Beyond its endowments of works of art, the foundation has several grant programs for projects or programs focused on European art from antiquity through the early nineteenth century: Resources of Scholarship, for development of essential resources for art historical research and the practice of art conservation; Sharing of Expertise, projects in which art historians and conservators share their professional skills and experience; Art Conservation Research, scientific investigation of problems in art conservation; Conservation and Restoration Projects, which support the care and conservation of works of art and the preservation of European monuments; and its Special Initiatives Program, which are projects that the foundation takes an active role in developing and implementing. Further information and application information on grant and fellowship programs is available on the foundation's Web site, along with further information on the foundation and a listing of locations where works from the Kress Collection are currently on exhibit.

Kronkosky Charitable Foundation (TX) (http://www.kronkosky.org)
The San Antonio, Texas-based, Kronkosky Charitable Foundation was established in 1991 with a mission "to produce profound good that is tangible and measurable in Bandera, Bexar, Comal, and Kendall Counties." The focus of the foundation is to support programs, projects, and collaborative efforts that reach as many people as possible; involve the persons served in developing solutions; raise expectations; build self-esteem; develop personal and organizational capacity; encourage innovation; and make use of technology. Funding areas are health and human services, including the elderly, youth, child abuse and neglect, and persons with disabilities; cultural activities; and other areas, such as wildlife preservation and animal issues. Consult the Web site for detailed information on each funding area, application information, FAQs, grants lists, the foundation's annual reports and recent tax returns, an online feedback/contact form, and contact information.

Kulas Foundation (OH) (http://fdncenter.org/grantmaker/kulas/)
The Cleveland, Ohio-based Kulas Foundation was established in 1937 and supports various aspects of music, including musical education, institutions and performances, and other groups that have similar priorities. Besides supporting programs designated by its founders, the foundation has a grantmaking program that distributes funds to Cleveland-area programs in four areas: arts and culture, education, social services, and

community. The last three categories are still music-oriented, focusing on arts programs in schools, the musical needs of social service organizations, and music or arts components of community projects. The foundation also supports research in music therapy. The foundation's Web site offers program descriptions and application guidelines, lists of trustees and officers, financial statements, and biographical information on the founders that provides important insight into the foundation's grantmaking decisions.

Ronald and Mary Ann Lachman Foundation (IL) (http://www.lachman.org)
The Ronald and Mary Ann Lachman Foundation is an outgrowth of the Lachman Associates Foundation, founded in 1987, which was established with the proceeds of the sale of Lachman Associates, a Chicago consulting firm, to Eastman Kodak. The foundation supports the causes of deaf education, especially literacy; technology for the deaf; technological development, especially for organizations that support technology education in computers or energy; and Jewish education. The foundation seldom grants unsolicited funding requests, preferring to establish a long-term relationship with particular organizations. Grant recipient organizations are listed on the foundation's Web site. A biography of the Lachman family, information on the foundation's grantmaking goals and interests, and contact information are also available online.

Laird Norton Endowment Foundation (WA) (http://www.lairdnorton.org/)
The Laird Norton Endowment Foundation was initiated in 1940 by descendants of three men who formed the Laird Norton Company, a lumber business: William Harris Laird, Matthew George Norton, and James Laird Norton. Through the foundation, the Laird Norton family seeks to honor and reflect a common heritage—the American forest and lumber industry—in programs of creative philanthropy. The mission of the Seattle-based Laird Norton Endowment Foundation is to fund distinctive programs in conservation and forestry education. The foundation is currently concentrating its efforts on sustainable forestry: the practice of forestry that restores, enhances, and then sustains a full range of forest values, both ecological and economic. Visit the Web site for grant information, application materials and procedures, guidelines, grants lists, and contact information.

The Lalor Foundation (RI) (http://www.lalorfound.org)
The Lalor Foundation, based in Providence, Rhode Island, was established in 1935 from bequests from members for the Lalor Family. The goal of the foundation is to give assistance and encouragement to capable investigators who have teaching and research careers in universities and colleges. The principal areas of support have been branches of life sciences, "wherein applications of chemical and physical methods of research could be expected to give useful and fruitful results." Since 1960, however, the foundation has concentrated its support on special aspects of reproductive physiology, which the foundation considers of "pressing importance." Its Web site states that, since resources must be conserved, "a finer understanding of all aspects of reproduction and the means to control population growth is an imperative." Visit the Web site for more information about the foundation's grant program, application instructions and a printable application form, links to related sites, a listing of current grant awardees and their projects, and contact information.

Jacob and Valeria Langeloth Foundation (NY) (http://www.langeloth.org)
The Jacob and Valeria Langeloth Foundation was established in 1914 to provide grants in the area of healthcare, primarily to hospitals and other health facilities. The foundation "supports programs designed to improve, speed, make more cost effective, and in other ways promote physical and emotional recovery from illness and accident." The New York City-based foundation seeks proposals that include one or more of the following: innovative approaches or model programs that can be replicated; new community models that reach out to empower communities that may normally be beyond the reach of good medical care; interdisciplinary and interagency collaboration; programs that promote among patients greater knowledge of their illnesses, paths to recovery, and rights as consumers of medical care, as well as involving families in the convalescence process; applied research that holds the promise of developing new knowledge and understanding about the field;

and humanization of relations between medical professionals and those in their care. Consult the Web site for application procedures, a sample budget template, a history of the foundation and its founder, staff listing, and contact information.

Lannan Foundation (NM) (http://www.lannan.org)

The Lannan Foundation, established in 1960, is headquartered in Santa Fe, New Mexico, and is dedicated to supporting contemporary artists and writers, as well as native activists in rural indigenous communities. The foundation's program areas include fellowships for contemporary visual artists, poets and fiction and nonfiction writers, as well as native community activists. Funding for the last category must be for programs that are "consistent with traditional values in the areas of education, native cultures, the revival and preservation of languages, legal rights, and environmental protection." Descriptions of the specific funding available for each area (prizes, exhibitions, and grants), as well as recipients of the awards, guidelines, and procedures, are available on the foundation's Web site. The foundation also sponsors the Prize for Cultural Freedom and residency program, which gives artists, curators, writers, and native community activists contemplative time to work. Applications and letters of inquiry are not accepted for these programs. The foundation's Web site includes details of all of its funding opportunities and links to other resources.

George A. and Dolly F. LaRue Trust (MO) (http://www.gkccf.org)

The George A. and Dolly F. LaRue Trust was established in 1971 after the deaths of its two founders. George A. LaRue was president of LaRue Printing Company, and he and his wife were active in charitable and civic programs in the Kansas City area. The trust supports religious, charitable, scientific, and educational purposes and operates as an affiliated trust of the Greater Kansas City Community Foundation. Visit the foundation's Web site to find a brief introduction to the LaRue Trust in the online annual report and contact information.

Albert & Mary Lasker Foundation, Inc. (NY) (Operating foundation) (http://www.laskerfoundation.org/index.html)

The Albert & Mary Lasker Foundation, Inc. is known for its Albert Lasker Awards. Philanthropists Albert and Mary Woodard Lasker inaugurated these awards in 1946. The mission of the foundation is "to elevate and sustain medical research as a universal priority so that the foundation's goals—to eradicate life threatening disease and disabilities and improve health standards—are strongly supported by national and international policies and resources." An international jury of top medical researchers annually selects the Lasker Award recipients, scientists, physicians, and public servants who have made major advances in the understanding, diagnosis, treatment, prevention, and cure of human disease. Currently, three awards are presented each year: the Albert Lasker Basic Medical Research Award, Clinical Medical Research Award, and Award for Special Medical Research Achievement. In addition to its awards programs, the foundation also has a program of public education aimed at encouraging federal financial support for biomedical research. The primary beneficiary this support has been the National Institutes of Health. Visit the foundation's Web site for more information about the foundation's award programs, past recipients, a searchable library of materials related to the awards and its past recipients, and press releases.

The Ronald S. Lauder Foundation (NY) (http://rslfoundation.org/)

Since its establishment in 1987, the Ronald S. Lauder Foundation has been committed to rebuilding Jewish life where destruction of the Holocaust in Europe was followed by the oppression of communism. In its mission, the Ronald S. Lauder Foundation hopes to make available to every Jewish child in Central and Eastern Europe the chance to develop pride in Jewish tradition by learning in a Jewish school, attending a Jewish summer camp, or participating in a Jewish youth center program. Visitors to the foundation's Web site will find detailed information of programs currently funded, information about the international student exchange program, a quarterly newsletter on the progress of the organization, and contact information.

Lavelle Fund for the Blind (NY) (http://fdncenter.org/grantmaker/lavellefund/)
The Lavelle Fund for the Blind of New York was established in 1999 and is "dedicated to supporting programs that promote the spiritual, moral, intellectual, and physical development of blind and low-vision people of all ages, together with programs that help people avoid vision loss." The fund concentrates on providing support for program creation or expansion or the improvement of qualified organizations. Please consult the fund's Web site to find information on the fund's giving priorities and limitations, application procedures, and contact information.

The Lawrence Foundation (CA) (http://www.thelawrencefoundation.org/)
The mission of the Santa Monica-based Lawrence Foundation is to "make a difference in the world by providing contributions and grants to organizations that are working to solve pressing educational, environmental, health, and other issues." In previous years, the foundation has supported education, environment, health, and disaster relief. Visitors to the foundation's Web site will find information on grant programs, restrictions, and application procedures; grant listings; and contact information.

Leader to Leader Institute (NY) (Operating foundation) (http://www.pfdf.org/)
The Leader to Leader Institute continues the work of the Peter F. Drucker Foundation for Nonprofit Management, which was founded in 1990 by Frances Hesselbein. The mission of the New York City-based institute is "to strengthen the leadership of the social sector." The institute supports social sector leaders of character and competence, forges cross-sector partnerships that deliver social sector results, and provides leadership resources that engage and inform social sector leaders. The Peter F. Drucker Award for Nonprofit Innovation looks "to find the innovators, whether small or large; to recognize and celebrate their example; and, to inspire others." The institute also, on occasion, seeks candidates for the Frances Hesselbein Community Innovation Fellows Program. Visitors to the institute's Web site will find institute guidelines and instructions, downloadable application forms, conference reports, an online feedback and information request form, descriptions of the institute's leadership publications and readers' guides, publications order forms, and contact information. The institute makes clear that it only provides programs and resources, and does not make grants, and cannot accept funding proposals.

Leeway Foundation (PA) (http://www.leeway.org/)
Artist Linda Lee Alter, to promote the welfare of women and to benefit the arts, established the Leeway Foundation in 1993. The foundation's primary grantmaking program supports individual women artists in the Philadelphia area and encourages their increased recognition and representation in the community. The foundation makes grants each year in a selected visual or literary discipline. Grants are awarded to artists who demonstrate exceptional creativity and vision in a body of work. In addition, two special grants recognizing artists at particular stages in their careers are available each year at the jurors' discretion. The foundation's Web site provides information about these programs, as well as the foundation's general program; application instructions (including the dates and locations of foundation-sponsored application workshops in the five-county Philadelphia metro region); the names of recent grantees and examples of their work; listings of the foundation's board and staff; and contact information.

The LEF Foundation (CA) (http://www.lef-foundation.org/)
Founded in 1985, the LEF Foundation supports the creation and presentation of contemporary work in the visual arts, performing arts, new media, literary arts, architecture, and design. Funds are given for projects, programs, and services that encourage "a positive interchange between the arts and the natural urban environment." Projects may also involve public and environmental art, architecture and landscape architecture, and be design and interdisciplinary collaborations. Within these areas, the foundation also considers projects that address critical community needs. Located in Cambridge, Massachusetts, and St. Helena, California, the foundation primarily sponsors projects in New England and northern

California, although applications may be open to relevant proposals outside of those areas. Consult the Web site for application instructions and guidelines and contact information.

The Lauren B. Leichtman and Arthur E. Levine Family Foundation (CA) (http://fdncenter.org/grantmaker/leichtmanlevine/990pf.pdf)
View the most recent tax return of the California-based Lauren B. Leichtman and Arthur E. Levine Family Foundation.

Lemelson Foundation (NV) (http://www.lemelson.org/)
The Lemelson Foundation was established to stimulate the U.S. economy and secure its position in the global marketplace by creating the next generation of inventors, innovators, and entrepreneurs. The Lemelson Foundation makes grants only to pre-selected charitable and educational organizations and does not accept unsolicited requests for funds. Visit the foundation's Web site to find a brief history of the organization, biographies of the founders, a FAQ section, grant application information, and contact information.

The Leonsis Foundation (DC) (http://www.leonsisfoundation.org)
The Leonsis Foundation, established in 2000, believes that for children, "education is the key to self-empowerment," and the foundation makes grants that allow children to "overcome obstacles and achieve their goals." Grants are made in the areas of academics and career mentoring, technological proficiency, health-related issues, and certain other social and extracurricular activities. Grant guidelines and application procedures, profiles of grantee organizations, a description of the foundation, and contact information are available online.

Levitt Foundation (NY) (http://fdncenter.org/grantmaker/levitt/)
The Levitt Foundation is an independent foundation incorporated in New York in 1949. The foundation is interested in the environment, as it relates to children and youth living in the five boroughs of New York City and on Long Island, New York. The foundation supports programs that help young people understand the value of their environment and to help young people build confidence, self-esteem, and leadership skills. Visit the foundation's Web site for information on the foundation's interests, a listing of recent grantees, and contact information.

The Cora T. Lewis Foundation (GA) (http://www.coratlewistrust.org)
The Cora T. Lewis Foundation of Georgia was established under the will of Jesse Lewis in memory of her mother, Cora Thurman Lewis. The foundation's funding priorities include children and the elderly, with "particular emphasis on those older people who by virtue of misfortune, illness, or divine providence are unable to fully provide for themselves, and for the benefit of young children, who by virtue of poverty, broken homes, lack of able parents, or other similar reasons, may not receive the same advantages in life customarily enjoyed by average children among their contemporaries." Visitors to the foundation's Web site will find information on average grant ranges, a listing of charities with missions similar to the foundation's application information and submission dates, a downloadable application form, and contact information.

Libra Foundation (ME) (http://www.librafoundation.org/)
Founded in Portland, Maine, in 1989, the Libra Foundation seeks to provide financial assistance, hope, and assurance to a broad spectrum of people in Maine. The foundation doesn't have formal grant guidelines online but believes that all areas and people need support. Broad subject areas that have been supported in the past include religion, health, education, human services, the arts, public/society benefit, and justice. The foundation accepts applications from all over the state of Maine and supports all sectors of Maine society. Information found on the foundation's Web site includes a complete grant history, a list of trustees, information on grant exclusions, and application procedures, and contact information.

Dolores Zohrab Liebmann Fund (NY) (http://fdncenter.org/grantmaker/liebmann/)
The Dolores Zohrab Liebmann Fund of New York provides graduate fellowships to universities in any recognized field of study in the humanities, social sciences, or natural sciences (including law, medicine, engineering, architecture, or other formal professional training) and scholarly publications focusing on Armenian studies and culture nationally. Visit the fund's Web site to find application procedures and restrictions, previous recipients, and contact information.

The Lifebridge Foundation, Inc. (NY) (http://www.lifebridge.org)
Established in 1992, the Lifebridge Foundation, Inc. supports organizations and individuals who are dedicated to creating bridges of understanding among all people by bringing to realization the concepts of one humanity and the interconnectedness of all life. The foundation, located in New York City, seeks to promote the concept of "one humanity and the interconnectedness of all life" and to foster a spirit of "inclusiveness and global vision leading to transformative action." Grantees cover a wide range of disciplines and social concerns and can be roughly divided into the following fields: arts and culture, youth/education, the environment, science, community service, world goodwill, and "inter-dimensional." The foundation generally pre-selects grantees, but it does accept letters of introduction. Visit the Web site for grant guidelines, lists of grantees, newsletters, links to related sites and projects, and contact information.

The Linden Foundation (MA) (http://www.lindenfoundation.org)
Located in Arlington, Massachusetts, the Linden Foundation is committed to helping needy and disadvantaged families improve their quality of life. The foundation primarily funds organizations that serve families, youth, the homeless, and the elderly in four specific regions of the Northeast. The foundation's geographic focus is outlined on its Web site, along with more specific details on types of grants, a listing of recent recipients, and a description of the foundation's funding interests. The application process and links to the online grant summary form and grant report forms are also available on the site, as is contact information.

Agnes M. Lindsay Trust (NH) (http://www.lindsaytrust.org/)
Located in Manchester, New Hampshire, the Agnes M. Lindsay Trust was founded when its namesake died in 1937. The mission of the trust is to provide grants in the areas of educating poor and deserving students from rural communities and child welfare. Grants are restricted to New Hampshire, Massachusetts, Maine, and Vermont. The trust's Web site provides contact information and guidelines and deadlines for grant applications.

Franklin Lindsay Student Aid Fund (TX) (http://www.franklinlindsay.org)
The Franklin Lindsay Student Aid Fund was provided for in the will of Franklin Lindsay, who died on May 3, 1954. He believed that "the greatest good that could be done for the country and the world was to educate its people." Accordingly, he arranged for his $2 million estate to be held and managed in a trust which would provide loans for students to further their education. Located in Austin, Texas, the fund makes loans to "worthy and deserving" students of either sex who wish to pursue an education at an institute of higher learning in the state of Texas. Loans are made per academic year and are non-interest bearing for up to four months after graduation, provided they comply with certain terms and conditions. Consult the Web site to learn more about the fund's program, terms, conditions, and application procedures, and for contact information. The site also features online application and feedback forms.

Albert A. List Foundation, Inc. (NY) (http://fdncenter.org/grantmaker/listfdn/index.html)
The New York City-based Albert A. List Foundation achieves its mission of supporting and enhancing citizen participation within our pluralistic society through grantmaking in three major program areas: democracy and citizen participation, freedom of expression, and new problems/new solutions. The foundation currently funds organizations that foster citizen participation in the democratic process and share its commitment to a society free of

ageism, classism, homophobia, racism, religious prejudice, sexism, and discrimination against those who are physically or mentally challenged; community involvement; economic justice; involving youth in the process of social change; alliances that go beyond traditional, short-term coalition building around a specific action; progressive, proactive policies that speak to the needs of broad sectors of society; and solutions to ongoing and emerging problems that enable us to live more harmoniously with our natural environment and with each other. The foundation does not accept any unsolicited proposals. The Web site provides descriptions of the foundation's three main programs, eligibility requirements, application procedures, and contact information.

John M. Lloyd Foundation (CA) (http://www.johnmlloyd.org)
John M. Lloyd was committed to seeking the root causes of problems, not just treating their symptoms. The John M. Lloyd Foundation, created at the time of its namesakes's death from AIDS-related complications in 1991, strives to fund programs related to the prevention, care, and public awareness of AIDS. Based in Santa Monica, California, the foundation supports two areas in the overall fight against HIV and AIDS: public policy and prevention and education/awareness. Previous grants in each category are listed on the foundation's Web site, along with grant guidelines, an outline of the application process, and contact information.

The John Locke Foundation (NC) (Operating foundation) (http://www.johnlocke.org)
The John Locke Foundation is a non-partisan public policy institute that opened its doors in 1990. Based in Raleigh, North Carolina, the foundation's purpose is to "conduct research, disseminate information, and advance public understanding of society based on the principles of individual liberty, the voluntary exchange of a free market economy, and limited government." The foundation also seeks to "foster a climate of innovative thinking and debate on issues facing North Carolinians." It operates a number of programs and services to provide information and observations to legislators, policymakers, business executives, citizen activists, civic and community leaders, and the news media. Among its activities are producing newsletters, journals, and policy research reports; holding public policy events; delivering speeches; and responding to requests for information. Visit the Web site to find information about the foundation services, a history of the foundation and biography of its namesake, and a description of its goals, purposes, and positions on issues.

Longview Foundation for Education in World Affairs and International Understanding, Inc. (MD) (http://fdncenter.org/grantmaker/longview/)
Founded in 1966, the Longview Foundation for Education in World Affairs and International Understanding, Inc. helps elementary and secondary students, teachers, and teacher educators in the United States develop the knowledge, attitudes, values, and skills for responsible citizenship in a complex, interdependent world. Visit the foundation's Web site for information on funding priorities, eligibility criteria, grants listings, and contact information.

Edward Lowe Foundation (MI) (Operating foundation) (http://edwardlowe.org)
The Edward Lowe Foundation, established by its namesake in 1985, champions the entrepreneurial spirit by encouraging second-stage business owners to get "PeerSpectives" on their businesses. To that end, the foundation encourages business owners to get involved with entrepreneurial peer-networking organizations and to think about their businesses in new and creative ways. In addition to its mission statement and a listing of officers and directors, the foundation's Web site offers a history of the foundation's grants, detailed program information, and a number of electronic information services related to its mission.

George Lucas Educational Foundation (CA) (http://glef.org/)
The George Lucas Educational Foundation uses various media, including its Web site, to promote and share the latest strategies, especially those that integrate technology with teaching or learning to change the K-12 educational system. Those strategies are based on the filmmaker's belief that "education is the most important investment we can make to

secure the future of our democracy." Visitors to the site can access the foundation's newsletter and "Learn & Live," the foundation's educational resource guide. Although the foundation is a private operating entity and does not make grants, its Web site visitors are encouraged to alert the foundation of any programs or resources that can advance the foundation's mission.

Henry Luce Foundation, Inc. (NY) (http://www.hluce.org/)
Established in 1936 by the late Henry R. Luce, co-founder of Time Inc., the New York City-based Henry Luce Foundation, Inc. today focuses its activities on the interdisciplinary exploration of higher education, increased understanding between Asia and the United States, the study of religion and theology, scholarship in American art, opportunities for women in science and engineering, and contributions to youth and public policy programs. Higher education has been a persistent theme for most of the foundation's programs, with an emphasis on innovation and scholarship. The foundation's Web site provides detailed information about a range of programs, including the Luce Fund in American Art, the American Collections Enhancement Initiative, the Clare Booth Luce Program, the Henry R. Luce Professorships, the Luce Scholars Program, the United States-China Cooperative Research Program, and the Asia Project; general application guidelines and guidelines for specific programs and grant restrictions; recent grants list organized by program area; a helpful FAQ section; listings of the foundation's board and staff; and contact information.

The Ludwick Family Foundation (CA) (http://www.ludwick.org/)
Founded in 1990, the Ludwick Family Foundation "seeks opportunities to encourage new and expanded projects and programs by providing grants to non-profit organizations for new equipment, equipment replacement and modernization, improvements to facilities, and educational materials." The foundation, which is located in Glendora, California, does not seek to provide continuing long-term support. Grants are limited to U.S. organizations or international organizations based in the United States. To apply for a grant, an organization must first provide a letter of inquiry and complete an information form, which is available online. Full proposals are only by invitation. Deadlines, contact information, and financial information are all available on the site.

Christopher Ludwick Foundation (http://www.ludwick.org/)
The Christopher Ludwick Foundation was founded by Christopher Ludwick (1720-1801), a Baker General of the Army of the United States during the American Revolution. His bequest of $13,000 was to be put in a trust for "the schooling and gratis, of poor children of all denominations, in the city and liberties of Philadelphia, without exception to the country, extraction, or religious principles of their parents and friends." The origins of the foundation can be traced back to the founding of the Philadelphia Society for Free Instruction of Indigent Boys in 1799, which over the course of two centuries bore different names until it became the Christopher Ludwick Foundation in 1995. The trust has grown to over $5 million over the intervening two hundred years, and approximately $250,000 in grants are awarded each year, with secondary school children a current funding priority. Programs must target children who reside in Philadelphia in order to receive funding. Visit the foundation's Web site for application information, further information on the foundation, listings of trustees, and grants list.

Lumina Foundation for Education (IN) (http://www.luminafoundation.org/)
The Lumina Foundation for Education of Indianapolis, Indiana, seeks to expand education beyond high school as a means of helping people achieve their potential. The foundation is based on the belief that "postsecondary education remains one of the most beneficial investments that individuals can make in themselves and that society can make in its people." The foundation focuses on three areas in its grantmaking: financial access, retention and attainment, and nontraditional learners and learning. Visitors to the foundation's Web site will find information on what is and is not funded, a FAQs section, a listing of recent grantees, application procedures, and contact information.

Lumpkin Foundation (IL) (http://www.lumpkinfoundation.org)
Established in 1953, the mission of the Illinois-based Lumpkin Foundation is "to provide leadership, individually and collectively, both locally and globally, to enrich [family members'] respective communities and in so doing preserve the tradition and goals of the [Lumpkin] family." The foundation is dedicated to supporting education, preserving and protecting the environment, and fostering opportunities for leadership, and it gives special consideration to its heritage in east central Illinois. In addition to a mission statement and officer and committee listings, the foundation's Web site provides grant application procedures and restrictions, a letter of conditions (for grant recipients), downloadable versions of its grant application cover sheet and post-evaluation grant report, and contact information.

The Louis R. Lurie Foundation (CA) (http://fdncenter.org/grantmaker/lurie/)
The mission of the San Francisco-based, Louis R. Lurie Foundation is to be an active instrument to improve the lives of youth and their families. In fulfilling its mission, the foundation intends to heighten skills that develop self-reliance, compassion, self-esteem, respect for diversity, and a strong desire to give back to others in the community. The foundation's funding priorities emphasize youth, focusing on family support, education, health, cultural enrichment, and recreation. The foundation accepts proposals by invitation only. Visitors to the foundation's Web site will find detailed information on funding priorities, restrictions, and contact information.

Lyndhurst Foundation (TN) (http://www.lyndhurstfoundation.org)
The Chattanooga, Tennessee-based, Lyndhurst Foundation, was founded in 1938 by Thomas Cartter Lupton, a pioneer in the Coca-Cola bottling business. The foundation has gone through many transformations. Initially the foundation focused on broad local and regional activities; however, upon Mr. Lupton's death, the priorities changed to concentrate on giving to more specific areas, including parks, inner-city neighborhoods, childhood development, education, and youth development. The foundation's priorities inside Chattanooga include: the development of Tennessee's state parks and natural environment, revitalization of inner-city neighborhoods, arts and culture, elementary and secondary public school education, housing, and urban issues. Outside of Chattanooga, the foundation holds an interest in the preservation of the South Appalachian Mountains, supporting Tennessee charter schools, and other interests of the trustees. The foundation's Web site includes board/staff list, a three-year financial history, and contact information.

Lynn Charitable Foundation, Nancy L. (CA) (http://www.nllcf.org/)
The Nancy L. Lynn Charitable Foundation was established to assist organizations in southern California. The foundation focuses on: organizations dedicated to helping children with life threatening illnesses through direct services, child abuse organizations providing direct services and prevention education, and missing children's organizations providing assistance through direct services and prevention education. Specific grant guidelines, applications, and instructions are available for download. Additionally, the site maintains a list of previous grants awarded, a list of resources, and links.

John D. and Catherine T. MacArthur Foundation (IL) (http://www.macfdn.org/)
Founded in 1978, the Chicago-based John D. and Catherine T. MacArthur Foundation is dedicated to helping groups and individuals foster lasting improvement in the human condition. The foundation seeks the development of healthy individuals and effective communities, peace within and among nations, responsible choices about human reproduction, and a global ecosystem capable of supporting healthy human societies. Among the many grantmaking initiatives set by the foundation are: human and community development; global security and sustainability; the MacArthur Fellowship Program; the General Program; and program-related investments that support its goals. Visitors to the foundation's Web site will find brief biographies of John D. and Catherine T. MacArthur, detailed program descriptions and application guidelines, financial statements, links to philanthropy resources, contact information, and a variety of other materials.

The MacDonnell Foundation (CA)
(http://www.pacificfoundationservices.com/macdonnell/index.html)
The MacDonnell Foundation was founded in 1989 in San Francisco, California, to support disadvantaged youth and families in the communities surrounding San Francisco. The foundation's primary interest centers on rewarding talent and achievement of low-income, disadvantaged youth in areas of education, recreation, and/or social activities. The foundation is also interested in literacy and learning disabilities, as well as programs that enhance children's self-esteem and self-awareness. The foundation will also support recreation and athletic programs, specifically for inner-city youth. Capital campaigns may also be considered by the foundation on a limited basis. The foundation's Web site features most recent grants list, contact information, a board of directors list, and application procedures.

The Maclellan Foundation, Inc. (TN) (http://www.maclellanfdn.org)
Dora Maclellan Brown, Robert J. Maclellan, and Robert L. Maclellan established the Maclellan Foundation, Inc., in Chattanooga, Tennessee, in 1945. The purpose of the foundation is "to contribute to and otherwise serve strategic national and international organizations committed to furthering the Kingdom of Christ; to contribute to and otherwise serve select local organizations which foster the spiritual welfare of the community; and to serve by providing financial and leadership resources to extend the Kingdom of God in accordance with the Great Commission." The foundation prefers to make project or seed grants, not operating grants. Visit the Web site for application instructions; information about the foundation's philosophy, policies, and guidelines; the grantmaking process, from board meetings to a site meeting checklist used by the foundation; grantee responsibilities; and contact information. The site also features a letter from one of the foundation's founders on the ideals the foundation was established upon, a grantmaking manual prepared by the foundation, a public discussion forum, and multimedia clips.

Josiah Macy, Jr., Foundation (NY) (http://www.josiahmacyfoundation.org/)
Established by Kate Macy Ladd in memory of her father in 1930, the Josiah Macy, Jr., Foundation has been committed to "improving the education of health professionals in the interest of the health of the public, and to enhancing the representation of minorities in the health profession," since the 1960s. To this end, the foundation funds numerous programs and research initiatives in the medical profession, as well as the yearly Macy Conference. Current and ongoing programs are detailed on the foundation's Web site, along with contact information, grant guidelines, and the foundation's recent publications and studies.

Maddie's Fund (CA) (http://www.maddies.org/)
Established in 1994 by David and Cheryl Duffield to honor the memory of their beloved miniature schnauzer, Maddie's Fund (formerly known as the Duffield Family Foundation) hopes "to revolutionize the status and well being of companion animals," by helping to build, community by community, a "no-kill movement," in which healthy, adoptable dogs and cats in animal shelters across the country are guaranteed loving homes. The fund is particularly interested in supporting animal welfare organizations capable of building alliances and developing collaborative pet-related projects within their communities. Successful projects will set forth comprehensive life-saving strategies that involve the participation of cooperating animal shelters, rescue groups, volunteer foster organizations, local animal control agencies, veterinarians, and others. In addition to the fund's philosophy and goals, the Maddie's Fund Web site provides detailed grant proposal guidelines and requirements, a hypothetical funding scenario, a downloadable application form, a letter from the fund's president, and contact information.

A.L. Mailman Family Foundation, Inc. (NY) (http://www.mailman.org)
Headquartered in White Plains, New York, the A.L. Mailman Family Foundation, Inc. focuses its grantmaking activities on children and families, with a special emphasis on early childhood. The foundation's current program is focused in the following areas: early care and education, family support, and moral education and social responsibility. Foundation grants generally are not awarded for ongoing direct services, general operating

expenses, individuals, capital expenditures, endowment campaigns, or for local services or programs. Visitors to the foundation's Web site will find general information and recent grant summary lists for each program area; grant application guidelines; a listing of directors, officers and staff; and contact information.

Manitou Foundation, Inc. (CO) (http://www.manitou.org/MF/mf_index.html)
Founded in 1988, the Manitou Foundation offers land grants in the Crestone/Baca area of Colorado to qualified U.S. nonprofit organizations in the following categories: religious organizations and spiritual projects, ecological and environmental sustainability projects, and related educational endeavors (youth and adult). The foundation also administers a land preservation program and seeks to network with individuals and organizations locally, nationally, and internationally to facilitate its mission objectives. The foundation's Web site includes guidelines, application procedures, and contact information.

John and Mary R. Markle Foundation (NY) (http://www.markle.org/)
The John and Mary R. Markle Foundation was established in 1927 "to promote the advancement and diffusion of knowledge and the general good of mankind." Today the foundation focuses its activities on the ways that emerging communications media and information technology create unprecedented opportunity to improve people's lives. Most of the foundation's current work is through the following programs: the Opportunity Fund, Policy for a Networked Society, Interactive Media for Children, and Information Technologies for Better Health. Visitors to the foundation's Web site will find information about the foundation's communications and technology, information on current programs, grant guidelines, the history of the foundation, board and staff listings, news, and contact information.

MARPAT Foundation (MD) (http://fdncenter.org/grantmaker/marpat/)
The Silver Spring, Maryland-based MARPAT Foundation provides support for organizations benefiting the greater Washington, D.C. metropolitan area. Projects related to education, healthcare, cultural affairs, and science constitute the foundation's funding priority. The foundation does not support endowment funds, individuals, medical research projects, or organizations based outside the United States. Visitors to the foundation's Web site will find an alphabetical listing of past grants, current grant guidelines and deadlines, a downloadable grant summary sheet, and contact information.

Carlos and Marguerite Mason Trust (GA)
(http://www.wachovia.com/charitable_services/masontrust_overview.asp)
The Carlos and Marguerite Mason Trust was established in 1991 with the purpose of "improving the process of organ transplantation for Georgians through the making of grants to Georgia 501(c)(3) organizations associated with the transplantation process." The foundation awards grants to qualified organizations and institutions. The Web site includes grant guidelines, downloadable grant application, a list of recent grants awarded, listings of committee members, and contact information.

Harriet McDaniel Marshall Trust (GA) (http://www.marshalltrust.org)
The Harriet McDaniel Marshall Trust was established in 1962 to honor Harriet McDaniel Marshall's father, Sanders McDaniel, Atlanta attorney and son of a former governor of Georgia. The trust benefits nonprofit organizations in the metropolitan Atlanta community. Brief grant guidelines and limitations are provided online, along with a link to the downloadable grant application form. The trust's funds and grants are administered by the SunTrust Bank Atlanta Foundation, and contact information can be found online.

Charlotte Martin Foundation (WA) (http://www.charlottemartin.org/)
The Charlotte Martin Foundation, located in Seattle, Washington, is dedicated to enriching the lives of youth in the areas of athletics, culture, and education and also to preserving and protecting wildlife and habitat. The foundation was established in 1987 and is committed to awarding grants, primarily in the Pacific Northwest Region. The foundation's Web site

provides detailed information about each program area. The site also explains how to apply for grants and includes the foundation's annual report, a list of previous grantees, and contact information can also be found on the site.

The Katharine Matthies Foundation (CT) (http://www.electronicvalley.org/matthies/)
Established in 1987, the Katharine Matthies Foundation supports programs in education, social service, sports recreation, healthcare, culture, prevention of cruelty to children and animals, and other programs that benefit local residents and improve the quality of life in Seymour, Ansonia, Derby, Oxford, Shelton, and Beacon Falls, Connecticut. The foundation is the legacy of Katharine Matthies, a lifelong Seymour resident whose family members were leading industrialists. Visitors to the site will find application guidelines and submission requirements, a list of grants, a short biography of the foundation's founder, and contact information.

Edmund F. Maxwell Foundation (WA) (http://www.maxwell.org)
The Edmund F. Maxwell Foundation, located in Seattle, Washington, "believing in the importance of acknowledging the fine accomplishments of high-achieving young people," offers the Edmund F. Maxwell Foundation Scholarships to residents of western Washington who require financial assistance to attend independent colleges or universities. The foundation's namesake, Edmund Maxwell, was the head of Blyth & Co., a premier investment firm in the region. Students who are residents of western Washington with a combined S.A.T. score over 1200 and a demonstrated financial need, and who meet other criteria, are eligible for the scholarship. Consult the foundation's Web site for application guidelines, printable forms, a recipients list, and contact information.

The Faye McBeath Foundation (WI) (http://www.fayemcbeath.org)
The Faye McBeath Foundation of Wisconsin was established in 1964 to support the community in which Ms. Mcbeath was born and raised. The foundation's major areas of interest include children, the elderly, healthcare, health education, and civic/governmental affairs organizations in the metro Milwaukee area. Visitors to the foundation's Web site will find information on the foundation's program priorities, information on special programs, application information, a history of grantees, and contact information.

McCarthy Family Foundation (CA) (http://fdncenter.org/grantmaker/mccarthy/)
Established in 1988, the San Diego-based McCarthy Family Foundation makes grants in four primary program areas: K-12 science education, HIV/AIDS, assistance to homeless people, and child abuse prevention. The foundation makes grants exclusively within San Diego County. The foundation does not make grants for individuals, scholarship funds, sectarian religious activities, general fundraising drives, or programs supporting political candidates or that influence legislation. The foundation's Web site provides visitors with program guidelines, application instructions, and a recent grants list.

The Edna McConnell Clark Foundation (NY) (http://www.emcf.org/)
The Edna McConnell Clark Foundation seeks to improve conditions and opportunities for people who live in poor and disadvantaged communities. Through its grantmaking, the foundation "assists nonprofit organizations and public agencies committed to advancing practices and policies that better the lives of children and families, [while supporting] initiatives that promise to help systems and institutions become more responsive to the needs of the people they serve." The current interests of the foundation fall into three separate program areas, each with specific goals, strategies, and grantmaking priorities: the Program for Children, the Program for New York Neighborhoods, and the Program for Student Achievement. Applicants may want to read the foundation's latest annual report to ensure that their projects fit within the above programs' very specific, site-based grantmaking strategies. Visitors to the foundation's Web site will find detailed program descriptions, application guidelines, a recent grants list organized by program area, a report from the foundation president, a list of foundation-sponsored publications, board and staff listings, and contact information.

Robert R. McCormick Tribune Foundation (IL) (http://www.rrmtf.org)

The Robert R. McCormick Tribune Foundation was established as a charitable trust in 1955 upon the death of Colonel Robert R. McCormick, longtime editor and publisher of the *Chicago Tribune,* and was restructured as a foundation in 1991, with an emphasis on four grantmaking areas: communities, journalism, education, and citizenship. Because each program has its own guidelines, geographic restrictions, and application procedures, grantseekers are encouraged to read carefully all information pertaining to their particular program of interest. In addition to the four program areas, the foundation also provides annual support to Cantigny, the Colonel's former estate in Wheaton, Illinois, which is now operated as a park for the "education, instruction, and welfare of the people of Illinois." The foundation's Web site provides program descriptions, grant summaries, and grant guidelines.

McCune Charitable Foundation (NM) (http://www.nmmccune.org/)

Perrine D. McCune founded the McCune Charitable Foundation in Sante Fe, New Mexico, in 1989 to continue the philanthropic legacy that she and her husband, Marshall Lockhart McCune, had established during their lifetimes. The couple was a significant part of the cultural and artistic life in the Sante Fe area, and they helped establish many organizations and institutions there. The mission of the McCune Charitable Foundation is "to memorialize the donors through grants which enrich the cultural life, health, education, environment, and spiritual life of the citizens of New Mexico." Funding is targeted for community-based, community-driven projects, with preference given to organizations that operate programs in Sante Fe or northern New Mexico. Visitors to the Web site will find grant application guidelines, staff listings, short descriptions of sample funded projects, and contact information.

James S. McDonnell Foundation (MO) (http://www.jsmf.org/)

The James S. McDonnell Foundation was established in 1950 by aerospace pioneer James S. McDonnell, "to explore methods for developing a stable world order and lasting peace." Today the foundation awards $11 million in grants annually, primarily in the areas of biomedical and behavioral sciences and research and innovation in education. The three programs the foundation currently supports are Bridging Brain, Mind, and Behavior; Studying Complex Systems; and Brain Cancer Research. The foundation's Web site provides program information, application guidelines, a listing of past grants, current financial reports, staff and board information, and contact information.

D.V. and Ida J. McEachern Charitable Trust (WA) (http://fdncenter.org/grantmaker/mceachern/)

The D.V. and Ida J. McEachern Charitable Trust was established in 1969 to help give a better start in life to all children, both educationally and physically. The trust supports social service agencies that allow children and youth to attain their basic needs. Artistic and cultural programs are also of interest to the trust. Visitors to the trust's Web site will find application guidelines, grant ranges, sample grants, restrictions, application deadlines, and contact information.

R.J. McElroy Trust (IA) (http://www.cedarnet.org/mcelroy)

R.J. McElroy was a pioneer Iowa broadcaster who founded the Black Hawk Broadcasting Company, KWWL, KWWL TV, and several other radio and television stations. When he died in 1965, a provision in his will provided for the establishment of a trust fund for the educational benefit of deserving young people. Located in Waterloo, Iowa, the R.J. McElroy Trust has since then funded a broad range of educational programs, such as scholarships, fellowships, internships, student loan funds, and other projects to benefit youth of all ages. Organizations located in the KWWL viewing area are preferred, and organizations located in Black Hawk County and the rural counties in that viewing area will receive higher priority. The trust will also give higher priority to grants that fund programs rather than capital projects. Consult the trust's Web site for grant application guidelines, policies, and contact information.

William G. McGowan Charitable Fund (DC) (http://www.mcgowanfund.org/)
The William G. McGowan Charitable Fund was established in 1992 in Washington, D.C., to further the vision of its founder, Bill McGowan. In 1968, McGowan organized the MCI Communications Corporation, effectively ending the telecommunications monopoly in the United States. The fund makes grants in the areas of healthcare and medical scientific research, the creation of educational opportunities, and the development of the gifts and talents of youth. Funding is limited to organizations in the following geographic areas: northeastern Pennsylvania, the Chicago metropolitan area, western New York, central and northern California, the Dallas/Houston/San Antonio region, Washington, D.C., northern Virginia, and the Kansas City metropolitan area. Details on the grantmaking process, guidelines, and a downloadable application are provided on the fund's Web site. More information on the fund and the vision and work of its founder is also available online.

McGregor Fund (MI) (http://www.mcgregorfund.org/)
Founded in 1925 by Michigan philanthropists Tracy and Katherine Whitney McGregor, the McGregor Fund was established to "relieve the misfortunes and promote the well being of mankind." The fund presently awards grants in the areas of human services, education, healthcare, arts and culture, and public benefit. Only organizations located in the metropolitan Detroit area, or projects that significantly benefit that area, are eligible for support. The fund does not award grants for individuals or student scholarships and generally does not support travel, conferences, seminars or workshops, film or video projects, or disease-specific organizations. Visitors to the fund's Web site will find brief descriptions of each program area, application procedures and guidelines, a grants list archive organized by program area, complete financial statements, a listing of fund trustees and staff, and contact information.

Robert E. and Evelyn McKee Foundation (TX) (http://www.mckeefoundation.org)
The Robert E. and Evelyn McKee Foundation was founded in 1952 in Texas. Robert E. McKee founded one of the nation's largest general contracting firms. He and his wife Evelyn, were noted local philanthropist. The foundation makes grants in the categories of civics, culture, and religion; education and scholarships; hospitals; medicine and medical research; welfare, rehabilitation, and mental health; the United Way; and youth activities. Scholarships are made to select local high school and universities that distribute the funds to individual students. Grants are mainly limited to local nonprofit organizations or national organizations with local affiliates. Grants in the area of religion are directed toward local Episcopal churches. The foundation's Web site provides a history of its founders, succinct grant guidelines, and contact information.

The McKnight Endowment Fund for Neuroscience (MN)
(http://www.mcknight.org/neuroscience)
The McKnight Endowment Fund for Neuroscience is an independent organization established in 1986 and funded by the McKnight Foundation to oversee its neuroscience research awards program, which dates back to 1977. The fund has its own board of directors but is administered by the McKnight Foundation. This research program is a direct legacy of founder William L. McKnight, who was interested in the biology of the brain, particularly diseases affecting memory. The board of directors makes funding decisions on the basis of recommendations by review committees. Visitors to the fund's Web site will find downloadable application forms and guidelines, list of awardees, announcements, a search engine for the site, and contact information.

The McKnight Foundation (MN) (http://www.mcknight.org)
The McKnight Foundation was established and endowed by William L. McKnight, one-time president and CEO of 3M, and Maude L. McKnight in 1953. The McKnight Foundation seeks to improve the quality of life for present and future generations by "supporting efforts to improve outcomes for children, families, and communities; contributing to the arts; encouraging preservation of the natural environment; and promoting scientific research in selected fields." The foundation has the following funding areas: children,

families, and communities; arts; the environment; international initiatives; and research and applied science. Located in Minneapolis, Minnesota, its primary geographic focus in its human services and arts grantmaking is the state of Minnesota. Consult the foundation's Web site for more information on grant and award programs for each funding area; downloadable guidelines; conditions and limitations; grants lists; financial information; online publications request; an annual report; and an online contact form.

The McLean Contributionship (PA) (http://fdncenter.org/grantmaker/mclean/)
The McLean Contributionship of Pennsylvania was originally established in 1951 as the Bulletin Contributionship for charitable, educational, and scientific purposes. Today, the contributionship interests include the environment, and encourages the ill and aging, and education, or medical, scientific, or on occasion, cultural developments enhancing the quality of life. Visitors to the organization's Web site will find detailed information on funding priorities, restrictions, application information, a copy of the most recent tax return and contact information.

Meadows Foundation, Inc. (TX) (http://www.mfi.org/)
The Meadows Foundation, Inc. was established in 1948 by Algur H. and Virginia Meadows to benefit the people of Texas by "working toward the elimination of ignorance, hopelessness and suffering, protecting the environment, providing cultural enrichment, encouraging excellence, and promoting understanding and cooperation among people." The foundation provides grants in the areas of art and culture, civic and public affairs, education, health, and human services. In addition to examples of grants awarded in each area of giving, visitors to the foundation's Web site can access grant guidelines (in Spanish and English); the foundation's financial information; a listing of officers, directors, and staff; and links to local and national nonprofit organizations. The site also describes the foundation's Wilson Historic District housing restoration project as well as its Awards for Charitable School project, which supports youth voluntarism.

Medina Foundation (WA) (http://www.medinafoundation.org/)
The Medina Foundation seeks to "aid in improving the human condition in the greater Puget Sound community by fostering positive change, growth and the improvement of people." The foundation makes grants to qualified charitable organizations, particularly those offering direct service delivery. No grants are made to individuals. The foundation supports four program areas: human services, education, persons with disabilities, and alcohol and drug abuse. The foundation's Web site includes program and financial guidelines, funding parameters and geographical restrictions, application procedures, FAQs, and contact information.

Mega Foundation (CT) (http://www.megafoundation.org)
The Mega Foundation, located in Norwalk, Connecticut, works toward the development and community of severely gifted people and their ideas. "Severely gifted" is defined as someone with an IQ of 164 or above, and the foundation posts some information about identifying these individuals. In order to keep severely gifted people from falling through the cracks of an educational system that may not nurture their "rage to learn," the Mega Foundation maintains a variety of programs and grants to encourage work by and about people who are severely gifted. The foundation has three program areas: giftedness development, science, and visual, literary, and performing arts. Additionally, the foundation runs Ultranet, a Web and mentoring community program for the severely gifted. The foundation's Web site includes a form for more information and links to more resources.

Mellam Family Foundation (NY) (http://www.mellam.org/)
The Mellam Family Foundation was established in 1987 to support medical and scientific research, education, the environment, and social services. The majority of the foundation's grant recipients are located in the San Francisco Bay Area, the New York metropolitan area, and Hawaii. The foundation does not accept unsolicited grant requests. Visitors to the

foundation's Web site will find grant guidelines, recent grants listings, recent financials, and contact information.

Edward Arthur Mellinger Educational Foundation (IL) (http://www.mellinger.org/)
Established in 1959, the Edward Arthur Mellinger Educational Foundation of Monmouth, Illinois, is committed to the support of education. The foundation devotes a major portion of its resources to providing scholarship and loan assistance to young men and women from western Illinois and eastern Iowa who attend colleges and universities throughout the nation. In addition, the foundation offers support to a variety of educational organizations and programs in its local area. Visit the foundation's Web site to find a brief history of the organization, a detailed FAQ section, grant application information, and contact information.

Andrew W. Mellon Foundation (NY) (http://www.mellon.org)
Under its broad charter, the New York City-based Andrew W. Mellon Foundation currently makes grants on a selective basis in the following areas of interest: higher education, cultural affairs and the performing arts, population, conservation and the environment, and cost-effective uses of technology in teaching. Although the foundation reviews proposals on a rolling basis, "prospective applicants are encouraged to explore their ideas informally with foundation staff (preferably in writing) before submitting formal proposals." The foundation does not make grants to individuals or to locally-based organizations. In addition to a range of general information, visitors to the foundation's Web site will find program descriptions, a list of foundation trustees and staff, and online reports from 1987 to present.

Richard King Mellon Foundation (PA) (http://fdncenter.org/grantmaker/rkmellon/)
Founded in 1947 by the financial giant, the Richard King Mellon Foundation is committed to improving the quality of life in Pittsburgh, Pennsylvania and to national land and wildlife conservation. Grants have been given in the following program categories: civic affairs, conservation, cultural activities, medicine, education, and human services. The organization considers support for operations, capital projects, programs, and start-up costs, but it prefers not to be the only donor. Most funding is distributed in southwestern Pennsylvania, except for the sponsored national land conservation program. The site has grant procedures, guidelines, and a downloadable application. There is a grants history and lists of the staff and board members. The foundation also accepts the Grantmakers of Western Pennsylvania's Common Grant Application Form.

Merck Family Fund (MA) (http://www.merckff.org/)
Established in 1954, the Merck Family Fund is a private family foundation with two goals: to restore and protect the natural environment, and to strengthen the social fabric and the physical landscape of the urban community. There are two areas of priority to help achieve a healthy planet: protecting of vital ecosystems in the eastern United States and supporting the shift towards environmentally sustainable economic systems, incentives, and behaviors. There are two areas of priority for strengthening the urban community: creating green and open space and supporting youth as agents of social change. The Milton, Massachusetts-based fund limits grants to grassroots programs in New York City; Providence, Rhode Island; and Boston, Massachusetts. Visit the fund's Web site for more information on funding areas and priorities, grant application guidelines, financial information, a grant lists with links to grantee organizations, related links, and contact information. The fund urges grantseekers to use the common proposal form (for invited proposals only) and provides a link to a site where it can be downloaded.

The Merck Genome Research Institute (PA) (Operating foundation) (http://www.mgri.org)
The Merck Genome Research Institute, located in West Point, Pennsylvania, is dedicated to "improving techniques to the linkage of human genetic traits and resolving biological function of disease genes." The organization gives special interest to the "development of

methods which tend to accelerate predictions of gene function independent of linkage." Associated with Merck & Co., the organization provides funding for two types of grants: research proposals (one to two years duration) and pilot proposals for high-risk projects (one year duration). The organization's Web site provides eligibility requirements, a description of the selection process, application guidelines, and terms of the grants. Contact information and more details about the Institute are also available at the site.

Mertz Gilmore Foundation (NY) (http://www.mertzgilmore.org)
The Mertz Gilmore Foundation makes grants to nonprofit organizations active in the areas of the environment, human rights, peace and security, and New York City civic and cultural life. The foundation currently sponsors seven grantmaking programs: international human rights; immigrant rights in the United States; lesbian and gay rights in the United States; Israel and Palestine; dance in New York City; New York City human and built environment; and energy. The foundation does not typically make grants for endowments or annual fund appeals; capital projects; political activities such as lobbying; conferences or workshops; sectarian religious concerns; individual scholarships, research, fellowships, loans, or travel; film or media projects; or publications. Visitors to the foundation's Web site will find program guidelines and restrictions, a listing of selected grants by program area, recent financial statements, application instructions, and a listing of the foundation's staff and board of directors.

Meru Foundation (MA) (Operating foundation) (http://www.meru.org)
The Meru Foundation is a private nonprofit research and educational corporation founded in 1983 to "study ancient alphabets and texts from a modern mathematical perspective, with emphasis on their self-organizing whole systems." Its work is based on 20 years of research by Stan Tenen into the origin and nature of the Hebrew alphabet and the mathematical structure underlying the sequence of letters of the Hebrew text of Genesis. Visit the Web site for articles and papers describing Mr. Tenen's work.

MetroWest Community Health Care Foundation Inc. (MA) (http://www.mchcf.org)
Established in 1999, the MetroWest Community Health Care Foundation Inc. provides annual financial support to meet the unmet health needs of the twenty-five communities in the MetroWest area of Massachusetts. Visit the foundation's Web site to view counties that qualify for support, recent grants listings, a staff list, and contact information.

Eugene and Agnes E. Meyer Foundation (DC) (http://www.meyerfdn.org/)
Founded in Washington, D.C., in 1944, the Eugene and Agnes E. Meyer Foundation invests in nonprofit entrepreneurs and community-based organizations that meet emerging social needs and strengthen the region's communities. The foundation is interested in a variety of programs, including arts and humanities, community service, education, health and mental health, law and justice, neighborhood development, and housing. The foundation also strongly supports the metropolitan Washington, D.C., area through the Management Assistance Program, cash flow loans, the Technology Circuit Rider Program, and sector capacity-building. The foundation's Web site includes a searchable database of grant recipients, with extended profiles of each organization; a set of links and resources; staff/board listings; grant guidelines and applications; and contact information.

Meyer Memorial Trust (OR) (http://www.mmt.org/)
Founded by retail-store magnate Fred G. Meyer, the Portland-based Meyer Memorial Trust operates three grantmaking programs—general purpose grants, small grants, and support for teacher initiatives—to benefit qualified tax-exempt applicants in Oregon and Clark County, Washington. The trust does not provide grants, loans, or scholarships to individuals, nor does it provide assistance to for-profit businesses. Visitors to the trust's Web site will find application guidelines, restrictions, and downloadable cover sheets; grants lists organized by subject area; a listing of trustees and staff; a brief biography of trust founder Fred Meyer; and a short list of links to other online resources.

Allen H. and Nydia Meyers Foundation (MI) (http://www.meyersfoundation.org/)
The Allen H. and Nydia Meyers Foundation, located in Adrian, Michigan, was founded in 1966 by the Meyers family to encourage, support, and stimulate scientific education, teaching, research, and related efforts such in engineering and aerospace study and design. The goal of the foundation is to provide early financial support for young men and women interested in post-secondary education for aeronautics or scientific careers. The foundation generally grants awards to Lenawee County, Michigan School District high school graduates planning college studies in the sciences and allied fields. The foundation also makes grants to institutions of learning and research that are engaging in projects that will generally help fulfill the goals of the foundation. A downloadable application and detailed history of the foundation are posted on the Web site.

The Michelson Foundation (CA) (http://www.pacificfoundationservices.com/michelson/)
Founded in California in 1991, the Michelson Foundation is committed to provide disadvantaged individuals and families with support through education, human services, healthcare, and teen pregnancy prevention in San Mateo County. Other areas of interest include support for psychiatric disabilities and organizations that support the arts for youth. The foundation will also consider requests involving capital improvements and equipment acquisitions. The foundation's Web site features a list of the most recent grants, contact information, a board of directors list, and application procedures.

Milbank Memorial Fund (NY) (http://www.milbank.org)
The Milbank Memorial Fund, based in New York City, supports nonpartisan analysis, study, research, and communication on significant issues in health policy. It makes the results of its work available in meetings with decisionmakers, reports, books, and the *Milbank Quarterly,* a peer-reviewed journal of public health and healthcare policy. Access bibliographies, abstracts, and articles on the fund's Web site.

Milken Family Foundation (CA) (http://www.mff.org/)
Established in 1982 by Lowell and Michael Milken, the California-based Milken Family Foundation advances its mission of "helping people help themselves and those around them to lead productive and satisfying lives" by focusing its activities on education and medicine (specifically prostate cancer and epilepsy). The foundation's Web site features information about the foundation's areas of interest and programs, including the American Epilepsy Society/Milken Family Foundation Epilepsy Research Award Grants and Fellowship Program, which recognizes outstanding physicians and scientists working to improve the lives of people with epilepsy; Mike's Math Club, a mentoring program for fifth- and sixth-graders; and the Milken Family National Educator Awards, offering financial recognition to outstanding educators in schools affiliated with the Bureau of Jewish Education of Greater Los Angeles.

The Miller Foundation (MI) (http://www.willard.lib.mi.us/npa/miller)
The Miller Foundation was established in Battle Creek, Michigan, in 1963 by Robert Miller, newspaperman and noted philanthropist. The foundation seeks to improve the Battle Creek community and serve as an example to other philanthropic groups. Through grants and partnerships with other organizations, the foundation focuses on the areas of economic development, neighborhood improvement, improving educational outcomes for youth, and eliminating barriers to employment for all in Battle Creek, Michigan, and the surrounding area. The foundation's Web site features a short biography of founder Robert Miller, a list of past grantees, related links, guidelines for letter that should be sent to the foundation by interested grantseekers. The foundation strictly limits funding to the Battle Creek area.

Minnesota Masonic Foundation, Inc. (MN) (http://mn-mason.org/)
The Minnesota Masonic Foundation, Inc. was created in 1970 to meet the needs of Minnesota Masonry. The St. Paul, Minnesota-based foundation is focused on Minnesota's youth, matching local lodge scholarships up to a pre-set limit that varies from year to year. Local

lodges administer their programs as they wish, and the foundation augments the contributions for the education of young Minnesotans. Visitors to the site will find printable scholarship applications, links to contact information, and application instructions.

The Joan Mitchell Foundation (NY) (http://fdncenter.org/grantmaker/joanmitchellfdn/)
The mission of the New York-based Joan Mitchell Foundation seeks to demonstrate that painting and sculpture are significant cultural necessities. The foundation provides grants, stipends, and scholarships for painters and sculptors and it also seeks out avenues to meet the needs of artists through colloquiums and workshops, classes, and other resource facilities. Each year the foundation's giving program awards twenty grants to outstanding artists who are in need of financial aid. The foundation has established free art classes for artistically inclined young people in grades seven through twelve. Visit the foundation's Web site to learn more about the history of Joan Mitchell and the foundation. Also at the site, visitors will find further information about the scholarship programs, recent grant recipient lists, and contact information.

The Ambrose Monell Foundation (NY) (http://www.monellvetlesen.org/)
The Ambrose Monell Foundation's mission is to "voluntarily aid and contribute to religious, charitable, scientific, literary, and educational uses and purposes, in New York, elsewhere in the United States, and throughout the world." Grants are made to qualified nonprofit organizations; no individual grants are given. The foundation's Web site contains a downloadable copy of its latest tax return, previous annual reports, and lists of recent grants awarded.

Gordon E. and Betty I. Moore Foundation (CA) (http://www.moore.org)
The Gordon E. and Betty I. Moore Foundation was founded in San Francisco in 2000 by the co-founder of the Intel corporation and his wife, and is dedicated "to the improvement of the quality of life through education, science, and conservation." Specific project areas of interest include education, scientific research, the environment, and select San Francisco Bay Area projects. Interested applicants should check the foundation's Web site for grant instructions and forms and contact information.

The Burton D. Morgan Foundation (OH) (http://www.bdmorganfdn.org)
Established in 1967, the mission of the Akron, Ohio-based Burton D. Morgan Foundation is to preserve and encourage America's greatest asset, the free enterprise system. Other areas of interest include economics, education, and mental health. The foundation prefers to make grants to organizations located in northeastern Ohio and does not make grants to social service organizations or programs. It is recommended that grantseekers contact the foundation regarding any proposals before sending a formal grant request letter. Visitors to the site will find a brief history of the foundation, grant application guidelines, and contact information.

Morino Foundation/Institute (VA) (http://www.morino.org)
Founded by business leader and "social entrepreneur" Mario Marino, the Morino Foundation/Institute is dedicated to "opening the doors of opportunity—economic, civic, health, and education—and empowering people to improve their lives and communities in the communications age." Grants are normally made from the Morino Foundation, on behalf of the institute, in support of initiatives or focus areas in which the institute is actively engaged—youth advocacy and services, entrepreneurship, social networking, and community services. In all of its grantmaking activities, the institute, which does not accept unsolicited proposals, emphasizes the emerging medium of electronic communications and how it can be applied to further positive social change and community improvement. The institute's Web site offers information about the institute's core beliefs and funding philosophy, general program and grant information, links to a variety of institute-sponsored projects and partners, and contact information.

The John Motley Morehead Foundation (NC) (http://www.moreheadfoundation.org)
Based in Chapel Hill, North Carolina, the John Motley Morehead Foundation sponsors the Morehead Award, a full four-year scholarship award to attend the University of North Carolina at Chapel Hill. It includes a stipend covering all educational and living expenses during the recipient's four years of undergraduate study, as well as a leadership training program during each of their four undergraduate summers. It is not possible to apply for the award; candidates are nominated by committees at their high schools. All high schools in North Carolina, 73 schools outside of North Carolina, 31 schools in Great Britain, and all high schools and cégeps in Canada are eligible to nominate students. A list of eligible schools is provided on the site. Visitors to the site will also find eligibility criteria, a history of the award, an alumni directory and profiles, and contact information.

Charles Stewart Mott Foundation (MI) (http://www.mott.org/)
Established in 1926, the Flint, Michigan-based Charles Stewart Mott Foundation makes grants in the United States and, on a limited geographic basis, internationally, in four broad program areas: civil society; the environment; philanthropy in Flint, Michigan; and poverty. These programs, in turn, are divided into more specific areas: the civil society program focuses on the United States, South Africa, Central/Eastern Europe, Russia, and the newly created Republics; the environment program is devoted to reform of international lending and trade policies, prevention of toxic pollution, protection of the Great Lakes ecosystem, and special initiatives; the Flint program concentrates on institutional capacity building, arts and recreation, economic and community development, and education; and the poverty program focuses on building communities, strengthening families, improving education, economic opportunity, and cross-cutting initiatives. In addition to detailed application guidelines and a biography of Charles Stewart Mott, the foundation's Web site offers a searchable grants database, dozens of links to grantee Web sites, a list of publications available through the foundation, copies of the latest annual reports, and related stories in each broad program area.

MSMS Foundation (MI)
(http://www.msms.org/msmsto/msmsfoundation/foundation.html)
The MSMS Foundation is sponsored by the Michigan State Medical Society. Its purpose is to "advance the field of health for the public good." Specifically, the foundation works to support and/or initiate education, research programs, and projects in the field of health; encourage the advancement of healthy lifestyles and the prevention of disease; and develop and administer funds for the support of health education and research. The foundation supports both research programs and demonstration programs with short-term or start-up costs. The foundation accepts the Council of Michigan Foundations Common Grant Application Form, which can be downloaded from the site. The Web site also provides information about the foundation's board of directors, recent news, contact information, and a list of recent grant recipients.

M.J. Murdock Charitable Trust (WA) (http://www.murdock-trust.org/)
The Vancouver, Washington-headquartered M.J. Murdock Charitable Trust was established by the will of Melvin J. Murdock, co-founder of the Oregon electronic instruments company, Tektronix, Inc., in 1975. The trust focuses its grantmaking efforts in the five states of the Pacific Northwest: Alaska, Idaho, Montana, Oregon, and Washington, with an emphasis on programs in education and scientific research, the arts, public affairs, health and medicine, human services, and people with disabilities. The trust makes grants in the four general areas of education, scientific research, arts and culture, and health and human services. The trust's Web site provides grant guidelines, limitations, and application requirements; a listing of recent grantees; a history of the trust; financial statements; and contact information.

John P. Murphy Foundation (OH) (http://fdncenter.org/grantmaker/jpmurphy/)
The John P. Murphy Foundation was established in 1960 in Cleveland, Ohio, by Murphy, to provide funding for "charitable, educational, scientific, literary, and religious purposes."

The foundation today continues to follow the pattern of giving established by its namesake: supporting the areas of education, the arts and culture, social service, community, health, and religion. The foundation's Web site provides a short biography of John Murphy, details on the spirit in which the foundation makes grants, grant application requirements and guidelines, a contact address, a list of board members and officers, and financial statements.

Musicians Foundation, Inc. (NY) (http://www.musiciansfoundation.org)
The Musicians Foundation, Inc. aims to foster the interests and advance the conditions and social welfare of professional musicians and their families in case of need. Based in New York City, the foundation provides financial assistance to musicians who need help in meeting current living, medical, and allied expenses. Visitors to the foundation's Web site will find a downloadable grant application, board listings, a letter from the president, annotated links to related sites, and contact information.

Musser Fund (MN) (http://www.musserfund.org)
The Musser Fund was established in 1989 in Minnesota and provides grants to qualifying organizations in areas where trustees live or have an interest and in rural areas, including the Little Falls, Minnesota, area where Laura Jane Musser made her lifelong home. The fund makes grants in the domains of children and youth, music and fine art, intercultural harmony, rural life, and the environment. The fund places priority on organizations that are creative or innovative in approach, community based and/or community initiated, self-sustaining, offer replicable possibilities, and have smaller budgets The fund does not make grants toward general operating support. Visit the fund's Web site to find application guidelines and printable application.

The Mustard Seed Foundation (VA) (Operating foundation) (http://www.msfdn.org)
Dennis and Eileen Harvey Bakke established the Mustard Seed Foundation in 1983 as "an expression of their desire to advance the Kingdom of God through faithful stewardship." The foundation provides grants to Christians who are engaged in or preparing for evangelism, stewardship, ministry, education, and relieving human suffering. Individuals and organizations receiving Mustard Seed grants must demonstrate personal faith in Christ and must desire "to serve and witness in His name." The foundation places highest priority on funding projects that "seek to draw disciples to Jesus from every 'unreached' community, city, and culture and which attempt to redeem society's structures and institutions. Consult the Web site for detailed information on each grant and scholarship program, a downloadable application form, online contact forms, a description of the foundation's principles, an annual report, and financial information.

E. Nakamichi Foundation (CA) (http://www.enfoundation.com)
The E. Nakamichi Foundation was established in Los Angeles, California in 1982, to encourage the propagation and appreciation of baroque and other fine forms of classical music that are generally not available on a commercial basis. The foundation underwrites performances or broadcasts of performances on public television or radio. It does not make grants to individuals, nor does it make multi-year grants. Extensive information on the guidelines and limitations of funding are available at the foundation's Web site. On the site, grantseekers may register their organizations and apply for grants directly online; the foundation allows applicants to check the status of their preliminary applications, read a list of previously funded organizations and institutions, and access contact information.

The National Academy of Education (NY) (Operating foundation) (http://www.nae.nyu.edu)
The National Academy of Education was founded in 1965 to "promote scholarly inquiry and discussion concerning the ends and means of education, in all its forms, in the United States and abroad." The New York City-based organization has sponsored a variety of commissions and study panels that have published proceedings and reports. In keeping with its mission, the academy seeks to fund proposals that promise to make significant scholarly

contributions to the field of education as well as to advance the careers of the recipients. The academy also administers a Postdoctoral Fellowship Program, funded by the Spencer Foundation, which is designed to insure the future of research in education by supporting young scholars working in critical areas of educational scholarship. Visitors to the site will find downloadable fellowship applications, grant application instructions and guidelines, and links to affiliated Web sites.

National Association of Chain Drug Stores Foundation, Inc. (VA) (http://www.nacdsfoundation.org/)
Based in Alexandria, Virginia, the chief purpose of the National Association of Chain Drug Stores Foundation, Inc. is to represent the views and policy positions of member chain drug companies. The foundation seeks to address pharmacy and health-related issues, promote the value and role of community retail pharmacy in the healthcare system, ensure that the community retail pharmacy perspective is communicated to and understood by legislators and policymakers, provide appropriate forums for retailers to interact with their suppliers and business partners, create a favorable political and business climate in which the foundation's member companies can carry out their business plans, and develop and promote policies and programs aimed at improving merchandise distribution and retail operations efficiency. The foundation provides members with a library, publications, meetings and conferences, and programs, such as an interactive education for pharmacy technician training programs. Visitors to the Web site will find online membership applications.

National Video Resources, Inc. (NY) (Operating foundation) (http://www.nvr.org)
National Video Resources, Inc. was established in 1990 by the Rockefeller Foundation. Its goal is to "assist in increasing the public's awareness of and access to independently produced media & film and video as well as motion media delivered through the new digital technologies." The organization designs and implements projects that help enable individuals and organizations, such as public libraries, colleges and universities, and other nonprofits, to acquire and use independent film and video. The organization also commissions and publishes research on issues of concern to independent media makers, distributors, educators, activists, and individuals. Visitors to the site will find information on publications and projects. The organization manages the Film/Video/Multimedia Fellowships Program for the Rockefeller and John D. and Catherine T. MacArthur Foundations, which supports media artists from the United States (funded by Rockefeller) and Latin America (funded by Rockefeller and MacArthur). Fellowships are awarded through a nomination process; applications are not accepted. The organization's Web site features information on programs and publications.

Needmor Fund (CO) (http://fdncenter.org/grantmaker/needmor/)
Established in Toledo, Ohio, in 1956, the Colorado-based Needmor Fund today works to change the social, economic, and political conditions that bar access to participation in a democratic society. The fund is committed to the idea that "citizens should be free and equal to determine the actions of government and the terms of public policy, and thus assuring their right to justice, political liberty, the basic necessities of life, an education that enables them to be contributing members of society, and the opportunity to secure productive work with just and decent wages, benefits, and decent working conditions." Visitors to the fund's Web site will find a statement of the fund's mission and values, detailed application guidelines and restrictions, and a recent listing of grants.

The Nemours Foundation (FL) (http://www.nemours.org/no/)
The Nemours Foundation of Florida was created in 1936, following a bequest from Alfred I. DuPont. The foundation's mission is to "execute prudently and effectively the wills of Alfred I. duPont and [his brother-in-law] Edward Ball in perpetuity;" since 1940 this mission has manifested itself in the operation of health institutions. These institutions provide services for children in Delaware and Florida and the surrounding areas and for the elderly in Delaware. Foundation funding goes toward staff education and research. The organization also sponsors continuing medical education conferences throughout the country. The

foundation funds KidsHealth.org, which is full of information on infections, behavior and emotions, food and fitness, and children's health. The site includes information on the history of the foundation, each of the sponsored institutions, and the offered conferences.

New England Biolabs Foundation (MA) (http://www.nebf.org/)
Established in 1982, the New England Biolabs Foundation supports grassroots organizations working in the areas of the environment, social change, the arts, elementary education, and limited scientific research. Ordinarily, the foundation limits its domestic grantmaking to the greater Boston/North Shore area, but the foundation does encourage proposals from or about developing countries with an emphasis on assisting community organizations in their endeavors. Due to its size, it restricts these activities to specific countries. Visitors to the foundation's site will find detailed application guidelines and reporting requirements, proposal tips from the foundation's director, a history of grantees, and contact information. The foundation accepts the National Network of Grantmakers' Common Grant Application Form.

New York Foundation (NY) (http://www.nyf.org)
One of the first foundations in the country, the New York City-based New York Foundation was established in 1909. The group's mission is to "support groups in New York City that are working on problems of urgent concern to residents of disadvantaged communities and neighborhoods . . . . [with a particular interest] in start-up grants to new, untested programs that have few other sources of support." The types of programs that the foundation likes to support include services and advocacy for various issues facing minority communities; education, hunger, and youth organizations; and coalitions of community groups. The foundation holds regular meetings between its board and its grantees. The staff also supports the grantees through site visits and technical assistance. The foundation's Web site offers application guidelines; grant, staff, and board lists; and a news section. The foundation accepts the New York/New Jersey Common Application Form.

New York Foundation for Architecture, Inc. (NY)
(http://www.aiany.org/nyfoundation.org/index.html)
The New York Foundation for Architecture, Inc. is the sister organization of the New York Chapter of the American Institute of Architects. The two groups work together to provide scholarship and educational opportunities to students and the general public. The New York Chapter of the AIA offers two types of grants: Eleanor Allwork Scholarship Grant and the Douglas Haskell Award for Student Journalism. Each year, the foundation's grant selection committee supervises the selection of scholarship recipients and distributes the awards. Information about these grants and how to apply is available on the foundation's Web site.

Newman's Own (CT) (http://www.newmansown.com/)
Established in 1982 in Westport, Connecticut, by actor Paul Newman, Newman's Own produces a wide variety of comestibles, donating 100 percent of the post-tax revenue to charity. The organization holds an interest in the arts, affordable housing, children, disaster relief, education, elderly groups, environmental causes, and hunger relief. Grant guidelines and a downloadable grant application are available on the site.

Laura J. Niles Foundation (CT) (http://www.laurajnilesfoundation.org)
The mission of the Connecticut-based, Laura J. Niles Foundation is to encourage and support efforts to improve the lives of both people and animals. Program interests of the foundation include education, economic self-sufficiency, and animals. The foundation favors programs addressing long-term solutions to the causes of problems, as opposed to programs that simply treat the symptoms. Visitors to the foundation's Web site will locate guiding principles, grant guidelines, a printable grant application, and contact information.

Nine Tuna Foundation (MI) (http://www.ninetuna.org/)
Based in Lansing, Michigan, the Nine Tuna Foundation has made grants in past years to local nonprofits in the areas of science education, the arts, the environment/animals, and rehabilitative engineering. The foundation does not accept unsolicited grant proposals. Visit the foundation's Web site to find how to view the most recent tax filing and find contact information.

Samuel Roberts Noble Foundation (OK) (http://www.noble.org/)
Established in 1945 by oil industrialist Lloyd Noble in honor of his father, the Samuel Roberts Noble Foundation seeks "to assist humanity in reaching its maximum usefulness." To that end, the Ardmore, Oklahoma-based foundation focuses on basic plant biology and agricultural research, consultation, demonstration projects that enable farmers and ranchers to achieve their goals, enhancing plant productivity through fundamental research and applied biotechnology, and assisting community, health, and educational organizations through grants and employee involvement. Among other offerings, the foundation's Web site provides grant guidelines and procedures; an overview of activities in the foundation's Plant Biology and Agricultural divisions; links to a variety of local, regional, and Internet resources; and contact information.

The Nokomis Foundation (MI) (http://www.nokomisfoundation.org/)
The Nokomis Foundation exists to "make a difference in the lives of women and girls by advocating for women-friendly policies, celebrating women's accomplishments, instilling economic self-sufficiency, and promoting healthy choices." The foundation is located in Grand Rapids, Michigan, and primarily funds grants in the west Michigan area, but it will consider applications for programs with a state or national focus, provided they include a west Michigan component. The foundation is particularly interested in pilot programs and gives priority to organizations that do not have access to traditional sources of funding. The foundation funds programs that have similar focus to its mission, that show innovation and creativity, and that intend to foster collaboration among groups and accomplish long-term social change. To apply for a grant, an interested party should send a concise letter or e-mail describing the program; details are listed on the Web site. Lists of previous grants awarded are available on the site as is the most recent edition of the foundation's newsletter.

Norcross Wildlife Foundation, Inc. (MA) (Operating foundation) (http://www.norcrossws.org/)
The Norcross Wildlife Foundation, Inc. was established in 1965 by Arthur D. Norcross, a native of Massachusetts and founder and manager of the Norcross Greeting Card Company. He established the Wales, Massachusetts-based foundation to ensure the future well-being of the Norcross Wildlife Sanctuary, which began as a 100-acre woodlot-pasture that Arthur Norcross inherited from his father in 1916, and presently covers 4000 acres. Around 1930, he began purchasing nearby woodlands, and other parcels with the goal of establishing the sanctuary. It was formally dedicated in 1939 as "a place where wildlife may be encouraged not just to survive but also to propagate and spread naturally, so that specific species, threatened with extinction, might again attain more normal distribution." In addition to maintaining the sanctuary, the foundation also has a grantmaking program. The foundation prefers to place grants with organizations that ask for specific amounts. The foundation generally supports projects that have finite completion dates. Consult the foundation's Web site for grant request guidelines and contact information. Visitors to the Web site will also find histories of the foundation and sanctuary, descriptions of the programs and exhibits at the sanctuary, schedules, and horticultural and animal facts.

Nord Family Foundation (OH) (http://www.nordff.org)
The Nord Family Foundation was originally the Nordson Foundation, a trust created in 1952 by Walter G. Nord, founder of the Nordson Corporation in Ohio. The Nordson Foundation was dissolved in 1988 and the Nord Family Foundation was created. In the tradition of its original founders Walter and Virginia Nord, the foundation, located in Elyria, Ohio, seeks to build community by supporting projects that bring opportunity to the

disadvantaged, strengthen family bonds, and improve quality of life. Grants are awarded in the fields of social service, health, education, the arts, and civic affairs. High priority is given to programs that address the needs of economically or socially disadvantaged families and projects that address the root causes of problems. Most grants are made to organizations or for projects in Lorain County, Ohio, with a small number of grants to organizations in Cuyahoga County, Ohio; Denver, Colorado; Columbia, South Carolina; and to national organizations that address the foundation's priorities. Consult the foundation's Web site for application instructions and contact information.

Norman Foundation (NY) (http://www.normanfdn.org/)
Established in 1970, the New York-based Norman Foundation is committed to a strategy of seeking and supporting grassroots efforts that strengthen the ability of communities to determine their economic, environmental, and civic well-being; promote community-based economic development efforts that experiment with new ownership structures and financing mechanisms; work to prevent the use of toxins and their disposal into the environment; build bridges across issues and constituencies and organize to counter the "radical right" in all its forms; promote civil rights by fighting discrimination and violence and working for ethnic, religious, and sexual equity and for reproductive freedom; challenge the power of money over the political process; and/or seek to improve government's and business' accountability to the public, especially to those affected by their actions. The foundation also seeks to address "the profound civic disengagement in society," and is particularly interested in strategies that "engage more Americans in their civic lives to increase their faith and involvement in community institutions." The foundation's Web site provides a description of the application process, grant guidelines and restrictions, basic financial information, and a list of the grants the foundation recently awarded; listings of officers, directors, and staff; and contact information.

The Noyce Foundation (CA) (http://www.noycefdn.org)
Based in Palo Alto, California, the Noyce Foundation is committed "to stimulating ideas and supporting initiatives designed to produce significant improvement in the academic achievement of public school students in grades K-12." With a strong interest in rethinking and reconfiguring curriculum, pedagogy, and resources in schools and school districts, the foundation focuses on programs that work for long-term improvement in literacy, mathematics, and science. The foundation does not accept unsolicited proposals, rather it lists and describes the organizations that it does fund on its Web site. Visitors to the site will also find events lists, the foundation's downloadable version of annual reports, and regional contact information.

The Kenneth T. and Eileen L. Norris Foundation (CA) (http://www.norrisfoundation.org)
Kenneth T. and Eileen L. Norris owned Norris Stamping and Manufacturing Companies, later called Norris Industries. Kenneth Norris was a metallurgist who discovered a way to make steel casings for bullets, which led to a key role for the family business during World War II. Established in 1963, the foundation funds in the areas of medicine, education and science, youth, community, and cultural arts. Located in Long Beach, California, the foundation funds organizations in the Los Angeles County area. Unsolicited grant applications are not accepted. Visitors to the Web site will find information about the founders, a downloadable annual report, and contact information.

Northwest Area Foundation (MN) (http://www.nwaf.org/)
The Northwest Area Foundation was established in 1934 by Louis W. Hill, son of James, J. Hill, the founder of the Great Northern Railroad, and renamed in 1975 to reflect its "commitment to the region that provided its original resources and its growth beyond the scope of the traditional family foundation." The foundation's mission is to help communities most in need in Minnesota, Iowa, North Dakota, South Dakota, Montana, Idaho, Washington, and Oregon to create positive futures—economically, ecologically, and socially. To implement that mission, the foundation will help communities "work toward a balanced and sustainable system that will reduce poverty; stimulate economic growth; sustain the

natural environment; and develop effective institutions, relationships, and individuals." In addition to contact information, a brief history of the foundation, staff and trustee listings, and a copy of the most recent annual report, the foundation's Web site provides an overview of the foundation's new direction and the decision-making process that led to it.

Northwest Fund for the Environment (WA) (http://www.nwfund.org/)
The Northwest Fund for the Environment was established in 1971 to "promote change in the uses of natural resources which will increase their protection and preservation in the State of Washington," with special emphasis placed on "the protection of wild fish, native wildlife, natural forests, wetlands and shorelines, and the preservation of pure and free-flowing waters." Located in Seattle, Washington, the fund supports actions to preserve threatened and endangered species and/or ecosystems, implement and enforce environmental laws and regulations, fund research directly relevant to Washington State, and strengthen the effectiveness of nonprofit environmental groups. Visit the Web site for grant guidelines, printable and downloadable application forms, selections from annual reports, a report of the fund's grantmaking trends, and contact information.

Northwest Health Foundation (OR) (http://www.nwhf.org/)
The Northwest Health Foundation was founded in late 1997 from the proceeds of the sale of PACC Health Plans and PACC HMO. The Northwest Health Foundation exists to "advance, support, and promote the health of the people of Oregon and southwest Washington." The foundation supports innovative programs that address the following issues: health protection; quality of healthcare; access to healthcare; basic and applied biomedical, health, and socio-behavioral research; education for health professionals and consumers; and mental health. In addition, the foundation gives preference to projects that deal with children, rural or diverse communities, and specifically projects and programs that benefit Clackamas County. More details about the types of programs and projects funded are available on the foundation's Web site, as are lists of previous grants awarded. Those interested in applying should first send a letter of inquiry. Deadlines and information about what should be included in the letter and the downloadable application cover sheet available on the Web site.

Jessie Smith Noyes Foundation, Inc. (NY) (http://www.noyes.org)
The Jessie Smith Noyes Foundation, Inc. was established in 1947 by Charles F. Noyes as a memorial to his wife. Charles F. Noyes owned a real estate brokerage firm in New York City, and his most famous deal was the 1951 sale of the Empire State Building, "previously regarded as a white elephant," for the largest price at the time in real estate history. Located in New York City, the foundation is committed to "protecting and restoring Earth's natural systems and promoting a sustainable society by strengthening individuals, institutions and communities pledged to pursuing those goals." Currently, the foundation makes grants primarily in the areas of the environment and reproductive rights, with the following program areas: toxins, sustainable agriculture, sustainable communities, reproductive rights, metro New York environment, and related interests, which are activities outside of the five areas but that still further the foundation's goals. Projects that receive preference are ones that address the connections between these concerns and their broader implications, have potential for widespread impact or applicability, and that address the connections between environmental and social justice issues. Visit the Web site for program and application guidelines, grants lists, annual reports, financial information, staff listings, and contact information.

John M. Olin Foundation, Inc. (NY) (http://www.jmof.org/)
The John M. Olin Foundation, Inc. was established in 1953 by the industrialist John Merrill Olin (1892-1982). Mr. Olin was committed to "the preservation of the principles of political and economic liberty as they have been expressed in American thought, institutions, and practice." Accordingly, the purpose of the foundation is to provide support for projects that "reflect or are intended to strengthen the economic, political, and cultural institutions upon which the American heritage of constitutional government and private enterprise is

based." Within this context, the foundation has authorized grants in the areas of American institutions, law and the legal system, public policy research, and strategic and international studies. In each of these areas, it attempts to advance its objectives through support of research, institutional support, fellowships, professorships, lectures and lectures series, books, scholarly journals, journals of opinion, conferences and seminars, and, on occasion, television and radio programs. While no longer accepting unsolicited proposals, thc foundation's Web site provides general information about its programs and grantmaking policies, a schedule of the foundation's recent grants, listings of the foundation's trustees and staff, and contact information.

Onan Family Foundation (MN) (http://www.onanfamily.org/foundation.htm)
The Onan Family Foundation was founded by David Warren Onan, an entrepreneur in Minneapolis who wanted to give back to the community where his business thrived and where he lived. Located in Minneapolis, Minnesota, the foundation has a strong interest in programs that focus on Minneapolis and St. Paul, Minnesota. Funding areas are education, social welfare, cultural and civic affairs, and religion. Consult the Web site for grant guidelines, grants lists, staff listings, financial information, and contact information. Grant requests are to be made using the Minnesota Common Grant Application Form which can be downloaded from the site.

The William J. and Dorothy K. O'Neill Foundation, Inc. (OH) (http://www.oneillfdn.org/)
The William J. and Dorothy K. O'Neill Foundation, Inc. of Cleveland, Ohio, was established in 1987. The foundation strives to continue the family's philanthropy in a manner in which the founders would be proud. Gifts are made through three different channels. The first is through its focus program which centers on families. Through RFPs to institutions in cities where family members live, the foundation is currently sponsoring "fathering" programs as part of its effort to find the root cause of the family unit's disintegration. The general grantmaking program supports groups that fall under the following areas of interest: family, health, education, employment, housing, poverty, children, and the elderly. Finally, there is a matching gifts program with organizations in which family members are active. The Web site includes application guidelines and deadlines, grants lists, financial statements, and lists of trustees and officers.

Open Society Institute (NY) (http://www.soros.org)
The Open Society Institute "promotes the development and maintenance of open societies around the world by supporting an array of programs dealing with educational, social, and legal reform." There are Open Society Institutes in countries around the world that all share a similar mission: "to support the development of an open society." The Open Society Institute in New York specifically works with the Open Society Institute in Budapest to assist the other organizations in the Soros Foundations Network by providing programmatic, administrative, financial, and technical support. There are links to each institute in every country on the site, along with contact information.

Oringer Foundation (CA) (http://www.oringerfoundation.org)
The mission of the San Francisco-based, Oringer Foundation is to "provide opportunity and means to enable politically, economically, and socially disadvantaged people to become more self-sufficient and productive in their lives and communities." Established in 2000, the foundation funds organizations that maintain a focus on immigrant rights and prisoner advocacy. Visitors to the foundation's Web site will find information about the application process, a downloadable grant application, a listing of grant recipients, and contact information.

Ottinger Foundation (NY) (http://www.ottingerfoundation.org)
The Ottinger Foundation, located in New York City, supports "organizations that develop innovative public policy and new ways of grassroots organizing to build a movement for social change." The foundation generally funds groups that promote grassroots citizen activism with national significance. Letters of inquiry are not accepted. Grant guidelines

and a listing of recent grantees are posted on the foundation's Web site, along with contact information.

Oxford Foundation, Inc. (PA) (http://www.oxfordfoundation.org/)
The Oxford Foundation, Inc. of Pennsylvania was founded in 1947 to promote excellence in health, human services, education, early childhood development, historic and environmental preservation, arts and culture, and public policy planning. The foundation provides funds to a wide variety of organizations in the geographic areas of interest to the board of directors. Visit the foundation's Web site to find a history of the organization and its founder, funding criteria, application procedures, grants listings, board/staff listings, and contact information.

Pacific Northwest Foundation (OR) (http://www.pnf.org)
Established in 1988, the Pacific Northwest Foundation of Portland, Oregon, is a nonprofit venture capitalist organization whose mission is to "respond quickly to unique nonprofit ventures, focusing particularly on their efforts to expand and become self-sustaining through broad support from within their respective communities." Recent multi-year grant recipients have included an organization that provides technical assistance and grants research information to those interested in nonprofit pursuits, a project alerting the public to latex sensitivities, and an environmental pollution project. The site includes a recent annual report, board and staff lists, information on individual giving and how to make the most of nonprofit boards, summaries of insurance and policy issues, and health reports based on two case studies on pollution and allergies. The foundation does not accept unsolicited applications.

Pacific Pioneer Fund (CA) (http://www.pacificpioneerfund.com)
The Pacific Pioneer Fund exists to support emerging documentary filmmakers. "The term 'emerging' is intended to denote a person committed to the craft of making documentaries [and] who has demonstrated that commitment by several years of practical film or video experience." Grants are limited to persons and organizations in California, Oregon, and Washington. Printable application forms, contact information, and details about restrictions and limitations are all available on this site.

David and Lucile Packard Foundation (CA) (http://www.packard.org)
The David and Lucile Packard Foundation was created in 1964 by David Packard (1912-1996), a co-founder (with his Stanford classmate William Hewlett) of the Hewlett-Packard Company, and his wife, Lucile Salter Packard (1914-1987). The foundation supports nonprofit organizations with the hope that it can help people through the improvement of scientific knowledge, education, health, culture, employment opportunities, the environment, and quality of life. To that end, the foundation makes grants (with a special focus on San Mateo, Santa Clara, Santa Cruz, and Monterey Counties) nationally and internationally in the following broad program areas: conservation and science, population, and children, families, and communities. In addition to a history of the foundation and a biography of David Packard, the foundation's Web site provides detailed program descriptions and application guidelines, recent grants in a number of program areas, a listing of the foundation's officers and trustees, foundation contact names by program area, and the foundation's annual report.

PADI Foundation (CA) (http://www.padi.com)
The PADI [Professional Association of Diving Instructors] Foundation's headquarters are located in California, but there are PADI service offices around the world. PADI is the world's largest recreational diving membership organization, with a membership including diving businesses, resort facilities, academic institutions, instructor trainers, diving educators, divers, snorklers, and other watersports enthusiasts. The foundation exists to "develop programs that encourage and fulfill the public interest in recreational scuba and snorkel diving worldwide." The foundation encourages and supports underwater science, environmental projects, and education, and its funds projects that will enrich mankind's

understanding of the aquatic environment and encourage sensitivity to and protection of the delicate ecological balance of underwater life. In addition, the foundation funds projects to increase understanding of sport diving physics and physiology that will benefit the general diving public and add to the scientific understanding of man's relationship and ability to survive in the underwater environment. Instructions on how to apply for grants and whom to contact are available on the site, as is more information about other PADI programs, including its diving projects around the world.

Parker Foundation (VA) (http://www.parkerfoundation.org)
Established in 1995, the mission of the Richmond, Virginia-based Parker Foundation "is to assist strategic international, national, and local Christian organizations whose primary focus is advancing the Gospel of Jesus Christ." To this end, the foundation maintains a number of general funding concerns, including world evangelism, evangelical leadership development, and Christian social relief and public persuasion. The foundation tends to support a few specific organizations already established as grant recipients, as well as some startup projects or organizations with special projects intended to increase their effectiveness. The foundation's Web site includes grant guidelines and restrictions, links, contact information, the foundation's grant application form, and a self-evaluation form for grant requests.

Patrina Foundation (NY) (http://www.patrinafoundation.org/)
The Patrina Foundation was established in 1990 with the mission of expanding women's educational opportunities and creating scholarship opportunities for women in the Northeast. The foundation's interests focus on research and in curriculum development. Recipients of the foundation's giving are mostly educational and cultural organizations, but the foundation also occasionally funds social service organizations that build on skills and leadership qualities. The foundation does not make grants for general operating support, and it does not fund individuals. Visitors to the foundation's Web site will find detailed applications procedures, guidelines, and contact information.

Alicia Patterson Foundation (DC) (Operating foundation) (http://www.aliciapatterson.org)
The Alicia Patterson Foundation was established in 1965 in memory of Alicia Patterson, editor and publisher of *Newsday* for 23 years before her death in 1963. The Washington, D.C.-based foundation has a fellowship program, in which one-year grants are awarded to working journalists to pursue independent projects of "significant interest." Recipients spend that year traveling, researching, and writing articles based on their investigations for *The APF Reporter,* a quarterly magazine published by the foundation. The foundation's Web site features a downloadable application form, instructions, *The APF Reporter* archive, biography of Alicia Patterson, grant application instructions, listings of past fellows, related links, and contact information.

Pegasus Foundation (MA) (http://www.pegasusfoundation.org/)
The Pegasus Foundation, established in 1997 for the purpose of animal protection, environmental preservation, and public education, mainly provides funding to programs in the West and Southwest (Arizona and Montana), Florida, and Cape Cod, Massachusetts. The foundation partners with other nonprofit environmental and animal protection groups to support various projects. It also maintains programs in wildlife protection, companion animal and equine rescue programs, and land conservation and preservation. Unsolicited proposals are not accepted, as the foundation works with projects where they have already established a personal connection. The foundation's Web site provides a detailed description of each of its three projects, a listing of its partnership organizations with links to their Web sites, an annual report, and contact information.

William Penn Foundation (PA) (http://www.wpennfdn.org/)
The William Penn Foundation, a private grantmaking organization created in 1945 by Otto Haas and his wife, Phoebe, strives to improve the quality of life in the greater Philadelphia

area, Particularly for its neediest residents. The foundation makes grants ranging from a few thousand dollars to several million dollars in three main categories: children, youth and families; arts and culture; and the environment and communities. The foundation's grantmaking is limited to the six-county Philadelphia area (Bucks, Chester, Delaware, Montgomery, and Philadelphia Counties in Pennsylvania and Camden County, especially the City of Camden, in New Jersey) unless initiated by the foundation. Grants for school-based programs in Philadelphia are generally limited to the Martin Luther King, Jr. and west Philadelphia clusters. The Web site provides detailed program descriptions, application guidelines and restrictions, searchable grants lists, statements of the foundation's mission and grantmaking values, a history of the foundation, board and staff listings, and contact information.

Pew Charitable Trusts (PA) (http://www.pewtrusts.com/)
The Philadelphia-based Pew Charitable Trusts are a group of seven individual charitable funds established by the children of Sun Oil Company founder Joseph N. Pew and his wife, Mary Anderson Pew. Each year, the trusts make grants to qualifying organizations in the areas of culture, education, the environment, health and human services, public policy, and religion, as well as through its Venture Fund. In addition to a strong national giving program, the trusts maintain a particular commitment to their local community. The trusts' Web site provides program guidelines and limitations, application procedures, searchable grants lists, grantee Web links, publications, news, a staff list, and contact information.

Gustavus and Louise Pfeiffer Research Foundation (NJ) (http://fdncenter.org/grantmaker/pfeiffer/)
The Gustavus and Louise Pfeiffer Research Foundation, located in Denville, New Jersey, funds healthcare research. The foundation's grant program supports "projects or programs carried out in the United States for advancement of medicine and pharmacy, including scientific research, post-graduate scholarship, and fellowship assistance, and studies in nutrition, blindness, deafness, and other physical disabilities." Funding for basic research is restricted to breast, ovarian, and prostate cancer. Projects involving animal experimentation are not funded. The foundation publishes a biennial report that includes program descriptions and lists of grant recipients. Potential applicants can request a copy of the report. The foundation's Web site includes application guidelines and restrictions and instructions on submitting a letter of inquiry.

Ellis L. Phillips Foundation (MA) (http://www.ellislphillipsfndn.org/)
The Ellis L. Phillips Foundation was established by its namesake, the president and founder of the Long Island Lighting Company, in New York in 1930. Now headquartered in Boston, the foundation seeks to enhance the communities where its directors live, in fields of particular interest to the foundation. The foundation focuses the majority of its giving on its ongoing Catalogue for Philanthropy project and on the promotion of philanthropy. The foundation does not accept unsolicited proposals. The foundation's Web site includes grant guidelines, board/staff listings, and explanation of the foundation's grant evaluation process and criteria, lists of past grant recipients, and contact information.

Louie M. & Betty M. Phillips Foundation (TN) (http://www.phillipsfoundation.org)
Located in Nashville, Tennessee, the Louie M. & Betty M. Phillips Foundation was established in 1978 after the death of Mrs. Phillips, but it was not fully funded until the death of Mr. Phillips in 1986. The foundation supports a variety of organizations in the fields of health, human services, civic affairs, education, and the arts. The foundation's Web site features funding information, application guidelines, information about the foundation, and details about previous grants.

Pickett & Hatcher Educational Fund, Inc. (GA) (http://www.pickettandhatcher.org)
The Pickett & Hatcher Educational Fund, Inc. was established in 1938 through the generosity of Claud A. Hatcher, president of the Nehi Corporation that later became the Royal Crown Cola Company. Located in Columbus, Georgia, the fund is a private foundation that

grants loans to students who otherwise might not be able to attend college. To be eligible, students should be United States citizens and legal residents of Alabama, Florida, Georgia, Kentucky, Mississippi, North Carolina, South Carolina, Tennessee, or Virginia. Consult the fund's Web site for complete eligibility requirements, loan limits, interest rates, renewal requirements, application instructions, and contact information.

Pinkerton Foundation (NY) (http://fdncenter.org/grantmaker/pinkerton/)

The New York-based Pinkerton Foundation was established in 1966 with the mission of reducing crime and preventing juvenile delinquency. In order to work towards its mission, the foundation makes grants to organizations that strengthen youth programs in poor communities. The foundation supports programs that develop individual competencies, instill values, and increase opportunities to participate in society. Visitor's to the foundation's Web site will find further information on the foundation's programs, a listing of recent grants, staff and board information, grant guidelines, and contact information.

The Virginia G. Piper Charitable Trust (AZ) (http://www.pipertrust.org)

Established in 1995, the Virginia G. Piper Charitable Trust is committed to enhancing the lives of the people in Maricopa County, Arizona, believing that dynamic and creative people lead effective and vital organizations. Areas of interest to the trust include: early childhood, youth, elderly, and arts and culture. Visitors to the trust's Web site will find further details on the trust's grantmaking program; a FAQ section; a trustees, officers, and staff listing; and contact information.

The Piton Foundation (CO) (Operating foundation) (http://www.piton.org)

The mission of the Denver-based, Piton Foundation is to help children and families in Denver move from poverty and dependence to self-reliance. The operating foundation was established in 1976 and is principally funded by the Gary-Williams Energy Corporation. The foundation generally provides support for public education, youth development, economic opportunity, and neighborhood leadership. The foundation also maintains the Charter Fund Scholarship program, which supports Colorado students in their first year of undergraduate study. The foundation also maintains a database that includes maps and graphs on the population, housing, economic, and education characteristics of each of Denver's 79 neighborhoods. The database is available through the foundation's Web site, as well as many downloadable reports and articles.

William I.H. and Lula E. Pitts Foundation (GA) (http://www.pittsfoundation.org/)

The William I.H. and Lula E. Pitts Foundation was established in 1941 to "support charities within the state of Georgia that are affiliated with the Methodist Church." Major areas of interest for the foundation include education, children's homes, charitable hospitals, and care of the elderly. The foundation's Web site gives a detailed history of the Pitts and their organization, lists recent grant recipients, grant application guidelines, and a downloadable application.

Plan for Social Excellence, Inc. (NY) (Operating foundation) (http://www.pfse.org)

Established in 1990, the Plan for Social Excellence, Inc., located in Mt. Kisco, New York, creates and supports innovative pilot projects in education in the United States. The organization pursues its goals through five major activities: grantmaking, 'coinvestments' (collaboration and co-investment with other foundations and corporations in funding programs), technical assistance, scholarships, and dissemination. In addition, the organization disseminates the results of many of its funded projects to organizations that may have an interest in replicating the project. The organization also administers a last-dollar scholarship program for high school students who have participated in select plan-supported projects. Consult the organization's Web site for more complete information on activities and programs and for application information, instructions, and guidelines.

Carl and Eloise Pohlad Family Foundation (MN) (http://www.pohladfamilycharities.org)
Based in Minneapolis, Minnesota, the Carl and Eloise Pohlad Family Foundation is one-third of the Pohlad Family Charities. The foundation seeks to improve and enrich the lives of economically disadvantaged children, youth, and families. The foundation makes grants to organizations that maintain a focus on serving the citizens of the Minneapolis/St. Paul metropolitan area. Grants are made to human services, education, and enrichment programs for the economically disadvantaged. The foundation does not fund research or demonstration projects or programs that will need ongoing support. Unsolicited applications are not considered for Family-Directed Grants. The foundation's Web site offers grantmaking guidelines and application, an annual report, grants listings, and contact information.

The Howard and Geraldine Polinger Family Foundation (MD) (http://fdncenter.org/grantmaker/polinger/)
The Howard and Geraldine Polinger Family Foundation's mission is to improve the quality of life for individuals, families, and communities through support of ongoing programs and innovative projects that create positive outcomes. The foundation places major emphasis on support of organizations that strengthen Jewish life locally and in Israel. Foundation grants focus primarily on the Washington, D.C., metropolitan area, and concentrate on providing opportunity and access to quality education, cultural arts, and services to enhance family well-being. Visitors to the foundation's Web site will find submission guidelines and information on the application procedure, a listing of recent grant recipients, and contact information.

Polk Brothers Foundation (IL) (http://www.polkbrosfdn.org/)
The Chicago-based, Polk Brothers Foundation's mission is to "strengthen the city's children and families [as well as] bolster social service, education, cultural and healthcare programs that provide direct service to low-income Chicagoans." The foundation directs its funding toward four main categories: social service, including employment, families, and children and youth; education, including programs in the classroom, beyond the classroom, and full service schools; culture, including school programming and neighborhood outreach; and health, including facilities enhancement and mothers and newborns. All proposals should address the goals of increased access to services and the improvement of the quality of life for Chicago-area residents. The foundation has both large and small grants programs, for which applications are accepted year-round. Visitors to the foundation's Web site will find application guidelines, grant limitations, a list of recent grantees, a pre-application form, request for proposals, the foundation's financial report, and contact information.

Pollock-Krasner Foundation, Inc. (NY) (http://www.pkf.org/)
Established in 1985 by Lee Krasner, widow of the painter Jackson Pollock and a celebrated artist in her own right, the Pollock-Krasner Foundation's mission is to aid, internationally, those individuals who have worked as professional artists over a significant period of time. Potential grant recipients must demonstrate a combination of recognizable artistic merit and financial need relating to either work, living, or medical expenses. The foundation provides support exclusively to visual artists—painters, sculptors, and artists who work on paper, including printmakers—and will not accept applications from commercial artists, photographers, video artists, performance artists, filmmakers, crafts-makers, or any artist whose work primarily falls into one of these categories. The foundation's Web site provides a brief history of the foundation, a downloadable application, a list of grant restrictions, officer and staff listings, and contact information.

Irwin Andrew Porter Foundation (MI) (http://www.iapfoundation.org/)
The Michigan-based, Irwin Andrew Porter Foundation's mission is to "support projects and programs fostering connections to ourselves, our community, our environment, our world." The foundation places primary importance in the areas of the arts, education, the environment, and social programs; however, it believes that the quality and innovativeness

of the specific program is more important than broad topic areas. The foundation does not provide funding for general operating costs, capital campaigns, fundraising events, political or religious causes, or to individuals. The foundation gives preference to organizations in Minnesota, Wisconsin, Illinois, and Michigan. Visit the foundation's Web site to find a list of selected recent grants, information on grant and geographic restrictions, a grant application, and contact information.

Portsmouth General Hospital Foundation (VA) (http://www.pghfoundation.org)
The Portsmouth General Hospital Foundation of Virginia was established in 1988 to support new and innovative or established programs that improve the health and quality of life of the Portsmouth, Virginia, community. The foundation limits its grant program to six areas: substance abuse prevention, teen pregnancy prevention, health and the family, health education and preventive health programs, research and coordination of indigent care, and the environment, education, and the arts as they positively impact the health and quality of life of the community. Visit the foundation's Web site to find further information on the organization's programs, proposal guidelines, a downloadable grant application, a list of recent grant recipients, board of directors listings, and contact information.

Pottruck-Scott Family Foundation (CA) (http://www.ps-ff.org/)
The Pottruck-Scott Family Foundation was established in 1995 to "improve the lives of disadvantaged children and youth, and to support volunteer-driven organizations, with a primary focus in San Francisco." The foundation funds organizations that support education, youth services, and civic/community initiatives. The foundation is particularly interested in youth development programs that promote success in school, engagement in community life, self-reliance, and general health and well-being, as well as programs that use voluntarism as a vehicle for community engagement and participation. Visitors to the foundation's Web site will find a listing of recent grants, a downloadable version of the foundation's latest tax return, board and staff listings, and contact information.

Poudre Valley Hospital Foundation (CO) (http://www.foundation.pvhs.org/index.php3)
The Poudre Valley Hospital Foundation's mission is to "philanthropically support and promote activities that best serve the health interests of the community." The foundation receives, administers, and distributes funds for community health initiatives that target prevention, health promotion, wellness, disease management, and educational and charitable purposes. Visitors to the foundation's Web site will find further information on the grantmaking program, a downloadable version of the foundation's most recent tax return, staff listings, and contact information.

Power of Attorney, Inc. (NY) (Operating foundation) (http://www.powerofattorney.org)
Power of Attorney, Inc. awards a small number of grants to local programs across the United States each year. With a mission of helping qualified *pro bono* business law providers increase their capacities and enhance their ability to serve their communities, the organization's grants are targeted to *pro bono* organizations that offer the greatest potential to expand their capacities within a reasonable time frame. Visit the organization's Web site to obtain more information about the grantmaking program, services, and contact information.

Priddy Foundation (TX) (http://www.priddyfdn.org/)
Founded in 1963 in Wichita Falls, Texas, the Priddy Foundation is dedicated to the support of programs that offer significant potential for individual development and community improvement in human services, education, the arts, and health. Specific areas of interest considered by the foundation include: arts and culture, community enhancement, education, health, human services, and youth programs. Grants are made to select organizations in the Wichita Falls, Texas, area. To a limited degree, grants are made to organizations in the Dallas/Fort Worth area, but such grants are initiated by the foundation board and are not considered in the regular grant review process. Visitors to the foundation's Web site will

find grant guidelines and policies, an online application form, a complete listing of recent grant recipients, and an online contact form for more information.

Prince Charitable Trusts (IL) (http://fdncenter.org/grantmaker/prince/)
The Prince Charitable Trusts were established in 1947 and support three separate states. The trusts have unique interests in each of the three geographic locations. In Chicago, the trust supports arts and culture, education, the environment, health, and social services. In Washington, D.C., the trust supports the environment, arts and culture, social services, health, and youth programs. In Rhode Island, the trust supports the environment, arts and culture, social services, and health. Visitors to the trusts' Web site will find grant guidelines, application information, and contact information.

The Prospect Hill Foundation (NY) (http://fdncenter.org/grantmaker/prospecthill/)
The Prospect Hill Foundation was established in New York in 1960 by William S. Beinecke, former president and chairman of the Sperry and Hutchinson Company. In 1983, the Prospect Hill Foundation merged with the Frederick W. Beinecke Fund. The foundation has a broad range of philanthropic interests, but recently has made grants to support organizations active in environmental conservation, nuclear weapons control, and family planning in Latin America, as well as selected social service, arts, cultural, and educational institutions. The foundation's Web site provides an introduction to the foundation, grant program descriptions, a grants list, and application guidelines.

Public Domain Foundation (VT) (http://www.pdfoundation.org)
The Public Domain Foundation was founded in Vermont by folk artist, Noel Paul Stookey of Peter, Paul, and Mary fame. After Mr. Stookey wrote "The Wedding Song" in 1971, he felt as if the inspiration had come from some distant place. Because of this, Noel decided to donate all the royalties of this song to his new foundation, whose belief is that "into every songwriter's life comes a song, the source of which cannot be explained by personal experience." The foundation encourages other folk singers who experience this type of inspiration to follow his lead. The foundation is mainly interested in supporting children's and family services. Visitors to the foundation's Web site will find information on how to get involved and how to contact the foundation.

Public Welfare Foundation, Inc. (DC) (http://www.publicwelfare.org/)
Established and incorporated in Texas in 1947 and reincorporated in Washington, D.C., in 1960, the Public Welfare Foundation, Inc. is dedicated "to supporting organizations that provide services to disadvantaged populations and work for lasting improvements in the delivery of services that meet basic human needs." The foundation's wide-ranging interests include criminal justice, disadvantaged elderly and youth, the environment, population, health, community and economic development, human rights, and technology assistance. The foundation's Web site provides a short history of the foundation, FAQs, detailed program information, financial statements, application procedures, grants lists organized by specific funding area, and contact information.

The Puffin Foundation, Ltd. (NJ) (http://www.puffinfoundation.org/)
The Puffin Foundation, Ltd. was established in 1983 with the mission of "continuing the dialogue between art and the lives of ordinary people." The foundation seeks to "open the doors of artistic expression to those who are often excluded because of their race, gender, or social philosophy," and to "ensure that the arts not merely survive, but flourish at all levels of our society." The foundation provides seed grants to artists and arts organizations across the spectrum of visual and performing arts. It has established two exhibition, performance, and discussion spaces: the Puffin Room in SoHo, in New York City, and the Puffin Cultural Forum in Teaneck, New Jersey, where the foundation is located. It also has a publishing branch to produce books that otherwise might not come to life. Consult the foundation's Web site for instructions on obtaining an application packet. The site also contains a link to the Puffin Cultural Forum's site, which provides a schedule of upcoming events.

The Cyrus M. Quigley Foundation (CT) (http://fdncenter.org/grantmaker/quigley/)
The Cyrus M. Quigley Foundation of Connecticut focuses on experiences that emphasize physical challenge and service to others. Cyrus M. Quigley demonstrated a commitment to live a courageous life and to help others in that pursuit. Mr. Quigley believed that a courageous life includes the attributes of initiative, self-reliance, self-respect, a sense of humor, and a dedication to effecting positive change in the lives of others. Mr. Quigley also believed that these attributes are best developed by testing one's limits and questioning assumptions about oneself and the larger world. The foundation's Web site includes application information and guidelines, grants histories, a listing of board members, and contact information.

The Radford Foundation (CA) (http://www.radfordfoundation.org/)
Established in 2000 in Los Altos, California, to support innovative ideas and programs that show the promise of making a positive and long-term contributions to the community at large or to economically disadvantaged individuals, especially children. The foundation places priority on smaller nonprofit organizations. The foundation is no longer accepting unsolicited grant applications or inquiries. Visitors to the foundation's Web site will find a brief history of the organization, further information on funding priorities, and contact information.

John G. Rangos Charitable Foundation (PA) (http://www.rangosfoundation.org/)
The John G. Rangos Charitable Foundation is dedicated to helping children by supporting various healthcare and educational programs. The foundation's Web site includes descriptions of some of the organizations it supports, including the Children's Hospital of Pittsburgh, the Pittsburgh Children's Museum, and the International Orthodox Christian Charities. Additionally, a biography of John G. Rangos and an online contact form are available.

Bernard and Audre Rapoport Foundation (TX) (http://www.rapoportfdn.org/)
The mission of the Bernard and Audre Rapoport Foundation is "meeting basic human needs while building individual and social resiliency." Located in Waco, Texas, the foundation's current program priorities are education, focusing on early learning; cultural enrichment, especially programs that encourage the participation of children and the disadvantaged; healthcare, to improve the quality and delivery of services to all citizens, especially women, children, and the disadvantaged; community building, to improve quality of life and foster the growth and development of children; and building democratic opportunities and encouraging democratic citizenship, to make governments more responsive and to encourage citizens to take a more active interest and role in political life. Consult the Web site for grant application instructions, an update on the foundation's activities, and contact information.

The Paul Rapoport Foundation (NY) (http://fdncenter.org/grantmaker/rapoport/)
The New York-based Paul Rapoport Foundation was established in 1987 as memorial to its namesake and his life. Mr. Rapoport was deeply committed to supporting the lesbian, gay, bisexual, and transgender (LGBT) communities, with a particular focus on efforts to eliminate homophobia and discrimination. The foundation supports projects in the greater New York area concerned with social services, healthcare, and legal rights and issues for the LGBT community. Visitors to the foundation's Web site will find more specific information on the foundation's areas of interest, application guidelines, a grants list, a board listing, and contact information.

The Bill Raskob Foundation, Inc. (MD) (http://www.billraskob.org/)
The Bill Raskob Foundation provides no-interest loans to deserving undergraduate or graduate students attending an accredited school in the United States. To apply for a loan, an applicant must be an American citizen; have completed his or her first year at an accredited college or university or medical school; and demonstrate financial need. The foundation's Web site features scholarship criteria, restrictions, a downloadable application, and contact information.

Rasmuson Foundation (AK) (http://www.rasmuson.org)
The Rasmuson Foundation was established in 1955 to help Alaska's nonprofit community improve the quality of life for all Alaskans. The foundation prefers to assist organizations with specific needs and focuses on requests that will enable the organizations to become more efficient and effective. The foundation's Web site provides further information on the grants program, detailed guidelines, recent grants lists, a downloadable copy of the foundation's most recent tax return, FAQs, and contact information.

V. Kann Rasmussen Foundation (MA) (http://www.vkrf.org/)
Established in 1991, the V. Kann Rasmussen Foundation of Boston, Massachusetts, makes grants in three areas: the environment; Greenwood, South Carolina, and the state of South Carolina; and medical research. Visit the foundation's Web site to learn more about the foundation's mission and grantmaking programs, detailed funding history, profiles of new grantees, application procedures, and contact information.

A.C. Ratshesky Foundation (MA) (http://www.grantsmanagement.com/ratshesky.html)
A.C. Ratshesky celebrated his 50th birthday in 1916 by establishing this charitable foundation in his own name. Currently, the Boston, Massachusetts-based foundation has three program areas: childcare, education and training, and arts and culture. Support is generally limited to Boston and adjacent communities and is focused on children, teens, immigrants, "linguistic minorities," the gifted and talented, and the Jewish community. Support for programs that service disadvantaged Jewish populations or Jewish cultural institutions are of special interest. From time to time, the trustees may also give consideration to programs that fall outside of the usual geographic or program limitations. Visit the Web site for application procedures, grants list, and contact information.

Michael Reese Health Trust (IL) (http://fdncenter.org/grantmaker/health/)
The Michael Reese Health Trust seeks to improve the health of people in Chicago's metropolitan communities through effective grantmaking in healthcare, health education, and health research. The trust, which funds exclusively in metropolitan Chicago, with an emphasis on the City of Chicago, seeks to address the needs of the most vulnerable in society, particularly through programs that serve the medically indigent and underserved, immigrants, refugees, the elderly, the mentally and physically disabled, and children and youth. To emphasize the trust's Jewish heritage, special consideration is given to programs that serve those who fall within these populations in the Jewish community. The trust does not fund capital needs (such as buildings, vehicles, and equipment), endowments, fundraising events, debt reduction, individuals, or scholarships. The trust's Web site includes a mission statement, recent grants lists, program guidelines, application procedures, and contact information.

Paul E. & Klare N. Reinhold Foundation, Inc. (FL) (http://www.Reinhold.org)
Located in Orange Park, Florida, the Paul E. & Klare N. Reinhold Foundation was established in 1954. The organization's mission is to continue to support programs that are involved in the founders' areas of interests, including the church, youth, and healthcare. Awards are made to nonprofits in northeast Florida, with major emphasis in Clay and Duval Counties. The grants program makes gifts in six categories: healthcare, religion, children and youth services, music appreciation and education, art appreciation and education, and projects for public improvement and enjoyment. Applications are reviewed once a year by the board. Potential grantees will find short, basic application guidelines and a downloadable application cover letter. The site, which is hosted by the Reinhold Corporation, also includes a list of all grantees and basic contact information.

Research Corporation (AZ) (http://www.rescorp.org/)
The Research Corporation, one of the first private foundations in the United States, is the only domestic foundation wholly devoted to the advancement of science and technology. Its unique philanthropic mission is to make inventions and patent rights "more available and effective in the useful arts and manufactures," and to devote any new resources there

"to provide means for the advancement and extension of technical and scientific investigation, research, and experimentation" at scholarly institutions. The foundation makes between 200 and 300 awards annually for original research in chemistry, physics, and astronomy at colleges and universities throughout the United States and Canada. Visitors to the Web site will find guidelines for foundation-supported programs, recent news releases, contact information, and a downloadable version of the the current issue of the *Research Corporation Report.*

Research Institute for the Study of Man (NY) (Operating foundation) (http://www.rism.org/sft.html)

Incorporated in 1955, the Research Institute for the Study of Man "conducts research and training programs to foster the development and dissemination of basic knowledge in the behavioral sciences." The organization provides institutional grants related to race and ethnic relations and/or issues in political economy. The Web site contains information about the application procedure and provides contact information.

Retirement Research Foundation (IL) (http://www.rrf.org)

The Chicago-based Retirement Research Foundation is the nation's largest private foundation exclusively devoted to aging and retirement issues. Founded by the late John D. MacArthur, it makes grants each year to nonprofit and educational organizations to support programs, research, and public policy studies to improve the quality of life of older Americans. The foundation operates a general grants program and two award programs (the Organizational Capacity Building Program and the Congregation Connection Program) that are open to Chicago-area nonprofits only. Visitors to the foundation's Web site will find a variety of materials, including an overview of the foundation and its funding interests, program descriptions, grants lists, program-related FAQs, board/staff lists, application information, and a number of press releases.

Reuter Foundation (OH) (http://www.reuterfdn.org)

Founded in 1988, the Cleveland, Ohio-based Reuter Foundation provides human services to the disadvantaged, as well as supporting other organizations that share the same mission. The foundation's primary charitable grantmaking remains centered around helping the needy, homeless, and disadvantaged in the Cleveland, Ohio, and Dallas, Texas, areas. The foundation maintains a strong interest in services to the elderly and the physically, mentally, or developmentally disabled. Application guidelines, details on grant awards, an annual report, and contact information are available at the foundation's Web site.

Charles H. Revson Foundation (NY) (http://www.revsonfoundation.org)

The New York-based Charles H. Revson Foundation was founded in 1956 by Charles H. Revson, the founder of Revlon, Inc., as a vehicle for his charitable giving. The mission of the foundation is to "spread knowledge" and to "improve human life." Areas of interest include urban affairs, education, biomedical research policy, and Jewish philanthropy and education. Visitors to the foundation's site will find detailed information about the organization and its grantmaking programs, board/staff listings, grants listings, grant guidelines, and contact information.

Kate B. Reynolds Charitable Trust (NC) (http://www.kbr.org)

Located in Winston-Salem, North Carolina, the Kate B. Reynolds Charitable Trust is named after the late Kate Gertrude Bitting Reynolds, wife of William Neal Reynolds, chairman of R.J. Reynolds Tobacco Company. She created the trust in 1947 in her will, designating that one-fourth of the income from the trust be used for the poor and needy in Winston-Salem and Forsyth County and that the remaining three-fourths be used for charity patients in North Carolina hospitals. The trust's grantmaking is limited to North Carolina. The trust also has satellite offices in different areas of the state, to make themselves more accessible to those who can benefit most from their grantmaking and to help the trust gather information on different areas of the state. Guidelines, applications, downloadable expenditure and program report forms, and contact information are on the trust's

Web site. Information on outreach programs and special initiatives, grants lists, advisory board and staff listings, FAQs, and press releases are also included.

The Christopher Reynolds Foundation Inc. (NY) (http://www.creynolds.org)
The Christopher Reynolds Foundation Inc. of New York was established in 1952. It is currently interested in supporting U.S. relations with Cuba and needs in Cuba as defined by Cubans themselves. The foundation does not accept proposals that have not been requested by its staff or been approved for receipt by the executive director. Visitors to the foundation's Web site will find an extensive archive of grant recipients, grant guidelines, board/staff listings, and contact information.

Donald W. Reynolds Foundation (NV) (http://www.dwreynolds.org)
The Donald W. Reynolds Foundation was established in 1954 by Donald W. Reynolds, a pioneer in the American communications industry and the founder of Donrey Media Group. The foundation's current programs, however, did not begin taking shape until 1993, when Mr. Reynolds died and left a generous bequest. The mission statement of the Las Vegas-based foundation is to make grants in "Arkansas, Nevada, and Oklahoma to qualified charitable organizations which demonstrate a sustainable program, exhibit an entrepreneurial spirit, and assist those served to be healthy, self-sufficient, and productive members of the community." The foundation's programs include: the Capital Grants Program, the Aging and Quality of Life Initiative, the Clinical Cardiovascular Research Program, the Community Services Center Program, and Donald W. Reynolds Special Initiatives. Some programs solicit applications; others are driven exclusively by trustee initiative. Guidelines for the Capital Grants and Community Services Center Programs, annual reports, grants lists, staff listings, and contact information are available at the foundation's Web site.

Z. Smith Reynolds Foundation (NC) (http://www.zsr.org/)
Created in 1963 to serve the people of North Carolina, the Z. Smith Reynolds Foundation is one of the country's largest general purpose foundations with a mandate to make grants within a single state. The foundation focuses its activities in the areas of community-building and economic development; the environment; governance, public policy, and civic engagement; pre-collegiate education; and social justice and equality. However, the foundation will consider proposals that fall outside these areas as long as they are consistent with the foundation's mission. The foundation's Web site provides general information about the foundation, detailed grant application procedures, information on special publications and programs, a helpful FAQ section, a list of recent grants awarded, and links to grantee Web sites.

RGK Foundation (TX) (http://www.rgkfoundation.org)
Ronya and George Kozmetsky established the RGK Foundation in 1966 to support medical and educational research. Since then, the Austin, Texas-based foundation has broadened its focus and "community" is now the third component to the foundation's grantmaking. Grants in these three areas support research in several areas of national and international concern, including health, corporate governance, energy, economic analysis, and technology transfer; conferences, which are designed to enhance information exchange and maintain an "interlinkage" among business, academia, the community, and government; programs that promote academic excellence in institutions of higher learning, raise literacy levels, attract minority and women students into the math, science, and technology fields; and promote the well-being of children. There are no geographic limitations to the foundation's grantmaking. Visitors to the Web site will find application guidelines, a printable and downloadable application form, online contact form, grant lists, related links, a list of publications resulting from foundation-sponsored research, financial data, staff listing, and contact information.

The Walter H. and Marjory M. Rich Memorial Fund (GA) (http://www.richmemorialfund.org)
The Walter H. and Marjory M. Rich Memorial Fund was founded in 1959 by a local businessman and his wife to benefit the metropolitan Atlanta area. Brief grant guidelines and

limitations are provided online, along with a link to a downloadable grant application form. The foundation's funds and grants are administered by the SunTrust Bank Atlanta Foundation. Contact information can be found online.

The Richards Foundation (GA) (http://www.rrichards.org/)
Located in Carrolton, Georgia, the Richards Foundation was established in 1990 by Roy Richards, Jr. to extend his Christian beliefs. The organization's mission is to "support programs which address the root causes rather than the symptoms of social needs." Areas of interest include art and culture; elementary, secondary, and higher education; human services for children and youth; medical and hospice care; and religion. The foundation is looking for projects that will have a lasting effect on Carrolton and the surrounding areas and that will break the cycles that keep people deprived. Programs outside of Carrolton are considered if they fall strictly within the foundation's goals. There is no application available online, but the Web site includes proposal guidelines and deadlines, a list of past grant recipients, and financial data.

Smith Richardson Foundation, Inc. (CT) (http://www.srf.org)
H. Smith Richardson and his wife, Grace Jones Richardson, created the Smith Richardson Foundation, Inc. in 1935. H. Smith Richardson helped build a "world-wide medicinal empire" with Vicks Family Remedies. Located in Westport, Connecticut, the foundation seeks to "help ensure the vitality of our social, economic, and governmental institutions," and "assist with the development of effective policies to compete internationally and advance U.S. interests and values abroad." The foundation has two grant programs: the International Security and Foreign Policy Program, which supports research and policy projects on issues central to the strategic interests of the United States, and the Domestic Public Policy Program, which supports research, writing, and analysis that informs the thinking of policymakers and the public on domestic issues. The foundation also makes small grants to organizations that provide innovative services for children and families at risk in North Carolina and Connecticut. The foundation's governors customarily solicit these grants. Consult the Web site for information about the foundation's grant programs and grant guidelines, proposal templates (for those who are invited to submit a proposal after an initial inquiry has been made), grant reporting requirements, FAQs, staff listings, and contact information.

Ringing Rocks Foundation (PA) (http://www.ringingrocks.org/)
The Ringing Rocks Foundation of Pennsylvania was established in 1995 to explore, document, and preserve indigenous cultures and their healing practices. Each year grants are awarded to organizations throughout the world that promote indigenous healing, work with indigenous cultures, and educate the public at large about these topics. Grants are used for startup costs, program development, special projects, and general operating expenses. Each grant will have a strategic impact in an indigenous community. The foundation's Web site features a history of the foundation, description of the foundation's current interests, lists of recent publications, information on current initiatives, grants data, and contact information.

The Riordan Foundation (CA) (http://www.riordanfoundation.org)
Richard J. Riordan founded The Riordan Foundation in 1981 "to ensure that all children become successful readers and writers while they are still young." The foundation also seeks to use its funds as a "catalyst to encourage a broad base of support for early childhood education." The foundation chartered Rx for Reading in 1989, a public foundation through which many donations are distributed, to enhance and support the goals of the foundation. Through Rx for Reading, the foundation makes challenge grants to schools that wish to participate in Writing to Read, Computers in the Classroom, and English Language Development grants. Visit the foundation's Web site for more information on the foundation's grant programs and guidelines, downloadable grant applications, FAQs, and contact information.

Fannie E. Rippel Foundation (NJ) (http://fdncenter.org/grantmaker/rippel/)
The Fannie E. Rippel Foundation's objectives are to support the relief and care of aged women, the erection and maintenance of hospitals, and the treatment of and/or research concerning heart disease and cancer. Although strict geographic limitations are not imposed, emphasis is given to institutions located in New Jersey and the greater New York metropolitan area, the general Northeast, and the Mid–Atlantic states. The foundation's Web site features an online version of the foundation's most recent annual report, application guidelines, messages from the foundation's president and chairman, recent grants listings, financial statements, description of foundation's activities, and listings of trustees and staff.

The Roberts Foundation (CA) (http://www.pacificfoundationservices.com/roberts/)
Established in 1985, the San Francisco-based Roberts Foundation encompasses distinct grant programs supporting northern California. The Roberts Foundation grant program supports children and youth services, education, higher education, and wildlife preservation and animal welfare. As this time, the Roberts Foundation has suspended its grantmaking; however, the Roberts Enterprise Development Fund's grant program continues and seeks to "raise the standards of excellence and integrity in the nonprofit and philanthropic community nationwide through the development and dissemination of innovative approaches to address critical social issues." The foundation's Web features a recent grants list, contact information, and board of directors list.

Edward C. and Ann T. Roberts Foundation (CT)
(http://fdncenter.org/grantmaker/e&aroberts/)
The Edward C. and Ann T. Roberts Foundation supports and encourages excellence in the arts in Hartford, Connecticut, and the surrounding area. The foundation focuses its support on the creation, presentation, and performance of works of art. Visitors to the foundation's Web site will find grant limitations and guidelines, recent grants lists, application requirements, and contact information.

Robins Foundation (VA) (http://www.robins-foundation.org/)
The Richmond, Virginia-based Robins Foundation seeks to improve the lives and opportunities of Virginians through grants to nonprofit organizations. It is particularly interested in helping with emerging issues and underfunded areas where its grants can act as catalysts and also help established organizations sustain and build on past successes. Funds are given in the form of program support, capital expenditures, or endowments. The early childhood/quality improvement grants program specifically supports organizations that devote a major portion of their resources to young children and their families. Grantmaking is normally limited to the central Virginia area, but the foundation may consider proposals from other areas of the Commonwealth. The foundation's Web site features downloadable application materials and guidelines, and contact information.

Rockefeller Brothers Fund (NY) (http://www.rbf.org/)
Since 1984, the Rockefeller Brothers Fund has promoted social change that contributes to a more just, sustainable, and peaceful world. The fund's grantmaking focuses on four areas: democratic practice, sustainable development, peace and security, and the Charles E. Culpeper Human Advancement Program. The fund's programs are intended to develop leaders, strengthen institutions, engage citizens, build communities, and foster partnerships that include government, business, and civil society. Visitors to the fund's Web site will find program guidelines and comprehensive lists of recent grants, application procedures and grant restrictions, a list of fund publications, a listing of trustees and officers, and links to the fund's non-grantmaking programs and affiliations.

Rockefeller Foundation (NY) (http://www.rockfound.org/)
Endowed by John D. Rockefeller and chartered in 1913 for "the well-being of people throughout the world," the Rockefeller Foundation is one of America's oldest private foundations and one of the few with strong international interests. The foundation focuses its

activities on creativity and culture, food security, health equity, working communities, global inclusions, and a number of special programs all over the world. The balance of the foundation's grant and fellowship programs supports work in building democracy, international security, international philanthropy, and other special interests and initiatives. Visitors to the foundation's Web site will find information about the foundation's programs, funding priorities, fellowships, and recent grants; recent annual reports; a listing of the foundation's trustees; and a letter from the foundation's president.

Winthrop Rockefeller Foundation (AR) (http://www.wrockefellerfoundation.org/)
The Winthrop Rockefeller Foundation's vision is for Arkansas to be a state where economic, racial, and social justice are universally valued and practiced. The foundation seeks to build and sustain strong communities by supporting and strengthening organizations that serve Arkansans. The foundation concentrates its resources in the following areas: economic development, education, and economic, racial, and social justice. The foundation does not make grants for capital purposes, deficit operations, individuals, or endowments. Visitors to the foundation's Web site can find information on the geographic areas that will be considered, application guidelines, a downloadable application form, and contact information.

Rockwell Fund (TX) (http://www.rockfund.org/)
The Houston, Texas-based, Rockwell Fund was established 1931 upon the death of James M. Rockwell, owner and manager of Rockwell Lumber Company. The Rockwell Fund is dedicated to the charitable purposes set forth by its founder and the Rockwell family. The fund is most interested in education, although other areas, such as the arts and health, civic, religion, and social services, are also occasionally supported. The fund awards most grants in the city of Houston; however funding is not completely limited to that singular area. The fund makes grants in the form of scholarships (through schools, colleges, and universities), general operating support, new buildings, building renovations, endowments, equipment, professorships, academic chairs, special projects, operation of existing programs, and seed money. The fund's Web site features financial information, a most recent grant list, printable application guidelines and applications and contact information.

Rosenberg Foundation (CA) (http://www.rosenbergfdn.org/)
The Rosenberg Foundation was established in 1935 by relatives and associates of Max L. Rosenberg, a San Francisco businessman and philanthropist. Since the 1940s, the foundation has emphasized the health, education, and recreation of California's children and communities. Today, the foundation accepts grant requests in three priority areas: the Changing Population of California Program, which includes activities that "promote the full social, economic, and cultural integration of immigrants and minorities into a pluralistic society"; the Children and Families in Poverty Program, which includes activities that "reduce dependency, promote self-help, create access to the economic mainstream, or address the causes of poverty among children and families"; and the Child Support Reform Program, a multi-year initiative aimed at increasing "economic security for children, particularly children in low-income families, through the development of a public system that is effective in establishing paternity, fair in awarding support, efficient and effective in collecting and distributing payments, and build[s] toward a national program of child support assurance." Visitors to the foundation's Web site will find thorough program descriptions, recent grants lists organized by program area, application guidelines and procedures, current financial information, a brief history of the foundation, and contact information.

Henry and Ruth Blaustein Rosenberg Foundation (MD) (http://fdncenter.org/grantmaker/rosenberg/)
The mission of the Henry and Ruth Blaustein Rosenberg Foundation is to improve the human condition through promoting life-long educational opportunities, research advances, and a spectrum of cultural programming. The foundation focuses its grantmaking primarily in the Baltimore, Maryland, area, providing support in three general program areas: education and adult self-sufficiency, arts and culture, and health and youth

development. Details about grant guidelines and restrictions can be found on the foundation's Web site. Organizations interested in applying for grants should submit a letter of intent or a short proposal. The Web site contains information about what details should be included and where the letter should be sent. The site also contains a list of previous grants awarded, including a description and dollar amount for each grant.

Sunny & Abe Rosenberg Foundation (NY) (http://www.rosenbergfoundation.org)
Founded in 1966 by Abraham Rosenberg, a successful New York City businessman, "to promote a wide variety of philanthropic interests both in New York and Israel," the Sunny & Abe Rosenberg Foundation mainly funds organizations in New York City, but it does consider worthwhile grant requests from other geographic areas. The foundation concentrates its giving in six areas. Health organizations include mental health programs, cancer research, programs for the young and elderly, and programs serving persons with physical or sensory impairments. Education includes public education, libraries, and organizations that promote tolerance and combat discrimination. Artistic and cultural programs include art museums, performing arts, and education in public schools. Recreation includes city parks programs and youth camps. Social services includes food distribution to the needy and elderly, AIDS prevention, family planning, youth employment services, and alcohol and drug rehabilitation programs. International includes schools, orphanages, and libraries. The foundation's Web site provides funding guidelines, contact information, and useful links.

The Judith Rothschild Foundation (NY) (http://fdncenter.org/grantmaker/rothschild/)
The Judith Rothschild Foundation seeks to stimulate interest in recently deceased American painters, sculptors, and photographers whose work is of the highest quality but lacks wide recognition. The New York City-based foundation makes grants to present, preserve, or interpret work of the highest aesthetic merit by lesser known American artists who have died after 1976, as stipulated in Rothschild's will. Rothschild's goal for the foundation was "to increase the public understanding of such lesser known and insufficiently appreciated artists—affording their work the opportunity for public viewing, institutional acquisition, and critical reassessment." The foundation's Web site contains a description of the foundation's mission, grant application instructions, a listing of grants, a short biography of Rothschild, and contact information.

The Shelley and Donald Rubin Foundation (NY) (http://www.sdrubin.org)
The New York City-based Shelley and Donald Rubin Foundation is dedicated to "encouraging and supporting policy analysis, advocacy, and research as well as educational and artistic activities that address issues around society's changing family structure and its cultural and ethnic diversity." The grant areas of interest include: at-risk children, healthcare, AIDS and its effects, the environment, developing community identity, and preserving ancient Tibetan art. Interested organizations should contact the foundation with a letter of inquiry in order to receive a grant application. Projects will be monitored by phone, correspondence, and site visits throughout the grant period. The foundation's Web site includes contact information and a list of grant recipients, with brief descriptions of many projects.

Helena Rubinstein Foundation (NY) (http://fdncenter.org/grantmaker/rubinstein/)
The Helena Rubinstein Foundation of New York was established in 1953 to encourage young women to undertake higher education and to pursue nontraditional careers. Today, the foundation supports programs in education, community services, arts/arts in education, and health, with emphasis on projects which benefit women and children. Grants are primarily targeted to organizations in New York City. Although general operating grants are made, the foundation prefers to support specific programs. Visitors to the foundation's Web site will find a brief biography of Ms. Rubinstein, funding guidelines and restrictions, recent grants lists, staff/board listings, and contact information.

The Ruddie Memorial Youth Foundation (MD) (http://www.rmyf.org)
The mission of the Maryland-based Ruddie Memorial Youth Foundation is to "identify and disseminate innovative and effective ways for youths to reach their full potential." The foundation maintains two grant programs. Evaluation Grants fund the identification and evaluation process used to select productive programs for underprivileged youth. Dissemination Grants fund thc implcmcntation and dissemination of selected programs. Visitors to the foundation's Web site will find detailed information about each grant program, criteria information, online grant applications, and contact information.

Rural Kentucky Medical Scholarship Fund (KY) (http://www.kyma.org/rural.stm)
The Rural Kentucky Medical Scholarship Fund has distributed millions of dollars to medical students since its establishment in 1951. The fund works "to provide better distribution of physicians to rural areas of Kentucky." This is done by awarding loans for a year of medical school for every year that the recipient practices in a designated rural area. Those who practice in rural areas receive very low interest rates; those who practice in areas of critical need are forgiven their loans. Currently the fund is not accepting applications. The fund's Web site includes a table of the counties in Kentucky with designations of whether they qualify for this program.

Russell Family Foundation (WA) (http://www.russellfamilyfdn.org)
The Russell Family Foundation of Seattle, Washington, was established in 1994 by the founders of the Frank Russell Company, an investment management and advisory firm. The foundation "exists to enhance family and improve community" in the Puget Sound region. While the grantmaking focus is on western Washington, the foundation accepts proposals from nonprofits throughout the state that fall in its major funding categories: values-based education and a healthy, sustainable environment. Proposals are accepted outside of these categories from nonprofits that are located in Pierce County. The foundation's Web site includes application deadlines and instructions on the first step of the process; submitting a letter of inquiry.

Ida Alice Ryan Trust (GA)
(http://www.wachovia.com/charitable_services/idaryan_overview.asp)
The Ida Alice Ryan Trust was established in Georgia after the death of Miss Ida Alice Ryan in 1953. The trust supports charitable institutions in the vicinity of Atlanta, Georgia. The split-interest trust makes grants to metropolitan Atlanta nonprofits primarily for capital needs in the areas of health, human services, and community welfare. Special consideration is given to ministries of the Catholic Church. Visit the trust's Web site to find grant guidelines, a downloadable grant application, a recent grants list, and a listing of committee members.

Sachs Foundation (CO) (http://www.frii.com/~sachs)
The Sachs Foundation was established in Colorado Springs, Colorado, in 1931. The organization is committed to awarding scholarships to graduating African-American high school seniors who have lived in Colorado for at least five years. Applicants cannot be currently attending college but may have graduated high school within three years of applying. Applicants are screened for both financial need and academic achievement, and the foundation attempts to keep the ratio of men and women even. The average scholarship is $4,000 a year and continues for the four years of college. The site includes an application and a financial statement, both of which must be printed, filled in, and mailed to the foundation for consideration.

Russell Sage Foundation (NY) (Operating foundation) (http://www.russellsage.org/)
The Russell Sage Foundation is dedicated "to strengthening the methods, data, and theoretical core of the social sciences as a means of improving social policies." It does this through its Visiting Scholars Program and by funding studies by scholars at academic and research institutions. The foundation currently is focusing on four areas: the future of work, immigration, literacy and disadvantaged children, and the psychology of cultural contact.

Offerings at its Web site include program descriptions, grants lists, application guidelines, information about projects of special interest to the foundation, and a searchable listing of foundation publications, all of which can be ordered online.

Sailors' Snug Harbor of Boston (MA) (http://www.sailorssnugharbor.org)
Sailors' Snug Harbor of Boston helps current and retired fishing families in Massachusetts achieve sustainable self-sufficiency during this period of transition in their industry. The organization was established in 1852 to provide homes to sailors who were "broken down by infirmities brought on by disease in foreign clinics, expenses, and hardships." In recent years, the organization has made grants to support the needs of low-income elderly sailors and their families. Since 1995, the trustees have focused funds specifically toward programs addressing the needs of Massachusetts fishing families, primarily in Gloucester, New Bedford, and Cape Cod. Visitors to the foundation's Web site will find a list of past grants, lists of trustees/staff, contact information, and a downloadable grant proposal form.

Salomon Family Foundation (NY) (http://fdncenter.org/grantmaker/salomon/)
The New York-based Salomon Family Foundation supports the treatment of child abuse, with special emphasis on sexual abuse and programs that provide the intensive and extensive treatment needed. The foundation's Web site features an introduction on the foundation's purpose, grant proposal guidelines, information on grant cycles, a downloadable copy of the foundation's latest tax return, and contact information.

The Grace Ford Salvatori Foundation (CA) (http://fdncenter.org/grantmaker/salvatori/)
The California-based, Grace Ford Salvatori Foundation's Web site includes a copy of the foundation's three most recent tax returns.

The Fan Fox and Leslie R. Samuels Foundation, Inc. (NY) (http://www.samuels.org)
Although founded in Utah in 1959, the Fan Fox and Leslie R. Samuels Foundation, Inc. is now located in New York City. The foundation supports performing arts programs and organizations or projects working to improve the delivery of high quality healthcare throughout the metropolitan New York area. The healthcare program is focused on supporting elderly and chronically ill patients and making sure they receive the treatment to which they are entitled. Grants are made to support "demonstrations, evaluations, and other types of studies that directly impact the users of healthcare." The performing arts program supports the highest level companies and presenters, along with arts education programs in the public schools and support for those pursuing careers in the arts. Disciplines eligible for support include dance, music, opera, and theater. Special project grants are made to support programs addressing important issues in the arts community. Application guidelines for each program, lists of past grant recipients organized by category, and a staff list are included on the foundation's Web site.

San Juan Island Community Foundation (WA) (http://www.sjicf.org/)
Established in 1994, the mission of the San Juan Island Community Foundation is to ensure and enhance the quality of life on San Juan Island. The foundation has been achieving its mission by encouraging philanthropy, growing an endowment for purposeful grants to community charitable organizations, and building partnerships that effectively connect donors with island nonprofit organizations. Grants are made for the arts, health and social services, youth and education, and the environment and conservation. Visitors to the foundation's Web site will find further grant details, application information, FAQs, a board listing, and contact information.

Sarkeys Foundation (OK) (http://www.sarkeys.org/)
Established in 1962, the Sarkeys Foundation provides grants to nonprofit and charitable organizations that are committed to improving the quality of life in Oklahoma. The foundation focuses its grantmaking in the areas of education, healthcare and medical research, and cultural and humanitarian programs of regional significance. Complete application instructions and guidelines are available from the foundation's Web site, including a

downloadable application. Currently the foundation is not accepting new proposals. Additional details about the Sarkeys Foundation's history and facilities, along with contact information, can be found online.

Santos Family Foundation (DC) (http://fdncenter.org/grantmaker/santos/)
The Santos Family Foundation of Washington, D.C., focuses on improving automobile safety, Particularly the crash-worthiness of passenger vehicles. The leaders of the foundation hope that an improved standard will reduce rollover deaths and injuries from roof crush, which now represent a significant portion of all injuries and fatalities due to rollovers. The foundation does not allow submissions from the public. Visit the foundation's Web site for contact information and a number of reports based on crash and rollover statistics.

Sarah Scaife Foundation, Inc. (PA) (http://www.scaife.com)
Located in Pittsburgh, Pennsylvania, the Sarah Scaife Foundation, Inc. is one of four Scaife foundations. The Sarah Scaife Foundation's grant program is "primarily directed toward public policy programs that address major domestic and international issues." There are no geographical restrictions, but only nonprofit organizations are eligible for grants. To apply, organizations should send letters with brief descriptions of their programs and several supporting documents, which are described on the Web site. The site also has contact and mailing information as well as downloadable financial information.

Scaife Family Foundation (PA) (http://www.scaife.com)
The Scaife Family Foundation is located in Pittsburgh, Pennsylvania, and is one of four Scaife foundations. The foundation awards grants to programs that "support and develop programs that promote the well-being of the family and traditional values." Applications for projects in southwestern Pennsylvania are given special priority. Initial inquiries to the foundation should be in letter form signed by the organization's president, or authorized representative, and have the approval of the board of directors. Specifics about the letter and necessary attachments are described on the foundation's Web site. Contact and financial information and downloadable annual reports are also available on the site.

Robert Schalkenbach Foundation (NY) (http://www.schalkenbach.org)
The Robert Schalkenbach Foundation of New York was created in 1925 to teach, expound, and propagate the ideas of Henry George as set forth in his book, *Progress and Poverty,* and other works. The foundation and its supporters are convinced that the principles expounded by Henry George will, to the extent that they are enacted into law, give equal opportunity to all and lead to the betterment of society. These principles will free labor, exchange, and capital formation to create a world of greater abundance coupled with lesser demands on scarce natural resources, leading to the elimination of poverty. The foundation makes grants to individuals and organizations that show an interest in progressing the public dialogue of Henry George's philosophy and ideas. Specific areas of interest are support for publications dealing with Henry George's ideas, support for individuals and organizations that educate the public in principles of economics and public finance related to Henry George's ideas, and for support of research towards a more just and productive society. Visitor's to the foundation's Web site will find information on the foundation's grant program, a listing of directors and staff, and contact information.

The Karla Scherer Foundation (IL) (http://www.comnet.org/local/orgs/kschererf/)
Appalled by how badly she was treated during the proxy fight to sell her father's company in 1988, the result, she felt, of being a woman in a male-dominated business world, Karla Schere "resolved to do her utmost to enable more women to attain positions of power in business. With this resolve, and $4 million dollars from the sale of the company, the Karla Scherer Foundation was born." Located in Chicago, Illinois, the Karla Scherer Foundation awards scholarships to female students majoring in finance or economics with plans for a corporate business career. Applications must be requested in writing; the address and other

necessary information are provided on the site. There are no geographic restrictions, and those awarded scholarships may apply for renewals.

The Scholarships Foundation (NY) (http://fdncenter.org/grantmaker/scholarships/)
The Scholarships Foundation, founded in 1921 by Maria Bowen Chapin, is based in New York and awards grants to undergraduate and graduate students enrolled in full-time or part-time academic programs. Priority is given to students who do not fit into defined scholarship categories, and grants are based on merit and need. The foundation's Web site features a mission statement, FAQs, and information on who should apply for a grant and how to do so.

Caroline & Sigmund Schott Foundation (MA) (http://www.schottfoundation.org/)
The mission of the Massachusetts-based Caroline & Sigmund Schott Foundation is to develop and strengthen the movement for equality in education and childcare. The foundation believes that "a child's intellectual, emotional, social, and moral development is significantly shaped by the quality of their educational experiences." The Schott Foundation emphasizes three areas of education, including creating better public schools in underserved communities; making schools "gender healthy" by supporting professional development for teachers, counselors, and administrators and by strengthening and expanding the network of activists and advocates for gender equality; and to assure universal and accessible high-quality early care and education. To meet the goals, the foundation's grant program assists in raising public awareness, increasing understanding of complex issues, and strengthens grassroots advocacy networks. Specific areas of interest supported by the foundation include leadership development programs, grassroots organizing, partnership with policy makers, media campaigns for public awareness, voter education, litigation, research, and coalition building. Visitors to the foundation's Web site will find information on the organizations the foundation supports, application guidelines, staff listings, and contact information.

The Eulalie Bloedel Schneider Foundation (WA) (http://fdncenter.org/grantmaker/schneider/)
The Eulalie Bloedel Schneider Foundation of Seattle, Washington, is primarily interested in creative educational programs and community-based grassroots programs that contain in-depth experiential learning and skills training for family members of all ages. The foundation also shows an interest in the environment, natural sciences, and artistic and cultural programs. Visit the foundation's Web site for further information on grants guidelines and restrictions, application procedures, and contact information.

The Arthur B. Schultz Foundation (NV) (http://www.absfoundation.org)
Located in Incline Village, Nevada, the Arthur B. Schultz Foundation supports "improved understanding between nations of previously differing political systems through trade in an interdependent global economy; education of a new generation of students within the framework of an interdependent global economy and environment; and organizations and initiatives promoting environmental protection and natural resource conservation." The foundation's grants support improved facilities and specific programs in "visionary educational institutions." The foundation also supports environmental conservation and habitat protection. Visit the Web site for details on program areas, grant guidelines, grants lists, financial information, and contact information.

The Schumann Fund for New Jersey (NJ) (http://fdncenter.org/grantmaker/schumann/)
The Schumann Fund for New Jersey was created in 1988 by Florence Schumann and her children to continue the lifelong philanthropy of Mrs. Schumann and her husband John. The fund's areas of interest include early childhood development, environmental protection, public policy, and grants to Essex County. Visit the foundation's Web site to find a brief history of the fund, program guidelines, a recent grants list, financial information, and contact information.

Charles and Lynn Schusterman Family Foundation (OK) (http://www.schusterman.org)
Located in Tulsa, Oklahoma, the Charles and Lynn Schusterman Family Foundation was founded in 1987 to support programs that enhance Jewish life in the United States, Israel, and the former Soviet Union. It also funds Oklahoma-based, non-sectarian charitable groups that focus on education, children, and community service. Visit the Web site for grant guidelines, a downloadable preliminary application form, news and media stories about the foundation, contact information, and related links.

Charles and Helen Schwab Family Foundation (CA) (http://www.schwabfamilyfdn.org/)
The San Mateo, California-based Charles and Helen Schwab Family Foundation maintains a number of formal grant programs, including capacity building, homelessness, poverty prevention, substance abuse, and learning differences. Special emphasis is placed on helping individuals and families achieve a sense of self-sufficiency. The foundation's Web site describes the types of grants made, and provides specific application information, individual grant histories, financial information, staff/trustee lists, and contact information.

Schwab Foundation for Learning (CA) (Operating foundation) (http://www.schwablearning.org)
The Schwab Foundation for Learning is a nonprofit operating foundation founded by discount brokerage pioneer Charles R. Schwab and his wife, Helen O'Neill Schwab, in 1988. The foundation established a resource center in San Mateo, California, that is dedicated to raising awareness and providing parents and teachers with information, resources, and support to improve the lives of children with learning differences. Questions about learning differences can be asked online for free, and more extensive help is offered if you become a member, which gives you access to personalized resources and addresses your specific concerns. The Web site also features a list of resources for parents and educators, online bulletin boards, an online feedback form, online membership sign-up, and contact information.

The Self Family Foundation (SC) (http://www.selffoundation.org/)
The Self Family Foundation has its roots in the Self Foundation, which was incorporated by James C. Self, founder of Greenwood Mills, in 1942. Its primary goal then was to build a hospital. Today, the foundation's mission is "to encourage self-sufficiency in people and the communities in which they live." The foundation's grantmaking program is concerned with enhancing life, encouraging self-sufficiency, and "providing cures rather than treatments," in the following target areas: education, healthcare, and human services; civic and community life; and arts, culture, and history. The foundation's primary geographic area of interest is Greenwood, South Carolina, where the foundation is located, the surrounding counties, and upper Piedmont region. The foundation will consider providing seed money for creative and innovative projects in other regions of South Carolina, if they have the potential to be replicated in or have a positive impact on the Greenwood area. Visit the foundation's Web site for grant guidelines and application procedures, grants lists, and contact information.

Shared Earth Foundation (MD) (http://www.sharedearth.org/)
The Shared Earth Foundation of Maryland is committed to the tenet that all creatures have an enduring claim to sustainable space on this planet. The foundation believes that today's human beings have the responsibility to share Earth's resources with other creatures and future generations by limiting their adverse impact on the planet and by enriching and protecting Earth's wildlife and the places they inhabit. Visit the foundation's Web site for further details on funding priorities, application guidelines, information on programs funded in the most recent cycle, and contact information.

Emma A. Sheafer Charitable Trust (NY) (http://fdncenter.org/grantmaker/sheafer/)
The Emma A. Sheafer Charitable Trust of New York supports the performance arts in the New York City metropolitan area. Types of support provided by the foundation include projects, capital, capacity building, and special projects. No grants are made to individuals,

private foundations, governmental organizations, or for matching gifts or loans. Visit the trust's Web site to locate application procedures, lists of previous grant recipients, and contact information.

Siebert Lutheran Foundation (WI) (http://www.siebertfoundation.org/)
The mission of the Wisconsin-based, Siebert Lutheran Foundation is "to be wise stewards enabling Lutheran congregations, associations, and institutions to be more responsible, creative, compassionate, and effective in sharing God's word serving people." Although the funding interests of the foundation change, it is currently supporting education and training, community development and outreach, aging and health services, evangelism, and youth programs. Visit the foundation's Web site to find a brief history of the organization, a detailed FAQ section, grant application information, and contact information.

Sierra Health Foundation (CA) (http://www.sierrahealth.org)
The Sierra Health Foundation, headquartered in Sacramento, California, awards grants in support of health and health-related activities in a 26-county region of northern California. It was established in 1984 when Foundation Health Plan, now part of HealthNet of California, converted from nonprofit to for-profit corporate status. The Sierra Health Foundation was created and endowed with the proceeds from the sale. The foundation seeks to provide monetary support for local and regional health-related programs and services, influence public health policy and choices, and stimulate improvement in California's healthcare system. Visit the foundation's Web site to view program information, grant guidelines, and recent awards; download applications; view and download publications; request information online; and to access contact information.

William E. Simon Foundation, Inc. (NJ) (http://www.wesimonfoundation.org)
The William E. Simon Foundation, Inc., located in Morristown, New Jersey, is named after its principal benefactor. It supports programs that strengthen the free enterprise system and "the moral and spiritual values on which it rests: individual freedom, initiative, thrift, self-discipline, and faith in God." The main charitable purpose of the foundation is to assist those in need by providing the means through which they may help themselves; accordingly, the foundation seeks to fund programs that promote independence and personal responsibility among those in need. Its funding areas include, but are not limited to, education, family, and faith. Visit the foundation's Web site for details about funding areas and for contact information.

Harry Singer Foundation (CA) (Operating foundation) (http://www.singerfoundation.org/)
Founded in 1987, the California-based Harry Singer Foundation focuses on promoting "responsibility and involving people more fully in public policy." As a private operating foundation, it supports and administers active programs but does not make grants. Current programs focus on government spending, personal responsibility, values, and emotional intelligence. The foundation's Web site provides information about a range of foundation programs, including current and past essay contests, a teacher's mentor program, a workbook series, and an electronic lending library.

The Siragusa Foundation (IL) (http://www.siragusa.org/index.html)
The Siragusa Foundation was founded in 1950 by Ross D. Siragusa, a Chicago philanthropist whose charitable interests included child development, social services, education, healthcare, cultural endeavors, and the environment. The Siragusa Foundation follows the original interests of its founder in its funding today, basing most of its grantmaking in the Chicago area. Currently, the foundation is not accepting proposals; in general, the foundation does not accept unsolicited proposals from outside the Chicago area. Visitors to the foundation's Web site will find application guidelines, listings of past and recent grantees; the foundation's annual report, links to philanthropic resources, a history of the organization and biography of its founder, a general introduction to philanthropy, and contact information.

Skillman Foundation (MI) (http://www.skillman.org/)
Founded in 1960 by Rose P. Skillman, widow of 3M vice president and director Robert H. Skillman, the Skillman Foundation seeks to improve the well-being of residents in southeastern Michigan and, in particular, the metropolitan Detroit area (Wayne, Oakland, and Macomb Counties). Developing children and youth to their maximum potential is the foundation's primary goal. To that end, it makes grants in the areas of child and family welfare, child and family health, education, juvenile justice, youth development, basic human needs, culture and the arts, and civil instituations that strengthen the community. The foundation's Web site provides information about the foundation's grantmaking policies and procedures; a list of grants organized by subject area; online versions of its most recent newsletters, reports, and publications; an evaluation guide; a listing of the foundation's trustees and staff; and contact information.

Alfred P. Sloan Foundation (NY) (http://www.sloan.org/)
Established in 1934 by longtime General Motors chairman and CEO Alfred P. Sloan, the New York City-based Alfred P. Sloan Foundation today concentrates its activities in four main areas: science and technology; standards of living, competitiveness, and economics; education and careers in science and technology; and selected national issues. The foundation has no deadlines or standard forms. Visitors to the foundation's Web site will find detailed program descriptions, application procedures, a directory of foundation officers and staff, and a brief biography of the foundation's founder.

The Christopher D. Smithers Foundation (NY) (http://www.smithersfoundation.org)
R. Brinkley Smithers established the Christopher D. Smithers Foundation in 1953 in memory of his father, who was one of the founders and a major stockholder of IBM. A recovered alcoholic, R. Brinkley Smithers made alcoholism the focus of the foundation's efforts. The foundation, located in Mills Valley, New York, seeks to educate the public that alcoholism is a "respectable, treatable disease from which people can and do recover." It also encourages prevention programs and activities, with an emphasis on high-risk populations, and aims to reduce and eliminate the stigma associated with alcoholism. Visitors to the Web site will find a history of the foundation, several biographies of its founder, related links, and contact information.

Sobrato Family Foundation (CA) (http://www.sobrato.com/foundation)
Ann and John A. Sobrato, and his wife, Susan, established the Sobrato Family Foundation in 1996. The Sobratos are owners of the Sobrato Development Companies which have led the real estate industry in innovation by developing and building facilities for more than 200 high-technology companies in the Santa Clara Valley in California. The mission of the Cupertino, California-based family foundation is "dedicated to helping create and sustain a vibrant and healthy community where all Silicon Valley residents have equal opportunity to live, work, and be enriched." The foundation provides rent-free office space grants in a nonprofit multi-tenant center located in Milpitas, California. It also operates the Sobrato Family Affordable Housing Fund which makes interest-free loans to local nonprofit housing developers to create affordable rental, homeless, and transitional housing. Visit the foundation's Web site for grant guidelines, grant program information, grant lists with links to grantee organizations, and contact information.

Society for Analytical Chemists of Pittsburgh (PA) (http://www.sacp.org/)
The Society for Analytical Chemists of Pittsburgh, founded in 1943, is dedicated to "the advancement of analytical chemistry through science education." The society is a professional membership organization that provides educational opportunities for its members and the community. The society provides a number of educational and scholarship programs for college, high school, and elementary students. Brief descriptions of the scholarship programs are provided on the site. Those who are interested are encouraged to contact the society directly. The site also has information about membership, monthly meetings, and related links.

The Paul & Daisy Soros Fellowships for New Americans (NY) (Operating foundation) (http://www.pdsoros.org)

The New York City-based, Paul & Daisy Soros Fellowships for New Americans was named after the founders who are "New Americans" themselves. The fellowships were established "in recognition of the contributions New Americans have made to American life and in gratitude for the opportunities the United States has afforded the donors and their family." They provide opportunities to "continuing generations of able and accomplished New Americans to achieve leadership in their chosen fields and to partake of the American Dream." Annually, thirty fellowships, consisting of grants for two years of graduate study in the United States, are awarded to "New Americans" who have shown at least two of the following three attributes: potential in the fields for which they seek further education; a capacity for creativity, persistence, and work; and a commitment to the values of the U.S. Constitution and Bill of Rights. A "New American" is an individual who is a resident alien, a naturalized U.S. citizen, or the child of two parents who are both naturalized citizens. Visit the fellowships' Web site for further program information and requirements, application instructions, printable application forms, profiles of past fellows, related links, and contact information.

Soros Foundations Network (NY) (http://www.soros.org)

Supported by financier-turned-philanthropist George Soros, the Soros Foundations Network comprises a number of national foundations located in the countries of Central and Eastern Europe, the former Soviet Union, South Africa, and Haiti, and the Open Society Institute, which promotes connections and cooperation among the various Soros-sponsored foundations. The network's member organizations "help build the infrastructure and institutions necessary for open societies" by supporting programs for education, children and youth, media and communications, civil society, human rights and humanitarian aid, science and medicine, arts and culture, and economic restructuring. The network's Web site offers a wide range of information, including general program categories and application guidelines, annotated bibliographies, newsletters, press releases, and contact information.

Southshore Foundation (AR) (http://www.southshore.com/foundation/)

The Southshore Foundation seeks to enhance the quality of life in the South Shore, Bull Shoals, Arkansas region. The SouthShore Foundation awards scholarships for academic success in surrounding school districts and promotes education for all ages. The foundation's mission is to "enhance the quality of life in the service area of Northern Arkansas Telephone Company through promoting the use of telecommunications technology to accomplish goals of educational advancement, environmental preservation, and economic development." The foundation's Web site features funding guidelines, a grant application form, grant restrictions, a recent grants listing, and the foundation's most recent tax return.

Space Shuttle Children's Trust Fund (MD) (http://www.spaceshuttlekidsfund.org/)

The Space Shuttle Children's Trust Fund of Maryland was founded on the day after the Space Shuttle Challenger tragedy in 1986, with the full support of NASA. Since 1986, the fund has served as a provider of health, education, and general support for the astronauts' children, almost all of whom are now college graduates. The fund is now accepting donations for the children of the astronauts killed in the 2003 Columbia disaster. Visit the fund's Web site for further details and contact information.

Spencer Foundation (IL) (http://www.spencer.org/)

Established in 1962 by Lyle M. Spencer, founder of the educational publishing firm Science Research Associates Inc., the Spencer Foundation investigates "ways in which education, broadly conceived, can be improved around the world." To this end, the foundation supports "high quality investigation of education through its research programs [and] strengthens and renews the educational research community through fellowship programs and related activities." Visitors to the foundation's Web site will find program descriptions, eligibility guidelines, application instructions, and contact information for each research grant program; the foundation's latest annual report; and a listing of directors, advisors, and staff.

The Stanley Foundation (IA) (Operating foundation) (http://www.stanleyfdn.org)
The Stanley Foundation is a non-partisan operating foundation based in Muscatine, Iowa. C. Maxwell and Elizabeth Stanley created the foundation in 1956 to pursue their longtime commitment to the effective management of global problems. The foundation strives to "provoke thought and encourage dialogue on world affairs" and to "secure peace with freedom and justice." It serves policy professionals through policy conferences, congressional staff programs, and conference reports; involves citizens through conferences, seminars, resource materials, and networking; and addresses the wider public through *Common Ground,* a weekly news radio program on world affairs, *World Press Review,* a monthly magazine, the *Courier,* a newsletter, and the foundation's Web site. Current topics are arms control and security, global economy and society, global education, human rights, regions and countries, United Nations, and U.S. foreign policy. Visitors to the foundaton's Web site will find conference reports, radio transcripts and live broadcasts, online publications, publications ordering information, and an online contact form.

Starr Foundation (NY) (http://fdncenter.org/grantmaker/starr/)
Located in New York City, the Starr Foundation was created by insurance entrepreneur Cornelius Vander Starr in 1955. The foundation focuses its funding on education, while also generously supporting projects in medicine and healthcare, human needs, public policy, and culture. In addition to having endowed scholarships at over 80 colleges, universities, and secondary schools, the foundation "funds organizations that provide need-based financial aid to students seeking to attend secondary and post-secondary schools" and occasionally supports foreign exchange programs. The foundation runs scholarship programs specifically for children of American International Group employees, students who live in Brewster, New York, and students at specified high schools in downtown Mahnattan. Funding in medicine and healthcare goes toward a variety of projects, including capital campaigns, research, and those programs providing care to underserved communities. Recipients of human needs awards range from literacy to housing to hunger programs. Outside of the tri-state area, most of the foundation's giving is done through community foundations. Public policy grants focus on international relations and funds institutions all over the world. Culture grants have gone to large museums and to small, community-based groups, but not to individual artists. There is no formal application and no deadlines, but the foundation's Web site lists proposal requirements and contact information.

Staunton Farm Foundation (PA) (http://www.stauntonfarm.org)
Located in Pittsburgh, Pennsylvania, the Staunton Farm Foundation was incorporated in 1937 as directed by the will of Mrs. Matilda S. McCready. She charged her executors to erect and maintain "a home for the treatment and care of persons suffering curable neurotic, mild mental, and kindred ailments, wherein persons undergoing treatment may have the benefit of fresh air, sunshine, and rural surroundings in ample grounds for work and recreation without being brought in contact with those suffering from incurable forms of the same trouble." In addition to the outpatient clinics the foundation has established, it awards grants in the field of mental health in southwestern Pennsylvania. The ten-county area is outlined on a map on the foundation's site. To apply for a grant, an initial letter of intent must be submitted. The foundation accepts the Common Grant Application for Western Pennsylvania and provides a link to this application on its Web site. Application guidelines, a recent grant recipients lists, and contact information are also available on the site.

Rudolph Steiner Foundation (CA) (http://www.rsfoundation.org)
The Rudolph Steiner Foundation was formed in 1984 in San Francisco and upholds Steiner's vision of a progressive financial service organization supporting social and environmental change. Through gifts, grants, and loans, the foundation supports education and the arts, science and caring for the earth, social responsibility and mutual support, medical

and religious renewal, and associative economic relationships, among others. The foundation's Web site provides client profiles, a listing of specific funds, descriptions of projects funded, links to affiliated associations, and an e-mail contact form.

Stern Family Fund (VA) (http://www.sternfund.org/)
The Arlington, Virginia-based Stern Family Fund supports policy-oriented government and corporate accountability projects. The fund is committed to guaranteeing the responsiveness of public and private institutions that wield substantial power over individuals' lives. The Stern Fund seeks to achieve these goals through two distinct grant programs: the Public Interest Pioneer Program, which provides large seed grants to spark the creation of new organizations, and Strategic Opportunity Grants, which are awarded to projects or organizations "at critical junctures in their development." The fund's Web site provides detailed program information, a list of grantees, application guidelines and procedures, FAQs, and a listing of the fund's board members.

The Stocker Foundation (OH) (http://www.stockerfoundation.org)
Founded in 1979 in Lorain, Ohio, the Stocker Foundation serves as a catalyst for constructive change to help build strong communities, strengthen families, support sound educational programs, and provide vital human services. The foundation focuses on the areas of art, community needs, education, health, social services, and women's issues in the regions where the foundation's trustees reside. The foundation's Web site features details on the foundation's funding interests, success stories of previously funded programs, a complete listing of recent grant recipients, detailed grant guidelines and restrictions, contact information, a foundation history, and information on geographic regions of support.

Lydia B. Stokes Foundation (NM) (http://www.lydiabstokesfoundation.org/)
The Lydia B. Stokes Foundation is committed to the Quaker philosophy of empowering people to help themselves. The foundation's grantmaking focuses on women's issues, the environment, children, education, and Quaker concerns. Grantmaking is centered in Colorado, New Mexico, New Hampshire, Massachusetts, and Florida, though not exclusively. The foundation does not accept unsolicited grant proposals. Visit the foundation's Web site for more about the foundation's mission and history, grant information, links, and contact information.

Stranahan Foundation (OH) (http://www.stranahanfoundation.org/)
Founded in 1944 by two brothers in Toledo, Ohio, the Stranahan Foundation supports organizations "that give people the tools to become educated, healthy, self-reliant, and contributing members of our society." The foundation focuses its giving in four main areas: education, healthcare, culture, and community. Visitors to the foundation's Web site will find details on the grantmaking process, information on the organization's guiding principles, a downloadable application, a list of current grantees, contact information, and the foundation's most recent annual report.

The Stuart Foundation (CA) (http://www.stuartfoundation.org)
The Stuart Foundation's purpose is to help the children and youth of California and Washington become responsible citizens. The foundation's approach to this purpose is to help strengthen the public systems and community supports that contribute to children's development. The foundation's three grant programs are: Strengthening the Public School System, Strengthening the Child Welfare System, and Strengthening Communities to Support Families. Visit the foundation's Web site for funding guidelines and program information, application guidelines and instructions, grant statistics and lists with short project descriptions and links to grantee organizations, lists of related links, an online feedback form, and contact information.

The Sudbury Foundation (MA) (http://www.sudburyfoundation.org/)
Herbert J. and Esther M. Atkinson established the Sudbury Foundation in 1952 to benefit the people of Sudbury, Massachusetts, and the organizations that serve them. The

foundation operates a number of programs: the Atkinson Scholarship Program, which recognizes and assists local, college-bound students; the Charitable Sudbury Program, which supports nonprofit organizations whose work improves the quality of life for Sudbury residents and their neighbors in surrounding towns; the Regional Program, which supports the neighboring counties with youth and community development; and the Environmental Program, which maintains ecological integrity and community sustainability in New York, Vermont, New Hampshire, and Maine. Visitors to the Web site will find funding guidelines for the two main programs, grant lists with program descriptions, application instructions, links to other sites of interest, and contact information.

Summerlee Foundation (TX) (http://www.summerlee.org/index.htm)
The Summerlee Foundation, located in Houston, Texas, was established in 1988 to support animal protection and preserve the history of Texas. The Animal Protection Program emphasizes research and dissemination of information on companion animals, cruelty investigations and rescue, feral cat issues, overpopulation, and reducing euthanasia. The Texas History Program focuses on research. The foundation also holds an interest in enhancing the programmatic needs of state agencies responsible for the promotion, preservation, and interpretation of the history of Texas. Visit the foundation's Web site for recent grants listings, grant guidelines, and contact information.

Surdna Foundation, Inc. (NY) (http://www.surdna.org/)
Established in 1917 by businessman John E. Andrus, the New York City-based Surdna Foundation, Inc. concentrates its grantmaking activities in five programmatic areas: the environment, biological diversity, human systems, transportation and urban/suburban land use, and energy. The foundation's Web site offers general information about the foundation and its approach to grantmaking, detailed program information, application guidelines and grant restrictions, a recent listing of grants, board and staff information, and contact information.

Swalm Foundation (TX) (http://www.swalm.org)
The Swalm Foundation, located in Houston, makes grants to human service organizations in Texas that serve the homeless, the educationally and economically disadvantaged, survivors of domestic violence, victims of child abuse and neglect, and the mentally or physically disabled. The foundation is especially interested in assisting organizations in parts of Texas that have very limited resources, including small towns and rural areas. The foundation's Web site features gant guidelines and restrictions, and an online application form.

Ralph and Eileen Swett Foundation (NJ) (http://www.swettfoundation.org/)
Founded in 1999, the Ralph and Eileen Swett Foundation aids orphaned children by promoting their adoption and intervention in the lives of troubled youths. Other areas of interest of the foundation includes the arts, the environment, loans and loan guarantees, unrestricted grants, endowments, awareness programs, and "bricks & mortar" grants for construction, education, and research. Visit the foundation's Web site for information on the foundation's grantmaking programs, lists of previous grantees, and contact information.

Teagle Foundation (NY) (http://fdncenter.org/grantmaker/teagle/)
Established in 1944, the Teagle Foundation of New York maintains a "major interest [in] strengthening private higher education, with a principal emphasis on small liberal arts colleges and a secondary emphasis on nursing education and theological education." Visit the foundation's Web site to learn more about the foundation's mission and funding priorities, grant guidelines, recent grant data, board listings, FAQs, and contact information.

John Templeton Foundation (PA) (http://www.templeton.org/)
The John Templeton Foundation was established in 1987 by international investment manager John Templeton "to explore and encourage the relationship between science and religion." The foundation's programs focus on five areas: spiritual information through

science, spirituality and health, free enterprise, character development, and the John Templeton Prize for Progress in Religion. In addition to general program and contact information, the foundation's Web site features a listing of the foundation's officers and trustees, winners of the Templeton Prize for Progress in Religion, information about other awards given by the foundation, a list of recent grants, and a request for proposals for scientific studies in the area of forgiveness, with downloadable application packets.

Virgil Thomson Foundation, Ltd. (NY) (http://www.virgilthomson.org)
The mission of the Virgil Thomson Foundation, Ltd. is to promote the performance, preservation, dissemination, and public appreciation of serious music in general and the music and writings of Virgil Thomson in particular. Qualifying nonprofits may request either general operating support or support for special projects. Visitors to the foundation's Web site will find a biography of Virgil Thomson and a listing of his works, funding guidelines, a downloadable application, and contact information.

Thrasher Research Fund (UT) (http://www.thrasherresearch.org)
The Thrasher Research Fund was established in 1977 to support medical research that will benefit children. Grants are also considered for research on major health problems such, as tobacco, alcohol, obesity, or drug use. The fund's Web site features a history of the fund, information on current projects, recent reports, grant guidelines and application procedures, staff listings, and contact information.

The Tiffany & Co. Foundation (NY) (http://www.tiffanyandcofoundation.org/)
Established in 2000, the Tiffany & Co. Foundation, which is based in New York City, supports the arts, including crafts and arts education; preservation and conservation; the decorative, performing, and visual arts; and environmental conservation. The foundation's Web site features grant proposal guidelines and limitations, recent grants listings, board of directors listings, and contact information.

Tinker Foundation, Inc. (NY) (http://fdncenter.org/grantmaker/tinker/)
Created in 1959 by Dr. Edward Larocque Tinker, the Tinker Foundation, Inc. has long focused its grantmaking activities on Latin America, Spain, and Portugal. More recently, it has included in its mandate the support of projects concerning Antarctica, "a region of significant interest on an international scale." The foundation awards institutional grants to organizations and institutions "that promote the interchange and exchange of information within the community of those concerned with the affairs of Spain, Portugal, Ibero-America and Antarctica." Within these parameters, the foundation looks for innovative projects in the areas of environmental policy, governance, or economic policy that have a strong public policy component. The foundation also awards field research grants to recognized institutes of Ibero-American or Latin American Studies graduate or doctoral programs at accredited U.S. universities. The foundation's Web site offers descriptions of both grant programs; application instructions, reporting requirements, and a downloadable proposal cover sheet; a recent grants list for the institutional grants program; and a listing of foundation officers and staff.

TKF Foundation (MD) (http://www.tkffdn.org)
Created in 1985 in Annapolis, Maryland, the TKF Foundation is committed to "creating urban greenspace, sponsoring public art, and championing urban agriculture with the goals of nurturing the human spirit and fostering a sense of community." Open to projects in the Annapolis and Baltimore, Maryland, and Washington, D.C., areas, the grants program has two major categories: Open Spaces/Sacred Places and Community Greening. The former funds community parks, healing gardens, recreation paths, and bay buffers that are available to a large segment of the population. The latter helps community-based initiatives with small-scale plantings and with funding for projects that include community-sustainable agriculture. The foundation only funds new projects and considers constant evaluation a very important part of each project. Grantseekers are required to submit a letter of inquiry with a series of required attachments. If the group is advised to submit a proposal, the

foundation accepts the Association of Baltimore Area Grantmakers' Common Application Format. The foundation's Web site includes application deadlines, lists of previous grant recipients, and a monthly feature on a successful project.

The Randall L. Tobias Foundation, Inc. (IN) (http://www.rltfound.org)
The Randall L. Tobias Foundation, Inc. is a family foundation located in Indianapolis, Indiana. Established in 1994, the foundation seeks to inspire excellence in education. Currently, the foundation is only funding its own programs. Unsolicited grant requests are not being accepted. Visit the foundation's Web site for contact information.

Tocker Foundation (TX) (http://www.tocker.org/)
The Tocker Foundation was established in 1964 to implement the philanthropic interests of Phillip Tocker, a Texas businessman and attorney, and his wife, Olive. In 1992 the foundation decided to focus its grantmaking on small rural libraries serving a population of 12,000 or less. The foundation partners with community libraries to make their services more accessible to individuals who by reason of distance, residence, handicap, age, literacy level, or other disadvantage are unable to receive the benefits of public library services. In recent years the foundation has made grants for outreach and "shut-in" programs, library automation, enhancement of services, adult reading classes, after school projects, bilingual material, and a variety of other projects initiated by community libraries. Visitors to the foundation's Web site will find a brief history of the foundation, detailed grant proposal guidelines, a downloadable grant application form, recent grants lists, a list of library automation projects in progress, and contact information.

Together Foundation (NY) (Operating foundation) (http://www.together.org/)
The New York City-based Together Foundation, a private operating foundation, was established in 1989 to foster "communication between individuals, groups, corporations, and governments working in service to the Earth and humanity." To this end, the foundation specializes in "providing assistance to non-profit organizations, United Nation agencies and other intergovernmental organizations with their computer, information, networking, database, and telecommunications needs." This is achieved through support to the areas of information technology, the organization and delivery of information, leadership training, and sustainable development. The foundation's Web site includes a past annual report, reference and past program area information, and contact information.

The Trellis Fund (DC) (http://fdncenter.org/grantmaker/trellis/)
The Washington, D.C.-based Trellis Fund is committed to making communities more responsive to and responsible for their residents and other constituents. The fund does not set specific funding foci. It is interested in supporting organizations that attempt to solve "complex problems." The fund prefers to fund organizations within the District of Columbia, although it is interested in funding "extraordinary funding opportunities" from outside the area.The fund has a special interest in local arts institutions that sponsor artistic talent that alters, refines, critiques, or in any way extends thinking beyond the status quo. Therefore, a small portion of the fund's annual budget will be made available to support the visual arts. Visitors to the fund's Web site will find application guidelines, a staff listing, application procedures and deadlines, a copy of the foundation's latest annual report, and contact information.

Emily Hall Tremaine Foundation (CT) (http://www.tremainefoundation.org/)
Established in 1986 in Meriden, Connecticut, the Emily Hall Tremaine Foundation seeks to fund innovative projects that advance solutions to basic and enduring problems. The foundation makes grants in the areas of art, the environment, and learning disabilities. Visit the foundation's Web site to find further information on individual programs, application policies, a listing of foundation board and associates, and contact information.

The Trio Foundation (CA) (http://fdncenter.org/grantmaker/trio/)
The Trio Foundation of Berkeley, California, funds organizations that serve young children and their families in the east San Francisco Bay Area. The primary focus of the Trio Foundation is to help young children of all cultures, who are growing up in poverty, achieve their fullest and brightest potential. The foundation's secondary focus is to fund projects sponsored by Jewish organizations that serve Jewish children in need or that serve a multi-cultural clientele. Visit the foundation's Web site for funding priorities, eligibility criteria, application procedures, and contact information.

The Trull Foundation (TX) (http://www.trullfoundation.org)
In 1967 the Trull Foundation was founded in Texas, continuing the legacy left by the B.W. Trull Foundation that was originally founded in 1948 to support religious and educational purposes. The Trull Foundation reprioritized and created a broader grant program supporting educational, religious, cultural, and social programs. The foundation makes grants primarily in the state of Texas. The foundation's priorities center around healthcare, children and families, substance abuse, and agriculture and farming in Texas communities. The foundation's Web site includes board/staff listing, grant guidelines, current grants list, a printable proposal fact sheet, and contact information.

Tucson Osteopathic Medical Foundation (AZ) (Operating foundation) (http://www.tomf.org/about.html)
The Tucson Osteopathic Medical Foundation is a "conversion" foundation that resulted from the sale of Tucson General Hospital to Summit Health, Ltd. in 1986. The foundation's mission is to advance postgraduate osteopathic medical education, improve the public's understanding of osteopathic medicine, and "elevate through education" the health and well-being of the community. The foundation has two grant programs: the Founders Awards, which are loans that become scholarships if recipient osteopathic medical students graduate and practice in southern Arizona for a specific period of time, and Trustee Awards, which are grants to local charitable organizations that can achieve significant results with small grants. Applicants to the Founders Awards must be Arizona residents, and applicants from southern Arizona will be given special consideration. The foundation's Web site features a printable application, selection criteria, and application instructions for the Founders Awards; information on the foundations's operating programs; information on osteopathic medicine; related links; a searchable directory of physicians; and a continuing education events calendar.

The Turner Foundation (OH) (http://hmturnerfoundation.org/)
Establish in 2000, the Turner Foundation of Ohio supports the communities of Springfield and Clark Counties. The foundation provides support for organizations with an interest in community development, education, healthcare, and leadership. The Turner Foundation does not fund individuals, churches, legislative action groups, annual fundraising campaigns, scholarships, fraternal groups, or political groups or issues. The foundation's Web site features grant guidelines, downloadable applications, a helpful FAQ section, and contact information.

Turner Foundation, Inc. (GA) (http://www.turnerfoundation.org/)
Founded in 1990, the Turner Foundation, Inc. supports activities directed toward preservation of the environment, conservation of natural resources, protection of wildlife, and sound population policies. The foundation supports organizations that "provide education and activism on preservation activities and seek to instill in all citizens a sense of common responsibility for the fate of life on Earth." Please note: the Turner Foundation has suspended its grantmaking activities until 2004. The foundation's Web site provides detailed program guidelines, lists of recent grants awarded in four main program areas (i.e., water/toxics, energy/transportation, habitat, and population), application procedures and limitations, messages from founder Ted Turner and the foundation's executive director, and contact information.

Turrell Fund (NJ) (http://fdncenter.org/grantmaker/turrell/index.html)
The main purpose of the New Jersey-based Turrell Fund is to support social and educational activities that will contribute to the development of young people from families that could not afford these services without help. Programs that focus on children under the age of twelve are given highest priority; requests for capital support, while considered, are of secondary priority. The fund supports programs in Vermont and in Essex, Hudson, Passaic, and Union Counties in New Jersey. Visitors to the fund's Web site will find a brief description of the fund's program interests; application instructions; a listing of officers, trustees, and staff; FAQs; and a downloadable summary request form.

Isaac H. Tuttle Fund (NY) (http://www.tuttlefund.org)
Established in 1872, the New York-based Isaac H. Tuttle Fund's mission is to "provide temporal and spiritual welfare of aged persons." The organization supports both individuals and organizations that service the elderly population of the New York City borough of Manhattan, with a goal of enabling this population to continue living in their own homes "so long as they are physically and mentally able to do so." Support is provided through a stipendiary program, which provides financial help to elderly persons whose financial stability had been eroded by illness, inflation, or other factors, and through the foundation's grants to organizations program. The fund's Web site to find further details about the grantmaking initiatives, a brief history of the fund, a listing of recent grants, and contact information.

United States-Japan Foundation (NY) (http://www.us-jf.org/)
The principle mission of the United States-Japan Foundation is "to promote greater mutual knowledge between the United States and Japan and to contribute to a strengthened understanding of important public policy issues of interest to both countries." The foundation currently focuses its grantmaking in the areas of pre-college education and policy studies. It does not award grants to capital campaigns, endowment funds, or deficit operations; for the construction or maintenance of buildings; or for the purchase of equipment. Visitors to the foundation's Web site will find basic program descriptions, application procedures, a limitations statement, and contact information.

Until There's A Cure Foundation (CA) (http://www.utac.org/)
The Until There's A Cure Foundation was established in 1993 by Dana Cappiello and Kathleen Scutchfield. The foundation derives its funds from the sale of "The Bracelet," a bracelet bearing the design of the AIDS ribbon. The foundation has four priority areas: direct care services, prevention education, vaccine research development, and policy development. The foundation also has a partnership program in which qualified organizations keep 25 percent of the total revenues they generate from sales of "The Bracelet." Visitors to the Web site will find grant application instructions, grants lists, and contact information.

W.E. Upjohn Institute for Employment Research (MI) (Operating foundation) (http://www.upjohninst.org)
The W.E. Upjohn Institute for Employment Research has its roots in the W.E. Upjohn Unemployment Trustee Corporation, which maintained a cooperative farm for laid-off workers to maintain their income and their dignity. Dr. W.E. Upjohn, founder and head of the Upjohn Company, had conceived of the idea during the Depression in 1932, when he was concerned about the prospects of laying off his workers and the broader problems and hardships of the unemployed. The farm program did not last long, but concern over unemployment remained a top priority. In 1945 the trustees established the W.E. Upjohn Institute, located in Kalamazoo, Michigan, today a research organization devoted to finding, evaluating, and promoting solutions to employment-related problems. The foundation's grant program funds proposals to conduct policy-relevant research on employment issues. Although proposals on any policy-relevant labor market issue will be considered, the foundation gives higher priority to proposals addressing employment relationships, low wages and public policy, and social insurance. Visit the Web site for grant and award program

information, application instructions, a history of the foundation, information and publications on employment issues, and contact information.

Valentine Foundation (PA) (http://www.valentinefoundation.org/)
Located in Haveford, Pennsylvania, the Valentine Foundation was founded in 1985 and today advocates for social change in issues concerning women and girls. The foundation supports nonprofit organizations or programs in the greater Philadelphia area and those that are national in scope that "empower women and girls to recognize and develop their full potential or which work to change established attitudes that discourage them from recognizing that potential." The foundation's Web site includes a complete history of the organization, guidelines and limitations for grants, a listing of past grants to girls and women, publications that can be ordered from the foundation, and contact information.

Valley Foundation (CA) (http://www.valley.org/)
Formed in 1984 from the proceeds of sale of the Community Hospital of Los Gatos, California, and Saratoga, Inc., the Valley Foundation provides funding for nonprofit organizations in Santa Clara County, with an emphasis in the medical field. Although the foundation's primary interest is in medical services and healthcare for lower-income households, it also supports programs in the areas of youth, the arts, seniors, and general medical services. Visitors to the foundation's Web site will find a listing of sample grants awarded in each of the foundation's program areas, application procedures and limitations, a financial summary of the foundation's activities, a listing of the foundation's board, and an electronic application form.

van Ameringen Foundation (NY) (http://fdncenter.org/grantmaker/vanameringen/)
The van Ameringen Foundation is located in New York City and gives in the urban Northeast United States. The organization "promotes mental health through preventive measures, treatment, and rehabilitation and supports the field of psychiatry." Areas of interest are mental health, treatment, and mental health/crisis services. The foundation's web site has basic application instructions and deadlines. The foundation does publish an annual report.

VanLobenSels/RembeRock Foundation (CA) (http://www.vlsrr.org/)
The VanLobenSels/RembeRock Foundation's goal is to promote social justice and the well-being of the residents and communities in northern California. The foundation is interested in providing critical funding for programs that serve low-income youth and adults and other vulnerable and underserved populations. Programs most likely to be supported by the foundation tend to have programs focusing on low-income youth, families and adults, the elderly, the disabled, immigrants, refugees, and newcomers. Visitors to the foundation's Web site will find grant guidelines, detailed application information, the foundation's most recent annual report, brief biographies of the trustees, and contact information.

The Varsavsky Foundation (NY) (http://www.varsavskyfoundation.org/)
The Varsavsky Foundation was established in 2000 in New York City (with an office in Madrid, Spain,) with the mission "to broaden access to, and improve the quality of, education world-wide." Founded in honor of David Varsavsky, a young man who disappeared and was presumed killed by the Argentine military in the 1976, the foundation especially focuses on children's access to technology and the Internet as a learning tool. The foundation makes a number of grants to institutions and organizations in the United States, Latin America, and Spain in support of extending the availability of education and computer access for educational purposes. Details on specific grants and the history of the foundation can be found on the foundation's Web site, along with grant application guidelines. The site is available in Spanish and English.

The G. Unger Vetlesen Foundation (NY) (http://www.monellvetlesen.org/)
The G. Unger Vetlesen Foundation's mission is to "voluntarily aid and contribute to religious, charitable, scientific, literary, and educational uses and purposes, in New York,

elsewhere in the United States, and throughout the world." The foundation concentrates its grants in the fields of oceanographies, climate studies, and other earth sciences. Interested parties should submit a request for funding to the foundation; guidelines and information about what should be included can be found on the foundation's Web site. The foundation's Web site also provides a downloadable copy of its tax return, previous annual reports, and a listing of recent grants awarded.

Victoria Foundation (NJ) (http://www.victoriafoundation.org/)
Established in 1924, the Victoria Foundation strives to improve opportunities for poor and disadvantaged families in New Jersey. Areas of support considered by the foundation include education, the environment, neighborhood development and urban activities, and youth and family. The foundation places priority on the city of Newark and the urgent environmental problems within New Jersey. Visitors to the foundation's Web site will find a history of the organization, its most recent annual report, grants listings, application guidelines, and contact information.

Virginia Environmental Endowment (VA) (http://www.vee.org)
The Virginia Environmental Endowment aims to improve the quality of the environment by encouraging all sectors to work together to prevent pollution, conserve natural resources, and promote environmental literacy. It was created through a court order in 1977, when a portion of the fine that the Allied Chemical Corporation was ordered to pay for polluting the James River was used to create the Virginia Environmental Endowment. Located in Richmond, Virginia, the endowment currently limits awards to programs conducted in Virginia and in the Kanawha and Ohio River Valleys of Kentucky and West Virginia. Visit the Web site for grant application procedures, grant lists with links to grantee organizations, links to other useful resources, and application procedures for the Virginia mini-grants program.

VNA Foundation (IL) (http://www.vnafoundation.net/)
The Visiting Nurse Association of Chicago, an organization with a hundred-year history as an active healthcare service, founded the VNA Foundation to finance nonprofit organizations offering home and community-based healthcare to the underserved in Cook County, Illinois, and the surrounding area, with an emphasis on Chicago. Grants are given to groups working mainly in three areas: home healthcare services, prevention and health promotion, and early intervention. Priority is given to care services provided by nurses. The VNA Foundation's Web site provides a message from the foundation's executive director, grant guidelines, application procedures, a listing of past grants, a financial report, and contact information.

The Laura B. Vogler Foundation, Inc. (NY) (http://fdncenter.org/grantmaker/vogler/)
Established in 1959, the Laura B. Vogler Foundation awards one-time, non-renewable grants for new programs in the areas of health, youth, child welfare, the disadvantaged, the elderly, and other related services. The foundation favors specific programs or projects, rather than general operating support or capital programs. The foundation does not make grants for conferences, seminars, or loans. The foundation is a member of the New York Regional Association of Grantmakers and the Association of Small Foundations. Visitors to the foundation's Web site will find a brief description of the foundation's program interests, a listing of trustees, a sampling of recent grants, application instructions, and a copy of the New York/New Jersey Area Common Application Form.

The William J. Von Liebig Foundation, Inc. (FL) (Operating foundation) (http://www.vonliebigfoundation.com)
The William J. Von Liebig Foundation, based in Naples, Florida, "encourage[s] the movement of technical innovation and relevant clinical findings from the laboratory to the vascular surgical community." The foundation awards a prize to the resident or fellow with the best essay on a problem in general vascular surgery. Prizes are also awarded to manuscripts with high ratings and to the research mentors of award winners. The foundation also

presents research grants to universities and to noted presidents of vascular societies. The foundation's Web site lists past residents and fellows award winners, general requirements for awards, links to vascular resources, and contact information to request application materials.

Waitt Family Foundation (SD) (http://www.waittfoundation.org/)
The Waitt Family Foundation was founded in 1993 by Ted Waitt, the founder of the Gateway Computer Company, and his wife Joan. The foundation is based in Sioux City, South Dakota, and the foundation focuses its funding on the surrounding Siouxland area. The foundation does fund some national programs, but the Siouxland area takes priority. Funding areas include education, non-violence, child advocacy, and community enhancement. The foundation supports other programs and initiatives as well. A guide to grant and funding limitations and an application request form are available on the foundation's Web site.

Waksman Foundation for Microbiology (MI) (http://www.waksmanfoundation.org)
The mission of the Waksman Foundation for Microbiology is "to promote, encourage, and aid scientific research in microbiology; to provide and assist in providing the funds and facilities by which scientific discoveries, inventions, and processes in microbiology may be developed all to the end that the science of microbiology shall progress in the service of mankind." The foundation today supports research and education in the general field of microbiology, including medical disciplines, agricultural and soil microbiology, marine microbiology, and the diverse environmental interactions of microbes. The foundation's Web site features information about the foundation's mission, application procedures and guidelines, and contact information.

Wallace Global Fund (DC) (http://www.wgf.org)
The mission of the Washington, D.C.-based Wallace Global Fund is "to catalyze and leverage critically needed global progress towards an equitable and environmentally sustainable society." The fund is guided by the vision of the late Henry A. Wallace, former Secretary of Agriculture and Vice-President under Franklin D. Roosevelt. The fund supports initiatives that advance globally-sustainable development in some fundamental way. Grants have been made to a wide range of projects that address obstacles to a sustainable future, including, but not limited to, population growth, over-consumption, global climate change, imperfect economic policies and inadequate analytic tools, and deforestation. Visitors to the Web site will find program information, application procedures, grants lists with links to grantee organizations, financial information, staff and trustee listings, and contact information.

Wallace-Reader's Digest Funds (NY) (http://www.wallacefunds.org/)
Founded in 1987 as the Dewitt Wallace-Reader's Digest Fund and the Lila Wallace-Reader's Digest Fund, the Wallace-Reader's Digest Funds now operate under a common goal of "enriching people through better schools, enhanced community activities, and participation in the arts." The funds have pooled their resources to concentrate and continue its support of New York City programs in education, the arts, and communities. The Dewitt Wallace-Reader's Digest Fund focuses on education and career development of low-income youth, while the Lila Wallace Reader's Digest Fund focuses on making the arts part of individuals' daily lives, promoting literacy programs for adults, and creating or improving urban parks. While continuing these programs, the Wallace-Reader's Digest Funds will work to find more effective superintendents and principals to improve the quality of public schools, engage more people in the arts and cultural institutions, and promote informal learning for adults and children in low-income areas. The funds' Web site contains information on past and present grant recipients, along with evaluations of these programs; downloadable annual reports and articles about the funds' work; links to related resources; and contact information.

Walton Family Foundation, Inc. (AR) (http://www.wffhome.com)

The Bentonville, Arkansas-based Walton Family Foundation was established by Sam M. (founder of Wal-Mart stores) and Helen R. Walton. The foundation is principally involved in programs of its own initiative and does not accept unsolicited proposals, but from time to time grants are made to organizations whose work embodies one or more of the goals of the foundation. Applicants are asked to send a brief letter of inquiry to the foundation prior to submitting a complete application. The foundation has a primary focus on education, specifically systemic reform, with special emphasis on primary and secondary education. Consult the Web site for program and scholarship information, geographic restrictions, funding guidelines, application procedures, links to programs the foundaiton supports, and contact information.

Wagnalls Memorial Foundation (OH) (http://www.wagnalls.org/)

The Wagnalls Memorial Foundation was established by the co-founders of the Funk and Wagnalls Publishing Company who designed and built the Wagnalls Memorial Library and Community Center for the people of Lithopolis and Bloom Township, Ohio. The foundation also established scholarships in 1948 for higher education in institutions of "learning, music, and art" for individuals of these Ohio towns. The foundation's Web site features information on the foundation's two specific scholarships, contact information, descriptions of the Memorial Library and Museum, a history of the foundation, and more details on the projects and institutions sponsored by the foundation.

The Andy Warhol Foundation for the Visual Arts (NY) (http://www.warholfoundation.org/)

The Andy Warhol Foundation for the Visual Arts was established in 1987 with the mission of advancing the visual arts. The foundation is committed to the idea that "arts are essential to an open, enlightened democracy," and seeks to foster innovative artistic expression and the creative process by encouraging and supporting cultural organizations that directly or indirectly support artists and their work. The foundation also supports efforts to strengthen areas that directly affect the context in which artists work, such as freedom of artistic expression and equitable access to resources. Grants are made on a project basis to curatorial programs at museums, artists' organizations, and other cultural institutions to assist in innovative and scholarly presentations of contemporary visual arts. Consult the Web site of this New York City-based foundation for grant guidelines, application information, and contact information. Visitors to the site will also find a brief biography of Andy Warhol; a calendar of funded projects; grants lists; a series of papers from the foundation's project on the arts, culture, and society (whose purpose is to ensure public debate about the global, economic, and societal forces affecting the arts); and FAQs.

The Warner Foundation (NC) (http://www.thewarnerfoundation.org)

The Warner Foundation was established in Durham, North Carolina, in 1996 "to help disadvantaged people and communities improve their economic circumstances and works to promote racial harmony." These goals manifest themselves in the foundation's areas of focus for its grants: the improvement of economic opportunities for disadvantaged individuals and communities and the improvement of race relations. Visitors to the foundation's Web site will find detailed grant guidelines, procedures, and instructions; resources for successful grantwriting; links to other resources; and contact information.

Warren Memorial Foundation (ME) (Operating foundation) (http://users.rcn.com/warren.javanet/board.html)

The Warren Memorial Foundation was established in 1929 with a bequest from Susan Warren, wife of Samuel Warren who was the president of S.D. Warren Mill and founder of the Warren Memorial Library. The foundation is the sole funder of the Warren Memorial Library of Westbrook, Maine. The goal of the Warren Memorial Library is "to provide a collection of materials appropriate to meet the informational, educational, cultural, and recreational needs of community residents." The foundation is also a strong advocate of literacy and encourages reading as a family activity. The library has a program of services designed to encourage an interest in reading and learning in children, and to facilitate the use of the library of senior citizens. Visitors to the foundatoin's Web site can read about the library's history, its programs and policies, and collections. Links to related sites and contact information are also provided.

Warsh-Mott Legacy Foundation (CA) (http://www.csfund.org)
The Warsh-Mott Legacy Foundation is interested in preserving biodiversity, defending democracy, preventing the commodification of life, and protecting human and environmental health. The foundation's grantmaking is forward thinking and guided by a belief in consistent and long-term support. Requests for support should be made by letter of inquiry. The foundation's Web site includes detailed information on the foundation's grantmaking programs, a board and staff listing, application procedures, grants listings, proposal deadlines, and contact information.

Washington Research Foundation (WA) (http://www.wrfseattle.org)
The Washington Research Foundation, based in Seattle, Washington, was established in 1981 to help Washington State research institutions capture value from their emerging technologies. The foundation initially focused on patenting inventions and licensing them to companies. With its proceeds from licensing, the foundation built a seed venture fund, that creates and invests in technology-based start-up companies that have strong ties to the University of Washington and other nonprofit research institutions in Washington State. It also established the WRF Venture Center, which leases office space to technology-based start-ups and provides them with business support. The foundation continues to pursue its licensing activities, and revenues generated from licensing and investments are used to make gifts to support scholarship and research at Washington State research institutions. The foundation's Web site features information on the services offered by the foundation, contact information, and a list of the foundation's past gifts.

Washington Square Health Foundation Inc. (IL) (http://www.wshf.org)
The Washington Square Health Foundation, Inc. grants funds in order to promote and maintain access to adequate healthcare for all people in the Chicagoland area. Located in Chicago, Illinois, the foundation makes grants for medical and nursing education, medical research, and direct healthcare services. The Web site contains grantmaking policies and guidelines, annual reports, grants listings, downloadable grant applications, and links to other foundation resources.

The Thomas J. Watson Foundation (RI) (http://watsonfellowship.org/)
The Thomas J. Watson Foundation was founded in 1961 as a charitable trust by Mrs. Thomas J. Watson, Sr., in honor of her late husband. Based in Providence, Rhode Island, the foundation initially used its resources in support of a variety of programs, but in 1968, in recognition of Mr. and Mrs. Watson's long-standing interest in education and world affairs, their children decided that the major activity of the foundation would be to support a fellowship that would give college graduates of "unusual promise" the freedom to engage in a year of independent study and travel abroad after graduation. Individual colleges and universities participating in the Watson Fellowship Program establish their own procedures and deadlines for the application process. Visit the Web site for a list of links to participating colleges and universities and a list of recent fellows.

Watson-Brown Foundation (GA) (http://www.watson-brown.org/)
The Watson-Brown Foundation of Thomson, Georgia, was established in 1970 to provide college scholarships for students from the Central Savannah River Area of Georgia and South Carolina. In addition to providing college scholarships, the Watson-Brown Foundation periodically provides grants for worthwhile educational and scholarly projects. Visitors to the foundation's Web site will find application guidelines, an application form, FAQs, and information about the foundation's institutional grant program and application restrictions.

Weaver Foundation (NC) (http://www.weaverfoundation.com)
The Weaver Foundation was founded in 1967 by W. Herman Weaver and H. Michael Weaver with the intention of supporting activities and causes that benefit the greater Greensboro, North Carolina, area. Since its establishment, the directors have been interested in supporting community improvement, environmental activities, educational development, helping the disadvantaged, and advancing human and civil rights, racial tolerance, and diversity. Specifically, the foundation's mission is to "help the greater Greensboro community enhance and improve the quality of life and the economic environment for its citizens while developing a sense of philanthropy, civic education, and commitment in current and future generations of the founders' families." The Weaver Foundation does not maintain a grant application cycle, nor does it accept unsolicited grant applications. However, inquiries are welcome via phone, letter, and e-mail. All grants are limited to programs that are designed to help the greater Greensboro community. Details on the foundation's grant program, grant highlights, annual reports, financial data, and contact information can all be found on the foundation's Web site.

The Weber Family Foundation (GA) (http://www.weberfoundation.org/)
Established in 1995, the Weber Family Foundation is committed to supporting organizations and programs that improve the quality of life in the city of Atlanta and its surrounding communities. Areas of interest include children and youth, education, health associations, human services, and arts and culture. The foundation's Web site maintains information on the foundation's grant program, grants listings, the foundation's latest tax return, foundation news, and contact information.

W.E.D. Educational Fund (VA) (http://members.aol.com/wedfund/index.html)
The W.E.D. Educational Fund was established in 1998 to help American citizens of Armenian ancestry to pursue studies and training in the United States or Canada. The fund provides grants and/or loans of up to $5,000 to worthy students regardless of age, gender, or level of education or training. Visit the fund's Web site to find information on eligibility, a recent recipient listing, application information, a downloadable application, and contact information.

Weeden Foundation (NY) (http://www.weedenfdn.org/)
From its inception in 1963, the New York City-based Weeden Foundation (formerly the Frank Weeden Foundation) embraced the protection of biodiversity as its main priority. More recently, the foundation has sought "to equalize distribution of grants between conservation and population programs in order to more fully address the factors driving biological impoverishment." The foundation's Web site offers visitors a mission statement, application guidelines, an index to and summary of the foundation's grant awards, and contact information.

Kurt Weill Foundation for Music, Inc. (NY) (http://www.kwf.org)
The Kurt Weill Foundation for Music, Inc. is chartered to preserve and perpetuate the legacies of composer Kurt Weill (1900-1950) and actress-singer Lotte Lenya (1898-1981). The foundation awards grants to individuals and nonprofit organizations "for projects related to Weill or Lenya" in the following categories: research and travel, publication assistance, dissertation fellowships, professional and regional performance and production, college and university performance and production, recording projects, and broadcasts. In addition to detailed guidelines, application information, and a listing of grants awarded by the foundation, visitors to the Web site can read about the Weill-Lenya Research Center, the *Kurt Weill Edition* (collected critical editions of Weill's works), and the Kurt Weill Prize. Listings of foundation staff and board members, information about copyright and licensing permissions, and contact information are also provided.

Weingart Foundation (CA) (http://www.weingartfnd.org)
The Weingart Foundation focuses its grantmaking efforts on programs serving children and youth in the southern California area, with secondary attention paid to institutions and

agencies benefiting the southern California community in general. The foundation's Web site features an online version of the foundation's current annual report, a biography of founder Ben Weingart, financial statements, brief profiles of eight grantees, grant guidelines and application procedures, downloadable application forms, descriptions of grants (in the following categories: crisis intervention, education, health and medicine, community youth programs, higher education, culture and the arts, and adult community services), and a bulletin board service for grantseekers.

The Welborn Foundations (IN) (http://www.welbornfdn.org)
The Welborn Foundation of Evansville, Indiana, makes grants to nonprofit organizations in counties formerly served by Welborn Baptist Hospital. Consistent with the stated mission of the Welborn Foundation, all grants will be in the areas addressing improvements in the status of health and the quality of life. For purposes of grantmaking, the foundation embraces a broad definition of health including the physiological, social, and environmental factors that influence health. The foundation defines quality of life as the physical, spiritual, cultural, and economic conditions that combine to support a life. Visitors to the foundation's Web site will find detailed information on the foundation's programs, geographic restrictions, application procedures and deadlines, and contact information.

The Robert A. Welch Foundation (TX) (http://www.welch1.org)
The Robert A. Welch Foundation was established in 1952 with the estate of Robert A. Welch, who made his fortune in oil and minerals. From his association with scientists, geologists, and petroleum engineers, Robert Welch determined that the pursuit of chemistry and chemical research held "great potential for the vast good and would continue to have a valuable impact on business, industry, global leadership, and the human condition." Accordingly, his Houston, Texas-based foundation supports fundamental chemical research at educational institutions within the state of Texas. It has a research grant program, a department grant program, the Welch Award in Chemistry, which recognizes important chemical contributions that have a significantly positive influence on mankind. In addition the foundation has established the Norman Hackerman Award in Chemical Research for chemical scientists "40 years old or younger doing research in Texas." Consult their Web site for grant guidelines, application instructions, newsletter, and contact information.

Richard C. Welden Foundation (NY) (http://www.welden.org)
The purpose of the New York-based Richard C. Welden Foundation is to support nature conservation projects and contribute towards research and education in the field. The foundation's grantmaking program centers on the areas of the environment and humanitarian initiatives. With regards to the environment, the foundation tends to support preservation of wetlands and other bird and wildlife habitats and general education. Humanitarian support comes by way of international assistance to areas in conflict. Visit the foundation's Web site to find out more about the foundation's program interest and find contact information.

Wellmark Foundation (IA)
(http://www.wellmark.com/community/wellmark_foundation/wellmark_foundation.htm)
The Wellmark Foundation, established in 1992 in Des Moines, Iowa, is a joint venture between the Wellmark Blue Cross/Blue Shields of Iowa and South Dakota, concentrating on health-related projects in those two states. The foundation's mission is to "efficiently and effectively facilitate the continuous improvement of health status within Iowa and South Dakota communities," mainly by providing seed money to organizations that will establish or expand healthcare in local communities. Other specific areas of interest to the foundation are quality care for chronic conditions, prevention of acute episodes of disease, cancer screenings, tobacco use, and immunizations. The Wellmark Foundation's Web site includes an overview of the foundation's activities, publications, and conferences; information for grantseekers: including proposal review criteria and application instructions; a list of past grantees; and contact information.

Wender-Weis Foundation for Children (CA) (http://www.wenderweis.org)
Based in Palo Alto, California, the Wender-Weis Foundation for Children was founded in 1994 by Amy Wender to provide charitable relief and assistance to at-risk, disadvantaged children throughout the San Francisco Bay Area. The foundation does not accept unsolicited grant proposals, nor does it fund individuals, travel, films, videos, religious organizations, political causes, campaigns, or candidates. Visit their site for contact information.

Wenner-Gren Foundation for Anthropological Research, Inc. (NY) (Operating foundation) (http://www.wennergren.org)
The Wenner-Gren Foundation for Anthropological Research, Inc. was created and endowed in 1941 by Axel Leonard Wenner-Gren, and was originally known as the Viking Fund, Inc. Its mission is to "advance significant and innovative research about humanity's cultural and biological origins, development, and variation, and to foster the creation of an international community of research scholars in anthropology." The foundation supports research in all branches of anthropology, including cultural/social anthropology, ethnology, biological/physical anthropology, archaeology, anthropological linguistics, and closely-related disciplines concerned with human origins, development, and variation. The New York City-based foundation also sponsors *Current Anthropology,* an international journal of general anthropology. Visit their Web site for further program information; application instructions; grants lists; contact information; listing of trustees, staff, and advisory council; and list of related links.

Whitaker Foundation (VA) (http://www.whitaker.org/)
The Whitaker Foundation primarily supports research and education in biomedical engineering. Since its inception in 1975, the foundation has awarded hundreds of millions of dollars to colleges and universities for faculty research, graduate fellowships, and program development. In the field of biomedical engineering, the foundation funds research grants, graduate fellowships, development awards, special opportunity awards, a teaching materials program, industrial internships, leadership awards, and conference awards. Visitors to the foundation's Web site will find program announcements and application guidelines, a copy of the foundation's most recent annual report, research grants program abstracts, and news.

The Thomas H. White Foundation (OH) (http://www.fmscleveland.com/thomaswhite/)
Established in 1913, the Thomas H. White Foundation maintains an interest in education and human services, while responding to new opportunities to make the greater Cleveland area a better place for children and families. Formal programs maintained by the foundation include human services, education, arts/culture, and public/society benefit. The foundation considers qualifying organizations in Cuyahoga County. The foundation's Web site features information about the foundation's grantmaking interests, guidelines, application information, staff/board listings, and contact numbers.

Whitehall Foundation, Inc. (FL) (http://www.whitehall.org)
The Whitehall Foundation, located in Palm Beach, Florida, assists scholarly research in the life sciences. Currently, it is focused exclusively on assisting basic research (excluding clinical) in vertebrate and invertebrate neurobiology in the United States. Research should specifically concern neural mechanisms involved in sensory, motor, and other complex functions of the whole organism as these relate to behavior, and the overall goal should be to understand behavioral output or brain mechanisms of behavior. Funding is provided through the research grants and grants-in-aid programs. Research grants are available to established scientists of all ages working at accredited institutions in the U.S., and are provided for up to three years. Grants-in-aid are designed for researchers at the assistant professor level who because they are not yet firmly established, have difficulties in competing for research funds. Applications will be judged on their scientific merit and innovative aspects. Consult the foundation's Web site for further program information, application procedures, grants lists, and contact information.

Helen Hay Whitney Foundation (NY) (http://www.hhwf.org/)
The Helen Hay Whitney Foundation was established and endowed by Mrs. Charles S. Payson, the former Joan Whitney, in 1943 and named in honor of her mother, Helen Hay Whitney. Originally established to stimulate and support research in the area of rheumatic fever and rheumatic heart disease, the foundation later expanded its interests to include diseases of connective tissue and, ultimately, all basic biomedical sciences. The Helen Hay Whitney Foundation supports early post-doctoral research training in all basic biomedical sciences. To attain its ultimate goal of increasing the number of imaginative, well-trained, and dedicated medical scientists, the foundation makes grants of financial support of sufficient duration to help further the careers of young men and women engaged in biological or medical research. The foundation's Web site includes a board list, an annual report, listings of fellowship recipients, eligibility information, and contact information.

The Claude R. and Ethel B. Whittenberger Foundation (ID) (http://www.whittenbergerfoundation.org)
Established in 1973, the Claude R. and Ethel B. Whittenberger Foundation of Caldwell, Idaho seeks to improve the quality of life for children and young people. The foundation's areas of interest relating to children and young people are education, arts and culture, health, social welfare, and recreation. Visit the foundation's Web site to learn more about the foundation's mission, application guidelines and procedures, grant limitations, grants listing, financial data, board and staff lists, and contact information.

Wilburforce Foundation (WA) (http://www.wilburforce.org/)
The Seattle-based Wilburforce Foundation awards grants in the areas of the environment and population stabilization to nonprofit organizations operating in the Pacific Northwest, Alaska, and the Canadian province of British Columbia. The foundation's Web site offers detailed information on the types of grants and support awarded, grant proposal guidelines and application information, a list of the foundation's recent grants, a map of the foundation's funding regions and a list of grants made in each region, links to similar organizations, and online news articles about the planet.

Catherine Holmes Wilkins Foundation (WA) (http://fdncenter.org/grantmaker/wilkins/)
The Seattle, Washington-based Catherine Holmes Wilkins Foundation was created by the will of Catherine Holmes Wilkins to provide charitable grants to qualified medical research and social service agencies in the Puget Sound region. Funding priorities of the foundation include medical research and education, the physically handicapped and mentally ill, and services for the needy. Visitors to the foundation's Web site will find specific information on the foundation's areas of interest, description of the foundation's funding policies, application procedures, and contact information.

The Wilkins Family Foundation (KS) (http://fdncenter.org/grantmaker/wilkinsfamily/)
The Wilkins Family Foundation of Kansas funds projects, community service organizations, economic development activities, and cultural organizations in the United States involved with education and health issues of children 17 years of age and younger. The foundation focuses on reinforcing organizations and projects with an established system of accountability by adding a strong entrepreneurial component to the donation process, promoting opportunities for self-empowerment and personal growth. Visitors to the foundation's Web site will find a listing of recent grant recipients, application procedures, and contact information.

Willary Foundation (PA) (http://www.willary.org)
The Willary Foundation, a small family foundation based in Scranton, Pennsylvania, makes grants for organizations and individuals in Lackawanna and Luzerne Counties. The foundation seeks to foster both individuals and groups with unique, innovative, or unusual ideas and efforts, and is disposed to leveraging the impact of its grants by encouraging efforts that could have a ripple effect in the community or by supporting projects in conjunction with other sources of funding. The foundation is particularly interested in projects

that support leadership and the development of leadership in business, the economy, education, human services, government, the arts, media, and research. In addition to a mission statement, visitors to the foundation's Web site will find a history of the foundation's recent grantmaking activities and financial activity, the foundation's latest tax return, a discussion board, printable grant application and grant evaluation forms, a listing of the foundation's board and staff, and contact information.

The Windham Foundation, Inc. (VT) (http://www.windham-foundation.org)
The Windham Foundation was established in 1963 by Dean Mathey, a prominent investment banker who had long family ties to Grafton, Vermont. The Grafton-based foundation was established with "a three-fold purpose: to restore buildings and economic vitality in the village of Grafton; to provide financial support for education and private charities; and to develop projects that will benefit the general welfare of Vermont and Vermonters." Links are provided on the site to some of the foundation's restoration projects. The foundation also awards scholarships to Windham County residents who are studying at the undergraduate level or who are high school graduates pursuing a certificate in a trade or technical setting. Application instructions and an electronic scholarship application are available on the foundation's Web site. The foundation also maintains a grants program that supports elementary and secondary educational organizations in Vermont. Prospective applicants will find application instructions and a downloadable grant application cover sheet on the foundation's site. Visitors to the Web site will also find a history of the foundation, its annual report, a search engine for the site, links to foundation projects, and an online contact form.

The Wolf Aviation Fund (PA) (http://www.wolf-aviation.org)
Located in Philadelphia, Pennsylvania, the Wolf Aviation Fund was created to help individuals work together to support general aviation. The fund's mission is to "promote and support the advancement of personal air transportation by seeking and funding the most promising individuals and worthy projects which advance the field of general aviation; by increasing the public's knowledge of aviation through publications, seminars, and other information media; [and] by informing the aviation and scientific community of the existence and purpose of the fund." The programs sponsored by the fund include: developing public policy and airports; networking and mutual support; development and alternative resources; communications, media, and community relations; general aviation technology, safety, and noise; outreach: improving public understanding and perceptions; and aviation and space education. The fund's Web site includes lists of previous grants, related links, specific grant guidelines and procedures, staff/board listings, and contact information.

The Wood Family Foundation (WA) (http://fdncenter.org/grantmaker/wood/)
The Wood Family Foundation of Seattle, Washington, was established in 1997 to enhance the lives of women and children. Specifically, the foundation provides support for at-risk teens and young adults living in poverty, preventing domestic violence and sexual assault, improving lives of low-income women, and encouraging philanthropy among teens and young people. Visitors to the foundation's Web site will find application guidelines, a listing of officers, grant restrictions, application deadlines, and contact information.

Jeffris Wood Foundation (WA) (http://fdncenter.org/grantmaker/jeffriswood/)
The Jeffris Wood Foundation is a small private foundation formed in 1994. Grants are made to community-based organizations working to provide opportunities for street youth and extremely poor individuals. The foundation supports creative, grassroots programs that successfully activate community volunteers. The foundation is interested in programs that support street youth, youth creativity, Native American youth, teen pregnancy prevention, and environmental programs, as well as other basic programs. Visit the foundation's Web site for information on the foundation's interests, application guidelines, and contact information.

Woodruff Foundation (OH) (http://www.fmscleveland.com/woodruff)
Founded in 1986, the Woodruff Foundation works to "address the unmet needs in mental health and chemical dependency in Cuyahoga County, Ohio." To this end, the foundation works with local hospitals and charitable groups to meet its mission. Specifically, the foundation supports the treatment of persons affected by mental disorders and chemical dependency, educational programs related to mental health, the coordination of mental health resources in the community, and research into the causes, nature, and recurrence of mental illness. Visitors to the foundation's Web site will find application guidelines and instructions, details on special initiatives, a listing of recent grant recipients, financial information, and contact information.

Robert W. Woodruff Foundation, Inc. (GA) (http://www.woodruff.org/)
Known for the first fifty years of its existence as the Trebor Foundation, the Robert W. Woodruff Foundation, Inc. was renamed in 1985 in honor of the man who, over six decades, guided the Coca-Cola Company from regional soft-drink enterprise to a multinational conglomerate with one of the most recognizable trademarks in the world and who, through the foundation, gave generously to a wide range of charitable and cultural organizations in Atlanta, the state of Georgia, and nationwide. Today, the Atlanta-based Woodruff Foundation, Inc. focuses its giving in the areas of elementary, secondary, and higher education; healthcare; human services, particularly for children and youth; economic development and civic affairs; art and cultural activities; and conservation of natural resources and environmental protection. It also has been seeking ways in which it can help achieve "systemic improvement in public education, healthcare access, and family, children, and youth services at the state and local levels." Most, but not all, of the foundation's grantmaking is limited to tax-exempt organizations operating in Georgia; organizations seeking support are encouraged to make an informal inquiry before submitting a proposal. Visitors to the foundation's Web site will find general background information and a brief biography of Robert W. Woodruff, grant application guidelines, an analysis of the foundation's recent grants, the foundation's latest financial information, and contact information.

Woods Charitable Fund, Inc. (NE) (http://www.woodscharitable.org/)
Based in Lincoln, Nebraska, the Woods Charitable Fund, Inc. seeks to "strengthen the community by improving opportunities and life outcomes for all people in Lincoln." The fund supports organizations that "are exploring creative alternatives and promoting more just, effective approaches to meet community needs." Within its limited geographic scope, the fund's special funding interests are in the program areas of children, youth, and families; education; community development and housing; and arts and humanities. In addition to a history of the fund and the affiliated Woods Fund of Chicago, the fund's Web site provides general information on funding interests and limitations, a summary of grants by areas of interest, and a listing of the board of directors.

Woods Fund of Chicago (IL) (http://www.woodsfund.org/)
The Woods Fund of Chicago supports a range of nonprofit activities that seek increased opportunity for the area's less advantaged. The fund's primary mission is to serve "nonprofits in their important roles of engaging people in civic life, addressing the causes of poverty and other challenges facing the region, promoting more effective public policies, reducing barriers to equal opportunity, and building a sense of community and common ground." The fund limits most of its grantmaking to metropolitan Chicago. Visit the fund's Web site to view information on the grantmaking programs, program guidelines, funding limitations, application procedures and forms, and contact information.

David, Helen, and Marian Woodward Fund-Atlanta (GA) (http://www.wachovia.com/charitable_services/woodward_overview.asp)
The David, Helen, and Marian Woodward Fund-Atlanta was established in 1974 to "benefit nonprofit institutions, corporations, and associations which are located in Georgia or one of its neighboring states, and which are organized and operated exclusively for religious, educational and charitable and scientific purposes and to governmental agencies to

which contributions by individuals are made deductible from income by the Internal Revenue laws." The fund's Web site includes grant guidelines, a downloadable grant application, recent grants awarded, and a listing of committee members.

The Frank Lloyd Wright Foundation (AZ) (http://www.franklloydwright.org)
Frank Lloyd Wright, "one of the 20th Century's greatest architects," established the Frank Lloyd Wright Foundation in 1940 to perpetuate the Taliesen Fellowship, a "self-sustaining community of apprentices and architects who would learn and practice the philosophy of organic architecture by sharing in architectural work, building construction, and the related arts." Located in Scottsdale, Arizona, the foundation is "committed to advancing the ideas and principles of organic architecture, organic education, and conservation of the natural environment," and "seeks to preserve and enhance the lifetime contributions and ideas of Frank Lloyd Wright and make available to the public opportunities to study and experience organic architecture." The foundation provides for the continued operation, maintenance, and reservation of Taliesin (Spring Green, Wisconsin) and Taliesin West (Scottsdale, Arizona), which were Wright residences during his life, as architectural, educational, environmental, and cultural centers, where public outreach and apprenticeship programs take place. Taliesen and Taliesen West also serve as the campuses of the Frank Lloyd Wright School of Architecture. Visit the Web site to learn more about the activities of the foundation, a bio of its founder's life and works, links to related sites, and contact information.

Xeric Foundation (MA) (http://www.xericfoundation.com)
Based in Northampton, Massachusetts, the Xeric Foundation was established by Peter A. Laird, co-creator of the Teenage Mutant Ninja Turtles and Planet Racers. The foundation offers financial assistance to self-publishing comic book creators in the United States and Canada and to nonprofit organizations in western Massachusetts. The Xeric Foundation assists comic book creators with some of the costs in self-publishing their work, though "it is not the foundation's intention to fully support an artist/writer through the entire process of self- publishing, but to encourage creators to experience the learning process involved in working towards such a goal." The foundation provides funds to charitable and nonprofit organizations for unique projects or services and for leveraging other funds. The foundation does not assist with operating budgets or capital costs. Visitors to the foundation's Web site can find a grants lists, application instructions and forms, and contact information.

Youth Foundation (NY) (http://fdncenter.org/grantmaker/youthfdn/)
Established in 1994, the Youth Foundation of New York awards scholarships to exceptionally worthy, financially needy, secondary school seniors for their undergraduate college education. The Youth Foundation encourages young people to establish permanent attitudes of self-reliance, confidence, self-discipline, responsibility, voluntarism, and exemplary character to benefit their own lives and the lives of others. The foundation's Web site features funding priorities, eligibility criteria, board listings, and contact information.

The Zimmer Family Foundation (FL) (http://www.zimmerfamilyfoundation.com)
The Zimmer Family Foundation is a private foundation located in Sarasota, Florida that supports religious, educational, and social programs—locally, nationally, and internationally—that bring help and hope to the less fortunate, primarily by seeding short-term pilot projects that have the potential of self-support. Visitors to the foundation's Web site will find information on granting criteria, guidelines, past recipients, and contact information.

APPENDIX C

Grantmaking Public Charities on the Web

AAA Foundation for Traffic Safety (DC) (http://www.aaafoundation.org)
Located in Washington, D.C., the AAA Foundation for Traffic Safety was founded in 1947 by the American Automobile Association. The group works to "identify traffic safety problems, foster research that seeks solutions, and disseminate information and educational materials." The foundation makes grants to support research and education in a broad spectrum of traffic safety issues, including child passenger safety, teen driver safety, truck safety, distracted driving, and senior driving issues. The foundation's Web site offers a variety of resources, including videos and publications, research reports, quizzes on safe driving, and guidelines for solicited and unsolicited proposals, application information, and deadlines.

Abraham Fund (NY) (http://www.coexistence.org/)
The Abraham Fund promotes constructive coexistence between Jews and Arabs within Israeli society. Named for Abraham, the common ancestor of both Jews and Arabs, the fund was established in 1989 as a funding source for programs aimed at developing coexistence opportunities. The fund awards grants in the following categories for projects that aim to strengthen coexistence: educational, community-based projects with children, teenagers, and adults; public advocacy projects; and best practices in the field of Jewish-Arab coexistence. The fund's Web site, which is available in English, Hebrew, and Arabic, includes a description of the fund and its activities, a listing of funded coexistence projects, newsletter excerpts, contact information for the fund in the United States and Israel, and links to related Web sites.

The Frederick B. Abramson Memorial Foundation (DC) (http://www.abramsonfoundation.org)
Located in Washington, D.C., the Frederick B. Abramson Memorial Foundation was created in 1991 to honor the respected member of the local legal community. The organization works to continue Abramson's commitment to young people and education through two scholarship funds. The Frederick B. Abramson Memorial Scholarships are awarded to economically disadvantaged District of Columbia public high school seniors to attend

four-year institutions. The Frederick B. Abramson Public Service Award is a fellowship for graduating law students, judicial law clerks, or practicing attorneys to help support a year's employment at a nonprofit or a public interest law firm. The foundation's Web site offers guidelines, deadlines, and application forms for both programs; a board member list; lists of past recipients; and a list of the foundation's funders.

Academic Distinction Fund (LA) (http://www.adfbr.org)
The Louisiana-based Academic Distinction Fund was established in 1989 "to raise and invest private funds to support innovative actions that lead to academic excellence for students in East Baton Rouge Parish Public Schools." The fund represents a collaboration among schools, businesses, and the community, working for private sector leadership in advancing public education. Visitors to the fund's Web site will find information on various grants for teachers and students; online application forms; details on a partnership with the National Football League Players Association to benefit area education; descriptions of special projects and events, including grantwriting and networking opportunities; links to outside grant resources and education sites; an online response form; and contact information.

Academy of American Poets (NY) (http://www.poets.org/)
The Academy of American Poets was founded in New York City in 1934 to "support American poets at all stages of their careers and to foster the appreciation of contemporary poetry." The academy awards prizes ranging from $1,000 to $150,000 to poets at different levels of achievement, and distributes university and college poetry prizes at more than 170 schools. Funding is also available through the Greenwall Fund, which supports the publication of poetry, and the American Poets Fund, which assists poets in the event of an illness or other emergency. Applications are not accepted for the latter—selected academy members and awardees can submit nominations. Each award listing includes submission guidelines (where applicable), a list of past recipients, and a list of judges. The academy's Web site also includes information on more than 450 poets, the texts of more than 1,200 poems, a poetry listening booth, events calendars, literary links, and information on becoming a member or donor.

ACCION New York, Inc. (NY) (http://www.accionnewyork.org)
Located in Brooklyn, New York, ACCION New York, Inc., was launched in 1991 as a part of an international nonprofit organization. The group works with self-employed individuals, or "microentrepreneurs," who lack access to traditional forms of business credit. Businesses can apply for loans using an online form. ACCION New York's Web site also provides links to small business resources, a calendar of upcoming events, a newsletter, an annual report, and contact information.

Achievement Rewards for College Scientists Foundation, Inc. (CA) (http://www.arcsfoundation.org/default.asp)
Founded in 1958 in Los Angeles as a reaction to the Soviet launching of Sputnik and the need for scientific advancement in the United States, the Achievement Rewards for College Scientists Foundation, Inc., is a "national volunteer women's organization dedicated to helping the best and brightest U.S. graduate and undergraduate students by providing scholarships in natural sciences, medicine, and engineering." Through its twelve chapters, the foundation supports scholars at more than 40 universities, all of which are listed on the foundation's Web site. Scholarship awards are given to the universities which then distribute the funds to individual students. The foundation's Web site includes an e-mail address for each chapter, general information about the scholarships, answers to frequently asked questions, and an alumni network page.

ACMP Foundation (NY) (http://www.acmp.net)
The Amateur Chamber Music Players, Inc. created the ACMP Foundation in New York City in 1993. The foundation provides funding toward the goal of "fostering the playing and singing of chamber music by people of all ages and skill levels." Grants are given

internationally in four program areas: home coaching awards for amateurs; weekend workshops awards for amateur players; community music grants for schools, youth symphonies, and similar institutions; and support for special events and projects. Board membership and contact information is available in the About ACMP section of the foundation's Web site.

Adhesive and Sealant Council Education Foundation (MD) (http://www.ascouncil.org/educationfoundation/)

The Bethesda, Maryland-based Adhesive and Sealant Council Education Foundation was created in 1987 to support a partnership between the adhesive and sealant industry and the Virginia Tech Center for Adhesive and Sealant Science. The partnership seeks to attract and train potential new employees for the adhesive and sealant industry, provide access to an academic environment and state-of-the-art equipment, offer continuing education opportunities, encourage research in adhesive and sealant science, and foster communication and exchange of ideas with academia. The Advancement Fund, an annual fundraising appeal, supports many elements of the program, including a scholarship program for summer, undergraduate, and graduate students; conventions; educational programs; meetings; campus tours; and a summer employment program within the industry. The site includes a list of contributors, information on plans for the foundation, and a description of services to the industry.

Advertising Women of New York Foundation, Inc. (NY) (http://www.awny.org/found.html)

Advertising Women of New York Foundation, Inc., was founded in 1912 in New York City as the first women's association in the communications industry. With a mission of providing a forum for personal and professional growth, serving as a catalyst for the advancement of women in the communications field, and promoting philanthropic endeavors, the foundation provides financial aid to educate future industry leaders and to support selected local charitable organizations that focus on improving the quality of life for women and children. The foundation's Web site offers information about the organization's charitable programs, a history of the organization, staff listings, and contact information.

Aerospace Legacy Foundation (CA) (http://www.aerospacelegacyfoundation.org/)

The Aerospace Legacy Foundation was founded in 1995 to work for "historical integrity and educational use of a portion of the NASA/Boeing site in Downey, California," which rose to fame as a center of the U.S./Russian space race in the 1960s. Today, the foundation seeks to preserve Downey's space-related history. Visitors to the foundation's Web site will find a detailed history of the Downey area and its importance in the space race, information on upcoming foundation events and meetings, and links to related resources.

AFC Foundation (GA) (http://www.afc-online.com/culture/foundation.html)

The AFC Foundation is the giving arm of AFC Enterprises, an organization of restaurant franchises based in Atlanta, Georgia. The foundation "gives its time, resources, and money to national and international charities that are aligned with [its] business strategies." The foundation collaborates with a number of national community service programs and organizations, including Save the Music and Habitat for Humanity. Further information on the foundation and links to these partner organizations are posted on the foundation's Web site. The AFC Foundation does not accept unsolicited requests for support.

Agape Foundation (CA) (http://www.agapefn.org)

The Agape Foundation, established by pacifists and anti-war activists in Palo Alto, California, in 1969, funds nonviolent grassroots projects in the western United States. The foundation strives to support "projects which challenge the root causes of war and bring fresh energy and new perspectives to the ongoing movement for peace and justice." Along with a loan program, the foundation offers funding through the Emergency Grant Fund; the Emmy Lefson Memorial Fund for Peace, Social Justice and Human Rights; and other programs. The foundation's Web site gives a brief history of the foundation, including previous grantees; an annual report; funding priorities; details on the grant application process; and a short FAQs section.

AHP Foundation (VA) (http://go-ahp.org/foundation)
The AHP Foundation was established in 1974 as the charitable arm of the Association for Healthcare Philanthropy. The foundation's programs include the study and dissemination of information regarding healthcare development, continuing education for healthcare resource development professionals, and grants to individuals and organizations. The foundation also provides scholarships for members to attend the Association for Healthcare Philanthropy's annual conferences. The foundation's Web site offers a number of publications on giving trends, information on the Pooled Income Fund for nonprofit healthcare organizations, and contact information.

Aid to Artisans, Inc. (CT) (http://www.aidtoartisans.org/)
Aid to Artisans, Inc., a nonprofit organization founded in 1976 to create economic opportunities for craftspeople around the world, offers design consultation, on-site workshops, business training, and links to markets where craft products are sold. It awards grants every year to emerging artisans and craft-based associations worldwide. The organization's Web site offers information about its direct service programs, a bulletin board of events, a description of its work and projects, and listings of officers, directors, and staff.

The AIDS Action Committee of Massachusetts, Inc. (MA) (http://www.aac.org)
Established in 1983, the AIDS Action Committee of Massachusetts, Inc., provides support services to men, women, and children with AIDS and HIV. The committee's mission is three-fold: to provide support services for people living with AIDS and HIV; to educate the public and health professionals about HIV transmission, treatment, and prevention; and to advocate for fair and effective AIDS policy at the city, state, and federal levels. The committee's Web site features its mission, a downloadable copy of the most recent annual report, and contact information.

AIDS Foundation of Chicago (IL) (http://www.aidschicago.org)
The AIDS Foundation of Chicago was established in 1985 and is now the largest private sector AIDS network in the Midwest. The foundation works "to develop and support a comprehensive system of HIV prevention and care, bringing together public and private resources, advocating for sound and compassionate public policy, and coordinating the activities of AIDS service providers." The foundation focuses on five main areas of funding interest: HIV service delivery systems, work with policymakers, technical support, AIDS service providers, and increasing private sector support. The foundation annually offers funding for HIV-related programs through a request for proposals process. The foundation's Web site contains a vast amount of information and links to resources on many topics related to HIV/AIDS, including information on prevention, case management, and provider services.

AIDS Foundation of St. Louis, Inc. (MO) (http://aidstl.org/home.htm)
Established in 1987, the mission of the AIDS Foundation of St. Louis is to create financial support for local organizations dedicated to providing high-quality direct services and educational programs to all people affected by the growing HIV/AIDS epidemic. The foundation also strives to facilitate cooperation and mutual support among area HIV/AIDS service organizations. Funding is considered for organizations that assist in the establishment and ongoing development of direct care and education in the metropolitan St. Louis area. Visit the foundation's Web site to learn more about the foundation's mission and find out how to obtain a grant application.

Alabama Humanities Foundation (AL) (http://www.ahf.net)
Based in Birmingham, Alabama, the Alabama Humanities Foundation (AHF) was founded in 1975 as the state's affiliate of the National Endowment for the Humanities. The foundation's mission is "to create and foster opportunities, through grants and AHF-conducted programs, for scholars and the public together to explore human values and meanings through the humanities." The foundation sponsors a number of programs related to the humanities, including grants for public humanities projects. Funding policies, grant

categories, and application and budget instructions are provided on the foundation's Web site, along with application forms for major and small grants, details on other programs sponsored by the foundation, upcoming events, and contact information.

Alabama Law Foundation, Inc. (AL) (http://www.alfinc.org/)
The Alabama Law Foundation, Inc., was established in 1987 to be the recipient of funds generated by the Interest on Lawyers' Trust Accounts (IOLTA) Program. The foundation distributes IOLTA grants each year in support of legal aid to the poor, to help maintain public law libraries, and to provide law-related education to the public. The foundation also administers the Cabaniss, Johnston Scholarship Fund; the Fellows Program; and the Kids' Chance Scholarship Program. The foundation's Web site offers descriptions of these programs and application information for funding.

Alabama Textile Education Foundation, Inc. (AL) (http://www.eng.auburn.edu/department/te/resources/scho.html)
The Alabama Textile Education Foundation, Inc., is associated with Auburn University's Textile Engineering Department, whose mission is to perform research and prepare students for the textile industry. The foundation, along with other textile companies and organizations, provides financial aid based on need to students in the field. Scholarship applications can be downloaded from the Auburn University Textile Engineering Department's home page, which also describes current careers, advancements, and available resources in the textile industry.

Alaska Humanities Forum (AK) (http://www.akhf.org/)
Founded in 1972 as the state's affiliate of the National Endowment for the Humanities, the Alaska Humanities Forum seeks to enrich the civic, intellectual, and cultural lives of Alaskans through the humanities. The forum's grant program funds a variety of innovative humanities-based projects, including publications, films, lectures, exhibits, conferences, scholarly research, and public discussions. The forum's Web site provides information about the its activities, grant guidelines and downloadable application forms, a listing of recent grant recipients, and a collection of links to related resources on the Web.

Alaska Wilderness League (DC) (http://www.alaskawild.org)
The Alaska Wilderness League was founded in 1993 in Washington, D.C., with the mission of protecting the environment of Alaska. The league promotes and protects Alaska's land and water resources by supporting legislative and administrative initiatives, promoting national and local education, strengthening grassroots activism, and providing leadership within the environmental community. The league's Web site features extensive background information on Alaska's natural resources and the league's current protection campaigns, current news items, information on sending messages on environmental issues to Congress, links to other conservation organizations, and league contact and membership information.

Albany-Schenectady League of Arts, Inc. (NY) (http://www.artsleague.org/)
Founded in 1946, the Albany-Schenectady League of Arts, Inc., is the oldest continually operating regional arts council in the United States. It provides technical and administrative services to artists and arts organizations in the 11 counties of the Capital Region of New York State. The league provides funding opportunities for the arts in Albany and Schenectady Counties; grant opportunities are posted on the league's site. Those interested in learning more about the grants are encouraged to call the league directly. Contact information, relevant links, a special events calendar, and information on league programs can also be found on the organization's Web site.

The Horatio Alger Association of Distinguished Americans (VA) (http://www.horatioalger.org)
Since 1947, the Horatio Alger Association of Distinguished Americans has been dedicated to honoring the accomplishments and achievements of outstanding individuals in our society who have succeeded in the face of adversity, and to encourage young people to pursue

their dreams with determination and perseverance. The association assists students who have demonstrated integrity, perseverance in overcoming adversity, strength of character, financial need, a good academic record, a commitment to pursue a college education, and a desire to contribute to society. The association's Web site features information on its various scholarship programs, application criteria, and contact information.

All Children's Hospital Foundation, Inc. (FL) (http://www.allkids.org/Foundation/FoundHome.html)

The All Children's Hospital Foundation, Inc., located in St. Petersburg, Florida, strives "to help meet the operational needs of the Children's Hospital and secure the future needs of our young patients through funding research and teaching programs." The hospital itself was established in 1926, and the associated foundation has worked to build specialty treatment centers and establish research chairs at the University of South Florida College of Medicine, among other programs. The foundation's Web site includes an overview of the organization, information on donor and volunteer opportunities, and contact information.

Alliance for Quality Education (SC) (http://www.allianceforqualityed.org)

Established in 1985, the Alliance for Quality Education was created to improve the quality of education in every public classroom in Greenville County, South Carolina. The grants program is made up of three components: the Mini-Grant Awards Program, which makes grants to districts, schools, and teachers to enhance student learning; the Professional Development Leadership Institute, a seminar run during the summer by the alliance to create professional development plans for the improvement of student learning; and the Healthy Schools, Healthy Communities program, which makes school-wide grants to improve the physical health of public school employees. Applications for each program, a list of staff and board members, and links to related resources are available on the alliance's Web site.

Alliance of Resident Theatres/New York (NY) (http://www.offbroadwayonline.com/aboutartny.php)

Founded in 1972, the Alliance of Resident Theatres/New York (A.R.T./New York) serves hundreds of nonprofit theatres and related organizations. A.R.T./New York provides low-cost office space for theater organizations, management-related technical assistance grants to small and emerging theaters, capital financing, and more. Details about A.R.T./New York's programs and funds, as well as contact information, are provided on the alliance's Web site. A.R.T./New York also promotes audience development through OffBroadwayOnline.com, which offers information on Off Broadway theatre companies.

Allied Arts Foundation (WA) (http://www.alliedarts-seattle.org)

Created in Seattle, Washington, in 1954, the Allied Arts Foundation works to "enhance the cultural livability of Seattle" through a network of those interested in the arts, architecture, urban design, and historic preservation. The foundation is a membership organization that supports and initiates arts groups, offers community reviews of projects, and makes grants to or sponsors select organizations. Grant and sponsorship guidelines are posted on the foundation's Web site, along with downloadable applications, contracts, membership details, and upcoming events.

Alpha Delta Kappa (MO) (http://www.alphadeltakappa.org)

Headquartered in Kansas City, Missouri, Alpha Delta Kappa is an international honorary sorority for women educators. The organization funds an International Teacher Education Scholarship Program, which provides foreign students with the opportunity to study educational systems in the United States. More information about this scholarship, as well as the member activities of Alpha Delta Kappa, are available through the group's Web site.

Alpha Kappa Psi Foundation, Inc. (IN) (http://www.akpsi.com/Foundation.cfm)

The Alpha Kappa Psi Foundation, Inc., was established in 1951 to "provide resources for enhancing the educational experience of future business leaders." Alpha Kappa Psi is a professional business fraternity and, as such, its foundation provides grants and scholarships to undergraduate and graduate students, supports educational programs in leadership and professional development, manages alumni chapters, and publishes a newsletter. The foundation's Web site provides more details and an opportunity to make a contribution online.

Alpha Omicron Pi Foundation (TN) (http://www.aoiifoundation.org/)

Based in Brentwood, Tennessee, the Alpha Omicron Pi Foundation was established in 1977 to "fund programs, which promote the intellectual, ethical, and leadership development of members of Alpha Omicron Pi Fraternity and, through its philanthropic efforts, benefit the larger society." The foundation offers grants to Alpha Omicron Pi members for scholarships, educational and leadership programming, and emergency aid to those in dire need. The foundation also provides charitable grants for arthritis research and education. The foundation's site provides an opportunity to contribute online and includes lists of staff and board members.

Alpha-1 Foundation, Inc. (FL) (http://www.alphaone.org/main.htm)

The Miami-based Alpha-1 Foundation, Inc., is a not-for-profit corporation founded in early 1995 by three individuals diagnosed with alpha 1-antitrypsin deficiency (Alpha-1), a genetic disorder that can cause liver and lung disease in children and adults. The foundation's mission is to "advance the means to control and cure Alpha-1 and to improve the quality of life for those with the disorder." The foundation supports educational programs and activities in the field of alpha 1-antitrypsin deficiency. The foundation also offers grants and awards to fund a broad range of Alpha-1 related research. Details about each program can be found on the foundation's Web site.

Alphapointe Association for the Blind (MO) (http://www.alphapointe.org)

The Alphapointe Association for the Blind was incorporated in 1916 in Kansas City, Missouri. The association's mission is to "assist blind and visually impaired persons in the greater Kansas City area to maintain dignity and independence" through rehabilitation, employment, advocacy and support services. Each of these services is explained in greater detail on the association's Web site. Links to additional resources, publications for sale, and contact information are also provided online.

Alzheimer's Association (IL) (http://www.alz.org/)

Founded in 1980 by family caregivers, the Chicago-based Alzheimer's Association and its more than 200 local chapters across the United States work to eliminate Alzheimer's disease through the advancement of research, while enhancing care and support services for individuals and their families. The Research area of the association's Web site describes its Research and Conference Grants programs, lists past grant recipients by year and state, and provides an overview of the Ronald and Nancy Reagan Research Institute. The remainder of the association's site offers news, contact information, and information on care and medical issues related to Alzheimer's disease.

America the Beautiful Fund (DC) (http://www.freeseeds.org)

The America the Beautiful Fund was founded in 1965 "for the preservation and restoration of the natural wonders of America." The Washington, D.C.-based fund's mission is "to preserve our national heritage by assisting community-level programs and projects to save the natural and historic environment and improve the quality of life." The fund supports volunteer community projects in all 50 states, and the fund's Web site provides details on the organization's programs and accomplishments.

American Academy of Dermatology, Inc. (IL) (http://www.aad.org)

The American Academy of Dermatology is dedicated "to achieving the highest quality of dermatologic care for everyone." The academy's Web site details upcoming events and conferences, current news in dermatology, and links to a variety of educational sites for children and adults on skin and skin conditions. Scholarships are available for young dermatologist students in developing countries to attend upcoming International Investigative Dermatology conferences. More information on the academy's scholarship, activities, and membership can be found at the academy's Web site.

American Academy of Family Physicians Foundation (KS) (http://www.aafpfoundation.org/)

Located in Leawood, Kansas, the American Academy of Family Physicians Foundation is the philanthropic arm of the American Academy of Family Physicians. The foundation is committed to "enhancing the healthcare delivered to the American people by developing and providing philanthropic resources for the promotion and support of family practice." The Web site provides detailed information on the foundation's many programs, awards, and research grants related to family medicine; electronic versions of the foundation's newsletter; and contact information.

American Academy of Otolaryngic Allergy Foundation (DC) (http://www.aaoaf.org)

Founded in 1941, the American Academy of Otolaryngic Allergy Foundation provides member training, education, and research opportunities toward the diagnosis, treatment, and prevention of allergic diseases. The foundation's Web site features information on the foundation's Research Funding program, including a grant application form and contact information; a history of the organization; board and staff member listings; and a range of resources for members, physicians, and patients.

American Antiquarian Society (MA) (http://www.americanantiquarian.org)

Established in Worcester, Massachusetts, in 1812, the American Antiquarian Society is an independent research library devoted to "documenting the life of America's people from the colonial era through the Civil War and Reconstruction," using collections including books, pamphlets, newspapers, periodicals, broadsides, manuscripts, music, children's literature, graphic arts, genealogy, and local histories. The society awards three different visiting fellowships: the Visiting Academic Research Fellowships, the Mellon Post-Dissertation Fellowships, and the Fellowships for Creative Artists and Writers. The society's Web site features detailed information and application guidelines for each of these programs, information on using the society's library, programs and publications offered by the society, and access to the collection's online catalog.

The American Architectural Foundation, Inc. (DC) (http://archfoundation.org/)

The American Architectural Foundation, Inc., is a public outreach and educational organization dedicated to helping people understand the importance of architecture in their lives. In addition to its education efforts and programs, the foundation offers scholarships, fellowships, and grants. Scholarships and fellowships are provided to undergraduates, graduates, and professionals in the United States and Canada. Descriptions of each scholarship and nomination forms are available on the foundation's Web site. The foundation's Accent on Architecture Grant Program assists local architectural foundations, AIA components, and other local design and civic organizations in producing innovative public education programming. Deadlines, guidelines, the application, educational materials, news updates, and staff information are also available on the Web site.

American Association for World Health, Inc. (DC) (http://www.thebody.com/aawh/aawhpage.html)

Located in Washington, D.C., the American Association for World Health boasts former president Jimmy Carter as its honorary chairman. The association is dedicated to grassroots health initiatives and providing the help local leaders need to influence positive health practices in their own home towns. Working with urban and rural local leaders in distributing information on public health to those who may not otherwise have access to healthcare, the association seeks to stimulate global and national action on health problems in order to "achieve a lasting impact on public health for U.S. citizens." The association advocates for international collaboration in order to focus further attention on health issues. The association's Web site provides details on the organization's goals, programs, and international supporters; information on the association's internship program, accompanied by a downloadable application; links to affiliated and co-sponsoring organizations; and contact information.

American Association of Airport Executives Foundation (VA) (http://www.airportnet.org/depts/membership/acad_rel/scholarship.htm)
The Alexandria, Virginia-based American Association of Airport Executives was founded in 1928 to represent the interests of managers and directors of U.S. and international airports. The foundation offers a scholarship to full-time undergraduate or graduate students who are attending accredited colleges or universities, one is available only to association members, and one for Native Americans. The foundation's Web site provides guidelines and contact information for these programs.

American Association of Higher Education (DC) (http://www.aahe.org)
Formed in 1969, the American Association of Higher Education is a membership organization that works to allow members, other individuals, communities, and institutions in the higher education community "to learn, organize for learning, and contribute to the common good." The association organizes conferences, publications, special programs, and partnerships. Visitors to the Web site will find information on the association's mission, activities, partners, programs, and special interest groups for members, along with current news about the organization.

American Association of Museums (DC) (http://www.aam-us.org)
The Washington, D.C.-based American Association of Museums was founded in 1906 "to promote excellence within the museum community." The association represents all types of museums and both paid and unpaid staff, and runs a variety of programs and services to foster communication and partnerships among distinct museum communities. The association's Web site includes descriptions of its services, guidelines and downloadable application materials for the association's professional education fellowships, upcoming events and initiatives, additional resources for members, and contact information.

American Association of School Administrators (VA) (http://www.aasa.org/)
The American Association of School Administrators, an international professional organization for education leaders, focuses on preparing schools and school systems for the 21st century, connecting schools and communities, and enhancing the quality and effectiveness of school leaders. The association offers numerous awards and scholarships, which are listed and described in the Awards and Scholarships area of its Web site.

American Association of Spinal Cord Nurses (NY) (http://www.aascin.org)
The Jackson Heights, New York-based American Association of Spinal Cord Nurses is dedicated to promoting quality care for individuals with Spinal Cord Impairment (SCI). Founded in 1983, the association advances nursing practice through education, research, advocacy, healthcare policy, and collaboration with consumers and healthcare delivery systems. The association's research grants program encourages nurses to conduct research related to SCI nursing practice and to evaluate the effectiveness of existing programs and delivery systems related to SCI. Grant application materials and guidelines; legislative updates; position statements; contact information; and information about upcoming conferences, the association's awards program, and membership are available on the association's Web site.

American Association of University Women (DC) (http://www.aauw.org/)
The American Association of University Women (AAUW) promotes education and equity for women and girls through a membership organization, the AAUW Educational Foundation, and the AAUW Legal Advocacy Fund. The foundation funds research on girls and education, community action projects, and fellowships and grants for outstanding women around the globe, and the fund provides funds and a support system for women seeking judicial redress for sex discrimination in higher education. The associations's Web site

describes the organization's fellowships, grants, and awards and provides application instructions for each category. Visitors to the site will also find membership information, AAUW research, a detailed overview of public policy issues of concern to organization members, and contact information.

American Bar Association Fund for Justice and Education (IL) (http://www.abanet.org/fje)
The American Bar Association Fund for Justice and Education was created in Chicago in 1961 to support American Bar Association (ABA) programs "that improve the legal system and educate the public about the role of law in our society." The fund supports a wide variety of law-related programs, including educational workshops; technical assistance to bar associations; *pro bono* assistance on behalf of elderly, youth, disabled, and low-income populations; publications; workshops; and a number of nonprofit legal aid organizations. The fund also grants three-year law school scholarships to racial and ethnic minority students through the ABA Legal Opportunity Scholarship Fund. A complete, downloadable application packet for the scholarship, additional details on the fund, and contact information are available at the fund's Web site.

American Bar Foundation (IL) (http://www.abf-sociolegal.org/)
The Chicago-based American Bar Foundation supports basic empirical research into the theory and functioning of the law, legal institutions, and the legal profession. The foundation sponsors fellowship programs for postdoctoral scholars, doctoral candidates, and minority undergraduate students. The foundation's Web site outlines each of these programs and provides a downloadable application form. The site also offers an overview of current areas of research, information for prospective donors, online versions of recent annual reports, and a directory of staff members with e-mail links.

The American Berlin Opera Foundation, Inc. (NY) (http://www.operafoundation.org)
The New York City-based American Berlin Opera Foundation, Inc., was created by opera enthusiasts in 1985 to send promising Americans to study and perform opera in Berlin and to then pursue professional careers in Europe. The foundation offers the Curt Engelhorn Scholarship supporting singers at the Deutsche Oper Berlin. The scholarship competition is open to American citizens or permanent residents between the ages of 18 and 30 who are beginning their professional careers. A downloadable application and information on the foundation's founders, trustees, and annual gala are available on the Web site.

American Cancer Society, Inc. (GA) (http://www.cancer.org/)
The American Cancer Society, Inc., the largest non-government funder of cancer research in the United States, has committed more than $2 billion since 1946 to finding a cure for cancer. The society offers a variety of research grants, training grants for health professionals, fellowships, and a clinical research professorship. Detailed information on the society's programs, including downloadable application forms in multiple formats, is provided in the Research Programs area of the society's Web site. Visitors to the site will also find listings by state of currently funded projects and information on different cancers, cancer treatments, statistics, alternative therapies, and a comprehensive set of links to related resources.

American College of Laboratory Animal Medicine Foundation (MD) (http://www.aclam.org)
The American College of Laboratory Animal Medicine (ACLAM) promotes the advancement of knowledge in the humane, proper, and safe care of laboratory animals by veterinary medical specialists through professional continuing education activities, educational materials, and research in laboratory animal medicine and science. The ACLAM Foundation funds research projects, specifically in the areas of analgesia/anesthesia, animal behavior/well-being, diagnostics/diseases of laboratory animals, laboratory animal husbandry, and refinement of animal models. Interested applicants will find information on current research grants, guidelines, the application process, grant application tips, recently funded

grants, grant reports, and further details about the organization itself are available in the Foundation area of the ACLAM Web site.

American College of Obstetricians and Gynecologists (DC) (http://www.acog.org/)
The American College of Obstetricians and Gynecologists (ACOG) is "the nation's leading group of professionals providing health care for women." It was founded in Chicago, Illinois, in 1951 and is now based in Washington, D.C. The college serves as a strong advocate for quality health care for women; maintains the highest standards of clinical practice and continuing education of its members; promotes patient education and stimulating patient understanding of, and involvement in, medical care; and increases awareness among its members and the public of the changing issues facing women's healthcare. Visitors to the college's Web site will find membership information, listings of ACOG events and seminars, news releases, and patient education resources.

American Council of Learned Societies (NY) (http://www.acls.org/jshome.htm)
The American Council of Learned Societies (ACLS) is a federation of 66 national scholarly organizations that seeks to "advance humanistic studies in all fields of learning in the humanities and the related social sciences and to maintain and strengthen relations among the national societies devoted to such studies." The council administers several grant and fellowship programs, which are explained in detail at its Web site. Visitors to the site can also request, through an electronic order form, a brochure on the current year's competitions, and will find information about ACLS affiliates and publications and a nice list of links to funding, research, and institutional resources.

American Council of the Blind (DC) (http://www.acb.org/)
Founded in Washington, D.C., in 1961, the American Council of the Blind strives "to improve the well-being of all blind and visually impaired people." This mission is accomplished through a variety of programs and efforts in education, public awareness, rehabilitation, cooperation with lawmakers and institutions, and a general advocacy on behalf of the blind and visually impaired. The council also offers scholarships to post-secondary students. Application guidelines and an online application form are available at the council's site, along with a number of other resources and services.

American Diabetes Association (VA) (http://www.diabetes.org/research)
The Alexandria, Virginia-based American Diabetes Association was founded in 1940 as a nonprofit health organization providing diabetes research, information, and advocacy. The association supports a large number of grants and awards for diabetes investigations and innovative research strategies. The association's Web site provides a wealth of diabetes-related resources; news on past grant recipients; deadlines for upcoming grants; downloadable forms, applications, and guidelines for funding; and contact information.

American Dietetic Association Foundation (IL) (http://www.adaf.org)
Established in 1966 to promote good nutrition, the American Dietetic Association Foundation focuses on public awareness, education, and research in the science of dietetics. The foundation provides grants and scholarships to dietetics students and professionals in the United States and internationally. Details about the foundation's scholarship and grant programs, current news and events, the *Insider's Report* publication, and contact information are available at the foundation's Web site.

The American Endowment Foundation (OH) (http://www.aef-fund.org)
The American Endowment Foundation (AEF), based in Hudson, Ohio, seeks "to expand the capacity of American philanthropy," especially focusing on family foundations and giving. The foundation maintains the Social Capital Fund as its donor-advised program and posts a list of charitable funding priorities on its Web site. A downloadable grant recommendation form and program description/application form, additional links, program details, and items of interest for donors can also be found at the site.

American Federation for Aging Research, Inc. (NY) (http://www.afar.org/)
Founded in 1981, the American Federation for Aging Research, Inc., helps scientists launch and further their careers in aging research and geriatric medicine in order to promote healthier aging. The federation administers a number of grant programs each year to provide medical students and junior scientists with research funding. The federation's Web site describes each grant program in detail and provides an interactive form for access to downloadable applications or to request hard copies of applications and brochures. Visitors to the site will also find donor, meeting, and conference information, and a listing of the federation's board members.

American Federation of Riders (OH) (http://www.afr1982.org)
The American Federation of Riders, founded in 1982 in Cincinnati, Ohio, is a federation of motorcyclists dedicated to helping needy, orphaned, handicapped, abused, and/or neglected children through support of individual children and organizations. The federation has provided trust funds for orphaned children, medical grants to families, Christmas gifts and meals, and recently started a scholarship fund for college-bound, high school seniors. The federation's Web site describes its support in general terms, gives a history of the organization, and provides contact information.

American Floral Endowment (IL) (http://www.endowment.org/)
The American Floral Endowment funds research and educational development in floriculture and provides development funding for the advancement of the floral industry. The endowment also offers scholarships and paid internships to horticulture students. Information on all funding programs is provided at the endowment's Web site, along with downloadable applications, news, research reports, and donor information.

American Foundation (AZ) (http://www.americanfoundation.org)
The Phoenix, Arizona-based American Foundation was established in 1997. The foundation's mission is to "energetically promote and help create vast amounts of new and more effective philanthropy." This is done in three ways: helping others to establish charitable trusts and foundations; helping these, and other, foundations become more successful and efficient; and building networks between the grantees, foundations, and donors. The foundation also makes grants to assist charities in developing their governance and organizational structure, improve equipment and facilities, and improve human resources. The foundation's Web site includes a list of grant recipients, extensive information on establishing a private or corporate foundation, and a special area for advisors (attorneys, accountants, etc.) to nonprofits.

American Foundation for AIDS Research, Inc. (NY) (http://www.amfar.org/)
Formed in 1985, the American Foundation for AIDS Research, Inc., (AmFAR) works to prevent death and disease associated with HIV/AIDS and to foster sound AIDS-related public policies—a goal it seeks to achieve through support of scientific and social research, advocacy, and public information programs. Requests for proposals are posted at AmFAR's Web site, along with information on the grantmaking process and past grants, press releases, publications, information about upcoming events and conferences, and donor information.

American Foundation for the Blind (NY) (http://www.afb.org)
Established in 1921, the American Foundation for the Blind is "dedicated to addressing the critical issues of literacy, independent living, employment, and access through technology for the ten million Americans who are blind or visually impaired." Helen Keller worked with this foundation for over 40 years. The foundation's Web site provides information and resources on Helen Keller, advocacy, aging and vision loss, education, employment, literacy, technology, and Web accessibility for the visually impaired. Additionally, the Web site offers access to journals, listings of upcoming events, subscriber services, and community message boards.

American Geriatric Society, Inc. (NY) (http://www.americangeriatrics.org)
Founded in New York City in 1942, the American Geriatric Society, Inc., is a "professional organization of health care providers dedicated to improving the health and well-being of all older adults" through education, public policy, culturally sensitive interdisciplinary geriatric clinical care, and research. The society's Web site provides a wealth of topical information for geriatrics healthcare professionals, the public, and other concerned individuals, including health links, information for students, job and training listings, and current public policy briefings. A page with funding opportunities is updated monthly with brief descriptions and contact information for further details and applications.

American Health Assistance Foundation (MD) (http://www.ahaf.org)
Founded in 1973, the American Health Assistance Foundation funds research on age-related and degenerative diseases, educates the public about these diseases, and offers assistance to Alzheimer's patients and their caregivers. The foundation provides funding for research into Alzheimer's disease, macular degeneration, glaucoma, heart disease, and stroke. It also funds the Alzheimer Family Relief Program, which provides direct financial assistance and resources to Alzheimer's patients and their caregivers. The foundation's Web site provides access to guidelines and applications for both the research grant programs and the Alzheimer Family Relief Program, information on making a donation, a list of publications, and links to organizations in each area of research.

American Heart Association (TX) (http://www.americanheart.org)
Established in 1924, the American Heart Association (AHA) provides information on heart disease and stroke and supports scientific research that will help fight these life-threatening medical conditions. The association offers numerous national and regional-affiliate research grant and fellowship programs. The Science and Professionals area of its Web site provides guidelines for all research programs, and access to application forms and instructions. The Web site also provides educational and scientific information on heart disease, links to AHA affiliates and other resources, online advocacy, and donor and volunteer information.

American Hotel Foundation (DC) (http://www.ei-ahma.org/ahf/ahf.htm)
The American Hotel Foundation serves the lodging industry by providing resources for projects that ensure continued growth and opportunities for the industry. The foundation awards scholarships to students pursuing an undergraduate degree in hospitality management and awards grants for research that will benefit the industry. Both programs are described on the foundation's Web site.

American Humane Association (CO)
(http://www.americanhumane.org/site/PageServer?pagename=pa_shelter_services)
Founded in 1877, the American Humane Association (AHA) works to "prevent cruelty, abuse, neglect, and exploitation of children and animals and to assure that their interests and well-being are fully, effectively, and humanely guaranteed by an aware and caring society." The organization supports improvements of animal care facilities through the Meacham Foundation Memorial Grant and provides scholarships for its Agency Members to attend AHA training workshops. The Web site provides information on grant programs, detailed program descriptions, the organization's most recent annual report, and contact information.

American Institute of Indian Studies (IL) (http://humanities.uchicago.edu/orgs/aiis)
Established in 1961, the Chicago-based American Institute of Indian Studies is a consortium of universities and colleges in the United States at which scholars engage in teaching and research about India. The group offers fellowship support to scholars, ranging from graduate students to established specialists, for periods of study in India. The institute also offers language, research, and training programs. The institute's Web site includes detailed program information, downloadable application forms, and a list of member organizations.

American Jewish World Service (NY) (http://www.ajws.org)
American Jewish World Service was founded in 1985 "to help alleviate poverty, hunger, and disease among the people of the world" regardless of religion or race. This mission is accomplished through technical support, humanitarian aid, emergency relief, and volunteer efforts in the areas of health, education, civil society, women's empowerment, agriculture, HIV/AIDS, and micro-credit. The organization offers support to grassroots non-governmental organizations with small grants. Its Web site provides grant application procedures, information on its worldwide programs, current news, and contact information.

American Kennel Club Canine Health Foundation (OH) (http://www.akcchf.org/)
Located in Aurora, Ohio, the American Kennel Club Canine Health Foundation's mission is "to develop significant resources for basic and applied health programs with emphasis on canine genetics to improve the quality of life for dogs and their owners." The foundation sponsors research into canine diseases, breeds, and related subjects. The foundation's Web site provides information on its research programs, current news, newsletters, upcoming events, links to resources, and contact information.

American Legacy Foundation (DC) (http://www.americanlegacy.org/)
The American Legacy Foundation was formed in 1998 as a part of the settlement reached between tobacco companies and the American public. The foundation is "committed to working with other organizations that are interested in decreasing the use of tobacco by Americans." Its two main goals are to reduce tobacco usage by young people and to help individuals of all ages quit smoking. The foundation maintains three strategies to accomplish these goals: state tobacco prevention programs; public education including the Truth advertising campaign; and evaluation and applied research projects. Visitors to the foundation's Web site will find complete details on each aspect of the organization's campaigns, a requests for proposals page for research projects, downloadable guidelines and applications, a message board, links to further tobacco resources, a calendar of regional events, and contact information.

American Library Association (IL) (http://www.ala.org)
The Chicago-based American Library Association "provides leadership for the development, promotion, and improvement of library and information services and the profession of librarianship in order to enhance learning and ensure access to information for all." The association has numerous areas of interest and activity, but its key action areas are diversity, education and continuous learning, equity of access, intellectual freedom, and 21st century literacy. The association's Web site provides program descriptions, application criteria, instructions, and application forms for its numerous grants, scholarships, and awards; job listings; a calendar of events and conferences; news; and contact information.

American Lung Association of California (CA)
(http://www.californialung.org/research/awards.html)
Headquartered in Oakland, California, with regional offices throughout the state, the American Lung Association of California works to prevent lung disease and promote lung health. The association's Web site provides comprehensive information on lung diseases and related issues, such as air quality and smoking; details on local programs and events; current research and advocacy; research grant and scholarship guidelines; FAQs; and applications. A portion of the Web site is translated into Spanish.

American Lung Association of Gulfcoast Florida (FL)
(http://www.lungusa.org/gulfcoastfl/)
Headquartered in St. Petersburg, Florida, with regional offices throughout the state, the American Lung Association of Gulfcoast Florida works to prevent lung disease and promote lung health. The association's Web site provides information on lung diseases and related issues, such as tobacco control and asthma. Additionally, visitors to the site will find details on local programs and services, current research, and advocacy. A portion of the Web site is translated into Spanish.

American Medical Women's Association Foundation (VA) (http://www.amwa-doc.org/foundation2.html)

Founded in 1915, the American Medical Women's Association (AMWA) strives "to advance women in medicine and improve women's health." To accomplish the association's charitable and education goals, the AMWA Foundation was established in 1990. The foundation seeks to educate physicians, medical students, and the general public on the issues of women's health through a variety of programs and services, including scholarship funds, the Reproductive Health Initiative, and grants to members of the association for projects associated with the organization's goals. The foundation's Web site details specific funding programs, provides a link to the *Foundation Watch* newsletter, and includes contact information.

American Meterological Society (MA) (http://www.ametsoc.org/ams)

The Web site of the Boston, Massachusetts-based American Meteorological Society is a clearinghouse of information on the meteorological sciences. Information on upcoming conferences, current news and trends in meteorology, journals and publications, and educational opportunities are available online. Under the Education Programs and Resources link, the society provides information on minority and other undergraduate scholarships and graduate fellowships for future meteorologists, oceanographers, hydrologists, and climatologists, as well as information on initiatives that promote science literacy in the nation's schools.

American Music Center (NY) (http://www.amc.net/)

Created in New York City in 1939 by a musical group headed by Aaron Copland, the American Music Center works to "foster and encourage the composition of contemporary music and to promote its production, publication, distribution, and performance in every way possible through the Western Hemisphere" and to build a national community for new American music. The center supports four grant programs: the Margaret Fairbank Jory Copying Assistance Program, the Live Music for Dance Program, the Aaron Copland Fund for Music Performing Ensembles Program, and the Aaron Copland Fund for Music Recording Program. The center's Web site includes information and applications for each program and features details on the center's workshops, networking groups, publications, and library.

American Music Therapy Association (MD) (http://www.musictherapy.org/about.html)

Founded in 1998, the American Music Therapy Association promotes the progressive development of the therapeutic use of music in rehabilitation, special education, and community settings. The association is committed to the advancement of education, training, professional standards, credentials, and research in support of the music therapy profession. The organization's Web site offers information on membership, publications, and conferences, as well as contact information.

American Occupational Therapy Foundation (MD) (http://www.aotf.org)

The American Occupational Therapy Foundation, based in Bethesda, Maryland, seeks to advance the practice of occupational therapy. The foundation offers scholarships for students pursuing entry-level occupational therapy or occupational therapy assistant degrees. The foundation's Web site provides a listing of scholarships and application instructions, additional sources of financial aid, information on its educational and research programs, and a listing of scholarship winners. The site also features a link to the Wilma L. West Library, a national clearinghouse of occupational therapy information; events; and contact information.

American Osteopathic Association (IL) (http://www.aoa-net.org)

The mission of the American Osteopathic Association is "to advance the philosophy and practice of osteopathic medicine by promoting excellence in education, research, and the delivery of quality, cost-effective healthcare in a distinct, unified profession." The association's Bureau of Research offers various grant programs, research fellowships, and awards.

Downloadable grant and fellowship applications, program descriptions, information on internships and residency programs for students, links to external resources, the Bureau of Research annual report, press releases, publications, and contact information are available on the association's Web site.

American Osteopathic Foundation (IL) (http://www.osteopathic.org)
The Chicago-based American Osteopathic Foundation's mission is "to serve the osteopathic medical profession and the public to improve healthcare outcomes." This goal is achieved through the distribution of a number of grants, awards, and scholarships, which are described on the foundation's Web site. The Osteopathic Seals Program and the Osteopathic Progress Fund also support student loans and research programs in the field. The site provides details on upcoming events and conferences, as well as contact information for interested grant applicants.

American Paint Horse Association Youth Development Foundation (TX) (http://www.apha.com/ydf/)
The Youth Development Foundation was established in 1980 by the American Paint Horse Association to help reward and educate young horsemen and women and to support scientific research in the equine industry. The foundation administers youth scholarships and provides research grants, in accordance with its educational and scientific goals. Visitors to the foundation's Web site will find more information on past scholarship recipients, downloadable application and recommendation forms, and contact information.

American Parkinson's Disease Association (NY) (http://www.apdaparkinson.com)
Founded in 1961, the American Parkinson's Disease Association, with offices in Staten Island, New York, and Los Angeles, California, seeks "to 'Ease the Burden and Find the Cure' for Parkinson's Disease through research, patient and family support, and education." The association funds fellowships and grants for Parkinson's research; distributes educational publications, some of which can be downloaded online; and administers information and referral offices throughout the United States. Fellowship and grant guidelines and application materials can be downloaded from the association's Web site.

American Pharmaceutical Association Foundation (DC) (http://www.aphafoundation.org)
Based in Washington, D.C., the American Pharmaceutical Association Foundation was created in 1952 "to enhance the quality of consumer health outcomes that are affected by pharmacy, positively affecting consumer health outcomes through research, public education, issue forums, and awards and recognition programs." The foundation's programs include grants for pharmacists to implement pharmaceutical care projects, student scholarships, and the Advance Practice Institute, a weekend program teaching new techniques and perspectives. Guidelines for each program are available online. The foundation's Web site also features research papers, descriptions of models developed from research projects, information on contributing, and a list of publications.

American Philosophical Society (PA) (http://www.amphilsoc.org)
Established in 1743 in Philadelphia with the support of, among others, Benjamin Franklin, the American Philosophical Society "promotes useful knowledge in the sciences and humanities through excellence in scholarly research, professional meetings, publications, library resources, and community outreach." The society's grants program supports research by U.S. residents, U.S. citizens working for foreign institutions, and foreign nationals whose research can only take place in America. The society's Web site provides information about each award program, including details on eligibility, guidelines, and downloadable applications. The site also includes announcements of upcoming meetings, a publications section, and information on the group's library.

American Physicians Fellowship for Medicine in Israel (MA) (http://www.apfmed.org/)
The American Physicians Fellowship for Medicine in Israel, established in 1950, is an organization of North American physicians and others dedicated to advancing the state of

medical education, research, and care in Israel. The core of the fellowship's funding is a program for Israeli physicians training in the United States and Canada. In recent years, the fellowship has expanded its support to include various awards and programs benefiting the medical community in Israel. Funding areas include research projects, a trauma program, training for Russian immigrant physicians and pathology technicians, the Solomon Hirsh Nurse Fund, and programs focused on women's health. The fellowship's Web site features descriptions of its funding programs, contact information, information on recent fellows, news, donor and membership information, a discussion forum, and a listing of staff and board members.

American Psychiatric Foundation (VA)
(http://www.psychfoundation.org/apfhome/default.asp)
The charitable arm of the American Psychiatric Association, the Arlington, Virginia-based American Psychiatric Foundation awards grants for public education programs to increase awareness and understanding of mental illness, advocacy on behalf of patients with mental illnesses and their families, and research focusing on access to and the quality of treatment for mental illness. The foundation also administers several annual fellowships that educate psychiatry residents about the development of public policy related to the care of the mentally ill and awards that recognize excellence in psychiatric research. The foundation's Web site features information on these programs, application guidelines and deadlines, information on upcoming events, and a mental illness resource center.

American Psychological Foundation (DC) (http://www.apa.org/apf/)
The Washington, D.C.-based American Psychological Foundation was created in 1953 to "advance the science and practice of psychology for the understanding of behavior and the benefit of human welfare." The foundation awards assorted scholarships to high school and graduate school students demonstrating achievement in areas of psychology, offers grants for research in specific areas and to reward outstanding research accomplishments, and sponsors an annual lecture series. The foundation's Web site contains application instructions and restrictions for each of the scholarships and awards, and a list of the board of trustees.

American Road and Transportation Builders Association (DC) (http://www.artba.org)
The American Road and Transportation Builders Association was established in 1902 as an advocate for "strong federal investment in the nation's transportation infrastructure to meet public demand for safe and efficient travel and shipment of goods." Working with the U.S. transportation construction industry, the association has a long history of advocating for improvement in the nation's infrastructure. The association's Transportation Development Foundation offers awards and scholarship programs, which are described on the association's Web site. The site also offers resources for members and the transportation builders profession in general and information on upcoming events, governmental affairs, and research projects.

American Skin Association (NY) (http://skinassn.org/research.htm)
Founded in 1987, the American Skin Association supports public education and medical research focused on skin disorders. The association provides support to qualifying organizations, professorships, and laboratories interested in skin research and educating children about the care and protection of their skin. The association's Web site provides information and guidelines on various programs, as well as contact information.

American Society for Industrial Security Foundation (VA)
(http://www.asisonline.org/foundation/index.xml)
Located in Alexandria, Virginia, the American Society for Industrial Security (ASIS) serves as a link between the academic and professional communities with the ultimate goal of "academic, strategic, and professional development" and the "evolution of the security field as a profession and a management science." The society's Web site features information on the ASIS Foundation, which provides funding at the national and local levels to

individuals seeking educational opportunities and funds researchers through grants and sponsorships, among other activities. The main ASIS Web site also provides news updates and publications, information on education courses, and links to further academic and professional resources in the industrial security field.

American Society for the Prevention of Cruelty to Animals (ASPCA) (NY) (http://www.aspca.org)
Founded in 1866, the American Society for the Prevention of Cruelty to Animals (ASPCA) was one of the first humane organizations in the Western Hemisphere. Its mission is "to prevent cruelty and alleviate the pain, fear, and suffering of animals through nationwide education, awareness, and legislative programs." Headquartered in New York City, the organization oversees various local animal services and serves as the parent organization for nationwide animal advocacy groups. The ASPCA Web site provides a host of information on advocacy, education, shelters, and pet care; links to similar organizations working for animal rights; numerous educational brochures; a free online newsletter; a special Web site geared toward children; and contact information.

American Society of Consultant Pharmacists Research and Education Foundation (http://www.ascpfoundation.org/) (VA)
The American Society of Consultant Pharmacists Research and Education Foundation of Alexandria, Virginia, was founded in 1982 by the American Society of Consultant Pharmacists to support educational programs and research. The foundation is made up of two institutes that each administer programs in their specific area of interest: the Niemerov Institute, which works on long-term care and consultant pharmacy practice; and the Geriatric Drug Therapy Research Institute, which supports the study of diseases that disable elderly people and the use of drugs to treat these conditions. The foundation funds research and traineeships in relevant areas of pharmacology. The foundation's Web site includes information, guidelines, and applications on the traineeships; information on electronic and print publications; and a collection of press releases.

American Society of Health-System Pharmacists Research and Education Foundation (http://www.ashpfoundation.org) Foundation (MD)
The Bethesda, Maryland-based American Society of Health-System Pharmacists Research and Education Foundation was established in 1968 "to foster research and educational activities that enable health-system pharmacists to expand their capacity to help people make the best use of medicines." The foundation funds various awards, grants, and traineeships related to this goal. The foundation's Literature Awards Program recognizes important contributions to the literature of pharmacy practice in health systems. The foundation's Web site provides information on its current research grants, traineeships, and advocacy programs; supporters; and news.

American Society of Interior Designers (DC) (http://www.asid.org)
The American Society of Interior Designers (ASID) was founded in Washington, D.C., in 1975 as a nonprofit professional organization representing the interests of interior designers and the interior design community. The society sponsors the ASID Educational Foundation, which provides grants to undergraduate design students and for special projects of an educational or historical nature. Descriptions of the scholarships are provided on the society's Web site, along with downloadable applications. Visitors to the society's Web site will also find a variety of resources on interior design, including information on events, employment opportunities, news on trends, and continuing education services.

American Society of Newspaper Editors (VA) (http://www.asne.org)
Based in Reston, Virginia, the American Society of Newspaper Editors is made up of directing editors of daily newspapers. The organization is "committed to fostering the public discourse essential to democracy; helping editors maintain the highest standards of quality, improving their craft, and better serving their communities; and preserving and promoting core journalistic values, while embracing and exploring change." The associated

foundation, along with member contributions and a long-standing endowment, fund the society's writing and photography awards. Award guidelines and entry forms are available on the society's Web site along with extensive information on the society, including a list of board members, annual convention information, publications, an events calendar, and links to related sites.

American Speech-Language-Hearing Association Foundation (MD) (http://www.ashfoundation.org)
The American Speech-Language-Hearing Association Foundation of Rockville, Maryland, was established in 1946 to "advance knowledge about the causes and treatment of hearing, speech, and language problems." The three primary giving programs are Research Grants, for research in communication sciences and disorders; Graduate Scholarships, including scholarships for minority students and students with disabilities; and Clinical Recognition Awards, which include awards for Outstanding Lifetime Achievement, Outstanding Recent Achievement, and Outstanding Schools-Related. Guidelines, applications, and nomination forms for grants and awards programs; a list of board members; opportunities to contribute; a list of current sponsors; and an events calendar are available on the foundation's Web site.

American Symphony Orchestra League (NY) (http://www.symphony.org)
Established in 1942, the American Symphony Orchestra League is a member organization headquartered in New York City committed to "providing leadership and service to American orchestras while communicating to the public the value and importance of orchestras and the music they perform." The league organizes conferences and meetings, research and analysis, professional development, and career opportunities in the field. The league's Orchestra Management Fellowship Program annually offers a limited number of highly qualified individuals the opportunity to learn about being executive directors of orchestras. The league's Web site includes fellowship guidelines and applications, information on its various programs, a special section for children, and links to related sites created by the league.

American Thyroid Association, Inc. (VA) (http://www.thyroid.org/)
Founded in 1932, the American Thyroid Association, Inc., provides outstanding leadership in thyroidology by promoting excellence and innovation in clinical care, research, education, and public policy. The association provides support to a limited number of research projects in thyroid function and disease. The association's Web site offers information on the grant program and eligibility, the association's mission, publications, staff/board lists, and contact information.

Americans Helping Americans, Inc. (IL) (http://www.helpingamericans.org/)
Located in Lorton, Virginia, Americans Helping Americans, Inc., supports the needs of various communities in the United States, particularly the Appalachian community. Its mission is "to join communities, build and strengthen neighbor relations, and work side by side with residences to address local concerns, linking resources supportive of a healthy, safe, and economically vibrant standard of living" through various charitable programs. Project areas include community housing, water, safe houses for victims of domestic abuse, disaster relief, and school supplies, among others. Information about the group's programs can be found online, along with contact information, current news and events, a children's page, and letters from previous program recipients.

AmeriCares (CT) (http://www.americares.org)
AmeriCares was established in 1982 as a nonprofit disaster relief and humanitarian aid organization for individuals and communities worldwide. AmeriCares acts as an intermediary between U.S. and international manufacturers and indigenous health and welfare professionals in countries around the world, thus providing immediate response to emergency medical needs and supporting long-term healthcare programs in these countries. The organization's Web site provides details on specific disaster and humanitarian programs

undertaken by AmeriCares, current news about the organization, a newsletter, and online donation opportunities.

Amit Women, Inc. (NY) (http://www.amitchildren.org)
Based in New York City, Amit Women, Inc., was founded in 1925 to support Israel and the Jewish people. The organization's goals include: "nurturing and educating Israel's children to become self-reliant and self-respecting; educating thousands of unprivileged youngsters throughout the length and breadth of Israel; instilling a love of Torah and Jewish tradition; providing children from dysfunctional homes with joy of real family life in family group homes; absorbing and training Ethiopian and Russian youngsters; and developing Israel's young scientific talent." The organization supports many schools and educational programs in Israel, as a result of successful fundraising and organizing at chapters throughout the United States. The organization's Web site provides contact information, a list of schools supported in Israel, selected articles from the online newsletter, and press releases.

The Amyotrophic Lateral Sclerosis Association (CA) (http://www.alsa.org)
The Amyotrophic Lateral Sclerosis Association is dedicated to the fight against amyotrophic lateral sclerosis (ALS; often called Lou Gehrig's disease). The association's patient education programs provide support groups; a telephone information/referral service; equipment loans; augmentative communication devices; respite, information, and support for caregivers and family members; referrals to ALS clinics and physicians; and support for nationally directed research programs. The association's Research Grant Program offers funding for scientific and clinical management research. The association's Web site provides research program guidelines, information about the disease and ways to help find a cure, and contact information.

Irene W. and Guy L. Anderson Children's Foundation (CA) (http://www.andersongrants.org)
The Irene W. and Guy L. Anderson Children's Foundation was established in 1970 to serve the needs of the children of Coachella Valley, near Palm Springs, California. The foundation makes grants to a wide variety of nonprofit organizations serving children in the area. The foundation's Web site includes reports on recipients of past grants, grantwriting tips, current grants and application procedures, contact information, and downloadable applications.

ANGELCARE (CA) (http://www.angelcare.org/)
Based in San Diego, California, ANGELCARE was incorporated in 1977 as Children's ANGELCARE Aid International by a Vietnam War veteran who wanted to help the Vietnamese refugees. The organization's goal is to "provide worldwide help to poor and needy children and families with food, clothing, medical care, medicines, parenting skills, schooling, and anti-drug programs through Child Sponsorship and emergency relief." One of the organization's primary programs is its Child Sponsorship Program, in which "angels" donate a set amount per month for the benefit of a particular child who receives food, education, health and dental assistance, and other support. ANGELCARE has sponsorship programs in communities throughout the world. The organization's Web site provides many opportunities for visitors to donate a one-time gift or begin a sponsorship. There are also descriptions of the various projects, features on needy children, and information on volunteer opportunities.

Animal Protection Institute (CA) (http://www.api4animals.org/)
Founded in 1968 in Sacramento, California, the Animal Protection Institute advocates for the protection of animals from cruelty and exploitation. The institute's campaigns and programs address issues ranging from animals used in the entertainment industry to wildlife protection; each is described in detail on the institute's Web site. Additional information and resources pertaining to animal welfare, including current legislation, publications, and Action Alerts are posted on the site.

Animal Umbrella, Inc. (MA) (http://www.animalumbrella.org/)
Founded in 1986, Animal Umbrella, Inc., is a volunteer, nonprofit organization dedicated to the rescue, spay/neuter, adoption, and overall welfare of homeless cats and kittens in Massachusetts. Since its inception, the organization has spayed/neutered several thousand cats, adopted thousands of cats/kittens through its shelter and network of volunteers, responded to thousands of rescue calls from concerned animal lovers, and worked to educate the public on animal welfare issues. The organization's Web site provides information about its cause and contact information.

Ann Arbor Film Festival (MI) (http://aafilmfest.org)
The Ann Arbor Film Festival is a nonprofit arts organization that showcases 16mm independent and experimental film. The festival's mission is "to provide a worldwide public forum for 16mm film screenings, to encourage and showcase independent and experimental film artists, to promote film as art, and to offer educational outreach." The festival is open to films in all categories that demonstrate a high regard for film as an art form. Those interested in entering the festival must submit an application and an entry fee along with their film. The festival's Web site contains contact information, deadlines and festival dates, and festival procedures.

Aplastic Anemia and MDS International Foundation (MD) (http://www.aamds.org/)
The Aplastic Anemia and MDS International Foundation works to find the causes of and cures for aplastic anemia, myelodysplastic syndromes, and other kinds of bone marrow failure. The foundation funds scientific research into these conditions. A description of foundation's Research Awards and other programs, downloadable applications, educational resources, newsletters, donor information, and related links are available on the foundation's Web site.

Appalachian Community Fund (TN) (http://www.kornet.org/appafund/)
Created in Knoxville, Tennessee, in 1986, the Appalachian Community Fund supports organizations in Central Appalachia (eastern Kentucky, southwest Virginia, east Tennessee, and all of West Virginia). The fund is "a regionally based and controlled grantmaking organization for work on economic, environmental, social, and racial justice issues." The fund supports programs that are directly tied to grassroots organizing for social change, and the fund's areas of interest include workers' rights, race and affirmative action, gender and sexual preference issues, domestic violence, training indigenous leaders and young people as activists, environmental justice, and alternative arts and media. The fund's Web site includes downloadable guidelines and application, a list of current grantees, information on contributing, and a staff list.

Arby's Foundation, Inc. (FL) (http://www.arby.com/arb07.html)
The Arby's restaurant chain established the Arby's Foundation, Inc., in 1986 to support education and youth development. The foundation maintains partnerships with Big Brothers Big Sisters and the Boys and Girls Clubs of America, providing sponsorships and fundraising efforts for the organizations' programs and services. The foundation also grants annual college scholarships to Big Brothers Big Sisters participants. Details on the foundation's programs, recent scholarship recipients, upcoming fundraising events, and contact information are provided on the foundation's Web site.

Arizona Cardinals Charities (AZ) (http://www.azcardinals.com/community/charities.php)
Founded in 1990, Arizona Cardinals Charities, established by the Arizona Cardinals football organization, supports programs designed to improve the quality of life and enhance opportunities for children, women, and minorities in the state of Arizona. Grant proposals are only considered from qualifying organizations that intend to use at least 75 percent of the funds in the state of Arizona. Visit the organization's Web site to learn more about its mission, view a grants listing, and obtain contact information.

Arizona Diamondbacks Charities, Inc. (AZ) (http://diamondbacks.mlb.com)
Arizona Diamondbacks Charities, Inc., is a nonprofit corporation established by the Diamondbacks baseball organization to generate and distribute contributions to nonprofit organizations that provide services to promote positive growth and development for residents of Arizona. The organization directs its efforts to helping the homeless, the indigent, and children. Visit the charities' Web site for contact information.

Arizona Humanities Council (AZ) (http://www.azhumanities.org/)
The Arizona Humanities Council, founded in 1973 as the state's affiliate of the National Endowment for the Humanities, directs and supports programs that promote understanding of "human thoughts, actions, creations, and values." The council provides support for humanities projects in a variety of formats through its General Grant program. Application guidelines and the Intent to Apply Form are provided on the council's Web site, as are guidelines and forms for other programs, and features a database of Arizona humanities scholars, news, a calendar, resources, and donor information.

Arkansas Humanities Council (AR) (http://www.arkhums.org/)
The Arkansas Humanities Council, established in 1974 as the state's affiliate of the National Endowment for the Humanities, promotes understanding, appreciation, and use of the humanities in Arkansas. To achieve its goal, the council awards grants to groups and organizations to plan, conduct, and evaluate projects in the humanities. Funding is provided for public programs, research, publications, media projects, and planning, as well as occasional matching grants. Downloadable major grant and mini-grant applications and descriptions of materials held in the council's Resource Center are available on the council's Web site.

Art Against AIDS Foundation, Inc. (FL) (http://www.artagainstaidspensacola.com)
Formed in 1990 in Pensacola, Florida, the Art Against AIDS Foundation, Inc., organizes fundraising events and programs to aid in the funding of local community organizations that serve people affected by HIV and AIDS. The foundation takes a creative approach to fundraising by using arts and crafts, as well as musical and theatrical productions to support its cause. The foundation's Web site provides a history of the foundation, a listing of the organizations it funds, financial information, upcoming events, sponsorships details, and contact information.

Art Alliance for Contemporary Glass (NJ) (http://www.contempglass.org)
The mission of the Art Alliance for Contemporary Glass is "to further the development and appreciation of art made from glass." The alliance supports and encourages museums, glass education, regional collectors, and public seminars. The alliance also makes grants to arts organizations for educational purposes relating to contemporary glass and provides select organizations with an unrestricted grant. A list of previous grantees and award recipients, grant guidelines, an application form, links to museums and local groups, membership information, and details on upcoming events are available on the alliance's Web site.

Art League of Marco Island, Inc. (FL) (http://www.marcoislandart.com)
The Art League of Marco Island, Inc., was formed in 1969 on Marco Island, Florida, as a nonprofit organization that promotes art and local artists. The league brings artists to Marco Island for educational programs; it also promotes local artists through cultural events, such as gallery shows and art fairs. Details on programs and events, as well as membership and contact information are provided on the league's Web site.

Art Omi International Art Center (NY) (http://www.artomi.org)
Located in Omi, New York, the Art Omi International Art Center is an "international arts center for visual artists, writers, and musicians as well as the site for the Fields Sculpture Park, a year round public exhibition space for contemporary sculpture." The center houses three residency programs: the Art Omi International Artists' Colony, the Ledig House International Writers' Colony, and Music Omi International Residency, all of which are

described on the center's Web site. The center also hosts public and educational programs throughout the year. Application guidelines; details on current residents, programs, fellowships, and prizes associated with the artists' and writers' colonies; and contact information are available on the center's Web site.

Arthritis Foundation, Inc. (GA) (http://www.arthritis.org/)
The Arthritis Foundation, Inc., originally established in 1948 as the Arthritis and Rheumatism Foundation, supports research to help find causes, treatments, and ways to prevent and cure the condition. The foundation's Web site details its grants, training awards, and career development awards and provides online applications; information on awards for achievement in research and quality of life; and information on the foundation's programs, publications, and advocacy work.

Arts and Cultural Council for Greater Rochester (NY) (http://www.artsrochester.org)
The Arts and Cultural Council for Greater Rochester was formed "to develop, promote, and strengthen the cultural industry for the benefit of the people of the Rochester, New York, region." The council offers grants through several programs: Community Arts Grants, Education Through the Arts, Individual Artists Projects, Culture Builds Communities, and Special Opportunity Stipends. Grant programs are described on the council's Web site with application information and recipients. The site also offers information on the board, staff, and membership.

Arts and Education Council of Greater St. Louis (MO) (http://www.stlartsanded.org)
The Arts and Education Council of Greater St. Louis, Missouri, works to support and promote "song, dance, drama, and creative energy in schools, on stages, and in performances throughout the region." The Council's Web site provides a downloadable application for its Project Grants program and offers arts organizations links, an events calendar, and contact information.

Arts Council of Greater Kalamazoo (MI) (http://www.kazooart.org/)
The Arts Council of Greater Kalamazoo, founded in 1969, supports the arts in Kalamazoo County, Michigan. Funds are granted on the basis of high artistic quality and merit to artists and organizations in the region. The council's Web site offers a list of its various grant programs and includes applications and deadlines. Visitors to the site will also find membership information, press releases, an events calendar, information on council activities, an arts directory, and contact information.

Arts Council of Indianapolis, Inc. (IN) (http://www.indyarts.org/)
The Arts Council of Indianapolis, Inc., works to "build the community through the arts by developing visibility, funding, audiences, information, and partnerships." The council's grant program supports local arts and cultural institutions and projects. Guidelines and downloadable applications, information and tickets for art events throughout the city, details on workshops and seminars for organizations, and a publications list are available on the council's Web site.

The Arts Council of Northwest Florida, Inc. (FL) (http://www.artsnwfl.org/)
The Arts Council of Northwest Florida, Inc., supports quality, diversity, and economic growth in the region's cultural community. The council awards grants to organizations to improve, extend, preserve, create, and plan cultural programs. Brief descriptions of the council's grant programs and activities, links to northwest Florida cultural institutions, news articles, and donor information are available on the council's Web site.

Arts Midwest (MN) (http://www.artsmidwest.org/)
Formed in 1985, Arts Midwest provides funding, training, publications, information services, and conferences to arts and cultural organizations, artists, art administrators, and art enthusiasts in Illinois, Indiana, Iowa, Michigan, Minnesota, North Dakota, Ohio, South Dakota, and Wisconsin. The organization's main granting program is the Heartland Arts

Fund, which supports and initiates tours in the 15-state heartland region by regional, national, and international artists and companies in dance, music, and theater. Arts Midwest also offers registration scholarships to the Midwest Arts Conference to individuals representing nonprofit organizations. The organization's Web site includes information on its programs, conference details, and links to arts organizations.

Arts United of Greater Fort Wayne, Inc. (IN) (http://www.artsunited.org)
The third-oldest united arts fund in the country, Arts United of Greater Fort Wayne, Inc., was established in 1955 as an umbrella organization to raise funds and awareness of the area's cultural organizations. The organization primarily provides funding to member and affiliate organizations, but it also considers requests from other organizations and individual artists. The organization's Web site provides information on its funding programs; staff, board, and fundraising committee lists; a list of funded/affiliate organizations; information on ways to contribute; and links to related resources.

ArtServe Michigan (MI) (http://artservemichigan.org/)
ArtServe Michigan serves, supports, and advocates for an enriched cultural environment, and promotes the arts as a valuable state and community resource. It assists and informs individuals and organizations in the state of Michigan through education, professional services, networking, support of artists and cultural organizations, volunteer assistance, and collaborations. The organization's Web site includes information on grants and awards for individual artists, a listing of the board of directors, and news about arts advocacy.

ArtsFund (WA) (http://www.artsfund.org)
Located in Seattle, Washington, ArtsFund has been supporting the city's nonprofit arts groups since 1969. The fund distributes sustaining and discretionary grants to groups in King and Pierce Counties for arts projects in a wide variety of disciplines. The ArtsFund Web site includes grant descriptions and guidelines, an online grant application form, information on donors, opportunities to contribute, grants lists, staff and board lists, and contact information.

The ASCAP Foundation (NY) (http://www.ascapfoundation.org)
Located in New York City, the ASCAP Foundation is "dedicated to nurturing the music talent of tomorrow, preserving the legacy of the past, and sustaining the creative incentive for today's musically gifted through a variety of educational, professional, and humanitarian programs and activities which serve the entire music community." The foundation funds a series of scholarships, which are administered by schools, colleges, conservatories, and other institutions; makes awards to exemplary composers and songwriters; funds educational programs for aspiring songwriters and composers; sponsors workshops, development programs, and residencies in affiliation with institutions around the country; and organizes performances to entertain assorted elderly and sick audiences. The foundation's Web site includes descriptions of its programs, a list of foundation officers and board members, and contact information.

Ashoka (VA) (http://www.ashoka.org)
Headquartered in Arlington, Virginia, and with offices around the world, Ashoka is dedicated to supporting social entrepreneurs through individual fellowships. Ashoka Fellows concentrate on leading global social change in the areas of education and youth development, healthcare, the environment, human rights, access to technology, and economic development. The Ashoka Web site is a resource for individuals involved or interested in social entrepreneurship, with descriptions of the fellowship program, details of Ashoka's various projects in more than 40 countries, general information on social change and leadership, resources for getting involved in the organization's volunteer and internship programs, and national and international contact information.

Asia Foundation (CA) (http://www.asiafoundation.com/)
The Asia Foundation is a private, nonprofit, nongovernmental organization working to build leadership, improve policies, and strengthen institutions to foster greater openness and shared prosperity in the Asia-Pacific region. The foundation currently has program priorities in four areas: governance, law, and civil society; economic reform and development; international relations; and women's political participation. The foundation's Web site offers detailed information on the foundation's programs in Asia, including environmental programs, the Asian-American Exchange, Books for Asia, and the Luce Scholars program, which offers scholars work experience in Asia; contact information for representatives in Asia and the United States; lists of trustees, officers, and senior staff; and links to Web resources in Asia.

The Asia Society (NY) (http://www.asiasociety.org/)
Founded in 1956 by John D. Rockefeller III, and headquartered in New York City, the Asia Society is a nonpolitical educational institution that was originally formed to "foster understanding between Asians and Americans" and has expanded to include programs affecting Asian American issues. The society presents art exhibitions and performances, films, lectures, seminars and conferences, publications, and educational materials and programs that present different aspects of Asia to Americans. The society's Web site includes information on current programs, forums for roundtable discussions, links to sites concerning Asia, information on contributing to the society, speech transcripts, and publications.

Asian American Arts Alliance (NY) (http://www.aaartsalliance.org/)
The Asian American Arts Alliance, located in New York City, is committed to "increasing the support, recognition, and appreciation of Asian American Arts." The alliance administers grant programs, including the JPMorgan Chase Regrant Program. Through other programs and services, the alliance strives to provide managerial and artist assistance, inform and educate the public, facilitate connections between artists and groups, and advocate for increased visibility and opportunities for Asian American artists and groups. More details on these programs, an events calendar, directory of Asian arts organizations, and contact information are available on the alliance's Web site.

Asian and Pacific Islander Wellness Center: Community HIV/AIDS Services (CA) (http://www.apiwellness.org)
The Asian and Pacific Islander Wellness Center in San Francisco, California, is committed to "educating, supporting, empowering, and advocating for Asian and Pacific Islander (A&PI) communities—particularly A&PIs living with, or at-risk for, HIV/AIDS." The center supplies many care services including treatment case management, peer advocacy, treatment advocacy, and counseling for HIV-positive Asian and Pacific Islanders. The center's Research and Technical Assistance Department offers training and technical assistance to community-based organizations throughout the United States in the form of grants, facilitation, and consultation on organizational development and program planning. The department has also developed various curricula for developing and running peer organizations, support groups, and prevention interventions. The center's Web site includes information on all these services and opportunities to volunteer and contribute.

Asian Cultural Council (NY) (http://www.asianculturalcouncil.org)
Created as a grantmaking organization in 1963 by John D. Rockefeller, III, the Asian Cultural Council is committed to "supporting cultural exchange in the visual and performing arts between the United States and the countries of Asia." With headquarters in New York City and regional offices in Tokyo, Hong Kong, and Taipei, the council's grants cover a large geographic area in Asia. The council aids individuals working in traditional and contemporary arts with fellowships as well as services and other forms of support. The council's Web site contains specific information on fellowships and grants, information for new applicants, news on recent grantees and activities, and contact information.

Assistance League of Austin (TX) (http://www.alaustin.org)
The Assistance League of Austin addresses specific needs of the Austin, Texas, community through six philanthropic projects and a network of volunteers. Projects range from scholarships to the Austin Community College to material donations to local schools. Details on the league's philanthropic projects and community donations, a membership page, contact information, and descriptions of fundraising activities are available on the league's Web site.

Association for the Cure of Cancer of the Prostate (CA) (http://www.capcure.org)
Founded in 1993 by Michael Milken, the Association for the Cure of Cancer of the Prostate is a private source of funding for prostate cancer research. Also known as CaP CURE, the group's mission is to "identify and support prostate cancer research that will rapidly translate into treatments and cures." The Santa Monica, California-based association, which takes a business approach to its crusade for a cure to prostate cancer, offers research funding through its Competitive Awards and Special Awards (for projects selected by donors). Grant guidelines and applications, information about prostate cancer, upcoming events, current research areas, news on clinical trials, and links to other resources are available on CaP CURE's Web site.

Association of Trial Lawyers of America (DC) (http://www.atlanet.org/)
The Association of Trial Lawyers of America "promotes justice and fairness for injured persons, safeguards victims' rights—particularly the right to trial by jury—and strengthens the civil justice system through education and disclosure of information critical to public health and safety." With more than 56,000 members worldwide, and a network of U.S. and Canadian affiliates involved in diverse areas of trial advocacy, the association provides lawyers with the information and professional assistance needed to serve clients successfully and protect the democratic values inherent in the civil justice system. Visit the association's Web site for information on law student education programs, awards and scholarships, and events.

Asthma and Allergy Foundation of America (DC) (http://www.aafa.org)
Founded in 1953, the Washington, D.C.-based Asthma and Allergy Foundation of America is dedicated to improving the quality of life for people with asthma and allergies through education, advocacy, and research. The foundation sponsors research toward better treatments and a cure for asthma and allergic diseases through its AAFA Investigator Research Grant Award and the Health Services Research Grant. The foundation's Web site offers a brief overview of its grant program as well as a board/staff listing, an annual report, an events calendar, educational resources, and contact information.

Astraea National Lesbian Action Foundation (NY) (http://www.astraea.org/)
The Astraea National Lesbian Action Foundation, established in 1977, works to promote the economic, political, educational, and cultural well-being of lesbians and provides financial support for organizations and projects that are lesbian-led or focused. Astraea administers six grants programs: the U.S. Grants Program, the International Fund for Sexual Minorities, the Lesbian Writers Fund, the Astraea Visual Arts Fund, the Margot Karle Scholarship, and Donor-Advised Funds. The foundation's Web site provides grant guidelines, membership and volunteer information, events, news, and contact information.

The Atlantic Philanthropies (NY) (http://www.atlanticphilanthropies.org)
The Atlantic Philanthropies seek to "identify and support leaders, institutions, and organizations dedicated to learning, knowledge-building, and solving pressing social problems." Made up of the Atlantic Foundation and the Atlantic Trust, both located in Bermuda, the Atlantic Philanthropies support several smaller philanthropies based principally in the United States and Great Britain. The organization provides support in the areas of higher education, pre-collegiate education, the nonprofit sector, health, aging, and human rights. The organization does not accept unsolicited applications for funding. Visitors to the Web site will find detailed information about the individual areas of support, a statistical

breakdown of past grants, a listing of executives and officers, and contact information for the various offices.

Atlas Economic Research Foundation (VA) (http://www.atlas-fdn.org/)
The Atlas Economic Research Foundation, incorporated in 1981, helps to create, develop, advise, and support independent public policy research institutes by providing "intellectual entrepreneurs" with advice, financial support, workshops, and access to a network of leaders who share a commitment to achieving a free society. The foundation's Sir Antony Fisher International Memorial Awards recognize outstanding publications produced by independent public policy research institutes. The foundation also provides startup grants to new public policy institutes. Award and grant guidelines, a Management Toolkit for independent public policy institutes, a directory of think tanks, and upcoming conference information are provided on the foundation's Web site.

Austin Film Society (TX) (http://www.austinfilm.org)
The Austin Film Society was incorporated in May 1986 to "make rarely seen works of film accessible to the Austin community [and to] serve as a nucleus of support and information for regional media production." The Texas Filmmakers' Production Fund makes grants to emerging film and video artists throughout the state. The society also sponsors exhibition programs and movie screenings. The society's Web site features a calendar of events; information on staff members; an online edition of the group's newsletter, *Persistence of Vision*; and a grant application.

Austin Young Lawyers Association (TX) (http://www.ayla.org)
The Austin Young Lawyers Association (AYLA) was formed in 1958 "to further professional, charitable and educational purposes" among this group of young or beginning lawyers in the Austin, Texas area. The association strives to provide charitable service within the community through collaborative efforts with governmental entities, other specialty bar associations and nonprofit organizations. More information can be obtained on the association's Web site, along with a contact email address and phone number for the AYLA Foundation.

The Autism Foundation of New York (NY) (http://www.afny.org)
Based in Staten Island, New York, the Autism Foundation of New York is comprised of family and friends of people afflicted with autism. The foundation's goal is to "advocate for appropriate, scientifically proven treatments and educational methodologies to help these individuals achieve their fullest potential." To this end, the foundation operates a number of events throughout the year and supports educational programs about autism. The foundation's Web site lists upcoming events, links to resources on autism, and contact information.

Averitt Express (TN) (http://www.averittexpress.com/AverittCares.htm)
Averitt Express, a delivery service located in Cookeville, Tennessee, supports local and national healthcare organizations and charities. The Averitt Cares area of the company's Web site provides details of recent contributions, a list of giving since 1987, and contact information.

Bainbridge Arts and Crafts, Inc. (WA) (http://www.bainbridgeartscrafts.org)
Bainbridge Arts and Crafts Inc., was founded in 1948 on Bainbridge Island, Washington, "to inspire interest in the visual arts, advance creative achievement in craft and fine art, support the development of local and regional artists, and fund arts education." The nonprofit organization and gallery offer a wide variety of charitable support and programs, including scholarships for local arts students, educational programs and funds for the community, a cultural grant to individuals and community arts organizations, an Art Apprentice Program and the quarterly *ART NEWS* publication. The organization's Web site features information on current and upcoming exhibits, general news on the organization, and contact information.

Bainbridge Foundation, Inc. (WA) (http://www.bainbridgefoundation.org/)
The Bainbridge Foundation, Inc., supports community organizations on and near Bainbridge Island, Washington. The foundation runs the "One Call for All" funding drive, which supports these organizations. The foundation's Web site lists the Island and off-Island organizations it funds, and maintains an online pledge form for donors.

Bainbridge Island Arts and Humanities Council (WA) (http://www.artshum.org/)
The Bainbridge Island Arts and Humanities Council was established in Washington in 1986. The council's mission is to "provide access to the arts and humanities for every Island citizen, and to assist individuals and organizations delivering cultural services and programs." The council's Web site includes a searchable database of cultural resources and artists in the area, information on current exhibits and events, a calendar of cultural events in the community, a page of links to related sites, and a membership form.

Bainbridge-Ometepe Sister Islands Association (WA) (http://www.bosia.org)
Founded in 1986, the Bainbridge-Ometepe Sister Islands Association forms connections between Bainbridge Island, Washington, and the island community of Ometepe, Nicaragua. The association's project to improve the quality of life in Ometepe includes the Sí a la Vida program and the sale of fair trade organic coffee from Ometepe. The association's quarterly newsletter, annual report, information on the history of the two sister cities, related links, and contact information can be found on the association's Web site.

Banner Health Foundation of Arizona (AZ) (http://www.bannerhealth.com/channels/Donors+and+Volunteers/arizona/arizona.asp)
The Phoenix-based Banner Health Foundation of Arizona has been providing philanthropic support for Banner Health medical facilities since 1978. The foundation's Web site provides an overview of the foundation's work, contact information, and information on the Banner Health Foundation's sister foundations, the Lutheran Foundation and the McKee Medical Center Foundation.

Barberton Community Foundation (OH) (http://www.bcfcharity.org/)
The Barberton Community Foundation was created in 1996 to improve the quality of life for the citizens of Barberton, Ohio. Grants are intended "for charitable endeavors, education, public health, public recreation, and to lessen the burden of government." Grants are distributed quarterly, with the Small Grants Program administered every month. The foundation awards scholarships to local students, has a business and home improvement loan program to invest in the community, and sponsors assorted local philanthropic events. The foundation's Web site includes downloadable grant applications, scholarship application guidelines, staff e-mail addresses, information on donating to the foundation, and links to other Barberton-related sites.

Barlow Foundation (CA) (http://www.barlow2000.org/foundation/default.htm)
The Barlow Foundation's mission is "to improve the quality of life for the patient population with respiratory and other diseases in the Southern California region," specifically through the support of the Barlow Respiratory Hospital and Research Center, in the Los Angeles area. The foundation's Web site provides directions to the Barlow Hospital, general information about the organization itself, an e-mail address for further inquiries, and details on the foundation's fundraising events and activities.

Barth Syndrome Foundation, Inc. (FL) (http://www.barthsyndrome.org/)
The Perry, Florida-based Barth Syndrome Foundation, Inc., was established in 1997 to support boys afflicted with Barth Syndrome and their families, fund research, promote awareness of the syndrome, and support other charitable causes with similar goals. The foundation's Web site provides a wealth of information on the syndrome, its history, and treatment; grant guidelines and forms; information on foundation programs; professional resources; and links to resources for families.

Beaumont Foundation of America (MI) (http://www.bmtfoundation.com/)
The mission of the Michigan-based Beaumont Foundation of America is "to fulfill the promise of the Information Age by providing access to technology and the skills to use it." The foundation makes community grants of technology equipment to community-based organizations, education grants for schools, and individual grants directly to individuals. The foundation's Web site provides grant guidelines, an application worksheet, and contact information.

Bedford Community Health Foundation (VA) (http://www.bchf.org)
Organized in 1978, the Bedford Community Health Foundation serves the "health-related needs of the citizens of Bedford City and Bedford County, Virginia," through financial grants to nonprofit health service organizations serving the community. The foundation's Web site offers descriptions of the foundation's grant and scholarship programs, instructions for potential applicants, a list of recent and past grants, information for donors and volunteers, a listing of health-related services in the Bedford community, and contact information.

Belgian American Educational Foundation (CT) (http://www.baef.be/)
The Belgian American Educational Foundation began as part of the Commission for Relief in Belgium, which was created in 1914. Today, the foundation is dedicated to "fostering the higher education of deserving Belgians and Americans" through its fellowships for Belgian citizens to study or perform investigations in the United States and for Americans to study in Belgium. The foundation also grants an Alumni Award for research in a variety of fields. The foundation's Web site offers descriptions of the various fellowships, detailed instructions for applicants, a preliminary online application, a history of the foundation, and contact information.

Bellona Foundation (DC) (http://www.bellona.no)
Formed in 1986 in Oslo, Norway, the Bellona Foundation maintains offices worldwide, including Washington, D.C. The foundation is dedicated to working on international environmental issues with business and political leaders. The foundation's Web site features details on the foundation's numerous current campaigns, downloadable publications, breaking environmental news, and contact information for the Washington, D.C., office.

The Bernardine Franciscan Sisters Foundation (VA) (http://www.bfranfound.org/)
The Virginia-based Bernardine Franciscan Sisters Foundation was established in 1996 to serve Newport News, Hampton, Poquoson, Gloucester, and York Counties in Virginia. The foundation "enables the Bernardine Sisters of the Third Order of St. Francis to continue and to increase its services to the poor." The foundation mainly focuses its giving in the area of healthcare, specifically care to the sick and injured, health promotion, general health in local communities, and resources for health restoration and disease prevention. The foundation's Web site provides grantmaking policies and limitations, recent grants, a list of the foundation's directors and staff, and contact information.

Betaseron Multiple Sclerosis Champions of Courage (DC) (http://www.championsofcourage.org/)
The Betaseron Multiple Sclerosis Champions of Courage program intends to show that "quality healthcare, combined with a positive attitude and the support of others, can be empowering forces that enable people with MS to enhance their quality of life." The program funds grants of up to $7,000 to recognize the achievements of people with MS and support their inspirational work. Grant applicants must be taking Betaseron, participate in community service work, and outline how they would use the grant to demonstrate courage and inspire others with MS. The organization's Web site provides grant guidelines and applications, answers to frequently asked questions about the program, contact information, news, links, and descriptions of past grant recipients and their projects.

The Amy Biehl Foundation (CA) (http://www.amybiehl.org)
Established to honor a young American Fulbright Scholar who was killed in South Africa in 1993, the Amy Biehl Foundation "works to prevent youth-perpetrated violence in South Africa and the United States through providing program opportunities in education, sports and recreation, arts, employable skills, and safety." The foundation's Web site provides information on a number of events and projects, including the foundation's after-school programs, first aid training, and the Amy Biehl Fun Run and Walk; a biography and news accounts of Amy Biehl's life and struggles; and the foundation's newsletter.

Bingham Program (ME) (http://www.megrants.org/BProgram.htm)
The Bingham Program was founded in 1932 "to promote the advancement of medicine and healthcare in Maine." The program grew out of a strong need for rural doctors to be connected to the latest information and support services that are available in urban areas. The Bingham Program initiates funds and programs in three high priority areas: health profession development, community health programs, and public health policy development. The program's Web site features recent grant lists, guidelines, deadlines, proposal information, and contact information.

Mary Black Foundation, Inc. (SC) (http://www.maryblackfoundation.org)
Founded in 1985, the Mary Black Foundation, Inc., serves Spartanburg County, South Carolina, with occasional support to upstate organizations that directly relate to the goals and mission in Spartanburg. The foundation provides grants to health-related, nonprofit organizations in the community,with a focus on selected physical activity and early childhood development. The foundation's Web site includes funding guidelines, a list of trustees and staff, and an applicant feedback form.

Blue Cross Blue Shield of Michigan Foundation (MI) (http://www.bcbsm.com/foundation)
The Blue Cross Blue Shield of Michigan Foundation seeks to improve healthcare in Michigan by "enhancing the quality and appropriate use of healthcare; improving access to appropriate health services; and controlling healthcare costs." Its grant programs support research and community healthcare solutions, acknowledge excellence in research, and support medical education. The foundation's Web site provides information on the foundation's grant and award programs, downloadable applications, contact information, and an online version of the foundation's most recent annual report.

Boat U.S. Foundation for Boating Safety (VA) (http://www.boatus.com/foundation/)
In 1989, the Boat U.S. Foundation for Boating Safety began its Grassroots Grants Program to support community-based boating safety programs and services. The foundation makes grants to "local, volunteer organizations that use innovative approaches to educate boaters about safe boating practices." The foundation also makes Clean Water Grants to fund education and hands-on efforts aimed at cleaning up the boating environment. The foundation's Web site hosts a wealth of resources for boaters and grantseekers, including grant program descriptions, news and resources on boating safety, a history of past grant recipients, and contact information.

Boston Adult Literacy Fund (MA) (http://www.balf.net/home.htm)
The Boston Adult Literacy Fund was founded in 1988 to provide access to basic education for adults in the Boston metro area and to raise awareness of the need for basic education and literacy. Grants are awarded to community-based literacy programs. The fund also awards scholarships to adults who have completed their basic education and wish to continue on to higher education or vocational training. In addition to descriptions of its programs, the fund's Web site provides a list of recent grant recipients, links to literacy-related Web sites, and contact information.

Boston Film and Video Foundation (MA) (http://www.bfvf.org)
The Boston Film and Video Foundation was established in 1976 to support local filmmakers. Today, the foundation's mission is "to provide an organizational support system to

artists for the understanding and the creation of new work, facilitate the discussion and critique of work and issues, and to pool human and equipment resources." The foundation offers programs to assist filmmakers in finding funding and obtaining access to equipment. The foundation's Web site describes the foundation's programs and services and offers information on membership and upcoming events.

Boston Foundation for Architecture (MA) (http://www.bfagrants.org/)
The Boston Foundation for Architecture was established in 1984 by the Boston Society of Architecture to support public education programs related to the field. Through its grantmaking program, the foundation encourages greater public awareness of the value of well-designed public places. The foundation's Web site provides downloadable grant guidelines and applications, lists of other architecture foundations, press releases, and contact information.

Boston Women's Fund (MA) (http://www.bostonwomensfund.org)
As the oldest women-run organization in Massachusetts, the Boston Women's Fund is a "progressive fund that links people who have resources with women who have ideas and solutions." To this end, the organization raises funds and collects contributions from donors to distribute to hundreds of women's organizations in the Boston area. Funding priority is toward projects developed and led by girls, women of color, lesbians, older women, women with disabilities, and low-income women. The fund's Web site offers further information on its programs.

Boulder County Arts Alliance (CO) (http://www.bouldercountyarts.org)
The Boulder County Arts Alliance of Boulder, Colorado, works to "provide leadership and resources for arts organizations, artists, educators, and the Boulder County community." Funding is available to artists and arts organizations for all arts disciplines, including visual arts, theater, dance, music, storytelling, film, literature, book arts, and more. The alliance also provides a range of artist services. The alliance's Web site offers information on the organization's programs, grant guidelines, links to member artists and organizations and other arts resources, a list of contributors, and alerts for upcoming events.

The Brandywiners, Ltd. (DE) (http://www.brandywiners.org)
The Brandywiners, Ltd., is a theater group started in 1932 that presents musical productions at Longwood Gardens in Kennett Square, Pennsylvania, and contributes the proceeds to cultural, educational, and civic causes throughout the Delaware Valley. The organization uses a portion of ticket proceeds to fund a variety of arts, cultural, and educational organizations. The organization's Web site features recent grants lists, a history of the group, upcoming and past productions, and contact information.

Bread and Roses Community Fund (PA) (http://www.breadrosesfund.org)
The Philadelphia-based Bread and Roses Community Fund "is a unique partnership of donors and activists committed to building a permanent base for social change in the Delaware Valley." The fund awards general fund grants to organizations working against a problem that affects many aspects of society; discretionary grants, which are distributed monthly for special projects, emergencies, technical assistance, and organizational development; the Jonathan Lax Scholarship, which is offered to gay men seeking further education; and the Phoebus Criminal Justice Initiative, which offers funding for work to address problems within the criminal justice system. The fund's Web site includes grant guidelines and applications, lists of staff members and grant recipients, and donor guidelines.

The Breast Cancer Research Foundation (NY) (http://www.bcrfcure.org)
The Breast Cancer Research Foundation, established in 1993, is committed to finding a cure for breast cancer through clinical and genetic research. The foundation's Web site serves as a resource center for information on breast cancer, research grants, and research facilities. Grant procedures are detailed online, along with the information on the

foundation's research partnerships, previously funded projects, upcoming events, general links, and answers to commonly asked questions about the disease.

Brewster Education Foundation, Inc. (NY) (http://www.bef.org)
Based in Brewster, New York, the Brewster Education Foundation, Inc., was established in 1984 to raise funds to foster, encourage, and promote public education programs for Brewster Central Schools. The foundation raises and disburses funds for projects beyond those supported by regular school sources and helps fill the gap that exists between the programs teachers would like to have and those available to them through district budgeting. The foundation funds scholarships, financial aid counseling, a dinner recognizing academic achievement, and other projects. The Web site includes information on the foundation's history and programs.

Bright Horizons Foundation for Children (TN) (http://www.brighthorizons.com/foundation/)
The Bright Horizons Foundation for Children was established in 1999 and supports nonprofit organizations focused on children, child, and youth education, and childcare in the communities where Bright Horizons Family Solutions employees live and work. Information, guidelines, limitations, and applications; additional details on donating and volunteering; and links to related community resources are available on the foundation's Web site.

Broadcast Education Association (DC) (http://www.beaweb.org)
Established in 1955, the Washington, D.C.-based Broadcast Education Association is an academic organization of professors, industry professionals, and graduate students who are committed to broadcast and electronic media education. The association annually administers a series of scholarships for undergraduate and graduate students. The association's Web site provides scholarship application instructions, printable application materials, and a scholarship recipient list; links to additional scholarship sites; information on grants for research in broadcasting, including guidelines and application forms; information on joining the association; publication subscription forms; information on the association's conventions; links to media sites; listings of industry and academic job openings; listings of individual, associate, and institutional members; a news archive; and contact information.

Broadway Cares/Equity Fights AIDS (NY) (http://www.bcefa.org/)
Founded in 1988, Broadway Cares/Equity Fights AIDS leverages the talents and resources of the American theater community to raise funds for AIDS-related causes in the United States. The organization also awards grants through its National Grants Program for direct care and services to people with HIV/AIDS. Projects funded in the past have provided meals, shelter, transportation, emergency financial aid, emotional/practical support, and payment of non-reimbursable medical expenses. The organization's Web site provides a description and guidelines for the National Grants Program, including contact information for requesting an application; information on other programs and events; a list of the organization's affiliates; links to Web resources; and an e-mail list for receiving information and updates.

Bronx Council on the Arts (NY) (http://www.bronxarts.org/)
The Bronx Council on the Arts serves the New York City borough of the Bronx by developing programs that provide for public participation in the arts, nurture arts organizations' development, publicize and promote the arts, and generate financial support and new initiatives. The council offers several types of grants. The council's Web site provides information on its arts activities; grant descriptions, guidelines, and downloadable applications; and membership, funding, staff, and contact information.

Brother Help Thyself, Inc. (DC) (http://www.dcpride.org/bht)
Brother Help Thyself, Inc., was formed in 1978 as one of the first groups to support gay and lesbian organizations in Washington, D.C., and Baltimore, Maryland. The organization has expanded to include support to AIDS service providers and health clinics in the area, as

well. The organization's Web site includes information on upcoming events and meetings, descriptions of educational programs, a listing of other member clubs, a downloadable grant application, and contact information for both locations.

The Brother's Brother Foundation (PA) (http://www.brothersbrother.com/)
Founded in 1958, the Pittsburgh, Pennsylvania-based Brother's Brother Foundation donates needed resources to millions of people internationally—in over 100 countries on five continents. This disaster relief organization focuses its efforts in the areas of educational, medical, humanitarian, and agricultural aid. The foundation's Web site includes an application form for requesting assistance, information and opportunities for organizations and individuals to donate money or in-kind gifts, an archive of newsletters, updates on the foundation's work around the world, a list of country recipients, and information on membership interaction.

Burger King/McLamore Foundation, Inc. (FL) (http://www.burgerking.com/community/BKscholars)
Formed in 1997 in Miami, the Burger King/McLamore Foundation, Inc., provides educational opportunities through scholarships for college or post-secondary vocational students in the United States, Canada, and Puerto Rico. The foundation's Web site offers testimonies from previous scholarship winners, a description of the program and application information, and contact information.

The Barbara Bush Foundation for Family Literacy (DC) (http://www.barbarabushfoundation.com)
Launched in March 1989, the Barbara Bush Foundation for Family Literacy works "to establish literacy as a value in every family in America, by helping every family in the nation understand that the home is the child's first school, that the parent is the child's first teacher, and that reading is the child's first subject; and to break the intergenerational cycle of illiteracy, by supporting the development of family literacy programs where parents and children can learn and read together." The foundation awards approximately $650,00 in funding each year through its National Grant Program. The foundation's Web site provides grant guidelines and application information, a grants list, news releases, publications, and descriptions of state literacy initiatives.

The Business and Professional Women's Foundation (DC) (http://www.bpwusa.org/content/BPWFoundation/foundation_introtext.htm)
The Business and Professional Women's Foundation, established in 1956, promotes equity for working women through education, information, and research. Headquartered in Washington, D.C., the foundation provides financial assistance to women seeking education to advance in their careers or re-enter the workforce. The foundation also collects, conducts, and analyzes research on issues affecting women in the workplace. The foundation's Web site provides scholarship application instructions and forms, details on other foundation events and programs, and contact information.

Business Consortium for Arts Support (VA) (http://www.norfolkfoundation.org/bcas)
The Business Consortium for Arts Support was founded in 1987 in Norfolk, Virginia, to fund grants to arts and cultural organizations. The consortium considers "organizations that regularly perform or exhibit in the south Hampton Roads area of Virginia." The consortium's Web site features a list of recently funded organizations, grant policies, financial information, and membership opportunities.

California Council for the Humanities (CA) (http://www.calhum.org/)
The California Council for the Humanities is a non-governmental affiliate of the National Endowment for the Humanities that looks for ways to make the knowledge and insights of the humanities available to all Californians. The council's Web site provides guidelines for current grant programs, a newsletter, announcements, information on past council-funded projects, and information on making contributions.

California HealthCare Foundation (CA) (http://www.chcf.org/)
The California HealthCare Foundation was established in May 1996 as a result of the conversion of Blue Cross of California from a nonprofit health plan to a for-profit corporation. The foundation's work focuses on "informing health policy decisions, advancing efficient business practices, improving the quality and efficiency of care delivery, and promoting informed health care and coverage decisions." Through its grant program, the foundation funds the development of programs and models aimed at improving the healthcare delivery and financing systems in California. The foundation's Web site provides grant guidelines and limitations, a list of recent grants, RFPs, an electronic form for ordering foundation publications, a comprehensive set of links to health-related Web sites, listings of the board and staff, and contact information.

Calvert Social Investment Foundation (MD) (http://www.calvertgroup.com/foundation)
The Bethesda, Maryland-based Calvert Social Investment Foundation is a community investment facility offering options for individuals and institutions to invest in community lenders globally. By raising funds and making investments into community development finance institutions and other community development nonprofits, the foundation aims to "end poverty through investment." Loans are made to community development loan funds, micro-enterprise and small business loan funds, affordable housing loan funds, community development banks and credit unions, nonprofit facilities funds, nonprofit enterprises, community development corporations, cooperatives, community development intermediaries, micro-finance institutions, and international financial intermediaries working in developing countries. The foundation's Web site provides information on the foundation's various investment programs, with lending guidelines for community organizations; information for potential investors; annual reports; a resource center for community investing; and contact information.

Cancer Aid and Research Fund (AZ) (http://www.canceraidresearch.org/)
The Cancer Aid and Research Fund, based in Phoenix, Arizona, strives to give aid and support to victims of cancer and their families. The fund has two main funding priorities: providing educational material about nutrition and alternative cancer treatments and providing medical equipment and supplies to clinics and hospitals that use alternative cancer treatments. The fund also works to establish and maintain cancer support groups and educate the public about preventative cancer measures. The fund's Web page provides contact information and an online donation form.

Cancer Care, Inc. (NY) (http://www.cancercare.org/)
Cancer Care, Inc., helps cancer patients and their loved ones cope with the impact of cancer. Services include counseling for cancer patients and their loved ones; limited grants for certain kinds of cancers and for people in some locations; information and referrals to home and child care services, hospices, hospitals, and other community resources; and teleconference and educational workshops. The organization's Web site includes details about the organization's financial assistance programs and other services, a full annual report, information about how to contribute, and contact information.

Cancer Research and Prevention Foundation (VA) (http://www.preventcancer.org/)
The Cancer Research and Prevention Foundation, formerly the Cancer Research Foundation of America, founded in 1985, supports education and research to help prevent cancer. Since its inception, the foundation has funded more than 200 scientists at leading medical centers, recognizing scientific excellence, new and innovative projects, and young scientists interested in cancer prevention research. Grant and fellowship details, past recipients, sample application forms, facts on preventing cancer, information on education programs, online versions of publications, and links to cancer resources are available on the foundation's Web site.

Cardinals Care (MO)
(http://stlouis.cardinals.mlb.com/NASApp/mlb/stl/community/stl_community_option1.jsp?story_page=promotion_grants_community)
Cardinals Care, the community foundation of the St. Louis Cardinals funds organizations that support youths under 20 years of age that are located in "Cardinals Country." The organization's Web site offers a downloadable application, other ways the organization gives back to its community, and contact information.

Caring Foundation of Wyoming (WY) (http://www.bcbswy.com/wyoming/caringprog.html)
The Caring Foundation of Wyoming was established in 1989 in Casper by the Blue Cross Blue Shield of Wyoming to address the basic healthcare needs of Wyoming's children. The foundation compliments federal aid programs and provides children with basic, primary, and acute healthcare and dental care. The foundation's Web site provides contact information and details on how to enroll a child in the program.

The Carter Center, Inc. (GA) (http://www.cartercenter.org/)
The Atlanta-based Carter Center, Inc., established by former President Jimmy Carter and his wife Rosalynn, is "guided by a fundamental commitment to human rights and the alleviation of human suffering; it seeks to prevent and resolve conflicts, enhance freedom and democracy, and improve health." The center achieves these goals through numerous programs and initiatives, including Peace Initiatives, Health Initiatives, and International Activities. The center also administers internship programs for students; a Graduate Assistant Program, which supplies a $3,000 stipend for select interns; and the Rosalynn Carter Fellowships for Mental Health Journalism. Guidelines and application procedures for the internship and fellowship are available on the center's Web site, along with information on the center's many events and programs and details on making a donation.

Carver International Project (CA) (http://www.carverworld.org/)
The California-based, Carver International Project exists with a purpose to be an "economic and intellectual asset stimulating philanthropy in communities throughout the world, contributing to lasting positive change." Areas of interest to the project include organizations that focus on civil society, education, media, public health, and human and women's rights. The project's Web site features information on the project's funding programs, application instructions, a board list, and contact information.

Cascadia Revolving Fund (WA) (http://www.cascadiafund.org)
Located in Seattle, Washington, the Cascadia Revolving Fund is a community development loan fund that provides loans and technical support to small businesses that have been unable to access financing through traditional sources. The fund seeks to bring much-needed jobs and economic prosperity to distressed communities throughout Washington and Oregon. The fund lends to women, minority, and low-income entrepreneurs; businesses that are located in distressed urban and rural communities that have a significant potential for job creation; businesses that act to preserve or restore the environment; nonprofit organizations; and more. The fund's Web site offers information on loan activity, application information, and instructions; information on making a donation to or investing in the fund; and contact information.

Catholic Campaign for Human Development (DC)
(http://www.nccbuscc.org/cchd/index.htm)
Established in 1969 by the National Conference of Catholic Bishops, the Catholic Campaign for Human Development works to empower the poor and encourage their participation in the decisions and actions that affect their lives in order to move beyond poverty. The organization funds community organizing and economic development projects to assist poor and marginalized people. Guidelines and application forms for both types of projects are available on the campaign's Web site, as is a list of currently funded projects organized by state, local contact information (also by state), and a form for requesting more information.

Catholic Community Foundation in the Archdiocese of St. Paul and Minneapolis (http://www.catholiccommunityfoundation.org/) (MN)
Founded in 1992, the Catholic Community Foundation in the Archdiocese of St. Paul and Minneapolis supports the spiritual, educational, and social needs of the Catholic community. The foundation provides support for those organizations seeking endowment funds that support the mission of helping parishes, schools, and Catholic organizations meet their long-term financial needs. The foundation's Web site provides information on its grant program, board and staff listings, a downloadable copy of the foundation's annual, and contact information.

The Catholic Diocese of Cleveland Foundation (OH) (http://www.cdcf.org/)
The Catholic Diocese of Cleveland Foundation provides funds and social services in the greater Cleveland, Ohio, area. Since 1996, the foundation has administered the Church in the City Grants Program, which distributes funds to Diocesan institutions for projects in the areas of social justice, urban redevelopment, interdependence, restructuring, and support for the poor. Other contributions from the foundation are from restricted funds that are not open to unsolicited applicants. Further details about the foundation and its structure and services within the Catholic church, as well as contact information, are provided on the foundation's Web site.

Center for Ecoliteracy (CA) (http://www.ecoliteracy.org/)
The Center for Ecoliteracy is dedicated to fostering the experience and understanding of the natural world in the San Francisco Bay Area. The center was founded in 1995 to support a network of northern California organizations engaged in habitat restoration and agriculturally-related programs. The grant program at the center encourages school districts and educational organizations in the region to engage in the fostering and understanding of the natural world. The center is a public foundation that sponsors donor-advised funds and shelters projects consistent with its mission. The center also publishes resources that provide research and education about the mission and the state of today's environment. The center's Web site offers downloadable publications, a board list, grant application information, a list of previous grant recipients, and contact information.

The Center for Photography of Woodstock, Inc. (NY) (http://www.cpw.org)
The Center for Photography at Woodstock, Inc., was founded in 1977 and provides an artistic home for contemporary creative photographers. The Woodstock, New York-based center sponsors programs in education, exhibition, publication, and services, such as access to a darkroom, a library, archives, portfolio reviews, and computers. The center's Web site provides information on current artist opportunities, the photographers' fellowship fund, internships, exhibitions and workshops, events, links to other photography Web sites and resources, and contact information.

Center for the Study of the Presidency (DC) (http://www.thepresidency.org)
The Washington, D.C.-based Center for the Study of the Presidency was created in 1969, inspired by President Eisenhower's call for programs on the American presidency. The center is the foremost institution devoted to the study of the presidency and related governmental and political institutions. A nonprofit, non-partisan institution, the center provides educational resources and also offers grants and fellowships for scholars and students studying related fields. The center's Web site offers descriptions of the center's fellowships and research grants, information on other programs, and contact information.

Central Coast Commission for Senior Citizens (CA) (http://www.slonet.org/~seniors/)
The Central Coast Commission for Senior Citizens was created in 1975 as a part of a national network of organizations that serve senior citizens with social, nutritional, and health services. The commission's Web site provides information about its programs, including the Senior Connection phone referral line, job placement advice, and online resource guides for San Luis Obispo and Santa Barbara Counties; links to additional

programs for senior citizens; the commission's national network of organizations on aging; and contact information.

Central Minnesota Arts Board (MN) (http://www.cmab.org)
The Central Minnesota Arts Board was founded in St. Cloud, Minnesota, in 1977. The board stimulates and encourages the creation, performance, and appreciation of the arts in Benton, Sherburne, Stearns, and Wright Counties. The board funds local arts-producing and sponsoring organizations, educational institutions, or individuals and will also provide other assistance to help further develop the arts in central Minnesota. Among its programs are project grants, which include furthering arts education and after-school and summer arts educational programming; the Technical Development and Education Fund, which provides training funds for nonprofit arts organizations staff to attend management workshops, seminars, or conferences; scholarships designed to help graduating high school seniors who want to further their education in the areas of music, dance, literature, visual art, or performance art; individual artist awards; general operation support; an individual artist directory, which is an Internet listing of artists to increase awareness of artists in the area and to encourage schools, galleries, performing and art centers to utilize those artists' skills; and grant writing assistance. The board's Web site offers online quarterly newsletters, the board's directory of artists, links to other arts-related sites, and contact information.

Central Missouri Counties Human Development Corporation (MO) (http://www.cmchdc.org/)
Established in 1965 in Columbia, Missouri, the Central Missouri Counties Human Development Corporation works to develop affordable housing opportunities for low-income people in Audrain, Boone, Callaway, Cole, Cooper, Howard, Moniteau, and Osage Counties. The organization's Web site provides information about its mission, staff and board listings, and contact information.

Chamber Music America (NY) (http://www.chamber-music.org)
Located in New York City, Chamber Music America is a national member organization that was created in 1978 "to make chamber music a vital part of American culture . . . [by] designing programs and services to help those who perform and present professional chamber music . . . [and by] the advancement of chamber music education." The organization's grant programs, which are only open to members of the organization, include the Residency Partnership Program, the Commissioning Program, New Works: Creation and Presentation Grant Program for jazz artists, Consulting Awards, and other awards recognizing excellence in teaching, service, and programming. The organization's Web site provides guidelines and applications for each grant program, information on membership, upcoming events, a publication center, and board and staff lists.

Changemakers Fund (CA) (http://www.changemakersfund.org/)
The Changemakers Fund is a national foundation that promotes community-based philanthropy through fundraising, grantmaking, donor education, and special programs. The fund awards capacity-building and collaborative grants to public foundations and fundraising organizations committed to the principles of community-based philanthropy and to other supportive organizations that serve to strengthen the sector and help transform the field of philanthropy by making it more responsive to groups working for social, economic, and environmental justice and equality for all. The fund's Web site provides grant guidelines, information on community-based philanthropy, donor education programs, staff/board list, and contact information.

Charities Aid Foundation America (VA) (http://www.cafonline.org/cafamerica)
Charities Aid Foundation America (CAFAmerica) was founded in 1992 through support from the United Kingdom's Charities Aid Foundation, which manages over $1 billion in charitable funds, to promote global philanthropy. CAFAmerica has developed Global Gifts, a program to ensure that U.S. citizens receive full tax-deductibility on their donations

to overseas charitable organizations. The foundation's Web site outlines the foundation's goals and provides information for nonprofit groups wishing to be included on the foundation's eligibility list to receive grants, an FAQ section, information for donors, and contact information.

Charlotte-Mecklenburg Education Foundation (NC) (http://www.cmef.org)
The Charlotte-Mecklenburg Education Foundation was established in 1991 to "define the issues and advocate for the changes required to permanently improve the quality of public education in Mecklenburg County" in North Carolina. Through programs and conferences, partnerships with other nonprofit organizations, and research and policy initiatives, the foundation strives to build awareness and understanding of the need for high-quality public education in its community. The foundation's Web site provides its goals, information on upcoming events and activities, links to other education resources, publications, and contact information.

Chattanooga Christian Community Foundation (TN) (http://www.cccfdn.org)
The Chattanooga Christian Community Foundation was established in 1992 to encourage Christian philanthropy through the support of "local ministries, students, causes, and events which will advance the Gospel and work of Jesus Christ primarily in the Chattanooga area." The foundation offers two basic grants: the Dora Maclellan Brown Community Priority Grant, which is made to area nonprofit ministries, and the Alpha Fund Grant, which is made to area projects and ministries that have not yet obtained nonprofit status. Additionally, the foundation provides theology and ministry-related scholarships. Grant and scholarship guidelines and applications, past annual reports, more details about the organization, and contact information are available on the foundation's Web site.

Chesapeake Bay Trust (MD) (http://www.chesapeakebaytrust.org)
The Chesapeake Bay Trust, created in 1985, "funds nonprofit organizations, civic and community groups, schools, and public agencies that promote public awareness and participation in the restoration and protection of the Chesapeake Bay." The trust's Web site provides grant guidelines, criteria, and deadlines; a summary of operations; environmental and Chesapeake Bay-specific links; contact information; and printable grant application forms.

Chicago Foundation for Education (IL) (http://www.chgofdneduc.org)
The Chicago Foundation for Education was established in 1985 and is dedicated to "improving and enhancing the educational experiences provided to Chicago's public elementary school children by the educators who serve, guide, and teach them." The foundation's grant programs include the Mentor and Adaptor Grants, which support the dissemination of successful projects to classrooms across the city, and the Small Grants program, which enables teachers to implement hands-on learning projects with their students. The foundation's Web site offers information on the foundation's programs, applications, a board list, links to related resources, information for volunteers, and an online survey.

The Chicago Foundation for Women (IL) (http://www.cfw.org)
The Chicago Foundation for Women focuses on three issues: economic self-sufficiency, freedom from violence, and access to health information and services. These issues are described on the foundation's Web site, which also provides the foundation's newsletter, information on upcoming events and programs, grant policies, details on making a contribution or volunteering, and contact information.

Chicago White Sox Charities, Inc. (IL)
(http://chicago.whitesox.mlb.com/NASApp/mlb/cws/community/cws_community_programs.jsp)
The Chicago White Sox Charities, Inc., established in 1990 to fund cancer research and treatment, have enlarged their efforts to include youth education and athletic programs and senior citizens services. Grants go toward programs and events that often involve Chicago White Sox players in youth education, athletics, and at-risk programs. The charities' Web

site includes information on past grant recipients, details on some of the programs and events the organization hosts, and information on fundraising efforts.

Child Abuse Prevention Foundation (CA) (http://www.capfsd.com/capf.htm)
The Child Abuse Prevention Foundation was established in 1981 by a group of concerned citizens to help the San Diego area's abused children. The foundation supports many programs and projects at the Polinsky Children's Center, giving up to $500,000 per year in cash and in-kind support for the nearly 5,000 children who stay at the center each year. The foundation also offers a Foster Fund scholarship program to assist San Diego foster youth in furthering their education. The foundation also supports local programs that work to break the cycle of child abuse in the San Diego community. The foundation's Web site provides information on the foundation's programs, board and staff lists, information on making a donation and volunteering, and contact information.

Child Care Capital Investment Fund (MA) (http://www.cccif.org/)
The Child Care Capital Investment Fund helps child care providers in Massachusetts improve or expand their physical space. To achieve its goal, the fund provides financial and technical assistance for large and small projects. The fund's Web site provides information about the fund's various grant options, geographic restrictions, and contact information.

Child Care of Southwest Florida, Inc. (FL) (http://www.ccswfl.org)
Established in 1967, the mission of Child Care of Southwest Florida, Inc., is "to initiate, coordinate, promote, and provide high quality child care through leadership, service, and education for families and businesses in Southwest Florida." The organization provides child care services to children in Lee, Collier, Hendry, and Glades Counties. Extensive information on parent and provider services, including referrals, legal obligations, and specific child care centers are provided on the organization's Web site. The organization's calendar of events and newsletter are also available on the site.

Child Health Foundation (MD) (http://www.childhealthfoundation.org/)
The Child Health Foundation was established in 1985 to prevent and treat life-threatening communicable diseases in infants and children through support of clinical research, medical outreach, public education, and collaborative research partnerships in the United States and throughout the world. The foundation's Web site provides information on its funding programs, including the Innovative Small Grants program; the foundation's newsletter and annual report; and general information about the foundation's formal partnership agreements with a number of educational and medical organizations.

Children Affected by AIDS Foundation (CA) (http://www.caaf4kids.org)
The Los Angeles-based Children Affected by AIDS Foundation is dedicated to supporting organizations that provide day-to-day needs for children infected with HIV or AIDS. The foundation focuses on funding direct care needs, educating the public, advocating on the children's behalf, and bringing joy and fun into the children's lives. The foundation's Web site lists funding initiatives, grant application procedures, specific programs and events sponsored by the foundation, links to Internet resources, contact information, and information for donors and volunteers.

Children's Aid Society (NY) (http://www.childrensaidsociety.org)
The Children's Aid Society was founded in 1853 to serve the physical and mental health of children and families with services throughout New York City. The society works with a network of child service providers in the five boroughs of New York City. Locations and specific descriptions of these partner organizations are listed in the Services Index of the society's Web site and include the areas of health, education, adoption, arts and recreation, housing, and juvenile justice advocacy, among others. The society's Web site also provides information on volunteer and donation opportunities, a calendar of upcoming meetings and campaigns, and the society's newsletter.

Children's Brittle Bone Foundation (WI) (http://www.cbbf.org)
The mission of the Children's Brittle Bone Foundation is to provide funds for research into the causes, diagnosis, treatment, prevention, and eventual cure for osteogenesis omperfecta (OI). The foundation supports programs that improve the quality of life for people afflicted with OI and promotes awareness and educates the public. The foundation's Web site provides a mission statement, the foundation's newsletter, details on how to make a donation, and contact information.

Children's Health Fund (NY) (http://www.childrenshealthfund.org)
The Children's Health Fund is committed to providing healthcare to the nation's most medically underserved children through the development and support of innovative primary care medical programs and the promotion of guaranteed access to appropriate healthcare for all children. Specifically, the fund works to ensure support of its flagship pediatric programs for homeless and underprivileged children in New York City, develop and support a national network of pediatric programs in some of the United States' poorest communities, advocate for policies and programs to ensure access to medical homes for all children, and educate health professionals, policy makers, and the general public about the needs and barriers to healthcare experienced by disadvantaged children. The foundation's Web site provides information on its programs, details on making a donation, a press center, and more.

Children's Scholarship Fund (NY) (http://www.scholarshipfund.org)
The Children's Scholarship Fund seeks to expand educational opportunities for low-income families, providing partial assistance to fund a child's private or parochial school tuition. Founded in 1998, the national fund intends to give disadvantaged families more options in their children's education. The fund's Web site features a school search, which includes a database of private American schools; application instructions and procedures; a contact form for more information; and a board listing, which includes members of Congress, CEOs, and education advocates from all walks of life.

Children's Trust Fund of South Carolina (SC) (http://www.childrenstrustfundsc.org)
The mission of the Children's Trust Fund of South Carolina is to focus on long-term solutions to the problems facing South Carolina's children by working through local community coalitions for systems change. The fund is dedicated to helping abused and neglected children in South Carolina by providing the basic needs of protection and safety, shelter, food, and social and cognitive development. The fund's Web site provides a listing of recently funded organizations, grant information, a board listing, and contact information.

Chinook Fund (CO) (http://www.chinookfund.org/)
Created in Denver, Colorado, in 1988, the Chinook Fund supports cutting-edge organizations throughout the state that "are working to address the root causes of social problems such as racism, sexism, homophobia, and discrimination against people with disabilities." The fund's giving programs include grants through the Start-up Fund and the Established Fund, technical assistance grants, and critical response grants. Downloadable application guidelines, forms, and newsletters; a listing of grantee organizations; lists of the board of directors and committee members; links to related resources; and opportunities to donate to the fund are provided on the fund's Web site.

Christian Chiropractor's Association (CO) (http://www.christianchiropractors.org/)
The Christian Chiropractor's Association was established in Fort Collins, Colorado, in 1963. The association "offers the chiropractic profession a Christian fellowship in which believers of various denominational backgrounds can fellowship and serve the Lord Jesus Christ together" through world mission programs. The association's Web site provides details on the group's religious mission, as well as specifics on its programs, a guide to chiropractic techniques, membership pages, and contact information.

Christian Ministries Foundation (GA) (http://www.cmf-online.org)
The Brunswick, Georgia-based Christian Ministries Foundation "helps individuals, ministries, organizations, and foundations make effective gifts to the ministries and charitable agencies or organizations of their choice." The foundation's Web site provides information on funds for donors, answers to frequently asked questions, a list of gift fund recipients nationwide, and contact information.

Citizens Committee for New York City, Inc. (NY) (http://www.citizensnyc.org)
The Citizens Committee for New York City, Inc., was established in 1975 to "stimulate and support self-help and civic action that improves the quality of life in New York City and its neighborhoods" This is primarily achieved through work with over 12,000 associations representing over one million volunteers. The committee administers a number of small grants, including the Neighborhood Environmental Action Program Award, Youth for Youth Incentive Grants, the Neighborhood Safety Award, the Building Blocks Award, the Mollie Parnis Dress Up Your Neighborhood Award, and more. Guidelines and applications for these programs, information on the committee's other services, links to related resources, and a calendar and bulletin board are available on the committee's Web site.

City of Hope (CA) (http://www.cityofhope.org)
Located outside Los Angeles in Duarte, California, City of Hope is a biomedical research, treatment, and educational institution founded in 1913. The center works to help people with cancer and other life-threatening diseases through a variety of services. The City of Hope Web site provides information on the center's programs, facilities, and volunteer and donor opportunities; contact information; and an online donation form.

The Clarence Foundation (CA) (http://www.theclarencefoundation.org)
The Clarence Foundation was created in 1999 with the mission to seek out grassroots organizations that have been successful in the relief of poverty worldwide. The foundation promotes the practice of "engaged international philanthropy" by offering opportunities for personal involvement in global change work. The foundation has five areas of interest: children, education, health, human rights, and women, and relies on a global network of volunteer advisors to identify groups to receive assistance. The foundation does not accept unsolicited proposals. The foundation's Web site offers information on currently funded projects, an online donation area, and information on getting involved in engaged philanthropy.

Henry O. Clark, Jr. Foundation (MI) (http://www.hcstrokefoundation.org)
The Henry O. Clark, Jr. Foundation, located in Michigan, promotes stroke awareness through education and support of organizations that benefit a healthy community. In promoting stroke awareness, the foundation hopes to decrease the number of new stroke victims, reduce the number of second stroke victims, and reduce the number of stroke related deaths within our community. The foundation's Web site explains how the organization supports other nonprofits in the community.

Cleveland Education Fund (OH) (http://www.cleveland-ed-fund.org)
The Cleveland Education Fund, established with funding from the Cleveland Foundation in 1984, "furnishes teachers with current research and trends in their subject areas, encourages practices that have proven successful elsewhere, supports teachers who are themselves developing new instructional methods, and makes monetary grants to innovative teachers and schools." Grants are given in two major categories: Leadership Grants for teachers and collaborative teams to help implement instructional projects, and Project Achieve Grants for schools focusing on long-term capacity building. Interested parties are encouraged to write to the fund for application guidelines and deadlines. The Web site offers information on past funded projects, lists of officers and funders, and an events calendar.

Club Foundation (VA) (http://www.clubfoundation.org/)
The Club Foundation, a professional organization for the managers of private clubs, was established in 1988 to provide educational opportunities for future professionals of the club industry. Scholarships and grants are awarded to students enrolled in hospitality programs who are pursuing managerial careers in club management. The foundation's Web site provides descriptions of its programs and downloadable application forms.

Coalition for the Advancement of Jewish Education (NY) (http://www.caje.org)
The Coalition for the Advancement of Jewish Education seeks to advance Jewish education by supporting Jewish teachers; encouraging young people to go into the field professionally; and running national conferences and local in-service programs. The coalition's Web site provides information about its annual conference, a job bank, newsletters, membership, and advocacy. The site also provides information and applications for education innovation grants for coalition members and programs related to the annual conferences.

College Art Association (NY) (http://www.collegeart.org/)
The College Art Association, founded in 1911, promotes scholarship and teaching in the history and criticism of the visual arts, as well as creativity and technical skill in the teaching and practices of art. The association's Fellowships for Artists and Art Historians provide two-year grants to M.F.A., Ph.D., and terminal M.A. students to help bridge the gap between graduate study and professional careers. The association's Web site provides fellowship guidelines and applications; lists other opportunities for artists—including awards, calls for entries and manuscripts, grants and fellowships, internships, and residencies—offered by other organizations; publications; conference information; and membership information.

Colorado Endowment for the Humanities (CO) (http://www.ceh.org)
The Colorado Endowment for the Humanities, located in Denver, was established in 1974. The group "sponsors and provides support for humanities programming throughout the state . . . including local history exhibits, free public lectures, radio programs, and Chautauqua performances." The endowment's funding programs include Program and Planning Grants, Research Grants, and Packaged Program Grants. Guidelines, deadlines, application forms, and lists of previous grant recipients; information on the endowment's Teacher Institutes and annual publication prize; an events calendar for projects around the state; and features on assorted sponsored events are available on the endowment's Web site.

Colorado Springs Osteopathic Foundation and Family Medicine Center (CO) (http://www.csof.org)
The Colorado Springs Osteopathic Foundation and Family Medicine Center was founded in 1984. The foundation offers a variety of programs, including the Family Medicine Center, general health education, continuing medical education programs, internships and fellowships, a speaker's bureau and physician referral service, and more, to benefit the health of medically indigent and low-income families in Colorado Springs. The foundation's Web site includes information on the foundation's services and programs, details on how to make contributions, and contact information.

The Columbus Medical Association Foundation (http://www.cmaf-ohio.org)
The Columbus Medical Association Foundation was created by local physicians in 1958 to "improve the health of the people of greater Columbus, Ohio, by focusing resources on health promotion, health education, and access to health care." The foundation accepts proposals for projects whose proposed outcomes enable people to take actions and adopt behaviors that will give them better control over their own health, thus creating a more health-conscious community. The foundation's Web site provides application guidelines and an electronic pre-proposal summary form, a listing of the board of trustees, an electronic request for the annual report, information on specific initiatives, and publications.

Comic Relief, Inc. (CA) (http://www.comicrelief.org)
Founded by writer-producer Bob Zmuda in 1986, Comic Relief, Inc., is a nonprofit organization dedicated to helping America's homeless population. Based in Los Angeles, the group presents an annual broadcast of comedians and celebrities, including its original trio of comedians: Billy Crystal, Whoopi Goldberg, and Robin Williams. Proceeds from the telecasts support homeless projects in cities across the United States and provide healthcare services to homeless men, women, and children. The group's Web site includes a history of the show, answers to frequently asked questions, contact information, and details on upcoming shows.

Common Counsel Foundation (CA) (http://www.commoncounsel.org/)
The Common Counsel Foundation is an Oakland, California-based public charity that offers strategic philanthropic advisory services to a small group of family foundations and individual donors committed to funding economic, environmental, and social justice initiatives that seek to "give voice" to the needs of low-income people, women, youth, people of color, and others working for justice, equality, and a healthy, sustainable environment. Current member funds of the foundation include the Abelard Foundation West, the Acorn Foundation, and the Penney Family Fund. The foundation also administers the Grantee Exchange Fund and the Social and Economic Justice Fund and coordinates retreat programs for writers and social-change community organizers and activists. The foundation's Web site contains information about the goals and funding areas of each of the foundation's member funds and retreat programs, proposal guidelines, grants lists, and contact information.

James N. Jarvie Commonweal Service (NY) (http://www.jarvie.org/)
Established in 1925, the James N. Jarvie Commonweal Service is focused on supporting the independence and dignity of the elderly—age 65 and up—who are living at home. The service is affiliated with the Presbyterian Church and serves organizations and individuals in the New York City area. The service's Web site provides guidelines and limitations for the service's various grant programs, including details on the organization's main areas of interest: underserved minority communities, dementia and mental health, outreach and case management, advocacy, and capacity-building. The site also lists organizations that have recently received funding and provides application details and instructions.

Community College of Allegheny County Educational Foundation (PA) (http://www.ccac.edu/default.aspx?id=137254)
The Community College of Allegheny County Educational Foundation creates connections between the college and the community to ensure the ongoing viability of the college. The foundation provides funds that ensure the college's ability to offer varied programming, offers scholarships, and provides college employees with mini-grants to fund innovative approaches to classroom teaching and student services. The foundation's Web site provides application information, eligibility limitations, and contact information.

The Community Health Charities of Minnesota (MN) (http://www.healthcharitiesmn.org/)
Based in Minneapolis, the Community Health Charities of Minnesota was formed in 1986 to unite health-related charities "to provide one efficient fundraising vehicle with a focus on health." The organization raises funds to support research and education programs to combat chronic health conditions, educational opportunities for employees, and charity missions. The charities' Web site is a health resource, with monthly features and articles, health-related links, information on support groups, and details for donors. Contact information is also provided.

Community Health Charities of New York (NY) (http://www.healthcharitiesny.org)
The Community Health Charities of New York was established in 1971 "to promote and support member agencies' programs that improve the health and well-being of all people throughout New York State." The charities' Web site lists benefits of membership, including participation in one of the many fundraising and federal workplace giving campaigns

sponsored by the organization; links to member organizations and corporate partners; and recent financial information for the charities.

Community Progress Council, Inc. (PA) (http://www.yorkcpc.org)
The Community Progress Council, Inc., was established in 1965 to promote self-sufficiency among low-income residents of York County, Pennsylvania. Details on the council's programs and partnerships with similar service agencies—including Head Start, Foster Grandparent Program, and Women, Infants, and Children (WIC)—are provided on the council's Web site, along with volunteer and contact information.

Community Shares (TN) (http://www.korrnet.org/cshares/)
Formed in 1985 to provide a choice for employees in workplace charitable campaigns, Community Shares supports "social change organizations in Tennessee in order to promote a more just and caring community." The group maintains offices in Knoxville and Nashville, Tennessee, and funds groups locally and at the state level that work on such issues as hunger, healthcare, domestic violence, education, and the environment. The Community Shares Web site lists member organizations and details about the workplace program. Contact information is also available online for both offices.

Community Shares of Wisconsin, Inc. (WI) (http://communityshares.com)
Located in Madison, Community Shares of Wisconsin, Inc., works toward fundamental social change. The organization's Liesl Blockstein Community Grants are distributed to support organizations in south central Wisconsin for projects that encourage cooperation between groups; work toward basic human rights for all; work toward the end of racial, sexual, and economic discrimination; and promote systemic change. Interested organizations can join the application mailing list by e-mail. The organization's Web site includes staff profiles and contact information, basic financial statements, project information, information on membership organizations, and an events calendar.

Concern Foundation (CA) (http://www.concernfoundation.org)
The Beverly Hills, California-based Concern Foundation was created in 1968 and is "dedicated to funding promising cancer researchers in the fields of immunology, immunotherapy, and other closely related areas of basic cancer research." The foundation's name stands for "CONquer canCER Now." The foundation's grant program provides support to independent investigators at the level of assistant professor or equivalent for cancer research. Grant guidelines and applications, information on current research, information on volunteering or making a donation, and a list of the foundation's governing board are available on the foundation's Web site.

Concerned Women for America (DC) (http://www.cwfa.org)
Located in Washington, D.C., Concerned Women for America was founded in 1979 to "restore the family to its traditional purpose and thereby allow each member of the family to realize their God-given potential and be more responsible citizens." The organization awards two scholarships annually to women attending a conservative, Christian college or university and offers extensive resources and advocacy positions on topics that concern members, from education and religious freedom to United Nations and national sovereignty. The organization's Web site includes grant guidelines and downloadable applications.

Connecticut Humanities Council (CT) (http://www.ctculture.org)
The Connecticut Humanities Council was created in 1974 as an affiliate of the National Endowment for the Humanities to "provide opportunities for all people in Connecticut to rediscover the joy of lifelong learning, to see themselves in the full context of their history and heritage, and to explore the infinite varieties of human thought and experience contained in our literature and expressed in our arts that give shape and direction to our lives." The council's Web site provides information on its various grant programs, downloadable

guidelines and applications, information on programs funded by the council, a cultural calendar, board and staff lists, and a museum directory.

The Conservation Alliance (WA) (http://www.outdoorlink.com/consall/)
The Conservation Alliance is a group of outdoor businesses that support grassroots citizen-action groups in protecting rivers, trails, and wild lands. Grants are made to organizations for projects focused on direct action to protect and enhance natural resources for recreation, not for mainstream education or scientific research projects. Guidelines and application instructions, a history of grantmaking, success stories, news, and membership information are available on the alliance's Web site.

Conservation Treaty Support Fund (MD) (http://www.conservationalliance.com)
Located in Chevy Chase, Maryland, the Conservation Treaty Support Fund works with international wildlife resources conservation agreements. The fund "promotes awareness and understanding of conservation treaties and their goals, to enhance public support, compliance, and funding" through a wide variety of educational materials and grant projects. Brochures and educational materials, a listing of current and past grants, an overview of the role of international treaties in wildlife conservation, and contact information are available on the fund's Web site.

Consumer Health Foundation (DC) (http://www.consumerhealthfdn.org)
Created in 1994, the Consumer Health Foundation works "to improve the health status of Washington, D.C.-area communities and to support activities that enable people to be more actively involved in their own health." The foundation makes grants to community organizations that promote healthcare access, especially to the vulnerable. The foundation's Web site provides a request for proposals, descriptions of recently funded organizations, membership information, the foundation's newsletter, and contact information.

Cooperative Development Foundation (DC)
(http://www.coopdevelopment.org/funds.html)
The Washington, D.C.-based Cooperative Development Foundation maintains an unrestricted fund as well as a large number of specific funds that address such needs as rural development, welfare-to-work programs, and agricultural coops, among others. Funding categories include consumer, general, housing leadership, rural, seniors, and students. The foundation's Web site provides a link to each of its specific funds, details about each fund, descriptions of sample projects, funding guidelines, and contact information.

Cooperative Fund of New England, Inc. (CT) (http://www.cooperativefund.org)
The Cooperative Fund of New England, Inc., in Hartford, Connecticut, is a community development loan fund whose mission is "to advance community based, cooperative, and democratically owned or managed enterprises with preference to those that serve low-income communities through: provision of prompt financial assistance at reasonable rates; provision of an investment opportunity that promotes socially conscious enterprise; and development of a regional reservoir of business skills with which to assist and advise these groups." The program loans are available only to organizations operated on a cooperative or nonprofit basis within the New England states of Massachusetts, Vermont, New Hampshire, Maine, Connecticut, and Rhode Island, or within the adjacent parts of New York State. The fund's Web site features a printable loan application.

The William J. Copeland Fund (PA) (http://www.copelandfund.org/)
The William J. Copeland Fund, formerly the Forbes Fund, was created in 1982 as a supporting organization of the Pittsburgh Foundation, and is dedicated to "[increasing] the skills of nonprofit organization staff and [increasing] administrative efficiency." The fund's programs include the Management Enhancement Grants Program, to help develop efficient organizational structures in nonprofits; the Elmer J. Tropman Nonprofit Research Fund, which sponsors applied research on a variety of topics pertinent to nonprofit management; and the Alfred W. Wishart, Jr. Award for Excellence in Nonprofit Management. The fund's

Web site contains information on these and other programs, management and communication tools, and other related resources.

The Copley Society of Boston (MA) (http://www.copleysociety.org/)
The Copley Society of Boston is "committed to the public support and advancement of the visual arts in New England and beyond." Through its gallery in Boston, the society works with young and established artists alike through exhibitions, workshops, and special events. Information on upcoming events and membership, downloadable newsletters, and contact information are available on the society's Web site.

Cottonwood Foundation (MN) (http://www.cottonwoodfdn.org)
The Cottonwood Foundation is "dedicated to promoting empowerment of people, protection of the environment, and respect for cultural diversity." The foundation focuses its modest grantmaking activities on "committed, grass roots organizations that rely strongly on volunteer efforts and where foundation support will make a significant difference." The foundation typically awards grants in the $500 to $1,000 range to organizations in the United States and internationally that protect the environment, promote cultural diversity, empower people to meet their basic needs, and rely on volunteer efforts. The foundation's Web site provides grant guidelines, a downloadable grant application form, a list of recent grant recipients, the foundation's latest annual report, and general information about its activities.

Council for Advancement and Support of Education (DC) (http://www.case.org)
The Council for Advancement and Support of Education (CASE) in Washington, D.C., is the professional organization for the advancement of professionals at all levels who work in alumni relations, communications, and development. CASE helps its members build stronger relationships with their alumni and donors, raise funds for campus projects, produce recruitment materials, market their institutions to prospective students, diversify the profession, and foster public support of education. CASE sponsors a variety of fellowship and scholarship programs to serve its members and to enhance the field of advancement, and also offers a series of awards for its members to recognize excellence in the field. The CASE Web site offers detailed information on the organization's programs and services.

Council of Independent Colleges (DC) (http://www.cic.edu/)
The Council of Independent Colleges, founded in 1956 and based in Washington, D.C., is an association of independent liberal arts colleges and universities that helps to enhance educational programs, improve administrative and financial performance, and increase institutional visibility. The council offers funding and technical assistance programs, which are outlined in the Projects & Services area of its Web site. Additionally, the council's Consortium for the Advancement of Private Higher Education (CAPHE) helps corporations and foundations stimulate meaningful reform in private colleges and universities by designing and administering directed-grant competitions, offering technical assistance to funders, and disseminating ideas resulting from its programs. The council's Web site provides information about CAPHE, membership and sponsor information, board and staff listings, and an online version of its most recent annual report.

The Covenant Foundation (NY) (http://www.covenantfn.org)
The New York City-based Covenant Foundation was established in 1990 to build on existing strengths within the field of Jewish education in North America, across all denominations and in all educational settings. The foundation honors Jewish educators and supports creative approaches to programming in hopes of strengthening endeavors in education that perpetuate the identity and heritage of the Jewish people. The foundation supports pre-collegiate, adult, and family education through awards, grants, and other activities. Information about the foundation's grant and award programs, a list of the foundation's board of directors, and contact information are available on the foundation's Web site.

Craft Emergency Relief Fund, Inc. (VT) (http://www.craftemergency.org)
Located in Montpelier, Vermont, the Craft Emergency Relief Fund, Inc., was established in 1985 to "provide immediate support to professional craftspeople facing career threatening emergencies such as fire, theft, illness, and natural disaster." Fund assistance is granted in the form of loans, booth fee waivers at craft shows, discounts from suppliers, and marketing and promotional assistance. Guidelines, downloadable application forms, staff and board of directors lists, press releases, an appeal for contributions, and links to related resources are available on the fund's Web site.

CREATE Foundation (MS) (http://www.createfoundation.com)
Based in Tupelo, Mississippi, the CREATE Foundation, an acronym for Christian Research, Education, Action, Technical Enterprise, is a community foundation for northern Mississippi. CREATE awards grants to select organizations in the areas of community development, human development, and education. Description of the foundation's funding area, application instructions and guidelines, contact information, and details on CREATE's role as an endowment fund and its presence in northern Mississippi are available on the foundation's We site.

Creative Capital (NY) (http://www.creative-capital.org/)
Creative Capital is oriented towards supporting individual artists in the visual, performing, media, and emerging arts fields. The organization provides audience development, marketing, and other forms of assistance tailored to individual projects in exchange for a share of the proceeds generated, which are then reinvested into the work of other artists. The organization's description, history, application and guidelines, lists of staff and advisors, links to other arts resource organizations, and a mailing list are available on the organization's Web site.

Creative Time, Inc. (NY) (http://www.creativetime.org)
Based in New York City, Creative Time, Inc., is a nonprofit public art presenter whose mission is to foster artistic experimentation in the public realm. Projects are presented in unique and unusual public spaces throughout New York's five boroughs in a variety of media—from deli cups, billboards, and the Internet, to the Times Square Astrovision screen and the skies over Manhattan. The organization's public programs are multidisciplinary and feature work by visual artists, architects, designers, performers, musicians, poets, and choreographers. The Citywide Program is the organization's process for reviewing unsolicited artist proposals. Guidelines, information on recent projects and events, internship opportunities, information on ways to donate or volunteer, an archive of past Creative Time projects, and funder and sponsor information are available on Creative Time's Web site.

Crossroads Fund (IL) (http://www.crossroadsfund.org)
The Crossroads Fund is a public foundation that raises money to support organizations working on issues of social and economic justice in the Chicago metropolitan area. The fund's Web site provides descriptions of the fund's various grant programs, including the Seed Fund, Growth Fund, Technical Assistance, and the Emergency Fund; applications and deadlines; the fund's newsletter; upcoming events; news; a list of grantee organizations; and contact information.

Cruise Industry Charitable Foundation (DC) (http://www.iccl.org/foundation.htm)
The Washington, D.C.-based Cruise Industry Charitable Foundation was established in 1998 by the International Council of Cruise Lines to improve the quality of life in the communities where the cruise industry has a presence by providing charitable grants to local programs. The foundation supports programs designed to encourage job creation and training, improve access to community services, and provide youth and adult education, particularly for minority and disadvantaged students. The foundation also focuses on programs designed to improve literacy, teach basic life skills, and provide mentoring services. Within these focus areas, the foundation actively encourages and supports programs that meet the

needs of "at risk populations within the following categories of individuals: the economically disadvantaged, the young, the elderly, people with disabilities, women, and minorities." The foundation's Web site provides grant requirements and guidelines, lists of grant recipients, press releases, and contact information.

Cure Autism Now (CA) (http://www.canfoundation.org)
Cure Autism Now was founded in 1995 in Los Angeles as "an organization of parents, physicians, and researchers, dedicated to promoting and funding research with direct clinical implications for treatment and a cure for autism." The organization funds scientific research and the Autism Genetic Resource Exchange program. The organization's Web site provides autism resources; the organization's downloadable newsletter; lists events sponsored by the organization; descriptions of current awards, programs, and grants; and contact information.

Cystic Fibrosis Foundation (MD) (http://www.cff.org/)
Headquartered in Bethesda, Maryland, the Cystic Fibrosis Foundation was created in 1955 "to assure the development of the means to cure and control cystic fibrosis and to improve the quality of life for those with the disease." The foundation offers research grants covering the many issues addressing cystic fibrosis. These include the Therapeutics Development Program as well as training grants and research grants. The foundation's Web site offers applications; publications, including the annual report; information on clinical trials; updates on relevant public policy and the foundation's involvement in these efforts; information on the cystic fibrosis pharmacy service; and facts about the disease.

Dakota Medical Foundation (ND) (http://www.dakmedfdn.org)
Established in 1960 in Fargo, North Dakota, the Dakota Medical Foundation's mission is to improve the health of the people of the Red River Valley region of North Dakota and Minnesota. The foundation supports health-related research and educational and service-oriented programs. The foundation's Web site provides information on the application process, details on special programs, lists of past grants, the foundation's newsletter, and contact information.

The Dallas Morning News Charities (TX) (http://charities.dallasnews.com)
The Dallas Morning News Charities was founded in 1986 "to raise funds and distribute them through agencies that provide food, clothing, shelter, and other basic assistance to those individuals and families in the most desperate need" in the Dallas, Texas, area. The charities' Web site includes a listing of nonprofit agencies funded by the charities, profiles of some of the clients served by these programs, information on making a donation, and contact information.

Dallas Women's Foundation (TX) (http://www.dallaswomensfoundation.org)
Established in 1985, the Dallas Women's Foundation "raises money, responsibly funds community programs that help women and girls realize their full potential, and advocates increased philanthropy by and for women and girls" in the Dallas, Texas, area. This mission is achieved through grants to select nonprofit organizations that benefit women. The foundation's Web site includes grant guidelines and forms; lists of previous grant recipients; information on special events, donor and volunteer opportunities, and research projects; and contact information.

Dance Films Association, Inc. (NY) (http://www.dancefilmsassn.org)
Dance Films Association, Inc., is a membership organization that acts as an information clearinghouse and meeting ground for users, producers, and distributors of dance films and videos. In addition to sponsoring publications, a film festival, and a touring program, the New York City-based association serves as a "nonprofit umbrella" for independent filmmakers seeking funding and offers annual grants to its members for post-production expenses. The association's Web site includes a printable entry form for the Dance on Camera Festival, a printable membership form, and a database of dance films and videos.

Daughters of Charity West Central Region Foundation (MO) (http://www.daughtersofcharityfdn.org/dcwcrf/)
The St. Louis, Missouri-based Daughters of Charity West Central Region Foundation was formed in 1996 to "create healthier communities in the West Central Region of the Daughters of Charity, giving priority to projects that target poor and underserved persons." The foundation offers grants through three main areas of focus: Quality of Life for the Elderly, Stronger Families, and Healthier Lifestyles. Grants are also available for general funding projects addressing health and wellness education, primary/preventive medical services, and social services. The foundation's Web site provides funding guidelines and grant application procedures, news on special initiatives, answers to frequently asked questions, links to further resources, and contact information.

Deaconess Community Foundation (OH) (http://fdncenter.org/grantmaker/deaconess/)
Deaconess Community Foundation was created in 1997 following the sale of Deaconess Hospital of Cleveland. The foundation provides resources that help organizations empower people in greater Cleveland, Ohio, to become self-sufficient and is guided by the spiritual traditions of the United Church of Christ. Grants are provided to nonprofit organizations for charitable, health, education, welfare, community, or social services. The foundation's Web site provides a history of the foundation, grant guidelines and an application form, grants lists, and a listing of the board of trustees.

Deaconess Foundation (MO) (http://www.deaconess.org)
Originally established in 1972 as a supporting foundation for Deaconess Hospital, the Deaconess Foundation is today an independent faith-based health foundation dedicated to the improved health of metropolitan St. Louis, Missouri. The priority of the foundation is to increase the well-being of vulnerable children in the urban core areas of the region. The foundation defines the metropolitan St. Louis area as including St. Louis City and the following counties: St. Louis, Franklin, Jefferson, and St. Charles Counties in Missouri and Madison, Monroe, and St. Clair Counties in Illinois. The foundation's Web site offers a description of the grant application process, grant listings, links to related sites, news releases, and contact information.

Deafness Research Foundation (NY) (http://www.drf.org)
The New York City-based Deafness Research Foundation is a voluntary health organization committed to curing and preventing all forms of hearing loss and making lifelong hearing health a national priority. The foundation's grant program seeks to stimulate research in hearing and balance. Priority is given to new investigators in the field and to projects that are likely to open new lines of inquiry. New and innovative projects developed by established scientists will also be considered. The foundation's Web site provides information on the grant program and other foundation initiatives, contact information, publications, a resource directory, and information on hearing health.

Delaware Humanities Forum (DE) (http://www.dhf.org/)
The Delaware Humanities Forum, an adjunct of the Delaware Humanities Council, supports educational programs in the humanities through its own programs and sponsorship of a range of activities, including lectures, conferences, radio and television broadcasts, interpretive exhibits, and book and film discussions. Descriptions of the forum's programs, which include a Speakers Bureau, a Visiting Scholars Program, and an Annual Lecture; information about grant eligibility requirements and deadlines; answers to frequently asked questions; downloadable guidelines and application forms; a calendar of events; an online form for ordering forum materials; and contact information are available at the forum's Web site.

Delta Dental Fund (MI) (http://www.deltadentalmi.com/ddf/index.html)
Created in 1980, the Delta Dental Fund is the philanthropic arm of Delta Dental Plan of Michigan (DDPMI). The fund supports educational and research funding programs for the advancement of dental science, promotes the general oral health of the public through

educational and service activities, encourages civic and cultural activities, and enhances the relationship between DDPMI and its participating dentists. The foundation's Web site provides guidelines for the fund's contribution programs and information on the fund's other programs and activities.

Dental Health Foundation (CA) (http://www.dentalhealthfoundation.org/)
The Oakland, California-based Dental Health Foundation was formed in 1985 to improve the overall oral health of Californians. Consisting of educators, trainers, public health dentists, dental hygienists, researchers, and project administrators, the foundation has three main goals: "providing leadership, advocacy, education, and public policy development; promoting community-based prevention strategies; and improving access to and the quality of oral health services." The foundation's Web site provides information and publications on the foundation's initiatives, programs, and services; details of current research; news and events; and contact information.

Denver Broncos Charities Fund (CO)
(http://www.denverbroncos.com/offthefield/broncocharity.php3)
Founded in 1994 by the National Football League's Denver Broncos, the Denver Broncos Charities Fund aids nonprofit organizations in Colorado. The fund, which receives matching contributions from the Robert R. McCormick Tribune Foundation, supports programs in education, athletics, and life skills designed to impact disadvantaged and at-risk young people; programs devoted to physically and mentally challenged individuals; and programs for the hungry and homeless. The fund also sponsor a number of events, camps, and programs for the youth and families of Colorado, which are described in the Community Relations portion of the Web site.

The Design Industries Foundation Fighting AIDS (NY) (http://www.diffa.org)
Founded in 1984 in New York City, the Design Industries Foundation Fighting AIDS (DIFFA) is committed to supporting nonprofit organizations fighting AIDS and HIV. The foundation's actions include "preventive education programs targeted to populations at risk of infection, treatment and direct-care services for people living with AIDS, and public policy initiatives which add resources to private sector efforts." The foundation's Web site provides general grant guidelines, lists of previous grant recipients, an online form to receive requests for proposals, lists of DIFFA chapters and community partners, information about national events, publications, and related resources.

Detroit Lions Charities Fund (MI)
(http://www.detroitlions.com/section_display.cfm?section_id=5&top=1&level=2)
Established by the National Football League's Detroit Lions, the Detroit Lions Charities supports education, civic affairs, and health and human services in the state of Michigan. Particular emphasis is placed on programs that benefit the children and youth of Detroit. The charities' Web site offers a description of the charities' activities and provides funding request deadlines, a press release on current grants and annual giving totals, and contact information.

Detroit Youth Foundation (MI) (http://www.detroityouth.org/)
The Detroit Youth Foundation was founded in 1999 "to provide programs and activities at the community level that support children and guide youth development" in the Detroit area. The foundation is an offshoot of the W.K. Kellogg Foundation and currently funds in two main areas: the Mid East/West Fest, which promotes multicultural and collaborative learning experiences, and the Junior Achievement of Southeastern Michigan, which is a grant focused on business education. The foundation's Web site includes the foundation's mission and grant and contact information.

Diana Princess of Wales Memorial Fund (DC) (http://www.usdianafund.org)
The Diana Princess of Wales Memorial Fund, set up in response to thousands of letters and contributions from people around the world following the death of Diana, Princess of

Wales, in 1997, "works to galvanize support for young people who are living on the margins of society and to help create the social and political changes necessary to prevent this marginalization." The fund provides long-term financial support and other assistance to youth-driven organizations working to support young people who have experienced cultural and institutional prejudice in their lives. The fund's Web site provides information on the fund's philosophy and activities, information on youth issues, a list of the board of directors, information on requesting grant competition details and making a donation, and contact information.

A Different September Foundation, Inc. (MA) (http://www.bu.edu/chelsea/adiffere.htm)
The Boston-based A Different September Foundation, Inc., was established in 1991 "to reform public education in Chelsea, Massachusetts, and to create a national model of urban school reform." The foundation sponsors the Boston University/Chelsea Partnership, a program in which the university assumes responsibility for the administration of the Chelsea public school system. Information on the program, a recent annual report, and list of supporting organizations are provided on the foundation's Web site.

Digital Blackboard (CA) (http://www.learningspace.org/digitalblackboard)
Digital Blackboard is a program of the Learning Space designed "to create new opportunities for students, teachers, and communities" in Washington State. The organization works to help teachers integrate technology into their programs in order to improve the learning experience, particularly for at-risk student populations. Digital Blackboard provides seed grants to support teacher training and curriculum development plans that utilize classroom technology. It also offers Innovation in Teaching Awards to honor exemplary teachers who use technology to improve math and science instruction. The organization's Web site provides grant and award guidelines, applications, information on grant and award recipients, lists of donors, and contact information.

Direct Selling Education Foundation (DC) (http://www.dsef.org)
Founded in 1973, the Direct Selling Education Foundation builds bridges of communication and understanding with consumer advocates, academics, and members of the small business community in the United States and abroad. The foundation currently operates two major programs: the Consumer Institute, which sponsors conferences, seminars, training sessions, and other programs on issues related to the consumer movement; and the Academic Institute, which introduces university professors and students to the direct selling distribution system through academic seminars, instructional materials, research, grants to academic organizations, and other programs. The foundation's Web site offers information on the foundation's programs and initiatives, board and staff listings, and contact information.

Disabled American Veterans Charitable Service Trust (KY) (http://www.dav.org)
The Disabled American Veterans Charitable Service Trust is committed to building better lives for America's disabled veterans and their families. To accomplish its mission, the trust supports physical and psychological rehabilitation programs, meets the special needs of veterans with specific disabilities such as amputation and blindness, and aids and shelters homeless veterans. Grantmaking priorities are centered on long-term service projects that provide direct assistance to disabled veterans and their families. The trust's Web site provides grantmaking procedures, information about the trust's organizational concerns, and contact information.

Discovery Channel Global Education Fund (MD) (http://www.discoveryglobaled.org)
Based in Bethesda, Maryland, the Discovery Channel Global Education Fund is "dedicated to improving the educational opportunities of people in need around the world through the use of technology." To this end, the fund provides technology, equipment, and training to schools and other locations accessible to local community members in underserved regions internationally. The fund's goals are achieved through Learning Centers, educational and technological institutions established at the invitation of the community. The fund's Web

site describes its programs, lists its locations worldwide, and provides teacher resource guides and documentary programming as well as contact information.

Do Something, Inc. (NY) (http://www.dosomething.org/index.cfm)
Founded in 1993, Do Something, Inc., provides leadership training, guidance, and financial resources to young people committed to strengthening their communities. The organization awards grants to young people who have an idea for a community project. The Do Something Web site provides grant guidelines, information on programs and contests, details on community causes, discussion boards, and polls.

The Dollywood Foundation (TN) (http://www.dollywood.com/Foundation.htm)
Founded in 1988 by Dolly Parton and the Dollywood Company, the Pigeon Forge, Tennessee-based Dollywood Foundation "develops and administers educational programs for the children of Dolly's native Sevier County, Tennessee, to inspire them to Dream More . . . Learn More . . . Care More . . . Be More." The foundation awards three scholarships in the areas of music, academics, and the environment each year at the county's three high schools. The foundation's main project is the Imagination Library, which distributes a 60-volume collection of books to children in Sevier County. The foundation's Web site includes a contact address and other information on the foundation's activities.

The Murray Dranoff Foundation (FL) (http://www.dranoff2piano.org/)
The Miami, Florida-based Murray Dranoff Foundation was founded in 1987 to introduce, educate, and involve the largest possible audience in the renaissance and literature of four-hand chamber music for the piano. The foundation hosts two annual two-piano competitions, one being a new competition for young players. The foundation also sponsors an annual two-piano symposium, commissions new pieces to be played in competition finals, and sponsors a series of salon nights in preparation for the competition. The foundation's Web site includes deadlines and downloadable applications for the competitions.

Drug Policy Alliance (DC) (http://www.drugpolicy.org)
Formerly known as the Lindesmith Center - Drug Policy Foundation, the Drug Policy Alliance is the leading organization working to broaden the public debate on drug policy and to promote realistic alternatives to the war on drugs based on science, compassion, public health, and human rights. The guiding principle of the alliance is harm reduction, an alternative approach to drug policy and treatment that focuses on minimizing the adverse effects of both drug use and drug prohibition. The alliance's Web site offers a range of information on drug policy issues, a collection of online publications, news and action alerts, an events calendar, and membership information.

The Dunn Foundation (RI) (http://www.dunnfoundation.org/)
The mission of the Dunn Foundation is to promote the quality of the visual environment as a guiding principle for the growth and development of America's communities through education and philanthropy. This mission is fulfilled through increasing public understanding of the contribution community appearance makes to our quality of life, and by linking people to the tools they need to make positive aesthetic changes in their environment. Application guidelines, grants lists, grantmaking priorities, and information on the foundation's "visual literacy" programs are available on the foundation's Web site.

Dystonia Medical Research Foundation (IL) (http://www.dystonia-foundation.org/)
The Dystonia Medical Research Foundation, based in Chicago, Illinois, supports research on dystonia, increases public awareness, and provides support to those affected by the disease. An in-depth description of the foundation's research funding program, information on its education and awareness activities, donor information, listings of the board of directors and scientific advisory board, and contact information are available on the foundation's Web site. The foundation also provides Spanish and French versions of the Web site.

EAA Aviation Foundation, Inc. (WI) (http://www.eaa.org/education/scholarships/)
Located in Oshkosh, Wisconsin, the EAA Aviation Foundation, Inc., funds a variety of scholarships that encourage individuals studying aviation technologies and skills. The majority of scholarships are for students majoring in aviation-related studies. Scholarship descriptions, a downloadable application, additional information about aviation and educational opportunities, and contact information are available on the foundation's Web site.

Eagles Memorial Foundation, Inc. (FL) (http://www.foe.com/memorial/index.html)
Located in Bradenton, Florida, the Eagles Memorial Foundation, Inc., was founded in 1947 to provide medical and educational benefits to the children of Fraternal Order of Eagles members who lost their lives while serving their country during World War II. The foundation's Web site provides eligibility requirements, details on the disbursement of medical and educational funding, and a downloadable brochure.

Earthwatch Institute (MA) (http://www.earthwatch.org)
Based in Boston with offices worldwide, Earthwatch Institute works "to promote sustainable conservation of our natural resources and cultural heritage by creating partnerships between scientists, educators, and the general public." Earthwatch Institute strives to involve the general public in environmental areas usually dominated by scientists, and acts as a liaison between the scientific community, conservation and environmental organizations, policymakers, business, and the general public. The organization offers grants and fellowships for scientists, educators, and students. Guidelines, forms, and grants lists for specific funding programs; information on Earthwatch conservation programs; research expeditions; educational resources; and membership information are available on the organization's Web site.

The Education Enhancement Partnership (OH) (http://www.teep.org)
Created in 1989, the Education Enhancement Partnership is located in Canton, Ohio, and works to "foster private sector efforts in education reform to improve learning for all children, from pre-school through twelfth grade, in Stark County, Ohio." The partnership supports schools that are committed to reform and are working in conjunction with their administration and community. The Web site includes information on the partnership's programs, staff and board lists, and a page of helpful links.

The Education Foundation of Palm Beach County (FL)
(http://www.palmbeach.k12.fl.us/foundation/)
The Education Foundation of Palm Beach County was established in 1984 by a collection of business and community leaders with the goal of enhancing and enriching the educational experiences of public school students in Palm Beach County, Florida. The foundation works to provide financial and physical assistance to classroom and school programs and events. The foundation's Web site provides information on programs, lists of grants and awards given, downloadable applications, and donor and contact information.

EDUCAUSE (CO) (http://www.educause.edu)
The mission of EDUCAUSE is to advance higher education by promoting the intelligent use of information technology. The organization maintains fellowship and awards programs to recognize individual achievement and foster sharing of information about meritorious professional practices. The organization's Web site offers information on programs, publications, membership, conferences, and policy initiatives.

The Electrical Contracting Foundation, Inc. (MD) (http://www.ecfound.org)
Located in Bethesda, Maryland, the Electrical Contracting Foundation, Inc., (ELECTRI' 21) has been supporting the goals of the National Electrical Contractors Association since it was established in 1988. The foundation's mission is to "strengthen the fabric of the electrical industry through the development of information which will positively affect the future of the electrical industry and its service to the public." Research grants are made to accomplish this mission. The foundation's Web site features requests for proposals

that include deadlines, guidelines, and specific project interests; information on becoming a member of the foundation; descriptions of ongoing research and research reports; news; a calendar of events; and the foundation's annual report.

Emergency Nursing Foundation (IL) (http://www.ena.org/foundation/)
The Emergency Nursing Foundation was founded by the Emergency Nursing Association in 1991 in Des Plaines, Illinois. Fulfilling its mission to "enhance emergency health services available to the public through education and research," the foundation works to promote emergency nursing, enhance professional development, educate healthcare professionals and the public on subjects relating to emergency care, and provide research grants and scholarships. Scholarships are available for undergraduate and graduate nursing students, and grants are made for research that will advance the practice of emergency nursing. The foundation's Web site includes guidelines and downloadable applications for each funding program, news, a contribution form, answers to frequently asked questions, and contact information.

Energy Assistance Foundation (IL) (http://www.illinoispower.com/ip/warmneighbors.nsf)
The Energy Assistance Foundation, established in 1982 by Illinois Power, oversees the Warm Neighbors program, which provides bill payment assistance and home weatherization for customers who do not qualify for federal or state heating assistance. Details on how to qualify, current Illinois Power news, agent locations, and contribution opportunities are provided on the foundation's Web site.

Enterprise Foundation (MD) (http://www.enterprisefoundation.org/)
Launched by developer Jim Rouse and his wife Patty in 1982, the Enterprise Foundation focuses its activities on seeing that "all low-income people in the United States have the opportunity for fit and affordable housing." The foundation's Web site offers information about the awards, loans, investments, training programs, and technical assistance supported by the foundation and its subsidiaries; details on the foundation's annual Network Conference; foundation publications, news releases, and newsletters; and searchable resources, including the Resource Database and MoneyNet.

The Entertainment Industry Foundation (CA) (http://eifoundation.org)
Formed in 1942 by Samuel Goldwyn as the Motion Pictures Charity Committee, the Entertainment Industry Foundation of Los Angeles, California, works to "help raise awareness and funds for important causes such as childhood hunger, cancer research, creative arts, education, cardiovascular research, and much more." The foundation annually provides support to more than 300 charitable organizations within the greater Los Angeles area and throughout the United States. The foundation's Industry Community Grants program funds charitable organizations in the greater Los Angeles area, and its National Initiative Grants programs provide funding to pre-selected grantees from across the country. The foundation's Web site provides information on its funding programs, including a grants FAQ page; details on special events; and information on how to make a donation or contact the foundation.

Entomological Foundation (MD) (http://www.entfdn.org)
The Entomological Foundation was created in 1991 in Lanham, Maryland, as the resource development arm of the Entomological Society of America (ESA). The foundation's mission is "to serve the educational enterprise by leveraging science-community resources to educate youth in applying insect science for achieving a healthy environment." The foundation and ESA offer a series of awards, grants, and fellowships for scientists, educators, and students working in the field of insect science. The foundation's Web site provides descriptions and guidelines for the assorted funding opportunities, and also includes a board list, donor lists, and information on donor-advised funds.

Entrepreneurs Foundation (CA) (http://www.ef3.homestead.com)
The Entrepreneurs Foundation was created in 1998 to encourage entrepreneurs in the Silicon Valley/Bay Area to reinvest in their communities. The foundation works with young companies to help them develop and facilitate a community involvement plan. In return, each company gives equity stock to the foundation, which invests the capital gains from the appreciated stock in nonprofit leaders who engage in venture philanthropy practices. The foundation's Web site provides information on the foundation's brand of philanthropy, profiles on participating companies, and contact information.

Environmental Research and Education Foundation (VA) (http://www.erefdn.org)
The Environmental Research and Education Foundation of Alexandria, Virginia, was established in 1992 to "develop environmental solutions for the future through research and education." The foundation offers grants for research and education in topics related to aspects of solid waste management and provides a scholarship program for doctoral candidates in environmental research and education. Guidelines for these programs and the foundation's annual report, which provides a board list and a list of recent grant recipients, are available on the foundation's Web site.

Epilepsy Foundation of America (MD) (http://www.efa.org)
Founded in Landover, Maryland in 1968, the Epilepsy Foundation of America strives to "ensure that people with seizures are able to participate in all life experiences; and prevent, control, and cure epilepsy through research, education, advocacy, and services." The foundation's Web site is a comprehensive resource on epilepsy and provides information on research, advocacy, online communities, and specific answers from epilepsy experts; details on the foundation's research grants, including previous grants lists, guidelines, and downloadable applications; and further information and links to other resources.

Episcopal Charities (NY) (http://www.episcopalcharities-newyork.org)
Begun in 1995, Episcopal Charities work "to enhance the outreach efforts of Episcopal congregations in the Diocese of New York" through fund development, grantmaking, and educational development. The charities maintain two main funding recipients: the Basic Human Needs and Keystone Partnership for Youth grants. Guidelines, application procedures, application forms, and information about the board of directors and advisors to the charities are available on the organization's Web site.

Episcopal Community Services Foundation (OH)
(http://www.episcopal-dso.org/pages/ecsf)
Based in Cincinnati, Ohio, the Episcopal Community Services Foundation was established in 1989 to "assist the Episcopal Church within the Diocese of Southern Ohio in response to the Christian imperative that the hungry be fed, the naked clothed, the homeless housed, and that others who are less fortunate share in the Good News of the Gospel." To this end, the foundation provides services and funds in a wide variety of areas and to different charitable groups. The foundation's Web site provides general information about the organization and its goals, a listing of recent grants, an online application form, and contact information.

Equipment Leasing and Finance Foundation (VA)
(http://www.leasefoundation.org/index.htm)
The Equipment Leasing and Finance Foundation was established in Arlington, Virginia, in 1989 as a means to "promote the growth and effectiveness of equipment leasing and finance" through the development and enhanced recognition of the lease financing industry. The foundation makes grants for research projects that have a practical application to professionals in the leasing and finance business. Internships in the industry are also available. The foundation's Web site offers grant guidelines, information about internships, publications and industry resources, and contact information.

Equity Foundation, Inc. (OR) (http://www.equityfoundation.org)
Based in Portland, Oregon, the Equity Foundation, Inc., works to promote the welfare of the gay, lesbian, bisexual, and transgendered communities and of the people of Oregon in general by providing support to nonprofit organizations throughout the state. The foundation provides funding through its annual granting cycle, individual donor-advised funds, and scholarship and event funds. Key issues for the foundation include human dignity, youth and family programs, health and social services, and arts and culture. The foundation's Web site provides a thorough description of its grantmaking activities, a list of recent grants, information for donors, answers to frequently asked questions, brief biographies of the foundation's board and staff, and contact information.

Boomer Esiason Foundation (NY) (http://www.esiason.org)
Based in New York City, the Boomer Esiason Foundation was founded by the football great in 1993 after his son was born with cystic fibrosis. The foundation is committed to "heightening awareness of cystic fibrosis and to providing a better quality of life for those affected by cystic fibrosis." The foundation supports research, makes sure that doctors have access to the most innovative treatments, educates the public on the disease, and helps patients combat the disease. The foundation's Web site includes information on its Lung Transplant Grants Program, which is designed to help families with expenses that are not covered by their insurance; updates on legislative issues; news on medical research; a basic definition of the disease; board and staff lists; fundraising information; and a listing of upcoming events.

Eurasia Foundation (DC) (http://www.eurasia.org/)
The Washington, D.C.-based Eurasia Foundation is a privately managed grantmaking organization dedicated to funding programs that build democratic and free market institutions in independent states of the former Soviet Union—Armenia, Azerbaijan, Belarus, Georgia, Kazakstan, Kyrgyzstan, Moldova, Russia, Tajikistan, Turkmenistan, Ukraine, and Uzbekistan. The foundation concentrates its support in the areas of private enterprise development, public administration and policy, and civil society. The foundation's Web provides program descriptions and application guidelines; a searchable database of grants; a directory of foundation offices, staff, and board members; links to Web sites of interest; job opportunities; news; and contact information.

Lettie Pate Evans Foundation, Inc. (GA) (http://www.lpevans.org)
Created in 1945 by the wife of one of the original bottlers of Coca-Cola, the Lettie Pate Evans Foundation, Inc., works for the "promotion of charity," with a grant program reflecting a strong emphasis in private secondary and higher education, arts and culture, and museums and historic preservation. Grants awarded by this Atlanta, Georgia-based foundation are limited to organizations in Georgia and Virginia. Grant proposals submitted to the foundation may be also be considered by one or more of the four other foundations sharing staff and offices with the Lettie Pate Evans Foundation. The foundation's Web site includes grant application guidelines, an analysis of previously awarded grants, financial information, a list of officers and trustees, contact information, and a short biography of the founder.

Experimental Television Center (NY) (http://www.experimentaltvcenter.org)
Founded in 1971, the Experimental Television Center's mission is "to support the creation of new work using electronic media technologies," through programs, grants, and services that encourage education, research, and preservation. The center offers a residency program and grants—including Finishing Funds, Presentation Funds, and the Media Arts Technical Assistance Fund—to electronic media and film artists. The residency and grant programs are explained in detail on the center's Web site, along with grant guidelines and downloadable applications, a history of the center, an introduction to its facilities, and contact information.

Family Care Foundation, Inc. (CA) (http://www.familycare.org)
The Family Care Foundation, Inc., located in Spring Valley, California, provides support and training for grassroots organizations in developing countries. The foundation concentrates its grantmaking in areas including emergency relief, vocational training, youth services, and drug prevention for communities, families, and children in 50 countries. The foundation's Web includes information on the foundation's grant process and giving programs, information about donor-advised funds, volunteer opportunities, and contact information.

Family Office Exchange Foundation (IL) (http://www.foxfoundation.org)
Based in Oak Park, Illinois, the Family Office Exchange Foundation (known as the FOX Foundation) is committed to lifelong family learning and a family-centered curriculum based on human, intellectual, financial, and social capital. These areas of interest are explained in detail on the foundation's Web site, along with an outline of the foundation's curriculum, with course descriptions and syllabi for each course, and contact information.

Farm Foundation (IL) (http://www.farmfoundation.org)
Created in 1933, the Farm Foundation of Oak Brook, Illinois, is an operating foundation that works "to improve the economic and social well-being of U.S. agriculture and rural people by helping private and public sector decision makers identify and understand forces that will shape the future." The foundation focuses its program funding in six priority areas: globalization, environmental and natural resource issues, new technologies, the role of agricultural institutions, consumer issues, and rural community viability. The foundation also awards Extension Fellowships to state and federal cooperative extension employees pursuing additional training. Guidelines and forms, research and public policy resources, lists of board and staff members, and publications, including the annual report, are available on the foundation's Web site.

Fidelity Investments Charitable Gift Fund (MA) (http://www.charitable-gift.org/)
The Fidelity Investments Charitable Gift Fund permits individuals to create donor-advised funds to make tax-exempt donations to nonprofit organizations of their own choosing. There are two programs: a Giving Account and a Pooled Income Fund. Grants are made to organizations selected by investors. There is no application process, as participants are encouraged to research areas of interest to find recipients. The fund's Web site describes the fund's operations, details giving options, offers information on researching charities, and provides financial information and an annual report.

Film Arts Foundation (CA) (http://www.filmarts.org)
The Film Arts Foundation was founded in San Francisco, California, in 1976 and is committed to supporting the development of independent films in the Bay Area with equipment and education, the screening of independent films, and support for the community that creates these films. Since 1984, the foundation has distributed grants for development, completion, and distribution of independent film/video works. Grant descriptions, lists of previous recipients, information on screenings and an annual film festival, and an extensive list of seminars are available on the foundation's Web site.

Film Society of Lincoln Center (NY) (http://www.filmlinc.com)
The Film Society of Lincoln Center's Web site, called filmlinc, is an online resource for filmmakers and individuals interested in the film arts in the New York City area. The site provides details on specific programming, such as the New York Film Festival, New York Video Festival, Walter Reade Theater events. The society's Web site also offers information on the Grand and Marnier Film Fellowships Competition, a calendar of upcoming film events, information on membership, and an e-mail list for further updates.

Fine Arts Work Center (MA) (http://www.fawc.org)
The Fine Arts Work Center in Provincetown, Massachusetts, was established in 1968 to support talented artists at the beginning of their careers. This greatly esteemed organization

is "devoted to encouraging and supporting young artists and is built on the belief that freedom and community are the best means and natural conditions for artistic growth." The center's core program is the seven-month Winter Fellowship for writers and visual artists. The center also sponsors summer and fall workshops, a returning residency program, and a program for senior fellows. The center's Web site offers application guidelines, deadlines, a printable online application, and a list of past recipients; an events calendar; staff and board lists; and organization updates.

First Nations Development Institute (VA) (http://www.firstnations.org/)
The First Nations Development Institute was formed in 1980 to help Native American tribes build sound, sustainable reservation communities by linking grassroots projects with national programs. The institute offers grants and technical assistance for asset-based development projects through the Eagle Staff Fund, as well as other donor-advised and donor-designated funds. The institute also supports policy and research projects, Native American philanthropy programs, and more. Information on these programs, information on publications and conferences, a list of related links, and contact information are available on the institute's Web site.

FishAmerica Foundation (VA) (http://www.fishamerica.org)
The philanthropic arm of the American Sportfishing Association, the FishAmerica Foundation was established in 1983 in Alexandria, Virginia, to "provide funding . . . for hands on-projects . . . to enhance fish populations, water quality, and/or applied fisheries research in North America " The foundation offers grants to encourage volunteer activity and to support the programmatic efforts of grassroots organizations in all fifty states and Canada. The foundation supports habitat improvement, streambank stabilization, reef projects, litter cleanups and prevention, and hands-on education. The foundation's Web site provides grant applications, guidelines, and lists of funded projects.

The Flatiron Foundation (NY) (http://www.flatironpartners.com/index_foundation.html)
The New York-based Flatiron Foundation is a grantmaking public charity whose mission is to encourage social entrepreneurship in the digital economy. The foundation provides grants to early-stage nonprofits and concentrates its work in three program areas: Children and Readiness, helping children be ready for life in a digital society; Minorities and Women's Entrepreneurship, educating and encouraging entrepreneurship among minorities, women, and others with less traditional access to capital; and New Entrepreneurial Solutions, finding ways to encourage new and experienced entrepreneurs to turn their attention to social problems. The foundation's Web site includes information on current funding opportunities, a brief history of the foundation, information on selected grantees, and contact information.

Alisa Flatow Memorial Scholarship Fund (NJ) (http://www.alisafund.org/)
The Alisa Flatow Memorial Scholarship Fund of Whippany, New Jersey, was created to "encourage others to follow in Alisa's footsteps by studying Judaism at schools in the State of Israel." Scholarships are granted for post-high school secular and Jewish study at institutions in Israel—recipients can simultaneously earn college credits. The scholarship is administered through the Jewish Community Foundation of MetroWest. The fund's Web site contains contact information and a list of present and past scholarship recipients.

A.J. Fletcher Foundation (NC) (http://www.ajf.org/)
Originally formed to provide operating support for A.J. Fletcher's Grass Roots Opera, which later evolved into the National Opera Company, the A.J. Fletcher Foundation today supports "nonprofit organizations in their endeavors to enrich the people of North Carolina." The foundation provides funding for education, the arts, human service needs, and support for strengthening the infrastructure of nonprofit organizations. Due to recent changes in its policies, the foundation discourages unsolicited proposals and will instead continue to fund its existing multi-year commitments and "explore opportunities for

effective grantmaking in the future." The foundation's Web site provides a description of the foundation, a biography of A.J. Fletcher, and information on current commitments.

Florida Children's Forum (FL) (http://www.fcforum.org/)
Founded in 1989, the Florida Children's Forum, headquartered in Tallahassee, Florida, provides leadership, program development, research, data collection and analysis, training, technical assistance and advocacy on behalf of children, families, childcare providers and employers throughout the state. The forum offers intense, focused training for the following specific initiatives: Child Care Resource and Referral, Caring for Kids, Infant and Toddler, Inclusive Child Care, School-Age Child Care, and Latino Providers. The forum's Web site offers information about the mission and how to get involved.

Florida Humanities Council (FL) (http://www.flahum.org/)
Founded in 1971, the Florida Humanities Council awards funds to community and educational organizations in support of public humanities programs. The council's grantmaking is divided into three main categories: Major Grants, Mini Grants, and Scholar/Humanist Fellowships. In addition to detailed funding guidelines and information on the council's activities and membership, the Web site provides a downloadable application, independent evaluator forms, a calendar of council-sponsored and -funded events, and links to dozens of state humanities councils and humanities resources on the Web.

The For All Kids Foundation, Inc. (NJ) (http://www.forallkids.org)
The For All Kids Foundation, Inc., was established in 1997 in Allendale, New Jersey, by talk show host Rosie O'Donnell. Its mission is to "help support the intellectual, social, and cultural development of disadvantaged children throughout the United States." The foundation focuses on supporting at-risk children through child care, healthcare, and education programs in underserved communities. A key interest is in organizations that provide direct child care services. The foundation's Web site includes application guidelines and a list of grant recipients.

Foundation for Chiropractic Education and Research, Inc. (IA) (http://www.fcer.org)
The Foundation for Chiropractic Education and Research, Inc., was established in 1944 and is committed to "promoting the public's health by encouraging and supporting research and education relative to the field of chiropractic care, and serving the needs of practicing chiropractors worldwide." Research grants are made in a number of major categories, including basic and educational research; verification of instruments, design, and data processing techniques; and economic and practice patterns of chiropractic care. The foundation also offers fellowship and residency programs. Application guidelines and restrictions, news and articles, lists of staff and board members, and contact information are available on the foundation's Web site.

Foundation for National Progress (CA) (http://www.motherjones.com)
Located in San Francisco, the Foundation for National Progress was established in 1975 "to educate and empower people through media to work toward progressive change." Along with a training program for interns in investigative journalism, the foundation has been publishing the magazine *Mother Jones* since 1976. The *Mother Jones* Web site includes Web-exclusive articles, discussion groups, and breaking news. Information on the Foundation for National Progress and the *Mother Jones* Investigative Reporting Internship Program can be found in the About Us section of the site.

Foundation for Physical Therapy (VA) (http://www.apta.org/Foundation)
The Foundation for Physical Therapy, located in Alexandria, Virginia, was established in 1979 to support the physical therapy profession's research needs in three areas: scientific research, clinical research, and health services research. The foundation aims to assist clinicians, researchers, and academicians in their doctoral programs; expand funding for emerging researchers; support clinically relevant research; and strengthen the foundation's capacity to promote the profession's research agenda. Information for requesting funding

application packets, contact information, a listing of staff members and the board of directors, and lists of recent grant and scholarship awardees can be found on the foundation's Web site.

Foundation for Saline Area Schools (MI) (http://saline.lib.mi.us/fsas)

The Foundation for Saline Area Schools was established in 1987 to help provide enrichment programs and other projects aimed at enhancing the quality of education and educational opportunities at schools in Saline, Michigan. Specifically, the foundation promotes student learning opportunities, encourages excellence and growth of all staff, and facilitates community/school partnerships. It receives and reviews grant proposals from Saline Area Schools teachers and staff members. The foundation's Web site provides grant guidelines and contact information for potential applicants, a list of board members and advisors, and lists of previous grants awarded.

The Foundation for Technology Education, Inc. (VA) (http://www.iteawww.org/I1.html)

Based in Reston, Virginia, the Foundation for Technology Education, Inc., was created in 1986 by the International Technology Education Association (ITEA) to "support the advancement of technology education through teacher scholarships and grants." The foundation's support programs are designed to: "make our children technologically literate; transfer industrial and corporate research into our schools; produce models of excellence in technology teaching; create public awareness regarding the nature of technology education; and help technology teachers maintain a competitive edge in technology." The programs, which are only open to members of the ITEA, are described on the foundation's Web site. Application guidelines and deadlines are also included.

Foundation for the Roman Catholic Diocese of Altoona-Johnstown (PA) (http://www.fdtndioceseaj.org)

The Foundation for the Roman Catholic Diocese of Altoona-Johnstown, located in Hollisdayburg, Pennsylvania, was established in 1990 "to provide funding for this Diocesan Church" of Altoona-Johnstown. The foundation works toward long-term investments in Catholic institutions within the eight-county Diocese of Altoona-Johnstown. The foundation's Web site offers a listing of various endowed funds, as well as information on the Misciagna Challenge Scholarship Program, which supports motivated students at one of the Diocesan schools. Information on giving opportunities and a form to contact the foundation are also included.

Michael J. Fox Foundation for Parkinson's Research (NY) (http://www.michaeljfox.org)

Founded in 2000 in New York City, two years after actor Michael J. Fox publicly announced his diagnosis of young-onset Parkinson's disease, the Michael J. Fox Foundation for Parkinson's Research is "dedicated to ensuring the development of a cure for Parkinson's disease within this decade through an aggressively funded research agenda." The foundation's Web site provides general information about Parkinson's disease, current research updates, information about Michael J. Fox, foundation news, events listings, and information on current research funding opportunities and funded research projects.

Frameline, Inc. (CA) (http://www.frameline.org/fund/)

Frameline, Inc., is dedicated to the exhibition, distribution, promotion, and funding of lesbian and gay film and video and presents the annual San Francisco International Lesbian and Gay Film Festival. Frameline's grant program, the Horizons/Frameline Completion Fund, helps artists to complete their film and video projects. Funding guidelines, information about the festival, film/video distribution, membership, events, and resources are available on the organization's Web site.

FRAXA Research Foundation (MA) (http://www.fraxa.org)

The FRAXA Research Foundation supports in-depth research leading to the treatment or a cure for Fragile X syndrome, a genetic, inherited cause of mental retardation. The foundation funds grants and fellowships that research timely and practical treatment of Fragile X, especially "preclinical studies of potential pharmaceutical and genetic treatments and studies aimed at understanding the function of the FMR1 gene." The foundation's Web site provides answers to questions about Fragile X; information on joining FRAXA; publications; events listings; links to other resources; lists of past fellows and grantees, with abstracts of their work; and grant guidelines, including the application process and obligations of fellows.

Freedom to Read Foundation (IL) (http://www.ftrf.org/)
The Freedom to Read Foundation was established in 1969 to protect and support the First Amendment rights of libraries and librarians. The foundation's Web site provides resources in the areas of advocacy, education, employment, and activities; legal documents; a history of the foundation; links to partner organizations; and membership and contact information.

French American Charitable Trust (CA) (http://www.factservices.org/)
The French American Charitable Trust (FACT) was established in San Francisco in 1989 by a French-American family "to address fundamental inequalities and injustices in society." The trust's program areas include social and economic justice, environmental health, and infrastructure, however it does not accept unsolicited proposals. The FACT Web site provides details on recent grantees, grantmaking strategies, downloadable guidelines, and information on the trust's partner organization in France.

French-American Foundation (NY) (http://www.frenchamerican.org)
Established in 1976, the French-American Foundation has been committed to strengthening French-American relations and encouraging an active dialogue between the two nations. To this end, the foundation arranges a wide variety of programs, including conferences, lectures, exchanges, and study tours designed to identify and share innovative practices from both societies. The foundation's Web site offers helpful links to American and French resources, a staff listing, and contact information.

Milton and Rose D. Friedman Foundation (IN) (http://www.friedmanfoundation.org/)
The Milton and Rose D. Friedman Foundation, established in 1996 by two economists concerned about the quality of public schools, works to encourage competition in the market for educational services and to give parents more choices about the schools their children attend. The foundation promotes the use of educational vouchers to fund tuition at private schools. The foundation funds research into the judicial and legislative decisions on school choice and the social and economic impact of voucher programs. The foundation's Web site offers opinions and answers to questions on this issue and provides donor information, links to related Web sites, and an contact information.

Friends of Bosnia (MA) (http://friendsofbosnia.org/)
Friends of Bosnia, located in Boston, Massachusetts, provides reconstruction and humanitarian aid to the Balkans and educates the American public about the wars, reconstruction, reconciliation, and peace. Efforts are focused on reconstruction and public education. The organization's Web site provides details about the organization's current projects, program information, a history of initiatives, board listings, and contact information.

Richard D. Frisbee III Foundation (CT) (http://frisbeefoundation.com/)
The Richard D. Frisbee III Foundation, located in New Canaan, Connecticut, was created to support education and research in the fields of childhood and adult cancers, leukemia, and stem cell transplantation. The foundation also makes grants to support patients and patients' needs. The foundation's Web site provides information about the foundation's giving interests, listings of recent grants, staff and board listings, and contact information.

Frontier Village Foundation (CO) (http://rmmc.org/mcmc/FVF/FVF.main.htm)
The Frontier Village Foundation is based in Palmer Lake, Colorado, and focuses its giving in the Rocky Mountain region. The foundation is associated with the Mountain Community Mennonite Church and mainly grants one-time startup funding for programs that

follow the foundation's mission: "to fund community service programs of a preventive nature which reflects our collective understanding of Jesus Christ's teaching to reach out to those in need among us." The foundation's Web site includes grant guidelines, lists of past grant recipients, the foundation's guiding philosophy, and a link to the foundation's parent church Web site.

The Fund for American Studies (DC) (http://www.TFAS.org)
The Fund for American Studies, located in Washington, D.C., is dedicated to "preparing young people for honorable leadership by educating them in the theory, practice, and benefits of a free society." This is done by sponsoring summer institutes for college students on economic concepts, political systems, and moral philosophy. The fund's Web site includes details on these competitive, international programs, as well as application information and testaments from former participants; the most recent fund newsletter; lists of the board and corporate sponsors; organization news; and a link to an alumni Web site.

Fund for an Open Society (PA) (http://www.libertynet.org/~open)
The Fund for an Open Society is a Philadelphia-based national nonprofit mortgage fund and a Pennsylvania mortgage broker. The fund provides financially advantageous loans to qualified borrowers seeking to purchase owner-occupied housing, thereby helping to sustain or promote racially integrated neighborhoods. Loans are made to people buying where their races are underrepresented. The fund's Web site provides loan guidelines and requirements, a mortgage loan prequalification form, newsletters, articles, brochures, related resources, and contact information.

Fund for Santa Barbara (CA) (http://www.fundforsantabarbara.org/)
Created in California in 1980, the Fund for Santa Barbara, supports progressive social change and is "dedicated to finding solutions to current and emerging social problems and issues that challenge our society as a whole." The fund encourages like-minded organizations in South Santa Barbara County to apply for grants and/or technical support. The fund's areas of interest include discrimination based on race, sex, age, religion, economic status, etc.; the rights of workers; self-determination in low-income communities; the environment; and operating in a democratic manner. The fund's Web site includes application guidelines, limitations, deadlines, and online application forms; information on contributing; a grant history; a newsletter; and contact information.

Fund for Southern Communities (GA) (http://www.fund4south.org)
The Fund for Southern Communities, located in Decatur, Georgia, was created in 1981 to "build safe, equitable communities that are free of oppression and that embrace and celebrate all people." These goals are being met today through grants to groups in Georgia, North Carolina, and South Carolina. The grant program supports organizations that work against discrimination, support the rights of workers, promote self-determination in low-income communities, and protect the environment. The fund's Web site includes extensive funding guidelines, deadlines, and downloadable applications; grants lists; and information on donor involvement.

The Fund for Wild Nature (OR) (http://www.fundwildnature.org/)
Located in Portland, Oregon, the Fund for Wild Nature works "to fund grassroots projects that protect biodiversity, which would not otherwise be funded through mainstream sources." The fund's general areas of support include wilderness defense, teaching the ethics of biocentrism, human population growth and commodity consumption reduction efforts, cultural arts that encourage action, and indigenous peoples' activism. The fund is particularly interested in funding proposals related to countering corporate globalization, public lands grazing, and genetic engineering. The fund's Web site includes application guidelines and restrictions, grants lists, and selections from the fund's annual report.

Funding Exchange (NY) (http://www.fex.org/home.html)
Funding Exchange is a network of 16 community foundations throughout the United States with a national office in New York City. These foundations support community-based efforts addressing a wide range of social problems, with emphasis on grassroots organizing. The group seeks to fund projects that work for a more equitable distribution of power and wealth in society; organize in communities and workplaces around basic economic and social issues; work for a society without discrimination on the basis of race, gender, sexual orientation, or age; operate in a democratic manner and involve the constituencies they serve; and have relatively little access to traditional sources of funds. The group's Web site provides links to its member organizations, grant application information, grants lists, and contact information.

Gamma Mu Foundation (FL) (http://www.GMFOUND.org)
Established by the Gamma Mu Fraternity in 1989, the Gamma Mu Foundation supports the unmet needs of the gay community on a nationwide and continuing basis. The foundation provides graduate-level scholarships to college and university students whose degree programs have a positive influence on gay acceptance in the community at large. The foundation also provides financial assistance for the needs of individuals suffering from HIV/AIDS in rural America. The foundation's Web site contains a grant listing, application instructions, and an e-mail link.

Gay and Lesbian Foundation of South Florida (FL) (http://www.glfsf.org)
The Miami-based Gay and Lesbian Foundation of South Florida, formerly the Dade Human Rights Foundation, was established in 1994 to advance education and public awareness with respect to Gay, Lesbian, Bisexual, and Transgendered (GLBT) issues and to support the local GLBT community. This is accomplished through an annual grant program for GLBT programming and organizations, a separate grant program administered by the foundation's Women's Fund, and other programs and services. The foundation's Web site includes grant guidelines, lists of recent and previous grant recipients, a listing of related organizations, listings of upcoming community events, and contact information.

Gay and Lesbian Medical Association (CA) (http://www.glma.org/)
The Gay and Lesbian Medical Association, located in San Francisco, California, was formed in 1981 to "promote quality healthcare for LGBT and HIV-positive people; to foster a professional climate in which our diverse members can achieve their full potential; and to support members challenged by discrimination on the basis of sexual orientation." Grant programs include the Lesbian Health Fund, which supports research and advocacy in creating better healthcare for lesbians and their families; the Medical Expertise Retention Plan, which addresses the issue of HIV-positive healthcare workers; and scholarships for medical students to attend the annual conference. The association's Web site provides application guidelines and materials, information on membership and conferences, publications, and a list of the board of directors.

General Health System Foundation (LA) (http://www.generalhealth.org/giving.php)
Based in Baton Rouge, Louisiana, the General Health System Foundation is committed to improving that community's access to healthcare services. The organization provides opportunities for education and assistance, as well as support for affiliates of the General Health System (GHS), a network of healthcare providers. The foundation is described briefly on a page of the GHS Web site.

Genesis Health Services Foundation (IA) (http://www.genesishealth.com)
The Genesis Health System, based in Davenport, Iowa, supports its Health Services Foundation in order to enhance services at the Genesis Medical Centers. Visitors to the Genesis Health System Web site will find detailed information on the Medical Centers and Health System organizations. Limited information about the foundation is available in recent articles through the Volunteer/Donate link. Contact information is provided for further details.

Georgia Humanities Council (GA) (http://www.georgiahumanities.org/)
The Georgia Humanities Council, the state affiliate of the National Endowment for the Humanities, was founded in 1970 to support and conduct local and statewide educational programs in the humanities. In addition to descriptions of and guidelines for its four grant programs—Special Program Grants, Public Program Grants, Planning/Consultant Grants, and Teacher Enrichment Grants—the council's Web site also provides information about a range of humanities resources (Web sites, book discussion groups, video resources, etc.) and contact information.

The German Marshall Fund of the United States (DC) (http://www.gmfus.org)
The German Marshall Fund of the United States was created in 1972 by the German people to memorialize post-WWII aid from the Marshall Plan. Headquartered in Washington, D.C., in the United States and in Berlin, Germany, the fund's goal "is to promote cooperation and networking between the United States, Western Europe, and the newly democratic countries of Central and Eastern Europe in the areas of political, economic, and environmental reforms." The fund's areas of interest include economics, the environment, foreign policy, and immigration and integration. Funding is made through grants and fellowship programs, both of which are detailed extensively on the fund's Web site and are designed to involve people and efforts on both sides of the Atlantic. Past grant and fellowship recipients, guidelines and limitations to funding, transatlantic resource links, the annual report, and board and staff information are all available on the fund's Web site.

Gifts In Kind International (VA) (http://www.giftsinkind.org/)
Gifts In Kind helps businesses to effectively and efficiently donate their products to charities. Its donation programs include the areas of technology, community service, community rebuilding, and youth/education. The organization's Web site provides information on the donation process for nonprofits wishing to receive products. The site also provides donor and partnership information, as well as information on new products, programs, and reports.

Elizabeth Glaser Pediatric AIDS Foundation (CA) (http://www.pedaids.org/)
Established in 1988, the Elizabeth Glaser Pediatric AIDS Foundation works to "identify, fund, and conduct critical pediatric research that will lead to better treatments and prevention of HIV infection in infants and children, to reduce and prevent HIV transmission from mother to child, and to accelerate the discovery of new treatments for other serious and life-threatening pediatric diseases." The foundation supports a number of research grant programs, including the Elizabeth Glaser Scientist Awards, Basic Research Grants, Scholar Awards, Short-Term Awards, and Student Intern Awards, all of which are described on the foundation's Web site, including application guidelines and forms. The site also provides a brief history of the foundation, facts about pediatric AIDS, staff and board listings, foundation-related news, and information for donors.

The Glaucoma Foundation (NY) (http://www.glaucomafoundation.org)
Established in 1984, the Glaucoma Foundation is dedicated to glaucoma research and public education worldwide. The New York City-based foundation's mission is "to create a world without blindness." The foundation funds research specifically in the areas of optic nerve rescue and restoration and the molecular genetics of glaucoma. The foundation also sponsors outreach and educational programs designed to raise awareness about prevention of the disease and assist those who have been diagnosed with glaucoma. The foundation's Web site offers grant guidelines and applications; a guide for glaucoma patients and their families; an online version of the foundation's newsletter, *Eye to Eye*; a calendar of events; press releases; and information on support groups for glaucoma patients.

Glaucoma Research Foundation (CA) (http://www.glaucoma.org/)
The Glaucoma Research Foundation funds research to find a cure for glaucoma. Funding goes to research in the United States and in other countries, particularly collaborative projects across disciplines. Current research explores such subjects as genetic links to

glaucoma, optic nerve analysis, new medications, and laser treatments. The Research area of the foundation's Web site provides information on the grants policy, grantees list, and program details. The Web site also provides information on the disease, a support network, a link to online donation opportunities, and contact information.

Global Fund for Women (CA) (http://www.globalfundforwomen.org)
The San Francisco-based Global Fund for Women is an international network of women and men "committed to a world of equality and social justice," which makes grants to support women's groups outside of the United States. The fund provides support to address human rights issues including literacy, domestic violence, economic autonomy, the international trafficking of women, and more. The fund's Web site, which is available in a number of languages, provides program descriptions, grant application guidelines and criteria, grantee profiles, a listing of the fund's board of directors and advisory council, detailed accounts of recent activities, links to nonprofit resources and sites concerned with women's issues, and an electronic donation pledge form.

Global Greengrants Fund (CO) (http://www.greengrants.org/)
The Boulder, Colorado-based Global Greengrants Fund "supports grassroots groups working for environmental justice and sustainability around the world." The organization helps fund a wide range of community-based initiatives that protect the environment in the most underserved and threatened regions on earth. Grants are made to pre-selected organizations recommended by volunteers and regional advisory committees of local environmental leaders. The fund's Web site contains a grants list based on region, background information on members of the advisory board and links to their organizations, links to related resources, and contact information. Any page on the site can be translated into French, German, Italian, Spanish, or Portuguese.

The Arnold P. Gold Foundation (NJ) (http://www.humanism-in-medicine.org/)
Established in 1988, the Englewood, New Jersey-based Arnold P. Gold Foundation works to "foster humanism in medicine" and emphasize the tradition of compassion in the doctor-patient relationship. The foundation raises funds to support advances in the development, implementation, evaluation, and replication of innovative medical educational programs and projects to influence the way physicians are trained. The foundation accepts grant applications from schools of medicine, osteopathy, and naturopathy to support medical education programs emphasizing humanism in the educational process. The foundation's Web site provides information about the foundation's programs for medical students, residents, and educators; grant application procedures; a printable grant request form; lists of past award recipients; a public forum and bulletin board; and contact information.

Golden Apple Foundation (IL) (http://www.goldenapple.org/)
The Chicago-based Golden Apple Foundation was created in 1985 to recognize excellence in teaching and seeks to "publicly honor excellent (Pre-K-12) teachers and provide them the means to have an impact on their profession." The foundation recognizes ten outstanding teachers a year, who then become fellows that participate in programs administered by the foundation. The foundation's Web site provides details on its awards programs and benefits to winners, a calendar of upcoming events, news, and donation information.

Good Samaritan Foundation, Inc. (KY) (http://www.gsfky.org/)
The Good Samaritan Foundation, Inc., of Lexington, Kentucky, is committed to "initiating, participating in, and supporting activities which focus on improving the health status of Kentuckians." The foundation supports county-wide surveys, local and statewide needs assessment programs, rural and urban healthcare programs, nursing scholarships and internships, and various clinics. The foundation's Web site includes grant guidelines, a printable grant application, a list of the officers and trustees, and information about the foundation's programs.

Grace Children's Foundation (NY) (http://www.gracechildren.org/GCF_Home.html)
The Grace Children's Foundation is a New York-based organization that seeks to improve the lives of China's orphans through directed health, education, and humanitarian aid programs in cooperation with the Chinese officials responsible for their care. The three distinct programs are geared towards making the lives of these children more positive and giving them opportunities for the future. The foundation's Web site provides information about the foundation's mission and contact information.

Grammy Awards Grant Program (CA) (http://grammy.com/grants.html)
The Grammy Awards Grant Program was established in California by the Recording Academy to distribute grants to organizations and individuals to support efforts that advance: the archiving and preservation of the music and recorded sound heritage of the Americas; research and research implementation projects related to music such as teaching methodology in early childhood and the impact of music study on early childhood and human development; and the medical and occupational well-being of music professionals. The Grammy Awards' Web site includes application procedures, downloadable grant applications, and contact information.

Grantmakers in Health (DC) (http://www.gih.org)
Formed in 1982, Grantmakers in Health (GIH) is a resource in the field of health philanthropy, "dedicated to helping foundations and corporate giving programs improve the nation's health." The organization disseminates information on health philanthropy and grantmaking through consultations, studies, workshops, and publications, among other resources. The GIH Web site features a members-only database of grants and grantmakers, a resource center for health foundations, a calendar of events, and publications.

Great Lakes Fishery Trust (MI) (http://www.glft.org/)
The Lansing, Michigan-based Great Lakes Fishery Trust was created in 1996 to "provide funding to enhance, protect, and rehabilitate Great Lakes fishery resources." The trust provides funding to nonprofit organizations, educational institutions, and government agencies for projects related to Great Lakes fisheries to provide mitigation for fish losses. The trust funds programs in education, research on Great Lakes fisheries and population rehabilitation, fishing access, fisheries habitat protection and restoration, and other projects. The trust's Web site provides detailed information about current funding programs, deadlines, and downloadable request for proposals; lists of previous grants; information about trustees and the trust's advisory team; recent press releases; and annual reports.

Great Lakes Protection Fund (IL) (http://www.glpf.org/)
The Great Lakes Protection Fund was established by the Council of Great Lakes Governors and the Center for the Great Lakes in 1989 as a "permanent environmental endowment that supports collaborative actions to improve the health of the Great Lakes ecosystem." Headquartered in Chicago, the fund maintains state programs in Michigan, New York, Pennsylvania, Wisconsin, Ohio, and Minnesota. The fund finances projects that lead to tangible improvements in the health of the Great Lakes ecosystem, promote the interdependence of healthy ecological and economic systems, and are innovative, creative, and venturesome. The fund provides financial support to nonprofit organizations, for-profit businesses, government agencies, and individuals. The fund's Web site provides funding guidelines, annual reports, an extensive archive of past grants, links to other resources, and contact information.

Greater Augusta Arts Council, Inc. (GA) (http://www.augustaarts.com)
Founded in 1968, the mission of the Greater Augusta Arts Council, Inc., is "to advance the arts and enrich the quality of life in Augusta and the Central Savannah River Area" of Georgia. The council sponsors art and literary competitions and showcases; information and downloadable applications are available on the council's Web site. The site also provides information on upcoming events, membership, local opportunities for artists, and the council's ongoing services.

Greater Seattle Business Association (WA) (http://www.the-GSBA.org)
The Greater Seattle Business Association (GSBA), "sometimes called the 'Gay and Lesbian Chamber of Commerce,' includes over 800 members who join together to promote and support the lesbian and gay business and professional community." GSBA offers two scholarship programs to provide support to lesbian, gay, bisexual, transgender (LGBT) and questioning students and children from LGBT families: the GSBA Scholarship Fund, which targets undergraduates in Washington State who demonstrate need and potential leadership for the LGBT community, and the Pride Foundation scholarships, which provide support for undergraduate and graduate students in Washington, Oregon, Idaho, Montana, and Alaska. The association's Web site provides scholarship guidelines, information on the association's other activities, and a business and community resource directory.

Green Empowerment (OR) (http://www.greenempowerment.org)
Established in 1997 in Portland, Oregon, Green Empowerment works "to promote community-based renewable energy projects internationally to generate social and environmental progress." Through environmentally-friendly energy sources, the organization's projects provide residential lighting and electricity, power for schools and clinics, and energy for income-generating equipment in international communities. The Green Empowerment Web site includes descriptions of these projects and their host communities, links to green energy resources, downloadable newsletters, and contact information.

Greensboro Justice Fund, Inc. (MA) (http://www.gjf.org)
Based in Northampton, Massachusetts, the Greensboro Justice Fund, Inc., is dedicated to the service of those fighting for human dignity against bigotry in the South today. The fund supports grassroots organizations and activists in the South that works for economic justice, workers' rights, and political empowerment and work to end racism, homophobic discrimination, violence, religious intolerance, police brutality, right-wing attacks, and environmental injustice. The fund particularly supports groups that seek to address root causes of economic and social injustice and that develop links between issues and across diverse communities. Projects must be located in Virginia, North Carolina, South Carolina, Georgia, Florida, Alabama, Mississippi, Kentucky, Tennessee, Louisiana, or Arkansas. The fund's Web site provides grant guidelines and an application form, related links, an online newsletter, a history of the organization, and contact information.

Group Health Community Foundation (WA) (http://www.ghcfoundation.org)
The Group Health Community Foundation was founded in 1983 and works "to transform communities through philanthropy, healthcare innovation, research, and community partnerships" in the Pacific Northwest. The foundation focuses its work on improving the health of children and adolescents and promoting diversity within healthcare. The foundation's Web site provides information on its grants, community programs, and health evaluation services; news and events; and contact information.

Harris County Hospital District Foundation (TX) (http://hchdfoundation.org/)
With headquarters in Houston, Texas, the Harris County Hospital District Foundation was founded in 1992 "to operate a charitable, scientific, and educational entity solely for the benefit of the Harris County Hospital District," which mainly involves "serving the medically indigent population with high quality care and serving the general population with unique healthcare programs and services." Some of the foundation's ongoing projects include funding a mobile health unit, literacy program, and immunization van. Other healthcare-related projects and services are described on the foundation's Web site along with upcoming events, a list of the board of trustees, and contact information.

Harvard-Yenching Institute (MA) (http://www.harvard-yenching.org)
The Harvard-Yenching Institute was founded in Cambridge, Massachusetts, in 1928 and is "dedicated to the advancement of higher education in the humanities and social sciences in East and Southeast Asia." This dedication manifests itself through the institute's support of the Harvard-Yenching Library, the publication of journals and books on East Asian

literature and history, and scholarships to students and faculty from East and Southeast Asian universities. The institute's Web site provides information on three types of scholarships: the Doctoral Scholars Program, Visiting Scholars Program, and Visiting Fellows Program. The site also includes details on current scholars and alumni.

Hawai'i Committee for the Humanities (HI) (http://www.hihumanities.org)
The Hawai'i Committee for the Humanities was founded in 1972 to promote and support public awareness in Hawai'i of the humanities. The committee offers grants primarily to nonprofit organizations that operate humanities programs, although a limited number of smaller grants are temporarily available for research by individuals and preservation and publications projects by nonprofits. The committee's Web site provides grant program information, including downloadable applications and instructions; humanities resources; information on Hawai'i History Day and other programs; and contact information.

Haymarket People's Fund (MA) (http://www.haymarket.org/)
Established in 1974, the Haymarket People's Fund in Boston, Massachusetts, is committed to providing funding and other assistance to groups that believe social change is possible and are working for solutions that address the causes of social problems. Applicants must conduct work within New England (Connecticut, Maine, Massachusetts, New Hampshire, Rhode Island, and Vermont); engage in grassroots organizing; or provide resources for grassroots organizing efforts. The fund's Web site provides grant guidelines and information on recent grantees, as well as details on the fund's other programs and activities.

Headwaters Fund (MN) (http://www.headwatersfund.org)
The Minneapolis-based Headwaters Fund is "a catalyst for social change that supports grassroots communities working to create social, economic, and racial justice." Through the Social Change Fund, the organization provides financial and organizational resources to grassroots organizations primarily in the Minneapolis/St. Paul metropolitan area whose programs address the root causes of social, political, environmental, and economic injustice. Support is also offered through the Fund of the Sacred Circle, which is directed toward grassroots groups or projects in Minnesota or Wisconsin engaged in social change organizing. The fund's Web site provides grant guidelines, information about donor opportunities, community and capacity building tools and events, and contact information.

Health Education Resource Organization, Inc. (MD) (http://www.hero-mcrc.org/index.html)
Founded in 1983 in Baltimore, Maryland, the Health Education Resource Organization, Inc.'s (HERO) mission is "to advocate for and provide direct care to people affected by HIV disease and to educate the community about HIV disease." The organization provides a range of services, including a community resource center, prevention education services, legal services, and case management to individuals with HIV/AIDS in the greater Baltimore area. The HERO Web site includes details on the organization's programs; a listing of upcoming community events; opportunities for volunteers; and information about the AIDSWALK, the group's largest fundraising event; and contact information.

Health Foundation of South Florida (FL) (http://www.hfsf.org/)
Created in 1993, the Health Foundation of South Florida exists for charitable, scientific, and educational purposes to advance the health and well-being of the people of Broward, Miami-Dade, and Monroe Counties. The foundation awards funding to support efforts at the neighborhood, county, and regional levels to improve the health of underserved individuals and families. Goals of the grant program include increasing access to healthcare services, promoting healthy lifestyles, and improving the effectiveness of the healthcare system for the poor and uninsured. The foundation's Web site offers a list of grant recipients, application guidelines and information for requesting an application, updates on special event fundraisers, and the foundation's newsletter.

Health Professions Education Foundation (CA) (http://www.healthprofessions.ca.gov/applications.htm)

The mission of the Health Professions Education Foundation is to improve healthcare in underserved areas of California by providing grants to health professional students dedicated to serving the underserved. The foundation awards scholarship and loan repayment grants to health professional students from economically disadvantaged backgrounds and demographically underrepresented groups, who are committed to practicing in underserved areas. The foundation's Web site describes the scholarship programs and other funding opportunities, and provides contact information.

Health Trust of Santa Clara Valley (CA) (http://www.healthtrust.org/)

The Health Trust of Santa Clara Valley was formed in 1996 with proceeds from the sale of the Good Samaritan Health System. The trust makes grants to nonprofit organizations that provide direct preventive health and wellness services, and operates community health programs that fill gaps in current health prevention services. Funding is offered through Good Samaritan Grants, which support grassroots health projects; Health Partnership Grants, for medically related services delivered by hospitals or by community-based organizations; and other award programs. The trust's Web site provides details on the trust's grant programs and other activities, donor and volunteer information, a listing of board and staff members, and contact information.

HealthONE Alliance (CO) (http://www.health1.org/)

Located in Denver, the HealthONE Alliance is dedicated to "supporting medical education, research, and philanthropy" designed to address the healthcare needs of citizens in metro Denver and throughout Colorado. Through its grant program, the alliance seeks to fund "innovative start-up programs led by dedicated people working to improve the health and well-being of Colorado's citizens." In addition to grantmaking, the alliance offers advanced training for healthcare professionals, administers research projects and clinical trials, and sponsors community health programs. The alliance's Web site provides grant guidelines and procedures, descriptions of current programs and priorities, and contact information.

The Daniel Heumann Fund for Spinal Cord Research, Inc. (VA) (http://www.heumannfund.org)

Founded in 1986, the Daniel Heumann Fund for Spinal Cord Research, Inc., provides funding for projects deemed worthy of financial support in the field of spinal research and neurosciences. The fund supports qualifying institutions performing ongoing research in the field. The fund's Web site provides a listing of organizations supported by the fund, information on how to become a contributor, a board listing, and contact information.

Hispanic Federation of New York City (NY) (http://www.hispanicfederation.org)

The Hispanic Federation of New York City, a membership organization of health and human services agencies, serves Latinos in the tri-state area of New York, New Jersey, and Connecticut. The federation's mission is "to build and strengthen community-based organizations which provide Latinos with a host of services, including immigration services, healthcare, economic development, job training, AIDS prevention, youth services, leadership development, and housing." The federation provides support through fund development and grantmaking, advocacy, and technical assistance for nonprofits. The federation's Web site offers details on its support programs, an extensive list of links to related resources, a local arts calendar, details on publications, and contact information.

Hispanic Scholarship Fund, Inc. (CA) (http://www.hsf.net/)

The Hispanic Scholarship Fund, Inc., was established in 1975 in San Francisco, California, to "recognize and reward outstanding Hispanic students in higher education throughout the United States and Puerto Rico." Scholarships are given in three major categories to American citizens and permanent residents of Hispanic background: the College Retention/General Program is for students at four-year colleges; the High School Program supports graduating seniors who have been accepted at a college; and the Community College Transfer

Program is for community college attendees or graduates who have the potential to succeed at a four-year college. The fund's Web site includes information and application procedures for each of these programs, as well as for other partnership and internship opportunities; information on general college aid; a list of other organizations offering scholarships to Latino students; a list of internship programs that seek Latinos; and information on the fund's operations and sponsors.

Hogg Foundation for Mental Health (TX) (http://hogg1.lac.utexas.edu/Default.html)
Since 1940, the mission of the Hogg Foundation for Mental Health has been "to develop and conduct . . . a broad mental health program of great benefit to the people of Texas" through education and grants supporting mental health service projects and research efforts. The foundation gives priority to projects in the areas of children and their families, youth development, and minority mental health. The foundation's Web site includes a short history of the Hogg family, grant restrictions and application guidelines, grants listings, a publications list, a staff listing with e-mail addresses, and information about the Regional Foundation Library, a longtime member of the Foundation Center's Cooperating Collections network.

The Holy Land Foundation (DC) (http://www.d-holliday.com/holyland/default.htm)
The Holy Land Foundation was founded in 1994 "to raise funds and provide motivation and incentives for Christians to remain in the land of their birth" through a scholarship program, job employment opportunities, subsidized housing, and a medical clinic in Jericho. The foundation's Web site provides a history of the Holy Land, the foundation, and its founding by the Franciscan Order; details on the foundation's current programs and academic ecumenical activities; and contact information.

The Horizon Foundation of Howard County, Inc. (MD) (http://www.thehorizonfoundation.org)
Established in 1998, the Horizon Foundation of Howard County, Inc., promotes and enhances the health and wellness of the Howard County, Maryland, community. The foundation provides grants in the areas of adolescent health and wellness, substance abuse, and older adult health. The grantmaking program provides support through proactive grants, capacity building grants, Strategic Initiatives Program grants, Community Health Issues Program grants, and discretionary grants. The foundation's Web site provides a description of current initiatives, a review of current publications, board and staff listings, and contact information.

Hospice Foundation for the Central Coast (CA) (http://www.hffcc.org)
The Monterey, California-based Hospice Foundation for the Central Coast "helps hospice care providers close the gap between decreasing healthcare reimbursement from insurance payers, such as Medicare, and the cost to provide this specialized, highly personal form of care." The foundation raises and distributes funds to support hospice care in Monterey and San Benito Counties. The foundation's Web site provides guidelines, priorities, limitations, and deadlines for grants; information on current grant recipients; a form to request publications; and contact information.

Hospice Foundation of America (FL) (http://www.hospicefoundation.org/)
The mission of the Hospice Foundation of America is to "provide leadership in the development and application of hospice and its philosophy of care for terminally ill people, with the goal of enhancing the American healthcare system and the role of hospice within it." The foundation designs and implements programs that assist hospices and the terminally ill. The foundation's Web site serves as an online resource for hospice care, providing excerpts from the foundation's own publications, numerous links to online hospice resources, information on an array of foundation projects, and contact information.

The Whitney Houston Foundation for Children (NJ) (http://www.whfoundation.com/)
The Whitney Houston Foundation for Children is dedicated to promoting a positive self-image in children and youth by providing opportunities for them to learn and express themselves in safe, supportive environments. The foundation's Web site includes grant guidelines, application instructions, and donor information.

Houston Regional HIV/AIDS Resource Group, Inc. (TX) (http://hivresourcegroup.org)
The Houston Regional HIV/AIDS Resource Group, Inc., was created in 1993 to "maximize all possible medical, psychosocial, and educational resources to help persons affected by or at risk of HIV/AIDS in the ten county area surrounding Houston, Texas." The group provides services and information to the community through a number of programs, including general HIV services, specific services for women and families, programs for adolescents, and rural services. The group's Web site offers information on eligibility, service providers, funders, feedback forms, a housing database, and more.

HSC Foundation (DC) (http://www.hscfoundation.org/)
The Washington, D.C.-based HSC Foundation seeks to "facilitate access to appropriate care and services for children with special needs and their families in the Washington, D.C., metropolitan area, while conducting regional and national projects with governmental, private, and philanthropic organizations." The foundation's Web site outlines the organization's activities and plans for future programs and provides a staff directory and contact information. The site also offers a Community Services Resource Directory to help families with children with special needs and healthcare professionals find listings for community services throughout the District of Columbia.

Hudson River Foundation (NY) (http://www.hudsonriver.org)
The Hudson River Foundation, located in New York City, was established in 1981 to support "scientific and public policy research, education, and public access projects involving the Hudson River with a focus on making scientific research integral in any decisions made about the River." The foundation's grantmaking program is made up of three funds: the Hudson River Fund, which supports scientific, ecological, and related public policy research; the Hudson River Improvement Fund, which funds projects that enhance public use and enjoyment of the river; and the New York City Environmental Fund, which supports the more general area of the city and Westchester County's public resources. The foundation's Web site provides grant guidelines and application materials, information on the foundation's education and research programs, and contact information.

Howard Hughes Medical Institute (MD) (http://www.hhmi.org/)
In addition to supporting more than 60 medical research laboratories worldwide, the Howard Hughes Medical Institute (HHMI), the nation's largest philanthropy, awards both institutional and individual grants to strengthen education in medicine, biology, and related sciences. The institute's grants program also supports the research of biomedical scientists outside the United States. The institute's Web site provides detailed program descriptions, application guidelines and requirements, a short history of the organization, press releases, the *HHMI Bulletin,* annual reports, a map of HHMI locations, and contact information.

Human Rights Campaign Foundation (DC) (http://www.hrc.org)
The Washington, D.C.-based Human Rights Campaign was founded in 1980 to serve as a national voice for gay and lesbian issues. The campaign "lobbies Congress; mobilizes grassroots action in diverse communities; invests strategically to elect a fair-minded Congress; and increases public understanding through innovative education and communication strategies." As a part of the campaign, the Human Rights Campaign Foundation focuses on educational programs and publications, including the National Coming Out Project, FamilyNet, and WorkNet, which all provide in-depth information on gay and lesbian family and workplace issues, laws, and policies. The campaign's Web site provides a wealth of links and resources on gay and lesbian topics, news, events, priorities of the campaign, and membership information.

The Humana Foundation, Inc. (KY) (http://www.humanafoundation.org/)
Based in Louisville, Kentucky, the Humana Foundation, Inc., is the philanthropic arm of Humana, Inc., one of the nation's largest managed healthcare companies. Established in 1981, the foundation supports charitable organizations and institutions that promote education, health and human services, community development, and the arts in communities where Humana has a business presence. In 1991 the foundation started its scholarship program, designed to assist Humana associates in meeting the cost of sending their children to college. The foundation's Web site provides scholarship and grant application guidelines and instructions, application forms, an aid recipient list, a breakdown of fund distribution by area, descriptions of projects, and contact information.

Humanities Council of Washington, D.C. (DC) (http://wdchumanities.org)
The Humanities Council of Washington, D.C., is the District of Columbia's affiliate of the National Endowment for the Humanities. The council annually supports 60-70 humanities programs in the nation's capitol through its grants program. The council's Web site provides grant information and deadlines, contact information, a calendar of events, information about the council's activities, newsletter subscription information, and donor information.

Humanities Iowa (IA) (http://www.uiowa.edu/~humiowa/)
Humanities Iowa was founded in Iowa City in 1971 as an affiliate of the National Endowment for the Humanities. The group provides grants to support other nonprofit organizations in furthering the humanities in Iowa as well as conducting its own humanities programs across the state. The organization's Web site provides grant guidelines and application materials, a calendar of events, and other humanities resources and publications.

Huntington's Disease Society of America, Inc. (NY) (http://www.hdsa.org)
The New York City-based Huntington's Disease Society of America, Inc., is a national health agency whose mission is to "promote and support research to find a cure for HD, help those affected by the disease and their families, and educate the public and healthcare professionals about HD." The society offers fellowships and grants in two main areas: laboratory research and clinical and epidemiological research. Research funding guidelines, information on requesting applications, information and research about Huntington's disease, a calendar of events, information on local chapters, opportunities to contribute, and board and staff lists are available on the society's Web site.

Idaho Humanities Council (ID) (http://www.idahohumanities.org)
The Idaho Humanities Council partners with civic groups, citizens, and educators to expand public humanities programs in the state. It accomplishes this mission by supporting educational programs for the general public and various target audiences. Grant guidelines and forms, news, information on programs for teachers, humanities resources, and contact and donor information are available on the council's Web site.

Illinois Arts Council Foundation (IL) (http://www.state.il.us/agency/iac/default.htm)
The Illinois Arts Council Foundation was established in 1965 in Chicago to support the development of the arts in Illinois. To this end, the foundation provides financial and technical assistance to artists, arts organizations, and other community organizations that present arts programming. Information on the foundation's grants and programs—including artists fellowships, literary awards, and grants to schools, among others—as well as current news and events, links to related sites, the foundation's newsletter, recent grant recipients, and contact information are available on the foundation's Web site.

Illinois Humanities Council, Inc. (IL) (http://www.prairie.org)
The Illinois Humanities Council, Inc., located in Chicago, was established as an affiliate of the National Endowment for the Arts in 1974. The council is "dedicated to fostering a culture in which the humanities are a vital part of the lives of individuals and communities."

The council's Web site provides funding guidelines, application materials, information on grant workshops, information on ongoing council programs, board and staff lists, an events calendar, maps, and information on exhibits and programs throughout the state.

Illinois State Historical Society (IL) (http://www.prairienet.org/ishs/)
Created in 1899 to support libraries, writing, and research on Illinois, the Springfield-based Illinois State Historical Society works to "foster in citizens a deeper understanding of and appreciation for all Illinois history through programs and publications" and to coordinate and support programs that further this goal. The society offers a series of awards for activities related to the history of Illinois. The society's Web site offers award guidelines, an events calendar, lists of books and other related publications, lists of directors and staff, and information on becoming a member.

Immune Deficiency Foundation (MD) (http://www.primaryimmune.org/)
The Towson, Maryland-based Immune Deficiency Foundation was founded in 1980 "to improve the diagnosis and treatment of patients with primary immunodeficiency diseases through research and education." The foundation funds a scholarship program for individuals with a diagnosed primary immune deficiency and a fellowship program for research into primary immunodeficiency diseases. The foundation's Web site provides program guidelines; information for families, patients, and researchers; and details on the foundation's services, such as free consultations, advocacy groups, discussion groups, and expert advice.

Independent Television Service (CA) (http://www.ITVS.org)
The San Francisco-based Independent Television Service was created by Congress to "create and promote independent media that will expand civic participation by bringing new voices and expressiveness into the public discourse," especially by addressing the needs of underserved minority and youth audiences. The service funds, distributes, and promotes new programs that show diversity, and a range of subjects, viewpoints, and forms. The organization offers a variety of funding programs that are described on its Web site. The site also provides downloadable guidelines and applications, a production manual, links to related resources, and descriptions of recently produced programs.

Indiana Humanities Council (IN) (http://www.ihc4u.org/)
The Indiana Humanities Council supports the humanities in Indiana in cooperation with educational, cultural, and community organizations. The council's grant programs include Humanities Initiative Grants, Indiana Heritage Research Grants, and Historic Preservation Education Grants. The council's Web site offers descriptions of its grant programs, listings of recent grant recipients, information on the organization's activities, articles about the humanities, a listing of humanities resources available to Indiana residents, and contact information.

Information Technology Community Foundation (VA) (http://www.itcf.org/)
The Information Technology Community Foundation, based in Washington, D.C., strives "to help make the greater Washington area a stronger community by providing a platform for charitable giving, voluntarism, and community leadership within the region's technology industry." The foundation's various committees address the need for community investment, development, education, and special events, among other areas. The foundation's Web site provides resources for nonprofit groups and information technology professionals, news about the foundation, information for members, and details about the foundation's partners.

Initiative Foundation (MN) (http://www.ifound.org)
Based in Little Falls, Minnesota, the Initiative Foundation was established in 1986 by the Knight Foundation to improve the quality of life for residents, families, and communities in central Minnesota through integrated community planning, promoting leadership training, and addressing barriers to economic development. The foundation's service area includes

the 14-county area of Benton, Cass, Chisago, Crow Wing, Isanti, Kanabec, Mille Lacs, Morrison, Pine, Sherburne, Stearns, Todd, Wadena, and Wright Counties. The foundation offers funding for innovative projects "that identify and mobilize existing resources and involve local people in creative problem solving." The foundation's Web site includes guidelines and downloadable grant applications for the foundation's funding programs, information on business investment and community planning, and an online contact form.

Initiative Fund of Southeastern and South Central Minnesota (MN) (http://www.semif.org/)

The Initiative Fund of Southeastern and South Central Minnesota is a regional economic and community development fund serving 20 counties in southeastern and south central Minnesota. The fund offers ongoing grant and mini-grant programs, and periodically issues request for proposals to address changing needs within the region. The fund also runs a loan program to help finance new business start-ups and to expand existing businesses. The fund's Web site provides grant and loan guidelines, downloadable applications, business and community resources, links to special projects, and contact information.

Institute for Community Economics, Inc. (MA) (http://www.iceclt.org)

Founded in Springfield, Massachusetts in 1967, the Institute for Community Economics, Inc., is a "national organization that promotes the just allocation of resources in communities in ways that address the needs of low-income families." The institute focuses on affordable housing and community economic development especially through the use of community land trusts (CLTs), a type of nonprofit corporation that was developed by the founders of the institute in the 1960s to acquire and hold land for the benefit of a community. The institute maintains a Revolving Loan Fund, supporting community organizations and CLTs nationwide. The institute's Web site provides a detailed explanation of CLTs and the organization, educational and technical resources on the trusts, and contact and donor information.

Institute of International Education, Inc. (NY) (http://www.iie.org/)

Created in 1919, the renowned Institute of International Education, Inc., is headquartered in New York City, but has offices all over the United States and internationally. The institute's purpose is "strengthening international understanding and cooperation by enabling men and women of talent and enterprise to study, conduct research, and receive practical training outside their own countries." Created in 1946, the Fulbright Program is principally administered by the institute and sponsored by the U.S. Department of State. Grants are made to Americans and residents of other participating countries for university teaching, advanced research, graduate study, and teaching in elementary and secondary schools. The institute also administers over 250 programs internationally. The institute's Web site offers a list of these programs, downloadable applications, information on membership, news, publications, and statistical and policy research.

International Affiliation of Independent Accounting Firms Educational Foundation, Inc. (http://www.iai.org/education/) (FL)

The International Affiliation of Independent Accounting Firms Educational Foundation, Inc., administers the Robert Kaufman Memorial Scholarship Fund to assist member firm employees in pursuing internships. The scholarship program is described on the foundation's Web site.

The International Association of Culinary Professionals Foundation (KY) (http://www.iacpfoundation.com)

The International Association of Culinary Professionals (IACP) Foundation was established in 1984 in Louisville, Kentucky, as the philanthropic partner of IACP. The foundation provides "funds for educational and charitable work related to the culinary profession." Scholarships are a priority of the IACP; the foundation provides funds to qualified applicants for education courses at culinary schools worldwide, as well as for independent study for research projects. The foundation also offers travel grants for food writers and other funding programs. The association's Web site provides information on these opportunities, as well as details on other foundation programs and events.

International Center for Research on Women (DC) (http://www.icrw.org/)
The International Center for Research on Women, founded in 1976, focuses its activities on women's productive and reproductive roles, family status, leadership in society, and management of environmental resources in developing countries. The center's Fellows Program gives development researchers and practitioners from developing countries the opportunity to spend time in Washington, D.C., to conduct independent research, meet policymakers, and refine their skills in data analysis and program development. The center's Web site provides fellowship details, a list of current fellows, news, information on the center's activities, current projects and research, publications, and listings of board, staff, and partners.

The International Center of Journalists, Inc. (DC) (http://www.icfj.org)
Established in 1984 in Washington, D.C., the mission of the International Center of Journalists, Inc., is "to improve the quality of journalism in nations where there is little or no tradition of independent journalism." The center's multilingual Web site provides details on current programs, a variety of fellowships for both journalists abroad and in the United States, media publications, fellowship guidelines, applications, and contact and donor information.

International Community Foundation (CA) (http://www.icfdn.org/)
Established in 1990, the International Community Foundation is committed to fostering lasting philanthropy to benefit international communities throughout the Americas and Asia, with emphasis on Mexico. The foundation supports sustainable communities, the environment, health, education, and culture. The foundation's grant awards have supported projects in Mexico, China, Ecuador, and Canada. The foundation's Web site offers information about its grantmaking activities, geographic restrictions, and contact information.

International Eye Foundation (MD) (http://www.iefusa.org)
Founded in 1961, the International Eye Foundation is dedicated to helping people see by expanding eye care services for those in need; supporting programs targeting avoidable blindness (cataract, trachoma, river blindness, and childhood blindness); providing affordable ophthalmic supplies, equipment, and medicines; and enhancing financial self-sufficiency of eye care providers to reduce dependence on aid. The foundation's Web site includes information about the various programs, board/staff listing, answers to frequently asked questions, and contact information.

**International Foundation of Employee Benefit Plans (WI)
(http://www.ifebp.org/interns/instudnt.asp)**
Based in Brookfield, Wisconsin, the members of the International Foundation of Employee Benefit Plans have been representing employees and their benefit interests since 1954. One of the main services of the foundation is its internship program. Potential interns can review guidelines and eligibility requirements for the programs, as well as available internships listed by state, on the foundation's Web site. Further details on internships and the foundation in general are also available on the site.

**International Franchise Association Educational Foundation (DC)
(http://www.franchise.org/edufound/edufound.asp)**
The Washington, D.C.-based International Franchise Association Educational Foundation is committed "to advancing the highest professional standards for franchising through education and research." The foundation achieves this goal through educational and certificate programs, some of which are offered online, as well as scholarships. Details on scholarships and special programs are available at the foundation's Web site.

International Fund for Animal Welfare (MA) (http://www.ifaw.org)
Located in Yarmouth Port, Massachusetts, the International Fund for Animal Welfare began as an effort to save endangered harp seals on the eastern coast of Canada three decades ago and has grown into an international animal welfare advocacy organization for thousands of animal species. The fund's mission is to "improve the welfare of wild and domestic animals throughout the world by reducing commercial exploitation of animals, protecting wildlife habitats, and assisting animals in distress." Information on the fund's component goals, including details on specific campaigns, animals, and countries of action; publications; information on aiding the fund's projects; campaign results; and worldwide contact information are available on the fund's Web site.

International Life Sciences Institute (DC) (http://www.ilsi.org)
Founded in 1978, the International Life Sciences Institute's goal is to "further the understanding of scientific issues relating to nutrition, food safety, toxicology, risk assessment, and the environment" and improve the well-being of the general public. Based in Washington, D.C., with operations worldwide, the institute works toward its goal through a variety of programs and partnerships with health-related nonprofit organizations. The institute's Web site includes descriptions and links to these programs and institutes, as well as details on ongoing activities and events, numerous publications, membership information, and contact information.

International Partners in Mission (OH) (http://www.clmission.org)
The International Partners in Mission was founded in 1974 in Cleveland Heights, Ohio, to provide "funding and technical assistance to community- and faith-based programs around the world." The organization works with five program areas including children and youth, community building, environmental justice, health, and women. The organization's Web site provides information on the organization's projects; an online archive of current and past issues of *Connections,* the organization's newsletter; and contact information.

International Reading Association, Inc. (DE) (http://www.reading.org)
The International Reading Association, Inc., is a professional membership organization dedicated to promoting high levels of literacy for all by improving the quality of reading instruction, disseminating research and information about reading, and encouraging the lifetime reading habit. Members of the association gain access to a broad range of professional meetings, publications, and other resources, designed to further five goals: professional development, advocacy, partnerships, research, and global literacy development. The association honors educators, authors, and others involved in reading and literacy efforts through its award and grant programs. The association's Web site offers information on these programs as well as a wealth of information on literacy, including news articles, calendar of events, outreach agendas, and contact information.

International Rescue Committee (NY) (http://www.theirc.org/)
Founded in 1933, the International Rescue Committee provides assistance to refugees fleeing racial, religious, and ethnic persecution, as well as those uprooted by war and violence. Areas of interest include children and youth, health, emergency response, resettlement, advocacy, protection, women's issue, immigration, and community collaboration. The committee's Web site provides detailed information about the mission and the areas served.

International Transactional Analysis Association (CA) (http://www.ITAA-NET.org)
The International Transactional Analysis Association was founded to help advance the theory, methods, and principles of transactional analysis. The organization maintains a number of scholarship and grant programs, including the Eric Berne Fund for the Future, Scholarship Grant Fund, and the TAlent Program. The organization's Web site contains grant program overviews, application information, board listings, and contact information.

International Youth Foundation (MD) (http://www.iyfnet.org/)
The International Youth Foundation promotes the positive development of children and youth, ages 5 to 25, around the world by supporting programs that focus on such areas as vocational training, health education, recreation, cultural tolerance, environmental awareness, and the development of leadership, conflict resolution, and decision-making skills. The foundation's Web site provides a listing of international partners, the foundation's programs, contact information, and detailed information about its work.

Irvine Senior Foundation (CA) (http://www.irvineseniors.com)
The Irvine Senior Foundation strives to meet the needs of seniors and their families in the Irvine, California, area. The foundation maintains partnerships with local service providers, and focuses its interests in the areas of adult day healthcare, low-income housing, transportation, nutrition, education, employment, and health. The foundation's Web site offers news on partnerships, details on programs and services, tips and links to further resources, and contact information.

The Izumi Foundation (MA) (http://www.izumi.org/)
Based in Boston, Massachusetts, the Izumi Foundation was created in hopes of alleviating human suffering through improving and extending healthcare to all living creatures. The foundation's goals are to "address the root causes of human suffering, to increase compassion and caring among all human beings, and to promote a society that respects all living things." Support is given to projects that address the underlying causes of disease and persistent healthcare problems, use innovative and creative solutions to promote sustainable outcomes, recognize the inter-relationship between disease and poverty, develop/strengthen leadership in healthcare, and promote collaboration and partnership between healthcare providers. The foundation's Web site includes information on application procedures and contact information.

The Henry M. Jackson Foundation (WA) (http://www.hmjackson.org/)
The Seattle-based Henry M. Jackson Foundation was created in 1983 to address issues that were important to the late senator, including "promoting dialogue between the academic and policy worlds, between the public and private sectors, and between citizens and their government." The foundation makes grants in four program areas: Education and Advanced Research in International Affairs, Environment and Natural Resources Management, Public Service, and Human Rights. The foundation's Web site includes grant guidelines and restrictions, and grants lists by category.

Jefferson Foundation (CO) (http://www.jeffersonfoundation.org)
The Jefferson Foundation is based in Lakewood, Colorado, and is a public education foundation serving Jefferson County. The foundation provides various grants within the Jefferson School District for teachers and students. The foundation's Web site includes a listing of past grants, current grant guidelines, and resources for teachers and students.

Jewish Communal Fund (NY) (http://www.JewishCommunalFund.org)
Through its many donor-advised funds, the Jewish Communal Fund provides support to an array of voluntary organizations—sectarian and nonsectarian—that respond to needs in all sectors of society, including health, education, social services, the environment, religion, and the arts. The fund's Web site includes information on its operations and guidelines for those wishing to establish a donor-advised fund.

Jewish Community Federation of Cleveland (OH) (http://www.jewishcleveland.org/)
The Jewish Community Federation of Cleveland raises money and distributes it to member organizations in order to meet the various needs of the local Jewish community. The federation's Web site is directed at potential donors and people looking to learn about the Jewish community in Cleveland. The site features a guide to Jewish Cleveland, a page of links to Jewish resources, and the organization's annual report.

Jewish Community Foundation of MetroWest (NJ) (http://www.ujfmetrowest.org)
Located in Whippany, New Jersey, the Jewish Community Foundation of MetroWest is affiliated with the United Jewish Federation of MetroWest and is the central location for endowments, bequests, trusts, and other forms of planned giving in the MetroWest Jewish community. The foundation is made up of hundreds of family funds, many designated for specific programs or fields of interest. The foundation's Web site includes information on creating a fund or endowment and contact information.

Jewish Family and Children's Services of San Francisco, the Peninsula, Marin, and Sonoma Counties (http://www.jfcs.org) (CA)
Jewish Family and Children's Services (JFCS) of San Francisco, the Peninsula, Marin, and Sonoma Counties was founded in 1850 to serve the West Bay area of California. Located in San Francisco, JFCS provides "professional and volunteer services for the purposes of developing, restoring, and maintaining the competency of families and individuals of all ages." JFCS administers services for adults and families, children and youth, people with special needs, refugees and émigrés, and older adults. These programs and services are staffed by volunteers and are described on the organization's Web site. The site also includes research and publications, a feedback form, and featured service organizations.

Jewish Federation of Metropolitan Detroit (MI) (http://www.jfmd.org)
The Jewish Federation of Metropolitan Detroit plays a leadership role in identifying needs within the Jewish community, mobilizing human and financial resources, engaging in communal planning and allocation, and advocating to meet those needs. The federation works with numerous agencies to accomplish its mission and provides services for people in the Detroit Jewish community, including the elderly and youth. Funds raised by the federation through its annual campaign are distributed to many Detroit agencies and several national organizations. The federation does not accept grant proposals. The federation's Web site describes its programs in detail and provides contact information, descriptions of missions and trips, and a community calendar.

Jewish Foundation of Greater Los Angeles (CA) (http://www.jewishfoundationla.org)
The Jewish Foundation of Greater Los Angeles is a clearinghouse for Jewish philanthropists in southern California, directing funds toward a variety of nonprofit organizations and services in Los Angeles, across the United States, in Israel, and elsewhere around the world. Through Legacy Grants, the foundation supports the areas of social service and health agencies, art and cultural institutions, educational institutions and synagogues, among others. Comprehensive Development Grants pair the foundation with other organizations or family foundations mainly focused on Jewish identity and affiliation for youth. Family resources, information for donors, program and grant details, news and publications, answers to frequently asked questions, descriptions of specific grants, funding guidelines, previous recipients, and application procedures are available on the foundation's Web site.

Jewish Fund for Justice (NY) (http://www.jfjustice.org)
Founded in New York City in 1984, the Jewish Fund for Justice works with community-based organizations across the United States to address poverty and its causes. The fund's mission is to "act on the historic commitment of the Jewish people to *tzedakah* (righteous giving) and *tikkun olam* (repair of the world)" to fight poverty in the United States. This is done by making grants to grassroots organizations, sponsoring awareness programs directed at Jewish Americans, and encouraging direct Jewish involvement. The grants program focuses on economic justice; building community; investing in youth; and assisting new Americans, women in poverty, and Jewish social justice groups. The fund's Web site provides funding guidelines, an information request form, staff and board lists, educational materials, and links to grantee Web sites.

Elton John AIDS Foundation (CA) (http://www.ejaf.org/)
The London- and Los Angeles-based Elton John AIDS Foundation was founded in 1992 by entertainer Elton John to fund programs that "provide services to people living with

HIV/AIDS and educational programs targeted at AIDS prevention, and/or elimination of prejudice and discrimination against HIV affected individuals." Services supported by the foundation include food banks and meal programs, legal aid, hospice and housing, counseling and support groups, education outreach programs, at-home care, and pediatric treatment centers. The foundation's Web site provides a description of its programs, contact information for those seeking grants, and areas for purchasing merchandise or otherwise contributing to the foundation.

Magic Johnson Foundation (CA) (http://www.magicjohnson.org/)
Originally established to raise funds for HIV/AIDS education and prevention programs, the Magic Johnson Foundation now awards grants to community-based organizations involved with education, health, and social programs for inner-city youth. The foundation does not accept unsolicited grant proposals. The foundation also supports a variety of special initiatives related to health, education, and cultural programs. The foundation's Web site describes these programs and provides HIV/AIDS and general health information, a calendar of upcoming events, and donor and contact information.

Just Tzedakah (MD) (http://www.just-tzedakah.org)
Just Tzedakah's mission is to "provide tools and encouragement to increase the level and effectiveness of *tzedakah* (charity) among American Jews." To this end, the West Bethesda, Maryland-based group provides a wealth of resources on its Web site to promote thoughtful charitable donations among Jewish individuals. The site includes giving guidelines, reports on Jewish charitable organizations, excerpts from classical Jewish sources, and the opportunity to make donations online. Each section includes answers to frequently asked questions and links for further information and resources.

Kansas Humanities Council (KS) (http://www.kansashumanities.org)
The Kansas Humanities Council, located in Topeka, was created to "promote understanding of the history, traditions, and ideas that shape our lives and the communities in which we live." The council has two main grant programs: the Humanities Program, which supports programs that make the humanities accessible to all Kansans; and the Heritage Programs, which offer grants to community groups that preserve Kansas' history. The council's Web site offers grant application guidelines and deadlines, advice on contacting council staff in regard to proposed projects, a cultural events calendar, lists of the board of trustees and staff, information on making a gift to the council, and contact information.

Kapi'olani Health Foundation (HI) (http://www.kapiolani.org)
The Kapi'olani Health Foundation is dedicated to fulfilling the health needs of all the people of Hawaii. Since its inception, the foundation has developed a broad range of health and medical services to meet the needs of the men, women, and children of the community. The foundation works through its two flagship hospitals, the Kapi'olani Medical Center for Women and Children and the Kapi'olani Medical Center at Pali Momi, as well as other health-related companies such as the Kapi'olani Health Research Institute, and the Kapi'olani Women's Center. The foundation's Web site offers information about its mission and the ongoing programs.

Kelly for Kids Foundation (NY) (http://www.jimkelly.com/charities/charitable.html)
Jim Kelly of the Buffalo Bills founded the Kelly for Kids Foundation (KFK) in 1987 to provide funding and support to organizations that operate for the benefit of disadvantaged and handicapped youths throughout western New York. The foundation's Web site provides information on the charity as well as a link to the Hunter's Hope Foundation, which was established by Kelly and his wife to raise awareness of Krabbe's disease (globoid-cell leukodystrophy).

John F. Kennedy Center for the Performing Arts (DC) (http://www.kennedy-center.org)
The John F. Kennedy Center for the Performing Arts, located in Washington, D.C., serves as one of the nation's premier arts facilities. The center "strives to commission, produce,

and present performances reflecting the highest standards of excellence and diversity indicative of the world in which we live, and to make those performances accessible to the broadest possible audience through arts education." Education and arts outreach programs are a high priority for the Kennedy Center. The center runs professional development programs for teachers, administrators, arts supervisors, and schools; provides paid internships for college students; supplies teaching resources; teaches courses and classes; and supports school and community initiatives in the metropolitan Washington, D.C., area. Additionally, the Kennedy Center awards a number of prizes to artists annually, as well as awarding grants through the Fund for New American Plays. The center's Web site offers a wealth of information on all of the center's programs and performances, including application guidelines for its award and professional development programs.

John F. Kennedy Library Foundation (MA) (http://www.cs.umb.edu/jfklibrary/index.htm)
Boston's John F. Kennedy Library Foundation was founded in 1984 and retains the same mission as the library itself: "To capture, preserve, and exhibit for scholars and visitors of future generations the history and essence of President Kennedy's life and career, and to encourage understanding, respect for, and participation in public service." The foundation's Profile in Courage Award, inspired by the Pulitzer Prize-winning book of the same name by John F. Kennedy, honors public officials who demonstrate the kind of political courage outlined in the book. The Profile in Courage Essay, open to high school students, covers the same theme. Additionally, the foundation funds research grants to defray costs incurred while researching in the library and an archival internship in the library. Information and an online application for these grants can be found on the foundation's Web site, along with its newsletter and further details about the foundation's activities and awards.

Kentucky Humanities Council (KY) (http://www.kyhumanities.org/)
The Kentucky Humanities Council, an affiliate of the National Endowment for the Humanities, provides grants and services to nonprofit organizations seeking to foster greater understanding of the humanities. Programs traditionally funded by the council include, but are not limited to, conferences, lectures, radio and video productions, exhibits, teacher training and development of curricular materials, interpretive programs for festivals, book discussions, and planning for future projects. The council's Web site provides grant guidelines; information about its speakers bureau, living history performances, and book discussion programs; a listing of board and staff members; and contact information.

Kern County Youth Mariachi Foundation (CA) (http://www.kernmariachi.com)
Located in Bakersfield, California, the Kern County Youth Mariachi Foundation is dedicated to "ensuring that local youth have the opportunity to learn and carry on the rich traditions and culture of Mariachi and its music." As a cultural, youth-focused organization, the foundation works to provide adult role models, expose students ages 7 to 17 to the traditions of the Hispanic culture, and provide educational and academic scholarship assistance. Programs, scholarships, and upcoming events are detailed on the foundation's Web site, along with contact information.

The Kids Foundation for Developmental Disabilities (NY) (http://www.kfdd.org)
Established in 2000, the Kids Foundation for Developmental Disabilities was developed to provide critical funding to organizations that provide education and therapeutic services to children with developmental disabilities in the New York metropolitan area. The foundation's Web site provides a listing of recent grant recipients, downloadable grant applications, a board listing, and contact information.

Kingston Technology Company, Inc. (CA) (http://www.kingston.com/company/charity.asp)
The Fountain Valley, California-based Kingston Technology Company, Inc.'s Charitable Giving Program follows the core values of the company itself, focusing on organizations that support education, technology, and the well-being of citizens. Specific areas of interest are education, community service, and arts and culture. The company's Web site provides funding guidelines, limitations, general application procedures, and contact information.

KnowledgeWorks Foundation (OH) (http://www.kwfdn.org)

Formerly the Thomas L. Conlan Education Foundation, the KnowledgeWorks Foundation of Cincinnati, Ohio, is "committed to furthering universal access to educational opportunities for individuals to achieve success and for the betterment of society." The foundation focuses its work on college access, school facilities planning and design, school improvement, early childhood literacy, and the education needs of children in substitute care. Guidelines and eligibility information for grant programs in these areas are available on the foundation's Web site, which also provides a resource library, pressroom, and related links.

Susan G. Komen Breast Cancer Foundation (TX) (http://www.komen.org/)

Founded in 1982 and best known as the sponsor of the 5K Komen Race for the Cure runs to raise funds for national and local breast cancer initiatives, the Susan G. Komen Breast Cancer Foundation is the largest private funder of research dedicated solely to breast cancer in the United States. The foundation's National Grant Program awards grants and fellowships in basic and clinical research, as well as grants for breast cancer education, treatment, and screening projects for the medically underserved. Descriptions of the foundation's programs, downloadable application forms, a list of Komen affiliates awarding grants locally, information about the Komen Race for the Cure, and the foundation's annual report are available on the foundation's Web site. The site also provides access to BreastCancerInfo.com, which offers general health and breast cancer news and information, an online forum, and a calendar of events.

Kosciuszko Foundation, Inc. (NY) (http://www.kosciuszkofoundation.org/)

Headquartered in New York City, the national Kosciuszko Foundation, Inc., was founded in 1925 to "promote educational and cultural exchanges between the United States and Poland and to increase American understanding of Polish culture and history." The foundation offers graduate school scholarships to Americans of Polish descent and Americans whose studies primarily relate to Polish subjects, and offers a series of grants and scholarships to Polish citizens who wish to study in the United States. The foundation also sponsors a voice competition, a piano competition, and an award to recognize scholarly works on subjects of interest to the foundation. The foundation's Web site includes application guidelines, deadline information, and application forms for its scholarships and awards, as well as information on current events, cultural events, and summer programs in Poland.

Lambda Chi Alpha Educational Foundation, Inc. (IN)
(http://www.lambdachi.org/foundation/)

Formed in 1946 as the charitable arm of the Lambda Chi Alpha fraternity, the Lambda Chi Alpha Educational Foundation, Inc., seeks "to continue and expand leadership development and educational programs, and to perpetuate the existence of these programs for future generations of youth as a complement to higher education." This effort is centered on scholarships to undergraduate and graduate student brothers of the fraternity. Scholarship applications and guidelines are posted on the foundation's Web site, along with its annual report, the current foundation newsletter, and information for donors.

Landscape Architecture Foundation (DC)
(http://www.asla.org/nonmembers/laf_section.cfm)

The Landscape Architecture Foundation, located in Washington, D.C., is the philanthropic arm of the American Society of Landscape Architects, whose mission is to "lead, to educate, and to participate in the careful stewardship, wise planning, and artful design of our cultural and natural environments." The foundation offers a variety of fellowships and scholarships to undergraduate and graduate students in the landscape architecture field. Deadlines and details about how to apply and information about the foundation's officers, its recruitment Web site (LAprofession.org) aimed at bringing in new people to the landscape architecture field, and other initiatives are available on the foundation's Web site.

The Leaky Foundation (CA) (http://www.leakeyfoundation.org)
The San Francisco-based Leaky Foundation supports anthropological research, as envisioned by its namesake, anthropologist Louis Leaky. This mission includes a multidisciplinary approach to the study of human evolution. The foundation maintains general research grants and fellowships. The foundation's Web site provides downloadable guidelines and application forms, recent news articles, information on upcoming events and travel opportunities, and membership information.

Legal Foundation of Washington (WA) (http://www.legalfoundation.org)
The Legal Foundation of Washington, established in 1984, seeks to fund legal and educational programs for low-income persons. The Washington Supreme Court mandated the creation of the foundation to administer the Interest on Lawyer's Trust Accounts (IOLTA) and provide "free access to justice in civil cases for the poorest and most vulnerable families throughout Washington State." The foundation also supports community and education programs for lawyers, social service providers, and the public toward greater knowledge about and defense of civil legal assistance for the poor. The foundation's Web site provides a list of staff, financial information, information on grants and grant applications, information on IOLTA, events, information on internships at the foundation, community links, and contact information.

Legal Services Corporation (DC) (http://www.lsc.gov)
The Legal Services Corporation is a private, nonprofit corporation established by Congress in 1974 "to promote equal access to the system of justice and improve opportunities for low-income people throughout the United States by making grants for the provision of high-quality civil legal assistance to those who would be otherwise unable to afford legal counsel." The corporation provides grants to approximately 179 local legal aid programs that offer legal assistance to financially eligible clients throughout the United States. The corporation's Web site provides information on its grant competition, an online form to locate legal aid services, a resource library, annual reports, a pressroom, and a map and listing of regional legal service offices.

The Leukemia and Lymphoma Society (NY) (http://www.leukemia-lymphoma.org)
In addition to sponsoring a broad range of public conferences about leukemia treatment and research, the Leukemia and Lymphoma Society supports worldwide research efforts—both in the lab and clinical applications—toward controlling and finding a cure for leukemia, lymphoma, and myeloma. Grant information, guidelines, and application forms are available in the Science/Professionals area of the society's Web site. The site also includes sections on Patient Services, Disease Information, Advocacy, and How to Help.

Leukemia Research Foundation (IL) (http://www.leukemia-research.org)
Founded in 1946, the Evanston, Illinois-based Leukemia Research Foundation works to "conquer leukemia, lymphoma, and myelodysplastic syndromes by funding research into their causes and cures, and to enrich the quality of life of those touched by these diseases." The foundation's leukemia-related research grant program supports new investigators with preference given to applicants proposing new lines of investigation. Three types of grants are funded: new investigator research grants, postdoctoral fellowships, and physician-scientist postdoctoral fellowships. The foundation's Web site provides funding guidelines, downloadable applications, lists of grant recipients, a medical information resource center, information for patients and their families, an events listing, and opportunities to make a donation.

The Liberace Foundation for the Performing and Creative Arts (NV) (http://www.flashwaremedia.com/liberace/foundation.cfm)
Located in Las Vegas, Nevada, the Liberace Foundation for the Performing and Creative Arts was founded by the pianist and showman in 1976. The foundation's Scholarship Fund funnels support through colleges, universities, and conservatories to talented students in disciplines including music, theater, dance, and the visual arts. Only institutions, not

individuals, are eligible to apply for the scholarship grants through the foundation. The foundation's Web site includes scholarship guidelines and applications, as well as a history of the foundation.

Liberty Hill Foundation (CA) (http://www.libertyhill.org/)
Created in 1976, the Liberty Hill Foundation, located in Santa Monica, California, "promotes progressive social change by funding grassroots community organizations in Los Angeles that empower the disenfranchised and challenge the institutions and attitudes which create economic, social, and racial inequalities." The Grantseekers/Organizers section of the foundation's Web site features information on its funding programs, including the Seed Fund, the Fund for a New Los Angeles, the Environmental Justice Fund, the Social Entrepreneurial Fund, the Lesbian and Gay Community Fund, and the Special Opportunities Fund. The site provides guidelines for each fund with downloadable applications. The site also features an area for Donor/Activists, its annual report, news updates and an events calendar, and information on contributing, including establishing a donor-advised fund.

Library of Michigan Foundation (MI)
(http://www.michigan.gov/hal/0,1607,7-160-17445_19270_19410—-,00.html)
The Library of Michigan Foundation "supports major projects of the Library of Michigan, promotes library resources and services for all of the citizens of Michigan, and accepts private gifts to finance projects for local libraries throughout Michigan." The foundation fulfills its mission by providing support for library programs, including the Abrams Genealogy Collection, library services for the blind and physically handicapped, and cultural and historic preservation of Michigan's printed heritage. Information about foundation programs and its annual report can be found on the Web site.

Libri Foundation (OR) (http://www.librifoundation.org)
The Libri Foundation, located in Eugene, Oregon, was established in 1989 to help " rural libraries acquire quality children's books they could not otherwise afford to buy." The nationwide foundation donates new hardcover children's books to small, rural public libraries in the United States through its Books for Children program. The foundation's Web site includes application guidelines, deadlines, information for requesting an application packet, lists of grant recipients, links to related sites, fundraising tips, and information on making a donation.

LIFEbeat (NY) (http://www.lifebeat.org)
LIFEbeat, the Music Industry Fights AIDS, is a national nonprofit organization dedicated "to reaching America's youth with the message of HIV/AIDS prevention." The organization works to mobilize the music industry to raise awareness and to provide support to the AIDS community. LIFEbeat provides direct outreach to young people through programs tied to music tours, at concert venues and in clubs, and other events. Working with AIDS service organizations across the United States, LIFEbeat provides HIV/AIDS prevention materials and referrals to testing and counseling services. The organization's Web site provides information on programs and events, links to related resources, and information on volunteering and contributing.

Lifelong AIDS Alliance (WA) (http://www.nwaids.org)
Formed from the merger of Chicken Soup Brigade and the Northwest AIDS Foundation, the Seattle, Washington-based Lifelong AIDS Alliance is committed "to preventing the spread of HIV, and to providing practical support services and advocating for those whose lives are affected by HIV and AIDS." The organization's programs are designed to allow people with HIV/AIDS to live as independently as possible, maintain and improve their health and quality of life, and have access to medical, practical, and support services. The organization's Web site provides information on its support services, advocacy, and education and prevention programs, as well as donor and volunteer information, an events calendar, and contact information.

Charles A. and Anne Morrow Lindbergh Foundation (MN) (http://www.lindberghfoundation.org)
The Charles A. and Anne Morrow Lindbergh Foundation awards grants to individuals whose "initiative and work in a wide spectrum of disciplines furthers the Lindberghs' vision of a balance between the advance of technology and the preservation of the natural/human environment." The foundation pursues its mission through three major programs: Lindbergh Grants of up to $10,580 (a symbolic amount representing the cost of the "Spirit of St. Louis"), an awards program, and the sponsoring of educational programs and publications which advance the Lindberghs' vision. In addition to a brief history of the foundation, contact information, and application guidelines and forms, the foundation's Web site offers a list of past grant recipients; an online version of the foundation's most recent annual report; a listing of the foundation's officers, board, and staff; and links to related sites.

LMC Community Foundation (CO) (http://www.lmccf.org/)
Formerly the Lutheran Medical Center Foundation, the LMC Community Foundation of Arvada, Colorado, was created in 1975 to "help people and communities help themselves achieve better health in all dimensions." Initiatives include the Connecting Neighbors program, which distributes grants to support activities working for the health and well-being of local communities. The foundation's Web site provides program and application information, information on other foundation programs, a calendar of events, and opportunities to volunteer and donate.

Local Initiatives Support Corporation (NY) (http://www.liscnet.org)
Begun by a grant from the Ford Foundation and six Fortune 500 companies in 1979, the Local Initiatives Support Corporation (LISC) is committed to revitalizing neighborhoods through community services and affordable housing. The corporation channels "grants, investments, and technical support to community development corporations (CDCs) rebuilding neighborhoods and rural areas throughout the country." The corporation incorporates various program initiatives in the cities and communities it serves, including Public Housing Initiatives, Rural LISC, the Community Investment Collaborative for Kids, the Retail Initiative, and the Community Building Initiative. The corporation's Web site provides information about LISC's programs, funding sources, and projects, and a form to request more information on grants and programs.

The Loft, Inc. (MN) (http://www.loft.org/)
The Loft, Inc., was formed in Minneapolis, Minnesota, in 1974 by a group of writers who gathered together to give each other feedback, guidance, and support. The Loft is now one of the nation's largest, most comprehensive literary centers. The mission of the Loft is "to foster a writing community, the artistic development of individual writers, and an audience for literature." The Loft offers a variety of contests, grants, and fellowships. Grants and fellowships are given to writers, poets, and organizations and individuals that promote literature. In addition to information, guidelines, and application for grants and contests, the organization's Web site provides comprehensive information about the organization's history and mission, staff contact information, and a calendar of Loft events.

Los Angeles Women's Foundation (CA) (http://www.lawomen.org)
The Los Angeles Women's Foundation is a community-based foundation with a 15-year history of promoting women's philanthropy and granting funds to community-based organizations to support services to women and girls in the greater Los Angeles area. The foundation's strategic grantmaking focuses on women's health initiatives, economic literacy and justice, prevention of violence, self-determination, and technical assistance. The foundation's Web site provides details on areas supported, a history of the foundation, and contact information.

Louisiana Endowment for the Humanities (LA) (http://www.leh.org/)
The Louisiana Endowment for the Humanities was founded in 1971 to foster a deeper understanding and appreciation of the humanities throughout Louisiana and to broaden Louisianans' access to history, literature, philosophy, language, and culture. To that end, the endowment develops its own projects and makes grants to nonprofit organizations for public projects such as documentary films, museum exhibits, radio programs, conferences, lecture series, library reading programs, books, and interpretive folklife festivals. The endowment's Web site provides descriptions of its funding programs, grant guidelines, and application materials, as well as humanities links and information on special projects.

Lower Manhattan Cultural Council, Inc. (NY) (http://www.lmcc.net)
The mission of the Lower Manhattan Cultural Council, Inc., is to provide support for individual artists and arts organizations while fostering public participation in the arts through free events in the performing, visual, and new media arts. The council also produces a quarterly newsletter on the arts called *The Low Down,* which is available online. The council's Web site also provides grant and funding information, details on upcoming programs, information on supporting the council, staff and board listings, and contact information.

The Lutheran Church-Missouri Synod Foundation (MO) (http://www.lfnd.org/HTML/foundation.html)
The Lutheran Church-Missouri Synod Foundation was created in 1958 in St. Louis, Missouri, as the fundraising arm of the Lutheran Church-Missouri Synod (LCMS). The foundation allows donors, organizations, or individuals to set up funds to provide assistance to the ministries that LCMS supports. The foundation's Web site includes services and advice for donors and potential donors and a monthly success story.

Lutheran World Relief (MD) (http://www.lwr.org)
Located in Baltimore, Maryland, Lutheran World Relief "extends the hand of Christian love to people overcoming poverty and injustice in 50 countries." The Web site provides financial and contact information, a history of the organization, and stories about the work the organization does around the world.

Lymphoma Research Foundation of America, Inc. (CA) (http://www.lymphoma.org/)
Formed from the 2001 merger of the Cure For Lymphoma Foundation and the Lymphoma Research Foundation of America, the Lymphoma Research Foundation of America, Inc., funds lymphoma research and provides educational and support programs for lymphoma patients. Research funding is provided through fellowships and career development awards. The foundation's Web site provides guidelines, application forms, and instructions for these programs, as well as lists of past recipients; information on the foundation's education and advocacy activities; information about clinical trials; and links to various lymphoma-related resources on the Internet.

Terri Lynne Lokoff Child Care Foundation (PA) (http://www.childcareabc.org)
Located in King of Prussia, Pennsylvania, the Terri Lynne Lokoff Child Care Foundation was founded in 1986 by the parents of the foundation's namesake, a child care teacher who died in a car accident. The foundation's mission is to: "improve the quality of child care for all children; support and elevate the status of child care teachers and providers; raise awareness of the need for affordable, quality child care; and partner with business and government in making child care a priority." The foundation annually offers the Tylenol & TLLCCF National Child Care Teacher Awards to reward "outstanding child care teachers for their commitment and dedication." Childcare teachers from all 50 states and the District of Columbia are eligible for the award. The foundation's Web site provides information on the award program as well as resources to help parents find quality daycare, features on foundation events, and information on contributing or becoming a member.

James Madison Memorial Fellowship Foundation (DC) (http://jamesmadison.com/)
Established by Congress in 1986, the James Madison Memorial Fellowship Foundation seeks to "strengthen secondary school teaching of the principles, framing, and development of the U.S. Constitution" and works to foster the spirit of civic participation in teachers and students. The foundation annually awards fellowships for graduate study to teachers of American history, American government, and social studies in grades 7-12, as well as to college seniors and college graduates who plan to become secondary school teachers of these subjects. The foundation's Web site provides a thorough description of the application process; news announcements; a listing of staff, trustees, academic advisors, and faculty resentatives by state; and contact information.

Maine Humanities Council (ME) (http://www.mainehumanities.org)
The Portland-based Maine Humanities Council was founded in 1975 to promote "community programs in cultural heritage, contemporary issues, reading and literacy, as well as enrichment programs for teachers." The council's grants and programs are designed to encourage collaboration among cultural, educational, and community organizations, such as universities, colleges, schools, museums, libraries, professional associations, historical societies, social service agencies, and civic groups. The council's Web site provides extensive information on its grants program, as well as information on ongoing programs, such as the Maine Center for the Book.

Maine Initiatives (ME) (http://www.maineinitiatives.org/)
Maine Initiatives, founded in Augusta, Maine in 1993, works for economic, environmental, and social justice in the state of Maine. The group makes major fund contributions and supports the Harvest Fund, which focuses on sustainable agriculture and solutions to hunger. The organization's Web site provides further details about the organization, along with grant guidelines, deadlines, and downloadable application forms.

Maine Women's Fund (ME) (http://www.mainewomensfund.org/)
Founded in 1988, the Maine Women's Fund "envisions a world where women and girls have achieved political, economic, and social equality." To help achieve this goal, the fund supports policy, programs, and practices that help empower the girls and women of Maine. The fund supports start-up expenses, projects, programs, and general operating support of organizations that promote the empowerment, advancement, and full participation of women and girls in society. The priorities of the fund include economic self-sufficiency, health, prevention of violence, and building self-esteem. The fund's Web site provides grant guidelines, lists of recent grants, a board list, and contact information.

Manhattan Neighborhood Network (NY) (http://www.mnn.org)
The Manhattan Neighborhood Network (MNN) administers public access television in Manhattan. The network looks for programming that supports First Amendment rights and promotes social, political, ethnic, and artistic diversity. The network's Community Media Grant provides support to Manhattan-based nonprofit and grass roots community and cultural organizations to "help maintain a viable space for community media, build social capital in community media through a process of community development, and contribute towards a more media literate public." The network's Web site provides grant program information, as well as programming schedules and information on taking advantages of MNN's television production resources.

MAP International (GA) (http://www.map.org/)
MAP International is a Christian relief and development organization whose mission is to promote the total health of people living in the world's poorest communities. Founded over 45 years ago as an arm of the Christian Medical Society, MAP (Medical Assistance Programs) works to provide essential medicines, prevent and eradicate disease, and promote community health development. The MAP Web site provides eligibility requirements for receiving medicines and medical supplies, information on the MAP/Reader's Digest

International Fellowship program for medical students, information on MAP's international programs, press releases, newsletters, and contact information.

March of Dimes Birth Defects Foundation (NY) (http://www.modimes.org/)
President Franklin D. Roosevelt created the March of Dimes in 1938 at the height of the polio epidemic. With the advent of the polio vaccine in the late 1950s, the focus of the organization shifted to the reduction of birth defects and infant mortality rates through advocacy, education, and the support of community programs and research in genetics and neurobiology. The March of Dimes Birth Defects Foundation's Web site provides detailed information about its grants, scholarships, and application guidelines; information (some of it in Spanish) about the foundation's advocacy, education, and fundraising efforts (including Walk America); and information on various health issues affecting infants.

Mariners Care (WA)
(http://seattle.mariners.mlb.com/NASApp/mlb/sea/community/sea_community_programs.jsp)
Mariners Care, a nonprofit organization of the Seattle Mariners Baseball Club, is dedicated to supporting community service programs in the Pacific Northwest. The organization's Web site provides descriptions of the numerous programs the charity is involved in, along with a community calendar and information on Mariners Care promotions.

Mariposa County Arts Council (CA) (http://www.arts-mariposa.org/)
Founded in Mariposa, California, in 1981, the Mariposa County Arts Council strives "to promote and support all forms of the cultural arts, for all ages, throughout Mariposa County." The council sponsors a variety of workshops, lectures, exhibitions, and competitions, including the Young Masters Art Competition. Details on the council's programs, an entry form, and upcoming events can be found on the council's Web site.

Maryland 4-H Foundation, Inc. (MD)
(http://www.agnr.umd.edu/4-h/foundationhome.htm)
The Maryland 4-H Foundation, Inc., has as its mission to "build and manage the financial resources to support Maryland youth in reaching their fullest potential as competent, caring, responsible individuals through 4-H programs." The foundation supports 4-H members through scholarships, which are "made available through an endowment established by the 4-H families and friends of those for whom the scholarships are named." The foundation's Web site includes information on scholarship winners, a calendar, newsletter, and a list of its board of directors.

Maryland Humanities Council, Inc. (MD) (http://www.mdhc.org)
Based in Baltimore, the Maryland Humanities Council, Inc., supports programs and individuals working in the humanities. The council strives to promote the humanities in Maryland through public programs, including lectures and courses, grants, and awards. Grant funds are primarily intended to support programs aimed at out-of-school adult audiences; smaller grants are available to support programs for primary and secondary school students. The council's Web site provides extensive information on the grant program, including downloadable grant guidelines; information on upcoming events and the council's ongoing programs; and contact information.

Mary's Pence (NJ) (http://www.igc.apc.org/maryspence/)
Mary's Pence is dedicated to furthering the self-empowerment of all women and, through women's growth, the self-improvement of all humanity. In support of these goals, the organization provides seed money for creative programs designed to bring about systemic change in church and society. The organization offers two grant programs to support women of Catholic background in ministry: a Ministry Grant program and a Study Grant program. In addition to a detailed description of the organization's funding philosophy, the Mary's Pence Web site provides grant guidelines, a list of past recipients, information on how to get involved, and contact information.

Massachusetts Bar Foundation (MA) (http://www.massbarfoundation.org)
Founded in 1964, the Massachusetts Bar Foundation's mission is to "to improve the administration of justice, to promote an understanding of the law, and to ensure equal access to the legal system for all residents of the Commonwealth, particularly those most vulnerable." The foundation's grantmaking program, IOLTA, awards grants to nonprofit organizations in Massachusetts whose programs either provide civil legal services to the state's low-income population or improve the administration of justice in the Commonwealth. The foundation also provides support through its Legal Intern Fellowship Program. The foundation's Web site includes a listing of recent grantees, downloadable program instructions, application forms, information on grant cycles, and contact information.

Massachusetts Environmental Trust (MA) (http://www.massenvironmentaltrust.org)
The Massachusetts Environmental Trust was established in 1988 through the settlement of a federal lawsuit over the pollution of Boston Harbor. The trust funds grassroots environmental programs that will restore, protect, and improve the quality of Massachusetts' waterways. The trust offers a range of funding opportunities through its restricted and unrestricted grant programs. The trust's Web site provides grant guidelines, recent grant awards, and contact information.

Massachusetts Foundation for the Humanities, Inc. (MA) (http://www.mfh.org)
Founded in 1974 as the Massachusetts arm of the National Endowment for the Humanities, the Massachusetts Foundation for the Humanities, Inc., strives to bring the humanities "out of the classroom and into the community." Its mission is to "foster critical inquiry; promote understanding of our diverse cultural heritages; and provide forums for the citizens of [Massachusetts] to engage actively in thoughtful public discourse about matters of individual choice and collective responsibility." The foundation offers a range of grants for humanities projects. The foundation's Web site provides descriptions of funding opportunities, downloadable applications, humanities resources, links, contact information, and definitions of the humanities.

MATHCOUNTS Foundation (VA) (http://www.mathcounts.org/About/about.html)
The MATHCOUNTS Foundation, based in Alexandria,Virginia, is a national organization that has promoted math excellence among middle school students since 1984. The foundation's mission is to "increase interest and involvement in mathematics among all intermediate school students in order to assist in developing a technically literate population essential to U.S. global competitiveness and the quality of life." The foundation's Web site provides a copy of the foundation's annual report, a listing of board and staff, information on how the program is funded, and contact information.

The Joseph Matteucci Foundation (CA) (http://www.jmf4peace.org)
The Castro Valley, California-based Joseph Matteucci Foundation is dedicated to youth nonviolence. Joseph Matteucci was the victim of a senseless act of violence when another youth mistakenly hit him with a baseball bat after a little league game dispute. The foundation that bears his name strives to sponsor programs that promote nonviolence, especially in sports. The foundation's staff and supporters seek to use Joseph's story for positive change through meditation programs in schools, the Sportsmanship Program, the Stand for Peace workshop, a gun violence education program; and a speaking program. A scholarship program is also offered. The foundation's Web site provides information on its programs, events, links to further resources for youth nonviolence, and contact information.

MBE We Deliver Dreams Foundation (CA) (http://www.mbe.com/wddf)
The San Diego-based Mail Boxes Etc. (MBE) We Deliver Dreams Foundation was founded in 1998 "to deliver dreams to at-risk children primarily through MBE local centers around the world." The foundation fulfills dreams that would normally be unobtainable for individual children in MBE communities who are victims of violence, neglect, abuse, poverty, or illness. Guidelines, stories of dreams fulfilled through the program, descriptions of

the foundation's core values and mission, downloadable dream request forms, and contact information are available on the foundation's Web site.

W.H. "Howie" McClennan Scholarship Fund (DC) (http://www.iaff.org/academy/scholarships/mcclennan.html)
The W.H. "Howie" McClennan Scholarship Fund is one of the many charities of the International Association of Fire Fighters (IAFF). Named in honor of IAFF President Emeritus Howie McClennan, the fund exists to help the sons and daughters of fire fighters who have been killed in the line of duty. The annual award can be used by the recipient toward the expenses of any university, accredited college, or school of higher learning in the United States or Canada. Scholarships are awarded each year and can be renewed for up to four years. Guidelines and details on how to apply for the scholarship are posted on the fund's Web site.

Ronald McDonald House Charities (IL) (http://www.rmhc.org)
The Ronald McDonald House Charities, based in Illinois, is committed to "lifting children to a better tomorrow." The charities provide comfort and care to children and their families by supporting Ronald McDonald Houses in communities around the world and by making grants to other not-for-profit organizations whose programs help children in need. The organization has a network of over 170 local charities serving in 44 countries. The charities' Web site offers information for families who need a place to stay, volunteer opportunities, a history of Ronald McDonald Houses, information on grantmaking and scholarship programs, and contact information.

Ronald McDonald House Charities of New Mexico/Southern Colorado, Inc. (NM) (http://www.rmhc-nm.org)
The Ronald McDonald House Charities of New Mexico/Southern Colorado, Inc., were founded in 1982 to operate and fund the New Mexico Ronald McDonald House in Albuquerque. The upkeep of the house, grants, and scholarships are funded through financial donations and volunteer efforts. Information on scholarship programs, grant guidelines, details on volunteer and donation opportunities, instructions on staying in the house, Spanish-language information on the house, and contact information are provided on the charities' Web site.

McKenzie River Gathering Foundation (OR) (http://www.mrgf.org/)
The McKenzie River Gathering Foundation is a community-supported foundation established in 1976 to provide funding to Oregon grassroots groups challenging social, economic, and political inequities. The foundation's grantmaking focuses on human and civil rights, racial justice, economic justice, environmental protection, peace, and international solidarity. The foundation's Web site describes its mission and provides grant guidelines, contact information, donor information and a link to the Funding Exchange Network, of which the foundation is a member.

McStain Enterprises, Inc. (CO) (http://www.mcstain.com/ecology/grants.htm)
As a Colorado land developer and homebuilder, McStain Enterprises, Inc., maintains a community involvement program that seeks to find long-term solutions and establish educational programs dealing with land-use and environmental issues. The grant program is open to nonprofit organizations that "promote effective land or resource use that will enhance the environment, or have an education program that emphasizes land resource appreciation, environmental sustainability, and stewardship" in the communities where McStain builds homes. The program also offers discretionary funds for smaller grants. The organization's Web site provides criteria for eligibility, a funding timeline, proposal guidelines, and contact information.

MDC, Inc. (NC) (http://www.mdcinc.org/)
Located in Chapel Hill, North Carolina, MDC, Inc., was established in 1967 to help the state make the transition from an agricultural to an industrial economy and from a

segregated to an integrated workforce. The organization's mission is "to advance the South through strategies that expand opportunity, reduce poverty, and build inclusive communities." To that end, the organization publishes research and develops policies and programs with the goals of strengthening the workforce, fostering economic development, and removing employment barriers in the South. The organization's Web site provides downloadable publications and information on the organization's mission.

Mechanical Contracting Education & Research Foundation (MD) (http://www.mcaa.org/mcf)
The Mechanical Contracting Education & Research Foundation, located in Rockville, Maryland, is the philanthropic arm of the Mechanical Contractors Association of America. Among other projects, the foundation makes grants toward contracting-related research. The foundation's Web site describes recent grant recipients and their projects and provides contact information.

Media Alliance, Inc. (NY) (http://www.Mediaalliance.org)
Based in New York City, Media Alliance, Inc., is a resource for media amateurs and professionals. The group's mission is to advance "independent media—video, film, audio, radio, and computers—in New York State by expanding resources, support, and audiences for the media arts." The alliance awards the Independent Radio and Sound Art Fellowships to provide project support for the creation of works by individual artists working in radio or sound art. Fellowship guidelines; a list of previous recipients; contact information; a listing of resources, including New York State arts organizations; publications; and information on video preservation services and funding are available on the organization's Web site.

Meet the Composer (NY) (http://www.meetthecomposer.org/)
Meet The Composer was founded in 1974 as a project of the New York State Council on the Arts to increase artistic and financial opportunities for American composers, which the organization does by providing composer fees to nonprofit organizations that perform, present, or commission original works. Meet the Composer has several funding programs, which are detailed on its Web site with downloadable application forms and guidelines. The site also offers news, free publications, links to related Web sites, and donor and contact information.

Melanoma Research Foundation (CA) (http://www.melanoma.org)
Located in Lake Forest, California, the Melanoma Research Foundation funds melanoma research with the ultimate goal of finding a cure. The foundation's Research Grant Program funds a variety of grants, many of them multi-year. Details on specific grants, application information, a newsletter, a listing of comprehensive cancer care centers, links to further resources, and contact information can be found on the foundation's Web site.

The Memorial Foundation (TN) (http://www.memfoundation.org)
Established in 1994, the Memorial Foundation supports organizations that provide important services in the Middle Tennessee region. The foundation responds to diverse community needs, assisting agencies that focus on health and rehabilitation, youth and children, senior citizens, education, human services, and substance abuse. The foundation's Web site provides details on each program area, application guidelines, a listing of recent grants, and contact information.

Methodist Healthcare Ministries (TX) (http://www.mhm.org)
Since 1995, the Methodist Healthcare Ministries has worked "to provide innovative, effective and long-term physical, mental, and spiritual resources to promote healing and wellness and to nurture wholeness of body, mind, and spirit" to 72 counties of southern Texas. This goal takes the form of providing healthcare services and programs to underserved communities through parenting programs, clinical services, and health and wellness programs, among others. More details of these projects and a general description of the ministries' overall mission are available on the ministries' Web site.

Michigan AIDS Fund (MI) (http://www.michaidsfund.org/)
The Michigan AIDS Fund was established in Grand Rapids, Michigan, in 1990 to address the AIDS epidemic in the state. The organization aims to pool resources "to support efforts to stop the spread of HIV/AIDS and to alleviate the suffering of those infected and affected by the AIDS epidemic." The fund makes grants to groups that provide HIV/AIDS prevention and services. The fund's Web site includes funding guidelines, details on the fund's other programs, information on making donations to the fund, and information on the AIDS epidemic in Michigan.

Michigan Humanities Council (MI) (http://mihumanities.h-net.msu.edu/)
The Michigan Humanities Council, the state's affiliate of the National Endowment for the Humanities, encourages and supports activities that bring humanities scholars and the public together to promote understanding and appreciation of the humanities. The council's grants program supports organizations of different kinds, sizes, and varying levels of expertise. Grant guidelines and application forms are provided at the council's Web site, along with grant announcements, council newsletters, resources, and events listings.

Michigan State Bar Foundation (MI) (http://www.msbf.org/)
The Michigan State Bar Foundation was established in 1947 in Lansing to provide leadership and funding in order to improve Michigan's justice system. The foundation seeks to improve legal access and to better public understanding of the law through a number of programs and grants. Information on grants for law-related educational, charitable, and technology programs; downloadable grant criteria and applications; and further details on the foundation, its activities, and mission can be found on the foundation's Web site.

Michigan Women's Foundation (MI) (http://comnet.org/mwf)
Founded in 1986 on the anniversary of the ratification of the 19th Constitutional Amendment, which gave women the right to vote, the Grand Rapids-based Michigan Women's Foundation is committed to the interests of women and girls in the state. The foundation's goal is to "expand economic options for low-income women, to promote financial education for women, to sponsor leadership programs for women and girls, to help nonprofit organizations serving women and girls become more effective and efficient, and to increase women's participation in the philanthropic process." The foundation's Web site provides information on its grant programs, newsletters, donor information, events sponsored by the foundation, links to further resources, and a listing of the board and staff members with contact information.

Mid Atlantic Arts Foundation (MD) (http://www.midatlanticarts.org)
One of six regional arts organizations in the continental United States, the Mid Atlantic Arts Foundation addresses the support of the arts in a multi-state region comprised of Delaware, the District of Columbia, Maryland, New Jersey, New York, Pennsylvania, the U.S. Virgin Islands, Virginia, and West Virginia. The foundation, which is primarily concerned with providing increased access to quality arts programs, provides financial support, technical assistance, and information to artists and arts organizations through a variety of programs and services. The foundation's Web site provides information on the foundation's grant and service programs; recent grant awards and descriptions; listings of the foundation's board and staff; links to Mid-Atlantic state arts agencies' Web sites; and an online version of *ARTSINK,* the foundation's newsletter.

Milagro Foundation (CA) (http://www.milagrofoundation.org/)
Guitarist Carlos Santana and his wife Deborah began the Milagro Foundation in 1998 in Marin County, California, to support nonprofit organizations dedicated to children and youth in the arts, education, and health. The foundation supports programs in the San Francisco Bay Area, across the United States, and in countries where Santana performs. The foundation focuses on disadvantaged children and youth at risk due to factors such as poor health, illiteracy, or insufficient educational and cultural opportunities. The foundation's

Web site provides grant guidelines and a listing of previous grant recipients, answers to frequently asked questions, donor opportunities, and contact information.

Million Dollar Round Table Foundation (IL) (http://www.mdrtfoundation.org/)
The Million Dollar Round Table Foundation is the philanthropic arm of the Million Dollar Round Table, an international association of life insurance and financial services professionals. The mission of the foundation is "to encourage member voluntarism and to give funds to worthy charitable organizations throughout the world," with an emphasis on improving the quality of life for those in need. The foundation's Web site provides information on the its worldwide grant programs, lists of grant recipients, news updates, and contact information.

Minnesota Humanities Commission (MN) (http://www.thinkmhc.org/Grants/grants.htm)
The Minnesota Humanities Commission is dedicated solely to promoting the study of the humanities throughout Minnesota. The commission's Grant Program provides funding for Minnesota groups and organizations conducting public projects in the humanities. Grants are intended to foster connections among humanities scholars, cultural organizations, and community groups. Priority is given to senior citizen organizations, minority organizations, multi-site projects serving hard-to-reach audiences, and greater Minnesota organizations. The commission's Web site provides information on the grant program, application guidelines, recently awarded grants, details on other projects, and contact information.

Minnesota Independent School Forum (MN) (http://www.misf.org)
Located in St. Paul, the Minnesota Independent School Forum advocates for independent education through a consortium of 40 independent high schools in the state. The forum works to promote and improve independent education through scholarships for high schools students and programs related to multicultural education, research, and public policy. The forum's Web site provides an educators' toolkit, information for students, tips for parents, news and events for member schools, information on private schools, and contact information.

Minnesota Twins Community Fund (http://www.pohladfamilycharities.org/mtcf.html)
Founded in 1991, the Minnesota Twins Community Fund supports Minnesota nonprofits through direct funding and the volunteer efforts of Minnesota Twins baseball players and their families. Financial support is mainly directed toward youth recreation and education programs, particularly area baseball and softball leagues. The fund also makes in-kind donations of tickets and memorabilia to aid area nonprofit organizations. Further details and funding guidelines, downloadable application materials, general information for nonprofits, news releases, printer-friendly versions of documents, and contact information are available on the fund's Web site.

Mississippi Humanities Council (MS) (http://www.ihl.state.ms.us/mhc)
The Mississippi Humanities Council encourages and supports activities that make the humanities accessible to the people of Mississippi, primarily by awarding grants to nonprofits that plan and sponsor humanities activities. The council's Web site provides grant program descriptions and guidelines, contact information, information about the council, a calendar of events, and links to humanities resources and funding sources on the Web.

Missouri Humanities Council (MO) (http://www.mohumanities.org)
The Missouri Humanities Council promotes community, citizenship, and learning through humanities programs. The council makes grants for projects including cultural heritage development and initiatives that enhance knowledge of the cultural traditions of Missouri. Grant guidelines and downloadable applications are provided on the council's Web site, along with information on the humanities and the council's activities, links to Missouri Web sites, a listing of board members, and contact information.

Mr. Holland's Opus Foundation, Inc. (CA) (http://www.mhopus.org)
The Sherman Oaks, California-based Mr. Holland's Opus Foundation, Inc., was inspired by the movie of the same name and was founded by the movie's creative team: composer Michael Kamen, actor Richard Dreyfuss, and director Stephen Herek. The foundation is committed to "promoting instrumental music nationwide by partnering with businesses, schools, and communities to provide new and refurbished musical instruments to qualified schools and individual students." Three grants programs help attain this mission: the Melody Program, which supports school music programs threatened by budget cuts; the Solo Program, which grants instruments to financially limited student musicians; and the Special Project Program, which provides funding for community schools of the arts, hospitals, nursing homes, music therapy programs, and school districts. The foundation's Web site includes grant information, criteria, and requirements; lists of past grant and instrument recipients; and contact information for grant applications.

The Mockingbird Foundation (NY) (http://www.phish.net/mockingbird/)
The Mockingbird Foundation, located in Saratoga Springs, New York, was founded in 1997 by fans of the band Phish. It was originally founded to produce the most factually accurate and literary book on Phish's music. While the book is the main focus of the foundation, it now seeks to produce a wider range of resources for fans, including a Phish tribute album. Additionally, the foundation uses the proceeds from its books and albums to offer competitive grants to schools and nonprofit organizations with in the United States that effect improvements in areas of importance to the Phish fan community. These areas include music, education, and children. Grant guidelines, details about how to apply, and deadlines are all available on the foundation's Web site.

Monmouth County Arts Council, Inc. (NJ) (http://www.monmouthartscouncil.org/)
Established in 1971 to serve the cultural needs of the Monmouth County, New Jersey, community, the Monmouth County Arts Council, Inc., strives to "promote and assist a wide range of cultural organizations and programs within the county." This mission manifests itself in the form of programs and services that work to build community among the artists of the county; create partnerships among the council and local government, nonprofit organizations, businesses, and educational institutions; advocate for the arts to the general public; and provide artists and cultural organizations with technical assistance. The council's Web site provides details and instructions for potential grant applicants, a downloadable grant application, descriptions of the council's services, a calendar of events, and contact information.

Montana Committee for the Humanities (MT) (http://www.umt.edu/lastbest/)
The Montana Committee for the Humanities, the state's affiliate of the National Endowment for the Humanities was founded in 1972 and offers grants for public programs in history, literature, philosophy, and other disciplines of the humanities. It also awards fellowships for humanities research relating to Montana. The committee's Web site provides information on these programs, a speakers bureau, and a media collection; contact information; news; committee information; and a listing of humanities resources.

Morris Animal Foundation (CO) (http://www.morrisanimalfoundation.org)
The Morris Animal Foundation was established in 1948 in Englewood, Colorado, for the purpose of improving "the health and well-being of companion animals and wildlife by funding humane health studies and disseminating information about these studies." To this end, the foundation funds animal health research at veterinary institutions around the world. The foundation divides the projects it funds into five categories of study: canine, equine, feline, llama/alpaca, and wildlife/special species. The foundation's Web site provides information on current research projects, instructions for potential grant applicants, current special focus studies, animal health news, listings of upcoming events, and details on the foundation's history and general operation.

Philip Morris Employee Community Fund (NY) (http://www.pmusa.com/policies_practices/community_involvement/employee_funds.asp)
The Philip Morris Employee Community Fund is a workplace-giving program managed by employees of Philip Morris who elect focus areas for their charitable contributions. Programs and initiatives support causes such as hunger, homelessness, domestic violence, adult illiteracy, AIDS, after-school youth development, and seniors. More information on the fund can be found on the Philanthropy section of the Philip Morris Web site.

Moses Cone-Wesley Long Community Health Foundation (NC) (http://www.mcwlhealthfoundation.org)
The Moses Cone-Wesley Long Community Health Foundation was established in 1996 in Greensboro, North Carolina to "invest in the development and support of activities, programs and organizations that measurably improve the health of people in the geographic area traditionally served by the Moses Cone Health System." Specifically, the foundation seeks to fund disease prevention and health education programs, health services for the underserved, and community self-sufficiency programs. The foundation's Web site provides grant guidelines and instructions on applying and more general information on the Moses Cone Health System and its foundation.

Irving Moskowitz Foundation (CA) (http://www.moskowitzfoundation.org)
Established in Hawaiian Gardens, California, in 1968, the Irving Moskowitz Foundation exists to help people in need, regardless of race, creed, politics, or religion. The foundation supports a wide array of religious, educational, cultural, and emergency services organizations. Specific areas of interest include education, sports, religion, health, children, and individuals. The foundation's Web site offers a biography of Mr. Moskowitz, details on the founation's mission and areas of interest, lists of recent grantees, and contact information.

The Mt. Sinai Health Care Foundation (OH) (http://www.mtsinaifoundation.org)
The mission of the Cleveland, Ohio-based Mt. Sinai Health Care Foundation is to "assist greater Cleveland's organizations and leaders to improve the health and well-being of the Jewish and general communities now and for generations to come." The foundation's grantmaking program specifies four areas relating to its work within the health field: child development, the elderly, organizations, and the community. The foundation also considers proposals not covered within its specific areas to deserving applicants. The foundation's Web site offers details on the specific program areas, information on submitting proposals, restrictions, news on the foundation, and contact information.

Mount Zion Health Fund (CA) (http://www.mzhf.org/)
The San Francisco-based, Mount Zion Health Fund maintains a mission of "advancing programs designed to improve the physical, emotional, and spiritual health of vulnerable populations and that reflect the Jewish values and traditions of Mount Zion Hospital." The public charity primarily funds qualifying organizations in the San Francisco Bay Area. Grants to individuals are not made. The fund's Web site offers more information about the fund's grantmaking activities, restrictions, and application procedures; a grants history; board listings; and contact information.

The Mountain Institute (DC) (http://www.mountain.org)
The Mountain Institute is a scientific and educational organization committed to the preservation of mountain environments and the advancement of mountain cultures around the world. Since 1972, the organization has administered conservation, research, development, and education programs in the Andean, Appalachian, and Himalayan Mountain Ranges. The institute's programs work to improve the livelihoods of people living in and around mountain parks and protected areas; use the mountains as a learning environment for mountain leaders of all ages; and undertake rigorous research and protection of habitat for some of the world's most endangered and unique animals, such as the Andean Condor considered by the ancient Inca as a messenger of the gods, and the snow leopard of the

Himalayas. The organization's Web site provides more information on the institute's programs and contact information.

Ms. Foundation for Women (NY) (http://www.ms.foundation.org/)
The Ms. Foundation for Women, founded in 1972, supports the efforts of women and girls to govern their own lives and influence the world around them by funding women's self-help organizing efforts and by supporting changes in public consciousness, law, philanthropy, and social policy. The foundation awards grants through special initiatives in three issue areas —Women's Economic Security; Women's Health and Safety; and Girls, Young Women, and Leadership—and offers Movement Building Grants in two grant cycles. Grant guidelines, requests for proposals, application forms, information on the foundation's activities, such as "Take Our Daughters to Work Day" and collaborative funding are available on the foundation's Web site.

Multiple Sclerosis Foundation, Inc. (FL) (http://www.msfacts.org/)
Based in Fort Lauderdale, Florida, the Multiple Sclerosis Foundation, Inc., was founded in 1986 to provide both "complementary and conventional health care options to address the varied symptoms associated with MS." Among the services provided by the foundation are toll-free phone support, the home care assistance program (which provides temporary non-medical home care to people with MS who financially qualify for the relief), newsletters, MS updates, an in-house library, networking and referral services, and donated medical equipment program. The foundation provides gifts for research into the cause, treatment, prevention, and eventual cure of MS. The foundation also provides scholarships for student studies and special projects in the areas of quality of life and healthcare issues related to MS. The foundation's Web site provides related links, a directory of products and services provided by people with MS, and contact information.

Muscular Dystrophy Association (AZ) (http://www.mdausa.org/)
The Muscular Dystrophy Association seeks to find the causes of and cures for 40 neuromuscular diseases through sponsorship of 400 research projects worldwide. The association provides research grants to professionals or faculty members who are qualified to conduct and supervise a program of original research at appropriate educational, medical, or research institutions. Grant guidelines, an application form, and lists of current research grantees and projects; information on research developments and clinical trials; and listings of scientific meetings, symposia, and workshops are available on the association's Web site.

Music Associates of Aspen, Inc. (CO) (http://www.aspenmusicfestival.com)
The Music Associates of Aspen, Inc., founded the Aspen Music Festival and School in 1949. The Aspen Music Festival and School preserve and promote classical music through music education, public performance, visiting artists and faculty, and service to the community. The association sponsors artist residencies through its Musical Odysseys Reaching Everyone (M.O.R.E.) program in local schools. For more information on the Aspen Music Festival and School, including upcoming performances, contribution opportunities, and a contact address for further details, visit Aspen's Web site.

Music Institute of Chicago (IL) (http://www.musicinst.com)
The Music Institute of Chicago seeks to provide its students with "the foundation for a lifelong enjoyment of music." Details on the institute's programs and classes, including its Institute for Therapy through the Arts; upcoming performances; donation requests; application and financial aid opportunities; and contact information are provided on the institute's Web site.

MusiCares Foundation, Inc. (CA)
(http://www.grammy.com/academy/musicares/index.html)
The MusiCares Foundation, Inc., established in 1989 by the Recording Academy, "ensures that music people have a place to turn in times of financial, personal, or medical crisis. Its

primary purpose is to focus the resources and attention of the music industry on human service issues which directly impact the health and welfare of the music community." The foundation's programs include emergency financial assistance, addiction recovery, outreach and leadership activities, and senior housing. The foundation's Web site provides further details on the foundation's programs and services and contact information.

A.J. Muste Memorial Institute (NY) (http://www.ajmuste.org)
The A.J. Muste Memorial Institute explores the link between nonviolence and social change by applying its resources to the nonviolent struggle for social justice and a peaceful future. The institute awards grants for projects promoting its mission through peace and disarmament, social and economic justice, racial and sexual equality, and the labor movement. It also provides funding through its International Nonviolence Training Fund. Grant guidelines; contact information for interested grantseekers; a list of grantees since 1994; details of the institute's fiscal sponsorship program; a description of the Peace Pentagon, which offers low-cost office space in New York City for activists; information on publications; details on how to make contributions to the institute; and a biography of A.J. Muste.

Dikembe Mutombo Foundation, Inc. (GA) (http://www.dmf.org)
The mission of the Dikembe Mutombo Foundation is to improve the health, education, and quality of life for the people of the Democratic Republic of Congo in Central Africa. In conjunction with the work of the foundation, which was established in 1997, Dikembe Mutombo seeks to promote preventive, educational, and therapeutic approaches to health and well-being. The foundation's Web site provides information about Dikembe Mutombo, four-time NBA Defensive Player of the Year; information about the foundation's mission; press releases; and contact information.

NAACP Legal Defense and Educational Fund, Inc. (NY) (http://www.ldfla.org)
The NAACP Legal Defense and Educational Fund, Inc., was established in 1940 under the leadership of Thurgood Marshall. The fund has a national office in New York and regional offices in Washington, D.C., and Los Angeles. The fund "fights for equality and empowerment for African Americans and other disenfranchised groups in the areas of education, employment, criminal justice, voting rights, housing, health care, and environmental justice" through litigation and educational programs. The fund's Web site provides application information on its undergraduate and law school scholarship and training programs for African Americans, details on the fund's legal program, and information on events and how to make a contribution.

NAFSA: Association of International Educators (DC) (http://www.nafsa.org)
NAFSA: Association of International Educators, a membership organization created in 1948, promotes the international exchange of students and scholars through training programs, grants and scholarships, conferences, and a variety of overseas opportunities. The NAFSA Web site provides details on these programs as well as information about financial aid, a job registry, public policy resources, information on upcoming conferences, and publications by NAFSA members.

National AIDS Fund (DC) (http://www.aidsfund.org)
The Washington, D.C.-based National AIDS Fund pools its efforts with local community partners to lead community-based prevention, care, and support programs for people with HIV/AIDS. It seeks to provide "financial support, technical assistance, and compassionate guidance to communities seeking to build programs and services that meet the needs of local people hardest hit by the epidemic." The fund coordinates a range of programmatic activities to support community-based HIV prevention efforts, principally in its 29 partnership communities. The fund's Web site provides details on these programs, information on its partner communities and funders, links, and funding opportunities.

National Alliance for Autism Research (NJ) (http://www.naar.org)
Created in 1994 and based in Princeton, New Jersey, the National Alliance for Autism Research seeks "to determine the causes, prevention, effective treatments, and, ultimately, a cure for autism spectrum disorders." To this end, the alliance funds, promotes, and supports biomedical research into autism. Under the Grants and Research heading of its Web site, the alliance details current funding opportunities with instructions for submitting proposals online. The Web site also provides a wealth of autism-related information, including current news on research, upcoming events and meetings, and related links.

The National Alliance for Research on Schizophrenia and Depression (NY) (http://www.narsad.org)
The National Alliance for Research on Schizophrenia and Depression, located in Great Neck, New York, was incorporated in 1986 through the combined efforts of several mental health organizations. The alliance's purpose is to raise and distribute funds for scientific research into the causes, cures, preventions, and treatments of severe mental illnesses, primarily schizophrenia and depression. The alliance has three award programs: the Young Investigator Award, the Independent Investigator Award, and the Distinguished Investigator Award. Award descriptions, deadlines, guidelines, and application materials; information about the alliance and its mission, including press releases and publications; details about symposia and other events; and a list of staff contacts are all available on the alliance's Web site.

National Alopecia Areata Foundation (CA) (http://www.naaf.org)
Based in San Rafael, California, the National Alopecia Areata Foundation's mission is "to support research to find a cure or acceptable treatment for alopecia areata, to support those with the disease, and to educate the public about alopecia areata," a skin disease of the autoimmune system that results in the loss of scalp and body hair. This mission is accomplished through public education, research funding, and advocating for those afflicted with the disease. The foundation's Web site offers announcements on current research, recent grant recipients, grant instructions and application forms, a form for requesting further information on alopecia areata, news and events, and upcoming conference information.

National Association for the Exchange of Industrial Resources, Inc. (IL) (http://www.naeir.org)
Founded in 1977, the National Association for the Exchange of Industrial Resources, Inc., based in Galesburg, Illinois, is a nonprofit organization that collects and processes donations of new, top quality merchandise from American corporations, and then redistributes those goods to qualified schools and nonprofits across the United States. Schools and nonprofit organizations pay a membership fee to participate in the program. Donated merchandise must be used for the care of the ill, the needy or minors, and cannot be bartered, traded, or sold. Materials are offered to association members through a variety of programs, including catalogs and special offers. The association's Web site provides an online membership application and details on how the program works.

National Association of Child Advocates (DC) (http://www.childadvocacy.org)
The National Association of Child Advocates was created in 1984 in Washington, D.C., as a national network of child advocacy organizations. The association operates according to the belief that the United States has the resources to "lift all children out of poverty; end childhood hunger and homelessness; and ensure quality health care, early childhood, and school programs for every child." Ongoing initiatives include child welfare, early care and education, health, and income supports. The association's Web site provides a primer on child advocacy, information on membership and benefits to nonprofit organizations, a listing of current members, links, and downloadable publications, including "Child Advocates Making a Difference."

National Ataxia Foundation, Inc. (MN) (http://www.ataxia.org/)
The Minneapolis, Minnesota-based National Ataxia Foundation, Inc., was established in 1957 to support research into the causes and mechanisms of hereditary ataxia, a group of chronic and progressive neurological disorders affecting coordination. The foundation also works to locate families affected by ataxia or at risk for ataxia in order to offer information and education, identify needs and services for purposes of referral, create and disseminate educational programs, and increase public awareness. There are more than 45 affiliated chapters and support groups throughout the United States and Canada. The foundation's Web site provides a listing of the foundation's chapters and support groups, a chatroom, an online information request form, related links, and articles from the foundation's publication, *Generations*.

National Blood Foundation (MD) (http://www.aabb.org/About_the_AABB/Nbf/nbf2.htm)
The National Blood Foundation was established in 1983 as a program of the American Association of Blood Banks to fund "basic and applied scientific research, administrative/research projects, professional education, technical training, and public education in all aspects of blood banking, transfusion medicine, and tissue transplantation." The foundation's Scientific Research Grant Program provides grants for projects dealing with scientific, administrative, or educational aspects of blood banking and transfusion medicine. The foundation's Web site provides a list of grant recipients, donor information, and board and staff listings.

The National Catholic Community Foundation (MD) (http://www.nccfcommunity.org/)
Created in 1997 and based in Maryland, the National Catholic Community Foundation offers a donor-advised fund program to "address the needs of persons and organizations who wish to engage in philanthropic activities which support the ministries of the Catholic Church, but do not have the ability to organize a traditional private foundation." Donations can be made to Catholic organizations or to groups that support the Gospel in a larger way. The foundation's Web site includes a list of the individual funds, a list of grant recipients, a catalog of possible recipients for donors, testimonials from donors and grant recipients, a list of the board of trustees, information on how to establish a fund, and advice on all areas of giving.

National Center of Small Communities (DC) (http://www.natat.org/ncsc/Default.htm)
The National Center of Small Communities was formed in 1976 to serve the leaders of America's smaller communities. The center's programs and services strive to support smaller communities by re-orienting and expanding their economies and employment opportunities, developing skilled elected leadership, finding additional funding, complying with federal regulations, protecting rural and small-town character, and soliciting and receiving government and private grants. The center also administers an American Hometown Leadership Award, and works with the Environmental Protection Agency to protect small town water sources. The center's Web site includes links to related Web sites, updates on its national conference, publications, and contact information.

National Children's Cancer Society (MO) (http://www.children-cancer.com)
The St. Louis-based National Children's Cancer Society was created in 1987 to help children suffering from cancer and their families with emotional and financial support. The society's Web site offers information geared toward both adults and kids. Questions about financial support are addressed in the FAQ section of the society's Web site. Information about patient and family services, donations, voluntarism, special events, links, and contact information are also available on the site.

National Community Capital Association (PA) (http://www.communitycapital.org)
Established in 1986 in Philadelphia, the National Community Capital Association "helps institutions and individuals provide capital that increases resources and opportunities for economically disadvantaged people and communities." Through financing, training, consulting, and advocacy—in cooperation with a system of member community development

financial institutions (CDFIs)—the association works for social, economic, and political justice. The association's Web site provides information on its program areas, answers to frequently asked questions, links to resources, details on specific programs and publications, membership information, further details on the association, and contact information.

National Community Pharmacists Association Foundation (VA) (http://www.ncpanet.org)
Established in 1898 as the National Association of Retail Druggists, the National Community Pharmacists Association (NCPA) is located in Alexandria, Virginia. Elements of the association's mission include "representing the professional and proprietary interests of independent retail pharmacists and vigorously promoting and defending those interests; restoring, maintaining, and promoting the health and well-being of the public we serve; and ensuring the ability of independent retail pharmacists to compete in a free and fair marketplace." The NCPA Foundation offers a series of scholarships to NCPA student members. Information on these programs can be found in the Students section of the association's Web site, along with downloadable applications. The foundation also funds research grants for pharmacology school faculty; a list of past recipients can be found online. In addition to grant and scholarship information, the site includes information on the association's annual conference, publications, current public policy issues, and upcoming meetings and membership.

National Council for the Social Studies (DC) (http://www.ncuf.coop)
Founded in 1921, the National Council for the Social Studies (NSCC) supports social studies education at all levels. Through its awards programs, the council honors excellence in teaching, curriculum development, research, writing, and service. Grantmaking programs include the Grant for the Enhancement of Geographic Literacy, the Fund for Advancement of Social Studies Education Grant, and the Christa McAuliffe Reach for the Stars Award. The council's Web site provides information and application guidelines for the council's programs, professional development resources, publications, a discussion board, membership information, details on curriculum standards, information on state and local councils, and teaching resources. The site's NSCC DataBank offers additional resources for educators.

National Credit Union Foundation, Inc. (WI) (http://www.ncuf.coop)
The goal of the National Credit Union Foundation, Inc., is to promote consumer financial independence through credit unions. As the charitable arm of the U.S. credit union movement, the foundation raises "funds and make grants that promote consumer financial education, affordable mortgage lending, savings and asset accumulation," and more. The foundation provides grants to credit unions and related organizations for projects focused on building strategic partnerships and incubating national model programs. The foundation's Web site provides program information, board and staff listings, and contact information.

National Endowment for Democracy (DC) (http://www.ned.org)
Founded in 1983, the National Endowment for Democracy is a grantmaking organization created to strengthen democratic institutions around the world. Funded by an annual congressional appropriation, the endowment's grants program assists organizations abroad that are working for "political and economic freedom, a strong civil society, independent media, human rights, and the rule of law." The endowment also offers fellowship opportunities. The endowment's Web site offers funding program descriptions and application instructions, details on funded projects, information on the endowment's many other programs, publications, and contact information.

National Environmental Education and Training Foundation (DC) (http://www.neetf.org/)
Founded in Washington, D.C., the National Environmental Education and Training Foundation is committed to "helping America meet critical national challenges through environmental learning." Areas of interest include health and the environment, adult learning, education and the environment, business and the environment, and National Public Land Day. The foundation has ongoing projects in all of these areas and addresses them further by

sponsoring conferences and training sessions with assorted partners. The foundation also distributes Challenge Grants and the Environmental Education Teacher Professional Development Awards. The foundation's Web site provides program descriptions, grants lists, lists of award recipients, and links to related resources.

National Film Preservation Foundation (CA) (http://www.filmpreservation.org)
The National Film Preservation Foundation was created by the Congressional National Film Preservation Act of 1996 to save America's film heritage. Based in San Francisco, the foundation supports "preservation activities nationwide that ensure the physical survival of film and improve access to film for study, education, and exhibition." The foundation provides grants for organizations or individuals involved in the process of restoring and disseminating early American film work. The foundation's Web site offers grant guidelines and application information; background material on the necessity and process of preserving films; examples of projects the foundation has funded in the past, such as the preservation of Groucho Marx's home movies; details on the foundation's operations and projects; and board and staff listings.

National Fish and Wildlife Foundation (DC) (http://www.nfwf.org/)
The National Fish and Wildlife Foundation, located in Washington, D.C., seeks to conserve healthy populations of fish, wildlife and plants, on land and in the sea, through partnerships, sustainable solutions, and education. The foundation funds projects to conserve and restore fish, wildlife, and native plants through challenge grant programs and offers special grants, which are more specific in their criteria. The foundation's Web site provides descriptions of its grant programs, guidelines, grantee information, recipient lists, answers to frequently asked questions, and nationwide contact and location information.

National Foundation for Advancement in the Arts (FL) (http://www.nfaa.org/)
The Miami-based National Foundation for Advancement in the Arts was founded in 1981 to identify emerging artists and assist them at critical junctures in their educational and professional development, and to raise appreciation for and support of the arts in American society. The foundation operates the Arts Recognition and Talent Search (ARTS) program, which awards scholarships and financial support to young artists (high school seniors and other 17- and 18-year-old artists) in the disciplines of dance, film and video, jazz music, photography, theater visual arts, voice, and writing. Program participants are eligible for cash awards and programs, including ARTS Week, the Presidential Scholars in the Arts, and the Music for Youth Foundation awards. The foundation's Web site provides details and application information for the ARTS program, news updates, information on program alumni, and staff and contact information.

National Foundation for Infectious Diseases (MD) (http://www.nfid.org/)
The National Foundation for Infectious Diseases supports research and training in infectious diseases, aids in the prevention and cure of these diseases, and sponsors public and professional educational programs. In addition to its own research and education activities, the foundation awards grants and fellowships for research and specialization in infectious diseases. Detailed information about the foundation's various fellowship and grant programs can be found in the Awards and Fellowships area of the foundation's Web site. The site also offers information on infectious diseases, access to publications, links to related Web sites, information on conferences and courses, and contact information.

National Foundation for Jewish Culture (NY) (http://www.Jewishculture.org)
Based in New York City, the National Foundation for Jewish Culture was founded in 1960 by the Council of Jewish Federations. The foundation works with artists, scholars, cultural institutions, and community agencies to enrich local Jewish life, enhance educational opportunities, and foster a dynamic Jewish identity in a multicultural society. The foundation's grant programs include the Fund for Jewish Documentary Filmmaking, New Play Commissions in Jewish Theater, and Doctoral Dissertation Fellowships in Jewish Studies. The foundation also sponsors a series of awards for achievements in Jewish culture.

Visitors to the foundation's Web site will find information on its various grant and awards programs, application information, an events calendar, publications, board and staff listings, and contact information.

National Foundation for the Improvement of Education (DC) (http://www.nfie.org/)
The National Foundation for the Improvement of Education, created in 1969 by the National Education Association, provides grants and technical assistance to improve student learning in public schools. The foundation's Innovation Grants and Learning & Leadership Grants provide support for teachers, education support personnel, and higher education faculty and staff to engage in professional development activities and fund innovations designed to improve student achievement, particularly for economically disadvantaged students. The foundation's Web site provides guidelines and application forms for these funding programs and others; news and publications; links to related resources; and listings of staff, directors, and partners.

National 4-H Council (MD) (http://www.fourhcouncil.edu)
Headquartered in Chevy Chase, Maryland, the National 4-H Council is an organization that promotes the 4-H "youth development movement to build a world in which youth and adults learn, grow, and work together as catalysts for positive change." The council offers programs, grants, curricula and publications, initiatives, and projects in a variety of areas, including workforce preparation; the environment; health, wellness, and safety; and community development. The council's Web site provides information about the council's youth grants, including instructions and applications; details about National 4-H's programs; current events; membership information; and the council's annual report.

National Gallery of Art - Center for Advanced Study in the Visual Arts (DC) (http://www.nga.gov/resources/casva.htm)
The Center for Advanced Study in the Visual Arts is a research institute founded in 1979 as part of the National Gallery of Art. The center fosters study on the production, use, and cultural meaning of art, artifacts, and architecture from prehistoric times to the present, and encourages study of the visual arts from a variety of approaches by historians, critics, and theorists of art as well as by scholars in related disciplines of the humanities and social sciences. The center's fellowship programs include the Predoctoral Fellowship Program for Travel Abroad for Historians of American Art; the Paired Fellowship Program for Research in Conservation and the History of Art and Archaeology, the Predoctoral Fellowship Program, the Senior Fellowship Program, and the Visiting Senior Fellowship Program. Details on the fellowship programs, downloadable application forms, contact information, a list of the center's current fellows, and links to Web resources of the National Gallery of Art are available on the center's Web site.

National Gardening Association (VT) (http://www.garden.org)
The National Gardening Association, established in 1972 in Burlington, Vermont, seeks "to renew the fundamental links between people, plants, and the Earth." The association's mission is accomplished through programs in schools and communities to promote environmental stewardship, advance learning and science literacy, and create partnerships that enhance communities. The association administers a series of grant programs to support projects across the United States that involve children in gardening. The association's Web site provides details on each grant program, with application guidelines and forms; information on free services for gardeners, including regional garden reports, how-to instructions, online courses, and discussion boards, among other community and gardening resources; and a sister site dedicated to gardening for kids.

National Geographic Society Education Foundation (DC) (http://www.nationalgeographic.com/foundation/)
The National Geographic Society Education Foundation was established in 1988 "to prepare children to embrace a diverse world, succeed in a global economy, and steward the planet's resources." The foundation awards grants to teachers and educational institutions

for programs in the classroom, to not-for-profit institutions working within the classroom, and to organizations providing nontraditional education outside the classroom. Education grants are also available from special funds in Colorado, Mississippi, and Oklahoma. The foundation's Web site provides detailed descriptions of the foundation's grant programs, application guidelines and forms, a list of sample teacher grants, information on making a contribution or creating a state education fund, and contact information.

National Hemophilia Foundation (NY) (http://www.hemophilia.org/)
The National Hemophilia Foundation is dedicated to preventing, treating, and finding cures for inherited bleeding disorders through education, advocacy, and research. The foundation offers a series of research grant and fellowship programs, including Laboratory Grants and Career Development Awards; Judith Graham Pool Postdoctoral Fellowships for physicians and scientists embarking on research careers; Nursing Excellence, Social Work Excellence, and Physical Therapy Excellence Fellowships; and the National Hemophilia Foundation Clinical Fellowship Program. The foundation also offers the Kevin Child Scholarship for a young person with a bleeding disorder. Funding application guidelines and forms, information on bleeding disorders, foundation events and programs, publications, a listing of board members, contact information for regional chapters, links to related Web sites, and a listing of scholarship opportunities for individuals affected by bleeding disorders are available on the foundation's Web site.

National Heritage Foundation (VA) (http://www.nhf.org/)
The National Heritage Foundation, located in Falls Church, Virginia, helps individuals establish their own foundations in the areas of charitable, educational, scientific, or religious activities. Donors and applicants are provided with administrative, tax filing, and fundraising support. The foundation's Web site includes applications for participating in the foundation's programs, information on how the foundation can assist different types of organizations, and information on legal issues.

National Hispanic Scholarship Fund, Inc. (CA) (http://www.hsf.net/)
Established in 1975, the mission of the National Hispanic Scholarship Fund, Inc., headquartered in San Francisco, California, is "to double the rate of Hispanics earning college degrees." The fund offers a series of scholarships for students of various educational backgrounds. Applicants must be U.S. citizens or legal permanent residents of Hispanic heritage. The fund's Web site includes application information for the fund's scholarship and internship programs. The site's CyberCampus section includes a listing of scholarship programs for Hispanics offered by other organizations, information on applying to college, obtaining financial aid, information on careers, and a listing of Hispanic student organizations. The site also offers news, a calendar of events, publications, links to related resources, and contact information for each of the fund's regional offices.

National Hospice Foundation, Inc. (VA) (http://www.hospiceinfo.org)
The National Hospice Foundation, Inc., established in 1992 in Alexandria, Virginia, works "to broaden America's understanding of hospice through research and education" and by informing the public about the quality end-of-life care options provided by hospice programs. The foundation's Web site provides a general description of hospice care; downloadable brochures on choosing a hospice program and communicating end-of-life wishes; information on national hospice campaigns, including the foundation's Public Engagement Campaign; and contact information.

National Italian American Foundation, Inc. (DC) (http://www.niaf.org/)
Established in 1975, the National Italian American Foundation, Inc., serves as an advocate for Italian Americans. Through scholarships, grants, and other programs, the foundation seeks to "preserve and protect Italian American heritage and culture." The foundation offers scholarships for Italian American students and for students of any ethnic background majoring or minoring in Italian subjects. The foundation's grants are offered in three main areas: Italian language study, culture and heritage projects, and college/university club

activities. Scholarship application information and forms; grant program information and downloadable applications; information on other foundation programs, conventions, activities, news, and research; and membership information are available on the foundation's Web site.

The National Latina/o Lesbian, Gay, Bisexual, and Transgender Organization, Inc. (http://www.llego.org/) (DC)
The National Latina/o Lesbian, Gay, Bisexual, and Transgender Organization, Inc., or LLEG, was established in 1987 after the National March in Washington for Gay and Lesbian Rights. LLEG seeks to "build and strengthen the national network of Latina/o Lesbian, Gay, Bisexual and Transgender (LGBT) community-based organizations and to build their capacity to serve their local constituency." Available in English and Spanish, the organization's Web site provides information on services for the Latina/o LGBT community, with listings of publications, conferences, and organizations, including information geared toward specific population groups, such as Latina/o LGBT youth and Latinas/os living with HIV/AIDS.

National Medical Fellowships, Inc. (NY) (http://www.nmf-online.org)
Established in 1946, National Medical Fellowships, Inc., is committed to "improving the health of underserved communities by increasing the representation of minority physicians, educators, researchers, and policymakers in the United States," through the special training of minority medical students, and education on the health needs of underserved populations. Based in New York City, with regional offices in San Francisco and Washington, D.C., the organization offers a series of scholarships, fellowships, awards, and prizes for minority medical students. The Web site provides application guidelines and forms for available funding opportunities, news and events, background information on the organization, and donor information.

National Multiple Sclerosis Society (NY) (http://www.nationalmssociety.org)
The National Multiple Sclerosis Society promotes research, education, and advocacy on critical MS-related issues and organizes a range of programs for individuals living with MS and funds research and training grants. The society's Web site offers a wealth of MS-related resources, a background and history of the disease, discussions of treatments, brochures and breaking news, programs and events sponsored by the society, and information about current grants with downloadable applications.

National Music Foundation (FL) (http://www.usamusic.org)
The Orlando, Florida-based National Music Foundation is dedicated to American music and musicians. The foundation works "to preserve and celebrate American music through educational programs and performances and to provide retirement-related assistance to musicians and professionals from related fields." The foundation's educational work is focused on its American Music Education Initiative, which awards grants in recognition of the accomplishments of teachers who use American music in the classroom. Additionally, the foundation is in the process of establishing a fund to which American musicians may apply for retirement-related financial assistance. Guidelines and applications for the American Music Education Initiative, lesson plans for teachers, and contact information are available on the foundation's Web site.

National Park Foundation (DC) (http://www.nationalparks.org/)
The National Park Foundation was established in 1967 to help conserve, preserve, and enhance United States National Parks and to support education and outreach programs. The foundation makes grants in cash, services, or in-kind donations to the National Park Service and its partners. The foundation's Web site provides current grant guidelines, downloadable applications, sample grants, contact information, and details about the foundation's education, voluntarism, community engagement, and other programs.

National Press Foundation (DC) (http://www.nationalpress.org)
The National Press Foundation, located in Washington, D.C., was established by journalists and communicators in 1975 to "offer issue-oriented professional development programs and awards for journalists." The foundation presents a number of prestigious awards to journalists and helps administer journalism awards presented by other organizations. The foundation also offers competitive fellowships for working journalists to attend seminars run by both the foundation and by other groups. The foundation's Web site includes listings of available awards and award winners, fellowship application guidelines, information on seminars and other professional development programs, news and events, staff and board listings, contact information, and a cartoon gallery.

National Recycling Coalition (VA) (http://www.nrc-recycle.org)
Established in 1978, the Washington, D.C.-based National Recycling Coalition is committed to the development of recycling, reusing, source reduction, and composting through technical information, education, training, outreach, and advocacy services to its members. The coalition's ultimate goal is to conserve resources for the benefit of the environment. The coalition's Web site provides information on its programs, technical councils, partnerships, events, and publications; general information on recycling and its environmental impact; details on the coalition's various awards programs, which recognize achievements in the field; board and staff listings; and contact information.

National Repertory Theatre Foundation (CA) (http://www.nrtf.org)
Founded in 1961, the Los Angeles-based National Repertory Theatre Foundation is a theatre development agency that encourages new talent, creates new programs, and sponsors new organizations vital to the growth of American theater. The foundation sponsors the National Play Award (NPA), a competition for unproduced, unpublished full-length plays. The foundation also sponsors the Classical Theatre Lab, a group of professional actors dedicated to the exploration, preservation, and celebration of the classics, and the New Works Company, an association of producing artists who assist in script development. The foundation's Web site provides information about the foundation's programs and events, NPA guidelines, and contact information.

National Restaurant Association Educational Foundation (IL) (http://www.nraef.org)
The National Restaurant Association Educational Foundation was formed in 1987 to provide training and enrichment for individuals in the restaurant and food-service industry. The foundation runs various educational and certification programs, seminars, and research projects. Additionally, the foundation provides a series of scholarships for students and educators in restaurant/foodservice programs. Program descriptions, application instructions and contact information for scholarships, and resources on careers and training in the field are available on the foundation's Web site.

National Society of Accountants Scholarship Foundation (VA) (http://www.nsacct.org/)
The National Society of Accountants Scholarship Foundation, created in 1969 to ensure the future of the accounting profession, awards annual scholarships to undergraduate students majoring in accounting at two- or four-year colleges or universities. The foundation is also planning to launch a new educational grant program to fund professional development programs, research projects, and other educational activities benefiting accounting and tax professionals. The foundation's Web site provides information on the scholarship program, application instructions, a list of recipients, foundation news, and contact information.

National Society of Professional Engineers Educational Foundation (VA) (http://www.nspe.org/edfoundation/home.asp)
Founded in 1934, the National Society of Professional Engineers (NSPE) "strengthens the engineering profession by promoting engineering licensure and ethics, enhancing the engineer image, advocating and protecting PEs' legal rights at the national and state levels, publishing news of the profession, providing continuing education opportunities, and much

more." In 1960, the society established the NSPE Educational Foundation, which grants engineering scholarships to high school, college, and graduate students. The society's Web site includes online applications for these scholarships, details on NSPE programs and events, news and information related to engineering and careers in the field, links, and membership information.

National Tourism Foundation (KY) (http://www.ntfonline.org)
The Lexington, Kentucky-based National Tourism Foundation's mission is "to benefit society through the support of education and research contributing to the values of travel and tourism," including personal enrichment, community development, heritage and natural preservation, and cultural understanding. To this end, the foundation maintains services in the areas of education and research, including scholarships, internships, conferences, and other programs. The foundation funds a variety of scholarship programs, including general and state-specific educational funding. Application requirements and guidelines for each scholarship, information on visiting scholars, internships, research opportunities, and upcoming conferences, among other tourism-related resources are available on the foundation's Web site.

National Traders Charity Foundation (NY) (http://www.tradingforcharity.com)
The National Traders Charity Foundation, located in New York, is publicly funded through donations made by members of the financial services industry for the purpose of making grants to nonprofit organizations nationally and at the community level. The broker-dealers and other service providers donate a portion of their earnings from commissions, fees, and other revenue to the foundation for the benefit of various charitable causes around the United States. The foundation's Web site provides a brief mission overview, funding information, news, and contact information.

National Trust for Historic Preservation (DC) (http://www.nthp.org/)
The National Trust for Historic Preservation, founded in 1949, provides leadership, education, and advocacy to save diverse historic places and revitalize communities. The trust gives several awards in recognition of excellence in preservation and restoration. The National Preservation Awards page of the trust's Web site provides a brief description of each award category, a downloadable nomination form, and contact information for further details. The trust's Web site also offers a wealth of information on historic preservation, news, membership and donor information, and online publications.

National Urban League, Inc. (NY) (http://www.nul.org)
The National Urban League, Inc., was founded in New York City in 1910 "to enable African Americans to secure economic self-reliance, parity, power, and civil rights." These goals are obtained through a variety of programs in education, economic self-sufficiency, civil rights, and technology; community mobilization; advocacy; and research. The league's Web site features a career center, publications and speeches, a listing of Urban League Affiliates, and details on the league's programs and special events.

National Wildlife Federation (VA) (http://www.nwf.org)
Headquartered in Reston, Virginia, the National Wildlife Federation's mission is "to educate, inspire, and assist individuals and organizations of diverse cultures to conserve wildlife and other natural resources and to protect the Earth's environment in order to achieve a peaceful, equitable, and sustainable future." The federation was founded in 1936 as a network of grassroots environmental organizations and today combines action and education to further its mission. The federation's Campus Ecology Fellowship Program provides undergraduate and graduate students with the opportunity to create environmental projects for their campuses and communities. The federation also offers awards, including the National Conservation Achievement Award. The federation's Web site provides program and award information and guidelines, information on the federation's regional field offices and state affiliates, details on educational and other programs, events listings, job opportunities, publications, and advocacy information on specific environmental issues.

Native American Public Telecommunications, Inc. (NE) (http://www.nativetelecom.org)
Based in Lincoln, Nebraska, Native American Public Telecommunications, Inc., works "to inform, educate, and encourage the awareness of tribal histories, cultures, languages, opportunities, and aspirations through the fullest participation of American Indians and Alaska Natives in creating and employing all forms of educational and public telecommunications programs and services." This mission is achieved through the development and distribution of telecommunications programs, the formation of partnerships, and dissemination of educational and leadership programs in telecommunications fields for American Indians and Alaska Natives. The organization's Web site offers proposal guidelines, information on film festivals, links to Native American Web sites, details on major contributors and information for donors, details on the organization's radio and video services, and contact information.

The NATSO Foundation (VA) (http://www.natsofoundation.org)
The NATSO Foundation was established in 1990 in Alexandria, Virginia, as "the research, education, and public outreach affiliate of America's travel plaza and truckstop industry." The foundation provides services and support in its three main areas of interest: research, to benefit the travel plaza and truckstop industry; education, to provide opportunities to industry employees; and public outreach, through programs that benefit the general public and enhance the industry. The education program offers the Bill Moon Scholarship Program, which supports the education of travel plaza industry employees and their dependents. The foundation's Web site provides application guidelines and forms, news and publications, lists of current funders, and contact information.

Nebraska Humanities Council (NE) (http://lincolnne.com/nonprofit/nhc)
Founded in 1972, the Nebraska Humanities Council "works with numerous groups throughout the state to create high-quality programs that add to the understanding and appreciation of Nebraska and the world, and that foster a better understanding of the humanities." The council provides a variety of grants, which are described on the council's Web site, along with downloadable applications. The site also offers a humanities resource center, a calendar of events, links, and contact information.

Nellie Mae Education Foundation (MA) (http://www.nelliemaefoundation.org)
The Nellie Mae Education Foundation was launched in 1998 in Quincy, Massachusetts, to "promote accessibility, quality, and effectiveness of education from preschool through postsecondary levels, especially for underserved and low-income populations in the six New England states." The foundation supports educational and community-based organizations and programs in the areas of out-of-school time, minority high achievement, college preparation, and adult literacy. The foundation's Web site offers funding guidelines, helpful resources for nonprofit and education organizations, research, a newsroom, events listings, and contact information.

Nevada Humanities Committee (NV) (http://www.nevadahumanities.org)
The Reno-based Nevada Humanities Committee was established in 1971 to "enrich the lives of all Nevadans through the humanities." The committee's grants program is designed to provide financial support to organizations for exemplary public humanities programs. The committee's Web site provides grant proposal guidelines and forms, deadlines, staff contact information, information on the committee's other programs, a sponsored programs calendar, and contact information.

New England Forestry Foundation (MA) (http://www.newenglandforestry.org)
Located in Groton, Massachusetts, the New England Forestry Foundation was created in 1944 to promote "the conservation and sustainable management of the private and municipal forestlands of New England." The foundation works to conserve New England's forests by acquiring and protecting land, educating people about forest stewardship and land planning, managing foundation land as models, supporting regional policy that encourages private ownership, and conserving a working landscape to best benefit New England. The

foundation's Web site provides detailed information on a number of conservation programs, newsletters, a clothing and publications marketplace, and a membership and donations section.

New England Foundation for the Arts (MA) (http://www.nefa.org/)
One of six regional arts organizations in the continental United States, the New England Foundation for the Arts links the public and private sectors in a regional partnership to support the arts in Connecticut, Maine, Massachusetts, New Hampshire, Rhode Island, and Vermont, and on national and international levels. The foundation's programs are offered in two main areas: Creation and Distribution, to increase opportunity and accessibility for artists, arts organizations, and audiences; and Research and Learning, to inform cultural decision-making and to promote public understanding of the role of the arts in communities. The foundation's commissioning and touring grant programs are part of the Creation and Distribution program. The foundation's Web site provides descriptions of the foundation's programs, grant guidelines and deadlines, a calendar of events, publications, links, and a staff list with e-mail addresses.

The New Israel Fund (DC) (http://www.nif.org/)
The New Israel Fund was founded in 1979 to strengthen Israeli democracy and promote social justice. This is achieved through grants and technical assistance to Israeli public interest groups and through public education programs in Israel and abroad about the challenges of democracy in the Israeli state. The fund's Web site includes information on the programs and services the fund supports, including study tours, events, and Shatil (seedling in Hebrew), which provides technical assistance to social change organizations in Israel; an overview of the fund's grant program in Israel; and a listing of grantees.

New Jersey Council for the Humanities (NJ) (http://www.njch.org/)
The Trenton-based New Jersey Council for the Humanities was created in 1973 as a state council of the National Endowment for the Humanities. The organization works "to develop, support, and promote projects that explore and interpret the human experience, foster cross-cultural understanding, and engage people in dialogue about matters of individual choice and public responsibility." The council's Web site provides information on its grant and award programs, guidelines and forms, a newsletter, features on current programs, information on volunteering, and links to related sites.

New Jersey Historic Trust (NJ) (http://www.njht.org/)
Founded in 1967 in Trenton, the New Jersey Historic Trust was created "to advance the preservation of the state's historic properties through financial, educational, and stewardship programs." The trust supports numerous programs and initiatives; its main funding programs are the Garden State Historic Preservation Trust Fund, the Historic Preservation Bond Program, the Emergency Grant and Load Fund, the Revolving Loan Fund, the Preservation Easement Program, and the New Jersey Legacies. The trust's Web site provides detailed descriptions of each program, with links to other resources and related topics; information on funded projects; news; links to other history-focused sites; publications; and contact information.

New Mexico Endowment for the Humanities (NM) (http://www.nmeh.org)
The New Mexico Endowment for the Humanities was established in 1972 in partnership with the National Endowment for the Humanities. The endowment "encourages and supports the humanities in New Mexico [by] seeking out and funding quality humanities programs for presentation to public audiences throughout the state." The endowment achieves its goal through the distribution of grants and through other programs, including a Speakers Bureau and Teachers Institute. The endowment's Web site includes grant guidelines and deadlines, a list of currently funded programs, a list of the board of directors, information on available materials and resources, and information on how to donate to the endowment.

New Orleans Jazz and Heritage Foundation, Inc. (LA) (http://www.nojhf.org)
The New Orleans Jazz and Heritage Foundation, Inc., seeks "to promote, preserve, perpetuate, and encourage the music, arts, culture, and heritage indigenous to the New Orleans area." To accomplish its goals, the foundation offers a variety of programs, including grantmaking, music classes and clinics, seed money to economically disadvantaged Louisiana businesses, and more. The foundation's Web site offers details on its programs, application guidelines, and information on music and cultural resources in the New Orleans area.

New Schools Venture Fund (CA) (http://www.newschools.org)
Based in San Francisco, California, the New Schools Venture Fund pools the resources of technology venture capitalists and entrepreneurs to improve "public K-12 education by supporting a growing community of education entrepreneurs." The New Schools Network includes education entrepreneurs, organizations in which the fund has invested, and the fund's supporters. The fund's Web site provides investment criteria and business plan guidelines, links to recommended reading and related educational resources, news and events, and contact information.

New Visions for Public Schools (NY) (http://www.newvisions.org/)
New Visions for Public Schools works with the New York City school system, the private sector, and the New York community to improve the educational achievements of children. The organization's programs include creating new schools, renovating school libraries, bringing technology to classrooms, and training teachers in innovative instruction. The organization's Web site provides descriptions of the organization's programs, some of which award grants; an online version of its most recent annual report; publications; and links to (local and national) education-related resources.

The New World Foundation (NY) (http://www.newwf.org)
The New World Foundation has been supporting "organizations working to strengthen and expand civil rights and the active participation of citizens in American democracy" since 1954. Based in New York City, the foundation maintains four main areas of grantmaking: Political Participation (including the California Initiative and Southern Organizing programs), Environmental Justice, Economic Justice (the Phoenix Fund), and the Media and Education Fund. The New World Foundation does not accept unsolicited proposals. The foundation's Web site includes descriptions of its programs and grantmaking philosophy, information for donors, the foundation's financial statement, and an online form to request further information.

New York Foundation for the Arts (NY) (http://www.nyfa.org)
The New York Foundation for the Arts (NYFA) serves individual artists, promotes their freedom to develop and create, and provides the broader public with opportunities to experience and understand their work. NYFA accomplishes this by offering financial and informational assistance to artists and arts organizations, by supporting arts programming in schools and local communities, and by building collaborative relationships with others who advocate for the arts in New York State and throughout the country. The foundation's programs include artists' fellowships in 16 disciplines; fiscal sponsorship of artists' projects and emerging organizations; grant initiatives that support career advancement, organizational development, technology planning, and arts-in-education projects; informational services, including NYFA Source, an online national database of awards, services, and publications for artists of all disciplines; and a weekly online arts news publication and a quarterly arts magazine. NYFA's Web site offers detailed program information, downloadable application forms, links to related Web sites, and a range of informational resources.

The New York Women's Foundation (NY) (http://www.nywf.org)
The New York Women's Foundation was established in 1987 to "be a voice for women and a force for change." The foundation seeks to fund programs within the five boroughs of New York City that assist low-income women and girls in moving towards economic

self-sufficiency and self-reliance. The foundation awards grants in seven primary areas: sustainable economic self-sufficiency and self-reliance for low-income women, community organizing and advocacy, multi-year capacity building, collaborative activity, positive development programming for girls, violence against women; and health. The foundation has an annual grantmaking cycle. Downloadable applications and deadlines, information on foundation events, contact information, and an online feedback form are available on the foundation's Web site.

Newspaper Association of America Foundation (VA)
(http://www.naa.org/foundation/index.html)
Located in Vienna, Virginia, the Newspaper Association of America Foundation helps to "develop tomorrow's readers by encouraging students to acquire and value information from newspapers and new media." The foundation accomplishes these goals through three main programs: Newspaper in Education, a cooperative effort between schools and newspapers to promote the use of newspapers as an educational resource; youth content; and student newspapers. The foundation also sponsors a number of conferences and publications. The foundation's Web site includes information on the foundation's programs and events, contact information, and links to related resources.

NFL Charities (NY) (http://www.nfl.com)
The NFL Charities are "dedicated to serving communities and encouraging individuals to join National Football League clubs and players in volunteering to support community needs." This charitable support comes in many forms, such as community initiatives, grants to local charitable organizations, and team-related involvement in special events. From the home page of the NFL Web site, follow the In the Community link to read about the activities of the NFL Charities; links to details on donations, volunteer programs, and player and team involvement are provided. More information on charitable programs and volunteer involvement can also be found elsewhere on the NFL site.

1939 Club (CA) (http://www.1939club.com)
Taking its name from the year in which Hitler invaded Poland, the Los Angeles-based 1939 Club is an organization of Holocaust survivors promoting Holocaust education, documentation, and justice. The club maintains strong ties to UCLA, where it sponsors lecture series through the Holocaust Studies Program, and to Chapman University in Orange County, California. The club's Web site features lists of previously honored survivors; a wealth of resources on Holocaust survivors and related materials, including links to articles, recommended reading, other Holocaust-related nonprofit organizations, and activities; and membership and contact information.

Nonprofit Finance Fund (NY) (http://www.nonprofitfinancefund.org)
The Nonprofit Finance Fund is a nationwide community development financial institution that provides financial services—primarily loans—and advisory services to nonprofits across the country. The fund makes loans for facilities projects, such as new construction, leasehold improvements and relocation, and for other growth-related needs. The fund's Web site describes its services; lists its clients, projects, and funders; and provides contact information for the fund's national office in New York and its regional offices, articles and publications, and answers to frequently asked questions.

The Nonprofit Sector Research Fund (DC) (http://www.nonprofitresearch.org/)
Established by the Aspen Institute in 1991, the Nonprofit Sector Research Fund is based in Washington, D.C. The fund "awards research grants and organizes convenings to expand knowledge of the nonprofit sector and philanthropy, improve nonprofit practices, and inform public policy related to nonprofits." The fund focuses its work in three areas: nonprofits and public policy, nonprofit relations with business and government, and foundation policy and practice. The fund's Web site provides application guidelines for the fund's grant programs, including the national research program and a scholarship for

minority students; reports on funded research studies; a publications list; and staff and contact information.

North Capitol Neighborhood Development, Inc. (DC) (http://www.ncnd.org)
Since 1984, North Capitol Neighborhood Development, Inc., has been developing affordable housing, promoting small business, and empowering the community to improve neighborhoods in Washington, D.C. The organization takes a comprehensive approach to neighborhood revitalization by forecasting, planning, influencing, and executing programs that stimulate housing and economic development in its service areas. The organization's Web site provides information about its residential, community, and business development programs, as well as contact information.

North Carolina Rural Economic Development Center, Inc. (NC) (http://www.ncruralcenter.org)
Located in Raleigh, the North Carolina Rural Economic Development Center, Inc., was created in 1987 as a resource for rural people and communities. The center maintains a host of programs and services, including current research, grants and loans, and leadership development. Details on these programs, a rural data bank and online publications, rural-life related resources, guidelines for grant programs, downloadable applications, upcoming events, current news, and contact information are available on the center's Web site.

North Shore Health Care Foundation (MN) (http://www.boreal.org/nshcf)
Located in Grand Marais, Minnesota, the North Shore Health Care Foundation was established in 1993 "to benefit healthcare for all those who live, work, and visit in Cook County." To this end, the foundation supports a variety of services: providing information and education on healthcare issues, assisting with medical equipment purchases, sponsoring healthcare programs and conferences, and publishing the *Health Care Foundation Newsletter.* The foundation's Web site provides news on upcoming conferences and fundraising events, as well as membership and contact information.

North Star Fund (NY) (http://www.northstarfund.org/)
Founded in 1979, the New York City-based North Star Fund is a partnership of donors and community activists "dedicated to building a permanent institutional and financial base for progressive social change." The fund's grants are given to New York City organizations that organize poor and working communities to make a lasting change, are structured democratically and held accountable by their communities, and connect different forms of oppression. Funding categories include regular, interim, and emergency grants; strategic grantmaking initiatives; and a revolving loan fund. The fund's Web site includes grant guidelines, a list of funded organizations, information on the fund's mission and philosophy, a list of staff, and information on contributing to the fund.

Northern California Community Loan Fund (CA) (http://www.ncclf.org)
The Northern California Community Loan Fund, established in 1987 in San Francisco, California, is a nonprofit lender "dedicated to strengthening the economic base of low-income and minority communities." The fund lends to northern California community-based nonprofit organizations that have limited access to financing from traditional lenders. Loans support four types of projects: affordable housing, community facility, economic development, and operating lines of credit. Contact information is available on the fund's Web site, along with information about the types of programs and organizations to which the fund has made loans.

Northland Foundation (MN) (http://www.northlandfdn.org/)
The Northland Foundation, located in Duluth, Minnesota, seeks to address economic, social, and human needs in a rural seven-county area of northeastern Minnesota to accomplish greater self-sufficiency for communities, organizations, families, and individuals. The foundation achieves these goals through grants and business loan programs. Grants are awarded in three areas: Connecting Kids and Community, Aging with Independence, and

Opportunities for Self-Reliance. The foundation's Web site provides grant program information, application guidelines, information on the foundation's other activities, contact information, and a staff listing with e-mail links.

Northwest Children's Fund (WA) (http://www.nwcf.org)
The Northwest Children's Fund provides funding to human service agencies in western Washington, primarily in the Puget Sound region. Through its grants program, the fund supports agencies that concentrate on prevention and early intervention, with a focus on programs that attempt to break the cycle of abuse and neglect and address the problems of poverty, homelessness, teen pregnancy, illiteracy, and youth violence. The fund's Web site provides application guidelines, lists of recent grants, events, and contact information.

Northwest Danish Foundation (WA) (http://members.aol.com/_ht_a/DanesNW/nwdf/)
The Northwest Danish Foundation has two branches in Portland, Oregon, and in Seattle, Washington. The foundation is a human service organization "whose goal is to promote and preserve Danish heritage and social interaction in the Danish communities of Oregon and Washington through a variety of intergenerational cultural, educational, social, and support programs." The foundation awards scholarships each year to persons who participate in the Danish community or demonstrate interest in preserving Danish heritage. Applications may be downloaded at the foundation's Web site, or requested by e-mail, phone, or mail. Contact information is available on the site.

Northwest Osteopathic Medical Foundation (OR) (http://www.nwosteo.org/)
The Northwest Osteopathic Medical Foundation serves people of the Northwest United States (Alaska, Idaho, Montana, Oregon, and Washington) by providing resources for osteopathic education. Currently, the Portland, Oregon-based foundation has four grant programs: Professional Grants, which funds osteopathic professional enhancement; Community IMPACT Grants, which supports the health and safety of families; Osteopathic Education, a student scholarship program; and the Rural Rotation Program, which makes grants to assist osteopathic medical students who seek an experience in rural medicine in the Pacific Northwest. The foundation's Web site contains descriptions of and application information for each of its funding programs, osteopathic links, an events page, and an online contact form.

Northwestern Memorial Foundation (IL) (http://www.nmh.org/gifts/)
The Northwestern Memorial Foundation is the philanthropic arm of Chicago's Northwestern Memorial Hospital, supporting clinical programs, patient care, facilities, research, and education at the hospital. The foundation's Web site includes descriptions of partner community fundraising organizations, online donation services, further explanation of the foundation's mission and services, links to the Northwestern Memorial Hospital's Web site, and contact information.

The NRA Foundation, Inc. (VA) (http://www.nrafoundation.org/)
Since 1990, the NRA Foundation, Inc., located in Fairfax, Virginia, has "supported a wide range of firearm-related public interest activities of the National Rifle Association of America and other organizations that defend and foster the Second Amendment rights of all law-abiding Americans." Funding goes toward promoting firearm and hunting safety, supporting marksmanship for shooting sport participants, and educating the public on firearms. Grants are made through a national program and through state funds. The foundation's Web site provides guidelines for the national program, contact information for obtaining information on the state funds, a list of the board of trustees, news, and information on how to make donations.

Ohio Humanities Council (OH) (http://www.ohiohumanities.org)
Located in Columbus, Ohio, the Ohio Humanities Council was established in 1972 to "encourage all Ohioans to become explorers of the human story, to use history, philosophy, and the other humanities as the means to arrive at new insights." Funded in part by the

National Endowment for the Humanities, the council supports a wide range of projects in the humanities. The council's Web site provides a calendar of programs and events; links to humanities councils nationwide and details on the Ohio Forum; and details on the grant application process, including eligibility, deadlines, limitations, and a grant application cover sheet and budget report form.

Oklahoma Humanities Council (OK) (http://www.okhumanitiescouncil.org)
The Oklahoma City-based Oklahoma Humanities Council is the state's National Endowment for the Humanities affiliate whose mission is "to enrich the lives of individuals and communities by fostering access to and education in the humanities" statewide. The council administers a number of humanities-related programs and funds grants in the field. Descriptions of the council's programs and grants; grant guidelines, categories, limitations, and deadlines; links to national humanities resources; a calendar of events; and contact information can be found on the council's Web site.

Oklahoma State Medical Association - Education and Research Foundation (OK) (http://www.osmaonline.org/)
The Oklahoma State Medical Association (OSMA) is committed to the advancement of "science and the art of medicine for the betterment of Oklahoma physicians and the public they serve." The OSMA Education and Research Foundation was established in 1991 to promote "the betterment of public health through scientific and medical research, both directly and by the application of assets to the use of individuals for scientific and medical research, or to any corporation, trust, fund, or foundation whose purposes and operations are scientific, educational, or charitable." Information on the foundation is available on the association's Web site under OSMA Subsidiaries and includes information on the foundation's purpose and a listing of its board members.

100 Black Men of Greater Charlotte, Inc. (NC) (http://www.100blackmenofcharlotte.org)
100 Black Men was born in New York City in 1963, when a body of successful men from the fields of business, industry, public affairs, government, and other professions decided to pool their skills, experiences, and resources to improve the quality of life for Blacks and other minorities. In the 1970's, individual chapters in cities were established. The primary focus of the 100 Black Men of Greater Charlotte, Inc., in North Carolina, is "The Movement of Youth," a structured one-on-one and group mentoring program for at-risk middle school students. The organization seeks to assist African American male students to develop high self-esteem and an appreciation for the value of a good education by providing citizenship and leadership development, motivational workshops, cultural enrichment, and community activities. In addition, the organization also has a job shadowing program, a scholarship program, and a service-learning program. The organization's Web site describes it program activities and provides contact and membership information.

Operation Fuel, Inc. (CT) (http://www.operationfuel.org)
Operation Fuel, Inc., was established in 1977 to provide emergency energy assistance to individuals and families that do not qualify for government assistance in Connecticut. The organization's Web site includes specifics on the program, testimony from those who have received aid, an online donation form, and contact information. Operation Fuel is not affiliated with any specific energy provider in Connecticut.

Optical Society of America (DC) (http://www.osa.org)
The Washington, D.C.-based Optical Society of American serves as a resource for an association of optical scientists, engineers, and technicians worldwide. The society offers a series of awards, grants, and fellowships for education, research, and technical programs. The society's Web site provides resources for those in the field, including optics news, an industry calendar, and publications; funding guidelines, deadlines, and forms; and contact information for each of the society's awards, grants, and fellowships.

Oracle Help Us Help Foundation (http://www.helpushelp.org/)
Funded by the Oracle Corporation and other corporations and individuals, the Oracle Help Us Help Foundation "assists K-12 public schools and youth organizations in economically challenged communities through grants of computer equipment and software." The foundation's Web site provides complete online grant information including eligibility and criteria, grant timelines and status updates, support services—including instructions for software and hardware set-up—and downloadable grant applications, as well as information for donors and volunteers.

Order of the Alhambra Charity Fund, Inc. (MD) (http://www.OrderAlhambra.org)
Headquartered in Baltimore, Maryland, the Order of the Alhambra "provides assistance, education, and residences for persons developmentally disabled by mental retardation; identifies, marks, preserves, and commemorates Catholic historical places, events, and persons of international or regional importance; and promotes fraternalism and sociability among its members and their families." The Order of the Alhambra Charity Fund's programs include scholarships to undergraduate students, support for establishing residences for persons with developmental disabilities, and a medical research program dedicated to finding the causes of mental retardation. These programs are briefly described on the group's Web site, which also offers contact information for further details.

Oregon Law Foundation (DC) (http://www.osbar.org/2practice/olf.html)
The Oregon Law Foundation is the charitable arm of the Oregon State Bar. The foundation awards funding to provide legal aid to low-income Oregonians, for law school scholarships, and other law related charitable programs. The foundation's Web page outlines the organization's work and provides contact information for further details.

Oregon Lions Sight and Hearing Foundation, Inc. (OR) (http://www.orlions.org)
The Portland-based Oregon Lions Sight and Hearing Foundation, Inc., was founded by the Lion Clubs of Oregon in 1959 "to serve Lions Clubs by supporting their efforts in humanitarian assistance, including but not limited to sight, hearing, diabetes awareness, and positive youth development" for the people of Oregon. The foundation supports research to find the causes and cures of blindness and deafness, and administers various programs related to its mission, including the Lions Eyebank, the Mobile Preventative Health Screening Program, and the Indigent Patient Care Program. The foundation's Web site provides information on its programs and events and contact information.

Organization of Black Airline Pilots (GA) (http://www.obap.org)
The mission of the Organization of Black Airline Pilots is to enhance, advance, and promote educational opportunities in aviation; develop and sustain a process for the ongoing mentoring of youth; monitor the development of aviation projects; and protect the general interest of its members. The organization's programs include the Aviation Career Enrichment Program, the Professional Pilot Development Program, and the Type Rating Scholarship Program. The organization's Web site provides program details, a brief history of the group, organizational priorities, a board listing, links, and contact information.

Orthopaedic Research and Education Foundation (IL) (http://www.oref.org/)
The Orthopaedic Research and Education Foundation of Rosemont, Illinois, was established in 1955 to "support research and education on diseases and injuries of bones, joints, nerves, and muscles . . . leading to improved health, increased activity, and a better quality of life for patients." The foundation provides a series of grants, awards, and fellowships for individuals working at U.S. institutions as well as grants and awards for departments and organizations. The foundation's Web site includes deadlines and downloadable applications for each program, lists of past recipients, lists of board and staff members, links to related organizations, and opportunities to donate to the foundation.

Osteogenesis Imperfecta Foundation, Inc. (MD) (http://www.oif.org)
The Osteogenesis Imperfecta Foundation, Inc., located in Gaithersburg, Maryland, was created in 1970 to improve the quality of life for individuals affected by osteogenesis imperfecta (OI), a genetic disorder characterized by bones that break easily, through research, education, awareness, and support. The foundation offers fellowships for young investigators working to develop expertise in OI research, and seed grants for either basic or clinical studies with relevance to OI. The foundation's Web site provides funding guidelines, downloadable applications, details on current research projects, information on other foundation programs, resources for patients and their families, news and events, and contact information.

Osteopathic Heritage Foundations (OH) (http://www.osteopathicheritage.org/)
The Osteopathic Heritage Foundations, located in Columbus, Ohio, is comprised of three separately incorporated foundations: the Osteopathic Heritage Foundation, supporting community health and quality of life, primarily in central Ohio; the Osteopathic Heritage Foundation of Nelsonville, improving community health and quality of life in southeastern Ohio; and the DH Foundation, funding osteopathic medical education and research, as well as supporting the initiatives of the other two foundations. The foundations' Web site offers a map of counties eligible for funding, funding procedures, board and staff listings, and contact information.

Overture to the Cultural Season (LA) (http://www.overtureneworleans.org)
Formed in 1968, Overture to the Cultural Season is a nonprofit organization dedicated to supporting "the vitality of the arts in the New Orleans area by generating public awareness and involvement in the activities and performances of cultural organizations." Overture is a volunteer organization that maintains community programs, special events, and scholarship and award opportunities to primary, secondary, and college students in the arts. Overture's Web site provides descriptions of the organization's arts programs and events, with information on membership, member activities, and contact information.

Owl Research Institute, Inc. (MT) (http://www.owlinstitute.org/)
The Owl Research Institute, Inc., was founded in 1988 in Charlo, Montana, to "engage in scientific research of wildlife," with a focus on owls. In its desire to achieve conservation by informing the public, the institute supports a variety of research and educational projects and programs. The institute's Web site offers descriptions of recent research projects and collaborations with scientists across the world; details on educational programs, including the training of college and university students; a list of reference publications; links to related resources; and a newsletter sign-up form.

Oxfam America (MA) (http://www.oxfamamerica.org)
Initiated in 1970 in Boston, Oxfam America is one of 12 Oxfam organizations around the world that comprise Oxfam International. The organization's mission is to create "lasting solutions to hunger, poverty, and social injustice" through long-term partnerships with poor communities worldwide. To this end, Oxfam America operates emergency relief programs and humanitarian aid projects, and advocates for policy change. The organization's Web site provides descriptions of current programs and campaigns, news and updates on humanitarian emergencies, a youth action page, advocacy publications and toolkits, opportunities for individuals to get involved, and contact information.

Pacific Vision Foundation (CA) (http://www.cpmc.org/services/eye/pacific-vision.html)
The Pacific Vision Foundation has supported the California Pacific Medical Center Department of Ophthalmology since 1977. Located in San Francisco, the foundation strives to prevent blindness and improve vision through support of educational and research initiatives at the center. The foundation's areas of focus include training for medical students in the field of ophthalmology, continuing education for eye professionals in northern California, and clinical research. Contact information as well as donor and volunteer details are provided on the foundation's Web site.

Packaging Education Forum (VA) (http://www.pmmi.org/pef)
Located in Arlington, Virginia, the Packaging Education Forum is a corporate membership organization through which "industry guides the development of, establishes quality standards for, and provides financial assistance to packaging education program, curricula, and students at universities in the United States." The forum seeks to ensure the quality of college-level packaging education programs through: university relations, student assistance, faculty development, and expanded teaching materials. The forum's Web site provides information on the forum's funding programs for students, details on the organization's other programs, events, and related resources.

Lucile Packard Foundation for Children's Health (CA) (http://www.lpfch.org)
The Palo Alto, California-based Lucile Packard Foundation for Children's Health was founded in 1996 and works toward improving and protecting "the physical, mental, emotional, and behavioral health of children." The foundation fulfills its mission through three programs: serving as the fundraiser for Lucile Salter Packard Children's Hospital and pediatric programs at Stanford University School of Medicine, making grants to community health organizations in San Mateo and Santa Clara Counties, and providing a reliable source of information about the health of children in San Mateo and Santa Clara Counties. The foundation's Web site offers detailed information on its Community Grantmaking Program, downloadable application guidelines, information on the foundation's other programs, a feedback form, newsroom, and contact information.

Page Education Foundation (MN) (http://www.page-ed.org)
In 1988, Alan Page, NFL Hall of Fame Pro Football player, established the Page Education Foundation to encourage Minnesota youth of color to continue their education beyond high school. The foundation grants scholarships to students of color attending college in Minnesota, and these students in turn serve as mentors and role models to youth in Service-to-Children projects. Adult volunteers also participate in the program as mentors to the scholarship recipients. The foundation's Web site includes scholarship details and application guidelines, information on volunteering as a mentor, an FAQ page, a history of the foundation and its scholarship recipients, and contact information.

Pan-Icarian Foundation (PA) (http://www.pan-icarian.com/pan_icarian_foundation.htm)
The Pan-Icarian Foundation was established in 1961 as the charitable giving arm for the Philadelphia-based Pan-Icarian Brotherhood, the oldest Hellenic organization in the Western Hemisphere. The foundation makes charitable donations for "medical aid, scholarships, disaster relief, and other charitable causes in North America and Greece." A list of current officers of the foundation, contact information, and more details about the Pan-Icarian Brotherhood can be found on the foundation's Web site.

Paralysis Project of America (CA) (http://www.paralysisproject.org)
The Paralysis Project of America was formed in 1987 in Los Angeles, California, "to accelerate progress toward finding a cure for paralysis caused by spinal cord injury (SCI)." The project works toward its mission by funding select scientific and clinical studies researching spinal cord injuries and regeneration. The project's Web site provides information on its research funding program, a Call for Applications, updates on SCI research, links to other funding and scientific resources, and details on upcoming project events.

Parenteral Drug Association Foundation for Pharmaceutical Sciences, Inc. (NY) (http://www.pdafoundation.org)
The mission of the Parenteral Drug Association Foundation for Pharmaceutical Sciences, Inc., is to "promote the good of the public by identifying needs in the fields of parenteral and related sciences and technologies and by dispensing funds in support of research and educational activities that meet those needs." The foundation funds projects at colleges, universities, and medical schools. The foundation's Web site provides information on the foundation's current grant programs, application information, recent grants made, and a contact form and address.

The Park Nicollet Foundation (MN)
(http://www.parknicolletfoundation.org/Grants/grants.html)
The Park Nicollet Foundation is committed to improving the health of children and adults in the communities of Minneapolis and its suburbs. To this end, the foundation provides community grants to area nonprofit organizations that offer programs for families or children that improve health and build developmental assets. The foundation's Web site provides downloadable community grant application guidelines and forms, descriptions of previous grantees, and contact information.

Parkinson's Disease Research Foundation (NY) (http://www.pdf.org/)
The Parkinson's Disease Research Foundation, located in New York City is a national nonprofit organization dedicated to Parkinson's disease research, education, and public information. The foundation provides research funding through awards, grants, and fellowships to support research into the cause and cure of Parkinson's disease and the training of young scientists. The foundation is particularly interested in research proposals addressing the atiology, pathogenesis, and treatment of Parkinson's disease. The foundation's Web site provides information about the foundation's funding programs, grant guidelines, contact information, information on Parkinson's disease, foundation newsletters, and information on making a donation.

Paso del Norte Health Foundation (TX) (http://www.pdnhf.org)
The Paso del Norte Health Foundation was founded in 1995 "to carry on the work begun by Providence Memorial Hospital, and to improve the health and wellness of the people who live in the greater El Paso region through education and prevention." The foundation's programs work with the populations of west Texas and southern New Mexico in the United States, and Ciudad Jurez in Mexico. The foundation's Web site provides details on its initiatives, including recent grantees, and additional contact information for each program; links to health resources; news and upcoming events; and details on the areas the foundation serves. The foundation's Web site is also available in Spanish.

Pasteur Foundation (NY) (http://www.pasteurfoundation.org)
Originally known as the Rapkine French Scientist Fund, the New York City-based Pasteur Foundation works to "introduce the research conducted at the [Paris-based] Institut Pasteur to the American public, to develop exchanges between Pasteurian and U.S. scientists, and to raise funds for Pasteurian research." In collaboration with the Institut Pasteur, which is dedicated to the prevention and treatment of diseases through biological research and public health efforts, the Pasteur Foundation administers a program to bring U.S. post-doctoral researchers to work in Institut Pasteur laboratories in Paris. The foundation's Web site provides fellowship application guidelines, details on the foundation's history and current activities, newsletters, opportunities to make a contribution, and contact information.

The Gary Payton Foundation (WA) (http://www.gpfoundation.org/)
Established in 1996 by the All-Star NBA point guard and Olympic Gold Medalist, the Gary Payton Foundation works to benefit underprivileged youth. The foundation provides grants and supports community events in education, recreation, and overall wellness for at-risk youth who live in Seattle, Washington, or Oakland, California. Grant guidelines, information on beneficiaries, a section on foundation events, and contact information are available on the foundation's Web site.

Peace Development Fund (MA) (http://www.peacefund.org/)
Started in 1981 in Amherst, Massachusetts, the Peace Development Fund partners with organizations sharing a common vision to "strengthen a broad-based social justice movement that embodies, embraces, and honors many cultures to create the new systems and institutions essential to building a peaceful, just, and equitable world." Grants address three major issues: the relationship between the United States and other countries and people; relationships between people and groups within the United States; and the relationships between institutions, those who run them, and those that they serve. Funding is available

for projects, organizations, and national and international networks based in the United States, its territories, Canada, and Mexico. The fund's Web site includes instructions on submitting letters of intent, a list of the activist board and staff, and donation opportunities. Proposals are accepted by invitation only.

Pediatric Brain Tumor Foundation of the United States, Inc. (NC) (http://www.pbtfus.org)
The Asheville, North Carolina-based Pediatric Brian Tumor Foundation of the United States, Inc., "seeks to find the cause and cure of brain tumors in children by supporting medical research, increasing public awareness of the disease, and aiding in early detection and treatment of childhood brain tumors." The foundation funds basic scientific research grants to bring about new and improved therapies for children with brain tumors. The foundation's Web site provides the current call for research proposals with downloadable applications, a list of funded institutions and recent grants, contact information, information on the foundation's family support programs, fundraising events, and the Central Brain Tumor Registry of the United States.

Pediatric Cancer Research Foundation (CA) (http://www.pcrf-kids.com)
Located in Irvine, California, the Pediatric Cancer Research Foundation was formed in 1982 "to improve the care, quality of life, and survival rate of children with malignant diseases." To this end, the foundation sponsors special events and funds grants for research. The foundation's Web site offers stories of children, details on the areas of research funded, current foundation news and events, and contact information.

PEF Israel Endowment Funds, Inc. (NY) (http://www.pefisrael.org)
The PEF Israel Endowment Funds, Inc., was founded in 1922 "to enable the direct distribution of funds to selected and approved charitable organizations in Israel." The funds support a wide variety of programs and services in Israel, including primary and secondary education; scientific research; the special needs of women, children, and families in distress; and the promotion of "greater tolerance and understanding between religious and secular communities and between Arabs and Jews"; among others. The funds' Web site offers an overview of the organization, contact information, and details on how to make a contribution.

PEN American Center, Inc. (NY) (http://www.pen.org)
The New York-based PEN American Center, Inc., is a membership association of literary writers and editors who seek "to defend the freedom of expression wherever it may be threatened, and to promote and encourage the recognition and reading of contemporary literature." To this end, the PEN American Center funds a series of literary awards for American authors, translators, editors, and publishers; sponsors annual writing awards for prisoners; and administers programs such as the Readers and Writers Program, which sends writers and their books to low-income populations that have little access to literary culture, and Open Book, a program that promotes racial and ethnic diversity within the literary and publishing community. The center also offers two emergency funds: the PEN Writers Fund and the PEN Fund for Writers and Editors with HIV/AIDS, both of which makes grants to combat serious financial difficulties. The center's Web site provides detailed information on all of these programs, membership and contact information, and an order form for the center's Guide to Grants and Awards Available to American Writers.

Pen and Brush, Inc. (NY) (http://www.penandbrush.org)
Pen and Brush, Inc., is the oldest organization of women in the arts in the United States. Located in New York City, the organization works to "bring together the public and its female artist members to stimulate appreciation for their work and to encourage the participation of women in the arts." Activities include concerts, play readings, and exhibitions. Schedules and upcoming events are posted on the organization's Web site with contact information and directions.

PEN/Faulkner Foundation (DC) (http://www.penfaulkner.org)
The Washington, D.C.-based PEN/Faulkner Foundation was established in 1980 by writers to honor their peers. The foundation annually presents the largest juried fiction award in the United States, giving prizes to the authors of five exceptional published works of fiction each year. The winner of the PEN/Faulkner Award for Fiction receives $15,000, and four other nominees receive $5,000. The foundation also presents a series of readings by writers of fiction, and sponsors the Writers in Schools program in which writers teach classes in Washington, D.C., public high schools. The foundation's Web site includes a calendar of readings, lists of current and past winners of the award, submission guidelines, and contact information.

The PENCIL Foundation (TN) (http://www.pencilfoundation.org)
The PENCIL Foundation was established in 1982 "to link community resources with Nashville, Tennessee, public school to help young people achieve academic success and prepare for life." The foundation sponsors a variety of programs, including job training, science education, student writing, math and reading volunteer programs, and awards for educators, among others. The foundation's Web site provides details on each of its programs, guidelines for awards, newsletters, and contact information.

Pennsylvania Humanities Council (PA) (http://www.pahumanities.org/)
The Pennsylvania Humanities Council, the state affiliate of the National Endowment for the Humanities, conducts and supports public humanities programs that encourage lifelong learning in history, philosophy, literature, and related subjects. The council provides qualified nonprofit organizations with resources for developing humanities programs, including speakers, grants, and access to local scholars. The council's Web site provides grant guidelines and downloadable forms, details on other community resources and events, and contact information.

Perfect Storm Foundation (MA) (http://www.perfectstorm.org/)
The Perfect Storm Foundation, located in Gloucester, Massachusetts, was founded by author Sebastian Junger, who was inspired by the fisherman of Gloucester while writing his international best seller, *The Perfect Storm.* The mission of the foundation is to "provide educational and cultural opportunities to young people whose parents make their living in the commercial fishing industry and in working maritime communities." The foundation's Web site provides downloadable grant and scholarship application forms, background information on the foundation, a mailing address, and an online contact form.

The Pet Care Trust (WA) (http://petsforum.com/petcaretrust/)
The Pet Care Trust seeks to "to help promote public understanding regarding the value of and right to enjoy companion animals, to enhance knowledge about companion animals through research and education, and to promote professionalism among members of the companion animal community." The trust awards grants for education, research, and other projects related to its mission. The trust's Web site provides information on the trust's grant cycle and funding criteria, contact information for requesting an application, a list of grantees, information on the trust's other programs, a listing of the board of trustees, and selected program video clips.

Petroleum Research Fund (DC) (http://www.acs.org/prf/)
Established in 1944 by seven major oil companies, the Petroleum Research Fund exists to support "advanced scientific education and fundamental research in the 'petroleum field,' which may include any field of pure science which . . . may afford a basis for subsequent research directly connected with the petroleum field." Grants are made to nonprofit institutions in the United States and other countries. The fund's Web site provides an online form for requesting application materials, information about its funding programs, research assistance, databases, and links to other educational resources.

PETsMART Charities, Inc. (AZ) (http://www.petsmart.com/charities/petsmart_charities)
Established in 1994, PETsMART Charities, Inc., works "to improve the quality of life for all companion animals" by raising awareness of companion animal welfare issues, funding programs to further individual animal welfare society missions, and facilitating adoptions through in-store programs. The charities' Web site offers grant and sponsorship guidelines for animal welfare organizations, information on making a donation, answers to frequently asked questions, and details on the PETsMART charities' adoption centers.

Pharmaceutical Research and Manufacturers of America Foundation (DC) (http://www.phrmafoundation.org/)
The Pharmaceutical Research and Manufacturers of America (PhRMA) Foundation promotes public health through support of scientific and medical research. The foundation provides funding for research and for the education and training of young scientists and physicians who have chosen careers in pharmacology, pharmaceutics, toxicology, informatics, or health outcomes. The foundation's Web site provides downloadable grant and fellowship guidelines and applications and listings of the foundation's board, advisory committees, and benefactors.

Philanthrofund Foundation (MN) (http://www.scc.net/~philanth/)
The Philanthrofund Foundation provides financial and fundraising support to organizations that serve the needs and enhance the quality of life of the gay, lesbian, bisexual, transgender, and allied communities of the Upper Midwest. The foundation's Web site provides information on granting areas of interest, grant and scholarship guidelines and application instructions, a listing of previous grant recipients, and contact information.

Philanthropic Ventures Foundation (CA) (http://www.venturesfoundation.org/)
The Philanthropic Ventures Foundation, located in the San Francisco Bay Area, works with individuals, families, businesses, and foundations to create innovative giving programs to match the specific interests of donors. Adopting an investment model for charitable giving, the foundation seeks out quality people and programs doing outstanding human service work to maximize the impact of philanthropy. The foundation's Web site provides information on its grantmaking approach, grant programs, donor services, consulting, publications, and contact information.

Phoenix Suns Charities (AZ) (http://www1.nba.com/suns/community/)
A program of the National Basketball Association team, the Phoenix Suns Charities works to help improve the quality of life in Arizona. The charities offer various resources to nonprofits to help them fulfill their missions, including item donations, celebrity appearances, and financial donations. Suns Charities grants are awarded to nonprofit organizations operating youth- or family-related programs. The charities' Web provides contact information for requesting grant applications and information on the charities' philanthropic and community events.

Phoenixville Community Health Foundation (PA) (http://www.pchf1.org)
The Phoenixville Community Health Foundation, located in Valley Forge, Pennsylvania, was established in 1997 through the merger of the Phoenixville Hospital and the University of Pennsylvania Health System. Providing services in Chester and Montgomery Counties, the foundation seeks to improve the health and quality of life of the community. The foundation's Web site provides information on its service areas, a grantmaking overview, grant guidelines, contribution request forms, lists of previously awarded grants, and the foundation's annual report.

PKD Foundation (MO) (http://www.pkdcure.org/index.html)
Founded in Kansas City, Missouri, in 1982, the PKD Foundation is "devoted to determining the cause, improving clinical treatment, and discovering a cure for polycystic kidney disease (PKD)." The foundation supports PKD research grants and fellowships and disseminates a wealth of information on the disease. The foundation's Web site provides

funding guidelines, application procedures, detailed information on PDK, listings of the staff and board, membership and donor information, news items on PKD research, and links to other related resources.

The Ploughshares Fund (CA) (http://www.ploughshares.org/)
Founded in 1981, the San Francisco-based Ploughshares Fund was created to provide financial support to people and organizations working to eliminate the threat of nuclear war. Ploughshares has expanded its areas of support and currently offers grants for initiatives aimed at: ending the threat from nuclear, chemical, and biological weapons; stopping the spread of weapons of war; addressing the environmental legacy of the nuclear age; promoting public understanding and participation; and preventing global and regional conflict. The fund's Web site provides access to its grants database, grant application guidelines, the fund's newsletter and annual report, board and staff lists, and contact information.

Points of Light Foundation (DC) (http://www.pointsoflight.org/)
Created in 1990, the Washington, D.C.-based Points of Light Foundation is a "nonpartisan nonprofit organization devoted to promoting volunteerism." Through a partnership with the Volunteer Center National Network, the foundation advocates for volunteer service, helping to mobilize people and resources to address community problems. The foundation distributes a series of recognition awards including the Awards for Excellence in Corporate Community Service, the President's Community Volunteer Award, the National Family Volunteer Award, and the Daily Points of Light Award. The foundation's Web site includes awards program details; a wide range of information for volunteers, organizations, and volunteer managers; details on training and events; and a search tool to locate volunteer centers.

Police Foundation (DC) (http://www.policefoundation.org)
The Washington, D.C.-based Police Foundation was established in 1970 "to help the police be more effective in doing their job, whether it be deterring robberies, intervening in potentially injurious family disputes, or working to improve relationships between the police and the communities they serve." The foundation offers research, publications, and training in the field. It also administers the Police Fellowship Program for law enforcement personnel interested in police policy and the application of technology, research, and/or training development. The foundation's Web site provides details and application guidelines for the fellowship program, information and updates on research and other projects, lists of the staff and board members, opportunities to order publications, and contact information.

The Dorothy Rider Pool Health Care Trust (PA) (http://www.pooltrust.com)
The Dorothy Rider Pool Health Care Trust serves "as a resource that enables Lehigh Valley Hospital to be a superior regional hospital and improve the health of the citizens of the region it serves." The trust funds a variety of grants related to its mission. The trust's Web site provides application procedures; background information on the trust, including its annual report and history; and information regarding the associated Rider-Pool Foundation.

The Roscoe Pound Institute (DC) (http://www.roscoepound.org)
The Roscoe Pound Institute was established in 1956 by trial lawyers to honor and build upon the work of Roscoe Pound, Dean of the Harvard Law School from 1916-1936. Based in Washington, D.C., the institute strengthens the practice of trial law through its programs, publications, and research grants, which are designed to help judges, academics, and others understand a balanced view of the U.S. civil justice system. The institute's awards for law students include the Elaine Osborne Jacobson Scholarship for Women Working in Health Care Law, the Richard S. Jacobson Award for Excellence in Teaching Trial Advocacy, and the Roscoe Hogan Environmental Law Essay Contest. The institute's Web site provides descriptions of the institute's programs, publications, contact information, and links to related resources.

Prevent Blindness America (IL) (http://www.preventblindness.org/)
Prevent Blindness America was established in 1908 as a "volunteer eye health and safety organization dedicated to fighting blindness and saving sight." The organization is based in Schaumburg, Illinois, with regional offices throughout the United States. The organization's Web site provides news and information on health, safety, and current research related to optical health; details on requesting information packets; a Web forum; and searchable listings of local programs and services.

The Pride Foundation (WA) (http://www.pridefoundation.org/)
The Pride Foundation of Seattle, Washington, works to "strengthen [the] gay, lesbian, bisexual, transgender, and allied community today, and build an endowment fund for tomorrow." The foundation offers funding through its grants programs for a wide range of organizations and projects in Washington, Oregon, Montana, Idaho, and Alaska. The foundation also offers scholarships for gay, lesbian, bisexual, and transgender youth and adults; children raised in gay or lesbian families; leaders and activists in promoting the rights of sexual minorities; and others. The foundation's Web site includes current grant and scholarship guidelines and forms, links to related sites and funding opportunities, information on contributing and volunteering, a calendar of events, and a grants list from 1991 to the present.

Pridelights Foundation, Inc. (MA) (http://www.pridelights.org)
Located in Boston, Massachusetts, the Pridelights Foundation, Inc., was established in 1995 to "eliminating homophobia through collaborative efforts between the gay and straight communities." The foundation's Bridge Builder Grants Program works to strengthen these collaborative efforts by supporting such areas as education, the arts, and community outreach programs. The foundation also runs its annual Pridelights Festival, along with other activities and events that highlight the gay and lesbian community to gay and non-gay people alike. Grant criteria, a grant application form, information on volunteer opportunities, upcoming foundation-sponsored events, and contact information are available on the foundation's Web site.

Princess Grace Foundation-USA (NY) (http://www.pgfusa.com/)
Established in 1982 in memory of Princess Grace of Monaco, the Princess Grace Foundation-USA supports emerging young artists nationwide in the fields of theater, dance, and film. Students in their last year of schooling or training are eligible for tuition assistance through scholarships, while young artists working in the areas of theater and dance qualify for apprenticeships and fellowships. The foundation also recognizes exceptional and continuing professional achievement through the awarding of Princess Grace Statuettes, its highest honor, to two or three recipients annually. The foundation's Web site provides a fact sheet and background information about the foundation, application guidelines, a list of recent grantees, and contact information.

Pro-Choice Resources (MN) (http://www.sff.net/people/RobinR/pcr.htm)
Located in Minneapolis, Minnesota, Pro-Choice Resources was founded in 1967 to provide information and referral services for women facing an unwanted pregnancy. Its mission today is to "provide financial and educational resources to ensure access and expand reproductive options for all women including the right to choose and obtain a legal abortion." The organization's programs include education and outreach services; the Hersey Abortion Assistance Fund, which provides grants or loans to women who have no health insurance or face other hardships to obtain abortions; and the HLHV Medical Scholarship Fund, which provides tuition assistance for medical students who will provide abortions as part of their practice. Further program details and contact information are provided on the organization's Web site.

Professional Tennis Registry Foundation (SC) (http://www.ptrtennis.org/foundation.htm)
Based in Hilton Head Island, South Carolina, the Professional Tennis Registry Foundation was established in 1981 as the charitable arm of the United States Professional Tennis

Registry. The foundation raises, administers, and distributes funds for charitable activities. The foundation's primary focus is to bring tennis instruction and tennis equipment to children in inner cities and rural areas where the opportunity to play may not otherwise be available to them. The foundation's Web site offers an overview of the foundation's activities and contact information.

The Progeria Research Foundation, Inc. (MA) (http://www.progeriaresearch.org)
The Progeria Research Foundation, Inc., supports research to find the cause, treatment, and cure for Hutchinson-Gilford Progeria Syndrome (HGPS), a rare genetic condition which causes premature aging. The foundation also seeks to promote awareness of the disease, and to raise funds for research and education programs. The foundation's Web site provides research grant criteria, guidelines for interested applicants, a list of recent grant recipients, and information and research on the disease.

Project Tomorrow (CA) (http://www.tomorrow.org)
Founded in 1996, Project Tomorrow is a nonprofit collaborative of businesses and educators dedicated to improving K-12 science education in Orange County, California, schools. The organization seeks to accomplish its mission through programs for students, professional development for educators, and community involvement. The organization's Web site offers details about program interests, board/staff listings, an events calendar, and contact information.

Proliteracy Worldwide (NY) (http://www.proliteracy.org)
Formed from the 2002 merger of the world's two largest adult volunteer literacy organizations, Laubach Literacy International and Literacy Volunteers of America, Inc., ProLiteracy Worldwide works to "sponsor educational programs and services to empower adults and their families by assisting them to acquire the literacy practices and skills they need to function more effectively in their daily lives and participate in the transformation of their societies." The organization is active in 45 developing countries as well as in the United States and serves more than 350,000 new adult learners around the world each year. Its publishing division, New Readers Press, produces and distributes adult educational books and materials to literacy organizations, schools, libraries, and other institutions nationwide. The organization's Web site provides access to a database of literacy programs, a resource list, and the Web sites of its founding organizations.

Prosthetics for Diabetics Foundation (GA) (http://www.expage.com/page/pfdfoundation)
Created in 1999, the Prosthetics for Diabetics Foundation, located in Monroe, Georgia, works to meet "the needs of amputees and their families by providing them with not only prosthetics, but also rehabilitation and long-term care as well." The foundation assists diabetic patients with medical bills related to prosthetic costs and works to raise awareness of diabetes. The foundation's Web site offers links to related organizations and contact information.

Public Education Network, Inc. (DC) (http://www.publiceducation.org)
The Public Education Network, Inc., headquartered in Washington, D.C., is a nationwide association of local education funds (LEFs) and individuals working toward school reform in America's low-income communities. The network's mission is "to build public demand and mobilize resources for quality public education for all children." The network and its LEF members work to create policy initiatives in the areas of standards and accountability, teacher quality, and schools and community. Details on local education funds across the country, news and upcoming events, the network's annual report and other publications, and resources are available on the network's Web site.

Public Entity Risk Institute (VA) (http://www.riskinstitute.org/)
The Public Entity Risk Institute, located in Fairfax, Virginia, began working in 1997 to serve the risk management needs of local governments, small businesses, and small nonprofit entities through the provision of resources and information. The institute's Grant and

Research Program is designed "to improve the theory and practice of risk management." The institute's Web site provides current funding priorities, application procedures, information on funded projects and reports, publications and other resources, a news center, and contact information.

Pulmonary Fibrosis Foundation (CO) (http://www.pulmonaryfibrosis.org)
The Pulmonary Fibrosis Foundation, incorporated in Colorado and now headquartered in Chicago, Illinois, works to provide funding for research and treatment of pulmonary fibrosis. The foundation aims to "empower scientists and physicians to sufficiently increase biomedical knowledge to the point where having Pulmonary Fibrosis no longer implies a death sentence." The foundation is also an educational resource, providing access to the most recent studies on the disease. The foundation's Web provides guidelines for current funding opportunities, a range of information on pulmonary fibrosis, resource links, a listing of the foundation's board members, and contact information.

PVA Spinal Cord Research Foundation (DC) (http://www.pva.org/NEWPVASITE/research & education/scrf/scrf.htm)
Established after World War II to help veterans who had incurred spinal cord injuries during the war, Paralyzed Veterans of America (PVA) today works to "support research to alleviate, and ultimately end, the medical and functional consequences of paralysis." In 1975, the organization created the PVA Spinal Cord Research Foundation to carry out the responsibility of supporting research. In addition to supporting work that aims to find a cure to spinal cord dysfunction, the foundation also "supports grants designed to improve the current treatment and care for acute and chronic spinal cord dysfunction, develop innovative rehabilitative therapies and assistive devices for paralyzed individuals, and train talented researchers to focus on the problem of spinal cord dysfunction." Descriptions of foundation funding categories, downloadable guidelines and procedures, information on the funding review process, and the organization's annual report are available on the foundation's Web site.

Queens Council on the Arts (NY) (http://www.queenscouncilarts.org)
The Queens Council on the Arts was founded in 1966 to promote, support, and develop the arts in Queens County, New York. Specifically, its mission is to "assist arts organizations and individual artists and to present our diverse cultural resources to the two million residents of our borough, to residents of other boroughs, and to visitors to New York City." Through the Queens Community Arts Fund, the council offers funding to Queens-based artists and arts organizations. The council's Web site provides downloadable applications and guidelines, dates and locations of seminars for new applicants, a list of special events, publications, videos, and a calendar of performances and exhibitions throughout Queens.

Radio and Television News Directors Foundation (DC) (http://www.rtndf.org)
As the educational arm of the Radio and Television News Directors Association, the Radio and Television News Directors Foundation provides training programs, seminars, scholarship support, and research in areas of critical concern to electronic news professionals and their audience. The foundation offers a variety of scholarships, fellowships, and internships for journalism students and journalists in electronic media. The foundation's Web site provides descriptions of these programs, along with downloadable applications, contact information, and answers to frequently asked questions for each program; details on the foundation's other programs and resources; information on upcoming training workshops; and a list of the trustees and staff.

Rainforest Action Network (CA) (http://www.ran.org)
Founded in 1985 in San Francisco, the Rainforest Action Network works "to protect rainforests and the human rights of those living in and around those forests" through activism in the United States and in rainforest countries. The network's Web site provides detailed information on all of the network's campaigns; an Action Center, where visitors can contribute in a variety of ways, including sending e-mail messages to government officials;

resources for activists; activities for kids; and background information on the plight of the rainforests.

Rainforest Alliance, Inc. (NY) (http://www.rainforest-alliance.org)
The New York City-based Rainforest Alliance, Inc., is an international nonprofit organization that works "to protect ecosystems and the people and wildlife that live within them by implementing better business practices for biodiversity conservation and sustainability." The alliance pursues this mission through education, research in the social and natural sciences, and the establishment of cooperative partnerships with businesses, governments, and local peoples. The alliance's research projects and funding programs are designed to promote and support scientific and social research and new methods of tropical conservation. The alliance's Web site provides information on current funding programs and other alliance projects, annual reports, rainforest resources and facts, news, links to other resources, and contact information.

Rainforest Cafe Friends of the Future Foundation (MN) (http://www.rainforestcafe.com/RFC/IFriends.asp)
The Rainforest Cafe Friends of the Future Foundation, located in Hopkins, Minnesota, is dedicated to supporting environmental causes and causes that enrich the lives of children, their families, and the communities in which the Rainforest Cafe operates. An application form and instructions are available on the foundation's Web site, along with the contact information.

Ramakrishna Foundation (CA) (http://www.geocities.com/rkfoundation)
The Ramakrishna Foundation was established in 1996 to collect and distribute funds to "any religious organization that promotes religious harmony," foster religious cultural and educational activities, and aid organizations and individuals who support the foundation's objectives. The foundation aids organizations located in India. A list of religious organizations currently appealing for funds and details on the foundation's funding method, mission, and religious philosophy are available on the foundation's Web site.

The Ayn Rand Institute (CA) (http://www.aynrand.org/)
The Ayn Rand Institute was founded in 1985 to advance Objectivism, author Ayn Rand's philosophy of "reason and rationality; individualism and individual liberties; and free-market capitalism." The institute seeks to promote this philosophy through opinion pieces and its own media projects, a Campaign Against Servitude opposing voluntarism, essay contests for high school and college students, resources for college and university campus clubs, and materials and training on Objectivism. The institute's Web site provides information on Objectivism and Ayn Rand, and describes the activities of the institute.

Rapides Foundation (LA) (http://www.rapidesfoundation.org/)
The Rapides Foundation is centered in a nine-parish service area in central Louisiana. Founded in 1994, the foundation funds "opportunities that strengthen health and well-being, education, and the arts and humanities" through its grant programs. Initiative Grants focus on selected community health, arts, education, and community development issues; Responsive Grants fund innovative and effective approaches not covered in the Initiative Grants; and mini-grants provide funding of less than $10,000 for short-term projects. The foundation's Web site provides current grant guidelines, newsletters, contact information, and news on current foundation events.

Ravens Foundation for Families, Inc. (MD) (http://www.baltimoreravens.com/template.php?subsection=rff)
The Baltimore-based Ravens Foundation for Families, Inc., "seeks to help change fundamental ills with which Baltimore and area families must deal in the pursuit of healthy and productive lives for themselves and their community." Established by the Baltimore Raven's National Football League team, the foundation's funding priority is the physical and mental health of youth and the creation of environments for their positive social

development. The foundation's Web site provides information about the foundation, community programs, special events, and other charitable foundations established by Baltimore Raven's football players.

Reaching Heights (OH) (http://www.chuh.net/reachingheights)
Founded in 1989, Reaching Heights is a "citizen organization that supports the public schools serving Cleveland Heights and University Heights, Ohio." The organization's goal is to enhance local public education to meet the challenges of the 21st century. Reaching Heights provides grants to promote learning, to involve the public in the school system, and for music education projects. The organization's Web site provides grant guidelines, past grant recipients, links, and contact information.

Reader's Digest Partners for Sight Foundation (NY) (http://www.rd.com/corporate/rd_fundblind.html)
The Reader's Digest Partners for Sight Foundation was established in 1955 in Pleasantville, New York, to provide "support that directly improves the lives of the blind and visually impaired, helping them realize their full potential in society." The foundation publishes large-type editions of Reader's Digest magazines and funds two types of grants: large, multi-year grants and smaller annual grants to local organizations. Interested applicants can use the contact information provided on the foundation's Web site to inquire about further funding details.

Reading Musical Foundation (PA) (http://www.readingmusicalfoundation.org/)
The Reading Musical Foundation, located in Reading, Pennsylvania, is an umbrella funding resource for music and the allied arts in Berks County. The foundation supports music organizations and education programs, provides a series of music scholarships for future musicians, and funding opportunities for adults. Application guidelines and an application form for each scholarship, information on the foundation's programs, a schedule of concerts, listings of musical ensembles in the area, and contact information are available on the foundation's Web site.

Red Ribbon Charitable Foundation, Inc. (FL) (http://www.red-ribbon.org/)
Created in 1995, the Red Ribbon Charitable Foundation, Inc., is dedicated to protecting future generations from HIV and AIDS. Based in Pensacola, Florida, the foundation raises and provides funds for activities that reduce the impact of HIV/AIDS on the community. The foundation's Web site provides a downloadable funding application, a list of grant recipients, the foundation's annual report, a list of community resources, and contact information.

Donna Reed Foundation for the Performing Arts (IA) (http://www.donnareed.org/)
The Donna Reed Foundation for the Performing Arts was formed in 1987 in Denison, Iowa, to memorialize Ms. Reed's achievements and to perpetuate her commitments to youth, education, and the performing arts. The foundation supports talented youth through national, state, and local scholarships; conducts workshops by industry professionals; and promotes stage plays, concerts, and other cultural activities. The foundation's Web site provides information about the Donna Reed Scholarships for students of the performing arts, downloadable application forms, details on workshops, membership information, and press releases about the foundation and its activities.

Christopher Reeve Paralysis Foundation (NJ) (http://www.christopherreeve.org)
Created in 1999, the Springfield, New Jersey-based Christopher Reeve Paralysis Foundation is committed to funding research that develops treatments and cures for paralysis caused by spinal cord injury and other central nervous system disorders. The foundation also works to improve the quality of life for people living with disabilities through its Quality of Life Grants program and advocacy efforts. Information, guidelines, and downloadable applications for the foundation's research grants and Quality of Life Grants; information on research grant recipients; research updates and other news; resources for people

living with spinal cord injury; an online paralysis resource center; and a list of affiliated organizations are available on the foundation's Web site.

The Reinvestment Fund (PA) (http://www.trfund.com)
Based in Philadelphia, Pennsylvania, and founded in 1985, the Reinvestment Fund is a community development financial institution that works to alleviate poverty and create economic opportunity in a 21-county, three-state region centered in Philadelphia. The fund uses investments from individuals and institutions to make loans and equity investments in affordable housing, community facilities, small businesses, workforce development programs, and sustainable energy. Visit the fund's Web site for detailed information on each of the fund's lending areas and application instructions, details on other fund programs, information for investors, and contact information.

Research Foundation of the City University of New York (NY) (http://www.rfcuny.org)
The Research Foundation of the City University of New York (CUNY) was chartered in 1963 "to provide low-cost reliable post-award administration of sponsored programs for the university." The foundation administers all awards and contracts to CUNY faculty and staff for research, training, education, and services. The foundation's Web site provides information on grants offices at each CUNY branch, information on internal award programs and access to external funding sources, a range of administrative information and materials, and contact information.

Resist, Inc. (MA) (http://www.resistinc.org)
Originally formed in 1967 to oppose the war in Vietnam and to support draft resistance, the Somerville, Massachusetts-based Resist, Inc., funds activist organizing and education work within movements for social change. The organization provides "small but timely" grants and loans to grassroots organizations for both ongoing and new projects that address social and/or economic injustice. Resist is particularly interested in providing support to groups that are too radical to receive funding from traditional sources. Resist also offers emergency funding to help groups respond quickly to unexpected organizing needs and support to make projects or events accessible to people with disabilities. The organization's Web site includes application guidelines, a downloadable application form, information on past grantees, listings of the board and staff, newsletters, and an online guide to finding funding.

Rett Syndrome Association of Illinois (IL) (http://www.rettillinois.org/)
The Rett Syndrome Association of Illinois was established as a support network for families and a means of disseminating information about Rett Syndrome, a form of mental retardation in girls. The association hosts workshops and conferences, publishes a newsletter, and organizes support groups, all with the goal of promoting the general welfare and understanding of those with Rett Syndrome. The association's Web site provides information about the syndrome, a listing of upcoming events, news on current research, and a feedback form for more information.

Rett Syndrome Research Foundation (OH) (http://www.rsrf.org)
The Rett Syndrome Research Foundation (RSRF) was created in 1999 to find treatments and a cure for Rett Syndrome by engaging scientists and facilitating the exchange of information and data. The foundation offers research grants and post-doctoral fellowships for general research into the syndrome and research focusing on neurobiology or respiratory dysfunction. The foundation's Web site provides information about the syndrome, funding guidelines and applications, lists of award recipients, research findings, scientific meetings, newsletters, and contact information.

Rex Foundation (CA) (http://www.rexfoundation.org/index.html)
The Rex Foundation, a charitable foundation established by members and friends of the Grateful Dead, "aims to help secure a healthy environment, promote individuality in the arts, provide support to critical and necessary social services, assist others less fortunate

than ourselves, protect the rights of indigenous people and ensure their cultural survival, build a stronger community, and to educate children and adults everywhere." Grant recipients are selected through the personal knowledge of the foundation's decision makers; unsolicited requests will not be considered. The foundation's Web site provides annual reports, a listing of grant recipients, profiles of selected foundation beneficiaries, a listing of board members, and information about the Rex Awards for achievements in creativity and human rights.

Riverside Community Health Foundation (CA) (http://www.rchf.org)
The Riverside Community Health Foundation, in partnership with the Community Health Corporation, works "to identify, develop, and support opportunities to expand access to healthcare; foster health education and prevention; and provide programs and services that improve the health of the people in the community" of Riverside, California. Grant guidelines and applications, a list of past recipients, contact information, and links to related resources are available on the foundation's Web site.

The Robin Hood Foundation (NY) (http://www.robinhood.org/)
Established in 1988, the Robin Hood Foundation is committed to "ending poverty in New York City." To this end, the foundation supports organizations in the areas of youth and after-school programs, early childhood, education, job training, and survival. Additionally, the foundation established its Robin Hood Relief Fund to aid victims of the World Trade Center attacks. The foundation's Web site includes details on the group's investment strategies, funding application guidelines and a downloadable form, information on the organizations it funds, descriptions of funding priorities, an online donation system, and contact information.

Jackie Robinson Foundation (NY) (http://www.jackierobinson.org/)
The Jackie Robinson Foundation, founded in 1973 by Rachel Robinson, "provides education and leadership development opportunities for students of color with strong capabilities, but limited financial resources." The foundation awards four-year scholarships annually to minority students enrolled in higher education studies and offers leadership and career development programs. The foundation's Web site provides program information, scholarship guidelines, an application form, and alumni information.

Rockefeller Family Fund, Inc. (NY) (http://www.rffund.org/)
The New York City-based Rockefeller Family Fund, Inc., makes grants in five major program areas: citizen education and participation, economic justice for women, the environment, institutional responsiveness, and self-sufficiency. The fund supports tax-exempt organizations engaged in educational and charitable activities of national significance. In addition to general program descriptions, the fund's Web site provides a list of recent grantees and links to those with Web sites, application procedures, a listing of the fund's trustees and staff, and links to fund affiliates.

Rockefeller Philanthropy Advisors, Inc. (NY) (http://www.rockpa.org)
Located in New York City, Rockefeller Philanthropy Advisors, Inc., is an independent non-profit that develops, manages, and monitors all types of foundations and charitable organizations. The group works with individuals, families, collaborative organizations, foundations, and trusts on all aspects of their philanthropic endeavors. The group's Web site provides details on the group's services and special programs, links to further resources, and contact information.

Rocky Mountain Elk Foundation, Inc. (MT) (http://www.rmef.org)
The Rocky Mountain Elk Foundation, Inc., located in Missoula, Montana, was created by four hunters in 1984. The apolitical organization's mission is to "ensure the future of elk, other wildlife, and their habitat." This is accomplished through a number of educational outreach and conservation programs. The foundation annually offers a series of awards, including the Wildlife Leadership awards/scholarships to undergraduate wildlife students

and scholarships for the foundation's national conservation education program for high school students. Scholarship guidelines and forms, a range of information on the elk and its habitat, membership information, links to related Web sites, news, and board and staff lists are available at the foundation's Web site.

Roots of Peace (CA) (http://www.rootsofpeace.org)
Roots of Peace was established in 1997 in San Rafael, California, and is dedicated "to eradicating landmines worldwide and rehabilitating the land to make it productive once more." To this end, the organization helps countries no longer at war to turn "mines into vines," planting local produce in areas where mines once dominated the land. The organization's Web site provides information on current landmine projects, links to related organizations, and a contact address.

Rose Community Foundation (CO) (http://www.rcfdenver.org/)
The Rose Community Foundation, located in Denver, Colorado, was created in 1995 from the sale of Rose Medical Center. The organization "dedicates its resources towards enhancing the health and well being of the Greater Denver community." The foundation funds programs in five basic categories: aging, child and family development, education, health, and Jewish life. The foundation's Web site includes application guidelines, information on contributing, and answers to frequently asked questions.

The R.O.S.E. Fund (MA) (http://www.rosefund.org)
The R.O.S.E. (Regaining One's Self-Esteem) Fund is located in Boston, Massachusetts. The national nonprofit organization is devoted to ending violence against women and their children and assisting women survivors of violence to regain their self-esteem and rebuild their lives. Programs include grants for direct service agencies throughout the United States, awards and scholarships for survivors of abuse, and a reconstructive surgery program for women who have been disfigured by abuse. The fund's Web site includes award and scholarship guidelines and forms, grant program information, a list of grant recipients, links to related resources, and a staff list.

The Rose Hills Foundation (CA) (http://www.rosehillsfoundation.org/)
The Rose Hills Foundation, located in Los Angeles, California, supports charitable organizations for the benefit of the people of southern California, with an emphasis on San Gabriel Valley and East Los Angeles. Areas of interest include arts and culture, civics and community services, education, community-based health programs, and youth activities. The foundation's Web site provides grant guidelines, application procedures, and contact information.

The Rosenberg Fund for Children (MA) (http://www.rfc.org/)
In 1953 Ethel and Julius Rosenberg were controversially accused and executed for allegedly giving top-secret data on nuclear weapons to the Soviet Union. The Rosenberg Fund for Children was founded by their son, Robert Meeropol, in Easthampton, Massachusetts, to "provide for the educational and emotional needs of children of targeted progressive activists, and youth who are targeted activists themselves." The fund defines "targeted" as someone whom as a result of his or her activism, has lost a job, suffered physical or mental injury or disability, been harassed or discriminated against, been imprisoned, or died. The fund supports children and young adults in the following areas: school tuition, camp tuition, counseling, cultural lessons, outdoor programs, after-school programs, and supplies for college. The fund's Web site provides grant guidelines, downloadable applications, and contact information.

Rotary Club of Sacramento Foundation (CA) (http://www.rotarysacramento.com)
In 1971, the Rotary Club of Sacramento formed its foundation to aid underprivileged youth in the Sacramento area. The foundation manages two types of funds: Community Service and Endowment Service funds. The former supports community-based programs, such as the Youth Incentive Program, while the later supports the long-term charitable goals of the

foundation. The basic funding mission of the foundation, as well as contact information for further details, can be found on its Web site.

Rotary District 6360 Foundation (MI)
(http://www.district6360.com/district foundation.htm)
The Rotary District 6360 Foundation was founded in 1992 to provide the clubs in Rotary District 6360, headquartered in Kalamazoo, Michigan, with funding and other assistance for their service projects. The foundation makes grants only to Rotary clubs. Information on requesting an application is available on the foundation's Web site.

The Rotary Foundation (IL) (http://www.rotary.org/foundation/)
As the philanthropic arm of Rotary International, the Rotary Foundation supports efforts to "achieve world understanding and peace through local, national, and international humanitarian, educational, and cultural exchange programs." The foundation sponsors activities in two main areas: humanitarian programs, which fund projects designed to improve quality of life, primarily in the developing world; and educational programs, through which the foundation provides funding for students to study abroad, university professors to teach in developing countries, and exchanges of business and professional people. In addition to general program descriptions, the foundation area of Rotary International's Web site provides information on the foundation's history, support, and governance, including a list of trustees.

Damon Runyon Cancer Research Foundation (NY) (http://www.cancerresearchfund.org/)
The Damon Runyon Cancer Research Foundation was established in 1954 by radio personality Walter Winchell after his friend journalist Damon Runyon died from cancer. Winchell believed that "young scientists following their own best instincts would make the critical discoveries leading to the defeat of cancer." Following this belief, the fund grants postdoctoral Fellowship Awards, Scholar Awards, and Clinical Investigator Awards. The fund's Web site provides detailed guidelines and application forms and also provides donor information and a Science Spotlight.

Rural Community Assistance Corporation (CA) (http://www.rcac.org)
Located in West Sacramento, California, the Rural Community Assistance Corporation was certified as a Community Development Financial Institution in 1996. Designed to be a major resource for the rural west (serving Alaska, Arizona, California, Colorado, Hawaii, Idaho, Montana, Nevada, New Mexico, Oregon, Utah, Washington, and Wyoming), the corporation provides technical assistance and access to financing for programs in the areas of affordable housing, environmental infrastructure, and community facilities. The corporation's Web site includes guidelines and downloadable applications for its loan fund, publications, fact sheets on the programs in each of the 13 states the corporation serves, upcoming events, and contact information.

Albert B. Sabin Vaccine Institute (DC) (http://www.sabin.org)
The Albert B. Sabin Vaccine Institute was established to promote "rapid scientific advances in vaccine development, delivery, and distribution worldwide." (Albert B. Sabin developed the original polio vaccine.) In the field of vaccine development, the institute supports the academic development of scientists and physicians; provides grants for research, development, and testing; advocates for the integration of scientific advances and public policy; and promotes public awareness of vaccine research and the development of educational materials. The institute's Web site offers brief descriptions of its programs and activities and contact information.

Sacred Heart Foundation (FL) (http://www.sacred-heart.org/foundation.asp)
The Pensacola, Florida-based Sacred Heart Foundation was established in 1985 as the private fundraising arm of the Sacred Heart Health System to care for the sick, the poor, the young, and the aged. The foundation supports all areas of healthcare within the Sacred Heart Health System, including programs such as the Patient Aid Fund for Cancer Care and

the local Children's Miracle Network efforts. The foundation's Web site contains information on its work and projects, as well as contact information for further details.

St. Agnes Foundation (MD)
(http://www.stagnes.org/cportal/general/content.asp?cid=16)
The St. Agnes Foundation raises funds for St. Agnes HealthCare in Baltimore, Maryland. The foundation's Web site provides a newsletter, details on fundraising events, information for donors, and contact information.

St. Elmo Foundation (NY) (http://www.st-elmo.net/foundation)
Based in Pearl River, New York, the St. Elmo Foundation supports the literary, scientific, and charitable activities of the brothers of the Delta Phi Fraternity. To this end, the foundation offers grants and scholarships to Delta Phi members and other students enrolled in undergraduate or graduate programs, faculty and staff of those organizations, or student groups or departments at such institutions, such as fraternity chapters or sponsored programs. Grant and scholarship guidelines, application forms, and contact information are available from the foundation's Web site.

St. Louis Rams Foundation (MO) (http://news.stlouisrams.com/Community/)
Just one arm of the St. Louis Rams football team's community outreach program, the St. Louis Rams Foundation supports "efforts and organizations that inspire positive change in the greater St. Louis area with an emphasis on youth in the areas of education, literacy, health, and recreation." The foundation's Web site offers guidelines and applications for the Community First program, which seeks to encourage youth community service, as well as information and updates on other Rams community projects.

St. Luke's Foundation (WA) (http://www.stlukesfoundation.org)
St. Luke's Foundation supports health-related activities in the Bellingham, Washington, community through direct financial support to healthcare agencies and health education programs. The foundation looks for projects and programs designed to solve health-related problems and provide health education to the residents of Whatcom County. The foundation also offers nursing scholarships. The foundation's Web site offers a brief history, grant and scholarship guidelines, and contact information.

Saint Lukes Foundation of Cleveland, Ohio (OH) (http://www.saintlukesfoundation.org)
The Saint Lukes Foundation of Cleveland, Ohio, was created from the sale of Saint Lukes Medical Center in 1997. The foundation's mission is to "foster and improve the health status and well-being of the people of Northeast Ohio, with special emphasis on those living in the areas traditionally served by Saint Luke's Medical Center . . . [by] providing funding support for initiatives focused on general health and wellness, health and medical education, medical research, and healthcare delivery." The foundation makes grants to support programs that serve broadly defined health and well-being needs of the people of greater Cleveland. Application guidelines and procedures, lists of past grant recipients, and contact information are available on the foundation's Web site.

St. Luke' Health Initiatives (AZ) (http://www.slhi.org/)
St. Luke's Health Initiatives of Phoenix, Arizona, works to accomplish its mission of improving the health of people in Arizona in three general areas: community grants, medical assistance, and Arizona Health Futures, which focuses on health policy and education. The organization also makes Bridge Grants, which are small grants that allow organizations to move to a higher level of effectiveness. The organization's Web site provides information on its programs, issue briefs, research reports, and contact information.

San Angelo Health Foundation (TX) (http://www.sahfoundation.org/)
Established in 1995, the San Angelo Health Foundation focuses its support and funding on "community health in its broadest form" in the San Angelo and Concho Valley area of Texas. To this end, all community services are eligible for funding, with health-related

services a priority. The foundation's Web site provides grant guidelines, lists of recent grants, news, answers to frequently asked questions, and contact information.

San Diego Foundation for Change (CA) (http://www.foundation4change.org/)
Created in 1994, the San Diego Foundation for Change works to "promote positive, permanent change" to end discrimination, lack of opportunity, poverty, and environmental degradation in the San Diego/Tijuana border region. To fulfill its mission, the foundation provides funding and technical assistance to small, community-based organizations working to achieve social, economic, and environmental justice in San Diego County. The foundation also offers two special awards programs: the San Diego Lesbian, Gay, Bisexual, and Transgender Pride Awards and the James Mitsuo Cua Award for Lesbian, Gay, Bisexual, and Transgender San Diegans. Downloadable grant application guidelines, a board list, a list of recipient organizations, information on contributing, and links to related resources are available on the foundation's Web site.

San Francisco AIDS Foundation (CA) (http://www.sfaf.org)
The San Francisco AIDS Foundation was founded in 1982 in San Francisco's Castro District as an emergency response to a quickly emerging health crisis. Today the foundation is established as a global leader in the fight against AIDS. The foundation seeks to educate the public about the disease and works with those who need treatment. Services provided by the foundation include locating housing for those in need, treatment support, financial counseling, providing a help hotline, and advocating for better medical insurance and treatment options. The foundation's Web site provides a wealth of information on HIV/AIDS and on the foundation's work.

San Jose Center for Poetry and Literature (CA) (http://www.poetrycentersanjose.org)
Established in 1978, the San Jose Center for Poetry and Literature is a nonacademic, nonprofit organization dedicated to supporting the literary arts. Located in San Jose, California, the center sponsors readings, lectures, and literary contests. The center's Web site includes information on recent contest winners and selections of their written work, spotlights on area authors, a calendar of events, and membership and volunteer opportunities.

Stanley J. Sarnoff Endowment for Cardiovascular Science, Inc. (VA) (http://www.sarnoffendowment.org)
The mission of the Stanley J. Sarnoff Endowment for Cardiovascular Science, Inc., is to interest medical school students in careers in cardiovascular and biomedical research. The endowment administers a fellowship program that is open to students currently attending medical school, and a scholars program, which is open to former Sarnoff Fellows. Details of both programs are provided on the endowment's Web site along with application guidelines and forms, information about current and past Sarnoff Fellows and Scholars, a brief biography of Dr. Sarnoff, information about the endowment's scientific board and board of directors, and contact information.

Save the Dunes Conservation Fund (IN) (http://www.savedunes.org/html/stdcfund.html)
The Save the Dunes Conservation Fund was created in 1952 in Michigan City, Indiana to protect Indiana's Dunes and surrounding natural areas. The fund has also worked to create a "National Lakeshore" along Lake Michigan. The fund's Web site offers a history of the Indiana Dunes and their protection, information about current conservation efforts, newsletters, and membership and contact information.

Save-the-Redwoods League (CA) (http://www.savetheredwoods.org)
Created in 1918, the Save-the-Redwoods League in San Francisco is committed to conserving the ancient forests of California. The league's mission is "to rescue from destruction representative areas of primeval redwood forests, and to cooperate with state and national park services in establishing redwood parks." This is accomplished through four program areas: the Redwood Land Purchase supports buying and protecting redwood forests; Memorial and Honor Groves allow donors to create a living memorial by dedicating a

grove; the organization plants new redwoods through a Tree Planting Program; and the Granting Program supports research on redwoods and projects that inform people about the cause. Areas of interest include trail maintenance, interpretation, research, exhibits and books on redwood and sequoia trees and ecosystems. The league's Web site includes information on each program, including application guidelines for the grants; resources on redwoods and their environment; a description of the Master Plan for redwoods that the league is developing; the league's newsletters; and press releases.

The Scholarship Foundation of the Union League of Philadelphia (PA) (http://www.unionleague.org/guestframeset.html)

Established in 1955, the Scholarship Foundation is one of the charitable foundations affiliated with the Union League of Philadelphia. The scholarship for post secondary education is awarded to young people in Philadelphia on the basis of "character, scholastic ability, personality, leadership potential, financial need, service to society, and loyalty to American traditions and principals." The foundation's Web page in the Foundations section of the Union League's general Web site provides a history of the foundation, a list of endowed and named scholarships, and contact information.

Detlef Schrempf Foundation (WA) (http://www.detlef.com)

Formed in 1996, the Detlef Schrempf Foundation of Seattle, Washington, was created to involve the basketball player and his wife further in their community. The goal of the foundation is to support "organizations that provide hope, care, and assistance for children and families in the [Pacific] Northwest." The foundation's Web site includes a list of grantees, an events calendar, features on upcoming and past fundraisers, and contact information.

Schumpert Medical Center Foundation (LA) (http://www.schumpertfoundation.org/)

The Schumpert Medical Center Foundation in Shreveport, Louisiana, was established in 1992 to assist the humanitarian efforts of the Sisters of Charity of the Incarnate Word. The foundation's mission is "to further the Sisters' mission, and to support new and innovative healthcare programs for the benefit of our community, without regard for an individual's ability to pay." Projects supported by the foundation include a cancer treatment center, hospice care, physical medicine and rehabilitation programs, and women and children's health and radiology services. Detailed descriptions of each project, information on current fundraisers, ways to contribute, and a list of the board of directors are available on the foundation's Web site.

Schwab Fund for Charitable Giving (CA) (http://www.schwabcharitable.org/)

The San Francisco-based Schwab Fund for Charitable Giving strives "to increase charitable giving in the United States by providing useful information, unbiased guidance, and advantageous ways to give." The organization's Web site describes seven principles to guide charitable giving, and provides information on the fund's Charitable Gift Account program for donors. The site also offers a charity search, links to further resources on charitable giving, online account services, and contact information.

Scoring for Children (VA) (http://www.scoringforchildren.org)

Scoring for Children was founded by Washington Capitals hockey player Peter Bondra in 1996 to benefit children's charities throughout the Washington, D.C. region. The goal of the organization is to raise funds for critically ill children. The Scoring for Children Web site provides a listing of supported charitable organizations, upcoming special events, donation information, and a contact address.

Securities Industry Foundation for Economic Education (NY) (http://www.sia.com/about_sia/html/sifee.html)

Located in New York City's Financial District, the Securities Industry Foundation for Economic Education was established over two decades ago by the Securities Industry Association to "promote economic education and financial literacy among children and adults." The foundation's primary program is the Stock Market Game, a stock market simulation program designed for students of all ages. The Stock Market Game program has become a teaching resource for economic education and investment principles for 25,000 teachers in the United States and in countries worldwide. The foundation's Web site provides a link to the Stock Market Game site, the annual report, sample issues of foundation publications, and press releases.

Seedco and Non-Profit Assistance Corporation (NY) (http://www.seedco.org)
Established in 1986 with a grant from the Ford Foundation, the New York City-based Seedco and Non-Profit Assistance Corporation is a community development intermediary. The organization works to provide "financial and technical assistance, and management support, for the community-building efforts of nonprofit organizations and small businesses in targeted disadvantaged communities throughout the United States." Seedco, which affiliated with the Non-Profit Assistance Corporation in 1998, focuses its programs on workforce development, affordable homeownership, and entrepreneurship to achieve its community revitalization goals. The organization's Web site includes descriptions of the organization's programs, information on applying to one of its loan funds, contact information, news updates, and the group's newsletter.

Selena Foundation (TX) (http://www.q-productions.com/selenaf.htm)
The Selena Foundation was established in 1995 with funds donated to Selena's family following the death of the Tejano singer and songwriter. Based in Corpus Christi, Texas, the foundation's mission is to "offer the motivation that every child needs to complete their education, to live moral lives, to love their families, to respect human life, and to sing whatever song they were born to sing." The foundation's Web site provides information for donors, lists of contributors and grantees, and contact information.

Sertoma Foundation (MO) (http://www.sertoma.org)
Headquartered in Kansas City, Missouri, Sertoma (Service To Mankind) International is a volunteer civic service organization with member clubs in the United States, Canada, Puerto Rico, and Mexico. Sertoma's primary service project is assisting people with speech, hearing, and language disorders. The Sertoma Foundation was established in 1960 to " to support Sertoma's approved charitable and educational programs . . . through effective fundraising, investment of funds, and the distribution of proceeds." The foundation's Web site provides information on the latest club news, upcoming events, and service projects; membership and donor guidelines; and contact information.

Seva Foundation (CA) (http://www.seva.org/)
The Seva Foundation, located in Berkeley, California, was founded in 1978 and works to build "partnerships to respond to locally defined problems with culturally sustainable solutions throughout the world." The foundation's programs address a range of issues, including: avoidable blindness in India and other countries; indigenous culture, sustainable agriculture, and microenterprise in Guatemala and Chiapas; and the epidemic of diabetes on Native American reservations. Information on the foundation's philosophy and program areas, donor and volunteer information, publications, and contact information are available on the foundation's Web site.

Seventh Generation Fund (CA) (http://www.7genfund.org)
Formed in 1977 in Arcata, California, the Seventh Generation Fund works to promote and maintain the uniqueness of native peoples and nations in the Western Hemisphere. The fund's areas of interest include arts and cultural expression, environmental health and justice, indigenous peoples of the Americas, protection of sacred places, and sustainable communities. These interests are supported through advocacy, small grants, financial management services, and nonprofit administration, leadership training, and technical services. The fund's Web site provides details on its areas of focus, grant application guidelines, recent annual reports, a newsletter, a listing of upcoming events, and links to further resources.

Share Our Strength (DC) (http://www.strength.org/)
Created in 1984, the Washington, D.C.-based Share our Strength "mobilizes individuals and industries to use their talents to raise funds and awareness for the fight against hunger and poverty." Share our Strength focuses on both short- and long-term solutions to hunger and poverty issues, including food assistance, job training, economic development programs, and advocacy. The organization offers a range of programs and events. The organization's Web site provides descriptions of its programs; donor, volunteer, and contact information; details on programs that have received funding through the organization's projects; and information on Community Wealth Ventures, Inc., a for-profit subsidiary of Share Our Strength that provides consulting services for nonprofit organizations and corporations.

The Shefa Fund (PA) (http://www.shefafund.org/)
The Philadelphia, Pennsylvania-based Shefa Fund was founded in 1988 to "encourage American Jews to use their tzedakah (charitable resources) to create a more just society, and in the process, to transform Jewish life so that it becomes more socially conscious and spiritually invigorating." The fund acts as a charitable "bank," distributing funds in accordance with funder recommendations to address issues such as social and economic justice, including community and economic development; feminism and gender issues; Middle East peace and economic development; and the transformation of Jewish life, including youth funding and anti-homophobia work. The fund's Web site provides details on its general mission and funding strategies, as well as contact information.

Shinnyo-En Foundation (CA) (http://www.sef.org/)
Also known as Buddhists for World Harmony, the San Francisco-based Shinnyo-En Foundation was founded in 1994 as the grantmaking arm of the Shinnyo-En USA order. The foundation's mission is to "bring forth deeper compassion among humankind, to promote greater harmony, and to nurture future generations toward building a more ethical society." The foundation makes grants primarily for programs that benefit the ethical development of young people. The foundation's Web site features an overview of the foundation's funding program and process, a list of recent grants, contact information, and directions to the foundation.

The Sierra Club Foundation (CA) (http://www.sierraclub.org/foundation/)
The Sierra Club Foundation provides financial support to the Sierra Club and other environmental organizations. The foundation funds a range of environmental projects in the general categories of public education, litigation, and training. The section of the Sierra Club's Web site devoted to the foundation offers information on the organization and its programs, listings of trustees and staff, a list of supporters, annual reports, news, and contact information.

Sigma Chi Foundation (IL) (http://www.sigmachi.org)
The Sigma Chi Foundation serves as an educational funding resource for the undergraduate and graduate student members of the Sigma Chi Fraternity. The foundation offers awards, grants, and scholarships to qualified individuals and groups within the Sigma Chi Fraternity system. Scholarship and award details, downloadable applications, a history of the foundation, publications, donation opportunities, and information about the foundation's activities and programs are available on its Web site.

Silicon Valley Realtors Charitable Foundation (CA)
(http://www.siliconvalley-realtors.org/foundation.asp)
The Silicon Valley Realtors Charitable Foundation, located in Los Altos, California, provides funding to ensure "the welfare and prosperity of the communities where we live and work," and aims to "help create more productive and enriched communities." The foundation considers applications from all nonprofit organizations operating within the jurisdictional boundaries of the Silicon Valley Association of Realtors. Special consideration is given to organizations involved in housing or education issues. The foundation's Web site provides grant guidelines and a downloadable application.

Simon Youth Foundation (IN) (http://syf.simon.com/servlet/SYFViewer)
Founded in 1960 in Indianapolis, Indiana, the Simon Youth Foundation focuses its work on "improving educational opportunities, career development, and life skills for 'at risk' youth through focused programs and initiatives." The foundation supports programs for youth that take place in Simon malls across the country. The foundation also offers financial awards to help meet the financial needs of promising students in communities that host Simon malls. The foundation's Web site provides information about its philanthropic work throughout the country and contact information.

The Sisters of Charity Foundation of South Carolina (SC) (http://www.sistersofcharitysc.com)
The Sisters of Charity Foundation of South Carolina, a ministry of the Sisters of Charity of St. Augustine, works "to address the needs of the poor and underserved in South Carolina through a variety of programs, grant opportunities, and collaborative ventures." The foundation's grantmaking is limited to programs and projects located within South Carolina. Grant guidelines and procedures, links to related organizations, a publications list, news and events, and contact information are available at the foundation's Web site.

Sisters of St. Joseph Charitable Fund (WV) (http://www.ssjcharitablefund.org)
The Sisters of St. Joseph Charitable Fund was established to continue and to expand the health and wellness ministry of the Sisters of Saint Joseph of Wheeling, West Virginia. The fund's mission is to promote healthy and sustainable communities by providing financial assistance, strengthen collaborative relationships, and support local initiatives. Programs of interest include communities, families, and senior citizens. The fund's Web site provides information on its grant programs, a listing of recent grant activity, answers to frequently asked questions, and contact information.

Skoll Community Fund (CA) (http://www.skollfoundation.org/)
The Skoll Community Fund was founded in 1999 by Jeff Skoll, the first full-time employee and president of eBay, in San Jose, California. The fund supports innovative and established nonprofit organizations working "to produce significant, tangible benefits on a local, national, or global scale" in the specific program areas of education, philanthropy, micro-enterprise, and technology. Grant categories and application guidelines, grantee profiles, links to news and events, answers to frequently asked questions, links to related resources, and contact information are available on the fund's Web site.

Social Science Research Council (NY) (http://www.ssrc.org/)
The Social Science Research Council, located in New York City, was founded in 1923 and is devoted to the advancement of interdisciplinary research in the social sciences through a wide variety of interdisciplinary workshops and conferences, fellowships and grants, summer training institutes, scholarly exchanges, and publications. Fellowships and grants are given out on the pre-dissertation, dissertation, and post-doctoral levels and short-term programs are sponsored for younger students. The subject areas vary from European to Middle Eastern countries and from sexuality and migration to economics. Specific program descriptions, guidelines, and application deadlines; information on other council programs and resources; a staff list with phone numbers and e-mail addresses; and a publications list are provided on the council's Web site.

Society of Cosmetic Chemists (NY) (http://www.scconline.org)
The New York City-based Society of Cosmetic Chemists "promotes high standards of practice in the science and serves as a focus for the exchange of ideas and new developments in cosmetic research and technology." The society maintains chapters nationally and in Canada and publishes the *Journal of Cosmetic Science.* Additionally, the society offers a Graduate Research Fellowship Program as well as numerous award programs for members. The society's Web site provides a description of each program, as well as contact information.

Society of Manufacturing Engineers Education Foundation (MI) (http://www.sme.org/cgi-bin/smeefhtml.pl?/foundation/homepg.htm&SME&)
The Society of Manufacturing Engineers (SME) Education Foundation offers a variety of grant and award programs, including grants for university and college programs that target "competency gaps" in manufacturing identified by SME's Manufacturing Education Plan. The foundation also offers scholarships to students seeking degrees in manufacturing engineering and technology, or closely related fields. The foundation's Web site provides an outline of the foundation's funding programs, guidelines, application forms, recent funding results, a list of board members, donor information, related links, and contact information.

Society of Singers, Inc. (CA) (http://www.singers.org/default.htm)
The Society of Singers, Inc., was formed in 1984 in Los Angeles "to aid professional singers who face financial, medical, family, or other crises." The organization maintains regional offices in Las Vegas and New York and offers Singers' Assistance and Scholarships to singers and aspiring vocalists in need. The society's Web site provides details, contact information, news and upcoming events, and links to further resources.

Sons of Italy Foundation (DC) (http://www.osia.org/public/foundation.htm)
The Sons of Italy Foundation, established in 1959, supports programs to preserve Italian American culture, encourage educational excellence, and support transatlantic initiatives for diplomatic, economic, and educational exchanges. The foundation administers the National Leadership Grant Competition, which comprises several scholarship programs, as well as a grantmaking program for cultural preservation and advancement, disaster relief, education, medical research, and special projects. The foundation's Web site provides information on the National Leadership Grant Competition, with downloadable application forms; grant guidelines; information on the foundation's other programs; a list of grant recipients and supported charities; and contact information.

South Carolina Humanities Council (SC) (http://www.schumanities.org)
Located in Columbia, the South Carolina Humanities Council supports humanities-related projects and services such as "exhibits, documentaries, discussion forums, research, planning, workshops, dramatizations, and lectures," among others. Founded in 1965 as an affiliate of the National Endowment for the Humanities, the council offers a number of different grants, including major, mini, planning, and resource grants. The council's Web site provides application guidelines, downloadable applications, a description of featured projects, a calendar of events, a listing of affiliated organizations, and contact information.

South Dakota Humanities Council (SD) (http://web.sdstate.edu/humanities/)
The South Dakota Humanities Council, located in Brookings, was created by the National Endowment for the Humanities in 1972 to "explore and promote state, regional, and national programs focusing on ideas, history, and culture." The council awards funds to nonprofit groups for humanities activities to enhance public appreciation and use of the humanities in the state. The council's Web site includes information on its funding programs, grant guidelines, an online preliminary application form, grants lists, a list of publications, and a directory of scholars.

Southern Arts Federation (GA) (http://www.southarts.org)
The Atlanta, Georgia-based Southern Arts Federation is a regional arts organization that "promotes and supports arts regionally, nationally, and internationally and enhances the artistic excellence and professionalism of Southern arts organizations and artists so that they successfully connect with citizens and their communities." The federation's partner states are Alabama, Florida, Georgia, Kentucky, Louisiana, Mississippi, North Carolina, South Carolina, and Tennessee. The federation offers funding for performing arts presenters. Information on its current grant opportunities, details on the organization's other programs and services, links, and contact information are available on the federation's Web site.

Southern Education Foundation (GA) (http://www.sefatl.org/)
The Southern Education Foundation was formed in 1937 to "improve access to quality educational opportunity for all people of the South, especially those disadvantaged by race, gender, poverty, or color." The foundation's programs focus on teacher preparation, student opportunity and performance, educational equity and opportunity, socioeconomic factors affecting equity, and community enrichment. The foundation supports programs in collaboration with funding partners, which are listed on its Web site. The site also provides grant lists for each program, information on the foundation's activities, a history of the foundation, and contact information.

Southwest Minnesota Foundation (http://www.swmnfoundation.org/)
The Southwest Minnesota Foundation was created in the early 1980s to help Minnesota communities in need of support due to declining farming and mining economies. The foundation's mission is to facilitate opportunities for economic, social, and cultural growth by promoting philanthropy, leadership, innovation, and collaboration for the 18 counties of southwest Minnesota. Program interests include aging, inclusive communities, connecting youth and communities, and business and economic development. The foundation also offers loan programs aimed at start-up or expanding businesses to help create employment in southwest Minnesota. The foundation's Web site offers specific program information, grant guidelines, board/staff listings, and contact information.

Britney Spears Foundation (NY) (http://www.britneyspears.com/foundation)
The Britney Spears Foundation was founded by its pop star namesake to help children in need through "the restorative aspect of entertainment." The foundation runs the annual Britney Spears Camp for the Performing Arts for children in New England, New York, and Washington, D.C.; creates playrooms for kids in extended hospital stays; and donates funds to other children's causes. The foundation's Web site provides details on the camp, an online camp alumni forum, donation information, and contact information.

Special Libraries Association (DC) (http://www.sla.org/)
The Special Libraries Association seeks to be "a catalyst in the development of the information economy, and a strategic partner in the emerging information society." The association offers scholarships for graduate study in librarianship and related fields of study, grants to promote research on and the advancement of library science, and other funding programs. The association's Web site provides scholarship and grant guidelines, information on other programs and initiatives, publications, links to other funding sources, and contact information.

Spirits of the Land Foundation (OK) (http://greatspirit.earth.com/)
Incorporated under the laws of the Sac and Fox Nation of Oklahoma, Spirits of the Land Foundation supports education and activities benefiting Indian tribes, bands, and nations and supports scientific research to benefit humanity and earth. The foundation's Web site provides news, Indian resources and business opportunities, Indian attractions in Oklahoma, mailing addresses of tribes and their leaders, and foundation contact information.

Sponsors of Musical Enrichment, Inc. (CA) (http://www.someinc.com)
Sponsors of Musical Enrichment, Inc., was founded in California in 1978. It exists for the purpose of "supporting local youth organizations and the performing arts on a continuing basis." The organization also provides deserving students of the musical and performing arts with scholarships for career advancements and works with programs like the Drum Corps International, sponsoring national scholarships and underwriting competitions. The organization's Web site provides a list of the types of scholarships given, a calendar of events with upcoming concerts, information on how to obtain tickets, and contact information.

The Starbucks Foundation (WA) (http://www.starbucks.com/aboutus/foundation.asp)
The Starbucks Foundation makes grants to nonprofit organizations serving low-income, at-risk youth. Through the Youth Leadership grants program, the foundation focuses support on programs that involve writing, literacy, and the promotion of the voices of youth in public forums and that teach the value of societal diversity. Applicant programs must provide opportunities for Starbucks partners and stores to be integrated in a meaningful way. The foundation's Web site provides grant criteria, downloadable guidelines and applications, and contact information.

The Stark Education Partnership (OH) (http://www.edpartner.org)
The Stark Education Partnership was established in 1989 as a "catalyst for school change and a supporter of school-based initiatives to improve the education outcomes for all children, pre-school age through twelfth grade, in Stark County, Ohio." The partnership works with teachers, union associations, the business community, and parents to improve education in public and private schools in the region. Information about the partnership's specific education initiatives, events, news, an online contact form, and links to additional resources are available on the partnership's Web site.

State Medical Society Foundation, Inc. (WI) (http://www.wisconsinmedicalsociety.org/physician_resources/foundation)
The State Medical Society Foundation, Inc., was chartered by the Wisconsin State Medical Society in 1955 and works to "advance the health of the people of Wisconsin by supporting medical and health education." The foundation's Web site provides information on the foundation's current scholarship and grant programs with guidelines and downloadable applications, information on the foundation's student loan program, details on other foundation programs, and a list of contributors.

Rudolf Steiner Foundation (CA) (http://www.rsfoundation.org/)
Established in 1984, the Rudolf Steiner Foundation is a progressive financial service organization that supports social and environmental change. The foundation's basic work is to connect philanthropists and investors with projects in need of grants or loans. The foundation supports research and activities that include children and education, environment and science, arts and culture, sustainable agriculture, economic and social renewal, medicine, and spiritual renewal. The foundation, located in San Francisco, California, carries out its charitable activity on a worldwide basis through its gift, grant, and loan fund programs. The foundation's Web site provides information on the foundation's programs, as well as contact information.

Stonewall Community Foundation (NY) (http://www.stonewallfoundation.org/)
Founded in 1990, the Stonewall Community Foundation is an organization benefiting New York City's gay and lesbian community. The foundation's mission is to "strengthen programs and projects dealing with health and human services, civil liberties, HIV/AIDS, youth and senior advocacy, and the arts." The foundation makes one- and two-year grants for community nonprofit organizations serving the needs of the bisexual, lesbian, gay, and transgendered community in the five boroughs of New York City. The foundation's Web site provides a list of grant recipients, information on services, answers to frequently asked questions, news on upcoming events, donor information, and contact information.

Summerfair, Inc. (OH) (http://www.summerfair.org)
Summerfair, Inc., sponsors an annual exhibition of fine arts and crafts in Cincinnati, Ohio, and supports grants to individual artists, local arts organizations, and high school scholarships. The Summerfair Web site includes extensive information about the exhibition, including volunteer and artist participation opportunities; details on current grants and recent grant recipients; grant guidelines; and an online application form for the Aid to Individual Artists grant.

Summit Fund of Washington (DC) (http://www.summitfund.org)
Since 1993, the Summit Foundation of Washington has worked to improve the quality of life in the Washington, D.C.-area, focusing on two main projects: restoring and protecting the Anacostia River and preventing teen pregnancy in the District of Columbia. The organization's Web site provides data and news reports on both of these areas, grant guidelines, recent grants lists, and contact information for potential applicants.

Sundance Institute (UT) (http://institute.sundance.org)
Established in 1981 by Robert Redford, the Sundance Institute has administrative and programmatic offices in Salt Lake City, Utah, and Los Angeles, California, while most events take place in Utah. The organization is "dedicated to the support and development of emerging screenwriters and directors of vision, and to the national and international exhibition of new, independent dramatic and documentary films." In addition to sponsorship of the annual independent film festival that bears its name, the institute sponsors a variety of development and funding programs for filmmakers, including the Documentary Film Program, Screenwriting and Filmmaking Laboratories, and Film Music Composers Lab. Program descriptions, application guidelines, information on volunteer and donation opportunities, a calendar of events, and contact information are available on the institute's Web site.

Suntory Water Group, Inc. (GA)
(http://www.suntorywatergroup.com/about_us/cor1515_inthecom.asp)
The Atlanta, Georgia-based Suntory Water Group, Inc., maintains ties with the community by sponsoring a number of healthy living programs throughout the United States. These include Drink to Your Good Health Month, to encourage people to drink the proper amount of water each day; the Good Health Advisory Board, providing experts for health and medical advice; and a bottle recycling program. Information on these programs is available on the group's Web site.

Surfrider Foundation (CA) (http://www.surfrider.org/)
The Surfrider Foundation is a nonprofit environmental organization "dedicated to the protection and enjoyment of the world's oceans, waves, and beaches for all people through conservation, activism, research, and education." Founded in 1984 in San Clemente, California, the foundation accomplishes its mission through a variety of programs, including the Thomas Pratte Memorial Scholarship Fund, which promotes academic research of the coastal environment. The foundation's Web site offers descriptions of its programs, educational resources, membership and donation information, links to chapters, and contact information.

Survive AIDS! (CA) (http://www.surviveaids.org)
Based in San Francisco, Survive AIDS! was formerly known as ACT UP Golden Gate, part of the national coalition ACT UP (AIDS Coalition to Unleash Power) that was established in 1987. As Survive AIDS!, the group lobbies, communicates, educates, mentors, creates and maintains an infrastructure to support HIV/AIDS activism and research, working "to keep people with AIDS alive and improve and sustain their quality of life." The group's Web site includes a clarification on its name change, as well as recent information on the group and AIDS-related news.

TAPPI Foundation, Inc. (GA) (http://www.tappi.org/index.asp?pid=16129)
Created in 1990 by the Technical Association of the Pulp and Paper Industry, the TAPPI Foundation, Inc., "manages the funds and endowments of TAPPI awards and scholarships, distributes monetary awards, and funds TAPPI's public outreach activities." The foundation's Web site provides scholarship program guidelines and applications, information on award programs and public outreach efforts, a list of contributors, and information on contributing to the foundation.

The Elizabeth Taylor AIDS Foundation (CA) (http://www.elizabethtayloraidsfoundation.org)
The Elizabeth Taylor AIDS Foundation was founded in 1991 by the actress "to provide funding to organizations providing critically needed support service, prevention services, and education for people with HIV/AIDS." The foundation distributes funds to AIDS organizations around the world. Contact and donation information are provided on the foundation's Web site.

R.J. Taylor, Jr. Foundation (GA) (http://www.taylorfoundation.org/)
The R.J. Taylor, Jr. Foundation, based in Atlanta, Georgia, was founded in 1971 to promote "genealogical research in Georgia to secure information from public and private records and to preserve and publish the results of this work" Both organizations and individuals are eligible to apply for grants to publish books or databases of qualifying records. The foundation's Web site provides grant requirements, guidelines for producing publications, a grant application, a project map, and library resources for more information.

Teammates for Kids Foundation (CO) (http://www.teammates4kids.com)
Based in Littleton, Colorado, the Teammates for Kids Foundation was co-founded by country music performer Garth Brooks in 1999. Teaming with Major League Baseball players and National Hockey League players, the foundation makes grants and donations based on game performance (for instance, specific dollar amounts are donated for home runs, strikeouts, etc.). The foundation's emphasis is on children's charities, mainly in health, education, and inner-city needs. The foundation's Web site provides an overview of the foundation's operations, listings of the athletes and celebrities involved, grant guidelines and application, a list of grant recipients, a listing of board and staff members, and contact information.

Technology Student Association (VA) (http://www.tsawww.org)
The Technology Student Association promotes technological literacy, leadership, and problem solving and works to build personal growth and expand opportunities for students through its membership organization. K-12 students enrolled in technology education classes benefit from national competitive events, conferences, and special programs such as National TSA Week. Details on these activities can be found on the association's Web site, along with membership and contact information.

TEK Foundation (UT) (http://tekfoundation.org/)
Established in 2001 in Salt Lake City, Utah, the TEK Foundation works to improve the living and economic conditions of underprivileged people worldwide. To this end, the foundation is establishing international Educational Resource Centers that will provide education, food and healthcare services, thus aiding communities in becoming self-sufficient. The foundation's Web site provides details of the foundation's programs and resources, locations of Educational Resource Centers, a brochure, and contact information.

A Territory Resource Foundation (WA) (http://www.atrfoundation.org/)
Based in Seattle, Washington, A Territory Resource Foundation strives to "create a more equitable, just, and environmentally sound society for all" by providing limited financial support to activist, community-based organizations in the states of Idaho, Montana, Oregon, Washington, and Wyoming. In addition to grant guidelines and a list of recent grantees, the foundation's Web site offers a brief history of the foundation, a copy of the director's report, a short essay on socially responsible investing, and donor information.

Texas Bar Foundation (TX) (http://www.txbf.org)
The Texas Bar Foundation, located in Austin, is dedicated to "promoting the ends of justice through education and charitable activities which improve the administration of our legal system . . . which advance public education and understanding of our judicial system . . . and which are sensitive to the needs of the public as well as the legal profession." The foundation funds four program areas: legal assistance to the poor and disadvantaged, legal and

public education on the court system and legal process, legal aid facilities, and experimental projects in an area that needs seed money. The foundation's Web site includes application guidelines and forms, a list of various board and committee members, lists of previous grantees, and links to related sites.

Texas Council for the Humanities (TX) (http://www.public-humanities.org/)
The Texas Council for the Humanities, established in 1972 as an affiliate of the National Endowment for the Humanities, "provides opportunities for people to deepen their understanding of ideas, values, and human experiences and envisions Texas as a place where people enrich their lives and strengthen their communities through the joy of learning." The council's grant program provides financial support to nonprofit organizations and institutions for public humanities programming. The council's Web site provides grant guidelines and downloadable application forms, information about the council's activities, publications and other resources, an events calendar, related links, and contact information.

Texas Equal Access to Justice Foundation (TX) (http://www.txiolta.org)
The Texas Equal Access to Justice Foundation is an organization of the Supreme Court of Texas and the State Bar of Texas established in 1984 "to administer funds to create community capacity to provide civil legal services" for Texans. Located in Austin, Texas, the foundation works to "fund the provision of civil legal services to the poor in Texas." The foundation's Web site provides grant guidelines and applications, links to legal resources, a list of recent grantees throughout Texas, and a history of the foundation and how it operates.

Texas Neurofibromatosis Foundation (TX) (http://www.texasnf.org)
The Texas Neurofibromatosis Foundation, established in 1980, is "committed to meeting the needs of people challenged with neurofibromatosis by providing care, comfort, support, information, education, funding, and other resources for its treatment, prevention, and cure." The foundation's Web site provides general details on neurofibromatosis, information on research projects, the foundation's office locations throughout Texas, links, patient outreach services, and upcoming events.

Texas Nursery and Landscape Association Education and Research Foundation (http://www.txnla.org/green_industry/Foundation.html) (TX)
The Texas Nursery and Landscape Association Education and Research Foundation was formed in 1992 in Austin "to develop necessary educational and research resources for the Green Industry." The foundation provides scholarships to graduate and undergraduate students in horticulture, funds Texas-based research, and is creating a permanent endowment through the Horticultural Research Institute. The foundation's Web site includes a scholarship application, a grant proposal form, information for donors, contact information, and further details about the foundation.

Theatre Communications Group (NY) (http://www.tcg.org/)
Theatre Communications Group was founded in 1961 and offers a wide range of services designed to "strengthen, nurture, and promote the professional not-for-profit American theatre." The group's grant program provides support for early career and senior artists, the creation of new work by emerging and established playwrights, audience development and mentoring programs at small and large theaters, and other projects. Current grant program information, guidelines, and forms; information on the group's other programs; answers to frequently asked questions; information on grant recipients; and contact information are available on the group's Web site.

Third Wave, Inc. (NY) (http://www.thirdwavefoundation.org)
Third Wave, Inc., a New York City-based activist association that connects young women to "the resources necessary to counter attacks on their personal freedoms," strives to combat inequalities, and supports young women's activism. Third Wave offers scholarships for college students and grants focusing on reproductive rights and organizing and advocacy. Scholarships are available to students who are activists, artists, or cultural workers active

on issues of inequality. Grants fund projects headed by women 15 to 30 years old, with an emphasis on low-income women, differently-abled women, women of color, and lesbian and bisexual women. Scholarship and grant guidelines, applications, information on the organizations other programs, related resources, and contact information are available on the foundation's Web site.

Dave Thomas Foundation for Adoption (OH) (http://www.davethomasfoundationforadoption.com)

Established in 1992 by the founder of the Wendy's restaurant chain, the Dave Thomas Foundation for Adoption serves as a national advocate for adoption by working with national initiatives that directly impact waiting children and expanding the public's awareness of adoption. The foundation funds organizations that strive to increase adoptions of waiting children in North America. Grant guidelines, a downloadable grant application form, general resources on adoption, and links to organizations with similar interests are available on the foundation's Web site.

Three Guineas Fund (CA) (http://www.3gf.org/)

Founded in 1994, the Three Guineas Fund promotes social justice by expanding access to economic opportunity for women and girls. The foundation makes grants to and creates partnerships with organizations aligned with its mission. The foundation's Web site contains information on the application process, selected grants listings, links and resources, and contact information.

The Threshold Foundation (CA) (http://www.thresholdfoundation.org/)

The Threshold Foundation of California serves the social change movement through collaborating with and funding innovative American and international nonprofit organizations and individuals working toward social justice, environmental sustainability, humane economic systems, and peaceful coexistence. The foundation's Web site provides grant guidelines, a listing of recent grants, and contact information.

The TIA Foundation (DC) (http://www.tia.org/About/found.asp)

The TIA Foundation was founded in 1990 to benefit the U.S. travel industry by supporting education and research vital to the concerns of the industry. The foundation awards yearly graduate and undergraduate scholarships. The foundation's Web site provides a list of scholarship recipients, board members, and contact information.

The Tides Foundation (CA) (http://www.tidesfoundation.org)

The Tides Foundation, located in San Francisco, California, was established in 1976 as part of the Tides family of organizations. The group "partners with donors to increase and organize resources for social change." Funding areas include civic participation, economic and racial justice, the environment, HIV/AIDS, native communities, women's empowerment and reproductive health, and youth organizing. Most of the foundation's grants are made on the recommendation of donors interested in funding specific issues; the organization does not accept unsolicited proposals. The foundation's Web site includes current grant information and initiatives, details on organizations that have received foundation support, lists of directors and key staff, and information on creating a donor-advised fund at the foundation.

Tri-City Hospital Foundation (CA) (http://www.tricityhospitalfoundation.org)

The Tri-City Hospital Foundation was founded in 1964 to promote community and financial support of the Tri-City Medical Center located in San Diego. The foundation provides support for programs including Tri-City Hospice and scholarships for Tri-City Hospital nurses. The foundation's Web site includes information on the foundation's activities, a list of trustees, details for donors, and contact information.

Trust Fund for Children with Special Health Care Needs (MI) (http://www.mdch.state.mi.us/msa/cshcs/)
Created in 1944, the Trust Fund for Children with Special Health Care Needs "helps pay for services and projects for children with special healthcare needs not provided by other healthcare funds" in Michigan. The fund supports unique services and programs for special needs children, their families, and caregivers that promote optimal health and development. Specifically, the fund has three areas of giving: services for children, assistance to groups, and improving service systems. The fund's Web site provides details on the organization's funding programs, contact information for those wishing to apply, background information on the trust, and details on making a contribution.

Tucson Arts District (AZ) (http://tucsonartsdistrict.org/)
The Tucson Arts District serves artists in the downtown Tucson area. The organization's Web site includes descriptions of events, such as art walks and studio tours; opportunities for artists; a calendar of events; a listing of downtown galleries; links to resources on the arts in Arizona; and contact information.

Les Turner Amyotrophic Lateral Sclerosis Foundation (IL) (http://www.lesturnerals.org/)
The Les Turner Amyotrophic Lateral Sclerosis Foundation, located in Skokie, Illinois, was created in 1977 and is "devoted to the treatment and elimination of amyotrophic lateral sclerosis (ALS), better known as Lou Gehrig's disease" and supports the ALS community in Chicago and its suburbs. The foundation funds research programs, the Lois Insolia ALS Center (a clinic affiliated with Northwestern University Medical School), support groups, and many educational programs. The foundation's Web site includes information on the foundation's programs, links to resources on ALS, updates on research projects, an events calendar, and information on making a donation.

Uncommon Legacy Foundation, Inc. (NY) (http://www.uncommonlegacy.org/)
The Uncommon Legacy Foundation, Inc., was founded in 1990 to enhance the visibility, strength, and vitality of the lesbian community. The foundation awards scholarships to openly lesbian students with leadership potential and funds projects and organizations that contribute to the health, education, and culture of the lesbian community. The foundation's Web site provides guidelines, downloadable application forms, and lists of past recipients for the scholarship and grant programs; an online version of the foundation's newsletter; information for prospective donors; and contact information.

Union League Civic and Arts Foundation (IL) (http://www.civicandarts.org)
The Civic and Arts Foundation, one of three philanthropic efforts of the Union League Club of Chicago, was established in 1949 to contribute to the cultural and civic well-being of the Chicago metropolitan area. The foundation awards grants to community organizations and scholarships to young people enrolled in visual arts and music programs. The foundation's Web site provides a description of its activities, a list of grant recipients, information on current competitions for young people, details on making a donation, and contact information.

United Black Fund of Greater Cleveland (OH) (http://www.ubfogc.org)
The United Black Fund of Greater Cleveland was founded in 1981 to raise and distribute donations to charitable organizations in the Cleveland area for the benefit of children, families, and seniors in poor, African American, and minority communities. The fund's Web site includes a listing of the agencies it supports, information on grant procedures, an events calendar, answers to frequently asked questions, and contact information.

United Board for Christian Higher Education in Asia (NY) (http://www.unitedboard.org)
The United Board for Christian Higher Education in Asia was chartered in 1922 for "the support of higher education in Asia from the perspective of the Christian faith." The board works with selected schools in Asia on programs including scholarly exchanges within Asia and between Asia and the West; academic training for faculty; strengthening libraries, curricula, and research; and professional development for administrators. The board's Web

site includes lists of supported schools, the board and staff, selected programs, information on an alumni program, information on contributing, and contact information. The board does not accept unsolicited proposals.

United Hospital Fund (NY) (http://www.uhfnyc.org/)
Created in 1879, the United Hospital Fund is a "health services research and philanthropic organization that addresses critical issues affecting hospitals and healthcare in New York City." The fund provides a variety of grant programs for hospitals, nursing homes, and healthcare, academic, and public interest organizations. Funding is available "to examine emerging issues and stimulate innovative programs." The fund's online Grant Center provides grant guidelines and downloadable application forms. The fund's Web site also includes grant lists for each program, information on the fund's research and other programs, a publications list, and information on contributing.

United Methodist Health Ministry Fund (KS) (http://www.healthfund.org)
Formed in 1986 in Hutchinson, Kansas, the United Methodist Health Ministry Fund provides programs and services related to primary healthcare to people in the state of Kansas. Affiliated with the Methodist Church, the fund is "dedicated to the extension of health, healing, and wholeness to all people in all stations of life." To this end, the fund makes grants to health-related nonprofit organizations statewide. A complete description of grant guidelines, deadlines, evaluation forms, and previous grant recipients are posted on the fund's Web site. Additionally, the fund provides details on upcoming events and activities, current special initiatives, the annual report, health study-related publications, and contact information online.

United Nations Foundation (DC) (http://www.unfoundation.org)
The United Nations Foundation, located in Washington, D.C., was founded by Ted Turner to support the goals and objectives of the United Nations and its charter in order to promote "a more peaceful, prosperous, and just world." The foundation has four areas of particular interest: women and population, children's health, the environment, and humanitarian causes. The foundation engages in four primary activities in pursuit of its mission: providing additional funding for programs and people served by UN agencies, strengthening UN institutions and encouraging support for the UN and UN causes, sponsoring or conducting outreach efforts aimed at educating the public about the UN, and raising new funds to support UN programs and purposes. The foundation works collaboratively with the UN in program development and does not accept unsolicited proposals. The foundation's Web site provides information about the foundation's priority issues and projects, grants lists, news about the UN, links to the UN and its agencies, and an online contact form.

United States Institute of Peace (DC) (http://www.usip.org/)
The Washington, D.C.-based United States Institute of Peace was established in 1984 "to strengthen the nation's capabilities to promote the peaceful resolution of international conflicts." Grants support research, education, pilot projects, training, and the dissemination of information on international peace and conflict resolution. The institute accepts unsolicited grant proposals for any project that fits within its general mandate and solicited grant proposals related to specific topics or themes of special interest to the institute. The institute also sponsors the Jennings Randolph Program for International Peace, which offers fellowships to individuals conducting research on international conflict and peace. The institute's Web site includes application guidelines and forms for each funding program, a database of past grants, lists of former fellows, publications, descriptions of education and training programs, and links to related resources.

US Soccer Foundation (DC) (http://www.ussoccerfoundation.org/)
Based in Washington, D.C. the US Soccer Foundation was created in 1993 to "enhance, assist, and grow the sport of soccer." The foundation's grants program is open to anyone with a soccer-specific program or nonprofit project. Annual grant applications, guidelines, and answers to frequently asked questions; lists of staff, directors, and recent grantees; and

a resource center to assist in the development of soccer projects and programs are available on the foundation's Web site.

Utah Humanities Council (UT) (http://www.utahhumanities.org)
The Utah Humanities Council (UHC), the state affiliate of the National Endowment for the Humanities, promotes learning through the humanities. UHC provides grants and technical assistance to nonprofit organizations and a limited number of individual grants to teachers and scholars. The council's Web site provides grant guidelines, downloadable application forms, annual reports and newsletters, details on UHC's activities, and contact and donor information.

V Foundation (NC) (http://www.jimmyv.org/)
Founded by the late Jim Valvano (Jimmy V) and ESPN, the cable sports network, the V Foundation seeks to raise awareness of and support for cancer research. The foundation does not accept unsolicited funding applications. The foundation's Web site provides an overview of the foundation's research grants programs and funding procedures, a biography of Jimmy V, information about events staged in support of the foundation, and updates about the foundation and its activities.

Valerie Fund (NJ) (http://www.thevaleriefund.org)
Founded in 1976, the Maplewood, New Jersey-based Valerie Fund works "to provide comprehensive healthcare for children with cancer and blood disorders" in the greater New York, New Jersey, and Philadelphia metropolitan areas. The fund maintains four specific initiatives for children: projects dealing with sickle cell anemia; Sibshops, which are programs for siblings of afflicted children; school re-entry workshops; and Camp Happy Times. The fund's Web site provides news, information on regional service centers, details on community contributions to the fund, and contact, volunteer, and donation information.

Vanguard Charitable Endowment Program (PA) (http://www.vanguardcharitable.org)
The Vanguard Charitable Endowment Program is an independent public charity established "to support and increase philanthropy across the United States." Through its donor-advised funds, the program supports a wide range of nonprofit, charitable organizations and institutions, mainly in the areas of human services, education, the environment and wildlife, religion, health, arts and culture, and civic services. The program's Web site explains how the program operates and provides resources and information for potential donors, including answers to frequently asked questions, and a calculator for determining the tax benefits of a donation.

Vanguard Public Foundation (CA) (http://www.vanguardsf.org)
Created in 1972, the Vanguard Public Foundation is located in San Francisco, California. The organization is a "partnership of community activists and donors [that] has distributed [funds] to organizations and projects that work to achieve a more equitable distribution of power and resources in our society." Grantees are located in northern California, in counties north of Monterey. The foundation is interested in programs that try to change the underlying causes of injustice and poverty, involve the self-determination of low-income and working class people, work toward a prejudice-free society, and incorporate affirmative action practices. Areas of interest include issues of civil rights, economic justice, workers' rights, women's rights, education, disability, health, housing, the environment, cultural activism, indigenous people's rights, and international solidarity. The foundation's Web site includes application guidelines and instructions, information on donating to the foundation, and a staff list.

Viking Children's Fund, Inc. (MN)
(http://www.vikings.com/community/vikingchildrensfund.htm)
The Viking Children's Fund was established in 1978 as a means for players, their families, and staff of the Minnesota Vikings football team "to combine their time and resources with that of the corporate community and fans in an effort to support the many needs of children

in the Upper Midwest." Half of all funding is directed toward the University of Minnesota Department of Pediatrics, with the other half earmarked for nonprofit organizations in the fields of health education and family services serving the upper Midwest. Further details on fund's focus areas and contact information are available on its Web site.

Virgin Islands Humanities Council, Inc. (VI) (http://www.vihumanities.org/)
The Virgin Islands Humanities Council, Inc., was established in 1984 in St. Thomas with funding from the National Endowment for the Humanities "to provide opportunities for the diverse population of the Virgin Islands to participate in humanities programs which promote a love of learning, encourage dialogue, enhance understanding, and broaden people's judgment." The council provides grants to cultural and civic institutions, and other humanities-related organizations in the territory. The council's Web site provides information on specific grant programs and initiatives, the Humanities Resource Center, and the council's goals and objectives. Contact information is available for further details.

Virginia Foundation for the Humanities (VA) (http://www.virginia.edu/vfh)
Established in 1974, the Virginia Foundation for the Humanities is based at the University of Virginia in Charlottesville. The foundation is "dedicated to promoting the humanities, and to using the humanities to address issues of broad public concern." The foundation's Grant Program supports organizations in Virginia, or those that will have an impact on a large population of Virginians, involved in areas of the humanities. Grants provide financial support for a range of projects, such as exhibits, public forums and discussions, media programs, and publications. The foundation's Web site includes grant opportunities, grant guidelines, application instructions, information on other programs, ongoing research projects, and a list of featured grant recipients.

Virginia Health Care Foundation (VA) (http://www.vhcf.org/)
The Virginia Health Care Foundation funds local public-private partnerships that increase access to primary healthcare services for uninsured and medically underserved Virginians. The foundation supports projects that offer innovative primary and preventive care service delivery, increase primary care providers in target areas, incorporate telemedicine initiatives, or replicate the foundation's "Models That Made It"—programs that have proven to be cost effective and capable of sustaining themselves. The foundation's Web site offers descriptions of the foundation's funding categories, answers to frequently asked questions, grant guidelines, a listing of board and staff members, and information for donors.

Visual Aid (CA) (http://www.visualaid.org)
Visual Aid, located in San Francisco, California, is committed to "encouraging visual artists with life-threatening illness to continue their creative work by providing a variety of direct services." These services include a voucher program, which distributes certificates that can be redeemed at participating art and photo supply stores; the Art Bank, which distributes donated art supplies; exhibitions and workshops; studio assistants; and a resource center. The organization's Web site includes information on its programs, exhibitions, workshops, and lectures.

John D. Voelker Foundation (MI) (http://www.voelkerfdn.org/default.htm)
The John D. Voelker Foundation seeks to pay tribute to its namesake, a fly fisherman, author and former Michigan Supreme Court Justice, through scholarships and awards. The Native American Scholarship assists Native American students in the pursuit of a legal education. The Robert Traver Fly Fishing Fiction Award prizes a work of short fiction that somehow incorporates the theme of fly fishing. Information on this award and Voelker's exploits, eligibility and application instructions, membership and contact information, can be found on the foundation's Web site.

Wampum (WA) (http://www.wampum.org/)
Wampum of Spokane, Washington, is a nonprofit public charity interested in making the arts a part of everyday life to the people of Spokane. Around 20 Spokane area arts and culture

organizations receive grants from the charity annually. Wampum is also dedicated to providing opportunities for children in the community to participate in and realize the value of the arts. All grants made by Wampum are unrestricted and can be utilized for any purpose that supports the mission of the grantee's organization. Wampum's Web site includes a listing of officers and trustees, a listing of past grant recipients, and contact information.

Washington AIDS Partnership (DC) (http://www.washingtonaidspartnership.org)
Founded in 1989, the Washington AIDS Partnership is a philanthropic collaborative affiliated with the National AIDS Fund and Washington Grantmakers that funds a wide range of HIV/AIDS prevention, education, and service programs. The partnership provides grants in the areas of prevention, technical assistance, social/support services, medical morale, and public policy. Priority is given to organizations that effectively educate high-risk populations on HIV prevention. The partnership's Web site includes funding information and the current request for proposals, lists of grantees and funding partners, the latest annual report, and contact information.

Washington Commission for the Humanities (WA) (http://www.humanities.org/)
The Washington Commission for the Humanities supports humanities projects—which it defines as "the stories, ideas, and writings that help us make sense of our lives and enhance our ability to think creatively and critically about our world"—in Washington State. Grants are awarded for a range of programs and activities, including exhibits, public forums, school programs, lecture and discussion series, and cultural presentations. The commission's Web site provides grant guidelines, information about past recipients, information on sponsored programs, a calendar of events, and contact information.

Washington Health Foundation (WA) (http://www.whf.org)
Based in Olympia, the Washington Health Foundation is "dedicated to improving health and access to quality healthcare for the people of Washington state, including those residents who are medically underserved in both rural and urban communities." The foundation's programs include: referral and support for low-income families, pregnant women, and people living with HIV/AIDS; viability grants to healthcare providers to sustain vital medical services in rural communities; a statewide campaign with local efforts to enroll eligible children in public insurance programs; and Healthy Communities activities, including an annual symposium. The foundation's Web site includes viability grant guidelines and procedures, information on the foundation's other programs, publications, resource links, and contact information.

Washington Performing Arts Society (DC) (http://www.wpas.org)
The Washington Performing Arts Society was established in 1965 as a means of increasing the opportunity for artists and the public to share the performing arts. The society's mission is threefold: to bring performers to venues throughout Washington, D.C., to sponsor enriching educational projects for school children, and to showcase innovative art forms and emerging artists. The society's Web site provides information on upcoming performances and events; opportunities for artists, volunteers, and interns to get involved with the organization; and membership and contact information.

Water Environment Research Foundation (VA) (http://www.werf.org)
Based in Alexandria, Virginia, the Water Environment Research Foundation was created in 1989 and is dedicated "to advancing science and technology addressing water quality issues as they impact water resources, the atmosphere, the lands, and quality of life." The foundation accomplishes this by funding research and making the results available to its subscribers. Requests for proposals are regularly posted on the foundation's Web site, and the foundation encourages submissions from all qualified entities, including international organizations and disadvantaged business enterprises. The foundation's Web site also provides in-depth information on submitting a proposal, necessary forms, information on the foundation's publications and other resources, contact information, board and staff lists, and information on volunteering.

Wausau Health Foundation, Inc. (WI) (http://www.chcsys.org/wausau_health_foundation/)
Located in Wausau, Wisconsin, the Wausau Health Foundation, Inc., works to support philanthropy, clinical research, and health services projects in northern and central Wisconsin. The foundation's mission is to meet the health needs in its community by working with local healthcare systems. The foundation's Web site provides details of recent grants and gifts, current research and health services projects, application guidelines and limitations, the foundation's annual report, downloadable funding applications, and contact information.

Wender Weis Foundation for Children (http://www.wenderweis.org/)
Based in Palo Alto, California, the Wender Weis Foundation for Children was founded in 1994 to provide charitable relief and assistance to at-risk, disadvantaged children throughout the San Francisco Bay Area. The foundation uses the proceeds from fundraising efforts to sponsor various outreach programs that encourage confidence and self-esteem in children. The foundation does not accept unsolicited grant proposals. The foundation's Web site provides details on its programs and contact information.

West Central Initiative (MN) (http://www.wcif.org/)
The West Central Initiative was created to enhance the viability of the west central Minnesota region through funding initiatives including workforce, community, family, and leadership/management. The initiative's Web site provide details of these initiatives, downloadable application forms, and a variety of regional information, including links to community Web sites.

West Virginia Humanities Council (WV) (http://www.wvhumanities.org)
The West Virginia Humanities Council is a state affiliate of the National Endowment for the Humanities, providing lifelong learning opportunities to the state's citizens. The council works toward this goal by sponsoring humanities programs as well as specific grants and fellowships. Grant guidelines for an array of funding opportunities, downloadable applications, a calendar of events, publications, an online magazine, descriptions of a variety of current programs, and contact information are available on the council's Web site.

Western States Arts Federation (CO) (http://www.westaf.org/)
The Western States Arts Federation, also known as WESTAF, supports state arts agencies, arts organizations, and artists in the western United States to promote creative advancement and preservation of the arts. WESTAF is committed to programmatic work in the areas of multicultural arts, literature, folk arts, visual arts, and performing-arts presenting. The foundation's Web site provides information on the federation's grant programs and other projects, annotated art links, publications and research, information on the CultureGrants Online grant application system, and links to the Arts Registers featuring visual artists, writers, and performing artists.

WHAS Crusade for Children, Inc. (KY) (http://www.whas-crusade.org)
Based in Louisville, Kentucky, the WHAS Crusade for Children, Inc., was created in 1954 to raise money for agencies, schools, and hospitals that help special needs children in Kentucky and southern Indiana. The crusade is centered on an annual telethon, though donations are accepted year-round. Nonprofit agencies that help special children can apply for funds once a year from the crusade. The crusade's Web site provides contact information, grants lists, and a Report to the People, which provides financial information.

Wheat Ridge Ministries (IL) (http://www.wheatridge.org/)
Wheat Ridge Ministries is an independent Lutheran charitable organization that provides support for new church-related "health and hope" ministries that focus on "health of body, mind, and spirit." The ministries' funding programs include Major Grants, Special Short-Term Grants, and Congregation Health and Hope Grants. The ministries' Web site provides proposal guidelines, links to grant writing resources, and a list of recipients; news;

Web, video, and fax resources; information on Wheat Ridge awards; and a listing of board and staff members.

Joseph B. Whitehead Foundation (GA) (http://www.jbwhitehead.org)
The Joseph B. Whitehead Foundation was established in 1937 to support charitable activities in Atlanta, Georgia, where the foundation is located. The foundation's grant program has a particular interest in basic human services, especially organizations and programs that benefit children and youth in metropolitan Atlanta; a recent focus is improving public education and family, children, and youth services. Preference is given to one-time capital projects. The foundation's Web site provides grant guidelines and application procedures, grants lists, links to other foundation resources, a brief biography of Joseph B. Whitehead, links to other foundations with which the Joseph B. Whitehead Foundation shares a common administrative arrangement, and contact information.

Lettie Pate Whitehead Foundation, Inc. (GA) (http://www.lpwhitehead.org)
The Lettie Pate Whitehead Foundation, Inc., was chartered in 1946 to aid "poor and needy Christian girls and women" in Georgia, North Carolina, South Carolina, Virginia, Louisiana, Mississippi, Alabama, Tennessee, and Florida. Support is given in the form of grants to educational institutions in the nine states to fund scholarships for the education of women. In addition, operating grants are provided to a few select institutions serving the needs of elderly women. Applications for individual scholarship aid should be made directly to the educational institutions. The foundation's Web site provides information about the foundation's grant programs, a list of participating institutions, a biography of the foundation's namesake, links to other foundations with which the Lettie Pate Whitehead Foundation shares a common administrative arrangement, links to other resources, and contact information.

The Elie Wiesel Foundation for Humanity (NY) (http://www.eliewieselfoundation.org)
The Elie Wiesel Foundation for Humanity was established by Elie Wiesel and his wife, Marion, after he was awarded the 1986 Nobel Prize for Peace. Based in New York City, the foundation's mission is "to advance the cause of human rights by creating forums for the discussion and resolution of urgent ethical issues." In addition to international conferences and seminars that bring together leading scholars, artists, scientists, politicians, humanists, and young people from all over the world, the foundation also sponsors an annual undergraduate essay contest. Through all its activities, the foundation seeks to combat indifference, intolerance, and injustice. The foundation's Web site includes guidelines and forms for the essay contest, information on the foundation's other programs, giving opportunities, and contact information.

Wilson International Center for Scholars (DC) (http://wwics.si.edu/)
The Wilson International Center for Scholars was established by Congress in 1968 as a living memorial to President Woodrow Wilson and as a location for intellectual dialogue on current and future public policy challenges. The center offers internships to current undergraduate and graduate students, fellowships for the investigation of public policy issues, and the Woodrow Wilson Awards for Public Service. Guidelines, application forms, and instructions for the fellowship; information on events and programs; and news are provided on the center's Web site.

Woodrow Wilson National Fellowship Foundation (NJ) (http://www.woodrow.org/)
The Woodrow Wilson National Fellowship Foundation encourages excellence in education by developing and funding programs that target the needs of new teachers and scholars, encourage cooperation between academia and other sectors of society, improve the status and representation of minority groups and women, and help maintain the vitality of teachers. The foundation's programs include fellowships for graduate study, professional development for teachers, educational opportunities for women and minorities, relating the academy to society, and national service. Fellowship programs, application guidelines, the

foundation's annual report and newsletters, press releases, listings of board and staff, and contact information are available on the foundation's Web site.

The Wilson Research Foundation (MS) (http://www.mmrcrehab.org/wilson_foundation)
The Wilson Research Foundation is the research arm of the Jackson-based Mississippi Rehabilitation Center. Established in 1988, the foundation's mission is "to enhance the quality of life for the catastrophically disabled through medical, clinical, and educational research." The foundation awards grants for rehabilitation research in collaboration with the Methodist Rehabilitation Center for disabling illnesses and injuries including spinal cord injury, brain injury, stroke, and adult neurological diseases. The foundation's Web site includes grant proposal guidelines and contact information, a list of funded projects, and information on making a contribution.

The Windstar Foundation (CO) (http://www.wstar.org/)
Created in 1976 by singer/songwriter John Denver and Aikido master Tom Crum, the Windstar Foundation of Snowmass, Colorado, is an environmental education organization that works "to inspire individuals to make responsible choices and take direct personal actions to achieve a peaceful and environmentally sustainable future." Foundation programs include the Environmental Studies Scholarship Program; the Windstar Connection Program, a regional grassroots outreach program; the Earthcamp program for kids; and conferences and other programs. The foundation's Web site provides information on the foundation's founders, philosophy, and programs; details on the Windstar Land Conservancy and other projects; opportunities to contribute; and contact information.

Wireless Foundation (DC) (http://www.wirelessfoundation.org/)
The Wireless Foundation of Washington, D.C., "initiates and oversees philanthropic programs that utilize wireless technology to help American communities." The foundation's projects include Call to Protect, which distributes wireless phones to victims of domestic violence; ClassLink, in which wireless phones and airtime are donated to classrooms in order to advance learning; and Donate a Phone, which recycles used wireless phones to help the environment and raise funds for charities. The foundation's Web site includes an overview of its programs, information on donating phones, contact information for further details, board and staff lists, a list of contributors, and information on how organizations can raise funds for their programs by collecting used wireless phones.

Wisconsin Community Fund (WI) (http://www.wisconsincommunityfund.org/)
The Wisconsin Community Fund, which has offices in Madison and Milwaukee, was founded in 1982 to "raise and disburse money to progressive groups working for democracy, justice, and social and economic equality." The fund donates money and provides technical assistance and other support to a wide variety of social, political, and environmental programs throughout Wisconsin. The fund's Web site offers information on organizations the fund has supported in the past, grant guidelines and limitations, links to progressive organizations and grantmaking resources, and contact information.

Wisconsin Health Association Foundation (WI) (http://www.wha.org/about/foundation.aspx)
The Wisconsin Health Association Foundation was established in 1968 "to support the educational, research, and charitable programs of the Wisconsin Hospital Association and its members." The foundation has provided funding for efforts to increase the preparedness of the healthcare workforce, implement innovative methods of delivering services to vulnerable populations, expand curriculum for healthcare professionals, and provide resources to support conferences on healthcare issues. The foundation's page on the association's Web site provides an overview of the foundation's activities, a list of trustees, and an e-mail address to request further information on the foundation and its grantmaking priorities.

Wisconsin Humanities Council (WI) (http://www.danenet.wicip.org/whc/)
Created in 1972 as an affiliate of the National Endowment for the Humanities, the Madison-based Wisconsin Humanities Council supports "public programs that engage the people of Wisconsin in the exploration of human cultures, ideas, and values." As part of its mission, the council provides grants to support programs in libraries, museums, universities, historical societies, schools, and other nonprofit settings throughout the state. The council's Web site provides grant guidelines and forms, information on the council's Speakers Bureau and other programs, links to humanities resources, the council's newsletter, and a calendar of sponsored events.

Women's Community Foundation (OH) (http://www.wcfcleveland.org/)
Based in Cleveland, Ohio, the Women's Community Foundation was established in 1981 with $30,000 in proceeds from the exhibition of the artist Judy Chicago's "The Dinner Party." The foundation raises money and makes grants to groups serving women and girls in Cuyahoga County, Ohio. The foundation also administers the Creative Philanthropy Award, greater Cleveland's annual tribute to a woman who has demonstrated outstanding leadership in supporting programs that serve women and girls. The foundation's Web site provides funding guidelines, award and grant recipient lists, and contact information.

The Women's Foundation (CA) (http://www.twfusa.org)
Based in San Francisco, the Women's Foundation is a philanthropic fund for women in the western United States. Created in 1979 to address the inequity of funding directed towards women and girls throughout the United States, the foundation supports organizations that serve low-income women and girls throughout 50 counties in northern and central California and the Mexico side of the United States-Mexico border. The foundation funds programs for the prevention of violence against women and girls, girls' leadership, health, and economic justice. The foundation's Web site provides information about its programs, partnerships, and various grantmaking funds; downloadable grant applications; information on upcoming events; and details on making a donation.

The Women's Foundation of Colorado (CO) (http://www.wfco.org)
The Women's Foundation of Colorado, established in 1987, "works to create communities in which women's talents and abilities are valued as important assets in building a vital and strong society." The foundation's grantmaking focuses on removing barriers for girls and women in three areas: girls' futures; education, employment, and training; and technology. The foundation's Web site provides grant guidelines and downloadable applications, reports and research, grants lists, and news and events.

Women's Foundation of Minnesota (MN) (http://www.wfmn.org/)
Established in 1986, the Minneapolis-based Women's Foundation of Minnesota "empowers women and girls with the resources they need to organize for economic, political, and social equality and provides a vital voice for their cause." The foundation provides grants through its Social Change Fund to provide resources for "women and girls projects that are designed to have a significant impact on societal attitudes and behaviors or result in systems change." The foundation also offers a technical assistance program and a grantmaking and public awareness initiative focused on building the economic power of girls. The foundation's Web site provides current funding guidelines, research and education resources, links to related Web sites, lists of the staff and board of trustees, and contact information.

Women's Funding Alliance (WA) (http://www.wfalliance.org/)
The Women's Funding Alliance, located in Seattle, Washington, was created in 1983 to "promote justice, health, and opportunities by investing in the future of women and girls." The alliance provides ongoing support to a group of affiliated agencies and offers grants through the Community Fund to nonprofit organizations serving women and girls in the Puget Sound region of Washington State. The alliance also offers a scholarship to women who are involved with one of its affiliated agencies. The alliance's Web site includes

funding and scholarship guidelines, information on making donations or volunteering, features on special events, lists of the board of directors and staff, and contact information.

The Women's Resource of Greater Houston (TX) (http://www.thewomensresource.org/)
The Women's Resource of Greater Houston, located in Houston, Texas, seeks to help women become economically self-sufficient, encourage prevention and early intervention of problems affecting women and girls, support programs that help to develop and improve life skills, actively involve women in philanthropic decision-making, and educate women about charitable giving. Foundation grants have funded programs on literacy, job readiness and training, parenting skills, health education, and violence prevention. The foundation's Web site provides information on its grantmaking program, a list of previous grant recipients, information on the foundation's research and educational programs, and contact information.

Women's Sports Foundation (NY) (http://www.womenssportsfoundation.org/)
The Women's Sports Foundation, founded in 1974 by Billie Jean King and other female athletes, is dedicated to increasing opportunities for girls and women in sports and fitness through education, advocacy, recognition, and grants. The foundation's Web site provides detailed information and downloadable application forms for numerous grant and scholarship programs; details on membership and making a donation; and information on sports, athletes, and related issues.

Women's Studio Workshop, Inc. (NY) (http://www.wsworkshop.org/)
The Women's Studio Workshop, Inc., (WSW) located in Rosendale, New York, was begun in 1974 by four women artists committed to developing an alternative space for female artists to create new work and share skills. The organization supports a number of grants, fellowships, and special initiatives, most of which take place at the studio in Rosendale, with facilities for printmaking, papermaking, book arts, clay, and photographic media. Grants include the Artists Book Residency and the Artists Book Production Grant. Fellowships are generally for a reduction in cost of studio time at the WSW, and are either for general purposes or clay. Special initiatives include Residency for New Jersey Artists, Visiting Artist Project, Art-in-Education, and the Emerging Artist Project. The organization also sponsors six internships throughout the year. The organization's Web site includes details on resources available to artists at the studio, a literary journal, information on programs and grants, grant application forms, current news and events at the WSW, and a contact form.

Women's Way (PA) (http://www.womensway.org)
Formed in 1977 by a group of local women's agencies, Women's Way serves the greater Philadelphia area, including the Delaware Valley and southern New Jersey. Through its discretionary fund, Women's Way supports programs that are run by and serve women and that "advocate freedom from violence, guarantee equal opportunity, challenge discrimination in all forms, foster economic self-determination, and affirm reproductive freedom." The Women's Way Web site includes numerous listings of events and news, links to resources for women, current funding guidelines and forms, a list of recent grantees, information on making a contribution, and contact information.

The Tiger Woods Foundation, Inc. (OH) (http://www.twfound.org)
Golfer Tiger Woods created the Reynoldsburg, Ohio-based Tiger Woods Foundation in 1996 to "empower young people to reach their highest potential by initiating and supporting community-based programs that promote the health, education, and welfare of all of America's children." The foundation runs youth golf clinics; makes grants in urban American cities in the areas of child and family health and welfare, education, parenting, and youth development; awards college scholarships; and, in partnership with Target stores, sponsors the Start Something program for youth achievement. The foundation's Web site offers an overview of its programs, extensive grant application guidelines and procedures, information on scholarship recipients, news and details on upcoming events, and an online feedback form.

World Parks Endowment (DC) (http://www.worldparks.org/)
With offices in Washington, D.C., and San Francisco, California, the World Parks Endowment operates as an international conservation organization, working to preserve the Earth's threatened species and ecosystems. Partnering with local organizations, the endowment purchases and protects environmentally diverse and important lands. The endowment's Web site provides details on the organization's environmental mission, past projects, partner organizations, links to related publications, and contact information for both offices.

World Wildlife Fund (DC) (http://www.worldwildlife.org/)
The World Wildlife Fund, the largest privately supported international conservation organization in the world, directs its conservation efforts toward "protecting endangered spaces, saving endangered species, and addressing global threats." The fund's Web site provides information on its activities around the world and on issues related to conservation; information on the Russell E. Train Education for Nature Program, the foundation's initiative to foster a corps of conservation leaders in Africa, Asia, and Latin America through scholarships, fellowships, and grants; and the Guide to Funding Sources for Conservation and Education database.

World Wings International, Inc. (FL) (http://www.worldwingsinternational.org)
World Wings International, Inc., was established in 1959 as the philanthropic organization of the former flight attendants of Pan American World Airways. The organization's Web site provides a history of the group, upcoming member events, lists of charities that the group supports, newsletters, and contact information for officers and regional directors.

Worldstudio Foundation (http://www.worldstudio.org)
The Worldstudio Foundation provides scholarships to minority and economically disadvantaged students who are studying the design/arts disciplines in American colleges and universities. The foundation aims to increase diversity in the creative professions and to foster social responsibility in the artists and designers of tomorrow. Scholarship recipients are selected not only for their ability and their need, but also for their demonstrated commitment to giving back to the larger community. On its Web site, the foundation provides downloadable applications and information about its mentoring program.

Worldwide Christian Schools (MI) (http://www.gospelcom.net/wcs)
Worldwide Christian Schools is an international evangelical ministry located in Grand Rapids, Michigan, working to help "responsible Christian organizations worldwide to develop Christian schools." The organization helps develop schools "primarily among the world's poor children in areas where there are usually few or no options for education." The organization's Web site offers information on the organization's school projects and general philosophy, school development funding guidelines, volunteer opportunities, information on mission homes, news on special events, and contact information.

Wycliffe Associates, Inc. (CA) (http://www.wycliffeassociates.org)
Wycliffe Associates, Inc., was established in 1967 in Orange, California, as the lay ministry organization working to support the Wycliffe Bible Translators. The organization raises funds and provides volunteers and prayer support for the Wycliffe Bible Translators. Details on the group's beliefs, financial information, and upcoming events; service and donation opportunities; and contact information are available on the organization's Web site.

Wyoming Council for the Humanities (WY) (http://www.uwyo.edu/special/wch/)
The Wyoming Council for the Humanities fosters interaction between the public and humanities scholars on questions related to the "significant dimensions of our existence—personal, social, cultural, and political—from local, national, and international perspectives." The council awards grants to organizations for projects encouraging analysis and public discussion of issues in the humanities. The council's Web site provides information on the council's activities and events, grant guidelines and downloadable application

forms, a database of humanities scholars, an online newsletter, and information for prospective donors.

Kristi Yamaguchi's Always Dream Foundation (CA) (http://www.alwaysdream.org)
The Oakland, California-based Kristi Yamaguchi's Always Dream Foundation was founded by professional figure skater Kristi Yamaguchi to support organizations that have a positive influence on children in California, Nevada, or Hawaii. The foundation's Web site offers information on the foundation's mission, lists of past beneficiaries, details on making a donation, and contact information.

Yellow Jacket Foundation, Inc. (SD)
(http://www.bhsu.edu/alumni/yellowjacketfoundation/index.htm)
The Yellow Jacket Foundation, Inc., located in Spearfish, South Dakota, supports the athletic programs at Black Hills State University. The foundation's Web site includes upcoming university athletic events and news, a hall of fame, donation information, and contact information.

APPENDIX D
Community Foundations on the Web

ALABAMA

Calhoun County Community Foundation (http://www.cccfoundation.org)
Located in Anniston, Alabama, the Calhoun County Community Foundation is a family of funds that serve as a permanent endowment for the long-term benefit of Calhoun County in northeast Alabama. The foundation exists to "support nonprofit organizations targeting the most discernible needs and most promising opportunities within Calhoun County, Alabama." The foundation maintains the Stringfellow Health, Preventative Healthcare, and E.D. King Family Funds. The foundation's Web site features funding guidelines and downloadable applications, information about investments and planned giving opportunities, and news.

The Community Foundation of Greater Birmingham (http://www.foundationbirmingham.org)
Established in 1959, the Community Foundation of Greater Birmingham is made up of more than 200 grantmaking funds established by individuals, families, nonprofit agencies, private foundations, and businesses. Its mission is to connect caring people and key resources with community needs, today and tomorrow. The Women's Fund of Greater Birmingham is a component fund of the foundation and is dedicated to improving the status and quality of life for women and girls in the greater Birmingham area through purposeful philanthropy and the establishment of a permanent endowment. The foundation's Web site features a brief history of the foundation, application guidelines and procedures, information on becoming a donor, a listing of the foundation's board of directors and staff, FAQs, and contact information.

Community Foundation of South Alabama (http://communityendowment.com/)
The Community Foundation of South Alabama was established in 1975 to provide leadership to Mobile and surrounding communities by offering a flexible vehicle for donors with varied philanthropic desires to make gifts in perpetuity. The foundation responds to the needs of the growing community, providing leadership and direction through proactive

grants to nonprofit organizations in Mobile, Baldwin, Clarke, Conecuh, Washington, Choctaw, Escambia, and Monroe Counties. The foundation's Web site features information on the organization's giving priorities, an online copy of the latest annual report, and contact information.

ALASKA

Alaska Conservation Foundation (http://www.akcf.org)
Established in 1980, the Alaska Conservation Foundation receives funds and makes grants to protect the integrity of Alaska's ecosystems and to promote sustainable livelihoods among its communities and peoples. The foundation's areas of interest include advocacy, community development, public communications, public policy, and rural affairs. The foundation's guidelines favor approaches that convene diverse constituencies, promote citizen participation in public process, provide forums for increasing environmental awareness, and build capacity to implement sustainable futures. The foundation's Web site offers a mission statement, a brief history of the foundation and facts about the state of Alaska, board and staff listings, program descriptions, grant guidelines and application procedures, and contact and donor information.

The Homer Foundation (http://www.homerfund.org/)
The Homer Foundation was created in 1991 to enhance the quality of life for the citizens of Alaska's Southern Kenai Peninsula. The foundation maintains a number of permanent funds established to support a broad purpose or issue such as youth, arts, education, or human services. The foundation also makes scholarships to students in the community. The foundation's Web site features information about the funds, grant guidelines, geographic restrictions, staff/board listings, financial and contact information.

ARIZONA

Arizona Community Foundation (http://www.azfoundation.com)
The Phoenix-based Arizona Community Foundation was established in 1978 by a trio of local businessmen and has since become one of the fastest growing public charities in the nation. Through its grantmaking activities, the foundation aims to improve the lives of children and families and strengthen neighborhoods and communities across the state. The foundation supports programs that respond to the needs of low income and vulnerable older persons, disadvantaged and underserved children and youth, education, neighborhood- and community-based economic and social development, social justice, and the environment. The foundation's Web site features general program information, a board of directors listing, information for potential donors, and contact information for its affiliates in Flagstaff, the Green Valley area, Page, Scottsdale, Sedona, Tempe, and Cochise, Graham, and Yavapai Counties.

Community Foundation of Southern Arizona (http://www.cfsoaz.org)
The Community Foundation of Southern Arizona was established in 1980 to serve Tucson and southern Arizona. The foundation addresses wide range of the most critical charitable causes in its community in the areas of health, human services, education, the arts, and the environment. The foundation's Web site includes information about the grantmaking programs, application criteria, board and staff listings, and contact information.

ARKANSAS

Arkansas Community Foundation, Inc. (http://www.arcf.org)
The Arkansas Community Foundation, Inc., was established in 1976 in Little Rock to "provide and promote leadership as the premier builder of philanthropic funds to meet Arkansas' diverse grantmaking needs and challenges." The foundation's emphasis is placed on

projects that benefit rural and urban, communities, promote philanthropy throughout the state, and partner nonprofits together. The foundation is interested in projects that will have a long-term effect and can be replicated. The foundation prefers letter of inquiry as an initial approach. The foundation's Web site features a list of scholarships for students in post-secondary schools, including the very specific qualifications for each; board and staff lists; information on contributing or starting a fund; and an electronic form to request foundation publications.

Foundation for the Mid South (http://www.fndmidsouth.org/)
The Foundation for the Mid South makes grants "to build the capacity of communities, organizations, and individuals" throughout Arkansas, Louisiana, and Mississippi. Grants are made within the three primary program areas of economic development, education, and families and children. The foundation's Web site features detailed program descriptions, including types of funding provided within each program area; downloadable application forms; an interactive bulletin board through which regional grantseekers and grantmakers can communicate; and selections from the foundation's annual report, including listings of grants by program area.

CALIFORNIA

Berkeley Community Fund (http://www.netwiz.net/~bcf/)
The Berkeley Community Fund was established in 1992 to address local social problems. It seeks to narrow the inequities within the community, create hope and opportunity for disadvantaged youth, enhance cultural and intellectual diversity while building consensus to address common problems, and stimulate public and private investments to raise the quality of community life. The fund connects people and organizations to enhance planning and resource sharing, provides technical assistance, makes cash grants to community groups and gives college scholarships to deserving Berkeley High School seniors, and brings "public and private resources to bear on efforts that support the mission of the fund and the needs of the community." The fund's Web site features grantmaking criteria, FAQs, descriptions of some of the fund's current projects, contact information, a listing of the board of directors and staff, and contact information.

California Community Foundation (http://www.calfund.org/)
Established in 1915, the California Community Foundation was Los Angeles' first grantmaking institution and is the country's second-oldest community foundation. The foundation makes grants to organizations serving the greater Los Angeles region in human services, community development, civic affairs, community health, early education, and arts and culture. The foundation's Web site features general information, grant guidelines, a downloadable version of the foundation's grant application form, a list of recent grants, brief biographies of selected donors, a list of foundation-sponsored publications, and a calendar of upcoming foundation-related events and special initiatives.

Claremont Community Foundation (http://www.claremontfoundation.org/)
The Claremont Community Foundation was established in 1989 to serve the community of Claremont, California, a town within the larger Los Angeles metropolitan area. The foundation supports projects that preserve the local cultural heritage and has awarded grants to programs and special projects for the arts, health, welfare, education, and history. The foundation's Web site contains contact information and application guidelines.

Community Foundation for Monterey County (http://www.cfmco.org/)
Established in 1945, the Community Foundation for Monterey County seeks to improve the quality of life for all residents of Monterey County, and to strengthen the institutions that help build healthy communities. The foundation encourages applications that provide significant benefits to the community in the areas of health, education, social and community services, arts and culture, environmental and historic preservation, and animal welfare.

The foundation also has a Management Assistance Program, which is designed to improve and expand access to management assistance services and resources for nonprofit organizations in Monterey and San Benito Counties. Workshops, management, and technical assistance grants are available to nonprofits. The foundation's Web site features application materials, downloadable program guidelines, and other funding sources.

Community Foundation of Santa Cruz County (http://www.cfscc.org)
The Community Foundation of Santa Cruz County was established in 1982 to make "greater Santa Cruz County a better place to live, now, and in the future." The foundation builds permanent endowed funds contributed by individuals and institutions. The foundation's grants are made to organizations that hold an interest in health, human services, education, arts and humanities, historic preservation, community development, or the environment. The foundation also maintains a scholarship fund. Visitors to the foundation's Web site will more information on the grants program, board and staff listings, financial data, and contact information.

The Community Foundation Serving Riverside and San Bernardino Counties (http://www.thecommunityfoundation.net)
The Community Foundation Serving Riverside and San Bernardino Counties' mission is focused on "strengthening communities by meeting the needs and enhancing the lives of individuals in Riverside and San Bernardino Counties in partnership with philanthropic individuals, community leaders, and the nonprofit sector." The foundation maintains a number of funds including a variety of Field of Interest Funds, which makes up about a third of the foundation's giving grantmaking. The rest of the foundation's grantmaking is allocated for scholarships or for grants to agencies designated by the original fund donors. The foundation's Web site features information about the individual funds, listings of recent grant recipients, application information, and application forms, and contact information.

Community Foundation Silicon Valley (http://www.siliconvalleygives.org/)
Created in 1954, the Community Foundation of Santa Clara County changed its name in 1997 to the Community Foundation Silicon Valley to better reflect the entrepreneurial spirit, creativity, and diversity of the community it serves. The foundation supports programs that benefit the residents of Santa Clara County and southern San Mateo County in the following areas: education and lifelong learning, arts and cultural participation, neighborhoods and civic engagement, self-reliant individuals and families, and innovative application of technology. The foundation's Web site provides general program information, application guidelines, a foundation calendar, list of recent grants, an electronic form for ordering copies of the foundation's print publications, related links, contact information, the latest "Corporate Community Involvement Study," and an introduction to the foundation's Mayfair Neighborhood Improvement Initiative.

East Bay Community Foundation (http://www.eastbaycf.org/)
Founded in 1928, the Oakland-based East Bay Community Foundation is a permanent endowment of charitable funds dedicated to improving the human condition and enhancing the quality of life of the residents and communities of Alameda and Contra Costa Counties in California. Grantmaking is focused on education, youth development, human services, health and wellness, arts and culture, the environment, civic engagement, and organizational effectiveness. The foundation also sponsors the Art Education Initiative, which promotes arts education for local school children and brings together artists, teachers, parents, schools, community groups, and businesses to create sustainable arts education programs; the Livable Communities Initiative, which promotes smart growth in land use and transportation planning in rural, suburban, and urban areas of the East Bay; the East Bay Public Safety Corridor Partnership, which seeks solutions to the problems of local public safety; and Safe Passages (formerly the Oakland Child Health and Safety Initiative), which is a collaboration focusing on the health and safety of Oakland's youth. The foundation's Web

site features grant guidelines and application procedures, general information, contact information, and links to affiliate funds.

Fresno Regional Foundation (http://fresnoregfoundation.org/)
Established in 1966, the Fresno Regional Foundation is a community foundation serving the economic, educational, social, environmental, and cultural needs of California's San Joaquin Valley. The foundation's Web site contains information on the foundation's continuous and competitive grants and donor programs, grant guidelines, lists of previously funded organizations, information on the foundation's partnerships and funding goals, and a downloadable grant application.

Great Valley Center, Inc. (http://www.greatvalley.org)
Based in Modesto, California, the Great Valley Center, Inc. is a non-partisan organization committed to activities and organizations that support the economic, social, and environmental well-being of California's Great Central Valley. The center was established to foster collaboration, seek solutions, and be a voice for California's Great Central Valley. The center awards monetary grants to nonprofit groups, community organizations, and local governments that are working to improve the well-being of the Great Central Valley through initiatives in the areas of land use, the environment, growth, agriculture, conservation, and investment. The center also has a fellowship, the Institute for the Development of Emerging Area Leaders (IDEAL) Fellowship Program, whose goal is to provide access and information to emerging area leaders on issues relating to Great Central Valley land use, economics, agriculture, and conservation. The program is targeted to reach underrepresented groups, minorities, and local leaders from small rural communities. The center's Web site features downloadable applications, information on the counties in the Great Central Valley area, related links, and contact information.

Humboldt Area Foundation (http://www.hafoundation.org/)
The Humboldt Area Foundation was established in 1972 as a vehicle of and for the citizens of the north coast of California—Humboldt, Del Norte, and parts of Trinity and Siskiyou Counties. The foundation's Web site contains general information about the foundation, detailed grant application guidelines, and an overview of the resources available to nonprofit organizations at the foundation-operated William T. Rooney Resource Center.

Jewish Community Foundation (http://jcfsandiego.org/index.html)
The Jewish Community Foundation of San Diego, California, seeks to "promote philanthropy through meaningful partnerships with donors and community organizations in achieving charitable goals [and] to increase current and future support for a vibrant and secure Jewish community in San Diego, Israel, and around the world." The foundation's Web site contains information on the foundation's numerous funds and ways to get involved and contact information.

Los Altos Community Foundation (http://www.losaltoscf.org/)
The Los Altos Community Foundation serves Los Altos, Los Altos Hills, and the surrounding area "by promoting community building—those activities and facilities that give the community its favorable character, making it a desirable place to live and work." Community building includes projects that strengthen values, preserve the community's physical heritage, and enhance community-based philanthropic activities. The foundation makes grants to local programs, builds an endowment, and manages philanthropic activities for other organizations and individuals. The foundation's Web site features a description of the foundation's programs, information about the criteria for grantmaking, the foundation's financial statement, and contact information.

Marin Community Foundation (http://www.marincf.org/)
The Marin Community Foundation strives to encourage and apply philanthropic contributions to help improve the human condition, embrace diversity, promote a humane and democratic society, and enhance the community's quality of life. The foundation focuses its

grantmaking activities in the following areas: the arts, with an emphasis on arts in the community and arts education; community development; education and training, with an emphasis on drop-out prevention, improving literacy and basic skills, school restructuring and redesign, and lifelong learning; the environment; human services; and religion. The foundation's Web site features detailed program descriptions and application guidelines; additional information about the foundation's various community programs, donor-advised funds, and loan programs; FAQs; and links to related sites.

Orange County Community Foundation (http://www.oc-communityfoundation.org/)
Established in 1989, the mission of the Orange County Community Foundation is to encourage, support, and facilitate philanthropy in Orange County. The foundation makes discretionary grants in the following areas: children and youth, with a focus on ensuring the safety of young people in their homes and neighborhoods, child and foster care, early childhood development, school preparedness, arts and classical music education, and building self-esteem; family relationships, with a focus on improving family impact on children and youth, parenting, family economic self-sufficiency, and family violence; and diverse communities, with a focus on the promotion of mutual respect and understanding among diverse groups in Orange County. The foundation also awards a limited number of scholarships to high school juniors and seniors who are continuing their education in an accredited institution and are graduating from an Orange County high school and are residents of Orange County. The foundation's Web site provides information on the foundation's grantmaking activities, application guidelines and recent grants, FAQs for grantseekers and potential donors, a summary of foundation publications, and contact information.

Pasadena Foundation (http://www.pasadenafoundation.org/)
Founded in 1953, the Pasadena Foundation serves as a leader, catalyst, and resource for philanthropy in the community it serves. The foundation seeks to improve the lives of children, the disabled, and seniors in the Pasadena, Altadena and Sierra Madre areas of California. The foundation also sponsors various initiatives, including a Christmas present program for underprivileged children called "Yes, Virginia." The foundation's Web site features a grants list; information on donor services, including the Fellows Program; a message from the chairman; and contact information.

Peninsula Community Foundation (http://www.pcf.org/)
Created by residents of the San Francisco peninsula in 1964, the Peninsula Community Foundation today provides funding for nonprofit groups in San Mateo and Santa Clara Counties that address the needs of children, youth and families, or that work in the areas of education, health and human services, housing and homelessness, the arts, or civic and public benefit. Through its Center for Venture Philanthropy, the foundation is also forging partnerships of donor/investors "to make long-term, focused investments in complex programs . . . [such as] as school reform and welfare reform." In addition to information for potential donors, visitors to the foundation's Web site will find general program information, current grantmaking guidelines, a list of recent grants, board and staff listings, a calendar of deadline and events, information on the foundation's Strategic Philanthropy initiatives (i.e., the Center for Venture Philanthropy; the Peninsula Partnership for Children, Youth and Families; the Prenatal to Three Initiative; and the Neighborhood Grants Program), and contact information.

Sacramento Regional Foundation (http://www.sacregfoundation.org)
The Sacramento Regional Foundation is the community foundation for Sacramento, Placer, and Yolo Counties. It is committed to implementing donors' charitable wishes and creating an everlasting gift that will benefit the Sacramento area for generations. The foundation maintains the Community-Based Wildfire Prevention Program, which works to prevent wildland fire prevention in California. The foundation also maintains a number of scholarship programs. The foundation's Web site features examples of the foundation's grantmaking and contact information.

The San Diego Foundation (http://www.sdfoundation.org)
The San Diego Foundation was established in 1975 to "improve the quality of life within all of our communities by promoting and increasing responsible and effective philanthropy." The foundation's grantmaking programs support projects that encompass arts and culture, economic development, education, the environment, healthcare and human services, and religious endeavors. Interested organizations must submit a letter of intent and any requested additional information. While some funding is unrestricted, there are funds established to support specific areas, including the Civil Society Initiative, the Teachers Fund, and Community Endowment Grants. Applications and guidelines are posted as grants become available. The foundation also administers a large number of scholarships. These are listed in two categories, those that accept a common application and those with their own application. The latter include contact information to receive an application. The common application and a list of necessary supporting documents, board and staff lists, financial information, and information on how to make a donation are available on the foundation's Web site.

The San Francisco Foundation (http://www.sff.org/)
Established in 1948, the San Francisco Foundation mobilizes resources and acts as a catalyst for change to build strong communities, foster civic leadership, and promote philanthropy. As the community foundation serving Alameda, Contra Costa, Marin, San Francisco, and San Mateo Counties, it partners with diverse donors and organizations to mobilize resources in the promotion of vibrant, sustainable communities throughout the Bay Area. The foundation awards grants to nonprofit organizations in the fields of arts and humanities, community health, education, the environment, neighborhood and community development, social services, and philanthropy. The foundation's Web site features information about the foundation's grantmaking activities, including program priorities, selected grants in each program area, and grantee profiles; information about the Koshland Civic Unity Awards, the foundation's Special Awards Program, and the foundation's Community Initiative Funds; information for prospective donors; FAQs; a short list of foundation publications; and contact information.

Santa Barbara Foundation (http://www.sbfoundation.org)
The Santa Barbara Foundation was established in 1928 by Major Max Fleischmann to enrich the lives of the people of Santa Barbara County through philanthropy. With a mission of "benefiting the public good," the foundation funds the fields of the arts, education, recreation, the environment, community enhancement, health, human services, and youth. It also works to promote partnerships to address important community issues and leverage resources to meet community needs. In addition to grantmaking, the foundation also has several student aid programs in the form of loans and scholarships. Visit the foundation's Web site for grant application guidelines and contact information.

Shasta Regional Community Foundation (http://www.shastarcf.org/)
Located in Redding, California, the Shasta Regional Community Foundation works to "build resources to meet needs in Shasta and Siskiyou communities through philanthropy, education, and information." The grant program is defined by the ongoing needs of the community and the challenges the community is facing. Nonprofits serving the residents of either or both of the counties are eligible to apply for funding. The foundation's Web site offers application guidelines, an application and coversheet request form, deadlines and restrictions, a staff list and contact information.

Sonoma County Community Foundation (http://www.sonomacf.org/)
The Sonoma County Community Foundation administers and awards grants from a permanent endowment to eligible nonprofit organizations based and operating in Sonoma County, California, in the areas of health, social well-being, the economy, the environment, and culture. The foundation manages and distributes monies from several individual funds established to support the specific philanthropic interests of their donors. Also, the foundation's scholarship program offers financial assistance to Sonoma County residents

pursuing higher education through over fifteen separate scholarship funds. The Web site contains a listing and brief description of all individual funds, listings of the board of trustees and major donors, FAQs, and contact information.

Sonora Area Foundation (http://www.sonora-area.org/)
Established in 1989, the Sonora Area Foundation strives "to enhance the community and the quality of life of its residents through facilitating the philanthropic intentions of donors, and the needs of the surrounding communities." The foundation awards grants annually to nonprofit and public agencies throughout the Tuolumne County area. Grants have been made in the areas of human services; education; arts, culture, and humanities; health; public/society benefit; and environment/animals. The foundation does not make grants to individuals. The foundation's Web site offers a history of the foundation, descriptions of the foundation's programs and the individual donor funds administered by the foundation, a grants listing, grant application policies and instructions, a listing of board members, and contact information.

Truckee Tahoe Community Foundation (http://ttcf.net/)
Established in Truckee, California, in 1998, the Truckee Tahoe Community Foundation is committed to "matching philanthropic interests with charitable needs to enhance the quality of life in the Truckee-Tahoe community." Funding is considered in the areas of arts and culture, civic and public benefit, education, the environment, conservation and animal welfare, health and human services, recreation, and youth development. Geographic limitations are set for the areas of Donner Summit, Truckee, Squaw Valley, and the west and north shores of Lake Tahoe. The foundation's Web site features grant guidelines, a recent grants listing, application information, and contact numbers.

Ventura County Community Foundation (http://www.vccf.org)
Headquartered in Camarillo, California, the Ventura County Community Foundation "provides grantmaking opportunities for programs meeting the needs of children, youth, and families or programs focusing on education, health and human services, housing and homelessness, the arts, and civic and public benefit." The foundation funds nonprofit organizations serving Ventura County. The foundation, through its scholarship program, also funds individual. The foundation's Web site provides a list of the specific cities the foundation serves, a guide for grantseekers with limitations and deadlines, the foundation's Resource Center for Nonprofit Management, information regarding the annual report, nonprofit links, and contact information.

COLORADO

Aspen County Community Foundation (http://www.avcfoundation.org)
The Aspen County Community Foundation was established by the Aspen Skiing Company in 1980. Formerly known as the Aspen Foundation, the organization's goal is to "strengthen the community by expanding opportunities for individuals and families to live healthy and independent lives." The grant program funds nonprofits in the areas of health and human services, education, and community that support families and strengthen the community. Emphasis is placed on programs that eliminate risks to children and families and that create a permanent change in the way people live. Programs in Pitkin, Garfield, and west Eagle Counties are eligible to apply. Application guidelines, deadlines, specific descriptions of each funding category, lists of previous grantees, board and staff lists, articles from the foundation's newsletter, and information on the Executive Service Corps, a program that links retired professionals who volunteer their time as consultants with nonprofit programs, are available on the foundation's Web site.

The Broomfield Community Foundation (http://www.broomfieldfoundation.org)
The Broomfield Community Foundation has been "building a community with heart for present and future generations through creative philanthropy" in the Broomfield, Colorado,

area since 1993. The foundation's funding priorities include unmet educational needs of local schools, human service and emergency needs in the community, artistic and cultural opportunities, programs serving senior citizens, and civic projects that contribute to the sense of community. The foundation's Web site features information about current initiatives, grant criteria and restrictions, and contact information.

Community Foundation Serving Boulder County (http://www.commfound.org/)
Established in 1991, the Community Foundation Serving Boulder County generally supports the community of Boulder County, Colorado; however, "several donors have interests elsewhere which they fund through the community foundation." The foundation's areas of interest include arts, civic engagement, education, the environment, and health and human services. The foundation's Web site features the grant guidelines, application information, lists of past grantees, and contact information.

Community Foundation Serving Northern Colorado (http://www.fortnet.org/CF/)
Established in 1975, the Community Foundation Serving Northern Colorado's mission is to "build an endowment to meet the diverse needs of [the] community by attracting, managing, and distributing funds entrusted by donors." The foundation supports diverse projects throughout Berthoud, Estes Valley, Fort Collins, Longmont, and Loveland Counties, through its endowment and donor-directed funds. The foundation's Web site features includes contact information and a general description of the foundation's contribution to different populations (donors, community, and nonprofits).

The Denver Foundation (http://www.denverfoundation.org/)
Established in 1928, the Denver Foundation supports a range of community-based programs that make the metropolitan Denver area a better place to live. The foundation has awarded grants in the areas of arts and culture, community development, education, and health and human services to nonprofit organizations in Adams, Arapahoe, Boulder, Broomfield, Denver, Douglas, and Jefferson Counties. In addition, some donor funds help nonprofit organizations throughout Colorado and beyond. The foundation's Web site provides a mission statement, general program information, grant guidelines and application procedures, FAQs, information for potential donors, an electronic order form for foundation publications, and contact information.

The Summit Foundation (http://www.summitfoundation.org)
Established in 1984 as the Breckenridge Development Foundation by the Breckenridge Ski Area, the Summit Foundation added support from Copper Mountain, Keystone, and Arapahoe Basin Ski Resorts and assumed its current name in 1991. Based in Breckenridge, Colorado, the Summit Foundation is dedicated to improving the quality of life for residents and guests of Summit County. The foundation funds other Summit County nonprofit agencies that provide programs and services in arts and culture, health and human services, education, the environment, and sports. The foundation's Web site contains an online contact form and contact information.

Yampa Valley Community Foundation (http://www.yvcf.org/)
The Yampa Valley Community Foundation serves the residents of Routt County, Colorado. It was originally established in 1979 as the Yampa Valley Foundation to save Alpine College, Colorado. The new name was adopted in 1994 to reflect a reorganization and broadening of focus. The foundation's present areas of interest include arts and culture, education, health and human services, recreation, and the environment. Detailed application guidelines, FAQs, and a form for requesting more information are available on foundation's Web site.

CONNECTICUT

Community Foundation for Greater New Haven (http://www.cfgnh.org/)
Founded in 1928, the Community Foundation for Greater New Haven manages charitable funds in its 20-town region of Connecticut. The mission is to "to strengthen and protect the community's varied assets; to increase respect, understanding, and collaboration among its diverse stakeholders; and to enhance the quality of life for all." The foundation supports a wide range of interests, including the areas of education, health, youth development, community development, regionalism, and capacity building, through many distinct endowments funds. The foundation's latest annual report, current newsletter, and grant guidelines are available on the foundation's Web site.

The Community Foundation of Southeastern Connecticut (http://www.cfsect.org/)
The Community Foundation of Southeastern Connecticut, located in New London, Connecticut, focuses its giving on cultural, educational, health, social services, and other charitable organizations. High priority goes to programs that "strengthen families; improve access to area resources, especially for underserved populations; encourage residents to participate in the cultural life of the community; and add to the general well-being of the community." Additionally, the foundation provides numerous scholarships for college-bound students. A list of scholarships and downloadable applications; grant guidelines, limitations, a downloadable grant application, a listing of the southern Connecticut towns served by the foundation; donor information; and contact information are available on the foundation's Web site.

Fairfield County Foundation (http://www.fcfoundation.org/)
Established in 1982, the Wilton, Connecticut-based Fairfield County Foundation "promote[s] the growth of philanthropy to fulfill donor interests and strengthen the communities of Fairfield County." The foundation identifies and responds to the needs of the community through specific initiatives, partnerships with funders, and strategic grantmaking. The foundation's Web site provides grant guidelines, an overview of the application process, and contact information.

The Greater Bridgeport Area Foundation, Inc. (http://www.gbafoundation.org)
Established in 1967, the Bridgeport, Connecticut-based Greater Bridgeport Area Foundation, Inc. maintains the mission "to participate actively in shaping the well-being of the region by: raising resources entrusted to the foundation; distributing income effectively to arts and entertainment, education, health and human services, and other charitable organizations serving the community; and identifying the pressing needs of the community and responding with appropriate initiatives and financial support." The foundation primarily serves the communities of Bridgeport, Easton, Fairfield, Milford, Monroe, Shelton, Stratford, Trumbull, and Westport. The foundation's Web site contains grant guidelines, instructions, and application materials; scholarship listings, application instructions, and materials; a listing of scholarship recipients; and contact information.

Hartford Foundation for Public Giving (http://www.hfpg.org)
Established in 1925 to serve the changing needs of the residents of Connecticut's Capitol Region, the Hartford Foundation ranks among the largest of the country's community foundations. The foundation provides grants and other support to a broad range of nonprofits, helps donors make effective charitable giving decisions, and brings people together to discuss important community issues. The foundation's Web site provides general information about the foundation and its programs, information on the foundation's grantmaking policies, a searchable consultant database, information for donors about charitable giving, a searchable college scholarship directory and application form for students, grantee guidelines, and contact information.

The Waterbury Foundation (http://www.waterburyfoundation.org/)
The Waterbury Foundation, headquartered in Waterbury, Connecticut, "makes grants to support programs that improve the quality of life for residents of the Central Naugatuck Valley and Litchfield Hills." The foundation funds grants, a nonprofit management assistance initiative, and scholarships. Grants dealing with the art, humanities, and youth growth and development are given priority. The foundation's Nonprofit Assistance Initiative provides consulting or funding to help strengthen nonprofits in northwestern Connecticut. Scholarships are intended for residents of the foundation's 21-town service area. The foundation's Web site features scholarship application guidelines and downloadable forms, grant guidelines and limitations, information on donor services, and a reply form to request more information from the foundation.

DELAWARE

Delaware Community Foundation (http://www.delcf.org/)
Established in 1986, the Delaware Community Foundation focuses its unrestricted grantmaking resources on building a stronger community, in large part by supporting disadvantaged populations. Program grants have been awarded to address some of Delaware's most pressing challenges, including affordable housing, homelessness, healthcare, arts stabilization, adolescent needs, and violence prevention. The foundation's Web site provides application guidelines and deadlines for grantseekers; information for potential donors, friends, and supporters; general information on starting an endowment; selections from recent newsletters; a version of the foundation's most recent annual report; a listing of the foundation's board and staff; and contact information.

DISTRICT OF COLUMBIA

The Community Foundation for the National Capital Region (http://www.cfncr.org)
The Community Foundation for the National Capital Region was founded in 1973. Its mission is to build philanthropic capital and improve the quality of life in metropolitan Washington, D.C. It works to strengthen the region's nonprofit organizations and fund projects that offer new solutions to community needs. The foundation assists individuals with philanthropy by helping them to invest time, money, and commitment in building a stronger, better region. The foundation and its regional affiliates house hundreds of different funds, and each has its own set of guidelines for grantmaking. The foundation's Web site provides specific details about each fund's deadlines and application processes; information about the foundation's staff, history, and prior grantmaking; contact information; and an online version of the most recent annual report.

FLORIDA

The Community Foundation for Palm Beach and Martin Counties (http://www.cfpbmc.org/)
Founded in 1972, the Community Foundation for Palm Beach and Martin Counties offers insights into community needs and assists donors in their philanthropic goals of helping the community. The foundation's area of interest include; community needs, human and race relations, arts and culture, education, community development, health, human services, the environment, and the conservation and preservation of historical and cultural resources. The foundation's Web site features a mission statement; a brief history of the foundation; listings of the foundation's board, officers, and staff; program descriptions and information about the foundation's Dwight Allison Fellows Program; grant guidelines and eligibility requirements; a selection of recent grants; donation information; and information about the foundation's Funding Resource Center.

The Community Foundation in Jacksonville (http://www.jaxcf.org)
The Community Foundation in Jacksonville is a grantmaking foundation that receives gifts or bequests from individuals, families, or organizations interested in providing, through the foundation, financial support for charitable and public causes or institutions. The foundation's goals are to strengthen families with children, improve services to infants and young children, strengthen neighborhoods, encourage conversation on community values, and foster vitality in the arts. The foundation serves residents of the First Coast Region of northeast Florida, a five-county area including Baker, Clay, Duval, Nassau, and St. Johns Counties. The foundation's Web site features application instructions, a description of the application review process, contact information, and FAQs.

Community Foundation of Broward (http://www.cfbroward.org)
Based in Ft. Lauderdale, Florida, the Community Foundation of Broward was incorporated in 1984 and exists to enhance the quality of life for all residents of Broward County. Areas of interest include children and families, cultural and social environments, animal welfare, arthritis and cancer research/patient care, and adult literacy. The foundation also gives scholarships to individuals who want to pursue higher education. The foundation's Web site features a nonprofit job bank, an online discussion forum for topics related to nonprofit organizations, a resource library and nonprofit links, a printable application form, and contact information.

Community Foundation of Central Florida (http://www.cfcflorida.org/)
Established in 1994, the Community Foundation of Central Florida serves the needs of charities and communities throughout Orange, Osceola, and Seminole Counties. The foundation's mission is to build philanthropic capital dedicated to improving the region's quality of life, strengthen the region's nonprofit organizations, and fund projects and experiments offering new solutions to community needs. The foundation supports arts and culture, community building, seniors, children, youth and families, education, and special initiatives. Visit the foundation's Web site to learn more about funding criteria, geographic limitations, or to locate a copy of the most recent annual report and contact information.

The Community Foundation of Sarasota County (http://www.sarasota-foundation.org)
The Community Foundation of Sarasota County supports a variety of worthy causes throughout the west coast of Florida, including the arts and culture, community development, education, the environment, health, and human services. The foundation also administers a number of scholarship funds designated for students in Charlotte, Manatee, and Sarasota Counties, Florida. Scholarship recipients are selected on an objective, competitive basis that takes into account academic and non-academic factors and demonstrated financial need. Visitors to the foundation's Web site will find application guidelines, a current grants list, scholarship information, and information for donors.

Community Foundation of Tampa Bay (http://www.cftampabay.org)
The Community Foundation of Tampa Bay awards creative grants with the goal of fostering positive changes in the community. The foundation's interests include arts and culture, community enablement, education, the environment and animals, health and human services, history, neighborhoods, senior citizens, and youth and families. The foundation primarily serves Hillsborough and Pinellas Counties in Florida. Visit the foundation's Web site to see specific programs and areas not considered for funding, grant guidelines, a downloadable grant application, and contact information.

Dade Community Foundation (http://www.dadecommunityfoundation.org/)
Established in 1967, the Dade Community Foundation exists to enhance the quality of life for all residents of Miami-Dade County. It makes grants in the broad program areas of education, health, human services, arts and culture, the environment, and community and economic development. In addition to the unrestricted funds, grantmaking through field-of-interest funds addresses the economically disadvantaged, abused and neglected children, immigrant and refugee populations, people with HIV/AIDS, homelessness, social

justice, black affairs, care of animals, and heart disease. The foundation's Web site features the mission statement, guidelines and application procedures, scholarship information, a grants listing, and contact information.

Mount Dora Community Trust (http://www.fnbmd.com/_docs/com_trust.htm)
Established in 1972, the Mount Dora Community Trust of Mount Dora, Florida, is committed to supporting "community activities and charitable organizations providing services to the community." Two major grant categories are schools and the public. The schools category includes grants for scholarships, classroom equipment, computers, and sports teams. The public category encompasses libraries, parks, the arts, and public festivals. The trust's Web site includes a list of the members of the distribution committee, a list of past grants given, and an electronic request form for more information.

Pinellas County Community Foundation (http://fdncenter.org/grantmaker/pinellas/index.html)
Established in 1969, the Pinellas County Community Foundation's mission is to distribute the investment income from donated funds (or principal when directed by a donor) to recognized charitable organizations located in Pinellas County, Florida. If designated by a donor, charities located outside of the county can be beneficiaries of donated funds or income earned on those funds. The foundation carefully screens charities in the county that request funding through discretionary grants. The foundation favors programs that assist persons with handicaps or low or moderate incomes to become self-sufficient. Also favored are nonprofit organizations that assist persons who have been abused or neglected or have special needs. The foundation's Web site provides information about the foundation's structure, guidelines, donor funds, and financials; recent grants lists; reports from the foundation's chairman and executive director; and contact information.

The Southwest Florida Community Foundation, Inc. (http://www.floridacommunity.com)
Located in Fort Meyers, Florida, the Southwest Florida Community Foundation, Inc. was established in 1976 to serve the charitable needs of Charlotte, Lee, Glades, Hendry, and Collier Counties, Florida. The foundation's areas of interest include arts and culture, education, the environment, health and human services, community development, and historical and cultural resources. Of particular interest to the foundation is that a project demonstrate an innovative approach to a community problem that has measurable outcomes. Besides its major grant program, the foundation also distributes the Good Samaritan Fund, which addresses one-time emergencies that are not covered by any other funding. The foundation's Web site includes a printable application, detailed guidelines and deadlines and a list of past grantees, a board list, descriptions of the different types of funds that make up the foundation, and information on contributing to and joining the foundation.

GEORGIA

The Community Foundation for Greater Atlanta, Inc. (http://www.atlcf.org/)
The Community Foundation for Greater Atlanta, Inc. was established in 1951 to improve the quality of life in the metropolitan Atlanta area. The foundation benefits Barrow, Bartow, Butts, Carroll, Cherokee, Clayton, Cobb, Coweta, DeKalb, Douglas, Fayette, Forsyth, Fulton, Gwinnett, Hall, Henry, Newton, Paulding, Pickens, Rockdale, Spalding, and Walton Counties of greater Atlanta. The foundation's Unrestricted Grants Program considers and funds proposals in seven major program areas: arts and culture, civic affairs, education, health, religion, social services, and community development. The foundation emphasizes two of these areas each year. In addition to its application guidelines, the foundation's Web site provides information about the foundation's community scholarships, information for donors and professional advisors (including a planned giving design center), press releases, and contact information.

The Community Foundation for Northeast Georgia (http://gfi.actx.com/)
Established in 1985, the Community Foundation for Northeast Georgia (formerly the Gwinnett Foundation) strives to better the quality of life for the people of northeast Georgia, by serving as a "catalyst for constructive programs and initiatives." The foundation focuses on the areas of education, health and human services, community service, and the arts. The foundation's Web site features a listing of specific funds available; financial information; information for donors; grant policies, restrictions, and deadlines; information on the foundation's philanthropic advising programs, and contact information.

Community Foundation of Central Georgia (http://www.cfcgonline.org)
Established in Macon, Georgia, in 1993, the Community Foundation of Central Georgia helps individuals, families, businesses, and nonprofit organizations meet their charitable goals by providing technical expertise and charitable giving services and by connecting donors with the projects and organizations that serve their interests. The foundation grants benefit the entire central Georgia community. The foundation's Web site features downloadable grant applications and guidelines, a list of all the foundation's funds, board/staff members, and contact information.

CSRA Community Foundation, Inc. (http://csracf.com/)
The CSRA Community Foundation, Inc. of Augusta, Georgia, promotes philanthropy through education, responsible management of charitable contributions and the distribution of these funds, and provides the structure for this to be accomplished by individuals, companies, and organizations. Visitors to the foundation's Web site will learn more about the grant opportunities, obtain a listing of previous grant recipients, and view contact information.

East Lake Community Foundation (http://www.eastlakecommunityfdn.org/)
Established in 1995 in Atlanta, Georgia, the East Lake Community Foundation seeks "to redevelop Atlanta's troubled inner-city East Lake neighborhood through long-term educational, recreational, and self-sufficiency programs for community residents." The foundation's Web site provides details on physical redevelopment, programming, and the progress of the foundation's various community projects.

North Georgia Community Foundation (http://www.ngcf.org/)
Established as the Gainesville Community Foundation in 1985, the North Georgia Community Foundation today provides grants and serves donors in a 15-county area of northeast Georgia. The foundation is interested in organizations that can demonstrate they have planned their projects in light of overall community need, as well as in projects that can be replicated by other nonprofit organizations in other areas. The foundation generally does not provide funding for annual fund campaigns, lobbying activities, ongoing operating support, or to individuals. The foundation's Web site features information about the foundation and its activities, grant application guidelines, and information for potential donors.

HAWAII

Hawai'i Community Foundation (http://www.hcf-hawaii.org)
The Hawai'i Community Foundation was established in 1916, making it one of the oldest community foundations in the United States. The foundation supports nonprofit organizations in the following areas: culture and art, natural resources conservation, education, health and medical research, human services, disability, mentoring and media, and neighbor island assistance. The foundation also supports Hawaiian individuals through various scholarships. The foundation's Web features contact information, grant guidelines, a list of past grantees, a calendar with applicable deadlines, and descriptions of the resources the foundation offers for Hawaiian nonprofits.

IDAHO

Idaho Community Foundation (http://www.idcomfdn.org/)
The Boise-based Idaho Community Foundation was established in 1988 to enhance the quality of life for people in Idaho. The foundation makes grants in a variety of areas, including the fields of health, human services, arts and culture, education, public projects, and the environment. The foundation's Web site contains detailed instructions for grants, a listing of recent grant recipients, a number of general grant-related publications, services and resources for donors, a financial report, and contact information.

ILLINOIS

The Aurora Foundation (http://www.aurorafdn.org/)
Established in 1948, the Aurora Foundation provides scholarships to students and grants to nonprofit organizations in the City of Aurora, southern Kane County, and Kendall County in the state of Illinois. The foundation's areas of support of include education, social services, healthcare, and arts and humanities. The foundation also provides scholarships to students in the Fox Valley area. The foundation's Web site includes a mission statement, a "letter to the community," information on ways to give and benefits to donors, financial information, a summary of grants awarded in the previous year, and a listing of directors, officers, and staff.

The Chicago Community Trust and Affiliates (http://www.cct.org)
The Chicago Community Trust was established in 1915 "to improve the lives of the people of metropolitan Chicago." The trust focuses on five main areas of grantmaking: arts and culture, basic human needs, community development, education, and health. Within these broad areas, the trust's funding priorities include excellence in dance, leadership transition, and arts education. Additionally, the trust maintains a number of special programs and awards mainly for community service and service to developmentally disabled individuals. All funding is restricted to organizations that serve Cook County, Illinois, and its residents. The trust's Web site features details of each award and program, a listing of recent grants, an overview of the trust's organization, details for donors, contact information, grant guidelines, and a downloadable application form.

DuPage Community Foundation (http://www.dcfdn.org/)
The DuPage Community Foundation of Wheaton, Illinois, was created in 1986 by longtime DuPage residents. The organization's goals are "to develop and channel philanthropy to meet the emerging, changing, and ongoing needs of the people of DuPage County." The foundation funds qualifying organizations that support arts and culture, civic affairs, education, health, and human services. There are also a variety of donor-advised funds, scholarship programs, and an agency endowment fund for a local children's chorus. The foundation's Web site includes information on the history of community foundations and how to create or contribute to a fund, lists of the board of trustees and of all existing funds, contact information, and an electronic form to submit inquiries.

Evanston Community Foundation (http://www.evcommfdn.org/)
The Evanston Community Foundation was established in 1986 as a special project of Evanston United Way and began independent operations early in 2001. The foundation is dedicated to enriching Evanston and the lives of its people, now and in the future. The foundation builds and manages its own and other community endowments, addresses Evanston's changing needs through grantmaking, and provides leadership on important community issues. The foundation makes grants each year from its funds in the areas of the arts and culture, the environment, youth and family support, health and human services, housing, and community redevelopment. Its community programs include Leadership Evanston. The foundation makes no grants to individuals. The foundation's Web site

features information about the foundation and its board, contact information, and a list of current grants and guidelines for prospective grantees.

Oak Park-River Forest Community Foundation (http://www.oprfcommfd.org)
The Oak Park-River Forest Community Foundation was established in 1958 "to provide a tangible, permanent contribution" to the residents of Oak Park and River Forest, Illinois. The foundation focuses on supporting educational, cultural, and charitable organizations. Areas of interest include; arts and culture, health, neighborhoods, seniors, persons with disabilities, diversity, shelter, education, violence prevention, families, and youth. The foundation also provides scholarships and awards. Grant guidelines, FAQs, and contact information are available on the foundation's Web site.

INDIANA

Central Indiana Community Foundation (http://www.cicf.org/)
The Central Indiana Community Foundation is the product of a collaborative effort between community foundations serving Marion and Hamilton Counties. The founding partners of the foundation—the Hamilton County Legacy Fund and the Indianapolis Foundation—are "committed to a structure that sustains local engagement, leadership, and capacity while supporting an expanded level of philanthropic service and growth for the region." In addition to assisting the community in "convening, consensus building, and problem solving," the foundation supports and coordinates a variety of special projects, including the Neighborhood Preservation Initiative; the Youth, Sport, and Fitness Network; the Library Fund and Project Hi-Net; the Marion County Education Foundation Network; and the Partnership for National Service. The foundation's Web site features information about the foundation's mission, donor services, programs, and initiatives.

Community Foundation of Boone County (http://www.bccn.boone.in.us/cf/index.html)
The Community Foundation of Boone County was established in 1992 to serve residents of Boone County, Indiana, by providing a central philanthropic vehicle for donors of various interests and purposes, building and managing community capital, and serving a broad base of human service organizations. The foundation's main areas of interest are education, youth, culture, health and human services, civic affairs, the environment, and recreation. The foundation gives to individuals, in the form of scholarships, and to nonprofits. Detailed application guidelines and deadlines and contact information are available at the foundation's Web site.

Community Foundation of Grant County (http://www.nxco.net/community)
The Community Foundation of Grant County, located in Marion, Indiana, was established in 1984 to serve as a vehicle through which "those of us who have lived our lives and earned our livelihoods in Grant County could pool our resources for the benefit of our own community." The foundation offers financial support for several fields of interest, such as community development, community services, education, health, and human services. Downloadable grant and scholarship applications, and an online version of the foundation's annual report are available on the foundation's Web site.

The Community Foundation of Howard County, Inc. (http://www.cfhoward.org/)
The Community Foundation of Howard County, Inc. was established in 1992 in Kokomo, Indiana, to "serve the interest of donors of enduring charitable gifts" and to serve as a "catalyst for stimulating and funding initiatives that improve the quality of life for citizens of Howard, Carroll and Clinton Counties, Indiana." The grants program concentrates giving in the following areas: health and medicine, social services, education, cultural affairs, and civic affairs. The foundation prefers to make gifts with an emphasis on seed money and considers making grants of technical or staff assistance. The foundation also manages scholarship funds; award amounts and restrictions vary by fund. Printable application forms, contact information, basic grant application guidelines and restrictions, lists of past

grantees and scholarship recipients, board and staff lists, lists of funders, and information on creating a fund are available on the foundation's Web site.

Community Foundation of Morgan County (http://cfmconline.org/)
The Indiana-based, Community Foundation of Morgan County works with its citizens to enhance the quality of life for current and future generations. The foundation was created in 2000, with the merger of the Mooresville Community Foundation and the Morgan County Foundation. Visit the foundation's Web site to learn more about the mission and funding priorities, obtain a board listing, find out about upcoming events in the area, and get contact information.

Community Foundation of St. Joseph County (http://www.cfsjc.org/)
The Community Foundation of St. Joseph County was established in South Bend, Indiana, in 1992 with the support of the Eli Lilly Endowment G.I.F.T. Initiative. The foundation is a "charitable endowment to improve the quality of life for the citizens of St. Joseph County and their succeeding generations." The foundation maintains a number of grant programs and initiatives. Additionally, the foundation maintains scholarships for high school seniors bound for Indiana colleges. Visitors to the foundation's Web site will also find the foundation's most recent tax return, a financial statement, list of recent grants, sites for professional advising and charitable donor information, a calendar of events, and a form to request more information.

Community Foundation of Southern Indiana (http://cfsouthernindiana.com/)
The Community Foundation of Southern Indiana's mission is to build a permanent resource of funds to help meet community needs today and the changing needs of future generations by encouraging philanthropic leadership, providing flexible endowment opportunities, and practicing financial stewardship of bequeathed funds. The foundation serves Clark, Floyd, and Harrison Counties and has an affiliate in Crawford County. The foundation's Web site features information about grant and scholarship opportunities, downloadable grant applications, and staff and contact information.

Community Foundation of Wabash County (http://www.cfwabash.org)
The Community Foundation of Wabash County serves the residents of Wabash County, Indiana. The foundation's areas of interest include social services, education, civic affairs, cultural affairs, health and medicine, recreation, and the environment. The foundation's Web site features information on becoming a donor, application guidelines, board and staff lists, and contact information.

Dearborn County Community Foundation (http://www.dearborncounty.org/dccf)
Established in Lawrenceburg, Indiana, in 1997, the Dearborn County Community Foundation serves the needs and philanthropic aims of donors who wish to better the community, now and in the future. The foundation makes grants in the fields of community service, social service, education, health, the environment, and the arts. The foundation's Web site contains descriptions of various grant and scholarship programs, downloadable grant applications, and contact information.

Elkhart County Community Foundation, Inc. (http://www.elkhartccf.org/)
The Elkhart County Community Foundation, Inc., located in Elkhart, Indiana, exists to create permanent endowment funds, make grants in the community, address the charitable needs of the community, and serve as a leader in meeting those needs. The foundation provides funding in the following areas: arts and culture, community development, education, and health and human services. The foundation funds innovative programs or projects that address problems to be solved or opportunities to be seized in Elkhart. The foundation gives priority to programs in which communities and organizations work together towards a shared goal with shared responsibility and accountability. The foundation's Web site contains grant application deadlines and guidelines, information for donors about different funds, planned giving, and current events.

Fort Wayne Community Foundation (http://www.fwcfoundation.org)
The Indiana-based, Fort Wayne Community Foundation's mission is to "build public giving partnerships that effectively connect donors with nonprofit organizations and community projects to produce a brighter future for all people in Allen County." The foundation awards grants in the areas of health and human services, education, arts, and community development. Also available through the foundation are a number of scholarship opportunities for private elementary and high schools, technical schools, or colleges and universities. Visit the foundation's Web site to find more information about the foundation's grantmaking programs, application criteria, and contact information.

Hancock County Community Foundation, Inc. (http://www.hccf.cc/)
The Hancock County Community Foundation, Inc., established in Greenfield, Indiana, in 1992, seeks "to build and improve the quality of life within the community through culture, education, physical and mental healthfulness, art, social services, social awareness, and economic vitality." These goals are met through scholarships for post-secondary education through specific Hancock County high schools and grants. Grants fall into the following categories: health and human services, education, arts and culture, civic affairs, and youth. The foundation's Web site offers grant guidelines; a printable application form; an outline of the grant review process; a complete listing of scholarships, sorted by high school where they are available; information for donors; and a contact address.

Henry County Community Foundation, Inc. (http://www.newcastlein.com/hccf/)
Established in 1985, the mission of the Henry County Community Foundation, Inc., which is located in New Castle, Indiana, is to "help where the needs are the greatest and the benefits to the community and its citizens are most substantial, and to provide public-spirited donors a vehicle for using their gifts in the best possible way now and in the future as conditions inevitably change, and to provide excellent stewardship of those gifts which it receives." The foundation awards grants in the areas of health and medicine, social services, education, cultural affairs, and civic affairs. Those interested in applying for a grant should first submit a letter of inquiry; details are available on the foundation's Web site.

Indianapolis Foundation (http://www.indyfund.org/)
The Indianapolis Foundation was created in 1916 to serve the residents in and around Indianapolis, Indiana. The foundation's mission is "to help where the needs are greatest and the benefits to the community are most extensive; and to provide donors a vehicle for using their gifts in the best possible way now and in the future as conditions in the community change." The foundation funds programs in Marion County, and grants from its unrestricted Community Endowment Fund are made in the areas of arts, culture and humanities, civic and community development, education and libraries, health and human services, and information and technology. Grant guidelines, a list of the board of trustees, and the foundation's financial statement are available on the foundation's Web site.

Kosciusko County Foundation (http://www.kcfoundation.org)
The Kosciusko County Foundation was first organized in Warsaw, Indiana, in 1968, as the Greater Warsaw Community Foundation under the sponsorship of the Warsaw Chamber of Commerce. In 1973 the foundation was renamed for the county in which it is located. With help from the Indiana-based Lilly Endowment in 1990, the foundation's assets grew significantly. Grants are given in civic services, education, health, culture, the environment, and social services. Scholarship funds are also available for graduating high school seniors and adults returning to school. Grant guidelines, financial information, and contact information are available on the foundation's Web site.

Lawrence County Community Foundation (http://www.kiva.net/~lccf/)
The mission of the Lawrence County Community Foundation is to "enhance the quality of life for the citizens of Lawrence County, Indiana, in the areas of education, health and human services, civic and historical affairs, the arts and culture, and recreational activities." The foundation achieves its goals by attracting charitable donations from the community,

managing those funds, and helping donors turn their philanthropic desires into reality. The foundation works closely with other community organizations to meet the needs of the community, generally funding arts and cultural activities, civic and historical affairs, education, recreation, and health and human services. A more detailed description of the types of projects the foundation typically funds is available on the foundation's Web site, as are printable applications, contact information, financial information, and lists of past grants awarded.

Legacy Fund Community Foundation (http://www.legacyfundcf.org/)
The Legacy Fund Community Foundation was founded in 1991 to "strengthen the Hamilton County community by attracting charitable endowments, maximizing benefits to donors, making effective grants, and providing leadership to address community needs." The foundation awards grants in the areas of arts and culture, health and human services, education, and civic affairs. The foundation's Web site provides financial statements, a list of the board of directors and staff, information about grant restrictions and limitations, descriptions of the types of programs the foundation supports, and deadline information.

Madison County Community Foundation (http://www.madisonccf.org/Welcome.asp)
Established in 1992, the Anderson, Indiana-based Madison County Community Foundation supports the arts and culture, education, health, human services, economic development, and civic affairs locally in order to enhance the quality of life of Madison County residents. The foundation provides funding in the support of various named grants and scholarships. The foundation's Web site features grant procedures, downloadable grant cover sheets, listings of past grantees and scholarship recipients, financial information, recent events and programs at the foundation, and contact information.

Montgomery County Community Foundation (http://www.mc-cf.org/)
The Crawfordsville, Indiana-based Montgomery County Community Foundation, established in 1991, splits its funding between grants and scholarships in the local community. The foundation makes grants in five categories: health and medical; social services; education; arts, local history and historical preservation; and civic affairs. The foundation's Web site includes grant information, details of recent grants, information on scholarships to students attending colleges in Indiana, a list of applicable institutions, a downloadable application form, a listing of the board and staff members, and contact information.

Noble County Community Foundation (http://www.noblecounty.org)
The Noble County Community Foundation's primary mission is to improve the quality of life for the people of Noble County, Indiana. The foundation holds interests in children and youth development, jail intervention programs, and operating funds for organizations within Noble County. The foundation's Web site features contact information and a list of publications.

Northern Indiana Community Foundation (http://nicf.org/)
The Northern Indiana Community Foundation's mission is "to build a growing endowment in each county we serve though donor relationships and to provide ethical, philanthropic leadership for enrichment and assistance to human services, education, revitalization, social, art, and cultural endeavors." The areas supported by the foundation include Fulton, Miami, Pulaski, and Starke Counties. The foundation is a publicly supported philanthropic organization governed by a volunteer board from the member counties. The foundation seeks to enrich the quality of life of each of these communities by administering funds entrusted or bequeathed by individuals, corporations, and other organizations and agencies. Visit the foundation's Web site to view information on the types of funds supported, find downloadable grant forms and guidelines, and obtain contact information.

The Portland Foundation (http://www.portlandfoundation.org)
Created in 1951, the Portland Foundation is the second oldest community foundation in Indiana and works to "promote and assist donors in realizing their philanthropic intentions

through the establishment of permanently endowed funds designed to address the ever-changing needs of the community." The foundation's grant program funds nonprofits that serve the citizens of Jay County in areas including community improvement, arts and culture, health and human services, youth, economic development, and education. The foundation also awards scholarships to area students attending post-secondary schools. Applicants are judged by "academic accomplishment, financial need and resources available to the student, and activity and involvement in school, work, and the community." The foundation's Web site features proposal and scholarship guidelines and downloadable applications, excerpts from the foundation's current newsletter and annual report, information on creating a fund, and contact information.

Steuben County Community Foundation (http://www.steubenfoundation.org/)
The Steuben County Community Foundation serves the residents of Steuben County, Indiana. The foundation makes grants to support arts and culture, community development, education, and health and human services programs and projects. The foundation also helps community groups develop and manage special collaborative projects. Grant guidelines, staff/board listings, and contact information are available at the foundation's Web site.

Unity Foundation of LaPorte County (http://www.uflc.net/)
Founded in Michigan City, Indiana, in 1992, the Unity Foundation of LaPorte County supports the areas of the arts, education, health and human services, the environment, and the community in general for the benefit of the citizens of LaPorte County, Indiana. With various types of funds, including donor-advised funds and endowments, the foundation is able to support a wide range of programs and services. The foundation's Web site contains grant guidelines, downloadable grant applications, and contact information.

Wabash Valley Community Foundation, Inc. (http://www.wvcf.com)
Established in 1991, the Wabash Valley Community Foundation, Inc. is a public charity whose mission is "to enhance the quality of life in the Wabash Valley." The foundation receives gifts and administers an endowment comprised of numerous funds, large and small, from which it makes grants for community betterment. Downloadable grant and scholarship applications, deadline information, a calendar of upcoming community events, and contact information are available at the foundation's Web site.

Washington County Community Foundation (http://www.blueriver.net/~wcegp/foundation/index.html)
Founded in 1993, the Salem, Indiana-based, Washington County Community Foundation was created "to encourage philanthropy and the fostering of responsibility for the public good." The foundation seeks and accepts donations from public and private sources and manages these funds for the purpose of distributing the earned assets, which are used to provide grants to community enhancing projects. The foundation is a collection of separate charitable funds, each created by varied donors to fulfill a different purpose. To apply for a grant, interested organizations should submit a letter of inquiry. If the foundation is interested, it will mail a grant application to be completed. The foundation's Web site provides a list of grants approved in previous years and information about the types of funds that donors can create or contribute to.

IOWA

Community Foundation of the Great River Bend (http://www.cfgrb.org/)
Established in 1964, the Community Foundation of the Great River Bend operates in a number of counties in Iowa by providing services to donors who wish to support quality of life enhancement programs in the community. To this end, the foundation maintains grants and a number of scholarships. Visitors to the foundation's Web site will find a listing of

recent grants, downloadable grant and scholarship applications, a downloadable budget form, and an online contact form for further details.

Greater Cedar Rapids Community Foundation (http://www.gcrcf.org/)
The Cedar Rapids, Iowa-based, Greater Cedar Rapids Community Foundation is a collection of permanent and pass-through funds whose assets provide support to hundreds of nonprofit organizations and programs annually throughout Linn County, Iowa. The foundation's mission is "to assist in identifying unfulfilled needs of the community and to be a catalyst for solutions that have long-lasting impact." The foundation considers requests for funding in seven broad areas: arts and culture, health, community affairs and development, historic preservation, education, human services, and the environment. One year grants are made to organizations headquartered in or serving Johnson, Linn, or Black Hawk Counties. The foundation's Web site contains a funds chart with specific information on priorities, areas of interest, and application deadlines for each fund; information on the Iowa Community Aids Partnership, a collaboration with the National AIDS Fund focusing on HIV/AIDS education, prevention, and direct services in Iowa communities; printable application materials; grant lists; and contact information.

KANSAS

Greater Kansas City Community Foundation (http://www.gkccf.org/)
Established in 1978, the Greater Kansas City Community Foundation strives "to make a positive difference in the lives and future of the people in Greater Kansas City" [Jackson, Clay, and Platte Counties in Missouri and Johnson and Wyandotte Counties in Kansas] "through grant making, advocacy, support of the nonprofit sector, and promotion of philanthropy for the benefit of the community." The foundation's Web site features board and officers lists, contact information, links to other sites of interest, a listing of scholarships available through the foundation, information about important foundation initiatives in the areas of early childhood education and homelessness, application guidelines, a list of publications, and an online copy of the annual report.

Jewish Community Foundation of Greater Kansas City (http://www.jcfkc.org/)
Established in 1959, the Jewish Community Foundation of Greater Kansas City's mission is to "serve as the focal point for planned giving and to enhance and promote the continuity of the Jewish community through a broad range of innovative and charitable programs." The foundation works towards its mission by providing leadership and serving as a role model and teacher of family philanthropy; collaborating with all community funders; working with community estate planning, tax, legal, and financial planning professionals in providing expertise; developing endowment funds, which form a permanent base of support for the Jewish community; communicating, educating, and motivating donors by providing opportunities for philanthropy; and providing stewardship for donor funds and fostering donor relations. The foundation's Web site features information about the grant programs, a history of the organization, board and staff listings, and contact information.

KENTUCKY

Blue Grass Community Foundation (http://www.bgcf.org/)
Established in 1967, the Blue Grass Community Foundation is a permanent community endowment built with gifts from individuals, families, foundations, businesses, and organizations committed to meeting the changing needs of the many communities surrounding central and eastern Kentucky. The foundation holds several types of funds that provide grants for the community annually, makes scholarships, and provides funds to schools and universities. Funds can be set up in the form of discretionary funds, field-of-interest funds, scholarship funds, donor-advised funds, designated funds, agency endowment funds, and affiliate funds. The foundation's Web site features a copy of the latest tax return, a board

listing, specific information about the available funds, application requirements, and contact information.

The Community Foundation of Louisville, Inc. (http://www.cflouisville.org/)
Established in 1984, the Community Foundation of Louisville, Inc. promotes philanthropy in the Louisville, Kentucky area by enriching the quality of life of individuals and serving as a catalyst within the local community. In addition to its unrestricted grantmaking, the foundation awards community grants in support of programs designed to break the cycle of poverty in the Louisville neighborhoods of Algonquin, California, Chickasaw, Limerick, Old Louisville, Park DuValle, Park Hill, Parkland, Portland, Shawnee, and South Louisville; field of interest grants in the areas of the visual arts, crafts, theater, and historic preservation; donor endowment grants; nonprofit organization endowment grants; and scholarships. The foundation's Web site provides a brief overview of the foundation's activities, general program and application information, a list of recent community grants, an electronic order form for requesting print materials and application forms, a list of the foundation's board and officers, and contact information.

LOUISIANA

Baton Rouge Area Foundation (http://www.braf.org)
The Baton Rouge Area Foundation, established in 1964, "seeks to enhance the quality of life for all citizens now and for generations to come." The foundation makes grants in eight categories of interest: arts and humanities, community development, education, the environment, human services, medical health, religion, and scholarships. The foundation's Web site features guidelines for specific named grants, the annual report and financial reports, donor and membership information, a list of recent grants, and contact information.

Community Foundation of Shreveport-Bossier (http://www.comfoundsb.org/)
The Community Foundation of Shreveport-Bossier, established in 1961 in Shreveport, Louisiana, supports nonprofit organizations that serve the people of the Caddo and Bossier Parishes. Areas of funding include: education, the environment, arts, youth services, programs for the elderly, and other social and cultural areas as determined by donors to the foundation. Grants are made from a pool of funds: unrestricted, field of interest, designated, donor advised, and scholarships. The foundation's Web site features information on these funds; a list of past grants; application guidelines, limitations, instructions, and procedures; a model proposal, a calendar of events, a guide for donors, the annual report, and contact information.

Foundation for the Mid South (http://www.fndmidsouth.org/)
The Foundation for the Mid South makes grants "to build the capacity of communities, organizations, and individuals" throughout Arkansas, Louisiana, and Mississippi. Grants are made within the three primary program areas of economic development, education, and families and children. The foundation's Web site features detailed program descriptions, including types of funding provided within each program area; downloadable application forms; an interactive bulletin board through which regional grantseekers and grantmakers can communicate; and selections from the foundation's annual report, including listings of grants by program area.

The Greater New Orleans Foundation (http://www.gnof.org)
Founded in 1983 as successor to the Community Chest, the Greater New Orleans Foundation "improves the quality of life for all citizens of our area, now and for future generations." It serves as a catalyst and resource for philanthropy by awarding grants that invest in leaders and systemic change, building permanent endowments for the community, and serving as a vehicle for philanthropists to invest in the community. The foundation makes grants primarily to nonprofit organizations in the broad program categories of arts and

culture, education, health, human services, and public/society benefit. The foundation's Web site provides grant application guidelines and deadlines and contact information.

MAINE

Maine Community Foundation (http://www.mainecf.org/)
Established in 1983, the Maine Community Foundation administers a variety of individual funds established to support a wide range of organizations and programs within the state of Maine. Funds may be restricted by their donors to support specific programmatic or geographic interests or unrestricted and distributed at the foundation's discretion. The foundation also manages scholarship funds, provides technical assistance to guide grantseekers through the fundraising process, and is involved with a number of initiatives that provide major support to address specific issues within Maine. The foundation's Web site features general information about the foundation, application procedures, a staff listing, donor information, scholarship information, news, calendar of events, and contact information for other Maine-based philanthropic organizations.

MARYLAND

The Baltimore Community Foundation (http://www.bcf.org/)
The Baltimore Community Foundation serves the greater Baltimore region by raising, managing, and distributing funds for charitable purposes. The funds were established with a unique mission and purpose, which the foundation is pledged to carry out in perpetuity. The foundation is committed to helping donors plan and carry out their charitable giving, making grants that respond to community needs, and building a permanent source of charitable funds for the Baltimore region. The foundation's Web site features details about the foundation's mission, its donors, and board of directors.

The Columbia Foundation (http://www.columbiafoundation.org/)
The Columbia Foundation, the community foundation of Howard County, Maryland, was founded in 1969 by James W. Rouse. "The foundation's purpose is to enhance the quality of life in Howard County by helping to meet diverse needs and building a more caring, creative, and effective community." Grants are made in four major categories: human service, culture, education, and community affairs. Gifts are made in three different categories: project grants supports the development of innovative, new programs; operation grants go to groups that have existed for at least three years and during that time received and successfully used a grant from the foundation; and contingency grants are given to assist with unanticipated situations and crises. The foundation's Web site includes application guidelines and deadlines, printable applications, lists of past grantees and the board of directors, information on making contributions, and updates on news and events at the foundation.

Community Foundation of Frederick County (http://www.cffredco.org)
Founded in 1986 in Frederick, Maryland, the Community Foundation of Frederick County "strive[s] to build a lasting legacy of financial support for human services, civic causes, scholarships, healthcare, the arts, education, and historic preservation." The foundation focuses its giving on scholarships, which are given to full-time students who are residents of Frederick County, and a variety of grants, which are distributed in the fall of the year. The foundation's Web site features contact information; scholarship and grant guidelines, deadlines, and a printable application form; and FAQs.

Community Foundation of the Eastern Shore (http://www.cfes.org/)
The Community Foundation of the Eastern Shore is dedicated to improving the quality of life in Maryland's Worcester, Wicomico, and Somerset Counties. The foundation manages and distributes monies from individual funds in the areas of education, health and human services, arts and culture, community development and conservation, and historic preservation. Grants are awarded to nonprofit organizations located within or serving the three

counties for three general purposes: "as seed funding for special projects that meet priority needs; as expansion funding to enable successful programs to serve broader constituencies; and to strengthen small and moderate sized nonprofit agencies that are providing exemplary services within [foundation] areas of interest." The foundation's Web site features general information about the foundation, application guidelines and instructions, and contact information.

Prince George's Community Foundation, Inc. (http://www.pgcf.org/)
Incorporated in 1981 as the Prince George's County Parks and Recreation Foundation, in 1994 it became the Prince George's Community Foundation, Inc. It serves the residents of Prince George's County, Maryland. The foundation awards grants and services to community-based nonprofit groups, schools, and social services organizations that offer programs in the areas of human services, education, and children and youth. Contact information, application guidelines, and a community resource directory are available on the foundation's Web site.

MASSACHUSETTS

Berkshire Taconic Community Foundation (http://berkshiretaconic.org/)
Since 1987, the Berkshire Taconic Community Foundation of Massachusetts has sought to improve the quality of life in Berkshire, Litchfield, Columbia, and Dutchess Counties through organized philanthropy. The foundation manages grants related to individuals, nonprofits, scholarships, and school enrichment. The foundation's Web site features information about the foundation's grant opportunities, a listing of previous grant recipients, staff/board lists, and contact information.

The Boston Foundation (http://www.tbf.org/)
Founded in 1915, the Boston Foundation fosters active philanthropy, connecting donors to nonprofit organizations working to improve the lives of the residents of greater Boston. The current focus of the foundation's discretionary grantmaking is the Building Family and Community Initiative, which gives priority to community-building strategies that help children and their families overcome poverty. Special funding initiatives include the Boston Foundation Arts Fund, the Vision Fund, the Fund for the Environment, the Polaroid Fund at the Boston Foundation, and the Bruce J. Anderson Foundation. In addition to information about these initiatives and the foundation's discretionary grantmaking, the foundation's Web site provides application procedures and guidelines (in English and Spanish), a selection of recent grants, excerpts from past issues of the foundation's quarterly newsletter, and information for donors.

Community Foundation of Cape Cod (http://www.capecodfoundation.org/)
Established in 1989, the Community Foundation of Cape Cod serves the community of Cape Cod, Massachusetts. The mission of the foundation is to improve the quality of life for the people of Cape Cod through the support of educational and charitable programs. Areas in which grants are made include the arts, education, health and human services, conservation, the environment, and community development. The foundation also provides scholarships for local students through a number of scholarship funds. The foundation's Web site provides news, grant guidelines, a list of scholarship funds, grants lists, staff and board information, and an information request form.

Community Foundation of Southeastern Massachusetts (http://www.cfsema.com/)
The Community Foundation of Southeastern Massachusetts was established in 1995 to improve and protect the quality of life in the region. The foundation "is not dedicated to one specific cause, it can aid local charities and nonprofit organizations in a variety of areas—from the arts to education, from the environment to helping the needy." The geographic focus is southeastern Massachusetts which includes the cities and towns surrounding Fall River, Taunton, Attleboro, New Bedford, Brockton, Bridgewater, and Plymouth.

Grant guidelines, information on scholarships, and contact information are available at the foundation's Web site.

Crossroads Community Foundation (http://www.ccfdn.org/)
Established in Natick, Massachusetts, in 1995, the mission of the Crossroads Community Foundation is to "promote and encourage the value of philanthropy, serve as a resource and catalyst for charitable activities, fulfill the interests of donors, and enhance the quality of life for all of our citizens, in perpetuity." The foundation supports the following program areas through its many funds: community/civic, culture, education, the environment, housing/shelter, health/mental health, and social services. Visit the foundation's Web site to find an archive of grant recipients, information on becoming a donor, board and staff listings, and contact information.

Greater Lowell Community Foundation (http://www.glcfoundation.org/)
The Greater Lowell Community Foundation seeks to improve the quality of life in the greater Lowell, Massachusetts, community. The foundation is a "resource which attracts funds, distributes grants, makes loans, and serves as a catalyst and leader among funders, agencies, and individuals to address identified and emerging community needs." It seeks to strengthen the administrative and program management capacity of nonprofits so that they can more effectively address their mission, in a wide variety of fields, including health and social service, arts and culture, education, community development, recreation, and the environment. The foundation's Web site features grant guidelines, a printable proposal summary form, and contact information.

Greater Worcester Community Foundation (http://www.greaterworcester.org)
The Greater Worcester Community Foundation is a permanent charitable resource to build healthy and vibrant communities in central Massachusetts. The foundation achieves its mission by working with donors on tailored giving programs, distributing grants to projects conducted by local nonprofit organizations, convening people with shared goals to solve problems, and safeguarding the assets in its trust. Grants are made to a broad range of organizations, including those involved in arts and culture, the environment, health and human services, and youth and community development. The foundation also administers a scholarship program. For individuals, businesses, and private foundations, the Greater Worcester Community Foundation offers low-cost stewardship of gifts and professional grants management. The foundation's Web site features information for donors, grant guidelines and applications, and lists of scholarships and recent grants.

MICHIGAN

Albion Community Foundation (http://www.albionfoundation.org/)
The Albion Community Foundation has been serving the philanthropic needs of the Albion area since 1969. Its mission is to promote philanthropy, build a permanent community endowment, address community needs through grantmaking, and provide leadership on key community issues. The foundation's Web site includes grant applications and a cover sheet, deadlines, a recent grants list, the most recent tax return, and contact information.

Alger Regional Community Foundation (http://www.algercounty.com/communityfoundation/)
The Alger Regional Community Foundation was established in 1992. Located in Munising, Michigan, the foundation provides financial support through grants to qualified tax-exempt organizations for projects aimed at solving community problems or enhancing life in Alger County. Grants are made in the field of cultural arts, community service, education, the environment and conservation, health and human services, youth, and scholarships. Grant requests must have direct relevance to the residents of Alger County. The foundation makes no grants to individuals; in general, requests for sectarian religious purposes, budget deficits, routine operating expenses of existing organizations, and

endowments are not funded. Visit the foundation's Web site for grant guidelines, instructions, a downloadable application, and contact information.

Ann Arbor Area Community Foundation (http://www.aaacf.org/)
Since 1963, the Ann Arbor Area Community Foundation has been an agent for positive change in the Ann Arbor community. Specifically, its mission is to "enrich the quality of life in the greater Ann Arbor area." The foundation achieves this goal by building a permanent endowment for the community, providing a flexible vehicle for donors with varied philanthropic interests, and acting as a leader of the local philanthropic community. The foundation administers many funds and is most interested in funding projects that focus on education, social service, environmental awareness, culture, community development, or health and wellness. The foundation welcomes grant applications from organizations in Ann Arbor and the surrounding area. Prospective grant applicants are encouraged to contact the foundation to discuss their proposal and obtain more information about the grantmaking process. The foundation's Web site features details about the foundation's focus, information about special programs, and downloadable applications.

Barry Community Foundation (http://www.barrycf.org)
Established in 1995, the Hastings, Michigan-based, Barry Community Foundation "bridges community needs with donor interests, granting dollars to programs, projects, and organizations that fit our vision, to be a trusted resource for positive change." The foundation awards grants throughout Barry County for a wide variety of programs and projects that positively impact the lives of its residents. Visit the foundation's Web site to locate grants lists, printable application materials and instructions, a listing of funds, links to related sites, and contact information.

Battle Creek Community Foundation (http://www.bccfoundation.org/)
The Battle Creek Community Foundation supports organizations in the Battle Creek area through four grant categories: unrestricted, the health fund, special funds, and scholarships. The foundation funds programs and services in areas such as education, health, human services, the arts, public affairs, and community development. The Youth Alliance Committee, comprised of local high school students, reviews youth grant requests. The foundation's Web site contains an online database of scholarships, funding guidelines and limitations, and contact information.

Bay Area Community Foundation (http://www.bayfoundation.org/)
The Bay Area Community Foundation was created in 1982 by an endowment from the Kantzler Foundation. The foundation serves to improve the quality of life in the Bay Area community. The foundation maintains a number of funds, including family funds, field-of-interest funds, donor-advised funds, and scholarship funds. The foundation's Web site features information on the foundation's initiatives, board/staff listings, and contact information.

Berrien Community Foundation (http://www.qtm.net/~bcf)
The Berrien Community Foundation is a public charity established in 1952 to improve the quality of life for the people of Berrien County, Michigan. It is a permanent, growing endowment built by gifts from individuals, families, organizations, and businesses. The foundation promotes, builds, and maintains a permanent collection of endowment funds used to shape effective responses to community issues and opportunities. The foundation manages and awards grants from a number of individual endowments, ranging from field-of-interest funds to donor-advised funds. Grants are awarded in the general areas of the arts and culture, community development, education and scholarships, health and human services, restoration and preservation of historical resources, sustainable development, youth leadership and development, and strengthening the family, with an emphasis on the needs of children and women. The foundation's Web site features information about its grants, guidelines, and a wide range of donor services.

Cadillac Area Community Foundation (http://www.netonecom.net/~cavb/CACF.htm)
The Cadillac Area Community Foundation, established in 1988, supports the areas of arts and culture, education, healthcare, the environment, human services, economic development, and youth and recreation in the Cadillac community. The foundation's Web site provides information on past grantees, board listings, and contact information.

Capital Region Community Foundation (http://www.crcfoundation.org/)
The Michigan-based Capital Region Community Foundation's mission is to serve the charitable needs and enhance the quality of life in Ingham, Eaton, and Clinton Counties. The foundation's fields of interest include the humanities, education, the environment, healthcare, human services, and public benefit. The foundation's Web site features a history of the foundation, information on how to become a donor, grant guidelines, and contact information.

Community Foundation for Delta County (http://www.cffdc.org)
The Community Foundation for Delta County was established in Escanaba, Michigan, in 1989 to "better the lives of area residents, now and in the future." The foundation grows and manages permanent endowments from a wide range of donors and makes grants to meet changing community needs. Visitors to the foundation's Web site will find details on the foundation's programs, information on how to submit applications, staff and board listing, and contact information.

Community Foundation for Muskegon County (http://www.cffmc.org/)
The Community Foundation for Muskegon County was established in 1961 to serve the residents of Muskegon County, Michigan. The foundation supports projects in the areas of the arts, education, community development, health, human services, and youth issues to individuals available and operates its own performing arts center. There are also several scholarships available to individuals of the community of Muskegon County. The foundation's Web site includes a detailed description of the different types of support the foundation provides, application guidelines, and contact information.

Community Foundation for Southeastern Michigan (http://comnet.org/comfound/index.html)
The Community Foundation for Southeastern Michigan serves the residents of seven counties in southeastern Michigan. Its main areas of interest are education, arts and culture, health, human services, community development, and civic affairs. The foundation has major interest in improving the already existing cultural and economic infrastructure of its geographic area. The foundation's Web site features application guidelines, funding restrictions, and contact information.

Community Foundation of Greater Flint (http://www.cfgf.org/)
Through its support of "projects aimed at solving community problems or enhancing life in the county," the Community Foundation of Greater Flint is committed to improving the quality of life in Genesee County, Michigan. The foundation makes grants through a number of funds in the fields of the arts and humanities, advancing philanthropy, community services, education, conservation and the environment, and health, human, and social services. The foundation also makes limited grants from discretionary funds, with special priority given to programs addressing issues of persistent and pervasive poverty and children under the age of ten. The foundation does not make grants to individuals, for sectarian religious purposes, budget deficits, routine operating expenses of existing organizations, or endowments. Visitors to the foundation's Web site will find general information about the foundation and its funding priorities, downloadable application guidelines, and information for potential donors.

Community Foundation of Greater Rochester (http://www.cfound.org/)
The Community Foundation of Greater Rochester was established in Michigan in 1983 by Richard Huizenga, a local educator and community leader. The foundation is dedicated to

enhancing the quality of life for the citizens of the greater Rochester area by becoming a perpetual source of income to help meet the charitable needs of the community. The foundation distributes grants from restricted funds to designated groups and makes awards to applicants through unrestricted funds. Grants are given to innovative projects that support the arts, culture, youth, and other philanthropic activities. The foundation also awards a series of scholarships to local high school seniors. The foundation's Web site features scholarship descriptions and downloadable applications, information on contributing to or starting a fund, a list of existing funds, and a list of the board and staff.

The Community Foundation of the Holland/Zeeland Area (http://www.macatawa.org/~cfothza)
Formerly the Holland Community Foundation, the mission of the Community Foundation of the Holland/Zeeland Area is to make the greater Holland/Zeeland area a better place to live and work by enhancing the quality of life for all its citizens. The Holland, Michigan-based foundation is a community foundation that manages endowments, using the income to "meet the needs and enhance the quality of life in ways that are compatible with the wishes of the donor and the goals of the community" through a wide variety of funds and scholarships. The foundation's areas of interest are the arts and culture, education, health, recreation, youth, the elderly, affordable housing, social needs, the environment, and natural resources. Grants are focused on capital projects and "new, creative endeavors." Visitors to the foundation's Web site will find grant guidelines, application instructions, a downloadable application, a detailed listing of managed funds, a list of past grants, and contact information.

Dickinson Area Community Foundation (http://www.dcacf.org/)
The Dickinson Area Community Foundation is an independent nonprofit organization located in Iron Mountain, Michigan. Established in 1995 for the benefit of Dickinson County and surrounding Wisconsin communities, the foundation encourages philanthropic investment by building and managing permanent endowments and utilizing the income to enhance the community's quality of life. The foundation states that it "is not designed to compete with, nor duplicate, the efforts of other agencies which provide ongoing support for charitable organizations and services;" rather, it focuses on "one-time-only and start-up funding, support for innovative projects when there is an identified need that cannot be met by other means, and programs that enhance the quality of life in [the] community." While the foundation supports a broad range of activities, its current grantmaking is centered on youth. Visit the foundation's Web site for a printable grant application, contact information, and press releases.

Four County Community Foundation (http://www.4ccf.org/)
Established in 1987, the Four County Community Foundation serves the northeast corner of Oakland County, the southeast corner of Lapeer County, the southwest corner of St. Clair County, and the northwest corner of Macomb County, Michigan. The foundation is dedicated to bringing together human and financial resources to support progressive ideas in education, health, community, youth, and adult programs. Visit the foundation's Web site to find a brief history of the foundation, a staff listing, specific information on the grant programs, a downloadable grant application, and contact information.

Fremont Area Foundation (http://www.tfaf.org/)
Established in 1933, the Fremont Area Foundation serves the community interests of Newaygo County, Michigan, through a variety of grants, scholarships, and initiatives. Areas of interest include health, education, social welfare, civic responsibilities, the arts and culture, character building, and rehabilitation, all for the benefit of Newaygo residents and services. Other programs that the foundation supports include: a Summer Youth Initiative, for organizations providing summer youth programs; scholarships; the Leadership in Newaygo County Initiative; Newaygo County Youth Initiative; and the Salute to Educators Initiative. The foundation's Web site features links, financial information, contact

information, and information and applications for the foundation's many grants, scholarships, and initiatives.

The Grand Rapids Community Foundation (http://www.grfoundation.org/)
Established in 1922, the Grand Rapids Community Foundation serves Grand Rapids, Michigan, and its surrounding communities. With a mission to build and manage the community's permanent endowment and lead the community to strengthen the lives of its people, the foundation's fields of interest include education, arts and culture, health, community development, the environment, and human services. Each year the foundation also awards numerous scholarships to Kent County residents. Downloadable applications and contact information are provided at the foundation's Web site.

Grand Traverse Regional Community Foundation (http://www.gtrcf.org/)
The Grand Traverse Regional Community Foundation is committed to enhancing the quality of life in Antrim, Benzie, Grand Traverse, Kalkaska, and Leelanau Counties, all located in Michigan. It facilitates philanthropy by providing leadership that coordinates the use of resources for community improvement. The foundation establishes and develops permanent endowment funds; involves regional volunteers in developing, managing and distributing income; develops an understanding of the role of philanthropy in helping the community; and empowers individuals to make a difference through grantmaking and leadership. The foundation's Web site features a search feature that allows users to locate funds either by county or keyword, information about the foundation's staff and financials, the foundation's most recent annual report, a calendar of events, and recent press releases.

The Jackson County Community Foundation (http://www.jacksoncf.org/)
The Jackson County Community Foundation was founded in 1948 for the purpose of assisting the residents of Jackson, Michigan. The foundation provides support to the programs and services of nonprofits in areas such as the arts, community development, education, health, and human services. It "serves as a convener of individuals and organizations for the purpose of identifying community-wide challenges and opportunities as well as the resources to address both." Application guidelines, scholarship listings, and contact information are available on the foundation's Web site.

The Kalamazoo Community Foundation (http://www.kalfound.org/)
Founded in 1925, the Kalamazoo Community Foundation is dedicated to enhancing the spirit of community and quality of life in the greater Kalamazoo area through its stewardship of permanently endowed funds. The foundation's grantmaking priorities focus on the four areas of individuals and families, community engagement and youth development, education and learning, and economic development. The foundation also awards several scholarships each year, helping students in the greater Kalamazoo area pursue higher education. The foundation's Web site features information on the foundation's activities and grantmaking programs, a helpful resource section, and contact information.

Keweenaw Community Foundation (http://www.keweenaw-community-foundation.org/)
Established in 1994, the Keweenaw Community Foundation supports the communities of Houghton and Keweenaw Counties. The foundation's areas of interest include arts and culture, community and economic development, education, the environment, and historic preservation. The foundation does not participate in advocacy or lobbying. The foundation's Web site includes a list of current funds, information for donors and applicants, information on the foundation's Youth Advisory Committee, and contact information.

Mackinac Island Community Foundation (http://www.micf.org)
Established in 1994, the Mackinac Island Community Foundation serves the general well-being of island residents and visitors. The foundation, through a number of specific funds, supports the arts, health, social sciences, humanities, education, youth, senior citizens, beautification, the environment, and the conservation and preservation of historical

and cultural resources. The foundation's Web site features details on current funds, donor and grant applicant information, and contact information.

M & M Area Community Foundation (http://www.mmcommunityfoundation.org/)
Founded in 1994, the M & M Area Community Foundation strives to promote the spirit of philanthropy and meet the needs of the people of Menominee County, Michigan, and Marinette County, Wisconsin. A variety of funds provide support in the areas of education, the environment, and cultural, recreational, and charitable purposes. The foundation also maintains a number of scholarship funds for qualifying students in the counties of interest. The foundation's Web site features a list of current funds, donor and applicant information, and contact information.

Michigan Gateway Community Foundation (http://www.mgcf.org)
The Michigan Gateway Community Foundation was established to strengthen south Berrien and Cass Counties. The foundation supports organizations that strengthen families and youth by providing prevention-oriented social action programs; that assist families and youth to find quality of life in the arts, beautification, recreation, and other diverse family programs; and that help solve community problems. The foundation's Web site features information on the programs the foundation supports, deadlines, a list of recent grants recipients, financial information, and contact information.

The Midland Foundation (http://www.midlandfoundation.com)
Established in 1973, the Midland Foundation promotes and enables community-wide philanthropic giving to enrich and improve the lives of residents throughout the greater Midland County area. The foundation restricts its discretionary grantmaking to qualified nonprofit, educational nonprofit, or governmental nonprofit organizations, and to projects that have a direct relevance to the people of Midland County and the surrounding area. While the foundation does not make grants directly to individuals, it does administer two student loan funds and a general scholarship program for Midland County high school seniors, college students, or adults who are resuming undergraduate study or who are retraining to enter the job market. The foundation's Web site features general information about the foundation and its activities; general grant, student loan, and scholarship information; relevant application deadlines and a deadline calendar; information for donors; and contact information.

Petoskey-Harbor Springs Area Community Foundation (http://www.petoskey-harborspringsfoundation.org)
Founded in 1991, the Petoskey-Harbor Springs Area Community Foundation seeks to improve the quality of life for all people of Emmet County. The foundation supports arts and culture, educational enrichment, environmental awareness and preservation, community development, health and human services, youth programs, and various civic improvement projects. Scholarships are also made through a number of designated funds. The foundation's Web site provides information for donors and grantseekers, and contact information.

Saginaw Community Foundation (http://www.SaginawFoundation.org/)
Founded in 1984, the Saginaw Community Foundation is dedicated to improving the quality of life in Saginaw County, Michigan. Its donors are individuals, families, corporations, and organizations who establish permanent charitable funds within the foundation. From arts and education to human services and the environment, the foundation supports all types of community projects. Guided by the wishes of its donors, the foundation makes grants and awards scholarships to a wide variety of nonprofit organizations and individuals throughout Saginaw County. Visitors to the foundation's Web site can find detailed grant information, downloadable grant applications, board and staff listings, information on the foundation's scholarship program, and a special section for professional advisors.

Southfield Community Foundation (http://www.scfmi.org)
The Southfield Community Foundation was established by philanthropically active business, civic, and community leaders in 1989 to enhance the lives of those who work and live in Southfield and Lathrup Village. Through the development of permanent funds made by donations from individuals, corporations, and foundations, the foundation creates a flexible base of financial, informational, and human resources that can be used to effectively address the community's changing needs. Grantmaking priorities focus on six areas; community building, youth development, senior adults, public education, arts and culture, and diversity. The foundation's Web site features a history of the foundation, FAQs, grant program information, and contact information.

Upper Peninsula Community Foundation (http://www.upcfa.org/)
The Upper Peninsula Community Foundation, based in Galdstone, Michigan, provides financial support through grants to qualified tax-exempt organizations for projects aimed at solving community problems or enhancing life in the county. The foundation serves as a catalyst for change, an innovator to solve problems, a partner with other community organizations, and as a resource for solutions to emerging community needs. Grants are made in the fields of cultural arts, community service, education, the environment and conservation, health and human services, and youth and scholarships. Visit the foundation's Web site for contact information.

MINNESOTA

Duluth-Superior Area Community Foundation (http://www.dsacommunityfoundation.com)
Incorporated in 1983, the Duluth-Superior Area Community Foundation strives to improve the quality of life for the residents of Duluth, Minnesota; Superior, Wisconsin; and the surrounding areas. The foundation supports local projects and organizations in the arts, civic projects, education, the environment, and human services. The foundation also awards scholarships. The foundation's Web site features information on grants and scholarships, list of previous grantees, the foundation's most recent annual report, donor information, a contact form, a history of the foundation, and staff and board lists.

Grand Rapids Area Community Foundation (http://www.gracf.org/)
Founded in 1994, the Grand Rapids Area Community Foundation is a collection of endowment funds that are contributed by individuals, corporations, and community service organizations to benefit the geographical area of Grand Rapids, Minnesota. The foundation makes grants in the areas of the environment, arts and humanities, peace and safety, recreation, community initiatives, community health, education, operations/administration, and families. The foundation's Web site features information on applying for funding, geographic restrictions, information on scholarships to individuals, and contact information.

Northwest Minnesota Foundation (http://www.nwmf.org)
Established in 1986, the Northwest Minnesota Foundation's mission is "to improve the quality of life for the residents in the twelve counties of northwest Minnesota." The foundation provides grants to nonprofits, governmental units, and public institutions. Grants are awarded in the areas of technical assistance, youth entrepreneurship, and general grants, and are awarded only to organizations that work within the foundation's twelve-county area. To be considered for a grant, an organization must first submit a pre-proposal. The foundation's Web site features information on grant restrictions and downloadable application materials.

The Saint Paul Foundation (http://saintpaulfoundation.org/)
The Saint Paul Foundation was established in 1940 to help create a healthy and vital community in which all people have the opportunity to enhance the quality of their lives and the lives of others. To achieve its mission, the foundation makes grants in eight fields of

interest: arts and humanities, civic affairs, education, the environment and nature, health, human services, religion, and scholarships in the greater Saint Paul area. The foundation's Web site features grant and application guidelines, grants listings, information on starting a fund, information for scholarship seekers and prospective donors, board/staff listings, and contact information.

St. Croix Valley Community Foundation (http://www.scvcf.org/)
Founded in 1995, the St. Croix Valley Community Foundation serves the communities of St. Croix Valley in Wisconsin and Minnesota with a goal of "strengthening the community of communities." The foundation's fields of interest include education, arts, the environment, civic affairs, and emergency human needs. The foundation's Web site features the foundation's most recent annual report, financial data, board and staff lists, and a form to request more information.

MISSISSIPPI

Community Foundation of Greater Jackson (http://www.greaterjacksonfoundation.com)
The Community Foundation of Greater Jackson was established in 1994 to serve central Mississippi (Hinds, Madison, and Rankin Counties). Areas of interests include: arts and humanities, community building, education, the environment, families and children, health, and areas of particular interest to individual donors. The foundation also maintains a scholarship program for local high school students. The foundation's Web site features information on the foundation's most recent grant cycle, a brief history of the foundation, details on starting a fund, and contact information.

Foundation for the Mid South (http://www.fndmidsouth.org/)
The Foundation for the Mid South makes grants "to build the capacity of communities, organizations, and individuals" throughout Arkansas, Louisiana, and Mississippi. Grants are made within the three primary program areas of economic development, education, and families and children. The foundation's Web site features detailed program descriptions, including types of funding provided within each program area; downloadable application forms; an interactive bulletin board through which regional grantseekers and grantmakers can communicate; and selections from the foundation's annual report, including listings of grants by program area.

MISSOURI

Greater Kansas City Community Foundation (http://www.gkccf.org/)
Established in 1978, the Greater Kansas City Community Foundation strives "to make a positive difference in the lives and future of the people in Greater Kansas City" [Jackson, Clay, and Platte Counties in Missouri and Johnson and Wyandotte Counties in Kansas] "through grant making, advocacy, support of the nonprofit sector, and promotion of philanthropy for the benefit of the community." The foundation's Web site features board and officers lists, contact information, links to other sites of interest, a listing of scholarships available through the foundation, information about important foundation initiatives in the areas of early childhood education and homelessness, application guidelines, a list of publications, and an online copy of the annual report.

St. Louis Community Foundation (http://www.stlcf.org)
The St. Louis Community Foundation was established in 1915 to benefit the people and communities in the St. Louis region. The foundation's interests of include the arts, education, community development, conservation, health, and human services. The foundation's criteria for grant consideration includes an organization's ability to: "demonstrate new approaches to addressing unmet needs; enable people to move toward greater self-reliance; increase the effectiveness and efficiency of established organizations; and represent collaborative efforts among agencies or systems in order to better utilize resources." The

foundation's Web site features an online copy of the foundation's most recent annual report, financial reports, application procedures, board listings, and contact information.

MONTANA

The Lower Flathead Valley Community Foundation (http://www.lfvcf.org/)

The Lower Flathead Valley Community Foundation serves the community of Flathead Valley, Montana. The foundation's purpose "is to bring tribal and non-tribal members together to work on projects preserving and conserving the cultural, natural, and human resources of the region, with special emphasis on meeting the needs of children." The foundation's fields of interest include education, preservation and conservation, culture, arts, health, human services, and civic improvement. Contact information, lists of previous grant recipients, and detailed information on the funds are available on the foundation's Web site.

Montana Community Foundation (http://www.mtcf.org/)

Established in 1988, the Montana Community Foundation makes grants in seven areas: arts and culture, basic human needs, economic development, education, natural resources and conservation, leadership development, and tolerance. The foundation's Web site features an overview of the foundation and its activities; descriptions of its General Grants, Leadership Development, and Fund for Tolerance programs; grant application procedures and a grant application cover sheet; information for potential donors; a list of board members and staff; links to sites of interest; and contact information.

NEBRASKA

Grand Island Community Foundation (http://www.gicf.org/)

The Grand Island Community Foundation was established in 1960 to make a lasting difference in the quality of life for greater Hall County by orchestrating charitable activities within the community. The foundation's Web site features background information, information about a number of the foundation's endowed scholarship funds, and a forum for donors and charities to come together.

Lincoln Community Foundation (http://www.lcf.org/)

Established in 1955, the Lincoln Community Foundation makes grants to enrich the quality of life in Lincoln and Lancaster Counties, Nebraska. The foundation administers and disperses monies from a permanent unrestricted endowment, responds to emerging and changing community needs, and sustains existing organizations through grants for education, arts and culture, health, social services, economic development, and civic affairs. The foundation also manages a number of individual funds established by donors with specific philanthropic interests. The foundation's Web site features discretionary funding guidelines and restrictions, application instructions (including the common application form accepted by a number of area grantmakers), information for donors interested in establishing funds, a staff listing, a listing of recent grants, excerpts from the foundation's latest annual report, and descriptions of the foundation's grantmaking focus and programs.

Nebraska Community Foundation (http://www.nebcommfound.org/)

The Nebraska Community Foundation was established in 1993 to provide financial management, strategic development, and education/training services to communities, organizations, and donors throughout Nebraska. The foundation provides affiliated fund status which allows communities or organizations to achieve nonprofit charitable status without forming their own nonprofit corporation, and strategic development assistance in nearly 150 communities throughout Nebraska. The foundation also maintains the Rural Entrepreneurship Initiative which attempts to build stronger rural development strategies employing entrepreneurial opportunities. The foundation's Web site features information on how to start or support a current fund, a recent annual report, a listing of recent grant recipients, and contact information.

Omaha Community Foundation (http://www.omahacf.org/)
The Omaha Community Foundation was created to enhance the quality of life for the citizens of the greater Omaha community by identifying and addressing current and anticipated community needs, as well as raising, managing, and distributing funds for charitable purposes in the areas of education, health, and civic, cultural, and social services. The foundation's three primary grantmaking programs are the Fund for Omaha, Neighborhood Grants, and the Women's Fund Community Initiated Grants. Each program has a different process and timetable, though all limit their grants to organizations, not individuals, serving the greater Omaha area. The foundation's web site features information about the foundation's grantmaking, a downloadable version of the foundation's annual report, grant applications, staff listing, and contact information.

NEW HAMPSHIRE

New Hampshire Charitable Foundation (http://www.nhcf.org)
The New Hampshire Charitable Foundation, headquartered in Concord, was founded in 1962, making it the first community foundation in northern New England. The foundation makes grants and loans, from funds contributed by individuals, organizations, and corporations, to meet changing needs in the state. The foundation also has an extensive scholarship program for New Hampshire graduate, adult, undergraduate, and graduating high school students. The foundation's Web site features links to other regional foundations, instructions for requesting general grant information, a scholarship application guide, a listing of specific scholarships, and downloadable program application forms.

NEW JERSEY

Princeton Area Community Foundation (http://www.pacf.org)
The Princeton Area Community Foundation was established in 1991 to bring the services of a community foundation to the greater Mercer County area. Today, the foundation seeks "to enter into partnerships with nonprofit organizations that are actively involved in developing their community," while supporting "groups working to coordinate resources and strengthen relationships between residents, businesses, and institutions in a neighborhood." The foundation's Web site features a brief history of the foundation; information about the New Jersey AIDS Partnership; application guidelines; a listing of the foundation's various unrestricted, donor-advised, memorial, and scholarship funds; recent grants lists; brief trustee and associate profiles; and information for prospective donors.

Westfield Foundation (http://www.westfieldnj.com/wf/index.htm)
The Westfield Foundation, established in 1975 by local citizens and former mayor, H. Emerson Thomas, of Westfield, New Jersey, strives to improve the quality of life for the residents of its community. Grants are made in the areas of education; the arts and other cultural activities; civic, health, and human services; community development; and the conservation and preservation of historic resources. The foundation's Web site provides financial statements, grant guidelines and limitations, information for donors, an extensive list of the named funds available, a printable application form, and contact information.

NEW MEXICO

Albuquerque Community Foundation (http://www.albuquerquefoundation.org/)
Established in 1984, the Albuquerque Community Foundation manages a pool of charitable funds whose income is used to benefit the greater Albuquerque, New Mexico, community through grants to nonprofit organizations, educational programs, and scholarships. The general policy of the foundation is to allocate funds to nonprofits, including educational institutions, whose purpose and continuing work is in the areas of arts and culture, education, health and human services, and environmental and historic preservation. The

foundation's Web site features information about the foundation's grant policies and restrictions, detailed proposal guidelines, a section for prospective donors, board and staff listings, links to regional and national nonprofit resources, and contact information

New Mexico Community Foundation (http://www.nmcf.org/)
Established in 1983, the New Mexico Community Foundation supports residents of the State of New Mexico, primarily in rural areas. The foundation's focus is on "entrepreneurial enterprises which address environmental, water-related, youth service, or other community resource use issues," as well as technical assistance in the forms of organization and business development, marketing design, and financial management. The foundation's Web site contains detailed application guidelines and contact information.

Santa Fe Community Foundation (http://www.santafecf.org/)
Founded in 1981, the Santa Fe Community Foundation serves the general area of Santa Fe, New Mexico. Although priority is placed on projects and programs in the Santa Fe area, proposals from Rio Arriba, Los Alamos, Taos, San Miguel, and Mora Counties are also eligible. The foundation's fields of interest include arts, civic affairs, education, the environment, and health and human services; it also offers technical assistance grants and lesbian and gay initiative grants. The foundation's Web site provides detailed grant guidelines, a calendar with proposal deadlines, and contact information.

Taos Community Foundation (http://www.taoscf.org/)
The mission of the Taos Community Foundation is to create an active endowment supporting effective philanthropy to meet community needs. Established in 1994 in New Mexico, the foundation supports qualifying organizations in Taos and western Colfax Counties. The foundation's areas of interest include health and human services; education and activities for youth; visual, literary, and performing arts; community and economic development; natural environment; and historic preservation. The foundation's Web site features information on the foundation's various grant funds, board/staff listing, restrictions, and contact information.

NEW YORK

Chautauqua Region Community Foundation (http://www.crcfonline.org)
Established in 1978, the Chautauqua Region Community Foundation seeks to enrich the quality of life in the Chautauqua region of New York. The community foundation provides grants for a wide variety of arts, education, social service, and other noble purposes. Scholarship funds are available for students, primarily from the Chautauqua region, attending secondary, post-secondary, and graduate education programs. Awards may be for individuals pursuing a variety of educational pursuits, those demonstrating scholastic achievement, financial need, or any combination thereof. The foundation also gives out several different types of grants. The foundation's Web site features award, scholarship, and grant descriptions, deadlines, and downloadable applications; board and staff list; and an archive of previous newsletters and annual reports.

Community Foundation for the Capital Region (http://www.cfcr.org/)
The Community Foundation for the Capital Region was established in 1968 to serve residents of in the area of Albany, New York. The foundation gives grants to nonprofits and scholarships to individuals. The foundation is primarily interested in funding for health services, technology, and AIDS; however, other areas are not excluded. The foundation also makes donor-advised funds. The foundation's Web site features descriptions of the foundation's grantmaking activities, contact information, and application guidelines.

Community Foundation of Greater Buffalo (http://www.cfgb.org)
Established in 1919, the Community Foundation of Greater Buffalo serves the area of western New York. The foundation's mission is "to strengthen and improve the quality of

life in the greater Buffalo area by supporting and enhancing philanthropy and charitable activities." The foundation's areas of interest include education, humanities, civic needs, community development, health, the environment, science, and social needs. The foundation also has created a special initiative called the 21st Century Fund. The foundation's Web site contains grant guidelines and deadlines, information on scholarships, contact information, and a staff listing.

Long Island Community Foundation (http://www.licf.org/)
Founded in 1978, the New York-based Long Island Community Foundation serves as the Long Island arm of the New York Community Trust for the citizens of Nassau and Suffolk Counties. The foundation "prefers supporting efforts that: start, change, or accomplish something specific and concrete; solve problems rather than alleviate their symptoms; address the needs of people who are disadvantaged, economically or otherwise; address problems that have significance for large numbers of people; are undertaken by smaller organizations with limited access to other resources; [or] use the resources of the community to accomplish self-sustaining change." In addition, the foundation believes "that strong arts organizations form an integral part of healthy communities." FAQs, application guidelines, and contact information are available on the foundation's Web site.

New York Community Trust (http://www.nycommunitytrust.org)
The New York Community Trust was established in 1924 to "help New Yorkers fulfill their charitable goals and make grants that respond to the needs of our city." The trust is comprised of numerous charitable funds established by individuals, families, or businesses, and provides funding to organizations in New York City, on Long Island, in Westchester County, and across the country. The trust's Web site contains introductory information and resources for donors, including a guide to giving, a handbook for donor advisors, financial statements, a listing of the trust's board, and contact information.

Northern Chautauqua Community Foundation (http://www.nccfoundation.org)
The mission of the Northern Chautauqua Community Foundation is to enrich the area it serves. To that end, the foundation, which was established in 1986, has five primary goals: to be a catalyst for the establishment of endowments to benefit the community both now and in the future, to provide a vehicle for donors' varied interests, to promote local philanthropy, to serve as a steward of funds, and to provide leadership and resources in addressing local challenges and opportunities. The foundation's Web site provides lists of recent grants and scholarships awarded by the foundation, descriptions of the funds the foundation administers, financial statements, downloadable applications, and a roster of the foundation's board, staff, and members.

Rochester Area Community Foundation (http://www.racf.org/)
Established in 1972, the Rochester Area Community Foundation manages a number of funds that provide grants for a wide variety of arts, education, social service, and other civic purposes in the Genesee Valley region of upstate New York, including Orleans, Genesee, Monroe, Wayne, Livingston, and Ontario Counties. The foundation also administers scholarships mostly to students originating in the same geographic areas. The foundation's Web site features the foundation's most current annual report, grant guidelines, downloadable applications, staff and board listings, and contact information.

NORTH CAROLINA

Community Foundation of Greater Greensboro (http://www.cfgg.org/)
Since its inception in 1983, the Community Foundation of Greater Greensboro has "promoted philanthropy, built and maintained a permanent collection of endowment funds, and served as a trustworthy partner and leader in shaping effective responses" to issues and opportunities in the greater Greensboro, North Carolina area. The foundation's Web site provides information about the foundation's funds and endowments, grants information

organized by category, financial information, profiles of recent donors and grant recipients, listings of the foundation's board and staff, and current issues of *Horizon,* the foundation's seasonal newsletter.

The Community Foundation of Henderson County (http://www.cfhendersoncounty.org)
The Community Foundation of Henderson County was established in 1983 to serve the people of Henderson County, North Carolina. Through its numerous funds, the foundation makes grants to qualifying organizations in Henderson County. The foundation's programmatic interests include arts and culture, civic affairs, conservation, education, health, and human services. The foundation also maintains a scholarship program primarily for students graduating from high schools within Henderson County. The foundation's Web site features information on creating a fund, details on the foundation's funding interests and priorities, recent grants listings, board/staff listings, and contact information.

The Community Foundation of Western North Carolina (http://www.cfwnc.org/)
Established in 1978 to benefit 18 mountain counties, the Community Foundation of Western North Carolina comprises a number of charitable funds with a mission of promoting and expanding regional philanthropy. The foundation currently makes grants to support activities benefiting the arts, education, the environment, human services, and civic improvements. The foundation's Web site features information about the foundation's programs and affiliates, application guidelines and procedures, recent grants lists by category, information for donors, an online version of the foundation's quarterly newsletter, a calendar of upcoming events, staff and board listings, and contact information.

Foundation for the Carolinas (http://www.fftc.org/)
Established in 1958, the Foundation for the Carolinas is the one of the largest community foundations in the South. Building A Better Future, the foundation's major grantmaking program, awards grants only to organizations located in or serving the greater Charlotte area. Other grant opportunities are available through affiliated community foundations serving the Lexington area and Blowing Rock, Cabarrus, Cleveland, Iredell, and Union Counties in North Carolina and Cherokee, Lancaster, and York Counties in South Carolina. The foundation's specialized grants programs include the Salisbury Community Foundation (Salisbury and Rowan Counties), the African American Community Endowment Fund (Charlotte-Mecklenburg and surrounding communities), the Cole Foundation Endowment (Richmond County area), HIV/AIDS Consortium Grants (13 Charlotte-area counties), and the Medical Research Grants program (North and South Carolina). The foundation's Web site features information for potential donors; program information, guidelines, and deadlines; listings of senior management and board members; an electronic form for requesting copies of the foundation's publications; and contact information.

North Carolina Community Foundation (http://www.nccommf.org/)
The North Carolina Community Foundation, established in 1988, is a statewide foundation seeking gifts from individuals, corporations, and other foundations to build endowments and ensure financial security for nonprofit organizations and institutions throughout the state. Based in Raleigh, North Carolina, the foundation also manages a number of community affiliates throughout North Carolina, that make grants in the areas of human services, education, health, arts, religion, civic affairs, and the conservation and preservation of historical, cultural, and environmental resources. The foundation also manages various scholarship programs statewide.

Outer Banks Community Foundation (http://www.obcf.org)
The Outer Banks Community Foundation was organized in 1982 as a public charity to help meet local needs in Dare County and all of the Outer Banks communities from Corolla to Ocracoke Island in North Carolina. The foundation manages charitable funds for individuals and agencies and targets grants toward the community's most pressing needs and promising opportunities. Located in Kill Devil Hills, North Carolina, the foundation was organized to provide assistance to the Outer Banks areas of Dare and Currituck Counties and

Ocracoke Island (Hyde County). The foundation makes grants to qualifying nonprofit organizations, churches and government agencies, and to individuals for designated purposes through named funds established by donors. Each scholarship fund has its own criteria for selection, such as academic ability, career choice, financial need, athletic interests, or geographic location. The foundation's Web site features information on the foundation's grant and scholarship funds, details on the foundation's grantmaking policy, a grant recipient list, contact information, and printable grant scholarship application forms.

Triangle Community Foundation (http://www.trianglecf.org/)
The mission of the Triangle Community Foundation is to expand private philanthropy in the communities of the greater "Triangle region," including Wake, Durham, Orange, and Chatham Counties, North Carolina. The foundation is comprised of a number of individual philanthropic funds. The foundation also distributes discretionary monies for new initiatives or one-time special projects in cultural affairs and the arts, community development, education, environmental issues, health, social services, and other areas that benefit residents of the region. The foundation's Web site features eligibility guidelines, application procedures, a recent grants list, and articles from the foundation's current newsletter.

The Winston-Salem Foundation (http://www.wsfoundation.org)
Founded in 1919, the Winston-Salem Foundation is a community foundation dedicated to building a permanent pool of philanthropic funds to benefit the community. Based in Winston-Salem, North Carolina, the foundation provides resources and leadership to improve life for all people in the greater Forsyth County area. The foundation makes grants in the areas of children and families, education, health and well-being, arts and culture, and community improvement. The foundation's Web site features information on the foundation's current student aid fund, recent grants listings, FAQs, and contact information.

NORTH DAKOTA

Fargo-Moorhead Area Foundation (http://www.areafoundation.org/)
The Fargo-Moorhead Area Foundation, established in Fargo, North Dakota, in 1960, supports nonprofit organizations that serve the local community in the fields of the arts, civic affairs, education, health, and human services. Most grants are made to qualifying organizations in Cass County, North Dakota, and Clay County, Minnesota. Grants are made from a pool of funds including: unrestricted, field of interest, advised, designated, and organizational. Interested grantseekers should write or call the foundation for a grant application and guidelines. The foundation's Web site features financial information, a newsletter, and contact information.

OHIO

Akron Community Foundation (http://www.akroncommunityfdn.org/)
The Akron Community Foundation was established in 1955 to serve the communities of Summit County, Ohio, through grantmaking in civic affairs, culture and the humanities, education, and health and human services. A number of funds, such as the Women's Endowment Fund and the Medina County Fund, have been created to address the needs of distinct populations or a specific region. The former, the foundation's first affiliated fund, focuses on creating opportunities to support the educational, physical, emotional, social, artistic, and personal growth of women and girls. The latter, another affiliate fund, is laying the groundwork for the establishment of a Medina County community foundation in the future. The foundation's Web site features an overview of the foundation's activities, application guidelines, FAQs, information about the foundation's donor services, press releases and a calendar of events, links to sites of interest, and contact information.

Bowling Green Community Foundation (http://www.wcnet.org/~bgcf/)
The Bowling Green Community Foundation was created in 1994 to provide a perpetual endowment to support worthwhile projects benefiting the community and its citizens. The foundation has a diversified grant program supporting a variety of organizations within the Bowling Green area. The foundation also maintains a scholarship fund for students within the county. The foundation's Web site features grant guidelines, information on the board of trustees, a list of the foundation's current funds, a calendar of upcoming events, and contact information.

The Cleveland Foundation (http://www.clevelandfoundation.org/)
Founded in 1914, the Cleveland Foundation is the nation's oldest community foundation. It gives grants in support of projects in greater Cleveland or that benefit Clevelanders directly in the area of arts and culture, civic affairs, education, economic development, the environment, health, and social services. The foundation maintains a number of scholarship programs for high school seniors attending institutions of higher education. The foundation's Web site features program guidelines and application procedures, information for donors and on planned giving, an electronic publications order form, a listing of the foundation's board and executive staff, and contact information.

The Columbus Foundation (http://www.columbusfoundation.com)
The Columbus Foundation was established in 1943 "to serve as a leader, catalyst, and center for education on philanthropy; to broaden the base of philanthropic giving in central Ohio; to preserve and grow an endowment to address changing community needs in partnership with all stakeholders; and to strive for measurable community improvement through strategic grantmaking in the arts, community development, education, health, social services, and other community needs." Key grant categories include arts and humanities, conservation, education, health, social services, urban affairs, and advancing philanthropy. The foundation's Web site features a list of grant recipients, downloadable grant cover sheets, a staff directory, lists of committee members, and an version of the foundation's online newsletter.

Community Foundation of Delaware County (http://www.delawarecf.com/)
The Community Foundation of Delaware County was established in 1995 as a vehicle through which individuals, companies, foundations, and charitable organizations are able to make gifts and bequests to benefit the future of the community in Ohio. Visit the foundation's Web site to view the various forms of program support, geographic restrictions, listings of recent grant recipients and funds available, board listings, and contact information.

Community Foundation of Greater Lorain County (http://www.cfglc.org/)
The Community Foundation of Greater Lorain County was established in 1980 to serve the residents of Lorain County, Ohio. Every year the foundation makes numerous contributions to the community through many funds. The foundation's areas of interest include arts and culture, civic affairs, education, health, and social services. Diversity grants are awarded through its African American Community Fund and Hispanic Fund. The foundation also awards scholarships and tries to address "gaps in services" through funds for program development, capacity building, preventive endeavors, and "projects that enhance greater self-sufficiency" for individuals and organizations. The foundation's Web site features downloadable application forms.

Community Foundation of Shelby County (http://www.commfoun.com/)
The Community Foundation of Shelby County was established in 1952 to improve the quality of life in Shelby County, Ohio. The foundation supports education, arts, healthcare, and youth projects. A general fund was also established early in the foundation's history for the promotion of education and advancement of learning improvement of the health and physical well-being, enrichment of the moral and spiritual life, and betterment of community relationships. The foundation also makes scholarships to individuals. The foundation's

Web site features information on the foundation's giving program, a brief history of the foundation, a listing of trustees, and contact information.

Coshocton Foundation (http://www.coshoctonfoundation.org/)
The Ohio-based Coshocton Foundation was created in 1967 to "lend a helping hand" to the community of Coshocton County. The foundation makes grants to organizations that support areas of community improvement, literacy and education, encouragement of the arts, health and welfare, and parks and recreation. Visitors to the foundation's Web site will find a listing of officers and trustees, a summary of recent grants, application information, a printable application, and contact information.

Dayton Foundation (http://www.daytonfoundation.org/)
Established in 1921, the Ohio-based Dayton Foundation is "a community foundation designed for permanence and for the benefit of the Dayton/Miami Valley region." The foundation supports a wide range of interests. Its goal is to support projects "not addressed by existing organizations or to support special efforts of already-established nonprofit organizations in the Miami Valley." Grantseekers are encouraged to call for application guidelines. The foundation's Web site features contact information.

Foundation for Appalachian Ohio (http://www.appalachianohio.org/)
Established in 1998, the Foundation for Appalachian Ohio serves the residents of 29 Appalachian counties in Ohio. The foundation addresses a wide range of local needs, including employment opportunities (job creation/retention/training), overcoming the effects of poverty, education and training, human services, healthcare and prevention services, affordable and accessible housing, physical infrastructure (roads, bridges, power, communications, water, and sewer), preserving and improving the natural environment, enhancing arts and cultural opportunities, increasing philanthropic/charitable capital and leadership, and reducing out migration of human, capital, and natural resources. FAQs, contact information, and Ohio Appalachian resources and links are available on the foundation's Web site.

The Greater Cincinnati Foundation (http://www.greatercincinnatifdn.org/)
The Greater Cincinnati Foundation is a charitable organization that builds and preserves endowment funds, identifies opportunities to enhance the quality of community life, and responds with grants addressing six key areas: arts and culture, community progress, education, the environment, health, and human services. Formed in 1963, the foundation provides philanthropic leadership to eight counties in the Ohio-Kentucky-Indiana region. The foundation's Web site contains contact information for foundation representatives, who can provide information on applying for grants and on grant opportunities.

Greater Wayne County Foundation, Inc. (http://gwcf.net/)
Based in Wooster, Ohio, the Greater Wayne County Foundation, Inc. was established in 1978 to accept contributions, create and administer funds, and make grants for the benefit of the people of the greater Wayne County area. Grants are paid to a wide variety of organizations in the areas of arts, culture, and humanities; capital campaigns; civic and community; conservation and environment; education; health and wellness; human services; religion; and scholarships. The foundation's Web site features downloadable grant guidelines and applications, scholarships listings, and contact information.

Middletown Community Foundation (http://www.mcfoundation.org/)
Founded in 1976, the Middletown Community Foundation funds scholarships and grants in the Middletown, Monroe, Trenton, Franklin, Madison, and Lemon Township areas of Ohio. Scholarships are available for area high school and adult students. The foundation's grants focus on the arts, education, health, social services, recreation, and community development, among other needs. Additionally, the foundation gives the Crystal Apple Teacher Recognition Award, a prize for area educators, and the Summertime for Kids Award, a mini-grant program that funds nonprofit organizations that have activities catering to youth during the summer. The foundation's Web site provides charts on the

organization's growth, membership and donor information, links to other resources, contact information, and scholarship, grant, and award information and applications.

Muskingum County Community Foundation (http://www.mccf.org/)
The mission of the Muskingum County Community Foundation, established in 1985 in Zanesville, Ohio, is to "improve the quality of life and to serve the charitable needs of the community by attracting and administering charitable funds." The foundation's Web site features lists of available scholarships and past recipients, lists of available grants and past grantees; a list of restricted funds and recent donors, a listing of staff and officers, a report on the foundation's financial position, a strategic plan and donor guide, an online version of the foundation's newsletter, a nomination form for the Thomas Community Service Award, and contact information.

Parkersburg Area Community Foundation (http://pacf.wirefire.com)
The Parkersburg Area Community Foundation is committed to serving the people of the Mid-Ohio Valley (Wood, Pleasants, Ritchie, Doddridge, Gilmer, Wirt, Calhoun, Roane, and Jackson Counties in West Virginia and Washington County in Ohio) by linking community resources with community needs. The foundation focuses its grantmaking in the areas of arts and culture, education, health and human services, recreation, and youth and family services. The foundation also administers a variety of different scholarship funds, the majority of which are designated for students in Wood County, West Virginia. The foundation's Web site provides information about the foundation, application guidelines and scholarship information, and details about becoming a donor to the foundation.

Sandusky/Erie County Community Foundation (http://www.sanduskyfoundation.org/)
The Sandusky/Erie County Community Foundation was created in 1996 to enable people and organizations to make a positive impact on the Erie County community. The foundation is particularly interested in providing seed money for new programs that work to meet emerging needs of the community or to expand successful programs. The foundation's areas of interest include arts and culture, community development, education, environmental services, parks and recreation, safety, social services, and youth services. The foundation's Web site features information on the foundation's grant programs, news, a listing of recent grants by subject area, FAQs, and contact information.

Stark Community Foundation (http://www.starkcommunityfoundation.org/)
The Stark Community Foundation of Canton, Ohio, was established in 1963 to "promote the betterment of Stark County and enhance the quality of life for all of its citizens." In recent years, the foundation has provided support for education, leadership training, health, and social and community issues, including affordable housing and neighborhood revitalization. The foundation also maintains a number of active scholarship and loan funds benefiting Stark County students. The foundation's Web site features a history of the foundation, grant guidelines, application information, a downloadable grant application, and contact information.

Wapakoneta Area Community Foundation (http://www.wapakacf.org/)
Established in Wapakoneta, Ohio, in 1989, the Wapakoneta Area Community Foundation provides a perpetual endowment to support worthwhile projects benefiting the community and its citizens. Each year its funds provide the resources for grants to support the services and programs of many nonprofit organizations. The foundation's Web site features program support information, geographic restrictions, listings of recent grant recipients and funds available, board listings, and contact information.

OKLAHOMA

Oklahoma City Community Foundation, Inc. (http://www.occf.org)
Established in 1969 the Oklahoma City Community Foundation, Inc. serves the area of Oklahoma City, Oklahoma. As part of its mission, the foundation promotes community programs that address specific opportunities and issues within Oklahoma City and provides support for organizations interested and able to address these issues in effective ways. The foundation's areas of interest include arts, culture, education, rural development, and others. The foundation's Web site provides FAQs, a board of trustees listing, contact information, and community program descriptions.

OREGON

The Oregon Community Foundation (http://www.oregoncommunityfound.org)
The Oregon Community Foundation, established in 1973, funds a variety of grants, scholarships, and special initiative programs. The foundation's funding objectives for grants fall into four areas, all geared toward Oregonians: nurturing children, strengthening families, and fostering self-sufficiency; enhancing educational experience; increasing cultural opportunities; and preserving and improving Oregon's livability through citizen involvement. The foundation also funds a scholarship program for college-bound graduates of Oregon high schools or returning adults. The foundation's Web site provides grant and scholarship guidelines, limitations and deadlines, recent grants and scholarships, FAQs, downloadable forms and instructions, board and staff listings, related links, information for potential donors, and contact information.

PENNSYLVANIA

Berks County Community Foundation (http://www.bccf.org)
Established in 1994, the Reading, Pennsylvania-based Berks County Community Foundation seeks "to improve the quality of life for the residents of the county by providing funds to meet existing and emerging needs." The foundation disperses funds to social, educational, environmental, and cultural programs in Berks County. Visit the foundation's Web site for an overview of the foundation's grant activities, descriptions of its special programs and initiatives, a grants list, a list of established funds, news and press releases, links to related resources, downloadable financial information, and contact information.

Big Ben Foundation (http://www.lehigh.edu/~inifc/bbf/bbf.html)
Founded at Lehigh University in February 1995, the Big Ben Foundation is a cooperative between members of the Allentown, Bethlehem, and Easton, Pennsylvania, communities and the students of Lehigh University. The purpose of the foundation is "to raise and distribute funds to other nonprofit community-based organizations or individuals with specific economic hardships." The foundation provides nonprofits with supplemental funding, "so they in turn can maintain existing programs and provide new and better services for their local communities." The foundation does not accept applications. It operates its own programs and raises funds from the general public and local businesses. Visit the foundation's Web site to find contact information.

Centre County Community Foundation (http://centrecountycf.org/)
The Centre County Community Foundation was established in Pennsylvania, in 1981 and is dedicated to meeting changing needs and assisting individuals, families, and businesses throughout Centre County to plan and carry out their charitable giving. The foundation provides support for the arts, social and health concerns, education, and the environment. The foundation tries to target funds toward the community's most pressing needs and projects that will have the greatest impact. Visitors to the foundation's Web site will find more information about the foundation's mission, grant activities, types of funds, grant listings, board listings, and contact information.

Chester County Community Foundation (http://www.chescocf.org/)
Established in 1994, the Chester County Community Foundation's mission is lead, inspire, and encourage all individuals and organizations to create or contribute to lasting philanthropic charitable legacies, improving the quality of life, primarily in Chester County. The vast majority of grants that the foundation makes are donor-advised. The foundation maintains field-of-interest funds, donor-advised funds, memorial funds, scholarship funds, and dedicated nonprofit endowments. The foundation's Web site features information about the foundation's grantmaking programs, lists of available funds, board/staff lists, and contact information.

Community Foundation of Greene County, PA (http://www.cfgcpa.org)
Located in Waynesburg, Pennsylvania, the Community Foundation of Greene County works to manage charitable contributions in order to finance programs that will better the Greene County community. The foundation maintains and enhances the educational, social, cultural, health, and civic resources of the community. The foundation's Web site features an online request form for further information; nonprofit groups interested in grant guidelines and applications must contact the foundation directly.

Greater Harrisburg Foundation (http://www.ghf.org/)
Established in 1920 by Donald McCormick, the Greater Harrisburg Foundation serves Cumberland, Dauphin, Lebanon, Perry, and Franklin Counties in south central Pennsylvania. Field-of-interest funds held by the foundation include the arts, services for children, education, homelessness and hunger, health, the environment, dental care for the disadvantaged, head and spinal injury prevention, services to girls, mental health, mental retardation, and services for the needy, among others. The foundation's Web site provides FAQs, information on regional foundations, grant guidelines, and contact information.

Lehigh Valley Community Foundation (http://www.lehighvalleyfoundation.org/)
The Lehigh Valley Community Foundation, of Allentown, Pennsylvania, was established to "enhance the fabric of life in the Lehigh Valley." The foundation's areas of interest include arts and culture, community betterment, education, the environment, healthcare, history and heritage, human services, and science. The foundation's Web site contains information on program support, geographic restrictions, listings of recent grant recipients, links to local and regional organizations, and contact information.

The Luzerne Foundation (http://www.luzernefoundation.org/)
The Luzerne Foundation, of Wilkes-Barre, Pennsylvania, works to enhance and improve the Luzerne County community through permanent endowment funds. The foundation's areas of funding interest include the arts, education, community development, the environment, and health and human services. Funds are distributed through various donor-advised grants, scholarships, and general grants. The foundation's Web site provides information and benefits for donors, grant guidelines, a downloadable application, and contact information.

The Philadelphia Foundation (http://www.philafound.org/)
Established in 1918, the Philadelphia Foundation serves as a vehicle and resource for philanthropy in Bucks, Chester, Delaware, Montgomery, and Philadelphia Counties. It does this by developing, managing, and allocating community resources in partnership with donors and grantees, building on community assets, and promoting empowerment, leadership, and civic participation among underserved groups. Grant distributions are made according to the charitable interests and specifications of the individual fund donors, but the foundation also identifies emerging needs in the community and sets policies and priorities for distributing unrestricted dollars in the areas of children and families, community organizing and advocacy, culture, education, health, housing and economic development, and social services. The foundation's Web site features application guidelines, policy information, the foundation's financial management policies, listings of recipient organizations, recent press releases, and a donor information section.

The Pittsburgh Foundation (http://www.pittsburghfoundation.org)
The Pittsburgh Foundation was established in Pennsylvania in 1945 "to provide individuals, families, organizations, and corporations with an avenue for their charitable giving and to benefit the world around them—especially the people in the communities where they live." The foundation promotes the betterment of the greater Pittsburgh community and the quality of life for all its citizens. The foundation's Web site features general information about the foundation, guidelines and applications, information on how to establish a fund, a list of supporting organizations, and a link to the Planned Giving Design Center, which was created to provide professional advisors with resources to advise clients in matters of charitable giving and estate planning.

Scranton Area Foundation (http://www.safdn.org/)
The Scranton Area Foundation was founded in 1954 as a private foundation, becoming a community foundation in 1988, to serve the city of Scranton and Lackawanna County, Pennsylvania. The foundation's mission is to "enhance the quality of life for all people in Lackawanna County through the development of organized philanthropy." Areas of funding interest include health, education, arts, the environment, human services, and civic affairs. The foundation's Web site provides information for prospective donors and grantees, FAQs, links, and contact information.

Three Rivers Community Foundation (http://www.threeriverscommunityfoundation.org)
Established in 1989 by five donors, the Three Rivers Community Foundation is based in Pittsburgh, Pennsylvania, and helps the communities of southwestern Pennsylvania. The foundation "identifies and funds alternative methods of dealing with barriers in society that hinder education, employment opportunities, and community development." The foundation generally supports smaller groups not supported by the government or other foundations. The funding interests include children, youth, and families; global neighbors; progressive organizing; public accountability; racial divisions and racial pride; health concerns; and gay and lesbian issues. A newsletter, calendar of events, information about the foundation's proposal writing workshop, grant guidelines, lists of past grant recipients, application information, and contact information are available at the foundation's Web site.

Washington County Community Foundation (http://www.wccf.net)
The mission of the Pennsylvania-based Washington County Community Foundation is "to improve the quality of life in Washington County by making it possible for donors to receive philanthropic advantages otherwise available only to the wealthiest contributors." Areas of interest include the arts, education, the environment, health, human needs, and religion. The foundation's Web site offers information on the foundation's many funds, listings of recent grants, board listings, a publications section, and financial and contact information.

PUERTO RICO

Puerto Rico Community Foundation (http://www.fcpr.org)
Through its support of self-directed development of Puerto Rican community groups, the Puerto Rico Community Foundation "seeks to contribute to the growth of a healthier community, [acting] as a catalytic agent in fostering new and innovative solutions to the Island's problems." Although the foundation concentrates its efforts on the needs of Puerto Ricans on the island, it collaborates with Puerto Rican communities in the United States as well. Visitors to the foundation's Web site will find descriptions of the foundation's various programs, a listing of the foundation's board of directors and staff, and links to other philanthropic resources and organizations of interest on the Web.

RHODE ISLAND

The Rhode Island Foundation (http://www.rifoundation.org/)
Established in 1916, the Providence-based Rhode Island Foundation has grown to become one of the largest community foundations in the United States. The foundation focuses its discretionary grantmaking in the areas of children and families, economic/community development, and education, although it views those designations more as starting points than as fixed categories with fixed parameters. Visitors to the foundation's Web site will find a history of the foundation, program descriptions and recent grants in each program area, application guidelines and eligibility requirements, information for donors, a financial overview of the foundation, listings of the board and staff, and contact information.

SOUTH CAROLINA

Community Foundation of Greater Greenville (http://www.cfgg.com/)
Located in Greenville, South Carolina, the Community Foundation of Greater Greenville "exists to enhance the quality of life of the citizens of greater Greenville by linking philanthropic leadership, charitable resources, and civic influence with needs and opportunities in the community." The foundation makes grants to tax-exempt organizations to enhance community life through the support of a broad range of services, including health, education, religion, arts and humanities, and the environment. Some grants follow an open application process under published guidelines. Other noncompetitive grants reflect the charitable priorities of individual donors. The foundation's Web site features information for requesting an application, news about the foundation, and a list of previous grantees.

The Community Foundation Serving Coastal South Carolina (http://www.communityfoundationsc.org)
The Community Foundation Serving Coastal South Carolina was founded in Charleston in 1974 to serve the eight coastal counties of South Carolina. The foundation provides funding in various programs areas, including: arts, education, basic human needs, neighborhood and community development, health, conservation, historical preservation, and animal welfare. The foundation's Web site includes grant descriptions, guidelines, downloadable applications, a complete listing of scholarships, a detailed list of past grants, news and events, a donor guide, and a regional map covering funding possibilities in surrounding areas.

Foundation for the Carolinas (http://www.fftc.org/)
Established in 1958, the Foundation for the Carolinas is the one of the largest community foundations in the South. Building A Better Future, the foundation's major grantmaking program, awards grants only to organizations located in or serving the greater Charlotte area. Other grant opportunities are available through affiliated community foundations serving the Lexington area and Blowing Rock, Cabarrus, Cleveland, Iredell, and Union Counties in North Carolina and Cherokee, Lancaster, and York Counties in South Carolina. The foundation's specialized grants programs include the Salisbury Community Foundation (Salisbury and Rowan Counties), the African American Community Endowment Fund (Charlotte-Mecklenburg and surrounding communities), the Cole Foundation Endowment (Richmond County area), HIV/AIDS Consortium Grants (13 Charlotte-area counties), and the Medical Research Grants program (North and South Carolina). The foundation's Web site features information for potential donors; program information, guidelines, and deadlines; listings of senior management and board members; an electronic form for requesting copies of the foundation's publications; and contact information.

Hilton Head Island Foundation, Inc. (http://www.hhif.org)
South Carolina's Hilton Head Island Foundation, Inc., established in 1994, is "dedicated to the principles of fairness and caring stewardship so that [it] may provide opportunities of enduring value for the Hilton Head Island community area." The foundation's Web site

features a donor guide, a legal and financial advisors guide, news and events, a list of recent grants, related links, contact information for the foundation's staff and board, grant guidelines and deadlines, and a reply form to request more information.

SOUTH DAKOTA

Sioux Falls Area Community Foundation (http://www.sfacf.org)
The Sioux Falls Area Community Foundation is located in Sioux Falls, South Dakota, and works to support the needs of the surrounding region. The foundation is committed to "serving as a resource and catalyst for charitable purposes; building an endowment fund for the future; serving donors with many different interests; and assessing and responding to community needs." The foundation's areas of interest includes the arts and humanities, community affairs and development, education, the environment, health, human services, and religion. The foundation's Web site features grant guidelines, staff/board listing, and contact information.

TENNESSEE

Community Foundation of Greater Chattanooga (http://www.cfgc.org)
Established in 1962, the Community Foundation of Greater Chattanooga "encourages and invests in creative and long-term solutions to improve the community and the lives of its citizens." The foundation maintains a number of funds that make grants in many forms, including community funds, scholarship funds, project funds, agency funds, field-of-interest funds, designated funds, and donor-advised funds. The foundation's Web site features a grant history archive, grant guidelines and procedures, a board listing, information on scholarships, and contact information.

Community Foundation of Greater Memphis (http://www.cfgm.org/)
The Community Foundation of Greater Memphis was established in 1969 to serve communities in eastern Arkansas, northern Mississippi, and western Tennessee. The foundation's mission is to strengthen the community through philanthropy. The foundation supports a wide variety of causes, including serving children with disabilities and visually impaired individuals, organizing children's summer camps, and providing humane contraception for animals through several funds. Contact information, application guidelines, and staff and board listings are available on the foundation's Web site.

The Community Foundation of Middle Tennessee (http://www.cfmt.org/)
The Community Foundation of Middle Tennessee was created to enhance the quality of life in the 40 counties of the "Middle Tennessee area." In order to serve this community, the foundation has identified several broad categories in which needs exist and in which grant requests are encouraged. These categories include arts and humanities, civic affairs and community planning, conservation and environment, education, employment and training, health, historic preservation, housing and community development, and human services for citizens of all ages. The foundation's Web site provides information about the foundation's various funds (e.g., discretionary, donor-advised, scholarship, etc.), grant application guidelines, financial policies, board and staff listings, and contact information.

East Tennessee Foundation (http://www.easttennesseefoundation.org)
The East Tennessee Foundation was established in 1986 through a merger of the Community Foundation of East Tennessee and Business Trust for the Arts. The foundation's grantmaking interests include arts and culture, community development, education, youth-at-risk, or a particular east Tennessee county within the foundation's 24-county service area. The foundation also makes four-year scholarships to qualified Tennessee students. The foundation's Web site features information on the foundation's grant program, a detailed map outlining the 24 counties eligible for grant consideration, a list of foundation publications, a helpful links page, board and staff listings, and contact information.

TEXAS

Amarillo Area Foundation (http://www.aaf-hf.org/)
The Amarillo Area Foundation of Texas was established in 1957 to meet the needs of underserved communities in the northernmost 26 counties of the Texas Panhandle. The foundation does not limit its discretionary grantmaking to a particular area of interest. Rather, it seeks to support the entire range of human needs in the Panhandle. The foundation manages hundreds of funds in the form of donor-advised funds, scholarships, unrestricted funds, and project funds. In general, the foundation does not fund religious or political causes; private of parochial schools; national, state, or local fundraising activities; or general operating support for United Way agencies. The foundation's Web site features a history of the foundation, board/staff lists, grant application criteria, application guidelines, printable application form, deadlines, and FAQs.

Communities Foundation of Texas, Inc. (http://www.cftexas.org/)
Based in Dallas, the Communities Foundation of Texas, Inc. was formed in 1981 from the Dallas Community Chest Trust Fund, which was established in the 1950s. The foundation carries out the objectives of its donors through many funds as well as various external charitable projects and branch offices throughout Texas. The foundation's major areas of distribution include education, religion, culture and history, social services, youth, and inner city/community. The foundation gives locally in Texas and across the United States. The foundation's Web site features a year in review; listings of the board, advisory council, and staff members; profiles of grant recipients; a financial report; application guidelines; and a newsletter.

Community Foundation of Abilene (http://www.abilene.com/communityfoundation)
The Community Foundation of Abiline was created in 1985 "to establish permanent charitable endowments; to provide a vehicle for donors' varied interests; to promote local philanthropy; and to provide leadership and resources in addressing local challenges and opportunities." The foundation's giving program also has many components, including a grants program, scholarships, and a community leadership program. The foundation supports projects that benefit the community, with particular interest in those that promote voluntarism and community involvement, address emerging needs, include cooperation between nonprofits, and address prevention in addition to assistance. The scholarship program makes awards to area students at a variety of colleges. Interested students should speak with their high school counselor. In the community leadership area, the foundation offers a resource center and planning support. The foundation's Web site features staff and board lists; a grants history; an online newsletter; grant guidelines, restrictions, and deadlines; scholarship descriptions; and resources for community leaders.

The Community Foundation of North Texas (http://www.cfntx.org/)
The Community Foundation of North Texas, located in Fort Worth, Texas, was known as the Community Foundation of Metropolitan Tarrant County until 1999. The foundation makes grants to qualified organizations in the areas of human services, community programs and service, education, health, arts, and cultural affairs. The foundation's Web site includes information on the many funds available, application guidelines and deadlines, board and staff lists, and informaton on how to establish a fund.

Community Foundation of the Texas Hill Country (http://www.communityfoundation.net/)
In operation since 1982, the Community Foundation of the Texas Hill Country, formerly the Kerrville Area Community Trust, is a collection of individual funds and resources given by local citizens and organizations to enhance and support the quality of life in the Kerrville, Texas, area. The foundation's Web site provides information on the foundation; FAQs; a summary of the foundation's grants made since its inception; grant application guidelines, policies, deadlines, and a downloadable grant application form; information about the foundation's funds; a list of publications; and a calendar of events.

The Dallas Foundation (http://www.dallasfoundation.org)
The Dallas Foundation, established as a community foundation in 1929, serves as a leader, catalyst, and resource for philanthropy by providing donors with flexible means of making gifts to charitable causes that enhance the Dallas community. The foundation gives donors the ability to establish funds with specific charitable goals, guidance in developing effective grantmaking plans, and other services. The foundation also assists the nonprofit community through grantmaking and projects designed to strengthen agencies' operations. The foundation's site contains grant guidelines, grant lists, financials, FAQs, links, news and press releases, contact information, publications, and the most recent annual report.

El Paso Community Foundation (http://www.epcf.org/)
The El Paso Community Foundation was established in 1977 to address community challenges in the southwest Texas border region. Today, it awards funds twice a year (in May and November) to grant applicants from area nonprofit organizations or from community activist groups in the following areas of interest: arts and humanities, civic affairs/public benefit, environment/animal welfare, education, health and disabilities, and human services. Priority is given to more effective ways of doing things and ideas that require risk-taking; projects where a moderate amount of grant money can have an impact; and projects that show collaboration with other organizations. The foundation does not fund capital campaigns, fundraising events, projects of a religious nature, medical or academic research, annual appeals and membership contributions, organizations that are political or partisan in purpose, travel for individuals or groups, ongoing requests for general operating support, and requests from organizations outside the El Paso geographic area. The foundation's Web site features grant guidelines, a listing of the volunteers who serve as the foundation's board of directors, and contact information.

Lubbock Area Foundation, Inc. (http://www.lubbockareafoundation.org)
The Lubbock Area Foundation, Inc. was created in 1981 to help Texas South Plains residents realize their long-term philanthropic goals. The foundation manages a pool of charitable funds, the income from which is used to benefit the South Plains community through grants to qualified organizations; educational programs; and scholarships. Grants are made for start-up funding, general operating support, program support, and/or demonstration programs. The foundation does not make grants to individuals, for political purposes, to retire indebtedness, or for payment of interest or taxes. The foundation's Web site offers information on funding priorities and application procedures, a list of endowed scholarship funds, general information about the foundation's Mini-Grants for Teachers Program and its Funding Information Library (a Foundation Center Cooperating Collection), and contact information.

San Antonio Area Foundation (http://www.saafdn.org/)
The San Antonio Area Foundation was established in 1964 as a memorial to local community leader, visionary, and philanthropist Nat Goldsmith. The foundation does not state its areas of interest on its Web site. The foundation only reviews proposals from applicants whose letters of intent have been approved. In addition to a brief history of and general information about the foundation, the foundation's Web site features scholarship and grant application instructions, information for donors, and a board list.

The Waco Foundation (http://www.wacofdn.org/)
Established in 1958, the Waco Foundation serves the residents of Waco and McLennan Counties in Texas. Its fields of interest include childcare, medical facilities, education, and art and culture. Through its MAC Grant Scholarship Fund, the foundation helps local high school graduates attend a community college. The foundation's Web site features grant guidelines, downloadable applications, and contact information.

VERMONT

Vermont Community Foundation (http://www.vermontcf.org/)
The Vermont Community Foundation was established in 1986 to address the needs of Vermont, now and in the future, by building charitable capital and by providing services, resources, leadership, and encouragement to donors and to the nonprofit sector. In its role as a grantmaker, the foundation will consider any project that meets a clearly-defined community need in Vermont. Categories of support include, but are not limited to, the arts and humanities, education, the environment, historic resources, health, public affairs and community development, and social services. The foundation emphasizes small one-time grants rather than continuing support. It does not make grants for endowments, annual operating or capital campaigns, religious purposes, individuals, or equipment (unless it is an integral part of an otherwise eligible project). In addition to detailed grant guidelines, lists of recent grants, information for potential donors, and a list of links to related resources, the foundation's Web site provides general information about the Vermont Women's Fund and various TAP-VT technical assistance programs.

VIRGIN ISLANDS

Community Foundation of the Virgin Islands (http://fdncenter.org/grantmaker/cfvi/)
The Community Foundation of the Virgin Islands, based on the island of St. Thomas, was established in 1990 to "enhance the educational, physical, social, cultural, and environmental well-being of the islands' people." The foundation works to improve the quality of life for people in the Virgin Islands through programs, initiatives, funds, and scholarships. The foundation's Web site lists its numerous programs and specific funds, including the Technical Assistance Program, mini-grants which benefit children and families, and scholarship and scholar awards. The foundation's Web site also provides donor information, foundation news, a directory of Virgin Islands community services organizations, listings of recently-funded programs and scholarships, and contact information.

VIRGINIA

The Community Foundation Serving Richmond and Central Virginia (http://www.tcfrichmond.org/)
The Community Foundation Serving Richmond and Central Virginia was established in 1968 to enhance the lives of the citizens of central Virginia. Located in Richmond, the foundation "provides effective stewardship of philanthropic assets entrusted to its care by donors who wish to enhance the quality of community life." The foundation maintains a number of grantmaking funds that support a wide variety of interests to qualified organizations. The foundation also has several student scholarship funds. The foundation's Web site provides a grant list, listings of community foundations in Virginia by area, press releases, information on each fund, application information, and contact information.

DPC Community Foundation (http://www.dpccf.org/)
The DPC Community Foundation was established in 1996 to serve the charitable needs of the city of Danville and Pittsylvania and Caswell Counties, Virginia. The foundation maintains a number of funds that help to meet a variety of social, educational, health, and other area needs. The foundation also awards scholarships to qualifying students. Visit the foundation's Web site to find more information about the grantmaking programs, application criteria, the foundation's most recent tax return, and contact information.

Greater Lynchburg Community Trust (http://www.lynchburgtrust.org)
The Greater Lynchburg Community Trust was founded in 1972 by the Fidelity American Bank. It is located in Lynchburg, Virginia, and serves the cities of Lynchburg and Bedford and the counties of Amherst, Bedford, and Campbell. The trust exists "to promote local philanthropy and to simplify the process of giving." It provides for the administration and

the investment of gifts and bequests. Needs served are broad in scope, including human services to children, youth, the needy, and the elderly; education; health; the arts; and the humanities. The trust will consider applications from nonprofit organizations that work to help the communities the trust serves. Grant application informaton and deadlines are provided on the foundation's Web site.

The Norfolk Foundation (http://www.norfolkfoundation.org)
The Norfolk Foundation is a "permanent endowment created by the community for the community." Established in 1950, the foundation is dedicated to improving the quality of life in Norfolk and surrounding cities. Grants are made to students for financial aid and to nonprofit organizations in qualified communities within Virginia. Two important initiatives of the foundation are the Business Consortium for Arts Support, which provides operating support to dozens of arts organizations in the community, and the Planning Council's Homeless Prevention Program. The foundation's Web site features information on the foundation's funding restrictions, application information, recent grants lists, and contact information.

The Portsmouth Community Foundation (http://www.thepcf.org/)
Established in 1965, the Portsmouth Community Foundation is devoted to improving the quality of life in Portsmouth and surrounding cities. The foundation makes grants to qualifying organizations in the areas of health and human services, education, the arts, and economic development. Visitors to the foundation's Web site will find a board listings, grant guidelines, lists of recent grants, links and resources section, and contact information.

Staunton Augusta Waynesboro Community Foundation (http://personal.cfw.com/~sawfdtn/)
The mission of the Staunton Augusta Waynesboro Community Foundation is to "provide for the enrichment of the quality of life in the community by developing a permanent endowment in order to assess and respond to changing community needs today and in the future, and serving as a mechanism for donors at all levels of charitable giving." Local industrialist H.D. Dawbarn founded the foundation in 1992. Its area of service extends to the city of Staunton, county of Augusta, city of Waynesboro, and surrounding communities; the foundation itself is located in Waynesboro, Virginia. In addition to building endowments for the community, the foundation does award grants. Its areas of funding interest are education, health and human services, civic and community initiatives, arts and culture, and the environment. Those interested in receiving a grant are encouraged to first contact the foundation office for direct assistance. The foundation's Web site features grant guidelines and deadlines.

The Virginia Beach Foundation (http://vabeachfoundation.org/)
The Virginia Beach Foundation is a community foundation serving the people of Virginia Beach and their neighbors. Founded in 1987, the foundation's mission is to stimulate the establishment of endowments to serve the people of Virginia Beach now and in the future; respond to changing, emerging community needs; assist donors in achieving their charitable giving objectives; and serve as a resource, broker, catalyst, and leader in the community. The foundation's Web site features a history the foundation, FAQs, words from foundation supporters and grantees, and donor information.

WASHINGTON

Community Foundation for Southwest Washington (http://www.cfsww.org/)
The Community Foundation for Southwest Washington, located in Vancouver, has been assisting the surrounding community since 1984. The group's mission is to "shape the future of southwest Washington through philanthropy by supporting worthy projects in the areas of social and human services, arts and culture, education, and quality of life." Nonprofits serving the communities of Cowlitz, Clark, Skamania, and West Klickitat

Counties are eligible to receive funding. Areas of funding interest include social services, civic affairs, health, education, children's issues, and arts and cultural affairs. The public charity also hosts a series of special initiatives. These include a program to address welfare reform laws, assistance with electric bills during the winter, a sculpture garden, and a fund to support innovative ideas in the classroom. The foundation's Web site includes printable guidelines and applications, a list of board members, calendar of events, and contact information.

Greater Tacoma Community Foundation (http://www.tacomafoundation.org)
The Greater Tacoma Community Foundation was created in Tacoma, Washington, in 1981 to improve the quality of life for all people in Tacoma and Pierce Counties. In the past, the foundation has supported organizations with interests in arts and culture, education, health, civil society, the environment, religion, and social services. The foundation also maintains a number of scholarship programs for students in the qualifying region. The foundation's Web site features information about its giving priorities, grant application information, restrictions, and contact information.

Kitsap Community Foundation (http://www.kitsapfoundation.org)
The Kitsap Community Foundation of Washington State is committed to "enriching the community through creative and effective philanthropy." The foundation works to bring people together to discuss making the community a better place. The foundation makes grants to increase literacy, strengthen families, protect the environment, enhance fine and performing arts, build low-income housing, support elementary education projects, bring music into the lives of young people, and encourage self-sufficiency. Visitors to the foundation's Web site will find a sampling of recent grant activities, descriptive grant guidelines, a history of the foundation, and contact information.

The Seattle Foundation (http://www.seattlefoundation.org/)
Established in 1946, the Seattle Foundation today works to improve the quality of life for people in the Puget Sound region by nurturing a greater sense of community in the region and by serving as a catalyst for dialogue within the area's nonprofit community. Grants are awarded quarterly to organizations in the areas of arts, culture, and the humanities; health; human services; the environment; and public/society benefit. All applicant organizations must be qualified nonprofits and be located primarily in King County. Visitors to the foundation's Web site will find general information about the foundation and its activities, grant guidelines, and latest annual report, and contact information.

WEST VIRGINIA

Beckley Area Foundation, Inc. (http://beckleyareafoundation.com/)
The Beckley Area Foundation, Inc. of West Virginia seeks to build a better area in which all of its citizens can enjoy life—work, play, and retire. The foundation provides grants each year in the fields of education, health and human services, the arts, public recreation, and beautification. Programs funded through the annual community grant application process must be located in Raleigh County. Visit the foundation's Web site to learn more about the foundation's grantmaking processes; learn about priorities, restrictions, and scholarship opportunities; and find contact information.

The Greater Kanawha Valley Foundation (http://www.tgkvf.org)
The Greater Kanawha Valley Foundation was organized in Charleston, West Virginia, in 1962 to "accept contributions, create and administer funds, and make grants for the benefit of the people of the greater Kanawha Valley." The foundation makes grants to nonprofits with interests in arts and culture, economic development, education, health, human services, land use, and recreation. The foundation also maintains a number of scholarship programs for students who live in the area served. The foundation's Web site features

information about the foundation's grantmaking activities, a downloadable grant application, previous grant recipient lists, and contact information.

Parkersburg Area Community Foundation (http://pacf.wirefire.com)
The Parkersburg Area Community Foundation is committed to serving the people of the Mid-Ohio Valley (Wood, Pleasants, Ritchie, Doddridge, Gilmer, Wirt, Calhoun, Roane, and Jackson Counties in West Virginia and Washington County in Ohio) by linking community resources with community needs. The foundation focuses its grantmaking in the areas of arts and culture, education, health and human services, recreation, and youth and family services. The foundation also administers a variety of different scholarship funds, the majority of which are designated for students in Wood County, West Virginia. The foundation's Web site provides information about the foundation, application guidelines and scholarship information, and details about becoming a donor to the foundation.

WISCONSIN

Community Foundation for the Fox Valley Region (http://www.cffoxvalley.org)
Incorporated in 1986, the Community Foundation for the Fox Valley Region "exists to enhance the quality of life for all citizens" in the region of Wisconsin, from Neenah to Appleton to Kaukauna and into surrounding areas. The foundation's grants support five program areas: human services, arts and culture, healthcare, education, and community development. The foundation's Web site contains infromation on past programs, current grant guidelines and limitations, a printable common grant application, board and staff lists, financial information, press releases, donor information, and related links.

Dickinson Area Community Foundation (http://www.dcacf.org/)
The Dickinson Area Community Foundation is an independent nonprofit organization located in Iron Mountain, Michigan. Established in 1995 for the benefit of Dickinson County and surrounding Wisconsin communities, the foundation encourages philanthropic investment by building and managing permanent endowments and utilizing the income to enhance the community's quality of life. The foundation states that it "is not designed to compete with, nor duplicate, the efforts of other agencies which provide ongoing support for charitable organizations and services;" rather, it focuses on "one-time-only and start-up funding, support for innovative projects when there is an identified need that cannot be met by other means, and programs that enhance the quality of life in [the] community." While the foundation supports a broad range of activities, its current grantmaking is centered on youth. Visit the foundation's Web site for a printable grant application, contact information, and press releases.

Duluth-Superior Area Community Foundation (http://www.dsacommunityfoundation.com)
Incorporated in 1983, the Duluth-Superior Area Community Foundation strives to improve the quality of life for the residents of Duluth, Minnesota; Superior, Wisconsin; and the surrounding areas. The foundation supports local projects and organizations in the arts, civic projects, education, the environment, and human services. The foundation also awards scholarships. The foundation's Web site features information on grants and scholarships, list of previous grantees, the foundation's most recent annual report, donor information, a contact form, a history of the foundation, and staff and board lists.

The Eau Claire Area Foundation (http://www.ecareafoundation.org)
The Wisconsin-based, Eau Claire Area Foundation is committed to enriching area life by strengthening the community, encouraging volunteer participation and collaboration, and helping people help themselves. The foundation considers funding in education, culture, the environment, recreation, and social concerns. The foundation's Web site includes a grant application form, application guidelines, an annual report, a downloadable version of foundation's most recent tax return, and contact information.

Fond du Lac Area Foundation (http://www.fdlareafoundation.com)
Established in 1976, the Fond du Lac Foundation funds community endeavors in education, health and human services, youth services, arts and culture, and the environment. A number of named scholarships are available for area students. Grants are made to provide practical solutions to community problems, promote cooperation and volunteerism, stimulate stability and effectiveness, and encourage prevention as well as remediation. The foundation's Web site features current financial information, grant and scholarship guidelines and limitations, FAQs, recent foundation news, links to additional resources, donor information, a downloadable contributions form, and a contact form.

The Greater Green Bay Area Community Foundation (http://www.ggbcf.org)
The Greater Green Bay Area Community Foundation provides assistance to worthy charities serving the people of Brown, Door, Kewaunee, and Oconto Counties, Wisconsin. The foundation supports Personal Charitable Gift Funds which allows donors to direct their donations to nonprofits that fit their needs. The foundation also administers a number of scholarships to qualifying students. The foundation's Web site features listing of the available funds, scholarship details, recent grants lists, and contact information.

Greater Milwaukee Foundation (http://www.greatermilwaukeefoundation.org/)
Established in 1915, making it one of the first community foundations in the United States, the Greater Milwaukee Foundation is comprised of a number of individual funds. The foundation makes grants in six areas: arts and culture, education, employment and training, health and human services, community economic development, and conservation and historic preservation. The foundation limits its grantmaking "to projects that offer a significant improvement" to the lives of the people living in Milwaukee, Waukesha, Ozaukee, and Washington Counties. Grants made outside this area are based upon donor recommendations. The foundation's Web site features a history of the foundation, application procedures, recent grants lists, information for prospective donors, an electronic form for requesting the foundation's annual report, details on funding criteria, and contact information.

La Crosse Community Foundation (http://www.laxcommfoundation.com)
The La Crosse Community Foundation seeks to enrich the quality of life in the greater La Crosse, Wisconsin area. The foundation supports "programs and activities of economic, educational, social, and cultural nonprofit organizations" through grants and scholarships. During the quarterly foundation meetings, an issue of primary concern is decided upon, and grants strive to address this focus. The foundation's Web site includes a complete list of specific scholarships for individuals, donor and financial information, and an online contact form for grantseekers.

M & M Area Community Foundation (http://www.mmcommunityfoundation.org/)
M & M Area Community Foundation strives to promote the spirit of philanthropy and meet the needs of the people of Menominee County, Michigan, and Marinette County, Wisconsin. A variety of funds provide support in the areas of education, the environment, and cultural, recreational, and charitable purposes. The foundation's Web site features a list of current funds, donor and applicant information, and contact information.

Racine Community Foundation (http://www.racinecf.org)
The mission of the Racine Community Foundation is to serve all of Racine County by actively seeking, receiving, and administering philanthropic funds to meet changing community needs and to serve the charitable interests of donors. Current areas of interest include arts and culture, the environment, community development, health, education, and human services. The foundation's Web site features information about the foundation's grantmaking programs, application criteria, and contact information.

St. Croix Valley Community Foundation (http://www.scvcf.org/)
Founded in 1995, the St. Croix Valley Community Foundation serves the communities of St. Croix Valley in Wisconsin and Minnesota with a goal of "strengthening the community of communities." The foundation's fields of interest include education, arts, the environment, civic affairs, and emergency human needs. The foundation's Web site features the foundation's most recent annual report, financial data, board and staff lists, and a form to request more information.

WYOMING

Community Foundation of Jackson Hole (http://www.cfjacksonhole.org/)
The Community Foundation of Jackson Hole is committed to "enhancing philanthropy and strengthening the sense of community in the Jackson Hole, Wyoming area by providing a permanent source of funding and other support for nonprofit organizations and scholarship recipients." The foundation assists donors in maximizing the impact of their charitable giving, manages permanent endowments in response to donors' wishes, provides and monitors competitive grants, and holds workshops for local nonprofit organizations. The foundation's Web site features financial information, comprehensive listings of Jackson Hole-area charitable organizations, contact information, grantmaking guidelines, and application forms.

Wyoming Community Foundation (http://www.wycf.org)
The Wyoming Community Foundation, established in 1989, strives "to ensure and enhance the quality of life for present and future generations of Wyoming people." The foundation focuses its grants in the general areas of arts and culture, civic projects, education, conservation and natural resources, and health and human services. The foundation favors giving in two areas: prevention and early intervention for high-risk children and families and community-based organizations that address physical, social, and economic issues at the grassroots level. The foundation's Web site features application guidelines, information for donors, a list of the foundation's board and staff, related links, and contact information.

APPENDIX E

Corporate Grantmakers on the Web

Abbott Laboratories Fund (IL)
(http://www.abbott.com/community/community_relations.html)
The Abbott Laboratories Fund makes grants to nonprofit organizations in the areas of health and welfare, education, culture, art, and civic and public policy. Priority is given to organizations that serve Abbott communities, institutions that provide education or service to present or potential Abbott employees, and organizations with activities directed toward the support of professions that directly or indirectly provide healthcare or other services in fields related to Abbott's primary areas of operation, including the basic sciences, clinical and laboratory medicine, and pharmacy, nursing, and nutrition. The fund generally gives preference to requests for one-time contributions and for programmatic and operating purposes. Its guidelines preclude it from making grants for individuals, purely social organizations, political parties or candidates, religious organizations, advertising, symposia and conferences, ticket purchases, memberships, or business-related purposes. In addition to general facts about the fund's giving, the fund's Web site contains program guidelines, application instructions, and contact information.

Acme Markets (ID) (http://www.acmemarkets.com/acme/pr/pr_main.asp)
Acme Markets' community giving program includes the donation of funds, goods, and services to nonprofit organizations in the company's market area (Delaware, New Jersey, and Philadelphia) and national charitable organizations, such as the Ronald McDonald House and the Susan G. Komen Breast Cancer Foundation. Additionally, Acme Markets supports local charities and events through a gift certificate program and holiday food donations. Details on these philanthropic endeavors and contact information are available on Acme's Web site.

ADC Telecommunications (MN) (http://www.adc.com/About_ADC/community/index.jsp)
Based in Minneapolis, Minnesota, ADC Telecommunications is a global supplier of voice, video, and data systems and solutions for television, cable television, Internet, broadcast, wireless, and private communications networks. The ADC Foundation provides support in the areas of math, science, and technology education; access to technology; economic

self-sufficiency; and arts and culture within cities or municipalities where ADC Telecommunications has significant numbers of employees. The foundation also matches gifts by ADC Telecommunications employees and supports organizations where employees volunteer through the Dollars for Doers Program. The foundation's Web site provides information on eligible programs and geographic locations, guidelines for submitting a letter of inquiry, a grant recipient list, an online annual report, and contact information.

Adobe Systems, Inc. (CA) (http://www.adobe.com/aboutadobe/philanthropy/main.html)
The San Jose, California-based Adobe Systems, Inc. provides software solutions for network publishing. Through its giving programs, Adobe supports primary and secondary schools and qualified nonprofit organizations/NGOs in the United States and internationally with donations of its latest software. The program is managed in partnership with Gifts In Kind International, and a nominal processing and shipping fee is charged for all software donations. Adobe makes cash grants through its Community Investment Grant Program to nonprofit organizations dedicated to breaking the cycle of poverty, specifically hunger and homelessness, and to K–12 schools in San Jose/Silicon Valley, California, or Seattle/King County, Washington. Adobe also offers free software training programs for teachers and nonprofit organizations and a Volunteer Request Program through which schools and nonprofit organizations in select areas can request employee volunteer support for community activities. Adobe's Web site provides program descriptions, geographic restrictions, application guidelines, downloadable application forms, an online annual report, and contact information.

Aetna Foundation (CT) (http://www.aetna.com/foundation/)
As the Hartford-based insurance giant's primary philanthropic vehicle, the Aetna Foundation seeks "to help build healthy communities by funding initiatives that improve the quality of life where our employees and customers work and live." The foundation's giving focuses broadly on health, diversity, and voluntarism. The foundation's regional Community Grants Program supports organizations that address critical health issues in Aetna's six business regions. Grantmaking currently is limited to proposals submitted by a request for proposal or by invitation only. Aetna also matches its employees' gifts to charities and makes grants to organizations where employees volunteer. The foundation's Web site provides program overviews, funding guidelines, the current RFP for the Community Grants Program, grants lists, news features and updates on foundation initiatives, and a listing of business regions and foundation contacts.

AFC Enterprises, Inc.(GA) (http://www.afce.com/culture/community.html)
AFC Enterprises, Inc. is a restaurant and franchising company whose brands include Popeyes Chicken, Church's Chicken, Cinnabon, Seattle's Best Coffee, and Torrefazione Italia Coffee. AFC Enterprises provides time, resources, and money to national and international charities that are aligned with its business strategies. Giving is focused on housing, youth, and education. The AFC Foundation does not accept any unsolicited requests for support. The foundation's funding recipients include Habitat for Humanity, Boys and Girls Clubs of America, United Negro College Fund, and the Hispanic Association of Colleges and Universities. AFC's Web site provides an overview of the company's giving programs and details on specific programs offered by the different franchise brands.

Agilent Technologies, Inc. (CA) (http://www.agilent.com/philanthropy/)
Palo Alto, California-based Agilent Technologies, Inc.'s corporate giving programs are focused on improving science and mathematics education around the world. The Agilent Technologies Donations Program and the Agilent Technologies Foundation focus on elementary and secondary education and support programs that actively support the company's pre-university education objective: "to improve student achievement in mathematics and science, and increase the number of women and underrepresented populations who study and teach technical subjects." Agilent also offers a University Philanthropic Grants Program which provides equipment grants for universities and four-year colleges. Agilent's corporate education initiatives are international, national, and/or regional in

scope. The Agilent Technologies Foundation also provides disaster relief grants. Additionally, organizations near an Agilent Technologies location may be eligible for a local grant from that site. Grants from Agilent originate with invited proposals or through a request for proposals process; the company does not accept unsolicited proposals. Agilent's Web site provides details on the different funding programs and the donations process, guidelines for submitting letters of inquiry, lists of grant recipients, and regional contact information.

Alcoa Foundation (PA) (http://www.alcoa.com/global/en/community/foundation.asp)
The Alcoa Foundation is the philanthropic arm of Pittsburgh, Pennsylvania-based Alcoa, a leading producer of aluminum. The foundation gives priority consideration to programs and organizations in or near communities where Alcoa plants or offices are located. The foundation's global grantmaking is guided by "areas of excellence," including conservation and sustainability, safe and healthy children and families, global education and workplace skills, and business and community partnerships. Corporate contributions are also available for local grants in certain instances. The foundation generally does not respond to unsolicited proposals that are not recommended by an Alcoa location contact. The foundation's Web site provides giving guidelines; foundation news; details on special initiatives; the most recent "Community Investment Report," which includes a list of funded programs and information on employee volunteer programs and disaster relief grants; and a complete list of Alcoa operating locations with contact information.

The Aleut Foundation (AK) (http://www.aleutcorp.com/found.html)
The Aleut Foundation is a nonprofit organization funded by the Aleut Corporation, a Native corporation established in 1972 under the terms of the Alaska Native Claims Settlement Act. The Anchorage, Alaska-based foundation supports the economic and social needs of Alaska Natives, particularly those Natives living in the Aleut region, by offering programs that promote their socioeconomic stability and cultural awareness. These programs include: the Scholarship Program, the Job Referral Program, and the Cultural Preservation Program. Visitors to the Web site will find detailed eligibility criteria, scholarship application instructions and forms, and information on the Aleut Corporation and Aleut culture.

Alliant Energy Foundation (WI) (http://www.alliantenergy.com/community/charity.htm)
The Madison, Wisconsin-based Alliant Energy Foundation provides funding to organizations within the territory where Alliant Energy has a significant business presence and in communities where Alliant Energy employees live and work. The foundation focuses on the following areas: human needs, education, culture and the arts, civic service, and nature. The Web site provides eligibility guidelines, application instructions and a downloadable application form, the annual giving report, and contact information. The site also provides information on other Alliant community initiatives, including employee volunteer and matching gifts programs.

The Allstate Foundation (IL) (http://www.allstate.com/foundation/)
Founded in 1952, the Northbrook, Illinois-based Allstate Foundation is an independent corporation funded by contributions from Allstate Insurance Company. The foundation provides grants to nonprofit organizations across the United States in the areas of tolerance, inclusion, and diversity, which includes programs to teach tolerance to youth, alleviate discrimination, and reduce hate crimes; safe and vital communities, which includes programs focusing on catastrophe response and mitigation, school anti-violence, and revitalization of communities; and economic empowerment, which includes financial and insurance education, economic literacy, and entrepreneurial/small business skill development initiatives for women. The foundation's Web site provides funding guidelines and procedures, national and regional contact information, information on matching grants and volunteer programs for Allstate employees, and a map of local community initiatives.

Altera Corporation (CA)
(http://www.altera.com/corporate/news_room/community/co-index.html)
The Altera Corporation of San Jose, California, supports organizations that make a meaningful impact on the future of its employees and the local community. Current priorities include K–12 education, at-risk youth, and health and human services. Funding is generally limited to the Santa Clara, San Mateo, and Alameda Counties of California. Visit Altera's Web site to learn more about funding priorities and restrictions and to find an online application and contact information.

Altria Group, Inc. (NY)
(http://www.altria.com/responsibility/04_00_ResponsibilityOver.asp)
Altria Group, Inc. has been helping to support local, national, and international communities since 1956 with its corporate contributions program. Headquartered in New York City, Altria Group strives to help people in need through "a tradition of giving back to the communities where [they] do business, and a demonstrated commitment to creativity, excellence, innovation, and diversity." Altria Group's main funding concerns are hunger relief, assistance to victims of domestic violence, and the arts. In addition, it has programs in the areas of the environment, AIDS, and humanitarian assistance. Details of each funding area, grant guidelines, and application information are available on the Altria Group's Web site.

Ameren Corporation (MO)
(http://www.ameren.com/community/adc_cm_NonProfitGrants.asp)
Ameren, an energy provider based in St. Louis, Missouri, supports community groups and organizations in its Missouri and Illinois service area through the Ameren Corporation Charitable Trust and a direct corporate giving program. The trust makes grants focusing on education, services for the youth and elderly, and the environment. The company also provides grants to civic and nonprofit organizations for energy-efficient lighting projects in public places, makes grants to youth sports teams, and supports a program to help the needy pay their energy bills. Ameren's Web site provides details on each program, funding guidelines and application information, regional contact information, and a list of recent charitable contributions.

American Eagle Outfitters Foundation (PA) (http://www.ae.com/corp/foundation.htm)
Since 1998 the American Eagle Outfitters Foundation of Warrendale, Pennsylvania has been committed to giving back to the customers and communities that have contributed to the company's success. In the past, the foundation has supported teen and college student programs that either foster civic engagement, render safe and nourishing places for teens, embrace diversity, or encourages youth development. The foundation fulfills its mission by making grants in communities where the company operates. The foundation's Web site features information on program interests, restrictions, and contact information.

American Electric Power Company, Inc. (OH)
(http://www.aep.com/about/corpgivingandeduc/default.htm)
The Columbus, Ohio-based American Electric Power Company, Inc. (AEP) maintains corporate giving programs in the areas of education, the environment, and human services, such as hunger, housing, health, and safety. The company makes grants and in-kind donations to nonprofit organizations that benefit communities within AEP's service territory in Michigan, Indiana, Ohio, Kentucky, West Virginia, Virginia, Tennessee, Texas, Arkansas, Louisiana, Oklahoma, or communities with major AEP facilities. AEP's Web site provides grant guidelines, application procedures, contact information, an online version of the annual report, information on AEP employee volunteer and matching gifts programs, and details on the company's educational programs, including workshops, initiatives, and resources for teachers and students.

American Express Foundation (NY)
(http://home3.americanexpress.com/corp/philanthropy/)

The New York City-based American Express Company's philanthropic program includes the activities of the American Express Foundation and a direct corporate giving program, which provide support to U.S. nonprofits and organizations outside the United States that can document nonprofit status. The company makes grants in three program areas: community service, with funding primarily supporting the volunteer efforts of employees and advisors in their local communities; cultural heritage, with the twin themes of protecting the built and natural environment and supporting art and culture unique to countries and regions; and economic independence, with an emphasis on supporting initiatives that encourage, develop, and sustain economic self-reliance. In addition to general program information, application guidelines, and contact information, the foundation's Web site features a list of grant recipients, descriptions of current major initiatives, and the company's philanthropic contributions report.

American Express Minnesota Philanthropic Program (MN)
(http://home3.americanexpress.com/corp/philanthropy/)

Based in Minneapolis, Minnesota, the American Express Minnesota Philanthropic Program works to support the communities in which employees live and work. The three-part program is made up of community support, philanthropic giving, and a volunteer program. Community support includes donations to the United Way and supporting the community-oriented nonprofit efforts of financial advisors across the country. The grant program awards gifts in three areas of interest to nonprofits in the Twin Cities and throughout greater Minnesota: economic independence, particularly programs that serve youth, build awareness of career and job options, and educate people on the basics of business and economics; art/cultural heritage, focusing on arts and major cultural institutions and projects; and community service grants, which support employee volunteer efforts and selected service groups. The volunteer program supports employee volunteer efforts and organizes their participation. The program's Web site includes application guidelines, restrictions, and deadlines.

American Power Conversion Corporation (RI)
(http://www.apcc.com/corporate/contributions.cfm)

Based in West Kingston, Rhode Island, the American Power Conversion Corporation's Contributions Program supports organizations and services in regions where the corporation has a significant business presence. The program's main funding interest is technological education for primary, secondary, and university students, supported through financial aid to area school districts, equipment donation, and specific educational program support. The corporation's Web site provides funding criteria, limitations, and an online funding request form.

American Savings Foundation (CT) (http://www.americansavingsfoundation.org)

The American Savings Foundation was established by the board of directors of American Savings Bank (now part of Banknorth Connecticut) in 1995. Now an independent, permanent charitable endowment, the foundation awards grants and scholarships within the Connecticut towns served by American Savings Bank. The foundation's grant program supports organizations and programs that improve the quality of life for residents of the communities served by the foundation, with a special emphasis on the needs of children, youth, and families. Grant program priority areas are education, human services, and arts and culture. Scholarships are awarded to college, university, and technical/vocational program students. The foundation's Web site features funding and application guidelines, a list of the towns served by the foundation, and listings of recent grants.

AMERIGROUP Charitable Foundation (VA) (http://www.amerigroupcorp.com/Foundation/)

The Virginia-based AMERIGROUP Charitable Foundation is committed to communities where the company operates and fosters research and debate on healthcare policies affecting low-income families and people with disabilities. The foundation focuses on three areas of giving: fostering access to healthcare, safe and healthy children and families, and promoting community improvement and healthy neighborhoods. Visitors to the foundation's Web site can view funding priorities, grant limitations, a download a copy of the grant application, and contact information.

AMR/American Airlines Foundation (TX) (http://www.amrcorp.com/corpinfo.htm)
The AMR/American Airlines Foundation supports nonprofit organizations in the communities that the AMR Corporation serves, particularly its hub cities of Dallas/Fort Worth, Texas; Chicago, Illinois; Miami, Florida; and San Juan, Puerto Rico. The Texas-based foundation provides organizations with air transportation and monetary support, which is focused on four areas: community development, arts and culture, education, and health and welfare. Due to the financial crisis facing the airline industry, the foundation is forced to suspend all cash grants at this time. Requests for air transportation will be considered, albeit on a limited basis until the airline returns to profitability. The foundation's Web site provides grant guidelines, instructions for proposal submissions, and contact information.

Amway Corporation (MI) (http://www.amway.com/OurStory/o-comm.asp)
The Amway Corporation, a direct seller organization, supports the areas of human services, education, the environment, arts and culture, and sports through its charitable programs. Amway provides philanthropic benefits to a variety of organizations worldwide. The Community Involvement section of Amway's Web site features examples of funded projects and an online contact form for inquiries.

AOL Time Warner Foundation (NY) (http://www.aoltwfoundation.org/)
The New York City-based AOL Time Warner Foundation is dedicated "to helping young people acquire the 21st Century literacy skills they need to succeed at school, at work, and in their communities." Through grants, employee involvement, and other corporate contributions, the foundation works to promote awareness of the importance of a technology-enriched education and supports programs in the out-of-school hours that help young people ages 13-19 acquire technological and other skills. Except in very special circumstances, the foundation does not fund unsolicited proposals. The foundation's Web site features a list of organizations and projects that are not eligible for funding, information on the foundation's many programs, links to related resources, details on upcoming events, and contact information.

Apogee Enterprises, Inc. (MN) (http://www.apog.com/community_involvement.asp)
Apogee Enterprises, Inc. makes a variety of charitable contributions through employee involvement in the United Way, the Apogee & Subsidiaries In-Service Team (ASIST) program, and other charitable donations in the Minneapolis/St. Paul area, as well as other communities where Apogee is located. The Community page of Apogee's Web site features lists of recent events organized by the ASIST program and contact information.

Applied Materials, Inc. (CA) (http://www.appliedmaterials.com/about/community.html)
Applied Materials, Inc. of Santa Clara, California, created a corporate philanthropy program to make a positive social contribution in areas where the company has major operations. Grants are focused in three giving areas: education, civic development, and arts and culture. The company's Web site includes grant guidelines, a proposal resource kit that includes application instructions and contact information, an online version of the company's "Global Citizenship Report," and information on the company's giving initiatives.

ARAMARK Corporation (PA)
(http://www.aramark.com/aboutaramark.asp?topic=community)
ARAMARK Corporation, a Philadelphia-based managed services corporation, supports a wide range of projects in the communities where it is active. Many of these projects focus on youth development and education and include support of the Big Brothers Big Sisters of America, literacy programs, and college scholarships for the children of ARAMARK employees. The company's Web site features an overview of the company's community

involvement activities, an article featuring a recently funded organization, and contact information.

Ashland Inc. (KY) (http://www.ashland.com/community)
Ashland Inc. is a diversified company headquartered in Covington, Kentucky, with operations in specialty chemical production and distribution, motor oil and car care products, and highway construction. The Ashland Inc. Corporate Contributions is the company's focal point for philanthropic efforts. The foundation seeks to address social, educational, and community-related issues in the geographic regions where the company has facilities. Funding is focused on education, arts and culture, the environment, and health and human services. The foundation does not provide an application and does not seek requests for funding. The Web site offers an overview of the foundation's funding areas, a downloadable foundation brochure, contact information, and details on other corporate giving programs.

Aspect Telecommunications Corporation (CA) (http://www.aspect.com/company/community.cfm)
The San Jose, California-based Aspect Telecommunications Corporation, a supplier of call center products, created the Aspect Community Commitment Fund, a direct corporate giving program, to support the education and healthy development of children in the communities where Aspect employees live and work through grants to local nonprofit organizations and schools. The fund provides monetary support for projects that help children up to age 14 "achieve specific results indicative of healthy development and educational success." The Community Commitment area of the company's Web site features contact information and details on the company's giving program, educational partnerships, and employee giving and volunteering programs.

AT&T Foundation (NY) (http://www.att.com/foundation/)
As the principal philanthropic arm of the AT&T Corporation, the AT&T Foundation makes grants in the United States and throughout the world in the program areas of education, arts and culture, civic and community service, and local grants. The foundation focuses its grantmaking on programs that serve the needs of people in communities where AT&T has a significant business presence, use technology in inventive ways, and feature the participation of AT&T employees as contributors and/or volunteers. The foundation generally awards funds through invitational programs or through projects that it proactively develops with nonprofit organizations. Unsolicited applications are reviewed but rarely supported. The foundation's Web site features detailed program descriptions, application guidelines and procedures, a searchable index of funded organizations, FAQs, and contact information.

Attachmate Corporation (WA) (http://cooljobs.attachmate.com/cooljobs/community.asp)
The Bellevue, Washington-based Attachmate Corporation, a supplier of enterprise information access and management software and services, provides support through its corporate contributions program to "qualifying organizations that are worthy, relevant, and have a tangible impact on our community." Attachmate donates money and equipment to many different nonprofit organizations, including those focused on health, social services, education, the environment, the arts, and other areas. Attachmate's Web site features details on the company's giving programs, lists of funded organizations, and contact information.

Autodesk, Inc. (CA) (http://usa.autodesk.com/adsk/servlet/index?siteID=123112&id=1064603)
Design software and digital content company Autodesk, Inc., located in San Rafael, California, established its Community Relations Program in 1989 to support the communities where Autodesk employees live and work. The company provides monetary and product donations to nonprofit organizations focused on art and culture, civic and community issues, education and technology, the environment, and health and human services. The company's product donations program is managed by Gifts in Kind International.

Autodesk's Web site provides guidelines and application procedures for financial and product grants, information on the company's employee volunteer program, and contact information.

Aventis Foundation (http://www.aventis-foundation.org)
The Aventis Foundation, formerly the Hoechst Foundation, seeks "to promote international, interdisciplinary, and future-oriented projects at the interfaces between culture, science, business, politics, and society." The foundation funds projects that analyze "ways to create a sustainable future at international and interdisciplinary levels." The foundation's grant program generally provides support to major international and multi-year projects through its three key projects: fine arts, civil society, and science. The foundation's Web site features a mission statement, details on featured projects, annual reports, application procedures, and contact information.

Aventis Pharmaceuticals, Inc. (NJ)
(http://www.aventispharma-us.com/main/0,1003,EN-US-28671-45824—,00.html)
Aventis Pharmaceuticals, Inc. is actively committed to the improvement of public health. The company supports activities in the communities in which it operates and its employees live. The Aventis Pharmaceuticals Giving Program has two primary focus areas. Health Initiatives supports programs that provide health and educational resources to the underserved population in the areas of breast and lung cancer, deep vein thrombosis, diabetes, and osteoporosis. Education Initiatives supports programs to combat obesity in children and programs to promote tolerance and acceptance. Aventis' Web site provides grant guidelines, application procedures, contact information, and information on the company's donation of in-kind services and products, associate matching gifts program, and other initiatives.

Avista Corporation (WA) (http://www.avistacorp.com/about/community/programs.asp)
The Avista Corporation's Community Connection Programs include the Avista Foundation and the Minds in Motion Scholarship. The foundation is the company's primary charitable giving vehicle and provides support in the geographic areas served by Avista Utilities (eastern Washington; northern Idaho; southern Oregon; Sanders County, Montana; and South Lake Tahoe, California). The foundation focuses its support on programs in the areas of education, vulnerable and limited income populations, and economic and cultural vitality. The foundation's Web site features funding guidelines, application procedures, a downloadable application form, contact information, and scholarship program information, including participating colleges and universities.

Avon Products Foundation, Inc. (NY)
(http://www.avoncompany.com/women/avonfoundation)
The Avon Products Foundation, Inc., located in New York City, is dedicated to improving the lives of women and their families by supporting programs that help provide economic opportunity and physical and emotional well-being. The foundation also supports women's health through collaborative efforts with the Avon Breast Cancer Crusade, a cause-related marketing initiative of Avon Products. The foundation focuses on cities and regions with a large concentration of Avon representatives and business operations. Avon's Web site features guidelines for the foundation's economic opportunity and breast cancer funding programs, lists of funded programs, contact information, and information on the company's other giving programs.

Balance Bar Company (NY) (http://www.balance.com/grants/default.asp)
The Balance Bar Company makes "four-month grants of financial support for enthusiasts and amateur athletes who prioritize balancing mind and body." The program is open to U.S. residents over the age of 18, and both individuals and teams are eligible to apply. The company's Web site provides a definition of a mind/body activity with examples of such activities, terms and conditions of grants, guidelines for submitting an online statement of purpose, and descriptions and photos of current and previous grant recipients.

Bank of America Foundation (NC) (http://www.bankofamerica.com/foundation/)
The Bank of America Foundation directs charitable giving on behalf of the Bank of America Corporation. The foundation "focuses resources on helping children and families succeed in life and neighborhoods flourish" in the bank's service area. The foundation's primary funding focus is education, with grants going to nonprofit and educational organizations for early childhood development, financial literacy, and professional development for teachers. The foundation's secondary focus is community revitalization, with funding available to nonprofit organizations for affordable housing and workforce development projects. The foundation's Web site provides details on the foundation's funding focus, application guidelines and forms, regional contact information, lists of state-specific contributions, FAQs, and information on educational partnerships and community outreach initiatives.

C.R. Bard Foundation (NJ) (http://www.crbard.com/about/foundation.html)
The C.R. Bard Foundation, established in Murray Hill, New Jersey, in 1987, supports charitable organizations that benefit the community where the healthcare products company is located, as well as Bard's employees, their families, and organizations in which they are active. The foundation provides funding in the areas of healthcare and social welfare, education, and arts, cultural, and community life. Within the healthcare category, the foundation primarily supports organizations or programs specializing in the fields of vascular medicine, urology, and oncology. The foundation's Web site includes an overview of the foundation's giving interests, a list of donations, information on the company's employee matching gifts program, and company contact information.

Barnes & Noble, Inc. (NY)
(http://www.barnesandnobleinc.com/company/codonation/co_donation.html)
Barnes & Noble, Inc. supports nonprofit organizations in the areas of education (K–12), the arts, and literacy through donations, sponsorships, and advertising support in communities where the company operates bookstores. The company's Web site provides descriptions of supported programs; national, regional, and local proposal procedures and contact information; a searchable store locator; and information on community events organized and sponsored by the company.

Baseball Tomorrow Fund (NY) (http://www.baseballtomorrowfund.com)
A joint initiative between Major League Baseball and the Major League Baseball Players Association, the Baseball Tomorrow Fund works "to promote and enhance the growth of baseball in the United States, Canada, and throughout the world by funding programs, fields, and equipment purchases to encourage and maintain youth participation in the game." Grants from the fund may be used to finance a new program, expand or improve an existing program, undertake a new collaborative effort, or obtain facilities or equipment necessary for youth baseball or softball programs. The fund's Web site provides grant application guidelines and forms, a list of grant recipients, news updates and feature stories, and contact information. Visitors can also sign up to receive the fund's newsletter.

Eddie Bauer, Inc. (WA) (http://eddiebauer.com/about/eb_philanthropy.asp)
Based in Redmond, Washington, Eddie Bauer, Inc. makes grants and in-kind donations through its community relations and corporate giving programs in areas where the apparel and home furnishing company does business. Support is provided in the categories of education, the environment, and empowering women. Education initiatives include the Eddie Bauer Scholars Program, which provides support to college-bound youth with a financial need through partnerships with educational institutions. The company's Web site provides an overview of each funding area with examples of funded projects, instructions and contact information for submitting requests for funding or merchandise, and details on the company's community volunteering programs.

Baxter International, Inc. (IL)
(http://www.baxter.com/investors/citizenship/foundation/index.html)
Baxter International, Inc., located in Deerfield, Illinois, is a global medical products and services company. The Baxter International Foundation, the company's primary philanthropic vehicle, funds programs that benefit the entire health field, including projects that improve quality, cost-effectiveness, access, or education. The foundation makes grants in communities throughout the world, often where large numbers of Baxter employees live and work. The foundation also administers a prize program to recognize excellence in community service and research and offers programs to support the philanthropic efforts of Baxter employees. Baxter's Web site provides information on the foundation's priorities and application procedures, foundation news, and contact information.

Bayer Foundation (PA) (http://www.bayerus.com/about/community/index.html)
Bayer Corporation, headquartered in Pittsburgh, Pennsylvania, develops healthcare products, chemicals, and imaging technologies. The Bayer Foundation supports the communities where the company is located and awards grants in three areas: civic and community programs, science education and workforce development, and the arts, arts education, and culture. The grant application process is decentralized; requests are submitted to and reviewed by Site Contributions Committees at local Bayer facilities. The company's Web site includes grant application procedures, a list of Bayer sites with contact information, examples of funded projects, and information on other company and employee contributions programs.

BEA Foundation (NJ) (http://www.bea.com/about/community/index.shtml)
The Liberty Corner, New Jersey-based BEA Foundation is the philanthropic arm of the BEA Corporation, an application infrastructure software company. The foundation supports "innovative programs that give our youngest children a strong start in life and a solid foundation for their future success" through community programs and grants in areas where the company has a significant employee population. The foundation's community initiatives include corporate volunteer programs, software product donations, and employee matching gift programs. The foundation's grant program supports health and education initiatives for pre-school aged children. Visitors to foundation's the Web site will find grant eligibility requirements, a listing of recent grant recipients, an application timeline, a grant application checklist form, and information on the foundation's other initiatives.

Bechtel Foundation (CA) (http://www.bechtel.com/bechfoun.html)
Bechtel Group, Inc., located in San Francisco, California, develops and manages capital projects and facilities worldwide. The Bechtel Foundation supports communities where the company has offices or major projects. The foundation supports the volunteer activities of Bechtel employees; provides funding to business, technical, and engineering students at selected universities; offers college scholarships for the children of its employees; and matches the contributions its employees make to U.S. universities. The foundation also supports math and science education and global understanding programs. All grants are generated internally by Bechtel's office and project managers. The foundation's Web site features a brief overview of the foundation's activities, contact information, links to funded programs, and examples of other corporate community initiatives.

BellSouth Foundation (GA) (http://www.bellsouthcorp.com/bsf/)
The BellSouth Foundation seeks to improve outcomes and stimulate active learning for students in elementary and secondary education in Alabama, Florida, Georgia, Kentucky, Louisiana, Mississippi, North Carolina, South Carolina, and Tennessee. In its 2002-2005 grantmaking activity, the foundation "seeks imaginative strategies to drive deeper learning and increase opportunities that lead to better lives for all students." Although the foundation invests the majority of its grantmaking funds in Special Initiatives through a targeted request for proposal process, it also awards a limited number of Opportunity Grants each year in response to unsolicited proposals. BellSouth's Web site features information on the

foundation's activities, including detailed program descriptions; Opportunity Grant guidelines, deadlines, and online application forms; and a searchable database of funded projects.

The Ben & Jerry's Foundation (VT) (http://www.benjerry.com/foundation/index.html)
The giving arm of Ben & Jerry's Homemade, Inc. ice cream company, the Ben & Jerry's Foundation offers competitive grants to nonprofit grassroots organizations throughout the United States that facilitate progressive social change by addressing the underlying conditions of societal and environmental problems. Projects supported by the foundation must "help ameliorate an unjust or destructive situation by empowering constituents; facilitate leadership development and strengthen the self-empowerment efforts of those who have traditionally been disenfranchised in our society; and support movement building and collective action." The company's Community Action Teams also distribute small grants to community groups within the state of Vermont. The Foundation area of the Ben & Jerry's Web site features funding guidelines, application instructions, a downloadable letter of interest cover page, recent grants lists, and online versions of the foundation's annual reports.

Berkshire Hathaway, Inc. (NE) (http://www.berkshirehathaway.com/sholdqa.html)
Berkshire Hathaway, Inc. shareholders can make charitable contributions to designated organizations through the corporation's Shareholder-Designated Contributions Program. The company's Web site provides information about the program, including limitations and guidelines for shareholders making a contribution, and contact information.

Berlex Foundation, Inc. (NJ) (http://www.berlex-foundation.org/)
The Hackensack, New Jersey-based Berlex Foundation, Inc. was established in 1986 by Berlex Laboratories, Inc. as a nonprofit organization dedicated to fostering education and encouraging innovative research in the field of reproductive medicine. The foundation supports a wide spectrum of awards and educational programs, including the Berlex Scholar Award in Basic Science Research, the Berlex Scholar Award in Clinical Research, the Berlex Faculty Development Award, and the Reproductive Scientist Development Program. In addition, the foundation annually sponsors the C.D. Christian Lectureship at the annual meeting of the Society for Gynecologic Investigation. The foundation's Web site provides guidelines and application requirements for each program, lists of awardees, links to related resources, and contact information.

Berry Petroleum Company (CA) (http://www.bry.com/givingback.htm)
Since 1986, the Berry Petroleum Company of Bakersfield, California, has been awarding college scholarships to local high school students. The company's Web site features a listing of recent awardees, eligibility criteria, and contact information.

Best Buy (MN) (hhttp://communications.bestbuy.com/communityrelations/default.asp)
Minneapolis-based Best Buy's main philanthropic vehicle is the Best Buy Children's Foundation. The foundation "dedicates its resources in two primary ways: supporting the development and delivery of innovative, technology-based educational curriculum and content, and making education accessible to graduating high school seniors through Best Buy Scholarships." Grants are provided to nonprofit organizations for K–12 technology and youth programs. Scholarships are awarded on the basis of grades and community service to students in every U.S. Congressional District. The company's Web site features grant guidelines, proposal requirements, application forms, information on the scholarship program and other national partnerships, local funding programs within Minnesota, store donation programs, and other community initiatives.

BI-LO, Inc. (SC) (http://www.bi-lo.com/learn/community.htm)
BI-LO, Inc. chain of grocery stores, centers its charitable giving in South Carolina, North Carolina, Georgia, and Tennessee. BI-LO raises funds through an annual golf tournament to provide support for children's charities, hunger relief programs, and organizations that

provide educational opportunities. The BI-LO Boosters are customers who partner with the grocery store to donate funds to their favorite schools, churches, or community organizations. The company also sponsors a teacher awards program. The company's Web site provides details on BI-LO's charitable programs and contact information.

Birds Eye Foods Foundation (NY)
(http://www.birdseyefoods.com/corp/about/foundation.asp)
The Rochester, New York-based, Birds Eye Foods Foundation provides grants to nonprofit organizations operating in communities where the company has facilities or where employees are located. Primary giving areas are health, community services, education, youth, agricultural research, and cultural programs. Grant guidelines, restrictions, and contact information for various divisions and locations are included in the Philanthropy and Community Service section of the company's Web site.

Birkenstock Footprint Sandals, Inc. (CA)
(http://www.birkenstock.com/our_company/giving/community)
Located in Novato, California, Birkenstock Footprint Sandals, Inc. supports charitable causes through its corporate giving program. Birkenstock makes grants and product donations to local community nonprofits, maintains an employee matching gift program, and has a volunteer program. The Community section of Birkenstock's Web site highlights information on charitable groups that the company supports, descriptions of the company's three giving programs, guidelines and program requirements for grants and product donations, and contact information.

Blimpie International, Inc. (NY) (http://www.blimpie.com/content/more/community.php)
Since 1992, Blimpie International, Inc. sandwich franchise, has supported the Boys and Girls Club of America through its Doing Well by Doing Good program. Blimpie stores also make a variety of contributions to their local communities. These efforts are described on Blimpie's Web site, with spotlights on different community projects and events.

Blockbuster, Inc. (TX) (http://www.blockbuster.com/bb/about/community)
Blockbuster, Inc.'s community relations activities are designed to deliver mutually beneficial results for the communities it serves and the business it builds by supporting organizations that reflect a film/video focus, impact children/families, or fulfull a specific company operation objective related to diversity in employment. Blockbuster's Web site features examples of specific funding in each interest area, guidelines and limitations for funding, and contact information.

Blue Cross and Blue Shield of Massachusetts (MA)
(http://www.bcbsma.com/common/en_US/index.jsp)
The community giving programs of Blue Cross and Blue Shield of Massachusetts provide "resources to address health-related and social issues in cities and towns across Massachusetts and throughout the region." Programs such as Jump Up and Go, which helps children become more physically active and develop healthy behaviors; school partnerships; and the Blue Cross Blue Shield of Massachusetts Foundation work toward this goal. Complete grant guidelines, eligibility information, FAQs, downloadable application forms, and lists of recent grant recipients can be found on the company's Web site. Additional information is available in the About Us and Our Commitment to the Community sections of the organization's Web site.

Blue Cross and Blue Shield of Minnesota Foundation, Inc. (MI)
(http://www.bluecrossmn.com/foundation/foundation.html)
Blue Cross and Blue Shield of Minnesota began operations in 1933 and is Minnesota's oldest health plan and the nation's second oldest Blue plan. The Blue Cross and Blue Shield of Minnesota Foundation, Inc. "works with communities and organizations across the state to make a healthy difference in the lives of Minnesotans." In addition to awarding grants, the foundation also develops programs that target specific healthcare needs, including a

preventive care program for minority and ethnic youth and a program to reduce youth tobacco use. The foundation's Web site provides descriptions of the foundation's funding priorities and programs, eligibility information, application guidelines and forms, annual grants listings, and contact information.

Bob Evans Farms, Inc. (OH)
(http://www.bobevans.com/website/homepage.nsf/pages/philanthropy)
Bob Evans Farms, Inc.'s corporate giving program focuses on families and children in the communities where the restaurant and food products company does business, primarily in southeastern and central Ohio. The company is specifically interested in funding programs that "strive to provide the skills young people and adults need to become self-sufficient." Examples of funded organizations, an online corporate giving application, and contact information are available on the Bob Evans Farms Web site.

The Boeing Company (IL) (http://www.boeing.com/companyoffices/aboutus/community/)
The Chicago-headquartered Boeing Company, one of the world's leading aircraft manufacturers, aims to strengthen the communities where its employees live and work in four main areas of support: education, health and human services, arts and cultural organizations, and civic and environmental organizations. The education program receives the largest portion of company contributions and provides funding for K–12 projects and to colleges and universities. In addition to company contributions, Boeing offers the Employees Community Fund, "the world's largest employee-owned and -managed charitable fund," which provides support to programs in local communities. Employees also contribute through the company's matching gifts program. The company's Web site provides information on Boeing's many philanthropic activities, grant guidelines and application information, and contact information for local community relations offices.

Boston Globe Foundation, Inc. (MA)
(https://bostonglobe.com/community/foundation/index.stm)
The Boston Globe Foundation, Inc., one of the principal charitable arms of the Boston-based Globe Newspaper Company, focuses its funding on children and youth in the greater Boston area. As part of this mission, the foundation supports programs "that build youth leadership, support education, and forge friendships across racial, cultural, and neighborhood boundaries." Support is provided for both program and operating support, with preference given to program support. The foundation's Web site provides funding criteria, information on the application process, a description of foundation initiatives, and links to related Web sites.

BP Amoco (IL) (http://www.bp.com/environ_social/external/communities/social.asp)
Headquartered in London, England, with North American headquarters in Chicago, energy company BP Amoco supports sustainable progress programs, humanitarian efforts following natural disasters, and cultural and other major sponsorships in communities where it has operations around the world. The company's Global Social Investment program is designed to align with its business strategy; unsolicited requests for funding are not encouraged. The company's cultural and other sponsorships are limited to a small number of long-term relationships with major cultural and academic institutions. Support for community programs is provided by local business operations, which should be contacted directly for information. Additionally, through the BP Employee Matching Fund, BP Amoco supports programs to which company employees donate their money and time. The company's Web site provides details on the Employee Matching Fund, as well as examples of the company's international social investment and environmental programs.

The Bringing Hope Foundation (UT) (http://www.bringinghope.net)
The Bringing Hope Foundation was established in 1998 by the Greenbacks/All a Dollar company in Salt Lake City, Utah, as an organization dedicated to helping single mothers achieve self-reliance. The foundation currently operates programs in Utah and Arizona, with plans to expand regionally. The foundation's Web site features lists of programs and

services provided by the group, including workshops, mentoring programs, and upcoming conferences and events; true stories of single moms; an online version of the foundation's newsletter, and information on volunteer opportunities.

The Bristol-Myers Squibb Foundation, Inc. (NY)
(http://www.bms.com/sr/philanthropy/data/)
The Bristol-Myers Squibb Foundation, Inc. provides financial support in keeping with Bristol-Myers Squibb Company's commitment to extending and enhancing human life. The New York City-based foundation supports the following program areas: biomedical research, women's health education, science education, programs to help improve healthcare in developing countries, AIDS/HIV research and outreach, donations of pharmaceutical products to developing countries and victims of natural disasters, and community support in areas where the pharmaceutical company has a presence. The foundation's major initiatives include the Unrestricted Biomedical Research Grants Program, which provides funding in the areas of cancer; cardiovascular, infectious, and metabolic diseases; neuroscience; and nutrition. The foundation's Web site provides application guidelines, a list of contact addresses, information on each giving category, and details on employee matching gift and volunteer programs.

Brookshire Grocery Company (TX)
(http://www.brookshires.com/company/community.asp)
The Brookshire Grocery Company, based in Tyler, Texas, sponsors assorted community service projects, including adopt-a-school programs, food drives, and other programs, events, and organizations. Support is given in areas where Brookshire stores operate. The company's Web site provides an overview of supported programs and a telephone number for requesting further information.

Burger King Corporation (FL) (http://www.burgerking.com/community/index.html)
The Burger King Corporation contributions program sponsors the BK Academies, a national network of academies designed for students who have already dropped out of school or who are functioning below their potential in a traditional school setting. Through the Burger King/McLamore Foundation, the company helps provide college and vocational school scholarships to high school seniors throughout the United States, Puerto Rico, and Canada. Burger King also participates in Second Harvest, donating food products and paper goods to food banks. The company's Web site provides an overview of the company's community giving and service programs and application guidelines for the Burger King/McLamore Foundation and BK Scholars program.

Cadence Design Systems (CA)
(http://www.cadence.com/company/community-involvement.html)
Cadence Design Systems of San Jose, California, provides funding, in-kind donations, and volunteer support through its community affairs program. Direct corporate cash grants are focused on organizations that serve the communities in the greater Santa Clara Valley. General information on grant guidelines, applications, and the review process are available on the company's Web site. Additionally, Cadence Design sponsors a Matching Gift Program for organizations located where employees live and work that focuses on the areas of K–12 education, higher education, arts and culture, health and human services, the environment, and animal rights and welfare. The company also offers support to community programs through a bowling tournament and provides university donations and scholarships. The company's Web site provides details on each of these giving programs.

California Pizza Kitchen, Inc. (CA) (http://www.cpk.com/cpk.cfm?page=about)
As part of its community relations program, California Pizza Kitchen, Inc. provides schools with Student of the Month Certificates and Pizza Passes, which can be used to award exceptional students throughout the year. Additionally, California Pizza Kitchen helps schools raise money through CPKids fundraising programs. Interested parties should

contact the manager at the nearest restaurant location; a list of locations can be found on the company's Web site.

The Candle Foundation (CA)
(http://www.candle.com/www1/cnd/portal/CNDportal_Channel_Master/0,2179,2683_2923,00.ht ml)
Candle Corporation, a software and services company, makes contributions through the El Segundo, California-based Candle Foundation. The foundation provides funding for programs in the areas of community investment, education and information dissemination, hunger and homelessness, preventive healthcare, and medical research. Support is provided to grantseekers throughout North America, with some preference given to areas in which there are Candle offices. The foundation's Web site features funding guidelines, application procedures, and the online application form.

Canon USA, Inc. (NY) (http://www.usa.canon.com/cleanearth/index.html)
Since 1990, Canon USA, Inc. has been supporting environmental efforts through its Clean Earth Campaign, based in Lake Success, New York. The program sponsors a variety of initiatives, including the Canon National Parks Science Scholars program, which provides scholarships for doctoral students doing environmental research on National Park ecosystems; the Envirothon, an environmental competition for high school students; and PBS's *Nature* series. Canon's Web site features information on the company's environmental initiatives, links to sponsored programs, and details on other community programs and regional projects.

Capital City Bank Group Foundation (FL)
(http://www.ccbg.com/website/index.cfm?pageID=38)
The Capital City Bank Group of Tallahassee, Florida, created its foundation in 1983 to support organizations in the Big Bend area. Funding goes toward "special projects and community needs." The foundation's Web site includes application guidelines and an application form, which can be submitted electronically or mailed to the foundation.

The Cargill Foundation (MN) (http://www.cargill.com/commun/found.htm)
Established by Cargill Corporation, an agriculture and food company, the Cargill Foundation focuses its resources in Minneapolis/St. Paul, home to Cargill's world headquarters. The foundation targets youth in the Minneapolis area and funds organizations and programs that focus on educational success and the development of necessary life skills that "enable socio-economically disadvantaged young people to work and thrive in a rapidly changing world." In addition to the foundation, the Cargill Citizenship Committee works in partnership with Cargill businesses to provide strategic grants to organizations serving communities where Cargill has a presence. The company also administers a Higher Education Initiative, which works to build mutually beneficial relationships with key schools, and funds scholarship programs for students living in or around communities where Cargill has a presence and for children of Cargill employees. The foundation's Web site features details on the various giving programs, funding guidelines, application procedures, and contact information.

Ceridian Corporation (MN) (http://www.ceridian.com/corp/section/0,1337,291,00.html)
Minneapolis-based Ceridian Corporation, an information services company in human resources and other markets, supports its employees' community service efforts. The company encourages employee voluntarism through volunteer recognition programs, United Way campaign events, and the Community Action Field Program, which enables employees to direct grants of up to $500 to nonprofit organizations in which they are actively involved. The company's Web site provides information on various employee volunteer programs.

Chadwick's of Boston, Inc. (MA)
(http://www.chadwicks.com/chadwicks/teacher/teacher.asp)
The department store Chadwick's of Boston, Inc. sponsors an annual Teacher of the Year award. Each year's winner and his or her school receive a cash award, as do the regional winners of the contest. Current award recipients and their institutions are listed on Chadwick's Web site, along with contact numbers for further information.

ChevronTexaco Corporation (CA) (http://www.chevrontexaco.com/social_responsibility/)
Headquartered in San Ramon, California, ChevronTexaco Corporation conducts business in a "socially responsible and ethical manner," by protecting the environment, supporting the communities where the company operates, and promoting human rights. The company's Web site features information on community partnerships in locations around the world, community news, and an online copy of the company's annual report of contributions, which includes detailed funding information and grants lists. The Web site also provides information on sponsored programs, including the ChevronTexaco Conservation Awards program, which annually recognizes outstanding contributions by individuals and organizations to the conservation of natural resources.

CIGNA Corporation (PA) (http://www.cigna.com/general/about/community/index.html)
A national employee benefits company based in Philadelphia, Pennsylvania, and Hartford, Connecticut, CIGNA Corporation's contributions program is primarily focused on preventive healthcare and well-being, with a special emphasis on women's health issues. CIGNA also supports educational, cultural, and civic efforts in communities where the company operates. The company's Web site provides information on funding interests, application guidelines and forms, a contributions report with listings of grant recipients, a contact e-mail address, and details on other corporate and employee community service initiatives.

Cinergy Foundation, Inc. (http://www.cinergy.com/Community/default.asp)
Cinergy Foundation, Inc. is the philanthropic organization of Cinergy Corp. The foundation seeks to improve the quality of life in Indiana, southwestern Ohio, and northern Kentucky communities by supporting arts and culture, lifelong learning, and healthy communities. The foundation's Web site provides thorough program descriptions and grant guidelines, an online application form, geographic considerations, examples of exemplary projects, a listing of foundation officers, and contact information.

Cingular Wireless LLC (GA)
(http://www.cingular.com/cingular/about_us/community_involvement)
Cingular Wireless LLC supports community-based programs and organizations that address educational, cultural, and social issues that affect the quality of life in the communities were the company operates. The company's Web site provides information on Cingular's charitable interests and contributions guidelines.

Cisco Systems Foundation (CA) (http://www.cisco.com/warp/public/750/fdn_home.html)
Created in 1997 with a gift from California's Cisco Systems, Inc., the Cisco Systems Foundation provides grants to organizations with "long-lasting impact on a local or global scale." Grants are awarded in communities in which Cisco Systems has a significant business presence. The foundation's Impact Grants support work in the areas of basic human needs, access to education, responsible citizenship, and technology and innovation in nonprofits. The Cisco Product Grant Program awards Cisco products to nonprofit organizations and K–12 schools. The foundation's Web site provides information on funding areas, criteria for successful grant proposals, the foundation's latest tax return, a listing of grant recipients, and information on the company's community partnerships and matching gifts program for employee contributions.

Citigroup Foundation (NY) (http://www.citigroup.com/citigroup/corporate/community/)
The Citigroup Foundation is the philanthropic arm of Citigroup Inc., a leading financial services company. Working with a global network of colleagues and partners, the

foundation provides grants in the categories of financial education, to help individuals and organizations around the world develop personal financial management skills and create a more secure financial future for themselves and their families; educating the next generation, to strengthen the quality of teaching, improve student achievement, increase access to higher education, and encourage students' creativity through arts education programs; and building communities and entrepreneurs, to improve communities where the company operates. The foundation's Web site features details on each funding area and examples of funded programs, grant guidelines and information on submitting proposals, annual reports, and information on other Citigroup giving programs.

Clorox Company Foundation (CA) (http://www.clorox.com/company/foundation/)
The Clorox Company Foundation is dedicated to improving the quality of life in communities where employees of the Clorox Company live and work. The foundation makes grants primarily in Oakland, California, its headquarters community, and in areas where company facilities are located. The foundation currently has two focus areas: education/youth development and culture/civic programs. The foundation also offers an Arts Mini-Grants Initiative to provide small grants to assist the Oakland nonprofit cultural community. The foundation's Web site contains grant guidelines and application instructions, the foundation's annual report, and contact information.

CNET, Inc. Community Involvement Program (CA) (http://www.cnet.com/aboutcnet/0-13620.html)
Located in San Francisco, California, the CNET, Inc. Community Involvement Program is the philanthropic effort of technology media company CNET, Inc. The program is committed to assisting nonprofit organizations that work to improve the education and computer skills of members of the communities in which the company's employees live and work. The program concentrates its involvement on education, health and human services, arts and culture, and civic affairs and community service. Most contributions are made to San Francisco area organizations, while some support goes to national groups. CNET does not provide large financial donations or corporate sponsorship funds, but it does make in-kind gifts and organizes collections for Goodwill drives. The company's Web site provides program guidelines, application procedures, and contact information.

The Coca-Cola Foundation, Inc. (GA) (http://www2.coca-cola.com/citizenship/foundation_coke.html)
The philanthropic arm of the Coca-Cola Company, the Coca-Cola Foundation, Inc. is located in Atlanta, Georgia. The foundation's goal is to "improve the quality of life in the community and enhance individual opportunity through education." Funding is focused on education, particularly in higher education, classroom teaching and learning, and global education. The program provides support for public and private colleges and universities, elementary and secondary schools, teacher training programs, educational programs for minority students, and global education programs. The foundation's Web site offers an overview of the foundation's funding interests, grant guidelines, a downloadable application, and contact information. The Web site also features information and contact details on the company's various philanthropic efforts and organizations around the world, including the U.S.-based Coca-Cola Scholars Foundation, a merit-based scholarship program.

Colonial Life & Accident Insurance Company (SC) (http://www.coloniallife.com/about/ColonialCares.asp)
Located in Columbia, South Carolina, the Colonial Life & Accident Insurance Company supports efforts to improve the Columbia community. The company's Web site provides brief descriptions of various company-sponsored programs and employee volunteer projects.

Colonial Pipeline Company (GA) (http://www.colpipe.com/ab_com.asp)
Based in Atlanta, Georgia, the Colonial Pipeline Company believes in reinvesting in the communities it serves throughout the eastern United States. Colonial Pipeline provides

grants to environmental organizations in its communities through the Earth Year Fund. Decisions about grants from the fund are made by Colonial employees. The company's Web site contains an overview of the Earth Year Fund, information on other community programs, examples of supported projects, and contact information.

Columbia Gas of Ohio, Inc. (OH) (http://www.columbiagasohio.com/community/service/)
Headquartered in Columbus, Columbia Gas of Ohio, Inc. seeks to improve "the quality of life, diversity, and fullness of opportunity" in the Ohio communities where its customers and employees live and work. The company's Web site provides information on the company's partnerships with the United Way, Salvation Army, and other organizations; information on employee matching gifts and volunteer programs; and a link to the Environmental Challenge Fund of parent company NiSource.

Columbia Gas of Pennsylvania and Maryland (PA)
(http://www.columbiagaspamd.com/community_outreach/community_outreach.htm)
Columbia Gas of Pennsylvania and Maryland's Corporate Contributions Program "provides cash contributions and volunteerism to deliver hope to deserving individuals and organizations" in the communities served by the company. Giving is focused in the areas of education in the humanities, community development and safety, and health and human services. The company's Web site features application guidelines, information on the Wish List Program, FAQs, and a link to the Environmental Challenge Fund, a program of parent company NiSource.

Columbia Gas of Virginia, Inc. (VA) (http://www.columbiagasva.com/community)
Columbia Gas of Virginia, Inc.'s Community Support Program focuses on three main areas of interest: energy, education, and the environment. Columbia Gas of Virginia supports charitable organizations through donations, employee voluntarism, and community service in the communities in which the company operates. The company's Web site provides information on the grant application process, a list of supported organizations, FAQs, contact information, and a link to the Environmental Challenge Fund, a program of parent company NiSource.

Comcast Corp. (PA) (http://www.comcast.com/InTheCommunity/index.html)
The Comcast Foundation was established by the Philadelphia-based Comcast Corporation as the communications, media, and entertainment company's chief source of charitable support to nonprofit organizations in Comcast communities across the United States. The foundation primarily funds programs in the areas of education, literacy/reading, and voluntarism/community service. The majority of organizations that receive funding are proactively identified by the foundation in coordination with local Comcast systems, or they are part of national programs such as Comcast Cares and the Comcast Reading Network. Unsolicited proposals are strongly discouraged. The company also supports an annual scholarship program for high school students. The company's Web site provides grant criteria and procedures, information about grant recipients and partner projects, details on the Leaders of Tomorrow Scholarship Program, community news and events, the company's corporate responsibility report, and contact information.

Commercial Metals Company (TX) (http://www.commercialmetals.com/community.asp)
The Commercial Metals Company focuses its philanthropic giving in three main areas: health and social issues dealing with the family, arts and cultural organizations, and educational programs. The company's corporate giving program focuses on two schools in the Dallas area, the Notre Dame of Dallas School and the Dallas Arts Magnet School. The company's Web site features program details and contact information.

Computer Associates International, Inc. (CA) (http://www.cai.com/charity/)
Computer Associates International, Inc. headquartered in Islandia, New York, focuses its philanthropic efforts on "children and activities that help them build the confidence they need to succeed" in communities where the company employees live and work around the

world. Through its Community Grants program, the company donates money and time to charities for efforts that improve the lives of children (pre-K–grade 12) and for projects that benefit children of diverse cultural and ethnic backgrounds and/or children with developmental disabilities. The company also offers product donations for programs that assist young people in achieving career success. The company's Web site provides grant and product donation guidelines and forms, a map of communities where the company operates with contact information, information on nonprofit partnerships, details on the company's employee matching gifts and volunteer programs, and a list of FAQs.

ConAgra, Inc. (NE) (http://www.conagrafoods.com/leadership/leadership_community.jsp)
Through its company-sponsored foundation, Omaha, Nebraska-based ConAgra, Inc. seeks to improve the quality of life in communities where the diversified food company's employees work and live. To that end, the ConAgra Foods Foundation focuses its resources in the areas of arts and culture, civic and community betterment, education, health and human services, and hunger, nutrition, and food safety. The company also sponsors national programs to help end child hunger in the United States and to educate consumers about home food safety. The ConAgra Web site provides the foundation's guidelines and application procedures, examples of funded programs, and a contact address.

The Connecticut Light and Power Company (CT)
(http://www.cl-p.com/community/partners/indexpartners.asp)
The Hartford-based Connecticut Light and Power Company maintains a corporate giving arm to support the communities that the company serves. Areas of focus include education, energy conservation, safety, and environmental stewardship; programs for special-needs customers; employee volunteerism; and charitable contributions. These charitable aims are accomplished through a number of programs, including educational grants; corporate grants in the areas of education, civic service and community, human services, the environment, and culture and the arts; and participation in the Northeast Utilities Foundation for grants over $5,000. The company's Web site features program information, grant applications, details on the company's other charitable efforts, and contact information.

Constellation Energy Group (MD) (http://www.constellation.com/about/community.asp)
The Baltimore, Maryland-headquartered Constellation Energy Group, together with its subsidiaries and employees, provides support in communities where the company has significant business interests, in central Maryland, and beyond. The company's corporate contributions program focuses on the areas of education, economic development, and environmental initiatives. The program will consider three types of requests: grants, event sponsorships, and in-kind donations. The company's Web site provides giving guidelines, information on making a contribution request, a list of funded projects, and contact information.

The Consumers Energy Foundation (MI)
(http://www.consumersenergy.com/welcome.htm)
The Consumers Energy Foundation, based in Jackson, Michigan, is the philanthropic arm of Consumers Energy. The foundation supports nonprofit organizations in six main categories: education, the environment, Michigan growth and enhancement, culture and the arts, social services, and emerging issues. The Volunteer Investment Program and Matching Gifts Program also allow company employees and retirees to contribute to the foundation's funding. The foundation's Web site features grant eligibility and limitations, application guidelines, contact information, and an online version of the *Community Forum* newsletter.

Cooper Industries (TX) (http://www.cooperindustries.com/about/index.htm)
Houston-based Cooper Industries, a diversified manufacturing company with facilities around the world, makes contributions through the Cooper Industries Foundation in the areas of education, arts and culture, health and human services, and community and the environment in communities where the company has a strong presence. The company provides the Project Pace Education Awards to help enhance the quality of vocational

education in communities where Cooper has operations. The company's annual Volunteer Spirit Awards recognize employees' volunteer efforts with grants to nonprofit organizations. The company's Web site contains information on Cooper's community programs, contribution guidelines and application procedures, an online version of the company's annual giving report, and a listing of the communities in which the company has operations.

Corning Incorporated Foundation (NY)
(http://www.corning.com/inside_corning/foundation.asp)
The Corning Incorporated Foundation was founded in 1952 in Corning, New York, and works to "develop and administer projects in support of educational, cultural, community, and selected national organizations" in and near locations where Corning Incorporated is an active corporate citizen. Within education, the foundation supports elementary and secondary schools, community colleges, four-year institutions of higher learning, and other programs. The cultural program supports arts organizations, libraries, museums, and public broadcasting stations. The community service category covers hospitals, hospices, community foundations, youth and women's centers, and local chapters of several national organizations. The foundation's Web site features application directions, lists of restrictions, and a description of the company's employee matching gifts program.

Credit Suisse First Boston Foundation (NY)
(http://www.csfb.com/about_csfb/company_information/foundation/index.shtml)
The Credit Suisse First Boston Foundation of New York City supports educational initiatives and programs for inner-city youth, including a variety of community-based and after-school programs incorporating the arts, music, sports, recreation, and community building. Foundation funding is focused primarily on organizations in New York City, but funding also extends to organizations in Atlanta, Baltimore, Boston, Chicago, Houston, Los Angeles, Miami, Palo Alto, Philadelphia, San Francisco, and Washington, D.C. The foundation's Web site provides information on the foundation's funding interests, guidelines on applying for an initial or renewal grant, and contact information.

Curriculum Associates, Inc. Excellence in Teaching Cabinet Grant Program (MA)
(http://www.curriculumassociates.com/cabinet)
The Excellence in Teaching Cabinet Grant Program is Curriculum Associates, Inc.'s acknowledgement of outstanding K-8 teachers. The Teachers Who Publish award provides three cash and materials grants each year to teachers who then serve on the company's cabinet of resource educators. Teachers submit innovative proposals for projects to run for three months to a year that are judged on "creativity, educational goals and objectives, ability to incorporate technology and print materials, and ease of implementation." The company's Web site offers explicit "Official Rules," a list of past award recipients, updates on projects, and application guidelines and deadlines.

DaimlerChrysler Corporation Fund (MI) (http://www.fund.daimlerchrysler.com)
The DaimlerChrysler Corporation Fund is headquartered in Auburn Hills, Michigan, and strives to improve the communities where DaimlerChrysler has offices or facilities. The fund supports four main areas: future workforce, community vitality, employee involvement, and marketplace and public policy leadership. The fund's Web site provides details on the fund's areas of interest, grant guidelines, application procedures, a list of the company's facilities with contact information, and the fund's annual report. The Web site also features an online application tool for organizations located in southeastern Michigan or representing a national or international program. Organizations located outside of Michigan should apply directly to their local DaimlerChrysler facilities.

Datatel Scholars Foundation (VA)
(http://www.datatel.com/datatel/index_datatel.cfm/107)
The Datatel Scholars Foundation is the philanthropic organization of Datatel, Inc., a provider of information service solutions to higher education. The foundation awards

scholarships to students planning to attend higher learning institutions that are Datatel client sites in the United States, Canada, and other areas. The foundation's Web site provides details on the various scholarships, application guidelines and online forms, a list of eligible schools, and contact information.

John Deere & Company (IL) (http://www.deere.com/en_US/compinfo/johndeere_foundations/contributions_index.html)
Through the John Deere Foundation and a direct corporate giving program, John Deere & Company awards grants and provides support to a variety of nonprofit organizations nationwide, with an emphasis on education, health and human services, community improvement, and arts and culture. Projects supported are generally in communities where the company has a presence. The company's Web site features the company's "Report of Contributions," which includes examples of funded organizations, financial data, and the foundation's procedures for funding; a list of the company's worldwide locations; and contact information.

Dell Foundation (TX)
(http://www.dell.com/us/en/gen/corporate/vision_000_foundation.htm)
The giving arm of Dell Computer Corporation, the Dell Foundation supports community programs that "equip youth for success in the digital world." The foundation funds organizations that benefit children newborn to 18 years of age in Dell's principle U.S. locations (central Texas; middle Tennessee; Twin Falls, Idaho; and Roseburg, Oregon). Proposals are accepted in the categories of health and human services, education, and technology access, as well as an open grant category for organizations that provide direct services to children but do not fit into the above-mentioned categories. The Web site provides details on the foundation's giving interests, application procedures and deadlines, a list of nonprofit partners, and a contact e-mail address, as well as information on employee volunteer and giving programs.

Delta Air Lines Foundation (GA) (http://www.delta-air.com/inside/community/index.jsp)
The Delta Air Lines Foundation, based in Atlanta, was established in 1968 as Delta's company-managed giving system to contribute to the well-being of the communities Delta Air Lines serves. The foundation supports nonprofit organizations that promote youth in three key areas: wellness, leadership development, and cultural advocacy. The foundation's Web site includes foundation grant guidelines and a printable application form; information on requesting corporate, in-kind, or volunteer support; and a list of supported organizations.

Deluxe Corporation Foundation (MN)
(http://www.deluxe.com/dlxab/deluxe-foundation.jsp)
The Deluxe Corporation Foundation was founded in 1954 and makes grants to qualified organizations located near Deluxe Corporation facilities. The foundation's funding programs are focused on education, human services, culture, and an employee matching gifts program. Grants are normally designated for operating or program support, equipment, and capital needs. The foundation's Web site provides information on the grant application process, a listing of funded organizations, Deluxe Corporation facility locations listed by state, and details on the employee matching gift program.

Detroit Tigers, Inc. (MI)
(http://detroit.tigers.mlb.com/NASApp/mlb/det/community/det_community_news.jsp)
Through the Tigers Care program, the Detroit Tigers, Inc. baseball team operates a number of charitable initiatives, including donations of tickets and memorabilia, the Ambassadors for Education program, and the support of hundreds of charitable organizations in the Detroit metropolitan area. Every player and coach of the Detroit Tigers is involved in a local nonprofit organization. The team's Web site includes a listing of charitable groups affiliated with the team, information about upcoming events, donation guidelines, and contact information.

The Dialog Corporation (NC) (http://training.dialog.com/gep/scholarship.html)
The North Carolina-based, Dialog Corporation, awards the Roger K. Summit Scholarship annually to graduate students who have demonstrated outstanding interest or performance in electronic information services. The award was established to honor Dr. Roger K. Summit, the founder of Dialog, for his outstanding contributions to the field of information science. The corporation's Web site features information about application procedures and restrictions.

Disney Learning Partnership (CA) (http://disney.go.com/disneylearning/)
The Disney Learning Partnership grew from Disney's American Teacher Awards, begun in 1989 to recognize "creative, innovative teaching strategies." The partnership focuses on three program areas: teacher recognition and professional development, collaborative school-wide learning initiatives, and strengthened parent-teacher connections. Disney's American Teacher Awards are given annually to creative teachers across the United States. The partnership's Web site contains a nomination form for the award; profiles of former winners; the Teacher Center, a Web site with resources for creative teaching; and information on the partnership's other programs and activities.

Dollar Thrifty Automotive Group, Inc. (OK) (http://www.dtag.com/indexcommunity.html)
Dollar Thrifty Automotive Group, Inc., located in Tulsa, Oklahoma, supports its employees' "desire to enrich the lives of others" through volunteer programs and financial gifts to nonprofit organizations. Contributions typically provide quality of life enhancements or help improve the economic well-being of neighborhoods where the company's employees and customers live. The company's Web site features online versions of the company's annual reports, company information, and contact numbers.

Dominion Resources, Inc. (VA) (http://www.dom.com/about/community/)
The philanthropic arm of the Richmond, Virginia-based energy service provider Dominion Resources, Inc. works to improve its community through a variety of programs, including fuel assistance programs and volunteer efforts. The Dominion Foundation makes grants to nonprofit organizations that "improve the overall quality of life" in which Dominion provides electricity or natural gas service and where the company has significant facilities and business interests. Funding is available in the categories of the environment, education, culture and the arts, neighborhood and community development, and health and human services. The company's Web site provides foundation funding guidelines and application procedures, regional contact addresses, a list of recently awarded grants, and information on the company's other community programs.

Domino's Pizza LLC (MI) (http://www.dominos.com/C1256B420054FF48/vwContentByKey/W256UR6D198DENNEN)
Headquartered in Ann Arbor, Michigan, Domino's Pizza LLC supports initiatives and causes in its hometown while also participating in national programs such as the Make-A-Wish Foundation. In addition, the company's franchises provide support, including pizza donations, for local programs. The company's Web site features information about the company's charitable work and contact information.

R.R. Donnelley & Sons Company (IL) (http://www.rrdonnelley.com/cportal/public/home/publicaffairs/index.jsp)
R.R. Donnelley & Sons Company, an international printing and information management company headquartered in Chicago, Illinois, supports activities that enhance the quality of life in communities served by the company. The R.R. Donnelley Foundation, the company's primary contributions vehicle, provides funding to programs that promote the written word and serve children and youth at risk. Funding is also provided to organizations through employee matching gifts and volunteer programs. The company's Web site provides descriptions of the company's funding areas, grant guidelines, application instructions, a listing of R.R. Donnelley & Sons geographic locations, an online version of the "Community Relations" annual report, and contact information.

The Dow Chemical Company Foundation (MI) (http://www.dow.com/about/corp/social/social.htm)
The Dow Chemical Company is a worldwide provider of chemicals, plastics, energy, agricultural products, consumer goods, and environmental services. The Dow Chemical Company Foundation focuses its funding on community needs in locations where Dow Chemical has a presence. In North America, the company's support is focused on improving the quality of education for K–12 in math, science, and technology. Preferential treatment is given to charitable contributions requested by Dow Chemical employees. The foundation's Web site provides details on the company's community initiatives, general guidelines for education programs, examples of supported projects in locations around the world, and a copy of the corporate social responsibility report.

The Dow Jones Newspaper Fund, Inc. (NJ) (http://www.dj.com/newsfund/)
The Dow Jones Newspaper Fund, Inc. was founded in 1958 by editors of the *Wall Street Journal* to improve the quality of journalism education and the pool of applicants for jobs in the newspaper business. Based in Princeton, New Jersey, the fund is a nonprofit foundation supported by the Dow Jones Foundation, Dow Jones & Company, Inc., and other newspaper companies. The foundation provides internships and scholarships to college students, career literature, fellowships for high school journalism teachers and publications' advisers, and training for college journalism instructors. The fund also accepts grant applications for programs that further its mission. The fund's Web site features program descriptions, grant application guidelines, and contact information.

DP Foundation (NV) (http://www.partnerwithdp.com/Dermody/foundation.cfm)
The giving arm of DP Partners, a Reno, Nevada-based industrial real estate company, the DP Foundation seeks to give back to the communities in which the company does business through volunteer support and financial donations to nonprofit causes. The foundation's primary focus areas are family and children, education, services for seniors, and the arts. The foundation's Web site contains contact information and examples of organizations that have received support.

DTE Energy Foundation (MI) (http://www.dteenergy.com/community/foundation)
The DTE Energy Foundation, the principal philanthropic vehicle of the Michigan energy and energy technology provider, supports programs in communities served by the company. The foundation supports organizations and programs in the focus areas of leadership, education and the environment, achievement, and development and diversity. The foundation's Web site provides grant guidelines, application procedures, FAQs, and contact information.

Duke Energy Corporation (NC) (http://www.duke-energy.com/decorp/content/community/deip22.asp?RBU=1)
Charlotte, North Carolina-based Duke Energy Corporation makes charitable contributions through the Duke Energy Foundation, which focuses on the fields of education, community development, and voluntarism. Grants are typically made to pre-selected organizations. Unsolicited requests are unlikely to be funded and the foundation does not encourage such requests. The company also administers employee matching gifts and volunteer programs, and the Share the Warmth program, which helps low-income customers with their heating bills. The company's Web site provides foundation funding policies and procedures, and information on the company's other community programs and supported projects.

E.I. du Pont de Nemours and Company (DE) (http://www.dupont.com)
An international company with operations throughout the United States, the E.I. du Pont de Nemours and Company is committed "to improving the quality of life and enhancing the vitality of the communities in which it operates throughout the world." Areas of support include educational programs, culture and the arts, environmental initiatives, human and health service organizations, and civic and community activities. Contributions are made through a number of programs, including the DuPont Office of Education, which awards

grants geared toward primary, secondary, and higher education institutions and programs; the DuPont Community Fund, which matches donations made by DuPont sites; and the DuPont Volunteer Recognition Awards. The Social Commitment section of the company's Web site features an overview of the community programs, application guidelines for the education program and for non education-related requests, a directory of worldwide locations, and contact information.

Eastman Kodak Company (NY) (http://www.kodak.com/US/en/corp/community.shtml)
The Eastman Kodak Company, an imaging company headquartered in Rochester, New York, designs its philanthropic programs and initiatives to instill employee pride, build public trust, foster education, respond to community needs, and enhance the company image. The company's primary funding areas include community revitalization (economic development, the environment, culture, and the arts), education, and health and human services. The Community Relations and Contributions area of Eastman Kodak's Web site describes the company's corporate giving programs and provides grant guidelines, recent quarterly recipient lists, details and updates on special projects and awards, and information on the company's support for diversity and volunteerism.

Eaton Corporation (OH) (http://www.eaton.com)
Eaton Corporation, headquartered in Cleveland, Ohio, is a global manufacturer of products for industrial, vehicle, construction, commercial, and semiconductor markets. Eaton's corporate giving initiatives are directed toward making a difference in the quality of life in communities where the company operates and include cash grants, a matching gifts program, and support of the United Way. Grants are focused on community improvement, education, and arts and cultural programs. Under the Who We Are heading, the Social Commitment section of the company's Web site provides information on funding interests, application guidelines, and a report of contributions.

eBay Foundation (CA) (http://pages.ebay.com/aboutebay98/foundation/)
Created in 1998, the eBay Foundation supports "organizations that provide tools, hope, and direction to those who seek new skills" and "organizations that implement programs that have long-term implications and maximize the ability to do good in the world." The foundation's global/national grants program seeks partnerships with programs that are national in scope; these grants may be applied for on an invitation-only basis. The foundation's community grants initiative provides funding for programs in U.S. communities where eBay has a major employment base (currently San Jose, California, and Salt Lake City, Utah). The foundation's Web site features a mission statement and guiding principles, submission guidelines, and contact information.

Educational Communications Scholarship Foundation (IL) (http://www.eci-whoswho.com/highschool/scholar/)
The Educational Communications Scholarship Foundation was created in 1968 to offer financial support to those students recognized in *Who's Who Among American High School Seniors.* The foundation is primarily funded by the book's publishing company. Application is restricted to those students appearing in the book, who receive scholarship applications automatically. The foundation's Web site features a list of members on the decision-making committee, a searchable database of past award recipients, and a list of educational and youth organizations that have received support from the company.

EI Charitable Foundation (CO) (http://www.eicharity.org/)
The Colorado-based, EI Charitable Foundation provides charitable, scientific, literary, and educational assistance to individuals lacking the means to adequately provide such for themselves. The foundation maintains areas of interest in New York City relief, faith-based charity, books for children, higher education, Pahdiar Benefit Fund, and crisis support. The foundation's Web site features a mission statement, details on the current initiatives, and contact information.

Eileen Fisher, Inc. (NY) (http://www.eileenfisher.com/)
New York-based, Eileen Fisher, Inc. provides grants for women's issues in the Irvington, New York, area and also to organizations near subsidiary offices, retail stores, or showrooms. The company occasionally provides funding for programs dealing with children and families. The company's Web site features a mission statement and contact information.

Electronic Data Systems Corporation (TX) (http://www.eds.com/community_affairs/)
Through its Global Community Affairs Program, the Electronic Data Systems Corporation, an information technology provider headquartered in Plano, Texas, supports education programs and efforts to bridge the "digital divide" in communities where the company has a presence. The foundation provides funding to programs addressing the digital divide issue, as well as arts and culture, health and human services, and general education programs. The company's EDS Technology Grants Program aids teachers in purchasing information technology products, training, or services. The company's Web site features funding program descriptions, application instructions, details on other community outreach programs, and contact information.

Electronics for Imaging, Inc. (CA) (http://www.e-beam.com/links/techfund.html)
The eBeam Tech Fund was established by Electronics for Imaging, Inc. to provide technology grants to educational institutions, government agencies, and other nonprofit organizations. Grants consist of a free or discounted eBeam System, which scans handwritten notes or designs to a computer. Interested applicants can fill out an online registration and essay form; more details on the program are available on the fund's Web site.

Eli Lilly and Company Foundation (IN)
(http://www.lilly.com/about/community/foundation/index.html)
Created in 1968, the Indianapolis, Indiana-based Eli Lilly and Company Foundation is the primary vehicle for the pharmaceutical company's charitable contributions. The majority of the foundation's financial contributions are employee directed through the Matching Gifts Program and a United Way initiative. The remaining cash contributions are made on a discretionary basis to groups aligned with company interests and to programs in Indianapolis and several other communities where Lilly has a significant employee base. The foundation's product donation program distributes pharmaceuticals all over the world through the Lilly Cares Patient Assistance Program, which provides free medication through physicians to needy patients, and the Disaster Assistance and International Relief program. The foundation's Web site includes a summary of contributions, an overview of the foundation's giving interests and procedures, physician guidelines for the Lilly Cares Patient Assistance Program, and details on employee involvement programs.

Ernst & Young Foundation (NY)
(http://www.ey.com/GLOBAL/content.nsf/US/About_Ernst_Young_-_Foundation)
The Ernst & Young Foundation of New York City was founded in 1937 by the accounting, tax, and consulting firm. The foundation supports institutions of higher education primarily in accounting, information systems, tax, and other business areas. Most funding to higher education is distributed through the employee matching gifts program. Other programs include in-kind services to business schools and accounting programs, tax training and educator award programs, and accounting professorships. The foundation's Web site featues an overview of the foundation's programs and a contact information.

ExxonMobil Corporation (TX)
(http://www2.exxonmobil.com/Corporate/Notebook/Citizen/Corp_N_CitizenDetails.asp)
ExxonMobil Corporation supports charitable organizations in the United States through a direct corporate giving program and the ExxonMobil Foundation. Contributions are focused on education, the environment, public policy and public research, health, united appeals and civic and community-service organizations, minority and women-oriented service organizations, and arts, museums, and historical associations. Within the category of education, the company provides unrestricted general support of higher education by

matching employee gifts on a three-for-one basis. Other programs focus on improving mathematics and science education at both the pre-college and college levels. ExxonMobil's Web site provides funding guidelines and application procedures, a list of major ExxonMobil communities, contact information, and details on other corporate citizenship initiatives.

Fannie Mae Foundation (DC) (http://www.fanniemaefoundation.org/)

The mission of the Fannie Mae Foundation is to create "affordable homeownership and housing opportunities through innovative partnerships and initiatives that build healthy, vibrant communities across the United States." The foundation is particularly committed to improving the quality of life in its hometown of Washington, D.C. The foundation provides informational guides on the home-buying process; offers outreach programs for new Americans, Native Americans, and adult students; conducts research on housing and urban issues; and provides financial support to organizations addressing housing and community development issues. The foundation's Web site features educational program and publication information, funding priorities, grant application procedures, information on the foundation's award and fellowship programs, a searchable database of grants awarded, and a listing of the foundation's regional offices.

Farmers Insurance Group (CA)
(http://www.farmers.com/FarmComm/content/CC010153.jsp)

Farmers Insurance Group of Los Angeles, California, has a corporate giving program committed to improving the communities where its customers, agents, and employees live and work throughout its 41-state territory. The company provides support to programs that improve safety, enhance educational opportunity, and increase civic participation. The company's Web site provides an overview of the company's corporate giving initiatives; a list of funded organizations; information on special programs, including the American Promise citizenship education program and Young Americanos, a project honoring Hispanic culture; and a list of the company's regional offices with contact information.

Federated Department Store Foundation (OH)
(http://www.federated-fds.com/community/)

The mission of the Federated Department Store Foundation is based on the belief that "stronger, healthy, and more vibrant communities provide better environments for our stores to do business and for our employees and customers to live and work." The program funds charitable organizations, civic programs, community projects, arts/cultural and educational institutions in hundreds of communities across the United States. Women's issues (such as breast cancer and domestic violence) and HIV/AIDS are two areas of special focus. The foundation has a matching gift program and places a strong emphasis on voluntarism. The foundation's Web site provides a summary of the company's giving programs, contact information, an online version of "Responsibility in Action: A Report to the Community," a report on the company's volunteer program.

Fidelity Foundation (MA) (http://www.fidelityfoundation.org/)

Established in 1965, the Fidelity Foundation focuses its grant program on strengthening nonprofit organizations primarily in regions where Fidelity Investments operates. The foundation approaches grantmaking as an investment process, seeking to leverage its funding through challenge grants, outcome evaluation, and other methods. The grant program focuses on arts and culture, community development and social services, health, and education. The foundation's Web site features geographic restrictions, information on selection criteria, application procedures, FAQs, and contact information.

Fieldstone Foundation (CA) (http://www.fieldstone-homes.com/foundation/)

As the philanthropic vehicle of the Fieldstone Group, a home builder based in southern California, the Fieldstone Foundation supports nonprofit organizations serving the communities where it works: Orange, Riverside, San Bernardino, and San Diego Counties in southern California and Salt Lake City in Utah. Donations are focused in the areas of humanitarianism, community and education, cultural arts, and Christian ministries. The foundation is particularly interested in programs serving children and families. The foundation's Web site features a listing of the foundation's recent grants; grant guidelines and application procedures; information on the Fieldstone Leadership Network, which provides technical and management training to nonprofits in Fieldstone communities; and contact information.

FirstEnergy Companies (OH) (http://www.firstenergycorp.com/communitysupport/)
Through its community giving programs, the Akron, Ohio-based FirstEnergy Companies support nonprofit, tax-exempt health and human services agencies; educational organizations; cultural and arts programs and institutions; and civic groups in the areas served by FirstEnergy's electric operating companies in Ohio, Pennsylvania, New Jersey, and where the company has facilities. Funding is provided through the FirstEnergy Foundation's grants program and employee matching gifts program. Through their education initiative, the companies also offer mathematics, science, and technology education grants to educators at schools and community groups served by its operating companies. FirstEnergy's Web site contains grant application procedures, details on the matching gifts program, a list of area managers at FirstEnergy's operating companies, and contact information.

FleetBoston Financial Corporation (MA)
(http://www.fleet.com/about_inthecommunity_overview.asp)
Through its charitable giving programs, FleetBoston Financial Corporation seeks to initiate societal change, support social entrepreneurs, improve the quality of life in the communities served by the company, and encourage the involvement of its employees and partners in civic and community service. The FleetBoston Financial Foundation provides support to nonprofit organizations in the priority areas of economic opportunity, youth development, public education, and arts and culture. Giving is targeted to organizations in Massachusetts, Connecticut, Rhode Island, Maine, New Hampshire, New York, New Jersey, and Pennsylvania. The company's Web site provides details on funding priorities, proposal guidelines, the foundation's annual report, the Fleet community report, a list of regional contact addresses, and information on the company's other community programs and sponsorships.

FMC Corporation (PA)
(http://www.fmc.com/Corporate/V2/GeneralDetail/0,1577,29,00.html)
Philadelphia-based FMC Corporation, a chemicals manufacturer, maintains a corporate contributions and philanthropy program that benefits employees and the communities in which the company operates. The company matches financial contributions by its employees to educational and art and cultural institutions and provides grants to qualifying organizations where employees volunteer. Local contributions are provided at the discretion of individual manufacturing plants and operations. FMC also supports the United Way and the National Merit Scholarship Program. The company's Web site features an overview of the company's philanthropic activities and contact information for corporate headquarters and locations worldwide.

FMR Corp. (MA) (http://personal.fidelity.com/myfidelity/InsideFidelity/FidelityCares/FidCares_investing.html)
Headquartered in Boston, FMR Corp.'s Fidelity Investments supports community and civic initiatives in the communities where the corporation maintains a presence. Fidelity Cares, the philanthropic arm of Fidelity Investments, operates a workplace giving campaign, provides support for community organizations and events, and encourages employee voluntarism. The organization also teams with Reading is Fundamental to promote literacy. The company's Web site provides an overview of the company's community programs and details on applying for corporate sponsorships.

Ford Motor Company Fund (MI) (http://www.ford.com/en/dedication/fundingAndGrants)
The Ford Motor Company Fund of Detroit, Michigan, was established in 1949 to support "initiatives and institutions that enhance and improve opportunities for those who live in the communities where Ford Motor Company operates." The fund makes awards in the areas of education; the environment; public policy, health, and social programs; civic affairs and community development; and arts and humanities. In all funding areas, the fund places top priority on "the support and development of organizations that promote diversity." The fund's Web site features an online annual report, which includes detailed funding information; contribution guidelines and application form; corporate and fund sponsorship guidelines; examples of funded projects; contact information; and a special section on Ford's sponsorship of arts and humanities programs.

Freddie Mac Foundation (VA) (http://www.freddiemacfoundation.org)
The Freddie Mac Foundation, the principal charitable arm of McLean, Virginia-headquartered mortgage company Freddie Mac, is dedicated to helping children, youth, and families at risk. The foundation provides funds to nonprofit organizations in the metropolitan Washington, D.C., area and in cities where regional offices are located. It also supports statewide initiatives in Maryland and Virginia and programs that are national in scope. Giving areas include building strong families, early child development, foster care and adoption, building constituencies for children, assisting teen parents, and expanding childcare. The foundation's Web site provides funding information, a grant application packet, geographic locations of the company, details on special initiatives and volunteerism, news, annual reports, and grants lists.

Frito-Lay, Inc. (TX) (http://www.frito-lay.com/company/responsibilities/)
Frito-Lay, Inc. focuses its charitable giving on communities located near its headquarters in Dallas/Fort Worth, Texas. Its corporate contributions target programs and organizations with results-oriented approaches and direct community benefits. The company is particularly interested in programs that improve education, economic development, and interracial relations. Its community service efforts include direct program funding, as well as active involvement by employees and expert counsel provided by executives serving on community boards in volunteer roles. The company's Web site does not provide a contact address or information on how to apply for funding.

Gannett Foundation, Inc. (VA) (http://www.gannettfoundation.org)
The Gannett Foundation, Inc., the philanthropic organization of Gannett Co., Inc., a news and information concern headquartered in McLean, Virginia, funds programs to improve the education, health, and quality of life of people living in communities where Gannett has a local daily newspaper or television station. The foundation seeks to fund programs that provide creative solutions to issues such as education and neighborhood improvement, economic development, youth development, community problem solving, assistance to disadvantaged people, environmental conservation, and cultural enrichment. The foundation's Web site features grant guidelines, an application form, a Gannett local community contact list, specific guidelines for the Washington, D.C., metropolitan area, the foundation's annual report, and contact information.

Gap, Inc. (CA) (http://www.gapinc.com/social_resp/social_resp.htm)
Based in San Francisco, California, Gap, Inc. provides support to nonprofit organizations around the world through the Gap Foundation. The foundation's primary areas of focus are education and youth development. Funding is also contributed to health and social service agencies, local arts and civic organizations, and nonprofit organizations committed to protecting the environment. While the foundation does not accept unsolicited proposals for cash grants, it does donate a limited number of gift certificates to public schools and youth-serving nonprofits in the San Francisco Bay Area and New York City. The company's Web site features guidelines for requesting gift certificates, information on areas of giving, major community partnerships, and employee volunteer programs, FAQs, and contact information.

GATX Corporation (IL) (http://www.gatx.com/common/about/community.asp)
Chicago-based GATX Corporation, a specialized financing and leasing company, supports "organizations and projects that improve the quality of life in GATX communities across the United States." GATX provides support to nonprofit organizations in the areas of culture, education, the environment, families, healthcare, and social services. The company has community investment committees in Buffalo, Chicago, and San Francisco, as well as several other locations. The Company's Web site provides an overview of the GATX community investment initiative, details on location specific giving programs, and information on the company's employee matching gifts and volunteer programs.

GE Fund (CT) (http://www.gefund.org)
The GE Fund, the philanthropic foundation of the General Electric Company, "invests in improving educational quality and access and in strengthening community organizations in GE communities around the world." The fund's focus on education includes targeted initiatives supporting increased educational opportunity from pre-college through higher education and international and public policy programs. The company also matches gifts from employees to colleges and universities and supports the United Way. The fund invites proposals from pre-selected organizations and does not encourage unsolicited proposals. The fund's Web site includes information on each funding program, FAQs, details on the funding process, grants lists, program highlights, online publications, and contact information.

Genentech, Inc. (CA) (http://www.gene.com/gene/about/community)
Genentech, Inc., a biotechnology company headquartered in San Francisco, California, provides support through its corporate contributions program to national and local nonprofit organizations working in areas of healthcare and science and to targeted local giving in the communities in which it operates. Funding is provided through general support or project-specific grants to nonprofit organizations and through sponsorships of selected nonprofit events. Additionally, the Genentech Foundation for Biomedical Sciences supports biomedical science education and research in the San Francisco Bay Area. The company's Web site features program descriptions, application guidelines, and contact information.

General Communications, Inc. (AK) (http://www.gci.com/about/corpgive.htm)
General Communications, Inc., an Alaska-based communications company, "supports worthwhile charities and organizations which contribute to the quality of life for all Alaskans." The company's corporate giving program is especially interested in organizations with which its employees are involved and programs benefiting youth. A listing of current and past funding beneficiaries, grant application guidelines, and contact information are available on the company's Web site.

General Mills, Inc. (MN) (http://www.generalmills.com/corporate/about/community/)
General Mills, Inc. provides charitable support through the General Mills Foundation and a direct corporate giving program. Grants made through the foundation's Minneapolis headquarters focus on family life, youth nutrition and fitness, education, and arts and culture. Grantmaking priorities in communities outside the Twin Cities include improving youth nutrition and fitness and the United Way. Through the corporate contributions program, General Mills' partners with specific philanthropic efforts to provide financial support and increase awareness of the cause. The company's Web site contains the foundation's grant criteria, guidelines, and application form; a report on corporate citizenship; grants listings; a directory of community action staff and regional programs; and information on specific community initiatives and employee voluntarism.

General Motors Foundation (MI) (http://www.gm.com/company/gmability/philanthropy)
Founded in 1976, General Motors of Detroit, Michigan, provides community support through the General Motors Foundation and a corporate contributions program. The foundation focuses its giving in six areas: education, health, community relations, public policy, arts and culture, and the environment and energy, with a strong commitment to diversity in

all areas. Education receives the largest share of funding; higher education and K–12 programs both receive support. Health and human services is another priority area, with cancer research a major concern. The company's Web site includes grant guidelines and application procedures, the philanthropic annual report, descriptions of funded programs in each major category, and details on special initiatives, including the GM Cancer Research Foundation.

Georgia-Pacific Corporation (GA) (http://www.gp.com/center/community/index.html)
The philanthropic endeavors of the Atlanta, Georgia-based Georgia-Pacific Corporation, which manufactures paper and building materials, include cash and product donations in the communities where the corporation operates, an employee matching gifts program, volunteer time, and the Georgia-Pacific Foundation. The foundation, established in 1958, makes community grants in the areas of education, community enrichment, and the environment, as well as providing support to organizations with which employees are involved. Details on each of these grant and program areas are provided on the Georgia-Pacific Web site, along with grant application guidelines and contact information.

Giant Food, Inc. (MD) (http://www.giantfood.com/community.htm)
Landover, Maryland-based Giant Food, Inc., which serves customers in the Baltimore/Washington, D.C., area and in the Delaware Valley regions of New Jersey and Delaware, supports community initiatives in the regions where the company operates. Through charitable contributions, major partnerships, and the donation of food for events, among other initiatives, the company seeks to address homelessness and provide food for people in need, contribute to locally based neighborhood activities, and support young people. The company's Web site features applicants with basic application guidelines and limitations and contact information.

Giant Food Stores, Inc. (PA) (http://www.giantpa.com/giantheart/giantheart.html)
Pennsylvania-based Giant Food Stores, Inc. focuses its charitable giving and fundraising campaigns on feeding the hungry, helping children, and supporting community groups. Through in-store donations and funding drives, the company raises money for numerous children's hospital charities in and around Pennsylvania. Additionally, the stores support anti-hunger campaigns and distribute benches made out of recycled store bags to local schools during Earth Week. The company's Web site contains information on charitable programs and donation request procedures, contact information, a list of community partners, and program updates.

The Goodyear Tire & Rubber Company (OH)
(http://www.goodyear.com/corporate/community.html)
Based in Akron, Ohio, the Goodyear Tire & Rubber Company "seeks to be a socially aware and responsive global citizen, wherever it operates or does business." Goodyear participates in organizations that provide opportunities for the young and disadvantaged through summer work-study programs, scholarships, recreational offerings, and employment opportunities. The company's Web site provides program details and contact information.

Grand Circle Foundation (MA) (http://www.gct.com/gct/general/default.aspx?oid=200)
The Grand Circle Foundation was established in 1992 in Boston to support global and regional projects, environments, cultures, and communities where Grand Circle travelers visit. The institutions and projects that the foundation supports include environmental conservation, funding for museums and historical sites, and the construction of schools and hospitals in developing communities. The foundation's Web site contains a listing of beneficiaries, information on the foundation's board of directors, and contact information.

Grand Victoria Foundation (IL) (http://www.grandvictoriafdn.org/)
The Grand Victoria Foundation is the philanthropic arm of the Grand Victoria Casino which is located in Elgin, Illinois. The foundation supports nonprofit organizations in Illinois "to assist communities in their efforts to pursue systemic solutions to problems in

specific areas of education, economic development, and the environment." The foundation's Web site features details on the foundation's funding priorities, application guidelines, FAQs, a nonprofit reference library, grantee profiles and lists of recent grants, and contact information.

Green Bay Packers Foundation (WI)
(http://www.packers.com/community/foundation.html)
The Green Bay Packers Foundation, located in Green Bay, Wisconsin, was created to assist charitable and worthwhile causes throughout the state of Wisconsin. It assists in a wide variety of activities and programs in the areas of education, civic affairs, health services, human services, and youth-related programs. The foundation's Web site provides information about the types of grants the foundation makes, the annual deadline for applications, procedures and contact information for requesting an application, and a list of past grant recipients.

Greyhound Lines, Inc. (TX) (http://www.greyhound.com/company/charitable.shtml)
Greyhound Lines, Inc. maintains a charitable giving program focused on underserved constituencies such as minorities, women, the disabled, and the financially disadvantaged. The company provides assistance to qualified nonprofits that seek to help these populations develop "skills, knowledge, and confidence." The company's Web site features eligibility guidelines and restrictions, application procedures, the charitable request form, contact information, and details on the company's charitable discounts for transportation program.

GROWMARK, Inc. (IL) (http://www.growmark.com/GMK/Volunteer/community.htm)
GROWMARK, Inc., an agricultural cooperative network located in Bloomington, Illinois, provides products and services to member cooperatives in the Midwest and Ontario, Canada, and offers community support through a variety of initiatives. The GROWMARK Volunteer Network is made up of corporate employees and participates in local activities "to help those in need and to make the community a better place to live." GROWMARK also supports youth and young farmer programs including FFA, 4-H, Farm Bureau Young Farmers/Leaders, Junior Farmers Association, and scholarships at selected universities. The company's Web site provides an overview of the volunteer network's activities, details on programs for young farmers, and a list of colleges offering GROWMARK scholarships.

The Guardian Life Insurance Company of America (NY)
(http://www.glic.com/wc/ggp.html)
The Guardian Life Insurance Company of America sponsors an annual Girls Going Places College Scholarship Program to "reward the enterprising spirits of girls ages 12 to 16." To be considered for the scholarship, girls must be nominated. The company's Web site features a downloadable scholarship nomination form, along with the official contest rules, information on upcoming Girls Going Places Entrepreneurship Conferences, a listing of recent scholarship recipients, and contact information.

The H&R Block Foundation (MO) (http://www.hrblockfoundation.org)
The H&R Block Foundation focuses giving in the Kansas City, Missouri, area, where the tax firm is headquartered. The foundation invests "in people, organizations, and ideas that move the quality of life in the communities where we live and work." The foundation focuses its philanthropy in four categories: arts and culture, community development, education, and health and human services. The foundation's Web site contains details on the foundation's funding priorities and policies; application procedures, deadlines, and forms; news and the annual report; contact information; and details on H&R Block's corporate volunteer program.

Hale and Dorr LLP (MA) (http://www.haledorr.com/firm/community.asp)
The Boston-based law firm of Hale and Dorr LLP contributes to the community through four programs: professional development, involvement in its clients' industries, community giving, and *pro bono* legal services. The firm focuses its community giving in the areas

of children and education, mainly through local organizations in Boston and Washington, D.C. Further information on these programs, along with a downloadable report detailing Hale and Dorr's community giving, are available through the firm's Web site. Additional details on client organizations and *pro bono* services are also available online.

John Hancock Mutual Life Insurance Company (MA) (http://www.johnhancock.com/company/community/index.html)
The John Hancock Mutual Life Insurance Company, headquartered in Boston, Massachusetts, supports the Boston community by providing financial grants, matching gifts, and in-kind contributions focused on programs that serve Boston's youth, particularly educational, after-school, and sports programs. The Community Relations area of John Hancock's Web site describes the company's funding activities and provides application instructions and descriptions of its special initiatives.

Hannaford Bros. Company (ME) (http://www.hannaford.com/community/index.htm)
The Hannaford Bros. Company, a chain of grocery stores based in Portland, Maine, with stores throughout Maine, New Hampshire, Vermont, New York, and Massachusetts, provides community support through a number of initiatives. The Hannaford Charitable Foundation supports health and welfare organizations, educational institutions, civic and cultural organizations, and other local charitable organizations. Preference for funding is given to programs that involve Hannaford associates and that are located in Hannaford's marketing territory. The company also supports the United Way, provides sponsorships for community events, and donates to food banks. Additionally, each Hannaford store provides contributions to its local community. The company's Web site provides an overview of the company's community activities, foundation application guidelines, and contact information.

Harleysville Group, Inc. (PA) (http://www.harleysvillegroup.com/abo/abo_5_1.html)
The Harleysville Group, Inc. of Pennsylvania established the Care Force program, an employee-run initiative, to provide volunteer support to nonprofit community organizations. Projects generally focus on disadvantaged citizens, housing and neighborhood development, the environment, and education and safety programs. The company's Web site features details about the program and contact information.

Hasbro Foundation (NY) (http://www.hasbro.org)
Toy and game manufacturer Hasbro seeks to aid children worldwide through a variety of philanthropic programs. The New York City-based Hasbro Foundation supports the development and/or expansion of innovative programs for disadvantaged children throughout the United States and also helps fund the building of fully accessible playgrounds. The Hasbro Charitable Trust, located at Hasbro headquarters in Rhode Island, makes toy donations worldwide, provides support for health and welfare programs in communities where Hasbro has facilities, and coordinates Hasbro's matching gift and employee volunteer programs. The foundation's Web site provides information on the activities of the foundation and trust, funding guidelines and procedures, the trust's online donation applications, year-end reports, and contact information.

Hawaiian Electric Industries Charitable Foundation (HI) (http://www.hei.com/heicf/heicf.html)
The philanthropic arm of Hawaiian Electric Industries, the Honolulu-based Hawaiian Electric Industries Charitable Foundation was created in 1984 "to assume leadership in making our community a better place in which to live for all of Hawaii's people." The grants program distributes gifts in four primary areas: community development, education, the environment, and family services. The foundation prefers to make awards to projects that exist in communities where the company has, or plans to have, a significant presence; that will provide recognition and goodwill for the company; and that are actively supported by volunteers from within the company. The foundation's Web site provides the "HEI Charitable

Foundation Report on Corporate Citizenship," which includes details on programs in each of the major categories; application guidelines and procedures; and contact information.

Hewlett-Packard Company (CA) (http://thenew.hp.com/country/us/eng/companyinfo/globalcitizenship.html)

The global philanthropic efforts of technology company Hewlett-Packard are informed by its "vision of the future where technology is accessible to everyone in the world as a means to learn, work, and benefit from information." The company's philanthropy and education programs are focused on developing and supporting programs that promote educational opportunity and "e-Inclusion" for people in underserved communities in the United States and around the world. In the United States, Hewlett-Packard awards equipment and cash donations through three programs: the U.S. grants program, local contributions programs, and employee giving programs. The national grants program does not fund projects from unsolicited proposals. Local programs provide contributions to nonprofit organizations and K–12 schools. The company's Web site provides contribution policies and procedures, details on strategic grant initiatives, locations and guidelines for local grant programs, FAQs, philanthropy annual reports, and information on the company's charitable programs in other regions of the world.

The Hitachi Foundation (DC) (http://www.hitachifoundation.org)

The Washington, D.C.-based Hitachi Foundation, established in 1985 by Hitachi, Ltd. of Tokyo, Japan, "seeks to build the capacity of all Americans, particularly those underserved by traditional institutions." The foundation offers three programs to advance this purpose. The General Grants Program supports U.S. nonprofit organizations that help "strengthen the position of underserved people in society." This program invites applications through an annual request for proposals process and does not accept unsolicited proposals. The foundation's corporate Matching Funds Program/Community Action Committees seek to improve the community through financial, volunteer, and in-kind contributions. The Yoshiyama Award for Exemplary Community Service provides scholarships on the basis of community involvement. Nomination guidelines and forms for the award are available on the foundation's Web site, as are overviews of each giving program, current guidelines for grantseekers, FAQs, and contact information.

Hoffmann-La Roche, Inc. (NJ) (http://www.rocheusa.com/about/responsibility.html)

The Hoffmann-La Roche, Inc. corporate giving program, based in Nutley, New Jersey, seeks to enhance the quality of life for the pharmaceutical company's employees and residents of the communities where the company has a significant presence. Funding is considered for domestic, charitable institutions whose initiatives closely align with the company's business interests. The corporate giving program focuses on the areas of health promotion and health education—with an emphasis on cardiology, dermatology, infectious diseases, metabolic diseases, neurology, oncology, transplantation, and virology/HIV—and math and science education, focusing on teacher enrichment in grades K–12. The company's Web site contains funding priorities, application guidelines, and contact information.

The Home Depot, Inc. (GA) (http://www.homedepot.com/HDUS/EN_US/corporate/corp_respon/corp_respon.shtml)

The Home Depot, Inc., a chain of home improvement stores headquartered in Atlanta, Georgia, seeks to have a positive impact on communities in North America where the company's associates live and work. Community support is provided through the Home Depot Foundation, a corporate grants program, and an employee volunteer program. Foundation and corporate grants fund efforts to create or rehabilitate affordable housing, assist at-risk youth, protect the environment, and prepare for and respond to disasters. The company's Web site offers information on funding priorities, foundation application guidelines and procedures, details on funded programs and partnerships, social responsibility reports, and contact information.

Honeywell Foundation (NJ) (http://www.honeywell.com/about/foundation.html)
A giving program of Morristown, New Jersey-based Honeywell, a diversified technology and manufacturing company, the Honeywell Foundation provides contributions and volunteer support in communities around the world where the company has operations and where its employees live and work. Support is provided to address such issues as affordable housing, crime prevention, and economic development. The foundation's Web site provides an overview of the foundation's giving interests and employee volunteer programs and information on the company's Canadian community investment program.

Horizon Organic Dairy (CO) (http://www.horizonorganic.com/about/corporate/index.html)
Located in Boulder, Colorado, the Horizon Organic Dairy makes charitable contributions to organizations that champion environmental education and preservation, family farmers and rural issues, animal welfare, and organic research, education, and promotion. Funded organizations should have a mission similar to Horizon's own. The company's Web site provides a mission statement, downloadable funding application form, and contact information.

HSBC USA, Inc. (NY) (http://us.hsbc.com/inside/community/communities.asp)
HSBC USA, Inc. provides philanthropic support in the communities where the company does business through corporate contributions, community and economic development programs, and its HSBC in the Community Foundation. These programs focus on various interest areas, including education, the environment, and the revitalization of low-to-moderate income neighborhoods. Specific details on each program can be found on the company's Web site, along with grant guidelines, application procedures, and descriptions of recently funded organizations, contact information, and a brochure entitled *Sharing Our Success.*

The Humana Foundation, Inc. (KY) (http://www.humanafoundation.org/)
Based in Louisville, Kentucky, the Humana Foundation, Inc. is the philanthropic arm of Humana, Inc., one of the nation's largest managed healthcare companies. Established in 1981, the foundation supports charitable organizations and institutions that promote education, health and human services, community development, and the arts in communities where Humana has a business presence. The foundation also offers a scholarship program for the children of its associates. The foundation's Web site features application guidelines and instructions, a downloadable application form, examples of grant recipients, descriptions of projects, and contact information.

IBM Corporation (NY) (http://www.ibm.com/IBM/IBMGives/index.html)
The IBM Corporation provides corporate contributions of "cash, equipment, and people to nonprofit organizations and educational institutions across the U.S. and around the world." The company's primary giving focus is education. Through the Reinventing Education Program, the company forms partnerships with school districts in the United States and in countries throughout the world to "develop technology solutions designed to help support school reform efforts and raise student achievement." The company's Web site contains a description of the company's corporate giving strategy and a summary of current philanthropic initiatives, including K–12 education, workforce development, adult education and job training, and the environment; examples of funded programs in IBM communities worldwide; grant application policies and procedures; and online versions of the company's annual report and program updates.

ICG Communications, Inc. (CO) (http://www.icgcomm.com/)
ICG Communications, Inc., based in Englewood, Colorado, "encourages community support and the spirit of volunteerism to enrich the lives of children, bringing together technology and education through cooperation, communication, and collaboration." ICG's programs are centered in the communities where the company does business. The company also sponsors a number of charitable community events. The company's Web site provides program descriptions, proposal guidelines, and contact information.

Illinois Power Company (IL) (http://www.illinoispower.com/ip.nsf/web/OurCommunity)
The Illinois Power Company has provided philanthropic support to the communities it serves for over 75 years. The company's Community Grants program supports nonprofit organizations in the areas of education, minority affairs, special constituencies, health and safety/environment, and economic development. The Bright Ideas program annually funds innovative community-based projects and programs. Grants are made only to those communities in areas where the company operates. The company's Web site includes grant guidelines, application procedures, and contact information.

Independence Community Foundation (NY) (http://www.icfny.org)
The Independence Community Bank of Brooklyn, New York, founded the Independence Community Foundation in 1998 to promote the "renewal and revitalization of low-income and moderate-income neighborhoods of New York City, Nassau County, and northern New Jersey." Funding is provided in three major categories: neighborhood renewal; education, culture, and the arts; and community quality of life initiatives. The foundation's Web site includes eligibility information, application guidelines and procedures, and contact information.

InfoSpace, Inc. (WA) (http://www.infospace.com/info/about/infospace_foundation2.htm)
InfoSpace, Inc., with offices in Seattle and Bellevue, Washington, maintains a corporate giving program that includes the InfoSpace Foundation, employee matching gifts, and volunteer programs. The company's foundation was established in 2000 "to provide the resources needed to make a positive difference in the lives of people in communities where InfoSpace employees live and work." Funding areas include K–12 and higher education, the well-being of youth, and issues associated with poverty. The company's Web site contains funding guidelines, a list of recently awarded grants, downloadable grant application forms, and details on the other corporate giving programs.

Ingram Book Group (TN)
(http://www.ingrambook.com/Company_Info/HR0523/html/philantropy.asp)
The LaVergne, Tennessee-headquartered Ingram Book Group and its employees participate in all levels of local and national community action programs. The company makes financial and in-kind charitable contributions with a focus on helping people. The Ingram Community Access Network consists of independent teams of Ingram associates at each of the company's locations, which encourage local community involvement efforts and help allocate the corporate contributions budget. The company's Web site provides an overview of the company's community programs and contact information.

Inspiration Software (OR) (http://www.inspiration.com/scholarship.html)
Located in Portland, Oregon, Inspiration Software develops and supports visual learning and thinking tools. The company offers annual Inspired Teacher Scholarships for Visual Learning to encourage teachers' professional development in visual learning and education technology. Inspiration Software's Web site features a description of the company's visual learning philosophy, a listing of recent scholarship recipients, and contact information.

Intel Corporation (CA) (http://www.intel.com/community)
Intel Corporation and its employees "are dedicated to supporting community needs, educational initiatives, and environmental programs" in communities around the world in which Intel has a presence. The company's top priority is education, with support provided for K–12/higher education and programs that advance science, math, and technology education, particularly for women and underserved populations. The company's Web site provides grant guidelines, application materials, information on local community programs and international programs, contact information, and online versions of Intel's "Annual Report of Contributions" and related publications.

International Paper Company (NY)
(http://www.internationalpaper.com/our_world/philanthropy/index.html)
The New York-based International Paper Company, a paper and forest products company, provides contributions through the International Paper Company Foundation focused on existing and emerging educational needs, specifically environmental, economic, and literacy programs for young children, as well as short-term, critical civic needs within the communities where International Paper has operating facilities. The foundation also supports organizations where its employees actively volunteer. The company's Web site features an overview of the foundation's priorities and information on national, local, and regional initiatives.

IPALCO Enterprises, Inc. (IN)
(http://www.ipalco.com/ABOUTIPALCO/Community/Community.html)
IPALCO Enterprises, Inc., an energy company headquartered in Indianapolis, Indiana, supports programs that focus on education, the environment, health and welfare, and the arts. IPALCO administers the Golden Apple Award, which recognizes outstanding teachers who integrate math, science, and technology into classroom subjects. The company's Golden Eagle Grants program funds projects aimed at resource conservation and environmental awareness. IPALCO's charitable efforts are described on its Web site, which also features information on funded programs and award recipients.

ITT Industries, Inc. Corporate Giving Program (NY)
(http://www.ittind.com/news/comm.asp)
Headquartered in White Plains, New York, ITT Industries, Inc. sponsors an international Corporate Giving Program. The company provides leadership in environmental, educational, and other community activities where employees live and work. The company was part of the effort to found the Engineering Alliance, which works to "improve public awareness, understanding, and recognition of the engineering profession and to address the crisis with respect to the number of U.S. students pursuing engineering degrees." It also sponsors international awards recognizing issues related to the world's use of water and community policing. The company's Web site features an overview of the company's corporate citizenship programs.

Jacksonville Jaguars Foundation, Inc. (FL) (http://www.jaguars.com/)
The Jacksonville Jaguars Foundation, Inc., based in Jacksonville, Florida, is committed to serving the greater Jacksonville area through strategic financial, networking, and volunteer support benefiting economically and socially disadvantaged youth and families. Created by the National Football League team, the foundation's primary objective is to "help meet the needs of disadvantaged youth, striving to address the causes of those needs wherever possible, and therefore prevent problems before they begin." The foundation also seeks to support efforts to build understanding among different groups and promote cooperation. The foundation also has several programs, including Honor Rows, which rewards youths with game seats for academic achievement, behavioral improvement, and providing public service. The NIKE/Jaguars Foundation Community Scholars program, a scholarship program, offers full tuition and mentor support at the University of North Florida for select inner-city high school students who have participated in the Honor Rows or Let Us Play Camp program and have demonstrated a commitment to public service. The foundation's Web site contains downloadable guidelines and application forms for each grantmaking program, grants lists, and contact information.

J.C. Penney Company (TX) (http://www.jcpenney.net/company/commrel/index.htm)
The J.C. Penney Company makes grants to national organizations in the areas of health and welfare, education, civic betterment, and arts and culture. Special attention is given to the support and promotion of voluntarism and the improvement of pre-college education, with a focus on the areas of K–12 reform, restructuring, and dropout prevention. Funding emphasis is given to projects that serve a broad sector of a particular community, national projects that benefit local organizations across the country, organizations that provide

direct services, and organizations with a proven record of success. Grants for projects with a local scope, hospitals, museums, and individual colleges and universities are made by local units of the company. The Community Involvement area of the company's Web site features general funding guidelines, application procedures and limitations, detailed information on support for education, Golden Rule and National Volunteer Awards, and the company's "Community Partners Annual Report."

Jewel-Osco (ID) (http://www.jewelosco.com/jewel/pr/pr_main.asp)
The Jewel-Osco charitable giving program focuses on the communities in Chicagoland, northwest Indiana, Wisconsin, and the Quad Cities served by the Jewel-Osco supermarket chain. The Midwest division of Albertsons Inc., Jewel-Osco supports a wide variety of philanthropic projects, including employee scholarship and volunteer programs, the United Way, area museums, food donations, and grants to nonprofit organizations in the areas of education, hunger relief, and health and nutrition. The company's Web site provides a general overview of Jewel-Osco's charitable giving strategy and history, as well as details on funded programs.

The J. Jill Group, Inc. (MA) (http://www.jjill.com/about/community.asp)
The J. Jill Group, Inc., a Quincy, Massachusetts-based women's retailer, is committed to issues affecting disadvantaged women and children. The company channels its corporate giving efforts through the J. Jill Compassion Fund, a donor-advised fund of the Boston Foundation. U.S. organizations serving homeless or at-risk women and children that provide services including job training, transitional and/or affordable housing, education, and emergency shelter are eligible for funding. The company's Web site provides Compassion Fund grant guidelines, deadlines, details on the review process, and contact information.

Johnson & Johnson Corporate Giving Program (NJ) (http://www.jnj.com/community/index.htm)
Through its worldwide contributions efforts, the New Brunswick, New Jersey-based healthcare company Johnson & Johnson "aligns its philanthropic initiatives with its expertise in four key platforms for giving: Access to Healthcare, Children's Health, Professional Development and Education, and Community Responsibility." The majority of the company's support is directed to specific programs and organizations; the company does not accept or respond to unsolicited proposals. The company's Web site provides the company's "Contributions Annual Reports," information on the company's signature giving programs, and a community calendar.

S.C. Johnson Wax Fund (WI) (http://www.scjohnsonwax.com/community/)
S.C. Johnson Wax Fund, headquartered in Racine, Wisconsin, is a manufacturer of home cleaning, storage, personal care, and insect control products and a supplier of products and services for commercial, industrial, and institutional facilities. Through the S.C. Johnson Wax Fund and a direct corporate giving program, the company supports programs focused on "advancing the three legs of sustainability: economic vitality, social progress, and a healthy environment" in communities around the world where the company does business. The company's Web site features descriptions of the company's giving initiatives, examples of funded projects, and an online version of the "S.C. Johnson Public Report," which details the company's contributions.

J.P. Morgan Chase & Co. (NY) (http://www.jpmorganchase.com/cm/cs?pagename=Chase/Href&urlname=jpmc/community)
J.P. Morgan Chase & Co., the global financial services firm established more than 150 years ago, supports "the development and prosperity of the communities it serves" through community activities sponsored by the corporation and its subsidiaries, the J.P. Morgan Chase Foundation, and the company's employees. Support is provided to communities in the New York tri-state region, across the United States, and around the world. The foundation places primary emphasis on supporting arts and culture, community development and human services, and pre-collegiate public education. The company's Web site provides

specific grant guidelines, eligibility information, application procedures for each program area, and details on the company's other community support programs.

Just Born, Inc. (PA) (http://www.justborn.com/about/community.html)
Just Born, Inc. located in Lehigh Valley, Pennsylvania, makes grants in the areas of education and arts to qualified organizations where the company operates. The company's Web site features information on restrictions, a brief listing of previous grant recipients, and contact information.

KeySpan Foundation (NY)
(http://www.keyspanenergy.com/corpinfo/community/foundation_all_all.jsp)
The KeySpan Foundation, located in Hicksville, New York, was established in 1998 by an endowment to serve as a compliment to KeySpan Energy's corporate giving program. The foundation focuses its funding within the major areas of education and the environment. Grants are limited to charitable 501(c)(3) organizations that provide services within KeySpan's service territory. The foundation's Web site features grant guidelines and limitations, application instructions, information on the company's service territory, and contact information.

KFC Corporation (KY) (http://www.kfc.com/community/colway.htm)
The KFC Corporation established the Colonel's Way Award as an "opportunity for younger generations to learn more about past generations, and vice versa." Awards are given for outstanding essays written by elementary school students that pay tribute to seniors. The company's Web site contains a history of the award, official rules, a description of prizes, and contact information.

King Pharmaceuticals, Inc. (TN) (http://www.kingpharm.com/public_relations.htm)
King Pharmaceuticals, Inc., based in Bristol, Tennessee, focuses its philanthropic efforts in the areas of health, education, arts and culture, community improvement, youth development, and ministerial programs. Through monetary grants and employee community service projects, the company seeks to "improve the life, health, and welfare of the community." General information about King Pharmaceuticals' charitable programs and contact information are available at the company's Web site.

Kingston Technology Company, Inc. (CA) (http://www.kingston.com/company/charity.asp)
The Fountain Valley, California-based Kingston Technology Company, Inc.'s charitable giving program follows the core values of the company itself, focusing on organizations that support education, technology, and the well-being of citizens. Specific areas of interest are education, community service, and arts and culture. The company's Web site provides funding guidelines, limitations, application procedures, and contact information.

Kmart Corporation (MI) (http://www.kmartcorp.com/corp/community/index.stm)
Located in Troy, Michigan, the Kmart Corporation contributes to the community through a variety of programs, including the Leaders in Learning initiative, a program that supports learning initiatives; the Kmart School Spirit Program, a fundraising program for schools; employee volunteer efforts; holiday outreach programs; and support for the March of Dimes and the American Red Cross. The company's Web site provides an overview of these programs and contact information.

Kohl's Corporation (WI)
(http://www.kohlscorporation.com/communityrelations/community01.htm)
The Menomonee Falls, Wisconsin-based Kohl's Corporation supports a number of philanthropic activities designed to improve health and educational opportunities for children in Kohl's communities. The Kohl's Kids Who Care Recognition Program funds young people who volunteer in their communities; the Fundraising Card Program provides profits from electronic gift cards to nonprofit organizations; the Children's Hospital Program donates proceeds from select merchandise sold during holiday seasons; and the Associate

Volunteer Recognition Program matches employees' volunteer efforts with corporate grants. The company's Web site provides details on these programs, forms to apply for the Gift Card Program and to nominate a young person for the Kids Who Care Recognition Program, and contact information.

Komag, Inc. (CA) (http://www.komag.com/community/community.html)
Komag, Inc., a San Jose, California-based producer of thin-film media for disk drives, provides support for nonprofit organizations with an emphasis on youth and education programs in regions where the company does business. The company's U.S. Corporate Grant Program provides cash grants and equipment to schools and nonprofit organizations. Komag also matches the charitable donations of its employees. The company's Web site provides grant guidelines and restrictions, details on employee matching gifts and volunteer programs, contact information, and an overview of the company's community programs in Malaysia.

The KPMG Foundation (NJ) (http://www.kpmgfoundation.org/)
The KPMG Foundation, established in 1968, is committed to enhancing business education for four groups of people: primary and secondary students, undergraduates, graduate students, and faculty. For primary and secondary students, the foundation funds SIFE (Students in Free Enterprise), a program to teach business skills, and LEAD (Leadership Education and Development), a Summer Business Institute program for minority students. The foundation funds scholarships, internships, and Ph.D. programs for minority undergrad and graduate students in business. Faculty teaching, research, and development gains support through sponsored professorships, conferences, and associations. The foundation also promotes corporate voluntarism and community service. The foundation's Web site features program descriptions linked to individual Web sites and contact information.

Koch Industries, Inc. (KS) (http://www.kochind.com/community/default.asp)
Koch Industries, Inc., based in Wichita, Kansas, "supports a wide variety of nonprofit organizations that share [their] values and market-based philosophy." The company funds organizations in communities where it has employees and facilities. Funding is provided for education programs that apply scientific and economic principles to problem solving, innovative environmental stewardship programs, and human services projects that promote "self-sufficiency, individual responsibility, tolerance, and respect for others." The company's Web site includes application guidelines, a list of communities that the company serves, and regional contact information.

Kroger Company (OH) (http://www.kroger.com/corpnewsinfo_charitablegiving.htm)
Headquartered in Cincinnati, Ohio, the Kroger Company family of stores includes grocery and multi-department stores, convenience stores, and mall jewelry stores. Kroger contributes to charitable causes and local communities where the company operates stores or manufacturing facilities. The company's corporate giving includes donations made by Kroger and the company's three foundations (Kroger Co. Foundation, Fred Meyer Foundation, and Ralphs/Food 4 Less Foundation), employees, and through in-store fundraising. Kroger's charitable giving is focused in five key areas: being a "good neighbor," hunger relief, education, advancement of women and minorities, and women's health. The company also encourages its retail divisions to work with nonprofit organizations and programs in their local communities. The company's Web site includes information on the charitable giving programs and priorities of Kroger, the company's retail divisions, and foundations; a listing of the company's family of stores; and contact information.

Land O'Lakes Foundation (MN)
(http://www.landolakesinc.com/OurCompany/CompanyInformationIndex.cfm)
Supported by Land O'Lakes Inc., the Land O'Lakes Foundation works to improve the quality of life in communities where Land O'Lakes, Inc. has members, employees, plants, and facilities. The foundation's funding and volunteer programs are designed to help "rural communities prosper and prepare for tomorrow." The Community Grants Program

supports organizations that address hunger, rural youth leadership, civic concerns, and the arts. The Mid-Atlantic Grants program is a grassroots effort developed for Land O'Lakes dairy communities in Maryland, New Jersey, New York, Pennsylvania, and Virginia. The foundation also matches cash donations by its member cooperatives for local projects and matches gifts by its employees to education institutions. The foundation's Web site features eligibility information, application guidelines and forms, program updates, grants lists, contact information, and annual reports.

Lanoga Corporation (WA) (http://www.lanoga.com/community.htm)
The Lanoga Corporation, a building materials company, works with its regional subsidiaries and divisions to contribute to the communities where the company operates. Contributions by the company's subsidiaries and divisions are typically in the form of in-kind contributions and employee involvement. The company focuses its giving efforts on Habitat for Humanity, food banks, medical needs, educational opportunities, endowments for the arts, and children and community services. The company's Web site features information on Lanoga's involvement in the community, details on the company's Habitat for Humanity donation program, and contact information.

Lee Jeans (KS) (http://www.leejeans.com/about_community.asp)
The Merriam, Kansas-headquartered Lee Jeans, a subsidiary of the VF Corporation, is a sponsor of many charitable causes, and encourages all of its employees to be active in the community. The company's Web site features information on Lee National Denim Day, a fundraising program benefiting breast cancer research; a list of organizations supported by the company; and contact information.

Levi Strauss & Co. (CA) (http://www.levistrauss.com/responsibility)
The Levi Strauss Foundation was created in 1952 and, along with a corporate giving program, is part of Levi Strauss & Co.'s commitment to the needs of communities around the world where the company's employees and contractors' employees live and work. Giving programs are focused on HIV/AIDS prevention programs targeting women and youth, economic development programs for women and youth, and education access projects. Grants are also provided to community organizations located in sourcing communities for programs including basic healthcare access and workers' rights information. The company's Web site provides grant guidelines, application procedures, and a list of eligible communities and countries with contact information, grants lists organized by geographic area, and information on employee volunteer and matching gifts programs.

Liberty Bank Foundation (CT) (http://www.liberty-bank.com/Foundation/)
Established in 1997, the Liberty Bank Foundation works to provide financial support to nonprofit organizations throughout central, eastern, and shoreline Connecticut. Funding is focused on projects relating to community and economic development, education, health, human services, and the arts. The foundation's Web site features grant guidelines and eligibility information, a downloadable application, a listing of recently funded grants, links to resources for nonprofit organizations, and contact information.

LifeLine Communications (OK) (http://www.lifeline.net/company/sharing)
Oklahoma City-based LifeLine Communications maintains a giving program that contributes ten percent of long distance revenues to Christian ministries, charities, and nonprofit organizations. The company's Web site contains guidelines for organizations that wish to partner with the company and contact information.

Limited Brands, Inc. (OH) (http://www.limitedbrands.com/community/index.jsp)
Fashion retailer Limited Brands, Inc., headquartered in Columbus, Ohio, maintains a foundation and corporate giving program focused on issues important to women, including empowering women, nurturing and mentoring children, and improving education. Special consideration is given to organizations with which the company's associates are involved as board members and those that serve areas where the company's home offices are

located. The company's Web site features grant guidelines and application procedures, a list of funded organizations, and contact information.

Lincoln Financial Group (PA)
(http://www.lfg.com/LincolnPageServer?LFGPage=/lfg/ipc/abt/cgv/index.html)
Headquartered in Philadelphia, Lincoln Financial Group provides funding through corporate giving programs and through the Lincoln Financial Group Foundation to support philanthropic endeavors within the communities where the company has a strong business presence. Funds are distributed in three areas: arts and culture, education, and human services. Charitable contributions committees at the company's affiliate offices administer local charitable giving programs. The company's Web site provides an overview of the company's community efforts, grants guidelines and application forms, and a list of business locations with contact information.

Lorillard Tobacco Company (NC) (http://www.lorillard.net/card.html)
The Greensboro, North Carolina-based Lorillard Tobacco Company sponsors a Youth Smoking Prevention Program which focuses on consumer-directed initiatives that discourage youth smoking and that restrict underage smokers' access to tobacco products. Links to specific Web sites for these programs, including "We Card" and "Butt Out Now" are available on the company's Web site.

Lubrizol Foundation (OH) (http://www.lubrizol.com/Foundation/default.htm)
The Lubrizol Corporation, a fluid technologies company based in Wickliffe, Ohio, created the Lubrizol Foundation to "complement and support the interests and values of the Lubrizol Corporation by awarding financial support to educational institutions and charitable organizations in communities primarily within the United States where Lubrizol operates major facilities." Funding is distributed in the greater Houston, Texas, and Cleveland, Ohio, areas. The foundation's Web site features application guidelines, the latest annual report, and contact information.

Lucent Technologies Foundation (NJ) (http://www.lucent.com/news/foundation/)
Lucent Technologies, Inc., a communications technology company headquartered in Murray Hill, New Jersey, supports communities where it has a business presence through the Lucent Technologies Foundation, the Community Relations Corporate Contributions Program, and Lucent Cares, a global volunteer organization. The foundation's mission is "to improve education by enriching the practice of teaching and improving students' academic performance," with a primary focus on the physical sciences and mathematics. The Community Relations Corporate Contributions Program supports local projects in communities around the world where Lucent employees work and live. The foundation's Web site contains funding guidelines, application procedures, contact information, and details on company-sponsored scholarships in the sciences.

Lyondell Chemical Company (TX)
(http://www.lyondell.com/html/social/social_responsibility.shtml)
The community services department of the Lyondell Chemical Company, headquartered in Houston, Texas, sponsors numerous community events, initiatives, programs, and services. Funding priorities include pre-college education, environmental quality, and community sustainability. The company generally seeks to support nonprofit organizations that benefit a broad spectrum of people within its plant communities and prefers to support organizations in which the company has some direct involvement. The company's Web site features descriptions of the company's various community initiatives, contributions guidelines and limitations, and contact information.

Maine Health Access Foundation (ME) (http://www.mehaf.org)
Located in Augusta, the Maine Health Access Foundation was incorporated in 2000 to promote "affordable and timely access to comprehensive, quality health care for every Maine resident." To fulfill this mission, the foundation supports solutions to Maine's healthcare

needs through grants and other programs, particularly targeting those who are uninsured and medically underserved. The foundation's Web site provides information on the foundation's funding priorities and programs, requests for proposals, application forms, technical assistance publications, a list of application resources, and contact information.

Marathon Oil Company Foundation (TX)
(http://www.marathon.com/Values/Our_Values/Philanthropy/)
The Houston, Texas-based Marathon Oil Company Foundation, a giving program of Marathon Oil Company, was established in 2001 to provide support for educational, health and human services, civic and community, environmental, and social needs. Grants are awarded to nonprofit organizations whose programs operate within the United States, primarily in the major employing locations of Marathon Oil Company and Marathon Ashland Petroleum LLC. The foundation's Web site features an overview of the foundation's giving interests, downloadable funding guidelines, and contact information.

Maritz Inc. (MO) (http://www.maritz.com/maritz-community-involvement.html)
A provider of performance improvement, travel, and marketing research services, Maritz, Inc., and its employees dedicate time, expertise, and financial support to civic and charitable projects in communities around the world. The company's Web site features examples of community involvement projects, a listing of the company's worldwide locations, and contact information.

Marsh Supermarkets, Inc. (IN) (http://www.marsh.net/ce_cg.html)
Indianapolis, Indiana-based Marsh Supermarkets, Inc. contributes to the communities in which it operates throughout Indiana and Ohio. Specifically, the company supports food banks and nutrition programs for children with both financial contributions and in-kind donations. Operating grants or project support are given to human service agencies that provide services to people in need. Priority is given to projects that directly benefit children, promote the education of children, or encourage the positive development of children. The company also supports cultural and arts organizations, community and civic groups, and local, grassroots organizations focused on improving their immediate community. Donation request procedures and contact information are available on the company's Web site.

Master Brewers Association of the Americas Scholarship Foundation, Inc. (MN)
(http://www.mbaa.com/scholarship/scholarship.html)
In 1887, the Master Brewers Association of the Americas was formed for the purpose of advancing the professional interest of brew and malt house production and technical personnel. Located in St. Paul, Minnesota, the association disseminates technical and practical information, promotes training, encourages cooperation and interaction, and furthers knowledge through the exchange of ideas. The association provides scholarships for members in a scientific course of study directly related to the technical areas of malting and brewing. The foundation's Web site features an online application, scholarship provisions, and contact information.

Materials for the Future Foundation (CA) (http://www.materials4future.org/)
The Materials for the Future Foundation was founded in San Francisco in 1992 by a group of Bay Area funders and recycling advocates to "support community-based initiatives that integrate the environmental goals of resource conservation through waste prevention, reuse, and recycling with the economic development goals of job creation/retention, enterprise development, and local empowerment." The foundation focuses on low-income communities, communities of color, and communities with high numbers of unemployed persons, especially in the San Francisco Bay Area. The foundation accomplishes its goals through grantmaking, loans, providing business and technical assistance, referral services, community education, and other projects. The foundation's Web site features a mission statement, information on current projects, online publications, links to related resources, and contact information.

Mattel Children's Foundation (CA) (http://www.mattel.com/about_us/Comm_Involvement/ci_mcf_over.asp)
Based in El Segundo, California, the Mattel Children's Foundation, the philanthropic arm of Mattel, Inc., encourages community involvement among its employees and makes charitable investments aimed at furthering Mattel's goal to better the lives of children in need. The majority of the foundation's resources are directed toward national initiatives that creatively address relevant children's issues. Priorities include the Mattel Children's Hospital at UCLA, the Children Affected by AIDS Foundation, and the Mattel Family Learning Program, which establishes computer learning labs worldwide. (Due to major funding commitments, the foundation is not currently accepting new proposals.) The foundation also offers grants to match employee volunteer and financial contributions and provides toy donations to nonprofit organizations directly serving children in need. The foundation's Web site features details on these programs and contact information.

Mazda Foundation (DC) (http://www.mazdafoundation.org)
The Mazda Foundation was established in 1990 to help fulfill the social responsibility goals of Mazda North American Operations. The foundation awards grants to programs promoting education and literacy, environmental conservation, cross-cultural understanding, social welfare, and scientific research. Preference is given to nonprofit organizations that are national in scope. The foundation's Web site features grant guidelines, application procedures and deadlines, details on current programs, and contact information.

McGraw-Hill Companies (NY) (http://www.mcgraw-hill.com/community/community.html)
The McGraw-Hill Companies, based in New York City, maintain a Corporate Contributions and Community Relations Community Partners program to "use the fiscal and human resources of the company to help people around the world learn, grow, acquire new skills, better their lives and, in doing so, better their community." Priority consideration is given to 501(c)(3) nonprofit organizations that support excellence in education and learning, with a primary emphasis on financial literacy; further financial literacy in the communities where the company operates; utilize new technologies; extend their reach globally; can be evaluated and can serve as models elsewhere; and are staffed and administered by people with demonstrated competence in their fields. The company's Web site includes grant guidelines and restrictions, application procedures, contact information, information on employee matching gift and volunteer programs, profiles of funded programs, and details on the Harold W. McGraw, Jr. Prize for advances in education.

McKesson HBOC (CA) (http://www.mckesson.com/community.html)
McKesson HBOC, headquartered in San Francisco, California, is a provider of healthcare products and services to retail pharmacies, hospitals, and healthcare networks. The company's principal charitable arm, the McKesson Foundation, Inc., works to "enhance the health and quality of life in the communities where McKesson Corporation operates and its employees live." Programs include Adolescent Health, to increase access to quality health care for at-risk children and youth; Youth-at-Risk, to provide opportunities for youth to develop life skills necessary to become productive citizens; and Employee Involvement, to encourage and support employee involvement in the community. The company's Web site features descriptions of the foundation's funding philosophy, grant guidelines and application procedures, a list of sample grants, and information on educational matching gifts, scholarships, special youth initiatives, and volunteering.

Medtronic Foundation (MN) (http://www.medtronic.com/foundation/index.html)
The Medtronic Foundation is the principal worldwide philanthropy and community affairs vehicle of Minneapolis-based Medtronic, Inc., a manufacturer of medical equipment and devices. The foundation's focus areas include building partnerships and empowering people with chronic disease, encouraging students' interest in science, and contributing to the vitality of the communities where Medtronic operates. Programs that serve socioeconomically disadvantaged people are a top priority across all funding areas. The foundation's Web site includes program descriptions, grant guidelines and application procedures,

application forms, a list of foundation grants, a listing of Medtronic communities, a selection of press releases, an interactive correspondence page, and details on employee volunteer and matching gifts programs.

MEEMIC Foundation for the Future of Education (MI) (http://www.meemic.com/foundframe.htm)
The MEEMIC Foundation for the Future of Education, a nonprofit organization created in 1992 by the MEEMIC Insurance Company, offers financial assistance to Michigan schools and educators in the form of "mini-grants." The foundation's Web site features program support restrictions, application information, FAQs, printable application sheets, and contact information.

Meijer, Inc. (MI) (http://www.meijer.com/pr)
Meijer, Inc., a grocery and general merchandise retailer with stores throughout Illinois, Indiana, Kentucky, Michigan, and Ohio, supports organizations in communities where the company operates. Meijer seeks to contribute to the education of young people and provides support to learning programs in local schools. School programs include honor roll rewards, teacher of the month and athlete/scholar of the month programs, and an alcohol awareness program. The company's Web site features a complete list and descriptions of supported programs and contact information.

Merck & Co., Inc. (NJ) (http://www.merck.com/about/cr/policies_performance/social/philanthropy.html)
Pharmaceutical company Merck & Co., Inc. aims "to make a positive contribution to the communities in which we work and live by supporting a wide range of charitable, educational, and environmental initiatives worldwide." Merck's corporate philanthropy programs are designed to align with the company's business interests and include improving access to quality healthcare and medicines, strengthening capacity in the biomedical sciences through advancement of education and research, and contributing to local communities where Merck has major facilities. The Merck Company Foundation is Merck's chief source of funding support to qualified nonprofit charitable organizations. Funding is focused on improving healthcare, fostering biomedical and science education, and supporting charitable arts, social services, civic, environmental, and other organizations. The company's Web site provides an overview of the foundation's priorities, a breakdown of contributions by giving category, information on other company and employee giving programs and projects, and contact information.

Mercury Computer Systems, Inc. (MA) (http://www.mc.com/about/sponsorships.cfm)
Mercury Computer Systems, Inc. of Chelmsford, Massachusetts, supports cultural and educational organizations in areas where the company operates. The goal of the company's sponsorship program is to "promote understanding of science and technology, with a special focus on encouraging young people to explore the technical professions." The company's Web site features a listing of the organizations that the company actively supports.

Merrill Lynch & Co., Inc. (NY) (http://philanthropy.ml.com)
Merrill Lynch & Co., Inc., a global financial management and advisory company headquartered in New York City, makes charitable contributions through its branch offices, business units and subsidiaries, and through the Merrill Lynch Foundation. The company has adopted Children and Youth as its global cause for 2000 to 2005 and seeks to support programs that meet the educational needs and interests of underserved children and youth. The foundation gives priority to grant requests from New York City and national organizations that reflect its focus. Requests outside of New York City should be submitted to the branch managers of local offices. The company's Web site features funding guidelines and exclusions, application procedures, and contact information.

Mervyn's (CA) (http://target.com/mervyns_group/community/community_main.jhtml)
A subsidiary of Target Corporation, Mervyn's stores seek to improve local communities through financial support, volunteer activities, and involvement in nonprofit initiatives. Mervyn's stores partner with local schools and arts and social action organizations to help improve the quality of life for families, particularly children. Funding currently focuses on arts and education. The Mervyn's grantmaking program "begins and ends" at the store level. Store managers serve as the initial contact for nonprofit organizations making a grant request. The company's Web site provides funding eligibility guidelines, a store locator, details on the application process, and information on national giving programs, including the annual Local Hero Scholarship Program.

Metropolitan Life Foundation (NY)
(http://www.metlife.com/Companyinfo/Community/Found/index.html)
Established by insurance company Metropolitan Life in 1976, the New York City-based Metropolitan Life Foundation provides support for educational, health, civic, and cultural organizations toward the goals of strengthening communities, promoting good health, and improving education. The foundation's Web site features grant application guidelines, examples of funded projects in each program area, contact information, details on employee volunteer programs, and information on the company's Social Investment Program, which provides aid primarily in the form of loans to assist community development and related programs.

Metropolitan Water District of Southern California (CA)
(http://www.mwdh2o.com/mwdh2o/pages/yourwater/cpp/cpp.html)
The Metropolitan Water District of Southern California is seeking to fulfill its mission by encouraging the discussion of water quality, water conservation, and water reliability issues important to the region through research, educational collaborations at all levels, and policy forums. The company supports national, state, regional, and local organizations that meet the missions, goals, and objectives set. The company's Web site features information about qualifications and online applications.

MicrobiaLogic LLC (AZ) (http://www.microbialogic.com/donation.html)
Based in Phoenix, Arizona, MicrobiaLogic LLC initiated a product donation program in 1999 to donate its outdoor toilet products to nonprofit and nationally known organizations or schools with outdoor programs that "maintain high standards of environmental stewardship." The company's Web site includes a list of recipients, an online questionnaire form for applicants to the product donation program, and contact information.

Micron Technology, Inc. (ID)
(http://www.micron.com/content.jsp?path=/About+Micron/Micron+Giving)
Micron Technology, Inc., a Boise, Idaho-based manufacturer of semiconductor components, provides community and educational support through its foundation and corporate giving program. The Micron Foundation supports scholarships, higher education grants and programs, and community and K–12 grants. To be eligible for a community or K–12 grant, organizations must be located in a Micron manufacturing site community. The company's corporate giving program supports student programs, faculty, and institutions of higher education through a variety of efforts, including the Partners in Research program, sponsoring visiting faculty, and student design projects, and equipment. The company's Web site features program descriptions, application guidelines, FAQs, and contact information.

Microsoft Corporation (WA) (http://www.microsoft.com/giving/)
Through its corporate giving, the Microsoft Corporation is committed to empowering people to discover and achieve their goals. Microsoft's corporate philanthropic efforts fall into four main areas: expanding opportunities through technology access, strengthening nonprofits through technology, developing a diverse technology workforce, and building community through corporate funding and through matching employees' charitable

contributions. Contributions are made to communities throughout the United States and internationally through Microsoft field and subsidiary offices worldwide. The Community Affairs section of the company's Web site provides funding guidelines, applications procedures, program updates, and contact information.

Millipore Foundation (MA)
(http://www.millipore.com/corporate/milliporefoundation.nsf/home)
The Millipore Foundation works to foster advances in science and technology related to Millipore Corporation business objectives, which includes providing technologies, tools, and services for the development and production of new therapeutic drugs; improving the quality of life in those communities in which Millipore employees live and work, particularly in the state of Massachusetts; and stimulating voluntarism and active community involvement by Millipore employees. Through its grants program, the foundation supports projects in the areas of education and research, social services, healthcare, public policy, and the arts. The foundation's Web site features an overview of the foundation, program guidelines, application instructions, FAQs, the foundation's financial summary, and contact information.

Minnesota Power (MN) (http://www.mnpower.com/community/index.htm)
Located in Duluth, Minnesota Power, an Allete company, supports local nonprofit organizations that maintain and improve the quality of life in the communities of upper Minnesota. The company's contributions are made in the areas of community service, civics and culture, health, the environment, and education. Grant guidelines and application information are available online. Additionally, the Community Involvement Scholarship Program provides funds to graduating seniors residing in Minnesota Power's service territory. The company's Web site provides the most recent community investment annual review and service territory map; information on the company's economic development program, teacher programs, and other projects; and a downloadable scholarship application form.

Monsanto Fund (MO) (http://www.monsantofund.org/)
The mission of the Monsanto Fund, the principal philanthropic arm of the Monsanto Company, is "to bridge the gap between people's needs and their available resources." The fund's grants emanate from the company's headquarters community in St. Louis and from its facilities in the United States and around the world. The fund also provides matching gifts for employee contributions. All funding falls into four priority areas: agricultural abundance, the environment, science education, and Monsanto communities. The geographic focus of the fund's giving is generally in the communities where Monsanto employees live and work. The fund's Web site features details on the fund's priority areas, funding qualifications and procedures, examples of funded programs, the fund's contributions report, and contact information.

MONY Foundation (NY) (http://www.mony.com/AboutMONY/InsideMONY/Foundation/)
The MONY Foundation of New York City is funded by the MONY Group in order to support "innovative, strategically effective, community-based programs." Foundation funding goes to communities where MONY employees live, work, and do business. In New York City, the foundation supports after-school, community service, and volunteer programs for youth. In Syracuse, New York, the foundation supports after-school programs for children and teens at risk. The foundation also encourages employee community service through matching gifts and volunteer programs. The foundation's Web site features an overview of the foundation's programs, detailed information on the New York City and Syracuse programs, application procedures, grants lists, and contact information.

Morton International, Inc. (IL) (http://www.mortonsalt.com/como/commcomm.htm)
Morton International, Inc., producer of salt for household and other uses, contributes to the community through financial and educational support, as well as through the energy and talents of its employee volunteers. Examples of some of the programs Morton is involved with, including the Morton Arboretum, an employee matching gifts program, work on

combating iodine deficiency disorders, and United Way partnerships, are available on the company's Web site.

The Motley Fool, Inc. (VA) (http://www.fool.com/foolanthropy/foolanthropy.htm)
The Motley Fool, Inc., an Internet portal dedicated to educating its visitors on the topics of personal finance and investing, administers the Foolanthropy program to raise funds for charities during an annual funding drive. Readers nominate charities, and the company provides message boards for visitors to discuss the organizations. To be eligible for funding, charitable organizations should hold long-term expectations, provide complete details of finances, look for sustainable solutions, and involve the public in charitable programs. The company's Web site provides information related to the Foolanthropy program, including details on contributing.

Motorola, Inc. (IL) (http://www.motorola.com/MotorolaFoundation/)
The Motorola Foundation, founded in 1953 by Motorola, Inc., provides funds for higher education and primary and secondary education throughout the world where the company does business. Emphasis is also placed on assisting human services, primarily through support to local United Way organizations. The foundation's global priority giving areas include engineering, technical, and science programs at universities; programs reaching traditionally under-represented groups in the areas of math, science, engineering, and business; programs providing technical assistance, research, and statistical information on the state of science and engineering education; strengthening science and mathematics education at the pre-collegiate level; and educational programs that promote and support the environment. The company's Web site provides funding priorities and limitations, application guidelines, an eligibility quiz to access the online application, and information on the company's sponsorships of community, education, and environmental programs.

Nantucket Allserve, Inc. (MA) (http://www.juiceguys.com/community.php)
Nantucket Allserve, Inc., the maker of Nantucket Nectars, established Juice Guys Cares in 1998 to support "educational initiatives, community service, and youth involvement." The group provides support to charitable organizations through juice donations, funds, and marketing assistance. Additionally, Juice Guys Cares sponsors athletes and athletic events. The company's Web site features links to organizations that the company supports, sponsorship opportunities and guidelines for athletic events, a downloadable sponsorship form, and contact information.

National Healthcare Scholars Foundation (MI) (http://www.nhsfonline.org/)
Founded in 1987, the National Healthcare Scholars Foundation works to "serve the community by providing financial assistance to educate minority healthcare professionals through scholarships and to support those institutions and organizations dedicated to enriching the community through programs and education." The foundation awards grants to organizations or institutions for specific programs or activities that fall within the scope of the foundation's mission. The foundation's Web site features a mission statement, scholarship program details with a list of participating schools, and contact information.

National Semiconductor Corporation (CA) (http://www.national.com/community)
The National Semiconductor Corporation, based in Santa Clara, California, supports a number of corporate philanthropy programs and initiatives with the common goals of improving education and addressing critical community needs in the communities where National Semiconductor is located. The company's corporate commitment to education focuses on grades K–12 and provides school funding, volunteers, and technical assistance and equipment. The National Semiconductor Foundation, established in 2000 as a charitable fund with the Community Foundation of Silicon Valley, provides financial support to programs in the areas of higher education, primary/secondary education, and critical community needs. Employee volunteers and matching gifts are also integral parts of the company's giving program. The company's Web site features program details, a list of the company's key communities, and contact information.

Nationwide Foundation (OH) (http://www.nationwide.com/about_us/involve/fndatn.htm)
Nationwide is one of the largest diversified financial and insurance services providers in the United States. Based in Columbus, Ohio, the primary goal of the Nationwide Foundation since 1959 has been to provide financial support for organizations whose programs address basic human needs within the following categories: health and human services, education, culture and arts, and civic and community services. The foundation supports organizations that provide services in locations that have a large number of Nationwide employees and agents, such as state offices, service centers, or corporate headquarter sites. The foundation's Web site provides information on the foundation's funding priorities, application guidelines, the foundation's annual report, and contact information.

NEC Foundation of America (NY) (http://www.necus.com/company/foundation)
The NEC Foundation of America was established in 1991 by NEC and its U.S. subsidiaries to promote NEC's corporate philosophy of advancing society through technology and enabling individuals to realize their full potential. As of 2003, the foundation's sole focus is on technology for people with disabilities. Grants support programs that have national reach and impact. The foundation's Web site features program information, funding guidelines, application procedures, a list of grant recipients indexed by organization type, geographic restrictions, a financial statement, and contact information.

Net Cruiser Technologies, Inc. (PA)
(http://www.charityadvantage.com/techadvantage.htm)
Net Cruiser Technologies, Inc., through its CharityAdvantage Program, donates computer systems to nonprofit organizations and helps these organizations purchase low-cost refurbished computers to meet their technological objectives. All donations are handled by the American Non-Profit Technology Alliance, a technology advocacy organization sponsored by CharityAdvantage. An online order form and a link to the American Non-Profit Technology Alliance are available online.

New Century Energies Foundation (CO)
(http://www.ncenergies.com/CommunityProjects/Community.asp)
Located in Denver, Colorado, New Century Energies created the New Century Energies Foundation to demonstrate its commitment to charitable giving. The foundation focuses "on creating communities that are well-educated, affordable, economically sound, and that reflect the involvement of NCE employees." The foundation provides grants in the areas of affordable living, workforce readiness, and classroom connection. To be considered for a grant, a nonprofit organization must complete the request for proposal process. The foundation's Web site provides contact information.

New England Financial (MA) (http://www.nefn.com/Content/AboutUs/comminv.cfm)
New England Financial, an insurance and investment company headquartered in Boston, Massachusetts, supports public education and makes grants to nonprofit organizations in the areas of education, healthcare, social service, housing, and culture. The Community Involvement area of the company's Web site provides a description of the company's funding strategy, examples of organizations awarded grants, and contact information.

New York Life Foundation (NY) (http://www.newyorklife.com/foundation/)
New York Life Insurance Company created the New York Life Foundation in 1979 to support groups in many categories, including health and human services, education, civic and community affairs, and arts and culture. The foundation is currently focusing on programs that support children in three specific areas: mentoring, creating safe places for kids, and educational enhancement. The foundation funds projects in New York City and also considers multi-site projects implemented by national organizations involving a select group of communities. The foundation also offers an educational matching gift program for employees, employee volunteer programs, and special grant initiatives for programs submitted by employees. Program descriptions, application guidelines, contact information, and an online version of the foundation's annual report are available on the foundation's Web site.

Newport News Shipbuilding (VA) (http://www.nn.northropgrumman.com/about/community.stm)

Newport News Shipbuilding, based in Newport News, Virginia, supports educational and cultural arts programs and community service, health, and human services organizations. Grants are generally made in the geographic locations of company plants, primarily in Virginia. The Community Affairs area of the company's Web site features descriptions of the company's giving strategy, a breakdown of charitable giving, lists of grant recipients, and contact information.

Nike, Inc. (OR) (http://www.nike.com/nikebiz/nikebiz.jhtml?page=26)

Through its community affairs programs, Portland, Oregon-based Nike, Inc. supports a variety of giving initiatives. Nike and the Nike Foundation contribute cash and products for programs that "encourage the participation of young people in physical activity and programs that address innovative solutions to the challenges of globalization." In the United States, giving is focused on communities where Nike has a significant employee or Niketown retail presence. Nike also supports causes that are important to athletes who endorse the company's products. The company's Web site provides an overview of Nike giving and volunteering programs; application guidelines; details on specific funding programs, including the Bowerman Track Renovation Program, Jordan Fundamentals, a program to aid low-income schools, and the Casey Martin Award, which honors athletes who have overcome disabilities, and contact information.

Nordson Corporation Foundation (OH) (http://www.nordson.com/corporate/grants.html)

The Nordson Corporation Foundation was founded in 1988 to direct the philanthropic resources of the Nordson Corporation. The foundation "operates on the belief that business, as a corporate citizen, has a social responsibility to share its success with the communities where it operates and draws employees." The foundation makes grants to organizations based in geographic areas where Nordson facilities and employees are located, including Cuyahoga and Lorain Counties in Ohio; the greater Atlanta, Georgia area; San Diego, California; Rhode Island; and southeastern Massachusetts. The foundation's areas of interest in order of priority are: education, human welfare, arts and culture, and civics. The foundation's Web site features details on the specific giving interests of each location, eligibility guidelines and limitations, regional contact information, application guidelines, and a downloadable application form.

Norfolk Southern Foundation (VA) (http://www.nscorp.com/nscorp/html/foundation.html)

The Norfolk Southern Foundation was established in 1984 to direct and implement Norfolk Southern Corporation's charitable giving programs. Areas of interest include educational, cultural, environmental, and economic development opportunities within the region served by Norfolk Southern. The foundation seeks to raise the standards of such programming, thereby enhancing the quality of life for Norfolk Southern employees and the "livability" of the communities it serves, which enables the communities to attract additional business development. The foundation's Web site features grant program information, limitations, application guidelines, and contact information.

Northeast Utilities System (CT) (http://www.nu.com/aboutNU/foundation.asp)

The Northeast Utilities System, a Hartford, Connecticut-headquartered group of energy companies, works through its community relations program to help enrich communities through supporting education, energy efficiency and environmental stewardship, financial and in-kind contributions to community programs in the company's service territory, and employee volunteerism. The company also established the Northeast Utilities Foundation in 1998 to provide funding for community projects in locations served by Northeast's companies. Giving areas include education, civic and community, housing, human services, income aid, the environment, and culture and arts. The company's Web site includes an overview of the community relations program with a contact form, links to the community relations programs of the company's subsidiary companies, and foundation funding guidelines, application instructions, and forms.

Northfield Savings Bank (VT) (http://www.nsbvt.com/l-donations.html)
The Northfield Savings Bank established the NSB Foundation, Inc. in 2000 to provide funding for community projects in the central Vermont community. Giving is focused in the areas of human services, education, and civic projects. The company's corporate giving program provides smaller grants for educational, healthcare, human services, cultural, civic, recreational, and preservation programs. It also offers a scholarship fund. The bank's Web site contains grant and scholarship program information, a list of funded organizations, contact information, and a link to the foundation's Web site, which includes funding guidelines, application procedures, forms, and grants lists.

Northrop Grumman Corporation (CA)
(http://www.northgrum.com/who_we_are/who_community.html)
The Northrop Grumman Corporation of Los Angeles, California, seeks to support programs that improve education, human services, and culture and that address diversity. More specifically, the company's Charitable Giving Program supports such areas as career and employment counseling; pre-college education; human services organizations; environmental, civic, and cultural organizations; and the United Way of Greater Los Angeles. The company also provides education support through the Northrop Grumman Litton Foundation, which focuses on literacy, math, science, and technology programs spanning pre-college through collegiate levels. The company's Web site features contribution guidelines, information on employee giving and volunteer programs, the community report, and contact information.

Novell, Inc. (UT) (http://www.novell.com/company/cr/corporate_giving.html)
Novell, Inc.'s Corporate Giving Program works "to enable nonprofit organizations to develop and realize their visions through the power of technology." Support is provided through the company's Software Donation Program. Nonprofit organizations whose missions focus on education, the homeless and hungry, and/or arts and culture are encouraged to apply. The company's Web site provides application criteria, guidelines, and contact information.

OMNOVA Solutions Foundation (OH) (http://www.omnova.com/commfr.htm)
OMNOVA Solutions Inc., a Fairlawn, Ohio-headquartered provider of building products and specialty chemicals, offers funding through the OMNOVA Solutions Foundation to support programs in the areas of education, civic enhancement, health and welfare, and arts and culture. Most funding goes to organizations in U.S. communities where the company conducts business and where its employees live and work. Preference is given to community projects that involve OMNOVA employees or that are recommended by foundation coordinators at OMNOVA facilities. The foundation's Web site features program restrictions, geographic interests, application procedures, and contact information.

The Ondeo Nalco Foundation (IL)
(http://www.ondeo-nalco.com/ASP/about_us/about_us.asp)
The Ondeo Nalco Chemical Company is a water treatment and process chemicals company based in Naperville, Illinois. The company's charitable giving arm, the Ondeo Nalco Foundation, makes grants to nonprofit organizations in the areas of education, community services, health, and the arts. Grants support a variety of organizations, including groups supporting the disabled, childcare, battered women's shelters, hospitals, colleges and universities, employment programs, and symphonies and museums. The company's Web site features a description of the foundation and its programs and corporate contact information.

Oracle Corporation (CA) (http://www.oracle.com/corporate/community/index.html)
Through its giving program, the Redwood Shores, California-based Oracle Corporation is committed to "improving the quality of life in our global community by supporting concrete efforts that promise definite solutions." As part of its commitment to education, the Oracle Giving program invests in math, science, and technology programs; targets

low-income communities and encourages young innovators; and increases access to technology by donating hardware and software as well as providing training and curriculum to academic institutions. A major education initiative is the Help Us Help Foundation, which assists K–12 public schools and youth organizations in economically challenged communities to obtain information technology tools. Oracle also invests in environmental and endangered animal protection efforts, and medical research programs. The company's Web site provides information on the company's giving interests and application procedures, details on employee giving and volunteer programs, a list of grant recipients, and a special section featuring details on and links to the sites of Oracle's major education initiatives.

The Orchard Foundation (MA/ME) (http://www.orchardfoundation.org)
Created in 1990, the Orchard Foundation of South Portland, Maine, supports New York and New England groups that work with the environment and children, youth, and families. The foundation funds environmental programs in areas of air quality, biodiversity, fresh and coastal waters, forests, toxic substances, and pollution prevention, with advocacy projects given preference. The children, youth, and families category includes child and family advocacy, literacy, and pregnancy prevention. The foundation also funds, on a small scale, organizations concerned with campaign finance reform at the state level. The foundation's Web site includes application guidelines and grant lists for each category.

Osram Sylvania, Inc. (MA) (http://www.sylvania.com/aboutus/corpgiving/)
Headquartered in Danvers, Massachusetts, Osram Sylvania, Inc. is a manufacturer of lighting products whose philanthropic mission is to give back to the communities in which the company is based. The company's main philanthropic focus is math and science education programs for vocational and community colleges and K–12 students. Additionally, the company is interested in supporting health and human services, youth and safety-centered civic organizations, arts and culture, and the environment. The company's Web site provides information on grant guidelines and restrictions, and online initial applications for funding in each region where Osram Sylvania facilities are located.

PG&E Corporation (CA)
(http://www.pge.com/007_our_comm/our_community_index.shtml)
Through its corporate contributions program, PG&E Corporation makes grants to nonprofit organizations in northern and central California. Financial and in-kind donations are provided for a wide range of organizations and programs, including food banks, economic development groups, K–12 and higher education institutions, and other initiatives that provide services for utility customers. In addition to a general description of PG&E's philanthropic programs, the company's Web site contains details on grant application procedures and contact information.

Pacific Life Insurance Company (CA)
(http://www.pacificlife.com/about/community/index.asp)
The Pacific Life Insurance Company provides funding through its Newport Beach, California-based Pacific Life Foundation to organizations in the areas of health and human services, education, arts and culture, and civics, the community, and the environment. A considerable portion of the foundation's budget each year is directed to five to seven pre-determined issues. Contributions are made primarily in communities with large concentrations of Pacific Life employees; some California statewide and national organizations also receive support. The company's Web site features funding guidelines, a downloadable grant application, and contact information.

The PacifiCorp Foundation for Learning (OR)
(http://www.pacificorpfoundation.org/Article/Article16917.html)
The philanthropic arm of PacifiCorp, an electric utility in Oregon, Utah, Washington, Wyoming, Idaho, and northern California, the Portland, Oregon-based PacifiCorp Foundation for Learning seeks "to foster strategic sustainable learning initiatives that serve the best aspirations of individuals, organizations, and communities, and that enhance and develop

their capabilities to address significant challenges and opportunities." While a majority of the foundation's funding is focused on learning projects and alliances, a share of support also goes for other programs that serve community interests. The foundation provides support to communities within its six-state service territory. The foundation's Web site features funding priorities and guidelines, details on the application process, and contact information.

Packaging Corporation of America (IL)
(http://www.packagingcorp.com/who_community.html)
The Packaging Corporation of America, based in Lakeforest, Illinois, takes an active role in the communities where the company operates throughout the United States. The company supports a number of causes, primarily local grassroots programs. The company's Web site features examples of supported projects and contact information.

Padilla Speer Beardsley, Inc. Corporate Giving Program (MN)
(http://www.psbpr.com/whoWeAre/whoe_comm.html)
Padilla Speer Beardsley, Inc., a public relations firm with offices in Minneapolis-St. Paul, Minnesota, and New York City, annually selects community organizations to receive special assistance in public relations programming. In addition, the firm responds to emerging community needs by contributing public relations expertise and financial support to nonprofit groups. The firm primarily supports programs and organizations that encourage the development of health and social services, youth development, education, and the arts. The firm's Web site contains the community giving report, detailed descriptions of programs, and contact information.

Palm, Inc. (CA) (http://www.palm.com/about/corporate/donations.html)
Milpitas, California-headquartered Palm, Inc. established its Palm Products Donation Program in 1998 to provide Palm handheld technology products to nonprofits groups that serve community needs. The company's Web site provides an overview of the program and a list of recipient organizations. Currently, the program is on hold and a date for reinstatement has not been scheduled.

The Panasonic Foundation (NJ)
(http://www.panasonic.com/MECA/foundation/foundation.html)
Headquartered in Secaucus, New Jersey, the Panasonic Foundation was established in 1984 for "the enhancement and improvement of public education in the United States." The foundation's flagship initiative is the Panasonic Partnership Program to help public school districts restructure their education systems. The foundation's Web site includes a list of the systems currently taking part in the program, online foundation publications, and contact information.

Parametric Technology Corporation (MA) (http://www.ptc.com/for/education/index.htm)
The Parametric Technology Corporation works to help students and teachers at secondary schools and universities become more technologically literate, especially with the creative use of 3-D designs. Through various programs, the corporation provides software for free or at a reduced cost to educational institutions around the world. Program details, updates, and contact information are available on the company's Web site.

Patagonia, Inc. (CA) (http://www.patagonia.com/enviro/enviro_grants.shtml)
Patagonia, Inc. of Ventura, California, established its environmental grants program in 1985 to help protect habitat, wilderness, and biodiversity in the United States and internationally. The company gives preference to grassroots organizations that seek to address the root causes of environmental problems, approach issues with a commitment to long-term change, and build a strong base of citizen support. The company's Web site provides funding guidelines and restrictions, application procedures, lists of funded organizations by geographic location and category, and contact information.

Paymentech, Inc. (TX) (http://www.paymentech.net/abo_cominf_comser_page.jsp)
Paymentech, Inc. located in Dallas, Texas, is a provider of global electronic payment solutions. Through financial and in-kind contributions, the company provides support to organizations in the areas of education and health and human services. Preference for funding is given to organizations whose work impacts the citizens of those areas in which the company's offices are located. Eligibility information and application instructions, a list of office locations, and contact information are available on the company's Web site.

Pfizer, Inc. (NY) (http://www.pfizer.com/pfizerinc/philanthropy/)
Pfizer, Inc. and the Pfizer Foundation's charitable giving programs provide grants through targeted initiatives focused primarily on healthcare and science education. Grant program areas include global health projects, education programs in science, and community and cultural programs targeting the communities in which Pfizer operates. The company discourages organizations from submitting unsolicited proposals. The company's Web site provides guidelines for each program area, updated information on grant programs, profiles of supported projects, contact information, and details on the company's patient assistance and employee volunteer programs.

PGE-Enron Foundation (OR) (http://www.pge-enronfoundation.org/)
Formed in 1997, the Portland-based PGE-Enron Foundation is a corporate foundation permanently endowed by Portland General Electric and Enron Corp. to improve the quality of life for Oregonians. The foundation's giving program centers on education, healthy families, arts and culture, and the environment. The foundation also created a special initiative called Community 101, which "helps high school youth experience the value of community service learning and philanthropy." The foundation's Web site contains information on the Community 101 program and other grant initiatives, application information, an online version of the foundation's latest annual report, an archive of recent press releases and news on the foundation, board and staff listings, and contact information.

Phelps Dodge Foundation (AZ) (http://www.phelpsdodge.com/index-community.html)
Headquartered in Phoenix, Arizona, the Phelps Dodge Corporation and its Phelps Dodge Foundation provide support to community organizations in areas where the company has mining and manufacturing operations. Funding is provided in the following categories: education, community safety, the environment, arts and culture, and community development. Grant guidelines, limitations, and details for each program area; contact information; and a listing of communities where Phelps Dodge has operations are available on the foundation's Web site.

Phillips Plastics Corporation (WI)
(http://www.phillipsplastics.com/corporateoverview/community)
As part of Phillips Plastics Corporation's third operating principle, "to encourage corporate involvement in and commitment to the community," the company's individual facilities and employees offer support to their local communities in many ways, "from traditional monetary donations to innovative programs to educate youth." Giving initiatives include the company's AnnMarie Foundation, which provides monetary awards to local organizations; corporate support for educational efforts in the communities that surround each facility; and scholarships to full-time college students. The company's Web site features details on these initiatives and contact information.

Pioneer Hi-Bred International, Inc. (IA)
(http://www.pioneer.com/pioneer_info/corporate/ci.htm)
Pioneer Hi-Bred International, Inc. is committed to helping improve the quality of life through philanthropic investments in the communities where its customers and employees live and work. The company's areas of funding interest include agriculture, education, and the environment. The company also maintains an interest in supporting international organizations that generate social or economic value to the community and company

stakeholders. The company's Web site features information on grant guidelines, application information, and contact information.

Pizza Hut, Inc. (TX) (http://www.pizzahut.com/pr_bookithome.asp)
Pizza Hut, Inc. corporate giving is focused on the BOOK IT! National Reading Incentive Program, which encourages children in kindergarten through 6th grade to read by rewarding students for their reading accomplishments with free pizza and recognition. The company also supports the BOOK IT! Beginners Program, which encourages teachers to read aloud to young children in preschool and pre-kindergarten. The company's Web site contains a link to the BOOK IT! Web site, where parents and teachers will find background information on the program, reading lists, sample verification forms, and links to other organizations that encourage reading.

Playboy Foundation (IL) (http://www.playboyenterprises.com/home/content.cfm?content=t_template&packet=0007B308-45F5-1C7D-9B578 304E50A011A)
Through the Playboy Foundation, a direct corporate giving program, Playboy Enterprises, Inc. provides funding "to nonprofit organizations addressing critical issues in the areas of civil rights and civil liberties, freedom of expression, human sexuality, and reproductive rights and health." The company also supports documentary films and videos that address issues of social change, sponsors the Freedom of Expression Award given at the Sundance Film Festival each year to honor the documentary film that "best educates the public on an issue of social concern," and presents the Hugh M. Hefner First Amendment Awards for efforts to protect First Amendment rights. The foundation's Web site provides funding and award program information, grant application and award nomination procedures, examples of funded programs, and contact information.

Plum Creek Foundation (WA) (http://www.plumcreek.com/company/foundation.cfm)
Plum Creek Timber Company, Inc., a Seattle, Washington-headquartered timberland owner, provides support through Plum Creek Foundation to community-based organizations in the company's areas of operation. Funding categories include the arts, community, education, and the environment. The foundation's Web site features program support restrictions, application information, downloadable application forms, an online version of the most recent annual report, contact information, and a map of the company's holdings and facilities locations.

PNM Foundation, Inc. (NM) (http://www.pnm.com/community/home.htm)
The PNM Foundation, Inc. was established to 1983 to improve the quality of life in New Mexico. The Foundation's areas of interest include education, health, and human services. Proposals that involve children, senior citizens, minorities, and low or fixed income families receive special consideration. The foundation's Web site features program support restrictions, application information, downloadable applications, and contact information.

Polaroid Fund (MA) (http://www.polaroid.com/polinfo/foundation/index.jsp)
The Polaroid Fund is the philanthropic organization of the Polaroid Corporation, a manufacturer of instant imaging products headquartered in Cambridge, Massachusetts. The fund supports programs in the Massachusetts communities of greater Boston and greater New Bedford that help disadvantaged children and adults develop measurable skills to become more independent and realize their full potential. The fund's Web site contains an overview of the fund's giving program and contact information.

Polo Ralph Lauren Corporation (NY) (http://about.polo.com/philanthropy.asp)
The Polo Ralph Lauren Corporation maintains a charitable giving arm to support a variety of causes and organizations, including breast cancer research, cancer care and prevention for medically underserved communities, September 11th relief efforts, the preservation of the "Star-Spangled Banner," and an employee volunteer program. These programs are discussed in detail on the Web site. Proceeds from the sale of "philanthropy items," including

clothing and other merchandise, support the corporation's charitable efforts. These items can be purchased online.

PowerBar, Inc. (CA) (http://www.powerbar.com/pbsports/teamelite)
PowerBar, located in Berkeley, California, maintains its Team Elite Program to assist individual athletes across a variety of sports by providing products and gear. Visitors to the PowerBar Web site will find a description of the Team Elite Program, project and application guidelines, an application that can be downloaded in Adobe Acrobat format, and contact information.

PowerQuest Corporation (UT) (http://www.powerquest.com/company/givingpolicy.cfm)
Located in Orem, Utah, the PowerQuest Corporation's charitable giving arm focuses on software donations and financial contributions to organizations that serve the ill, needy, or youth. The company gives priority to charities focusing on education, health, and human services located along Utah's Wasatch Front. The Giving Policy section of the company's Web site features guidelines for organizations interested in applying for software donations or cash contributions, and contact information.

Premera Blue Cross (WA) (https://www.premera.com/stellent/groups/public/documents/xcpproject/community_relations.as p)
Premera Blue Cross, with offices in Alaska and Washington State, supports a range of community programs through employee voluntarism, Premera CARES (Community Action by Responsible Employees), financial contributions, and various other resources. The company's Web site features contribution program guidelines, reports, and contact information.

PricewaterhouseCoopers Foundation (NY) (http://www.pwcglobal.com/Extweb/career.nsf/docid/08FCA24AB2EC57FB85256AE7005E1A18)
Formed in 1998 as a result of the merger of professional services companies Price Waterhouse and Coopers & Lybrand, the PricewaterhouseCoopers Foundation contributes funds to U.S. institutions of higher education. The foundation's programs are designed to enhance the quality and diversity of graduates interested in the professional services industry, improve lifelong learning in business education and research, and provide real-world information and experience as an important part of faculty development. The foundation also provides support through its employee matching gift program. The foundation's Web site features an overview of the foundation's programs and contact information.

Principal Financial Group (IA) (http://www.principal.com/about/giving)
The Principal Financial Group Foundation, Inc. was created in 1987 by the Principal Financial Group of Des Moines, Iowa. The charitable grants program focuses on four giving areas: health and human services; education; arts and culture; and the environment, recreation, and tourism. The company also has a matching gifts program for employees and runs a volunteer network. All grants will be given in communities where Principal Financial Group has a strong employee presence. The company's Web site includes application guidelines and deadlines, an application form, and a report to the community.

Procter & Gamble Fund (OH) (http://www.pg.com/about_pg/corporate/community/community_submain.jhtml)
The Procter & Gamble Fund makes charitable contributions worldwide. A major portion of the company's annual contributions go to colleges and universities, public policy research programs, economic education organizations, and the company's scholarship program for employee children. The company also makes grants to health, social service, civic, cultural, environmental, and other organizations. The fund's Web site contains descriptions of the company's giving philosophy and programs, a downloadable giving report with program details and examples of supported projects, and contact information.

Progress Energy (NC)
(http://www.progress-energy.com/community/foundation/index.asp)
Headquartered in Raleigh, North Carolina, Progress Energy is an energy company serving customers in North Carolina, South Carolina, and Florida. Progress Energy is committed to improving the communities it serves through local, corporate, and foundation grant programs. Contributions are focused on nonprofit organizations that support education, economic development, and the environment. Funding is offered primarily in the geographic regions in which Progress Energy employees and customers live and work. The company's Web site features an overview of the company's giving programs, a list of the counties served by the company, an online version of the foundation's latest annual report, and contact information.

Providian Financial Corporation (CA) (http://www.providian.com/cg/index.htm)
The Providian Financial Corporation, a bankcard institution operating nationally and internationally, funds grants, educational matching gifts, and volunteer service matching gifts through its Community Giving Program. Contributions are made in regions where the company has offices and are primarily directed to child care, consumer education, consumer financial literacy, and credit awareness. Support is also provided to community organizations and programs such as emergency services for children and families, affordable housing, economic development, and a variety of social and cultural programs. Priority is given to requests whose primary purpose is to benefit low- and moderate-income individuals. The company's Web site includes state-and country-specific grant guidelines and contact information.

Prudential Insurance Co. (NJ) (http://www.prudential.com/community)
Newark, New Jersey-based Prudential Insurance Co. accomplishes its philanthropic goals through the following programs: the Prudential Foundation, which awards grants in areas including public elementary education, job and financial training, community development, human services, and youth development; a Social Investments Program, which initiates and manages neighborhood revitalization and minority entrepreneurship projects; and Local Initiatives, which coordinates efforts by Prudential employees to address needs in their communities. The company's Web site features activity information; grant guidelines; and information on the company's Spirit of Community Awards, which encourage young people to become involved in their communities.

Public Service Electric and Gas Company (NJ)
(http://www.pseg.com/community/overview.html)
The Public Service Electric and Gas Company of Newark, New Jersey, provides support through a corporate giving program and the Public Service Electric and Gas Foundation to assist community initiatives throughout New Jersey. Through resources for schools, employee contributions, community initiatives, and financial contributions, the company supports children's issues, economic development, and the environment in the company's service territory. The company's Web site features information on each giving program, descriptions of supported projects, grant guidelines and application forms, and contact details.

QUALCOMM Incorporated (CA) (http://www.qualcomm.com/Community/)
Based in San Diego, California, QUALCOMM Incorporated creates digital wireless communications products and services. Through QUALCOMM's corporate giving program, the company provides cash and in-kind donations and volunteer programs to support a variety of qualifying nonprofit organizations. Program support is limited to areas where the company has locations. Funding priorities include math and science education, arts and culture, and health and human services. The company's Web site provides details on the corporate giving and voluntarism programs, grant guidelines, application procedures, and contact information.

Raymond James Financial, Inc. (FL) (http://www.raymondjames.com/art)
Headquartered in St. Petersburg, Florida, Raymond James Financial, Inc. supports the arts in Florida through a variety of programs. The company is a sponsor of the annual Gasparilla Festival of the Arts in Tampa, as well as a number of exhibitions, shows, and museums. The company's Web site features a virtual art tour; details on past exhibits, currently sponsored events, and institutions; and contact information.

Raytheon Company (MA) (http://www.raytheon.com/community)
The Corporate Contributions programs of the Raytheon Company, a Lexington, Massachusetts-headquartered technology company, are committed to improving math and science education; increasing access and opportunity for minorities, women, the physically disabled, and economically disadvantaged; and improving the environment. Raytheon's grant programs serve communities where the company has facilities. The company's Web site features funding FAQs, details on each funding area, an online application form, information on the company's other community programs, and contact details.

RealNetworks, Inc. (WA) (http://www.realnetworks.com/company/giving/)
RealNetworks, Inc., located in Seattle, Washington, provides community support through financial and product donations. The company focuses its giving on programs that "enhance the quality of life in areas where RealNetworks' employees live and work, and to enable alternative voices or foster the right of free speech throughout the world." The company contributes to charitable endeavors through several programs, including the RealNetworks Foundation, a software donation program, and employee volunteer and matching gifts programs. Details on each giving program, application guidelines, lists of grant recipients, and contact information are available on the company's Web site.

Recreational Equipment, Inc. (WA)
(http://www.rei.com/aboutrei/gives02.html?stat=side_32)
Recreational Equipment, Inc. of Washington is dedicated to "helping build a lasting legacy of trails, rivers, and wildlands for generations to come and ensuring ongoing programs to help people of all ages and experiences participate." The company's charitable giving focuses support on projects that protect outdoor places for recreation and help increase participation in outdoor activities. The grant program supports organizations nominated by the company's employees; the company does not accept unsolicited requests for funding. The company's Web site features program descriptions, lists of recent grant recipients, contact information, and descriptions of the company's other community programs.

Regence BlueShield (WA) (http://www.wa.regence.com/ioc/ioc_index.html)
Based in Seattle, Washington, Regence BlueShield's corporate giving program focuses on the areas of health and human services and community-based programs, with preference given to organizations in which employees of the company are involved. The company's Web site contains criteria descriptions and guidelines for potential applicants, funding limitations, a listing of recently-supported Washington nonprofit organizations, and contact information.

Reynolds and Reynolds Company Foundation (OH)
(http://www.reyrey.com/about/community.asp)
The Reynolds and Reynolds Company Foundation currently makes grants in Dayton and Celina, Ohio. The foundation focuses its funding on arts and culture, K–12 education, and community betterment programs. Additionally, the Reynolds and Reynolds Associate Foundation provides a vehicle for Dayton-based associates to improve human services in the company's local communities through grants and volunteer service. The foundation's Web site provides program descriptions, details on funded projects, application guidelines, and contact information.

Rite Aid Corporation (PA) (http://www.riteaid.com/company_info/community/)
The Rite Aid Corporation, a chain of pharmacies headquartered in Harrisburg, Pennsylvania, supports programs and projects in communities served by the company. The company provides support to children's hospitals through its national support of the Children's Miracle Network. The company's Web site provides an overview of the company's giving efforts and examples of local projects.

Rohm and Haas Company (PA) (http://www.rohmhaas.com/community/index.html)
Rohm and Haas Company, a Philadelphia, Pennsylvania-based chemical technology company, is committed to being a "responsible neighbor" in the communities where it does business. As part of this mission, the company provides contributions that promote science, technology, and mathematics education; after-school programs; environmental and safety efforts; and employee voluntarism. The company's Web site includes application guidelines and contact information.

Romic Environmental Technologies Corporation (http://www.romic.com/romchart.html) (CA)
Romic Environmental Technologies Corporation, located in East Palo Alto, California, maintains a corporate giving program that supports local programs that keep children in school and build self-esteem, develop marketable job skills or job opportunities, and fight drug abuse and crime. Programs must serve primarily East Palo Alto residents. The company's Web site features a description of the company's giving interests, lists of funded programs, and contact information.

Roslyn Savings Foundation (NY) (http://www.roslynsavingsfoundation.org/)
The Roslyn Savings Bank maintains branches in New York City and Long Island. The Roslyn Savings Foundation is committed to providing grants designed to further community development, expand home ownership opportunities, and provide access to affordable housing in the communities served by the company. In addition, the foundation supports local community organizations, such as those in the health, education, and culture categories, which contribute to the quality of life. The foundation's Web site provides grant guidelines, application procedures, a list of funded organizations, and contact information.

SAFECO Corporation (WA) (http://www.safeco.com/safeco/about/giving/giving.asp)
The Seattle, Washington insurance company SAFECO Corporation is committed to supporting business goals, enhancing SAFECO's reputation as an active community partner, contributing to healthy economic development, and demonstrating its commitment to social responsibility by placing resources back into its communities. The company provides financial literacy/education to people who would traditionally not have access, including first-time home buyers. The company also works with neighborhood business and community groups to improve the appearance, economic vitality, and safety of their neighborhoods, and is interested in promoting the inclusion of cultural arts in communities. The company's Web site features grants program information, geographic restrictions, and contact information.

The St. Paul Companies, Inc. (MN) (http://www.stpaul.com/wwwcorporate/content/communities/)
The St. Paul Companies, Inc, a property-liability insurance company located in St. Paul, Minnesota, has a multi-program corporate giving program. The entire program's mission is to "support people and institutions to reach their full potential, thereby creating strong, healthy, vital communities." All support is focused in four areas: education, community development, arts and culture, and advancement of the nonprofit, voluntary sector. Created in 1999, the St. Paul Companies, Inc. Foundation shares the mission and focus areas of the larger program. Grants are given to nonprofits in the Twin City and Baltimore areas, specific regions in the United Kingdom, and select other communities where the company has a significant business presence. The company's Web site offers specific descriptions of

giving in each category and lists deadlines and extensive restrictions. Previous grant recipients can directly request application materials from foundation staff.

Sallie Mae (VA) (http://www.salliemae.com/about/salliemae_fund.html)
Sallie Mae's philanthropic mission continues to be that of "making college accessible because it strengthens relationships within our communities and touches society as a whole." Based in Reston, Virginia, the company has loan servicing centers in Killeen, Texas; Panama City, Florida; Lawrence, Kansas; and Wilkes-Barre, Pennsylvania. These are the communities where Sallie Mae tends to center its community giving. The Sallie Mae Fund provides access to a post-secondary education for America's children by supporting programs and initiatives that help open doors to higher education, prepare families for their investment, and bridge the gap where no one else can. Details about specific programs and contact information are available on Sallie Mae's Web site.

Samsung Semiconductor, Inc. (TX) (http://www.sas.samsung.com/philanthropy.htm)
Austin, Texas-based Samsung Semiconductor, Inc. is enriching the social, economic, and environmental prosperity of the communities in which the company operates by granting funds and providing volunteers to causes in the areas of education (primarily math and science), health and human services, arts and culture, and the environment. The company's Web site provides descriptions of each of these funding areas; information on the company's volunteer services; grant instructions, guidelines, deadlines and limitations; and a downloadable grant application.

San Diego Gas & Electric (CA) (http://www.sdge.com/community/)
The San Diego Gas & Electric Company Community Center is the philanthropic arm of this southern California energy company. The center's goal is to "provide funds for programs that allow it the opportunity to build partnerships with organizations, businesses, and community leaders to meet community needs." Grants are made in five main categories: education, the environment, business and community development, health and human services, and civic and community affairs. The program also includes a Speakers Bureau, a Tree Smart program, and a Virtual Power Plant Tour to teach visitors about the company. The company's Web site features application guidelines, lists of grant recipients in each category, and a list of cities and counties that the company serves and supports.

The San Jose Sharks (CA)
(http://www.sj-sharks.com/sharks/community/sharks_foundation/)
The San Jose Sharks and the Sharks Foundation support a broad range of community programs, but they are especially focused on the community's youth. The Sharks Foundation is dedicated to meeting the educational, social, and cultural needs of the community. To apply for a grant, an organization must be located in Santa Clara County and must support local youth. The Shark's Web site features a downloadable grant application, descriptions of the community programs that the Sharks are involved in, contact information, and descriptions of all the Sharks Foundation community-based programs, which include golf tournaments, street hockey programs, and food, toy, and book drives.

Sara Lee Corporation (IL) (http://www.saraleefoundation.org/)
The Sara Lee Foundation of Chicago, Illinois was founded in 1981, along with the company's corporate giving program, to support groups that best serve the needs of communities where Sara Lee Corporation facilities and employees are located. The foundation focuses its giving on organizations dealing with women, hunger, homelessness and affordable housing, job training, and arts and culture. The company's Web site features application guidelines, a list of current sponsorships, lists of past winners, and specific applications for each of the awards.

SAS Institute, Inc. (NC) (http://www.sas.com/corporate/community/index.html)
Cary, North Carolina-based SAS Institute, Inc. has a corporate philanthropy program that supports a caring environment in the community. Giving is focused in two areas:

organizations working with children and families in crisis and the education of children and adults. The company focuses on K–12 education, with special emphasis on the integration of technology and education. The company also has extensive projects that involve employees in voluntarism in the community. The Corporate Culture section of the company's Web site features program information and the company's annual report.

SBC Foundation (TX)
(http://www.sbc.com/corporate_citizenship/sbc_in_our_communities/sbc_foundation/)
Established in 1984, the SBC Foundation, the philanthropic unit of SBC Communications, Inc., seeks to help communities search for lasting solutions to critical and complex problems. To that end, the foundation focuses on education, community economic development, health and human services, and arts and culture. Most grants are directed toward regions served by the company—Arkansas, California, Connecticut, Nevada, Missouri, Oklahoma, and Texas—but the foundation does support a number of relevant initiatives that are national in scope. The foundation's Web site features overview of the grantseeking process, grantmaking guidelines, a grant application form, and contact information.

The Scotts Company (OH) (http://2001.scotts.com/community/GBTGNominationFB.cfm)
The Scotts Company of Ohio maintains the Give Back to Grow initiative, which supports and recognizes gardening organizations and activities. The Company's Web site features information on how to become involved, a downloadable nomination form, find information about parks that have been supported and how to qualify for support, and contact information.

Scripps Howard Foundation (OH) (http://www.scripps.com/foundation)
Established in 1963, the Scripps Howard Foundation is the corporate foundation of the E.W. Scripps Company. Its mission is to "advance the cause of a free press through support of excellence in journalism, quality journalism education, and professional development." The foundation's programs and projects include National Journalism Awards, scholarships and internships for journalism students, fellowships for practicing journalists, and a collegiate reporting competition. The foundation also has an employee program, which includes matching gifts and scholarship awards. The foundation's Web site features program details, articles, lists of past awards, contact information, program/grant guidelines, and annual reports.

Seagate Technology (CA)
(http://www.sears.com/sr/misc/sears/about/communities/index_community.jsp)
Seagate Technology is "committed to being a good corporate citizen in the communities in which its employees live and work." The company demonstrates its support through donations of funds, furniture, computer and office equipment, and by encouraging employee voluntarism. The company focuses its giving on science and technology initiatives that enhance creativity and diversity in grades K–12. The company also gives special consideration to programs that offer employee-volunteering opportunities and funds programs that affect communities in which Seagate operates or its employees live. Grant requests must be submitted in letter format. The company's Web site features a list of contacts for those who need more information; a scrapbook, which contains photos from different projects and programs that Seagate has been involved with around the globe; and grant application guidelines.

Sears, Roebuck and Co. (IL)
(http://www.sears.com/sr/misc/sears/about/communities/index_community.jsp)
The Chicago-based Sears, Roebuck, and Co.'s Web site maintains information on the corporate philanthropy efforts. As part of the national American Dream Campaign, the company helps people achieve and preserve, what many consider, the ultimate dream of home ownership. The Sears-Roebuck Foundation does not accept or review unsolicited funding requests. The company's Web site features information on current interests, grant guidelines, past recipients of support, and contact information.

Sega Foundation (CA) (http://www.sega.com/community/home_community.jhtml)
The Sega Youth Education & Health Foundation, also known as the Sega Foundation, is committed to improving the lives of young people and has a particular interest in children's education and health. The foundation initiates most of its funding discussions with non-profit organizations, but it accepts unsolicited proposals for small grants. The Foundation area of the company's Web site features information about foundation-funded projects and initiatives. Visitors funding information, grant application and eligibility guidelines, and lists of grants.

Sempra Energy (CA) (http://www.sempra.com/community.htm)
Located in San Diego, California, the Sempra Energy corporate giving program is "dedicated to taking a leadership role in promoting health, furthering education and environmental protection, and stimulating economic vitality, while enhancing the quality of life in communities where we do business." The Sempra Energy corporate giving program also includes an employee matching program and a volunteer incentive program for employees. The company's Web site features contact information.

Service Corporation International (TX)
(http://www.sci-corp.com/html/sci_community.html)
The philanthropic arm of the Houston, Texas-based Service Corporation International, a company of funeral homes and cemeteries, seeks to "protect families from the senseless tragedies that sometimes lead them" to use the company's services. The company supports four community service programs: Escape School, teaching children how to avoid abduction; Smart & Safe Seniors, providing seniors with information on a variety of criminal activities of which they are targets; support for a traveling Vietnam War Memorial; and free funeral services for police officers and fire fighters. The company's Web site provides more details on these programs and contact information.

Shaklee Corporation (CA) (http://www.shaklee.com/main/aboutCitizen)
Through its Corporate Citizenship section, the Shaklee Corporation strongly supports corporate social responsibility. It is devoted to enriching the communities in which its employees and distributors live and work and providing educational opportunities through a wide variety of partnership programs, corporate contributions, and employee volunteer projects. The company's Web site features program details, a history of the corporation's charitable giving, and contact information.

Shaw's Supermarkets (MA) (http://www.shaws.com/Public/environment/index.cfm)
Shaw's Supermarket's Community Commitment Program support the quality of life in the six New England states of company operation. Although Shaw's Supermarkets primarily makes donations to specified organizations on an annual basis, the company does make other grants. Shaw's supports numerous organizations in the company's market area by participating in charitable grants, community relations activities, sponsorships, and public relations activities. There are set priorities, funding sources, guidelines and goals for each of these specific programs. The company's Web site is limited and does not feature any specific information on their formal grantmaking program.

Shell Oil Company Foundation (TX)
(http://www.countonshell.com/community/involvement/shell_foundation.html)
Founded in 1953, the Shell Oil Company Foundation of Houston, Texas "focuses on making a difference in the communities where Shell people work and live." Broad-based support is given across the country to selected qualified organizations in areas such as civic and public policy, community involvement, culture and the arts, education, the environment, and health and human services. The company's Web site features contact information, information on employee volunteer programs, a list of selected grants, application requirements, and an online version of the company's latest annual report.

ShopKo Stores, Inc. (WI) (http://www.shopko.com/giving.html)
Wisconsin-based ShopKo Stores, Inc. is primarily interested in assisting people with disabilities, the underprivileged, and the disadvantaged; strengthening family values; encouraging and supporting programs aimed at educating youth; and supporting the arts. The Company's Web site features information on areas considered for funding, details on organizations that have received support in the past, and contact information.

Siemens Foundation (NY) (http://www.siemens-foundation.org)
The Siemens Foundation of New York City "embodies the Siemens commitment to education and research and builds on the company's history of encouraging and supporting young talent throughout the United States." These goals are accomplished by awarding scholarships for higher education to gifted science, math, and technology students in the United States. Foundation programs include an Advanced Placement Award, which gives scholarships to students scoring highest on the advanced placement tests for math and science courses and to schools that have greatly improved their scores. It also runs the Siemens Westinghouse Science and Technology Competition, which gives hundreds of thousands of dollars in scholarships to the winners of this research-based competition. The foundation's Web site features descriptions of each program, announcements and profiles of past winners, and lists of what each award entitles.

Silicon Graphics, Inc. (CA) (http://www.sgi.com/company_info/community/)
A leader in high performance computing technology, Silicon Graphics, Inc. of Mountain View, California, is dedicated to "being an active partner in the continuous improvement of our community through strategic investments in health and human services, education, the arts, and the environment." The company supports voluntarism in its employees and internal environmental and diversity efforts. Unsolicited proposals are not considered.

J.R. Simplot Company (ID) (http://www.simplot.com/)
The J.R. Simplot Company is an agribusiness corporation based in Boise, Idaho. Through the company's charitable involvement it supports organizations providing services in the areas of community needs, education, youth, and the arts. The company funds a wide variety of projects and institutions in Idaho, including the Future Farmers of America, Idaho Public Television, and the United Way, among many others. The company's Web site features lists of recent events, details on sponsored organizations and activities, and contact information.

Simpson Investment Company (WA) (http://www.simpson.com/communitymain.cfm)
The mission of the philanthropic arm of the Simpson Investment Company of Washington is to improve the quality of life in the communities where a significant number of Simpson employees live and work and to encourage employees to become involved and provide leadership in their communities. Interested in areas such as education, health services, economic development, and the arts, the grant program provides the majority of its funds to counties in Washington, Oregon, and areas of northern California. The company also maintains the Mark E. Reed Scholarship Program. The company's Web site contains details on the grantmaking program, a history of grant activity, and contact information.

Skadden Fellowship Foundation (NY) (http://216.44.201.143/skadweb/siteindex.htm)
Created in New York City in 1988, the Skadden Fellowship Foundation was formed to "affirm the firm's commitment to public interest law." The program awards 25 fellowships a year to graduating law students and outgoing judicial clerks. The fellows find a sponsoring public interest organization that they will spend two years working for. These organizations serve clients including the poor, elderly, homeless, disabled, and those deprived of their human or civil rights. The fellowships are awarded in December and begin the following fall. The foundation's Web site features a description of the application process, contact information, a list of trustees, a demographic breakdown by law school and by sponsoring organization, and a list of fellows.

Solectron (CA) (http://www.solectron.com/about/index.html)
Solectron, a worldwide provider of electronics manufacturing services, has locations around the world, but its corporate headquarters are in Milpitas, California. Solectron's commitment extends "beyond customers, into its communities, demonstrating the company's belief in social responsibility [and] striving to be an asset to its communities." The Social Responsibility section of the company's Web site features a list of organizations and programs Solectron works with and supports in the areas of education, human services, the environment, and the arts; contact information; and application information, restrictions, and a listing of organizations previously funded.

SOM Foundation (IL) (http://www.som.com/html/som_foundation.html)
The SOM Foundation of Chicago, Illinois, is the philanthropic arm of Skidmore, Owings & Merrill LLP. The foundation's mission is "to help young architects and engineers broaden their professional education, instill in them a heightened sense of their responsibility to improve the quality of the built and natural environments, and encourage them to appreciate the influences that place-making, culture, and technology have on the design of buildings and their settings." This end is met by awarding traveling scholarships to undergraduate and graduate students of accredited architecture schools. The Architecture Traveling Fellowship, the Interior Architecture Traveling Fellowship Program, the United Kingdom Award, and the Urban Design Traveling Fellowship award different grant sizes awards to students of these disciplines. The foundation also awards the Chicago Institute for Architecture and Urbanism Award, which "encourages writing and research on the question of how architecture, urban design, and physical planning can contribute to improving the quality of life of the American city." Applicants must be nominated by their accredited school. The foundation's Web site features contact information.

Sonoco Products Company (SC) (http://www.sonoco.com/bottomnav/about+us/environment+-+community+and+the.htm)
The South Carolina-based Sonoco Products Company focuses its giving on education, health and welfare, arts and culture, and the environment in locations where the company has operations. The majority of its grants are awarded to U.S. institutions with a local, rather than a national, perspective. The company's Web site features general policy, program, guidelines, and contact information.

Southwire Company (GA) (http://www.southwire.com/)
Southwire Company, a wire and cable manufacturer, supports education and environmental programs in several counties in Georgia, Illinois, Mississippi, Alabama, and Kentucky. The company's Web site contains descriptions of its education grant and environmental award programs and online application forms.

Sovereign Bank Foundation (PA) (http://www.sovereignbank.com/companyinfo/foundation.asp)
In 1988, the Sovereign Bank Foundation was incorporated in Reading, Pennsylvania, to improve the quality of life in communities served by Sovereign Bank. Areas of interest include community investment and economic development, youth and education, human service programs that improve the social needs of low- and moderate-income communities and individuals, and arts and culture. The foundation seeks to enhance the quality of life for individuals located in the communities served by the bank, including areas in Pennsylvania, New Jersey, Connecticut, Massachusetts, New Hampshire, and Rhode Island. The foundation's Web site features application procedures, granting policies, obligations of grant recipients, deadlines, and contact information.

Sprint Corporation (KS) (http://www.sprint.com/sprint/overview/commun.html)
Commitment to community, with an emphasis on "support of local and regional organizations in which the corporation has a major presence," is the basis for the Sprint Corporation's philanthropy. Through the Sprint Foundation and its direct corporate giving program, Sprint supports education, arts and culture, community improvement, and youth

development. The Community Service area of the company's Web site includes information on Sprint's employee giving programs, a brief overview of the Sprint Foundation's activities, application guidelines, contact information, and an online version of the company's annual report.

Stage Stores, Inc. (TX) (http://www.stagestoresinc.com/companyinfo/community.htm)
Stage Stores, Inc. supports the communities in which it operates and its employees live. Stage co-sponsors a variety of local events, sports teams, state fairs, and rodeos. The company also makes donations to children's organizations, schools, hospitals, and medical research programs. The company occasionally creates fashion-related events to help raise money for charitable causes. The company also supports the United Way and helps in disaster relief efforts in its communities. Those interested in seeking support from the company should contact a local store manager. The company's Web site contains contact information.

Stahl Construction Company (MN)
(http://www.stahlconstruction.com/Pages/Company/company-giving.htm)
The charitable giving arm of the Stahl Construction Company was formed in 1998 in Minnetonka, Minnesota. The Stahl Corporate Giving Program's goals are to "impact the image of the company in the community, enhance employee relations, keep our community vital, and achieve results within the organizations that receive our contributions." As a member of the Minnesota Keystone Program, Stahl donates a percentage of its profits to charitable, educational, and cultural organizations, and plans and performs a yearly special service project. Organizations impacted by the Stahl Corporate Giving Program are listed on the company's Web site, along with contact information.

State Farm Companies Foundation (IL)
(http://www.statefarm.com/foundati/foundati.htm)
The State Farm Companies Foundation of Bloomington, Illinois, was created in 1963 to address the many requests that State Farm was receiving from nonprofits for financial support. The foundation makes grants in education to priority schools and to K–12 education. In the priority schools program, awards are made for insurance studies, actuarial science, and business and related fields; university scholarships and leadership training; and financial services centers that offer course work and resources to students and professionals in the financial services arena. The K–12 program provides funding for regional, state, and local organizations that promote and support education reform initiatives that do not engage in lobbying as their primary activity. The foundation's Web site features application guidelines, scholarship eligibility information, online applications, and contact information for outside organizations that administer foundation scholarships.

State Street Foundation (MA)
(http://www.statestreet.com/company/community_affairs/overview.html)
The State Street Foundation is the nonprofit corporate giving program of the State Street Corporation that has been providing grants to qualifying charities in the Boston area since 1977. State Street was founded in 1792 and provides information services, custody, securities lending, investment management, performance and analytic measurement, cash management, and recordkeeping. The foundation manages the allocation and distribution of most of the company's corporate contributions. Its primary mission is to help the urban poor build a better future. The foundation has a Global Philanthropy Program, which addresses the local needs of the communities at State Street's worldwide locations. The Global Philanthropy Program provides grants primarily for education and job skills training, affordable housing development and neighborhood revitalization, youth programs, and to address other community needs that its local sites deem appropriate. The foundation's Web site contains a summary of community support.

SUMCO USA Corporation (CA) (http://www.sumcousa.com/community.asp)
The companies that formed SUMCO, Sumitomo Sitix and Mitsubishi Silicon America, have consistently provided financial and volunteer support to organizations in the communities in which they do business. The company participates in programs that focus on resource conservation, waste reduction, and pollution prevention. Visit the company's Web site to learn more about the environmental interests, areas of company operation, and contact information.

Sun Microsystems (CA)
(http://www.sun.com/aboutsun/comm_invest/giving/foundation.html)
Through its Community Development Grants Program, the Sun Microsystems Foundation, Inc. "invests in communities that are often characterized by low income, high unemployment, and disturbing school drop-out rates." Grants are awarded in the areas of education and employment and job development in the southern San Francisco Bay Area, the Merrimack Valley of Massachusetts, and the West Lothian District of Scotland. The company's Web site features information on the funding criteria (including limitations), application guidelines, and an online version of the company's latest annual report.

The SunTrust Bank Atlanta Foundation (GA) (http://www.suntrustatlantafoundation.org)
The SunTrust Bank Atlanta Foundation was founded in 1959 to serve the metropolitan Atlanta community in educational, cultural, and human service programs. With the charitable revenue of the SunTrust Bank, the foundation supports Atlanta community organizations. The foundation also manages four charitable funds. The foundation's Web site features grant guidelines and limitations, a downloadable grant application form, information on the four charitable funds, and contact information.

SUPERVALU Foundation (MN) (http://www.supervalu.com/community/comm_main.html)
The SUPERVALU Foundation, established in 1993 and based in Minneapolis, Minnesota, "provides support to local programs that address community needs, are measurable and are serving communities where SUPERVALU or one of its companies has a significant presence." In addition to a college and university matching gifts program, the foundation funds grants in the areas of education, social services, workforce development, hunger relief, and the fine arts. The foundation accepts both the Minnesota Common Grant Application Form and its own grant application. The foundation's Web site also includes grant guidelines and limitations, information on the matching gifts program, and a downloadable application.

Symantec Corporation (OR) (http://www.symantec.com/corporate/community.html)
Headquartered in Eugene, Oregon, the Symantec Corporation sponsors four areas of charitable giving: corporate grants, software donations, matching employee gifts, and used equipment donations. Begun in 1995, these programs are designed to provide aid locally in communities where Symantec is located, in the areas of education, community, social and human services, the arts and humanities, and the environment. The company's Web site features complete grant and donation guidelines, instructions and limitations for each type of support, and contact address information.

Symbol Technologies, Inc. (NY)
(http://www.symbol.com/about/overview/overview_community_affairs.html)
Symbol Technologies, Inc. focuses its corporate giving programs in four areas: education, diversity, the arts, and community organizations that provide aid for the hungry and homeless, various health initiatives, and children's organizations. As a global organization, Symbol provides monetary aid and equipment donations worldwide. Guidelines, details on Symbol's funding goals, and descriptions of some of the organizations supported are available on the company's Web site.

3Com Corporation (CA) (http://www.3com.com/inside/comm_affairs)
Computer networking company 3Com Corporation seeks to "reinforce connections where communications and community intersect" by donating networking equipment, sharing the

company's expertise, and encouraging community investment where the company's employees live and work. Specific areas of community investment often include the advancement of education and community economic development through networking technology. The company provides support through financial and in-kind contributions, and an employee gift matching program. The company's Web site features selected lists of past grants, grant guidelines, application procedures, and contact information.

Target Corporation (MN)
(http://www.targetcorp.com/targetcorp_group/community/foundation.jhtml)
The Minneapolis, Minnesota-based Target Corporation maintains corporate giving programs through Target, Marshall Field's, and Mervyn's stores. Each division has its own priorities and review process. Target stores provide funding to "fortify families, bring the arts to our schools, support families of children with life-threatening illnesses, help teens achieve their dreams, and more." Marshall Field's stores help support arts and cultural events, projects that encourage children to read, and programs that strengthen the lives of children and families. Mervyn's stores partner with local schools and arts and social action organizations to improve the quality of life for families and children. These store-based giving programs generally support projects in their local communities; organizations should contact store managers for application information. Additionally, the Target Foundation works to enhance the quality of life in the Minneapolis/St. Paul metropolitan area by supporting local arts and social service programs. The company's Web site features lists of each store's community programs, foundation application guidelines, and contact information.

TCF Financial Corporation (MN) (http://www.tcfbank.com/ab_commu.htm)
The Wayzata, Minnesota-based TCF Financial Corporation serves the banking needs of communities in Minnesota, Illinois, Michigan, Wisconsin, Colorado, and Indiana. The TCF corporate giving program makes grants to nonprofit, community-based organizations in areas where the company operates. The Web site provides state-specific funding guidelines, application procedures, and contact information.

Tesoro Petroleum Corporation (TX) (http://www.tesoropetroleum.com/community.html)
The Tesoro Corporate Contributions program is the charitable giving arm of Tesoro Petroleum Corporation and its subsidiaries, including Tesoro Hawaii and Tesoro Alaska. Based in San Antonio, Texas, the Corporate Contributions program focuses on support for education and improving the quality of life for children in the communities where Tesoro operates. The company's Web site contains an overview of the contributions program, a list of regional contact information, and information about Tesoro employee volunteer programs.

Textron, Inc. (RI) (http://www.textron.com/profile/community.html)
Providence, Rhode Island-based Textron, Inc. corporate giving program works to "help make our community a better place for employees to live and work." Programs include Workforce Development and Education, including job training and employment development, youth mentoring, and college/university support, and Healthy Families/Vibrant Communities, including support for arts and culture outreach programs, community revitalization, and health and human service organizations. The company's Web site features funding guidelines, application procedures and forms, and contact information.

Thomson Financial Services (MA)
(http://www.thomsonfinancial.com/site/about/community.aspx)
Boston-based Thomson Financial Services focuses its community programs on children and youth. Initiatives include an online youth mentoring program and employee community volunteer projects. The company's Web site features details on these programs and contact information.

3M (MN) (http://www.3m.com/about3m/community/index.jhtml)
The Minnesota Mining & Manufacturing Co. (3M) of St. Paul, Minnesota, works to "affect people's lives in meaningful ways to build on successes in our communities everywhere." Funding is primarily given in four areas. Education grants mainly go toward science, technology, and business higher education. Health and human services funding supports agencies or programs dealing with service delivery systems, especially for youth, parenting, and strengthening families. Arts funding is given to major arts organization that help people learn about the world around them. Civic initiatives funding is generally in the form of operating and program grants for organizations in 3M communities. The company's Web site features a page on each category with a featured grantee, a searchable archive of past features, and contact information.

TI Foundation (TX) (http://www.ti.com/corp/docs/company/citizen/foundation/index.shtml)
The TI Foundation is the principal charitable vehicle of Dallas-based Texas Instruments Incorporated. The foundation's major emphasis is education, including early childhood development programs and higher education, engineering in particular. In addition, funding is available for health, welfare, civic, and cultural projects in areas where the company has facilities. The company also offers cash and in-kind contributions through its Corporate Citizenship program. The foundation's Web site features grant guidelines, examples of funded programs, and information on the company's corporate citizenship initiatives, including the Tech Smart Big Heart Grant Program.

The Timberland Company (NH) (http://www.timberland.com/cgi-bin/timberland/timberland/corporate/tim_about.jsp?c=Community%20Service)
The Timberland Company supports various community grants and projects through its Community Service programs. The company's Path of Service program provides Timberland employees with up to 40 hours of paid time per year for community service. The company's Web site provides information on the company's community programs and examples of supported projects.

Times Mirror Foundation (CA) (http://www.timesmirrorfoundation.org/)
The Times Mirror Foundation of Los Angeles, California, is a program of the Tribune Company dedicated to supporting nonprofit organizations that "measurably improve the quality of life" in communities served by the company. Program areas of interest include journalism, education, literacy, community enrichment, and art and culture. The foundation's Web site features program support restrictions, application information, a downloadable grant summary sheet, an online version of the foundation's most recent annual report, and contact information.

Tollgrade Communications, Inc. (PA) (http://www.tollgrade.com/about/culture/i_community.html)
Tollgrade Communications, Inc., a Cheswick, Pennsylvania-based network support company, works with "local charities that support and assist minority students in furthering their education." Additionally, the Tollgrade Cares program pairs employees with community events sponsored by organizations such as the Red Cross and the Salvation Army. Program details and contact information are available on the company's Web site.

Tom's of Maine, Inc. (ME) (http://www.tomsofmaine.com/about/grants.asp)
Family-owned Tom's of Maine, Inc. produces natural toothpaste and other health and beauty products. The Kennebunk, Maine-based company's community giving program is designed to "address community concerns in Maine and around the globe, by devoting a portion of our time, talents, and resources to the environment, human needs, the arts, and education." The company also encourages its employees to spend a portion of their work week volunteering in a nonprofit setting. The company's Web site provides an overview of the company's mission and beliefs, information on general funding priorities, lists of yearly grant recipients, and details on the company's Common Good Partnerships, which include the National Rivers Awareness Program.

Tops Markets, Inc. (NY) (http://www.topsmarkets.com/About/Community/comhome.html)
Tops Markets, Inc. of Williamsville, New York, centers its philanthropic giving in the communities in New York, Philadelphia, and Ohio where the company does business. Much of the company's charitable donations are to food banks and pantries. The company's Web site features descriptions of the company's community programs, contact information, and printable request and donation forms.

Toshiba America Foundation (NY) (http://www.toshiba.com/about/taf.html)
As the principal charitable arm of consumer electronics company Toshiba America, Inc., the Toshiba America Foundation focuses on the improvement of classroom teaching in grades 7-12, especially in the areas of science, mathematics, and technology. In addition to information about the foundation's current program interests, the company's Web site provides a summary of funded projects, grant guidelines, detailed instructions on preparing a grant application, and contact information.

Toyota USA Foundation (CA) (http://www.toyota.com/about/community/)
Carmaker Toyota "believes in helping people improve the quality of life in their communities." The company's community giving program is focused on education, with emphasis on primary and secondary schooling. In addition to funding national programs, Toyota supports the social well-being of communities where it has major operations (California, Indiana, Kentucky, Michigan, New York, and West Virginia). This includes assistance for arts and culture and civic and community development. The Toyota USA Foundation is committed exclusively to improving the quality of K–12 education in the United States with a primary emphasis on improving the teaching and learning of mathematics and science. Grants are made to accredited colleges, universities, community colleges, vocational or trade schools, and to nonprofit organizations engaged in pre-collegiate math and/or science education. K–12 public and private schools may not apply directly to the foundation, though they may be the recipient of an independent nonprofit agency's funding request. The company's Web site contains information on the company's many giving and award programs, guidelines for both the corporate and foundation grant programs, news and updates, and contact information.

Tupperware US, Inc. (FL)
(http://www.tupperware.com/pls/htprod_www/tup_company.child)
Tupperware US, Inc. established its charitable giving arm, Give a Child a Chance, in 1995. The mission of the organization is "to provide children, especially those from disadvantaged situations, with resources to combat the negative affects of poverty, neglect, and abuse." Tupperware's objective is to establish long-term alliances with children's groups in a number of countries. In the United States, it supports the Boys & Girls Clubs of America. The company's Web site provides an overview of the program and its activities in different countries.

Tyco Electronics Foundation (http://www.tycoelectronics.com/about/foundation)
The Tyco Electronics Foundation, the charitable arm of the Tyco Electronics Corporation, focuses its giving on education, with an emphasis on pre-college math and science. Grants are awarded in geographic areas where the company has a significant employee population and for projects that are consistent with Tyco's corporate objectives. The company's Web site includes funding guidelines, application procedures and forms, and contact information.

Union Pacific Foundation (NE) (http://www.up.com/found/)
The Union Pacific Foundation is the philanthropic arm of Union Pacific Corporation and its subsidiaries. The Omaha, Nebraska-based foundation has distributed funds since 1959 to organizations for the improvement of quality of life in communities served by the company. The foundation's Web site provides an overview of the foundation's work and history, news releases, and contact information.

United Airlines Foundation (IL) (http://www.ual.com/page/article/0,1360,1359,00.html)
The United Airlines Foundation of Chicago, Illinois, was formed in 1952 to "support charitable organizations, as well as programs and activities that improve the communities where our customers and employees live and work." Giving is focused in five areas: education, health, arts and culture, voluntarism, and diversity. Funding is concentrated in United's U.S. hubs: Chicago, Denver, Los Angeles, San Francisco, and Washington, D.C. The foundation's Web site contains descriptions of the philanthropic areas of interest, application guidelines and restrictions, and contact information.

United Parcel Service of America, Inc. (GA) (http://www.community.ups.com)
The United Parcel Service of America, Inc. (UPS) is "committed to making a difference" in communities throughout the United States and maintains a number of different programs to address this goal. The UPS Foundation, located in Atlanta, Georgia, was founded in 1951 and funds programs that support family and workplace literacy, food distribution, and increased nationwide volunteerism. The foundation's Community Investment Grant Program allocates dollars directly to UPS region offices for distribution to local projects; funds must go to organizations with which UPS employees already have an established relationship. UPS community relations programs include the Region/District Grant Program, which involves UPS employees in nominating local organizations for funding, and the Neighbor to Neighbor employee volunteer program. The company's Web site features information on the company's volunteer and funding programs, giving policies and procedures, grant guidelines, the foundation's annual report, and contact information.

United Technologies (CT) (http://www.utc.com/social/index.htm)
United Technologies, a Hartford, Connecticut-based diversified company that provides high-technology products and services to the building systems and aerospace industries worldwide, makes grants to tax-exempt organizations in the areas of education, human services, arts and culture, community and public policy, and international programs. The company focuses its grantmaking in communities where it has a substantial corporate presence. The company's Web site provides guidelines and limitations for the company's grant and matching gift programs, application instructions, and an online application form.

Unocal Corporation (CA) (http://www.unocal.com/responsibility)
The El Segundo, California-based Unocal Corporation and the Unocal Foundation seek to build community relationships where the company has operations. Support is provided for community and humanitarian projects through direct corporate giving, contributions from the operating budgets of individual business units, and grants from the Unocal Foundation. Funding is focused on efforts that support the education and well-being of children and families, provide skills training and self-help initiatives to enhance livelihoods, and improve community conditions in the vicinity of company operations and areas of business interest. The company's Web site provides a "Corporate Responsibility Report" with information on Unocal's U.S. and international corporate giving programs.

US Bancorp (MN)
(http://www.usbank.com/about/community_relations/commun_relation.html)
US Bancorp, a financial firm based in Minneapolis, Minnesota, contributes to civic and charitable causes in its 24-state banking region through the US Bancorp Foundation and a direct corporate giving program. Contributions are provided to nonprofit organizations in the priority areas of affordable housing and economic opportunity, education, and artistic and cultural enrichment. The Community Involvement area of the company's Web site features descriptions of its philanthropic activities, foundation grant guidelines, a downloadable application form, and contact information.

US Trust Corporation Foundation (NY)
(http://ustrust.com/ustrust/html/aboutUs/community/)
The US Trust Corporation Foundation of New York makes grants to cultural and arts institutions and community services organizations. The foundation supports worthy

organizations in the company's primary market areas with corporate contributions. These organizations include cultural and arts institutions and human services, civic, housing-related and urban affairs organizations that improve the quality of life in their communities. The foundation's Web site features more information.

Varnum, Riddering, Schmidt & Howlett LLP (MI)
(http://www.varnumlaw.com/overview/community.html)
The law offices of Varnum, Riddering, Schmidt & Howlett LLP support nonprofit organizations primarily in the western Michigan community though *pro bono* legal work and corporate donations. The firm's Web site provides an overview of the firm's community efforts, downloadable yearly contributions reports, and contact information.

Verizon Foundation (NY) (http://foundation.verizon.com/)
The giving arm of Verizon Communications, the Verizon Foundation, was created with a mission of "transforming the way the private, public, and nonprofit sectors work together in building collaborative partnerships." The foundation's contributions programs include a technology training program, a volunteer program, and an in-kind gift program, which provides donated computers and other office equipment to qualifying organizations. The foundation's grant program provides funding to organizations and programs in fields including workforce development, literacy, and education. The foundation's bilingual (English and Spanish) Web site features information on each contribution program, a series of "best-in-class" technology success stories, a comprehensive technology resource guide, current requests for proposals, contribution guidelines, an online eligibility quiz, and a technology needs assessment section. Applications are only accepted through the foundation's Web site.

Visteon Fund (MI) (http://www.visteon.com/about/community/)
The Visteon Fund was created in 1999 to enrich the lives of children and improve the environment. The mission of the fund is to be the community citizen of choice by providing employees with the resources necessary to make a positive contribution in the areas where they work and live. The fund's Web site features information about areas of interest, a listing of news and initiatives, and contact information.

Vulcan Scholarships, Inc. (AL) (http://www.vulcaninc.com/plt0p04.htm)
Vulcan Scholarships, Inc. was created in 1984 by Vulcan, Inc. of Foley, Alabama, to "influence qualified Foley and Robertsdale High School students' career paths by providing financial assistance in the pursuit of study in a qualified engineering curriculum." The scholarships are available only to graduating seniors at the two specified high schools. The company's Web site includes a list of recipients, applications guidelines, and details on each scholarship.

Wachovia Foundation, Inc. (NC)
(http://www.wachovia.com/inside/page/0,,139_414_430,00.html)
The North Carolina-based, Wachovia Foundation, Inc.'s mission is to build strong and vibrant communities, improve the quality of life, and make a positive difference where the company and its employees work and live. The foundation places grantmaking priorities in the areas of education, community and economic development, and quality of life. The foundation's Web site features funding priorities, guidelines, a downloadable application, a board listing, and contact information.

Walgreen Co. (IL) (http://www.walgreens.com/about/community/)
Headquartered in Deerfield, Illinois, pharmacy chain Walgreen Co. is "committed to improving our customers' lives across America." Most Walgreens grants are made to eligible nonprofits working in local Walgreens communities. Grants are awarded in the areas of health and human services, education, civics and community, and arts and culture, with health receiving the majority of company support. A small portion of the budget is reserved for select national organizations. Major grants have been made to health-related national

organizations, such as the American Heart Association, the American Cancer Society, and the Juvenile Diabetes Foundation. The company's Web site includes information on the company's giving and fundraising programs, grant guidelines, and contact information.

Wal-Mart Foundation (AR) (http://www.walmartfoundation.org/)
The Wal-Mart Foundation of Arkansas "serves Wal-Mart Stores, Inc. with stewardship, compassion, and integrity by developing and implementing programs that support children and families through education, health, and economic development in our local communities." The vast majority of funding is distributed locally through Wal-Mart Stores, SAM'S CLUBS, Neighborhood Markets, and Distribution Centers. Funding is currently focused in four areas: community, education, children, and the environment. Eligible applicants include 501(c)(3) organizations, schools, churches, and government-funded agencies. The foundation also offers awards for teachers, scholarships, and other programs. The foundation's Web site features descriptions of current programs, examples of funded projects, grant guidelines and application procedures, and contact information.

Washington Gas Light Company (DC) (http://www.washgas.com/library/pdf/giving.pdf)
The Washington Gas Light Company seeks to provide a lasting impact on the communities it serves through contributions, in-kind gifts, and volunteer resources to qualified organizations within the Washington, D.C., metropolitan area. The company's corporate giving program focuses on three primary interests: primary and secondary education, the environment, and health. The company's Web site features downloadable guidelines and application information.

Washington Mutual Foundation (WA) (http://www.wamu.com/foundation)
Washington Mutual seeks to build stronger communities in locations where the company operates. The Washington Mutual Foundation makes grants in the areas of affordable housing/community development and K–12 public education. Washington Mutual also supports a limited number of community involvement, volunteer leadership development, and community service programs. The foundation's Web site provides information on funding areas, application information, eligibility criteria, and contact information.

Weirton Steel Corporation (WV)
(http://www.weirton.com/company/about/citizenship.html)
The Weirton, West Virginia-based Weirton Steel Corporation supports a wide range of local programs through its Corporate Citizenship program. The company's philanthropic interests include support for youth programs, law enforcement, the medical community, and the local network of United Way agencies. The company's Web site features program overviews.

Wells Fargo & Company (CA) (http://www.wellsfargo.com/about/charitable/index.jhtml)
Wells Fargo & Company, the San Francisco-based banking and financial services concern, directs the bulk of its corporate giving to three areas: community development, education, and human services. Support is generally directed to organizations and programs that assist low- and moderate-income individuals. Organizations in locations served by Wells Fargo are eligible to apply. The company also actively encourages the volunteer efforts of its employees in their local communities. The company's Web site provides a list of eligible states, state-specific guidelines and application procedures, and contact information.

Wendy's International, Inc. (OH) (http://www.wendys.com/w-7-0.shtml)
Wendy's International, Inc.'s In Touch with the Community initiative offers a number of programs to support communities nationally. Established in 1992, the Dave Thomas Foundation for Adoption works to raise awareness of children in the United States waiting for adoption and to educate prospective parents about the adoption process. Wendy's High School Heisman Program seeks to recognize "America's most outstanding and well-rounded high school seniors." The company's Web site features lists of past recipients

of the Heisman award, information on how to get involved, and a link to the Dave Thomas Foundation Web site.

West Group Community Partnership Program (MN) (http://www.westgroup.com/aboutus/communityaffairs.asp)

West Group, a provider of information to the U.S. legal market headquartered in Eagan, Minnesota, makes charitable contributions and encourages the community involvement of its employees in communities where the company does business. The West Community Partnership Program considers grant proposals for funding in the focus areas of educating the future workforce, providing arts and culture experience to the community, and developing and strengthening youth, families, and communities. The company's Web site contains details on funding focus areas and application guidelines, a list of supported programs, and contact information.

West Marine, Inc. (CA) (http://www.westmarine.com/webapp/wcs/stores/servlet/DisplayPageView?storeId=10001&langId=-1&catalogId=10001&page=DonationsAndSponsorships§=about_wm)

The California-based West Marine, Inc. works to "actively promote boating, reduce our impact on the environment, improve and protect marine habitats, and contribute to meeting social needs in the communities of operations." The company provides support for organizations focused on youth, communities, and the marine environment. The company's Web site features grant guidelines and contact information.

Westinghouse Electric Company (PA) (http://www.westinghouse.com/E.asp)

Located in Pittsburgh, Pennsylvania, the Westinghouse Charitable Giving Program serves as the principal funding entity for the Westinghouse Electric Company's social investments. The program makes charitable contributions to nonprofit organizations in southwestern Pennsylvania and other communities throughout the United States where Westinghouse has a presence. Areas of focus include health and welfare, education, and civic and social services. Within these areas, Westinghouse encourages programs that meet the needs of special populations, such as the disadvantaged, the young, and the elderly. The company's Web site provides eligibility information, funding guidelines, application procedures, and contact information.

Weyerhaeuser Company Foundation (WA) (http://www.weyerhaeuser.com/community)

Weyerhaeuser Company, a supplier of forest products based in Washington State, established the Weyerhaeuser Company Foundation in 1948 to improve the quality of life in company communities and to increase understanding of forests and the products they provide. The foundation supports education and programs that promote responsible natural resource management and dedicates a significant portion of its giving to industry-related projects. The foundation's Web site features information on the foundation's giving activities, guidelines, a list of eligible locations, and an online application form.

Whirlpool Foundation (MI) (http://www.whirlpoolcorp.com/whr/foundation/foundation.html)

Whirlpool Corporation, the appliance manufacturer, provides philanthropic support through the Whirlpool Foundation to "improve the quality of family life primarily in our communities, worldwide." The foundation's Strategic and Citizenship Grants programs support nonprofit organizations in U.S. communities with a Whirlpool Corporation manufacturing facility. Funding is available in the areas of lifelong learning, cultural diversity, and quality family life. The company's Web site contains descriptions of the foundation's areas of interest and contact information.

WHO Foundation (TX) (http://whofoundation.org)

The WHO (Women Helping Others) Foundation of Dallas, Texas, was created in 1993 by the chairman of BeautiControl, Inc. The mission of the foundation is to encourage women everywhere to help others through local community service; support organizations dedicated to women and children; and educate individuals about health and education issues. The foundation awards grants to projects and programs addressing the needs of women and children in the United States and Puerto Rico. Programs dealing with health, education, and social service needs are a priority. The foundation's Web site provides application guidelines, a downloadable application form, and information on foundation publications and other programs.

Whole Foods Market, Inc. (TX)
(http://www.wholefoodsmarket.com/company/communitygiving.html)
Located in Austin, Texas, Whole Foods Market, Inc. contributes to nonprofit and educational organizations and compensates team members for time spent in community service. Contributions have supported organizations such as public radio stations, museums, river and creek cleanups, hospices, literary councils, schools, recycling organizations, soup kitchens, playground rebuilding projects, and organizations promoting organic agriculture. The foundation's Web site provides examples of projects and causes the company has supported through its stores and contact information.

The Windermere Foundation (WA)
(http://home.windermere.com/about/foundation/thefoundation.htm)
The Windermere Foundation was created by Windermere Real Estate for the purpose of raising and providing funds to support homeless assistance programs throughout the Northwest. Social services agencies that help homeless families can apply for funds by contacting their neighborhood Windermere office for information. The foundation's Web site features a grant recipient list and contact information.

Windhover Foundation (WI) (http://www.qg.com/whoarewe/windhover.html)
The Windhover Foundation was founded in 1983 as the charitable arm of the Pewaukee, Wisconsin-based Quad/Graphics company to fund "organizations focused on meeting a pressing, unfilled need, whether social, educational, cultural, or otherwise." The foundation also grants seed money to upstarts of "maverick intent," along with organizations such as hospices, women's centers, libraries, playgrounds, parks, and arenas. The foundation's Web site features application guidelines and contact information.

Working Assets (CA) (http://www.workingassets.com)
Working Assets is a San Francisco-based long distance, credit card, Internet services, and broadcasting company "that was created to build a world that is more just, humane, and environmentally sustainable." The Working Assets funding service donates a portion of its revenue to progressive nonprofit groups working for peace, human rights, equality, education, and the environment. The company's Web site contains information about the company's programs and services, a list of currently supported organizations, details on how customers can nominate an organization to receive funding, contact information, and "WorkingForChange," an activism information and resource Web site.

WSFS Financial Corporation (DE) (http://www.wsfsbank.com/communityservice.asp)
The WSFS Financial Corporation focuses its charitable contributions and volunteer programs in the Wilmington and Delaware Valley areas of Delaware. The company is mainly interested in supporting education, health, adult and child services, and the arts. The company's Web site provides an overview of the company's corporate contributions and volunteer programs and contact information.

Xcel Energy, Inc. (MN)
(http://www.xcelenergy.com/XLWEB/CDA/0,2914,1-1-1_4359-3873-0_0_0-0,00.html)
Xcel Energy, Inc., established in 2000, is committed to using "its collective knowledge, resources, and skills to meet the needs of its communities, and ensure that Xcel Energy's service area is a highly desirable place for all citizens to live, work, or own a business." Specifically, the Xcel Energy Foundation makes grants to nonprofit organizations within its Western and Midwestern 12-state service region in the areas of education, arts and culture,

and strengthening communities. The company's Web site includes descriptions of each giving area and general funding criteria. The grant application process may be completed entirely online. The company provides an online letter of inquiry form, and applicants can check the status of their letter from the site.

xyz.net (AK) (http://www.xyz.net/corpgiving.shtml)

xyz.net, located in Anchorage, Alaska, is an Internet service provider. The company's corporate giving program helps nonprofit organizations through small cash donations and gifts of products and services for the betterment of the Alaskan community. Giving is focused on youth and youth sports, technical and medical research, women's issues, education, arts and culture, and voluntarism relating to any of these giving areas. The company's Web site features eligibility criteria, funding policies, application instructions, contact information, and a corporate giving application that can be completed online and submitted electronically.

APPENDIX F

Nonprofit Organizations on the Web

Categories Used in the Center's Links to Nonprofit Resources

The following is a presentation of the organization currently used in the Center's Links to Nonprofit Resources (http://fdncenter.org/research/npr_links/index.html), but we reserve the right to change this structure as new sites are established and new Internet trends take hold.

Philanthropy

Fundraising
General
Charity-Monitoring Organizations
Online Giving
Professional Associations

Nonprofit News and Publications

Nonprofit Management & Staffing Resources
General
Boards
Job Opportunities
Program Evaluation
Voluntarism
NPO Membership Organizations

Nonprofit Technology

Public Interest and Policy

Government
General
Federal Agencies
State Agencies

International Philanthropy
General
Africa
Asia
Australia
Canada
Europe/Eurasia
Georgia
Germany
India
Israel
Italy

Japan
Latin America
Middle East
Switzerland
Taiwan
United Kingdom

Nonprofit Resources, by Program Area
Aging
Arts
Children, Youth, & Families
Community Development
Crime Prevention
Disabilities
Disaster Relief
Education—General
Education—Elementary & Secondary
Education—Higher
Environment
Gay/Lesbian
Health
HIV/AIDS
Hunger
Military/Veterans
Multicultural/Minorities
Science
Social Change
Substance Abuse
Women and Girls

Philanthropy

Affinity Group Network (http://www.cof.org/index.cfm?containerid=72)
The Council on Foundations' Affinity Group Network is composed of nonprofit organizations that cover a range of issues and population groups focused on a specific area of interest, and that tend to be oriented towards grantmakers who want to fund efforts in those particular areas. Some groups primarily engage in networking and information exchange among members, while others emphasize advocacy efforts centered around an issue or cause within philanthropy and beyond. The Web site includes a list of affinity groups in a variety of fields, summaries of their work, key staff member contact information, and links to their individual Web sites.

American Association of FundRaising Counsel (http://www.aafrc.org/)
The American Association of Fundraising Counsel is a membership organization composed of consulting firms that advise nonprofits on fundraising matters. The association's Web site has useful data regarding trends in philanthropy, including sources and distribution of funding. A particularly helpful feature on the site is the How to Choose Counsel area, which elucidates various factors to consider in selecting the right firm.

Association of Small Foundations (http://www.smallfoundations.org/)
The goal of the Association of Small Foundations is to help foundations with few or no staff. The Web site offers program information, a calendar of events, links to philanthropy organizations, a listing of members by state, links to members' sites, an online version of the association's newsletter, and more.

Association for Research on Nonprofit Organizations and Voluntary Action (http://www.arnova.org/)
The Association for Research on Nonprofit Organizations and Voluntary Action is a neutral open forum that brings together researchers, scholars, and practitioners from around the world and works to strengthen the research community in the emerging field of nonprofit and philanthropic studies. Its main forms of outreach are an annual conference, a variety of publications, and electronic discussions and seminars. The association's Web site includes information about these various activities, as well as the option to register for a listserv-based discussion group.

CharityChannel (http://charitychannel.com/)
CharityChannel is a Web site that features reviews written by a volunteer community of nonprofit-sector professionals from the fundraising field of nonprofit periodicals, books,

and software; free discussion forums with thousands of participants; and a searchable career database.

The Chronicle of Philanthropy (http://philanthropy.com/)

Like its biweekly print analog, *The Chronicle of Philanthropy*'s Web site is full of useful information for fundraisers, grantmakers, nonprofit managers, and others. The site is organized into broad topic areas—Gifts and Grants, Fund Raising, Managing Nonprofit Groups, Technology, and Jobs. It includes a summary of the contents of the *Chronicle's* current issue, with an archive of articles since 1987; a database of all corporate and foundation grants listed in the *Chronicle* since 1995; a listing of award and RFP deadlines; surveys conducted by the *Chronicle* and reports of other surveys conducted by other organizations; job opportunities in the nonprofit sector; a listing of upcoming conferences and workshops; and annotated links to other nonprofit resources on the Internet. In-depth information on nonprofit employers, technology companies, fundraising service companies, consultants, and direct-marketing service companies is also available. Visitors can also sign-up for free e-mail updates about changes to the site and breaking news stories. Some of the material is available only to *Chronicle* subscribers.

Common Grant Applications (http://fdncenter.org/funders/cga/index.html)

The common grant application format has been adopted by groups of grantmakers to allow grant applicants to produce a single proposal for a specific community of funders, thereby saving time. Before applying to any funder that accepts a common grant application form, be sure to check that your project matches the funder's stated interests, and ascertain whether the funder would prefer a letter of inquiry in advance of receiving a proposal. Also be sure to check whether the funder has a deadline for proposals, as well as whether it requires multiple copies of your proposal.

Community Foundation Locator
(http://www.cof.org/Locator/index.cfm?menuContainerID=34&crumb=2)

This extremely useful tool from the Council on Foundations has links to community foundations that provide aid to specific communities in all 50 states.

Council on Foundations (http://www.cof.org)

The Council on Foundations (COF) is a membership organization for grantmakers, which serves the public good by promoting and enhancing responsible and effective philanthropy. It provides leadership expertise, legal services, and networking opportunities—among other services—to more than 2,000 members and to the general public. The COF Web site offers a wealth of information for and about foundations. Site features include: Networking, including links to member Web sites, colleague organizations, and affinity groups; Publications; Career Center, with job postings and resources; Finding Answers, where you can search the council's FAQs; Legal, which includes excerpts from select publications and special articles offering advice on legal issues of concern to foundations, as well as legislative analysis, IRS regulations, board issues, grantmaking legal issues, and international legal information; the Newsroom, featuring news, press releases, media alerts, and issue papers; Events, announcing council conferences and workshops; and Tools, featuring a collection of resources helpful to the work of grantmakers. The council also offers a wide range of services and programs for grantmakers; *Foundation News & Commentary,* COF's flagship magazine; and Breaking News, a current awareness service. Much of the site is for members only, and members are required to register to obtain a username and password.

Forum of Regional Associations of Grantmakers (http://www.givingforum.org/)

The Forum of Regional Associations of Grantmakers (RAGs) is a membership association of the nation's largest RAGs across the country that help more than 4,000 local grantmakers practice more effective philanthropy in their communities. The forum assists RAGs in providing local leadership to grantmakers on the issues of public policy, promoting the growth of new philanthropy, technology, and measuring effectiveness and impact.

The forum's Web site includes the Regional Association Locator, which lists contact information for each individual RAG in the United States.

Gift Planning Resources Center (http://www.cam.org/~gprc/)
The Gift Planning Resources Center Web site provides an alphabetical listing of links (in English, with some information provided in French) to organizations in the United States and Canada that deal directly with planned giving; or to sites that offer planned giving information. A short description of the linked resource is provided.

GrantCraft (http://www.grantcraft.org/)
GrantCraft is a resource for grantmakers, from the Ford Foundation, that is designed to encourage conversations and reflection about the practice of effective grantmaking. Among the tools available on the Web site are guides, videos, and case studies that present the practitioners view of philanthropy. These materials incorporate insights from grantmakers working at a range of foundations of different sizes and fields of interest.

GuideStar (http://www.guidestar.org/index.html)
Produced by Philanthropic Research, Inc., GuideStar offers a searchable database of more than 850,000 United States nonprofit organizations; nonprofit sector news and articles; an online marketplace to find requests for donations, in-kind gifts, volunteers, and job postings; a conference calendar; and additional resources for nonprofits.

INDEPENDENT SECTOR (http://www.independentsector.org/)
The INDEPENDENT SECTOR (IS) is committed to promoting, strengthening, and advancing the nonprofit and philanthropic community to foster private initiative for the public good. The Web site provides an overview of IS programs in the Issues section, including the Three Sector Initiative, Corporate-Nonprofit Partnerships, Emerging Leadership, Giving and Volunteering, Tax Policy, Nonprofit Advocacy and Lobbying, Accountability, Civil Society Education, and Faith-Based Organizations in the Nonprofit Sector. The Research directory includes the Nonprofit Almanac and Desk Reference, which provides facts and figures on the size and scope of the nonprofit sector; Giving and Volunteering in the United States, which covers the giving and volunteering habits of individuals; and the Measures Project which focuses on measuring the impact of the third sector on society. IS's Public Affairs program advocates on behalf of the nonprofit sector in areas such as tax issues, nonprofit advocacy and lobbying, government funding, accountability, and public policy. Click on GiveVoice.org to connect with your legislators and government officials about the issues affecting the nonprofit sector. The NonProfit Pathfinder, designed for scholars, researchers, practitioners, funders, and the media, gathers and organizes online information on philanthropy, the nonprofit sector, and civil society organizations.

Internet Prospector (http://www.internet-prospector.org/)
Internet Prospector is a nonprofit service to the prospect research community, produced by volunteers nationwide who "mine" the Web for prospect research "nuggets." Although designed for nonprofit fundraisers, anyone seeking tools for accessing corporate, foundation, biographical, international, and online news sources will find this Web site useful. You'll find an online newsletter and an archive of past issues. A search engine is also provided, allowing you to quickly search for information from back issues located on the site. An option to subscribe to the free monthly newsletter is also available.

National Center for Charitable Statistics—Resources on Nonprofits and Philanthropy (http://nccs.urban.org/resource.htm)
The National Center for Charitable Statistics' Resources on Nonprofits and Philanthropy serves as the national repository of statistical information on the nonprofit sector from the Internal Revenue Service (IRS) and other sources. The Web site has microdata on nonprofit organizations, database documentation and data dictionaries, and IRS forms and publications, from which most of the data is collected.

National Center for Family Philanthropy (http://www.ncfp.org/)
Established in 1997 by a group of family foundations, the goal of the National Center for Family Philanthropy (NCFP) is to serve as a resource for family philanthropists by publishing books, conducting research, and offering educational seminars on family foundations. The center's Web site includes a set of links to family foundations' Web sites, links to resources on foundations and nonprofit organizations, and NCFP publications that can be ordered online.

National Committee for Responsive Philanthropy (http://www.ncrp.org/)
The National Committee for Responsive Philanthropy (NCRP) promotes philanthropy that addresses the unmet needs of disadvantaged populations through action research, providing technical assistance to nonprofits, and engaging in policy advocacy. NCRP's reform activism targets foundations, corporate grantmakers, individual donors, and workplace giving programs. In addition to information about the committee's projects, publications, and advocacy program, the Web site has the current issue of the NCRP newsletter, *Responsive Philanthropy,* as well as a selection of articles from past issues.

Philanthropy Roundtable (http://www.philanthropyroundtable.org/)
The Philanthropy Roundtable is an association of grantmakers founded on the principle that "voluntary private action offers the best means of addressing many of society's needs, and that a vibrant private sector is critical to creating the wealth that makes philanthropy possible." The Web site features highlights of articles from current and past issues of *Philanthropy,* a journal that covers relevant topics in the philanthropy field, and provides information about the roundtable's publications, conferences, and events.

Quality 990 (http://www.qual990.org/)
Quality 990 was created to serve organizations and individuals concerned with improving the quality of financial reporting in the nonprofit sector. It is dedicated to improving the quality of IRS Forms 990 filed by nonprofit organizations. With new regulations and wider, simpler access to a nonprofit's tax form, this site offers many resources to assist the community involved in filing this form. There is information on forming or joining a Nonprofit Accountability Collaborative (990 NAC), which are forums consisting of accountants, nonprofit managers, regulators, and the general public. Local 990 NAC activities fall under two main categories: education and recommendations. Comprehensive guides to the form are available, along with links to information that help in understanding the form itself and the rules to its disclosure.

Regional Association Locator (http://www.givingforum.org/ralocator.html)
The Regional Association Locator, part of the Forum of RAGs Web site, lists contact information for each individual RAG in the United States.

Third Sector New England (http://www.tsne.org/)
Third Sector New England encourages active democracy and capacity building among the voluntary or independent sector. The organization publishes *The Nonprofit Quarterly* and sponsors programs, services, and conferences. Additionally, Third Sector New England makes grants to organizations in Massachusetts that are active in social and economic justice issues. Guidelines and applications for the grants are available on the Web site.

Women's Philanthropy Institute (http://www.women-philanthropy.org/)
The Women's Philanthropy Institute is a nonprofit educational institute that brings together philanthropists, volunteers, and professional funders to educate and empower women as philanthropists, donors, and volunteers. The institute's Web site provides information about the institute's programs and services, a bulletin board, and several related articles.

Worldwide Initiatives for Grantmaker Support (http://www.wingsweb.org/index.html)
Sponsored by the Council on Foundations, the Worldwide Initiatives for Grantmaker Support (WINGS) seeks to bring together grantmakers and support organizations serving

philanthropy from around the world to create a forum in which to discuss the variety of common issues related to their support of grantmakers worldwide. The Web site includes a directory of WINGS network organizations, case studies of organizations supporting community foundations, a directory of associations serving grantmakers, a quarterly newsletter, a calendar of events, and annotated links to related Web sites.

Fundraising

GENERAL

The Chronicle of Philanthropy (http://philanthropy.com/)
Like its biweekly print analog, *The Chronicle of Philanthropy*'s Web site is full of useful information for fundraisers, grantmakers, nonprofit managers, and others. The site is organized into broad topic areas—Gifts and Grants, Fund Raising, Managing Nonprofit Groups, Technology, and Jobs. It includes a summary of the contents of the *Chronicle's* current issue, with an archive of articles since 1987; a database of all corporate and foundation grants listed in the *Chronicle* since 1995; a listing of award and RFP deadlines; surveys conducted by the *Chronicle* and reports of other surveys conducted by other organizations; job opportunities in the nonprofit sector; a listing of upcoming conferences and workshops; and annotated links to other nonprofit resources on the Internet. In-depth information on nonprofit employers, technology companies, fundraising service companies, consultants, and direct-marketing service companies is also available. Visitors can also sign-up for free e-mail updates about changes to the site and breaking news stories. Some of the material is available only to *Chronicle* subscribers.

David Lamb's Prospect Research Page (http://www.lambresearch.com/)
Lamb, a former development officer at the University of Washington and Santa Clara University, has attempted to "separate the wheat from the chaff" in describing truly useful Internet sites for researching corporations, foundations, and individual donors. David Lamb's Prospect Research Page includes links to directories of doctors, judges, lawyers, and airplane owners; online news sources; and corporate and public records databases. What's nice about the Prospect Research Page is that Lamb has distilled the vast number of potential sources of information on the Internet into a relatively small selection of annotated sites.

FinAid (http://www.finaid.org/)
FinAid is a comprehensive collection of links to information about student financial aid on the Web. It includes links to and information on financial aid applications as well as links to the free FinAid newsletter, financial aid calculators, and FastWeb, a free scholarship search service.

Foundations On-Line (http://www.foundations.org/index.html)
Foundations On-line, a service of the Northern California Community Foundation, contains a directory of links to various foundations and grantmakers, government grants, scholarship resources, fundraising software vendors and consultants, nonprofit attorneys, and related sites.

Free Management Library (http://www.mapnp.org/library/)
The Free Management Library is a free community resource for nonprofit and for-profit organizations; and is contributed to by users and readers. The library is designed to be as user friendly as possible, with a focus on providing online management resources to organizations. Visitors to this well-organized Web site can conduct a category search of free, self-directed management courses in topics such as communications, finances, fundraising, program management, program evaluation, strategic planning, and consultants.

Fund-Raising.com (http://www.fund-raising.com/)
A service of NicheNET, Fund-Raising.com provides nonprofits with information about creative ways to generate contributions. Resources include fundraising-oriented products, a Web-based fundraising competition, related links, and an Idea Bank that features suggestions from site visitors.

Fund-Raising and Foundation Research (http://www.usc.edu/dept/source/found.htm)
The Fund-raising and Foundation Research Web site is sponsored by the University of Southern California Development Research Department, as part of their selected sites for prospect research on the Web. The site features a list of links to Web sites that pertain to fundraising, foundation research, and philanthropy news.

Fundraising Forum (http://www.raise-funds.com/forum.html)
The Fundraising Forum contains information related to annual campaign fundraising and nonprofit organizations. The Web site features the Fundraising Forum Library, where fundraising information can be found under several categories: planning for fundraising, funding sources and prospects, organizing a campaign, managing a campaign, post campaign activity, and developing the development team.

Fundsnet Services Online (http://www.fundsnetservices.com/)
Fundsnet Services Online is a comprehensive and searchable directory of funders, funding resources, and scholarship opportunities on the World Wide Web. Most links are annotated, and the Web site also includes a section organized by subject area.

GB3 Group Nonprofit Marketing (http://www.nonprofitmarketing.org/)
GB3 Group, a member of the Association of Fundraising Professionals, is a marketing, communications, publicity and public relations, and fundraising consulting and training firm that services clients across the United States. The company provides training, consulting, coaching, and resources in marketing, communications, and fundraising to nonprofit and education managers, staff, and volunteers. The GB3 Group Web site offers a variety of topical reference material and information about workshops, books, free marketing tips, and related job openings in the field.

Getting Started On Your Own (http://www.federmanconsulting.com/how_to_begin.htm)
The Getting Started On Your Own section of the Federman Consulting Web site provides "primers" on how to begin development work in the areas of research, strategy, program development, and grantwriting.

GrantsNet (http://www.grantsnet.org/)
Sponsored by the American Association for the Advancement of Science, GrantsNet is an online searchable database of funding opportunities in biomedical research and science education that is specifically geared towards scientists-in-training.

The Grantsmanship Center (http://www.tgci.com/)
The Grantsmanship Center (TGCI) is a clearinghouse of fundraising information and provides training in grantsmanship and proposal writing for nonprofit organizations and government agencies. In addition to training program and schedule information, the center's Web site offers grant source information on community foundations and federal, state, and international funding; current *Federal Register* grant funding information, including a daily summary; *TGCI Magazine*, an online publication; and a listing of publications for fundraisers, including TGCI proposal writing guides. The Web site also has a new resource, Winning Grant Proposals Online, with examples of effective proposal writing models for designing programs, consisting entirely of recent federally funded, top-ranked grant proposals in a wide variety of subject areas.

GrantSmart.org (http://www.grantsmart.org/)
A project of Canyon Research with support from the J.C. Downing Foundation, GrantSmart.org serves grantseekers, philanthropic organizations, and individual donors by providing an informational and interactive resource center for and about the nonprofit community. The Web site has data about private foundation activities, philanthropic organizations, and individual donors, and features a searchable database of tax-related information for more than 60,000 private foundations that file Form 990 with the IRS, including information from key fields within each tax return.

GrantsWeb (http://www.srainternational.org/newweb/grantsweb/index.cfm)
Aimed at the academic/scientific research community, the GrantsWeb section of the Society of Research Administrators' Web site contains a comprehensive links resource for locating government research grant opportunities, as well as some information related to private funding. The links are categorized by general resources, U.S. federal agencies, Canadian resources, and by international resources, which includes Australia, Europe, Great Britain, and Israel.

Hoover's Online (http://www.hoovers.com/)
Hoover's Online, the Austin, Texas-based publisher of corporate information, may not be the "Ultimate Source for Company Information," as it bills itself, but it sure is a good one. The Web site's free offerings center around Hoover's Company Capsules, which provide news and information—company profile, key personnel, full stock quote, selected press coverage—on thousands of public and private enterprises. Paying subscribers get the same, in much greater depth and detail.

Internet Nonprofit Center's "How Can We Use the Internet for Fundraising?" (http://www.nonprofits.org/misc/981027em.html)
The Internet Nonprofit Center's "How Can We Use the Internet for Fundraising?" is a comprehensive 1998 report by Eric Mercer designed to provide "an introduction and a classification scheme to help readers learn to effectively evaluate alternative methods of online fundraising."

Internet Prospector (http://www.internet-prospector.org/)
Internet Prospector is a nonprofit service to the prospect research community, produced by volunteers nationwide who "mine" the Web for prospect research "nuggets." Although designed for nonprofit fundraisers, anyone seeking tools for accessing corporate, foundation, biographical, international, and online news sources will find this Web site useful. You'll find an online newsletter and an archive of past issues. A search engine is also provided, allowing you to quickly search for information from back issues located on the site. An option to subscribe to the free monthly newsletter is also available.

Michigan State University Grants and Related Resources (http://www.lib.msu.edu/harris23/grants/grants.htm)
The amount of information available through the Michigan State University Grants and Related Resources site is nearly overwhelming, but Jon Harrison of the University of Michigan Library System has created a site that is well organized and cleanly designed. Start by clicking Grants for Nonprofits. Most valuable here are the annotated lists of resources (print, electronic, and online) for grant information in particular subject areas, from Arts and Cultural Activities to Religion and Social Change. For each subject area, Harrison provides abstracts of useful print resources, descriptions of databases, and links to online information. There is also a substantial section on grants to individuals, including financial aid. Harrison has even assembled an impressive bibliography, with links, on grantsmanship techniques, including lots of information on fundraising research and proposal writing.

Michigan State University Grants and Related Resources—Grants for Individuals (http://www.lib.msu.edu/harris23/grants/3subject.htm)
The Michigan State University Grants and Related Resources Web site includes a separate section for individuals that covers Web sites, databases, and print resources, including links to many federal, state, and university-based funding sources. Resource listings are organized by academic type, population group, and subject.

Nickel News (http://www.nickelnews.com/comp/resources/)
Nickel News is a resource for nonprofits to aid in their fundraising efforts, mainly through an online publication that nonprofit organizations can customize to include advertisements from sponsors. Additionally, the Web site provides numerous links to nonprofit news sites and publications, commercial and noncommercial software providers, books on nonprofit fundraising, volunteer opportunities, and Web hosting and design information for nonprofit organizations.

Nonprofits and the Internet (DMA Nonprofit Federation) (http://www.the-dma.org/nonprofitfederation/index.html)
The Nonprofits and the Internet section of the DMA Nonprofit Federation's Web site provides links to several full-text reports covering topics such as online fundraising regulation, creating and designing charity Web sites, and related issues facing every charity that has a Web site on the Internet. The site also has a set of links to related Web sites.

Nonprofit Charitable Organizations (http://nonprofit.about.com/index.htm)
Nonprofit Charitable Organizations is a mini-Web site within the comprehensive About.com site that serves as a useful guide to resources and information about nonprofit organizations, foundations, fundraising, technology, educational opportunities, jobs, and more. Visitors to the Web site can search feature archives as well as the entire About.com site, participate in chats, post a resume, and register to receive newsletters via e-mail.

Nonprofit Coordinating Committee of New York (http://www.npccny.org/)
The Nonprofit Coordinating Committee of New York (NPCC) is a membership organization dedicated to protecting and helping the nonprofit community of the New York metropolitan area. The committee's Web site provides Peter Swords' "How to Read the IRS Form 990 & Find Out What It Means," an employee benefits survey, and Who Does What?, a searchable database of nonprofits that offer technical assistance to other nonprofits. A listing of government grants; programs; New York *Nonprofits*, an online newsletter; and workshop calendars are available online.

Online Fundraising Mailing List (http://www.gilbert.org/fundraising)
The Online Fundraising Mailing List, the Gilbert Center's mailing list for online fundraising, provides a learning environment for fundraisers at all levels of experience. Visitors to the Web site can also subscribe to receive the Gilbert Center's *Nonprofit Online News.*

Online Fundraising Resources Center (http://www.fund-online.com/)
The Online Fundraising Resources Center is a collection of online fundraising resources from the book *Fundraising and Friend-raising on the Web.* The Web site includes excerpts from the book, with updates, and a good set of successful Web site examples. The site also has a list of links that include some general nonprofit, fundraising, and charity review sites; essays and published articles related to "cyber fundraising"; and teaching materials from Internet fundraising classes.

Peninsula Community Foundation's Philanthropy Center (http://www.philanthropycenter.org/)
The Peninsula Community Foundation created the Philanthropy Center Web site to serve as a gateway for local community investors who want to educate themselves about the charitable sector in San Mateo and Santa Clara Counties, California. Private nonprofit organizations are represented in listings that include budget and funding information,

number of staff or volunteers, a statement on immediate needs, scope and purpose of the agencies' services, and a vignette about the clients served.

Polaris (http://www.polarisgrantscentral.net/)
Polaris is a grant support organization dedicated to providing resources for educational institutions, governmental agencies, healthcare services, and nonprofit organizations. The Web site offers a wealth of grants-related information and links, including grant workshops across the country, links to resources for grantseekers, publications, news and events, information on scholarships, grantwriting tips, new ideas and organizations, and an online question and answer service.

Portico (http://indorgs.virginia.edu/portico/)
Portico is a collection of Web sites, containing publicly available information, compiled for the use of the advancement and fundraising communities. The Portico Web site has a comprehensive set of links to sites that provide information on biographies of individuals, occupations, personal property, salaries, stocks, businesses, media, nonprofits, international, and other resources. The site also has resources for and about the nonprofit community, nonprofit and philanthropy news, state and regional resources and databases, science and medical-related funding opportunities, and sources related to the international philanthropic community. The Other Resources section has links to prospect research pages, professional organizations, electronic libraries, and periodicals.

Quality 990 (http://www.qual990.org/)
Quality 990 was created to serve organizations and individuals concerned with improving the quality of financial reporting in the nonprofit sector. It is dedicated to improving the quality of IRS Forms 990 filed by nonprofit organizations. With new regulations and wider, simpler access to a nonprofit's tax form, this site offers many resources to assist the community involved in filing this form. There is information on forming or joining a Nonprofit Accountability Collaborative (990 NAC), which are forums consisting of accountants, nonprofit managers, regulators, and the general public. Local 990 NAC activities fall under two main categories: education and recommendations. Comprehensive guides to the form are available, along with links to information that help in understanding the form itself and the rules to its disclosure.

SEC Filings & Forms (EDGAR) (http://www.sec.gov/edgar.shtml)
The Securities and Exchange Commission's EDGAR (Electronic Data Gathering, Analysis, and Retrieval system) is a goldmine of basic but often-hard-to-find corporate information (e.g., fiscal data, officers, subsidiaries, and recent mergers and acquisitions activity). EDGAR on the Web allows visitors to retrieve publicly-available filings submitted to the SEC from January 1994 to the present.

Seliger & Associates—Free Grant Information (http://www.seliger.com/freeservices.cfm)
Seliger & Associates, a grantwriting consulting firm, provides access to two types of free grant availability information: the online *Seliger Funding Report,* which lists available federal, state, local, foundation, and corporate giving grant opportunities, and e-mail grant alerts. Registration is required.

UK Fundraising (http://www.fundraising.co.uk/)
UK Fundraising is a comprehensive resource for charities and nonprofit fundraisers in the UK and internationally. The Web site has a fundraising bookshop, lists of consultants, e-mail discussion lists, events, funding, grants, magazines, nonprofit resources, products, professional organizations, research papers, services, software, job opportunities, and an extensive collection of links to examples of online fundraising activities.

Virtual Foundation (http://www.virtualfoundation.org/)
The Virtual Foundation is an online program, founded in 1996 by ECOLOGIA, that supports grassroots initiatives and community improvement projects around the world. The foundation screens and posts small-scale proposals that are initiated by non-governmental organizations in the fields of the environment, health, and sustainable economic activity to its Web site, where they can be read by potential donors.

CHARITY-MONITORING ORGANIZATIONS

BBB Wise Giving Alliance—Give.org (http://www.give.org/)
The BBB (Better Business Bureau) Wise Giving Alliance collects and distributes information about the programs, governance, fundraising practices, and finances of hundreds of charitable organizations that solicit nationally and are the subject of donor inquiries. Besides reports on specific charities, the Give.org Web site has news and alerts, and several "Tips On..." publications, including one on standards for charitable solicitations and used car donations. The site also offers an area where you can inquire or complain about a charity.

Charities Review Council of Minnesota (http://www.crcmn.org/)
The Charities Review Council of Minnesota is an independent nonprofit organization that develops accountability standards for charities that solicit funds in Minnesota and conducts reviews based on those standards. The review information is provided to the potential donors and to the charitable organization, without charge. The Web site includes the council's accountability standards, organized by public disclosure, governance, financial activity, and fundraising, and a Giving Guide that contains the list of charities that have been reviewed, with information on ordering a full report. The site also has information for donors, resources for nonprofits, and a good set of annotated links to charity-monitoring related Web sites.

Evangelical Council for Financial Accountability (http://www.ecfa.org/)
Comprised of charitable, religious, missionary, social, and educational organizations, the Evangelical Council for Financial Accountability serves as a "Christian Better Business Bureau" by making appropriate public disclosure of its more than 1,000 members' financial practices and accomplishments, and by developing and maintaining standards of accountability. The Web site has a directory of council members that can be searched by name, state, or ministry type. The site also has a statement of responsible stewardship for charities to follow and a "bill of rights" for donors.

Operation Missed Giving (http://www.ftc.gov/bcp/conline/edcams/giving/index.html)
The Federal Trade Commission's (FTC) Operation Missed Giving Web site provides information to help donors give wisely. Included on the site are a list of cases filed by the FTC, a set of links to other charity-monitoring organizations, and the FTC's brochure "Charitable Donation$ Give or Take," which provides a charity checklist to use in order to avoid making contributions to fraudulent charities.

ONLINE GIVING

CharityWave (http://www.charitywave.com/)
CharityWave provides an online donation service for selected charities. The selection criteria include nonprofit status, a Web site that lists the organization's program and budget, a readily-available IRS Form 990, and recommendation by CharityWave's board of advisors. Organizations are listed alphabetically and by category. Profiles of the organizations are also available to help the donor make informed decisions. An annual audit is conducted to ensure that 100 percent of every donation goes to the charity for which it was intended.

e-Philanthropy (http://www.actknowledgeworks.net/ephil/index_html)
e-Philanthropy is the Web site for the W.K. Kellogg Foundation report, "e-Philanthropy v.2.001," which documents the phenomenon of interactive online services for philanthropy and voluntarism. This site allows you to access the report and a database of information related to e-philanthropy, which can be browsed by name or primary focus (shopping and profit sharing, fundraising services, knowledge and capacity building, donor services, auctions/events, advocacy, giving time/volunteering, and full service portals) or searched by name keyword.

Groundspring.org (http://www.groundspring.org/index_gs.cfm)
Created in 1999 by the Tides Foundation as eGrants.org, Groundspring.org is a forward-looking nonprofit that works to help progressive nonprofits increase their financial support through online fundraising. Groundspring.org's tool DonateNow allows organizations to accept credit card donations through online transactions. EmailNow gives nonprofits an affordable, ad-free tool to send e-newsletters, raise money online, and communicate with supporters. Groundspring.org also recently acquired ebase, a free community relationship management database developed by TechRocks. A workshop calendar is also available.

Independent Charities of America (http://www.independentcharities.org/)
Independent Charities of America is a nonprofit organization that pre-screens and certifies the charities it presents to potential donors via Web-based giving, workplace giving programs, and other low-cost fundraising methods. Charities are reviewed and certified annually.

Independent Givers of America (http://www.givedirect.org/)
The Independent Givers of America (IGA) is a "nonprofit tax-exempt charitable organization whose mission is to bring together generous people and deserving causes, principally but not exclusively by developing Internet-based systems that reduce the cost and increase the productivity of charitable solicitation." Its Web site gives philanthropists the opportunity to set up a personal, private, online foundation; accept e-mail proposals at any time; find an IGA-recommended charity; and contribute to any IRS-recognized charity, church, or school.

Local Independent Charities of America (http://www.lic.org/)
Local Independent Charities of America is a federation of more than 600 local nonprofit organizations. The Web site provides an online giving service, and potential donors can conduct a key word search to access information on member charitable organizations. Information provided includes mission statements, programs offered, and links to the Web sites of various nonprofit charitable organizations.

Resources for Fundraising Online
(http://www.nonprofits.org/npofaq/misc/990804olfr.html)
Part of the Internet Nonprofit Center Web site, Resources for Fundraising Online lists information and services provided by organizations related to online fundraising.

PROFESSIONAL ASSOCIATIONS

American Association of FundRaising Counsel (http://www.aafrc.org/)
The American Association of Fundraising Counsel is a membership organization composed of consulting firms that advise nonprofits on fundraising matters. The association's Web site has useful data regarding trends in philanthropy, including sources and distribution of funding. A particularly helpful feature on the site is the How to Choose Counsel area, which elucidates various factors to consider in selecting the right firm.

American Association of Grant Professionals (http://www.grantprofessionals.org/)
The American Association of Grant Professionals serves grant developers who work for public or private organizations. The Web site has information about the organization, including a code of ethics and credentialing; useful articles about grantseeking; and links to Web sites that contain information related to educational grant writing.

AssociationCentral.com (http://www.associationcentral.com/)
Serving as a portal site for professional associations, nonprofit networks, and special interest organizations, AssociationCentral.com is structured in a similar fashion to many popular search engines, breaking down its listings according to industry categories and providing advanced search capabilities.

Association of Fundraising Professionals (http://www.afpnet.org/)
The Association of Fundraising Professionals (AFP) consists of 26,000 individual members in 169 chapters throughout the United States, Canada, and Mexico, working to advance philanthropy through advocacy, research, education, and certification programs. Visitors to AFP's Web site will find extensive information on nonprofit philanthropy and AFP activities and publications, AFP's professional advancement programs and course information, and the full text of its Code of Ethical Principles and Standards of Professional Practice and the principles of an E-Donor Bill of Rights, created to address concerns and challenges arising from Internet charitable giving. In addition, job opportunity and member services modules are made available to AFP members. You can sign up for free e-mail updates on professional advancement and public policy.

Association of Professional Researchers for Advancement (http://www.aprahome.org/)
The Association of Professional Researchers for Advancement (APRA) is an international organization for fundraisers who specialize in research and information management. The Web site has information about membership, links to Web sites about advancement research, and APRA publications and conference information.

National Committee on Planned Giving (http://www.ncpg.org/)
The National Committee on Planned Giving is the association for planned giving professionals. The Web site includes the LEAVE A LEGACY program, created by the Central Ohio Planned Giving Council and distributed nationally, in order to encourage estate gifts to local charities. The site also includes information regarding education and training programs, planned giving conferences, and information on purchasing committee publications and products.

Nonprofit News and Publications

AScribe (http://www.ascribe.org/)
Ascribe is a low-cost national public interest newswire that includes hundreds of nonprofit organizations and governmental agencies, including universities, think tanks, medical and scientific research centers, public policy advocates, professional associations, public relations agencies, and private and corporate foundations that are sending news and information to the news media, Web sites, portals, and online services. News releases can be organized around specific topics or from particular institutions and can be customized for geographical regions or demographic groups. AScribe's Web site has an example of the Live Newswire, with news releases that have been issued by members during the past seven days.

Association for Research on Nonprofit Organizations and Voluntary Action (http://www.arnova.org/)
The Association for Research on Nonprofit Organizations and Voluntary Action is a neutral open forum that brings together researchers, scholars, and practitioners from around the

world and works to strengthen the research community in the emerging field of nonprofit and philanthropic studies. Its main forms of outreach are an annual conference, a variety of publications, and electronic discussions and seminars. The association's Web site includes information about these various activities, as well as the option to register for a listserv-based discussion group.

Board Cafe (http://www.boardcafe.org/)
Board Cafe, published by CompassPoint Nonprofit Services, is a monthly electronic newsletter for members of nonprofit boards. Each issue includes board information, opinions, news, and resources, with a "Main Course" article that can be applied to board work. The Web site also has access to past issues of the newsletter dating back to 2001.

CharityChannel (http://charitychannel.com/)
CharityChannel is a Web site that features reviews written by a volunteer community of nonprofit-sector professionals from the fundraising field of nonprofit periodicals, books, and software; free discussion forums with thousands of participants; and a searchable career database.

The Chronicle of Philanthropy (http://philanthropy.com/)
Like its biweekly print analog, *The Chronicle of Philanthropy*'s Web site is full of useful information for fundraisers, grantmakers, nonprofit managers, and others. The site is organized into broad topic areas—Gifts and Grants, Fund Raising, Managing Nonprofit Groups, Technology, and Jobs. It includes a summary of the contents of the *Chronicle's* current issue, with an archive of articles since 1987; a database of all corporate and foundation grants listed in the *Chronicle* since 1995; a listing of award and RFP deadlines; surveys conducted by the *Chronicle* and reports of other surveys conducted by other organizations; job opportunities in the nonprofit sector; a listing of upcoming conferences and workshops; and annotated links to other nonprofit resources on the Internet. In-depth information on nonprofit employers, technology companies, fundraising service companies, consultants, and direct-marketing service companies is also available. Visitors can also sign-up for free e-mail updates about changes to the site and breaking news stories. Some of the material is available only to *Chronicle* subscribers.

Common Wealth (http://tap.epn.org/commonwealth)
Updated weekly, the Common Wealth Web site provides online access to current and archived articles from *The American Prospect,* a progressive, liberal magazine of current issues in civil society. Included on the Web site are reports on issues affecting nonprofit organizations and philanthropy, original articles written for the site, and links to other organizations.

Contributions Magazine (http://www.contributionsmagazine.com/)
Contributions Magazine offers current and archived feature articles of its bimonthly print publication on the Web site, and an index of the current issue's other articles, available by subscription. The site also contains a list of articles pertaining to nonprofit issues, book reviews of its own current fundraising publications, and a "descriptive forum" of links to sites that offer services or products related to the nonprofit sector.

Fundsnet Services Online (http://www.fundsnetservices.com/)
Fundsnet Services Online is a comprehensive and searchable directory of funders, funding resources, and scholarship opportunities on the World Wide Web. Most links are annotated, and the Web site also includes a section organized by subject area.

GuideStar (http://www.guidestar.org/index.html)
Produced by Philanthropic Research, Inc., GuideStar offers a searchable database of more than 850,000 United States nonprofit organizations; nonprofit sector news and articles; an online marketplace to find requests for donations, in-kind gifts, volunteers, and job postings; a conference calendar; and additional resources for nonprofits.

HandsNet (http://www.handsnet.org/)
HandsNet is a membership organization of more than 5,000 public interest and human services organizations. The Web site features articles and alerts, which provide daily news updates on human services issues and legislation; the WebClipper news and delivery service, with human services headlines from hundreds of Web sites that can be tailored to your interests; and information on training and capacity building programs, including a Mobile Technology Classroom and information consulting and knowledge-management services.

Idealist (http://www.idealist.org/)
Idealist, a project of Action Without Borders, is available in English, Spanish, French, and Russian. It has a searchable network of more than 30,000 nonprofit and community organizations in 165 countries, which can be searched or browsed by name, location, or mission; a searchable list of volunteer opportunities; hundreds of job, consultant, and internship listings; and listings of events, programs, and publications. News articles, commentary, reports, and essays related to NGOs are updated frequently. My Idealist allows you to register for personalized e-mail updates, job and volunteer information, and connections to others with similar interests.

Interactive Knowledge for Nonprofits Worldwide (http://www.iknow.org/)
Developed and maintained by Raffa & Associates, P.C., Interactive Knowledge for Nonprofits Worldwide is a collection of links to online education, fringe benefits, fundraising, governance, human resources, legal issues, legislation, strategic planning, board governance, financial management, and voluntarism resources for nonprofit organizations.

Internet Nonprofit Center (http://www.nonprofits.org/)
A project of the Evergreen State Society in Seattle, Washington, the Internet Nonprofit Center is oriented toward providing information to and about nonprofit organizations. The Web site has an extensive Nonprofit FAQ section, with information on a wide range of topics of interest to leaders and managers of nonprofit organizations; a Library that offers longer essays, bibliographies, practical guides, and analysis of the nonprofit sector; and current nonprofit news. The Recent Changes link provides you with a list of the 50 most recent revisions and additions to the site. You can also sign-up for the weekly e-mail publication, Nonprofit Online News.

Internet Prospector (http://www.internet-prospector.org/)
Internet Prospector is a nonprofit service to the prospect research community, produced by volunteers nationwide who "mine" the Web for prospect research "nuggets." Although designed for nonprofit fundraisers, anyone seeking tools for accessing corporate, foundation, biographical, international, and online news sources will find this Web site useful. You'll find an online newsletter and an archive of past issues. A search engine is also provided, allowing you to quickly search for information from back issues located on the site. An option to subscribe to the free monthly newsletter is also available.

Internet Resources for Nonprofits (http://www.ucp-utica.org/uwlinks/directory.html)
Amassed by the United Cerebral Palsy Association, Greater Utica (NY) Area, Internet Resources for Nonprofits is a sizable collection of annotated links to resources all across the United States and is divided into more than twenty subcategories. In addition, there is a Featured Web Sites section, along with a News and Views section which features topical articles selected by the site editors.

IUPUI University Special Collections (http://www-lib.iupui.edu/special/)
The Special Collections department at the University Library of Indiana University-Purdue University Indianapolis (IUPUI) encompasses the manuscript collections, university archives, and rare books, and the Joseph and Matthew Payton Philanthropic Studies Library. The Web site has The Philanthropy Collections, which include the historical records of organizations and individuals that have worked as advocates for the nonprofit sector, fundraising firms that help nonprofit organizations raise money, foundations and

individual philanthropists, and nonprofit organizations that provide social services, particularly in central Indiana.

National Center for Charitable Statistics (http://nccs.urban.org/)
The National Center for Charitable Statistics (NCCS) works with the IRS and other government agencies, private sector service organizations, and the scholarly community to develop data on nonprofit organizations and their activities for use in research on the relationships between the nonprofit sector, government, the commercial sector, and the broader civil society. Visitors to the Web site can download microdata on nonprofit organizations, view or download database documentation and data dictionaries, and download IRS forms and publications, from which most of the data is collected.

New York Nonprofit Press (http://www.nynp.biz/)
New York Nonprofit Press provides comprehensive news and in-depth analysis on social services issues and events and is distributed on a monthly basis to nonprofit health and human services agencies throughout the New York metropolitan area. The Web site also has archived issues and job listings.

Nonprofit Charitable Organizations (http://nonprofit.about.com/index.htm)
Nonprofit Charitable Organizations is a mini-Web site within the comprehensive About.com site that serves as a useful guide to resources and information about nonprofit organizations, foundations, fundraising, technology, educational opportunities, jobs, and more. Visitors to the Web site can search feature archives as well as the entire About.com site, participate in chats, post a resume, and register to receive newsletters via e-mail.

Nonprofit FAQ (http://www.nonprofit-info.org/npofaq/)
The Nonprofit FAQ Web site is an online resource of information and advice about nonprofits, taken from discussions on e-mail lists and other sources. This frequently asked questions file has five main categories: organization, management, regulation, resources, and development, as well as several sections with a more specific focus.

Nonprofit Issues (http://www.nonprofitissues.com/)
Don Kramer's *Nonprofit Issues* is a newsletter that addresses legal developments and events that affect nonprofit organizations and employees. Visitors to the Web site can read selected highlights from past issues and purchase Ready Reference Pages, which summarize the rules and regulations governing various aspects of nonprofit organization. Trial and regular subscription orders can be placed online.

Nonprofit Prophets
(http://www.kn.pacbell.com/wired/prophets/prophets.res.topics.html)
Nonprofit Prophets was designed to empower students to understand and positively impact an issue they see in the world. The Web site has a comprehensive index of annotated links, organized by topic, to resources that aid in research and the investigation of problems. Categories include the environment/ecology; trees and animals; global conflict/politics; family issues; homelessness, hunger, and poverty; disasters; and major online news sources.

The Nonprofit Times (http://www.nptimes.com/)
The NonProfit Times is a biweekly print publication covering nonprofit management issues. The Web site has selected articles and features from current and archived past issues of the publication. Also included are a classified employment advertisement section and a resource directory that lists names and addresses of service-related organizations.

The Nonprofit Zone (http://www.nonprofitzone.com/)
Staffed by volunteers, the Nonprofit Zone Web site provides "free tools and resources to help nonprofits work better, smarter, and faster." The Answers Database feature contains a library of "interactive" answers and links to articles related to issues typically encountered by nonprofits, including topics added by participants. Some of the free services provided to

nonprofit organizations include fundraising, volunteer classifieds, media, lobbying, public relations, marketing, technology, and a donations database for donating materials to organizations.

Online Fundraising Mailing List (http://www.gilbert.org/fundraising)
Online Fundraising Mailing List, the Gilbert Center's mailing list for online fundraising, provides a learning environment for fundraisers at all levels of experience. Visitors to the Web site can also subscribe to receive the Gilbert Center's Nonprofit Online News.

Philanthropy Journal (http://www.philanthropyjournal.org/front.asp)
The *Philanthropy Journal* reports on state, national, and international nonprofit news. Published by the A.J. Fletcher Foundation, the *Journal* addresses issues of fundraising, donations, management, volunteering, and technology in the philanthropic and nonprofit community. A free weekly e-mail news bulletin and job postings are available through the Web site.

Philanthropy News Digest (http://fdncenter.org/pnd/)
The *Philanthropy News Digest* (*PND*) contains abstract summaries of original articles, press and news releases, grantmaker Web sites, and other items related to the world of philanthropy. *PND* also includes the RFP Bulletin, which provides a brief overview of current funding opportunities offered by foundations or other grantmaking organizations; Connections, a guide to Web sites containing cutting-edge issues related to philanthropy; the NPO Spotlight, which highlights the activities of a different nonprofit organization or NGO each week; newsmaker interviews; book and Web site reviews; a conference calendar; the Job Corner; a message board; and the searchable *PND* archive.

Planned Giving Today (http://www.pgtoday.com/)
Planned Giving Today offers resources for gift-planning professionals, including excerpts from its monthly print newsletter and a list of planned giving resources. The Web site also includes information about the Canadian edition of the newsletter *Gift Planning in Canada.*

Nonprofit Management & Staffing Resources

GENERAL

Alliance for Nonprofit Management (http://www.allianceonline.org/)
The Alliance for Nonprofit Management members include management support organizations, individual professionals, and a range of national/regional, umbrella, research and academic, publishing, and philanthropic organizations that provide training and consulting to nonprofits. The Web site has a resource center that includes Web sites, books, videos, and other resources relating to nonprofit management and governance; *Pulse!,* the alliance's online newsletter; and a database of alliance member providers, searchable by name, state, types of assistance offered and/or by services offered.

Aspen Institute (http://www.aspeninstitute.org/)
The Aspen Institute is a global forum for leaders from various disciplines to address critical issues that affect societies, organizations, and individuals. The Web site provides information on seminars, fellowship programs, and policy programs that the institute offers; application guidelines; a list of grant recipients; special initiatives; publication content and summaries; research abstracts; and links to nonprofit resources.

Association of Fundraising Professionals (http://www.afpnet.org/)
The Association of Fundraising Professionals (AFP) consists of 26,000 individual members in 169 chapters throughout the United States, Canada, and Mexico, working to

advance philanthropy through advocacy, research, education, and certification programs. Visitors to AFP's Web site will find extensive information on nonprofit philanthropy and AFP activities and publications, AFP's professional advancement programs and course information, and the full text of its Code of Ethical Principles and Standards of Professional Practice and the principles of an E-Donor Bill of Rights, created to address concerns and challenges arising from Internet charitable giving. In addition, job opportunity and member services modules are made available to AFP members. You can sign up for free e-mail updates on professional advancement and public policy.

The Chronicle of Philanthropy (http://philanthropy.com/)

Like its biweekly print analog, *The Chronicle of Philanthropy*'s Web site is full of useful information for fundraisers, grantmakers, nonprofit managers, and others. The site is organized into broad topic areas—Gifts and Grants, Fund Raising, Managing Nonprofit Groups, Technology, and Jobs. It includes a summary of the contents of the *Chronicle*'s current issue, with an archive of articles since 1987; a database of all corporate and foundation grants listed in the *Chronicle* since 1995; a listing of award and RFP deadlines; surveys conducted by the *Chronicle* and reports of other surveys conducted by other organizations; job opportunities in the nonprofit sector; a listing of upcoming conferences and workshops; and annotated links to other nonprofit resources on the Internet. In-depth information on nonprofit employers, technology companies, fundraising service companies, consultants, and direct-marketing service companies is also available. Visitors can also sign-up for free e-mail updates about changes to the site and breaking news stories. Some of the material is available only to *Chronicle* subscribers.

CompassPoint Nonprofit Services (http://www.compasspoint.org)

Funded by foundations, corporations, and individuals, CompassPoint Nonprofit Services provides affordable management consulting, training, and research information to the San Francisco Bay Area nonprofit sector. Web site visitors can access Nonprofit Genie, which has a list of answers to FAQs on such topics as strategic planning, financial management, volunteer management, and board development.

Coro (http://www.coro.org/)

Coro is a nonprofit leadership training organization that offers related workshops, internships, fellowships, and youth programs to the nonprofit community. The Web site has detailed information about the various programs, including application procedures, and an online application form.

Executive Service Corps of Southern California (http://www.escsc.org/)

The Executive Service Corps of Southern California is an innovative organization that links retired executives and professionals with nonprofit organizations to serve as management consultants and board members on a volunteer basis. The Web site includes information on volunteering, highlights current projects, and offers links to other sites relating to the California nonprofit world.

Free Management Library (http://www.mapnp.org/library/)

The Free Management Library is a free community resource for nonprofit and for-profit organizations; and is contributed to by users and readers. The library is designed to be as user friendly as possible, with a focus on providing online management resources to organizations. Visitors to this well-organized Web site can conduct a category search of free, self-directed management courses in topics such as communications, finances, fundraising, program management, program evaluation, strategic planning, and consultants.

The Grantsmanship Center (http://www.tgci.com/)

The Grantsmanship Center (TGCI) is a clearinghouse of fundraising information and provides training in grantsmanship and proposal writing for nonprofit organizations and government agencies. In addition to training program and schedule information, the center's Web site offers grant source information on community foundations and federal, state, and international funding; current *Federal Register* grant funding information, including a daily summary; *TGCI Magazine*, an online publication; and a listing of publications for fundraisers, including TGCI proposal writing guides. The Web site also has a new resource, Winning Grant Proposals Online, with examples of effective proposal writing models for designing programs, consisting entirely of recent federally funded, top-ranked grant proposals in a wide variety of subject areas.

Hauser Center for Nonprofit Organizations (http://www.ksghauser.harvard.edu/)
The Hauser Center for Nonprofit Organizations is a Harvard University research center focusing on nonprofit policy and leadership. The Web site has information about the center's programs, major research activities, and working papers.

InnoNet (http://www.innonet.org/)
InnoNet (Innovation Network, Inc.) is dedicated to building evaluation and learning skills, knowledge, and processes within public and nonprofit organizations through the use of participatory evaluation. The Web site provides a free, innovative Workstation tool to guide nonprofits and public agencies through a planning and evaluation process, resulting in a blueprint for designing, evaluating, and implementing a successful program, with a corresponding work plan. InnoNet also provides information on its consulting services and workshops and provides a wealth of evaluation resources in its Resource Center. The InnoNetworking section connects you to a message board, discussion group, news, and an opportunity to signup for e-mail updates.

Institute for Not-for-Profit Management (http://www.gsb.columbia.edu/execed/INM/index.html)
The Institute for Not-for-Profit Management at Columbia Business School provides graduate-level management training to executives of nonprofit organizations through a variety of programs: the Executive Level Program, Middle Management Programs, and Leadership Development Program. Each of these is an intensive, several-day course, rather than lasting a full semester. Customized programs for individual organizations are available, as are scholarships for eligible applicants whose agencies are unable to sponsor them fully.

Interactive Knowledge for Nonprofits Worldwide (http://www.iknow.org/)
Developed and maintained by Raffa & Associates, P.C., Interactive Knowledge for Nonprofits Worldwide is a collection of links to online education, fringe benefits, fundraising, governance, human resources, legal issues, legislation, strategic planning, board governance, financial management, and voluntarism resources for nonprofit organizations.

Leader to Leader Institute (http://www.pfdf.org/)
The Leader to Leader Institute, formerly the Peter F. Drucker Foundation, supports leadership in the nonprofit sector by providing educational opportunities and other resources to promising nonprofit leaders. The institute's Web site has articles about leadership and management, a self-assessment tool, workshop information, and the Nonprofit Innovation Discovery Site, a searchable database of nonprofit programs and projects.

Learner Resource Center (http://www.uwex.edu/li/learner/index.htm)
The Learner Resource Center has a number of resources on the Web that provide assistance in a variety of nonprofit management and leadership areas. The center's Web site includes a section with links to annotated resources organized by topic, and Web-based articles.

Mandel Center for Nonprofit Organizations (http://www.cwru.edu/mandelcenter/)
The Mandel Center for Nonprofit Organizations, affiliated with Case Western Reserve University, has been the standard-setter in graduate education for leaders of nonprofit organizations in the United States. The center's Web site contains information about its academic programs, conferences and lectures, career and alumni services, and publications. The site also has information about the Center's Strategic Alliances project, and its Youth Philanthropy and Service program, for which it provides mini-grants.

Milano Nonprofit Management Knowledge Hub (http://www.newschool.edu/milano/hub/)
The Milano Nonprofit Management Knowledge Hub provides a gateway to resources on the Internet for nonprofit managers, leaders, students, researchers, teachers, and interested individuals on leading and managing nonprofit organizations. The Web site is an extensive resource on nonprofit management, with research archives, a Manager's Toolbox containing information on a variety of nonprofit leadership issues, and links to related Web sites.

Museum Marketing Tips (http://www.museummarketingtips.com/)
The Museum Marketing Tips Web site has a collection of tips, tools, and resources to aid in the online marketing and management of museums, historic sites and heritage attractions. The Links Library contains hundreds of annotated links to reports, tutorials, case studies, and other resources. The Articles Index contains original articles on topics ranging from media and community relations to cultural heritage tourism marketing.

My Noodle (http://www.mynoodle.org/)
My Noodle is a clearinghouse of information, news, and resources for the nonprofit community in the United States and abroad. The Web site includes daily news on a variety of subjects of interest to nonprofit organizations; twice-monthly feature articles; an extensive resource directory; listings of events, classes, workshops, and seminars; a searchable job database; and special reports on issues that are important to the nonprofit community. Visitors to the Web site can also sign up for a free e-mail newsletter.

National Teacher Recruitment Clearinghouse (http://www.recruitingteachers.org/)
The National Teacher Recruitment Clearinghouse is a "one-stop shop" for information and resources about teacher recruitment and retention. Developed through a planning grant from the U.S. Department of Education, and hosted by Recruiting New Teachers, the Web site offers practical resources for recruiters, teachers seeking jobs, prospective teachers, and others looking for information about how to become a teacher and how to improve teacher recruitment and retention efforts. In addition to other resources, the clearinghouse has links to and profiles of hundreds of job banks.

Nonprofit Coordinating Committee of New York (http://www.npccny.org/)
The Nonprofit Coordinating Committee of New York (NPCC) is a membership organization dedicated to protecting and helping the nonprofit community of the New York metropolitan area. The committee's Web site provides Peter Swords' "How to Read the IRS Form 990 & Find Out What It Means," an employee benefits survey, and Who Does What?, a searchable database of nonprofits that offer technical assistance to other nonprofits. A listing of government grants; programs; New York *Nonprofits*, an online newsletter; and workshop calendars are available online.

Non-Profit Nuts & Bolts (http://www.nutsbolts.com/)
Non-Profit Nuts & Bolts provides nonprofit professionals with management tips that will help build better organizations. The Web site includes articles, reports, and resources that pertain to nonprofit management.

Nonprofit Resource Center (http://www.not-for-profit.org/)
The Nonprofit Resource Center is designed for managers, board members, and volunteers of nonprofit or tax-exempt organizations. The Web site contains links to resources for nonprofits, listed by category: legal, fundraising, marketing and people management, support organizations, and books for nonprofits.

The Online Nonprofit Information Center (http://www.socialworker.com/nonprofit/nphome.htm)
The Online Nonprofit Information Center provides tools to help nonprofit organizations. The center's Web site provides purchasing information for nonprofit handbooks and guides, along with content summaries. The site also has an annotated nonprofit links page.

Partnership on Nonprofit Ventures (http://ventures.yale.edu/)
The Partnership on Nonprofit Ventures (Yale School of Management—The Goldman Sachs Foundation) provides education and offers business planning assistance, cash awards, and access to the investment community for nonprofits. In May 2002, The partnership launched the National Business Plan Competition for Nonprofit Organizations to assist nonprofit organizations in the development of promising profit-making ventures. The Web site has details of the the national competition (how to enter, the judging process, a calendar of events, rules and policies), conference and class information, an online discussion group, publications, research projects, and links to other organizations.

Strategic Solutions (http://www.lapiana.org/)
Strategic Solutions, a collaborative effort of the David and Lucile Packard Foundation, the James Irvine Foundation, the WIlliam and Flora Hewlett Foundation, and La Piana Associates, is dedicated to educating the nonprofit sector about the potential value of strategic restructuring activities, including mergers, joint ventures, and administrative consolidations. The Web site includes information about the projects three primary activities: research and development, documentation and dissemination, and training and workshops. Visitors to the site can read and download reports on restructuring, access services for consultation and facilitation of partnership negotiations, find local partners, and learn about training and events.

Texas Nonprofit Management Assistance Network (http://www.texasnetwork.org/)
The Texas Nonprofit Management Assistance Network develops and connects centers and organizations that provide information, libraries, workshops, consulting services, and publications to the nonprofit sector. The Web site has membership criteria and benefits information; a list of current members, with links to their Web sites; news and events; and links to Web sites of Texas educational institutions that have programs which include the study of nonprofits or voluntarism.

BOARDS

Board Cafe (http://www.boardcafe.org/)
Board Cafe, published by CompassPoint Nonprofit Services, is a monthly electronic newsletter for members of nonprofit boards. Each issue includes board information, opinions, news, and resources, with a "Main Course" article that can be applied to board work. The Web site also has access to past issues of the newsletter dating back to 2001.

Board Match Plus (http://www.boardmatchplus.org/)
Board Match Plus is a program designed to introduce qualified candidates to nonprofit boards of directors. Visitors to the Web site can join a nonprofit board or get advice on board service. The site also contains a section which allows visitors to browse board openings and submit an application form to boards with openings.

BoardSource (http://www.boardsource.org/)
BoardSource, formerly the National Center for Nonprofit Boards, provides practical information, tools and best practices, training, and leadership development for board members of nonprofit organizations worldwide. BoardSource also publishes material on nonprofit governance, including more than 100 booklets, books, videos, and audiotapes. Visitors to the Web site will find feature articles; information on membership, consulting and training, and board resources; Boardtalk, a listserv for BoardSource members that explores governance issues; and *Board Member Online,* an abridged version of *Board Member,* the members-only periodical of BoardSource.

JOB OPPORTUNITIES

CareerBuilder.com (http://www.nonprofit.careerbuilder.com/)
CareerBuilder.com combines the classified sections of several leading newspapers across the United States. The job listings can be searched by keyword, city, or state.

CharityChannel Career Search Online (http://charitychannel.com/careersearch)
CharityChannel's Career Search Online allows you to search for jobs by location, classification, title, organization, keyword, and just submitted items. You can also search listings of executive recruitment firms.

CharityJobs (http://www.charityjobs.co.uk/)
CharityJobs, part of JobDirectory.co.uk, matches job seekers with employers in the United Kingdom's nonprofit sector. Job seekers can search for vacancies, register their resume, and sign-up to receive job listings by e-mail.

The Chronicle of Higher Education—Career Network (http://chronicle.com/jobs/)
The Chronicle of Higher Education's Career Network is a valuable resource for professionals seeking employment in the field of higher education. The Web site contains job announcements, employer profiles, a forum for discussion, career-related advice, and an option to receive free e-mail notification of new jobs.

The Chronicle of Philanthropy's Philanthropy Careers (http://www.philanthropy.com/jobs/)
The Chronicle of Philanthropy's Philanthropy Careers Web site is full of useful information for job seekers. Visitors to the site can browse job listings, sign-up for e-mail notification of new job listings, view articles about the job market, and get practical advice on seeking work at nonprofit organizations.

Community Career Center (http://www.nonprofitjobs.org/)
The Community Career Center Web site provides a place for employers and prospective employees in the nonprofit sector to find each other. Employers can post jobs, and candidates can submit their credentials and search job listings.

DeepSweep (http://www.deepsweep.com/)
DeepSweep provides a free resume-bank and searchable job postings, with listings from the nonprofit sector. Positions advertised include entry-level vacancies and career opportunities for seasoned, nonprofit staff.

ElfNetwork.com (http://www.elfnetwork.com/)
ElfNetwork.com is a service for job seekers, employers and schools interested or active in nonprofit careers and training. The ElfNetwork Web site provides online recruiting for nonprofit organizations, online job search capabilities, job fair listings, and nonprofit career advocacy.

ExecSearches.com (http://www.execsearches.com/)
ExecSearches.com is a resource for senior-level job seekers in nonprofit and public sector employment in the areas of higher education, the environment, health, advocacy, philanthropy, government, social and human services, and community and economic development. The Web site allows employers to post and edit job notices for a fee, while job seekers can post resumes, search employment notices, and receive weekly job updates free of charge.

The Foundation Center's Job Corner (http://fdncenter.org/pnd/jobs/)
The Foundation Center's Job Corner features some 500 current full-time job openings at U.S. foundations, corporate grantmakers, educational institutions, nonprofit infrastructure organizations, grantmaking public charities, and other nonprofit organizations. Jobs are

searchable by organizational type, job function, state, and keyword. The Job Corner is also available as a free weekly e-mail bulletin.

Idealist—Nonprofit Internships (http://www.idealist.org/ip/internshipSearch?MODULE=INTERNSHIP)
Idealist, a project of Action Without Borders, offers a Nonprofit Internships Web site, which is a one-stop shopping source for internship opportunities around the United States and around the world. Visitors to the Web site can conduct a keyword search of the database and subscribe to an internship mailing list for daily updates on new postings.

Idealist—Nonprofit Jobs (http://www.idealist.org/ip/jobSearch?MODULE=JOB)
Idealist, a project of Action Without Borders, has a Nonprofit Jobs Web site that provides a searchable database of nonprofit jobs around the world. Visitors can search the database by geography, area of focus, or job category, and can subscribe to a free daily, personalized job e-mail list. Nonprofits can register and post job openings at no charge.

Jobs.NET (http://www.jobs.net/)
Jobs.NET is a job-matching Web site where users establish a free job seeking account that allows them to search for national and international positions, create an online resume, match their interests and skills with the needs of potential employers, and browse company profiles. The Jobs.NET Career Center provides a number of online articles on career management, interviews, immigration news, letters, and legal issues.

Nonprofit Career Network (http://www.nonprofitcareer.com/)
Created to fill the needs of the nonprofit sector, the Nonprofit Career Network is a "one-stop resource center" for job seekers looking for employment within a nonprofit organization and for nonprofits seeking qualified candidates. Visitors to the Web site can post jobs or resumes, search national job listings, consult a nonprofit organization directory and corporate profiles, and find out about job fairs, conferences, and workshops going on around the country.

Opportunity NOCs (http://www.opportunitynocs.org/)
At the Opportunity NOCs Web site, job seekers can conduct free searches through a large database of available nonprofit jobs, and nonprofit organizations can post employment opportunities for a fee. The site also has links to Web sites with career development resources.

PNN Online—Career Center (http://pnnonline.org/jobs/)
The online version of the *Philanthropy Journal of North Carolina* is a comprehensive source of nonprofit news and information. Its Nonprofit Jobs area enables prospective employees to search current listings by region or title and to apply for positions with an online form.

Professionals for Nonprofits, Inc. (http://www.nonprofitstaffing.com/)
Professionals for Nonprofits, Inc. is a staffing center for temporary and permanent employment with nonprofit organizations. The Web site provides employment resources for job seekers and nonprofit employers, including job listings, employee profiles, information on temporary and permanent positions, a list of nonprofit organizations served by the company, and a downloadable salary survey.

PROGRAM EVALUATION

American Evaluation Association (http://www.eval.org/)
The American Evaluation Association (AEA) is an international professional association of evaluators who assess the effectiveness of programs, policies, personnel, technology products, and organizations. The AEA Web site has a variety of evaluation-related

resources, including information about the association's annual conference and other related events, topical interest groups, published books and journals, the full text of key documents for evaluators, a list of job postings and training institutions in the field, links to other sites of interest, a listing of ongoing degree programs of relevance to evaluation, and the EVALTALK Listserv, a discussion list devoted to issues in the field of evaluation. The AEA member newsletter, first published in the winter of 2001, is also available on the Web site.

United Way of America's Outcome Measurement Resource Network (http://www.unitedway.org/outcomes/)
The Outcome Measurement Resource Network section of the United Way of America's Web site provides an online resource library that contains the full text of selected papers and newsletter articles, information about current initiatives, survey results, a report on outcome measurement data management systems for agencies, and links to related resources.

VOLUNTARISM

Association for Volunteer Administration (http://www.avaintl.org/)
The Association for Volunteer Administration is an international professional membership association providing networking with colleagues, professional credentialling, opportunities for skills development, and resources to aid organizations in developing the involvement of volunteers. The association's Web site has sample position descriptions, information about specific colleges and universities offering courses in volunteer program management, a job bank, a bibliography of publications and Web sites related to many aspects of managing volunteer resources, and news and events.

Community Resource Connections (http://www.cr-connections.org/)
Community Resource Connections works for volunteers and nonprofits in northern Arizona. The Web site provides links to nonprofit, volunteer, and funding resources. Interested nonprofit groups can post their upcoming events on the organization's online community events calendar.

Corporation for National and Community Service (http://www.cns.gov/about/index.html)
The Corporation for National and Community Service works with governor-appointed state commissions, nonprofits, faith-based groups, schools, and other civic organizations to provide opportunities for Americans of all ages to serve their community and the nation. The Web site has program resources and research information on volunteer opportunities available with AmeriCorps, Senior Corps, and Learn and Serve, including program profiles, news and public service announcements, job announcements, and information on internships and fellowships.

Energize, Inc. (http://www.energizeinc.com/)
Energize, Inc. is an international training, consulting, and publishing firm, specializing in voluntarism "especially for leaders of volunteers." The Energize Web site has Hot Topics, a monthly essay by voluntarism expert Susan J. Ellis; Collective Wisdom, offering success stories and advice; a volunteer management library of articles and books; voluntarism information sources and links, with listings of conferences, classes, resource centers, Web sites, magazines, products, and services; and listings of paid volunteer management jobs, internships, and exchange opportunities.

International Association for Volunteer Effort (http://www.iave.org/)
The International Association for Volunteer Effort was created in 1970 by a small group of women from throughout the world who shared a common vision of how volunteers can contribute to the solution of human and social problems and to the development of bridges of understanding among people of all nations. The association's Web site has news and

events, as well as education, public awareness, youth involvement, and membership services information.

Marin Nexus (http://marinnexus.org/)
Marin Nexus offers a series of workshops and trainings, affinity groups, a resource library, and a referral service for volunteers to the Marin County, California nonprofit and volunteer community. The organization's Web site has searchable databases of volunteer opportunities for individuals, youth, families, and groups; an online form that organizations can use to post a volunteer opportunity; and a monthly newsletter.

NetAid (http://www.netaid.org/)
Through a global network of partners, NetAid connects individual and group volunteer efforts with nonprofit and charitable organizations. The Web site has detailed information about the organization's two flagship programs: NetAid World Schoolhouse and NetAid Online Volunteering. Potential volunteers can search NetAid's database of online volunteering opportunities and apply for an assignment online. The site also includes a newsletter, current international nonprofit news, and additional information on opportunities for volunteers and partners.

New York Cares (http://www.nycares.org/)
New York Cares organizes individuals and groups who wish to volunteer in the New York metropolitan area for a wide range of nonprofit and charitable groups and events. Through the Web site, individuals and groups will find information on seasonal projects, annual service events, and community service opportunities. These flexibly-scheduled, team-based service events, coordinate a wide body of volunteers and skills with organizations in need of volunteer time. Further details, service updates, and upcoming events are all available on the Web site.

Points of Light Foundation (http://www.pointsoflight.org/)
Dedicated to encouraging community service, the Points of Light Foundation provides assistance to businesses that institute employee volunteer programs, youth organizations that promote involvement in the welfare of their community, and nonprofit groups that recruit and coordinate volunteer efforts. The Web site has volunteer information for individuals, families, and organizations, including project ideas, service stories, publications, and additional resources.

SERVEnet (http://www.servenet.org/)
SERVEnet, a program of Youth Service America, was designed to encourage community involvement through volunteering, by providing volunteer-based nonprofit organizations with the best resources available to them in a quick and easy manner and to match the skills, experience, and enthusiasm of dedicated volunteers with nonprofit organizations who need their participation. Visitors to the Web site can post and find volunteer and career opportunities, service news, events, and other resources. Volunteer opportunities are listed by location, and can be searched by entering a zip code.

ServiceLeader.org's Virtual Volunteering (http://www.serviceleader.org/new/virtual/index.php)
ServiceLeader.org's Virtual Volunteering encourages and assists in the development of volunteer activities that can be completed via the Internet. The organization's Web site has a virtual volunteering program guidebook and volunteer manager resources that include an article about implementing a volunteer program, sample online assignments, advice for volunteers, handbooks, papers, and reports.

U.S. Department of Housing and Urban Development's Volunteering (http://www.hud.gov/volunteering/index.cfm)
The U.S. Department of Housing and Urban Development's Volunteering site provides a listing of volunteer opportunities, including federal, national, and local volunteer programs. The Web site also includes links to national volunteer clearinghouses.

VolunteerMatch (http://www.volunteermatch.org/)
VolunteerMatch helps individuals nationwide find on-site volunteer opportunities posted by local nonprofit and public sector organizations. Volunteers can search an online database of thousands of one-time and ongoing opportunities—including walk-a-thons, beach day cleanups, tutoring, home building, and meal deliveries—by zip code, distance, category, and duration, then sign up automatically by e-mail for those that fit their interest and schedule. The Web site also has an online newsletter and a listing of "virtual volunteering" opportunities for individuals, including those with disabilities, who wish to contribute their time via computer. Community service organizations with volunteer opportunities can also post their information with VolunteerMatch.

Volunteers of America (http://www.voa.org/)
Volunteers of America is a national, nonprofit, spiritually-based organization providing local human service programs and the opportunity for individual and community involvement through outreach programs that help youths at risk, frail elderly, abused and neglected children, people with disabilities, and homeless individuals. The Web site has a directory of community-based offices; a newsletter and magazine; advocacy information, including a weekly public policy update; as well as extensive program information.

Washington State University's Volunteer Management Certificate Program (http://vmcp.wsu.edu/)
Washington State University's Volunteer Management Certificate Program is a Web-based learning opportunity encompassing the training, recruiting, management, and recognition of volunteers. Prospective students visiting the Web site will find program and enrollment information, a description of program instructors, and a skills self-assessment test. Registered students have their own point of entry into the site, and have easy access to online help and support as needed.

World Volunteer Web (http://www.worldvolunteerweb.org/)
Building on the success of the United Nations International Year of Volunteers 2001, World Volunteer Web provides a portal for the sharing of information on global volunteer activities and issues. The Web site includes stories and experiences from volunteers worldwide, international development issues, policy and legislation, research publications, news, and events.

NPO MEMBERSHIP ORGANIZATIONS

AssociationCentral.com (http://www.associationcentral.com/)
Serving as a portal site for professional associations, nonprofit networks, and special interest organizations, AssociationCentral.com is structured in a similar fashion to many popular search engines, breaking down its listings according to industry categories and providing advanced search capabilities.

Colorado Association of Nonprofit Organizations (http://www.canpo.org/)
The Colorado Association of Nonprofit Organizations provides leadership and services to strengthen nonprofits' ability to build and sustain healthy communities in Colorado. The organization's Web site contains a directory of members and links to their sites, an online version of the organization's newsletter, information about current legislation, links to helpful resources, and a calendar of local events and forums.

Council of Community Services of New York State (http://www.ccsnys.org/)
The Council of Community Services of New York State is a membership based nonprofit providing nonprofit management, technical assistance and training, public policy, employee benefits, and group purchasing services to its members. The Web site has membership information, annual publications and newsletters, a public policy and advocacy section, technical assistance information, and useful links to nonprofit resources.

INDEPENDENT SECTOR (http://www.independentsector.org/)
The INDEPENDENT SECTOR (IS) is committed to promoting, strengthening, and advancing the nonprofit and philanthropic community to foster private initiative for the public good. The Web site provides an overview of IS programs in the Issues section, including the Three Sector Initiative, Corporate-Nonprofit Partnerships, Emerging Leadership, Giving and Volunteering, Tax Policy, Nonprofit Advocacy and Lobbying, Accountability, Civil Society Education, and Faith-Based Organizations in the Nonprofit Sector. The Research directory includes the Nonprofit Almanac and Desk Reference, which provides facts and figures on the size and scope of the nonprofit sector; Giving and Volunteering in the United States, which covers the giving and volunteering habits of individuals; and the Measures Project which focuses on measuring the impact of the third sector on society. IS's Public Affairs program advocates on behalf of the nonprofit sector in areas such as tax issues, nonprofit advocacy and lobbying, government funding, accountability, and public policy. Click on GiveVoice.org to connect with your legislators and government officials about the issues affecting the nonprofit sector. The NonProfit Pathfinder, designed for scholars, researchers, practitioners, funders, and the media, gathers and organizes online information on philanthropy, the nonprofit sector, and civil society organizations.

Michigan Comnet (http://comnet.org/index.html)
Michigan Comnet, a community of individuals and organizations concerned with increasing communication and information sharing within the state's nonprofit public service sector, offers free Web hosting to nonprofit organizations. The Web site has a searchable directory of key individuals and nonprofit organizations in the state, a list of nonprofit directories, technical training for nonprofits, and a news and announcements forum.

Minnesota Council of Nonprofits (http://www.mncn.org/)
The Minnesota Council of Nonprofits, a statewide membership association of nonprofit organizations, works to provide information and services to Minnesota's nonprofits by sharing information, services, and research in order to educate its members and the community. The Web site has many useful links and resources, including a public policy page that includes legislative updates, a nonprofit job board, and links to a number of searchable databases.

National Council of Nonprofit Organizations (http://www.ncna.org/)
The National Council of Nonprofit Organizations is a network of dozens of state and regional associations ranging from large to small, well-established to just starting up, in all fields, including social service, education, health, and cultural activities. The council's Web site contains information on the various state associations, conferences and meetings, job listings, and projects with which the council is currently involved.

National Voluntary Organizations Active in Disaster (http://www.nvoad.org/)
National Voluntary Organizations Active in Disaster coordinates the planning efforts of many state and national voluntary organizations, and assists these organizations in their efforts to work with government agencies in responding to disaster. The Web site has a list of links to member organizations, planning documents, an annual report, news, and a calendar of events.

Nonprofit Coordinating Committee of New York (http://www.npccny.org/)
The Nonprofit Coordinating Committee of New York (NPCC) is a membership organization dedicated to protecting and helping the nonprofit community of the New York

metropolitan area. The committee's Web site provides Peter Swords' "How to Read the IRS Form 990 & Find Out What It Means," an employee benefits survey, and Who Does What?, a searchable database of nonprofits that offer technical assistance to other nonprofits. A listing of government grants; programs; New York *Nonprofits*, an online newsletter; and workshop calendars are available online.

TechSoup (http://www.techsoup.org/)
TechSoup is a Web-based resource center that offers technology assistance and solutions for small to mid-size nonprofit organizations. The site offers nonprofit technology articles and news, and information on where to find donated or discounted software and equipment through its companion site, DiscounTech. The site also has information on computer training; advice on technology funding; information on technology planning; listings of available volunteers and consultants; and detailed information on recycled hardware, including how to find it. The Web site also has a free, monthly publication, *By the Cup,* with feature articles related to nonprofit technology.

Nonprofit Technology

Alliance for Community Technology (http://www.communitytechnology.org/)
The Alliance for Community Technology (ACT) is dedicated to advancing the use of computing and communication technology internationally, acting as a resource for people through community serving organizations. ACT works to build relationships among community organizations, social investors, and academia through its Web site. To this end, the ACT Web site features a virtual conference center, seminar room, and online discussion board. Visitors will also find links to lists and databases focused on communication technology; a monthly online newsletter with new technologies for online collaboration; community technology initiatives; conferences devoted to various aspects of community technology (e-learning, groupware, digital divide, etc.); and relevant online readings and events.

America Connects Consortium (http://www.americaconnects.net/)
The America Connects Consortium (ACC) is funded by the U.S. Department of Education to provide technical assistance to community technology centers (CTCs) in low-income communities around the country. The ACC Web site provides resources mainly for community technology center staff members on a wide range of topics, including education, program design, disability and inclusion, and workforce development, among other practical guides to starting a technology center. The site also includes current news articles and spotlights on CTCs nationwide.

Benton Foundation (http://www.benton.org/)
The Benton Foundation works to bring together philanthropy, public policy, and community action in the promotion of digital media to bring about social change. The foundation's Web site offers a virtual library with information on a range of issues, such as health, education, and industry, and their roles in the information age. Visitors to the site can sign up for electronic news services, order and view publications, and join online discussion groups, all focusing on a variety of technology and social change-related issues. Links to numerous foundation initiatives, including the Digital Divide Network, Connect for Kids, and OneWorld U.S., are also provided.

Center for Arts Management and Technology at Carnegie Mellon (http://www.artsnet.org/camt/)
The Center for Arts Management and Technology at Carnegie Mellon was established to investigate existing and emerging information and communication technologies and to stimulate thinking about the practical application of such technologies for arts managers. The Web site has information about the center's services, which include eGrant, a custom

tool for funding agencies that wish to offer Web-based grant applications to their constituents; technology needs assessment; and Web site development and hosting.

CEO Forum (http://www.ceoforum.org/)
The CEO Forum issued five annual assessments of the nation's progress toward integrating technology into American classrooms before the forum, a five-year project, closed its doors in December 2001. The forum's Web site continues to offer useful information, including annual assessment reports, as well as an interactive self-assessment tool for colleges of education. Links to forum member organizations are also available.

CharityFocus (http://www.charityfocus.org/)
CharityFocus is a California nonprofit that organizes volunteers to create and market Web sites for nonprofit organizations, free of charge. The Web site also has a list of organizations and resources for nonprofits, as well as a list of resources for volunteers who design Web pages.

Community Technology Centers' Network (http://www.ctcnet.org/)
The Community Technology Centers' Network is a national membership organization that promotes nonprofit and community-based efforts to provide equal access to technology skills and usage to the general public and to disadvantaged populations. The Web site has contact information for community technology centers in the United States, Ireland, Scotland, Spain, and the United Kingdom where access to computers and computer-related technology is available. The site also has relevant news, conference information, publications, and other resources.

CompuMentor (http://www.compumentor.org/)
CompuMentor works to provide technology resources—person-to-person services, low-cost software, and online resources—to nonprofits and schools serving low-income communities. The Web site has a link to DiscounTech, which offers software packages that can be ordered online for a fraction of the retail cost to organizations that qualify; a mentor matching program that matches skilled technical volunteers with community organizations and schools; a consulting program that includes technology planning for small and mid-size nonprofits; and information for nonprofits interested in developing a Community Technology Center to provide access and training to low-income or disadvantaged communities.

The Digital Divide Network (http://www.digitaldividenetwork.org/)
The Digital Divide Network, produced by the Benton Foundation, addresses the gap between those who can effectively use new information and communication tools, such as the Internet, and those who cannot. Visitors to the Web site will find news about efforts going on across the country, research, and funding information.

Dot Org e-newsletter (http://www.dotorgmedia.org/Team/Involved.cfm)
Dot Org e-newsletter is a free bimonthly e-mail newsletter, with selected topics such as application service providers, online advocacy, fundraising, and Internet presence. The newsletter presents case studies, effective practices, techniques, and tools to help nonprofits maximize their Internet presence.

Download.com (http://www.download.com/)
Hosted by CNET, the Download.com Web site serves as a virtual warehouse of software and shareware of all kinds. Application types include business, education, games, home and personal, Internet, multimedia and design, Web developer, utilities and drivers, mobile, and MP3 and audio.

ebase (http://www.ebase.org/)
ebase, part of Groundspring.org, is an integrated database designed to help nonprofits effectively manage interactive communications with their members, donors, citizen

activists, volunteers, and clients. The database is available for downloading free of charge from the Web site.

The Electronic Development and Environment Information System (http://nt1.ids.ac.uk/eldis/eldis.htm)
The Electronic Development and Environment Information System (ELDIS) offers the latest information on development and environmental issues. ELDIS provides descriptions and links to various sources of information, including Web sites, databases, library catalogues, and e-mail discussion lists.

Gifts in Kind International (http://www.giftsinkind.org/)
Gifts In Kind International links corporations (including 40 percent of Fortune 500 companies) and their product donations and services—including software and computer training—with a network of more than 50,000 nonprofit organizations. Nonprofit organizations with 501(c)(3) status (or an international equivalent), tax-exempt educational organizations, and U.S. Indian reservations are eligible to register with Gifts in Kind for donated products and discounted services. A Special Needs section is also available for individuals with disabilities. Gifts In Time, a free global online system, matches company volunteers with nonprofits needing assistance in areas such as community rebuilding, mentoring, coaching, technology planning, and other critically needed support.

Global Technology Corps (http://www.globaltechcorps.org/)
Global Technology Corps (GTC), in partnership with the U.S. State Department, seeks to bridge the global digital divide by recruiting high tech volunteers for international short-term public diplomacy projects. The Web site provides information on GTC private and public partnerships, details on current international projects open to private-sector partners, news items, and links to related organizations.

iComm (http://www.icomm.ca/)
iComm is a nonprofit Internet service provider that donates its services to other nonprofits, community organizations, and charities all over the world. The Web site lists the groups currently receiving assistance.

The IT Resource Guide for UK Charities (http://www.itforcharities.co.uk/)
The IT Resource Guide for UK Charities provides information on software products, hardware, and technological services of interest to charities and nonprofit organizations located and operating in the United Kingdom. The Web site contains a series of technology reports and news, along with access to a free e-mail newsletter for interested UK organizations.

Making the Net Work (http://www.makingthenetwork.org/)
Making The Net Work, a UK-U.S. initiative led by David Wilcox, Drew Mackie, and Terry Grunwald, aims to help those planning to get their organization or neighborhood online or to create local technology centers. The Web site offers the MTNW Toolbox, which provides information for communities and organizations seeking an online presence.

Morino Institute (http://www.morino.org/)
The Morino Institute is a nonprofit organization that explores the opportunities and risks of the Internet and the "new economy" to advance social change by stimulating entrepreneurship, advancing a more effective philanthropy, closing social divides, and understanding the relationship and impact of the Internet on our society. The Web site has speeches and publications, information on the institute's programs and venture philanthropy partners, plus additional resources.

National Cristina Foundation (http://www.cristina.org/)
The National Cristina Foundation provides computer technology and solutions to give people with disabilities, students at risk, and economically disadvantaged persons the opportunity, through training, to lead more independent and productive lives. The foundation

works to recycle computer technology resources, giving them a second life as tools for developing human potential. The Web site provides information on how to donate computer equipment, specifications, and an online form to initiate a donation.

NetDayCompass (http://www.netdaycompass.org/)
NetDay is a nonprofit organization dedicated to helping educators meet educational goals through the effective use of technology, thus enhancing children's learning. NetDayCompass, the organization's Web site, is a resource for education technology geared toward technology decisionmakers working in K-12 schools. The Web site features a variety of links to resources in the areas of planning, infrastructure, grants and funding, classroom support, and best practices, as well as an interactive research desk for further inquiries.

Nonprofit Tech (http://www.nonprofit-tech.org/)
Nonprofit Tech works to provide expertise in technology, nonprofit management, human-computer interactions, and the psychology of service-driven industries to the nonprofit community. The Web site features details on the organization's programs and services in eight main areas: education and policy; technology transfer and research; client and member services; community services and special programs; communications, networking and collaboration; publications, media and marketing; professional development; and administration and management.

NPower (http://www.npower.org/)
NPower, which started in Seattle, Washington, but now has expanded to more than 60 communities nationwide, helps other nonprofits use technology to better serve their communities. NPower offers a variety of technology-related services to area nonprofits, including technology assessments and planning, hands-on help with network implementation, database management, technology training classes, print and electronic technology resource libraries, and short-term technology project assistance. NPower's Tech Surveyor enables an organization to assess hardware, software, and staff technology skills. TechAtlas is a step-by-step Web-based planning tool that nonprofits can use to assess their current technology use and to receive recommendations on how to better implement technology to achieve their mission.

Npsoft.org (http://www.npsoft.org/)
Catering to nonprofit organizations and academic organizations, Npsoft.org offers discounted software for nonprofits and schools. Software programs range in scope from technical assistance, to educational, business, and communication tools. The Npsoft Web site includes a newsletter and FAQs from schools and nonprofits with practical information about the software.

Open Studio: The Arts Online (http://www.benton.org/openstudio)
From 1996-2000, Open Studio: The Arts Online, a national initiative of the Benton Foundation and National Endowment for the Arts, provided Internet access and training to artists and nonprofit arts organizations to ensure that the communications environment of the 21st century would thrive as a source of creative excellence and diversity. The project is no longer active, but the site is archived by the Benton Foundation as a resource to the nonprofit community.

Pew Internet & American Life Project (http://www.pewinternet.org/)
A project of the Pew Research Center for People and the Press, the Tides Center, and the Pew Charitable Trusts, the Pew Internet & American Life Project explores the growth of the Internet and its societal effects on families, communities, and work environments. The Web site provides research reports; a useful listing of links containing information, discussion, and/or data on the Internet and society; and information about new research by the Pew Internet & American Life Project or other organizations.

SeniorNet (http://www.seniornet.org/)
SeniorNet provides training for and access to computer technology for adults age 50 and older. The Web site offers online courses on a variety of technology-related topics, virtual discussion groups, discounts on technology products, digital galleries, a robust enrichment center, and information about local learning centers.

Strategic Technology Program (http://www.strategictechnology.net/)
The Strategic Technology Program works to help nonprofit organizations take advantage of technology through a series of courses. The Web site has course materials, including numerous lesson plans; a toolkit of program resources; partner information; and links to technology planning and management assistance related Web sites.

TechRocks (http://www.techrocks.org/)
TechRocks encourages and enables foundations, advocacy groups, and activists to use technology to achieve their goals. Visitors to the TechRocks Web site will find ebase, a free downloadable software program that enables nonprofit organizations to manage their relationships with their members, donors, activists, and volunteers, and TechAtlas which provides context specific technology recommendations and step-by-step guides to assist organizations with their individual technology issues. Various case studies and TechBits, two- to three-page primers on topics about which organizations consistently have questions, are also available.

TechSoup (http://www.techsoup.org/)
TechSoup is a Web-based resource center that offers technology assistance and solutions for small to mid-size nonprofit organizations. The site offers nonprofit technology articles and news, and information on where to find donated or discounted software and equipment through its companion site, DiscounTech. The site also has information on computer training; advice on technology funding; information on technology planning; listings of available volunteers and consultants; and detailed information on recycled hardware, including how to find it. The Web site also has a free, monthly publication, *By the Cup,* with feature articles related to nonprofit technology.

TechSoup: Recycled Hardware (http://www.techsoup.org/recycle/index.cfm)
TechSoup's Recycled Hardware page is a great place to go if you are looking for usable recycled computers for your nonprofit organization or if you are looking for a place to donate your old computer. There is a list of recycling/refurbishing organizations, tips on donating a computer, featured articles and resources, and a message board.

Technology Grant News (http://www.technologygrantnews.com/)
Technology Grant News, published four times a year, covers upcoming grant announcements by the government, technology funders, trade associations, and private foundations. Among the technology funding opportunities covered are creating an Internet presence for educational purposes, electronic publishing, and global nonprofits and emerging technology outreach. The Web site has a sample issue with links to featured grant sites and a Grants Index sampling. A discounted subscription is offered to nonprofits.

Technology Tip Sheets for Nonprofits (http://www.coyotecom.com/tips.html)
Technology Tip Sheets for Nonprofits was created by Jayne Cravens, of Coyote Communications, to help nonprofit and public sector organizations reap money-saving, program-enhancing benefits from technology. Most of the material is geared to community-serving organizations, but some materials are for a broader audience. The Web site includes a What's New section for frequent visitors.

University of Michigan School of Information's Community Connector (http://databases.si.umich.edu/cfdocs/community/index.cfm)
The University of Michigan School of Information's Community Connector works to support community-serving organizations, funders, academics, and students who are using

technology to enhance geographic communities. The Web site provides specific resources for each type of organization or individual. A variety of publications, technology tutorials, discussion forums, funding examples and guides, and links to further technology resources are available at the site.

The Web Developer's Toolkit (http://www.fund-online.com/alabook/links/resource.htm)
The Web Developer's Toolkit has links to authoring, design, graphics, and other resources for developing a Web site, from *Fundraising and Friend-Raising on the Web: A Handbook for Libraries and Other Nonprofit Organizations.*

Web Page Design for Designers (http://www.wpdfd.com/wpdres.htm)
The Web Page Design for Designers Web site serves as a portal to a vast array of free Web design-related resources on the Internet. The information on the Web site is searchable, and the links are broken down by subject area. Each link is annotated with a brief description.

World Wide Web Consortium (http://www.w3.org/)
Under the direction of Tim Berners-Lee, the World Wide Web Consortium (W3C) has played a leading role since 1994 in developing and articulating the specifications and protocols at the heart of the Web. The W3C develops interoperable technologies (specifications, guidelines, software, and tools) to lead the Web to its full potential as a forum for information, commerce, communication, and collective understanding. The Web site has W3C news and activities, links to information about W3C technologies, as well as information about "getting involved" in W3C activties.

Public Interest and Policy

The Brookings Institution (http://www.brook.edu/)
The Brookings Institution holds conferences and conducts and publishes independent research, analysis, and criticism related to public policy issues in the areas of economics, foreign policy, and governance, bringing new knowledge to the attention of decision makers and enhancing scholarly insight into public policy issues. Its economic studies, foreign policy studies, and governmental studies departments form the core of its program. The Web site includes a list of current scholars, publications, research projects, news, and events.

The Carter Center (http://www.cartercenter.org/)
Founded in 1982 by former President Jimmy Carter in partnership with Emory University, the Carter Center is committed to enhancing freedom, democracy, and human rights and to the alleviation of human suffering that results from war, disease, famine, and poverty by advancing peace and health in neighborhoods and nations worldwide. Towards this end, the center works to prevent and resolve armed and political conflicts, monitors elections, safeguards human rights, fights disease, increases food production, promotes preventive healthcare, and builds strong democracies through economic development around the globe. The Web site has detailed information about the center's many programs, initiatives, and activities.

Center for Responsive Politics (http://www.opensecrets.org/home/index.asp)
The Center for Responsive Politics is a nonpartisan Washington, D.C.-based research group that tracks money in politics, and its effect on elections and public policy. The Web site offers a searchable database of political donors, campaign contributions and donations to PACs, a lobbyists database, and "soft money" donations.

HandsNet (http://www.handsnet.org/)
HandsNet is a membership organization of more than 5,000 public interest and human services organizations. The Web site features articles and alerts, which provide daily news

updates on human services issues and legislation; the WebClipper news and delivery service, with human services headlines from hundreds of Web sites that can be tailored to your interests; and information on training and capacity building programs, including a Mobile Technology Classroom and information consulting and knowledge-management services.

Hoover Institution (http://www-hoover.stanford.edu/)
Before he became 31st President of the United States, Herbert Hoover founded the Hoover Institution, a public policy research center at Stanford University devoted to the advanced study of domestic and international affairs. Recognized as one of the first "think tanks" in the United States, the institution boasts one of the world's most complete libraries on political, economic, and social change in the 20th century. The institution's Web site offers information on the organization's research program, publications, and library collections.

Hudson Institute (http://www.hudson.org/)
The Hudson Institute provides a major forum for leading policymakers and others of national and international acclaim to discuss important issues. The Web site includes a comprehensive listing of more than 800 articles, op-eds, and book reviews; a complete list of the institute's scholars and their areas of expertise; a standalone Web site for all 10 policy centers, including subjects such as welfare, middle East, national security, European and Eurasian studies, global food issues, crime policy, and much more.

National Center for Youth Law (http://www.youthlaw.org/)
The National Center for Youth Law (NCYL) is a California-based private, nonprofit law office serving the legal needs of children and their families. The organization focuses particularly on children living in poverty, advocating for their protection from abuse, for their access to housing, healthcare, public benefits, and for improved methods of collecting child support. It also seeks to address the tendency to deal with youth behavior punitively. NCYL works towards these goals by publishing articles, manuals, books, and its bimonthly journal, *Youth Law News;* providing technical assistance and training; assisting legal advocates who represent poor children; and conducting administrative and legislative advocacy. The Web site includes pertinent news, an overview of the organization, online articles, analyses, publications, and links to related resources.

National Center on Poverty Law (http://www.povertylaw.org/)
The National Center on Poverty Law develops its advocacy agenda in accordance with the needs of the low-income communities that it serves. Through policy, advocacy, and legal resources, the organization "identifies, develops, and supports creative and collaborative approaches to help achieve social and economic justice." The major clearinghouse on poverty law, the center's Web site provides access to an enormous collection of publications and case studies. The site also has information about advocacy, news, and an advanced search function.

National Issues Forums (http://www.nifi.org/)
The National Issues Forums, a voluntary, nonpartisan, nationwide network of forums and study circles, is rooted in the notion that citizens need to come together to deliberate about common problems in order to act on them. The Web site has NIF Reports, discussion guides on such topics as "News Media and Society: How to Restore the Public Trust?," a schedule of workshops where citizens come together to learn more about convening and moderating forums, and a message board.

NetAction (http://www.netaction.org/)
NetAction is dedicated to promoting the use of the Internet for effective grassroots citizen action campaigns and to educating the public, policymakers, and the media about technology policy issues. The Web site provides the Virtual Activist, an online training program for Internet outreach and advocacy; Netaction's Online Buyer's Guide; additional reports focusing on cyber action issues; and the report "Our Stake in Cyberspace: The Future of the Internet and Communications As We Know It."

The New York Public Interest Research Group (http://www.nypirg.org/)
The New York Public Interest Research Group is a research and advocacy organization primarily focused on environmental preservation, consumer protection, government reform, and public health issues. The Web site has details of the programs and campaigns which the group is currently working on in New York State, news updates on issues of interest to the organization, and information about contacting New York State government officials.

NIRA's World Directory of Think Tanks (http://www.nira.go.jp/ice/nwdtt/index.html#1)
The Japan-based National Institute for Research Advancement provides a no-frills Web site with basic information on specially-selected think tanks from dozens of countries and regions. It also provides an index of institutes by English name and by country. Information available for each organization can include executive personnel, organizational history, areas of research, geographic focus, availability of research findings, and funding sources. Contact information is also available, as are individual Web site links.

Nonprofit Sector Research Fund (http://www.nonprofitresearch.org/)
A program of the Aspen Institute in Washington, D.C., the Nonprofit Sector Research Fund makes grants for researching and disseminating information about nonprofit activities, impacts, and values and promotes the use of that information to enhance nonprofit practices and inform public policy. The Web site includes application guidelines, findings from research studies carried out by fund grantees, publication content and summaries, research abstracts, and links to nonprofit resources.

ProgressivePubs.com (http://www.progressivepubs.com/)
ProgressivePubs.com was created in 1997 to supply activists, policymakers, and other interested parties with print and electronic resources that can assist in enacting progressive change. The Web site offers access to a database of hundreds of foundations that support progressive efforts. There is also an online bookstore that sells hard-to-find works of progressive thinkers and organizations.

Project to Strengthen Nonprofit-Government Relationships (http://www.nonprofit-gov.unc.edu/)
The Project to Strengthen Nonprofit-Government Relationships is geared toward staff members, volunteers, or elected officials of nonprofit organizations or local governments. Working with practitioners and academics, the project helps nonprofit and government agencies collaborate to serve the public more effectively. The project's Web site provides information about its activities, training exercises, publications, and access to a listserv facilitating communication among professionals in similar fields.

Project Vote Smart (http://www.vote-smart.org/)
Inaugurated in 1992, Project Vote Smart is a nonpartisan citizen's organization that researches, tracks, and provides information on candidates and elected officials. The Web site offers a searchable database of voting records, campaign issue positions, polling place and absentee ballot information, ballot measure descriptions, voter registration forms for each state, information about the project's outreach programs, and contact information for state and county election offices.

Public Agenda Online (http://www.publicagenda.org/)
Public Agenda Online is a nonpartisan resource for journalists and researchers interested in public opinion and public policy. The Web site features a collection of public opinion data on important issues facing the country, including abortion, campaign finance, healthcare, higher education, the economy, medical research, race, immigration, gay rights, the environment, social security, and the federal budget.

RAND (http://www.rand.org/)
RAND (an acronym for Research and Development) researchers assist public policymakers at all levels, private sector leaders in many industries, and the public at large

in efforts to strengthen the nation's economy, maintain its security, and improve its quality of life. The Web site offers information about the organization's research activities, areas of expertise, publications, educational opportunities, and board of trustees.

State Public Interest Research Groups (http://www.pirg.org/)
Composed of state-based, citizen-funded organizations that advocate for the public interest, the nonpartisan state Public Interest Research Groups (PIRGs) aim to protect consumers, preserve the environment, and encourage citizen participation in the democratic process. In addition to information about state PIRGs campaigns, the Web site has complete voting records for the delegates of each state.

UCLA Center for Civil Society (http://www.sppsr.ucla.edu/ccs/)
The Center for Civil Society was established by the UCLA School of Public Policy and Social Research, as the focal point for the school's programs and activities in nonprofit leadership and management, community organizations and advocacy, international nongovernmental organizations, and philanthropy. The Web site includes nonprofit sector publications; links to research reports; course offerings on public policy, social welfare, and urban planning; fellowships, internships, and faculty grants information; a listing of events; and a set of links to relevant Web sites.

USC Center on Philanthropy and Public Policy (http://www.usc.edu/schools/sppd/philanthropy/)
The USC Center on Philanthropy and Public Policy works to promote effective philanthropy and strengthen the nonprofit sector through research that informs philanthropic decision making and public policy; and brings together philanthropic, nonprofit, policy, business and community leaders through a variety of activities, including a Distinguished Lecture Series, roundtable discussions, and periodic research seminars. In addition to reports and research papers, the Web site has links to academic research centers that focus on nonprofits, public policy, or the study of philanthropy.

WebActive (http://www.webactive.com/)
WebActive offers progressive activists an up-to-date resource by providing streaming audio radio programs. The Web site features *RadioNation,* the weekly broadcast edition of *The Nation* magazine; *Pacifica Network News,* available every day; *Democracy NOW!,* available every week day; *Hightower Radio,* with Jim Hightower's daily two-minute commentaries on politics and progressive issues; *CounterSpin,* a weekly one-half hour program produced by Fairness and Accuracy in Reporting; and *Soapbox,* an op-ed program of WebActive. The Web site also has an annotated, searchable directory of 1,250 progressive organizations.

Government

GENERAL

Catalog of Federal Domestic Assistance (http://www.cfda.gov/)
The Catalog of Federal Domestic Assistance has information on a wide variety of financial and non-financial assistance programs, projects, services, and activities. The Web site provides access to a searchable database of all federal programs available to state and local governments (including the District of Columbia), federally-recognized Indian tribal governments, and Territories and possessions of the United States; domestic public, quasi-public, and private profit and nonprofit organizations and institutions; specialized groups; and individuals.

Federal Register (http://www.gpoaccess.gov/fr/index.html)
The *Federal Register* Web site, updated daily, provides access to presidential documents, executive orders, rules, and proposed rules from federal agencies and organizations, and information regarding government-funded projects and funding availability. Visitors to the Web site can search the database in a variety of ways, including using the "browse feature," and detailed instructions and sample searches are provided to facilitate the process.

FirstGov (http://www.firstgov.gov)
FirstGov is an initiative administered by the U.S. General Services Administration. It bills itself as "the official U.S. gateway to all government information," and has a powerful search engine that can search 51 million pages of government information. To search for information on funding for the arts, for example, simply enter "art grants" in the search field. Your search will return more than 1,000 relevant results. You can target your searches to federal or state resources, or search them both. You can also browse government information on FirstGov by topic, such as Federal Benefits and Grants.

Grants.gov (http://www.grants.gov)
Grants.gov is a new comprehensive site that calls itself "the electronic storefront for Federal grants." Managed by the U.S. Department of Health and Human Services, it brings together eleven departments and agencies "for the development of a one-stop electronic grant portal where potential grant recipients will receive full service electronic grant administration." Grant topics are divided into categories such as Agriculture, Education, and Housing. A click on Arts, for example, will lead you to the funding information pages of the National Endowment for the Arts, Institute of Museum and Library Services, and others, where you can find guidelines and grant applications online. There are also links to the Catalog of Federal Domestic Assistance and other key government funding sites available.

LSU Libraries Federal Agencies Directory (http://www.lib.lsu.edu/gov/fedgov.html)
A partnership of Louisiana State University and the Federal Depository Library Program, the LSU Libraries Federal Agencies Directory is a meta-index of U.S. federal government agencies on the Internet.

National Charter School Clearinghouse (http://www.ncsc.info/)
The National Charter School Clearinghouse provides funding and research information on critical issues facing the establishment and operation of charter schools. Funded by the U.S. Department of Education, the clearinghouse posts articles on a variety of topics, including charter school funding, educational technology, "how-to" resources, and school accountability, along with links to the original sources of these articles. Additionally, a newsletter, updates from the Department of Education, an events calendar, and links to further resources can be found online.

OMB Watch's Nonprofits' Policy and Technology (http://www.ombwatch.org/npt)
The goal of OMB (Office of Managemnet and Budget) Watch's Nonprofits' Policy and Technology is to improve communication within the nonprofit sector in order to strengthen public policy participation. The Web site provides information about the federal budget, regulatory matters, a data quality resource page, extensive links to related Web sites, reports, and other publications.

Smithsonian Institution (http://www.si.edu/)
Established in 1846, the Smithsonian Institution is an independent trust of the United States holding more than 142 million artifacts and specimens in trust for "the increase and diffusion of knowledge." The institution is also a center for research dedicated to public education, national service, and scholarship in the arts, sciences, and history. The Web site has a wide range of information on the institution's museums, exhibitions, research, and education and outreach programs, including fellowships and internships.

THOMAS: Legislative Information on the Internet (http://thomas.loc.gov/)
THOMAS: Legislative Information on the Internet is offered by the Library of Congress, providing up-to-date information on the legislative activities of both the House and Senate and searchable databases of current and historical legislative documents from the U.S. Congress. The Web site databases include Bill Text, Public Laws, Bill Summary and Status, the *Congressional Record Index,* and Committee Reports, along with historical Congressional documents.

United States Small Business Administration (http://www.sbaonline.sba.gov/)
As an independent agency of the U.S. government, the United States Small Business Administration assists small businesses in order to encourage free enterprise and improve the nation's overall economy. Visitors to the Web site can retrieve exhaustive information about a variety of financial assistance programs, including application and instruction forms, some of which can be filled out online.

United States House of Representatives (http://www.house.gov/)
The United States House of Representatives' Web site provides House schedules, a directory of members, links to House committee and representative Web sites, a searchable database of U.S. Code, the House Internet Law Library, and links to information related to the legislative process.

United States Senate (http://www.senate.gov/)
The United States Senate's Web site provides information about Senate activities and committees, a complete directory of members, the ability to view and track recent floor activity by date, and a legislative events calendar.

FEDERAL AGENCIES

Administration for Children and Families (http://www.acf.dhhs.gov/)
The Administration for Children and Families' Web site has information on the vast array of programs and services offered by this division of the Department of Health and Human Services, dedicated to promoting the economic and social well-being of families, children, individuals, and communities.

Administration on Aging (http://www.aoa.dhhs.gov/)
The Administration on Aging is an exhaustive online clearinghouse for senior citizens. The Web site provides a resource directory, statistics on aging, an Eldercare Locator, breaking news, and links to related sites.

Agency for Healthcare Research and Quality (http://www.ahcpr.gov/)
The Agency for Healthcare Research and Quality (AHRQ) provides evidence-based information on healthcare outcomes; quality; and cost, use, and access. The Web site contains information on consumer health, research findings, data and surveys, and quality assessments. The Funding Opportunities section of the Web site includes an overview of AHRQ's research agenda, grant announcements, policy notices, grant award resources, contract solicitations, and research training information.

Centers for Disease Control and Prevention (http://www.cdc.gov/)
The Centers for Disease Control and Prevention (CDC) serves as the national focus for developing and applying disease prevention and control, environmental health, and health promotion and education activities designed to improve the health of the people of the United States. The Web site includes comprehensive program and application information for the CDC's many health-related funding opportunities.

Department of Health and Human Services (http://www.os.dhhs.gov/)
The Department of Health and Human Services' Web site provides consumer and policy information, grants and funding information, employment opportunities, and links to related government agencies.

Department of Housing and Urban Development (HUD) (http://www.hud.gov/)
Among many other resources, the Web site of the Department of Housing and Urban Development (HUD) has information about various types of grants, including community development, affordable housing, and research.

Environmental Protection Agency (http://www.epa.gov/)
The Environmental Protection Agency's Web site includes material on virtually every aspect of U.S. environmental policy and protection, including funding information.

Health Resources and Services Administration (http://www.hrsa.gov/)
The Health Resources and Services Administration (HRSA) works to assure the availability of quality healthcare to low-income, uninsured, isolated, vulnerable, and special needs populations. HRSA's Web site provides detailed information about its programs, services, and grant opportunities.

Indian Health Service (http://www.ihs.gov/)
Dedicated to raising the health status of American Indians and Alaska Natives, the Indian Health Service Web site provides information on the agency's activities, including the Tribal Management Grant Program, and serves as an online resource for Native American communities.

Internal Revenue Service (http://www.irs.gov/)
The highly regarded Internal Revenue Service Web site provides comprehensive tax information, including information for charities and nonprofits, and has a site-wide search engine.

National Endowment for the Arts (http://arts.endow.gov/)
The National Endowment for the Arts' (NEA) Web site serves as a comprehensive resource for the arts community and its supporters. The Web site includes information, guidelines, and applications for grants and funding; NEA news and legislative updates; and arts-related features and interviews. In addition, NEA publications—many of which are free—can be ordered or downloaded through the site.

National Endowment for the Humanities (http://www.neh.fed.us/)
The National Endowment for the Humanities (NEH) supports learning in history, literature, philosophy, and other areas of the humanities through its support of research, education, documentaries, exhibits, and other programs that preserve and provide access to cultural resources. The information-packed NEH Web site is a good place to find out about funding opportunities, cultural events, publications, and exhibits.

National Institute on Alcohol Abuse and Alcoholism (http://www.niaaa.nih.gov/)
The National Institute on Alcohol Abuse and Alcoholism's Web site provides grants information, news releases, upcoming meetings and events, and links to related publications and databases.

National Institutes of Health (http://www.nih.gov/)
The National Institutes of Health (NIH) is the federal government's principle medical and behavioral research agency. The NIH Web site has information about clinical trials, health hotlines, and drugs; grants and funding opportunities; news and events; scientific resources; and NIH centers, institutes, and offices.

National Science Foundation (http://www.nsf.gov/)
The National Science Foundation's Web site is comprehensive and well-organized, with program information and funding opportunities in biology, computer and information sciences, education, engineering, geosciences, math and physical sciences, polar research, and social, behavioral, economic, and environmental sciences.

National Telecommunications and Information Administration (http://www.ntia.doc.gov/)
The National Telecommunications and Information Administration Web site includes application guidelines and a listing of recent grants awarded through the Technology Opportunities Program, and the Public Telecommunications Facilities Program.

National Women's Health Information Center (http://www.4woman.gov/)
Sponsored by the U.S. Department of Health and Human Services' Office on Women's Health, the National Women's Health Information Center provides access to information on all areas of women's health. The information on the Web site is obtained from a variety of federal and private sector resources and can be searched by health topic or by keyword. The site includes press releases, a good set of links to online medical dictionaries and journals, a directory of residency and fellowship programs, and a Hot Topics in Congress section which details women's health-related legislation in the U.S. Congress.

Oak Ridge Institute for Science and Education (http://www.orau.gov/orise.htm)
The Oak Ridge Institute for Science and Education supports national and international programs in education, training, health, and the environment. The Web site has program and research information, training opportunities, news, and publications.

Office of Disability Employment Policy (http://www.dol.gov/odep/welcome.html)
The Office of Disability Employment Policy, an office of the Department of Labor, provides national leadership to increase employment opportunities for adults and youth with disabilities while striving to eliminate barriers to employment. The Web site provides information about the office's programs and initiatives, including grant opportunities; services information; technical assistance materials; publications; and an extensive list of for-profit companies interested in employing people with disabilities.

Office of Minority Health (http://www.omhrc.gov/)
The Office of Minority Health's (OMH) Web site provides information on its programs and initiatives and a Resource Center that offers a large amount of easily navigable material, including OMH funding announcements; a searchable funding database; news releases; online publications; requests for proposals; requests for applications; internship, fellowship, and scholarship announcements; additional funding resources; and OMH's newsletter, *Closing the Gap.*

Substance Abuse and Mental Health Services Administration (http://www.samhsa.gov/)
The Substance Abuse and Mental Health Services Administration (SAMHSA) was established to strengthen the nation's healthcare capacity to provide prevention, diagnosis, and treatment services for substance abuse and mental illnesses and serves as the umbrella under which substance abuse and mental health service centers are housed. The Web site has information about SAMHSA's programs, grant funding opportunities, grant planning tools, legislative and policy information, a quarterly newsletter, and employment opportunities.

U.S. Census Bureau (http://www.census.gov/)
The U.S. Census Bureau's sprawling Web site is *the* source of social, demographic, and economic information about the United States on the Web. Offerings include Census Bureau publications, listed by subject; statistical profiles for states, congressional districts, and counties; current economic indicators; custom state and county maps; and much more.

STATE AGENCIES

Nebraska Arts Council (http://www.nebraskaartscouncil.org/)
The Nebraska Arts Council promotes the arts, cultivates resources, and supports excellence in artistic endeavors for all Nebraskans. The Web site provides general information about the council's grant programs and application requirements, an artists directory, artists' opportunities, advocacy information, contacts, and links to other art councils, state organizations, and art museums on the Web.

North Carolina Arts Council (http://www.ncarts.org/)
The mission of the North Carolina Arts Council is to enrich North Carolina's cultural life by supporting the arts. The council is a catalyst for the development of arts organizations and gives grants, organizational assistance, and guidance to groups and individuals statewide. The council's Web site provides, among other items, program and grant information, news, and a searchable database of artists, arts organizations, and arts events.

North Dakota Council on the Arts (http://www.state.nd.us/arts/)
Established in 1967 by the state legislature, the North Dakota Council on the Arts is responsible for the support and development of the arts and artists in North Dakota. In addition to making grants based on recommendations from artists, arts administrators, and board members, the council administers the Cultural Endowment Fund, through which it secures private and public funds to enhance existing programs. The council's Web site provides program information, application instructions, grantwriting tips, arts opportunities, related arts resource links, news, and events.

Ohio Arts Council (http://www.oac.state.oh.us/home.html)
Established in 1965 to "foster and encourage the development of the arts and assist the preservation of Ohio's cultural heritage," the Ohio Arts Council (OAC) funds programs to make arts activities available to the public and also supports Ohio artists through 25 different grant programs. The coucil's Web site provides information about all OAC programs, complete grant guidelines, a search engine, and links to both state and national arts resources.

South Dakota Arts Council (http://www.state.sd.us/deca/SDArts/)
The South Dakota Arts Council encourages and supports artists, strengthens arts organizations and arts education programs, and increases South Dakotans' awareness of the arts. As a state agency of the Department of Education and Cultural Affairs, the council makes grants to schools, individuals, and arts organizations. The council's Web site includes detailed grant application guidelines, a directory of arts festivals, and other resources.

International Philanthropy

GENERAL

American Councils (http://www.americancouncils.org/)
American Councils is a nonprofit organization that specializes in education, training, and consulting, with a focus on the United States, Russia, Eastern Europe, and Eurasia. The organization's programs include academic exchange, professional training, institution building, research, materials development, and technical assistance. The Web site includes information about grant and fellowship opportunities.

Ashoka (http://www.ashoka.org/)
Arlington, Virginia-based Ashoka searches the world for the best new ideas, championed by the most capable, innovative social entrepreneurs and invests in them financially and professionally by selecting them to be Ashoka Fellows. The organization currently has

fellows in Africa, Asia, Central Europe, Latin America, the United States, and Canada working in a range of fields, including learning/education, the environment, health, human rights, economic development, and civic participation. The Web site offers information on selection procedures, job and volunteer opportunities, and an online donation form.

Association for Volunteer Administration (http://www.avaintl.org/)
The Association for Volunteer Administration is an international professional membership association providing networking with colleagues, professional credentialling, opportunities for skills development, and resources to aid organizations in developing the involvement of volunteers. The association's Web site has sample position descriptions, information about specific colleges and universities offering courses in volunteer program management, a job bank, a bibliography of publications and Web sites related to many aspects of managing volunteer resources, and news and events.

Charities Aid Foundation (http://www.cafonline.org/)
Charities Aid Foundation (CAF), an international nonprofit based in the United Kingdom, encourages more efficient giving to charity. The Web site includes contact information for thousands of charities, serves as a technical assistance provider to both funders and nonprofits, and offers links to several charity-related specialty sites.

Civicus (http://www.civicus.org/)
Civicus is an international alliance dedicated to strengthening citizen action and the capacity of civil society throughout the world, especially in areas where participatory democracy, freedom of association of citizens, and funds for public benefit are threatened. The Web site has links to current civil society news, awards and scholarship information, descriptions of specific programming areas, and country reports from Belarus, Canada, Croatia, Estonia, Mexico, New Zealand, Pakistan, Romania, South Africa, Ukraine, Uruguay, and Wales.

CRInfo (http://www.crinfo.org/)
A free service regarding conflict resolution and peacemaking funded by the William and Flora Hewlett Foundation. CRInfo offers a clearinghouse of information, links, and educational materials on the topic. The site allows visitors to search or browse more than 20,000 links to Web, print, and organizational resources in the conflict resolution field with tools designed for adversaries, intermediaries, students, educators, practitioners, and researchers. Additionally, CRInfo maintains a number of special projects and partnerships with other nonprofit organizations, delivers current news on conflict resolution, and offers networking resources.

Cross-Cultural Solutions (http://www.crossculturalsolutions.org/)
Cross-cultural Solutions sends volunteers to provide humanitarian assistance in Brazil, China, Costa Rica, Ghana, India, Peru, Russia, Tanzania, and Thailand. The organization's programs, in which volunteers work side-by-side with local people, are intended to empower local communities, foster cultural sensitivity and understanding, and contribute grassroots solutions in providing healthcare, education, and social development. The Web site has descriptions of the various volunteer programs, including the Insight Cuba program, which offers trips to Cuba; information on how to get involved in global issues on a local level; and comments from the press.

Disaster Relief (http://www.disasterrelief.org/)
The Disaster Relief Web site provides an easy-to-navigate clearinghouse of worldwide news and information for the disaster relief community and others providing disaster aid.

Grantmakers Without Borders (http://www.internationaldonors.org/)
Grantmakers Without Borders, a collaborative project of the Tides Center and the International Working Group of the National Network of Grantmakers, works to expand and enrich progressive international philanthropy and to support international projects by

providing free advice, alternative sources of information, and increased opportunities for communication among donors. The Web site has an annotated set of links to resources for international philanthropy organized by donor organizations, organized philanthropy, international news, economics and finance, statistics, and think tanks.

Idealist (http://www.idealist.org/)
Idealist, a project of Action Without Borders, is available in English, Spanish, French, and Russian. It has a searchable network of more than 30,000 nonprofit and community organizations in 165 countries, which can be searched or browsed by name, location, or mission; a searchable list of volunteer opportunities; hundreds of job, consultant, and internship listings; and listings of events, programs, and publications. News articles, commentary, reports, and essays related to NGOs are updated frequently. My Idealist allows you to register for personalized e-mail updates, job and volunteer information, and connections to others with similar interests.

International Association for Volunteer Effort (http://www.iave.org/)
The International Association for Volunteer Effort was created in 1970 by a small group of women from throughout the world who shared a common vision of how volunteers can contribute to the solution of human and social problems and to the development of bridges of understanding among people of all nations. The association's Web site has news and events, as well as education, public awareness, youth involvement, and membership services information.

International Foundation for Election Systems (http://www.ifes.org/)
The International Foundation for Election Systems promotes democracy worldwide and serves as a clearinghouse for information about democratic development and elections by conducting research and providing nonpartisan technical assistance in more than 100 countries. The organization's Web site features a calendar of elections around the world, information about its library holdings and current projects, links to related organizations, past issues of its newsletter, contact information for its various field offices, and job opportunities.

International Law Institute (http://www.ili.org/)
The International Law Institute works toward finding practical solutions to the legal, economic, and financial problems of the international community. The institute's mission is carried out through scholarly research, publishing, and practical legal training and technical assistance regarding various components of international law, economic policy, and practice. The organization's Web site features news, descriptions of its courses and publications, and includes a long list of related links, organized by subject area.

International Opportunities (http://www.interopp.org/)
The International Opportunities' Web site was designed as an information source for volunteers, advisors, and consultants on short-term international projects in developing countries around the world. The site provides background information on international projects, a matching service to link interested individuals with international organizations and projects, and free guides to project preparation and destination countries. Additional publications are for sale online.

International Reading Association (http://www.reading.org/)
The International Reading Association, a professional membership organization with members and affiliates in 99 countries, is dedicated to promoting high levels of literacy for all by improving the quality of reading instruction, disseminating research and information about reading, and encouraging the lifetime reading habit. The organization's Web site includes a nice listing of grant opportunities.

International Research & Exchanges Board (http://www.irex.org/)
The International Research & Exchanges Board (IREX) administers programs supporting higher education, independent media, Internet development, and civil society in the United States, Europe, Eurasia, the Near East, and Asia. In its focus area of higher education, IREX offers research support, study abroad opportunities, professional training and leadership development, educational advising services, institutional development, and policy forums. The Web site provides detailed information about these programs and services, grant opportunities, job opportunities, and e-mail updates.

International Women's Health Coalition (http://www.iwhc.org/)
The International Women's Health Coalition works to generate health and population policies, programs, and funding that promote and protect the rights and health of girls and women worldwide, particularly in Africa, Asia, and Latin America. The coalition's Web site features articles and publications on women's health and rights, information on upcoming conferences, updates on current issues, and more detailed information on the national and international programs and services offered by the coalition.

Internet Law & Policy Forum (http://www.ilpf.org/)
The Internet Law & Policy Forum (ILPF) is dedicated to promoting global growth of e-commerce by contributing to a better understanding of the particular legal issues which arise from the cross-border nature of the electronic medium. ILPF offers a spectrum of resources to lawyers and legal policy experts and provides a neutral forum for discussion of legal and policy issues that will affect the growth of global electronic commerce.

Internet Prospector (http://www.internet-prospector.org/)
Internet Prospector is a nonprofit service to the prospect research community, produced by volunteers nationwide who "mine" the Web for prospect research "nuggets." Although designed for nonprofit fundraisers, anyone seeking tools for accessing corporate, foundation, biographical, international, and online news sources will find this Web site useful. You'll find an online newsletter and an archive of past issues. A search engine is also provided, allowing you to quickly search for information from back issues located on the site. An option to subscribe to the free monthly newsletter is also available.

Novartis Foundation for Sustainable Development (http://www.foundation.novartis.com/)
The Novartis Foundation for Sustainable Development supports programs for development in poor countries in the southern hemisphere through concrete development cooperation in the sectors of social development, health, and rural and agricultural development. The foundation's Web site also contributes to development policy discussions, by elaborating and providing scientific analyses and by organizing public events.

Organization for Economic Cooperation and Development (http://www.oecd.org/)
The Organization for Economic Cooperation and Development (OECD), an international think tank incorporating 30 member countries, does work in macroeconomics, trade, education, development, and science and innovation. The organization provides governments a setting in which to discuss, develop, and perfect economic and social policy. The Web site includes statistics, news, events, and information on OECD's main themes and activities.

Peace Corps (http://www.peacecorps.gov/)
The Peace Corps, a volunteer aid organization, currently works in Africa, Central and East Asia, Europe and the Mediterranean, Inter-America and the Caribbean, and the Pacific. The Web site has information about assignments and areas of focus, benefits, returned volunteers, an online library, an application toolkit, and information for teachers and students.

ReliefWeb (http://www.reliefweb.int/)
ReliefWeb, a project of the United Nations Office for the Coordination of Humanitarian Affairs, was designed specifically to help the international community improve its

humanitarian relief efforts through the timely dissemination of reliable information on prevention, preparedness, and disaster response. In addition to current news regarding international emergencies, the Web site provides financial figures on humanitarian assistance, country background information, a list of recent natural disasters worldwide, job openings, and a directory of humanitarian organizations.

Soros Foundations Network (http://www.soros.org/)
The Soros Foundations Network's Web site serves as a clearinghouse of information about—and gateway to—the foundations, programs, and initiatives that support the development and maintenance of "open societies" in Central and Eastern Europe, the former Soviet Union, Africa, Asia, and the Americas.

Trickle Up Program (http://www.trickleup.org/)
Based in New York City, Trickle Up works with local partner agencies to assist the most marginalized people in Africa, Asia, and the Americas in starting a microenterprise, by providing seed capital and business training. The Web site includes success stories from the field, program information, recent annual reports and financial statements, news, events, and links to related resources.

United Nations (http://www.un.org/)
Established in 1945, the United Nations (UN) conducts worldwide efforts encompassing peace and security, economic and social development, international law, human rights, humanitarian assistance, and development. The vast, multilingual Web site provides detailed information about the UN and its more than 30 affiliated organizations, committees, and task forces; a list of conferences and events; documents; news; a publications index; and access to several of its online databases.

United Nations Educational, Scientific and Cultural Organization (http://www.unesco.org/culture/)
The United Nations Educational, Scientific and Cultural Organization (UNESCO) was established to contribute to peace and security in the world by promoting collaboration among nations through education, science, culture, and communication in order to further universal respect for justice, for the rule of law, and for human rights and fundamental freedoms. The UNESCO Web site has documents and publications, program information, and a calendar of events.

USAID (http://www.usaid.gov/)
The United States Agency for International Development (USAID) is an independent government agency that provides economic development and humanitarian assistance to advance U.S. economic and political interests overseas. The Web site has information about the organization and its work, USAID publications, news, and numerous links to governmental and non-governmental organizations concerned with international development.

Village Banking (http://www.villagebanking.org/)
Village Banking is a program of the Foundation for International Community Assistance, that supports the economic and human development of families trapped in severe poverty by creating peer groups of 30 to 50 members, predominantly women, based on microcredit. The organization's Web site offers a detailed explanation of how the program works, program locations and statistics, news, and job opportunities and internships.

The World Bank Group (http://www.worldbank.org/)
The World Bank Group strives to reduce poverty and improve living standards by promoting sustainable growth and investment in developing countries. The World Bank Group includes the International Bank for Reconstruction and Development, the International Development Association, the International Finance Corporation, the Multilateral Investment Guarantee Agency, and the International Centre for the Settlement of Investment

Disputes. The Web site offers an imposing smorgasbord of economic facts and general information about the dozens of countries in which the World Bank Group does business.

AFRICA

African Centre for the Constructive Resolution of Disputes (http://www.accord.org.za/)
Founded in 1991, the African Centre for the Constructive Resolution of Disputes (ACCORD) is a South African-based non-governmental conflict management organization, working throughout Africa to bring appropriate African solutions to the challenges posed by conflict on the continent. The ACCORD Web site has program information, news, publications, and a calendar of events.

AllAfrica Global Media (http://allafrica.com/)
AllAfrica Global Media posts more than 700 stories daily in English and French and offers a diversity of multilingual streaming programming, as well as a searchable archive of more than 400,000 articles from more than 80 African media organizations. The Web site is a one-stop source for up-to-date information on all of Africa. With reports from Africa's leading newspapers, magazines, and news agencies, the site is an invaluable resource.

Lawyers' Environmental Action Team (http://www.leat.or.tz/)
The Lawyers' Environmental Action Team is a public interest environmental law organization that promotes sound natural resource management and environmental protection in Tanzania. The Web site contains the team's policy briefs on critical environmental issues facing Tanzania and East Africa.

Novartis Foundation for Sustainable Development (http://www.foundation.novartis.com/)
The Novartis Foundation for Sustainable Development supports programs for development in poor countries in the southern hemisphere through concrete development cooperation in the sectors of social development, health, and rural and agricultural development. The foundation's Web site also contributes to development policy discussions, by elaborating and providing scientific analyses and by organizing public events.

RAINBO (http://www.rainbo.org/)
RAINBO (the Research, Action and Information Network for the Bodily Integrity of Women) works directly with immigrant and refugee communities in the United States on issues that intersect women's health and human rights. The RAINBO Web site provides descriptions of national and international programs and activities, including AMANITARE, which works toward the recognition of African women's and girls' sexual and reproductive health rights.

ASIA

Asia Pacific Philanthropy Information Network (http://www.asianphilanthropy.org/)
A project of the Asia Pacific Philanthropy Consortium, the Asia Pacific Philanthropy Information Network consists of research centers in several Asia Pacific countries. The network provides details on philanthropy and the third sector within the Asia Pacific region and builds networks among researchers interested in philanthropy in Asia. The Web site provides information on fields of activities in various regions, a database of researchers, and links to other philanthropic organizations interested or based in the region.

Asia Society (http://www.asiasociety.org/)
Founded in 1956 by John D. Rockefeller III, the Asia Society builds awareness of the more than 30 countries broadly defined as the Asia Pacific region through a range of programs, including major art exhibitions, performances, international corporate conferences, and policy programs. The Web site has information about the Asia Society and its programs,

roundtable discussions, transcriptions of speeches presented at the Asia Society, and annotated links to hundreds of resources on Asia.

Bridge to Asia Foundation (http://www.bridge.org/)
The Bridge to Asia Foundation, a San Francisco-based nonprofit, supports education and research in developing countries in Asia through the donation of books and journals to universities, research services, and the development of in-country libraries and computer networks.

National Bureau of Asian Research (http://www.nbr.org/)
Founded in 1989 with a major grant from the Henry M. Jackson Foundation, the Seattle-based National Bureau of Asian Research conducts advanced research on policy-relevant issues affecting Asia. The Web site has information about the bureau's research programs and policy activities.

AUSTRALIA

Philanthropy Australia (http://www.philanthropy.org.au/)
Through a network of member organizations, Philanthropy Australia is dedicated to promoting and protecting the interests of family, private, corporate, and community giving in Australia. The Web site provides information and resources on grantmaking trusts and foundations; programs and services in the areas of education, networking, and advocacy; links to nonprofit organizations within Australia and internationally; and upcoming conferences and seminars.

CANADA

Canadian Centre for Philanthropy (http://www.ccp.ca/)
The Canadian Centre for Philanthropy's mission is to "advance the role and interests of the charitable sector for the benefit of Canadian communities." Web site resources include a foundation and grants directory of more than 1,700 foundations that are actively granting in Canada; information about centre publications; membership information, including the centre's annual symposium; an overview of the centre's Imagine initiative, which promotes public and corporate giving, volunteering, and community support on a national level; and results of various research studies, including volunteering statistics, trends, and comparative studies, mostly through the centre's sister sites, Nonprofitscan.ca and Givingandvolunteering.ca.

CATALIST (http://prometheus.cc.uregina.ca/catalist/)
CATALIST (the Canadian Network for Third Age Learning) is a project dedicated to fostering later life learning through a network of Canadian organizations. The Web site, in French and English, provides members with a newsletter; course information; a list of foundations and corporations that are interested in providing funding for education, research, and other important issues regarding seniors; and links to associations or networks of educational organizations for older adults. Membership applications can be completed online.

Charity Village (http://www.charityvillage.com/)
The Canadian-based Charity Village Web site has news, jobs, information and resources for nonprofit managers, staffers, fundraisers, donors, and volunteers. Visitors to the Web site can access a searchable directory of annotated links to Canadian charities and nonprofit organizations; career advancement and assessment tools, including job listings from more than 5,000 Canadian nonprofit organizations; the Marketplace, an online directory of products and services especially for nonprofit executives; and a listing of educational programs and professional development opportunities, including Charity Village's own workshops and online tutorials, as well as links to courses available across the country.

In Kind Canada (http://www.inkindcanada.ca/)
In Kind Canada, in English and French, functions as an intermediary between registered charities, Canadian corporations, charitable foundations, and other interested parties. It does this by facilitating the process with which the granting of goods and services in support of philanthropic initiatives at the local, regional or national level can take place in an efficient and cost effective manner.

London Community Foundation (http://www.lcf.on.ca/)
The London Community Foundation is a public foundation serving London and Middlesex County, Ontario. The foundation solicits and accepts charitable gifts to establish permanent endowment funds and distributes the earnings to local charitable organizations in support of arts and culture, social service, education, health and physical activity, or the environment. The Web site has information on the granting process, details on the granting cycle, a profile of recent grants, information for donors, and news and events.

Ontario Arts Council (http://www.arts.on.ca/)
The Ontario Arts Council (OAC) supports individual artists and arts organizations throughout the province of Ontario through project, operating, and annual grants. The Web site, in English and French, has a description of OAC arts programs; grants application information, including eligibility requirements and deadlines; and application forms.

The Ontario Trillium Foundation (http://www.trilliumfoundation.org/)
The Ontario Trillium Foundation awards grants to fund capital, operating, and/or specific project costs in support of arts and culture, the environment, human and social services, and sports and recreation in communities across Ontario. The Web site, in English and French, has program guidelines, grant application forms, a full listing of recently approved grants, and a story gallery, with profiles of the winners of the foundation's "great grants" awards.

Science's Next Wave (http://nextwave.sciencemag.org/ca/)
Science Magazine's Next Wave is a weekly online publication that covers scientific training, career development, and the science job market. The Web site features material written by and of interest to Canadian scientists, including science policy and academic issues. The site also has job market news; information for graduate students; and information on career transitions, job-hunting, diversity, and worklife.

EUROPE/EURASIA

European Foundation Centre (http://www.efc.be/)
The European Foundation Centre (EFC) promotes and underpins the work of foundations and corporate funders active in and with Europe. Established in 1989 by seven of Europe's leading foundations, the EFC today has a membership of more than 200 members, associates, and subscribers; 250 community philanthropy initiatives; and serves a further 48,000 organizations linked through networking centers in 37 countries across Europe. The Web site has a listing of member events; information on EFC's projects, activities, and publications; and EFC newsletters, including *Newsline*.

Funders Online (http://www.fundersonline.org/)
An initiative of the European Foundation Centre, Funders Online seeks to promote and strengthen philanthropy in Europe by facilitating access to online independent funding and information resources. The Web site's fully searchable directory contains profiles of funder Web sites that can be located by country or location and by field of activity.

International Research & Exchanges Board (http://www.irex.org/)
The International Research & Exchanges Board (IREX) administers programs supporting higher education, independent media, Internet development, and civil society in the United

States, Europe, Eurasia, the Near East, and Asia. In its focus area of higher education, IREX offers research support, study abroad opportunities, professional training and leadership development, educational advising services, institutional development, and policy forums. The Web site provides detailed information about these programs and services, grant opportunities, job opportunities, and e-mail updates.

NGONet (http://www.ngonet.org/)
Administered by Freedom House Budapest, NGONet provides information to, for, and about non-governmental organizations active in Central and Eastern Europe and the former Soviet Union. Visitors to the Web site will find directories that include a collection of links with information related to human rights issues, policy institutes, think tanks, and cross-border networks, as well as information on grants, publications, events, jobs, and training.

Regional Environmental Center for Central and Eastern Europe (http://www.rec.hu/e_index.html)
The Regional Environmental Center for Central and Eastern Europe supports different groups concerned with and involved in environmental protection and promotes public participation in environmental decision-making through surveys and research programs, publications, education projects, library and information services, and project grants. The Web site offers information on the center's programs and grantmaking activities, as well as several searchable databases.

GEORGIA

American Friends of Georgia (http://www.afgeorgia.org/)
American Friends of Georgia provides practical humanitarian assistance to the peoples of the country of Georgia and the Caucasus Mountain region in order to improve educational, economic, social, and medical conditions. The organization's Web site provides background information about the regions, details on programs and services that the organization sponsors, an online newsletter, and links to further resources.

GERMANY

German Foundation Index (http://www.stiftungsindex.de/)
A joint project of the Federal Foundation Association of Germany, the University of Goettingen, and the Koerber-Foundation, the German Foundation Index serves as a one-stop source of information about German foundations, with links to German foundation Web sites, recommendations for students applying for grants, addresses of foundation researchers, and links to a variety of international resources.

INDIA

Foundation of Occupational Development (http://www.xlweb.com/food)
The Foundation of Occupational Development (FOOD India) strives to foster sustainable development among the poor by conducting research on social development and implementing welfare programs in the field of employment generation, poverty alleviation, cost effective housing, education, health, water and sanitation, energy conservation, ICTs, electronic NGO networking, e-commerce, and institutional and capacity building for women's networks. The FOOD India Web site has information on recent projects and partnership programs.

The Indian National Trust for the Welfare of Tribals (http://www.helptribals.org/)
The Indian National Trust for the Welfare of Tribals (INTWOT) advocates and works on issues important to communities of tribal India. The INTWOT Web site provides visitors

with information on and for tribal India, including programs in health, education, and income generation; current research and projects; future plans; publications; news; and individual members of the organization.

ISRAEL

Giving Wisely: The Internet Directory of Israeli Nonprofit and Philanthropic Organizations (http://www.givingwisely.org.il/)
The Giving Wisely Web site is the online companion to the print directory, *Giving Wisely.* The site has browsable listings of Israeli foundations, trusts (*Hekdeshot*), and nonprofit organizations (*Amutot*). In addition to browsing, you can use the searchable database to view foundation or nonprofit profiles in full or partial format. The search feature works in both Hebrew and English.

ITALY

UnDo.Net (http://www.undo.net/)
UnDo.Net is an Italian network on contemporary art, serving as a point of reference for artists, critics, galleries, and art enthusiasts. Providing current art news, information on funding and events, links to magazines and exhibition spaces, and resources on contemporary Italian art projects, Undo.Net is an online service mainly in Italian. The site can be customized to the user who may create events, perform research, and expand projects through the Web.

JAPAN

Japan Center for International Exchange (http://www.jcie.or.jp/)
The Japan Center for International Exchange is an independent nonprofit organization dedicated to strengthening Japan's role in international networks of policy dialogue and cooperation. Major components of the Web site (in English and Japanese) include Global ThinkNet, a cluster of center-sponsored activities designed to broaden policy research and dialogue on issues pertaining to Japan's relationships with other countries, and CivilNet, which is designed to advance the cause of the nonprofit sector in the Asia Pacific region, with a special emphasis on the development of civil society in Japan.

LATIN AMERICA

ACCION International (http://www.accion.org/default.asp)
ACCION International fights poverty through the practice of microlending to self-employed individuals ranging from the very poor to those who have some assets but remain marginalized from the mainstream economy and society. In addition to its programs in a number of U.S. states, the organization operates In Latin America, the Caribbean, and Africa. The Web site (in English, Spanish, and French) has information about services and products, technical support, annual reports, and newsletters.

Organization of American States (http://www.oas.org/)
The Organization of American States (OAS), composed of 35 member countries from North, Central, and South America, seeks to strengthen and maintain peace, security, human rights, and democracy in the Americas. The Web site (in English, Spanish, French, and Portuguese) has extensive information about the sessions of the general assembly; publications and documents, including the OAS Charter; fellowship, internship, and job opportunities; and news reports that include multimedia resources.

MIDDLE EAST

Abraham Fund Initiatives (http://www.coexistence.org/)
Headquartered in New York City and Jerusalem, the Abraham Fund Initiatives works to foster increased dialogue, tolerance, and understanding between the Jewish and Arab citizens of Israel through advocacy and awareness campaigns and by sponsoring coexistence projects. The Web site (in Hebrew, Arabic, and English) has project descriptions, research and reports, grant applications and guidelines, news, and events.

American Near East Refugee Aid (http://www.anera.org/)
Founded in 1968, the American Near East Refugee Aid (ANERA) works with schools, universities, health facilities, cooperatives, municipalities, grassroots committees, and charitable associations to improve communities throughout the West Bank, Gaza, Lebanon, and Jordan. The Web site has information about ANERA's projects, programs, and local partners.

Economic Research Forum for the Arab Countries, Iran and Turkey (http://www.erf.org.eg/)
The Economic Research Forum for the Arab Countries, Iran and Turkey is an independent regional network of economists, policymakers, and business people that initiates, funds, and facilitates policy-relevant economic research on the Arab Region, Turkey, and Iran. The Web site has publications, conference proceedings, training workshops, and information about the fund's research competition.

Foundation for Middle East Peace (http://www.fmep.org/)
Established in 1979, the Washington, D.C.-based Foundation for Middle East Peace works to promote a just solution to the Israeli-Palestinian conflict that brings peace and security to both peoples. In addition to its role as an information clearinghouse, the foundation awards grants to organizations and projects that contribute significantly to a solution to the Israeli-Palestinian conflict. The bimonthly *Report on Israeli Settlement in the Occupied Territories* reports on Israeli settlement policies and negotiations with the Palestinians.

Middle East Media and Research Institute (http://www.memri.org/)
The Middle East Media and Research Institute is an independent U.S.-based nonprofit that provides translations of Arabic, Farsi, and Hebrew media, as well as original analysis of political, ideological, intellectual, social, cultural, and religious trends in the Middle East. The institute's Web site is arranged by subject, country, language, cartoons, and videos.

Middle East Policy Council (http://www.mepc.org/)
The Middle East Policy Council was founded in 1981 to expand public discussion and understanding of issues affecting U.S. policy in the Middle East. The Web site has information about upcoming conferences, forums, and workshops and a journal with full-text articles, an archive, and book reviews.

Middle East Research and Information Project (http://www.merip.org/)
The Washington, D.C.-based Middle East Research and Information Project provides news and perspectives about the Middle East not available from mainstream media outlets. This online news Web site is searchable and includes back issues.

SWITZERLAND

Mandat International (http://www.mandint.org/)
Based in Geneva, Switzerland, Mandat International seeks to make information available to international delegates with the goal of upholding delegate participation, bringing the various domains of international delegations closer together, and creating a network of those involved in international conferences. The organization's Web site (in English,

French, and Spanish) provides delegates with a Welcome Center, a detailed Delegate's Guide, a calendar of conferences, information on specific projects and areas of focus, and a *Tribune of Information* newsletter for which individuals may sign-up online.

TAIWAN

Himalaya Foundation (http://www.foundations.org.tw/)
The Himalaya Foundation's goal is to enable capable people of Chinese ancestry to develop their talents and participate broadly in the world community. The complete "Directory of 300 Major Foundations in Taiwan," published by the foundation, is available at this Web site, along with links to the foundation itself and the Taiwan Philanthropy Information Center. Each of these Web sites maintains information in English and Chinese.

UNITED KINGDOM

AbilityNet (http://www.abilitynet.org.uk/content/home.htm)
The AbilityNet Web site provides an abundance of information regarding various forms of adaptive technology for people with a wide range of disabilities.

Charitynet (http://www.charitynet.org/index.html)
Charities Aid Foundation, a British nonprofit whose aim is to encourage charitable giving in the United Kingdom as well as internationally, sponsors the Charitynet Web site, "designed to benefit anyone with an interest in philanthropy, wherever they are in the world." The Web site includes contact information for thousands of charities and serves as a technical assistance provider to both funders and nonprofits. Use the search engine to search more than 2,000 charity and nonprofit Web sites by keyword, country, theme, or category. The Web site also provides a news service of current happenings in philanthropy and can also be customized to your program and geographic interests when you register with the site.

Commonwealth Foundation (http://www.commonwealthfoundation.com/)
The Commonwealth Foundation supports professional and community development and exchange, training opportunities, and the sharing of skills, experience, and information in the British non-governmental sector, with membership open to all member countries of the Commonwealth. The Web site has news, including articles from *Commonwealth People Magazine;* other publications; events and program information; and a message board devoted to issues relating to the Commonwealth, civil society, sustainable development, and poverty eradication.

New Economics Foundation (http://www.neweconomics.org/)
Operating as an independent think tank in the United Kingdom, the New Economics Foundation works to construct a new economy centered on people and the environment through research, advocacy, training, and practical action. The foundation's Web site provides details on the organization's areas of work, practical tools for the new economy, a searchable database of links, the foundation's publications, current news, and an indexed news archive.

Oxfordshire Community Foundation (http://www.oxfordshire.org/)
The Oxfordshire Community Foundation was established in 1995 to raise funds locally to support the work of local voluntary groups with programs in education, disability, poverty, and health within Oxfordshire County. The foundation's Web site has information about the grants process and eligibility criteria for organizations and projects.

UK Fundraising (http://www.fundraising.co.uk/)
UK Fundraising is a comprehensive resource for charities and nonprofit fundraisers in the UK and internationally. The Web site has a fundraising bookshop, lists of consultants,

e-mail discussion lists, events, funding, grants, magazines, nonprofit resources, products, professional organizations, research papers, services, software, job opportunities, and an extensive collection of links to examples of online fundraising activities.

The Wellcome Trust (http://www.wellcome.ac.uk/)
The Wellcome Trust supports applied clinical research in biomedical science and the history of medicine with the goal of improving human and animal health and encourages the exploitation of research findings for medical benefit. The Web site has information about research grants, international health, science and art, genetics, education, exhibitions, publications, and a searchable catalog of Internet sites covering public engagement in science, science communication, and the interpretation of science in society.

Nonprofit Resources, by Program Area

AGING

Administration on Aging (http://www.aoa.dhhs.gov/)
The Administration on Aging is an exhaustive online clearinghouse for senior citizens. The Web site provides a resource directory, statistics on aging, an Eldercare Locator, breaking news, and links to related sites.

American Association of Retired Persons (http://www.aarp.org/)
Helping older Americans achieve lives of independence, dignity, and purpose, the American Association of Retired Persons advances the interests of its members through advocacy efforts on issues related to Medicare, health insurance, housing, consumer rights, Social Security, tax reform, and transportation. In addition to providing information and policy statements on these topics, the Web site includes articles on a wide range of subjects of interest to retired people, including computers and technology, learning, and travel and leisure.

American Society on Aging (http://www.asaging.org/)
The American Society on Aging is a membership organization dedicated to providing up-to-date information, research, training, and resources to professionals concerned with all aspects of aging. The Web site has educational resources, conference and event listings, training opportunities, and a job bank.

The National Council on the Aging (http://www.ncoa.org/)
The National Council on the Aging is an association of organizations and professionals—including senior centers, area agencies on aging, adult day services, faith congregations, senior housing, health centers, employment services, and consumer organizations—that help community organizations enhance the lives of older adults. The Web site has reports and research, news, program ideas, workforce development resources, conference information, extensive advocacy resources, and links to other Web sites containing information about elderly Americans.

Project on Death in America (http://www.soros.org/death/)
The Project on Death in America is dedicated to transforming the culture and understanding of dying and bereavement in the United States. The Web site provides information about project initiatives, research, scholarships, past funding, the provision of care, public education, professional education, and public policy, as well as an excellent annotated list of links to other sites.

SeniorNet (http://www.seniornet.org/)
SeniorNet provides training for and access to computer technology for adults age 50 and older. The Web site offers online courses on a variety of technology-related topics, virtual

discussion groups, discounts on technology products, digital galleries, a robust enrichment center, and information about local learning centers.

SPRY Foundation (http://www.spry.org/)
The SPRY (Setting Priorities for Retirement Years) Foundation helps older adults plan for a healthy and financially secure future by conducting research and developing education programs. The Web site provides information about the foundation's work, research, publications, and events.

ARTS

Alliance of Artists Communities (http://www.artistcommunities.org/)
The Alliance of Artists Communities is a national service organization that supports artists' communities by encouraging collaboration among members of the field, raising the visibility of these communities, and advocacy. Web site resources include background information about the alliance and its projects, contact information for member programs, a list of links to individual communities, information about the organization's directory and other publications, job listings, and other links.

American Association of Museums (http://www.aam-us.org/)
The American Association of Museums is dedicated to promoting excellence within the museum community. Through advocacy, professional education, information exchange, accreditation, and guidance on professional performance standards and ethics, the association assists museum staff, boards, and volunteers across the country to better serve the public. In addition to information about the association, the Web site has news, events information, and other resources.

American Craft Council (http://www.craftcouncil.org/)
The American Craft Council is a national nonprofit educational organization working to further the interests of artists working in the media of clay, fiber, glass, metal, wood, and other materials. The Web site has information about the council's programs, awards, grants, mentoring, and publications; a craft resource library; gallery; craft calendar; and show and market listings. Other resources include links to craft-related magazines, museums, organizations, and schools.

American Institute for Conservation of Historic and Artistic Works (http://aic.stanford.edu/)
The American Institute for Conservation of Historic and Artistic Works is a national membership organization of conservation professionals dedicated to preserving art and historic artifacts. Providing a forum for the exchange of ideas on conservation, the institute advances the practice and promotes the importance of the preservation of cultural property by coordinating the exchange of knowledge, research, and publications. In addition to general information about the institute, the Web site has information about becoming or selecting a conservator, conservation specialties, professional development, meetings and conferences, health and safety, caring for treasures, and disaster recovery.

Americans for the Arts (http://www.artsusa.org/)
Americans for the Arts is a nonprofit organization dedicated to advancing the arts nationwide through resource, leadership, and public policy development; information services; and education. The organization's Web site provides news; information on issues, events, and services; research; and a field directory.

Art Deadlines List (http://www.xensei.com/users/adl/)
Art Deadlines List is a monthly Web and e-mail newsletter listing art contests and competitions, scholarships, fellowships, and grants; juried exhibitions; jobs and internships; calls for entries/proposals/papers; writing and photo contests; residencies; design and

architecture competitions; auditions; casting calls; festivals; and other funding opportunities (including some that take place on the Web) for artists, art educators, and art students of all ages. Two versions are available, free and paid subscription. *Art Deadlines List Blog* provides listings in Web log format so you can see the announcements as they become available.

Artcareer Network (http://www.artcareer.net/)
The Artcareer Network is a resource for visual arts professionals. Visitors to the Web site can browse available positions at museums, libraries, educational institutions, and galleries; schedule a free career guidance consultation; read the perspectives of other individuals in the visual arts field; and find links to other career development resources.

Arts & Business Council Inc. (http://www.artsandbusiness.org/home.htm)
Through its local and national programs, the Arts & Business Council Inc. promotes mutually beneficial partnerships between corporations and nonprofit arts groups. The council's signature program, Business Volunteers for the Arts, places corporate executives as *pro bono* management consultants with nonprofit arts groups. The Web site includes information about programs and services, including a link to ArtsMarketing.org, a national arts marketing site addressing arts organizations' daily marketing needs and longer-term marketing issues. The *Arts & Business Quarterly* provides updates on happenings at the council; social, economic, and political trends affecting the arts; reviews of new publications and technology; and general news from the arts community.

Arts and Culture Indicators in Community Building Project (http://www.urbaninstitute.org/nnip/acip.html)
The Arts and Culture Indicators in Community Building Project is an experimental effort to develop arts and culture neighborhood indicators for use in local planning, policymaking, and community building. The Web site includes descriptions of the concepts, research framework, and current project activities, seminars, and meetings.

Arts Education Partnership (http://www.aep-arts.org/)
The Arts Education Partnership, administered by Council of Chief State School Officers and the National Assembly of State Arts Agencies, is a national coalition of arts, education, business, philanthropic, and government organizations that demonstrate and promote the essential role of the arts in the learning and development of every child and in the improvement of America's schools. The Web site has advocacy resources, funding opportunities, publications and resources, task force reports and updates, and arts education links.

Arts International (http://www.artsinternational.org/)
Arts International supports and promotes global connections and exchanges between international performing and visual arts communities. The Web site offers helpful tools and resources for artists seeking to expand into the international arena.

Arts Journal (http://www.artsjournal.com/)
Arts Journal is a free digest of arts and cultural news. Each day *Arts Journal* combs through more than 200 English-language newspapers, magazines, and publications and posts links to articles about arts and culture at its Web site.

Arts Resource Network (http://artsresourcenetwork.org/)
The Arts Resource Network is a portal Web site for the Seattle arts community. The Web site provides articles and links addressing the professional growth of artists, organizational growth, and arts education. Additionally, how-to guides for starting and maintaining public art projects and community arts groups, and many links to similar organizations on the regional, national, and global levels can be found on the Web site.

ArtsEdge (http://artsedge.kennedy-center.org/)
ArtsEdge ("the National Arts & Education Information Network"), a cooperative agreement between the National Endowment for the Arts, the U.S. Department of Education, and the John F. Kennedy Center for the Performing Arts, is dedicated to supporting the place of arts education at the center of the curriculum through creative and appropriate uses of technology. The Web site includes news, teaching materials, and professional resources designed to help educators teach in, through, and about the arts.

ArtsEdNet (http://www.getty.edu/artsednet/)
ArtsEdNet, the J. Paul Getty Trust's arts education Web site, offers an extensive array of resources, including lesson plans, image galleries, and teaching tools for various subjects. Visitors to the site can also access ArtsEdnet Talk, an online arts education discussion group.

Arts4AllPeople (http://www.arts4allpeople.org/index.html)
Arts4AllPeople is a resource for anyone or any group dedicated to the arts and culture, who wish to share or gain better insight into successful ways to build and enhance audience participation. The Web site includes success stories about how arts organizations met the challenge of building and engaging audiences; research and resources, with formal research, surveys, reports and bibliographies on audience outreach topics; and an interactive forum.

ArtSites (http://www.artsnet.org/artsites/)
ArtSites (formerly Art Quarry) is a database of artists groups' Web sites supported by the Center for Arts Management and Technology and the New York Foundation for the Arts. Visitors to the Web site can search or submit information to the database.

Artsnet (http://www.artsnet.org/)
The Artsnet Web site is the online home of the Center for Arts Management and Technology, a research, service, and training center at Carnegie Mellon University, devoted to the use of computer and information technology in the arts management process; the Master of Arts Management Program at Carnegie Mellon; ArtSites, a searchable database of arts related Web sites; and Arts Management Resources, a searchable database of online arts management resources.

Association of Independent Video and Filmmakers (http://www.aivf.org/)
The Association of Independent Video and Filmmakers is a membership organization for local and international film and video makers and serves as a clearinghouse for information on all aspects of filmmaking. The association sponsors events, publishes several books and a monthly magazine, and engages in advocacy efforts. The Web site has online discussion areas, information on the association's Regional Salons (member-organized networking opportunities), and many other resources, including links to useful film-related Web sites.

Association of Performing Arts Presenters (http://www.artspresenters.org/)
The Association of Performing Arts Presenters is an active arts service organization, providing resources for the performing arts community. The association's international membership ranges from large performing arts centers in major urban centers to small presenters in rural communities, and includes artists, artists' managers, and other performing arts professionals. The Web site has information on funding, government affairs, continuing education, a members' conference, and a job bank.

California Lawyers for the Arts (http://www.calawyersforthearts.org/)
California Lawyers for the Arts provides lawyer referrals, dispute resolution services, educational programs, publications, and a resource library for the state's artists and arts organizations. The Web site has information about these services, jobs and internships, and links to relevant sites.

Center for Arts Management and Technology at Carnegie Mellon (http://www.artsnet.org/camt/)

Center for Arts Management and Technology at Carnegie Mellon was established to investigate existing and emerging information and communication technologies and to stimulate thinking about the practical application of such technologies for arts managers. The Web site has information about the center's services, which include eGrant, a custom tool for funding agencies that wish to offer Web-based grant applications to their constituents; technology needs assessment; and Web site development and hosting.

Community Arts Network (http://www.communityarts.net/)

The Community Arts Network promotes information exchange, research, and dialogue within the field of community-based arts. The Web site includes a monthly newsletter, an essay and links Reading Room, and an extensive list of links to related sites.

Connecticut Commission on the Arts (http://www.ctarts.org/)

The Connecticut Commission on the Arts offers matching grants, professional development programs and fellowships, and a number of other services to Connecticut artists, cultural, and other nonprofit organizations. The Web site has news; information for the public, schools, artists, and organizations; and a directory of Connecticut-based performing artists and ensembles, designed to provide employment opportunities for artists who specialize in public performances, classroom residencies, and curriculum development.

Eloquent Evidence: Arts at the Core of Learning (http://www.nasaa-arts.org/new/nasaa/nasaanews/ee.pdf)

"Eloquent Evidence: Arts at the Core of Learning" is a downloadable brochure providing an overview of the issues involved in integrating the arts into a K-12 curriculum. It is designed for, and to be used by, parents, teachers, administrators, school board members, and other stakeholders interested in promoting the case for arts education in the schools.

The Estate Project for Artists with AIDS (http://www.artistswithaids.org/)

The Estate Project for Artists with AIDS was created by the Alliance for Arts primarily to preserve artworks and create archives of visual artworks, films, videos, musical scores, dances, and manuscripts. The Web site offers information on artists' resources, a journal and forum, a virtual art collection, specific strategies for arts preservation, and links to relevant arts organizations, many of which are national in scope.

Fundsnet Services List of Arts & Culture Funders (http://www.fundsnetservices.com/arts01.htm)

Fundsnet Services List of Arts & Culture Funders is an online listing of grantmakers and funding opportunities, providing a solid and useful alphabetized compilation of arts and culture funders, including corporations and private foundations.

Grantmakers in the Arts (http://www.giarts.org/)

Grantmakers in the Arts is a nonprofit membership organization comprised of private foundations, family foundations, community foundations, corporate foundations, corporate-giving programs, and nonprofit organizations that make arts grants. The Web site has information about the organization; research and publications, including its own periodical; conferences and meetings; and links.

Hands On (http://handson.org/)

Founded in 1982, New York-based Hands On is dedicated to providing greater accessibility to arts and cultural events for the deaf and hard-of-hearing community. The Web site has a calendar of arts and cultural events; sign language interpreted theater information, which includes current listings and ticket orders; information on the TOLA (Theatre Offers a Lifetime of Adventure) Program, which was developed to increase the number of accessible theater experiences for deaf school-age children and their families; consultations and services to theaters and interpreters; and deaf community Web links.

Intermedia Arts (http://www.intermediaarts.org/index.html)
The mission of Minneapolis-based Intermedia Arts, a nonprofit multi-disciplinary art center, is to foster dialogue between cultures through art by providing artist support, programs, and community education in the upper Midwest region. Among other features, the Web site includes an artist opportunities page that offers guidelines for fiscal sponsorship and a list of funding opportunities nationwide.

International Society for the Performing Arts (http://www.ispa.org/)
The International Society for the Performing Arts is an organization of executives and directors of concert and performance halls, festivals, performing companies, and artist competitions; government cultural officials; artists' managers; and others with a professional involvement in the performing arts from countries in every region of the world and in every arts discipline. The Web site has a searchable membership directory, a quarterly report on the society's activities, events listings, job postings, and other resources.

Meet the Composer (http://www.meetthecomposer.org/)
Meet the Composer is a national nonprofit organization serving composers of every kind of music throughout the United States, through commissioning, residency, education, and audience interaction programs. The Web site has program information, publications, and an extensive set of links to composers and related organizations.

National Alliance for Media Arts and Culture (http://www.namac.org/)
The National Alliance for Media Arts and Culture is a nonprofit association of organizations whose purpose is to encourage film, video, audio and online/multimedia arts and to promote the cultural contributions of individual media artists. The Web site has a directory of media arts agencies in the United States, featuring profiles of alliance member organizations; current news; job and event listings; information on funding opportunities; advocacy information of relevance to the field; an archive of quarterly newsletters; and other useful resources.

National Arts Strategies (http://www.artstrategies.org/)
National Arts Strategies (formerly National Arts Stabilization) is a nonprofit organization dedicated to helping strengthen arts organizations through the development of managerial and financial skills. The Web site offers information about the organization's programs, research, and consulting services.

National Assembly of State Arts Agencies (http://www.nasaa-arts.org/)
The National Assembly of State Arts Agencies (NASAA) is the membership organization of America's state and jurisdictional arts agencies. The Web site's Arts Over America section provides a directory of links to state arts agencies and regional arts organizations, an annotated list of arts-related Web sites, and links to major funders in the arts. The Artworks section has information on trends, issues, and activities influencing decision makers in the arts and government. The Web site also has a News from NASAA section, featuring news and legislative updates, and Publications, including a strategic planing toolkit.

National Endowment for the Arts (http://arts.endow.gov/)
The National Endowment for the Arts' (NEA) Web site serves as a comprehensive resource for the arts community and its supporters. The Web site includes information, guidelines, and applications for grants and funding; NEA news and legislative updates; and arts-related features and interviews. In addition, NEA publications—many of which are free—can be ordered or downloaded through the site.

National Endowment for the Humanities (http://www.neh.fed.us/)
The National Endowment for the Humanities (NEH) supports learning in history, literature, philosophy, and other areas of the humanities through its support of research, education, documentaries, exhibits, and other programs that preserve and provide access to cultural

resources. The information-packed NEH Web site is a good place to find out about funding opportunities, cultural events, publications, and exhibits.

National Gallery of Art (http://www.nga.gov/home.htm)
Created in 1937 for the people of the United States, the National Gallery of Art began with the private art collection of financier and art collector Andrew Mellon and today houses a growing number of world-class art collections. The Web site includes information on exhibitions, programs, and events; services and resources for teachers; information on internships and fellowships; and details about the Center for Advanced Study in the Visual Arts, a research institute promoting study of the history, theory, and criticism of art, architecture, and urbanism from prehistoric times to the present.

Nebraska Arts Council (http://www.nebraskaartscouncil.org/)
The Nebraska Arts Council promotes the arts, cultivates resources, and supports excellence in artistic endeavors for all Nebraskans. The Web site provides general information about the council's grant programs and application requirements, an artists directory, artists' opportunities, advocacy information, contacts, and links to other art councils, state organizations, and art museums on the Web.

New York Foundation for the Arts (http://www.nyfa.org/)
The New York Foundation for the Arts Web site provides the national arts community with weekly news, analysis of current issues, job listings, and databases of opportunities for artists and organizations.

NYFA Interactive: For Artists (http://www.nyfa.org/level1.asp?id=1)
The New York Foundation for the Arts (NYFA), a nonprofit arts service organization, provides grants and services to individual artists and arts-related organizations in all artistic disciplines in the United States. The Web site includes information on fellowship opportunities in writing and the visual arts and on fiscal sponsorship; access to NYFA Source, an extensive national database of awards, services, and publications for artists of all disciplines; and *NYFA Current,* a weekly digest of news in the arts.

North Carolina Arts Council (http://www.ncarts.org/)
The mission of the North Carolina Arts Council is to enrich North Carolina's cultural life by supporting the arts. The council is a catalyst for the development of arts organizations and gives grants, organizational assistance, and guidance to groups and individuals statewide. The council's Web site provides, among other items, program and grant information, news, and a searchable database of artists, arts organizations, and arts events.

North Dakota Council on the Arts (http://www.state.nd.us/arts/)
Established in 1967 by the state legislature, the North Dakota Council on the Arts is responsible for the support and development of the arts and artists in North Dakota. In addition to making grants based on recommendations from artists, arts administrators, and board members, the council administers the Cultural Endowment Fund, through which it secures private and public funds to enhance existing programs. The council's Web site provides program information, application instructions, grantwriting tips, arts opportunities, related arts resource links, news, and events.

Ohio Arts Council (http://www.oac.state.oh.us/home.html)
Established in 1965 to "foster and encourage the development of the arts and assist the preservation of Ohio's cultural heritage," the Ohio Arts Council (OAC) funds programs to make arts activities available to the public and also supports Ohio artists through 25 different grant programs. The council's Web site provides information about all OAC programs, complete grant guidelines, a search engine, and links to both state and national arts resources.

Open Studio: The Arts Online (http://www.benton.org/openstudio)
From 1996-2000, Open Studio: The Arts Online, a national initiative of the Benton Foundation and National Endowment for the Arts, provided Internet access and training to artists and nonprofit arts organizations to ensure that the communications environment of the 21st century would thrive as a source of creative excellence and diversity. The project is no longer active, but the site is archived by the Benton Foundation as a resource to the nonprofit community.

Smithsonian Institution (http://www.si.edu/)
Established in 1846, the Smithsonian Institution is an independent trust of the United States holding more than 142 million artifacts and specimens in trust for "the increase and diffusion of knowledge." The institution is also a center for research dedicated to public education, national service, and scholarship in the arts, sciences, and history. The Web site has a wide range of information on the institution's museums, exhibitions, research, and education and outreach programs, including fellowships and internships.

Sources for Information on the Arts and Civic Engagement (http://www.ksg.harvard.edu/saguaro/sources7.html)
Sources for Information on the Arts and Civic Engagement is a bibliography of publications and Web links on the arts and civic engagement from the Saguaro Seminar at the John F. Kennedy School of Government at Harvard University.

South Dakota Arts Council (http://www.state.sd.us/deca/SDArts/)
The South Dakota Arts Council encourages and supports artists, strengthens arts organizations and arts education programs, and increases South Dakotans' awareness of the arts. As a state agency of the Department of Education and Cultural Affairs, the council makes grants to schools, individuals, and arts organizations. The council's Web site includes detailed grant application guidelines, a directory of arts festivals, and other resources.

Teachers & Writers Collaborative (http://www.twc.org/)
Founded in 1967 by a group of writers and educators who believed that writers could make a unique contribution to the teaching of writing, the Teachers & Writers Collaborative brings writers and educators together to explore the connections between writing and reading literature. The Web site includes information about Writer-in-Residence Programs; workshops for students; staff development workshops; WriteNet, a resource for writers and teachers interested in teaching imaginative writing; and related links.

UnDo.Net (http://www.undo.net/)
UnDo.Net is an Italian network on contemporary art, serving as a point of reference for artists, critics, galleries, and art enthusiasts. Providing current art news, information on funding and events, links to magazines and exhibition spaces, and resources on contemporary Italian art projects, Undo.Net is an online service mainly in Italian. The site can be customized to the user who may create events, perform research, and expand projects through the Web.

United Nations Educational, Scientific and Cultural Organization (http://www.unesco.org/culture/)
The United Nations Educational, Scientific and Cultural Organization (UNESCO) was established to contribute to peace and security in the world by promoting collaboration among nations through education, science, culture, and communication in order to further universal respect for justice, for the rule of law, and for human rights and fundamental freedoms. The UNESCO Web site has documents and publications, program information, and a calendar of events.

Volunteer Lawyers for the Arts (http://www.vlany.com/)
Established in 1969, the New York City-based Volunteer Lawyers for the Arts works to help the New York arts community understand and deal with its legal problems, including

through the provision of *pro bono* legal services. The Web site provides information on the group's educational and advocacy work, as well as a schedule of upcoming seminars, a publications listing, news, and contact information for a legal advice hotline.

VSA Arts (http://www.vsarts.org/)
VSA Arts creates learning opportunities through the arts for people with disabilities. The organization operates arts-based programs in creative writing, dance, drama, music, and the visual arts, and its Web site offers an extensive database of Web resources for artists with disabilities.

Warshawski Fundraising Bibliography (http://www.warshawski.com/bibliography.html)
Morrie Warshawski's Fundraising Bibliography provides information related to fundraising in the arts and is organized by: books on fundraising, books on independent film/video, booklets and guides, magazines and newsletters, miscellaneous publications, information services, software, fundraising Web sites, and mailing lists.

World Wide Arts Resources (http://wwar.com/artslocator/)
World Wide Arts Resources is a gateway Web site that provides access to artists, museums, galleries, art history, arts education, performing arts, classified ads, resume postings, arts forums, news, and more. The Web site's Artslocator provides information on organizations and agencies in cities around the world.

CHILDREN, YOUTH, & FAMILIES

Administration for Children and Families (http://www.acf.dhhs.gov/)
The Administration for Children and Families' Web site has information on the vast array of programs and services offered by this division of the Department of Health and Human Services, dedicated to promoting the economic and social well-being of families, children, individuals, and communities.

American Legion Child Welfare Foundation (http://www.cwf-inc.org/)
The American Legion Child Welfare Foundation works to provide other nonprofit organizations with a means to educate the public about the needs of children by providing grants to nonprofit, youth-serving organizations throughout the United States. The foundation's Web site posts information on grants, including guidelines, limitations, and application procedures; news; and details on the foundation's publications.

Catholic Charities USA (http://www.catholiccharitiesusa.org/)
The mission of Catholic Charities USA is to reduce poverty, help families become self-sufficient, build communities, and to advocate for justice in social structures. The Web site has programs and advocacy information, news releases, conference information, a media page, and a disaster response section.

Child Trends DataBank (http://www.childtrendsdatabank.org/)
The Child Trends Databank provides national trends and research on key indicators of child and youth well-being, with new indicators added each month. The Web site offers information organized by health; social and emotional development; income, assets and work; education and skills; demographics; and family and community.

Child Welfare League of America (http://www.cwla.org/)
The Child Welfare League of America is devoted to the well-being of America's children and their families. In addition to an advocacy section and information about the organizations programs, the Web site offers links to more than a thousand member agencies.

Children Now (http://www.childrennow.org/)
Children Now is a research and action organization devoted to the nurturing, safety, and rights of children. The Web site offers news, action alerts, job listings, and a wealth of related links, many of which lead to funding opportunities in children's issues.

Children, Youth and Family Consortium (http://www.cyfc.umn.edu/)
The Children, Youth, and Family Consortium's electronic clearinghouse at the University of Minnesota is a bridge to information and resources on children, youth, and families. Among other things, visitors to the Web site will find a listing of events and activities, an experts database, a list of consortium publications, discussion groups, and links to related resources.

Children's Charities of America (http://www.childrenscharities.org/)
Children's Charities of America (CCA) is a coalition of national nonprofit organizations dedicated to meeting the needs of children through heightened public awareness of children's issues and the solutions to their problems, and by helping raise funds mainly through participation in workplace campaigns. CCA pre-screens and certifies national charities working to protect and assist children in the United States and internationally, and then presents this information to potential donors. The Web site provides contact information, mission statements, and e-mail and Web links for each member organization.

Children's Defense Fund (http://www.childrensdefense.org/)
A leader in child advocacy, the Children's Defense Fund provides a wealth of information and news about children's issues on its Web site. The Web site also offers state-by-state statistics; information on jobs, internships, volunteering; and conferences; and the Parents Resource Network, a collection of links to Web sites that offer parents information on caring for their own children and on getting involved in group efforts to help children in their communities or states.

Connect For Kids (http://www.connectforkids.org/)
Connect For Kids, a project of the Benton Foundation, was developed for parents, educators, and policymakers and provides solutions-oriented coverage of critical issues for children and families. The Web site provides a free weekly e-mail newsletter, *Connect for Kids Weekly*; a news archive; and Connections, a monthly highlight of articles, profiles, and interviews. The site also has resources for volunteering; a list of organizations working on behalf of children and families, searchable by name, topic, and geographic scope; a calendar of events; and a list of resources by state.

HandsNet (http://www.handsnet.org/)
HandsNet is a membership organization of more than 5,000 public interest and human services organizations. The Web site features articles and alerts, which provide daily news updates on human services issues and legislation; the WebClipper news and delivery service, with human services headlines from hundreds of Web sites that can be tailored to your interests; and information on training and capacity building programs, including a Mobile Technology Classroom and information consulting and knowledge-management services.

Lion's Quest (http://www.lions-quest.org/)
Lion's Quest provides curricula, products, training, and services to support adults in helping young people develop positive personal and social skills and character traits. The Web site offers extensive information about the organization's programs, a collection of articles on and about community-based service-learning, workshop information and registration, and links to relevant Web sites.

KidsHealth (http://kidshealth.org/)
Created by the medical experts at the Nemours Foundation, the KidsHealth Web site offers up-to-date health and medical information about children from before birth through

adolescence. The Web site has separate areas for kids, teens, and parents, with a wealth of in-depth educational features, articles, animations, games, and resources.

Mediascope (http://www.mediascope.org/)
The aim of Mediascope is to sensitize researchers, the government sector, and the producers and consumers of film, television, the Internet, video games, and music to social and health issues, particularly as they relate to children and adolescents, and to promote the production of constructive and responsible work without compromising creative freedom. The Web site features sections for parents and educators, journalists, entertainment industry professionals, public policymakers, researchers, and activists. The Media Research Library has more than 6,000 titles on a diverse range of media-related topics and is a good resource for researchers, screenwriters, journalists, teachers, legislators, and public policy analysts.

National Center for Children in Poverty (http://cpmcnet.columbia.edu/dept/nccp/index.html)
The National Center for Children in Poverty works to identify and promote strategies that prevent child poverty in the United States and that improve the lives of low-income children and their families. The center's Web site provides access to numerous articles on issues such as welfare reform, family support, and state and local information. A research forum, online newsletters, and other publications can be downloaded from the Web site.

National Center for Youth Law (http://www.youthlaw.org/)
The National Center for Youth Law (NCYL) is a California-based private, nonprofit law office serving the legal needs of children and their families. The organization focuses particularly on children living in poverty, advocating for their protection from abuse, for their access to housing, healthcare, public benefits, and for improved methods of collecting child support. It also seeks to address the tendency to deal with youth behavior punitively. NCYL works towards these goals by publishing articles, manuals, books, and its bimonthly journal, *Youth Law News;* providing technical assistance and training; assisting legal advocates who represent poor children; and conducting administrative and legislative advocacy. The Web site includes pertinent news, an overview of the organization, online articles, analyses, publications, and links to related resources.

National Parent Information Network (http://npin.org/)
The National Parent Information Network (a project of the ERIC system) provides access to research-based information for parents and those who work with parents, with a focus on family involvement in education. The Web site's Virtual Library includes a search engine to full-text resources, book summaries, descriptions of newsletters and magazines, and a collection of full-text resources for urban/minority families. The site also includes AskEric, a question and answering service for educators, librarians, and parents.

Parents Anonymous (http://www.parentsanonymous.org/)
Parents Anonymous is a national network organization dedicated to strengthening families and preventing child abuse with innovative strategies that promote mutual support and parent leadership. The organization's Web site provides a map and contact information for regional support groups, and details on initiating or referring someone to a group. Additionally, the site posts further resources, tips for parents, and volunteer opportunities.

Phoenix Data Center of Santa Clara County (http://www.phoenixdatacenter.org/)
The Phoenix Data Center of Santa Clara County maintains an index of all free and low-income services offered throughout Santa Clara County. The Web site is a resource of information and links to social service programs in the areas of housing, transportation, food and meal service, health, legal, and senior programs, among others. Specification sheets on various services are available online, along with links to programs in other counties in the region.

Save the Children (http://www.savethechildren.org/)
Save the Children works in 19 states across the United States, and in more than 45 developing countries around the world to provide education and aid to communities in need. Areas of focus include health and nutrition, education, economic opportunity, and emergencies. The Web site provides information about about Save the Children's programs, including how to take action, make a donation, or sponsor a child.

Starting Points: Meeting the Needs of Our Youngest Children (http://www.carnegie.org/starting_points/index.html)
Starting Points: Meeting the Needs of Our Youngest Children is an abridged version of the 150-page full report of the Carnegie Task Force on Meeting the Needs of Young Children. The Web site includes a table of contents and information about how to order the full text version of the report.

UNICEF (http://www.unicef.org/)
The United Nations Children's Fund (UNICEF) advocates and works for the protection of children's rights by collaborating with other United Nations bodies, governments, and non-governmental organizations to offer community-based services in primary healthcare, basic education, and sanitation in developing countries. In addition to organizational information, UNICEF's excellent Web site provides program highlights, statistics, job postings, and many other features.

WOW Online (http://www.wowusa.com/)
WOW Online is a nonprofit organization that works with kids in wheelchairs. The Web site is aimed at the kids themselves, but includes additional resources for parents and volunteers. The site provides an introduction to the Internet; games, activities, and Web sites for kids; and a bimonthly Internet newsletter. The site also has additional information and resources for parents, corporations, and volunteers, including FAQs, bulletin boards, chat rooms, and links to WOW organizations.

Youth Today (http://www.youthtoday.org/)
Youth Today is an independent national newspaper geared to people who work in the child and youth services field. The Web site has a calendar of conferences and workshops, reviews of books and videos for use with staff and kids, grants awarded in the youth field, and analysis of legislative issues.

COMMUNITY DEVELOPMENT

Catholic Charities USA (http://www.catholiccharitiesusa.org/)
The mission of Catholic Charities USA is to reduce poverty, help families become self-sufficient, build communities, and to advocate for justice in social structures. The Web site has programs and advocacy information, news releases, conference information, a media page, and a disaster response section.

Coalition for Healthier Cities and Communities (http://www.healthycommunities.org/)
The Coalition for Healthier Cities and Communities is a network of community partnerships working to improve the health and quality of life of the country's communities. Through its Web site, the coalition is compiling a database of people, organizations, and initiatives dedicated to the sustenance of healthy communities around the nation. The site also offers a library of materials, tools, and resources.

Communities by Choice (http://www.communitiesbychoice.org/)
Communities by Choice is a national network of individuals and communities committed to learning and practicing sustainable development. The network's Web site has a searchable resources section with information for communities, households, businesses, schools, and action teams. The site's Community Center includes a calendar where members can

add conferences, workshops, or other events that are open to the public and that deal with sustainable development; a section for working groups to conduct online planning and discussions around sustainable development issues; a resources exchange list of community group related tools and processes; and job listings.

Community Technology Centers' Network (http://www.ctcnet.org/)
The Community Technology Centers' Network is a national membership organization that promotes nonprofit and community-based efforts to provide equal access to technology skills and usage to the general public and to disadvantaged populations. The Web site has contact information for community technology centers in the United States, Ireland, Scotland, Spain, and the United Kingdom where access to computers and computer-related technology is available. The site also has relevant news, conference information, publications, and other resources.

Department of Housing and Urban Development (HUD) (http://www.hud.gov/)
Among many other resources, the Web site of the Department of Housing and Urban Development (HUD) has information about various types of grants, including community development, affordable housing, and research.

The Digital Divide Network (http://www.digitaldividenetwork.org/)
The Digital Divide Network, produced by the Benton Foundation, addresses the gap between those who can effectively use new information and communication tools, such as the Internet, and those who cannot. Visitors to the Web site will find news about efforts going on across the country, research, and funding information.

Digital Partners (http://www.digitalpartners.org/)
Seattle-based Digital Partners' mission is to tap the power of the digital economy to develop market-based solutions that benefit the world's poor. Among other projects, Digital Partners fosters a global leadership movement in which information technology entrepreneurs are linked with the poverty-alleviation activities of social entrepreneurs, foundations, and development institutions. The Web site has an overview of current projects and initiatives, a newsletter, and other publications.

Habitat for Humanity International (http://www.habitat.org/)
Habitat for Humanity International aims to eliminate homelessness and poor housing conditions around the world by building and rehabilitating simple, decent houses with the help of volunteer labor and tax-deductible donations of money and materials. Habitat houses are sold to families at no profit and financed with affordable, no-interest loans. The Web site features basic information about the organization, in many languages; a list of local affiliates; testimonials from Habitat for Humanity volunteers and homeowners; news; and events.

Local Initiative Support Corporation (http://www.liscnet.org/resources/)
Local Initiative Support Corporation works through local offices and affiliates nationwide to provide grants, loans, and equity investments to community development corporations for neighborhood redevelopment. The Web site includes an Online Resource Library with news; funding opportunities; events; resources on affordable housing, social and economic development, organizational development, planning and land use; a glossary; and Web links.

National Center on Poverty Law (http://www.povertylaw.org/)
The National Center on Poverty Law (NCPL) develops its advocacy agenda in accordance with the needs of the low-income communities that it serves. Through policy, advocacy, and legal resources, the organization "identifies, develops, and supports creative and collaborative approaches to help achieve social and economic justice." The major clearinghouse on poverty law, the NCPL Web site provides access to an enormous collection of

publications and case studies. The site also has information about advocacy, news, and an advanced search function.

National Congress for Community Economic Development (http://www.ncced.org/)
The National Congress for Community Economic Development is a membership organization of more than 3,600 community development corporations (CDCs), which support their communities' economic development through grants, loans, donations, and income-generating projects. The Funding section of the Web site provides links to government funding opportunities and awards programs, and the State Associations section gives contact information for state-based coalitions of CDCs across the nation.

National Low Income Housing Coalition (http://www.nlihc.org/)
The National Low Income Housing Coalition seeks to address America's affordable housing crisis through education, organization, and advocacy. The Web site contains action alerts, news, publications, events, a state coalition directory, answers to FAQs, and related links.

NeighborWorks Network (http://www.nw.org/)
The NeighborWorks Network promotes the creation of healthy communities through affordable housing, home ownership, and investment in neighborhood revitalization by supporting local partnerships of residents, nonprofits, lenders, the business community, and local government. The Web site includes extensive information about a range of programs, coalitions, and organizations, including the Neighborhood Reinvestment Corporation, the Neighborhood Housing Services of America, and the NeighborWorks Network. Other useful features include a site-wide search engine, news and events listings, and a library of links.

Pratt Area Community Council (http://www.prattarea.org/)
The Pratt Area Community Council serves the neighborhoods of Fort Greene, Clinton Hill, and Bedford-Stuyvesant in Brooklyn, New York, to maintain neighborhood diversity and stability. The council provides programs and services for tenants, homeowners and buyers, job seekers, and businesses. In addition to information about the council's work, the Web site has links to community development organizations specific to these neighborhoods in Brooklyn and many other resources.

Rensselaerville Institute (http://www.rinstitute.org/)
The Rensselaerville Institute acts as a consultant to communities and organizations by providing tools that use outcomes rather than process to drive change, solve problems, and seize opportunities. The Web site provides specific information on the institute's New York campus, conference center, and other offices; special programs, workshops, and seminars; publications; and the organization's recent annual reports.

CRIME PREVENTION

Join Together Online (http://www.jointogether.org/)
Join Together Online, a project of the Boston University School of Public Health, is a national resource for communities working to reduce substance abuse and gun violence nationwide, through the dissemination of public policy and community action information. The Web site offers news releases, funding news, grant announcements, resources (including a searchable and browsable resource database), facts, and Web links related to both substance abuse and gun violence. You can also sign up for *JTO Direct,* a free e-mail newsletter with news, alerts, and funding headlines. Daily and weekly versions are available.

Minnesota Center Against Violence and Abuse (http://www.mincava.umn.edu/)
The Minnesota Center Against Violence and Abuse is an electronic clearinghouse for violence-related resources available online. Links to information are organized by

category—including child abuse, elder abuse, hate crimes, multimedia resources, speakers and trainers, and violence prevention. Additional resources are available in the areas of education, healthcare, criminal justice, and social service. The Web site provides a variety of searching mechanism for locating clearinghouse material. The site also has an events calendar, discussion lists, electronic newsletters, and a What's New section.

Partnerships Against Violence Network (http://www.pavnet.org/)
Partnerships Against Violence Network is a coalition of federal agencies, including the U.S. Departments of Agriculture, Education, Health and Human Services, Housing and Urban Development, Justice, and Labor, that provides an online library of information about anti-violence and youth-at-risk programs. The Web site also has a calendar of events that lists conferences, workshops, seminars, and other information related to juvenile and criminal justice, crime victimization, and drug control policy. There is also a page of links to other anti-violence resources on the web.

The Amherst H. Wilder Foundation's Violence Prevention and Intervention Publications (http://www.wilder.org/pubs/index.html#Violence)
Although the Amherst H. Wilder Foundation publishes materials on widely ranging topics, its offerings in the area of violence prevention and domestic abuse are especially substantial. Along with its titles that can be purchased online, the foundation gives visitors the opportunity to download, for free, the *Little Book of Peace*—more than 250,000 copies of which are in use in schools, homes, churches, businesses, and prisons to increase awareness and open discussion of violence and abuse issues.

DISABILITIES

AbilityNet (http://www.abilitynet.co.uk/)
The AbilityNet Web site provides an abundance of information regarding various forms of adaptive technology for people with a wide range of disabilities.

Disability Resources (http://www.disabilityresources.org/)
This nonprofit Web site network, staffed by volunteers, provides an extensive online guide to information resources—searchable by state and by subject—designed to help people with disabilities live independently. The site also includes funding sources (click on Grants & Grant-Writing). The print newsletter, *Disability Resources Monthly,* is available by subscription through the site.

Hands On (http://handson.org/)
Founded in 1982, New York-based Hands On is dedicated to providing greater accessibility to arts and cultural events for the deaf and hard-of-hearing community. The Web site has a calendar of arts and cultural events; sign language interpreted theater information that includes current listings and ticket orders; information on the TOLA (Theatre Offers a Lifetime of Adventure) Program, which was developed to increase the number of accessible theater experiences for deaf school-age children and their families; consultations and services to theaters and interpreters; and deaf community Web links.

National Cristina Foundation (http://www.cristina.org/)
The National Cristina Foundation provides computer technology and solutions to give people with disabilities, students at risk, and economically disadvantaged persons the opportunity, through training, to lead more independent and productive lives. The foundation works to recycle computer technology resources, giving them a second life as tools for developing human potential. The Web site provides information on how to donate computer equipment, specifications, and an online form to initiate a donation.

National Organization on Disability (http://www.nod.org/)
Founded in 1982, the National Organization on Disability promotes the full and equal participation and contribution of American men, women, and children with disabilities in all aspects of life. The organization's Web site focuses on three main topics—community involvement, economic participation, and access to independence—and for each provides programs, projects, information, featured articles, and links.

Office of Disability Employment Policy (http://www.dol.gov/odep/welcome.html)
The Office of Disability Employment Policy, an office of the Department of Labor, provides national leadership to increase employment opportunities for adults and youth with disabilities while striving to eliminate barriers to employment. The Web site provides information about the office's programs and initiatives, including grant opportunities; services information; technical assistance materials; publications; and an extensive list of for-profit companies interested in employing people with disabilities.

W3C Web Accessibility Initiative (http://www.w3.org/WAI/)
The W3C Web Accessibility Initiative, promotes a high degree of usability for people with disabilities, and, in coordination with organizations around the world, pursues accessibility of the Web through five primary areas of work: technology, guidelines, tools, education and outreach, and research and development. The organization's Web site provides resources to aid in making a Web site accessible, including Web site evaluation tools, curriculum for Web content accessibility guidelines, and training and technical references. The Web site also has information on various working groups that produce accessibility guidelines for Web sites, Web authoring tools, evaluation, education, and outreach.

WOW Online (http://www.wowusa.com/)
WOW Online is a nonprofit organization that works with kids in wheelchairs. The Web site is aimed at the kids themselves, but includes additional resources for parents and volunteers. The site provides an introduction to the Internet; games, activities, and Web sites for kids; and a bimonthly Internet newsletter. The site also has additional information and resources for parents, corporations, and volunteers, including FAQs, bulletin boards, chat rooms, and links to WOW organizations.

DISASTER RELIEF

American Red Cross (http://www.redcross.org/)
The American Red Cross serves to aid disaster victims in the United States and abroad. Their Web site contains information on the services offered, current and archived news of worldwide disasters, information on how to help, sign-up for news and updates via e-mail, and access to local chapters.

Do Unto Others (DUO) (http://www.duo.org/)
Do Unto Others (DUO) works to ease the suffering of people who have suffered war, natural disaster, famine, or epidemic by screening and certifying charities with similar goals, and helping donors to find charities whose work they wish to support. This site provides links to those charities' Web sites.

EDUCATION—GENERAL

America Connects Consortium (http://www.americaconnects.net/)
The America Connects Consortium (ACC) is funded by the US Department of Education to provide technical assistance to community technology centers (CTCs) in low-income communities around the country. The ACC Web site provides resources mainly for community technology center staff members on a wide range of topics, including education, program design, disability and inclusion, and workforce development, among other

practical guides to starting a technology center. The site also includes current news articles and spotlights on CTCs nationwide.

Council for Advancement and Support of Education (http://www.case.org/)
The Council for Advancement and Support of Education (CASE) is an international association of education advancement officers, including alumni, administrators, fundraisers, public relations managers, publications editors, and government relations officers at more than 3,000 colleges, universities, and independent elementary and secondary schools. The CASE Web site contains job postings; discussion groups; information about awards and fellowships, training courses, member services, and related merchandise; the online magazine, *CURRENTS;* a matching gifts clearinghouse database; and news about issues facing institutional advancement at colleges, universities, and independent schools around the world.

CRInfo (http://www.crinfo.org/)
A free service regarding conflict resolution and peacemaking funded by the William and Flora Hewlett Foundation, CRInfo offers a clearinghouse of information, links, and educational materials on the topic. The site allows visitors to search or browse more than 20,000 links to Web, print, and organizational resources in the conflict resolution field with tools designed for adversaries, intermediaries, students, educators, practitioners, and researchers. Additionally, CRInfo maintains a number of special projects and partnerships with other nonprofit organizations, delivers current news on conflict resolution, and offers networking resources.

International Reading Association (http://www.reading.org/)
The International Reading Association, a professional membership organization with members and affiliates in 99 countries, is dedicated to promoting high levels of literacy for all by improving the quality of reading instruction, disseminating research and information about reading, and encouraging the lifetime reading habit. The organization's Web site includes a nice listing of grant opportunities.

National Charter School Clearinghouse (http://www.ncsc.info/)
The National Charter School Clearinghouse provides funding and research information on critical issues facing the establishment and operation of charter schools. Funded by the U.S. Department of Education, the clearinghouse posts articles on a variety of topics, including charter school funding, educational technology, "how-to" resources, and school accountability, along with links to the original sources of these articles. Additionally, a newsletter, updates from the Department of Education, an events calendar, and links to further resources can be found online.

PreservationDirectory.com (http://www.preservationdirectory.com/)
PreservationDirectory.com is an online resource for historic preservation, building restoration and cultural resource management in the United States and Canada, and focuses on the preservation of historic buildings, historic downtowns and neighborhoods, and cultural resources by facilitating communication among preservationists, historical societies, state and federal historic preservation offices, and the general public. PreservationDirectory.com provides listings for online historic societies by state, a bookstore with publications on historic and cultural resource preservation, a photo gallery of historic buildings and cultural objects, and a variety of links to educational programs, historic property listings, and main street organizations. Visitors can also sign-up for a free e-mail update online.

Project to Strengthen Nonprofit-Government Relationships (http://www.nonprofit-gov.unc.edu/)
The Project to Strengthen Nonprofit-Government Relationships is geared toward staff members, volunteers, or elected officials of nonprofit organizations or local governments. Working with practitioners and academics, the project helps nonprofit and government agencies collaborate to serve the public more effectively. The project's Web site provides

information about its activities, training exercises, publications, and access to a listserv facilitating communication among professionals in similar fields.

Teacher Focus (http://www.teacherfocus.com/)
Teacher Focus is a Web board community forum where educators can communicate with each other through threaded online discussions. Teachers can post questions to be discussed and answered by other educators on a variety of topics. Web boards on the site address a wide range of topics related to teaching, including specific subject areas, teaching levels, and general topics like school violence, technology, and special education, among others.

Teachers & Writers Collaborative (http://www.twc.org/)
Founded in 1967 by a group of writers and educators who believed that writers could make a unique contribution to the teaching of writing, the Teachers & Writers Collaborative brings writers and educators together to explore the connections between writing and reading literature. The Web site includes information about Writer-in-Residence Programs; workshops for students; staff development workshops; WriteNet, a resource for writers and teachers interested in teaching imaginative writing; and related links.

EDUCATION—ELEMENTARY & SECONDARY

Children First America (http://www.childrenfirstamerica.org/)
Children First America supports the right of parents to choose their children's schools and promotes parental choice in education through private tuition grants and tax-funded options. The organization's Web site offers information on scholarship programs, downloadable research reports, a speaker's bureau, an e-mail newsletter, and policy updates.

Computers 4 Kids (http://www.c4k.org/)
Computers 4 Kids accepts donated computers, refurbishes them, and donates them to schools and organizations in need. The Web site has a list of needed equipment, grant information, downloadable application forms, and news of upcoming events.

Education Week on the Web (http://www.edweek.org/)
Education Week on the Web, a clearinghouse of information about education reform, schools, and related policies, was created by Editorial Projects in Education Inc., publishers of *Education Week* and the monthly *Teacher Magazine.* The Web site offers online versions of both publications, a daily news section, a series of special reports, background essays on various education topics, state education facts, and links.

ERIC/EECE Clearinghouse on Elementary and Early Childhood Education (http://ericeece.org/)
ERIC/EECE, created at the University of Illinois at Urbana-Champaign and funded by the U.S. Department of Education, provides information to educators, parents and families, and those interested in the development, education, and care of children from birth through early adolescence. The Web site offers publications and articles on various topics related to childhood and education, education links, and discussion groups. It also provides access to the National Parent Information Network; the online journal, *Early Childhood Research & Practice*; and the Educational Resources Information Center (ERIC), a comprehensive national database of education-related literature administered by the National Library of Education.

LETSNet (http://commtechlab.msu.edu/sites/letsnet)
LETSNet (Learning Exchange for Teachers and Students through the Internet), a product of the Michigan State University College of Education, helps teachers to experience the potential value of the Web in the classroom. Resources include lesson plans, curriculum standards and guides, pointers to e-mail discussion lists, and many other online materials

provided by teachers who have successfully utilized the Internet as a way to fulfill their teaching objectives.

National Education Association (http://www.nea.org/)
The National Education Association was founded in 1857 "to elevate the character and advance the interests of the profession of teaching and to promote the cause of popular education in the United States," and its members include public school teachers, faculty members, education support professionals, retired educators, and students preparing to become teachers. The Web site offers links to local and state resources to help parents, publications and multimedia, legislation information, a bookstore, and access to OWL.org, an online community where educators connect to share their knowledge and experience.

National Institute for Early Education Research (http://nieer.org/)
Established at Rutgers University's Graduate School of Education, the National Institute for Early Education Research offers independent research-based advice and technical assistance to policymakers, journalists, researchers, and educators. The institute's Web site features new papers written by leading researchers in early education, current news and events, an online discussion forum, and a State Databank that lists pre-school standards and salaries for every state.

TechLEARNING.com (http://www.techlearning.com/)
TechLEARNING.com, produced by *Technology & Learning Magazine,* is an interactive publishing forum for the K–12 community where participants can read, write, and talk about educational technology. The Web site provides access to content from *Technology & Learning Magazine,* including articles and Web sites on many education topics, news, a grants database and funding tips, and upcoming events.

EDUCATION—HIGHER

American Association of Community Colleges (http://www.aacc.nche.edu/)
The American Association of Community Colleges works with other higher education associations, the federal government, and other national associations representing the public and private sectors to promote the goals of community colleges and higher education. The Web site includes facts about community colleges, a Community College Finder, legislative information, news, events, and a job bank.

American Council on Education (http://www.acenet.edu/)
The American Council on Education, a coordinating body for the nation's higher education institutions, seeks to provide leadership and influence public policy through advocacy, research, and program initiatives. The council's Web site provides information on policy issues, adult learning, training, international initiatives, women and minorities in education, upcoming events, and publications.

Beyond Bio 101: The Transformation of Undergraduate Biology Education (http://www.hhmi.org/BeyondBio101/)
"Beyond Bio 101: The Transformation of Undergraduate Biology Education" is a colorful, well-designed report from the Howard Hughes Medical Institute based on the experiences of many of the 220 colleges and universities that, since 1988, have been awarded grants by the institute's Undergraduate Biological Sciences Education Program.

The Chronicle of Higher Education (http://chronicle.com/)
Published weekly, *The Chronicle of Higher Education* has news and information for college and university faculty and administrators. Subscribers who register can receive access to the entire Web site, and to regular e-mail news updates. The full Web site includes a daily briefing on developments in higher education; reports on developments in information technology, including links to Internet resources for higher education; and the full text of

the current issue, with a fully searchable archive going back more than ten years. Much of the Web site is available only to subscribers, but some parts of the site are free, including an open online discussion on issues in higher education, job announcements, and some articles.

The College Board (http://www.collegeboard.com/)
The College Board is an association of schools, colleges, universities, and other educational organizations dedicated to putting college within the reach of all students. The Web site provides online registration and information about College Board tests, including the SAT. The site also offers a College Search, with information on about 3,500 schools, as well as online college applications and other information designed to aid in planning and paying for college.

College Is Possible (http://www.collegeispossible.org/)
The College Is Possible Web site offers guidance on preparing for, choosing, and paying for college. It serves parents, students, and education professionals on behalf of the Coalition of America's Colleges and Universities.

EDUCAUSE (http://www.educause.edu/)
EDUCAUSE is an international membership association whose mission is to help shape and enable change in higher education through the use of information technology in teaching, learning, scholarship, research, and institutional management. Visitors to the Web site can learn about award and fellowship opportunities, upcoming conferences, and current policy initiatives; search for and post job openings; download extended excerpts from relevant print publications; and join numerous online discussion lists.

FinAid (http://www.finaid.org/)
FinAid is a comprehensive collection of links to information about student financial aid on the Web. It includes links to and information on financial aid applications as well as links to the free FinAid newsletter, financial aid calculators, and FastWeb, a free scholarship search service.

International Research & Exchanges Board (http://www.irex.org/)
The International Research & Exchanges Board (IREX) administers programs supporting higher education, independent media, Internet development, and civil society in the United States, Europe, Eurasia, the Near East, and Asia. In its focus area of higher education, IREX offers research support, study abroad opportunities, professional training and leadership development, educational advising services, institutional development, and policy forums. The Web site provides detailed information about these programs and services, grant opportunities, job opportunities, and e-mail updates.

National Science Foundation (http://www.nsf.gov/)
The National Science Foundation's Web site is comprehensive and well-organized, with program information and funding opportunities in biology, computer and information sciences, education, engineering, geosciences, math and physical sciences, polar research, and social, behavioral, economic, and environmental sciences.

PEP Directory of Computer Recycling Programs
(http://www.microweb.com/pepsite/Recycle/recycle_index.html)
Sponsored by Children's Software Revue and Custom Computers for Kids, the PEP (Parents, Educators, and Publishers) Directory of Computer Recycling Programs Web site is a comprehensive guide to organizations that supply low-cost or donated computer equipment to nonprofits and schools. The annotated index is arranged by state and also includes national and international listings.

Science's Next Wave (http://nextwave.sciencemag.org/ca/)
Science magazine's Next Wave is a weekly online publication that covers scientific training, career development, and the science job market. The Web site features material written by and of interest to Canadian scientists, including science policy and academic issues. The site also has job market news; information for graduate students; and information on career transitions, job-hunting, diversity, and worklife.

ENVIRONMENT

Amazing Environmental Organization WebDirectory (http://www.webdirectory.com/)
The name says it all. The Amazing Environmental Organization WebDirectory is an enormous searchable directory of environmental organizations on the Web. It includes thousands of links to sites from 100 countries, organized into topics folders. The Web site also has a list of other places to search for environment-related information.

Conservation Action Network (http://takeaction.worldwildlife.org/)
Conservation Action Network is an electronic advocacy network created by the World Wildlife Fund. The network disseminates concise information on issues such as endangered species, global warming, forest protection, and fisheries conservation, and uses emerging communications technologies to facilitate communication between concerned individuals and members of Congress, state legislators, newspaper editors, corporations, foreign government leaders, and international agencies.

Earth Pledge Foundation (http://www.earthpledge.org/)
The Earth Pledge Foundation promotes sustainability in the agriculture, cuisine, architecture, and building industries through educational programs, communications efforts, demonstration projects, publications, and events. The foundation's Web site provides information about the foundation's programs (Green Roofs, Waste=Fuel, and Farm to Table), publications, and events.

Earth Share of Washington (http://www.esw.org/)
Earth Share of Washington is an alliance of environmental organizations working to conserve and protect the environment internationally, nationally, and in Washington State. The organization's Web site provides information on workplace giving and volunteer opportunities, links to member organizations, and resources and information on specific environmental concerns.

EE-Link (http://www.eelink.net/)
EE-Link provides environmental education resources on the Internet. The Web site offers a vast array of useful resources for the classroom, students and professionals, job seekers, grantseekers, organizations in the field, and those in search of relevant news and data. EELink also offers Web site, design, development, and hosting services, along with consulting services targeted specifically to the needs of environmental education organizations and projects.

EnviroLink (http://www.envirolink.org/)
The EnviroLink Network is an environmental information clearinghouse that lists hundreds of online environmental resources by topic and by type of resource. It also runs the EnviroWeb program, which offers Web site and domain name hosting, automated mailing lists, bulletin boards, and e-mail accounts to nonprofit organizations within the environmental and animal rights communities.

Environmental Defense (http://www.environmentaldefense.org/)
Founded in 1967, Environmental Defense represents more than 300,000 members, focusing on a broad range of regional, national, and international environmental issues. The organization's Web site has detailed information about its programs in biodiversity, climate

change, health, and oceans, and an Action Center with practical suggestions for taking action to make a difference in solving environmental problems. The site also has a library with reports, brochures, fact sheets, and more.

Environmental Grantmaker Association (http://www.ega.org/)
The Environmental Grantmakers Association (EGA), an affinity group of the Council on Foundations, is a voluntary association of foundations and giving programs concerned with the protection of the natural environment. The Web site provides brief information on membership, EGA working groups, and member-initiated projects.

Environmental Justice and Climate Change Initiative (http://www.ejcc.org/)
The Environmental Justice and Climate Change Initiative supports energy efficiency, renewable energy, and conservation policies while seeking equitable measures to protect and assist the communities most affected by climate change. The Web site has news stories, publications, climate justice links, a Media Room, and a For Members area.

Environmental News Network (http://www.enn.com/)
Environmental News Network, which began as a monthly print publication in 1993, is a portal for environmental conservation activity on the Web. The Web site offers monthly environmental news, including archives; in-depth information about various environmental topics; and access to interactive features such as online forums, legislation searches, and tools to search for and write to national or local press or legislators.

Environmental "NewsLink" (http://www.caprep.com/index.htm)
The Environmental "NewsLink" Web site has the latest environmental news, access to the *Federal Register,* and documents from federal and state agencies and courts, state legislatures, and Congress. It is an excellent place to track environmental legislation.

Environmental Protection Agency (http://www.epa.gov/)
The Environmental Protection Agency's Web site includes material on virtually every aspect of US environmental policy and protection, including funding information.

Lawyers' Environmental Action Team (http://www.leat.or.tz/)
The Lawyers' Environmental Action Team is a public interest environmental law organization that promotes sound natural resource management and environmental protection in Tanzania. The Web site contains the team's policy briefs on critical environmental issues facing Tanzania and East Africa.

National Audubon Society (http://www.audubon.org/)
The National Audubon Society is dedicated to conserving and restoring natural ecosystems and focuses on birds, other wildlife, and their habitats for the benefit of humanity and the earth's biological diversity. The society's Web site lists state centers and chapters and provides information about birds and science, current issues and how to take action, educational efforts, local resources, and news.

The Nature Conservancy (http://nature.org/)
The Nature Conservancy operates the largest private system of nature sanctuaries in the world and preserves threatened species by buying and putting into trust the habitats they need to survive. This environmental Web site outlines the conservancy's initiatives, describes its programs around the world, and lets visitors know how to help.

ONE/Northwest (http://www.onenw.org/)
ONE/Northwest (Online Networking for the Environment) is a Seattle-based nonprofit that provides technology resources and expertise to environmental groups in Alaska, British Columbia, Washington, Oregon, Montana and Idaho. Free resources at the organization's Web site include articles to help environmental nonprofits use their technology effectively, a monthly newsletter, and information about how to stay informed and make a difference.

TreeLink (http://treelink.org/)
Created to provide information, research, and networking for people working in urban and community forestry, TreeLink serves the field online through its Web site, with various learning centers, information on how to take action, tree-related resources, and news.

The Wilderness Society (http://www.wilderness.org/)
The Washington, D.C.-based Wilderness Society seeks to protect and restore America's wilderness areas. The organization's Web site includes news, locations, key issues, and an online library offering reports and scientific papers, policy and science briefs, maps and spatial analysis, fact sheets, testimony and legal documents, handbooks and guides, and e-newsletters.

GAY/LESBIAN

Human Rights Campaign (http://www.hrcusa.org/)
The Human Rights Campaign promotes equal rights for lesbian, gay, bisexual, and transgender Americans. The Web site offers tools for political activism as well as resources and support for coming out, family issues, and workplace issues.

Lambda Legal (http://www.lambdalegal.org/)
Lambda Legal is a national organization committed to achieving full recognition of the civil rights of lesbians, gay men, bisexuals, the transgendered, and people with HIV or AIDS through impact litigation, education, and public policy work. The Web site outlines key issues facing this population; lists the issues affecting each state; provides information on cases, events, and how to get involved; and offers online media and law libraries.

HEALTH

Agency for Healthcare Research and Quality (http://www.ahcpr.gov/)
The Agency for Healthcare Research and Quality (AHRQ) provides evidence-based information on healthcare outcomes; quality; and cost, use, and access. The Web site contains information on consumer health, research findings, data and surveys, and quality assessments. The Funding Opportunities section of the Web site includes an overview of AHRQ's research agenda, grant announcements, policy notices, grant award resources, contract solicitations, and research training information.

Center for School Mental Health Assistance (http://csmha.umaryland.edu/)
The University of Maryland School of Medicine's Center for School Mental Health Assistance works to improve the mental health status of the nation's children, adolescents, and families through the advancement of effective mental health programs in schools. The center offers technical assistance and consultation by telephone, e-mail, as well as on site. The center's Web site features a bulletin board; access to some of its materials; information about training, networking opportunities, and projects; and a list of related links.

Centers for Disease Control and Prevention (http://www.cdc.gov/)
The Centers for Disease Control and Prevention (CDC) serves as the national focus for developing and applying disease prevention and control, environmental health, and health promotion and education activities designed to improve the health of the people of the United States. The Web site includes comprehensive program and application information for the CDC's many health-related funding opportunities.

Coalition of Voluntary Mental Health Agencies, Inc. (http://www.cvmha.org/)
The Coalition of Voluntary Mental Health Agencies, Inc., is the umbrella advocacy organization of New York City's mental health community, representing nonprofit community-based mental health. The coalition's Web site provides a tool for locating New York State mental health programs.

Department of Health and Human Services (http://www.os.dhhs.gov/)
The Department of Health and Human Services' Web site provides consumer and policy information, grants and funding information, employment opportunities, and links to related government agencies.

Families USA (http://www.familiesusa.org/)
Families USA is a national nonprofit dedicated to the achievement of high-quality, affordable healthcare for all Americans and works to provide the consumer perspective in national and state debates on healthcare policy. The Web site provides information on key health issues and numerous resources, including state-by-state information, a media center, and a legislative action center.

Health Resources and Services Administration (http://www.hrsa.gov/)
The Health Resources and Services Administration (HRSA) works to assure the availability of quality healthcare to low-income, uninsured, isolated, vulnerable, and special needs populations. HRSA's Web site provides detailed information about its programs, services, and grant opportunities.

Healthfinder (http://www.healthfinder.gov/)
Healthfinder is a free Web portal to consumer health and human services information developed by the U.S. Department of Health and Human Services. Healthfinder can lead you to selected online publications, databases, Web sites, and support and self-help groups, as well as the government agencies and nonprofit organizations providing health information for the public.

Indian Health Service (http://www.ihs.gov/)
Dedicated to raising the health status of American Indians and Alaska Natives, the Indian Health Service Web site provides information on the agency's activities, including the Tribal Management Grant Program, and serves as an online resource for Native American communities.

International Women's Health Coalition (http://www.iwhc.org/)
The International Women's Health Coalition works to generate health and population policies, programs, and funding that promote and protect the rights and health of girls and women worldwide, particularly in Africa, Asia, and Latin America. The coalition's Web site features articles and publications on women's health and rights, information on upcoming conferences, updates on current issues, and more detailed information on the national and international programs and services offered by the coalition.

Journal of the American Medical Women's Association (http://www.jamwa.org/)
The *Journal of the American Medical Women's Association* is a quarterly, peer-reviewed journal on women's health issues. The Web site includes a Women's Health Link Library with links to organizations and information relevant to women's health; discussion questions and forums; and current and past issues of the journal.

Kaisernetwork.org (http://www.kaisernetwork.org/)
Kaisernetwork.org, a project of the Henry J. Kaiser Family Foundation, is a free multimedia news summary service intended to keep users informed about critical health policy issues. The Web site features include daily reports from major newspapers; HealthCast, live and archived webcasts of major health policy events and speeches; and Health Poll Search, a national archive for public opinion questions on health.

KidsHealth (http://kidshealth.org/)
Created by the medical experts at the Nemours Foundation, the KidsHealth Web site offers up-to-date health and medical information about children from before birth through adolescence. The Web site has separate areas for kids, teens, and parents, with a wealth of in-depth educational features, articles, animations, games, and resources.

Medicare (http://www.medicare.gov/)
The Medicare Web site offers detailed information about Medicare benefits and resources for beneficiaries. The Web site also has information on choosing a nursing home; publications that can be downloaded; fraud and abuse information; a health information section; and tools for locating health plans, nursing homes, dialysis facilities, Medigap policies, contacts, Medicare events, participating physicians, and prescription assistance programs.

MedWeb (http://www.medweb.emory.edu/MedWeb/)
Created and maintained by the staff of the Robert W. Woodruff Health Sciences Center Library of Emory University, MedWeb is a science and health Web portal offering a vast database of resources that can be browsed or searched. The site also provides access to Emory's Health Sciences Center Library.

National Health Information Center (http://www.health.gov/nhic/)
Established in 1979 by the U.S. Department of Health and Human Services, the National Health Information Center (NHIC) is a health information referral service for health professionals and consumers. NHIC's Web site offers access to the searchable Health Information Resource Database, which includes hundreds of organizations and government offices that provide health information upon request. Entries include contact information, short abstracts, and information about publications and services that the organizations provide.

National Institutes of Health (http://www.nih.gov/)
The National Institutes of Health (NIH) is the federal government's principle medical and behavioral research agency. The NIH Web site has information about clinical trials, health hotlines, and drugs; grants and funding opportunities; news and events; scientific resources; and NIH centers, institutes, and offices.

Office of Minority Health (http://www.omhrc.gov/)
The Office of Minority Health's (OMH) Web site provides information on its programs and initiatives and a Resource Center that offers a large amount of easily navigable material, including OMH funding announcements; a searchable funding database; news releases; online publications; requests for proposals; requests for applications; internship, fellowship, and scholarship announcements; additional funding resources; and OMH's newsletter, *Closing the Gap.*

World Health News (http://www.worldhealthnews.harvard.edu/)
World Health News is an online news digest from the Center for Health Communication at the Harvard School of Public Health. The Web site covers critical public health issues from around the world and is a resource for policymakers and journalists as well as public health researchers, practitioners, and advocates.

HIV/AIDS

Bailey House (http://www.baileyhouse.org/)
Bailey House, located in New York City, provides safe, comfortable, and permanent housing for people living with HIV/AIDS. In addition to housing, Bailey House offers vocational education, job training, and placements; drop-in services for food, clothing, and support; mental health and substance abuse services; healthcare coordination; and technical assistance. In addition to information about its programs and services, the Web site offers publications on the subject of AIDS housing and links to other HIV/AIDS resources.

The Body (http://www.thebody.com/)
The Body is a comprehensive HIV/AIDS information Web site offering information on giving and getting help, as well as treatment information from experts, policy updates, and bulletin board communities.

The Estate Project for Artists with AIDS (http://www.artistswithaids.org/)
The Estate Project for Artists with AIDS was created by the Alliance for Arts primarily to preserve artworks and create archives of visual artworks, films, videos, musical scores, dances, and manuscripts. The Web site offers information on artists' resources, a journal and forum, a virtual art collection, specific strategies for arts preservation, and links to relevant arts organizations, many of which are national in scope.

Funders Concerned About AIDS (http://www.fcaaids.org/)
Funders Concerned About AIDS is an affinity group of grantmakers working to mobilize philanthropic leadership and resources, domestically and internationally, to eradicate HIV/AIDS and address its social and economic consequences. As a resource to funders primarily working on HIV and AIDS-related issues, the Web site provides links to programs and workshops, information on conferences and briefings, AIDS funding updates, and related publications.

Gay Men's Health Crisis (http://www.gmhc.org/)
Founded by volunteers in 1981, Gay Men's Health Crisis offers AIDS education and political advocacy nationwide and direct services to men, women, and children with AIDS, as well as their families, in New York City. The organization's Web site is divided into three areas: Drugs, Sex, and HIV; Living with HIV; and Take Action. Each area summarizes the issues specific to it and directs visitors to practical information.

Technical Assistance Clearinghouse (http://www.taclearinghouse.org/)
The Technical Assistance Clearinghouse provides New York City HIV/AIDS organizations and individuals living with HIV/AIDS with technical assistance, information, and resources. The Web site offers access to these resources through guides, basic information, and a database covering New York City-area consultants and technical assistance providers. Additionally, users may access the organization's job bank, services for people living with HIV/AIDS, funding news, and links to publications, trainings, and Web sites.

HUNGER

America's Second Harvest (http://www.secondharvest.org/)
Through a network of hundreds of food banks and food-rescue programs, America's Second Harvest provides emergency food assistance to millions of hungry Americans each year. The organization's Web site provides hunger statistics and profiles of hungry Americans, public policy updates and research studies, contact information for its food banks, guidelines for making financial contributions and donating food, current news, and announcements of volunteer and lobbying opportunities. Visitors can also sign-up to receive updates on hunger-related issues.

The Hunger Site (http://www.thehungersite.com/)
The Hunger Site donates one cup of staple food to those in need for every click on a Give Free Food button on the site's home page. The staple food is paid for by site sponsors and is distributed to those in need by Mercy Corps and America's Second Harvest. Funds are split between these organizations and go to the aid of hungry people in over 74 countries, including those in Africa, Asia, Eastern Europe, the Middle East, Latin America, and North America.

MILITARY/VETERANS

Military, Veterans, & Patriotic Service Organizations of America (http://www.mvpsoa.org/)
The Military, Veterans, & Patriotic Service Organizations of America is a nonprofit organization that pre-screens and certifies national charities working to assist military personnel, veterans, and their families. The Web site's database of charitable organizations (look

under Quick Search) is a useful resource for anyone looking for information about services to current or former military personnel.

MULTICULTURAL/MINORITIES

Coalition for Asian American Children and Families (http://www.cacf.org/)
Established to challenge myths, break barriers, and advocate for change, the Coalition for Asian American Children and Families Web site contains local and national directories of organizations with ongoing policy and advocacy efforts around healthcare, social services, and education for Asian American children, as well as other valuable resources for members of the Asian American community.

Council of Latino Agencies/Consejo de Agencias Latinas (http://www.consejo.org/)
Composed of member organizations in the nation's capital, the Council of Latino Agencies/Consejo de Agencias Latinas promotes awareness of available services geared towards bettering the quality of life in the Latino community. The Web site includes policy research and advocacy information, volunteer and job opportunities, and a newsletter.

Foundation Funding Sources for Tribal Libraries (http://www.u.arizona.edu/~ecubbins/founfund.html)
The Foundation Funding Sources for Tribal Libraries Web site provides links to funding sources for North American Indian tribal libraries.

Indian Health Service (http://www.ihs.gov/)
Dedicated to raising the health status of American Indians and Alaska Natives, the Indian Health Service Web site provides information on the agency's activities, including the Tribal Management Grant Program, and serves as an online resource for Native American communities.

MEDLINEplus Health Information (http://www.nlm.nih.gov/medlineplus/)
The MEDLINEplus Health Information Web site provides specific health information for African American, Native American, Hispanic American, Asian American, and Pacific Islander populations. The site includes lists of hospitals and physicians, a medical encyclopedia and dictionary, health information in Spanish, extensive information on prescription and nonprescription drugs, and links to thousands of clinical trials.

National Association for the Advancement of Colored People (http://www.naacp.org/)
The primary focus of the National Association for the Advancement of Colored People (NAACP) is the protection and enhancement of the civil rights of African Americans and other minorities. The NAACP Web site includes a description of programs, news stories, a calendar of events, membership information, and links to relevant Web sites.

NativeWeb's Resource Center (http://www.nativeweb.org/resources)
NativeWeb's Resource Center is a comprehensive collection of Web links and other resources oriented towards the Native American community and those who want to learn about Native American culture.

Office of Minority Health (http://www.omhrc.gov/)
The Office of Minority Health's (OMH) Web site provides information on its programs and initiatives and a Resource Center that offers a large amount of easily navigable material, including OMH funding announcements; a searchable funding database; news releases; online publications; requests for proposals; requests for applications; internship, fellowship, and scholarship announcements; additional funding resources; and OMH's newsletter, *Closing the Gap.*

SCIENCE

American Association for the Advancement of Science (http://www.aaas.org/)
The American Association for the Advancement of Science's Web site provides information on science and policy programs, international programs, education, research, and a Careers in Science section that has fellowship and grant information.

Beyond Bio 101: The Transformation of Undergraduate Biology Education (http://www.hhmi.org/BeyondBio101/)
"Beyond Bio 101: The Transformation of Undergraduate Biology Education" is a colorful, well-designed report from the Howard Hughes Medical Institute based on the experiences of many of the 220 colleges and universities that, since 1988, have been awarded grants by the institute's Undergraduate Biological Sciences Education Program.

National Science Foundation (http://www.nsf.gov/)
The National Science Foundation's Web site is comprehensive and well-organized, with program information and funding opportunities in biology, computer and information sciences, education, engineering, geosciences, math and physical sciences, polar research, and social, behavioral, economic, and environmental sciences.

Science's Next Wave (http://nextwave.sciencemag.org/ca/)
Science magazine's Next Wave is a weekly online publication that covers scientific training, career development, and the science job market. The Web site features material written by and of interest to Canadian scientists, including science policy and academic issues. The site also has job market news; information for graduate students; and information on career transitions, job-hunting, diversity, and worklife.

SOCIAL CHANGE

Changemakers (http://www.changemakers.net/)
Changemakers, an initiative of Ashoka Innovators for the Public, focuses on the world of social entrepreneurship. Its mission is "to provide inspiration, resources, and opportunities for those interested in social change throughout the world." The organization's Web site has the *Changemakers Journal,* which covers education, health, the environment, and other topics; a library of global resources; examples for mobilizing support; advice; readings; and additional materials.

National Network of Grantmakers (http://www.nng.org/)
The National Network of Grantmakers (NNG) is a membership organization of individual donors, foundation staff, board members, and grantmaking committee members involved in funding social and economic justice by supporting organizations working for economic and social change. The Web site provides program information, including NNG's research study on diversity in philanthropy and their "1% More for Democracy" campaign; a section with information on events, meetings, and networking activities organized around specific themes or topics; and a section with nonprofit links, job lists, publications available to purchase, and the network's Common Grant Application.

SUBSTANCE ABUSE

The Alcoholic Beverage Medical Research Foundation (http://www.abmrf.org/)
The Alcoholic Beverage Medical Research Foundation supports research on the effects of alcohol on health, behavior, and prevention of alcohol-related problems. The Web site provides grant program information and guidelines, national and international news, and an online journal.

Join Together Online (http://www.jointogether.org/)
Join Together Online, a project of the Boston University School of Public Health, is a national resource for communities working to reduce substance abuse and gun violence nationwide, through the dissemination of public policy and community action information. The Web site offers news releases, funding news, grant announcements, resources (including a searchable and browsable resource database), facts, and Web links related to both substance abuse and gun violence. You can also sign up for *JTO Direct,* a free e-mail newsletter with news, alerts, and funding headlines. Daily and weekly versions are available.

National Institute on Alcohol Abuse and Alcoholism (http://www.niaaa.nih.gov/)
The National Institute on Alcohol Abuse and Alcoholism's Web site provides grants information, news releases, upcoming meetings and events, and links to related publications and databases.

Phoenix House (http://www.phoenixhouse.org/)
Phoenix House is devoted to the treatment and prevention of substance abuse, working to empower adults and adolescents with skills and self-confidence so that they can lead independent, productive, and rewarding lives. The Web site has information about treatment programs, prevention and education, and a treatment center locater.

Substance Abuse and Mental Health Services Administration (http://www.samhsa.gov/)
The Substance Abuse and Mental Health Services Administration (SAMHSA) was established to strengthen the nation's healthcare capacity to provide prevention, diagnosis, and treatment services for substance abuse and mental illnesses and serves as the umbrella under which substance abuse and mental health service centers are housed. The Web site has information about SAMHSA's programs, grant funding opportunities, grant planning tools, legislative and policy information, a quarterly newsletter, and employment opportunities.

WOMEN & GIRLS

The Empowered Women's Network (http://www.empoweredwomen.net/)
The Empowered Women's Network is dedicated to promoting social change through a sharing of solutions to personal and political problems and through referrals to women's training and services worldwide. The network's Web site offers basic information about the organization and its mission, links to organizations with similar interests, news on current issues, and contact information.

Feminist Internet Gateway (http://www.feminist.org/gateway/master2.html)
The Feminist Internet Gateway is a comprehensive list of women's Web sites, maintained by the Feminist Majority Foundation, and arranged by subject: general women's issues; global feminism; violence against women; clinic violence; women and work; affirmative action; women and girls in sports; women in politics; women's health; abortion rights; and women's studies and centers.

Institute for Women's Policy Research (http://www.iwpr.org/)
The Institute for Women's Policy Research is a public policy research organization, working with policymakers, scholars, and public interest groups to design, execute, and disseminate research that illuminates economics and social policy issues affecting women and families. The institute's Web site is an excellent resource on issues focuses on issues of poverty and welfare, employment and earnings, work and family issues, the economic and social aspects of health and safety, and women's civic and political participation.

International Women's Health Coalition (http://www.iwhc.org/)
The International Women's Health Coalition works to generate health and population policies, programs, and funding that promote and protect the rights and health of girls and

women worldwide, particularly in Africa, Asia, and Latin America. The coalition's Web site features articles and publications on women's health and rights, information on upcoming conferences, updates on current issues, and more detailed information on the national and international programs and services offered by the coalition.

Journal of the American Medical Women's Association (http://www.jamwa.org/)

The *Journal of the American Medical Women's Association* is a quarterly, peer-reviewed journal on women's health issues. The Web site includes a Women's Health Link Library with links to organizations and information relevant to women's health; discussion questions and forums; and current and past issues of the journal.

National Women's Health Information Center (http://www.4woman.gov/)

Sponsored by the U.S. Department of Health and Human Services' Office on Women's Health, the National Women's Health Information Center provides access to information on all areas of women's health. The information on the Web site is obtained from a variety of federal and private sector resources and can be searched by health topic or by keyword. The site includes press releases, a good set of links to online medical dictionaries and journals, a directory of residency and fellowship programs, and a Hot Topics in Congress section which details women's health-related legislation in the U.S. Congress.

RAINBO (http://www.rainbo.org/)

RAINBO (the Research, Action and Information Network for the Bodily Integrity of Women) works directly with immigrant and refugee communities in the United States on issues that intersect women's health and human rights. The RAINBO Web site provides descriptions of national and international programs and activities, including AMANITARE, which works toward the recognition of African women's and girls' sexual and reproductive health rights.

Women's Funding Network (http://www.wfnet.org/)

Describing itself as an "international partnership of women and girls' foundations, donors, and allies that works to strengthen funds and is committed to social justice," the Women's Funding Network was established to support women and girls by encouraging collaboration among women, donors, communities, and institutions. The network's Web site provides visitors with news and events, activities and programs, publications, grants information, member resources, and job opportunities.

Women's Philanthropy Institute (http://www.women-philanthropy.org/)

Women's Philanthropy Institute is a nonprofit educational institute that brings together philanthropists, volunteers, and professional funders to educate and empower women as philanthropists, donors, and volunteers. The institute's Web site provides information about the institute's programs and services, a bulletin board, and several related articles.

APPENDIX G

Bibliography: Suggestions For Further Reading

Compiled by Sarah Collins

The following is a reading list of books and periodical articles that supplement the information in *The Foundation Center's Guide to Grantseeking on the Web.* Citations have been selected from the Foundation Center's bibliographic database, available on our Web site as *Literature of the Nonprofit Sector Online* (*LNPS*) (http://lnps.fdncenter.org). Be sure to check *LNPS Online* regularly to keep abreast of new publications. You can start by selecting the terms "Internet" or "Fundraising—computer aided" from the subject index list.

General Works

Baker, Todd. *Nonprofit Websites: Cutting Through the Emaze.* Atlanta, GA: Grizzard Direct Marketing, 2001.

A primer on use of the Internet as a marketing tool for nonprofits. Starting from the point of view that "the Internet has become a direct marketer's dream," the book presents various strategies for the full realization of the medium's potential.

Bergan, Helen. *Where the Money Is: Advancement Research for Nonprofit Organizations.* Arlington, VA: BioGuide Press, 2001.

A book of techniques for using the Internet to find information on people, companies, and foundations. Names and describes hundreds of Web sites that are useful for fundraisers and advancement personnel. With bibliographic references and index.

Corson-Finnerty, Adam, and Laura Blanchard. *Fundraising and Friend-Raising on the Web.* Chicago, IL: American Library Association, 1998.

Intended for library administrators, but with approaches that will succeed for any nonprofit, the book offers advice on such topics as developing and measuring the impact of a Web site, creating donor recognition in cyberspace, delivering your site directly to potential donors on disk or CD-ROM, and fundraising with digital cash. Throughout, examples on the Web are provided.

"E-Philanthropy v2.001: From Entrepreneurial Adventure to an Online Community." Battle Creek, MI: W.K. Kellogg Foundation, 2001.

This Web-based publication updates the W.K. Kellogg Foundation's first report "E-Philanthropy, Volunteerism, and Social Changemaking" and expands the number of Web sites included in a searchable database. The report interprets the changes that have occurred in e-philanthropy, suggests a structural guide for the various types of Web sites, offers insights into the future, and provides a listing of additional resources. Available as a PDF file and searchable database at http://www.actknowledgeworks.net/ephil/red_cover.

Garvin, Peggy, ed. *Government Information on the Internet.* 5th ed. Lanham, MD: Bernan Press, 2002.

Covers nearly 4,500 government (federal, state, and local) Internet resources. Also includes some primary sites in other countries. Organized into 18 subject categories and indexed by primary and alternative access URLs, Superintendent of Documents (SuDocs) number, publication title, agency, and subject.

Grobman, Gary M. *The Nonprofit Organization's Guide to E-Commerce.* Harrisburg, PA: White Hat Communications, 2001.

The book discusses how nonprofits can capitalize on the Internet for marketing, fundraising, maintaining contact with members and donors, and publicity. Appendices include a glossary, information about copyright, and a sample code of ethics.

Gross, Marilyn L. *300 Top Web Sites for Fundraisers.* Suffern, NY: Educational Funding Strategies, 2001.

Organized into broad categories, such as capital campaigns, prospect research, and international grantseeking, each entry provides a synopsis of the content of the Web site and its URL.

Hopkins, Bruce R. *The Nonprofit's Guide to Internet Communications Law.* Hoboken, NJ: John Wiley & Sons, 2003.

Hopkins elucidates the relationship between laws affecting nonprofit organizations and their use of the Internet. Focusing on fundraising, lobbying, political activity, and management of charitable giving, he explains and footnotes with case citations the relevant legal precedents. He notes that there are three paramount issues from a legal perspective: the cost of Internet use, essence of hyperlinks, and record keeping. Includes a table of cases.

Lane, Carole A. *Naked in Cyberspace: How to Find Personal Information Online.* Edited by Helen Burwell and Owen B. Davies. Medford, NJ: Information Today, Inc., 2002.

Includes a chapter on prospect research that indicates how to use public records, telephone directory databases, motor vehicle records, news, and biographical databases to search for wealthy prospects.

Peterson, Susan. *The Grantwriter's Internet Companion: A Resource for Educators and Others Seeking Grants and Funding.* Thousand Oaks, CA: Corwin Press, Inc., 2001.
A primer covering basic Internet resources for grantseekers in the field of education. Includes government as well as private sources of funding. Also discusses other standard uses of the Internet, such as e-mail.

Warwick, Mal. Ed. *Fundraising on the Internet: The ePhilanthropyFoundation.org's Guide to Success Online.* 2nd ed. San Francisco, CA: Jossey-Bass Publishers, 2002.
A compendium by various specialists, chapters cover recruiting donors online, managing Web site content, use of charity portals, and electronic prospect research, among many other topics. Case studies of organizations making successful use of the medium feature Comic Relief; Harvard, Stanford, and Wake Forest Universities; and the Heifer Project International. Includes glossary and index.

Distance Learning

Eisinger, Jane. "Education Evolution." *Association Management,* vol. 52, December 2000, p. 52-9. Shows how associations can utilize the potential of distance learning to provide professional development to their members and others.

LeCavalier, Jacques. *Making E-Learning Work in the Nonprofit Sector.* Rev. ed. Sunnyvale, CA: Brandon-Hall, 2003.
A primer on the topic of e-learning, delving into the specific issues that are relevant to organizations. Explains how nonprofits can use the capability of the Internet to train employees, clients, and volunteers. Case studies and profiles of e-learning initiatives are included. With glossary.

Online Fundraising

Abshire, Michael. "E-philanthropy Continues to Grow." *Corporate Philanthropy Report,* vol. 17, April 2002, p. 1, 11.
Reports on the Third Annual E-Philanthropy Conference that took place in March 2002 in McLean, Virginia. The role of Internet fundraising after the attacks of September 11 took center stage, and several statistics about the amounts raised are provided. Other speakers focused on the role of the Internet in soliciting volunteers and in sharing information about corporate donations.

Allen, Kent. "On the Horizon." *Currents,* vol. 27, May-June 2001, p. 21–4.
This article reports that institutions of higher education are finding e-mail to be a boon for fundraising solicitations, but there are caveats as well.

Causer, Craig. "Online Boundaries: Cyber Solicitation Guidelines Govern Affiliates." *NonProfit Times,* vol. 16, October 1, 2002, p. 21–2.
Explains the rules that national organizations have developed to minimize conflicts among local chapters over the allocation of funds raised on the Internet. Describes the different approaches the American Heart Association and Special Olympics International use to distribute online proceeds to local affiliates.

Cohen, Todd. "Staying Connected: Schools Spinning Alumni Webs." *NonProfit Times,* vol. 16, November 1, 2002, p. 55–6.

Demonstrates how schools such as Wellesley College and Phillips Academy are building online communities to strengthen relationships with alumni.

Hudson, Michel. "Researching Donor Prospects Online." *Advancing Philanthropy,* vol. 8, September-October 2001, p. 33–4.

Techniques for using Internet search engines and online databases to find potential donors.

Lewis, Nicole. "Charities Find Perfect Place for Odd Donations: Online Auctions." *Chronicle of Philanthropy,* vol. 14, April 4, 2002, p. 34.

Explains how nonprofits are fundraising through online auction sites such as eBay and MissionFish.

Lewis, Nicole. "You've Got a Charity Solicitation." *Chronicle of Philanthropy,* vol. 13, November 30, 2000, p. 25–8.

E-mail can be an effective and cost-efficient way to maintain contact with donors, potential donors, alumni, and other interested parties. Techniques for online solicitation via e-mail, however, differ from those for traditional methods for direct mail, and suggestions are given here.

Lyttle, Jeni. "New Dimensions for Fundraising." *Nonprofits & Technology,* vol. 2, October 1999, p. 1, 3.

Some fundraisers are creating virtual tours of their planned facilities in order to raise capital funds.

Moore, Jennifer. "Internet Appeals and the Law: State Charity Regulators Issue Guidelines on When Charities that Solicit Online Must Register Locally." *Chronicle of Philanthropy,* vol. 12, September 7, 2000, p. 21–3.

Article describes proposed guidelines by the National Association of State Charity Officials on the monitoring of online fundraising appeals.

Olsen, Merritt, et al. "E-relationship Development Strategy for the Nonprofit Fundraising Professional." *International Journal of Nonprofit and Voluntary Sector Marketing,* vol. 6, November 2001, p. 364–73.

Provides a methodology for maintaining and enhancing donor relations through use of online resources, specifically e-mail. Also includes results of a survey of 14 large U.S. nonprofits about their online solicitation practices.

Schwinn, Elizabeth. "Click and Easy." *Chronicle of Philanthropy,* vol. 13, December 14, 2000, p. 27–9.

The pros and cons of online marketing and fundraising arrangements are revealed. Nonprofits are recognizing the appeal of their credibility to corporations but may be naive in forging deals and handling the complicated ancillary issues of online promotional campaigns with for-profits.

Wallace, Nicole. "Forging Links Online." *Chronicle of Philanthropy,* vol. 14, 13 June 2002, p. 23-4, 26–7.

Describes strategies nonprofits have used to improve the effectiveness of online fundraising. Some organizations have tried coordinating direct mail campaigns with e-mail messages. Other groups have reported mixed results when using rented lists of e-mail addresses. Organizations with many local affiliates have reduced costs by developing centralized online giving programs.

Williams, Grant. "Advocacy Group's Online Savvy Nets More Than Donations." *Chronicle of Philanthropy,* vol. 15, April 17, 2003, p. 23, 25–6.

Describes the success of online advocacy group MoveOn.org, whose e-mail appeal raised more than $500,000.

Williams, Grant. "Guidelines Show Charities How to Work with Internet Companies on Fund Raising." *Chronicle of Philanthropy,* vol. 13, November 2, 2000, p. 67.

Discusses a report published by the Association of Fundraising Professionals titled "Internet Transaction Guidelines." This report outlines a set of 22 guidelines that nonprofits can follow when working with Internet companies to raise money through Web-based resources. The guidelines can be located at http://www.afpnet.org/tier3_cd.cfm?folder_id=868&content_item_id=1260.

Philanthropy Portals

Berger, Jeff, et al. "NotForLong.com: Nonprofit Sector Not Immune from 'Dot-Bombs'." *NonProfit Times,* vol. 15, March 2001, p. 27–30.

Some of the dot.coms serving the nonprofit world have folded, including OnGiving, KickStart.com, Zoom2Net.com, ACUSA.com, IReachOut.com, and some others are struggling or changing their focus. Meanwhile ePhilanthropyFoundation.org has issued a code of ethics, reprinted here.

"The Dot-Com Shakeout: Where Does It Leave E-Philanthropy?" *Advancing Philanthropy,* vol. 8, May-June 2001, p. 14–5, 17–8, 41–3.

The demise of Charitableway and other dot-coms reinforces the fact that nonprofit alliances with philanthropy portals can be risky. Details about the dissolution are given by observers and Charitableway CEO Pete Mountanos. Offers suggestions for maintaining an Internet presence through application service providers (ASPs), and recommends several companies. Also provides guidelines for selecting a technology partner and adds several real-world examples.

Hall, Holly. "A Brave New World of Giving." *Chronicle of Philanthropy,* vol. 12, June 15, 2000, p.1, 33–7.

The rise of Internet donation portals, or "philanthropy portals" includes both nonprofits and businesses that seek to connect donors with charities. America Online Foundation, which established Helping.org, is one of the most active sites, but there are numerous competitors vying to register the big-name nonprofits. A comprehensive list describes the major giving portals.

Martin, Nita L. "You've Got Donations." *Corporate Philanthropy Report,* vol. 15, January 2000, p. 1–3, 5.

Examines online cause-related marketing and the relationship between e-philanthropy companies and nonprofit organizations. Profiles the e-philanthropy Web sites Shop2Give, IGive.com, GreaterGood.com, and Helping.org. Sidebar provides tips to nonprofits that seek to do fundraising on the Internet or to partner with e-philanthropy companies.

Prospect Research

Allen, Nick. "Using E-mail and the Web to Acquire and Cultivate Donors." *Nonprofit World,* vol. 21, January-February 2003, p. 27–8.

Discusses ways to raise money on the Internet—and which are working best.

Barber, Putnam. "Looking for New Supporters? Look Again—Try Forging New Connections with the Friends You Already Have." *Advancing Philanthropy,* vol. 8, September-October 2000, p. 34–6, 38.

Article describes ways that nonprofits can improve their online communications to current supporters via the Internet.

Hudson, Michel. "An Introduction to Prospect Research." *Grassroots Fundraising Journal,* vol. 22, January-February 2003, p. 7–10.

The author describes some low-cost or free research resources available via the Internet that can be useful for prospect research, covering biographical information, asset information, news, and company data. In a sidebar, Kim Klein assesses how useful (and accurate) some Internet information is.

Knight, Margo. "How Technology and Its Use by Our Field Has Changed." *Connections,* vol. 14, Summer 2002, p. 4–6.

A prospect researcher describes her favorite online search tools.

Robinson, Andy. "Direct Mail Alternatives: Finding New Donors in Manageable Numbers." *NonProfit Times,* vol. 13, April 1999, p. 45–6.

Discusses techniques for small community organizations for recruiting new contributions.

Scholarships

Guernsey, Lisa. *College.Edu: On-Line Resources for the Cyber-Savvy Student.* Version 6. Alexandria, VA: Octameron Associates, 2002.

Recommended Web sites, with descriptions of how they are helpful to students in assessing colleges and in their search for scholarship funds.

Technology

"2003 Non-Profit Software Guide." *Fund Raising Management,* vol. 33, October 2002, p. 13–33.

Annual guide to fundraising software for nonprofits. Also see "The 2003 Internet Software Guide" in the same issue.

"2003 Technology Guide for Nonprofits." *Chronicle of Philanthropy,* vol. 15, January 9, 2003, p. T1–8.

An advertising supplement listing 44 companies that provide computer products and services. Also available at the *Chronicle*'s Web site at http://philanthropy.com/techguide.

CNET Glossary.

Located at http://cnet.com/Resources/Info/Glossary. A comprehensive glossary of terms for Internet users.

Feller, Gordon. "Latest High-Tech Trends: One Giant Leap for Nonprofits." *Nonprofit World,* vol. 19, January-February, 2001, p. 25–9.
Recommends that nonprofits partner with application service providers (ASPs) as a way of keeping their Web sites current without the expense of hiring their own technical staff. Explains further benefits of such an arrangement, and how to locate more information.

Stein, Michael. "Application Service Providers: An Important New Technology Solution for Today's Nonprofit." *Grassroots Fundraising Journal,* vol. 21, May-June 2002, p. 10–3.
Explains how application service providers (ASPs) can be a big help to smaller nonprofits that do not have technical personnel on staff, and provides guidance about finding one. Also describes eleven free ASPs.

Volunteering

Causer, Craig. "Impulse Volunteers." *NonProfit Times,* vol. 17, April 1, 2003, p. 20–1.
Explains that more nonprofits are using the Web to expedite communications with prospective volunteers.

Mincemoyer, Claudia C. "4-H Volunteers and the Internet: A Partnership for the Future." *Journal of Volunteer Administration,* vol. 21, Number 1, 2003, p. 31–6.
A study of the extent to which 4-H volunteers would be willing to utilize the Internet to access training materials and other information pertinent to their volunteer work. The survey was conducted with volunteers in Pennsylvania.

Moy, Laurie. "Tapping Global Resources: A Guide to Involving and Managing Online Volunteers." *Journal of Volunteer Administration,* vol. 20, Number 2, 2002, p. 47–52.
The author is the Online Volunteer Manager for People with Disabilities Uganda, and this article recounts her experience in managing more than 150 online volunteers.

A Snapshot of Internet Innovation: Using E-philanthropy to Expand Volunteering, Giving and Community Building. Washington, D.C.: INDEPENDENT SECTOR. 2002. 36 p.
Profiles 27 organizations and foundations that are utilizing the Internet to accomplish their missions.

Wallace, Nicole. "A Virtual Army of Volunteers." *Chronicle of Philanthropy,* vol. 13, February 22, 2001, p. 37–9.
Increasing numbers of volunteers are finding that they can help charities and people in need through Internet-based programs such as VolunteerMatch. This organization pairs volunteers with suitable agencies in their communities, while others, such as International Telementor Center, match "virtual volunteers" with recipients from afar.

APPENDIX H

Glossary of Web-Related Terms

Adobe Acrobat* A program that lets you capture a document and then view it in its original format and appearance. To view an Acrobat document, which is called a Portable Document Format (PDF) file, you need Acrobat Reader. The Reader is free and can be downloaded from Adobe (http://www.adobe.com/products/acrobat/readstep2.html).

Architecture The structuring paradigms, style, and patterns that describe or make up either software systems or Internet/intranet systems. In particular, architectures can be overall structures for systems.

Blog See Weblog.

Bookmark A bookmark (often referred to as "favorites") is considered by some to be the best thing about surfing the Web. By bookmarking a Web site while you visit it, you can easily return to it at a later time with a simple mouse selection rather than remembering or typing in the URL.

Boolean logic A system of math that uses operators such as "and," "or," "not," "if . . . then," which permit computation. This system is named after George Boole, an English mathematician who introduced the logic in 1847.

Browser Short for Web browser, it's the tool (program) that allows you to surf the Web. The most popular Web browsers are Netscape Navigator and Internet Explorer.

Adapted from the High Density.com glossary (except as otherwise designated). Used by permission of High Density Computing.
*Adapted from whatis.com's online encyclopedia at http://whatis.techtarget.com. Copyrighted by and used by permission of whatis.com and TechTarget, Inc.

Bulletin Board System (BBS) An electronic service that can be accessed via the Internet. BBS typically includes collections of files, notes from other computer users, and many other services.

Button A graphic that a user can click to do something, such as download a program, submit information, or go to another Web page.

Cache A file on your computer where the system stores a copy of things asked for recently. Then, if you ask for the same thing again, instead of issuing another Internet request, your computer can simply use the copy from the cache. This has to do with trying to speed things up, since every request you send over the Internet for a picture or text takes time.

Command A way of telling an application or Windows to perform a major chore, such as running an application or utility program. Usually an option from an application's menus. Also refers to commands typed in from a command-prompt session or from the Run dialog box from the Start Menu in Windows.

Cookie The most common meaning of "cookie" on the Internet refers to a piece of information sent by a Web server to a Web browser that the browser software is expected to save and to send back to the server whenever the browser makes additional requests from the server. Cookies might contain information such as login or registration information, online "shopping cart" information, user preferences, etc.

Cursor The representation of the mouse on the screen. It may take many different shapes.

Database A file or group of related files that are designed to hold recurring data types as if the files were lists.

Desktop The screen area on which the windows are displayed.

Dial-up connection The most popular form of Internet connection for the home user, this is a connection from your computer to a host computer over standard telephone lines.

Dialog box An on-screen message box that conveys or requests information from the user.

Digital divide* Describes the fact that the world can be divided into those who do and do not have access to, and the capability to use, modern information technology.

Discussion group A group of people who exchange messages about particular topics. Often associated with newsgroups, discussion groups can also take the form of interactive message boards, thread message forums, and e-mailing lists.

Domain name The unique name that identifies an Internet site. Domain names always have two or more parts, separated by dots. The part on the left is the most specific, and the part on the right is the most general. (See also Suffix.)

Download The transfer of information from the Internet to your computer. Every time you instruct your computer system to retrieve your e-mail, you are downloading your e-mail to your computer.

Drop list or drop-down menu A list of options that drops down when you click on a down arrow button.

E-commerce* The buying and selling of goods and services on the Internet, especially the World Wide Web.

E-mail (electronic mail) Messages, usually text, sent from one person to another via computer. E-mail can also be sent automatically to a large number of addresses. (See Mailing list.)

Encryption A way of making data unreadable to everyone except the receiver. A common way of sending credit card numbers over the Internet when conducting commercial transactions.

Extranet The connecting of two or more intranets. If you think of an intranet as a company's internal Web site, which allows users inside the company to communicate and exchange information, imagine connecting that virtual space with another company's intranet, thus allowing these two (or more) companies to share resources and communicate over the Internet in their own virtual space. This technology greatly enhances business to business communications.

FAQ (frequently asked questions) FAQs are documents that list and answer the most common questions on a particular subject.

Forms HTML pages that pass variables back to the server. These pages are used to gather information from users.

Forum See Discussion group.

Frames A term used to describe a viewing and layout style of a World Wide Web site, it refers to the simultaneous loading of two or more Web pages at the same time within the same screen.

Gateway See Portal.

GIF (Graphics Interchange Format)* Developed by Compuserve, this image format is one of the two most common file formats for graphic images on the World Wide Web. The other is the JPEG.

Hit A search result.

Home page This has several meanings; originally, the Web page that your browser is set to use when it starts up. The more common meaning refers to the main Web page for a business, organization, person, or simply the main page out of a collection of Web pages.

HTML (hypertext markup language) The coding language used to create hypertext documents for use on the World Wide Web.

Hyperlink A link in a document that, when activated (often by clicking it), links or jumps to another document or graphic. (See also Link.)

Icon A small graphic symbol used to represent a folder, program, shortcut, resource, or document.

Interface The visible layer enabling a user to communicate with a computer. In DOS, the interface consisted largely of typed commands and character-based feedback. Windows is an entirely graphical interface, using a mouse, menus, windows, and icons to allow the user to communicate his instructions and requirements to the computer.

Internet connection The way one gains access to the Internet. For the average person a simple phone line is used. This is also known as a dial-up connection.

iPDF (Interactive Portable Document Format) PDF forms that are interactive and can be completed/printed from your computer. You must have Adobe Acrobat Reader to use iPDF forms.

ISP (Internet service provider) An organization that provides access to the Internet in some form, usually for a fee.

Javascript A scripting language for Web pages. Scripts written with Javascript can be embedded into HTML documents. With Javascript you have many possibilities for enhancing your Web page with interesting elements.

Keyword A word you might use to search for, or on, a Web site.

LAN (local area network) A computer network limited to the immediate area, usually the same building or floor of a building.

Link A link will transport you from one Internet site to another with a click of your mouse. Links can be text or graphic. Text links usually will be underlined and are often a different color than the rest of the text on the screen. A graphic link usually has a frame around it. (See also Hyperlink.)

Listserv The most common kind of electronic mailing list.

Logon The process of connecting to a network or remote system.

Mailing list A discussion forum where participants subscribe to a list and receive messages by e-mail.

Menu A list of available command options.

Menu bar Located under the title bar on a Web site's home page, the menu bar displays the names of all available menu lists.

Message board See Web board.

Moderated mailing list A mailing list where messages are first sent to the list owner for review before they are distributed to all subscribers.

MP3* (MPEG-1 Audio Layer-3) is a standard technology and format for compression of a sound file into a very small file (about one-twelfth the size of the original file) while preserving the original level of sound quality when it is played.

Navigate To move around on the World Wide Web by following hypertext paths from document to document.

Navigation bar See Menu bar.

Newsgroup The name for a discussion group on Usenet.

Password A code used to gain access to a locked system.

PDF format See Adobe Acrobat.

Personalization* The process of tailoring Web pages to individual users' characteristics or preferences.

Portal* A term, generally synonymous with gateway, for a World Wide Web site that is or proposes to be a major starting site for users.

Post Means the same as "to put up." It can refer to subscribers to newsgroups or mailing lists sending or posting their articles or comments online. It is also used to indicate content added to or "put up" on a Web site.

Posting A single message entered into a network communications system, such as a newsgroup or a message board.

Search engine A databased Web site containing information that can be used to find other sites of interest.

Server A computer, or a software package, that provides a specific kind of service to client software running on other computers. The term can refer to a particular piece of software, such as a WWW server, or to the machine on which the software is running.

Site (Web) A location on the Internet containing HTML documents that visitors can view using a browser.

Site map* A visual model of a Web site's content that allows users to navigate through the site to find the information they are looking for.

Spam An inappropriate attempt to use a mailing list, Usenet, or other networked communications facility as a broadcast medium by sending the same message to a large number of people who didn't ask for it.

Suffix (domain name) The three-digit suffix of a domain can be used to identify the type of organization. Suffixes include, but are not limited to:
.com = commercial
.edu = educational
.int = international
.gov = government
.mil = military
.net = network
.org = organization

Surf To browse or "look at" information on the World Wide Web by pointing and clicking and navigating in a nonlinear way.

Text file A file containing only ASCII text characters. ASCII text is a basic form of electronic communication.

Thread A group of related messages on an electronic bulletin board system or Web discussion group.

Thumbnail Describes the size of an image you frequently find on Web pages. Usually a photo or picture archive will present a thumbnail version of its contents (which makes the page load quicker), and when a user clicks on the small image, a larger version will appear.

URL (uniform resource locator) The standard way to give the address of any resource on the World Wide Web. URLs typically begin with http:// or www.

Usenet Often referred to as simply "newsgroups," Usenet is a distributed bulletin board system supported mainly by UNIX machines.

User ID (user name) This is the unique identifier (like your logon name) that you use to identify yourself on a computer.

Virtual Simulation of the real thing. This word appears before various computer terms to indicate simulation technology that enables you to cross boundaries and experience something without needing its physical presence.

Virus A virus is a computer program written to interrupt or destroy a user's work. A virus may do something as innocuous as display a message, or as destructive as reformatting one's hard drive. A computer can "catch" a virus from a floppy disk or even from a file downloaded from a remote source. Once a computer has become "infected," the virus may spread via connections on a network or floppy disks shared with others. A variety of virus-detecting software programs exist.

Web board A discussion group or forum, which is accessed via the World Wide Web.

Web host The computer or hard drive where a Web site(s) is hosted and accessible through the World Wide Web.

Web page A document on the World Wide Web. Each Web page has its own unique URL. Every time you are on the World Wide Web, you are looking at a Web page.

Web site A home page or group of pages either owned by an individual or a company and placed on the Web.

Weblog (Blog) A personal or non-commercial journal about a particular subject or range of subjects that is available on the World Wide Web and is updated frequently.

World Wide Web (WWW or the Web) A global (worldwide) hypertext system that uses the Internet as its transport mechanism. In a hypertext system, you navigate by clicking hyperlinks, which display other documents, which also contain hyperlinks. The Web relies upon the hypertext transport protocol (http), an Internet standard that specifies how an application can locate and acquire resources stored on another computer on the Internet. Most Web documents are created using hypertext markup language (html).

ZIP The most common file/program compression program. Especially useful for "zipping" groups of files together.

Index

Note: FC refers to the Foundation Center. See also the Appendices, which contain additional information about foundations.